Cape Cod Library

CAPE COD LIBRARY

of

Local History and Genealogy

A Facsimile Edition of 108 Pamphlets Published in the Early 20th Century

Compiled and Indexed by
Leonard H. Smith Jr., C.G.

Volume 1

CLEARFIELD

> **NOTICE**
>
> This work was reproduced from the original edition. A characteristic of this copy, from which the printer worked, was that the image was uneven. Every effort has been made by the printer to produce as fine a reprint of the original edition as possible.

Reprinted for
Clearfield Company, Inc. by
Genealogical Publishing Co., Inc.
Baltimore, Maryland
2004

Copyright © 1992
Leonard H. Smith Jr.
All Rights Reserved. No part of this publication
may be reproduced in any form without permission
of the Publisher.
Published by Genealogical Publishing Co., Inc.
1001 N. Calvert Street, Baltimore, MD 21202
Library of Congress Catalogue Card Number 91-76526
International Standard Book Number, Volume 1: 0-8063-1325-0
Set: 0-8063-1324-2
Made in the United States of America

PREFACE

Cape Cod families are difficult to trace. Only the probate records survived the burning of the Barnstable County Courthouse in 1827. Other disasters have affected town records. Many of Chatham's records were lost in a local fire. Yarmouth's records for the Revolutionary War period have been missing for years. With my own ancestry tracing to the founders of Chatham and including numerous other Cape Cod persons and communities it was inevitable that my search should disclose the series of pamphlets published at Yarmouthport, Mass., by Charles W. Swift early in the 20th century under the series name *Cape Cod Library of History and Genealogy*.

Many of these pamphlets are undated; most are dated during the 1911-1914 period; two are dated in the 1940s. Two pamphlets were each numbered 22; I have designated one, arbitrarily, as 22a. Some were merely a single page; others ran as large as 40 or 50 pages. Some of the content material seems to have been published earlier in an unidentified newspaper.

The pamphlet covers were on newsprint and the internal pages on paper of a little better quality. The covers have largely turned dark brown from the sulphite content of the paper and photocopies are very difficult to make, sometimes impossible. The interiors are showing signs of deterioration.

Accumulating a set of the pamphlets proved a considerable task. About 80 were purchased in their original form. A few were purchased as photocopies from the Eastham Historical Society. Others were obtained by photocopying issues found in different libraries. Even the Library of Congress set was incomplete; I am pleased to have been able to assist in correcting that situation. The gaps are not noticed by the libraries because the pamphlets are normally catalogued as individual items.

A check of the files of the U. S. Copyright Office discloses that all of the pamphlets are in the public domain. Such copyrights as were claimed have expired and not been renewed.

Locating information presented another serious problem. A number of the pamphlets are devoid of pagination. Finding an item of information is difficult; citing its location is often virtually impossible. Using this valuable source of information meant constructing an index, which this book contains.

Securing the basic material and preparing the index have involved more than ten years. If its users find it as helpful as I do I will be pleased.

This project could never have been accomplished alone. Uncounted hours of monotonous proof-reading of the index have been contributed by Dorothy Marvelle Boyer and Norma Helen Smith; their work is deeply appreciated.

In a project of this size it is inevitable that errors have crept in. I accept responsibility for them with the hope that they are few.

CONTENTS

No.	Dated	Title	Author	Page
1	1935	Cape Cod Byways	Joshua F. Crowell	3
2	1930	The Descendants of John Jenkins	Samuel B. Jenkins	67
3	1928	Plymouth Trading Corporation	Samuel D. Hannah	125
4	1928	Summer Street - Hawes Lane, Yarmouthport	Ellen H. Shields	133
5	1928	The Baker Zone in West Dennis	Sylvanus C. Evans	137
6	1927	Cape Cod Land Titles	Samuel D. Hannah	141
7	1927	Permissive Use of the Common Lands of Proprietary Plantations	Samuel D. Hannah	149
8	1927	"Cast-Up" Lands	Samuel D. Hannah	153
9	1927	The Prince-Howes Court Cupboard	-	157
10	1927	The Cape Type of House	Katherine Crosby	161
11	1925	Shipbuilding at East Dennis	Thomas F. Hall	169
12	1925	The Nye House at Sandwich	Bernard Peterson	179
13	1925	History of Sandwich Glass and the Deming Jarves Book of Designs	Charles Messer Stow	185
14	-	Description of the Farris Windmill in South Yarmouth	Daniel Wing	203
15	1923	William Swift and Descendants to the Sixth Generation	Eben Swift	219
16	-	Old Shipmasters	A. B. C.	289
17	1915	Church Councils	William C. Smith	295
18	1925	Homer	Amos Otis	299
19	1924	The South Dennis Meeting House	William B. Bragdon	303
20	1923	Old Indian Meeting House at Mashpee	-	325
21	1923	The Revolutionary War Service of Nathan Crosby	-	333
22	1923	The Revolutionary War Service of Ansel Taylor	-	337
22a	-	The Oldest Public Library Building in the United States	-	339
23	-	The Geological Formation of Cape Cod	Winthrop Packard	343
24	1922	Fast Runs of Clipper Ships	-	347
25	-	The Romance of a Barnstable Bell	-	353
26	-	Glass-Making in Sandwich	-	357
27	1922	Thomas Foster of Weymouth and His Descendants	Rev. by C. W. Swift	365
28	1917	The Robbins Family of Cape Cod	H. N. Latey	369
29	1917	Bangs Family Papers	-	393
30	1917	Puddington-Purrington-Purinton	Evelyn Rich	415
31	1917	Thomas Howes of Yarmouth, Mass., and Some of His Descendants, together with the Rev. John Mayo, Allied to Him by Marriage	James W. Hawes, Esq.	421
32	1916	Early Settlers of Eastham, Book 2	Josiah Paine	457

CONTENTS

33	1916	Early Settlers of Eastham, Book 1	Josiah Paine	489
34	1916	Nicholas Snow of Eastham and Some of His Descendants, together with Samuel Storrs, Thomas Huckins, Elder John Chipman, and Isaac Wells, Allied to the Snows by Marriage	James W. Hawes	523
35	1915	Edward Kenwrick, the Ancestor of the Kenricks or Kendricks of Barnstable County and Nova Scotia and His Descendants	Joseph Paine	549
36	1915	Early Chatham Settlers	William C. Smith, Esq.	571
37	1915	Stephen and Giles Hopkins, Mayflower Passengers, and Some of Their Descendants, Including an Eldridge Line	James W. Hawes	611
38	1915	Old Quaker Village, South Yarmouth, Massachusetts	E. Lawrence Jenkins	639
39	1915	West Yarmouth Houses Seventy-Five Years Ago, from Parker's River Westward	Daniel Wing	691
40	1914	A Mayflower Line: Hopkins-Snow-Cook	Grace Fielding Hall	713
41	1914	Atwood Genealogy	Grace Fielding Hall	719
42	1914	Newcombe Genealogy	Grace Fielding Hall	725
43	1914	Early Wheldens of Yarmouth	James W. Hawes	731
44	-	Descendants of William Hedge of Yarmouth	-	735
45	1914	Thomas Clarke, the Pilgrim, and His Descendants	Amos Otis	739
46	1914	Burgess	Amos Otis	745
47	1914	The Yarmouth Families of Eldredge	Amos Otis	751
48	1914	Richard Taylor, Tailor, and Some of His Descendants	James W. Hawes	757
49	1914	The Cross Families of Truro and Wellfleet	Shebnah Rich	795
50	1914	The Mayo Family of Truro	Shebnah Rich	801
51	1914	Deacon John Doane and the Doane Family	Hon. Jonn Doane	805
52	1914	A Brief Sketch of the Life of George Webb, a Cape Cod Captain in the Revolutionary War	Josiah Paine	811
53	1914	Genealogical Sketch of Descendants of Jeremiah Howes of Dennis, Mass.	Thomas Prince Howes	823
54	1914	The Lumbert or Lombard Family	Amos Otis	853
55	1914	Eastham and Orleans Historical Papers	Josiah Paine	867
56	1913	Richard Rich of Dover Neck	Shebnah Rich	897
57	1913	John Robinson of Leyden and His Descendants to the Sixth Generation	(John Jenkins)	905
58	1913	The Yarmouth Family of Gray	-	911
59	1913	The Yarmouth Family of Chase	-	915

MAP OF CAPE COD BEFORE 1620.

DESIGNED AND DRAWN FOR THIS BOOK.

REFERENCES.
① Burying Hill, Bournedale.
② Iyanough's Grave.
③ Indian Cemetery.
④ Indian Monument.
⑤ Ancient Graves.

S. L. Deyo, 1890.

(From Simeon L. Deyo, *History of Barnstable County, Massachusetts*)

CAPE COD EARLY TOWN DIVISIONS

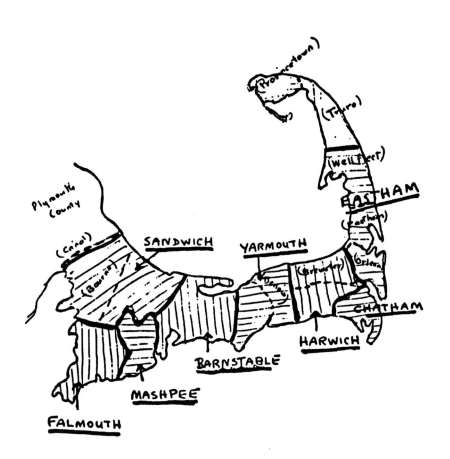

(From Pauline W. Derick, *The Nickerson Family*, Part 1, facing p. 6.)

CAPE COD BYWAYS

by

JOSHUA F. CROWELL

No. 1
Library of Cape Cod History and Genealogy

CAPE COD BYWAYS

by

Joshua F. Crowell

Author of "Garden Wise and Otherwise"

CHARLES W. SWIFT, Publisher
YARMOUTHPORT, MASS.
1920

Cape Cod Byways

As a roamer, who has for many years travelled the By-ways of Cape Cod, formerly a-foot, on horseback, with a one horse chaise, and later with a car; I wish to record a few impressions which may interest others.

Unless so expressed, all the roads mentioned are oiled and end with convenient turns, for I know only too well such adventures as: being stuck in the sand or having to turn on the edge of a marsh-hole, to inflict such upon other people. I will consider first the Safe and Sane Byways, dividing these into Shore-ways and Wood-ways and begin with—

The Shore-ways of Yarmouth

The south side of this town has eleven or more miles of beach with diversified charms.

Beginning at the eastern end of Hyannis we follow Bay View street to Bay View, a town landing provided with convenient parking and turning facilities. Here are extensive views of Lewis Bay and the Inner Bay or Cove, most intriguing at twilight or when the fishing boats come in.

Opposite are the Fish-hills, picturesque at all times, in the mists a Whistler etching, and in the bright sparkle of sun on wave, rising like a Pilgrim Land of Promise.

Across the Inner Bay, loom the buildings of the State College, and below the structure that was once a Yacht Club and now, by some modern magic, converts fish scales into pearls.

Distantly, at the left, is Point Gammon with its outwardly restored old lighthouse, visible in the daytime, yet soulless at night for nearly one hundred years, now a historical and legendary landmark.

The curving By-ways of this locality, called Hyannis Park though a part of Yarmouth, display an ideal location for a summer colony, now well established.

There are several beautiful gardens on Russo street, which has a blind end and requires a hitch or two for a turn, which I have taken a number of times and been amply repaid for the trouble.

Baxter Avenue, the next approach to Lewis Bay, has an extensive outlook over Mill Creek and at the end a narrow Town landing which gives a different overlook to the larger bay. Especially interesting because it is named for a family, once the aristocracy of the Cape, among whose members was Alexander Baxter, first President of the Cape Cod R. R. afterwards the Old Colony R. R. whose mansion, in the high pillared southern style, stood at the beginning of the road, opposite the picturesque Mill Pond; also Sylvester Baxter, a writer of national renown.

Colonial Acres, the next Shoreway, provides sunset views across Mill Creek, at the mouth of which was once located a famous controversial oyster-bed.

Here, at the end of the road, is an extensive view of Lewis Bay, landlocked by the irregular tree-line of that peninsular called Great Island, with its shining band of silver beach, by the yellow-white sands of Egg Island, reservation for gulls, and at the right the approaching almost embracing arm of Dunbar's Point. Below, as foreground, gleams the broad sand-tongue over the dark cut and curve of the rapid waters of the creek.

Near this road, once a cow pasture, now a modern and sophisticated tract of homes, was a bit of lowland, bright with scarlet meadow-lilies in summer, banked with shad and bayberry bushes, which served to hide a clay pit, now a memory only, which for many years supplied the surface material for hardening miles and miles of horse-highway.

It matters not which spot our hearts
    most praise:-
Pocasset to Wood End—along the
    line
The charm comes cooling from all
    creeks and bays,
Laden with salt and healing pine.

Berry Avenue in West Yarmouth, turning at the Old Windmill, leads directly to Englewood. This attractive summer resort, famous for its hotel and its tea-room, has a glamourous past. Looking out over the eastern curve of Lewis Bay to a few power boats and an occasional yacht, how can one realize the greater activity of former days?

At one time forty schooners made this their home-port, and sailed to all parts of the world.

Eighty years ago, to the Porgy factory for extracting oil, on the bluff where fine residences now stand, day after day came the train of heavily loaded dories, from the Menhaden fleet anchored in the bay.

Around the bay the salt-works stood,
    bounded by fields of grain,
A bit of pasture, and the sandy point
    beached about by many a boat
That belonged to the skippers of
    packets
    on the outer roads afloat.
For this was the port of the sailor,
    and vessels to Mobile and Spain
and carried off oil and grain.

On Route 28, in West Yarmouth, the next approach to the water is South Sea Avenue to Point Gammon. South Sea was once the village name, taken from the South Sea of the old sailor charts, now called Nantucket Sound.

This street was known as "The Lane" or "Lasses Lane", and, as the old Captains explained:- "The further down yer go the sweeter th' lasses!" In that age, skippers had big families, and it was not unusual for eighty or more lads and lasses to attend school at one time from The Lane.

Unfortunately, Point Gammon and Great Island are private property, and inaccessible to the general public, but no one should stop short of the sign, "Gate Closed, Turn Here", for the ocean or South Sea is close at hand and in the other direction are views of marsh and island, creek and bay and a western skyline of the church on the hill at Hyannisport.

Toward the south is Pine Island, covered with junipers, a place fortified in the war of 1812, and still showing the ammunition pits.

The Lane had its salt-works. No traces of them remain, nor of that famous Marsh Woods of lofty virgin pine felled for the building of many ships that sailed all seas.

The Shore Ways of Truro

The writer who said Cape Cod has no scenery may have been fresh from the grandeur of Colorado and The Rockies or from the spring flowering of the Carolina Mountains.

Cape Cod is not in competition with any other part of the world, for all who know, also love the bits of beauty on the byways, the varying vistas of creek and marsh, dune and sea, with here and there an old house reposing significantly, and the characteristic warm coloring of the landscape framed by the soft toning of sea and sky.

The Town of Truro is unique. Its one highway suggests, what its several byways prove, that a narrow land of rounded hilltops commands on one side the contours of Cape Cod Bay from Race Point to Manomet, and on the other side the majestic spectacle of the open ocean.

Of its shoreways, the road to Highland Light is most travelled because of the point of vantage of the Light itself, making it the sentinel for incoming craft and reporter of the moods of the ocean, which breaking into lines of foam one hundred and forty feet below the bluff, compels us to think of its other bound on the coast of Spain, three thousand miles away.

Below, from the beach, may be seen the inroads of pounding seas that have formed gullies and cut pinnacles in the side of this mountain of blue clay and marl, which, nevertheless, will remain for a few centuries more, a support to the Light and a barrier to the ocean.

The road in the other direction to Highland Light, across Grozier Square, leads to the North Truro R. R. station, where may be had at all times an excellent view of Provincetown Harbor, at the present time covered with the flotilla of the U. S. Navy.

On turning from this point, Highland Light is seen beyond the village in the valley with its pond bordered by willows, a significant picture of peace.

The Byways of Truro that lead to the Bay are all worthy of exploration, for although they have the same essentials of beauty, they vary in detail with each turn of the road.

Winding around hillsides, close to meadows or marshlands, abounding with cattails where cool creeks curve their way to the sea, through sweeps of bracken or bayberry or banks of glossy bearberry, there are glimpses of blue water through the rifts in the giant dunes, until at last emerging on some hilltop, a superb view of Provincetown Harbor presents itself.

In a progression from North Truro to South Truro, over the Bay-side dunes and the Church-topped hills, the outlook grows larger until it reaches its culmination in the plateau like position behind the abandoned church at South Truro.

From every point of Castle Road, the interest centers about the broad mouth of Pamet River and the peculiar dome of Corn Hill. Closing our eyes to the power boats for a moment, we may visualize the Pamet delta filled with Indian canoes. The name, Corn Hill, recalls its association with the Pilgrims. For a more detailed account of this interesting region and its memorials, there are numerous histories and an excellent and pleasing review of the whole region in Tarbell's Cape Cod Ahoy.

When we regard this landscape, it seems fitting that it was once chosen for a school of gliders.

The Head of Pamet South is a round-about with the Head of Pamet, North, and I recommend to others, what I generally do myself: make a complete circuit in each direction. Here the formal barrier to the ocean is green with bushes and tufts of beach grass but there are wind-torn rifts in the noble dunes with touches of the blue sea beyond.

Lunching on a knoll, by the roadside, where the outlook comprised the winding valley, the dunes and the sea, we were anxiously watched by the cottagers nearby. We threw down no cigarettes, we left behind no scrap of rubbish.

All along the winding ways of Truro, the Cape Cod houses, often as of old, sometimes remodelled into spacious summer homes, nestle under the hills. Occasionally a deep-in-the-valley bit of orchard, recalls the years when fruit exhibited from Truro captured the prizes at the Barnstable County Fair.

The peaceful valley called Longnook with its winding road to the beach, should not be missed by any lover of the Cape. Here are homes, one dated 1710, dooryards with flowers, situated in a charming and intimate valley with sides well clothed with growing green of oak and pine, ending at the ocean barrier of huge grass-topped, fantastic dunes.

And, may I say in the words of Walt Whitman:-

Is it a dream?
No! But the lack of it—a dream!

South Shore Ways of Dennis and Harwich

The Lower County Road from West Dennis to Harwichport parallels the Main Highway, Route 28. Simply to enjoy the bog, marsh, wood and sea views from this road, it is possible to traverse Fisk Street from Main in West Dennis, with a turn to the left at the sign: "To the Beach" and soon enter this coast-wise artery.

If your car must make sixty miles an hour, the whole thing is quickly done and you have missed fifteen or more delightful shoreways.

My mode differs radically, but from the many people, I have, in my way, introduced to these little herring-bone by-ways has come only enthusiasm and acclaim. Shall we go?

From Route 28 we will enter Uncle Barney's Road at the eastern end of Bass River Bridge. Here the water outlook is interesting, and I might hint what is at the end of this road, but that involves ruts and a narrow track, so we turn to the left at Uncle John's Road and soon another left upon Loring Avenue past the Giles Gardens and the next turn to the right gives a comprehensive picture of beautiful Kelley's Pond nestling under its green borders. There is another right turn at Fisk Street which leads in a pleasant but devious way across and around the marshes to The Beach. This, at West Dennis, is typical of all this section, with its open-face, honest spread of ocean and sky, and its generous supply of gleaming white sand.

Through Harwich the bluffs rise gradually and the outlook grows more extensive, but the general characteristics are of a safe, sane, sunny, open approach to the ocean and its benefits.

Alluring names, like Uncle Tinker's Road, Old Mill Point Riding Club, Swampum, Ocean Grove, Sea Street, Chase Avenue, Inman Road, all lead to the shore, but after passing the marshes where Swan River curves in a snake-like course, we choose Ocean Grove as the entrance to the circuitous following of the coast.

Passing Ocean Grove, where children of all ages from one to eighty-one may enjoy the breath of the pines and the touch of the sea, we cross Sea Street, special town byway from Dennisport to the beach, along Raycroft Road with its comfortable cottages, to Chase Avenue, then on and round about the Hotel Belmont.

Go in and out and round about this section as inclination and time allow but do not miss a V-shaped intersection of roads back of the Hotel, which overlooks a beautiful fenced-in garden to the picturesque wind-mill house, with Herring River blue below and the ocean bluer beyond and a skyline of towering and tossing pines.

Now back to the County Road cross Herring River with its charming outlook in either direction. This historic stream figures in legislative controversies as a navigable water

8

way, as a food supply, and has later assumed distinction as a source of fish-scale essence of pearls.

On its eastern bank is an unique settlement, Old Mill Point Club, which was recently pictured from the air in the Boston Evening Transcript.

As we go east from Herring River along the Lower County Road, each sea-way has its own characteristics.

Pleasant Road, with Mrs Phipps cottages, weaves through the pines near the bluff, with full evidence of the ever restless waves and that long silent, shining bar called Monomoy.

The shore roads named Grey Neck, Mirasol, Brooks, Wequasset, Hiawatha, all invite exploration.

When we have passed the neat, little, quiet cove of Allen's Harbor, with its boats and sea-horses, and noted the sweep of ocean beyond, oftentimes ridden by the wild sea-horses of Matthew Arnold's poem, we come to Wyndemere Bluffs, and the fun begins.

This portion of Harwichport is a checkerboard of narrow streets, some verging to the sea with a turn, others without a turn, a few crossing. Years ago, this was a campground, which could not have been a happier place than it is now, with its small cottages, side by side, close to the narrow driveways, under rustling trees, with everywhere a touch of the sea, expressed somewhat by the names over the doors, such as:—

    Shoreholm and Beachome
    Oceanside and Windelblo

Sea Gull and Sea Shell Soundings and Sunsetview

While we are playing pawn upon the checkerboard, as we move toward the east, we note a gradual increase in tone until we reach the pitch of larger comfort and even elegance.

As we wind about Satucket Road and Quason Lane, we come upon Flake-yard Road, and immediately a vision rises of that old industry of salting and drying fish that flourished here, and that furnished a livelihood for many a Cape Codder and a product called Cape Cod Turkey (Salt Cod) for the multitude.

In its place, we now have gardens and cottages of generous proportions, especially pleasing because of the nearness to the sea. We reluctantly leave the checkerboard, taking with us a delightful memory of a manse by the way, like a Quaker maiden in robes of grey, deserting the faith of her fathers for orange-pink decorations.

Ayer Lane returns us to Route 28 and Harwichport. Immediately at the right is Pilgrim Road, which, to take or not to take, I must leave to your better judgment. It is short, bordered on either side by cottages with very attractive dooryards and gardens, but at the end is the sea-edge and a fiendish heap of sand. I have accomplished a turn here many times in a narrow space between two fences but a long apprenticeship with many worse byways has compelled me to be an adept at half-hitching.

9

Harwichport has no more attractive feature than Wychmere Harbor, just a little jog-in of the ocean making a cosy mooring-place for pleasure boats. All around this bay used to be a race-track, where an older generation speeded their horses for a sweepstakes of fifty bushels of oats. Explore Wychmere Pines, Neel Road, if you wish, but if you prefer an uncultivated and unspoiled tangle of swamp and woodland take Julien Road and at the end turn left into Deep Hole Road which returns to Route 28.

We are in South Harwich now, near the locality that produced that sturdy character, Captain Jonathan Walker, the first slave liberator; afterward he became a personal friend of William Lloyd Garrison. The house where Captain Walker was born was moved to South Chatham.

Our grandfathers had a habit of moving their homes about by means of a number of yokes of oxen and rollers of unsplittable hornbeam, and sometimes they moved them over from Nantucket on schooners.

We come to the last south shore way of Harwich, Uncle Venie's Road, which features a number of rather fine summer homes and a beautiful pond.

We get varying impressions of Monomoy from points along the Harwich shore. If the day is clear and the ocean sparkling, the reality of that gleaming bar seems a mirage.

But we know that wraith of beauty becomes a terrible menace when the fog arises or as the Indians phrase it "When Giant Maushope smokes his pipe."

Around Wellfleet

As we enter Wellfleet from Eastham, we pass several sandy roads on the left that invite exploration by their names, such as, Private Way to the Ornithological Experimental Station, Four Winds, Cannon Hill, etc.; but our first essay will be Pleasant Point Road past a pond framed in rushes to the left through orderly pines to several pleasant points of view over the southern portion of the harbor, one point of such pretentions it might be called magnificent.

After the watch tower we find Spring Valley Road to Indian Neck where from across the harbor we catch our first glimpse of Wellfleet village, a hillside crescent of houses above a bay bounded by dazzling dunes, like a picture cluster of jewels set in a silver ring, centered with the blue depths of water, and resting in the velveting green of the forest beyond.

This oneness of Wellfleet and its harbor is seen from several angles and elevations from Nauhaugh Bluffs and other byways.

We soon realize that the little town of historical old houses and old willows, clustered around the hill, topped with the somewhat oriental tower of the church, ruling over the fair harbor with its protecting arm of silvery dunes and islands has been for generations, the homeport for the sailor:- for the oysterman, the fisherman, the whaler.

We recall the fact that at one time this old town was more famous than Nantucket or even New Bedford for its fleet of whaling vessels that sailed the seven seas.

The thousands that skim through this town every summer on the highway, have no idea of the historical and picturesque attractions of the by-ways.

Around the village and its shores there is a general impression of boats and boating, lobster-pots and bathing beaches, marshy valleys and sandy bluffs, distant dunes and Cape Cod Bay beyond.

We found the old hotel built out over the tide with its corner clipped by last winter's ice, a tiny lily pond in the midst of the dunes, a little valley village by itself, with weeping willows along the way, ending in a real old fashioned farm, and on the road to the Choquesset Golf Club a splendid outlook.

The town itself is full of old houses and old willows, both evidently treasured from the past. One very old, large, double Cape Cod House, memorable for its simplicity and strength and its opposite, a rather quaint octagonal structure belonging to a more ornate generation.

We leave reluctantly and find Pamet Point Road to Bound Brook Island, pleasant woodsy way leading to the Truro line which we could pursue into the highlands of South Truro and its generous outlook, but we turn back to Wellfleet, content with the vivid picture of an old white horse standing in the doorway of a red barn, framed with green foliage.

On the way back we take Gull Pond Road, note the many varieties of fine trees, locusts especially, look down and over the pond as we circle it, and see through the dunes the wonderful blue of the Atlantic.

On Cahoon's Hollow Road, we find a similar overlook of a pond, but a broader and closer touch with the ocean as we approach the famous Coast Guard Station.

Of the history of its name, of the first wireless station, of the blackfish that sometimes infest its sands, of the sturdy seamen themselves who made the place, and other matters I have not time to speak, for all who go to Wellfleet with open eyes will see answers written in the town itself.

Yarmouthport

South Shore Ways of Barnstable

Hyannis, Hyannisport, Craigville, Centerville, Osterville, Wianno and Cotuit are familiar names to natives of the Cape and to thousands of visitors, yet I am constantly finding people of both classes who have missed certain points of interest or beauty.

By taking Lewis Bay Road at Park Square in Hyannis, we approach the most picturesque overlook of the harbor. Irregular contours of shore and fish-hills surround the inner bay crowded with boats, with the ocean gleaming beyond, all touched with different light and color every hour of the day and every day of the year.

Along South Street, there are delightful vignettes of water and sky at the foot of School and Pleasant Streets, and turning left at Ocean Street we may sometimes visualize a superb etching of the harbor fringed with the silver tracery of masts and sails of fishing boats and drying nets against the sepia of descending twilight.

You may choose the bright daylight aspect of the same harbor, gay with colorful bathers, yachts and flags.

Old Harbor Road is sandy or gritty, but acceptable for a harbor-front view of the town and a very brief but actual close touch with the sea.

Beyond the tent houses of the Teachers College, at the left is the new town park, where the view is a complete panorama of Lewis Bay shores from Hyannis Park to the old Point Gammon Light.

From Gosnold Street we may take the sand road to the tip of Dunbar's Point or dip into the pleasant little colony on Hawes Avenue, or a little farther along take Harbor Road to the blue-roofed lighthouse.

Here are traces of the railroad where trains ran to the wharf to connect with boats for the Vineyard and Nantucket.

At Sea Street we follow the coast line around the marshes and as we will through Hyannisport, not neglecting Sunset Hill and its commanding view of winding creeks, deep green marshes and the sweep of ocean graphically limited by the headlands of Wianno and Popponesset and Martha's Vineyard.

Hyannisport is debonnair;
For sea and season place aright,
With pleasing features that invite
The restless world to loiter there.
True named, for wanderers, free of care,
Find you safe harbor, day or night, Hyannisport!
Now, for the ozone in the air,
For beauties seen in sunset light,
For all of summer's keen delight,
Few places with you can compare, Hyannisport!

Before leaving Sunset (or Sunrise) Hill at Hyannisport begin the fascinating game of locating The Vineyard, which may be played on every shore-way from here to the tip of Woods Hole. At night, fifteen miles

13

out beyond the rocks where the seals play, may be seen each thirty seconds, the powerful flash of light from the famous Cross Rip Lightship.

On the road to Craigville, First and Third Avenues of West Hyannisport present certain attractive features of pineland, creek and meadow.

The real Craigville is not the Beach but a sequestered hamlet situated on a well wooded ridge overlooking toward the east, two lovely ponds, and on the west, emerald salt meadows cut by curving creeks, spreading to the pines at the north, to the ocean at the south.

By taking the road at the right through the pines as we approach Craigville, and crossing the bridge between the two ponds, one famous as the source of the original pink water-lily, we may walk the Midway and stand a moment on the bluff absorbing the significance of the place and its individual charm. Craigville Beach was once but is not now a part of this secluded and peaceful retreat.

This beach, seen on a Sunday afternoon in August presents an overwhelming kaleidoscope of color and motion. In contrast, last winter, it was a spectacle of transcendent beauty, with its crescent of pure white sand clasping a silent ocean of alabaster.

Long Beach astonishes the casual visitor with the great number of fine spacious residences crowded into so small an area.

On the curve over the marshes toward Centerville at the left is a beautiful thicket of tupelo trees, not unlike hornbeam in their lateral growth. In spring they make a pastel of lacey branches blooming a dove-colored mist, in autumn they flare with deep but brilliant red.

Through Centerville to Osterville there are glimpses of the ocean, none more compelling than from the bridge over Bump's River, where one is reminded of places in Florida on the Halifax river.

The road by East Bay through Wianno to the very end where Oyster Harbors can be seen is too well known for detailed description, as is also Eel River Road to the West Bay where may be visited the Crosby Boathouses, where the famous cat boat originated or where one may cross over to Oyster Harbors for a circuit of that extensive and exclusive colony.

On returning from Wianno by the West Bay at the left near the highway is Bay Street, partly a shell road leading to a waterside knoll, where spread before us are the Crosby watercraft with a picturesque backing of boatshops, drawbridge and the shores of Little Oyster Island. An interesting and satisfactory marine view.

Saint Mary's Island and the Sepuit Golf Links afford delightful glimpses of the same bay. I have often wondered why the purveyors of Golf Links on the Cape preempt the choicest bits of scenery. Possibly to give inspiration or at least solace to those who follow the ball.

At Marstons Mills is a dirt road,

Prince Avenue, with a few houses, masses of Joe Pye, Meadow Rue and tall grasses adorning the swamps and a creek curling out to the sea.

On the way to Cotuit we pass the Old Post Road and take Little River Road instead, which threads its white shelled surface through the pines, edged with tall white sweet-clover and ends on the inner Oyster Bay at the fish houses opposite the hotel and residences of Oyster Harbors. Going back, we turn into the Old Post Road, pass the turkey farm and reach the very pleasant village of Cotuit.

Near the red houses of the Lowell Farm is a leafy shaded lane that I have long desired to explore but never have, and now I think it is enough to remember it always as a delightful picture.

Through the town to the bathing beach we pass many fine homes to one, cresting a slope of ocean bank, which by its position mostly, recalls Mount Vernon.

We go on, taking a sharp left turn through the Highlands, past an attractive garden of iris and hedges, across the swamp lands with pools of lilies surrounded by rushes and tussocks of dainty white flag, along the inland water way, where above the silver sand is the blue ocean gleaming beyond the feathering pines.

The Barnstable South Shore does not end here but the good road does, and we must wait for the finish until this byway is continued around Popponessett Bay or bridged to the Mashpee shore.

North Shore Ways of Barnstable

The village of Barnstable, with its abundance of stone walls winding along above a rock-ridged foundation, commands an outlook unique in character and unexcelled in beauty. Sandy Neck, seven miles of irregular glistening dunes forming a giant protecting arm, gives the bay within a distinction and charm which can only be measured by frequent visits with varying tide, cloud, sun and seasonable effects.

One space along the highway presents a beatiful picture, signifying that the few but choice approaches to Barnstable Bay will amply repay investigation.

Of these approaches, beginning at the Yarmouth end of the highway through Barnstable, Keveney Lane is rural and picturesque, Indian Trail compelling but almost too narrow for comfort and Commerce Road has advantages not to be denied. Besides the fact it is a fishing village as the signs at the sandy lanes disclose with gleaming touches of bay and dune in the distance it is primarily a long curving sweep around the edge of thicket, swamp growth, marshes and creek.

Pausing at the bridge over the creek, with the storage plant opposite, we try to locate the ship-yards of the older days, a leading industry here as well as in several other localities on the Cape.

Rendezvous Lane pleasantly meanders to a broad but intimate pastel of bay, dune and lighthouse.

Scudder Lane, taken slowly with frequent stops, gives many comprehensive and enthralling vistas of green fields sloping down to the rock-edged but placid bay, landlocked with silver dunes, and the long crescent of the Cape coast pencilled into the distance.

Through West Barnstable, across the Great Marshes spreads the influence of that great beneficent bar.

Knowing that only from the top of Scorton Hill can we complete the panorama, we turn to the left opposite the Great Marshes, and another left turn into a sandy but easy ascent and soon find our horizon enlarged to include not only extensive stretches of countryside on the one hand but on the other an almost unlimited prospect of colorful meadow

The pearl white sands,
The fields and marshes of a thousand tints,
Yield no tones that are crude or harsh,
But wield enchantment; while the creeks and bays
Mirror a blue, that only the fairest skies hold true.

Flowering Waysides in September

Now is the time to seek color from flowering fields, roadsides, swamps and marshes.

Mallows in pomegranate, pink and white, bordering the highway through Sandwich, have delighted thousands.

Asters and Michaelmas Daisies spread lavender, purple and white along woodland ways and across fields. The bright golden stars of the dwarf variety dot the dryer places.

Goldenrod is everywhere, the tall plumed variety especially transforming the ditching across the marshes.

Sea-lavender or Marsh-rosemary delicately colors many a marsh corner.

Blueberry leaves are reddening the swamps and woods.

The Ailanthus or Tree-of-Heaven is showing its great tawny-pink fluffs of bloom in many places, noteworthy along the mill-brook Road in Brewster.

Viburnums are heavily loaded with their clusters of dark slate-colored berries, profusely along the Thacher Road.

For one locality of great variety and interest, I have chosen the Weir Road at the eastern section of Yarmouth on the highway to Dennis. After a brief oiled surface, the lower or left sandy fork soon leads a winding way of enchantment.

Here the climbing False Buckwheat trails over shrubs and trees like threads strung with greenish-white three-cornered sequins, showing its cousinship to the cultivated Fleece or Lace Vine.

Along this bountiful byway may be found:- the yellow-buttoned Tansy, white tipped Snakeroot, curious wild Lettuce, tall spikes of purpled Liatris or Blazing-star often mistaken for thistle, and the similar but branching Ironwood, which is even more thistle-like; pink Ragged-sailor with the heart or arrowhead stamped on its leaf, silvery Everlasting, lacey Wild-carrot, Bouncing Bet, Poke Berry with its distinctive purple arching stems of glossy black berries, tall nodding pale Evening Primroses, and on the edges of the bogs thick masses of colorful Joe Pye Weed and a few greyish-white panicles of bitter Thoroughwort or Boneset.

Here as elsewhere the Staghorn Sumach pushes up its deep red pyramids of bloom and the Tupelos with spreading lateral arms are unfurling banners of color.

We note:- dainty white or pink Sand-knotweed, charming blue Chicory, pale yellow Butter-and-eggs, wild Mustard, Bindweed or wild morning-glory, tall seedpods of Meadow Rue and those of the sepia colored Marsh-dock, an occasional Silverrod, some escaped Honeysuckle in bloom, and a few late Clethera or Sweet Pepper-bush.

Jewel-weed dangles a profusion of dainty golden eardrops, not only here but around the very center of Sandwich and other villages wherever it may find a place for wet feet.

the bay within the elbow of the Cape.

After the bridge over the creek, in the very midst of salt marshes, we pass several square, flat-topped houses built by the captains of an older age, who brought home some memory of foreign architecture.

This whole land is replete with associations of the past and never fails to awaken new interest.

Wellfleet

Flowering Waysides in September

Now is the time to seek color from flowering fields, roadsides, swamps and marshes.

Mallows in pomegranate, pink and white, bordering the highway through Sandwich, have delighted thousands.

Asters and Michaelmas Daisies spread lavender, purple and white along woodland ways and across fields. The bright golden stars of the dwarf variety dot the dryer places.

Goldenrod is everywhere, the tall plumed variety especially transforming the ditching across the marshes.

Sea-lavender or Marsh-rosemary delicately colors many a marsh corner.

Blueberry leaves are reddening the swamps and woods.

The Ailanthus or Tree-of-Heaven is showing its great tawny-pink fluffs of bloom in many places, noteworthy along the mill-brook Road in Brewster.

Viburnums are heavily loaded with their clusters of dark slate-colored berries, profusely along the Thacher Road.

For one locality of great variety and interest, I have chosen the Weir Road at the eastern section of Yarmouth on the highway to Dennis. After a brief oiled surface, the lower or left sandy fork soon leads a winding way of enchantment.

Here the climbing False Buckwheat trails over shrubs and trees like threads strung with greenish-white three-cornered sequins, showing its cousinship to the cultivated Fleece or Lace Vine.

Along this bountiful byway may be found:- the yellow-buttoned Tansy, white tipped Snakeroot, curious wild Lettuce, tall spikes of purpled Liatris or Blazing-star often mistaken for thistle, and the similar but branching Ironwood, which is even more thistle-like; pink Ragged-sailor with the heart or arrowhead stamped on its leaf, silvery Everlasting, lacey Wild-carrot, Bouncing Bet, Poke Berry with its distinctive purple arching stems of glossy black berries, tall nodding pale Evening Primroses, and on the edges of the bogs thick masses of colorful Joe Pye Weed and a few greyish-white panicles of bitter Thoroughwort or Boneset.

Here as elsewhere the Staghorn Sumach pushes up its deep red pyramids of bloom and the Tupelos with spreading lateral arms are unfurling banners of color.

We note:- dainty white or pink Sand-knotweed, charming blue Chicory, pale yellow Butter-and-eggs, wild Mustard, Bindweed or wild morning-glory, tall seedpods of Meadow Rue and those of the sepia colored Marsh-dock, an occasional Silverrod, some escaped Honeysuckle in bloom, and a few late Clethera or Sweet Pepper-bush.

Jewel-weed dangles a profusion of dainty golden eardrops, not only here but around the very center of Sandwich and other villages wherever it may find a place for wet feet.

19

Here is a small portion of the many miles of sturdy Cattails, tall brown Reeds and Grasses that abound on the Cape.

Several of the bogs display patches or stretches of a flower gloriously yellow, reminding us of the Coreopsis of early summer fields; this is the Burr Marigold, one of that strange family of Begger-ticks that at seed time steal a ride by hooking into anything that passes.

At this season, not only Yarmouth, but every town has its flowering byway. However, not all is beauty, the evil Ragweed is in our midst with its menace to health, despoiler of our roadsides, and should be destroyed.

Hallet St., Yarmouthport

Wood Ways around Wakeby

From Marstons Mills continue west on Route 28 to the light at the Tavern in the Town, where on the lawn ofttimes posed a lady of ancient regime.

The right fork here leads into Mashpee past the beautiful Southern-style Mansion, through the lowly village of the dusky races to the right turn marked Wakeby.

This and other ways will soon be showing the gorgeous oak coloring, while even now reddening maples and tupelos are in evidence and the five-leaf woodbine and the three-leaf poison-ivy bright with color. If you are tempted to pick, beware the three-divided leaf.

On this road, we pass Santuit Lake with its development, and soon at the left across a cranberry-bog is charming Wakeby showing its wooded island and placid waters, seen from several angles as we move along.

A few years ago, at a point close to the lake, now a private way, at sunset, I stood with my uncle, Captain Thomas F. Hall of East Dennis and Omaha, recalling the association of two famous fishermen, President Cleveland and Joseph Jefferson, with this lake, when a white heron (Egret) slowly arose from the bank and glided across our vision, and we both remembered that Swift's History of Cape Cod has noted the fact that this bird, common enough in Florida and occasionally seen farther north, had been at home for many years at Wakeby.

On this oiled road, near the northern end of the lake we turn to the left into a sandy lane which allows us glimpses of the water from a higher level and leads us into another land.

Here are shallow dingles of white birches, deep dales of mingled oak and maple, deepened with dark masses of holly and made distinctive by the number of smooth-barked beeches all closely carpeted with fern and sarsaparilla.

The road winds, dips down suddenly into a vale, and after many a deliberate curve ending with a miniature Ashtabula Cut, passes Ascension Pond, with its well wooded banks, known on the old maps as Pimlico Pond.

We pass the bent-knees in stumps of growing trees formerly used as boundaries and come to Forestdale on the Mashpee-Sandwich highway. We may cross here into the Pocasset road, nearly opposite for a survey of Snake Pond, a picturesque bit a mile or so west of Forestdale.

To complete the tour of Wakeby return on the Forestdale road toward Mashpee, where we may catch a glimpse of the west side from the highway, or approach that lower part of the same water known as Mashpee Pond. Here are boat houses and the means of pursuing the delightful study of this sheet of water and its islands without, or with rod and line a la Jefferson and Cleveland.

21

Some Mid-Cape Woods Ways

East of Yarmouth on Route 6, enter the oiled road marked Mayfair to begin a woodsy circuit of four or five towns. Soon, on the right, is a distant view of Follen's Pond or Head-waters of Bass River. For a time, omitting Mayfair and its alluring situation on Follen's, we follow the left fork, cross Route 134 (South Dennis to East Dennis) and just beyond the Brewster line turn left and soon back into Dennis again, follow down the wandering valley among picturesque Devonshire hills, by a pastel of leafy-banked pond and icehouse, through colorful swamps; then, with Quivet Neck and the churchspire of East Dennis straight ahead, turn to right upon Route 6 as it crosses the extensive bogs and swamps where "Cape Cod Color Never Dies".

Very soon we take the right hand road up over the hills crowned with a few old houses, one the "Packet", and many stone walls, which somewhat interrept but also add to many charming views of rolling landscape, with the blue of Cape Cod Bay beyond, the white outline of the Cape itself, especially the great dunes outside Wellfleet Harbor, and often the shaft of the Pilgrim Monument, like a lone grey sentinel of the sea.

Along this road Locusts abound, many stately Alanthus bloom, as truly the Tree-of-heaven should and in the midst of little hills laced with stone walls, we dip down into the valley of Factory Village, as it was called in the old days.

Here is the bridge over Stony Brook, age old willows, and a water wheel to remind us of an earlier and more primitive one. Here in the spring the herring run in myriads against the rapids, where years ago another activity existed, manufacturing, with five mills making woolen goods and leather and copper products.

The ancient house, buttressed against the wall of stone, yellow with lichens, edged with ferns, and topped in spring with overflowing lilacs,—this house or its forerunner, was the Inn of stage coach days, once entertaining Charles Sumner.

Before this road reaches Route 6, one of the seven ponds that feed the mill stream is seen. We touch the highway briefly, for on Breezy Hill is Tubman road to explore.

Here we find more locusts and stone walls with rocky pastures and an asparagus farm before we cross Route 24 (Pleasant Lake road) and after that many silver-leafed poplars. When they show white, is a sign of rain.

On Route 24, by the Brewster Railroad station, we see over the rolling hills at the right the Long Pond part of Pleasant Lake region, but we stop at the roadside where the ravine shows on the right, for here at the left is the deepest sink hole of the glacial age on Cape Cod, shown on the old maps as No Bottom Pond.

Farther on, beyond the lawn so large and immaculately shorn, the road winds between two plashes or low ponds as we cross the town line into Harwich. Soon we reach the cross roads; shall we continue straight ahead on Route 25 into East Harwich and Harwich Center and the wood ways beyond, or turn to the left into the road that leads to Pleasant Bay and either Orleans or Chatham?

If you cannot make a choice, wait at the crossroads for me to lead the way.

All those left last week at the all-woods crossroads on Route 25 between Brewster and East Harwich, will, I hope, be ready to continue in the way I have planned.

Please leave Route 25 by turning left in order to reach the north end of East Harwich where a right turn leads to the workshop of a true artist, the bird carver, A. E. Crowell.

This second stretch of three sides of a rectangle which composes this village shows a picturesque stream and weir in the valley before we come out by the church where there is another turn right along the village street high above a pond or two, then stretches of woods with a pond and a plash to Harwich Center. This plash, and others at this season, are bordered with a peculiar glow of reddish or pinkish leaves from a plant belonging to the loosestrife family.

The central village of Harwich is little known to the users of Routes 6 and 28. It has a number of interesting features: A tree bordered public park for ball games and band concerts, a free Public Library which contains an unusual, almost complete collection of the historical and fanciful Roger's Groups; a homestead set with yellow weeping willows, glorious in spring; an engraved stone, souvenir from Harwich, England, set in the sidewalk before the tall Exchange Building, and a Christopher Wren Church spire.

Shall we go straight through this village, cross the bridge over the R. R. track and on to North Harwich, regaled with glimpses of cranberry bogs, and of small members of dusky families that labor on them, both of which abound in this region?

At North Harwich crossroad, take left before the ancient cemetery, on across the R. R. track at the N. H. station and the town line into Dennis. We are attracted by Swan Lake and its islands, a beauty spot not yet overcrowded.

Just a block before Route 28 at Dennisport we turn right into a parallel back road and cross Swan River, where, as at many other bridges, whole families are lined up for fishing or crabbing.

Entering South Dennis from this direction, take the left fork, cross Route 134 to the toll bridge or upper bridge over Bass River, which marks a picturesque bend as it widens out below into a bay and a cove.

As we go on, Bass River continues to display its charming contours, and if we wish to complete the panorama, a turn into the golf links to the club house and a short walk, with or without a golf club will be worth while.

Entering South Yarmouth by this route we pass the old Quaker Meet-

ing-house with its severely simple burial ground and I am reminded of many sweet and gentle characters of long ago, of whom I might say:
The heart of truth beats not upon the street,
Nor in a war-mad nation's strife;
But in such simple schemes of life,
As tune the worship of the eager soul
To strains of nature, soft and sweet!

Seasonable Comments — Autumn

Swamps are vivid, bogs and meadows glowing with yellow, brown and even scarlet, and woodways reaching new notes of intensity every day.

Once more the generous autumn
Has painted earth with joy,
And color's eager ecstasies
The woods and fields employ!

All ways are attractive, and highways compete with byways. Swamp and red maples vie with stag-horn sumac and the oaks are beginning their winter-long story of color but at the moment the tupelos hold first rank.

Because of their lateral branching and similarity in structure to the hornbeam all the older residents and not a few younger ones consider them as hornbeams. As a matter of fact, analysis of their fruit, shows them to be the tupelo or sour-gum of the middle south, well established here, one more proof of the mildness of this climate.

The wood of the two varieties has the same characteristics of long, smooth, tough fiber, useful in the making of rollers, hubs of wheels, etc.

By whatever name known, its beauty is unexcelled at this season. With its peculiar outspreading growth of right-angular branches, covered with foliage varying from clear brilliant red to deep toned mixtures of maroon, green and purple, it is the outstanding feature of many localities.

Among these I note three: On the road from Craigville Beach to Centerville, just before entering the village, the sweep around the marsh to the left; crossing Parker's River in West Yarmouth, and along the swamps back of the Great Marshes of Barnstable and Sandwich.

Other delights for the eye include the many marshes being touched with scarlet or purple shades of the samphire, and highways and byways alike dominated by the soft indescribable coloring of that abundant and feathery grass, which appears at one time yellow and even orange, at another time pink or red, and even when undetermined is always a symphony of color.

Beyond the glowing meadows
Crimson flames arise;
A pageantry of fantasies
Against untroubled skies.

Woodways and Ponds

While all the wood-ways are a riot of color, the natural beauties of lake and pond are abundantly enhanced. A difficulty arises; of the three hundred odd inland water gems of Cape Cod, which to select for the moment. The temptation is to try: ride, ride from morn to night, day after day and view them every one. Time interposes, as always. As first choice, there are the South Sandwich ponds, fully rewarding at any season.

Lawrence Pond may be approached variously, but to enjoy its aspect fully, I prefer to take the West Barnstable-Marstons Mills road, Route 49, and enter the sandy lane at the north side of the historical old church of West Barnstable. We follow an enchanting winding way of leafy forest, which by avoiding any sharp turns, leads to the eastern and longer side of Lawrence pond, a name marking the early association of that family with this region.

A map of 1850 shows here houses and farms with such familiar Cape names as: Crocker, Percival, Stevens, Jones and quite a number of Meigs. Skirting this pond with a view across to the well wooded hills beyond, the oiled surface of Race Lane is soon reached. We follow west with a parting glance at the Lawrence stretched lengthwise, on to the pathetic fragments of a former village, including an abandoned district school building, a tiny ancient cemetery on the roadside, and a few old houses.

Across the fields towards the south is a little gem of a pond with buildings massed among old trees beyond, making a perfect picture of the old Cape Cod. If this pond has a name, and is one of the two with porcine titles, (Upper Hog and Lower Hog) it shall still remain beautiful but nameless to me.

Triangle pond is most interesting. After passing Lakewood Camp, a historic hostelry, noted for its abundant hospitality and long line of famous names included among its guests, we begin to catch glimpses of this picturesque sheet of water and by continuing on the road provided around it, varying prospects from different levels furnish a clearer understanding of its peculiar and intimate charm. Camps and fine cottages are finding this locality.

For full enjoyment of any byway it should be retraced in the opposite direction. I can particularly recommend a complete circuit of Triangle pond in both directions.

Peter's Pond in Farmersville or South Sandwich.

Continuing from Lakewood Camps on the extension of Race Lane to the road sign of Wakeby we are confronted with a wide spreading field of formerly cleared land and buildings of an abandoned farm. Across this field, on the banks of the pond, at times arise the tents of a soldiers' summer camp. At this point of vantage, a long deep grassy slope, strewn with violets in the spring, bends to the dark waters below which

25

reflect from the opposite shore the intense green of the pines at all times and the changing colors of the oak in the fall.

Shawme Pond! Not only the well known delightful prospect as seen from the center of Sandwich village, but another and finer one. Passing from the Farmersville road into the Forestdale-Sandwich road Route 130 along the great Shawme forest, we see not only picturesque ravine and hill formation, so often fire swept in the past, but also evidence of recent road construction for fire prevention by the C. C. C. When these up-hill and down-dale roads are completed they will add not only to the safety but to the scenic development of the Cape.

Just after a glimpse of Cape Cod Bay and the Plymouth shore from a curve in the road and before entering the village, is Shawme road at the left leading over the hills around Shawme pond. Here is a touch of the tall wild forest mingled with shrubby slopes and vine tangled dales, until almost without premonition we stop suddenly at the perfect picture. Far below lies the blue shimmer of Shawme reflecting the village clustered about the church with the beautiful Christopher Wren spire and the broad bay beyond for background.

If we can leave this spot, as we go on we realize we are passing the hills and leas of the Dexter estate, famous for its extensive plantings of azalea, laurel and rhododendron.

Across the waters of Shawme soon the white spire is pictured more intimately. It is an ancient inspiration of beauty arresting and holding the attention of this modern but distracted age.

Pleasant Lake, between Harwich and Brewster on Route 24 is so obvious on every map, and so accessible, it should be known to every visitor. Evidently not, for I sometimes hear remarks like this: "Cranberry bogs! Where are they? I go up and down the Cape and never see one!"

Probably the art of not seeing things, or not knowing them when seen, has been unduly developed by the motor vehicle.

To all cranberry bog inquiring minds I recommend Route 24, where three large lakes cluster, Bangs pond and Pleasant Lake toward the west and Long pond to the east, bounded and bordered by the oriental carpets of the cranberry, and the highway tangles itself with the railroad, presenting certain aspects of beauty to careful drivers.

An interesting seasonable feature is the turkey farm on the banks of Long pond, where the big birds proudly strut all day long, or run in battalions at feeding time, hiding their heads in the bushes when a plane goes over, and seeking the tall trees or roosts at night, often making a somewhat symphonic music with a thousand gobbles.

Other seasonable features here are a field of Japanese Iris abloom in summer, and one of the earliest plantings of trailing roses on a bank to which year after year we made a special visit in the days before Cape Cod became so remarkably the home of ramblers.

All along this woodway, now, as at all times, the oaks are telling a part of their year-long story of color.

Ashumet Lake

South of Forestdale on Route 130 is a pleasant woodway to Hatchville, via Ashumet. Along here, wonderful giant goldenrod has been covering the devastation caused by forest fires and now new growth is green with promise. Great oaks, marvellously bent for boundary purposes border the roadbed which is mostly excellent, except when we take the left or worst turn at the fork and purposely choose to "shimmy" around Ashumet, so as not to miss any of this "Smiling Water" of the Mashpees, or the little old house on its own green pastured point and farther on the big farm with fields of golden pumpkins and nursery plants.

Here turn toward Hatchville, on a bit of stony or gritty road, soon covered; straight ahead at crossroads by the golf links and fire gutted greenhouse, polo field, and delightfully situated club-house to

Coonemesset Lake

With its foreground of cranberry bog and bushy ravine and background of forest, this inland gem dominates the locality, being the very core of that farm land formerly known as the largest east of the Mississippi, and of all the present day dairying features of cows, barns and pastures.

At Braeburn Farms' corner, follow Waquoit road with Deep Pond close by, but unseen, past St Armand estate of the prize Guernsey fame and exclaim at the quantity of little undressed pines (untrimmed by trimming). Good English, all the same!

Crooked Pond and its poultry farm, we pass, and Kensington Farms and Pine Knot Camp are on the way to the old Congregational Church of East Falmouth dating from 1796 with its simple dignified lines and twenty-four-small-paned windows.

From here we wind our way to Route 28 by left turns, passing a gentle side-hill effect, a meandering brook widening into a pond and extensive bogs, details which furnish so little pleasure to the reader and so much to the observer.

Wequaket (or Chequaquet) Lake.

There seems to be some confusion in the name of this big pond, called Ninemile Pond by our fathers and Iyanough Lake by our great-grandfathers in honor of that gentle and courteous Indian Sachem. On the map distributed by the Cape Cod Chamber of Commerce, it appears Chequaquet and on the margin of the same Wequaquet; showing how easily the Indian meaning is lost: Che— We— utterly different to the red man, all the same to the white.

Now the nine miles around is a pleasant short diversion with an automobile over the same ways that made a long tiresome day's journey in an ox-cart.

From Routes 28 or 132 or from Phinney's Lane there are easy approaches over modernized dust roads contrasting vividly with the deep rut-tracks used by an older generation, who, not liking the feel of the ocean on their bodies, or memories of disasters from its winds whistling in their ears, built their summer camps on Nine-mile Pond for relaxation from the social activities of Hyannis. The larger cottages and hotel of the present day attest to its continued popularity.

Well known to the Indians was Shoot-flying Hill, named by the duck-hunters, which, from its fire tower affords a commanding view of this lake, the stretch of the Cape to the east and north and the spread to the west and of all the waters about it. Not the highest point (220 ft), Bourne Hill (280 ft) having that distinction, but one of the three high spots of the Cape, and according to legendary lore, one of the footholds of his Satanic Majesty as he stepped from knoll to knoll and spilled an apronful of boulders in Pocasset woods and dribbles of rock all along the ridges to Scargo. For proof search the top of Shoot-flying Hill for the triangular imprint of his hoof in the stone, and when found, refuse to believe in tales of the prehistoric dinasaurus.

Mystic Lake. The Cotuit ponds lie nestling among the hills as if transported magically from Scottish scenery to Cape Cod

Clear Lake or Hamblin's pond, the companion of Mystic, may be seen gleaming through the trees along the road from Marstons Mills to West Barnstable, Route 49.

But Mystic itself will be most enjoyed from Race Lane, just west of the aviation field.

From the bridge built over a six foot viaduct for the exclusive use of cows on their way to drink, we look along down the grassy slope to the foreground vividly outlined by evergreens, the irregular middle-distance and the mysterious far-away of a charming lake.

At sunrise, at sunset, by sunlight or moonlight, in mist or in rain, it rests in beauty like a special gift from Nature's bounty.

It is no wonder that years ago, some one with Scott's Lady of the Lake in mind, named its beautiful island, Ellen's Isle. A little further along, the road approaches the sandy edge and the wider expanse of this sheet of water, and beyond that is a smaller companion pond which has a remarkable border of glowing pink from the fall loosestrife leaves; but we go back to the focal point of the Mystic view and stand where we have stood many times before and watch the blue depths touched with light and shadow.

John's Pond. The Indian town of Mashpee is favored with several good-sized attractive lakes, Santuit, Mashpee and Wakeby, already commented upon, and now, to complete the quartet, John's Pond.

The ride to Mashpee Centre either from Santuit or from Forestdale, Route 130, is replete with charm for we are in the midst of that country so ably described by a native son, Nelson D. Simons, ((Indian name—Wabun Annung, Chief of the Mashpees) in "Cape Cod in Poetry."

"Only my little village—the woods
Unbroken for ages surrounding—
Lies as it lay in the long ago,
The Indian village of Mashpee."

From the village center the old macadam road to Falmouth leads into the Quashnet region, where we take the turn at John's Pond Estates over wide smooth dirt roads, following all signs to John's Pond.

"Across the forest unbroken—"

I find no better way of recording impression than by quoting the native poet.

"Vast and awesome the forest
That stretched from ocean to ocean—"

"Oh! dear little hills of my people,
What long ago secrets ar't hiding,
What fears and hopes long expended
When all the forests were virgin?"

We ride up and down "the little hills of my people," by the big clean crimson cranberry bogs, over the Quashnet stream, through a modern development, marked with a feast of ancient Indian names, such as:—

Algonquin, Hobonock, Pemaquid, Sachem, Sassacus, Cappawack, Wampanoag, Massasoit, Tuspaquin,—until at last we go down the Old Brickyard Road to the edge of John's Pond. Visitors familiar with Pleasant Lake or Wequaquet or Wakeby may not know this large, serene, white bordered lake, with its slim pointed contours, sleeping in the virgin forest, surrounded by smaller satellites, Will's and Moody's and Deborah Bottles' Ponds, and many little locks, turns, pools and plashes.

"And you, little lakes of my people
So often mirrored the passing
Of warriors out to battle
In days that shall be no more"

We may go back to the old Falmouth road and move west from here following the left fork to East Falmouth, through a region of well-kept colorful cranberry-bogs and big farms where glorious long lines of brilliant sunburned-red strawberry leaves suggest next season's bounty of fruit, but memory will often return to the picture of the serene Lake of the Indian People surrounded by forest primeval.

The Christmas Woodways

Let us with Emerson invoke the mood of the evergreen woods, whether we walk or ride among them.

"Around me stood the oaks and firs,
Pine cones and acorns lay on the ground,
Over me soared the eternal sky,
Full of light and deity;
Beauty through my senses stole,
I yielded myself to the perfect whole."

Of the native pines, may I quote from "The Pilgrim Land":

The native pines sing sturdy songs;
Their branching candelabras
Of resinous tapers
Chant winter madrigals to health.
To celebrate the generous season,
They spread their broad branched brotherhood.

The White Pines, with their soft green gentleness, are planted here and there, but the tall, dark, mysterious cedar of the swamps has almost all vanished into cranberry bogs. The Savin or Juniper dots the old pastures around abandoned farms, and sometimes on a hillside we may see—

The blue, blue berries bright
On the green, green tree.

In a few localities, Black Spruces brought from Europe by our sea-faring ancestry, still flourish.

All the evergreens make a seasonable background for the colorful berries—the soft pearly-grey clusters of bayberry, the steely-blue buttons of inkberry, and the gay scarlet balls of the black alder. Holly, with or without berries, is beautiful in its native setting.

For all these lovely growing things, I ask consideration for the preservation of their beauty. If we must cut and destroy to bring within doors to a perishing atmosphere, let it be of the more plentiful bayberry, juniper and pine.

For the others may we have the fine feeling so ably expressed by Emerson in

FORBEARANCE

"Hast thou named all the birds without a gun,
Loved the wood rose and left it on its stalk?"

Shall we go out into the Christmas woodways and enjoy the festival of the native pines?

Billows of green,
Deep glossy green!
Green crests glowing
Above the black shadows!
Never a note of doubt
Or grieving!
Always the green giving
Of health and cheer,
And the strong faith
Of green growing!

Woodways and Ponds

For an all-season's ride, from the Centerville-to-West-Barnstable highway just before reaching the old Barnstable Townhouse a dirt road on the right soon leads up over the crest of the hill to that point where directly ahead is the stretch of great marshes outlining the irregular inner bay, and beyond the serrated dunes of Sandy Neck looming against the vast blue of Cape Cod Bay.

Directly opposite is the Osterville shore and Vineyard Sound. The only point this side of Wellfleet where from a car both sides of the Cape may be seen.

This road passes the Pelton Peach Farm, especially attractive at two seasons; in the spring for a sight of the multitudinous pink blossoms and in late summer or early fall for the delicious odor and taste of the ripened fruit. Attractive also in the neat, well-trimmed winter aspect of smooth grey bark and light but vigorous growth.

The third great feature of this all-season's road is Steward's Pond. At any time it is a delight to gaze down the long green slope of rock-strewn pasture to the placid lake filling the valley, up along the spreading village of West Barnstable, with its historic old white church standing like a sentinel at one side, and beyond to the far away purple hills of Manomet.

We can imagine it silvering in the moonlight, or blackened by a sudden storm; veiled in ice and framed in snow; rising out of the mists of Maushope's smoking, touched with the soft tints of dawn, or gorgeous in the sunset's glow, always with its individual charm.

The Great Marshes, West Barnstable

The Little Ponds

All over Cape Cod are scattered the tiny unmapped ponds, too small to arouse the interest of the fisherman or the tourist, too permanent in the life of the people to be overlooked

Considering their glacial formation, it is not so remarkable that all the larger ponds have satellites as that there exist so many lone tiny bits of water, often persistent and unvarying.

Of this class, there are two, one each side of the road soon after leaving Marston's Mills on Route 49. Like gems set deeply into the green pastured slopes, they reflect in cameo, cows and willows, clouds and sky.

On the West Barnstable to Centerville Road, a trifle beyond the left fork of macadam, an almost hidden sign, Pine Road, if not fallen, shows the way into an enchanting old-time byway of stone walls. Well built stone walls, well kept, showing the pride and hard labor of more than one generation.

Stone walls everywhere, over the hills, along the road, around the old houses, barns and cow yards, and as a climax, four lines of stone leading down into a tiny pond.

Possibly, this may be the only wall-crossed pond.

The building of fine roads has destroyed many a permanent pool as was the case of the Holy Water in West Yarmouth. So small and font-like it received its name in derision, it had nevertheless, a long and interesting history before it was filled with stumps, roots and sand from clearing the highway. We cannot tell how many centuries the frogs piped there in the spring, but for one century at least, dogs gratefully lapped its surface and oxen, then horses were watered there. It actually served as a baptistry for early members of the village church. There, for generations the children sailed their boats, and surreptitiously bathed in summer and safely skated there in winter.

The tallest man in town reports that once when the ice was thin he went through, under and came up in another place, proving the pond's depth and extent.

Another man, returning to his birthplace after sixty years in the West, said, that of all the changes, he missed most the Holy Water for that had been his childhood delight and a cherished memory all his days.

Highway construction has eliminated some of the smaller ponds but the great change in locomotion from horse to motor has left many former well-known landmarks remote and inaccessible as in the case of the Half-way Pond between West Yarmouth and North Yarmouth. The sandy woodway opposite Berry Avenue and the old mill in West Yarmouth was once the highway to the North-side and the little pond, two miles from either end, was important to the early settlers as a boundary, to the children of several generations as the resting place on the four mile walk to church and near the pond, a bent oak stood as late as 1900, marking the spot where grandmother dismounted from the pillion behind grandfather for relaxation.

The old pond saw many sights:- Ox-teams loaded with golden corn on their way to the packet that sailed from Yarmouth Port to Boston Port,—weddings and funerals wending slowly the dusty way, for all church activities belonged to the North-side for many years,—the gentle ladies of the sixties, gay with their enormous crinolined flounces, India shawls and tiny bright parasols, riding to their semi-yearly shopping in the cradle-swinging leather-springed carryall, the elegant vehicle of that period.

But best of all the old pond liked the passing of the sturdy children of a Sunday, barefoot, trudging through the mellow sand, carrying their socks, knit by mother, and their shoes, cobbled by father, to be put upon their feet only in sight of church, where they were doubtless worn in agony for the two sermons of three hours each, and the gossipy noon hour between.

There are many of these smaller unmapped ponds, now isolated, unvisited, yet memorials of vital activities of the past.

We must not overlook one tiny offering of nature, perhaps its smallest permanent pool.

Almost at the beginning of Tubman Road on Breezy Hill in Brewster is the miniature of waters, so diminutive we fear a thirsty cow might quaff it all away, yet with a look of permanence as if the Pilgrim settlers might have known and cherished it. From the road between stone walls, over a bit of old-time rail fence, we may watch this little circle of blue accommodate delicate reflections of true Japanese arrangement:- a cloud, a pine tree and a duck or two,- a willow tree, two woolly lambs and a gorgeous red-berried bush,-a rock, a blue bottom-up boat and a many-postured small flock of dark reddish-brown fowl, -or a red maple, a tousled grape vine, with spreading bayberries, all behind the delicate soft grey of a cedar post and rail.

There seems to be no end to the combinations, and best of all, these cameo compositions of beauty may be found at any season of the year.

Old Tupper House, Sandwich

Short Woodways

Bump's River. A few rods along the road from Centerville Square, back of the Monument and Post Office is the sign Bump's River Road, leading into a gritty or sandy way full of real country charm. It winds mostly through oaks, across a weir, along the twisty beginnings of the river, by an old farmhouse, and reaches the macadam again in Osterville, where we may turn backward to cross the bridge over the bigger Bump's River, flowing quietly by the fine residences on either side and making its way to the sea through the marshes that divide Long Beach from Centerville.

Shallow Pond. This seems insignificant from Route 132 but from the road that circles Wequaquet Lake it presents irregular and extended bayou effects of swamp and water, a scenic transportation from Louisana or Florida to Cape Cod.

There are a number of plashes with features of the Southland scattered through the deep woods between Pocasset and Chatham with this advantage to the Cape,—none of its swampy ponds have that unhealthy looking surface, out of which may rise a deadly watermoccasin or a monster alligator.

Parker Road, Pine Road and Church Street.

In Barnstable, turning from Route 6 by the interesting church of somewhat Russian architecture, past the Parker Inn, and the old Parker Farm, a family location of many generations, we soon achieve a beautiful wide expanse of field and swamp, netted with stone walls, marked with clumps of tupelo, distinctive at all times, and little knolls edged with bayberry and bracken with the remarkable dunes of Sandy Neck far to the right, and the old white church straight ahead, rising against a background of pines.

If the dirt is dry, we may take Pine Road through the stone-walliest byway hereabouts, but under any circumstances we must not fail to explore Church Street for its natural beauties and historical memories.

Here dwelt the famous Whelden sisters, superior teachers of a gone-by generation, and a little farther on the big house with its old box walk, stone walls and inscribed tablet, all telling of Lemuel Shaw, Chief Justice of Massachusetts.

This place and the Lemuel Shaw Lane, opposite, retain much of their charming simplicity.

The Wheldons and Shaws are gone but the descendents of the third prominent family of Church Street, the Jenkins, continue the traditions of rural life.

Some Short Byways

Lombard Avenue. A little south of West Barnstable R. R. Station is a cross street overlooking the rolling country to the west which has the distinction of being the boyhood playground of that world adventurous character, "Mad Jack" or Captain John Percival, who, after a long, busy naval career, which included Trafalgar, made his last voyage in Old Ironsides in 1844 to 1846, circling the globe in 495 days at sea. His grave may be found near the highway in West Barnstable almost where the Great Marshes begin.

The byways of the Cape are replete with memories of world-famous mariners who were born and bred on this "Narrow Land".

Maple Street. Easily found in West Barnstable from Route 6, this byway leads to the old Whitman Place, picturesque ideal of that well-known Music Master of the Piano age, who surrounded his home with plantings of unusual shrubs and trees. Nothing could be more graphically beautiful than the long lines of dark green spruces leading down to the charming pond.

Willow Street. From the Whitman Place a woodsy way meanders on to the famous old Congregational Church at the junction of several highways and byways. One of the latter, Willow Street, regains Route 6 across a pleasant bit of country, touched here and there with such signs of comfort as ample door-yards, gardens, and woodpiles can provide.

Camp Street, West Yarmouth. Another Camp Street in Hyannis testifies to the fact that some sixty years ago all roads led to the Yarmouth Camp Ground, the great summer religious-meeting and recreational place of the Cape. On Big Sunday people poured in by the hundred, sometimes well up into the thousands, by special trains from Boston and Provincetown, but mostly in buggies, wagons, carryalls and caravans behind horses plodding the sandy, dusty roads.

Because the South Shore-ers from Chatham to Yarmouth had to plod to Camp Street, Hyannis, for the turn, a cut-off was devised near the mill-pond in West Yarmouth. Then, as now, it started pleasantly down over the brook where wild ducks winter and hylas and water cress advent the spring. and wound on past the old houses where some of the sea-faring Baxters began, along the swamp of tall dark cedars edged with the red maples, spring and fall, to about where the Log Cabin Farm is now. Beyond that was a chaos of crooked and sandy ruts. There was much town controversy about the possibility of straightening this winding and doubling road, but my father, Isaiah Crowell, road commissioner at the time, took his compass in hand, and as he had done many times at sea, went straight for his goal. As we were taking a well known Cape woman through here recently, she recalled how as a little girl of five she sat all day at her grandmother's in South Yarmouth, making groups of five, four straight lines and one across, totalling the teams that passed on Camp Meeting Sunday.

Fearful of losing a count, her dinner was brought to her post of observation, a devotion to duty exemplifying future activities.

37

Yarmouthport is famous for its magnificent elms, planted nearly a century ago, now a living monument to the vision of our forefathers. The byways of Yarmouth cannot compete with its main street, but have compelling interests of their own.

Wharf Lane introduces that intimate touch with the inner coast life of the Great Right Arm of Massachusetts embracing Cape Cod Bay. The pictures here, and all along the connecting Thacher Road, are of swamp and marsh, creek, sky and sea with natural plant growth and wild bird life.

Thacher Street, turning by the old Thacher House, 1680, has an arching canopy of trees, with trunks luxuriously tangled with honeysuckle, framing a vista of farm and farmhouse at the end. Long may this charming byway continue in its present state of overgrown beauty.

THE THACHER ROAD
(Yarmouthport)

A winding way of Nature's never
    finished story,
Of tender spring delights and
    Autumn's generous glory;
Where Summer gives each hour
    a brighter sheen
To its great throbbing pulse
    of growing green.

Here lives no memory of worlds
    of noise and speed,
But that completely satisfying
    greater need
Of quiet fields, of creeks and marshes
    by the sea,
Of tangled leafage, vine and bracken,
    bush and tree.

Here are the treasures of the wild
    that please the eye,
That touch the heart and rest the mind.
    Against the sky
The ruddy tassels of the maple
    blend and lace
With flowing birch and brier
    in unspoiled grace.

Across the bay gleams Sandy Neck,
    soft silvering in the sun,
And verdant islets, from the marshes
    are rising, one by one.
From the cattails, red-wings o-kla-chee.
    Beyond the reeds
A heron moves, while a-far a meadow
    lark
    mysteriously pleads.

Warblers flit among the blossoms
    that promise berries in the Fall,
When over marshland touched with red
    will again the curlews call.
Here is pageantry of beauty,
    crowded, full and free,
The tangled overflowing of bracken,
    bush and tree.

Pageantry of music, of the shore birds
    fluting cry,
To viols of the wind and cellos of the sea
    that softly sigh.
Pageantry of color, from sweet-gale
    to golden-rod:-
For here the hand of man does not impair
    the work of God.

Church Street, in a dignified way, overlooks the sea meadows and leads back to the Thacher Road.

Winter Street affords one unique feature in its part-brick house with an aggressive, cobble-stone-arched entrance.

Center Street, as a byway, has a historical importance equal to or beyond any on the Cape or even in America.

Beyond those strange mounds of earth

among the pines, called Indian forts, whose story needs a separate chapter; beyond the ancient farms and the turn in the road where once the Town Farm stood, which always recalls to me, how as a little boy, I went there to dinner with my father at the all-day annual school-committee meeting, and ever afterward maintained the food to be the best ever;- beyond all this the road crosses a broad plain that commands an unparalleled view of Cape Cod Bay, with all the coast to Wellfleet on the right, with the shaft of The Pilgrim Monument in the middle distance, and at the west, the contours of the dunes and hills rising beyond the point of Sandy Neck Light through Barnstable, Sandwich, Bourne, to Manomet.

Here, at the town landing, we look over the Bass Hole, over the marsh and hillock of that country of the Indian Hockanoms where nearly five hundred years before Columbus and six hundred before The Pilgrims, one Thorwald, son of Eric, The Red, and brother of the true discoverer of America, Ericsson; harbored his ship, landed and encamped with his men, encountered the Screllings, as they called the Indians, was wounded and buried.

The seventeen-year old Thorwald's last words were: "Bury me here, place a cross at my head, another at my feet, call it CROSSNESS forevermore."

This information of the Norse youth, the first white man to be buried in America, comes to us through the researches of Edward F. Gray, whose book, "Lief Ericsson, Discoverer of America, 1003," records the facts, which have been ably transcribed by Tarbell in his "Cape Cod Ahoy!" also by Elizabeth Reynard in "The Narrow Land."

Old Yarmouth continues to interest beyond Center Street, for Playground Lane and Old Church Street leave impressions of story-book houses on quaint byways that lead again to the Indian Forts, and in the woods on the road to Dennis, is a sand-rutted road marked Hockanom, which explored to the fullest would repeat the tale of Thorwald in 1007, and some later lore of our ancestral pioneers of 1639.

Above the frail memorials of a sturdy race.

Tall pine trees answer to the breeze.

Where ivy trails and clings with poisonous grace,

White trilliums bring soft sweetnesses to spring.

Along Route 6 the entrance to Dennis is arresting, with its broad sweep of meadows and downs to the left, and gentle slope of hills and 'ups' at the right. (If 'downs', why not 'ups'?)

Can we recall, for a moment, an evening at the Tobey Farm sixty years ago? The great bell clangs to bring the farm hands from the cornfield and the cow-barn to the bountiful supper of fried ham and eggs, fried corn cake, baked apples, hulled corn and milk, with head cheese, sage cheese and cottage cheese pies and gingerbread, preserved quince and pickles galore; all home products. It was early bedtime for tired workers, after a few jokes and stories, and the nightly dignified service of scripture and prayer. In those days, not a byway but the full highway of life.

Quaker Meeting House, East Sandwich

In Dennis, at the triangular junction of roads we may wander far to the left through dirt roads, across the fields to come in touch once more with the borders of that mysterious and fascinating country of the English Bass Hole or the Indian Hockanom.

In Dennis village, the bend in the highway is the focal point for the spread of several interesting spoke-like shoreways.

Beach Street threads its way through willows, elms and poplars, overlooks stone walls, fields and meadows and commands at the end, the shore line of dunes and inlets, and on the return, an impressive view of the oak wooded hills massed beyond the town with solemn Scargo as sentinel. From this road and from many others yet to be considered there are shorter byways more or less desirable for exploration, which the finger of the guide may not touch while there are so many impressions of the more important byways to consider.

Nobscussett Road leads to the old hotel, where at one time Chicago millionaires displayed their diamonds in summer time, and now, as then, the sightly bluff commands the bay.

Hope Lane cuts through the picturesque swamp and lowland back of the famous Cinema.

Whig Street, crossing the shoreways, is quaintly and quietly residential.

From Corporation Road, just beyond the Playhouse, we review the country already passed and discover that what seemed a tree-covered hill in the distance, is actually a well rounded hill-like growth of silver poplars, formed from the dumping of discarded roots years ago. So Nature takes a hand in turning a pest of one generation into a delight for another. To fully appreciate this fact, capture the gorgeous glow of sunset shining through the dark pencilled trunks and soft grey-white fluttering leaves. At the end of Corporation Road is a superb view of Cape Cod Bay, usually intense blue with coast fringes of white, but unbelievably and solidly white like an alabaster sea in February, 1934.

Along this road, I look in vain for a picture of forty years ago. Then on the sunny side of a high stone wall, was spread a unique village playground, where, each in her own cranny or section, many dolls were keeping house; some of high degree in silk or satin surrounded with elaborate furniture, china and cooking utensils; others of lowly or rag estate with clam-shell dishes and pathetic attempts at broken box furniture: a miniature village with table set in every home with vases of wild flowers, pebble-plummed cakes and realistic mud-pies: waiting, waiting for the return of the human child mothers. The village that displayed such a remarkable child's playhouse long ago, has as remarkable a grown-up Playhouse now.

Sea Side Avenue, from Corporation Road, leads back to the State highway, granting meanwhile across the fallow fields, a gracious expanse of bay and a comprehensive view of Bleak House (why Bleak?), shared for many years by two friends of the pasture, a cow and an old white horse.

Dr Lord's Road is an up-hill and

41

down-dale nook by the sea completing the sextant of shoreways dominated by the heights of Scargo.

The ascent of Scargo from the west and descent to the east provides a gem of byways. The panorama from the Tobey memorial tower embraces the eighty mile sweep of Cape Cod Bay beyond the village nestling around the shadowy depths of Scargo Lake, and a forest world of oak and pine attuned to an atmosphere of Indian lore, including the legend of the Princess Scargo.

On the Dennis highway east of Dr Lord's Road, where a fork divides the great swamp, by following the left road —presumably Sesuit, though unmarked —passing a noble post-and-rail gateway, recalling that ancient structure, the pound, used for locking up stray cattle, beyond a real farm, a neat pinepark triangle, a few comfortable residences, we find the Shiverick memorial. At this point, looking down on the inlets of Sesuit Harbor, and reading the inscription on the tablet erected by Captain Thomas F. Hall and David Shiverick, descendants of the famous Cape Cod builders of clipper ships; it is not difficult to recreate the busy activities of 1810-1860.

For here arose The Flying Cloud, Witch of the Waves, Sovereign of the Seas and other sailing craft, which designed for beauty and for speed have never been surpassed.

And the captains of that era. Shall I quote briefly from a Cape Cod poet, Carol Wight of Chatham, in his "From a Scallop Shanty"—

Cape Cod Captains

Companions of the winds that sway the sea

We haunt the ports and highways of the world.

* * *

We grasp the God that rides upon the storm,

While feelings fathomless as an ocean grave

Surge in our souls, the souls of Cape Cod men.

Stamping as with a die into our lives

The wonder and the mystery of the sea.

East Dennis—Quivett Neck—Friendship Village

This part of East Dennis is a community in itself and a nest of charming byways; in winter practically an island when the bogs and swamps are flooded, and at all seasons, notably in spring, separated from the highway by a colorful growth of water shrubs and grasses. Beginning with six or more Cape styled homes charmingly facing the winter sun and following out all the ways around and across, we rejoice that to a modern village so much of old-time character remains. From the center, around which cluster the names of Shiverick and Hall, Crowell and Sears, shipbuilders, owners and master mariners, we recall some lines from a longer tribute to his native town, written by Thomas F. Hall.

High Scargo's dome in silhouette
Upon the glowing western sky,
Which may with Orient beauties vie,
Adds its true splendor to this scene,

* * *

The rising tide! Majestic sight!
How proudly its broad bosom swells
As stately up the creek it moves,
And closes up the caves and dells!

Interior of East Dennis Church

An East Dennis Doorway

Brewster, with its northern outlook, has the seaside atmosphere of the aristocracy and opulence of the Clippership days. The main street and the byways also display the homes of the ninety-nine captains who proved themselves famous sailors, excellent Yankee traders and providers and in some cases notable mixers in international affairs.

In West Brewster, we pass the two distinguished Dillingham houses, one built in 1660, the other of the salt-box type, holding beautifully to the present day a mirroring of the past. In an open space, we may see the low hillocks of Wing's Island close to the sea and cut off from the main land by marshes and creeks where the first great salt industry was created on the Cape.

* * *

Here were the salt-works, cities of salthouses,
Raising on stilts, wooly fibered wood vats
With quaint pivoted roofs gaping to sunshine.
Blue pools of ocean that slowly, in beauty,
Whitened to crystal! Acres of salt
Drawn from the sea wealth, for the health of the nation.
Savour of life! Symbol of wisdom!

* * *

By taking the lower road in West Brewster and following the sea lanes we gather impressions of:- taller grasses in colorful swamps, tangles of catbrier, locusts draped with honeysuckle, roadsides and yards matted with glossy green myrtle, an old boat shop surrounded by locusts, twisted and tied together, looped and laced with wistaria vines, in the blooming season a bit of old Japan. Interesting old houses, including the famous Cobb mansion, several with captain's walks, accompany this back road which ends at the big yellow manse with its lookout atop, and pleasant backyard below with trees and grassy slopes.

We may find interest and charm, whether we turn into the road between the fountain in the park and the church to bathing beach, or follow out the Point of Rocks Landing and the woodway back, or try Ellis Landing at the old wind-mill sight, or twist about the attractive shore cuts of Brewster Park or visit Monomoy Camp where youth in summer may learn a few things preparatory to life and good sportsmanship.

At Crosby Landing, we find the somewhat pathetic survival of an ideal. The adventurous Albert Crosby found gold enough in California to indulge his taste for music in founding an opera house in Chicago, and also to create a Romanesque castle on Cape Cod which completely encloses the cottage of his grandfather, his birthplace; and at one time housed another hobby of its owner, an art collection of old world pretentions.

Shoreways of Orleans

From the top of Woods Hill may be seen the water bounds of the town:—west and north, the curves of Cape Cod Bay,—northeast, the contours of Town Cove and Nauset Harbor,—at the east, ocean unlimited,—and on the south, glamorous Pleasant Bay. This top-of-the-world view necessitates a scramble through the forest. Better take the alternative and drive all around.

Namskaket Creek (variously:—Skaket, Scaquet, Skacut, Skaget) separates Orleans from Brewster and tallies with the inside of the elbow of the Cape; the shoreway here reaches the Bay along a stretch of moors and marshes from which rises the massive summer home of an artist with its brick-walled garden.

From here, following the left turns, we pass the long hedge of Scotch (?) Pines and the outlying western downs to

Rock Harbor. This creek, serving as an artery to the great marshes which almost cut the Cape in two, figures conspicuously in history. Always important in the palmy days of the packet and the salt trade, its fame began when the great storm of 1717, driving through the marshes, made it the first Cape Cod Canal. It is chronicled that at least one vessel went through, another was stranded and buried only to be found a century later. In 1804 a real canal was dug here for salt transportation, called Jeremiah's Gulley. In 1812 Lord Howe was here outwitted by the Cape Codders in a naval encounter.

To complete a survey of this interesting region, we may follow Bridge Road, the bay shoreway to Eastham, or cross the lowlands to the Town Cove and the Highway.

Tonset, Weeset and Nauset. Around the Cove to East Orleans, taking the Tonset Road and its tributaries, gives changing vistas of distant town and inlet across rolling hills footed with little ponds and topped with old houses, one of which bears the Massachusetts coat-of-arms, which once decorated the old State House in Boston.

At Weeset, we pass the old house of Joshua Crosby, gunner of Old Ironsides, with its remarkable display of whale vertebrae, and stop at last at one of the most thrilling and comprehensive views of the Nauset region.

On the rifted dunes beyond, half hidden in the sand, is the house where Henry Beston lived alone with the Atlantic for a year and wrote The Outermost House.

In the distance, above the vivid March blue of the creeks and the gleaming dunes rises the Nauset Light in Eastham. The land lines and water lanes of the vast lowlands form an indescribable picture. Beyond the dunes, where now the unbroken majesty of the ocean rules, once stood the great Isle Nauset which extended from Eastham to Chatham with a harbor of quiet water within, which was found by Leif Ericsson in 1003. It is difficult to say, whether here at Weeset, or a mile farther on at the top of the hill beyond the Mayo Duck Farm and the road to Nauset Beach, is the more perfect out-

45

look. Each position views the water-embroidered lowlands, the wind-and-wave-torn dunes and the tossing Atlantic in all their diversity of mood. Each place will fill the memory with a lasting impression of the Cape Cod of Thoreau or of the artist's Cape Cod Beautiful.

We may, at Nauset Beach, wade across the sands to get in closer touch with the mighty ocean, and to locate a peaty fragment of the lost Isle Nauset; we may take the up-hills and down-dales of Pochet for the many fine glimpses of the ocean, before we go back through the quiet wide street of East Orleans and around the woodway to South Orleans.

There are several charming ponds on this route. We pass Namequoit Road leading to a popular boys' camp, the famous old Kendrick house, and taking first the Portanumicutt Road then the Quanset Road we find the green-wooded hills about which the little ends of Pleasant Bay seem to cluster with bright waters.

Back again on the main road to Chatham, stop a moment at the top, or at least, slowly descend Winslow Hill, for here is the whole spread of beautiful Pleasant Bay.

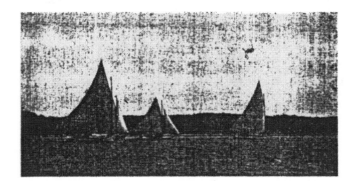

Chatham Shoreways

Forest Beach Road at South Chatham winds its wild woodsy way to the shore, where, at the top of a steep declivity, beyond the spread of lowly marshes and shining water is the slender grey line of Monomoy.

Buck's Cove is a marine artist's dream! Turning in by the dark stained church up over the wooded bluffs to the higher lookout, then down to the lower level among the picturesque scallop shanties, everywhere is the atmosphere of the sea;—boats stranded and afloat, oars and anchors, seines drying, heaps of shells, quahaug rakes, fishermen in oil skins and rubber boats, quaint huts with diminutive doors and windows and tiny rakish chimneys emitting slender wraiths of smoke,—fanciful sketches and pastels of a life of grim reality for the men who haunt the tides and fight the sea for a precarious living.

Cockle Cove is a minor repeat of the above and Ridgevale Road sounds well, but—.

Barnhill Road in West Chatham is a first magnitude star byway. After crossing the rolling country with a fine view of the town in evidence, down the slope of the hill as we approach the cove is a concentrated and intimate scene. The ducks in the foreground, in or out of the water, are as much a feature as the men in their dories, the boats riding at anchor or bottom up on the beach, or the curving cove itself with its background of dark cliff topped with houses. The shanties and sheds teem with activity and seem to grow out of the shell heaps. With the changing tide, it is an alluring place at all times especially when touched with the bright tints and rich shadows of sunset.

Chatham Light. For this outlook, second to none in popularity, proved by the cars parking here, winter and summer, day and night, storm or calm; instead of the regular way through the town, start with Queen Anne's Road, the first shoreway at the west end of the village. Curve about Oyster Pond, where children decorate the beach in summer, by the big place fenced in with ramblers, (June for this or perhaps July), take Cedar Street for the all-around drive, which is dominated by the old wind mill on the hill-top on one side and many shore views on the other.

Pause on the bluff that overlooks Oyster Harbor, with Harding Beach Light beyond, while from out behind the wooded islands streams the long lonely line of Monomoy, then go down around the sharp curve, past the wind-bent and frayed old willow, which somehow has survived the storms of years to serve the children with four swings, on to the landings at Stage Harbor, where lobsters abound in summer and fine sea-craft are moored in winter.

A bit beyond is the tablet marking Champlain's landing in 1606. The byway back to town passes two distinguished features; the mill, serene on its hill-top, and the Atwood house, oldest hereabout; but by following Bridge Street across the loop of the creek, the banks of Scotch broom and hedges of swamp willows and wild roses, we approach the Atlantic step by step, note

47

by the sea-horses with their manes of foam, before reaching the space between where the old lights went down and where the one light, formerly twin lights, now stands.

We see the sand bars, continually shifting, once a part of that Great Isle Nauset, and give a thought to Pollock Lightship with its many crews of hardy men and its many years of riding the boiling seas, seven miles off shore.

Monomoy may be explored its full length, ten miles of sand, on foot if you choose, more easily by special car; either way an unique experience.

From this elbow of the Cape, we may follow the ocean-side past Joe Lincoln's place and along the Chatham Bars.

North Chatham, in and out and round about its byways, affords many charming scenes of land-locked waters and sea touched shores, not forgetting the house, garage and whole estate covered with ramblers.

On toward Orleans we may explore the road to "Eastward Ho!" devoted now to Golf, where in the world war, seaplanes and blimps were in evidence, and long years before that, the famous Chatham Hotel stood, favorite week-end resort for Boston elite.

One by one we meet the slender arm-like coves, and at last the full-bodied sweep of Pleasant Bay and find that in four minutes we have passed the bounds of four towns:—Chatham, Harwich, Brewster, Orleans.

Sandwich Shoreways

Along the Great Marshes, entering Sandwich from Barnstable, the old-time city of salt-hay stacks raised on stilts is gone, but the old-time mansion surrounded by trees under the hillside where the road winds around to Sandy Neck, still remains. That long series of dunes, with its mingling of wind, water, sand and wild birds, affords a most interesting exploration, yet, like Monomoy, is an adventure outside the modern refinements for motoring.

In East Sandwich, the highway has a wide outlook, not only across the changing colorful marshes and swamps beyond the cultivated blueberry fields to the little wooded hills; but along the threading of Scorton Creek to the little harbor and Scorton Neck. The fast motorist will miss the very old and very large Box Tree by the wayside.

Past the double-fronted old Quaker house, serenely sedate back from the road, we come to Villa Vesta, a modern name and colony for an old family situation and the Beach Road continuation with evident summer attractions.

Spring Hill. Half hidden by trees a fork in the highway leads across the R. R. track and through bright cranberry bogs to the assembling place of other generations, the old Quaker Meeting House of Spring Hill.

The abiding spirit of this severely plain House-of-the-past is ably expressed in the following lines by Phoebe T. Chamberlain in "Cape Cod in Poetry":

As in meeting I sat with a worthy Friend,
The spirit of peace seemed on me to descend,

The lure of the world for awhile was done,
With its cares and worries, frets and wrong.
The quiet, the silence, the blessed calm,
Fell on my soul like healing balm.

A little farther around Spring Hill is the tablet to Stephen Wing, the first Quaker, who came in 1637, founded the Society of Friends; also the house he built in 1641.

Next is a fine house of the Cape Cod type, set in an orchard garden with an extensive marsh outlook. Here may be seen part of the hull of a vessel protruding from the great yellow house on the hill, called Mast Head, the home of John Foster, who for many years taught dancing as a fine art, to opera stars and to most of the royalty of Europe. Very few of the whole British Empire had his opportunities, for in his official capacity he could truly say: "I've had my arm around Queen Mary."

Soon after passing the two gates with roofs of thatch into the highway, we come to an old cattle-run between two tumble-down stone walls, white with snow-drifts of beachplum blossom in May.

At the cut-off of Sandwich village, by veering to the right we may visit the location of the once great Sandwich Glass Works.

Before the hill at the end of the marshway at the right is the Beach Road, winding past the Common Fields, to the broad bay outlook over the entrance to the Canal, where may at times be seen not only vessels of many types

Christopher Wren Spire, Sandwich

going through, but birds of many kinds going over, this being their chosen migratory crossing. Back on the lower road, we miss that old land mark, the Tupper House, and welcome the new, a glimpse of the imposing Sagamore Bridge.

As Old Sandwich itself is now a byway, at the Bourne line we turn back along the curving village street, past the grave of Joseph Jefferson, the interesting and picturesque houses to that ideal center where lined up and down the sides are beautiful old homes, among them the very ancient Huxie house, presumably dating back to 1637.

Not only from the pivot of the town in front of the Grecian-pillared town hall but from all sides, and especially from the opposite side of Shawme Lake, even from a clearing in the woods back of Shawme; from all directions are pictures graced with the outlines of that beautiful white church with its Christopher Wren spire.

Shawme Lake, Sandwich

Around Bourne

Sagamore Beach. In the casual minds of some people, Cape Cod extends to Middleborough, Plymouth or even Scituate. Its natural limit should be the Canal, but its political and historical boundary is the line separating the town of Bourne from the towns of Plymouth and Wareham.

North of the Canal, just off the Plymouth Highway, is Sagamore Beach, a delightful resort, where in the past, the master minds of the nation gathered for important social and peace conferences. A superior situation, where now many cottages cluster about the winding ways and sudden turns of woodland hill and dales, with intimate approaches to the beach with its broad outlook over the bay. Here back and forth, as well as around, will amply repay the motorist.

Great Herring Pond and Cedarville. From Bournedale, a village that once nestled comfortably among the hills until cut in two by the Canal and now about to be still more mutilated by the widening proposed:—from this remnant of a village, take the road to Plymouth for an interesting ride along beautiful Great Herring Pond to the quaint Cedarville, which, though actually outside the Cape lines, figured back in "the eighties" as the sensation of the day because the people of that section resented being put into the book "Cape Cod Folks" by Sarah Pratt MacLean. In the center may be found the little church and schoolhouse and the "Ark" where "Teacher" boarded and where Grandma used the Lotion, the Potion, the Setter and the Dye to Grandpa's hair every Sunday morning.

Buttermilk Bay. These picturesque head waters of the great Buzzard's Bay may be encircled by taking a road in the eastern part of the village, which meanders by the fine houses of the Garland Estates and along the frothy indentures of the bay with its fresh sweet winds and sunny waters, so beloved by Joseph Jefferson, that he built his Crow's Nest on its banks and then went fishing with Grover Cleveland who had raised his Gray Gables farther down on more open waters. For Buttermilk is but a baylet, though a charming place to meet the salty sea breeze roistering through on a summer day.

At the end of this circuit we are off the Cape in Wareham and turning back should take a look at the new Landing Pier by going up over the narrow bridge above the railroad tracks. The Pier itself is impressive with its fine structure, seeming to be architecturally a healthy great-grandchild of the old State House in Boston. The outlook here across the commingling waters of Canal and Bay across to Gray Gables and down the lines of the widening Bay recalls what that Sachem of the Comassakumkanet Indians proclaimed to Richard Bourne: "Much pleasant land! Much pleasant water!"

The whole western shore of Cape Cod on Buzzards Bay from Gray Gables to Penzance is a fascinating network of byways almost unknown to the through-route motorist.

Aptucxet. Soon after entering the

Shore Road at Bourne is a narrow underpass leading to the Indian Aptucxet (Little Trap by River), replica of the Pilgrim-Dutch Trading Post of 1627, called the Cradle of American Commerce. Of great historical interest, this quaint structure of hand-wrought woodwork, small-pane leaded windows, stone steps and nail-studded doors; houses many relics of the Indians and the Pilgrims and of the customs of their days. The Spring from which they drank remains, the beautiful situation has not changed, except that what was then the Bourne River is now the Cape Cod Canal.

Gray Gables. Once the summer Whitehouse, now an attractive resort for a number of families, which can be proved by taking in turn Jefferson, Gilder, and President Roads, named in honor of the three famous fishermen—a great actor, a great editor and a great president. Incidentally several points here command fine views of the Landing Pier on the opposite side of the Canal.

Monument Beach. On the Shore Road, crossing the bridge over Buck River, we see a scattering of the boulders that fell from Maushope's apron before he tripped and spilled them all along the hills and valleys.

Monument Beach! What a place! After a long train ride ending hectic months of city life, to land at a railroad station facing the open bay and the vitalizing touch of its fresh breezes! Here an old boat-shop, there a scattered boulder wall around an estate, and all along the shore road to Pocasset, often rural and wildwoodsy, are unexpected and charming water views.

Wing's Neck. Wenaumet. From Pocasset, this trail out over the marshes, across the creek, through the greenwood, around the harbor, accomplishes Wing's Neck Light on a rock strewn shore of a promontory, way out in the bay. On the way back to Barlow's Landing along Kenwood Road, rises a wonderful field of juvenile junipers; from the tiniest tot to the tall and tapering—a sturdy race, thriving on the thinnest soil, ever green and growing, and holding their own against the biting blizzards of winter and the dry siroccos of summer.

A little beyond this locality, a square yellow house was the boyhood home of Leonard Wood. A stone from this homestead is placed in the monument erected to him by the Cuban government.

Patuisset Road. Delightfully different is the drive around this rocky beach where the dark green barrier of mature clustering junipers protects the cosy cottages and allows enough prospectives of the inner and outer bays.

Along the shore road:—Pocasset Heights on Red Brook Harbor, bridging the stream where may be seen the windmill home of Agnes Edwards, a writer who gave Cape Cod a book, up the hill with a sharp turn to the right, around Cataumet with its circling roads——

Scraggy Neck. Another out-in-the-bay settlement, approached by a causeway with a fine outlook on each side.

Amrita Island. Near the Falmouth

line may be seen across a turreted stone bridge the small tree covered isle, left as a bird sanctuary to Harvard College by the Baxendales, who loved this spot as they loved all peaceful and beautiful things. Thus they passed on the legend of the Hindu name. "Youth Renewing Waters" to those seeking the quiet satisfying lore of nature.

———————

54

Falmouth Shoreways.

Meganset. On the Bay Shore-road below Cataumet is Meganset, one of the older settlements, its ample cottages on gentle woodsey slopes around a pond, or along the beach, mingling the advantages of the water-side with the comforts of modern innorovements. One is immediately convinced of the merits of the place.

Wild Harbor. Another excursion out into the Bay. Coming back, any one of three oiled roads reaches:

Silver Beach. Here the colonists have a broad outlook with Quisset and Penzance miles below and Dartmouth shores miles across the Bay.

Old Silver Beach.

The grasping waves forever reach For the glittering sands of Silver Beach. Here natural beauties abound, but all who demand other attractions, may find dining, dancing, and in season, performances at the famous Beach Theater.

Somewhere along the silver beaches North Falmouth merges into West Falmouth.

Spring Cove and Little Island. Near a stone-walled perennial garden, charmingly abloom through the summer months, we may chance to meet the Suckanesset clammers with pail and hoe going down the Spring Cove Road to their boats. Suckanesset, the Indian name for Falmouth, came from the purple shelled clam or quahaug from which the "black wampum" was made, the highest denomination of money to the Red-man.

The outer side of the Little Island has a cement seawall to keep in bounds the shifting sands of a riotous beach. Nonamesett Road leads to this same region.

On the beachways will be missed some of the landmarks of the North and West Falmouth throughway; among them the fine old house of the door light with its gilded sunburst and the severely plain Friend's Meeting House with the horse sheds still standing opposite, and a very ornate building near by, seemingly the reaction of the third or fourth generation to the simplicity of the past.

But all roads merge into one as we pass the stone walls that edge the Saconessett Hills and the Downs like those of Dorsetshire spreading far and wide against the water view.

Take the old road under the "Cape Codder" arch and beyond turn right into Sippiwisset Road.

From here to Woods Hole is a progression, a gradual enlarging of a different country side. The trees thicken, more varieties abound including the beeches and flowering dogwoods. There are many fine views from sightly elevations.

Beginning with a turn into the grounds of the "Cape Codder" once the Hotel Sippiwisset with the same commanding situation, along the rural woodway with ponds and thickets, perhaps with a visit to Racing Beach below the hills, we come to Quisset Road with its wind around the harbor to the site of the Yacht Club and back to the Shore Road curving on past fine estates with larger houses and gardens, until beyond the smooth green of the golfing course rise the per-

55

fect proportions of the water tower, like a monument; and we turn into the entrance of the Golf Club, and around the elevated curve, where, through fringes of birches is the most superb outlook of the whole Bay Shore.

From here with winding and changing features, the Gansett Road leads to Woods Hole.

56

The heel of the Cape spurns the waters of Buzzards Bay, and its foot steps firmly upon the Vineyard and Nantucket Sounds. It is this apex of the land separating the tides and the winds that has become the focal point for present realities that were dreams of the past.

Penzance or Long Neck. Entering Woods Hole from Quisset by the Ganset Road, we follow the indentures of the bay as the logical approach to this promontory with its chain of summer homes linked to the winding road with patches of the native heath or lawns, gardens, walls and gateways. It is a dreamland, privately owned, yet accessible at times and the nearest approach to the looming Great Isle Naushon. From the drive-around a picture of the village of Woods Hole rises above the wharves where the neat government boats are moored.

Marine Biological Laboratories. These buildings dominate the shore road, and are working out today for the nation the sixty year ago dream of Louis Agassiz. The modern history of this place, including the romance of the glass-bottomed boats and the adventures of the great depths of the sea as well as the congress of scientists and biologists from all over the world, recalls that a century ago this place was prominent in the activities of the whaling industry. The old stone building of 1829, now used for storage, was once a factory for turning whale oil into spermaceti candles and the wooden building near was the bake shop for "hard tack", daily bread for the crews of the whalers.

Back of the government buildings, on Millfield Street, opposite the Catholic Church is a charming bit of dreamland, where inside a peaceful close, is a shrine and Saint Joseph's Belltower.

Going on through quiet Quisset Avenue, we reach the water front again and find the byway over the Railroad out to the Boat Landing. The boats, buoys, and other naval paraphernalia make a colorful display like a gigantic toyland, yet speaking in no uncertain terms of the hard labor and often bitter experience of those who follow the sea. In contrast, quiet and restful is the turn Juniper Point with its attractive homes and garden slopes.

Opposite the Boat Slip and Landing is the little white gate that leads to another dreamland, the Fay Rose Gardens famous for many years as the first and largest display on the Cape, where that super-horticulturist, Michel Walsh, originated varieties of ramblers now known all over the world.

Just beyond the Little Harbor a sharp turn to the right passes several estates, beautiful for situation, including the Whitney Gardens, around and across the mole with its quiet waters within and its rock bound, wave washed shore without.

Nobska Point.

From the bluff where Nobska Light has flashed since 1828 one may watch the busy sea lanes of travel, where in one year thirty thousand craft move by from Long Island Sound or Buzzards Bay and from Nantucket Sound in the opposite direction. The Elizabeth Islands and the Vineyard stand like sentinels in review and we may locate by day or by night: Dumpling Rock, Gay Head, West Chop, East Chop, Cape Poge, and Hedge Fence Lightship.

Before we travel the rural and pleasant shore road from here to Falmouth, we must give a thought to No Man's Land behind the Vineyard, the island settlement of Leif Ericsson in 1003 and a few years later the birthplace of the first white man in America.

Some South Shoreways.

Poponesset Beach. From Route 28 in South Mashpee, through the virgin forest of the Indian Land, is a long trail to this open, broad-spreading beach, mostly undeveloped, formerly known as the Sage Lots and as a paradise for hunters. From here a well travelled road crosses the region known as Monica to beautiful Waquoit Bay and—

Seconett Island. This delightful short drive along the juniper-edged shore of Waquoit Bay, cottage bordered and island bounded, where the Indian Land merges into Falmouth; may also be taken from the highway at Waquoit village.

Menauhant (Pronounced Men-aunt). This drive on the Falmouth shore, along the Sound with the Vineyard always in evidence, and often suggesting Tennyson's "Magical city of Arras", bridging the indentures of the coast and ending with the expansive outlook at Falmouth Heights; is an unforgettable experience. Everywhere is felt an intimacy with that clean, refreshing touch of the sea.

Some time, no doubt, a bridge will be built across the creek at Falmouth Heights; at present we must drive around and in the village take the Shore Street to pass some of the fine old mansions. The Bathing Beach is noteworthy and the road along to Woods Hole touches the Sound closely. Around "The Moors" is a pleasing diversion.

All the byways and streets of Falmouth are interesting. Noteworthy are its fine public buildings, its charming village green, its stately churches, one dark in its splendid architectural proportions, the other with its white tower holding the bell cast by Paul Revere, one of the two of his workmanship still in use.

And last but not least the many fine old houses, in one of which was born Katherine Lee Bates, who wrote "America the Beautiful" and immortalized her home town in the following lines:

"Never was there lovelier town
Than Falmouth by the sea.
Tender curves of sky look down
On her grace of knoll and lea."

Stephen Wing Homestead, East Sandwich

The Airway

There are many woodways and shoreways I have failed to record; among the former are interesting trails around Newtown, Forestdale and Farmersville, also among the hills of Chatham, Harwich, Dennis, Orleans and Brewster that hide so many charming lakes, including Cliff Pond and the Seven Mill Ponds.

There are also several public parks in Yarmouth, some the gift of citizens, that deserve more than this passing notice.

After ten years and one hundred thousand miles along the Capeways, I often discover a new byway, or a new point of view on an old one.

To all those who will not or cannot traverse the innumerable byways, I suggest the one and only throughway, the airway; a possibility to all fliers with the ability and the means and to all others who have imagination.

Shall we rise above the Canal, where two of the new bridges show far below like grey webs spun across a tiny stream, then move over the Shawme Forest toward Falmouth, with the soft serrated shores of Buzzards trailing off into a chain of islands beyond Woods Hole and pass along the wooded center of the Cape. A few of the many auto roads show like slender threads knotted with little white villages, and the whole area is dotted with blue ponds and attending ribbons of river and creek.

The general impression is of unlimited forest surrounded by a magnificent coast line. This three hundred miles of beach washed by bay, sound and ocean is the frame for all the beauties and activities of the Cape,—the silver frame of the present popularity, of the future development and of its past in lore and legend. Outside the silver frame are neighbors, Nantucket and Martha's Vineyard, but within Cape Cod remains the unit of adventure, the right arm of Massachusetts held strongly out into and against the sea. This outline is not only beautiful and wonderful, but is a symbol of the rugged story of every whaler, every sailor, every fisherman, who has gone out from this shore.

From the air, we get the gleam of Monomoy, the glint of Pleasant Bay, the outlines of fair Nauset and the ocean-breasted bluffs of Highland Light and all too soon reach the real beginning of American history at Provincetown. The byways here, whether we find them afoot, by car or plane, are of narrow streets, of wharves and piers, the climb to the top of the Monument, and the ocean drive over the dunes.

We agree with Alma Martin:
"A heavenly town is Provincetown,
Its streets go winding up and down."

The enduring way of knowing Cape Cod is to see it with the eyes of others. Its literature comprises many books, short articles and poems, of which I can only mention a few. Swift's "Cape Cod" and Tarbell's "Cape Cod Ahoy!" review the history, and Reynard's "The Narrow Land" the folk-lore of the Cape. Important books are Brigham's "Cape Cod and the Old Colony" for geological information, and both "Cape Cod" and "Cape Cod Shipmasters" by Henry C. Kittredge.

Thoreau and Henry Beston have pictured life on the ocean front and innumerable poets have sung the charms of this Pilgrim Land.

For my final tribute to Cape Cod Byways, I have chosen a few significant lines.

"Come to the Cape, in Spring, with me, in May,
The beach plum blossom time!"
                                    Florence H. Crowell

"Yes, Summer's dead and Autumn's old
Winds are blustering and bold;
But, beneath the wintry skies
Life and warmth still meet your eyes
Cape Cod's color never dies."
                                    Helen L. Bayley

"You're more than a strip of land
Into the ocean run,
You're a race of men
Who have sailed the seas
To the edge of the setting sun."
                                    Sarah A. Dixon

(A loving to the tune of Auld Lang Syne:-

"The shores and woods, their peace we share
    with all from far and near,
Who come to change their load of care
    for life's content and cheer!
For old, for old Cape Cod, so dear,
    For old, for old Cape Cod.
We'll raise a thankful song of praise
    For old, for old Cape Cod."
                                    F. H. Crowell

Index

	Page
AIRWAY	61-62

BARNSTABLE

North Shore   16
  Sandy Neck, Scorton Hill

South Shore   13-14-15
  Hyannis, Hyannisport, Craigville,
  Wianno, Eel River, Oyster Harbors, Marston's Mills, Cotuit.

Woodways and Ponds
  Chequaket Lake   27
  Mystic Lake   28
  Shoot-flying Hill   28
  Short Byways   37
  Short Woodways   36
  Steward's Pond   31

BOURNE

North Shore   52
  Sagamore Beach, Cedarville, Buttermilk Bay.

West Shore   52-53
  Aptucxet, Gray Gables, Monument Beach, Wing's Neck, Patuisset, Pocasset, Amrita Island.

BREWSTER

North Shore   44
  Lower Road, Point of Rocks, Brewster Park, Crosby Landing

Woodways   22
  Stony Brook, Factory Village, Tubman Road, No Bottom Pond

CHATHAM

Shoreways   47-48
  Forest Beach, Buck's Cove, Barn Hill Road, Chatham Light, Monomoy, North Chatham.

CHRISTMAS WOODWAYS   30

DENNIS

North Shore   41-42
  Nobscusset, Scargo, East Dennis, Quivet Neck.

South Shore   8-9
  West Dennis, Dennisport.

Woodways   23
  Swan Lake, South Dennis, Bass River.

EASTHAM

Bay Shores   18
Ocean Side   17
  Nauset Light

FALMOUTH

Buzzards Bay Shore   55-56
  Megansett, Silver Beach, Spring Cove, Little Island, Saconessett Hills, Quisset.

South Shore   59
  Menauhant, Falmouth Heights.

Woods Hole   57-58
  Penzance, Marine Laboratories, Juniper Point, Nobska Point.

Woodways   27
  Ashumet, Coonemesset

FLOWERING WAYSIDES   19-20

HARWICH

Shoreways   8-9-10

Woodways   23
  Harwich Center, North Harwich. Pleasant Lake, Long Pond   26

MASHPEE

Shoreways   59
  Popenesset, Seconett Island

MASHPEE (Continued)

Woodways
John's Pond 28
Wakeby and Mashpee Ponds 21

MID-CAPE WOODWAYS 22-23-24

ORLEANS

Shoreways 45-46
Skaket, Rock Harbor, Tonset, Weeset, Nauset Heights, Pochet, Namequoit, Quanset, Pleasant Bay.

PONDS, THE LITTLE 33-34

PONDS AND WOODWAYS 25-29

PROVINCETOWN 61

SANDWICH

Byways 49-51
Great Marshes, Spring Hill, Glass Works, Old Sandwich.
Woodways
Shawme Pond, Shawme Forest 26
Lawrence, Triangle and Peter Ponds 25

SEASONABLE COMMENTS,
AUTUMN 24

SHORT WOODWAYS 36

TRURO

Ocean and Bay Shores 6-7.
Highland Light, Provincetown Harbor, Cornhill, Pamet and Long Nook.

WELLFLEET 11-12

Harbor and Village, Gull Pond, Candon's Harbor, Cahoon's Hollow Roads.

YARMOUTH

North Shore 38-39
Wharf Lane, Center Street, CROSSNESS, Playground Lane, Hockanom.
South Shore 4-5
Lewis Bay, All Around
Woodways
Camp Street 37
Little Ponds 33-34
Thacher Road 38
Weir Road 19

No. 2.

LIBRARY of
Cape Cod
HISTORY & GENEALOGY

THE DESCENDANTS OF
JOHN JENKINS

By

SAMUEL B. JENKINS

YARMOUTHPORT, MASS.
C. W. SWIFT, Publisher and Printer,
The "Register" Press,
1930

THE DESCENDANTS OF JOHN JENKINS

GENEALOGY and NOTES

By

SAMUEL B. JENKINS

West Barnstable, Mass.

1929

PREFACE

As no comprehensive record of this family has been printed it is hoped that this genealogy will be acceptable and useful; so far as it goes it is believed to be correct.

It is mainly from the Plymouth records, the town records of Barnstable, Yarmouth, Falmouth and Sandwich, wills in the Probate office at Barnstable, grave stones, the records of the West Parish church in Barnstable and those of the Friends' Society at East Sandwich.

The earliest locations are given as well as could be determined from old maps, wills, deeds, and traditions, compared with the writings of Freeman, Otis, Rev. Mr. Pratt and others. Later locations are quite exactly given.

To ensure the fullness and accuracy, valuable assistance has been received from Mrs. W. M. Lancaster, of Worcester, Mrs. Daniel Fritchie Summey of Cincinnati, Mrs. Robert M. Jenkins of Madison, Wis., Rev. John W. Suter of Boston, and others who furnished data from family records and research.

Mr. Gustavus A. Hinckley of Barnstable deciphered and recorded the inscriptions on the old gravestones in the Town of Barnstable, and his collected writings are in the custody of the Historical Society at Boston, where the original records of the West Parish church are deposited, a photostatic copy of which is held by the church officer at West Barnstable.

ABBREVIATIONS OF AUTHORITIES

P. R. Plymouth Colony Records
B. T. R. Barnstable Town Records
F. R. Family Records
F. S. R. Friends Society Records
C. R. Church (Parish) Records, W. Barnstable
W. R. Worcester, Mass. City Records

W. Wills, in the Probate Office at Barnstable
O. P. "Otis Papers"
F. T. R. Falmouth Town Records
S. T. R. Sandwich (Mass.) Town Records

Cape Cod, the ancestral point of the establishment of the family of John Jenkins in America, lies wholly in the County of Barnstable, Massachusetts.

At first, the name of Cape Cod was given to the arm of land which extends from Provincetown enclosing that harbor and which is now called Long Point.

The earliest mention of this cape is that of Verazano, who called it "Syrtis". Cabot called it "Cabo de Arecife" from the shoals near it. In 1542 Mercator named it "Cabo de Malabrigo", and in 1598 it was known to the Dutch and French navigators as "Malabar".

The name "Cape Cod" was given it, in 1602, by Gosnold because of the codfish that he found so numerous in the waters thereabout, and that name first appears in 1624 on the map of Alexander.

"Mourts Relation", London 1622, describes Cape Cod as "so goodly a land and wooded to the brink of the sea, the ground excellent black earth, the wood for the most part open and without underwood, fit either to go or ride in." But this should be understood as applying to the most of Cape Cod as now defined, for it was not true of that arm enclosing Provincetown harbor.

In time the original forest was all cut or burned over so that very few even of the old oaks may now be found. The light, rather superficial soil was planted for many years with little or no fertilization and large tracts became exhausted and comparatively sterile. Through individual foresight and private enterprise a few plantings of shade trees were made about one hundred years ago which grew to noble size. The largest trees ever grown on Cape Cod were the sycamore called "buttonwood" which attained a height of ninety feet, with limbs extending, almost horizontally, a distance of fifty-five feet. There are some fine elms in the villages and the white pine has grown to a maximum size until ravaged by insects. Reforestation is now being systematically carried on.

The wild flowers are numerous, brilliant and varied, and all fruits produced here have a very full and pronounced flavor, perhaps due to the humid and salty air.

There are beautiful bits of landscape and many broad and majestic views of the ocean, by which Cape Cod is surrounded.

A rather surprising feature of Cape Cod is the considerable area of fresh water; two hundred and seventy-seven ponds and small lakes dot its surface from which pickerel, black bass and perch are taken. In the Spring of the year many alewives ascend the brooks which are the outlets of some of these ponds to spawn, and great catches of the fish are annually made. This fishery is principally carried on in streams in Mashpee, Falmouth and between Yarmouth and Dennis, and has existed since the "memory of man".

The largest single farm this side of the Mississippi river is in the town of Falmouth, it is called the "Coonamesset Ranch". The oldest person born in Barnstable lived 105 years, 6 months and twenty days—a woman.

As the Jenkins family is so identified with the territory now known as the Town of Barnstable and, as the church in early times was the focus of all the social, religious and political activities, it is of interest to note some particulars about the first church buildings and their locations in this town.

The first meeting house was erected at Barnstable in 1646; prior to about 1700 this First Church was the only one in town; it had jurisdiction over the whole territory between Sandwich and Yarmouth as well as Mashpee and Falmouth; its location was in all probability, West of the old burying ground in Barnstable, opposite the residence of Marcus Harris. After 1700, when the town was divided into two parishes, a church building was erected in West Barnstable and that division was designated the "West Parish in Barnstable". All in Falmouth then came to this church until a separate parish was established in that town. The building in the West Parish was erected in 1717 and the first service was held on Thanksgiving day, November, 1719, by Rev Jonathan Russel, 2nd. Col. James Otis gave a bell cast by Paul Revere and a donation of eighty pounds sterling, the interest of which was to be distributed to the poorer members of the church forever. The bell was put up about 1807 and was the first in Barnstable County. It cracked and was replaced with another Revere bell in October, 1833, which is still in use. The gilded cock on the steeple was made in England and put in place in 1723. The frame and some of the original church structure remain though it has been modified several times.

Allusion may be made to the very influential Otis family whose ancestral home was in West Barnstable where the patriot James Otis was born, grew up and taught school. Governor Hinckley resided here on the lane which bears his name; the location of his house is shown by the cellar hole on the right side of the lane when going toward the railroad from the south just beyond the small pond passed on the left. This historic old highway is now narrow, crooked and almost impassable, but is to be improved

Parker Lumbart owned the land in West Barnstable from the brook at the present "Infirmary" to "Spring Creek", lying parallel to Centre street. A part of this land was added to the burying ground and, in May, 1798, more was taken to construct a lane, or public way, known as the "dock road" running from the main highway at the burying ground to the "Town Dock", or landing, on Spring Creek where the small "packet" coming from Boston was occasionally moored. In his will of

Nov. 13, 1754, he conveyed the residue of his land, after the settlement of prior claims, to the Town, the income from the land "shall be for the use and benefit of the poor of the Town, from one generation to another forever, and the land is never to be sold". When settled in 1755 the value of the real estate was £400.

The procedure in occupation and settlement of the new country, outside of Plymouth and within the limits of the Patent to Plymouth Colony, has been well set forth, in a digest of law by Samuel D. Hannah of Buzzard's Bay, Mass., as follows:

"A group of about ten men would come together for the purpose of establishing a plantation or new settlement. The next step was to appoint a 'Committee' of three or more men to act for the group in receiving the contributions of the members, buying the land from the Indians and in closing the bargain with Plymouth Corporation for the desired territory; this concluded the grant was entered on the Corporation records. These grants were made, as a rule, to the members of the Committee acting for a group and stated in form that the grant was made to three or four persons, named as 'fee officers' in trust, to form a society—meaning a corporation—to erect a plantation. The next step taken by the Committee or trustees was to prepare for the settlement so that all the families could occupy the territory at the same time as a measure of security and convenience. A community block house was first erected sufficient in size to accommodate all the families. Supplies were collected and stored and the Committee then laid out the home sites for the head of each family upon which rude log cabins were built as quickly as possible; these cabins were built in and about the block house so that it afforded protection in case of attack by the Indians. Later the blockhouse was also used for religious worship, for Freemen's meetings and general community purposes. Building the homes and getting settled was quickly accomplished. The community life then became more active, the church was organized under the direction of the minister and proprietors meetings were frequently held."

John Jenkins, with others, formed one of the groups described and the group received the grants on Cape Cod as noted. They secured the Indian title by purchase through their Committee which then set off sections or parts of the land within the grant to the shareholders.

The Cape Cod Indians were quite friendly but blockhouses were erected here in 1643. One at West Barnstable (of which the Indian name was Mos-ke-tuck-et) is to be located by the remains of the stone foundations on the property now owned by Mr. Roger Horton of Providence, R. I., this land originally belonged to the Crockers.

Houses for single families were first put up at Sandwich, Yarmouth and Barnstable in the order named, and a little later in Falmouth. An interesting and quite detailed account of the construction of these houses may be found in Vol. 2 of the "Otis Papers".

This Jenkins family is undoubtedly of Welsh origin; there are now, in South Wales, some of the name of John Jenkins but of the ancestry of the one who came early to Plymouth nothing is known up to 1929. The times were turbulent, and the Pilgrims were more concerned with what they were to do than with what had been done so left few recorded references to their former life.

"Of Noble Race is Shenkin" is the national song of Wales. Chorley, in his "History of Music"—an old work—speaks enthusiastically of a famous double bass player, John Jenkins by name, who played on his instrument all the tunes that the violin players of his time could play on theirs and who was a celebrity in England and in Paris

The John Jenkins who was the progenitor of those herein named came from London to Boston in 1635, in the "Defense" and remained in Boston for a time before going to Plymouth in 1637 He was no stranger to the authorities and wa evidently possessed of means for he at once bought land, purchased shares in Plymouth Corporation, became a "Proprietor" and received grants of land for his residence and use. His first residence was on land bought of Anthony Snow at Hobbs' Hole, Scituate—now Marshfield; this property consisted of a house and eight acres of land, and he received the title December 29, 1640. He soon became prominent in the developement of new territory by prospecting extensively and cooperating with others in acquiring the Indian titles to lands for new plantations.

A "Committee", consisting of Thomas Hinckley, Samuel Hinckley, Henry Cobb, John Jenkins and Nathaniel Bacon, was appointed by the Court, in 1659, to acquire lands in Suckinesset by purchase from the Indians. They secured the lands which were then set off, by the Council, to John Jenkins, Peter Blossom, Thomas Blossom, Thomas Hinckley and Samuel Hinckley. These tracts were in the present towns of Barnstable and Falmouth; they sold parts of their lands to later "comers" and thus became relatively wealthy through the moneys received therefor and the enhanced values of their remaining properties.

FIRST GENERATION

John Jenkins¹, the ancestor of those whom this record concerns, was born in England in 1614, and was united in marriage to Mary Ewer on Feb. 2, 1652 at Barnstable. She was a Quakeress and the widow of Henry Ewer who was born in London in 1629, came to America with his father Thomas and died very soon after his marriage to Mary. John and Mary probably resided on the Ewer farm in Barnstable near "Coggins Pond" as it was then called; this pond is passed on the left in going into the village of Barnstable from West Barnstable on the State highway. A consideration of all tradition and evidence inclines one to the belief that John Jenkins" remains rest in the old burying ground at Barnstable previously noted.

SECOND GENERATION

JOHN JENKINS¹ and Mary (Ewer) had
Sarah² b. Nov. 15, 1653
Mehitabel² b. Mar. 2, 1655; m. Eleazer Hamblin Oct. 15, 1675; d. 1684. She bore four children.
Samuel² b. Sept. 12, 1657; d. early
John² "of Barnstable" b. Nov. 13, 1659. First m. Mary Parker of West Barnstable the daughter of Robert Parker. Second m. widow Patience Paine Nov. 23, 1715 who was a granddaughter of Gov. Prence and had previously married Joseph Paine. She d. Oct. 28, 1745. John² became a "Freeman" at Plymouth June 24, 1689, owned shares and was "a man of note entitled to be called Mister". He went from Barnstable to Falmouth where he remained for a time occupying, defining and developing the lands previously acquired by his father from the Indians. About 1692 he returned to Barnstable, settled in the East Parish and died suddenly on July 8, 1736. His children were all born in Falmouth during his residence there.
Mary² b. Oct. 1, 1662 m. Thomas Parker

Thomas² b. July 15. 1666 d. 1745 m. Experience Hamblin Aug. 24, 1687. She was the daughter of James Hamblin Jr. About 1688 he built a house and fixed his domicile, on land at West Barnstable which was a part of his father's original purchase; this house was on the spot where now stands the house of William F. Jenkins¹, the third one there; the second one was that of Maj. Nathaniel Jenkins¹. Another house was built about 1736, a part of which is now standing, and is owned by Fred. S. Jenkins; this house was probably put up for, occupied, and became the property of Josiah³. Josiah probably left it by will to Lot⁴ and Nathan⁴, his nephews, it then passed to Philemon—Lot's son and heir—who sold it to Ebenezer Whelden in 1793 when Philemon appeared to have moved out of town. For his second wife Thomas² married Mercy............His will was made Nov. 9, 1737; probated Feb. 1745-6

Joseph² b. Mar. 31, 1669 at Barnstable; m. Lydia Howland, the daughter of John Howland, the son of Mayflower John Howland. Joseph² and Lydia resided at West Barnstable and were admitted to the church in Jan. 1717. He executed his will Jan. 24. 1733, it was probated Nov. 3, 1734 and is recorded in Vol. 5, p. 233, Barnstable Probate Office.

THIRD GENERATION

JOHN² and Patience (Mrs.) Paine had
John³ b. 1687; m. Abigail Whiston, of West Barnstable. Sept. 3, 1708. This John³ was the ancestor of the Falmouth Jenkinses. He made his will Mar. 3, 1760.
Sarah³ b. Nov. 15. 1693; m. William Bassett Jan. 31. 1722-3
Mehitable³ b. Sept. 24, 1694; m. James Chapman
Mary³ bapt. Nov. 3. 1694; m. Studley
Samuel³ b. July 15, 1697; m. Dorothy; d. soon without issue.
Philip³ b. July 6, 1699; m. Elizabeth White Dec. 13, 1721 B. T. R.
Joseph³ b. Aug. 13, 1701; m. Dorcas Paine Jan.

31, 1722-3; d. Jan. 16, 1749; made his will Nov. 22, 1745 Vol. 8, p. 90 Probate.

Ruth' b. 1704; m. Dr. Sackville West, Yarmouth, May, 1729

Dorothy'

Patience' The youngest daughter, by the will. Two daughters were born to Mrs Patience Paine— Experience and Dorcas, before she married John Jenkins'.

THOMAS' and Experience (Hamblin) had
Thankful' b. May 19, 1691; m. Israel Taylor
Experience' b. Mar. 28, 1693; m. John Pope Oct. 3, 1717
Mercy' b. Jan. 5, 1695; m. John White Dec. 23, 1718
Ebenezer' b. Dec. 5, 1697; d. June, 1750; m. Judith White Nov. 9, 1721. She d. Ap, 1729. m. Elizabeth Tupper July 25, 1731. His will was executed June 19, 1750. Vol. 8, p. 254. His children were all born of his second wife except Thomas', see Ebenezer'.
Samuel' b. Jan. 7, 1699 (B. T. R.), will 1811; m. Mary Hinckley Nov. 9, 1721 who was the daughter, by his second wife, of Ensign John Hinckley who was the son of Samuel Hinckley. Mary was half-sister to Ichabod Hinckley. Samuel', when a baby, was carried by his mother Experience to the near by "raising" of the house of Ichabod Hinckley. When Samuel' became of age he first resided at Skonkonet, on land received by his father and later owned by Lemuel Lumbart. When Ichabod Hinckley sold his property in West Barnstable and moved to Tolland, Conn. in 1732, Samuel bought this Hinckley estate for £140 and thus acquired for his residence the house he had seen raised when a child. This property was located on Hinckley's lane, West Barnstable, so called because it afforded access, from the old trail and main highway to the South, to the original grant to the Hinckleys. The property referred to passed in succession to Samuel's son Simeon', his grandson Braley' and his

great grandson Braley⁴. The house was taken down in 1914; some alterations had been made to it but the first construction with its heavy hewn timbers, pine paneling, mouldings, latches, etc. remained until its demolition. About 1820-25 there were four enormous sycamore trees in front of this house whose branches reached above the roof.

Josiah³ b. Ap. 16. 1702; d. 1750; m. Mary (Mrs.) Ellis of Middleboro Sept. 4. 1737; will Dec. 29. 1749 Vol. 8 pp. 361-2. There was no issue. Josiah³ left his property mainly to his brothers, sisters and nephew Nathan⁴, giving very little to his wife Mary. He dressed fashionably and spent much on dress; in short, was a fop. In 1755 Mary (resuming her former name Ellis) made her will (Vol. 9 p 230) giving her property to her children, William and Maria Ellis, by her first husband.

Hope⁴ b. July 5, 1704; m. Thomas White Ap. 19, 1727.

Sarah³ b. Dec. 1, 1706 (B. T. R.); m. Lemuel Nye 1737.

JOSEPH² and Lydia Howland had

Abigail³ b. July, 1695; m. Benjamin Hinckley Nov. 2, 1716. They had eleven children.

Bathsheba³ b. July, 1696; d. young

Ann³ b. May, 1701; m. Joseph Lothrop 1721; soon d.

Joseph³ b. Feb. 29, 1703; m. Mercy Howland July 15, 1736 by Rev Jonathan Russel. She was b. 1710. Joseph³ d. Oct. 13, 1793, "in his ninety-third year" (Grave Stone)

Lydia³ b. June 30, 1705; d. Aug. 5, 1773; m. Cornelius Crocker.

Benjamin³ b. June 30, 1707; m. Mehitable Blish Oct. 29, 1730, by Rev. Jonathan Russel. Benjamin³ was born and grew to manhood in West Barnstable. He inherited considerable land and property from his father Joseph² and his mother Lydia. He built the house, now standing in West Barnstable, where afterward lived for many years the Rev Oakes

Shaw, the father of the first Chief Justice of Massachusetts, Lemuel Shaw, the noted jurist to whose memory the Mass. Bar Association erected a tablet with appropriate ceremonies at a distinguished gathering. Benjamin also built another house near by and on his estate which is still standing. Both houses are in excellent condition and much the same as when first put up. About the time when his three sons were grown up, he visited Worcester, Mass. and, liking that country, he bought three hundred acres in the Western part of that town of Nathaniel Jennison, disposed of his Cape Cod properties and moved his family, with their effects, to Barre, near Worcester; there he lived the rest of his life, died and was buried on that farm which was reputed to be the finest and best equipped in that section. Before his death he divided his estate into three equal farms and had commodious buildings constructed thus establishing his sons "who all lived, died and were buried, on the paternal acres".

Reliance[8] b. Ap. 6, 1709; d. young.

Prudence[9] bapt. Ap. 6, 1718; b. about 1711-12; m. Samuel Baker May 30, 1732; moved to Windham, Conn. Had 5 children.

Hannah[1] b. Ap. 6, 1718; m. Stephen Freeman Oct. 22, 1736.

The name of the mother, Blish so spelled, came very early to be known as the correct spelling, though it appears in the earliest records spelled Blush.

The family had no part in making those early records, which were none too accurate, and the correction was not made 'til later. This is tradition received, from Mrs Braley Jenkins born Eunice Hopkins in 1776, by the writer. A manifesto was issued June 26, 1776, setting forth the position of the Barnstable townsmen in regard to their opposition to English oppression; this was signed by John Blish. It is also found that Joseph Blish was of a "committee", at about the same time; at no time after was the name recorded as other than Blish—not "Blush".

JOHN² and Abigail Whiston had, in Falmouth,
John⁴ b. June 27, 1709; m. Rebeca Green Oct. 30, 1734; made his will Mar. 3, 1760.
Joshua⁴ b. June 5, 1712; m. Hannah Handy Aug. 20, 1736; and m. Reliance Lawrence of Sandwich July 17, 1766; made his will July 5, 1794.
Abigail⁴ b. Mar. 27, 1715; m. Benjamin Crocker Jr. May 15, 1738.
Mary⁴ b. Feb. 10, 1717; m. Eben Swift Sept. 5, 1739; a "Ruth" and "son James" are named in his will—perhaps "daughter in law" and "son in law" of John².

PHILIP² and Elizabeth White had
David⁴ b. Sept. 22, 1722, at Barnstable.

JOSEPH² and Dorcas Paine had
Joseph⁴ b. Nov. 4, 1727; m. Remember Stewart Dec. 9, 1762.
Mary⁴ b. June 11, 1729.
Dorcas⁴ b. Ap. 10, 1731.
Keziah⁴ b. Mar. 30, 1733.
Rebecca⁴ b. Aug. 27, 1735; d. 1735.
Experience⁴ b. Mar. 11, 1738.
Rebecca⁴ b. Sept. 19, 1740; m. Ebenezer Bacon Sept. 22, 1782.
Patience⁴ b. Sept. 1, 1742; will 1783 Vol. 21, p. 205.

EBENEZER² and Judith White had
Thomas⁴ b. Mar. 8, 1725; m. Thankful Wing of Harwich 1752; m. Mercy............
Ebenezer², by his second wife, Elizabeth Tupper of Sandwich, had
Capt Ebenezer⁴ b. July 6, 1733, at West Barnstable. Rep. from Barnstable to the General Court in 1777.
Nathan⁴ b. Oct 21, 1734; d. Nov, 1782; will 21

p 175; m. Rachel Howland Dec 9, 1762. She was an "innholder" and made her will in 1792.
Martha⁴ b. Dec 4, 1736
Elizabeth⁴ b. May 9, 1740; m. William Fuller Mar. 1781.

SAMUEL³ (of Thomas and Experience Hamblin) and Mary Hinckley had
Experience⁴ b. Dec. 4, 1722; m. Lewis Hamblin.
Mary⁴ b. Sept. 7, 1725; d. June 7, 1727.
Samuel Jr⁴ b. Oct 20, 1727; m. Mary Chipman Mar. 11, 1749; was town clerk in 1770.
Nathaniel⁴ b. Dec. 6, 1729.
Simeon⁴ b. Sept. 18, 1733; d. Aug. 19, 1808; m. Hodiah Hinckley Mar. 25, 1762, who was born Oct. 6, 1738 of Capt John and Bethia Robinson Hinckley. Bethia was descended from Rev John Robinson. The marriage rite was performed by Pastor Green at the First Church at Barnstable.
Simeon⁴ and Hodiah resided and all of their children grew up in the Ichabod Hinckley house at West Barnstable. Hodiah d. May 14, 1808.
Lot⁴ b. Mar. 13, 1737.

JOSEPH³ and Mercy Howland had
Mercy⁴ b. May 25, 1737; Bapt. May 28; m. Lazarus Holmes Nov. 3, 1759.
Joseph⁴ (third of the name) b. May 3, 1739; d. Jan. 28. 1823, G. S.; will 1823; m. Bethia Bursley Mar. 15, 1786; m. Lydia Ewer Nov. 26, 1789, sister of Isaac Ewer.
Bathsheba⁴ b. Oct. 22, 1741; m. Daniel Crocker Oct. 9, 1766.
Abigail⁴ b. Sept. 6, 1745; m. Solomon Stuart Dec. 11, 1788.
Zacheus⁴ b. Feb. 8, 1748; d. 1837. W. Vol. 60; m. Sarah Hinckley who d. Oct. 24, 1795; m. Mrs Olive Conant who previously had a son Barnabas.
Mary⁴ b. Mar. 13, 1743; d. Dec. 14, 1810.

BENJAMIN³ and Mehitable Blish had

Anne⁴ b. Oct. 3, 1731; m. Isaac Goodspeed Oct.
17, 1754. Resided in West Barnstable.
Hannah' b. Jan. 25, 1733; m. Job Howland Dec.
6, 1753. She had eleven children.
Lydia⁴ b. Mar. 16, 1735; m. Joshua Nye in 1756.
Mehitable⁴ b. Feb. 24, 1737; m. Benjamin Lee.
Benjamin Jr.' b. Ap. 12, 1740 (C. R.). He was
strong and vigorous in body, of clear understanding and became a magistrate of some distinction.
His farm and farm buildings were called the best
in Western Massachusetts.
Southworth⁴ b. at West Barnstable, Nov. 29, 1742
in the house now (1929) standing which is owned
and occupied by Miss Elizabeth C. Jenkins'. He
was baptized in the old church on Dec. 4, 1742.
From the writing of his second son, Abraham', we
read that "at the age of sixteen he entered the
army that took and reduced the French Fortress
Louisberg, Cape Breton; his sufferings during that
campaign were severe. He was a man of few
words and fond of reading. Addison's works and
an old book called 'The Guardian' were his favorites. While he lived he was my 'book of reference' about the geography of the world, the history of the old French war, the Revolution, the
formation of our government both State and National, our laws, our institutions and our duties.
Morse's old geography he studied and Adam's Defense of the U. S. Constitution was as household
words to him. He had little chance for an education; a soldier in his sixteenth year and then coming to this place (Hardwick, Mass.) to enter upon
the severe labors of a young pioneer. He enjoyed
the teachings of a kind, wise mother which can
never be too highly prized. When a boy (at West
Barnstable) he had for a schoolmaster that venerated statesman James Otis and the seeds then
planted have shown the 'full corn in the ear'. The
characteristics of the family were perseverance,
self possession and a mind to grapple with difficulties and overcome obstacles". He married

Huldah Wright⁴ at Greenwich, Mass., and d. Dec.
13, 1820. She d. Nov. 19, 1810.
  Timothy⁴ b. Jan. 28, 1744; d. 1817 at Barre,
Mass.; m. Mary Cunningham of Barre Jan. 24,
1770. She d. Feb. 9, 1789, having borne six children. m. Abigail Perry, who was born in Martha's
Vineyard, Mass., (and who had come to Barre)
on June 11, 1789. She bore seven children at
Barre.
  Bethiah⁴ b. June 4, 1747.
  Sarah⁴ b. Mar. 1, 1750; m. George Lewis, Barnstable, Mass.
  Tabitha⁴ b. Mar. 31, 1733.

FIFTH GENERATION

JOHN⁴ (of John and Abigail Whiston) and Rebecca Green had   F. T. R.
  James⁵ b. Dec. 9, 1735; d. Ap. 10, 1807; m. Mary
Price Oct. 18, 1762; she d. Ap. 10, 1817.
  Ruth⁵

JOSHUA⁴ (of Falmouth) and Hannah Handy had
  Samuel⁵ b. July 27, 1744; d. Jan. 25, 1812 F. T.
R.; m. Rest Snow, of Rochester, 1768.
  Joanna⁵
  Joseph⁵ m. Elizabeth

THOMAS⁴ (of Ebenezer³ and Judith White) and
Thankful Wing had
  Thomas⁵ b. 1741 Barnstable; d. Sept. 10, 1808, in
Hudson, N. Y.; m. Judith Folger. Moved to Hudson, N. Y.
  Amial⁵ d. Nov. 25, 1764.

EBENEZER⁴ (of Ebenezer³ and Elizabeth Tupper)
and.................had (F. R.)
  Capt Ebenezer⁵ b. 1765; m. Lydia Smith Aug.
25, 1790; m. Mrs Catherine Hussey Connett 1816,
d. in Indiana in 1823.
  Priscilla⁵ bapt. Sept. 1771.

NATHAN⁴ and Rachel Howland had (B. T. R.)
Rebecca⁵ b. Nov. 5, 1763; m. Ebenezer Bacon
Aug. 22, 1782.
Asa⁵ b. July 4, 1767; m. Hannah Hamblin Mar. 13. 1793; d. Feb. 1847. She d. Mar. 21, 1838.

SAMUEL JR.⁴ (of Samuel³ and Mary Hinckley) and Mary Chipman had (O. P.)
Capt. Josiah⁵ b. Sept. 30, 1750; d. 1831; m. Prudence Davis of Barnstable.
Deborah⁵ b. Feb. 2, 1732; m............ and had three children Hannah, Elizabeth, Ebenezer.
Abiah⁵ b. Jan. 21, 1754 m.............and had Josiah, Prudence.
Samuel⁵ b. Sept. 24. 1755; m. Lydia Dyer, of Truro, Mass., and had Lydia b. 1776-8.
Mary⁵ b. Jan. 16, 1758; m.............and had Abiah, Elizabeth.
Joseph⁵ b. June 6, 1760; d. Ap. 20, 1783.
This family moved from Barnstable to Gorham, Me., at some time just previous to July 26, 1778. The children were all born in Barnstable.

NATHANIEL⁴ and Maria Ellis had, in West Barnstable,
Olive⁵ b. May 24, 1752; m. Daniel Lovell Jr, Mar. 2, 1772.
Ellis⁵ b. Mar. 2, 1755; administrator 1777.
Alven⁵ b. Feb. 27, 1763; d. Aug. 5, 1846; m. Mary Lawrence July 1, 1786.
Nathaniel Jr⁵ b.   d. 1825; m. Abigail Crocker June 2, 1786 "Major Nat", as he was familiarly known, was highly esteemed in youth and manhood. A very able, talented man, he served as selectman longer than any one but James Otis who served fourteen years. Abigail, his wife, d. in 1825.

SIMEON⁴ (of Samuel and Mary Hinckley) and Hodiah Hinckley had, in West Barnstable
Simeon Jr⁵ b. 1763; d. at Nantucket, July 5, 1831.

John⁴ b. Oct. 7, 1767; d. at Nantucket June 2, 1826; m. Susanna Holmes, of Osterville, Dec. 25, 1787. She d. Oct. 25, 1825, at Nantucket, their residence.

Prince⁴ b. Ap. 17, 1770; d. Aug. 19, 1815, in Cincinnati, Ohio; m. Lydia Crocker 1795, who d. 1796; m. Anna Bassett 1797. He owned land adjoining that of Loring and Ebenezer Crocker, Jr, at the "Common Fields", Barnstable, where he at first resided. He kept a general store and was school agent of the fifth school district in 1813. About 1814 he "treked" toward Cincinnati in a cart with wheels six feet high, which he built for the journey, taking the family with him. He was accompanied by several others from Barnstable.

Some of the Nyes, Snows and the Hinckleys, of Barnstable, settled in Indiana about this time. A Dr. Hinckley practiced in Oxford, O., at a later date.

Perez⁴ b. Dec. 29, 1772; d. Jan. 10, 1832; m. Sarah Blossom. He lived at Nantucket where all his children were born.

Braley⁴ b. Feb. 7, 1775; m. Eunice Hopkins Oct., 1798. She was the daughter of Edward Hopkins of Brewster, Mass., and a direct descendent of Stephen Hopkins¹, through Giles², Stephen³, Moses⁴ and Edward⁵. The land where Edward lived and Eunice grew up was on the North side of the "Sheep Pond", and was a part of that originally set off to Stephen Hopkins¹. Eunice was taught all the duties and numerous operations common to the households of the time and was proficient in the limited schooling then available. Of sunny disposition, ready wit, active mind and sound and vigorous body, she was well fitted to become the mate, for nearly seventy-four years, of Braley Jenkins. He was a carpenter by trade and often worked fourteen hours a day. He was the acting administrator of his father's estate for his three brothers and himself. He received large salt works, in which sea water was evaporated and from which quite an income was derived. In the Spring of 1811 he built salt works, for the Tudors of Boston, at Hull where the Hotel Pemberton stands; he also built houses and salt works in Barnstable and Brewster. He built a three story house in Nantucket and so well estimated and economically used the lumber first ordered that all the refuse was carried away in a single large basket when the job was completed. His old account book is in existence and contains curious items and references. The "watchers" in his father's last illness during a period of three weeks were provided with, and presumably consumed, a 'flood of "Westinjie" and other liquors and they were all "good people" too.

About 1811 Braley Jenkins', with his son Freeman' and his son-in-law, Sewall Short, had a bakery on his property which had been operated for many years. In this bakery was, what is believed to be, the earliest continuous bread oven, the loaves entering at one end and emerging baked at the other. This was devised by Mr Short.

Braley Jenkins' and Eunice Hopkins were united in marriage by the Rev Mr Dunster and they lived in the Ichabod Hinckley house at West Barnstable. In the winter of 1811-12 they were in Nantucket, renting the house for six months to Johnathan Nye for the sum of nine and a quarter dollars. They were again in Nantucket in 1835 at the height of the whaling industry when carpenters and builders were in demand at high wages. They soon returned to the old home and there remained the rest of their lives. He was esteemed for his integrity, thoroughness and fine workmanship, was deacon of the West Barnstable church for nearly 48 years, and died July 3, 1875, at the age of ninety-eight years and four months. Children instinctively recognized in Eunice a friend and ally and gave her an abiding love. She died July 3, 1872, at the age of ninety-six after a married life of seventy-three years and nine months.

Hodiah⁵ m. Samuel Crocker.
Lucy⁵
William⁵ b. Jan. 13, 1793; m. Susan Jenkins (daughter of John⁵ and Susanna Jenkins, his niece) Mar. 18, 1810. He was known as William Jenkins, Esq, and was a citizen of Boston in July, 1846.

LOT⁴ and Mary Howland had
Chloe⁵ b. Mar. 16, 1762; m. Nymphas Hinckley 1782.
Lot⁵ b. Sept. 28, 1765.
Philemon⁵ b. Feb. 26, 1767; m. Sarah Childs May 7, 1789. He owned the standing, old, Jenkins house and sold it to Ebenezer Whelden when he moved away in 1793.
Achsa⁵ b. Aug. 19, 1769; m. Jonathan Nye Dec. 23, 1788.
Mary⁵ b. Aug. 15, 1773.

JOSEPH, JR.⁴ (of Joseph⁵ and Mercy Howland) and Lydia Ewer had
Charles W⁵. b. July 27, 1793; m. Eunice N. Gardner; m. Love Pease, who d. at Nantucket Ap. 1829.
Mary⁵ b. July 9, 1796; d. July 9, 1876, in Osterville, Mass., called "Polly". Unmarried. Will No 6915, 1-386.
Joseph⁵ b. Aug. 8, 1803; d. 1823. Will made 1823.

ZACHEUS⁴ and Sarah Hinckley had
Ellis⁵ b. July 22, 1781; m. Susanna Goodspeed Nov. 30, 1809. Executor and residuary legatee of his father's estate. He died Jan. 23, 1859. She d. Mar. 3, 1869.
Eliphalet⁵ b. Oct. 4, 1784.
Distinguish between this Ellis⁵, son of Zacheus⁴, and Ellis⁵, the son of Nathaniel⁴, who was born twenty-six years earlier.

BENJAMIN JR.⁴ (of Benjamin⁵ and Mehitable Blish) and............had

Timothy⁴

SOUTHWORTH¹ and Huldah Wright had eleven children, all born in Barnstable.
Tabitha² b. Nov. 3, 1771; m. Amasa Smith.
Abraham² b. June 25, 1773; m. Mary Lord.
Southworth Jr². b. Jan. 11, 1775; d. Feb. 10, 1834.
Sarah² b. Dec. 19, 1776; m. Asa Mann at Hanover, Mass.; d. Feb. 2, 1850.
Patience² b. July 21, 1778; d. Dec. 19, 1779.
James Wright² b. Feb. 2, 1780; d. Sept. 19, 1866; m. Betsy Elizabeth Whipple Ap. 4, 1804, at Hardwick. She was the daughter of James Whipple, Lieut. in Col. Artemas Ward's regiment which marched from Grafton to Lexington in 1775.
Joseph² b. Nov. 11, 1782; d. in Boston Oct. 11, 1851; m. Mary Peabody; was Grand Master of Masons in Mass. from 1830 to 1832.
Benjamin² b. Sept. 10, 1784; d. Mar. 8, 1814; m. Hannah Atwood.
Charles² b. Aug. 28, 1786; d. Dec. 28, 1831; m. Amelia Leavitt.
Huldah² b. Dec. 13, 1788; unmarried; d. Dec. 9, 1831.
Lucy² b. Mar. 9, 1793; m. Joseph Libby.

TIMOTHY⁴ (of Benjamin³ and Mehitable Blish) and Mary Cunningham had, in Barre,
Robert² b. May 13, 1771.
Anna² b. June 3, 1773; d. Oct. 30, 1781.
Mary² b. Ap, 9, 1775; d. Sept. 5, 1849; m. Pelatiah Mann Hawes. She bore ten children in Barre.
Hannah (or Harriet)² b. July 30, 1777; d. Mar. 28, 1833; m. Haven Spooner of Hardwick Ap. 14, 1805. She bore eight children in Hardwick.
Sarah² b. Aug. 13, 1779 in Barre; d. 1854; m. Benjamin Cobb of Hardwick. She bore eight children.
Lydia² b. Sept. 13, 1781.

TIMOTHY⁴ (continued) and Abigail Perry had

Timothy⁶ b. Feb. 25, 1790; d. in infancy.
Lot⁶ b. Sept. 25, 1791; d. in infancy.
Mehitable Blish⁶ b. Mar. 2, 1793; d. unmarried Mar. 18, 1855, at Oneida Castle, Oneida Co. N. Y.
Mercy Freeman⁶ b. Aug. 14, 1794; m. Ira Ellis.
Josiah⁶ b. July 28, 1796; unmarried.
Timothy⁶ b. Jan. 29, 1799; d. Dec. 24, 1859, at Oneida Castle, N. Y. First m. Florilla Tuttle, at Vernon, N. Y., in 1828; second m. Harriet Tuttle, at Vernon, in 1829. She d. at Oneida Castle Dec. 28, 1886.

At the age of eighteen Timothy Jenkins⁶ went to New York state and studied law in Utica. He began the practice of law in the village of Vernon. In 1832 he moved to Oneida Castle where he remained until his death. He was district attorney from 1840 to 1845, and attorney for the Indians for ten years under appointment of the state. Elected to Congress in 1844-46 & 48 he thus served six years in that capacity. Though a democrat he often opposed party measures. He is believed to have been one of those who devised the "Wilmot Proviso". In 1856 he joined the "Freemont Movement" and was a "delegate at large to the convention which met in Philadelphia in 1856 to form the Republican party and ever after acted with that party.

His law library was given to Hamilton College, Clinton, N. Y., and many of his letters, written during his terms in Congress, are in the N. Y. State Library at Albany.

Abigail⁶ b. Ap. 13, 1801; d. unmarried Ap. 16, 1885; "A woman of talent, intelligence, culture, social excellence and exemplary piety".

JAMES⁵ (of John and Rebecca Green) and Mary Price had
Zilpha⁶ b. 1763.
Mary⁶
John⁶ b. May 7, 1766; d. at sea Nov. 8, 1793.
Weston⁶ b. Aug. 21, 1768; d. Feb. 13, 1834; m. Elizabeth Robinson, widow of Joseph⁶, a descendant

of Rev John Robinson of Leyden and a relative of Bethia Robinson, who married Capt John Hinckley of Barnstable, and who was the mother of Simeon Jenkins'" wife, Hodiah.

Rebecca*
Mehitable*
Thankful*

SAMUEL* (of Joshua and Hannah Handy) and Rest Snow had

Eli* b. June 26, 1769; m. Bethia.
Lydia* b. Dec. 11, 1770.
Elihu* b. Sept. 14, 1772; non compos auris et linguis.
Benjamin* b. June 4, 1774; d. Oct. 22, 1814; m. Temperance: served in War of 1812.
Samuel* b. May 24, 1776.
Thomas* Non compos auris et linguis.
Ivory*
Hannah*
Abner* m. Phoebe
Charles*

JOSEPH* (of Joshua and Hannah Handy) (F. T. R.) and Elizabeth had (who was Weston's wife too)

Daniel* b. June 17, 1776; m. Susanna.
Anna* b. Mar. 7, 1779.
Philip* b. May 29, 1781; m; Anna Hatch Jan. 11, 1816; m. Sarah Wicks Sept. 20, 1834.
Joshua* b. Aug. 24, 1784; m. Hannah Baker Feb. 10, 1814.
Sally* b. Jan. 15, 1787.
Prince* b. Mar. 15, 1789; d. Mar. 21, 1869; m. Susan E. Fish Aug. 30, 1820.
Rachel* b. Ap. 7, 1792.
Joseph Jr*. b. Dec., 1795.

EBENEZER* (of Ebenezer* and Elizabeth Tupper) and Lydia Smith had (F. R.)

Henry William* b. July 27, 1792; m. Jerusha Eddy 1824; d. 1850 at Panama.

Nathan° b. Mar. 25, 1794; m. Catherine Orton 1850; m. Eliza I. Purdy; d. Feb. 4, 1867, in Kentucky.
Josiah° b. Jan. 22, 1796,; m. Claretta Lois Crofoot in 1831; d. 1838 at Buffalo, N. Y.
Ebenezer° b. Nov. 4, 1798; m. Abigail Bartlett Feb. 8, 1836; d. June 28, 1878 at Chicago, Ill.
Lydia° b. Oct. 26, 1800; m. Rev. Edmund O'Flyng Oct. 9, 1822; d. at Bucyrus, O., in 1882.
Elizabeth° b. July 5, 1802; unmarried; d. at Bucyrus, O., in 1880.
Warren° b. Aug. 12, 1804; m. Marian Dutilh Dec. 2, 1825; m. Mrs Anna Howard at Matamoras; m. Mrs Mary Curtis at Columbus, O., where he d. May 11, 1866.
Marshall° b. 1806; d. 1822.
An unnamed babe° born and d. 1808.
Lucinda° b. 1810; d. in infancy.
Louisa° b. June 10, 1833; m. Rev John N. Goshorn at Cincinnati May 20, 1833; and d. at Galveston, Texas, in 1864.
Martha° b. 1812; d. 1813.

THOMAS° (of Thomas and Thankful Wing) and Judith Folger had, in Nantucket,
Benjamin° d, in W. I. in 1782; m. Deborah.
Sarah° b. Mar. 1, 1759; m. Samuel Gardner May 8, 1813; m. Benjamin Starbuck. She was a twin child with Seth.
Seth° b. Mar. 1, 1759; m. Dinah Folger; resided in Nantucket.

ASA° (of Nathan and Rachel Howland) and Hannah Humblin had
Nathan° b. Dec. 27, 1793; d. Nov. 7, 1865; m. Betsy Howland, who d. Feb. 27, 1875. She was a sister to Shadrach N. Howland, who was the sixth postmaster at West Barnstable and who held that office for many years, in connection with a general store. The first postmaster was Samuel Bassett in 1816. He made the first map of Barnstable town. The first postoffice was in the tavern on Howland

land, on the North side of the highway and diagonally opposite the corner of the old "Burying Ground". Nathan⁵ and Betsy always resided at and died in West Barnstable.

Charles⁶ b. Feb. 4, 1795; d. Dec. 27, 1861; m. Mary D. Bragg of the old Virginia family. She brought into this New England community many of the Southern customs, traditions and sentiments. They resided at "Hamblin's Plains" and were married Dec. 22, 1832. She d. Aug. 11, 1869.

Rachel⁶ b. Feb. 8, 1802; m. Jonas Whitman.

George⁶ b. June 10, 1805; d. Dec. 20, 1861; m. Eliza Hinckley Ap. 25, 1830. She d. Aug. 26, 1859; resided at "Hamblin's Plains".

CAPT. JOSIAH⁵ (of Samuel, Jr., and Mary Chipman) and Prudence Davis had
Sarah⁶ b. 1772 m. Daniel Lovell Nov. 6, 1817.
Mary⁶ d. soon.
Aurelia⁶
Josiah, Jr⁶.
Nancy⁶
Katherine⁶ b. 1785-8.

ALVEN⁵ (of Nathaniel⁴ and Maria Ellis) and Mary Lawrence had
Sally⁶ b. Nov. 22, 1794; m. Reuben Jones of Falmouth.
Elisha⁶ b. Oct. 8, 1797 (1st d. young, 2nd lived).
Amial⁶ b. Nov. 24, 1802.
Eliza Ellis⁶ b. Oct. 4, 1805.

MAJ. NATHANIEL, JR.⁵ (of Nathaniel⁴ and Maria Ellis) and Abigail, called "Nabby", Crocker had
Ellis⁶ b. Nov. 2, 1786; d. young.
Temperance⁶ b. Sept. 20, 1788, called "Tempy"; m. Ansel Wood; had six children.
Barker⁶ b. Jan. 20, 1791; d. young.
Lydia⁶ b. Feb. 29, 1793; d. young.
Nathaniel⁶ b. Jan. 6, 1796; d. old, in Cambridge, Mass. m. When a boy, Nathaniel⁶ was very active and agile. One of his feats was to

climb the steering pole of the large windmill where corn was ground for the neighborhood and ride around on the arms as the mill turned, his positions changing from head up to heels up. Another feat, and a difficult one, was to place five hogsheads, without top heads, in a row and touching one another. Then he would jump, standing into and out of them in succession and out upon the ground from the last, without pause or touching anything. He would stretch a cord between two upright stakes just high enough from the ground to permit his walking under it and then make a standing jump clear over it. In later life he built lighthouses. He resided in Cambridge, Mass.

Lydia* b. Mar. 9, 1798.

Ellis* b. Mar. 1, 1800.

Barker* b. July 17, 1802.

The second son by the name of Ellis* sold the property of his father, Maj. Nathaniel*, to Braley* and Freeman H. Jenkins*, and the latter built his house where "Maj. Nat's" stood and where that of Thomas* stood in 1686.

SIMEON, Jr.* (of Simeon and Hodiah Hinckley) had

Simeon* b. Aug. 23, 1807; d. July 12, 1891, in Somerville; m. Mary Keen Mar. 20, 1831.

JOHN* (of Simeon and Hodiah Hinckley) and Susanna Holmes had

John, Jr*., b. Sept. 22, 1788; m. Amelia Stubbs, Nantucket, Mar. 18, 1810.

Bartlett* (a carpenter) b. Feb. 4, 1791; d. May 17, 1821; m. Mary Crosby, daughter of Jesse and Susan Crosby, Aug. 25, 1818.

Samuel* b. Oct. 16, 1792—twin

Susan* b. Oct. 16, 1792—twin; m. William Jenkins, her uncle, Mar. 18, 1810. Susan* and her brother John, Jr., had a double wedding.

Nancy⁴ b. July 9, 1797; d. Dec., 1830.
Lucy⁴ b. Oct. 7, 1798; d. Sept. 16, 1839; m. Samuel R. Bartlett, of Lynn, Sept. 9, 1816.
Daniel W⁴. b. Oct. 23, 1808; m. Elizabeth J. Sprague July 11, 1836, in Salem.
Two children, Josiah⁵ and Warren⁵, d. very young.

PRINCE³ (of Simeon and Hodiah) and Anna Bassett had
Crocker⁴ b. Feb. 15, 1799; d. Oct. 7, 1866, in Franklin Co., Ind.; m. Mary Hussey Snow Sept. 16, 1821, a daughter of Lemuel Snow, a Revolutionary soldier.
Prince⁵ b. Ap. 17, 1770; d. 1857.
Oren⁵ b. 1806; d. 1868.
Elisha Bassett⁵ b. 1808; d. 1887.
Lydia⁵ b. 1813; d. 1862; m. Millspaugh.

PEREZ³ and Sarah Blossom had, in Nantucket,
Irad⁴ b. Oct. 19, 1798; d. Jan. 4, 1820 G. S.
Sarah⁴ b. Oct. 7, 1800.
Perez, Jr⁴. b. Oct. 22, 1801; d. Aug. 20, 1835; m. Eliza; d. 1835 in Kennebunk, Me.; m. Jane T. Taber, N. Bedford, 1837.
Josiah⁴ b. Jan. 27, 1810.
Lydia⁴ b. Ap. 19, 1812; m. Joseph B. Brown; resided in Worcester.
Simeon⁴ b. Aug. 23, 1807; m. Mary Keene Mar. 20, 1831.
Edward⁴ b. Mar. 22, 1805; m. Betsey H. Hamilton of Chatham Feb. 4, 1844.
Elizabeth⁴ b. 1803? m. Chandler Lee Hussey.

BRALEY³. and Eunice Hopkins had
Lucy⁴ b. Jan. 10, 1800, at Nantucket; d. May 28, 1896, at West Barnstable; m. Moses Alley, son of Richard and Martha Alley, 1820; m. Rev Enoch Pratt of Brewster.
Eunice⁴ b. Dec. 25, 1802; d. at an advanced age, at Morgan Park, Ill., and was buried there; m. Sewall Short Dec. 20, 1821. Resided in New Lon-

Jon, Conn., for many years, where her seven children were born.

Mary[6] b. June 19, 1805; d. in youth.

Dorcas b. June 19, 1807; d. Oct. 10, 1841; m. Jabez Howland, Jr., a fine character, much beloved. They had Ellen and Pomroy Belden Howland.

Braley[6] b. May 22, 1810; d. Mar. 27, 1894. Unmarried, he was a carpenter by trade, stout in figure, slow in movement, thorough in workmanship. He was scrupulously honest in all transactions and statements. The first to grow commercially and market "Cape Cod Cranberries" as such. A large grower of pears and other fruit. Built a large catboat, "Pomona", to transport cranberries in.

Freeman Hopkins[6] b. Dec. 25, 1815,; d. Jan. 4, 1902; m. Hannah Sexton Blossom May 3, 1854. She was the youngest daughter of Samuel and Sarah (Goodspeed) Blossom, and was born at E. Sandwich Nov. 20, 1832, and d. July 27, 1907, at West Barnstable.

Freeman H. was born in the Ichabod Hinckley house at West Barnstable and acquired a good common school education. He graduated from Harvard Medical School in 1844 and began practice in Harwich, soon returning to West Barnstable, where he continued until about 1861, when he, with his family, moved to Neponset, Dorchester, remaining there until 1865, when he returned to West Barnstable and continued in practice until of advanced age. High authorities in the profession pronounced him a diagnostician of superior ability. He was of sanguine temperament, "sandy complexion", medium height and average build. Active, nimble and resourceful, he could always extricate himself from any difficulty in which he found himself. He had a keen sense of the ludicrous and hugely enjoyed a good joke of which he had full store. Cheerful and courteous in manner, he was esteemed as a friend and associate and in early middle life provided, together with Capt. Benj. Weeks, a neighbor, and the local school master, much and frequent entertainment by singing, without accompaniment, old English glees. An intense liking for music and excellent taste were cultivated during the residence of the family in Nantucket in his youth where there were good musicians—singers, a string quartette, organists and players on various wind instruments. On the return of the family to West Barnstable, and after his marriage, he was interested in and took a prominent part in all musical activities, with the assistance of Mrs. Jenkins—usually at the harmonium then being introduced.

In 1844 while residing at West Harwich, he devised and directed the construction of the effective jetties at the mouth of the river, to divert the silt from the channel and keep it open for the passage of fishing craft.

Prince[6] b. Jan. 7, 1817; d. July 31, 1818.

WILLIAM[6] (of Simeon and Hodiah) and Susan Jenkins had

Susan H[7]. b. Feb. 28, 1811; m. George G. Cathcart Jan. 1, 1829.

Betsy[7] b. Oct. 15, 1813; m. Frederick Marchant, Edgartown, 1832. There was no issue.

CHARLES W.[6] (of Joseph, Jr.[5] and Lydia Ewer) and Love Pease, his first wife, had, in Nantucket,

Silvanus[7] b. Ap., 1822; m. Ann Barnard, daughter of Charles and Lucy Barnard.

JOSEPH[6] (of Joseph, Jr., and Lydia Ewer) and ....had, in W. Barnstable,

Lemuel[7]   m. Olive Crocker; m. Elizabeth Atkins. Made his will in 1734.

ELLIS[6] (of Zacheus and Sarah Hinckley) and Susanna Goodspeed had

Sarah[7] b. Feb. 18, 1813; d. Ap. 2, 1884; m. Eliphalet Loring Jan. 23, 1833.

Charles C⁶. b. Jan. 23, 1815; single; d. Jan. 26, 1907.
Ellis⁶ b. June 6, 1817; d. Dec. 7, 1891; m. Mary Ann Fish.
Susanna⁶ b. Oct. 28, 1819; single; d. Feb. 28, 1898.
Betsey Russel⁶ b. Ap. 27, 1822; d. Dec. 11, 1886; m. Jacob Kimball. Resided in Salem, Mass.
Lucy Ann⁶ b. Mar. 18, 1828; d. 1907; m. John Matthews. Resided in Dennis, Mass.

ABRAHAM⁴ and Mary Lord had

SOUTHWORTH, JR.⁵ (of Southworth and Huldah Wright) and had

JAMES WRIGHT⁶ and Elizabeth Whipple had
Josiah Whipple⁶ b. Oct. 6, 1805, at Hardwick, Mass; m. Electa Janetta Tuttle June 24, 1835; d. Oct. 10, 1852, at Vernon, N. Y.
James Wright⁶ b. Nov. 24, 1807, at Hardwick; m. Louisa Washburn Thompson, daughter of Dr. James Thompson, May 6, 1833. He d. Feb. 7, 1888.
Elizabeth⁶ b. Jan. 25, 1810, at Barre, Mass.; m. Jason Martin Gorham, a lawyer. She d. Mar. 24, 1895.
Elisha Warren⁶ b. Jan. 12, 1812, at Barre; d. young.
Caroline⁶ b. April 23, 1813, at Barre; d. Dec. 26, 1851; m. Alden Bradford Smith June 3, 1839.
Benjamin⁶ b. May 16, 1815, at Barre; m. Frances L. Riddle Nov. 23, 1840; he d. May 19, 1903, at Chittenango, N. Y. She d. 1889.
Huldah⁶ b. May 12, 1817, at Barre; d. Dec. 22, 1858,; m. Samuel Wadsworth May 20, 1841.
Lucy Ellen⁶ b. July 19, 1819, at Barre; d. Jan. 19, 1892,; m. Joel Benjamin Howe Nov. 26, 1846.
Sarah Bruce⁶ b. Feb. 6, 1822, at Barre; d. Dec. 9, 1903; m. J. Henry Hill Aug. 7, 1845.
Charles Southworth⁶ b. Mar. 28, 1824, in Barre; d. Nov. 28, 1873, at Stockton, Cal.

Capt Joseph William Herschel⁶ b. Dec. 8, 1829, at Barre; d. Oct. 27, 1874; m. Katherine Elizabeth Rockwood, the daughter of Rev Otis Rockwood. She was b. Nov. 4, 1831, and d. Mar. 3, 1903.

JOSEPH⁶ (of Southworth⁴ and Huldah Wright) and Mary Peabody had
 Joseph⁶; m. Mary Willis, sister of N. P. Willis.
 Catherine⁶

BENJAMIN⁶ (of Southworth⁴ and Huldah Wright) and Hannah Atwood had
 Charlot⁶ m. Anselm Parker, Falmouth, Nov., 1812.
 Daniel⁶ bapt. Sept., 1803.
 Henry⁶

REV. CHARLES⁵ (of Southworth⁴ and Huldah Wright) and Amelia Leavitt had
 Rev. Jonathan Leavitt⁶ b.   at Portland, Me.; m. Sarah Maria Eaton Oct. 15, 1862, at Lowell, Mass.; ordained in Portland, Me., 1825.
 Amelia Leavitt⁶ m. Dr. Charles Cheney Foote, of New Haven, Conn.

TIMOTHY⁵ (of Timothy and Abigail Pery) and Harriet Tuttle had
 Charles Montgomery⁶ b. at Vernon, N. Y., 1830; d. at Naussau, Bahama, I., Dec. 20, 1856; m. Ann Elizabeth Stevens. There was no issue.
 Hiram Tuttle⁶ b. 1833; d. 1870 at Utica, N. Y.; m. Cornelia D'Auby. He was a graduate of Hamilton College, Madison, N. Y., in 1854; practiced law in Utica, N. Y., and was, at one time, district attorney of Oneida County.
 Florilla⁶ b. Sept. 15, 1838, at Oneida Castle, N. Y., and d. there Nov. 26, 1919; m. W. Jerome Hickox, at Oneida Castle in 1875. The homestead where she lived and died has long been noted for its attractiveness and hospitality. She was the last of her family and "a worthy representative of those patriotic Americans who stabilized and influenced the affairs of her generation". "Like her

father she was distinguished for learning and industry, her great personal resolution and perseverance, her charitable interests and her fine mental attitude."

DANIEL⁶ (of Joseph and Elizabeth) and Susanna Childs had
Hannah Childs' b. Jan. 3, 1807.
Sophronia' b. Ap. 27, 1810.
Nathaniel William' b. June 5, 1812; m. Sophronia Chase.

PHILIP⁶ (of Joseph and Elizabeth) and Anna Hatch had
Augustus' b. Nov. 20, 1819.
Henry Dunham' b. May 3, 1872.

JOSHUA⁶ (of Joseph and Elizabeth) and Hannah Baker had

PRINCE⁶ (of Joseph and Elizabeth) and Susan E. Fish had
Foster H'. b. Mar. 9, 1829.
Joseph H'. b. Oct. 15, 1835.

JOSEPH, JR.⁶ (of Joseph and Elizabeth) and had

ELI⁶ (of Samuel and Rest Snow) and Bethia had (F. T. R.)
Maria' b. Dec. 31, 1789.
Reuben Eldred' b. Ap. 2, 1792; d. young.
Eli Jr.' b. July 9, 1794; m. Polly Swinerton 1817.
Rest Snow b. June 25, 1797.
John E.' b. Feb. 13, 1800; m. Harriet Swift Jan. 5, 1825 (?).
Lydia' b. Mar. 3, 1802; m. Davis Baker Jan. 27, 1819.
Hannah' b. July 6, 1804,; m. Nathan Davis Fish.
Shadrach Nye' b. Jan. 7, 1809.

BENJAMIN⁵ (of Samuel and Rest Snow) and Temperance had (F. T. R.)
Lydia⁶ b. Dec. 3, 1798.
Wilson Rawson⁶ b. Aug. 15, 1801; m. Betsey Smalley Oct. 13, 1822.
Desire Snow⁶ b. Oct. 18, 1805.
Benjamin Franklin⁶ b. Sept. 7, 1807.
Sabewan⁶ b. Sept. 7, 1809.
Henry B⁶ b. Dec. 14, 1811.
Wally R⁶. b. May 31, 1815.

SAMUEL, JR.⁵ (of Samuel and Rest Snow) and Rebecca Fish had (F. T. R.)
Alden Fish⁶ b. Aug. 1, 1808; m. Caroline E. Price.
Mary Ann⁶ b. Ap. 28, 1813.

ABNER⁵ (of Samuel and Rest Snow) and Phoebe had (F. T. R.)
Mary R⁶. b. Aug. 6, 1810; m. Ansel Lawrence.
Braddock G⁶. b. Ap. 26, 1811; m. Adeline...........
(?)
Martha S⁶. b. Aug. 4, 1812; m. Mitchell
Susan S⁶. b. Aug. 30, 1814; m. Thomas G. Nye.
Ameline⁶ b. Ap. 6, 1817.
Reuben⁶ b. Feb. 8, 1820.
Joseph G.⁶ b. June 4, 1823.
Phoebe Ann⁶ b. May 4, 1826.
Samuel⁶ b. July 7, 1828; m. Olive Fuller.

CHARLES⁵ (of Samuel and Rest Snow) and Eliza .... had
Mary

CAPT. WESTON⁵ (of James and Mary Price) (F. T. R.) and Elizabeth Robinson had
Hon. John⁶ b. Mar. 18, 1798; d. Aug. 10, 1859; m. Harriet Swift Jan. 5, 1825; m. Chloe Thompson.
Rebecca⁶ b. Mar. 19, 1800; m. J. H. Parker; m .... Thompson.
Mehitable⁶ b. May 3, 1802.

Charles Weston' b. July 31, 1805; d. Oct. 29, 1862; m. Phoebe Bishop. Residence, Bangor, Me.
Elizabeth Robinson' b. July 4, 1807; m. Oliver C. Swift July 4, 1827.
Capt. James' b. June 24, 1809; m. Phebe B. Donaldson Aug. 15, 1833; m. Eliza .... Moved West. Conn?
Eunice Robinson' b. July 23, 1812; m. Rev J. D. Davis.
Harriet Francis' b. Sept. 20, 1816; m. Rev F. Morton. She was called "Hetty".
Weston'

HENRY WILLIAM' (of Ebenezer' and Lydia Smith) and Jerusha Eddy had
William' b. 1825; d. 1826.
Ann Eliza' b. 1827; d. 1829.
Francis Louisa' b. 1829; m. T. R. Dole 1849.
William Henry' b. 1822.
Frank'

NATHAN' (of Ebenezer' and Lydia Smith) and Catherine Orton had
A son' b. 1831; drowned in 1836.
A son' b. 1832; drowned in 1836.
Caroline Electa' b. 1834.
Catherine' b. 1837; d. 1840.

JOSIAH' (of Ebenezer' and Lydia Smith) and Claretta Lois Crofoot had
Mary Jane' b. Jan. 24, 1833; d. Ap. 15, 1895 in Louisiana; m. Charles E. Hambleton Sept. 3, 1855; m. L. S. Hopkins Dec., 1865; m. Dr Hercules Sanche Nov., 1878.
Frances' b. Sept, 27, 1834; m. Nat. C. Stanley Jan., 1861; m. John E. McAllister Dec., 1867.
Josiah Henry' b. Feb. 23, 1836,; d. Oct. 22, 1924, at Cincinnati, O.; m. Abigail Augusta Fay Aug. 6, 1864; she was a descendant of John Fay of Sudbury.
Louisa Eliza' b. Ap. 6, 1838; d. June, 1868, in

Kentucky; m. Thomas V. Rodman Sept. 18, 1867.

EBENEZER⁶ (of Ebenezer⁵ and Lydia Smith) and Abigail Bartlett had
Lydia Jane⁷ b. Nov. 10, 1826; d. Aug. 10, 1827.
Jane S.⁷ b. Sept. 1, 1828.
William Henry⁷ b. Nov. 7, 1830.
Sarah E⁷. b. Sept. 26, 1833; d. Jan. 1, 1849.

WARREN⁶ (of Ebenezer⁵ and Lydia Smith) and Marion Dutilh (pronounced Duteel) had
Eliza Dutilh⁷ b. Dec. 24, 1826.
Henry⁷ b. May 25, 1828.
Warren⁷ b. 1830; d. in infancy.
Owen⁷ b. Mar. 9, 1832; d. Aug. 31, 1848.
Charles⁷ b. Sept. 2, 1834; d. Feb. 24, 1835.
Louisa⁷ b. Ap., 1836; d. May 26, 1848.
Hermon Dutilh⁷ b. Jan. 14, 1842; d. Oct. 31, 1918, at Madison, Wis. Rev. Hermon D. Jenkins was born in Columbus, O., but grew up in New York state. He graduated at Hamilton College in 1864 and Union Seminary in 1867. In the summer of 1863 he was a volunteer in the Pennsylvania Reserves; in 1867 he traveled in Europe. He was ordained in September, 1868, and on the 28th of the next month was married to Harriet Newell Burrill at Utica, N. Y. He was settled over important churches in Joliet and Freeport, Ill., Sioux City, Iowa, Kansas City and Riverside, Ill. He was a prolific contributor to the religious press and a correspondent for Boston journals when traveling.
Anna Calkins⁷ b. June 9, 1846.
Warren⁷ b. Sept. 27, 1838; d. May 3, 1876; m.
Two children⁷ who d. in infancy.

SETH⁶ (of Thomas and Judith Folger) and Dinah Folger had, in Nantucket,
Sarah⁷ unmarried.
Seth, Jr⁷. m. Sally Hathaway, daughter of John Hathaway.

Robert⁷ b. 1777; lost in Hudson River 1819; m. Hitty Dayton.
Amial⁷ d. 1795 of yellow fever; m. Nancy Lawrence.
John F⁷. d. Ap. 28, 1866; m. Eliza Pepoon.

NATHAN⁶ (of Asa⁵ and Hannah Hamblin) and Betsy Howland had
Francis⁷ b. July 9, 1824; d. young.
Joseph H⁷. b. July 30, 1826; d. Ap. 1, 1900; m. Persis Howes. Resided at West Barnstable.
Henry⁷ b. Mar. 31, 1828.
Charles E⁷ b. July 30, 1830; d. July 20, 1909; m. Mercy N. Bursley Nov. 25, 1863. She d. Feb. 7, 1911. Resided at West Barnstable. No issue.
Rachel⁷ b. July 3, 1832; d. young.
Francis⁷ b. July 22, 1838; d.   ; m. Mercy P. Nye. Resided at West Barnstable.
Hannah A⁷. b. July 14, 1836; m. Heman C. Crocker. Resided on the "Parson Shaw" estate, West Barnstable.

CHARLES⁶ (of Asa⁵ and Hannah Hamblin) and Mary D. Bragg had
William Bragg⁷ b. May 17, 1833; d. m. Chloe Wiley Sept. 27, 1862.
Asa⁷ b. Ap. 11, 1838; d. Ap. 23, 1903; m. Mrs. Martha Josephine Hamblin, the daughter of Eben Whelden. She d. Sept. 14, 1920. Resided at West Barnstable.

GEORGE⁶ (of Asa⁵ and Hannah Hamblin) and Eliza Hinckley had
James Hamblin⁷ b. Ap. 18, 1830; d. May 13, 1902; m. Ruth Jaques Fish of West Barnstable. He began a seafaring life at the age of fourteen, and became captain before he was twenty-one. His first ship to command was the "Van Couver", to India and to Chile. Later and for some years he was captain of the "Hoogly" in the China trade. After sixteen years as captain, without a shipwreck, he retired to the old home at "Hamblin's Plains".

Elizabeth Crocker' b. Mar. 24, 1835; d. Dec. 9.
1909; m. Charles W. Shattuck. Resided in Winchester, Mass.
John' b. Feb. 18, 1845; d. 1876.

JOSIAH' (of Capt. Josiah' and Prudence Davis) and had in Maine

LEMUEL' and Olive Crocker had
Olive Crocker' b. Jan. 16, 1804; d. Mar. 5, 1806. The mother died at the birth. Lemuel' then m. Elizabeth Atkins and they had
Elizabeth Atkins' b. Nov. 26, 1807; d. Sept. 15, 1881; m. Moses Burgess. Resided at West Barnstable.
Bethia Bursley' b. Ap. 17, 1811; m. Nathan Hamblin. Resided at "Hamblin's Plains".
Lemuel' b. Dec. 13, 1813. Killed by the fall of a tree on Mar. 18, 1842; m. Abby Crocker.
Content Atkins' b. Ap. 6, 1816; m. Seth Weeks. Resided at Osterville.
John James' b. Aug. 28, 1819; d. Ap. 13, 1903; m. Rebecca B. Brown, who d. Jan. 13, 1881, by whom he had his children. He then m. Fear H. Jones, who died Mar. 24, 1896. His education, as to schools, was limited, but he was a keen and accurate observer. His remarkable memory enabled him to recall an event with singular precision as to circumstance and time of occurence, so that to ask "Neighbor John" was as conclusive as to consult records with their possible, clerical errors.

ELISHA' (of Alven' and Mary Lawrence) and Laura had
Mary E'. b. Feb. 22, 1852.
Henry A'. b. Nov. 21, 1854; d. Mar. 24, 1861.
Howard P'. b. May 20, 1859.

AMIAL' (of Alven' and Mary Lawrence) and Sarah had
Elisha' b. May 2, 1828; (1800 Y. T. R.); d. Ap.

7, 1881, 81 yrs., 2 mo., 26 d. (Y. T. R.); m. Mary
G. Crowell, who d. Nov. 13, 1892. Resided in Yarmouth, Mass. Will Sept. 25, 1872.

NATHANIEL' (of Nathaniel, Jr.' and Abigail Crocker) and had
A son and two daughters.

ELLIS' (of Nathaniel, Jr.' and Abigail Crocker)

BARKER' (of Nathaniel, Jr.' and Abigail Crocker)

JOHN, JR.' (of John and Susanna Holmes) and Amelia Stubbs had
Sophronia' b. Ap. 5, 1811; m. William Baker Nov. 8, 1829.
John (third)' b. June 7, 1813; m. Abby Hammond, daughter of Caleb Hammond of Rochester.
Charles S'. b. Nov. 15, 1815; m. Mary J. Bailey Sept. 18, 1836; divorced; m. Clarinda S. Gardner of Newport 1844; m. Angeline, widow of Chas. G. Coffin.
Samuel' b. Mar. 18, 1817; m. Susan Hammond of Rochester.
Bartlett' b. Mar. 1, 1821; m. Josephine Eliot.
William' b. Feb. 23, 1822.
William' b. Aug. 7, 1826.

SIMEON' (of Simeon') and Mary Keen had
Sarah Blossom' b. Aug. 28, 1832; d. Dec. 25, 1864; m. Moses Coleman Vinal who d. 1907 in Scituate, Mass.
Washington Adams' b. July 4, 1835; d. Aug. 5, 1922, in Florida; m. Sarah Davis Mar. 24, 1859.
Howard' b. Jan. 10, 1839; d. Dec. 11, 1913, in Hyde Park, Mass.; m. Eliza Brayton Folger July 28, 1863.
George William' b. Jan. 29, 1842; d. Ap. 5, 1926, in Malden; m. Harriet Ellen Chase, of Brunswick, Me.; m. June 5, 1877. No issue. Residence, Malden, Mass.

Charlotte Abby⁷ b. Oct. 29, 1845; d. Nov. 25, 1921, in Medford, Mass.; m. William Henry Pitman June 5, 1867, who d. 1919.

PEREZ, JR.⁵ (of Perez and Sarah Blossom) and Jane T. Taber had
George Beman'; d. Oct. 23, 1832

FREEMAN HOPKINS, M. D.⁵ and Hannah S. Blossom had
Samuel Blossom' b. June 14, 1855, in the East chamber of the old Ichabod Hinckley house in West Barnstable. He was trained in music from the age of four. He taught piano pupils 1874-81. He was educated in the common and high schools. Engaged with piano firms in Boston and Washington, D. C., in middle life. Returned to the old home in 1814. Unmarried. In later life engaged in historical research.
William Freeman' b. June 10, 1858, in West Barnstable. Acquired a good common school education. He was delicate in childhood but robust in later life. Very fond of the out-of-doors, the open spaces, birds, trees, plants and all growing things. In 1920 the Barnstable (Town) Park Commission was established and he was chosen commissioner and served several terms. Resided in Boston; and in Winchester, N. H., in charge of a tannery, from 1881 to 1889. Then returned to West Barnstable. Was elected deacon of the old church in 1923. Unmarried. Inherited his father's enjoyment of fine music, and his father's property at West Barnstable.
Grace' b. Mar. 30, 1857; d. in infancy.

ELLIS⁵ (of Ellis and Susanna Goodspeed) and Mary A. Fish had
Mary Ann' b. May 10, 1862; m. Harry W. Jenkins Jan. 27, 1892.

JOSIAH WHIPPLE⁵ (of James Wright and Betsey E. Whipple) and Electa Janetta Tuttle had, in Vernon, N. Y.,

David Tuttle' b. May 4, 1836; d. in the Battle of the Wilderness; Lieut. Col. of 146th N. Y. Regiment.

Jennette' b. Feb. 2, 1838; d. Sept. 13, 1843.

Amelia' b. Aug. 24, 1840; d. 1840.

James Edgar' b. July 22, 1842; d. Sept. 14, 1888 in Vernon, N. Y.; m. Elizabeth Washburn at Worcester, Mass., 1870; treasurer of Brule Co. Dakota, 1883-8. Adjutant General of Dakota for a time.

Mary Elizabeth' b. June 9, 1844; m. M. P. Brewer, Minneapolis, Minn.

Josiah Whipple' b. Dec. 25, 1846; m. Alice S.; d. 1918; a well known civil engineer; residence, Coudersport, Pa.

JAMES WRIGHT° (of James Wright and Betsey E. Whipple) and Louisa Washburn Thompson had

Frederick William' b. Ap. 23, 1834; d. Oct. 11, 1895.

Henry Thompson' b. Nov. 25, 1835; d. Ap. 14, 1836.

Laura Elvira' b. Mar. 22, 1837.

JOSEPH° (of Joseph° and Mary Peabody) and Mary Willis had

Joseph Henry' unmarried.

Josephine' unmarried.

BENJAMIN (of James Wright and Betsey E. Whipple) and Frances L. Riddle had

Benjamin Riddle' b. Aug. 20, 1841; d. Oct. 8, 1913, at Cleveland, O.; m. Theresa A. Barnes; resided at Chittenango, N. Y.

James Whipple' b. Aug. 20, 1841; d. 1841; twin.

Charles Whipple' b. Nov. 3, 1843; d. 1857 in California.

Henry Bradford' b. June 15, 1849; m. Millie C. Gifford.

Frank H.' b. Mar. 15, 1855; residence Bloomsburg, Pa.; m. Anna M. Bittenbender, Dec. 22, 1880. Hannah Elizabeth' b. Jan. 9, 1857; d. June 8, 1920; m. J. Pearl Peck Oct. 15, 1884.

CAPT. JOSEPH W. HERSCHEL* (of James W. and Betsey E. Whipple) and Katherine Rockwood had

Katherine Rockwood' b. June 13, 1858; d. June 2, 1871.
Frank Wadsworth' b. Ap. 10, 1862; m. Ruth de Koven Prescott of Boston; residence Madison, Conn.
Joseph Herschel' b. Ap. 30, 1867, at Worcester, Mass.; m. Jane Schuyler Davis of Schnectady, N. Y., 1898. Residence Schnectady, N. Y.
Helen' b. Aug. 1, 1864; m. Rev. John W. Suter. Residence Boston.
Rev. James Rockwood' b. Feb. 25, 1869, at Worcester, Mass.; unmarried. Residence Phoenix, Arizona.
Lucy Howe' b. June 18, 1874, at Petersham, Mass.; unmarried. Residence Phoenix, Arizona.

CROCKER* (of Prince* and Anna Basset) and Mary Hussey Snow had

Lemuel Snow' b. Nov. 24, 1822; d. Mar. 30, 1909; m. Elizabeth Crocker 1853.
Elmira' b. 1824; d. 1887; m. Isaac LaRue Case 1841; bore five or more children.
Mary Wakefield' b. 1827; d. 1909; m. John Thompson 1847.
Alfred Crocker' b. 1830; d. 1897; m. Lydia Ann Rigsby 1854.
Samuel Bassett' b. 1832; d. 1864; m. Sarah Jane Hillyard 1853; bore two daughters.
Salome Ferguson' b. 1836; living in 1909; m. John Herron; bore two children.
Elhanan Winchester' b. 1839; d. 1888, Mt. Carmel, Ind; m. Indiana Seal 1869. He was a soldier in the Civil War; studied medicine in Cincinnati and practiced his profession in Mt. Carmel. After

his death Mrs. Indiana Jenkins moved, with her five children, to Iowa.

REV. JONATHAN LEAVITT⁶ (of Charles and Amelia Leavitt) and Sarah M. Eaton had
 MacGregor⁷ b. Ap. 14, 1869, at Amherst, Mass.; m. Alice Boorum Duncan.
 Sarah Eaton⁷ b. July 17, 1865; m. Grant Squires of New York Jan. 1, 1891.
 Austin Dickinson⁷ b. Jan. 19, 1879; m. Martha Frothingham Ritchie June 3, 1911. Residence Hubbard's Woods, Ill.

NATHANIEL W.⁶ (of Daniel and Susan   of Falmouth) and Sophronia Chase had
 Phoebe Jane⁶ b. May 28, 1838; d. infant, Nantucket.

HENRY B.⁶ (of Benjamin and Temperance   ) and   had

WALLY R.⁶ (of Benjamin and Temperance) and Mary Ann   had
 Sarah S.⁶ b. Jan. 26, 1838.

ELI JR.⁶ (of Eli and Bethia) and Polly Swinerton had

JOHN E.⁶ (of Eli and Bethia) and Harriet Swift had

SHADRACH NYE⁶ (of Eli and Bethia) and   had

WILSON RAWSON⁷ (of Benjamin and Temperance   ) and Betsy Smalley had
 Benjamin F.⁸ b. Sept. 14, 1824, in New Bedford; m. Sophia C.
 Charles⁸ b. Jan. 24, 1827.
 Henry W.⁸ b. Feb. 24, 1829, in Falmouth; m. Elvira Nickerson (of Harwich?)
 Joseph⁸ b. Nov. 2, 1831, in Falmouth; unmarried.

Elizabeth⁸ b. July 19, 1834; m.   ; no issue.
Edwin⁸ b. May 21, 1837.
William F.⁸ b. May 19, 1840.
Kesiah S.⁸ b. Dec. 28, 1842; d. 1844.

BENJAMIN FRANKLIN⁷ (of Benjamin and Temperance   ) and   had

LEMUEL SNOW⁷ (of Crocker and Mary Hussey Snow) and Elizabeth Crocker had
   David Crocker⁸ b. Feb. 20, 1865; m. Myrta Hetrick June 24, 1896. Residence Bringhurst, Ind.

ALFRED CROCKER⁷ (of Crocker and Mary Hussey Snow) and Lydia Ann Rigsby had
   William⁸ b.   ; d. 1914 at St. Paul, Ind.; m.   Taught in the public schools in Indiana for many years.
   Myron Crocker⁸ b.   m.   . Residence, Greensburg, Ind. Taught in the public schools; is now a lawyer by profession.

ELHANAN WINCHESTER⁷ (of Crocker and Mary Hussey Snow) and Indiana Seal had
   Phoebe⁸. m. Frank Montgomery. Residence Bagley, Iowa.
   William⁸ unmarried; Bagley, Iowa.
   Freeman Hawes⁸, m.
   Irvin⁸, m. Residence, Des Moines, Iowa.
   Carl⁸ b. 1885; m. Residence, Iowa.

CHARLES WESTON⁷ (of Capt. Weston and Elizabeth Robinson) and Phoebe Bishop had
   Emily Hart⁸ b. Jan. 23, 1836.
   Eliza Bishop⁸ b. June 4, 1839.
   Newell S   M   ⁸ b. Dec. 29, 1840; d. 1856 a. Williamstown.
   Herbert Morton⁸ b. Nov. 1842.

HON. JOHN⁷ (of Weston and Elizabeth Robinson) and Harriet Swift had

John Foster' b. Ap. 15, 1826.
Harriet Swift' b. Dec. 13, 1830.
Charles Weston' b. Feb. 13, 1838.

(John⁷) by his second wife, Chloe Thompson, had
Augustus Thompson' b. May 19, 1843.
Weston' b. Dec. 20, 1845.
Edward Hopkins' b. May 31, 1850.
William Thompson' b. Nov. 9, 1852.

CHARLES WESTON' (of Capt. Weston and Elizabeth Robinson) and Phoebe Bishop had, in Bangor, Me., 1825-8

CAPT. JAMES' (of Capt. Weston and Elizabeth Robinson) and Phebe B. Donaldson had
By second wife Eliza   had

WESTON' (of Capt. Weston and Elizabeth Robinson) and   had

WILLIAM HENRY' (of Henry William' and Jerusha Eddy) and

FRANK' (of Henry William' and Jerusha Eddy) and

JOSIAH HENRY' (of Josiah and Claretta Lois Crofoot) and   had
Helen Fay' b. July 24, 1868; m. Daniel Fritchie Summey, of Falls Church, Va. Residence Cincinnati, O.
Louise Babbitt' b. June 3, 1872; d. in infancy.

WILLIAM HENRY' (of Ebenezer' and Abigail Bartlett) and   had
Robert Moore' b. Ap. 24, 1873; b. Chicago; m. Ruth Dutilh Jenkins Mar. 24, 1908. Residence, Madison, Wis.
Luella' b. Oct. 20, 1870; m. George R. Brandon, who d. Dec. 4, 1928. Residence, Chicago, Ill.

Guy Springer⁸ b. Ap. 23, 1877; m. Mary Desmond, 1913. Residence, N. Y.

HERMON DUTILH⁷ and Harriet N. Burrill had
Anna Spalding⁸ b. Aug. 12, 1869.
Paul Burrill⁸ b. Aug. 25, 1872; m. Gertrude M. Halbert, Kansas City, Nov. 23, 1897.
Ruth Dutilh⁸ b. Jan. 2, 1872, at Freeport, Ill.; m. Robert M. Jenkins, Riverside, Ill., Mar. 24, 1908.

WARREN⁷ (of Warren⁶)

JOHN F.⁷ (of Seth and Dinah Folger) and Eliza Pepoon had, in Nantucket,

Matilda⁸ b. July 27, 1814; m. George Campbell of Pittsfield, Mass.
Elizabeth (first)⁸ b. 1815; d. young.
Augustus⁸ b. Feb. 27, 1817; m. Anna F. Lane at Jersey City, N. J.
Amiel⁸ b. Jan. 28, 1819; d. young.
Frances Mary⁸ b. Jan. 25, 1821; m. Theodore Olcott, Oct. 1, 1880, at Albany, N. Y.
Caroline Pepoon⁸ b. Sept. 11, 1822; m. George L. Ward of Boston.
Robert⁸ b. Oct. 20, 1824.
Elizabeth (second)⁸ b. July 21, 1827.

JOSEPH H.⁷ (of Nathan⁶ and Betsy Howland) and Persis Howes had
Harry Weston⁸ b. Aug. 12, 1860; m. Mary Ann Jenkins (of Ellis⁸ and Mary A. Fish) in 1892. Residence, West Barnstable.
Rachel F.
Zebina Howes⁸ b. Jan. 17, 1863; m. Ida B. E. Eldridge.
Gilbert Shaw⁸ b. Mar. 12, 1868; d. June 23, 1924; m. Nellie May Stopford.

FRANCIS⁷ (of Nathan⁶) and Mercy P. Nye had
Parker Nye⁸ b. Sept. 30, 1864; m. Cora Eldridge.
Julia Watts⁸ b. Oct. 20, 1866.

Frank Howland' b. July 30, 1868; m. Jane Louise Riley, June 16, 1898. Residence, Braintree, Mass.

WILLIAM B.' and Chloe C. Wiley had
Nellie' b. June 3, 1870; d. Ap. 2, 1926.

ASA' and Martha Josephine (Mrs. Hamblin) had
Thornton' b. June 4, 1873, at West Barnstable; m. Kate P. Chase of Hyannis, June 26, 1901.
Frederick Stanley' b. Feb. 29, 1876, at West Barnstable; m. Frances L. Kellough.

JAMES H.' and Ruth Jaques Fish had
Mary Eliza' b. July 18, 1861, at West Barnstable; m. Rev. E. L. Marsh; d. July 3, 1925.
Ruth Stanley' b. Jan. 10. 1871, at West Barnstable; m. Dr. E. S. Talbot; d. Dec. 8, 1900.
Elizabeth Crocker' b. Nov. 30, 1874, at West Barnstable. Owns and resides on (1929) the Shaw place at West Barnstable.

CHARLES S.' (of John Jr. and Amelia Stubbs) and Clarinda S. Gardner had, in Nantucket,
Sarah E.' b. April 19, 1845; d. infant.
Mary E.' b. 1846; m. Tilden Hall of Marshfield.
Charles S. Jr.' b. 1848; d. young.

LEMUEL' (of Lemuel' and Elizabeth Atkins) and Abby Crocker had
Lemuel H.' b. 1834; m. Susan F. Crocker of Barnstable, July 22, 1858, daughter of Joseph W. and Persis S. Crocker. Residence in Harwich.

ELISHA' (of Amial' and Sarah) and Mary G. Crowell had
James D.' b. Mar. 12, 1830; d. before Sept. 1872.
Alvin J.' b. Nov. 9, 1843; d. Ap. 6, 1909.
Elisha L.' b. Dec. 4, 1849; unmarried; d. May, 1923, at South Yarmouth.
Eliza' b. Dec. 24, 1828; m. Joseph Dudley.
Mary Crowell' b. Mar. 12, 1837; d. June 15, 1895.

Sophia Crowell b. Sept. 28, 1835; d. Jan. 17, 1909; m. Horace Freeman.
Sarah' b. Jan. 16, 1833; d. Mar. 16, 1852.

JOHN JAMES' and Rebecca B. Brown had
Content W.' b. Feb. 1849; d. Oct. 13, 1904; a school teacher; unmarried.
Joseph W.' b. Mar. 16, 1851; d. May 5, 1925; m. Alice L. Cook.

HOWARD P.' of Elisha and Laura.

MAJ. JAMES EDGAR' (of Josiah W. and Electa J. Tuttle) and Elizabeth Washburn had
Mabel' m. H. W. Bates, W. R.
David'
Alice Southworth' m. G. Elmer Allen.
Marshall'; in the Spanish war; d. some years after.
Jeannette'
And another child, between 1883 and 1889.

JOSIAH WHIPPLE' (of Josiah and Electa J. Tuttle) and Alice S   had
James' d. 1917. A civil engineer, by profession.

BENJAMIN RIDDLE' (of Benjamin and Frances L.) and Theresa A. Barnes had
Charles A.' b. May 15, 1871; d. July 19, 1924; m. Virginia S. Sauton.
Harry S.' b. Oct. 29, 1874; m. Jasmine O'Neil. Residence, Midway, Fla.
Frances Estelle' b. July 14   7; m. Charles Osborn. Residence, near Bost

HENRY BRADFORD' (o'   ajamin and Frances L.) and Millie C. Gifford
Alice'
Bradford'
Louise'

FRANK H.' (of Benjamin and Frances L.) and Anna M. Bittenbender had
Margaret' b. Sept. 22, 1887, at Bloomsburg, Pa.

FRANK WADSWORTH' (of Capt. Joseph W. H. and Katherine E.) and Ruth deKoven Prescott had
Helen' b. May 30, 1903; m. Edward Calhoun Smith. Residence, New York.

JOSEPH HERSCHEL' (of Capt. Joseph W. H. and Katherine E.) and Jane Schuyler Davis had
Caroline Schuyler' b. Sept. 8, 1902, in Schnectady, N. Y.
Katherine Rockwood' b. July 2, 1906; d. in infancy.
Schuyler Davis' b. Nov. 5, 1909.
Rockwood' b. Jan. 11, 1914.

MacGREGOR' and Alice B. Duncan had
Julia Duncan' b. June 22, 1912.
Sarah Eaton' b. Aug. 27, 1914.

AUSTIN DICKINSON' and Martha F. Ritchie had
Martha Williams' b. Dec. 25, 1913, in Chicago.
Ann' b. Jan. 14, 1916, in Winnetka.
Janet Ritchie' b. Aug. 6, 1921, in South Dartmouth, Mass.

BENJAMIN FRANKLIN' (of Wilson Rawson and Betsy Smalley) and Sophia C   had
Nathan Thacher' b. Jan. 11, 1834.
Walley Robinson' b. Aug. 29, 1835; d. 1840.
Joshua Turner' b. Oct. 27, 1837; d. 1840.
Benjamin Franklin Jr.' b. Oct. 25, 1840.
Simeon T.' b. Oct. 23, 1841.
Lydia A.' b. 1843.
Harrison G.' b. Dec. 15, 1845.
Pamelia O.' b. Oct. 27, 1848.
Susan H.' b. 1851.

CHARLES⁴ (of Wilson Rawson and Betsy Smalley) and   had

HENRY W.⁴ (of Wilson Rawson and Betsy Smalley) and Elvira Nickerson had
  Wilson Rawson⁵ b. Oct. 13, 1857; d. 1915; m. Aldana I. Fisher.
  Bessie Maud⁵ b. Mar. 12, 1868; m. Elijah P. Barrows of Quincy, Mass.
  Elvie M.⁵ b. May 24, 1867; m. William P. Holmes of Waquoit, Mass.
  Angie⁵ b. in Harwich.

EDWIN⁴ (of Wilson Rawson and Betsy Smalley) and   had

WILLIAM F.⁴ (of Wilson Rawson and Betsy Smalley) and   had

ALDEN FISH⁴ (of Samuel Jr. and Rebecca Fish) and Caroline E. Price had
  Louisa P.⁵ b. Jan. 7, 1830.
  Henry C.⁵ m. Sophia Baker, Yarmouth, Dec. 30, 1860.
  Maria Frances⁵ b. June 23, 1831.

BRADDOCK G.⁴ (of Abner and Phoebe   ) and Adeline   had
  Celia H.⁵ b. July 11, 1841. (FTR)
  Willard R.⁵ b. Oct. 1, 1844.

ROBERT M.⁴ and Ruth D. Jenkins had
  Barbara Burrill⁵ b. Sept. 25, 1912.

JOSEPH W.⁴ and Alice L. Cook had
  Ralph Leon⁵ m. Agnes Dillman, of Nova Scotia.

ZEBINA H.⁴ and Ida B. E., had
  Anne Louise⁵ b. Jan. 3, 1888.

HARRY WESTON⁴ and Mary Ann Jenkins had
  Weston Ellis⁵ b. Mar. 18, 1893, in West Barnsta-

ble; m. D. Josephine Hynes May 20, 1814; m. Gladys Vivian Shattuck Feb. 22, 1918.
Persis Howes' b. Jan. 15, 1903; m. Rupert William Marsters. Residence, Randolph.

GILBERT SHAW" and Nellie May Stopford had
Gilbert Shaw Jr.' b. July 27, 1906.
Ruth Hall' b. May 22, 1910.

THORNTON" (of Asa and M. Josephine) had
William Whelden' b. Oct. 5, 1902, in Hyannis, Mass.
Josephine' b. Jan. 29, 1904; m. William Leonard of Malden, Mass.
Peter Pineo' b. Oct. 12, 1908, in Malden, Mass.

FREDERICK STANLEY" and Frances L. Kellough had
Frederick Stanley Jr.' b. Sept. 9, 1910, in West Barnstable.
Eunice Lillian' b. July 21, 1913; d. in childhood of acidosis. A gifted, lovable child with a singing voice of great promise.

CHARLES A.' (of Benjamin Riddle and Theresa A. Barnes) and Virginia S. Santon had
Frances Elizabeth' b. Dec. 5, 1909.
Virginia Cora' b. Ap. 23, 1911.

HARRY S.' (of Benjamin Riddle and Theresa A. Barnes) and Jasmine O'Neil had
Robert' b. Oct. 28, 1912, Midway, Fla.

WILSON RAWSON' (of Henry W. and Elmira Nickerson) and Aldana I. Fisher had
Rawson C." b. July 28, 1885; m. Evalena Dimock, 1905. Residence, Falmouth, Mass.

WESTON ELLIS' (of Harry W. and Mary Ann Jenkins) and D. Josephine Hynes had
Weston Ellis Jr." b. Feb. 24, 1915.

Mary Josephine" b. May 7, 1917; d. infant.

RAWSON C." (of Wilson R. and Aldana Fisher) and Evalena Dimock had
    Delmar Rawson" b. Ap. 25, 1911.
    Harold Wilson" b. Nov. 22, 1912.
    Isabel Aldana" b. June 17, 1916.
    Bertha Louise" b. Ap. 16, 1918.

Lest some confusion or uncertainty arise in regard to a John Jenkins who married Roanna (or Rowena) Jones, the daughter of Hiram Jones of Sandwich on Dec. 5, 1858, and who is recorded as born in Italy (Nice, by tradition), it may be stated that he came to this country as a boy, alone and unconnected. He was brought up by Ellis Jenkins' who gave him the name "John Jenkins" by which he was known.

APPENDIX

Several others of the name Jenkins came to America than the John Jenkins whose descendants have been the concern of this record. Very prominent among them was Edward Jenkins who came to Plymouth later than John. Their relationship is not disclosed in the records.

Edward was the uncle of Joseph and John Whiston and was guardian of the latter in his youth. Turning back in this record it will appear that John Jenkins', the son of John' and Patience Paine, married Abigail Whiston, a sister of this Joseph and John Whiston, as his first wife. Edward's sister Sarah married George Lewes (the ancestor of the Lewes, or Lewis, family) in County Kent, England, and came with him and their five children to America. Edward died in 1699.

Edward Jenkins soon established himself in the confidence of his associates as a man of ability, probity and sound judgment, was made a Freeman May 4, 1647, and occupied various offices, was a member of the Council in 1667 and an advisor in contested divisions of land. Though he was not active or aggressive as a Quaker and took the "oath of allegiance" to the King, his family were all Quakers and he sympathized later with that sect. This accounts for the fact that after several years the Colony Records contain so little about him and nothing about his family except of his daughter's summons to Court as a Quaker.

The only further, authentic information here given has been gleaned from the Sandwich town records and those of the Friends Society in East Sandwich, Mass., which, though austere, are well preserved and wholly reliable. They contain many details of the fines and the abominable persecutions to which the Quakers were subjected.

The Pilgrims came to America under a primal and human impulse to secure their own liberty in religious matters; when militant Quakers came, hoping to enjoy the same freedom, a clash was inevitable, as there were radical differences of views and practices between the groups and, owing to their former repression in England, the Pilgrims demanded exclusive rights in their new abode and insisted on full compliance with their views, laws and regulations, re-enacting similar restrictions on others to those which they had experienced themselves in England.

EDWARD JENKINS[1] of Plymouth and Sandwich had

Elizabeth[2] b. Ap. 30, 1649, at Sandwich, Mass. T. R. She was summoned before the Council at Plymouth and fined for refusing to take the oath of allegiance. Though professing her loyalty and allegiance she adhered to the Quaker practice "swear not at all."

Mary[2] b. 1647 (?); m. Marmaduke Atkinson; divorced after seven years.

Sarah[2] b. Nov. 15, 1652.

John[2] b. 1672 "of Sandwich"; m. Susanna Cooke. A prominent Quaker. Resided at Sandwich, Mass. Made his will in 1708, the estate amounting to £116, 10s. 0d.

Job¹ b. 1681; m. Hannah Taylor of Yarmouth, Mass.

The Quakers of Barnstable County resided almost wholly at Sandwich and Yarmouth, with the headquarters, or "Mother Church", at Sandwich, now called East Sandwich.

In 1676 there was at Plymouth Edward Jenkins' and a Thomas Jenkins'—not the son of John'. This Thomas' may have been the brother of Edward'. Also there was a Samuel' contemporaneous with these.

JOHN² "of Sandwich" and Susanna Cooke had
Zacheriah' b. July, 1651; m. Abiah Allen in 1686, daughter of Francis Allen and Mary Barlow of Sandwich. Administrator of his father's estate; d. in N. Kingstown.
Job Coock² b. 1655 Ap. 14; d. just prior to 1708.
Thomas²

JOB¹ and Hannah Taylor had
Daniel²
Desire S².
Job³ b. 1681.

ZACHERIAH² and Abiah Allen had (S. T. R.)
Mary⁴ b. Jan. 5, 1689, in Sandwich, Mass.
Hannah⁴ b. Oct. 9. 1691.
Abiah⁴ b. July 14, 1693.
Susan⁴ b. May 28, 1695.
John⁴ b. Ap. 5, 1697; m. Lydia.
Job⁴ b. June 5, 1699.
Jedediah⁴ b. Ap. 2, 1701.
Dinah⁴ b. May 17, 1703.
Zephonia⁴ b. Dec. 10, 1704.

A number of persons of the surname, Jenkins, were resident in Nantucket, Mass. The names and births of some of these are here given, though only partly coordinated or the line of descent shown. The data were kindly given by Miss Clara Parker of the Atheneum from the original records, and may be found useful in the future, even if only fragmentary.

MATTHEW² and Mary Gardner had, in Nantucket
Joseph³ b. about 1718; m. Anna Macy.
Peter³ b. about 1724; m. Abigail Gardner, and m. Mrs. Christian Folger, daughter of John Swain.

JOSEPH³ (of Matthew and Mary Gardner) and Anna Macy had, in Nantucket,
Miriam⁴ b. Aug. 4, 1738; d. July 4, 1755.
Jonathan⁴ b. Nov. 14, 1748-9; d. at sea 1768.
Joseph Jr⁴. b. Mar. 4, 1753; d. Feb. 20, 1830; m. Bethia

PETER³ (of Matthew and Mary Gardner) and Abigail Gardner had, in Nantucket,
Tristram⁴ b. Mar. 20, 1745; d. Sept. 10, 1808; m. Anna Macy (of Francis and Judith Macy).
David⁴ b. Mar. 24, 1754; d. at sea 1780.
Matthew⁴ b. Sept. 2, 1734; m. Lydia Macy; d. at sea 1757.

TRISTRAM⁴ (of Peter and Abigail Gardner) and Anna Macy had, in Nantucket,
Peter⁵ b. Aug. 8, 1775; d. June 24, 1828; m. Rose Patty-Messiton, a widow from England.
Judith⁵ b. Nov. 28, 1777; m. David Coffin. No issue.
Matthew⁵ b. Nov. 27, 1780; m. Betsey Caborn of N. Y.
David⁵ b. 1782; m. Polly Doane of Fairhaven, Mass.; m. Betsy Folger (of Thaddeus Folger).
Francis⁵ b. 1785; single.
Hannah⁵ b. Oct. 14, 1788; d. Sept. 20, 1833.
Deborah⁵ b. 1791; m. Isaac Myrick; m. Wm. Clark Jr.
Reuben⁵ b. Mar. 14, 1794; m. Lydia Folger.

PETER⁵ (of Tristram and Anna Macy) and Rose Patty—Mrs. Messiton—had, in Nantucket,
David⁶ b. Feb. 21, 1811; d. 1832.

William C. b. Nov. 20, 1815; single; d. Jan. 29, 1836.
Caroline' b. 1809; m. Daniel Emmons of N. Y.
Ann Maria' b. 1813; m. Wm. Coggeshall.

WILLIAM and Martha had
John b. Dec. 5, 1737.
William Jr. b. Dec. 30, 1738.
George b. May 24, 1743.
Martha bap. May 25, 1746.
Stephen b. May, 1753.
Lemuel and Martha had, in Nantucket,
Prudence b. Feb. 27, 1737.
Thomas b. Oct. 22, 1741.
Sarah bap. Sept. 6, 1747.
Leonard bap. Sept. 6, 1747.
Nanne bap. Sept. 6, 1747.
Sarah b. Oct. 30, 1748.
Robert b. July 28, 1740.
Elizabeth bap. Feb. 5, 1748-9.

JOHN W. (of Charles and Hannah) and Hannah Barton (of Joseph) had, in Nantucket,
Sarah W.
John W. Jr.
Hannah
Samuel, m. Mary Coffin.
William
Anna
Edward
(John W. Sr. also m. Hannah Alsop of Boston)

SAMUEL (of John W. and Hannah Barton) and Mary Coffin had, in Nantucket,
Sarah, m. John Price.

JOSEPH (Jr.'?) and Bethia had, in Nantucket,
Southard b. Aug. 31, 1778; d. June 29, 1827; m. Anna Raymond, widow of John Bocot.

WILLIAM W. b. Wellfleet; d. July 19, 1880; m. Lucy

59
CHARLES and Mary Sherman had, in Yarmouth, Mass.,
Mary A. m. Abraham Baker July 8, 1860.

William Jenkins was of Newbury (Mass.) in 1759. See Weeden. Vol. II, P. 647.

No. 3.

LIBRARY of
Cape Cod
HISTORY & GENEALOGY

PLYMOUTH CORPORATION, A TRADING COMPANY, LOCATED AT PLYMOUTH, A PROPRIETARY PLANTATION
By SAMUEL D. HANNAH

YARMOUTHPORT, MASS.:
C. W. SWIFT, Publisher and Printer,
The "Register" Press,
1928

PLYMOUTH CORPORATION, A TRADING COMPANY, LOCATED AT PLYMOUTH, A PROPRIETARY PLANTATION.

—From The Yarmouth Register, May 5, 1928.

That there is at this time much interest manifested in the early history of Massachusetts is indicated by the numerous inquiries made of Samuel D. Hannah of Buzzards Bay because of articles that have appeared in The Register, because of various cases that have been in the courts, and in addition a lot of space has been devoted to these cases by the daily newspapers, some of which articles are a fair statement of what is happening while other articles which have appeared in one or two papers in Boston deliberately twist truths into false meanings; thereby deceiving many of their readers, causing unnecessary alarm as to titles to settled properties which are in no way involved in the Proprietary question or in any of the cases that have been or are now being considered by the courts.

False alarms, inciting persons to group action and possibly riot may be a legitimate process in politics in order to push some one person or a party into power, but as an attempt to stampede the courts and secure decisions contrary to well-established principles of law, such methods have rarely had much influence.

The average citizen does not seem to know how important a place matters of history occupy in certain types of cases to be considered by the higher courts, the opinions of which establish the law for the states or nation as a whole.

There may be found in various states early decisions which may stand as law for a half century, even longer, yet it happens that even after so long a time because of the discovery of more correct historical data such decisions have been set aside and a change in the law is made to conform with correct information.

Then in certain types of cases extending throughout the entire history of a court, from the time of its creation, a line of decisions will impress a careful student that there is a state of uncertainty in the minds of the judges as to this particular question, but why it is so one is not able to discover from the opinions.

One of these perplexing questions in Massachusetts is and has been the so-called "common or public right" on the sea shores.

Mr Hannah believes this question is mainly a historical problem and a clean cut presentation to the courts of a complete history of the subject from 1620 in Massachusetts to the present day can easily establish certainty where uncertainty exists.

He contends also that this question as well as the question concerning the wild and waste lands in this commonwealth are purely historical problems to be worked out and cleared up by a careful study of the early practices of the Proprietary Plantations of Plymouth and Massachusetts Bay colonies. The Proprietary Plantations, group settlements which occupied all the lands in both colonies and which early in their history created and built up the central governments of each colony, established the common law for each.

Mr Hannah admits he as not made

a careful study of Proprietary Plantations of Massachusetts Bay colony but that his interest has been particularly centered on Plymouth colony and that five years' study for the average mind is not too much time to devote to the subject. Not only must all the records of Plymouth colony be read and reread but all the records of the Proprietary Plantations and a lot of other proprietors' records which were subordinate organizations within the plantations. Unlike the colony records, which were printed about 1858, the proprietors' records are not printed but written in the style of their day and spelling that is not the same as our own; they used words not familiar to us and there are instances where words as used did not have the same meaning as we use them.

Average intelligence, education, and penmanship compared favorably with the average of our day. There are examples of handwriting in these ancient records which would indicate that the writer may have been the settlement school teacher, and one who wrote wills, deeds, and other legal instruments.

In reading opinions in court cases of late years, we find statements by judges that grants of lands, deeds, etc., of the early period must be construed liberally because of the lack of knowledge or significance of legal terms required in such instruments during the early period of the colonies; but one who makes a study of the ancient proprietary grants, deeds and legal instruments of that time will soon discover that there has never been a time in all the history of our country when such matters were as well understood and that this knowledge continued almost all through the period when Proprietors were functioning but that after they ceased to be a dominating factor in affairs almost the entire population lost this knowledge and from that period until the lawyer became a factor in conveyancing they made a terrible mess of things connected with land titles; even the lawyers of the later period failed to grasp the fact that the Proprietors had laid a foundation for a conveyancing system that was one of the most remarkable accomplishments of these pioneers, a system of record titles which if carried on would have eliminated nine-tenths of the title complications of today.

And thus we find ourselves standing at the base and facing a high wall which we must scale and go back to 1620 and step by step follow the stages of development and the progress of events in order to correct certain theories of law that are known to be uncertain, but just why is not known.

Without question the only mystery is easily determinable by a careful study of the early history of the colonies of the commonwealth and the Proprietary land system.

At this point we are confronted with the one question upon which historians disagree. Was Plymouth colony created a government upon the signing of the Provincetown Pact? If not when did the colony develop into a government?

The natural way to determine these matters would be to read the opinions of historians and then decide, but the best way is to discard what historians have to say and sift the records and continue to sift and analize until one can form an opinion

3

of his own, then read what historians have to say and check points of disagreement.

Naturally Plymouth colony history is of most interest to Cape Cod property owners because much false information has been circulated, perhaps not alone for selfish motives but in the main because few persons have made any study of the subject or know anything about it.

Most persons know who the Pilgrims were, why they came to America, and how they suffered many hardships during the early years after their arrival, but few do know the processes by which they established a government.

Historians tell us that the coming of the Pilgrims to the place they named Plymouth was a matter of accident, or misadventure at sea, forcing a landing at Cape Cod, now called Provincetown. Even the Pilgrims themselves indicate that their purpose was to settle elsewhere, but Mr Hannah believes that while this may have been the belief of most of the passengers on the Mayflower, he is of the opinion that some of the leaders of the enterprise, either the English capitalists interested or the leaders of the Pilgrims or possibly the two interests in combination knew exactly what they had in mind to do and did it. There were numerous reasons why they should do what was done, but this is not important at this time except perhaps to indicate how they acted in reference to the title and ownership of the land on which they established themselves at Plymouth.

They had no authority from the English government to settle where they did, which fact they well knew, but they assumed the attitude that the true ownership of the soil was in the Indian occupants from whom they acquired the title. This applied only to the land in about Plymouth and appears to have included what is now Duxbury and Scituate or a portion of these areas.

This area was acquired from Massasoyte either by purchase or as a gift and is described by Gov Bradford as Plymouth Plantation.

It seems to be fairly clear that Plymouth corporation which was the trading or colonizing company, formed with English capitalists and shipowners, did not at first make any claims of territory or territorial jurisdiction beyond the limits of Plymouth Plantation, and it was not till some years later that a patent was secured which appeared to define the jurisdiction of the corporation as covering what became the entire area of Plymouth colony.

According to the agreement made with the English capitalists and shipowners, the Pilgrims and settlers could purchase the English rights in the corporation and in 1627, 58 men gave a bond to pay a sum agreed upon.

Having secured the patent enlarging their jurisdiction, the purchasers of the corporation found themselves confronted with the difficult problem of meeting their obligation. The Plymouth settlement had increased in numbers and about 1638 groups began to form wishing to establish new settlements or plantations within the territory controlled by the corporation—accordingly the right to settle and establish new plantations was granted for a money consideration which sums would enable the Purchasers to meet their bond. These grants carried with them the obligation to purchase the Indian title to the areas granted. Thus Sandwich, Barnstable and Yarmouth Plantations were established. About this time there seems to have developed much dissatisfaction as to the governing authority exercised by the corporation, which in fact was only a trading company and without any political or civil control over the plantations beyond Plymouth Plantation.

In order to establish some kind of governmental authority over the entire territory of the colony it was agreed that the purchasers of the corporation should choose definite areas of land for themselves and their children and surrender the remainder of their lands, not then granted and that which they chose for themselves, to the body of Freemen and thus establish a government. This was brought about in 1640 and finally completed several years later.

All that section of the Cape east of Yarmouth passed to the purchasers of the patent as one of the three places selected for themselves and their children. From this area developed the plantations of Nauset (Eastham, now Wellfleet, Eastham and Orleans), Sautucket (now Brewster and a portion of Harwich), Monumoit or Monumoi (now Chatham and part of Harwich). Monumoiett as it appears from Plymouth colony records took in all Chatham and all of Harwich extending up to Herring river on the Sound, which must have been the boundary between early Yarmouth and Monumoiett.

Also in this area was Paomet, now Truro, and Provincetown. But at the tip end of Paomet was Cape Cod, a point of land extending perhaps a half mile beyond Cape Head. Joining Cape Cod was an arm or pothook which formed Cape Cod harbor. This point or arm was purchased in 1650 by the colony for the fishing privileges, by Thomas Prince. This became known as "Colony" or "People's land" and later when the Province was created it was called "Province land."

There arose a dispute between the purchasers of the patent and the colony as to just how far the purchasers' area extended, but this was quite a complicated situation and not important to discuss in detail at this time.

After the formation of a real government there seems to have been some radical changes in policy.

The earlier plantations seem to have been entirely independent of Plymouth corporation, made their own laws, orders, etc., but the new government became recognized as a medium necessary to development and control of interproprietary relations, particularly Indian affairs, the sale of liquor which became a very serious problem, also highways and bridges as between the various plantations.

Plymouth Plantation, which at first was synonymous with the Corporation, became separated and functioned in the same way as other plantations. About this time the plantations began to be classed as townships, which indicates that the plantation idea was undergoing a change because the idea or name "plantation" was more like a colony which had no super government over it. It was purely proprietary in that it exercised all the governmental functions, the ecclesiastical or religious function and land ownership and control.

When the government of the colony was established, and the plantations recognized its authority, the change to township in name meant a recognition of a superior authority.

The township continued proprietary in form but as time passed the central government began to make laws and orders which had to do with the civil affairs of the townships.

One of the early orders passed by the government about 1650 was that the freemen of the townships should meet together and make town laws, another order was passed that the town clerks should keep record books for recording deeds, deaths, marriages, etc.

Another early order was that the freemen should meet together and compare all rules, orders and laws as passed by plantations, from which were to be selected such as were important and these were to be established as a body of laws for the colony. Thus the laws of the colony were built up from the customs and common practices of the various plantations, and recognized as the common law.

The Proprietary townships having submitted to a higher governing body, soon discovered that they no longer exercised the same authortiy they did as plantations. The civil function began to be classed as the town, subject to government orders, the church occupied the same position, but jurisdiction over the land remained as before.

These distinctions were not suddenly made but extended over many years.

It was during the early period of the Province that the Proprietors began to lose their influence with the General Court and laws were enacted giving the non-proprietor element greater privileges in civil or town affairs, particularly in town meetings. As townships increased in population and the Proprietor class lost political power the Proprietors retained control of their lands by separate and exclusive meetings of Proprietors and in some instances their records continued a part of the town records or in the same book. The town clerk and proprietors' clerk were usually the same person.

It is not difficult to understand why this should happen, because the Proprietors from their beginning had created a system of record titles to land.

Land, in order to pass to private owners, had to come from the Proprietors by grant.

Then about 1650 Plymouth colony passed a law that each town should have a book for recording of deeds, so that with Proprietors' grants entered in town records and as well all deeds of this land from individual owner to subsequent owners, the system was complete within each township. Later the registry of deeds was created in the counties, which eliminated the necessity of town recording. But even if the recording of deeds passed to the county registry, the Proprietors' records still remained the place of record for new titles which they created even after the county registry was established.

6

When the towns separated from the Proprietors, taking the religious function with it, it became in fact a municipal corporation with both the civil and religious functions; later the religious function separated from the town and became the parish or church corporation.

Thus it was the Proprietary Plantation or township which combined the three functions of property ownership and control, the civil function and the religious function, became divided into three distinct corporate bodies.

Our Supreme judicial court has over a long period of time and by numerous decisions clearly defined the status of each of these bodies and has outlined the steps leading up to the final separation.

Even at this late date the claim is sometimes made that the towns of today are the successors of the Proprietary township and own any land never disposed of by the Proprietors, but our Supreme court has definitely settled this question and in several cases of fairly recent date. Chief Justice Holmes while a member of our Supreme judicial court stated in a case in which this question was raised that these grants made by Plymouth colony were a sale of land to private individuals and not grants establishing municipal corporations, which followed in line with all other decisions of this court.

Whether Plymouth colony in its earlier stages was a real government or not, it assumed the right to make such grants and they have been fully sustained. How the grantees conducted their affairs determined their status as corporations and that they were corporations was definitely settled both by statute and by court decisions. Such corporations cannot die so long as they own land.

The grants made by Plymouth colony to the persons named, for which money was paid, were contracts which can neither be altered or abridged by legislative acts or by court decisions—which principles of law are established beyond doubt.

The only question of doubt is how these corporations can be made to function and how they may convey any lands they own at this time. This question is now being considered by the Supreme judicial court and may soon be definitely determined.

Another interesting matter concerning the common law or practices of the Plantations of Plymouth colony as distinct and separate from the action of Plymouth colony as a government is not understood.

Among the early orders established in Plymouth Plantation and before any other plantations existed was that hunting, fowling and fishing should be free and that every man should have access to the water no matter where he lived. This was a regulation applying only to Plymouth Plantation and to the common lands of this Plantation.

Later in the history of the colony after it became a full governing authority, an order was passed by the General court that common lands of Proprietors should remain untaxed so long as they were allowed to be used by the public generally. This law was later enacted by the Province and continued in force by the Commonwealth, so that such lands have never been taxed and are not at the present day. The general uses permitted to the public were hunting, fowling, fishing, and many other

7

uses permitted to townspeople, erection of salt works, flaking and drying areas for fish, whaling grounds, drying salt hay, etc.,

From such practices in dealing with common lands of the Proprietary township grew the theory in law of a common or public right, which theory is correct, but it is only a permissive right extending to the public so long as the Proprietors as owners of such areas were exempt from taxation and so long as they wished to enjoy freedom from taxation.

Such laws are by their nature contracts and irrepealable.

Another theory in law is quite common and that is that such grants as were made to Proprietors were franchises from the government and if not exercised for many years were subject to forfeiture, by legal process, setting up non use or abuse.

It is also a well established principle in law that non use alone is not sufficient grounds for forfeiture and must be coupled with abuse, but to enforce forfeiture there must have been reserved in the original grant the right to declare a forfeiture for non use. There were no reservations in the Plymouth grants.

Again, if at any time the government has passed any law recognising non use then no forfeiture can be declared. The statutes of Plymouth colony and later the Province, stating that common lands shall not be taxed, if thrown open to the use of the public, is sufficient recognition on the part of the Commonwealth to prevent any claim of forfeiture for non use of a franchise of such a nature even if all other reasons for declaration of forfeiture were of no avail.

Therefore there is no foundation to the claim that the Proprietors have long since ceased to exist. So long as they own land they must exist.

No. 4.

LIBRARY *of*
Cape Cod
HISTORY & GENEALOGY

SUMMER STREET—HAWES LANE
Yarmouthport

By ELLEN H. SHIELDS

YARMOUTHPORT, MASS.:
C. W. SWIFT, Publisher and Printer,
The "Register" Press,
1928

SUMMER STREET—HAWES LANE
Yarmouthport

It is not generally known among the younger generation and many of the older that Summer street was in the early days of the town known as Hawes lane.

Many years ago a philanthropic old gentleman, whose family owned a goodly part of the land, probably thought he would dignify this thoroughfare by changing "lane" to "street." He erected a sign on the corner by the town pump on which was painted "Summer Street." This change was accepted by the town so from that fact it is still Summer street and not Hawes lane.

This name, I am told, was derived from Edmond Hawes, who occupied a house on the corner of the lane and the main street. The opposite side of the street was mostly owned by the Sears estate.

In the early 60's the upper end of the west side from the Morgan place to Dennis pond was owned by the late Edward B. Hallett. On deeds of the property sold at that time and on insurance papers taken out the location is given as Hawes lane.

In early years of the town this way was used as a means of the citizens to reach Dennis pond, where they were wont to take their cattle for water, and it was through this source that the way was often referred to as "Cow lane."

Of the seventeen houses that were formerly on this street, nearly 50 per cent. were moved from another location.

At one time there was an old Cape Cod house, a much desired present day style of architecture, standing on the ground in front of but more to the north of where The Cupboard is now. This old house was removed and a new two and a half story house erected further back from the street, by the late James Knowles. This house was always occupied by Mr. Knowles's family until a few years ago, after the death of Mrs. Knowles, the family vacated it. It was then occupied in the rear for a short period when it was finally destroyed by fire. Later the house known as The Cupboard was built on the same site and is occupied at the present time by the Misses Knowles.

The next house, occupied by Mr. and Mrs. B. W. Ellis, was

formerly on the Simpkins estate just east of the bank building or property, and was the property of the late Matthews C. Hallet, father of Thacher T. Hallet. Mr. Hallet carried on a tin or hardware business in the front room. When Mrs. Simpkins acquired this property, the house was purchased by the late James A. Cash, who moved it to its present location, and it is now owned and occupied by his daughter, Mrs. B. W. Ellis.

The house now occupied by Mrs. Phebe Vincent was built by her father, the late Calvin Hallett. Mr. Hallett was a staunch Methodist and when the church of that denomination ceased to exist, Mr. Hallett, probably for a souvenir, removed a few of the numbers from the pews. These he put on his house—16 to designate the street number and 1845 to indicate the year the house was built.

The next house was built on the ground on which it stands and was occupied for many years by the family of Mr. and Mrs. Benjamin Hamblin, parents of Brevet-Major Joseph Hamblin, a distinguished officer in the Civil War. It is now owned by C. R. Simpkins.

The next house in line was at one time a part of the store of James Knowles, who moved it up to this site to make room for the erection of a new store, the one that is now the property of A. A. Knowles. Another small house, also a part of the old Knowles store, was moved to the adjoining lot and was occupied at one time by Thomas G. Cook. This house was demolished several years ago, and the land on which both sections of the old store stood is now also the property of Mr. Simpkins.

It will be interesting to many of our readers of The Register to know that these two buildings originally were situated on the land where the Thacher Annex now stands. They were the property and used as a store by the late Henry Thacher, grandfather of Messrs. T. C. and L. B. Thacher. They passed into the hands of Mr. Knowles and were moved from this location to where the Knowles store stands and were moved again to make room for the new building above referred to.

There were two small buildings in the next lot, which were the property of Anthony Howard, father of the late Mrs. Patrick Morgan. Both of these houses were torn down some years ago as they gave way to decay. The first one was formerly used as a postoffice in Yarmouth. The second house in this same lot was moved, I have been told, from the western end of the grounds of Captain Frederic Howes, near where the house of Mrs. Joanna White stood, now the property of Mrs. Sophia Wolfe. The land on which these houses stood is still owned by the heirs of Mrs. Morgan.

The next house was built by the late William Shields and is now owned and occupied by his heirs.

On the other side of the street, I know of but one house that was moved from another site. The house owned and occupied by the Misses Coffey is said to have been moved to its present location, but this information is unauthentic. The next house, however, was moved from a lot of land diagonally across the street between the Ellis and Knowles estates. It was originally owned and probably built by Otis Crowell, who sold it to Frederic Matthews, who in turn sold it to James Gorham. It was then moved and finally it passed into the hands of the Misses Coffey, who are the present owners.

The remaining houses on the street, that of the heirs of Benjamin Hallett, the summer homes of Charles Lincoln and James Knowles, the Sears Arms Annex (built by Ebenezer Sears of Revolutionary fame) and the Sears Arms, which was originally the property of J. Montgomery Sears of Boston, it is safe to say, were all built on the ground on which they stand.

The above notes were derived some time ago from an old resident of the town, who for many years lived on this street.

No. 5.

LIBRARY *of* Cape Cod HISTORY & GENEALOGY

THE BAKER ZONE IN WEST DENNIS

By SYLVANUS C. EVANS

YARMOUTHPORT, MASS.:
C. W. SWIFT, Publisher and Printer,
The "Register" Press,
1928

THE BAKER ZONE IN WEST DENNIS

West Dennis, Mass., March 30, 1928.
To the Editor of The Yarmouth Register,
Dear Mr. Swift:

I make no pretence as a historian; should I do so you doubtless would have good reason to impeach my claim. I do, however, have an ardent taste for local history and I assume others may find something of interest in my revelations.

Fate decreed that I should be born in West Dennis, in the part which I choose to term the Baker Zone. The zone is about one mile in distance and scarcely a home in this Zone was without Baker blood three-quarters of a century ago and more, and it is of these that I write.

Beginning at the lower part of the village of South Dennis lived Uncle Peter Baker, a character well known in southeastern Massachusetts in his time. He had a large family, among whom were C. and J. F. Baker, well-known Boston merchants. Across the street from his home lived John Baker (a merchant), succeeded by his son James. Next lived Sukey Baker Harding, daughter of John. Across the street lived Peter Baker, Jr. Crossing the street diagonally lived Joshua Baker. Circling the triangular lot formerly known as the flag staff lot, lived Benjamin Thacher, Sr., whose wife was Sukey Baker, daughter of Judah Baker, Sr. Next was the homestead of Judah Baker, Sr., later owned by his son, Ezra H. Baker, and is still owned by his heirs. Ezra H. was one of Boston's leading men in commerce. The next house in order was that of Howes Baker, Sr. This property is still owned by his heirs. Next was the home of Theophilus Baker, Sr., later of Archelus, his son, and yet owned by his heirs.

Across the street in the present home of Mrs. Jessie Rogers, lived William Baker. This property, however, was owned by his brother, Ezra H. Later it was owned by Elkanah S. Baker. The next was the home of Samuel Baker; this house was razed and his son, Colin C., erected a house for summer occupancy. This house has since been moved to a location near the Hotel Belmont in West Harwich. Across the street lived Elnathan Kelley, whose wife was Harriet Baker; this house, however, is of more recent date. Next was the home of Coleman Small, whose wife was Betsey Baker. Across the street in the present home of the Edwards family stood the home of Henry White; this house was moved to South Yarmouth many years since. Mrs. White was the daughter of Benjamin Thacher and Sukey Baker. Next was the home of Joseph Thacher, a son of Benjamin Thacher and Sukey Baker.

Across the street lived Ezra Thacher, a brother of Joseph. Ezra's wife was Lucy Baker. This house is still owned and occupied by their daughter, Mrs. Seth Russell Baker. Across the street was the home of Crowell Baker, father of Mrs. Julia Ann Crowell and Mrs. Ruth Child et al. Later this house was owned by Peleg Howes, whose wife was a daughter of Judah Baker, Sr. Still later this property was acquired by my father, William Evans, and was my home from the age of six years until I married. On this lot today stands the fine residence of Dr. Hall.

The next in order, the house now owned by Mr. Marshall, was the home fo Sidney Baker. Across the street, the house of Mrs. Atcherly is of more recent origin. The next house to Sidney Baker's, the present home of Mrs. Heckman, was owned by Isaiah Baker. The next, now owned by Mrs. King, was the home of Daniel Baker. The next now owned by Mrs. Irving Rogers, was the home of Joseph and Jarius Baker. The next, now owned by Dr. Sears, was the home of Elisha Baker, the father of Elisha and John Baker, who were well-known merchants in Philadelphia. Next was the home of Zeno Gage; while there is no trace of Baker blood here we will attach a little because Zeno Gage's mother married Samuel Baker (second marriage). Across the street the home of Solomon F. Davis was originally built by Coleman Small, whose wife was Betsey Baker previously mentioned.

The next, the present home of Benjamin Davis, was that of his grandfather, Solomon Davis, and wife Phebe Baker. Across the street was the home of Deacon Samuel Small and his wife, Hetty Baker, daughter of Uncle Peter Baker. The next was the home of Arunah Small, whose wife was the daughter of Judah Baker, Sr. This house is now owned by Arthur Wade, but is radically changed from the original. The next, the present home of Isaiah Sherman, was the home of Lincoln Baker, the father of Mrs. Angeline Crowell. In the two Rogers houses across the street I find no trace of Baker blood, nor at the former home of Allen S. Crowell. Next to Lincoln Baker's was the home of Julius Baker, later owned by my father and the one in which I was born and lived until about six years of age. This is the lot on which now stands the residence of Mrs. Grace Gaylord. The next house, now owned by Mrs. Grace L. Greenleaf, was the home of Moses Small, whose wife, Love, was a sister of Zeno Gage, whose mother married Samuel Baker before mentioned.

Across the street was the home of Caleb Howes, who married a Baker, a sister of Alpheus Baker, Sr., of South Dennis. The next was the home of my grandfather, Sylvanus Crowell, my present home. A daughter of Sylvanus Crowell, Sarah, married Alexander Baker and made her home there many years. The next, the present home of Dr. Osborne, was the home of Calvin F. Baker. This house, however, is of more recent origin. In the next, formerly the home of Allen B. Crowell, now owned by the heirs of Henry H. Fisk, has lived for many years Cynthia J. (Baker) Fisk. In the next, the present home of Hiram C. Crowell, Baker blood still flows as Mrs. Crowell's maiden name was Susan K. Baker. The next, the home of J. H. Jenks, was the home of Joshua Howes, whose mother, Mrs. Ruth Child, was the daughter of Crowell Baker.

The next house, the present home of Mrs. L. C. Keith, was the home of her father, Obed Baker, 3rd. Across the street the property known as the Luther Child estate was purchased by Captain Child from Isaiah Baker, the same Isaiah previously mentioned.

About all of the houses that I have mentioned were built by the ones named and were the original houses within this zone. It is here that the Baker zone ends and the Crowell begins.

I trust these annals may be of interest to some, as it is to me to narrate them.

      Yours very truly,
       Sylvanus C. Evans,
        West Dennis, Mass.

No. 6.

LIBRARY of
Cape Cod
HISTORY & GENEALOGY

CAPE COD LAND TITLES
By SAMUEL D. HANNAH

YARMOUTHPORT, MASS.:
C. W. SWIFT, Publisher and Printer,
The "Register" Press,
1927

CAPE COD LAND TITLES

By SAMUEL D. HANNAH

[From The Yarmouth Register, September 24, 1927.]

A recent interview with Samuel D. Hannah of Buzzards Bay disclosed a situation of importance to all real estate owners in Barnstable county and to those interested in buying property.

It seems that his purpose in trying by legal process to establish the rights of the Proprietary Corporations of the Ancient Cape towns, is to discover if possible a method to create marketable titles to the wild and undeveloped lands, beaches, flats, etc., which areas at this time have but few claimants and if there are persons making such claims, they are of such a flimsy nature that no one should be imposed upon and led to give up their money for nothing in return.

Mr Hannah stated emphatically that he was not concerned and had in no instance made any attempt to disturb titles to types of property classed as settled and occupied lands, furthermore that the burning of the Barnstable County Registry of Deeds about a century ago could in no way have any effect on such titles because twenty years use and occupation of farms, houses, cultivated, fenced and occupied lands was generally speaking sufficient evidence of real ownership. Therefore, such properties are entirely excluded in the question of Proprietary rights.

Mr Hannah claims that because of his experience of buying and selling land in all parts of Barnstable county for the past twenty-five years and having thoroughly investigated the titles and claims to thousands of areas or tracts of land, coupled with the advice of a number of expert conveyancers of recognized standing, that he is in a better position to judge the situation than anyone who had had but a limited view of the general situation.

In the towns of Sandwich, Bourne, Falmouth and Mashpee, he purchased and sold to a single corporation more than twelve thousand acres. It took ten years to discover the ownership of the hundreds of separate areas, to buy the land and correct title defects to make a marketable title. In this area alone there were several thousand acres not assessed to anyone and even the persons discovered to be the owners by inheritance did not know they owned it.

During the effort to unravel the mystery of titles to this large area, it became necessary frequently to consult the Ancient Proprietary Records to discover ancient land marks described in deeds, to learn family history and local history. Had it not been that a progressive surveyor by the name of Jesse Boyden of Sandwich, who lived and worked about a century ago, had made a careful study of the Ancient Sandwich Proprietors' records and constructed a general plan of the Proprietors' land divisions, including most all the wood lands of Sandwich--which then included Bourne, it would have made the task of acquiring the bulk of this area almost impossible.

The experience and good fortune in the study of the Sandwich Proprietary records naturally gave him a clue to the mystery of the titles in other sections of Cape Cod to which it became necessary to resort in order to work out similar problems. It was thus he discovered that it was possible to construct maps of areas of Proprietors' divided lands in each town which would serve the same purpose as the Jesse Boyden map of Sandwich and Bourne wood lands.

It was by making a general outline of the divided lands that it was discovered that in every town certain types of land were never divided or sold to anyone because such lands then had no value,—such types as sand beaches or beach upland, broken lands which were areas of shifting sands partly covered with a growth of scrub or beach grass. These areas were sometimes called general fields— which meant that certain times of year grazing animals must be fenced out to protect the growth and hold the sand. Yet, other times pasturing was permitted to the generality of the Proprietary, hence the name "General Field."

These different types of land held in reservation, together with the home plots, salt meadow divisions and wood land divisions, covered practically the entire area and to construct such a plan of a town is not difficult. Neither is it so difficult to place the ancient land marks, roads, brooks, ponds, rivers, etc., according to their ancient names, which is the key to the solution of many difficult Cape titles.

In purchasing land Mr Hannah says that in many parts of the Cape at least half the titles to unoccupied lands could not be accepted as marketable and many claims to ownership were made without any evidence to support them. It later developed that the doubtful titles generally proved to be in areas within Proprietary towns which had never been disposed of to any one by the Proprietors.

Naturally persons buying real estate have an idea that the assessors of a town is the place to get information about all the land in the towns, but generally the assessors of Cape towns, when it comes to giving information as to wild and unoccupied lands are at sea, for an early method of assessing and still in general use taxes John Doe fifty acres of wood land, twenty acres of salt meadow, etc., but they have no record to show where it is—or there may be areas of land assessed to no one and the information given is that "No one owns it or it probably belongs to the town or to the State or United States—any way it is not assessed and has no value." The real reason why it has no value is because there is apparently no title in any known owner with whom a purchaser can deal.

It is only within the past twenty-five or thirty years that shore property on the Cape has been developing to the point of a real market. Buzzards Bay shores started earlier but down Cape there was little activity.

During the past five or ten years even these lower sections have been developing rapidly with the result that old deeds that have been in attic trunks for a half century or more are being recorded and many persons are asking the assessors to assess to them lands which have not before been discovered.

Many excuses are made for the poor titles of Cape Cod because of the burning of the Registry; but it was years ago, as late as 1800, the common practice not to record deeds and from 1800 to the Registry fire 1828, probably as many were not recorded as were.

Many of the early deeds of Cape lands were not drawn by lawyers but by the seller and warranty deeds were always given. Yet the descriptions of the land are so indefinite and crude that no one can tell where the land is except the buyer, "because the seller showed him the bounds." It frequently happened that if the owner cut off the wood and later needed another wood lot he would change locations, or if there was a locality where land was selling, particularly during the demand for shore locations, he would move down in a shore section and dispose of it at a fancy price.

Only within recent years have the Cape towns made any systematic effort to correctly assess property. A card index system of copies of all deeds are now sent to the towns and filed with their records for reference for descriptions for assessing. This property now changing hands is assessed with considerable accuracy but properties that have not been conveyed for some years past may have an assessors record that can give no one an idea of its location, or the land may not be assessed at all.

Only recently has it been the practice to have surveys made of land and such plans recorded with the Registry. Even the making of surveys may lead to considerable confusion. Unless the ancient land marks commonly mentioned in deeds can be located, one is apt to consider local hearsay as authority, which is as a rule not to be relied upon. Changing names and locations of ancient land marks, rivers, creeks, roads, etc., will very often create such confusion as to upset an entire neighborhood.

Mr Hannah contends that the courts in determining disputes as to titles can only decide on evidence and the facts presented by title examiners and attorneys in the cases.

It has been the practice in conveyancing to rely on information found in the Registry of Deeds. For settled lands this theory is no doubt as a general principle correct, but it will not answer in the examination of titles to wild lands.

As the courts can only determine questions of title from evidence and

3

information furnished, Mr Hannah's method has been in Land Court cases to raise questions as to several titles in scattered sections of each town, present to the court all the information as to the record title in the Registry of Deeds, also information contained in the Proprietors records. When these several cases have been presented then there is in the possession of the court full information both as to the ancient title situation and the recent record title—if any exists.

If courts are in error in making decisions it is generally not the fault of the courts but in the presentation of a case. Courts must have information and it is an attorney's job to furnish it no matter how tedious the work of preparation is. Historical data often plays an important part in securing correct court opinions and if not presented serious consequences may follow.

About a century ago the courts took the position that certain ordinances of a Massachusetts Bay colony, 1641 to 1647, applied to Plymouth Colony, but the justice who rendered the opinion stated he was not familiar with the history of the Plymouth Colony. This opinion established the law for many years when, by a decision made fairly recently, the Supreme Court decided that these ordinances did not apply to Plymouth Colony until 1692 when it was annexed to Massachusetts Bay Colony and the Province created. The reason for the change of attitude on the part of the Court was as stated because of the presentation of new facts or information. Plymouth Colony records had by the time of the late decision been printed so that it was not a difficult matter to acquire information concerning Plymouth Colony.

Another decision rendered about the same time established in law what may be called the Common or Public Right in the shell fisheries. This opinion and many since have left this question more or less surrounded by a haziness, that it is difficult to know just what this Common or Public Right is.

Had there been presented to the Courts the historical data contained in the Ancient Proprietary Records concerning this particular question, it would have been discovered that there was no such thing as a Common or Public Right in the shell fisheries, but it was a Right of Common belonging to the Proprietors owning the Proprietary townships. No one other than Proprietors of a township was allowed to trespass for the purpose of taking shellfish on the flats of another town. This was the same practice of the Indian tribes and had been from time unknown until the coming of the white man and the purchase by him of the Indian rights and property.

By presenting to the Land Court all the history and records available, Mr Hannah believes that there is thus accumulated a fund of information so complete and valuable and of so much importance in determining titles, rights of indivduals and the public, that in time the best legal minds will realize that for several

4

145

centuries students of history and law have overlooked much. Even now one is frequently asked why it was a Japanese, Roy H. Akagi, made such a careful study of the early history of New England in reference to land titles and discovered facts never before collected and presented in book form and why our own historians and legal minds failed to uncover the long lost information.

Mr Akagi dealt only with a general historical situation discovered here and there in the various New England states and in a few Proprietary towns. To have gone into the various details of all the Proprietary towns would have taken many years. Mr Hannah has confined his efforts entirely to the Proprietary towns lying within Barnstable county and originally only a part of the land held by New Plymouth Corporation.

Each Proprietary town must be separately studied because each town had the right to make its own laws and orders concerning their lands and in some particulars these methods, while similar, were quite different and there is no fixed rule to be applied to all.

A single decision of the courts cannot settle all the questions involved. The entire subject though ancient is entirely new to the legislative bodies and the courts in general. The usual practice in these Land Court cases is for the opposing attorneys to undertake to cite laws and decisions but nowhere in the laws of Plymouth Colony, the Province and the Commonwealth can laws be found applicable to the Ancient Proprietary Township Corporations and but few of the Court decisions deal with the Plymouth Proprietary Corporations and this phase of the subject.

There are laws and there are decisions dealing with Proprietors and Common Lands but there were numerous types of Proprietees, differing in status from the ancient Plymouth Proprietary Corporations or townships.

Even in the court of Plymouth Colony, where frequently cases were brought in which Proprietors' rights were concerned, this court finally ruled it had no authority to deal with questions of title concerning such lands and referred all such disputes back to the Proprietors themselves to settle in their regular way. Practically all such suits were non suited. This situation existed up to the time the Province was established and Plymouth Colony annexed to it. The government of the Province seemed to have but little knowledge of the situation in Plymouth Colony and later the Commonwealth seems to have known less about it.

One of the early cases before the Supreme Court of the Commonwealth was the Monamoi Great Beach Proprietors. These Proprietees in the first instance consisted of meadow owners in severalty who came together and by agreement established a common field by a fencing agreement,—then probably one hundred years later as was the custom, incorporated under the law of the Commonwealth. This was not a Proprietary township of the earlier form.

5

The court in rendering its opinion stated that such corporations were meant to die, which was very true because the only way to dissolve a Common field where the land originally was held in severalty, was to "lay it down"—in other words the Corporation merely gave up group management. This kind of a corporation could not by vote convey the meadow lots held in severalty. The agreements and organization was not for land ownership but for common fencing, protection and management. Yet in this same case the court states that the Proprietors of Common and undivided lands are not abridged but enlarged by statute.

Just what meaning the learned judge meant to convey by this statement is not clear. An enlargement of rights might prove to be an abridgement. But as to the ancient Proprietary Corporations or township, none were ever incorporated under the Province laws or under the laws of the Commonwealth.

These ancient associated groups of individuals owned land acquired by purchases from two sources,—the parent Colonial Corporation and the Indians. They held these lands through grants and by deeds. These grants were without doubt contracts which neither the legislative bodies or the courts could abridge by laws enacted or by court decisions.

The corporation of New Plymouth made three types of grants: first, to individuals; second, Proprietary townships or Plantations, most of which were made prior to 1640—sometimes called, early in Plymouth records, Colonies—and officials of the Corporation of New Plymouth were sometimes designated as the government of the United Colonies; third, later in its history grants were made to a limited group, two or more, of a tract of land not in any township, which areas were to be divided to the individuals of the group in equal proportions. The purpose of the later grants was immediate division, but, it sometimes happened, this intended division was not made and later in the history of the Colony about 1682 a law was passed providing how a meeting of such groups could be called for the purposes of carrying out the divisions of such areas, then held in common. This law had nothing to do with the Proprietary Townships.

The question is sometimes asked how many Proprietors now have an ownership in the ancient township corporations? This question is difficult to answer but Mr Hannah states it is safe to estimate a number of from a quarter to a half million in each township corporation; that these Proprietors are scattered all over the world, but that it is an easy matter to pick out a Proprietor if a person's ancestry can be traced back three generations and the name is the same as an Ancient Proprietor's surname. In Cape Cod a half century ago it was a common practice to have family trees made. The trunk of the tree represented the founders of the family and the branches the descendants. These family trees are not now difficult to find on the Cape.

According to custom and according to later laws Proprietary share interests descended from one generation to another and were not willed or administered upon. Unless the Proprietary records show transfers of share interests which were sometimes disposed of by sale, there would be no change in ownership except from generation to generation — the interest of each descendant would diminish according to the number of heirs, but in all cases a descendant would have some fractional interest of the original share in the corporation. For practical purposes of participation in Proprietary affairs, a thousandth part of a share is equal to a whole share for the owner of the fractional part is a Proprietee the same today as was his first ancestor Proprietor. A person holding a fractional Proprietary interest had a vote in all meetings when present.

It frequently happens that a present day Proprietor's original ancestor had a share interest in a particular Cape township, but by inter-Proprietary marriages of succeeding generations, the present day Proprietor not only has a share interest in one township but may have in all of them in Barnstable county.

The estimated average number of lineal descendants of a couple married about 1630 and extended down to the present or ninth generation, will be over two hundred thousand—and if all the living descendants of the early Cape Proprietors decided at one time to visit the home sites of their early ancestors, there would be land enough on the Cape for standing room only.

7

No. 7.

LIBRARY *of*
Cape Cod
HISTORY & GENEALOGY

PERMISSIVE USES OF THE COMMON LANDS OF PROPRIETARY PLANTATIONS

By Samuel D. Hannah

YARMOUTHPORT, MASS.:
C. W. SWIFT, Publisher and Printer,
The "Register" Press,
1927

PERMISSIVE USES OF THE COMMON LANDS OF PROPRIETARY PLANTATIONS

By Samuel D. Hannah

Because of the recent article in The Yarmouth Register, Samuel D. Hannah of Buzzards Bay has been asked "If adverse possession ran against Common Lands." Mr Hannah's theory is that there was no adverse use of such lands because all Proprietors in a township were allowed to use the land for their own private purposes so long as there were no permanent structures erected and maintained beyond a period when the land and building could be used with profit. This permission often extended to the use of the inhabitants although they were not Proprietors.

The uses made of common areas, particularly beach, meaning what in modern terms is called beach upland, were numerous. The most common use was the drying and stacking of salt hay, sedge and thatch; then there were stages for the curing of fish in the air and sun—or the drying places called "flake fields," where the fish after splitting and salting were spread out over a large area on sticks or boards. Then there were landing places—sometimes docks built of piling and boarding. Later the salt industry developed and salt works were erected, usually on the back side of a beach near salt water ponds, from which the salt water was pumped into evaporating vats.

Try houses where fish and blubber were boiled in order to procure the oil was a common process in the early days, and extended to a time not beyond the memory of some persons now living. Sometimes this process was carried on under the shelter of a roofed structure or it might be done in the open.

Still another use was the burning of lime from shells which were in large heaps, left by the Indians over a period of centuries.

The making of tar at one time was not an uncommon industry. The Proprietors of the common wood land frequently gave permission within restricted areas to box the pines, collect the sap and treat it on the premises to separate the resin and the tar, or it might be done by a heating process applied to pine knots. For this privilege a rental was sometimes paid to the Proprietee and distributed to the Proprietors.

Because of these permissive uses of common lands allowed to the public in general no taxes were ever paid by the Proprietary corporations within Plymouth Colony even after the creation of the Province and the Commonwealth.

The same general practice was followed as to the Proprietors' flats between high and low water. The taking of shellfish, sedge, thatch, etc., was a use permissive to all Proprietors and at times extended to admitted inhabitants, subject however to special regulation by the Proprietors.

Many instances may be found in the ancient proprietary records where uses of flats were parceled out to the Proprietors for specific purposes during the will of the Proprietee and subject to such regulations as a Proprietors' committee might make or such regulations as were voted at regular or special meetings of Proprietors.

The whole question of shellfishing which has grown into a tangle of legal questions, indefinite in most respects, has been caused largely because little attention has been paid to the early history of Plymouth Colony by legislative bodies. Even the courts in earlier days made rulings not consistent with the conditions that existed in early colonial times. Later the judicial department of our state government became better informed and in part corrected former errors.

The earlier rulings were not errors when considered in the light of historical data presented to the court,— these rulings only prove to have been an error when there was clearer presentation of early colonial conditions.

Our Selectmen of the present day is of ancient origin. Select men was a special and important committee of the ancient Proprietary corporations or Townships. This committee was really the executive committee of the corporation and as such exercised much authority, one of its special duties being the control of the taking of shellfish, which was exclusively a proprietary right.

In the gradual development of the towns, in time becoming municipal corporations as distinct from the proprietary corporations, selectmen became exclusively municipal officials. The Proprietors' clerk, the selectmen, acted at first in a double capacity—as a Proprietors' clerk and Proprietors' committee, also as Town clerk and Town selectmen.

As selectmen, officials of the town, they assumed they were acting as a Proprietors' committee in their authority to regulate the shellfisheries and so continued to act so long as the inhabitants were made up largely of Proprietors.

But as the towns grew in population and the admitted inhabitants outnumbered the Proprietors—when the office of selectman was a salaried position paid by public taxation—there was a scramble for the job with a struggle to win votes. At this time it became more popular to appeal to the non-Proprietor element and to do such things for this restricted class as had not been done when the town was dominated by the Proprietors.

The rights of Proprietors to exclusive fishing, pastorage in general fields, etc., which were protected by the selectmen acting as an executive committee for the Proprietors, were in time ignored by the selectmen elected as municipal officers by popular vote.

The selectmen acting in the capacity as municipal officials could act

3

only as such but they assumed authority to act in the control of shellfisheries because they were also acting for the Proprietors.

In time, Proprietors' meetings ceased, their interests and rights forgotten. Even selectmen as time passed never knew that the only authority they ever had to regulate shellfisheries was when this board was acting in the capacity as a Proprietors' executive committee: that as officers of the municipal corporation they acted under the authority of law and their authority carried only to the constitutional limit of such laws.

In other words, if the owner of tidal flats exercises his right to use them by raising shellfish, no law can be enacted that will deprive him of this right. To make a profit from his soil is his own right which certainly cannot be taken from him and turned over to others for the purpose of conducting a business for profit.

The supreme right of a government is to receive money for its support from taxation of property. Certainly no one can offer a sound argument that it is public policy to destroy by law the value of privately owned land in order that a few persons may conduct enterprise on land privately owned for private gain to the exclusion of the owner of the soil.

The problem of how to increase government income to keep pace with increased costs is a serious one always.

We have reached a stage where the industry of shellfish culture particularly as applied to clams can be carried on as a private enterprise with profit and if so a vast area of new property will be available for taxation, but so long as there exists the theory in law that there is a common or public right to take clams anywhere on tidal flats then there can be no private industry created.

It is only when it is legally established that a private owner of tidal flats has the exclusive right to cultivate the soil by planting and growing shellfish, that such areas will have value and will produce a new source of tax income to the government.

4

No. 8.

LIBRARY *of* Cape Cod HISTORY & GENEALOGY

"Cast-Up" Lands

By Samuel D. Hannah

YARMOUTHPORT, MASS.:
C. W. SWIFT, Publisher and Printer,
The "Register" Press,
1927

"Cast-Up" Lands

By Samuel D. Hannah

Several weeks ago The Register printed rather a lengthy description of the ancient Proprietary corporations called plantations, townships or towns by Samuel D. Hannah of Buzzards Bay.

Much interest is shown by Cape Cod property owners who write to Mr Hannah asking him to explain in detail certain customs and practices of these proprietary organizatons. Mr Hannah has expressed a willingness to answer through The Yarmouth Register rather than by individual letters which would require a lot of time to go into all details.

One of the questions asked is an explanation of the phrase "cast up lands." Some understand its meaning to apply to lands cast up by the sea from time to time, but "cast up lands" as used in the early Proprietors' records and those of Plymouth Colony have reference to lands granted to the settlers within the jurisdiction of the colony or proprietary plantations.

One of the early declarations of the Plymouth Corporation was that lands were granted for use and occupation and for the betterment of society but if the lands were not used or occupied and the bounds not kept up they were declared "cast up," reverting to the government in general or the townships in particular, meaning that the lands lotted to individuals by Plymouth Corporation and within its jurisdiction returned to this corporation, but if within the granted areas of the Proprietary townships then the lands returned to the Proprietaries.

It is not uncommon to find in the early records where lands once divided were later redivided to a different group of persons within the plantation.

There is usually a lapse of years between divisions which would indicate that a group might settle in a particular locality and finding the land of poor quality or too remote from a settled section would abandon the land and go elsewhere. This frequently happened when trouble was threatened with the Indians and a settlement of a large number in one village made life more secure.

It must be seen that life in the 17th century in the townships of Plymouth colony was a simple process and that there was little or no government to bother anyone and that there were no courts or lawyers to work out a complicated system of laws.

The Proprietary organizations were a simple and direct plan to handle any and all situations that might arise. The land question and ownership might create disputes but the organization through its regular elected committees soon settled

2

these questions and there was no expense to the process:

The "cast up" theory was simplicity to the extreme and was necessary to prevent constant complications. There was but slight chance to sell land in that time because it had but little value except to actually use it. Should an owner abandon it the Proprietors' committee assigned it to another wishing to use it. If no one wanted it then it was subject to the disposal of the committee any time or it could lie as part of the common lands of the Proprietors.

In most all of the Plantations areas were assigned to the use of Indians in order to keep them all together. The Proprietors' cattle and horses ran at large and naturally trespassed on Indian lands, eating their corn. Often the Proprietors had to aid the Indians in fencing their lands. An entire group of Indians would sometimes move out and join another Indian tribe or settlement. Such lands when so "cast up" returned to the Proprietary, were divided or held as common, or even at a much later time sold or divided.

The whole theory of Proprietary control of lands seems to have been not unlike the present theory in law on which our Land Court is based.

The Proprietors claimed and it can hardly be doubted that the paramount or original title to land in their boundaries was in the Proprietary corporation,—that it remained in it if no proof could be produced to show it had passed to others by grant; that if there was a dispute as to title, the claimants must prove that the Proprietors had granted the land and the grantees from the Proprietors had passed their title on to the then claimants but if the grantees from the Proprietors had not passed their title and did not appear to defend it then the land was "cast up" and was still in the Proprietors subject to determination by judicial process,—the Proprietors' committee regularly chosen for such purposes to hear the evidence and make final disposition of the matter.

The general plan followed would seem to have been as it is with our Land Court, a proceeding in rem —a process against the land. All claimants were notified to appear with their witnesses before the committee at a specified time and notices of hearings might be posted in a public place, usually the churches or schools in the proprietary.

At such a hearing the questions were disposed of. There were no attorneys to raise technical points for appeal—for there was no other court to which to appeal. The questioning appears to have been carried on by members of the committee. The committee might find that the land belonged to the Proprietee because it had not been lotted to anyone,—that it may have been lotted and abandoned, therefore "cast up," or that some particular person may have believed he owned it and had made use of it or needed it and under some such circumstance give it to a claimant which in result was a new grant from the Proprietors.

It would seem that the Common-

3

wealth in creating the Land Court an agency for establishing titles to land within the state had a similar theory, namely, that the original or paramount title to all the land within its bounds, Plymouth Colony included, rested in the government whether in Massachusetts Bay Colony or Plymouth Colony, and that the Commonwealth as successor to the governments of both colonies now holds the original or paramount title to all lands and if a claimant seeks to perfect his title the Land Court is the legal agency established by the Commonwealth through which by a Proceeding in Rem the Commonwealth authorizes the Land Court to grant a title by decree exactly in the same way in which the Proprietary Committee granted by its decree.

4

No. 9.

LIBRARY *of*
Cape Cod
HISTORY & GENEALOGY

The Prince-Howes Court Cupboard

YARMOUTHPORT, MASS.:
C. W. SWIFT, Publisher and Printer,
The "Register" Press,
1927

The Prince-Howes Court Cupboard

"The Prince-Howes Court Cupboard," owned by Miss Abby W. Howes, formerly of Dennis, is one of the oldest and rarest pieces of early Colonial furniture.

Miss Howes is a direct descendant of Thomas Prince (Prence), governor of Plymouth colony, who died in 1673, and the antique was at one time the property of Governor Prince.

Early Colonial history, shows that Thomas Prince reached America and his majority at the same time, on the Fortune, the ship following the Mayflower. His character so impressed the Pilgrims that, in 1634, he became governor.

He had, ten years before, married the daughter of Elder William Brewster. In 1635, being widowed, he married Mary, the daughter of William Collier, of Duxbury. At the time there was a general emigration to settle new and often remote towns. Eastham, otherwise known as Nauset, on the forearm of the Cape, was one of these, and to it Prince went, remaining at his "seat" there until 1665.

Elected governor for the third time in 1657, he was granted a dispensation to live apart from Plymouth until 1665. In that year the permission was cancelled, and, to induce the Governor's continuance in office, he was granted a "seat" a mile north of Plymouth, called the Lothrop farm. Governor Prince was continuously re-elected from 1657 till his death in 1673.

The Governor's fourth and last wife was Mary, widow of Thomas Howes, who was an original settler of Dennis, then part of Yarmouth. It is in his will that we find the now litigated antique mentioned. His will, of March 13, 1673, has the following items:

"My will is that Mary, my beloved wife, shall have such household goods of Any kind as were hers, before we married, Returned to her againe.

"Item I give unto my said loveing wife my best bed and the furniture there unto appertaining, and the Court Cubberd that stnds in the new Parlour with the Cloth and Cushen that is on it."

The reference in the will to the "new Parlour" is, evidently, to an extension to and embellishment of the Governor's "seat." It is likely that this addition was built about the time of his fourth venture into matrimony, which event occurred not long before Aug. 1, 1668. The cupboard which adorned the parlor may, therefore, be attributed to the period of 1665-1670.

The Governor's widow, Mary Howes Prince, returned to Dennis with the cupboard. Following her death the inventory of her personal estate, dated Dec. 23, 1695, mentions "an old chest and cupboard at Prence Howes's."

2

This Prence Howes was Mary Prence's grandson, by virtue of curious intermarriage, for Sarah Prence, daughter of Gov. Prince by his second wife, had married Jeremiah Howes, son of Thomas Howes and his wife Mary, who, following her widowhood, had become fourth wife of Gov Prince. The second son of Jeremiah Howes and Sarah Prence united the names as well as the blood of two families, for he was christened Prence Howes. It was only natural that he should become the guardian of the ancestral cupboard.

Prence Howes died in 1753. Elkanah Howes, it is reliably reported, moved a house, with the cupboard in it, in 1783, from Kiah's Pond, to a point near the center of Dennis. In 1849 Joshua C. and Polly Howes, grandchildren of Elkanah, retrieved the cupboard, which was then in the house in Dennis. The cupboard was too large to pass out of the chamber door and parts had to be removed. From this it can be inferred that the cupboard had been brought in before the house was finished, as few houses reach the age of 200 years without some change of partitions.

After some slight repairs, marked by zeal rather than knowledge, Joshua C. and Polly Howes affixed a legend to the inside of the cupboard doors, rehearsing what was known and what was surmised about the piece, and charging their posterity with its sacred preservation and retention in the family. Abby W. Howes was its next owner.

The court cupboard was the important central piece of furniture in Pilgrim days. Its name, singularly bears no reference to courts. Court here is merely "curt," spelled long, and refers to the short cupboard on the main shelf, an invariable characteristic. It was the sideboard and safe in the 16th and 17th centuries, and its possession was always a mark of social position. Its elaboration, size and cost singled it out as a kind of badge of family.

Court cupboards very strictly speaking, are open below the main shelf. When closed they are called press cupboards. Except a few much later imitations in pine, the court cupboard has an oak frame, and mostly oak panels, at least in front. The small mouldings are often of cedar and turnings soft maple, all features of the Prince cupboard. The knobs are always of wood, and small. The backs and interiors are generally of soft wood, like pine.

The Prince cupboard, like most, knobs are always of wood, and small is in two sections. Each, in the back, has four panels. These panels as well as drawer bottoms, drawer backs, the inside cupboard bottoms, divisions and shelves, and the upper outside end panels are of riven pine. As always, the mortised frame is fastened with pins, in this instance oak.

The lower section consists of a heavy oak frame containing two short end-to-end drawers, and below them two long drawers. There is the usual side groove, on the oak drawer ends, to run on the slides nailed to the frame ends.

3

The small mouldings applied to the drawers and to all the panels are cedar. The heavy serrated or toothed moulding between drawers, and on the upper section is oak. It is an ancient device handed down from Norman Gothic. The drawers are alike in style and depth.

There are two long vertical panels in each outside end of the lower section. The upper section has characteristic little panels and large outside end panels. The great posts have dowels of oak engaging in sockets at top and bottom; similar short dowels near the back fit upper and lower sections together.

The original locks, one having a keyhole side-wise rather than up and down; the pintle hinges, consisting of dowels on which the door swings and are fascinating to observe. The stiles and rails of the panels in the back are all carefully chamfered. In restoring, the back has been left absolutely as found, even to its mouse holes.

The main body of the cupboard is in oak, which was never painted. It is somewhat darkened by age and oil, but is much lighter than English oak. The great posts and all applied ornaments, the channel mouldings, the drawer panels and the flat section of the lintel are a very dark bottle green. The dentils and their toothed points are in the same color, but the opposing cut-out serrations are in red.

The cupboard is 56 inches high, 51 inches wide, across the front; 22½ inches deep on the cap shelf and 22 inches on the main shelf. The width of the body is 47½ inches. The depth, 21 inches. The cupboard section, above the main shelf, is 23¾ inches in diameter, and the overhang of the canopy is 6¾ inches. The drawers are 6 inches deep. The doors, including the hidden portion on the hinge side, are 13¼ inches wide and 14½ inches high. The stiles are 2¼ by 3½ inches.

No. 10.

LIBRARY *of*
Cape Cod
HISTORY & GENEALOGY

The Cape Type *of* House
By Katherine Crosby

YARMOUTHPORT, MASS.:
C. W. SWIFT, Publisher and Printer,
The "Register" Press,
1927

The Cape Type of House
By Katherine Crosby

All over the country there has been a sudden awakening of interest among architects and homebuilders in what is called the Cape Cod type of house. Even in far-away Texas they are putting up what they fondly believe to be examples of this kind of dwelling. Around home, near-Cape houses are springing up in every direction. As a rule, anything along Colonial lines, so long as it is shingled, goes.

Now the true Cape house is a little gem. Its builders had the genius to take a box and make it a thing of beauty. More than that, they made it a home. It is probably this quality, more than its excellence of design and proportion, which gives it its peculiar lure for women. There is something very sweet and sheltering, an air of comfort, or "home at last!" This charm is difficult to analyze, and is apt to be lacking in even the more faithful imitations that are being erected. One wonders if the building of these houses is perhaps a lost art, while one ardently hopes it is not.

When I started collecting old houses on the Cape last spring — which means collecting the delights of them, and not the actual deeds and all — I soon graduated from the early primitives, because they were few and far between, and went on to the later development which we call the Cape type. These were being built before 1700, but reached their climax about 1825. From then on, it is not too much to say that nothing good was built on the Cape until within the last four or five years, and even since then much that was good has been ruined by summer "restorations." But for a full century and a half the isolated people of Cape Cod, from Sandwich down to Provincetown, built for themselves these little houses of white pine and other local woods, suited them to their needs and to the small-scale scenery of their environment, moved them when they pleased from one location to another, added on an ell, cut through a window, changed the shutters, did what seemed good to them. But rarely did they lose the charm which goes with the type.

Men of the Cape have always been strongly individual, and their houses reflect that quality, even when they are of the same style and architecture. No two little Cape houses are just alike, just as no two families are alike — each house was built to meet the special needs of its particular family, and according to their particular taste. Variety in size and shape, in window-grouping, in combination of features, is so great that one cannot pick out one house and say it is THE type, for no one combines all the characteristics.

Certain features are common to all. They are one story and a half

1

high. They sit side to the road. Their roofs are free of dormers or other excrescences. They have good big chimneys, usually opposite the front door. They are low to the ground, with no foundation showing. They have no projecting eaves anywhere. Their front windows set close up to the roof, that is, in what I feel to be the true Cape type, although there are some rather beguiling ones with higher fronts. Common also to these houses is their excellence of proportion.

But now the fun begins. Take windows. Two on each side of the door. One on each side of the door. Two on one side, one on the other. Two on one side, none on the other. Even a door and one window. So much for the front of the house. Go round to the end and look up at the gable. Two windows up there, just enough smaller than the downstairs ones to make them look right. (That's a detail the modern copyist often overlooks.) Or, one window. Or, two windows with a tiny one each side, under the eaves, and perhaps a third one in the peak overhead. Or, one window with the two or the three little ones grouped about it. I notice that in the seven pictures I have chosen to go with this article, five different window arrangements appear in the gables. Also, five different ones in the facades.

Take front doors. The very oldest, I suspect, had no lights. One in a house about two hundred years old has none. Sometimes the upper panels in the almost inevitable Huguenot cross door have had glass substituted for the wood. Then, my guess is, they began putting a row of small window-panes along above the door, if there was room between it and the roof. I have seen these panes, evidently about four-by-sixes, cut in two and set horizontally, and the effect is entrancing. This was done where the roof came down very low indeed, and the doorway had to be high enough for a six-foot husband.

Room was often made for a fan-light, occasionally with side-lights but more often without, for here, too, the element of size had to be considered. A wide doorway would have looked crowded in many of these houses, but the builders knew when to use it and when not to. Blinds are common for the doors, sometimes shaped to fit the fan-light. Elaborate doorways are rare, though the door was always the center of interest and given whatever ornamentation a man's circumstances allowed.

Take roofs. I am inclined to think the secret of the Cape-house charm is largely in the roof. There is a low, brooding spread to it, a sort of mothering effect, that promises all the things which we mean when we say "home". The reason I feel sure the charm is here is because I have seen so many old houses lose this quality, the quality for which they were purchased, when their purchasers stuck in dormers. They became merely summer cottages.

Here let me say, as politely as possible, that if people want upstairs chambers with head-room and special ventilation, let them build their houses that way, not take our precious homes and ruin them. A Cape house, when being adapted to city standards of living, should be regarded as a bungalow, any rooms above the first floor not being taken seriously. A dormer on the back of the house, if it doesn't show from the side of the house, is forgiveable, and allows two good rooms and a bath upstairs, anyway. But on the front it is straight vandalism. I have photographs which would show what I mean, and abundantly prove my point, but it wouldn't be polite to use them.

And such attics as one finds in untroubled houses! Floor boards twenty inches wide. Rafters hewn out with an ax, mortised and held with wooden pegs. Ridgepoles resting in pockets left by the mason in the brickwork of the chimney. Roofs made of boards—even of planks—laid up and down instead of across. (These warp with age, and outside, the shingles following their curves, give a lovely ruffled effect to the roof—but try copying that!) These boards are rabbited together, and shed the rain even when you can see daylight through the cracks. I know a man who bought such a house, and thinking to build him a more serviceable dwelling, put up a modern imitation near by, with the roof boarded up in orthodox horizontal fashion; he told me the new roof leaked like a sieve, but that old one, for all it showed the sky, never leaked a drop all summer.

A beautiful variation found in Cape houses is the bowed roof. I know of only three extreme examples, but have seen many that were slightly bowed. One of the best is that of the old "Crooked House," which also has an interesting grouping of door and windows. Another is on the little Hoxie house, whose gentle quakeress owner died only a short time ago.

Just how these roofs were made is a much debated matter. One hears of timbers cut green and bent by great weights fastened to their middles, their ends being suspended, or by being laid over rocks and their ends weighted down. But I have myself seen the rafters of the Hoxie house, which is said to be 300 years old, and they were hewn out with an ax into their present shape. On the other hand, one does hear of a bowed roof that has "gone back" to straight, which would indicate a timber that had been bent rather than cut. It was undoubtedly a ship-builder's trick, and meant perhaps to give greater strength as well as beauty. This is a feature which one never finds being copied, by the way.

The little Hoxie house has its story, like so many, for its owner was as individual as her dwelling. In her youth Aunt Marthy had been betrothed to the Quaker minister. But he had died, and so she never married, but lived there all alone. She had plenty of money, and often kept it in kegs out in the shed—thousands of dollars at a time, and she wasn't too fussy about locking her doors either. Every year the railroad used to give her free passes to a stockholders' meeting in Boston; her frugal soul could not bear to waste those passes, and so when the day came around she would put on her best gray silk gown, with its white 'kerchief, and her best gray silk Quaker bonnet with its white satin lining, and off she would go to Boston on her pass. But do you think she would risk her life on the streets of that awful city? Well, no.

All day she would stay safely within the shelter of the railroad station, till the Cape train was made up for its return trip, and then back home she would go, with a sigh of relief and a clear conscience.

The fireplace in that house—the largest of its three fireplaces—is interesting, for it has a brick oven in the back, behind the fire. It is the only one of that sort I happen to have seen. In other houses they are out flush with the mantel, at one side or the other of the fireplace opening. Sometimes the fire for cooking was built in the oven, sometimes in a separate compartment beneath. But nearly always the Cape oven is covered with a cupboard door, shutting it away neatly from our sight.

A typical floor plan is that of the Kenrick house—it would probably fit any of the full-sized houses shown in the pictures, unless their partitions have been changed. This house was built in 1790, and is connected with Captain John Kenrick, the first American to circumnavigate the globe, and the man who discovered and possibly named the State of Washington and the Columbia River.

Entering the front door, one stands in a small square entry, facing a blank wall where the chimney is. But at either side is a door leading into a square front room with a fireplace. Both rooms open into a long room at the back, whose fireplace is larger and has a brick oven. This long room, originally the kitchen, has two small rooms at each end, a chamber and a buttery. In this house the attic stairs go up between one chamber and the buttery, and the cellar is reached by a trap in the buttery floor. Some houses have only one room at each end of the long room; many have an ell. Often the stairs go up from the entry, in front of the chimney.

It was fairly common, long ago, for a man to build himself a half-house, just the entry and one room wide. There would be the kitchen, a chamber and a buttery downstairs, besides the front room, and upstairs a finished room for himself and good wife to sleep. When the children were old enough to need more sleeping places, little windows were put in under the eaves, and the youngsters slept in these unfinished cubbies—this accounts for the tiny windows in so many Cape Cod gables, I am told.

When the oldest son got married, instead of building himself a house he could add on to his father's, another room in front, a lengthening of the kitchen, another chamber and buttery. Mother and daughter-in-law could cook over the same fire, presumably, though one sometimes finds a second kitchen.

Occasionally, with the originality of the true Caper, this process was reversed. I know of one house that was cut in two. It had been inherited by two brothers who couldn't get along, so one of them took his half of the house and moved it across the street. One of them had to build on a new chimney, I suppose. The half that was moved away is quite cunning, with its gray shingles and red trim.

Color is an element not to be forgotten. Left to itself, a shingle weathers silver-gray in the Cape air. Most of the Cape houses are shingled all or part. Clapboarded fronts,

4

painted white, often have gray-shingled ends. Sometimes the shingles are whitewashed, sometimes painted white, or even yellow. But typically they are gray, and when very old have on the north side an almost opalescent mixture of green and violet and rose with the silver, from the long weathering.

Sometimes the trim is painted, often it is not. White is most modern, pale green most effective, red not so bad as it sounds. This trim, by the way, always includes cornerboards and verge-boards, but never anything along the ridge-pole. An intriguing detail, one of the many subtleties which give these houses their special beauty, is that of the tapering verge-board, which is often just a bit narrower at the peak of the gable than it is down at the lower end, where it joins the corner boards.

Returning to paint, the old blinds that have been let alone have a wonderful blue-green that conscientious copyists go nearly mad trying to imitate. It is of course a faded green, but it has faded to blue in spots, and is truly lovely. Sometimes doors turn that way, too. I met a woman last summer who had found the old wooden shutters — the rare one paneled kind—that belonged on her house, and she was trying to get the painter to match up the front door to them. They weren't either of them happy, though she, at least, was still hopeful.

There is a fad for blue blinds on the Cape, when the house is white, and I suppose it started with the old Blue-Blind House, so long a landmark in its village. One hears that an early owner stipulated in his will that the color of the blinds should never be changed. The blue isn't so bad, except that it looks tearoomy, but when they try purple—well, fortunately they don't try it twice. Many old houses have no blinds at all, and get along very well.

I shall be glad when the furor over the white and ivory paint indoors and out has subsided. I am sure so much of it would have set ill with our forefathers. Left to themselves they had color galore. There is nothing homelike or cosy about white; it is the color of hospitals and bathroom fittings; neat is the most you can say for it. One often finds an old room with robin's-egg blue paint on the woodwork, and yellow was common. Furniture in light red, yellow, green, blue and black was common too. As a matter of fact, much of the early woodwork in small houses was probably unpainted, just the natural pine which is so much lovelier than any paint. But so far I haven't seen a single old house on the Cape, restored or otherwise, with this natural finish.

Not being an architect, I can't go very deep into the construction of the houses. A few things I have noticed, however, may be helpful. The foundations are often stoned, dry set, which gives plenty of ventilation beneath the house and prolongs its life. (In the winter you could bank it with seaweed to keep out the cold.) The cellar is small, usually round and lined with brick, with one small window.

Sills are laid on this foundation, which is so low that it does not show unless the grass is clipped very short. Corner posts are likely to be of the gun-stock or butt-end sort, widening at the top the better to support the floor joists above; sometimes they are cased in, where they show in a room, often not. One long room in an old house has a row of these square gun-stocks all along its back wall, which gives it a strangely nautical look, as if it were the cabin of a ship. Incidentally, as most of the old house builders were also ship builders, it is not surprising now and then to find an attic with the rafters and joists braced with knees as if it were a vessel.

The peculiar effect which the windows often have, as if they stuck out from the walls, is due to their having plank frames instead of box frames. Two-inch planks are nailed onto the boarding, and the shingles come up to them. The sashes are set into this plank frame, which brings them out at least flush with the shingling, if not beyond. These sashes, by the way, are likely to be uneven, the upper three panes deep, the lower two, or vice versa. Another piquant detail. Where the sashes are even, twenty-four panes is the older, twelve the more common, style.

Floors are of wide planking, sometimes eighteen or twenty inches. They are rarely even or level. Sometimes they tip one way. Sometimes they tip four ways—oh yes, I know one that does! Not uncommon are the planks cut from a short thick tree, tapering narrower at one end than the other and laid alternately so they fit together.

Details of interior finish I am going to leave. One hears tales of paneling from the cabins of vessels wrecked off the coast, but most that I have seen is the usual early American thing. Wainscots vary from 18 to 40 inches; rarely paneled, usually a single wide board with a plain moulding at the top. The mantlepieces are often paneled horizontally to the ceiling, the oldest ones with no shelf, a moulding surrounding the fireplace. The ceiling of the larger room is likely to have a summer-tree across the middle, but not often more than one beam. Crossbeams of course, one never sees. Cornices are rare. Interior doors are nearly always of the Huguenot cross pattern, often with glass lights in the upper panels even between rooms. Battened doors are common in back rooms. Chimney cupboards with doors of small-paned sash are the rule.

But all this is a story in itself and needs much more space for the telling. Some day I am going to make a round of calls on all the houses in my collection and take pictures of their insides. But their beauty will lie in their simplicity and their line. Poverty enforced a wholesome restraint when it came to ornamentation, and native good taste—in its way perhaps the best our country has produced—did the rest.

No. 11.

LIBRARY of
Cape Cod
HISTORY & GENEALOGY

SHIPBUILDING at EAST DENNIS

BY THOMAS F. HALL

YARMOUTHPORT, MASS.:
C. W. SWIFT, Publisher and Printer,
The "Register" Press,
1925

THE SIGNIFICANCE OF THE MONUMENT AND TABLET RECENTLY ERECTED AT THE SHIVERICK SHIPYARD SITE IN EAST DENNIS, MASSACHUSETTS.

By Thomas F. Hall

Some disappointment has been expressed that a public dedication was found inconvenient at the time the monument and tablet were completed.

It would have been gratifying to have had at that time, publicly recorded for future reference, such facts, incidents, and perhaps anecdotes as were remembered in connection with the enterprise, by those now living.

I will attempt to remedy this misfortune in part by a fragmentary statement from a defective memory.

It is doubtful if there are many living who remember that prior to 1848 there was a shipyard in operation about a half mile farther up the meadows, from the monument. It was operated by Asa Shiverick, the grandfather of David Shiverick who is yet with us. From that yard sloops, schooners and brigs were launched, and possibly vessels of other rigs.

In 1848 the three sons of Asa: David, Asa, Jr., and Paul, closed that yard and constructed another and larger one directly below the spot where the monument stands, with its launching dock yet to be seen extending eastward into Sesuit Creek.

From this shipyard, deep water, square-rig ships were launched, averaging in size about 1000 tons register. It required a high degree of enterprise, of skill and of courage, at that early date, for such an undertaking.

It is a realization of that requirement that has impelled the descendants of those active men to erect a simple yet enduring monument to perpetuate the memory of their deeds.

I can well remember when the atmosphere of Quivet village, (unlike today) reverberated to the music of mechanics' hammers and axes, broadcasted from the grounds on which the monument now stands.

Farther down the creek a wharf was constructed at the same time as the shipyard, and it was a part of the same enterprise. The safe, convenient harbor which the wharf created presented almost as busy a scene as the shipyard itself.

That wharf was on the east side of the creek, extending from the "Island" creek bridge to the end of the present stone jetty. It had a heavy plank floor covering from its upper end, down to about high water mark on the beach. This floor was often covered its whole length with merchandise incidental to the commerce of the harbor. Mackerel that had been packed in barrels for the market constituted a large part of this merchandise.

The harbor was the home port of a fleet of more than a score of vessels. Some of them, in summer time, were arriving and departing daily; some to and from the mackerel grounds; some to and from the codfish grounds farther away. Others were chartered crafts which brought materials for the construction of the ships. One schooner, the "David Porter," as a packet, made constant trips back and forth to Boston, and one sloop, the "Star," freighted salt, that was manufactured in this village, to all the harbors in Massachusetts bay. Local fishing boats, and boats for pleasure, as a result of the prevailing maritime interest, were quite numerous. Taken altogether this village was in those days a busy place indeed.

Adjoining the wharf were two large general stores, the only stores in Quivet village. One of them, managed by Kelley and Sears, was primarily a supply house for the mackerel fishermen. The other was primarily for the codfishermen, managed by Dean Sears, but both of them supplied the needs of the village.

A steaming plant at the shipyard, for preparing timbers for bending, was located south of the road below the bluffs, a little to the west of the monument. The main shops were located north of the road. They consisted of a blacksmith shop, in charge of Heman G. Sears; an inboard joiner shop, in charge of James A. Smalley; a general carpenter shop operated by power, and a calkers' shop located at the foot of the hill below the other shops.

Most of the workmen crossed the meadows to their homes on Quivet Neck over a foot bridge. Some of the stakes to that foot bridge are still to be seen across the meadow.

On launching days, neighbors from surrounding towns flocked to the shipyard to witness a completed ship make her first plunge. Many of the men visitors took positions on the ship's deck, ready to man the capstans and ropes as soon as the ship reached the water, in order to hurry her down the stream during the brief time that she was afloat.

It required several days of tugging and hauling to get a ship out of the creek, safely into the bay. The sharp bend in the creek, just below the present cold storage building, (which was then midway the wharf), caused some trouble in getting the ships around it, delaying them usually over a tide, or a day. But, strangely enough, it so happened that the "Webfoot," the largest ship of them all, was the easiest to get around that corner.

There was some hesitation about locating the shipyard at the place where the monument stands, on that account. Some regret was afterwards expressed that it was not located farther down the creek, so that the ships could have been launched into the stream below the bend.

The first two ships built, "Revenue" and "Hippogriffe," were provided with jury masts, yards and sails; and sailed to Boston under their own rig. In Boston they were permanently sparred and rigged for sea.

Voyaging to Boston, on those two ships, were interesting events to many. Each ship was several days on the passage. The "Revenue" was delayed because she encountered a strong northwest gale, causing her to beat against it, under reefs, all the way to Boston. It would indeed be a strange sight today to see a square-rigged ship beating to windward in Cape Cod bay.

The "Hippogriffe" made two separate attempts to get to Boston. She was about a week

3

altogether in getting there. After two days' absence on the first attempt she returned and anchored off the harbor, to land Prince S. Crowell (one of the owners) who had suddenly been taken sick on the second day out.

None of the other ships had a full jury rig. Instead a tugboat came down from Boston, backed up into the creek as far as the wharf, took the ship in tow, and returned with her to Boston.

The launchings always occurred during the high course tides in the early spring or fall. Even then there was not a great surplus of water, only enough really to float the larger ships for about one-half to three-quarters of an hour at each tide.

Launching such large vessels into such a small stream was, therefore, at that time, and would be at this time, considered by the inexperienced a venturesome, daring undertaking. But those responsible for the outcome were competent men, who knew their business thoroughly, and they made a complete success of the undertaking in all respects.

The "Revenue," however, (the first ship) broke down her "ways" and did not reach the water on the first attempt to launch her. The second attempt succeeded.

The captains of the ships were appointed to their positions long before the ships were launched; sometimes before the keel was laid. It was, therefore, customary to say that the ship was built for the designated captain. These captains assumed command as soon as the ship reached the water.

Captain William Frederick Howes of this village was appointed captain of the "Belle of the West" early in her construction, and was in command as soon as she was launched. When the tugboat attempted to pull her out of the creek, the hawser parted. The flying end of it struck Captain Howes and broke his leg, incapacitating hime from further service until after the ship reached Boston.

In May (1857) my father died. The ship that was being built at the time of his death was

4

launched on Sept. 1 of that year and named for him, "Christopher Hall."

No ship was built after his death for five years. Then only one more.

In 1862-3 the Shivericks built a ship (and the last one) on their own account, being sole owners. She was sold before launching, and named by the purchasers "Ellen Sears." This event ended shipbuilding at East Dennis.

Every ship that was built while my father lived was commanded by an East Dennis man. Every one was officered and apprenticed, on every voyage, largely by East Dennis men and boys. The boys usually started on their seafaring career at about the age of 15. It will be seen, therefore, even across this long distance in time, that such an enterprise, located in such a small village, naturally conferred unnumbered blessings on every one of its inhabitants.

The enterprise was also instrumental in carrying many of their names, their thoughts, and their memories, over the seven seas, to almost every seaport in the world. The ships themselves were as well known in Europe, South America, California, Japan, China, India and Australia, as they were in Boston or New York, and perhaps they were, in some ports, as well known as in East Dennis.

I can write about the joint enterprise of the shipyard, wharf and maritime commerce, with perhaps a pardonable pride, and with some sentiment, because my father was the capitalist, the promoter and prime mover in it all. He was the sole owner of the first ship, the "Revenue," and he determined the location of the shipyard.

I can write about the ships themselves from individual experience. Six years of my youth, commencing at the age of 15, were spent at sea on two of those beautiful ships, the "Wild Hunter" and the "Belle of the West," circumnavigating the globe in each.

To understand clearly the high standard reached in developing those ships, it should be remembered that they were built during the years when the American Mercantile Marine itself was in the very zenith of its fame and glory. The

5

merchant ships of the United States eclipsed those of all nations in the world, in swiftness, in beauty, in seaworthiness, in stability, and in the standing of its builders and commanders. This fact is not an overdrawn statement; it is universally acknowledged history. When, therefore, it is realized that ships from the Shiverick yard were not only equal, but in some technical respects, superior to any in the American fleet, it is more than gratifying to local pride; it is touching very closely the immortal, to truthfully say that no loftier pitch of the shipbuilder's art has ever been attained than that which was reached through the skill of the Shivericks, made manifest in the ships they launched from that very yard, in the sixteen memorable maritime years between 1849 and 1863.

The world has seen no finer ships. None ever floated on the sea that were more staunch, more lovely, swift, or more beautiful; none that made a grander sight when their transient beauties blended with the eternal beauty of the sea.

Those were great years; great events; great men.

It was a masterful undertaking, as I have said, to establish such an enterprise in such a quiet spot, on the banks of such a small stream. Yet it is due entirely to the modesty and reticence of those giant intellects that this village is not renowned for the masterpieces it sent out, that challenged the admiration of the maritime world.

It is to be hoped that the original drawings of the "Belle of the West" may yet be found among the papers left by her brilliant designer, Samuel Hartt Pooke of Boston. She was, in my opinion, the finest specimen of naval architecture ever seen. Every line in her hull was grace and beauty.

It was my good fortune, at one time, in a foreign port, to see that beautiful ship, full rigged, hauled out of the water, to be recoppered.

I still suffer the regret I then felt, on observing for a week or two that beautiful picture, silhouetted against a fleecy Indian sky, in a grand panoramic view, that it could not at that time have been wrought in marble, to vie in artistic beauty through the ages with the choicest Phidian statues.

and to immortalize the name of her designer, the youthful Samuel Hartt Pooke of Boston, the Praxiletes of his time.

The cabin of the "Belle of the West" was my home for four and one-half years. She at last became my sweetheart, my idol. She was a graven image before which, for years, I daily bowed and worshipped, and although she has been lying in her grave at the bottom of the sea in the Bay of Bengal for sixty years, I would delight, if it were possible, to erect a marble shaft over the spot where her sacred bones are resting.

"I knew what master laid her keel,
What workmen wrought her ribs of steel,
Who made each mast, and sail, and rope,
What anvils rang, what hammers beat,
In what a forge, in what a heat
Were shaped the anchors of her hope."

It is doubtful if there is any other inanimate thing in existence, except the home, that has such a grasp upon ones affection as a merchant sailing ship. One must study Joseph Conrad to understand fully the cause and meaning of that peculiar influence. A few years ago a Mr. Lewis, who was at the time mayor of Duluth, Minn., spent a day at my home. He had, in his early life, been the chief mate of the ship "Kit Carson," which ship was launched from this yard. He had traced her career and learned that she had been sunk to block the harbor of Rio Janeiro during a Brazilian war. "If it were practical," he said, "and I could afford it, I would have her raised, and towed into the harbor of Duluth, where I could look at her all the remaining days of my life, and make her my summer home."

It was a beautiful sight, in New York and Boston harbors in those days, to see the laden ships almost daily unfold their wings, to furl them in a foreign clime. But change is the order of the universe.

The perilous task of doubling Cape Horn to westward; or "running down the easting in the roaring forties," will hereafter gradually become a memory and a legend, to be known only in song

7

and story, by the Masefields and Conrads of the future.

It will, therefore, be seen that in a brief quarter of a century, the glory of sail has passed away. Sailing ships that at one time were the pride and wonder of their age, have become a reverie and a dream. The sound of foaming waters tumbling beneath their advancing prows; the winds of the trades and westerlies, whistling and singing through their standing rigging, have died into the silence of eternity.

The ships, the owners, the builders, the seamen, are gone. The queens of sail, in all their splendor, that contributed for so many years to such glorious ocean scenes, whitening every sea, are gone.

As of the ships so of the men. They are a race never again to be needed. Individuality in builders, in owners and in captains, has given way to corporation and combinations of corporations.

Invention has, by cable and radio, not only shrunken the size of the ocean, it has shrunken the importance of ship captains. A captain today of a fifty-thousand-ton liner is not so absolute a king as was the master of a little thousand-ton clipper, in the years of sail.

So has passed the romance, the fascinating glamour, and the glory of sailing ships. They have had their day. They have met the fate of all things earthly, and have passed to the beyond.

The monument, of which I write to dedicate, has been erected in the hope that it may be a reminder of greater days and greater men; that it may halt, even though temporarily, the vanishing memory of noble deeds; that its tablet may tell to future passerby some part of the story of a great local industry that has passed away.

8

No. 12.

LIBRARY of
Cape Cod
HISTORY & GENEALOGY

The NYE HOUSE at SANDWICH
BY BERNARD PETERSON

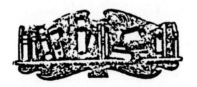

YARMOUTHPORT, MASS.:
C. W. SWIFT, Publisher and Printer,
The "Register" Press,
1925

HOME OF THE NYE FAMILY

CAPE COD ESTATE BECOMES STATE SANCTUARY FOR WILD LIFE

The Nye Homestead at East Sandwich, Occupied by Eight Generations of the Family Since 1685, Is Presented to the Commonwealth by Mr Ray Nye.

By Bernard Peterson

An estate of Colonial fame has come into the possession of the Commonwealth of Massachusetts through the generosity of Mr Ray Nye of Sheboygan, Wis., whose ancestral home it has been for nearly three hundred years, and by the Commonwealth's acceptance of the gift it now becomes a perpetual sanctuary for birds and other wild life.

The property in question is the historic Nye estate, located in East Sandwich. It has sheltered eight successive generations of the Nye family, since the erection of the present house in 1685. A bronze tablet, authorized by the state, tells the story concisely:

> Home of the Nye Family
> Founded by Benjamin Nye 1685
> Presented to
> The Commonwealth of Massachusetts
> In the Year 1924
> by Ray Nye
> One of the Lineal Descendants
> For the Protection and Propagation
> of Wild Life

As long as the house, which still stands on the old road from East Sandwich to Barnstable, shall endure, this tablet will keep the wayfarers informed of the origin, history and destiny of the estate and when the perishable structure shall have disappeared the thirty-seven acres of wood-covered land, plain fields, underbrush and pond will continue as a protected home for fish and fowl, under the tablet's seal.

Negotiations that led to the presentation of this property to the Commonwealth have been going on for a long time, says the Boston Transcript, but it now becomes apparent that long before these negotiations started Mr Ray Nye entertained a hope that when the cherished homestead should pass out of the Nye family, if it ever did, it might be dedicated to permanent service for the perpetuation of wild life. For at a recent date Mr Nye wrote to William C. Adams of the Division of Fisheries and Game, Department of Conservation:

Permit me to assure you, your associates in the Department of Conservation, Division of Fisheries and Game, and the Commonwealth of Massachusetts, that in this case, as in all others, it is more pleasure to give than to receive. Let me assure you, also, that it will add to the comfort and happiness of my declining years to know that the old "Nye Estate" is to be forever used as a game and fish reserve by the Commonwealth of Massachusetts. It seems particularly fitting in that all my life I have had a love for the "out of doors," been a follower of Isaak Walton and a lover of birds and game

Mr. Nye bought the property in 1911 from Helen F. Holway to save it from the inglorious fate of passing out of the Nye lineage. He was then living in Nebraska, and planned an occasional visit to the estate, but the idea possessed him that its perpetuation in a worthy cause would be assured by having the title pass to the Commonwealth, through sale or otherwise. Because of the adaptability of the property for the protection and propagation of game it was leased to the Department of Conservation, at a nominal annual rental, as there was no law under which the Commonwealth could accept land as a free gift until 1923. It has been used by the Division of Fisheries and Game a number of years for pheasant breeding and fish hatcheries. Thus it already has become a well-known reservation which contributes fish and fowl for liberation in other parts of the state. In the opinion of the authorities, it was the most suitable spot on the Cape for this specific purpose, and has been instrumental in the development of this highly appreciated support of rod and gun sports in Massachusetts.

The Nye house is one of the oldest houses in Massachusetts, built in 1685 for Benjamin Nye, the founder of the Nye family in America, who came to this country in 1635, and who died in that house. According to the records it was given to his son, Jonathan, by a deed dated 1704, "if he will take care of me and Katherine Nye, my wife." Evidently Jonathan observed this condition in the will and held the title to the property, for he deeded it to his son, Joseph, in 1724, with a corresponding stipulation that Joseph should take care of his father and mother as long as they should live.

Joseph was a clothier and had three sons, Joseph, Sylvanus and Samuel, all of whom became distinguished, for they all fought in the Revolutionary war. Samuel was a graduate of Harvard college, and became a noted surgeon. Sylvanus became the owner of the house through purchase of his brothers' equities in it, and he gave it to his sons, Samuel and Joseph. Samuel's daughter, Helen, later came into possession of it and lived in it with her husband, Augustus Holway. Her son, Jerome Holway, and his sons have also lived in the house, so that for eight successive generations the historic estate has been owned and occupied by Nye descendants. It appears never to have been out of the Nye family until title was executed transferring it to the Commonwealth of Massachusetts.

Hanging in the house, perhaps from its earliest days down to the time of its occupancy by Helen Holway, was the Nye coat-of-arms, framed in a crudely carved oak frame. This was treasured in the Nye family like a family Bible, but was never conspicuously displayed. It was mentioned in wills which disposed of it from generation to generation, and a colored copy of it is now in the possession of the Nye Family association. It presumably was brought over from England by the young Benjamin Nye in 1635, though that has not been established by records.

There is little doubt as to the age of the house, because the county records show that the county road was laid out across Benjamin Nye's mill dam in 1664, and a record of May 17, 1682, shows that this property was already fenced in. Hence it is evident that the house was built not later than 1685, as it has always been told in the family that the house was built before the present highway. The mill dam referred to was used for a corn mill, and there was also a carding mill, both of which were operated by several generations.

Commissioner Adams naturally is highly pleased with the results of his long negotiations with Mr Nye, which might have been terminated much earlier had it been possible for the state to accept land as a gift. Legislation is now effective which serves just such situations.

Speaking of this property and the use which will be made of it, Mr Adams said:

The property consists of the old Nye homestead, a fine example of Cape Cod architecture, together with land lying around the East Sandwich Fish Hatchery. This will be retained in order to give complete control over the waters and surrounding site, in order that the property may be utilized to the best advantage for the hatching and rearing of fish. There is an additional tract lying on the opposite side of the New York, New Haven & Hartford railroad and on which is now located the Sandwich Game farm. This property will be devoted entirely to the uses of the farm, and is of sufficient extent to permit of a satisfactorily sized complete game farm being developed."

Both Sandwich and East Sandwich are making a substantial contribution to the wild-life stock of Massachusetts, and the perpetuation of the Nye estate in this service is a most important development. Almost 1,500,000 eggs are taken from the brood stock at the East Sandwich Fish Hatchery in the course of a year and distributed to rearing stations at Palmer, Amherst, Worcester, Canton, and to the public waters in various parts of the state.

Pheasants are favored for breeding stock at Sandwich, because it is a very game and interesting bird, with which Commissioner Adams would like to restock the forests of the state. When the laying season began in 1924 there were 543 pheasants in the brood stock at Sandwich and 16,011 eggs were collected and set, with a hatch of 9119 chicks. From these were raised 4298, of which 3880 were distributed in the covers and 258 late-hatched birds held over winter.

Following is a copy of the oldest Nye deed in existence, covering the transfer of the house of Jonathan to his son, Joseph, in 1724, when Jonathan Nye appeared before "His Majesty's Justice of the Peace" and acknowledged "the above written instrument to be his act and Deed":

To all Christian people, to whom these presence shall come, Greeting: Know ye that I, Jonathan Nye, of the town of Sandwich, in the county of Barnstable, within ye Government of the Massachusetts Bay, in New England, yeoman, for and in consideration of the love and good will which I have toward my son, Joseph Nye, of the town of Sandwich, and in ye county and Province aforesaid, clothier, and for further consideration as hereafter mentioned; do by these presence, give, grant, bargain, aliene and convey and confirm unto him, my said son, Joseph Nye, to him his heirs and assigns forever all my housing and Land where I now dwell, the Corn Mill and Fulling Mill and the pond and the stream which carries said mills, the upland and swampy ground containing about six acres, be it more or less according to the known and accustomed bound thereof: and half my Lott or parcele of marsh lying in Barnstable, near the marsh of Ralphe Jones adjoining thereunto, southeasterly and then round by the upland and beachland being in a cove and containing in the whole, ten acres, be it more or less, and also my piece of Upland lying southerly from said mill pond and adjoining thereunto except three acres adjoining westerly to said mill pond, and northeasterly on the highway which I already on this day have disposed of to my son, Benjamin Nye, the sd Benjamin Nye allowing a convenient Highway over it for his brother Joseph, next Samuel Sandersons, his land, and also two small Lotts in the last Division of the Comons in Sandwich aforesaid, the one is the twenty-third Lott and the other 140th Lott, according to the boundaries thereof on record in the town of Sandwich, Reference thereunto be had; and all the upland and marsh which I bought of Henry Sanderson with that marsh which I bought of my son Jonathan that he purchased of sd Samuel Sanderson, or be the same however otherwise Butted or Bounded with all the appurtenances thereunto belonging; to him his heirs or Assigns forever. To have and To Hold the sd Joseph Nye, his heirs and Assigns above granted premises to Him the Use, Benefit and Behoof forever; and I, sd Jonathan Nye, for myself, my heirs, executors and administrators do promise and grant unto and with the sd Joseph Nye, his heirs and Assigns forever; that at the time of ensealing hereof, I am the lawful and sole owner of the above Given and granted Premises; he the sd Joseph Nye upon the further consideration as above said, performing a covenant made the date hereof; with the sd forever to his and theirs own proper Jonathan Nye for the support of himself and wife as therein Expresst. In witness whereof, I, ye sd Jonathan Nye, have hereunto sett my hand and seal, this seventh day of August Anno Domini 1724.

Signed, sealed and delivered in presence of
NATH'L OTIS.
  (Signed) JONATHAN NYE

No. 13.

LIBRARY of
Cape Cod
HISTORY & GENEALOGY

HISTORY of SANDWICH GLASS
By Bangs Burgess

The Deming Jarves Book of Designs
By Charles Messer Stow

YARMOUTHPORT, MASS.:
C. W. SWIFT, Publisher and Printer,
The "Register" Press,
1925

HISTORY of SANDWICH GLASS

Thirty-seven years after the Sandwich, Mass., glass factory fires were drawn, never to be rekindled, Sandwich glass today is all the rage. Odd pieces of the famous old product which was known throughout the world are bringing high prices and the collector goes far abroad to obtain them. July 4, this year, will mark the 100th anniversary of the founding of the Boston-Sandwich Glass Company, and the town of Sandwich plans to celebrate the event with fitting ceremonies. For almost two-score years the furnaces have been out, yet the romance of the old glass industry still lives. Bangs Burgess of Sandwich here tells the story.

By Bangs Burgess

On many visits as a child to my grandmother in Sandwich, where living and thought were centered in the Glass house, I unceasingly questioned my Uncle Tom, who was Thomas Heffernan of Sandwich, about glass making. He had worked all his life in the Boston-Sandwich glass factory. My father began working there when the factory was 18 years old and my grandfather had worked there before his marriage, which must have been in the infancy of the industry. It was, however, all novel and strange to me, for I went away from Sandwich when I was three.

As my Uncle Tom talked, my eyes turned from the pretty glass book, bell and bellows on the whatnot to the mantel with its glass vases, row of glass lamps, and the black bear which is now so much hunted that when you bag his head you cannot get his body to match. These glass bears of various colors were originally made for a bear-ointment concern. I was told, and at that time one could be had for the asking. The best that mantel contained is now in my possession: a set of doll flatirons made of blue glass nearly 80 years ago for a little girl.

Uncle had a way of chaffing me, but much that he told me I have since learned to have been the truth fashioned to fit my youthful understanding.

"Glass making," he said, "was a gentleman's job; in fact, in France at first only noblemen were allowed to make glass, for it was considered a high art."

"Who made the first glass?" I asked.

"Why, glass making goes back beyond the beginning of history," he answered.

"What did they first make it out of?"

"Elements of the earth the same as they do now, only fewer were used. Before flint glass the product was dull and dark."

"Why do they call it flint glass?"

"Because in England flints were calcined and pulverised to make silica, which is the principal constituent of glass. In France they ground up pure rock crystal; before that it was translucent like glass that comes through a

1

fire. You have heard of that fiddling fellow Nero? Well he drank wine from the first clear glass.

"In our factory," he continued "they used potash, nitre, sand, oxide of lead, and many other minerals. And let me tell you, we used the very best lead. Just listen," he said, snapping his fingers against the side of a goblet, or ringing the glass bell, whose tongue was a shoe button on a string. I now know that the tone of a glass bell is clearer, more sonorous, and travels further than that of metallic bells. My next question was, "Do they use the sand from the beach?"

Uncle Tom said, "Shoo! People a good deal bigger than you think the factory was built in Sandwich on account of sand, which isn't so. Our sand comes from Berkshire county. At one time it came from Plymouth beach and after that a better grade from Morris River, New Jersey, and now the best sand in the world comes from Cheshire, Mass."

"If it was not for the sand, what made them build the factory here, uncle?" I pursued.

"Make a guess." he said.

"The sea," was my ready answer, predicated on my previous knowledge that the company at one time owned the Packet Polly and later built and operated the steamer Acorn.

"The pine woods," he answered.

It seems that a man came down from Boston and bought a huge tract of land covered with pine trees, after he had a consultation with the townspeople and told them how much money they could earn in a glass factory he proposed to build.

As a result, a century ago, on the lower border of the most beautiful town I have ever seen, by the side of the colorful marshes that stretch away to the golden and green dunes by the sea, Cape Cod witnessed, on a bright 19th of April, the tossing out of the first shovelful of earth at the command of the Boston man, Deming Jarves, who then began the building of an industry whose products were destined to travel over the whole world and in color vie with the jewels "Balkis brought unto his king." Possibly some of these were glass, for long ago Egyptians made necklaces of jewel-like glass, and what jewel could surpass in color some of the old Sandwich glass which found its way into every court in Europe.

From lumber taken from the pine woods houses were erected for the workmen, who were allowed to move into them as soon as finished and pay for them by instalments. The great elms planted then still comprise a park in front of the old factory site and stand in full health and vigor, although they have seen the factory and all its projectors pass away.

The following Fourth of July saw 60 employes cross the threshold of the new plant; the next year a stock company was formed by Deming Jarves, the original owner; Henry Rice, Andrew T. Hall and Edward Munro. It was incorporated on Feb. 22, 1826, as the Boston & Sandwich Glass Company and the fires burned until Jan. 1, 1888.

The furnaces were always in full blast; formerly the factory operated with two shifts. A watchman went through the town and rapped on the houses with a stick to call up the glassmakers for the nightly shifts.

In the palmy days of the Sandwich glass factory, all the workmen wore the very best clothes that could be purchased in Boston. Gaffers were known to pay $100 for an overcoat and $20 a pair for high kid boots, and their wives had bonnets and coats made of velvet that cost $20 a yard. The annual glassmaker's ball was one of the principal social functions of the town, and the rivalry of the wives and daughters to be belle of the ball often furnished the chief topic of discussion, sometimes acrimonious, for many weeks. The ladies were bedecked with costumes expressly designed for this event, and many dusted their hair and dresses with powdered glass

The original workmen were nearly all English. Then came Belgians and French, and subsequently native-born of all races played their different parts. A large proportion of the substantial citizens of the town were glassmakers or connected with the industry in one way or another. I remember my father telling of an itinerant preacher who exercised his lungs during the week as a glass blower and on Sunday exercised them in the pulpit. Every man had a nickname, the origin of which was in most cases obscure, but the name persisted to the exclusion of his Christian or legal name.

It was a source of infinite amusement to me to look through the glasshouse windows into the gloomy interior and watch the men walk right up to the mouth of the white hot pots, thrust in an iron tube, and draw it forth with a ball of molten glass on the end, the iron being continually turned to keep the semi-liquid mass from running down to the ground. When I returned to my home in Ware, where all the industrial power was furnished by the Ware river, I fear my description of the glass factory to my schoolmates minimized the technical salamander.

At last one day, to satisfy my unsated curiosity, my uncle took me to the glass house with him. The regulations regarding visitors were very stringent, but worked no inconvenience as no one paid them the slightest heed. Accordingly, I was free to wander about as I willed, keeping a sharp lookout for pieces of hot glass on the floor, flying splinters, and the workmen themselves each armed with a blowing iron on which was some glass in process of manufacture

I saw Gaffer Mathews, a large and rotund Englishman, making the tiniest of wine glasses; Gaffer Lutz was making gypsy kettles of flint glass wound about by ruby glass thread, and yonder was Gaffer Quinn rubbing tumblers.

3

In another part of the factory Gaffer Lovett was working on large and very thick glass dishes, which were subsequently to be cut. Gaffer Grady, a true naturalist, who knew more woods lore than many an eminent writer on the subject, was turning out the white globes that were then so commonly used on gas lights; and huge electric light globes, almost as big as a barrel, fell to the lot of Gaffer Kinney. As each article took shape, it was kept soft enough to work by heating in the glory hole.

A glory hole was like a little furnace but without pots. Around its circumference was a series of round holes of various sizes, according to the size of the article to be heated, through which the fiercest flames rolled and roared in their progress up the chimney pipe. As the article in process of hand manufacture cools, it is heated at one of the openings by the Gaffer, who turns the iron constantly to keep the article in shape. The fuel for the glory hole was pulverized rosin, which an old man seated on a stool and known as a rosin monkey threw into the fire with a very small shovel-like scoop. In later years rosin as a fuel was superseded by a coal tar and afterwards by crude petroleum.

When Gaffer Kinney had made an electric light globe to a certain stage of completion he took a glass instrument very much like an enormous plumb bob with a handle called a stop pipe, and with it entirely closed the open end of the globe. At the same time a small boy applied his mouth to the other end of the iron and blew into it most prodigiously, until the globe swelled to the required size. It astonished me that so small a boy was able to blow the globe to a size which seemed to me to be as big as the boy himself. My imagination exaggerated the boy's effort, for the rapid expansion of the air thus introduced into and confined in the hot globe played a very large part in the process.

Childlike, I was, of course, more interested in what Uncle Tom was doing and I watched closely his every move. A young man known as a gatherer took a blowing iron which at its tip was heated red hot, thrust the end into the pot of white hot glass, turning it many times until he drew it out with a mass of semi-liquid glass adhering to it. He continually turned the iron in his hand to keep the glass from running down onto the floor. That operation was what was called gathering. The iron got hot from being in the furnace, so he laid it across a butt of water, turning it all the time with one hand and splashing water on the iron with the other.

He then rolled the glass on a smooth rectangular iron table called a marver, until it was the shape of a short cylinder. After it was cool enough to retain some semblance of shape, he raised the iron perpendicularly over his head, allowing the molten mass to settle somewhat, in the meantime blowing through the iron, which increased the size of the

4

glass and made it hollow instead of solid. Now I would see what he was going to make.

In the meantime, like a small black imp seated on a soap box in the glow of the furnace, was another member of the shop, in this case a boy, before whom was a mold. This mold was made of a heavy block of iron in two equal hinged sections and the exterior design of the article to be blown was cut out of the iron. The mold rested on an iron plate which constituted its bottom, and it was opened and closed by means of two iron handles. The mold was always heated before use by being filled with hot glass; otherwise the article blown in it would have a rough and dull finish.

The glass being now blown in a more or less globular form and still so soft and ductile that the iron had to be constantly rotated,. Uncle Tom took it, and placed the glass globe in the open mold, which was tightly closed and so held by the mold boy. Then uncle put the end of the iron in his mouth and continued to blow until the glass completely filled the mold. Then he stretched the glass upward from the opening in the top of the mold, still blowing. The part of the glass which was not confined became inflated and much thinner. Then the mold boy opened the mold, the hot and newly made article was removed and passed to the gaffer The mold boy then immersed the mold in a large tub of water, for it is important that the mold shall not get too hot, else the glass will stick to it.

It must be understood that several boys and men collaborated in the making of every article, and the aggregation constituted a shop. The gaffer was the foreman, of the shop, its most skilled workman, and he put the finishing touches on every article the shop made. The gaffer sat on a bench from which a long arm-like projection extended on either end on which he could roll his iron back and forth.

While all this was going on another man of the shop had gathered from the furnace a small quantity of glass which he in turn rolled on the marver until it was about the shape and size of a very short fat snake. With his iron perpendicular and the red-hot snake hanging down, he approached the gaffer. The gaffer seized the end of the rapidly lengthening glass with pincers and fastened the end to the molded article; measuring the required length with his eye, he cut the glass off with a large pair of scissors somewhat resembling pruning shears. It seemed wonderful to me to see him cut red-hot glass, as you would a strip of soft molasses candy. Then seizing the loose end with the pincers, the gaffer also fastened that end to the molded article, and before one could draw another breath it was a little handle.

The gaffer then wet the pincers in a butt of water by his side, and, applying them to the thin glass, caused it to crack and break away from the iron, and, behold, a little kerosene lamp dropped into a tray of sand. It was no longer red, and looked just like the lamp I see before me now. A boy took it up by inserting a piece of wood into the opening, placed it on a sort of wooden paddle covered with asbestos, and departed in an impudent sort of way.

I followed to see what he did with it. At the farther end of the great factory room were several arched, oven-like structures some 40 or 50 feet long. At the opening of each of these annealing ovens, which were called leers, was a very hot fire, the object being to have the temperature as near as possible to that of the newly made glass. In each of these ovens was a series of large, square, sheet-iron pans, attached to each other by hooks. These pans moved by means of little wheels on tracks, and the entire train was moved through the oven by a windlass on the other end of the leer.

Our young man, arriving at one of these leers, deposited his little board containing the lamp on a shelf at its mouth. Then picking up the lamp with a two-pronged fork some six or eight feet long, he placed it in a row of many other such lamps at the farther end of the first pan. This process was repeated a great many times, and eventually the pan at the mouth of the leer was completely covered with similar lamps arranged in rows; but no two lamps touched each other, separation being necessary to prevent them from sticking together.

As soon as a pan was filled, the windlass at the other end of the leer moved the whole train along, and an empty pan was again placed first in the line, a process repeated as rapidly as the first pan in the train was filled. The idea of all this was that, as the pans were intermittently drawn through the leer, the temperature gradually became cooler. This process was known as annealing. If it were not for this, of course, the lamps would have cracked or broken as rapidly as they became cold, by reason of too rapid contraction.

I was very curious to know what was to happen to my little lamp; they told me it would not come through the leer perhaps for a day or two, but I could as well find out by seeing what happened to other similar little lamps. So one of the workmen took me into another room in which there were innumerable identical lamps laid in paper divided layers in great boxes.

A man with huge gray whiskers sat on a nail keg. He wore a long apron of blue and white ticking. On his head was a sort of square turban artfully designed from a paper bag. He rapidly chipped off those flakes of thin glass which still adhered to the opening in the lamp where it broke from the iron and smoothed it by drawing across it a large flat file such as machinists use. As fast as he did this he placed them in a box similar to that from which he took them. When a box was filled it was removed to an upper floor by means of rope and tackle and thence to the cutting shop, where rough openings of the lamps were ground smooth.

Manufacturing processes were more deliberate and less efficient in those days than they are now. It was a common thing for wares to be hauled back and forth through different stages of manufacture. I followed by way of the stairs, to the next floor where there was another man with a striped apron sitting on a keg, also wearing a paper turban and long whiskers and with iron spectacles well down on the end of his nose. He was busily engaged in fastening on the lamps what appeared to be round brass bands that shone like gold rings. He cemented them with plaster of paris on the opening of the lamps, which had now been ground smooth in the cutting shop.

He was a very nice old man and showed me how he did it. Laughing he said they were not rings but collars, because they went around the necks of the lamps, and the burners of the lamps would be screwed into these collars. Our little lamp was now finished.

It was then packed and eventually sold to a farmer's wife for 15 or 20 cents by a tin peddler or traded for rags or bones, and afterwards relegated to a barn, cellar or attic. But then these sad features were only stepping stones to its final repository years after in a safety vault in Tiffany's, from which it was resurrected and offered to me in exchange for a king's ransom.

The Boston and Sandwich Glass Company early adopted the press, so called, and made rapid and great improvement in pressing machinery, thus early beginning to make the pressed glass which is now so fabulously valuable. A press consists of a mold made in two and sometimes three sections into which is put the molten glass, which is forced into the pattern of the mold by a plunger or die operated by a long handle or lever. In most cases the glass was gathered in the usual manner on an iron and allowed to run from the iron into the mold. When a sufficient quantity was in the mold the presser cut the glass off with a pair of scissors. In some instances the glass was taken from the pot with heavy, long-handled iron ladles and poured into the press mold.

I have often seen bankers inks, so called, made in this way. A bankers ink is a cubical block of glass about six inches on the square with a comparatively small depression or well for ink made by the plunger of the press. These were made of the best metal, the designation for flint glass with a large proportion of red lead in its composition. It was a soft glass, very brilliant, and was adapted to cutting. These inks were smoothed to all their surfaces and highly polished in the cutting shop. The ladle was used in their making, as they have to be free from bubbles, which result is more readily insured when the glass is taken from the pot with a ladle.

7

The pressing of candlesticks in the form of crucifixes was always to me an interesting performance. These were made in Sandwich in flint, opal and colors. They were pressed upside down, a generous quantity of glass being put in the top or large opening in the mold. The plunger was brought down and forced the glass from the large hollow base to the very tips of the design and into the finest tracery of the mold.

I have mentioned some of these processes, as there is a tendency in the popular mind to make the whole case for Sandwich glass a matter of cup plates, which were also pressed glass. These derive their chief value as relics of a time and usage so long past as to seem queer to us today. They are merely good examples of the then state of the art of pressing glass, by no means perfect.

Years ago it was good form to drink tea or coffee from the saucer. To protect from stains the linen of those days, china and porcelain manufacturers in England provided little cup plates with their dinner and tea sets. Sandwich began to manufacture them in glass. These became so much the vogue that china and porcelain manufacturers continued making them.

These cup plates commemorated everything and everybody of any note. The completion of Bunker Hill monument was signalized by so many Bunker Hills that all moldmakers turned to making Bunker Hill designs. When the bridge which spans Niagara river was completed the cup plate, "Maid of the Mist," became fashionable. The politics of the country was reflected in them. The Henry Clay group became well known, and extra money is placed on Henry's head for facing the other way. George Washington was more than cup-plated. Major Ringold, who fell at the battle of Palo Alto, was very popular on the tea table for awhile. Everyone knew that Harrison was born in a log cabin, and one could cite the exploitation in this way of many heroes and statesmen. In fact, it might be said the fame of national heroes was then perpetuated by cup plates instead of the cigar-box labels, which latterly translated their fame to the world.

The miscellaneous designs are almost unnumbered. Some wag made the unhappy marriage with two heads facing each other and the inscription "The Wedding Day" the outlet for his satire. Invert this cup plate, and the same heads have visages distorted as if they might bite each other, and the words, "Three Weeks After." Some of the cup plates ran to color, but were never very popular in the old days, as they were too expensive to manufacture. Other unusual specimens are merely the result of a cold mold. I have now in possession a set of doll's cup plates, 80 years old, the only ones I have ever seen.

These off-shades of cup plates that are so prized and valued today were caused by an overdose of one or more of the ingredients. For the same reason the lavender and over-green window panes on Beacon street are the result of incorrect compounding of ingredients aggravated by action of the weather. So much is sold for Sandwich glass that never saw the sea that it is a pleasure when one comes upon the real old glass candlesticks. They were made in two separate molds and fused together. A fraction of an inch difference on the sides of the stick will often be noticed. The seams could not be kept in straight line as the two pieces were slightly rotated while being joined.

Now that all the glass which ever was or could possibly have been made in Sandwich together with the output of contemporary factories, to say nothing of a quantity of imitations thrown in, has been sold and resold until no one but a profiteer or a bootlegger can afford to buy it, we have arrived at the point where fragments are offered to the public to be worn as jewelry. Most of this is made from cullet, which was of no value whatever, except for remelting. Cullet is simply broken or imperfect glass which leaked from a broken pot or was scraped from a pot that was being prepared for melting a new batch. Some of it also came from breaking from the blowing irons the small amount of glass that always adhered after an article was blown. Another source of these gems was a pot of glass which, by reason of deficient or uneven heat, was improperly melted. The result was that there was present much unfused silicate, causing the glass to be seedy. At other times the pot of glass was not of uniform consistency and was said to be cordy. In either case the glass was removed from the pot by means of great iron ladles and poured into huge iron kettles filled with water. The sudden immersion of the molten glass in cold water caused it to break in small pieces resembling in appearance granulation on a large scale. As glass, it was without value; as jewelry, its price is appreciably greater.

Many very beautiful and unique pieces were made for the Centennial exposition in 1876. Sandwich always did itself proud in its presentation pieces. The Prince of Wales on his first visit to the United States carried home Sandwich glass. Queen Victoria had a cup plate and other beautiful pieces sent to her. Gladstone was commemorated, and the last presentation piece was for President Garfield.

There was one lovely old man whom I remember as a child called Mr Bonique, who was the gaffer of the Castor place shop, so-called. What he really did was to make odds and ends from patterns. I once saw him copying a perfumery bottle, that had a broken stopper, of a then celebrated actress. Her order was that they were to drill a hole in the old bottle and get the perfumery out without waste.

In the old days each glassmaker was in close touch with his neighbor in factory, home and church, and there was much vieing and secrecy to excel in original pieces. Sometimes he talked his ideas over at home and would be surprised to find that someone else had made a piece which was a good imitation of what he was thinking of, for his children's boastful pride of their father's accomplishment would many times be the cause of a rival piece.

A glassmaker wishing to make something entirely different from what had been made before, as a gift to friend or family, would ask the superintendent for leave to work overtime and pay for the material used. Strange and beautiful pieces were evolved in this way, such as glass canoes, of all colors and tints, whose hollow interior filled with beet water made a beautiful ruby core. Speaking of ruby, Sandwich made the most beautiful ruby glass in the world; the exquisite coloring being obtained by the use of purple of Crassus, which was produced from gold coins that were an accurate measure of quantity and quality.

Gaffer Lutz once made for me a glass pipe that held a pound of tobacco. I remember my brother and I playing with glass balls of various colors. We sat on the floor with our legs apart and rolled the balls from one to the other. Sometimes they met and broke, but we did not mind, for they were plentiful and we merely swept up the pieces.

When speaking of Sandwich glass one should not omit a mention of Edward Swan, one of the artists. Any one who possesses a piece of glass painted by him has an art treasure. I have stood before the originals of some of his flower designs and it seemed impossible to believe they were paintings on glass rather than living flowers.

To a native of Sandwich, it seems a pity that so much cheap, tawdry, crude and worthless glassware, all of uncertain origin, should be exploited as Sandwich glass, when, in truth, the reputation of Sandwich glass was made by its wonderful hand-made, decorated, engraved, etched and cut glassware of all colors, the best examples of which remain today unrivalled.

A few days ago I interviewed a retired blower, an "old-timer" he styled himself, who told me that of all the blowers who laid down their tools at the end only four now survive. He did not take Sandwich glass as seriously as some of the collectors, and told the following story, with which he was immensely pleased:

A woman resident of Sandwich possessed much Sandwich glass. Its steadily rising value made her somewhat timid about using it. So she made an excursion to a nearby city and acquired at the five-and-ten-cent store a stock of glassware for common use. One day a collector appeared at her house and said he understood she had some Sandwich glass, to which she assented. His eye caught a pressed glass dish on the table, and he immediately identified it as a rare specimen. He told her that he was an expert on the subject and wished to purchase the dish; that he knew all about values; that he would give her $20 for the dish, and no haggling. The woman tried to explain the origin of the glassware, but the expert would not listen. Finally, she reluctantly accepted a $20 bill in exchange for the dish that cost her 20 cents a few days before.

He was regretfully reminiscent of the old time when, after the working week of five and one-half days, the glass makers fished in the bay for mackerel or tramped the woods or marshes for a shot at a rabbit or marsh bird.

The glass factory is no more. The furnace fires were drawn, never to be rekindled, Jan. 1, 1888. Jarves, Waterman, the Fessendens, and Henry F. Spurr, its last manager; Swan, the master decorator; the Laphans, the engravers; Packard, the cutter; Dillaway, the moldmaker; Chapoul, the bookkeeper of 60 years' service, and the long line of gaffers and blowers who were part and parcel of the institution in its days of greatness, have gone to their reward.

The town itself, largely the product of their lives and labors, has year by year receded from the industrial to the rural. Its charm of location, comfortably nestled in the palm of nature's hand, lulled by the rippling wavelets and the sound of singing sands, still makes it, as Joseph Jefferson said, "The most beautiful town in all the world, except the town in England it was named for."

11

The Deming Jarves Book of Designs

By Charles Messer Stow

July 4, 1925, was the hundredth anniversary of the date of the opening by Deming Jarves of the Boston and Sandwich Glass Company's works at Sandwich on Cape Cod. For sixty-two and a half years the factory ran, becoming the chief industry of the town, furnishing prosperity for hundreds of workers, making an enviable reputation for itself as a producer of good glass and paying good dividends to the backers of the concern. Then labor troubles developed and on Jan. 1, 1888, the fires were drawn and the affairs of the company were wound up.

During the period of its activity the factory turned out glassware of every description except window glass and bottles. It had several notable achievements to its credit. It was the first factory in the United States to make pressed glass. It has been credited, though this is probably erroneous, with being the first American factory to make cut glass. Its ruby glass had no equal on this continent. Its flint glass was of notably fine quality. Its colors were deep and pure. It used good metal in its product and the ring when a piece is struck is loud and clear. Deming Jarves, the founder and moving spirit, knew how to make glass.

It is only natural that the present deep interest in antiques that is noticeable all over the country should catch up Sandwich glass in its rush and send the values of authentic pieces soaring. It is only natural also that much glass that was made in the New England Glass Company's factory in Cambridge, or in the western factories at Pittsburgh and farther down the Ohio River, or in Ireland and England, which was imported into this country in staggering amounts, should be attributed to the factory at Sandwich. The absence of factory mark, save in a few rare instances, and the similarity between the products of all glass factories of the period, because of the migratory habits of glass blowers, make the attribution of genuine Sandwich glass an extremely difficult matter. Almost it is true that one man's guess is as good as another's. Still, enormous quantities were turned out and shipped all over the United States. Not only that, but there were foreign exports as well, so that Sandwich glass may be found in almost every part of the world.

Collectors have bewailed the fact that there existed no record of the patterns, or anything that might serve as a reliable guide to identification. There have, however, come into my hands two most valuable bits of Americana in the form of a book of patterns used in the Sandwich factory and another little book in the handwriting of Deming Jarves giving some of the formulas he used to produce his colors. These are the property of P. J. McCarthy, a dealer in glassware at 146 Summer street, Boston, and a glass man all his life. They came into his possession when he was superintendent of one of the glass factories that were started at Sandwich after the dissolution of the Boston and Sandwich Company. They are slender records to be the only documentary attestation of the immense business done by this Cape Cod industry, but so far they are the only ones to come to light.

The notebook of Deming Jarves was written possibly for some trusted workman, possibly for his son, Deming Jarves, who also followed the glass business. In the early 1850s Deming Jarves is said to have built near Boston a factory for his son which was the best laid out plant of the kind known in America, and into which he put all his knowledge of processes and convenient arrangement. In 1860 he built another plant at a little distance from the Boston and Sandwich factory alongside the railroad. Here under the name of the Cape Cod Glass Company, he carried on the business of glass manufacturing for some years, having left the old company in 1858.

Of most interest in the little book to the general collector at least, are the directions for firing glass. Deming Jarves says:

Having completed the kiln according to the model and dried it well by having the fire under it for several days, according to the size you have it built, and having it warm when you set in your glass, either crown of flint, cover each plate about one-eighth of an inch thick with whiting by means of a sieve about eighteen meshes to an inch, which will be quite as fine as the whiting will pass through easy. Place your glass, if crown, flat on the plate, laying it so that the edge is two inches from the outside of the plate and so fill each plate, putting those pieces you wish of the deepest color at the top and bottom part of the kiln, as they are sure to be a little hotter than the middle, never placing anything on the bottom plate.

If flint glass, put them to stand about three inches from the bottom and in which way each article will stand best to support itself whilst hot. Liquor goods as wines, etc., to be bedded in sifted quick lime and whiting, equal parts, up to the bowl of each, never using the lime, etc., twice, but always having fresh for each firing, as small portions of the stain getting into it will speck the goods (if you wish to leave any part plain as the stem, foot, etc.). After each firing when you draw the goods out of the kiln and whilst the plates, etc., are warm, wash the inside of the kiln and the plates with thin whiting and water. It prevents the glass from being specked or sulphured. If a little sulphur should get on the flint goods, which it seldom does, it may

13

be taken off by the cutters with a wood or brush and putty.

The successful firing of glass depends to a great extent on the personal equation. A man in the glass business can tell at a glance usually from what factory a piece comes, even in these days of machine-made goods. Collectors soon learn to distinguish by feel and appearance the source of an article. Certain characteristics appertain to the product of certain factories, and they are brought about by individual methods. This is proved by the directions Deming Jarves gives for regulating the heat necessary. He says:

Heat depends entirely on the size, thickness of kiln, quality of coal or fuel, kind of glass and color you want it. The deeper you wish it the hotter it must be, which practice and attention alone can teach. My own method, and I have tried a great many and I seldom fail, is partly by the eye through the holes for so doing and by placing nothing in the middle of the plate opposite the center of the door-plate, and introducing an iron rod down the middle of that plate to the back of the kiln by cutting a corner off the half brick that stops up that sight-hole to allow the iron rod to slide through. The rod is about three-eighths diameter.

My kiln takes about five or six hours to fire. I always fire so as to have the heat up to its right pitch about two hours after sunset as you can see the degree of heat better after dark and as soon as I percieve by drawing the iron rod out in a dark place that it is just red all along it, I draw the bars and take the fire away immediately, letting the kiln remain till the next evening when it will be cool to take the glass out without danger of its breaking. For flint goods you must draw the fire as soon as you find the least trace of red heat, however faint it may be, so that you just perceive it along the rod, as they will not stand so much heat as crown glass or they will drop, always looking at the rod in a dark place. By attending to these I have no doubt but you will be able at three or four firings to fire a kiln upon a certainty. I cannot possibly give the directions more distinct or in more simple terms.

However simple Deming Jarves may have thought he made his directions, they are not for a novice. They presuppose a knowledge and experience in making glass. Jarves had this experience. After setting down in his notebook formulas for red stain for crown glass, orange stain, amber, yellow stain for crown glass and yellow stain for flint glass, he adds:

These are as concise as possible, not theoretical, but the result of experiments and ten years' practice. I have no doubt you will succeed well, I trust to your honor in never divulging how you obtained these and likewise keeping them entirely to yourself.

The head of the Sandwich glass

factory was eminently a progressive man. This is attested by the enormous variety of the products he turned out. He willingly developed anything that the trade called for and he even tried to keep ahead of the trade by originating new designs. When kerosene replaced "burning fluid." camphene or sperm oil in the early sixties, the factory at Sandwich immediately got a hold on the market with its kerosene lamps. This it retained and lamps of all sorts were manufactured in tremendous quantities. The book of designs owned by Mr McCarthy shows a number of pencil drawings with proportions noted for lamp bases. Production of these articles almost reached a "quantity basis" in this factory. Since it closed new machine methods have been applied to the manufacture of glass and its daily output would not be able to compete with that of a modern factory. Up to the limit of invention, however, the Sandwich factory used machine methods.

That period of the stilted, the bizarre and the ugly which we are accustomed to call the Victorian era drew on and its standards of decoration caught up the Sandwich factory together with all other makers of household goods or decorations and swept them along into artistic darkness but financial brilliance. The book of designs used in the Sandwich factory which I discovered is unfortunately of the Victorian period. It is impossible from any internal evidence to ascribe a date to these patterns, but about 1870 would, I think, be a safe attribution. The designs are for epergnes, for table ornaments such as fish bowls, for ornaments with no ostensible purpose, and for a few lamps. These designs show rather hints to the workman than specific working drawings. They show no great skill in invention and certainly no great artistic ability. They were of that period in the factory's history which succeeded the years of pressed glass making when the types we are accustomed to denominate lace glass were turned out. These designs are all for blown glass Unfortunately this book of designs represents the artistic decadence of the Sandwich factory. The objects pictured may be classed as antiques only by courtesy, because they were made considerably less than a hundred years ago, and one hundred years seems to have been informally adopted generally—as marking the age-limit of an antique. They have an interest for collectors, however, partly because they are the output of a famous factory, partly because by the time they may be properly called antiques they will be of exceeding rarity and partly because they are interesting as indicating the artistic trend of a certain period of American development. The real fame of the Sandwich factory will properly, I think, rest on its pressed glass, that type which goes by the name of lace glass. Search has been made unsuccessfully for some of the molds that were used in the Sandwich factory. Mr McCarthy accounts for their disappearance. The iron molds, he says, were all taken by William Nye, a former state senator of Massachusetts, who had a factory at Bournedale, on the Cape. Mr Nye melted them all down. The wooden molds, of which there were a great number, were stored about the plant until it was purchased about 1906 by Captain Robert Hammond, who dismantled it. The wooden molds, Mr McCarthy believes, were used for firewood at that time.

After the old Boston & Sandwich Glass Company disintegrated, ten of the old employees formed the Sandwich Co-operative Glass Company in 1888, but the venture did not succeed. At another time William Swansey, son of the Patrick Swansey who made the first piece of pressed glass at Sandwich, a piece which he made for himself after hours, using a wooden mold, started a glass business there with Jules Bergin. This was about 1897, but it was a failure. Again about 1903 the Sandwich Glass Company was started by New York capital, but this also did not endure. Once again an attempt was made about 1905 when Gardenio F. King started the Alton Manufacturing Company. This went the way of the others. Now the glass industry is not represented at Sandwich.

No. 14.

LIBRARY *of*
Cape Cod
HISTORY & GENEALOGY

DESCRIPTION OF
THE FARRIS WINDMILL
IN SOUTH YARMOUTH

By
Daniel Wing

YARMOUTHPORT, MASS.:
C. W. SWIFT, Publisher and Printer,
The "Register" Press,

OLD CAPE COD WINDMILLS

By Daniel Wing.

DESCRIPTION OF THE FARRIS WINDMILL IN SOUTH YARMOUTH

Living, as the writer of this article did, for almost fifty years quite near this interesting structure, and often as a boy having visited it for its products or for play, it is not strange that he became interested in its operation, its architecture and history, and ultimately in other mills as well.

The boys of sixty odd years ago found great pleasure at times, when the wind was light, in grasping the end of a mill arm when near the ground, and holding on until their courage failed; and they came to earth always ready to "stump" their companions to go to a greater height.

The experience of the writer which cured him of taking part in that dangerous sport, came at a time when he feared to go higher and was almost as much afraid to let go his hold.

I have known some of the more reckless boys to braid themselves between the slats of a mill arm and make the entire circuit, with their heads downward when at its highest point, which must have been fifty or more feet above the ground level; hastily untangling themselves in order to escape a blow from the following arm, and then earnestly inviting others to do likewise.

The frame of this old building was of heavy timbers well secured by firmly driven trenails of the same material. There were two doors so placed that one or the other of them would always be accessible, free from danger from the revolving arms.

On entering the eastern door, one would see at his right hand, the long, deep trough into which the meal came pouring down through a wooden spout which received it from the floor above where it had been crushed and ground between the upper and nether millstones.

I now can seem to see the old miller, (he could not have been much over sixty), as he sat upon his elevated seat at the farther end of the trough, occasionally allowing the meal to run between the thumb and fingers of one hand to ascertain its degree of fineness, while the other hand grasped the lever for controlling the same by elevating or lowering the upper millstone as conditions required.

On the wall, within his reach, was a sort of little wooden windlass having several short spokes but no rim, around which were wound a few turns of codline with a weight attached to the free end. I believe, to "hold the slack." This was to control the flow of grain as it passed from the hopper on its way to the space between the millstones.

The other end of the codline was carried over several pulleys on the second floor and attached to the lower end of a narrow trough, which, by its downward pitch passed the grain along with greater or less speed as controlled by the miller below.

There was an opening some six or eight inches in diameter through the chamber floor nearly over the miller's seat, through which sev-

2

oral substantial ropes came down and were belayed to cleats upon the wall. These ropes tightened or released an immense wooden friction clutch which passed around the main driving wheel and were used in bringing the revolving mill arms to a standstill. Through the opening the miller could see by the position of the main driving wheel, whether the arms were in position for shortening sail, or were "crotched," which was the signal for notifying the villagers that all grists had been ground and the mill was awaiting further business.

At the left end of the big meal trough was an opening with hooks on its margin for holding bags, into which the miller, from time to time, pushed the meal by use of a broad wooden paddle made for the purpose. Behind a wooden partition and back of the big meal trough, stood the heavy oak frame which supported the weight of both millstones, the vertical shaft and the wooden lantern pinion near its upper end.

I remember that at one time, power was taken from the lower end of this shaft to run a jig saw for sawing plank for wheelwright's use.

At the right of the miller's seat was the winding stairway which led to the second floor. On that level stood the octagonal woodwork which surrounded the millstones, and which in turn supported the hopper and narrow trough already referred to. At the level of the latter, the upright shaft was of iron somewhat flattened rather than round, and when the mill was in action, the trough, which was so suspended as to lean against it, was made to shake from side to side, thus helping the grain onward with greater speed. The octagonal surrounding of the millstones was made more nearly circular by wooden chocks fitted into the angles, thus leaving a uniformly narrow space, which, when filled with meal, made the long spout the only available exit.

One of the interesting features of the second

story, was the arrangement for raising the upper millstone, and swinging it to one side so that the grinding surface of each stone could be reached and sharpened whenever necessary.

Inasmuch as the upper millstone, sometimes called the "runstone," probably weighed more than five tons, the apparatus for handling it had to be correspondingly solid and secure. A derrick, made of oak and strapped with iron, was permanently placed in position to lift the stone and swing it outward over an opening or hatchway in the floor.

Two long, heavy iron caut-hooks which fitted into holes drilled into opposite sides of the stone, were suspended from this derrick in such a manner as to allow the stone to be turned over and the grinding surfaces of both made accessible for the sharpening process.

In each of these surfaces eight shallow channels were cut, diverging from the center, with shorter channels in the intermediate spaces so arranged that, when in motion, the meal resulting from the grinding would be forced outward, clear from the stone itself; and, as the only place of egress was at the upper end of the long spout leading to the big trough below, it found its way there as already described.

The sharpening was done by the use of highly tempered picks; the channels being made a little deeper, and the flat surfaces between, roughened; care being taken to keep the same as a whole, perfectly level.

The shape of the mill was hexagonal; but, as the sides sloped inward, each floor space was smaller than the next lower.

There was a marginal gallery at the third story, which was seldom used I think, except as a platform when lubricating or repairing the runway on which the revolving roof rested. The roof itself was elongated, had two gables, and the circular track on which it moved allowed it to be turned in any direction from which the wind might blow.

The shaft which carried the mill arms was projected from one gable, and from the other a long spar extended nearly to the ground with a heavy cart wheel attached for the purpose of turning the vanes to the wind by revolving the whole roof. The track on which the roof rested had to be lubricated freely; and ultimately, in its old age, it became so difficult to turn that wooden rollers were put in; but these proved to be of little advantage, I believe.

The vanes of the mill arms were of slats arranged ladder-like, and when the wind blew very strong no further surface was needed. Strips of canvas were provided however, two for each arm, which were fully spread when the wind was light by hooking them over pegs at the top, and by weaving them in and out between the lower cross bars and securing them by stout strings to the lowest one.

Shortening sail was accomplished by twisting the lower half or more of each canvas so as to expose less surface and securing as before.

There was a chain for securing the mill arms from turning; but sometimes the miller depended upon lowering the upper millstone upon the lower for that purpose, and upon one occasion when he had climbed part way up, a gust of wind started the mill into action and he fell to the ground and was lame ever after.

Whenever the wind veered in either direction, the wheel at the end of the long spar was manned and the right direction was determined when a person standing there could feel the breeze coming on both sides of the mill with equal force.

The above description of the Farris mill applies in most respects to most of the wind grist mills of which I have knowledge, although the details of the interior arrangements may have varied somewhat.

HISTORY OF THE FARRIS MILL
IN SOUTH YARMOUTH

When and by whom this structure was built, are facts unknown to the present generation; but the following account is believed to be authentic.

In 1883, David K. Akin, who was born in 1799, told the writer of this article that it formerly stood in the open field back of the old Ichabod Sherman homestead in the lower village (now known as Bass River). He, himself, had seen the circle described by the big wheel as it swung round to different points of the compass to keep the mill arms "in the eye of the wind;" and the memoranda made at the time of that interview are still in my possession.

Capt. Howes Berry (1805-1890), late of South Yarmouth, a man well posted as to ownership of lands in that part of the town, confirmed the above statement and said the mill belonged to Lot Crowell (1730-1809), who "moved it from the north side of the Cape."

David Kelley, late of South Yarmouth, stated to a friend of mine that he, David, had a tax bill made in the 18th century to his grandfather David (1744-1816), for the tax on that mill, and that it then stood in South Yarmouth (Friends' Village), but that it did formerly stand near the mouth of Bass river.

This seems to be conclusive evidence as far back as it reaches in point of time. I have also been credibly informed that David Kelley, Senior, and Capt. Samuel Farris who died in 1825, moved the mill from its location near the mouth of Bass river in 1782 to the spot in Indian Town, later known as Friends' Village, where it stood for 112 years; that the initials "T. G." and the date "1782" painted in black upon the inner wall or frame, stand for Thomas Greenough, a half breed

Indian, and the year when he probably took some part in the moving process, but never owned it.

The motive power, according to the testimony handed down from an eye witness, "was forty yoke of oxen," and help came from all directions, as may easily be imagined; especially as at a "house raising," there was likely to be a plentiful supply of spirits for lubricating purposes. And there was; for the same eye witness further declared that "a barrel of rum," (New England, we may presume,) "stood on end with head knocked out; the contents free for all, with the natural result that, as the spirits of the workers rose, those in the barrel fell in like ratio, and "there was a noisy, drunken crowd in the vicinity that night composed of both Indians and white men."

The owners and tenders of this mill while in Friends' Village, have been Samuel Farris, Reuben his son, and Samuel his grandson; William Haffards, and finally Remegio Lewis, whose heirs sold it in 1894 to F. A. Abell who moved it to West Yarmouth, where it now stands.

A memorial tablet might very appropriately be placed on the spot which it occupied for five score and twelve years, in recognition of its long and faithful service.

AN OLD YARMOUTH MILL

In the year 1747, the town of Yarmouth granted leave to Thomas Howes, Lot Howes and Samuel Eldridge "to build a windmill on a piece of land in the East Parish, near the schoolhouse." This location is in Dennis, which at that time was a part of Yarmouth.

I quote some extracts from the story of this mill as told by the late Capt. Thomas Prince Howes:

"The mill was built shortly after, and stood until 1869 near the old meetinghouse and within a few rods of the district schoolhouse.

"There it stood a period of 122 years when it was sold to Mr. Edmund Matthews, who removed it to the top of Newcomb's hill. It was used for mill purposes until 1882, when Mr. Matthews took it down and used its timber for other purposes. Mr. Perez Howes was an owner in my young days, and tended mill more than anyone else. I remember him fingering the meal as it poured down the spout from the floor above, where it passed under the mill stones. Mr. Abner Howes was the miller for eight or ten years, a sturdy seaman of the old school, with whom I was shipmate for two seasons on board a mackerel fisherman some sixty years gone by.

"Mr. Henry Hall, also an old shipmate of mine for one season, was for several years in attendance at the mill. On one occasion he passed through a dangerous experience. He had stopped his mill to shorten sail; but had neglected to hook the chain to the spindle of the mill arm. A sudden flaw of wind came, and he felt the arm which he was standing on, moving around. He was too high up to jump off, and with singular activity for a man of seventy years, slid down when the arm was in the right position, to the shaft, and kept astride of that by shifting his position as it turned over, until some one came to his assistance and stopped the mill.

"Much more might be said about our old mill if time allowed, and of the customers who brought their bags of corn and rye to the mill to be ground.

"Many a time, after a long calm spell, the bags would accumulate in the upper chamber of the mill, where the unground grain was carried, to wait its turn. There have I often been to wait my turn to get my grist into the hopper. Others, too, whose meal chests were empty at home, had to go to the mill and wait for their turns.

"To the scholars who attended the old district school, for generations the mill was a never ending source of amusement and instruction. With what hearts of glee and noise did they sally out of the schoolhouse door and rush across the road to the mill; and various were the sports the boys indulged in. There was good fun for some to cling to the mill arms as they swung around, and get a hoist in the air as far as they dared go, and then let go. One young fellow, so the story goes, was carried quite around, getting so high that he feared to let go, and so held on and went around and came down unharmed. There too, was the delightful sport sometimes indulged in, of walking up the tail from the wheel at the lower end, to the upper end where it was inserted into the mill top."

THE SCORTON MILL.

About the year 1796, Bennett Wing, my great-grandfather, built a mill of the usual type not far from his residence in that part of Sandwich known as Scorton, quite near the road which led to and faded out among the sand dunes of Sandy Neck.

The fact that there were few trees and fewer houses in that vicinity goes to show that the location was favorable for the vanes of the mill to catch the full force of the winds; from whatever points of the compass they might come.

The writer has but few dates in the history of this structure or in that of the owner; but the record shows that the latter was born in 1758, was married in 1782, and "died comparatively young." As the mill was built when the proprietor was 38 years old; and as he died "comparatively young," we may reasonably infer that it was subsequent to his decease, in the early part of the last century, that Isaac Bassett purchased

9

it and moved it to a spot in the lower village of South Yarmouth.

Later, it was owned and managed by Roland Lewis, a resident of that section, and still later, by Freeman Crowell 2d. and Seth Collins, who moved it to West Dennis and placed it in an open field near the old road which led to "Uncle Elihu's Ferry."

There it was tended by the owners for some years; but men and mills grow old together: time passed on, and in 1884, the mill which had done its duty well for nearly a century, was purchased and dismantled by Uriah H. Sears, and the mill stones, later purchased by the writer of this article, now rest upon the grounds of the Owl Club, his former home, in South Yarmouth, the upper supporting a large bomb picked up on Morris Island, Charleston harbor, just after the close of the Civil war; and the nether mill stone still doing duty in holding the foot of the club's flagstaff.

THE PETER BAKER MILL.

This mill was built in South Dennis by Peter Baker, father of the Peter Baker who was well known as the keeper of an inn during the middle of the last century, and stood quite near his residence for many years. I have seen it there, and the fact that it stood so near dwelling houses and the street, seemed to make an impression upon my memory; for usually, windmills were placed at a distance from residences and from much frequented highways.

In fact, the law in at least one of the New England states required all windmills to be located away from public highways, to lessen the danger of frightening horses.

Captain Braddock Matthews purchased this mill in October 1866, and moved it to the lower village of South Yarmouth, near the mouth of Bass river, where, as I have recently been informed, it remains to this day; not used however for grinding grain, but kept as a memorial of the times when thirty-two quarts made a bushel, and when men worked from sun to sun with apparently as much comfort and contentment as are manifest now-a-days.

The roof of this mill differs from some others in that it is conical in form and has two dormers, through one of which the big, horizontal shaft which bears the arms, extends; while through the other the long spar reaches down to the wheel used in turning the mill to the wind.

It bears upon one of its timbers within, the date "1797, 11th Decem."

I am told that the present owner is Mr. Stone.

Long may this interesting structure which has weathered the storms of a century and a quarter, remain where it now is, to gratify the antiquarian, and to remind the present generation of the period when gasoline was unknown, and people travelled mostly on foot or on horseback.

THE OLD MILL IN CHATHAM.

The following is quoted from the Chatham Monitor:

"In 1797, the year that John Adams became the second president of the United States, what is familiarly known as the "Old Mill" came to occupy the hill overlooking Stage harbor, the Mill pond and farther away Altantic ocean. The date 1797, said to be the year the mill was built, is covered on the stair casing with some others which are supposed to be the dates when the mill changed owners; at least that is what is told by Capt. George F. Harding, who was born and lived over eighty years within a stone's throw of the mill.

11

The first owner was Col. Benjamin Godfrey, who owned and operated it during his lifetime.

In 1818 it was acquired by Christopher Taylor, who inherited the mill and property adjoining, including the dwelling house now owned and occupied by Charles R. Atwood; as the saying was in those days, C. Taylor was 'brought up' in Col. Godfrey's family, and inherited his property.

Near the time of the close of the Civil war, Christopher Taylor sold the mill property to Oliver Eldrodge, who kept it in operation during his lifetime.

After his death it was again sold in the year 1884 to Zenas Nickerson and was used by him in his grain and grocery business, and later by the firm known as Zenas Nickerson & Sons.

Zenas A. Nickerson acted as miller for a period of nineteen years and George H. Nickerson 2d for about four years; or until in the year 1907, in a northwest gale, the outer end of the shaft with all of the arms was blown off and completely demolished.

In the year 1908 the mill and land adjoining were sold to Nelson Floyd of Winthrop, who bought the property on which to erect a summer home and who later sold it to Charles Hardy, who put a new shaft in the mill, added new arms and otherwise repaired the building; but the summer suns and the storms of winter, (and one might add the jackknife carvers) are now fast destroying what was once one of the largest and best of the old windmills of Cape Cod."

"Note—The last miller tells us that a day's work was a varying amount of meal. In a high wind, ten minutes would reduce a bag or corn to meal; while again it might require a whole day to accomplish the same amount."

The issue of the Chatham Monitor dated April 8, 1924, states that "The gale of last Tuesday night and Wednesday did serious damage to one of our most favored landmarks, the old mill.

12

It struck it in the tail and so tipped the head out, wrecking the trundle top and one arm. . . Mr. Hardy has had it inspected and hopes to be able to repair it."

In our youth we greatly enjoyed the humorous story of Don Quixote's planned attack upon a group of innocent windmills which he mistook for giants; but really, a windmill when in vigorous action, is no mean antagonist, if one ventures too near its huge, swinging arms.

Among the victims of the old Farris mill can be counted two creatures slain, (a horse and a cow), a man maimed for life, and at least one boy wounded while engaged in the favorite pastime of running between the revolving arms.

While writing this series of articles on old windmills, the ancient story has frequently come to mind, of a certain legislator who had gained notoriety for his dry, long-winded speeches to the extent that he had become a bore to his hearers. On one occasion, the length and dryness of his harangue had so parched his tongue that he ordered a page to bring a glass of water. Just as he raised it to his lips, a fellow member arose and in a very dignified manner addressed the chair: "Mr. Speaker, I rise to a point of order."

The chair: "The gentleman will state his point of order."

The member: "Mr. Speaker, my point of order is this:—that it is highly improper to run a windmill by water power."

THE THACHER MILL IN YARMOUTH.

The windmill known as the Thacher Mill was built in 1794. Thomas Thacher financed the enterprise and Capt. Hallett supervised the construction.

The carpenters began work on the structure August 4, 1794, and it was finished and the first bushel of grain ground January 14, 1795. The whole expense of the mill was £303:18:1.

13

An old print definitely discloses its exact location on a plot of land near Summer street in the rear of the homestead now occupied by Mr. Nathan H. Matthews. The tract is designated as the Mill Lot. A right-of-way between the adjoining land of Miss Lilla T. Arey and the Knowles estate from Summer street to the mill lot, is of record and is known as Mill Lane.

That this mill was later moved to a site at the rear of the present public school building opposite the Congregational church is quite generally thought to be true.

If so, there was at one time some competition in the grist-mill business, for the same authorities give the record of the building and ownership of another mill situated nearby, which was owned in eighths by the following citizens: William Taylor, Richard Taylor, John Taylor, Isaac Hall, Ebenezer Hallett, Ansel Hallett, Chandler Gray, Timothy Hallett. William Taylor, Ansel Hallett and John Taylor hewed the timbers at Great Island. The stones were quarried from the huge boulders of Scargo Hill by Richard and John Taylor.

William Taylor finally bought out the heirs of the former owners of the mill. Mr. William Anderson, Benjamin (Nat.) Matthews and Seth Hamblin were successive owners.

Mr. Hamblin moved it to the eminence back of "Charles's Folley" hill, and George Ryder was the miller. In fact through all the years we find the name of Ryder associated with the milling business.

Mrs. Bayard Thayer purchased it after it had been unused for a number of years in order to preserve the landmark. It was probably not in active operation after 1880.

Now all that remains of this mill is the millstone, bearing a most fitting epitaph of service chiselled deep and worn smooth, to endure after all those frail creatures of humanity of today who are interested in this environment and its early activities have shuffled off.   C. W. S.

TO THE FARRIS WINDMILL.

Now take thy rest, thou good old mill,
From peak of roof to oaken sill;
No more thine arms go circling round,
Thy noisome gears emit no sound.
No more thy vanes point to the breeze;
For now thou tak'st thy well earned ease;
While millers known to thee of yore
Have lived their lives and gone before.
Long time ago, thy oaken frame
Out from the native forest came;
Those massive grinders brought from far,
E'en to this day, thy pride they are.
That iron shaft made strong to stand
The weight above, was forged by hand;
For hammers then weren't run by steam
To work on shaft, or band, or beam.
Then, workers toiled from sun to sun;
Their daily wage was fully won;
They did not quit at three or four
And go right home to work no more.
Thou'st done thy duty long and well:
We would today thy praises swell;
For good example thou hast set
Which mortal man should not forget.
Though winds blew high or winds blew low,
Thy steady course did onward go:
With sails adjusted to the breeze,
Thy work was always done to please.
Man raised the grain; thou mad'st it fit
To make the "staff of life" of it.
In this, thou'st nobly done thy part;
So thou, a benefactor art,
* * * *

The mealy stream no more runs out
Into the trough from wooden spout;
  For the grinding has ceased,
    The meal does not flow;
  Memories only remain
    Of those scenes long ago.

Hingham Center.   Daniel Wing.

No. 15

LIBRARY *of*
Cape Cod
HISTORY & GENEALOGY

WILLIAM SWIFT
and
Descendants to the Sixth Generation
BY
EBEN SWIFT

YARMOUTHPORT, MASS.:
C. W. SWIFT, Publisher and Printer,
The "Register" Press,
1921

WILLIAM SWIFT

and

Descendants To *The* Sixth Generation.

By EBEN SWIFT

In 1890 George H. Swift, Esq., of Amenia, N. Y., published under the title of "William Swyft of Sandwitch and Some of His Descendants, 1637-1899;" a genealogical record of the Swifts.

The chronicler who was 80 years of age when he put between covers the result of his life work found, as is usual in genealogical production, that the task was, even in the face of persistent, intelligent and tireless effort, somewhat crude.

Yet let us console those who have been associated with him in this work, with the fact that the first objective was reached and in many instances, even when the wrong road was taken, the true path was indicated by the error of way. Mr. Swift has furnished the basis of a structure on which the later generations must build.

Mr. Swift had notes of many families which during his life he had not been able to connect. This correspondence is unfortunately destroyed. It included some twenty thousand of the unidentified Swifts.

Major General Eber Swift of Fort Leavenworth, Kansas, took up the thread where it ended by the death of this early chronicler. He has revised and added to the original draft, safeguarding his efforts with unusual care and skill.

And these are the chronicles herewith presented in part, with such revision or amendment as seemed meet and fitting.

It is with pardonable delicacy that the present publisher, who has brought out many of the original genealogical records of Cape Cod families, under the collective title of the "Library of Cape Cod History and Genealogy," enters into a field involving his own line of ancestry. But as these records are familiar in antiquarian circles throughout the United States, it seems necessary in order to complete as nearly as possible the Cape Cod lines, to add these Swift records to those of the other familiar names of the Old Colony stock.

Inspired by the text of the family motto—Festina Lente—we

3

have assumed the responsibility of going forward with the publication of the Swift memoranda, as another step towards which the original translator of the records bravely trod the paths of uncertainty in virgin fields of research with an intelligence and a patience that upheld the family traditions and set an example that it will. be satisfactory to follow.

Charles W. Swift

Yarmouthport, Mass.
March 3, 1923.

Bocking Deanery, Braintree, England.
May 12, 1874.

Dear Sir:

My father, the Dean of Bocking (having a great deal of work on his hands when he received your letter), gave me access to the parish records in his keeping so that I might ascertain all possible information relating to your Bocking forefathers.

The enclosed statement is the result of my search.

Swift is a very uncommon name in this part of the country; which is an indirect proof that Messrs. Thomas, James and James Swift were of your family. The oldest inhabitants have no recollection of anyone so called—which leads me to think that with their deaths, the Bocking Swifts became extinct.

The parish clerk has, at my request, hunted throughout the church and church yard for monuments or inscriptions to members of the Swift family but he has found none. This is strange, since T., J. and J. Swift were evidently gentlemen of position and property.

I desired him also to make every inquiry amongst the village people in order to find out if any of them remembered the name. All that he was able to gather was a melancholy tradition of a person named Swift who committed suicide and was (in accordance with the barbarous custom of our ancestors) buried where three roads met with a stake through his heart. They say the place is yet called "Swift's Corner."

Mordant's History of Essex is the best work on the subject. Mr. Thomas Wright has more recently written a history in two or three quarto volumes. I think you could get a map of the county from Edward Stanford, agent for the ordnance maps, etc., 6 Charing Cross, London.

I should always be happy to be of service to a citizen of your great republic, and I beg you to believe, that if I am not able to

Your obedient servant,
Evelyn Carrington

Charles F. Swift, Esq.

The first Book of Registers of the Church of St. Mary, Bocking, which is still in preservation, begins in the year 1655. The writing has become extremely faint and I have not been able to discover the name of Swift in its pages although it is probable they contain it more than once.

In the second book, I find the following registers:

"Mary, daughter of James Swift, baptized August 5, 1671."

"A daughter of Tho. Swift, burned Nov. 3rd, 1671."

In a book of records of the parish rates and containing other memoranda, the statement which follows is among the first entries;

	£	s.	d.
"Herein is underwritten the names and sums of all which gave towards the ransoming of English men out of Turkish slavery. The sum was. Collected by William Lane and Thomas Howe, church wardens and paid to Richard Colebraud, dean and rector of the parish, 1670."	11	10	4
Among the subscriptions are those of			
Thomas Swift		1	6
James Swift			6
The rating of the Swifts, as recorded in this book, is as follows:			
Rate for repairing the church and other necessaries in 1670, Thomas Swift,	6	6	2
Rate in 1673, Thomas Swift,		8	
Rate in 1675 and 1676, Thomas Swift, Bradford street, Bocking,		6	7
Rate in 1677, Thomas Swift,		5	2
Rate in 1678, Thomas Swift,		2	11

6

Rate in 1679, Thomas Swift,		5	11
Rate in 1682, Thomas Swift,	1	6	3
Rate in 1684, Thomas Swift,		8	9
Rate in 1685, Thomas Swift,		17	6
Rate in 1685, James Swift,		9	
Rate in 1686, Thomas Swift,		5	4
Rate in 1686, James Swift,		8	
Rate in 1687, Thomas Swift,		2	8
Rate in 1687, James Swift,		1	8

On consulting the registers I find this year, 1687, the entry: "Thomas Smith buried November 3rd."

Rate in 1699, James Swift, for the Resting Seat,		3	
ditto James Swift,		11	3
Rate in 1700, James Swift, for Resting Seat,		2	
ditto James Swift,		7	6
Rate in 1701, James Swift, for Resting Seat,		1	8
ditto James Swift,		6	3
Rate in 1703, James Swift, for Resting Seat,		4	
ditto James Swift,		15	
Rate in 1704, James Swift, for Resting Seat,			10
ditto James Swift,		3	1½

Here occurs a gap in the record, and the rates do not appear again in the book till 1720, when there is no longer any mention of the name of Swift. I referred to the registers and found the two entries which follow:

"James Swift: buried June 7, 1713."

"James Swift: buried October 5, 1713."

The Rate book contains the written signatures of Thomas Swift affixed (together with the names of other notables of the parish) to the reckoning up of the accounts for the year 1685.

It is interesting to observe that Thomas Swift paid higher rates than any save four or five out of two hundred on the lists. The precise value of Thomas and James Swift's landed property (which of course need not represent their whole wealth) may be ascertained by an easy calculation. In 1687—the year in which

7

Thomas Swift died—the rates are described as having been down at one penny in the pound. Therefore—(seeing that the reckoning is done by quarters)—Thomas Swift's rating being 2-8 the quarter, his property in land was worth £128 per year, in itself a handsome income at that period. James Swift, who paid 1-3 in the same year for a quarter's rating must have possessed land valued at £80 per annum.

In Bradford street there are still several houses dating from 1500 and 1600—especially a large and very fine old gabled house which used to be the Woolpack Inn, and which is one of many existing proofs that Bocking was a place of considerable importance 300 years ago.

The standard work on the "History of the County of Essex" is that by Philip Morant in three large folio volumes, published in MDCCLXVIII. I have searched in vain in this work for the name of Swift; but I found in the list which Morant gives of the sheriffs for Essex in the year 1509 (Henry VIII) the name of "John Sewfter Esq." and I strongly suspect this is the same name as Swift, only differently spelt. The more so, as James Swift appears once as "James Swefte" in the registers. There was a great deal of variety in the spelling of proper names in those days.

The Heating Seat is a nice house, which I have always understood took its name from having been the halting place of the Roundheads in the Commonwealth times. It has a garden and attached to it is a malting house. It now belongs (or is hired) by a family named Wyatt.

EARLY SWIFTS.

The name of Swift, Swithern, Swyft, Swyfte, Swifte, Swift, appears in the early annals of England.

Sir Francis Palgrave gives the name in his rolls of Norfolk and adjoining countries as early as the year 1164.

Burke's Landed Gentry says that the ancestor of the family was of Belgian origin and came to England about the fourteenth

8

century. and that from the difficulty of pronouncing the name D'Suivo it was changed through the forms Suyfo, Swyf, Swyfte, till it reached Swift. Bardsley's Dictionary of English and Welsh names suggests that they originated in the effort to describe personal characteristics or occupations. He gives other names having the same meaning as Swift, as Purchas, Shearwinde, Lightfoot, Golightly, Bullet, etc. From all of this it becomes quite evident that family names were derived in various ways of which the above are examples of a particular case.

The branch of the name at Allergill and Rotherham in Yorkshire traces back to Bryan Swift who lived in 1333, at which time Burke says they were settled in County Durham. From them descended many persons of note, among them the famous Dean of St. Patrick's, whom Addison addressed as: "The most Agreeable Companion. The Truest Friend, and the Greatest Genius of his Age."

Some account of the Rotherham family is given in the fragment of an autobiography by Dr. Jonathan Swift, 1667-1714. Further accounts will be found in the Life of Major General Richard Deane, 1870; in "Historic Notices of Rotherham" by John Guest, F. S. A.; in "South Yorkshire" by Rev. Joseph Hunter.

Among early settlers in America a considerable number bore the name of Swift. In many cases they made their homes in widely separated parts of the Colonies, while some lived in close proximity with others of the name, without leaving a trace or record of family relationship. Some of the most notable of these are the following:

(1) Thomas Swift of Dorchester, Mass., came to Massachusetts Bay soon after the first Colony landed at Plymouth. They claimed relationship with the Rotherham family. From them descended General Joseph G. Swift, first graduate of the West Point Military Academy, distinguished soldier in the War of 1812, and officer of Engineers. His published Memoirs (1890) include a short genealogy by Harrison Ellery.

(2) John and Jerusha Swift lived in the state of New York

about 1743. Their two sons Thomas and John, and their seven daughters had a numerous progeny.

(3) John and Elizabeth Swift lived in Caswell County, North Carolina, towards the close of the eighteenth century. They had five sons and three daughters, most of whom moved to Missouri in early days. To this family belonged Hon. John F. Swift of San Francisco, formerly U. S. minister to China. A record of this branch with the title "Tree Book of the Swift and Orr Families" is said to have been printed some years ago.

(4) John Swift married Abigail Sage, 1774, at Middletown Upper Houses, now Cromwell, Conn. They had fourteen children, of whom nine sons reached manhood and left many descendants. Search for further information as to the antecedents of John has been without result, except a tradition that his father had also been seen near Derby, Conn., on some ancient day. Among the family relics is an old seal resembling the crest of the Rotherham family.

(5) James Swift, an officer of the English Army, born in England in 1739, wounded in the Colonial wars, married Mehitable Merwin and lived at Wilmingford, Conn., blessed with a large family.

(6) Morton Swift married Belinda Barlow and lived at Dover, N. Y., in early days.

(7) Captain James Swift of Leeds, England, came to Virginia with Captain John Smith, 1620. After some years he returned to England and his son John came to Philadelphia in 1662. The family prospered and became prominent. Among his descendants was Dr. Samuel Swift of the Manor of Moreland, Philadelphia County, a friend of Benjamin Franklin.

(8) John or "Jack" Swift came from Bristol, England, to Philadelphia, 1737-8, where members of the family were already established. One of his descendants was collector of the port under the British regime, another was mayor of the city, another a wealthy merchant, others were the "Ladies Swift of Digby

10

Hall." The families of Captain James and John Swift were connected by marriage in later generations.

(9) William and Joane Swift of Sandwich, 1637, were the progenitors of by far the most numerous of all these Swift families. Their descendants have been estimated to number many thousands. Among them are Senator Benjamin Swift of Vermont; Chief Justice Zephaniah Swift of Connecticut; Professor Lewis Swift, the astronomer; Gustavus Franklin Swift of Chicago, whose practical use of the refrigerator car made the packing industry what it is today; Alexander Swift of Cincinnati, a leader in the iron and steel business; Isaac and Ivan Swift, authors and writers; Lemuel Swift, newspaperman. Great numbers were soldiers, serving in every war from the early campaigns against the savages to the World war. Among them were General Heman Swift of the Revolution; Generals John and Philetus Swift of the War of 1812; General Ebenezer Swift of the Mexican and Civil wars; General Frederick W. Swift of the Civil war; General Eben Swift of the latest war. Generals Lewis, Lindsay and Richard K. Swift served in state troops.

In apparent contradiction to this military record is the fact that many of the Swift family were Quakers, and were inter-married with many of the prominent families belonging to that sect. During the years when persecution of the Quakers was at its most vicious point they stubbornly maintained their faith. At a time when, from their barren heritage, a meagre provision was the best could ever be gotten, a fine, that would sweep away the entire product of a year of toil, was given for such an offence as wearing one's hat at meeting or "for disturbing the public peace by his silent worship." Widow Joan herself was fined "for being at Quakers' meetings."

Perhaps the sailors were even more numerous than the soldiers, for in the brief annals of the family we often see the record "Lost at Sea," repeated from generation to generation. Rear Admiral William Swift during an important period was at the head of the navy of the country.

11

The widow Joan survived her husband for twenty years. A note in "The Wing Family of America" tells us that "Joana was a prominent person in Sandwich, she being esteemed wealthy, and is the only woman who seems to have been accorded the privilege of uniting with the men in calls to pastors and like public business."

Although William bought the largest farm in Sandwich, he died heavily in debt, too soon perhaps to establish himself firmly. His will shows that he owned "two shuites of apparell," one "coate," "two ruffbauds and four playne bands"—all appraised at something less than fifteen dollars of our money. It gives us pause to read of two muskets, two bandoliers, a "french bill and cosset," and a "hallbeard," but whether they show him to have been a man of war or whether they were the ordinary equipment of a settler of his day, we do not know. A "prcoll of bookes" calls our attention, small as it evidently was.

In this record of the descendants of William we find a number of the Swift name who are connected by marriage but who have not been further identified up to the present. Some of them are:

(1) Seth Swift, who married Rebecca Swift (144) in 1777. See 91A (2) Ephraim Swift, Jr., "of Sandwich," whose son Ezra married Lucy Swift of Falmouth, November 30, 1797.

(3) Elizabeth Swift of Sandwich, who married Jesse Swift (115) on April 7, 1763.

(4) Ezra W. Swift, who married Elmira O. Swift (780a) on July 18, 1858.

(5) Henry E. Swift, who married Bathsheba Leech Swift, November 9, 1843.

(6) Frances Augusta Swift, who married James H. Swift (707) February 4, 1847.

(7) John H. Swift married Isaphene Swift, daughter of Philander (779).

Records of Births in Church in Rotherham, England.

Memo of George H. Swift

S. Swyft, October 13, 1585.
John Swyft, October 24, 1589.
Elizabeth Swyft, September 27, 1579.
Alexander Swyft, March 23, 1577-8.
Robert Swyft, March 25, 1575-6.
Thomas Swyft, January 7, 1575-6.
Elizabeth Swyft, Feb. 24, 1573-4.
Martyn Swyft, November 15, 1573.
John Swyft, October 4, 1573.
Alice Swyft, March 17, 1570-1.
Ann Swyft, December 17, 1570.
Ralph Swyft, November 12, 1569.
Alexander Swyft, June 27, 1568.
John Swyft, May 23, 1568.
Robert Swyft, June 12, 1564.
Margaret Swvft, November 30, 1561.

Baptisms at Rotherham.

Ellen, dau. of Nicholas Swifte, February 10, 1627-8.
William, son of Hugh Swift, December 24, 1626.
Thomas, son of George Swift, March 4, 1624.
Edward, son of Seth Swift, January 20, 1623-4.
Ann, dau. of Nicholas Swift, December 11, 1623.
William, son of William Swift, July 28, 1622.
Thomas, son of Seth Swift, January 20, 1620-1.
Elizabeth, dau. of Nicholas Swift, June 11, 1622.
Anne, dau. of William Swift, alias Savige, July 5, 1618.
Ann, dau. of William Swift, November 20, 1614.
Richard, son of Thomas Swift, May 2, 1613.
Ellen, dau. of William Swift, March 22, 1611-12.
Robert, son of Robert Swift, March 22, 1610-12.
An (?), dau. of Robert Swift, January 25, 1609-10.

Ralph, son of Thomas Swift, September 20, 1607.
—d, son of Robert Swift, May 18, 1608.
Ann Swift, September 29, 1604.
—— Swift, September 3, 1603.
Hugh Swift, July 7, 1602.
John Swift, April 5, 1602.
Francis Swift, December 1. 1601.
Nicholas Swift, May 15, 1600.
Ann Swift, September 7, 1599.
Katharine Swift, April 4, 1598.
Elizabeth Swift, March 19, 1596-7.
—— Swift, April 5, 1596.
George Swift, November 1, 1594.
Thomas Swift, June 22, 1593.
Thomas Swift, April 13, 1592.
Alexander Swift, April 18, 1591.
Elizabeth Swift, August 17, 1589.

Marriages at Rotherham Church.

Thomas Swift and Rosamonde Beck, June 23, 1636.
Hugh Swift and Margery ——, February 1624-5.
Nicholas Swyft and Anne Bothomeley, June 4, 1622.
Seth Swift and ——, May 29, 1617.
George Marshall and Issabell Swifte, January 24, 1612.
William Swift and Issabell ——, January 27, 1608.
Richard Swyft and Issabell Barton, December 14, 1595.
Alexander Swyft and Alice Wood, April 15, 1580.
John Swyft and Ellen Turton, February 10, 1576-7.
Henry Swyft and Elizabeth Ingle, February 30, 1572-3.
Henry Swyfte and Margaret Walker, October 2, 1569.
Hugh Swift and Jane Duke, July 20, 1567.

John Guest's notices at Rotherham. M. Bolton, High Street.

WILLIAM SWIFT

and Some of His Descendants.

It seems quite certain that "William Swyft of Sandwitch," with his family, came from England to America in the great "Boston Immigration" of 1630-1. Savage says that he "probably came from Bocking County, Essex, or its vicinity; was in Watertown, Mass., in 1634; had been there some time. Sold his property in Watertown in 1637, and probably moved to Sandwitch, where he died in January, 1644." Rev. F. Freeman says that he died in 1642. But the Plymouth Colony Record says:
"In Probate office, Plymouth,"
"William Swyft, Sandwitch."
"1643.—Administration by Joane his wife."
** Jan. 1643, the Inventory was shown at Court. Amount 72 pounds 11 shillings."

Search in Bocking for traces of the first William has proved fruitless, as the Parish Records were burned about the time of the Restoration. Dr. Henry Bond in his History of Watertown and its early settlers, says: "William Swyft, proprietor, 1636-7, sold his house and land in Watertown to Thomas White of Sudbury, who sold it March 31, 1640, to John Knight. In 1636

---

*The year then began in March, and January was the 11th month of the year. —

Vol. 1. Folio 14, Plymouth County Wills and Inventories.
Vol. 1. Folio 45, same. Amount £72 17s. 00d. for "goods and cattels," £10 00s. 00d. for house and meadow land.
A house and land at Sudbury mortgaged to secure debt of £20 10s.
Debts, including funeral charges, £245 15s. 18d.

15

233

William Swift mortgaged his house and lands in Watertown to John Haines, attorney of Andrew Coleman, in England, to whom Swift has given his name as joint security in a matter where Roger Spring was the principal debtor. Col. Rec. Sout. 1, 1640."
He also says, that in the third Great Dividends of Town Lands owned by the proprietors, made July 25th, 1636, William Swift drew No. 14, being a 40-acre lot, and Feb. 28, 1636-7, he also drew a 5-acre lot in "Beaver Brook Plowlands." At another division of proprietors' lands in June, 1637, his grantee, Thomas White, received a lot, proving that William sold out in Watertown and removed to Sandwich in the spring of that year. The farm which he then bought in Sandwich, the largest in the town, was in 1887 owned and occupied by his lineal descendant, Shadrach Freeman Swift, Esq.

His widow Joan survived him twenty years. Jedediah Allen, on of Ralph and Easter (or Esther) writes in the family Bible as follows: "Jone Swift, my grandmother deceased ye 26 day,——" the rest is torn off with the leaf. As her will bears date Oct. 12, 1662, and the inventory of her estate was taken Dec. 25, 1663, she probably died Nov. 26, 1663.

The following is a copy of her will from Plymouth Colony Records. The amount of inventory is £105 6s.

"The 12th day of the 8th month, 1662.

"I, Jone Swift of Sandwich, being sicke of body, but of perfect memory, do make my last will.

"I do give unto Daniel Winges, his sons Samuel and John, a mare foal of a year old. Item, I give unto my grandchild Hannah Swift, the old mare, if she be alive, if not, the next to her. Item, 1 give unto my grandchild Experience Allen, a chest with drawers and my bible. Item, I give unto my two grandchildren Hannah Swift and Experience Allen, all my linen and my pewter to be equally divided between them. Item, I give unto Mary Darboy my wearing clothes. Item, I give unto Hannah Winge the Elder my best hat, and forty shillings to her daughters to be divided amongst them. Item, I give unto Jedediah Allen and Experience Allen the third part of my estate, this house and garden being part of the third. I give unto my son William's children, each of them a mare foal; my debts being discharged, and my funeral being paid, I give the rest of my estate to my son William, whom I make my Executor. I make John Dincent and Benjamin Hammond my overseers of this my will and give them twenty shillings apiece.

Witness
John Dincent   the   mark of
Benjamin Hammond   JONE   SWIFT

"Benjamin Hammond gave oath to this Will the third of March 1663, before the General Court, then held at Plymouth.

"Mr. John Dincent was deposed to this Will of Jone Swift above said this seventh of April, 1664, before me, Thomas Hinckley, Assistant, by order from the Court."

Rev. F. Freeman in his "History of Cape Cod" writing of the inhabitants of Sandwich, and the Rev. C. P. Wing in his "Register of John Wing of Sandwich, Mass., and his Descendants" each speaks of this will as the will of "John Swift," evidently having been misled by the peculiar spelling of the name; and yet, the merest reference to the heading of the inventory of her estate recorded with the will (a copy of which heading is given below), would have dispelled the erroneous idea:

"An Inventory of the Estate of Mistriss Joane Swift deceased taken by us, whose names are underwritten being this 25 of the 10 month, 1663, and exhibited to the Court held at Plymouth, the 3d of March 1663, on the oath of William Swift..

17

FIRST GENERATION.

1 WILLIAM SWIFT, born in England, d. 1642-3, married Joan ——, d Nov. 26, 1663. Their children were:
2 Hannah, born   , married Daniel Wing, Nov. 5, 1641, d. Jan. 1, 1664.
3 Easter (or Esther), b.   , married Ralph Allen 1645.
4 William, Jr., born   , died Jan. 1705-6, married Ruth ——.

SECOND GENERATION.

2 HANNAH, daughter of William and Joan Swift (1), born in England, was married at Sandwich, Mass., to Daniel Wing of that town on 9 mo. (Nov.) 5, 1641, and died there 10th mo. 1, 1664. Her husband married again on 6 mo. 2, 1666, Anna, daughter of Thomas and Sarah (Learned) Ewer, and died in 1678-9.

3 EASTER (ESTHER), a daughter of William and Joan Swift (1), born in England, was married in 1645 at Sandwich, Mass., to Ralph Allen, who was a native of that place. Two of her children, Jedediah and Experience, are named in the will of their grandmother Joan Swift.

4 WILLIAM, only son of William and Joan Swift (1), born in England and accompanying his father until he settled at Sandwich in the spring of 1637, married Ruth ——, and lived at Sandwich until his death in Jan. 1705-6. Their children were:
5 Hannah, born March 11, 1651, married —— Tobey.
6 William, born Aug. 28, 1654, married Elizabeth ——.
Ruth, born 1652, died in infancy.
7 Ephraim, born June 6, 1656, married Sarah ——.
8 Mary, born April 7, 1659, married Shubael Smith of Sandwich, Feb. 6, 1677.
9 Samuel, born Aug. 10, 1662, married Mary —— about 1688.
10 Jireh, born 1665, married Abigail Gibbs (Sandwich) Nov. 26, 1697.

11 Temperance, born   , married Deacon Timothy Bourne.
12 Esther, born   , married John Gibbs.
13 Dinah, born   , married Ezra Perry, Jan. 11, 1704.
14 Josiah, born   , married Mary Bodfish April 19, 1706, married Experience Nye June 23, 1718.

On the Sandwich Records William Swift's name appears in 1643 as "able to bear arms." In 1655 he unites in a call to a pastor, together with his mother "Johana." In 1658 record is made of the boundaries of his land. In 1675 he is recorded among the 52 freemen of Sandwich, and in 1702 his name appears on a list of freemen ordered June 25, and his son Jirch also appears on the same list. His will is dated Dec. 15, 1705, and was presented in court Jan. 29, 1705-6.

1643, Enrolled as between 16 and 60. Able to bear arms—therefore born at least as early as 1627, and beyond doubt, in England.

1681, The names of Ephraim Swift and William Jr. recorded as additional townsmen to vote for officers, and Ephraim and William Jr. and Samuel took the oath of fidelity.

William Swift held many offices and his name is found quite often in the Colony Records. "Att the Court held att Plymouth the fift day of July Anno 1669, Liberty is granted by the Court unto William Swift to keep an ordinary for the entertainment of strangers att Sandwich." He was fined for being absent from "The Grand Enquest," at the meeting of June 7, 1652. His name appears as on the Grand Inquest June 1, 1680, and June 6, 1682, and as on the jury March 1, 1663-4, March 5, 1667-8, March 1, 1669-70, July 5, 1670, July 5, 1671, and July 6, 1680. At a meeting of the General Court June 8, 1655, his name appears as "Survayor for the Highwaies Sandwidge," and he also held the same office in 1679 and 1683. He was constable in Sandwich in 1660 and 1668, selectman in Sandwich 15 years, and deputy to the General Court in 1673, 1676, 1677 and 1678. Freeman on list of May 29, 1670, and also in 1689.

General Court July 5, 1670. "Whereas the Court hath or-

dered that all tho tarr made in the goument shalbe sold to some psons within tho collonie, if any such will giue eight shillings in mony for euery smale barrell, and twelue shillings for enery great barrell, during the full tearme of two years, and that during the said tearme noe tarr shallbe transported or sold out of the collonie by any pson whatsoeuer but by or under those that engage to giue us aforesaid, vnder the forfeiture of all such tarr so transported or sold, or the vallue of it; the one halfe to the collonie, the other halfe to the psons engageing as aforsaid. Wee whosenames are heer vnderwritten, takeing the sence of the Court to be that the aforsaid tarr shalbe deliuered to some one of vs, or some one of our order, att the water syde in each towne, whervnto it shalbe brought in good, marchantable caske, and upon due tryall made found to be marchantable tarr, doe engage to pay or cause to be payed the said sume of eight shillings p smale barrell, and twelue shillings p great barrell, for all such tarr made, conditioned and deliuered as aforsaid vntill the full tearme of two yeares aforsaid shalbe expired."
Dated the 24th of June, 1670.

                                    Thomas Hinckley,
                                    John Freeman,
                                    Richard Bourne,
                                    Thomas Huckens,
                                    Wilam Clarke,
            The marke of   Edw. Gray
                                    Samuel Sturgis,
                                    Wilam Swift.

By order from some of the majestrates this last clause was added August 11th, 1670. "This Court doth accept of the abouemensioned engagement and doe heerby order and declare the Court order a'iouesaid relating therevnto to take place according to the sence therof declared imediately from and after the 10th of this instant July vntill the tearme of two yeares shalbe fully expired; alsoe, Mr John Freeman being to take of all the tarr made within the liberties of Eastham which shalbe brought to him or his order and to pay the prise abonenamed p barrell to such as shall deliuer it conditioned as abouesaid; and Samuel Sturgis to doe the like for the liberties of Yarmouth; and Mr Thomas Hinckley and Thomas Huckens to doe the like att Barnstable; and Richard Bourne and Wilam Swift to doe the like att Sandwich and Edward Gray and Wilam Clarke to doe the like for Plymouth and all the westeren townes of the collonie; John Cobbs of Taunton being the place of deliuery of what tarr shalbe made within the liberties thereof, And for the better pformance of the p'mises and the advancement of the publicke good therin this Court doth charge and require all coopers respectively to see that all the caske they make be sufficiently good and tite and according to the accustomed size of late in vse amongst us, as they will answare the contrary att their p'rills; and that all that shall bring in and deliuer any tarr as aforsaid doe see to it that they deliuer theire tarr in good, sufficient, tite caske as aforsaid, which said caske are not to be less than will contain sixteen gallons beer measure."

Colonial Records (Shurtleff) Vol. 5, pp. 45-47.

General Court, Oct. 29, 1672. "It is ordered by this Court that an Indian named Old John, allies Mopes, shall pay vnto Wilam Swift six pound, to be deliuered in tarr att Sandwich att or before the first of May next with the charges which hath arisen about a suite comenced att the Court of the Celect Men of the town of Barnstable against the said Swift; and in defect of payment as aforsaid, then the said Swift is heerby impowered to sieze on the said body of the said Old John, allies Mopes, and to bring him or cause him to be brought before the Gou' or Court whoe will take such a due course as that his just dues shalbe satisfyed by the seruice or sale of him the said Old John, allies Mopes, and upon the Courts graunt of this order the said Wilam Swift did engage to acquitt and release Jedadia Lumbard from that engagement of his to the said Wilam Swift on that account of the said Old John or any other Indians whoe were his cecuritie."

Col. Records (Shurtloff) Vol. 5.

21

General Court, July 13, 1677. "A comittee appointed by the Generall Court to meet the second Tusday in August next whoe are appointed and impowered to heare and determine all matters respecting debts due from the Collonie to all p'sons whatsoeuer and ballence the accompts between the seuerall townes of this Collonie concerning the late warr, not before ballenced and each towne to pay them for theire time, and theire expences to be bourne by the collonie." Among the names of this ccmmittee of 12 was that of William Swift.

1705, William (2) made his will Dec. 15 of this year, which was presented at Court Jan. 29, 1705-6, and which was as follows:

"I, William Swift, senior, of the Town of Sandwich in the County of Barnstable in New England being weak in body, but in good and perfect memory do make this my last will and Testament making null and void all other and former will and wills which has by me been made whether written or verbal.

"I commend my soul unto the hands of Almighty God and Jesus Christ his only son in and through his merits I hope for Salvation. First my mind and will is that after my decease my body deceutly buried by the advice of my friends at the comon burial place of our Town. Secondly that all my just debts be payed by my executor hereafter named. Thirdly I make my son in law Timothy Bourn my whole and sole executor. Item I do give unto my loveing wife Ruth Swift fifty pounds in money of my estate after my decease. Fifthly I do give unto my son Josiah Swift this house and land I now live in andpossess excepting that piece of land about the picket clifts I bought of Jonathan Morie. Sixthly I do give unto the three sons of William Swift my son deceased Thomas Swift, Josiah Swift and Ebenezer Swift that tract of land I bought of Jonathan Morie iying upon the Clifts as ye go to Plymouth as appears by adeed equally to be divided among the three brothers and not to be sold or any way disposed of but to the Swifts. Seventhly I do give unto my son Jirie Swift Twenty pounds in moveables of my estate. Eighthly I do give unto my grandson William Swift son of the deceased William Swift twenty abillings. Ninthly I do give unto my daughter Hannah Tobie and to my daughter Temperance Bourn and to my daughter Hester Gibs and to my daughter Dina Perry the rest of my moveables to be equally divided amongst them four sisters and will that all things herein contained and mentioned be faithfully and truly performed written this fifteenth day of December, one thousand seven hundred and five years.

William Swift, Senior (Seal).

Signed and sealed in presence of us.
   Thomas Gibs,
   Samuel O Gibs,
      his mark
   James Stewart.

THIRD GENERATION.

5 HANNAH, a daughter of William and Ruth Swift (4), born March 11, 1651, is named as Hannah Tobey in her father's will and nothing beyond this is known of her.

6 WILLIAM, eldest son of William and Ruth Swift (4), born Aug. 28, 1654, was a carpenter by trade, married Elizabeth ——, and died at Sandwich in April or May, 1701. His will dated June 17, 1700, and presented at Court May 12, 1701, names his wife Elizabeth, his sons William, Benjamin and Joseph, and "their brothers and sisters." His sons William, Thomas, Josiah and Ebenezer are named in their grandfather's will. The children were:

15 William, born Jan. 24, 1679, married Lydia Weeks (Falmouth) Oct. 9, 1707.
16 Benjamin, born 1682, married Hannah Wing (Sandwich) Feb. 24, 1703-4.
17 Joseph, born Nov. 1687, married 1st Mercy Morton, Sandwich, married 2nd Mrs. Rebecca Clark Ellis March 4, 1730-1.
18 Samuel, born Dec. 1690, married Abigail ——.
19 Joanna, born March 9, 1692, married Thomas Gibbs (Sandwich) Oct. 22, 1714.

23

20 Thomas, born December 169—, married Thankful Morey (Plymouth) Jan. 23, 1718-19.
21 Elizabeth, gem., born Jan. 11, 1696, married John Gibbs, Sandwich, Nov. 9, 1716.
22 Thankful, gem., born Jun. 11, 1696, married Benj. Morey, Plymouth, Nov. 3, 1715.
23 Josiah, born
24 Ebenezer, born , married Abigail Gibbs (S.) Feb. 13, 1723-4.

7 EPHRAIM, second son of William and Ruth Swift (4), born June 6, 1656, married Sarah —— (who died before him, Aug. 13, 1734) and died at Sandwich, where he had always lived, in 1742. He was a carpenter and cooper by trade. His will dated April 10, 1735, and presented at Court Feb. 17, 1742, names all his children except Ephraim Jr., who died in childhood. Their names were:
25 Elizabeth, born Dec. 29, 1679, married Joshua Lawrence. Sandwich, Dec. 15, 1702.
26 Joanna, born July 7, 1683, married Roger Haskell (Hascal), Rochester, Feb. 25, 1707-8.
27 Samuel, born April 9, 1686, married Ruth Hatch, Falmouth, Dec. 24, 1712.
Ephraim, Jr., born Dec. 9, 1688, died young.
28 Sarah, born April 12, 1692, married ——Kirby.
29 Hannah, born May 19, 1695, married Allen Marshall, March 18, 1723-4.
30 Moses, born Sept. 15, 1699, married Mary Foster, Sandwich Dec. 24, 1719.

8 MARY, a daughter of William and Ruth Swift (4), born April 7, 1659, married Shubael Smith Feb. 6, 1677.

9 SAMUEL, third son of William and Ruth Swift (4), born Aug. 10, 1662, married about 1688 Mary ——, who survived him, being named with all their children in his will dated Oct. 5, 1730, and presented at court June 6, 1733. He died at Sandwich, Mass., May 25, 1733. Their children were:

31 Mary, born March 18, 1690-1.
32 Seth, born March 17, 1692-3, married Maria
33 Jemima, born October 12, 1695.
34 Ebenezer of Yarmouth, born June 17, 1698, married Mary Gibbs, Sandwich, June 8, 1721.
35 Keturah, born April 30, 1700, married Nathaniel Hatch, Falmouth, Sept. 14, 1727.
36 Zaccheus, born Feb. 5, 1701-2, married 1st Abigail Foster, Sandwich, May 15, 1735; married 2nd Susannah Nye, Sandwich, May 7, 1752.
37 Temperance, born May 7, 1704.
38 Ephraim, born June 17, 1706.
39 Elizabeth, born April 7, 1708, married Jonathan Morey, Plymouth, Oct. 13, 1728.
40 Samuel, Jr., born.

10 JIREH, fourth son of William and Ruth Swift (4), born 1665, married Abigail Gibbs of Sandwich, daughter of Thomas Gibbs and Allis Warren, November 26, 1697, and had by her twelve children. After her death he married Mary Besse of Wareham Nov. 19, 1741, who survived him and is named with all his children and Catharine "Curby" (probably a daughter of his niece, Sarah Kirby) in his will dated March 29, 1744, and presented at Court May 1, 1749. Jireh died after a busy and prominent life at Wareham in April, 1749, aged 84. His children were:

41 Alice, born July 23, 1698, married James Crocker, Barnstable, Nov. 21, 1721, died July 15, 1783.
42 Susannah, born Oct. 6, 1699, married Joseph Isham, Sandwich, Dec. 11, 1730.
43 Jabez, born March 16, 1700-1, married Abigail Pope, Sandwich, Oct. 9, 1729, died Kent, Conn., Nov. 12, 1769.
44 Zephaniah, born March 6, 1702-3, married Lydia Chipman, Sandwich, Sept. 30, 1725, died May 9, 1781.
45 William, born July 5, 1705, died between Oct. 2 and Dec. 20, 1748; married 1st Kezia ——, who died March 23, 1735-6, 2nd Abigail Burgess of Sandwich.

25

46 Captain Nathaniel, born March 14, 1707-8, died March 13, 1790, at Warren, Conn.; married Abia Tucker, Sandwich, Sept. 14, 1730.
47 Jireh Jr., born Nov. 23, 1709, died Acushnet, Mass., March 16, 1782; married Deborah Hathaway, Oct. 9, 1730, born 1711, died Jan. 7, 1794.
48 Job, born Oct. 3, 1711, died Sharon, Mass., Feb. 14, 1801; married Sarah Blackwell, Sandwich, Jan. 20, 1733-4, died April 12, 1772.
49 Silas, born Aug. 2, 1713, died Lebanon, Conn., Sept. 24, 1794; married Abigail Tucker at Lebanon, Oct. 16, 1735, born 1716, died Feb. 15, 1811.
50 Lydia, born July 26, 1715, married Hammond.
51 Isaac, born May 3, 1720, died Bridgewater, Nov. 22, 1811; married 1749 Mrs. Susanna (Keith) Ames, born 1714 died May 23, 1795.
52 Rowland, born March 24, 1721-2, died Lebanon, Conn., Feb. 13. 1795; married Mary Dexter, 1745, died Oct. 19. 1798.

11 TEMPERANCE, a daughter of William and Ruth Swift (4), married Deacon Timothy Bourne of Sandwich (born April 18, 1666), a prominent man in his day and much engaged in public business. Their children were Job, Benjamin, Joanna, Mehitable and last Timothy Jr., born Dec. 5, 1703, who married Elizabeth Bourne and died Oct. 5, 1780.

12 ESTHER, a daughter of William and Ruth Swift (4) is named as Esther Gibs in her father's will, but leaves no record.

13 DINAH, a daughter of William and Ruth Swift (4), is called in her father's will Dina Perry; married Ezra Perry, Jan. 11, 1704.

14 JOSIAH, youngest son of William and Ruth Swift (4), married April 19, 1706, Mary Bodfish of Barnstable, and had by her four children. She died in 1715, and Josiah married Experience Nye of Sandwich June 23, 1718, by whom he also had four children. She survived him, and is named in his will (dated Oct. 23, 1753, and presented at Court Dec. 6, 1757) with seven children, one:

26

having died in childhood. Josiah died between 1753 and 1757. The children's names were:

53 William, born Aug. 22, 1707, married Elizabeth Wheeler, Lebanon, Nov. 8, 1734.
54 Mary, born Oct. 1710, married Nathan Barlow, Sandwich, June 30, 1732.
55 Josiah Jr., born Nov. 1712, married Mrs. Mary Morey, Plymouth, May 26, 1738.
Joanna, born Feb. 1714, died a babe.
56 Mercy, born April 19, 1719, died 1815, married John Pope Oct. 25, 1775.
57 Hannah, born Feb. 15, 1720-1, married Nathan Davis, Rochester, Dec. 24, 1740.
58 Joanna, born Aug. 25, 1723.
59 John, born Oct. 3, 1727, married Desire Swift, Falmouth, Sept. 21. 1752.

FOURTH GENERATION.

15 WILLIAM, eldest son of William and Elizabeth Swift (6), born Jan. 24, 1679, married Lydia Weeks of Falmouth Oct. 9, 1707, and lived in that town until his death in 1750. Administration upon his estate was granted to his widow Lydia Oct. 13, 1750. No entry of the birth of any children appears on the Town Records and yet I enter as their child,

60 William, born April 1719, died Aug. 7, 1809-10, married Dorcas Hatch Nov. 29, 1744, married Mehitable Hallet Sept. 1, 1772.

This is the only entry ever made by me which is not based upon absolute record, either family or public, and the following is the authority upon which it is made.

The Record says that William Swift, Junior, married Dorcas Hatch. This is a strong proof that his father's name also was William, since the Record attaches "Jr." almost invariably when the son is named for the father, and "2nd" when named for some other living relative.

27

Again, Elijah, grandson of William and Dorcas, left on record a statement from his aunt that her brother William's son was the fourth of the name in lineal descent. This again shows that the father of William (60) was also named William,

Now, William (15), the husband of Lydia Weeks, was the only William in all the family according to the Records, who, regarding age, time of marriage, etc., could have been the father of William who married Dorcas Hatch. Q. E. D.

Since writing the above, I find that Mr. Davis in his "Landmarks of Plymouth, Mass.," quotes as from the Old Colony Records the fact that "William Swift and his wife Lydia had Solomon, born 1715, and William, born 1719." This Solomon was doubtless he who married Love Shiverick Sept. 21, 1740 (Falmouth Rec.).

    60a Solomon, son of William and Lydia (Weeks) Swift, born 1715, married Love Shiverick Sept. 21, 1740.

16 BENJAMIN, second son of William and Elizabeth Swift (6), was born in Sandwich, Mass., in 1682 and married Hannah Wing, also of that place, Feb. 24, 1703-4. The Wings were Quakers from the days of John (the first immigrant of the name, who married Deborah Batchelder), whose son Daniel married Hannah Swift (2) in 1641; and his wife's influence and that of her family, probably brought Benjamin over to that faith. He was the first of the name who was accounted a Quaker, his name appearing among the Quaker remonstrants in 1731, and was fined many times for disturbing the public peace by his silent worship. All his children married in the connexion. They were:

    61 Samuel, born Sept. 11, 1704, married Mercy Wing, Sandwich, May 18, 1741.

    Mary, born Oct. 11, 1706, married William Gifford, Aug. 3, 1727.

    62 Content, born Dec. 12, 1708, married Zaccheus Wing, Sandwich, March 15, 1731-2.

    63 Zebulon, born April 15, 1712, married Rebekah Wings, Nov. 15, 1739.

Hannah, born , married Benjamin Collins, Lebanon,
Aug. 8, 1743.
Elizabeth, born , married Reuben Landers July 4, 1746.
64 Benjamin Jr., born , married Waitstill Bowerman,
F., Sept. 4, 1741.
17 JOSEPH, third son of William and Elizabeth Swift (6), was born Nov. 1687, in Sandwich and was twice married. His first wife was named Mercy, by whom he had six children; and after her death he married Mrs. Rebecca (Clark, Ellis) Morton, March 4, 1730-1, by whom he had one son. His children's names were:
 65 William, born Feb. 26, 1711, married Lydia Gibbs, S., March 2, 1731-2.
 Joan, born Dec. 4, 1713, married Thomas Glover, Wareham, Feb. 10, 1743-4.
 66 Joseph Jr., born Sept. 4, 1716, married Mrs. Sarah (Bartlett) LeBaron. Plymouth, Jan. 21, 1736-7.
 67 Joshua, born Feb. 14, 1717-8, married Jane Faunce, Plymouth, March 21, 1738-9.
 Martha, born May 4, 1719.
 Mercy, born March 16, 1721-2.
 68 Thomas born   married Abigail Phillips, Sandwich, Nov. 15, 1752.
18 SAMUEL, fourth son of William and Elizabeth Swift (6), born Dec. 1690, married Abigail —— in Sandwich and removed to Plymouth in 1716, where he died. His children were:
 Mary, born April 28, 1715.
 Elizabeth, born Jan. 22, 1717-8.
 69 James, born March 1, 1720-1.
 70 Samuel Jr., born Jan. 16, 1723-4, married Thankful Ashley; Rochester, Nov. 7, 1751.
19 JOANNA, a daughter of William and Elizabeth Swift (6), born March 9, 1692, married Thomas Gibbs of Sandwich Oct. 22, 1714. The record of her descendants has not been searched.
20 THOMAS, fifth son of William and Elizabeth Swift (6), born Dec. 169--, married Thankful Morey of Plymouth Jan. 23, 1718-19,

and lived in that town until his death. Their children were:
- Lydia, born Sept. 1, 1720.
- Deborah, born May 28, 1723, married Jon. Tobey, Sandwich, Feb. 19, 1740.
- Elizabeth, born Jan. 11, 1724-5.
- 71 Thomas Jr., born May 11, 1727, married Rebekah Clark, Plymouth, Oct. 21, 1746.
- Jerusha, born Feb. 25, 1731-2, married John Morey, Plymouth, Oct. 17, 1751.
- 72 Phineas, born March 10, 1733-4, married Rebekah Phillips, Sandwich, April 9, 1752.
- Rhoda, born 1735, married Benjamin Cornish Jr., Plymouth, Oct. 22, 1750.
- 72b Thankful, gem., born Feb. 26, 1737-8, married Nathaniel Wing, Plymouth, May 22, 1755.
- 73 Lemuel, gem., Feb. 26, 1737-8, married Rebecca Whitfield, Rochester, Dec. 8, 1756.

21 ELIZABETH, a daughter of William and Elizabeth Swift (6), born Jan. 11, 1696, married John Gibbs of Sandwich Nov. 9, 1716. Her descendants are not traced.

22 THANKFUL, a daughter of William and Elizabeth Swift (6), born Jan. 11, 1696, married Benjamin Morey of Plymouth Nov. 3, 1715. Her descendants are not traced.

23 JOSIAH, sixth son of William and Elizabeth Swift (6), leaves no trace in this world save the entry of his name in his grandfather's will, made Dec. 15, 1705. No record of his birth or marriage or death is found and conjecture is out of place, or we might suppose that he was foolish enough to live and die unmarried.

24 EBENEZER, youngest son of William and Elizabeth Swift (6), married Abigail Gibbs of Sandwich Feb. 13, 1723-4, and settled in Wareham. He died Sept. 2, 1775. Their children were:
- Abigail, born
- 74 Jabez, born Feb. 1732, married Hannah Perry, Sandwich, Jan. 30, 1755, married Lydia Nye, Sandwich, Sept. 19, 1765.

75 Ebenezer Jr., born July 1, 1733, married Jedidah —— of Wareham, 1753.

25 ELIZABETH, a daughter of Ephraim and Sarah Swift (7), born Dec. 29, 1679, married Joshua Lawrence of Sandwich Dec. 15, 1702, and is named in her father's will dated April 10, 1735. Her descendants are not traced.

26 JOANNA, a daughter of Ephraim and Sarah Swift (7), born July 7, 1683, married Roger Haskell of Rochester Feb. 25, 1707-8, and her name also appears in her father's will.

27 SAMUEL, eldest son of Ephraim and Sarah Swift (7), born April 9, 1686, married Ruth Hatch of Falmouth Dec. 24, 1712. Ruth was born in 1693. Samuel was a blacksmith and carpenter and owned two farms, one in Falmouth, and the other in Scusset, as the western part of Sandwich was then called. His will names his eight children and his grandson Joshua Gibbs. It was dated Oct. 18, 1756, and proved Jan. 3, 1758. Their children were:

76 Ephraim 2nd, born Oct. 11, 1713, married Anna Robinson, F., Feb. 17, 1735-6.
77 Manasseh, born March 24, 1714-5,. married Ruth Robinson, F., Dec. 15, 1743, married Tamar Dexter, F., July 3, 1764.
78 Judah, born Sept. 3, 1716, married Elizabeth Morton, F., Dec. 14, 1738.
79 Reuben, born Oct. 27, 1717, married Hannah Dexter, daughter of Samuel Dexter and Elizabeth Burgess of Falmouth, Jan. 27, 1741-2. Hannah was born Sept. 17, 1726.
80 Moses, born Oct. 4, 1720, married Mary Robinson, F., Oct. 29, 1746, married Rachel Parker, F., May 17, 1772.
Mary, born March 11, 1722-3, married Benjamin Nye, 3d, F., Dec. 1, 1740.
Joanna, born April 9, 1725, died a babe.
81 Joan, born May 8, 1728, married Benjamin Gibbs, Jr., F., Jan. 10, 1744-5, married Nathan Barlow, F., Feb. 9, 1748-9.
81b Lydia, born   , married Seth Swift (85), F., Aug. 29, 1751.

31

28 SARAH, a daughter of Ephraim and Sarah Swift (7), born April 12, 1692, is named in her father's will as Sarah Kirby. No other trace or record of her is found, except that Ephraim's brother Jirch names in his will Catharine "Curby," who may have been Sarah's daughter.

29 HANNAH, a daughter of Epnraim and Sarah Swift (7), born May 19, 1695, married Allen Marshall of Rochester March 18, 1723-4, and suryived her father, who names her in his will. No record.

30 MOSES, youngest son of Ephraim and Sarah Swift (7), born Sept. 15, 1699, married Dec. 24, 1719, Mary Foster of Sandwich, born Sept. 1, 1697. She was a sister of Abigail Foster, who married Moses' cousin Zaccheus Swift. Their children were;

    Ruth, born Oct. 10, 1720, married Melatiah Nye, F., Dec. 18, 1740.

    Bathsheba, born March 8, 1721-2, married George Lewis, F., July 12, 1744.

    Sarah, born Oct. 17, 1723, married David Crowell, F., March 21, 1743-4.

    Hannah, born May 7, 1725, married Israel Fearing, Jr., Wareham, Nov. 13, 1746.

8&. Elizabeth, born Jan. 10, 1727-8, married Jehosaphat Eldridge, Jr., F., Dec. 17, 1747.

    Dorcas, born March 10, 1730-1, married John Fearing, Wareham, March 23, 1758.

83 Samuel, born March 6, 1733-4.

84 Captain Ward, born Dec. 1, 1735. married Rememper Tobey, S., Jan. 9, 1755.

    Content, born May 15, 1743.

31 MARY, a daughter of Samuel and Mary Swift (9), was born March 18, 1690-1. We have the record of her birth and "ne plus ultra."

32 SETH, oldest son of Samuel and Mary Swift (9), born March 17, 1692-3, married Maria —— and removed to Plymouth, where his children were born. They were:

32

Mary, born May 17, 1723, married Zaccheus Mendell, S., Oct. 26, 1749.

85 Seth Jr., born Dec. 2, 1724, married 1st Desire Holmes, P., March 29, 1749, married 2nd Lydia Swift (816) Aug. 29, 1751.

Hannah, born Sept. 17, 1727, married James Clark, Jr., P., Aug. 6, 1747.

33 JEMIMA, a daughter of Samuel and Mary Swift (9), born Oct. 12, 1695, leaves no record beyond that of her birth. She survived her father, who died May 25, 1733, being named in his will.

34 EBENEZER, second son of Samuel and Mary Swift (9), commonly called "of Yarmouth," born June 7, 1698, married Mary Gibbs of Sandwich June 8, 1721. He soon removed to Plymouth, where all his children were born and where he died about 1765. His children were:

Elizabeth, born Aug. 22. 1722.
86 Judah, born Feb. 26, 1723-4.
87 Job, born July 17, 1726.
88 Enoch, gem., born July 25, 1735, married Esther Sampson, Wareham, July 21, 1757.
89 Micah, gem., born July 25, 1735, married Abigail Swift (of Joshua, of Joseph, of William 3), P., March 29, 1758.

35 KETURAH, a daughter of Samuel and Mary Swift (9), born April 30, 1700, married Nathaniel Hatch of Falmouth Sept. 14, 1727, and leaves no record save her name in her father's will made Oct. 5, 1730.

36 ZACCHEUS, third son of Samuel and Mary Swift (9), born Feb. 5, 1701-2, was twice married. His first wife was Abigail Foster of Sandwich, born Feb. 27, 1708-9, (sister of his cousin Ebenezer's wife) whom he married May 15, 1735, and by whom he had at least two children. He married his second wife, Susannah Nye, May 7, 1752, who had no issue. His business transactions were extensive, he owning lands in Plymouth, Falmouth and Sandwich, Mass., Lebanon, Conn., and Amenia Precinct, N. Y. His children were:

90 Elisha, born May 22, 1736, married Susanna Davis April 9, 1761.

91 Stephen, born   , married Ruth ——.

37 TEMPERANCE, a daughter of Samuel and Mary Swift (9), was born May 7, 1704, and leaves no further record than her name in her father's will.

38 EPHRAIM, fourth son of Samuel and Mary Swift (9), born June 17, 1706, was living in 1730, being then named in his father's will, died after 1744, married Pheby ——, who died after 1744. His children were:

91a Epheram, born between 1728 and 1744, living in 1744.

91b Ebenezer, born between 1728 and 1744, living in 1744.

Sarah, born between 1728 and 1744, living in 1744.

Will of Samuel Swift, Senior, of Sandwich, dated Oct. 5, 1730. Extract:

"I give and bequieve to my three sons Zaccheus, Ephram and Samuel, all my real estate and personal both housing and lands and meadow that I have In the Town of Sandwich to be equally divided between them."

Ephram above is spelled Ephream three times elsewhere in the will.

Will of Epheram Swift of White Oak and Onslow County, North Carolina, planter, dated November 4, 1744. Extract:

"I bequeathe to my son Ephream, what land I have in Sandwich, in the County of Barnstable in New England in parinership. My desire is likewise that the profits of what is left amongst the three children may be for their bringing up and education until they are of age."

The will also provides for wife Pheby, son Ebenezer and daughter Sarah.

34

1823 Nineteenth Street, N. W., Washington, D. C.
May 13, '92.

Charles W. Swift, Esq.

My dear Mr. Swift: When you publish the new Swift book, I hope you may find a place for the two Ephraims or Ephrams, whose records I enclose.

I have been hunting for the elder of the two for a long time, and I found him only recently. As the book of George H. Swift gave only the female line of Lucy Swift (of Asa, of Samuel, of William, of William, of William) and not that of Ezra Swift, her husband, I sought to connect him with the same line if he was really of the same descent. It was easy to find that Ezra was son of Ephraim Swift, Jr., of Sandwich who married Sarah Bourne of Falmouth (East) in 1761, but there the record stopped. George H. Swift wrote me that all his efforts to trace Ephraim, Junior, had been without result and that he must be. "like Melchisidik, without father or mother." I did not forget, however, that my father told me many years ago that his name Ebenezer was not for one of the Wareham Swifts but for an uncle—his father's family, which came from North Carolina. My aunt was Sarah Ann Bourne Swift Robinson, who told me the same.

Ephraim Swift, Jr., had a daughter Phebe, the other children, with the exception of one, being named for the family of Sarah Bourne, his wife.

The will of Ephraim Swift of North Carolina seems to confirm the family tradition. The names Pheby, Sarah, Ephraim and Ebenezer point to the Falmouth family, as well as the property in Sandwich.

The name Pheby is not a common one in the Swift family. This will also points to New England ancestry for the North Carolina Ephraim. Every child born on the records of Sandwich or Falmouth is otherwise accounted for except Ephraim, who was born in 1706. The words "in partnership" in his will can be explained by the terms of the will of Samuel in 1730. The family of Samuel seems to have left Sandwich for the most part. Only

35

seven out of ten children left any trace. Although all were living in 1730, only Samuel Jr., the youngest, was on Fessenden's list in 1730.

The biblical method of spelling Ephraim in the Swift book and in most practical records is misleading. Samuel Swift spells it Ephram, Epharam. Epheram spells it so, Falmouth seems to spell it Ephream.

I am far better satisfied with this line than I am with the other line, as given by G. H. Swift for Lucy Swift (of Asa, of Samuel and Mercy Wing, of Benjamin, etc.). He wrote me that his authority was Freeman, the historian of Cape Cod. But Asa Swift wrote in his Bible, "Father Swift died February 15, 1798, 77 years old. Mother Swift died May 4, 1790, 72 years old." Some one has written to the Boston Evening Transcript giving these dates as those of Mercy Young. Possibly Wing is misread Young in this case. George H. Swift did not change his opinion when I quoted Asa Swift's Bible.

(Signed) Eben Swift

39 ELIZABETH, a daughter of Samuel and Mary Swift (9), born April 7, 1708, married Jonathan Morey of Plymouth Oct. 13, 1728, and then disappears from this record.

40 SAMUEL JR., fifth and youngest son of Samuel and Mary Swift (9), makes no appearance at all upon the records, the only mention of his name being in his father's will as one of his residuary devisees.

41 ALICE, eldest daughter of Jireh and Abigail Swift (10), born July 23, 1698, married James Crocker of Barnstable Nov. 21, 1721, and died in Connecticut July 15, 1783. James, born Sept. 3, 1699, son of Jonathan and Hannah (Howland) Crocker, removed soon after his marriage to Connecticut with several of his brothers and sisters. Their children are omitted, not being within the scope of this record.

42 SUSANNAH, daughter of Jireh and Abigail Swift (10), born Oct. 6, 1699, married Joseph Isham of Sandwich Dec. 11, 1730.

She with all Jireh's other children, is named in his will dated 1744. No further record.

43 JABEZ, the eldest son of Jireh and Abigail Swift (10), born March 16, 1700-1, married Abigail Pope of Sandwich Oct. 9, 1729. In 1743 he reomved to Kent in Litchfield County, Conn., where he died Nov. 2, 1767. His widow survived him nine years. Their children were:

 92 Elisha, born May 14, 1737, married Mary Ransom Dec. 30, 1756.
 93 Gen. Heman, born Oct. 14, 1733, married four times. (See his number.)
 Jabez Jr., born April 14, 1736, married ——.
 95 Captain Jireh, born Aug. 20, 1738, married Sarah Delano Oct. 4, 1759.
 Abigail, born Dec. 1. 1740, married Peleg Chamberlain Oct. 4, 1759.
 96 Rev. Job, born June 15, 1743, married Mary Ann Sedgwick of Sharon, Conn., Nov. 6, 1769.
 Hannah, born Aug. 31, 1745, married Dr. Bird.
 Bathsheba, born July 28. 1747, married 1st Reuben Smith, 2nd Dr. Ephraim Croker, 3rd —— Rose.
 97 Rev. Seth, born Nov. 14. 1749, married Lucy Elliott Sept. 27, 1781.
 Patience. born , unmarried.

44 ZEPHANIAH, second son of Jireh and Abigail Swift (10), born March 6, 1702-3, married Sept. 30, 1725, Lydia Chipman, born June 9, 1708, in Sandwich, a twin to Stephen, and daughter of Hon. John (born 1670) and Mary (Skiff) Chipman and granddaughter of Elder John Chipman, who came to Boston in 1631. She died June 23, 1790. Zephaniah had much of a wandering spirit, married and living in Sandwich in 1725, in Plymouth in 1728, at Lebanon in 1739, at Groton in 1743 and in Lebanon again in 1746, where he sold 100 acres of land in 1764. He died May 9, 1781, at Wilmington, Vt. Their children were:

 98 Perez, born Feb. 14, 1725-6, in Sandwich, married Mary Fox,

Groton, Conn., Nov. 3, 1746.
Lydia, born Sept. 13, 1728, in Plymouth, married William Young of Lebanon Jan. 15, 1761.
Alice, born April 25, 1731, in Plymouth, married Samuel Davis, Lebanon, Conn., Oct. 22, 1747.
Mary, born   in Plymouth, married Rev. Judah Moore May 24, 1753.
99 Silas, born   , not mentioned in father's will.
100 Chipman, born   , baptized July 8, 1750, at Lebanon, died at Derby, Conn., March 8, 1825; married 1st Mary Lane, who died in Wilmington, Vt., June 22, 1813, married 2nd at Derby, Conn., May 6, 1819, Mrs. Sarah (Humphrey) Mills, who died Sept. 27, 1840.

45 WILLIAM, third son of Jirch and Abigail Swift (10), born July 5, 1705, married Keziah ——, who died March 23, 1735-6, and for his second wife Abigail Burgess of Sandwich. His two sons by Abigail, Stephen and Jacob, probably died young, as they are not mentioned in their father's will, dated Oct. 2, 1748, and proved Dec. 20, 1748. His children were:
Anna, born Jan. 18, 1733-4.
Keziah, born Jan. 22, 1735-6, married Thomas Mitchell, Bridgewater, Dec. 6, 1757.
Stephen, born June 5, 1741.
Jacob, born Oct. 16, 1742.
Abigail, born April 24, 1744, married Eliab Fish Jan. 1, 1764.
Mary, born June 23, 1746, married Josiah Ellis Oct. 20, 1765.

46 CAPT. NATHANIEL, fourth son of Jirch and Abigail Swift (10) born March 14, 1707-8, married Abia Tucker of Sandwich Sept. 14, 1730. Abia was a daughter of Eliakim and Joanna Tucker, born Nov. 1, 1713, and died in Warren, Conn., April 4, 1782, where Nathaniel also died, March 13, 1790. Nathaniel was also a wanderer, having lived in Sandwich, Plymouth and Rochester, Mass., and Kent and Warren in Connecticut. His children were:
Innominatus, born April, 1731, and died three days old.
Rufus, born Nov. 24, 1734, in Plymouth, died an infant.

38

Joanna, born July 17, 1737, in Rochester, died young.
Abigail, born Nov. 12, 1746, married Dr. Sturtevant.
101 Nathaniel Jr., born Sept. 18, 1749, married Sarah Thomas Dec. 21, 1769.
102 Dr. Isaac, born Feb. 27, 1753, married Patience Cass, Jan. 3, 1775.
Rufus, born Oct. 3, 1756, died Dec. 16, 1760.

47 JIREH JR., fifth son of Jireh and Abigail Swift (10), born Nov. 23, 1709, died March 16, 1782, married Oct. 9, 1730, Deborah Hathaway, born 1711, who died Jan. 7, 1794. He lived and died at Acushnet, Mass., and is known in the history of his times as "Deacon" Jireh. Their children were:

103 Jonathan, born 1732, married Elizabeth Bourne, Falmouth, Oct. 16, 1753.
Susan, born 1734, married Samuel Perry.
Lois, born 1736, married Manasseh Kempton.
104 Jireh 3rd, born 1740, married Elizabeth Haskell, Rochester, Jan 6, 1763.
105 Silas, born March 15, 1743, married Deborah Tobey, Sandwich, 1766.
Deborah, born 1748, married Gamaliel Bryant.
106 Paul, born 1753, married Jemima ———.
Sophia, born 1757, died young.

48 JOB, sixth son of Jireh and Abigail Swift (10), born Oct. 3, 1711, married Sarah Blackwell, daughter of Joshua Blackwell and Sarah Ellis, of Sandwich, at Wareham, Jan. 20, 1733-4. Job died at Sharon, Mass., Feb. 14, 1801. Sarah was born Feb. 6, 1713, and died at Sharon April 2, 1772. This Job was a member of the first board of selectmen of the town of Sharon, 1765. Was one of the committee of safety, 1774. Was delegate to Provincial Congress, 1774-5. Was a member of Ebenezer Tilden's Co., who marched from District of Stoningham, now Sharon, April 19, 1775. His three boys were also members of militia companies. Their children were:

106a Joshua, born Aug. 28, 1744, married Mary Hewins at Sharon, June 14, 1769.
106b Job, born Sept. 5, 1746, married 1st Rebecca Cummins; Sept. 14, 1768, 2nd Elizabeth Guild, April 5, 1779
106c Jireh, born June 4, 1748, married Waitstill Lyon, July 31, 1769.
    Abigail, born   , married William Lewis, Feb. 17, 1774.
    Lusanna, born   , married 1st Nathaniel Capen, published Oct. 21, 1758, 2nd —— Price.
    Sarah, born   , married John Johnson, March 13, 1755.
    Temperance, born   , married Thomas Manley, Jr., Dec. 20. 1759.
    Unity, born Sept. 13, 1752, married William Randall of Easton, May 26. 1771-2.
    Patience, baptized May 8, 1743, died at Sharon Feb. 12, 1768.
    Charity, baptized Nov. 11, 1750, buried Nov. 15, 1754.
    Philip, baptized Sept. 1, 1754, buried Oct. 15, 1754.
49 SILAS, seventh son of Jireh and Abigail Swift (10), born Aug. 2, 1713, married Oct. 16, 1733, at Lebanon, Conn., Abigail Tucker, daughter of Eliakim Tucker, and sister of his brother Nathaniel's wife, Abia. He settled in Lebanon, Conn., went to Windham in 1750, but returned in a year or two to Lebanon, where he died Sept. 24, 1794. His widow, born 1716, survived him more than 16 years and died in Lebanon, Feb. 15, 1811, at the great age of 94 years. Their children were:
    Elias, born June 10, 1736, in Rochester, died young.
    Lydia, born May, 1740, in Lebanon, died young.
107 Deacon Charles, born March 16, 1742, in Lebanon, married Deborah Clark, L., May 26, 1763.
    Abigail, born July 19, 1745, in Lebanon, married John Thacher, L., May 31, 1764.
    Susanna, born July 28, 1747, in Lebanon, unmarried.
    Silas Jr., born Nov. 17, 1749, in Lebanon, unmarried
    William, born Dec. 14, 1751, in Windham, unmarried.
    Darius, born Nov. 23, 1757, in Lebanon, unmarried.

Roxalana, born Oct. 8, 1761, in Lebanon, unmarried.

50 LYDIA, a daughter of Jireh and Abigail Swift (10), born July 26, 1715, is called Lydia Hammond in Jireh's will. Nothing further appears of her.

51 ISAAC, eighth son of Jireh and Abigail Swift (10), born May 3, 1720, married in 1749 Mrs. Susannah (Keith) Ames of Bridgewater. He settled in that place when married and died Nov. 22, 1811. His wife, born 1714, died May 23, 1795. Their children were:

 108 Jireh, born 1749, married Lucy Keith, 1772.
 109 William, born 1752, married Rachel Leonard, 1795.
  Susannah, born 1754, married Elijah Storrs, 1782, died Oct. 27, 1813.
  Mary, born 1759 married Capt. Jacob Leonard, 1788, died April 8, 1843.

52 ROWLAND, ninth and youngest son of Jireh and Abigail Swift (10), born March 24, 1721-2, married Mary Dexter of Wareham, Dec 5, 1745. Mary, born June 3, 1728, daughter of Samuel Dexter, Falmouth, was sister of Hannah Dexter, who married Reuben Swift (29). Rowland's children were all born at Wareham, but in after life he removed to Lebanon, Conn., where he died Feb. 13, 1795, and Mary Oct. 19, 1798. Their children were:

110 Barzillai, born Jan. 9, 1747, married Sarah Fearing, Wareham, Dec. 21, 1769.
 Abigail, born Feb. 3, 1749, died Feb. 9, 1749.
 Abigail, born July 8, 1751, married Amos Peabody, Oct. 24, 1770.
111 Rowland Jr., born Dec. 10, 1753, married Betsey Larned, Lebanon.
112 Jiren, born Dec. 6, 1755, unmarried, drowned at sea.
113 Zephaniah, born Feb. 27, 1759, married 1st Jerusha Watrous of Colchester, 2nd Lucretia Webb, Windham, March 14, 1794.
 Mary, born March 1, 1761, died 1845, married Feb. 3, 1780,

1st Lothrop Davis of Barnstable, who was lost at sea, 2nd Jesse Wing of Sandwich, Sept. 27, 1790.
114 William, born Jan. 19, 1764, married Abigail Clarke.
Thankful, born Oct. 14, 1766, died 1805, married —— Terrill.

53 WILLIAM, eldest son of Josiah and Mary Swift (14), born Aug. 22, 1707, married Elizabeth Wheeler of Lebanon, Conn., Nov. 8, 1734. No record is found of any children, and he doubtless died childless, as his father's will dated Oct. 23, 1753, nineteen years after William's marriage, contained this clause: "I give and bequeath to my son William of Lebanon in Connecticut, all my housing and land which he improves or which I have or ought to have in sd Lebanon to him, his heirs and assigns forever, in case he shall have any issue lawfull begotten of his body, but my will is that if said William dye without any such issue &c."

54 MARY, a daughter of Josiah and Mary Swift (14), born Oct. 1710, married Nathan Barlow of Sandwich, June 30, 1732. Her family not traced.

55 JOSIAH JR., second son of Josiah and Mary Swift (14), born Nov. 1712, married Mrs. Mary Morey of Plymouth, May 26, 1738. He settled in Wareham, where his children were born. They were:
    115 Jesse, born Oct. 3, 1739, married Elizh. Swift, S., April 7, 1763.
    Mary, born Sept. 8, 1743, married Elisha Ellis of Wareham, Nov. 5, 1761.
    Hannah, born Oct. 21, 1745.
    116 Elisha, gem., born Jan. 31, 1747-8, married Martha Briggs, R., Dec. 18, 1775.
    117 Benjamin, gem., born Jan. 31, 1747-8.

56 MERCY, a daughter of Josiah and Experience Swift (14), born April 19, 1719, married John Pope, Oct. 25, 1775.

57 HANNAH, a daughter of Josiah and Experience Swift (14), born Feb. 15, 1720-1, married Nathan Davis of Sandwich, Dec. 24, 1740, and leaves no further record.

58 JOANNA, a daughter of Josiah and Experience Swift (14), born Aug. 25, 1723, leaves no record.

59 JOHN, youngest son of Josiah and Experience Swift (14), born

42

Oct. 3, 1727, married Desire Swift of Plymouth, Sept. 21, 1752, and then disappears beyond all search of mine.

REVISION

It is apparent from depositions which follow that the record of Samuel Swift, who married Mercy Wing, should be changed as follows:

"Of Samuel and Mary, of William (2), of William (1).

Samuel Swift, Jr., born 1711, died F., June 4, 1788, married May 18, 1741, Mercy Wing, born 1718, died May 5, 1790; and had issue as indicated by 124.

124 Asa, born Dec. 30, 1742, married Lucy Briggs, March 9, 1765."

This is in brief the result of much correspondence and investigation through a considerable period of time.

I received the following letter from George H. Swift, written March 10, 1891:

"I have no doubt that 'Father Swift' and 'Mother Swift' refer to Samuel Swift and Mercy Wing, and if your records were made as the births and deaths occurred, I should feel assured that they were right. But the Reverend Frederick Freeman, the historian of Cape Cod, assured me that the Samuel Swift, Jr., who married Mercy Wing, was the son of Benjamin Wing, the first Quaker. (The Wings were all Quakers). I pointed out to him that if this were true, Samuel must have been 37 years of age when married, which was an unusual thing in those days. But he declared that other descendants of Benjamin, through Benjamin Junior, his son, were all Quakers and kept faithful traditions, and that their family records pointed to Samuel, son of Benjamin, as husband of Mercy Wing, and I had no knowledge of any facts in opposition to his claim. Yet always a current of uncertainty has run through my mind upon the subject.

"Then again there was no Samuel in the family, so far as I know, who could take the place of Benjamin's Samuel, as the husband of Mercy, except Samuel Jr., son of Samuel, whose birth does not appear upon the town records, as do all of Samuel's other children, but I only find him mentioned in his father's will dated in 1730 as one of the three to whom he gives his real estate. Your record would make Samuel, husband of Mercy, born in 1720 and 21 when he was married.

"My faith in Samuel, son of Benjamin, was settled, but is now shaken.

"Ephraim 13 has not been traced at all.

* * * * * * *

"If this Samuel Junior married Mercy Wing he must have been born 12 years after Elizabeth, or in 1720, when his father was 58 years old and his mother at least 48."

"The record of 'Father Swift' and 'Mother Swift, to which George H. Swift refers, was the following, taken from the Bible of Asa Swift, son of Samuel, in possession of General E. Swift.

"Deaths

"Father Swift, Feb. 15, 1798, 77 years old.

"Mother Swift, May 4, 1790, 72 years old."

It seemed perfectly plain then that Samuel Swift, the husband of Mercy Wing, could not be son of Benjamin. Who was he? Was the date of the death of "Father Swift" wrong?.

On this point the following was to be noted;

(1) The Bible was published in 1801.

(2) All entries between 1766 and 1825 having references to Asa Swift and his children show that they were written by Asa Swift himself, at the same time.

(3) They were therefore written by him after 1825, at which time he was 82 years old.

(4) The entries were made in sequence of dates, except the date of the death of "Father Swift" in 1798, which appears after an entry of 1784, and before one of 1790.

(5) The census of 1790 does not give Samuel as an inhabitant of Wareham. The family declare that Samuel Swift lived in the old Swift farm near Wareham, still owned by the family, where

44

the position of the house, and the broad stone at the front door, are pointed out today. His name appears as holder of certain town offices in the year preceding 1790.

Now we clear up the whole matter by the following record, which I got from my relative, Mrs. Eunice Swift Thomas Resor, granddaughter of Briggs Swift of Cincinnati, Ohio. Mrs. Resor copied it from the records of the First Congregational Church of Wareham. The record says:

"Samuel Swift died of a pectoral decay F. 6|4 1788 aged 77.

"Mercy Swift died of a dropsical Consumption May 5, 1790, aged 73."

Therefore George H. Swift was right in supposing that Asa Swift's record was not accurate. The date of death of Samuel was ten years earlier. The other dates were nearly correct.

Thus Samuel Junior of Wareham, who married Mercy Wing, was evidently son of Samuel, not Benjamin Swift. He was born in 1711, three years younger than his sister Elizabeth, when his father was 51 and his mother under 40, and he married at the age of 30. He died before the census of 1790. The family tradition as to his living on the old Swift farm at Wareham is correct.

The Freeman story that Samuel Junior was son of Benjamin looks doubtful to say the least. The Wing family traditions to which he refers do not seem to have been known to Rev. Conway Wing when he published his Wing Book in 1888. Mercy is mentioned by name only and nothing more. The president of the Wing family of America, George W. Wing, wrote me on Sept. 12, 1910:

"I am unable at this date to locate Mercy who married Samuel, but I am inclined to think she was a daughter of Nathaniel Wing, son of Stephen, who lived in that part of Sandwich now known as Pocasset." He later located Mercy as daughter of Nathaniel, who was son of the above mentioned Nathaniel.

I believe the Wings of Pocasset were not "all Quakers" as stated by Freeman. These records were not well kept, according to their latest historians.

Again Old Pocasset deeds show that —— 1757, Zaccheus Swift

45

sold a number of pieces of land in Pocasset to Nathaniel and Meltiah Wing, probably the father and brother of Mercy. Zaccheus was brother of Samuel and Ephraim who inherited the estate of Samuel. Zaccheus was executor of the estate and at least a portion of the land sold thus was a portion of the estate, being so stated in the deed. Probably Samuel and Mercy were residents of Pocasset before their marriage.

I believe I have now cleared up my double line to Ephraim Jr., and to Samuel Jr., sons of Samuel.

(Signed) Eben Swift

Copy of Family Record.

Deaths	Age
Peleg Swift, April 9, 1772,	4 years, 11 months, 6 days
Lot Swift, July 19, 1784,	17 years, 8 months, 7 days
Father Swift, Feb. 15, 1798,	77 years
Mother Swift, May 4, 1790,	72 years
Ausel Swift, Dec. 10, 1804, Made a watery grave	23 years, 9 months, 11 days
Seth Swift, July 7, 1804, Made a watery grave	18 years, 4 months, 16 days
Lucy Swift, wife of Asa Swift, Sr., died May 3, 1825,	80 years, 5 months,
Asa Swift, Junior, Sept. 3, 1833,	89 years, 8 months,
Hallet Swift, June 18, 1835,	63 years, 5 months,
Charles O. Swift, May 19, 1837,	24 years, 2 months,
Harriet N. Swift, Jan. 1, 1839,	21 years

FIFTH GENERATION

60 WILLIAM, son of William and Lydia Swift (15), born 1719 in Falmouth, married Dorcas Hatch of Falmouth Nov. 29, 1744, by whom he had seven children. After her death he married Mehitabel Hallet of Yarmouth, youngest daughter of Jonathan Hallet, Sept. 1, 1772, and had three children by her. He died Aug. 7, 1809, aged 90 years. His children were:

118 Solomon, born Oct. 15, 1745, married Susanna Childs, F., Nov. 23, 1769.
119 William Jr., born Feb. 17, 1747, married Martha Eldred, F., Oct. 6. 1773.
    John, born , unmarried, died on a prison ship during the Revolution.
    Thomas, born , unmarried, died on a prison ship during the Revolution.
    Mary, born , married Richard Weeks, 1777.
120 Job, born 1759, married 1st Elizabeth Eldridge, 2nd Charlotte Brightman Mosher.
121 Jethro, born Mar. 25, 1763, married Rosanna Phinney, F., March 12, 1789.
122 Hallet, born 1774, married Hannah Phinney, F., Jan. 28, 1803.
    Lydia, born , married Walter Turner, Sippican, Sept. 5, 1799.
123 John, born July 10, 1780, married Melinda Leonard, F., March 7, 1805.

60a SOLOMON, son of William and Lydia (Weeks) Swift, born 1715, married Love Shiverick, Sept. 21, 1740, Falmouth.

61 SAMUEL, eldest son of Benjamin and Hannah Swift (16), born Sept. 11, 1704, married Mercy Wing of Sandwich May 18, 1741. Samuel died Feb. 15, 1798. Mercy died May 4, 1790, aged 72 years. He removed to Wareham, where his children were born. They were:

    124 Capt. Asa, born Dec. 30, 1742, married Lucy Briggs, Wareham, daughter of Ebenezer Briggs, March 9, 1765.
    Martha, born May 3, 1744, married Simeon Bates, Rochester, Feb. 10, 1763.
    125 Willard, born May 15, 1746, married Zilpah Hamblin, W., Dec. 1, 1768.
    126 David, born Nov. 25, 1750, married Lydia Savery, W., June 4, 1772.

127 Lemuel, born Oct. 31, 1752, married Betty Briggs, W., April 17, 1773.
128 Samuel, Jr., born Nov. 19, 1757, married Eleanor Sherman, Rochester, Dec. 4, 1793.
129 Jesse, 2nd, born Feb. 20, 1760, married Mercy Bates, W., Aug. 28, 1783.
62 CONTENT, a daughter of Benjamin and Hannah Swift (16), born Dec. 12, 1708, married, March 15, 1731-2, Zaccheus Wing, a grandson of Hannah Swift (2) who married Daniel Wing Nov. 5, 1641. They lived and died in Sandwich and their children were Hannah, Beulah, Paul, Benjamin and Deborah.
63 ZEBULON, second son of Benjamin and Hannah Swift (16), born April 15, 1712, married Rebekah Winge of Sandwich Nov. 15, 1739. They settled in Falmouth, where their children were born and were named:
130 Joseph, born July 16, 1741, married Martha Crowell, F., Nov. 19, 1772.
131 Samuel, born Sept. 12, 1743.
132 Abraham, born Dec. 31, 1745, married Johana Sisson, Nine Partners, N. Y.

Hannah, born , married —— Dillingham.
Dorothy, born . , married Nathan Hatch, F., April 3, 1779.
Elizabeth, born , married —— Gifford.
Rebecca, born
Deborah, born ,. married Stephen Tripp.
Huldah, born , married Clifton Bowerman.
Jemima. born , married Richard Landers; publ. Dec. 6, 1793.
133 Barnabas, born , married Cynthia Carrington.

64 BENJAMIN, JR., youngest son of Benjamin and Hannah Swift (16), married Waitstill Bowerman, Sept. 4, 1741. Waitstill Bowerman was another of the Wing connection closely related to Rebecca, Zaccheus and Mercy. They lived and died in Falmouth, and their children were:

48

134 Sylvanus, born Aug. 28, 1743, married 1st, Elizabeth Tripp, Nov. 19, 1764, 2nd, Experience Landers, 1799.
135 Paul, born Jan. 15, 1744-5, married Chloe Wing, Jan. 15, 1778.
136 Silas, born July 18, .746, married Elizabeth Bumpus, Nov. 11, 1772.
  Rest, born Oct. 15, 1748, married Joseph Bowerman.
  Mary, born June 7, 1750, married Benjamin Coleman.
137 Hannah, born June 1, 1752, married Presbury Wing, June 2, 1780.
  Rosanna, born Aug. 24, 1754, married William Allen, May 27, 1775.
  Sarah, born June 16, 1756.
  Lydia, born May 10. 1759, married Isaac Weekes, Nov. 11, 1791.
  Waitstill, 2nd, born Oct. 1, 1762.
138 "Capt." Benjamin, born Sept. 24. 1764, married Elizabeth Swaim, Oct. 6, 1791.

65 WILLIAM, eldest son of Joseph and Mercy Swift (17), born Feb. 26, 1711, married Lydia Gibbs of Sandwich, March 2, 1731-2. He removed to Lebanon, Conn., about 1745 or 1746, where two of his children died. He then went to Plymouth, where two more were born and died. His children were:

139 Job, born Jan. 14, 1732-3.
  Mercy, born April 11, 1734.
  Rebekah, born March 13, 1735-6.
  William, born Feb. 27, 1737-8, died June 16, 1749, at Lebanon, Conn.
  Joshua, born March 29, 1743, died June 21, 1749, at Lebanon, Conn.
  Solomon, born Dec. 12, 1750, at Plymouth, died young.
  William; born Oct. 31, 1752, at Plymouth, died young.

66 JOSEPH, JR., second son of Joseph and Mercy Swift (17), born Sept. 4, 1716, married Mrs. Sarah (Bartlett) LeBaron of

Plymouth, Jan. 21, 1736-7, where their only child was born. No record of their deaths has been found.

    Mary, born Aug. 1738, died Dec. 1738.

67 JOSHUA, third son of Joseph and Mercy Swift (17), born Feb. 14, 1717-18, married Jane Faunce of Plymouth, March 21, 1738-9, and settled in that place, where their children were born. Their names were:

140 Abigail, born March 8, 1739-40, married Micah Swift (89), March 29, 1758.

141 Joseph, born Feb. 5, 1742-3.

    Joan, born June 6, 1744, married —— Rider.

142 John, born Sept. 15, 1746, married Elizabeth Gibbs, publ. Jan. 1770.

    Susannah, born Feb. 1748.

142b Joshua, Jr., born   , married Mary Cornish, 1780.

    Joanna, born

    Rebecca, born

    Mercy, born

68 THOMAS, only son of Joseph and Rebecca Swift (17), married Abigail Phillips of Sandwich, Nov. 15, 1752, and lived in that town until his death in 1803. Their children were:

    William, born Sept. 4, 1753, died young.

143 Clark, born Sept, 23, 1755, married 1st, Mary Gibbs, 2nd, Phebe Freeman, Aug. 16, 1789.

144 Rebecca, born Feb. 12, 1760, married Seth Swift, 1777.

145 Joseph, born June 30, 1762, married Anna Freeman, S., 1785.

146 Nathaniel, born Dec. 31, 1764, married Elizabeth Ellis, Plymouth, Nov. 24, 1785.

    Maria, born April 28, 1767, married Jonathan Beale, Braintree, Nov. 29, 1787.

147 Thomas, Jr., born May 13, 1772, married Cynthia Blackwell. S., Oct. 3, 1793.

148 William, born May 1, 1777, married Katy T. Gibbs, S., April 12, 1804.

149 Levi, born May 13, 1780, married 1st, Rebecca Ryder,

50

Kingston, 1803, 2nd, Mrs. Phebe Cushman, widow of Dr. Bartholomew.

69 JAMES, eldest son of Samuel and Abigail Swift (18), born March 1, 1720-1, in Plymouth, leaves no record save that of his birth.

70 SAMUEL, JR., youngest son of Samuel and Abigail Swift (18), born at Plymouth Jan. 16, 1723-4, married Thankful Ashley of Rochester, Nov. 7, 1751. No further trace of him is given by any records as yet found.

71 THOMAS, JR., eldest son of Thomas and Thankful Swift (20), born May 11, 1727, at Plymouth, married Rebekah Clark of Plymouth, Oct. 21, 1746, and lived in that town two years. In 1748 he removed to Rochester, where the rest of his children were born. They were:

    150 Jonathan, born July 7, 1747, at Plymouth.
    Lucy, born Feb. 14, 1749, at Rochester.
    Meribah, born Aug. 8, 1753, at Rochester.
    151 Thomas, born Aug. 8, 1755, at Rochester.
    152 James, born Dec. 24, 1758, at Rochester.
    Mary, gem., born Aug. 12, 1764, at Rochester.
    153 Joseph, gem., born Aug. 12, 1764, at Rochester.

72 PHINEAS, second son of Thomas and Thankful Swift (20), born March 10, 1733-4, married Rebekah Phillips of Sandwich, April 9, 1752. Their children were:

    Jedidah, born June 5, 1753, married Samuel Norris, Wareham, May 28, 1770.
    Abia, born March 17, 1756, married Benjamin Morey, Jr., Sandwich, March 30, 1786.
    154 Phineas, Jr., born 1758, married Sarah Ellis, Sandwich, publ. April 1780.
    155 Stephen, born June 17, 1760, married Phebe Mendell, Plymouth, publ. May 1782.

72½ THANKFUL, 2nd, a daughter of Thomas and Thankful Swift 20); born Feb. 26, 1737-8, married Nathaniel Wing of Pocasset,

51

May 22, 1755. Children, Lemuel, Noah, Mary, Olive, Barnabas, Jesse, William, Judah.

73 LEMUEL, youngest son of Thomas and Thankful Swift (20) and twin to Thankful above, married Rebecca Whitfield of Rochester, Dec. 8, 1756. No further trace of them or of any descendants has yet been found.

74 JABEZ, eldest son of Ebenezer and Abigail Swift (24), born February, 1732, married Mrs. Hannah Perry of Sandwich, Jan. 30, 1755, by whom he had three children. After her death in 1764 he married Lydia Nye of Sandwich. Sept. 19, 1765, by whom he had four children, and died Jan. 25, 1810, buried at Falmouth. Lydia, born Nov. 1729, died Aug. 12, 1822, age 92 years, 9 months. Jabez' children were:

    Jemima, born
156 Abram, born 1762, married Olive Lawrence, Sandwich, May 1, 1799.
    Hannah, born
157 Heman, born   , died in Vermont, age 90.
    Mary, born   , married John Perry, 4th, Sandwich, Jan. 20, 1793,
    Abigail, born   married John Lawrence, Sandwich, April 3, 1795.
158 Ebenezer, born   lived at Barnstable.

75 EBENEZER, JR. youngest son of Ebenezer and Abigail Swift (24), born July 1, 1733, married Jedidah ―― of Wareham, 1753. Their children were:

    Lydia, born Aug. 5, 1754, married Freeman Wing, Sandwich, April 9, 1773.
159 Judah, born Feb. 6, 1756, in Revolutionary war.
160 Benjamin, gem., born March 30, 1758, in Revolutionary war, married 1st, Eunice Morey, W., 1779-80, 2nd, Susannah Foster, S., 1787, 3rd, Hannah Cornish, Plymouth, 1790.
161 Joseph, gem., born March 30, 1758, in Revolutionary war.
    Ann, born Jan. 20, 1760.

76 EPHRAIM, eldest son of Samuel and Ruth Swift (27), born Oct. 11, 1713, at Sandwich, married Feb. 17, 1735-6, Anna Robinson of Falmouth, born 1718. They settled in Falmouth at Woods Hole, where Ephraim died Dec. 22, 1801, and his widow Jan. 18, 1804. Their only child was
  Mercy, born , who died unmarried in 1802.
77 MANASSEH, second son of Samuel and Ruth Swift (27), born March 24, 1714-5, married Ruth Robinson of Falmouth, Dec. 15, 1743. Ruth, born in 1721, bore eight children to Manasseh and died in 1761. Manasseh married Tamar Dexter of Falmouth July 3, 1764, who bore to him four children. In 1779, during the Revolutionary war, the British visited the houses of Ephraim and Manasseh at Woods Hole in search of fresh provisions, having learned that they had fine dairies. A refugee led two soldiers to Mrs. Tamar's cheese room and each speared a cheese with his bayonet, expecting to bear away the booty in triumph, but Mrs. Swift met them at the door and recovered her cheeses in spite of the bayonets, and drove off the soldiers, whether with her tongue or a more weighty weapon, History saith not. Manasseh's children were:
  Bethia, born , married Job Parker, Sandwich, Nov. 13, 1766.
162 Ephraim, born 1749, married 1st, Elinor Chadwick, F., publ. April 13, 1776, 2nd, Sarah Davis.
163 Asaph, born 1750, married Elizabeth Hincks, F., Dec. 25, 1783.
  Anner, born , married Abiel Eldred, F., publ., April 27, 1776.
  Abigail, born , married Barnabas Hatch, F., publ. June 29, 1776.
164 Reuben, born , married Temperance Weeks, F., publ. June 8, 1777.
165 Joseph, born , married
  Joanna, born , married Holland Nye, F., Sept. 20, 1779.
  Ruth, born , unmarried.

53

166 Philip, born   , married Ruth Butler, May 16, 1787.
167 Manasseh, Jr., born   , married Tryphemia Gifford, F., Dec. 9, 1789.
Tamar, born

78 JUDAH, third son of Samuel and Ruth Swift (27), born Sept. 3, 1716, in Sandwich, married Dec. 14, 1738, Elizabeth Morton of Falmouth, born Nov. 22, 1720. They lived in Falmouth till 1769 when Judah, having made $3,000 by buying heavy standing timber on Naushon Island, which no one else could get out from the bowl-like valley in which it grew, and building a winding road around the sides by which means he got the timber to market. They removed to Amenia, Dutchess County, N. Y., travelling with ox teams the whole distance, where Elizabeth died Nov. 12, 1802, and Judah Jan. 17, 1807. Their children were:
    Lois, born Jan. 24, 1740, married Josiah Burgess, Sandwich, Dec. 13, 1764. Lois died Dec. 12, 1768.
168 Samuel, born June 11, 1744, married Mrs. Mary (Phillips) Crosby, Aug. 31, 1773.
169 Nathaniel, born March 19, 1747, married Deborah Smith, Falmouth, Oct. 30, 1771.
    Moses, born May 15, 1752, died Dec. 24, 1758.
    Rebecca, born March 16, 1754, died Jan. 17, 1759.
170 Seth, born March 16, 1757, married Mary Wells of Franklin, Conn., 1782.
171 Elizabeth, born Oct. 19, 1760, married 1st, Samuel Jarvis, Amenia, N. Y., Sept. 4, 1774. 2nd, Andrew Hawkins.
172 Moses, born March 10, 1763, married Hannah Hurd, Dover, N. Y., June 9, 1785.

79 REUBEN, fourth son of Samuel and Ruth Swift (27), born Oct. 27, 1717, in Sandwich, married Hannah Dexter, sister of Mary (52), of Falmouth, Jan. 21, 1741-2. In 1743 he removed to Kent, Conn., where all his children were born and where he died March 2, 1773. Hannah survived him 22 years, dying in Feb. 1795. Their children were:
    Joanna, born Nov. 8, 1743, married Aaron Payne.

54

173 Barzillai, born Sept. 21, 1745, married Prudence Hopson of Kent, Conn., March 22, 1770.
    Ruth, born June 30, 1747, married David Beardsley.
    Elizabeth, born March 18, 1749, married Asa Hall.
    Chloe, born Feb. 6, 1751, married William Trapp.
    Hannah, born March 26, 1753, married Job Giddings.
    Sarah, born March 26, 1755, married Timothy Pearl.
    Moses, born April 1, 1757, died unmarried.
    Lydia, born March 31, 1759, married John Hopson of Kent, Conn.
173b Asaph, born March 24, 1763, married Theodosia Hopson of Kent, Conn., 1781.
80 MOSES, youngest son of Samuel and Ruth Swift (27), born Oct. 4, 1720, at Sandwich, married Oct. 29, 1746, Mary Robinson of Falmouth born 1723, who died without issue in 1771. He then married May 17, 1772, Rachel Parker of Falmouth, born 1736, who also died without issue March 10, 1807. Moses died June 28, 1809, age 88 years, 8 months. He was a member of the Provincial Congress. Buried at Falmouth.
81 JOAN, a daughter of Samuel and Ruth Swift (27), born May 8, 1728, married Benjamin Gibbs, Jr., son of Joshua Gibbs, of Falmouth Jan. 10, 1744-5, and had by him one son, Joshua, named in his grandfather's will. Benjamin died soon after his marriage, and Joan married Nathan Barlow of Falmouth, Feb. 9, 1748-9. In 1756 they removed to Amenia, N. Y., and after many years removed again to Duanesburgh, N. Y., where they died. Their children were: Mary, Sarah, Samuel, Nathan. These four were baptized with their mother in the Presbyterian church at Amenia South, Sept. 15, 1776.
81b LYDIA, a daughter of Samuel and Ruth Swift (27), married Seth Swift (85), of Falmouth, Aug. 29, 1751. The record of their marriage and the mention of their names in her father's will were the only traces found of either until recently, when the family records gave us the names of their children as follows:
174 Seth, born

Ruth, born   . , married Joseph Merrick.
Mary, born   , married Ezra Wade.
174b Lot, born March 13, 1758, married Elizabeth Barlow, Dec. 10, 1778.
Abigail, born 1760, married John Moffet, Jr., July 14, 1782.
Rebecca, born   , married Benjamin Whiting.
Lois, born   , married Abijah Lee.
Hannah, born   , married Games Dean.

82 ELIZABETH, a daughter of Moses and Mary Swift (30), born Jan. 10, 1727-8, married Jehosaphat Eldridge or Eldred, Jr., of Falmouth, Dec. 17, 1747. They soon removed to Litchfield County, Conn., where their children were born and their daughter Joanna married Rufus Swift (192), son of Gen. Homan (93).

83 SAMUEL, eldest son of Moses and Mary Swift (30), born March 3, 1733-4, leaves no trace on the records except the date of his birth.

84 "CAPT." WARD, youngest son of Moses and Mary Swift (30), born Dec. 1, 1735, married Remember Toney of Sandwich, Jan. 9, 1755. He was a prominent man in the town and took an active part in raising men and serving his country during the Revolution. His children were:

175 Moses, born 1765, married Rebecca Nye, Falmouth, Jan. 6, 1791.
176 Ward, Jr., born   , married Fear Nye, Falmouth, Jan. 13, 1799.
177 Samuel, born   married ―― Perry.
    Betsey, born   , married 1st, Nathan Barlow, 2nd, John Freeman.
    Bathsheba, born   married Joshua Crowell, Falmouth,
    Jan. 28, 1796.
    Mary, born   , married Samuel Eldred, Falmouth, Oct. 25, 1787.
    Hannah, born   married Charles Bourne, Sandwich,
    1798.

56

178 Heman, born   , married Hannah Hinds, Middleboro, publ. May 18, 1798.
179 Alvan, born 1783, married Patience Coleman, Nov. 29, 1809. Alvin died March 2, 1854.
85 SETH, JR., son of Seth and Maria Swift (32), born Dec. 2, 1724, married Desire Holmes of Plymouth, March 29, 1749. Nothing further has been learned of him positively, but it is believed that, Desire dying soon after her marriage, Seth then married his third cousin, Lydia Swift (81b), daughter of Samuel and Ruth Swift (27), Aug. 29, 1751.
86 JUDAH, eldest son of Ebenezer and Mary Swift (34), born Feb. 26, 1723-4, leaves no other trace than the date of his birth upon the record.
87 JOB, second son of Ebenezer and Mary Swift (34), born July 17, 1726. As of his brother Judah we find of him "only this and nothing more."
88 ENOCH, third son of Ebenezer and Mary Swift (34), born in Plymouth, July 25, 1735, married Esther Sampson of Wareham, July 21, 1757, and settled in Wareham. Their children were:
   180 Enoch, Jr., born Nov. 29, 1758, married Olive Wing of Sandwich.
   Esther, 2nd, born March 21, 1761.
   181 Ichabod, born Nov. 15, 1763, married Charlotte Barlow, S., publ. Nov. 12, 1790.
   Mercy, born Sept. 8, 1766, went to Maine with Enoch, Jr.
   182 Obadiah, born June 28, 1769, married Phebe Ann Blackwell, S., Oct. 28, 1791.
   Sarah, born Oct. 26, 1771.
   183 Hazadiah, born Feb. 25, 1776.
89 MICAH, twin to Enoch and fourth son of Ebenezer and Mary Swift (34), born July 25, 1735, married March 29, 1758, Abigail Swift of Plymouth, daughter of Joshua and Jane Swift (67), and settled in Wareham, where their children were born. Those children were:
   Mercy, born July 10, 1760.

Abigail, born July 26, 1763.
184 Micah, Jr., born Feb. 26, 1766, married 1st, Temperance Blackwell, W., Aug. 6, 1807, 2nd, Fear Hathaway, Middleboro, April 16, 1812.
184a William, born April 23, 1775.

90 ELISHA, eldest son of Zaccheus and Abigail Swift (36), born at Sandwich, May 22, 1736, married Susanna Davis of Falmouth, April 9, 1761, and died at Charleston, S. C., Aug. 20, 1807... The children were:
  184b Stephen, born 1762, married Rebecca Pease, April 19, 1785, died Dec. 30, 1835.
  Mary, born 1760, married Demas Strong, Feb, 4, 1787, died Aug. 26, 1883.

91 Stephen, second son of Zaccheus and Abigail Swift (36), born at Sandwich, married Ruth —— and had at least one son. He removed to Amenia, N. Y., in 1760 and in 1763 or later again removed to the western part of New York state and died at Yates, Orleans C., N. Y. His son was:
  185 Zaccheus, born   , married Amy Green.

91a EPHERAM, JR., son of Ephraim and Pheby Swift (38), married May 14, 1761, Sarah Bourne, and had issue:
  Martha, born Jan. 14, 1762.
  Phebe, born May 30, 1763.
  Sarah, born April 7, 1765.
185a Ephraim, born Sept. 10, 1766.
185b Ezra, born July 28, 1768, died Dec. 23, 1849, married Lucy Swift (267b), Nov. 30, 1797. Lucy was daughter of Asa (124) of Wareham (of Benjamin, of William 3).

92 ELISHA, eldest son of Jabez and Abigail Swift (43), born May 16, 1737, in Sandwich, married Dec. 30, 1756, Mary Ransom of Kent, Conn., born Dec. 4, 1737, died Aug. 24, 1807.. Elisha died July 2, 1777. Their children were:
  186 Heman, born Nov. 15, 1757, died Feb. 1813.
  Roxalana, born Aug. 25, 1759, died Feb. 5, 1761.
187 Gen. John, born June 17, 1761, married 1st, Rhoda Sawyer,

March 6, 1784, 2nd, Hepsibah Treat Davidson.
188 Gen. Philetus, born June 26, 1763, married 1st, Sally Deane, 2nd, Mrs. Fannia Cole Swift, widow of Capt. Asa R.
 Alice, born July 19, 1765, married Zach Blackman, died Jan. 17, 1813.
 Philae, born Aug. 1, 1767, married —— Hart, Jan. 19, 1813.
 Jabez, born July 20, 1769, died unmarried Sept. 9, 1795.
189 Severus, born Sept. 15, 1773, married.
190 Lewis, born Nov. 12, 1774, married.
191 Elisha, Jr., born July 5, 1777, married Delane Truesdale, Oct. 8, 1798.

93 GEN. HEMAN, second son of Jabez and Abigail Swift (43), born Oct. 14, 1733, in Sandwich, married, Feb. 29, 1760, Mary Skiff of Kent, Conn., born August 1736, and had by her eleven children. She died March 18, 1788, and he afterwards married Mrs. Eleanor (Marvin) Johnson, mother-in-law to his son Jabez. After her death, which occurred March 24, 1790, he married Mrs. Sarah (Robinson) Fay of Bennington, Vt., who died April 17, 1804. His fourth wife was Mrs. Hannah (Hopson) Pratt of Kent, Conn. His children were:
192 Rufus, born Jan. 15, 1761, married Joanna Eldred of Warren, Conn.
193 Philo, born Nov. 10, 1762, married 1st, Eunice Buel, Nov. 8, 1792, 2nd, Sarah Johnson Cogswell, Sept. 29, 1824.
194 Elisha, born Aug. 14, 1764, married Betsey Carter Sackett.
195 Jabez, born Sept. 11, 1766, married Abigail Johnson, Nov. 28, 1787.
196 Heman, Jr., gem., born Sept. 23, 1768, married Elizabeth Wood.
 Innom., gem., born Sept. 23, 1768, died an infant.
 Denis, born Aug. 26, 1770, married William Kellogg.
 Polly, born April 28, 1772, marrid Dr. John Calhoun, Oct. 4, 1801.
 Rhoda, born Sept. 27, 1774, married Miles Lewis, Oct. 5, 1794.
197 Ira, born Feb. 17, 1778, married Grace Rogers, Oct. 2, 1800.

59

198 Erastus, born Jan. 6, 1781, married Sarah Lewis.
94 JABEZ, Jr., third son of Jabez and Abigail Swift (43), born April 14, 1736, in Sandwich, died 1775. He graduated at Yale, was an attorney and settled in Salisbury, Conn. Died in camp in Boston and left one son, Amos Bird Swift. He was a man of position and promise. He must have been prosperous, as he built a large and expensive stone house which is still standing in Salisbury, though in a somewhat delapidated condition. His child was:
   198a Amos Bird.
95 CAPT. JIREH, fourth son of Jabez and Abigail Swift (43) born Aug. 20, 1735. at Sandwich, married Sarah Delano of Kent, Conn., Oct. 4, 1759. He lived in Kent, where his children were born, and the inscription on his tombstone tells the end.
   "Here lies the body of Capt. Jireh Swift, who departed this life July ye 28, 1776 in the 29th year of his age.
   "I, in the prime of life must quit ye stage,
   Nor see ye end of all ye Briton's rage.
   Farewell my wife and my 8 children dear,
   God will be gracious, never yield to fear.
   "He was one of the unfortunate soldiers who went to the northward and died on his return."
   He took part in Arnold's Campaign against Quebec in the autumn of 1775. His children were:
   Salome, born Aug. 7, 1760.
   Tressenda, born Feb. 8, 1762, married Barnabas Berry, born July 13, 1759.
   Pope, born Jan. 4, 1764, died 1768.
   Prudence Abigail, born Oct. 27, 1765.
   Susannah, born Nov. 12, 1767, married Jehiel Berry.
199 Anson Pope, born July 25, 1769, went to Bridport, Addison County, Vermont. Married Hannah Berry, Kent., Conn. Children: Julia, married —— Kent; Lucinda, married Amasa Williams; Lucretia, married Montgomery Crofoot; Jirah, married 1st —— Church, 2nd —— Baldwin.
200 Hibert, born May 1, 1771, died young
201 Jireh, Jr., born May 15, 1773, went to Bridport, Addison

County, Vermont, married Hannah Ferguson, Starksboro, Vt., April 15, 1798.

202 Jabez, born June 10, 1775, went to Bridport, Vermont, married Polly Bostwick, Aug. 20, 1797.

96 REV. JOB, fifth son of Jabez and Abigail Swift (43), born June 15, 1743, at Kent, Conn., married Nov. 5, 1769, Mary Ann Sedgwick of Sharon, Conn., born July 27, 1749. He graduated at Yale in 1765, was settled in the ministry at Richmond, Mass., 1767, and continued there seven years. Then settled in Amenia, N. Y., in 1774 and removed to Bennington, Vt., in 1783, where he lived to the end of his life, Oct. 20, 1804. His widow survived him 21 years, dying Feb. 6, 1826. Their children were:

Sarah Gold, born Nov. 13, 1770, died Oct. 23, 1863, married Elisha Strong, Sept. 18, 1814.

Clarinda, born July 18, 1772, died April 12, 1851, unmarried.

203 Sereuus, born May 27, 1774 married Rachael Bulkley, Aug. 11, 1805.

204 Noadiah, born Feb. 24, 1776, married Janette Henderson, March 28, 1802.

205 Erastus, born Feb. 9, 1778, married Louisa Everest, March 1, 1804.

206 Benjamin, born April 9, 1780, married Rebecca Brown, Sept. 1809.

207 Judge Samuel, born Aug. 5, 1782, married Mary B. Young, Nov. 17, 1817, lived at Middlebury, Vt.

Mary Ann, born July 22, 1784, died March, 1790.

Semantha, born May 12, 1786, died June 20, 1805, unmarried.

Persis, born May 28, 1788, married Rev. Allen Greely, Aug. 19, 1813.

Laura, born March 6, 1790, died April 17, 1790.

208 Heman, born Sept. 30, 1791, married Ruth Robinson, Dec. 3, 1818.

209 Job Sedgewick, born April 11, 1794, died 1859, unmarried.

Mary Ann, 2nd, born Aug. 18, 1796, married Hiram Everest, July 1, 1819.

97 REV. SETH, youngest son of Jabez and Abigail Swift (43),

born Nov. 14, 1749, at Kent, Conn., married Lucy Elliot of Kent, Sept. 21, 1781. He was settled at Williamstown, Mass., for many years and was a prominent man in his denomination. Their children were:
- 210 Rev. Ephraim Griswold, born Aug. 14, 1782, married Sarah Keziah Beach.
- Clarinda, born April 23, 1785, married Philo Clark, Nov. 25, 1810.
- Lucy, born May 18, 1788, married Rev. Sylvester Selden, June 1813.
- 211 Nathan Elliot, born July 10, 1790, died Oct. 6, 1855, unmarried.
- 212 Rev. Elisha Pope, born Aug. 12, 1792, married Elizh. Darling Beach, Oct. 2, 1817.
- 213 Joseph, born Dec. 20, 1794, married Eliza Root, Aug. 22, 1818.
- Sabrina, born Nov. 2, 1798, died March 9, 1868, married Joshua Logan, April, 1825.

98 PEREZ, eldest son of Zephaniah and Lydia Swift (44), born Feb. 14, 1725-6, in Sandwich, married Mary Fox of Groton, Conn., Nov. 3, 1746. Their children born in Lebanon, Conn., were: -
- 214 Perez, Jr., born July 4, 1749, married Hannah Fairchild, Oct. 11, 1770, in Mansfield, Conn.
- Deborah, born Sept. 21, 1751.
- 215 Jesse, born March 25, 1754, married Lydia Storrs, Dec. 23, 1779.

99 SILAS, second son of Zephaniah and Lydia Swift (44), born at Lebanon, Conn., leaves no trace to be found anywhere.

100 CHIPMAN, third son of Zephaniah and Lydia Swift (44), born in 1750 at Lebanon (baptized July 8) married Mary Lane and removed to Wilmington, Vt., where his children were born. Mary died June 22, 1813. Soon after in 1816 Chipman went to Derby, Conn., to reside with his son, Rev. Zephaniah S. He there married Mrs. Sarah Humphrey Mills, May 6, 1819, and died March 8, 1825. Sarah died Sept. 27, 1840, in 68th year. His children were:
- 216 Rev. Zephaniah, born 1771, married Sarah Packard, 1793.

Lucy, born 1773, died April 12, 1790.
Lydia, born 1775, died Dec. 29, 1828.
Polly, born 1779, died Dec. 23, 1781.
Chipman, Jr., born 1782, died April 5, 1784.
Cynthia, born   , married Alanson Parmalee, Wilmington.
Sally, born 1787, died Oct. 2, 1825.
Polly, born   , married Rev. Urbane H. Hitchcock of Charlestown, Mass.

101 NATHANIEL, JR., second son of Capt. Nathaniel and Abia Swift (46), born Sept. 18, 1749, at Warren, Conn., married Sarah Thomas, Dec. 22, 1769. Their children were:

Joanna, born Aug. 30, 1770.
Abigail, born 1772, married —— Comstock.
217 Rufus, born Feb. 5, 1774, married Lydia Carter, Jan. 1, 1799.
Sarah, born July 8, 1776, married Amasa Peters.
Lucinda, born April 30, 1779.
Huldah, born Aug. 29, 1780.
218 Rev. Nathaniel, born Feb. 8, 1783, married Elizabeth Wakeman.
Chloe, born 1785, married Rev. Worthington Wright. Chloe died June 29, 1815.
Aner, born 1789, died Jan. 5, 1807, age 17.
219 Julius, born 1792, married 1st, Betsey ——, 2nd, ——.

102 DR. ISAAC of Cornwall, third son of Capt. Nathaniel and Abia Swift (46), born Feb. 27, 1753, at Warren, Conn., married Jan. 3, 1775, Patience Cass and died at Cornwall, July 29, 1802. Patience, daughter of Moses and Phoebe (Peters) Cass., born Dec. 17, 1754, died at Warren, Conn., Oct. 29, 1808. Their children were:

220 Adoniram, born 1776, married Lodemia Peck, Nov. 9, 1805.
Lura, born   , married —— Dexter.
Abia, born 1782, married Jesse Conklin Crissey.
Patience, born 1784, married Rev. Dr. Thomas Lippincott, died 1819.

221 Isaac, Jr., born Jan. 30, 1790, married Eliza Thompson, Jan. 15, 1818.

103 JONATHAN, eldest son of Jireh, Jr., and Deborah Swift (47), born in 1732, called "of Dartmouth" in his marriage record, married Elizabeth Bourne of Falmouth, Oct. 16, 1753. He died Jan. 31, 1763, age 30. Their children were:
222 John, born July 30, 1754.
223 David, born Jan. 31, 1756.
    Abigail, born Nov. 8, 1757 married Zebulon Haskell, Middleboro, Mass., died July 6, 1811.

104 JIREH, 3d, second son of Jireh, Jr, and Deborah Swift (47), born in 1740, married in Wareham, Jan. 6, 1763, Elizabeth Haskell of Rochester, born 1740. Jireh died July 16, 1817. Elizabeth died Aug. 10, 1794. Their children were:
224 Jonathan, born 1763, married 1st, Love Bassett, Oct. 21, 1792, 2nd, Hannah Marshall, Rochester, April 5, 1815. Jonathan died Sept. 19, 1834.
    Ruth, born 1765, died 1838, married William Ross, 1790.
    Betsey, born   , married John Briggs.
225 Jireh, Jr., born Sept. 26, 1773, married Elizabeth Hathaway, Nov. 10, 1805. Jireh died Oct. 15, 1857, Elizabeth died 1860.
    Lydia, born 1780, died 1828, married Elisha Tobey, 1808 Elisha born 1783.
    Nancy, born 1785, died 1878, married Loum Snow 1806, who died 1823.

105 SILAS, third son of Jireh, Jr., and Deborah Swift (47), born March 15, 1743, at Acushnet, Mass., married Deborah Tobey of Sandwich, 1766, daughter of Dr. Elisha Tobey, and settled at Cheshire, Mass., where he died Jan. 12, 1803, just one month after the death of Deborah. He was a miller and did the best of work. Their children were:
226 Lemuel, born April 28, 1767, went to Maine.
    Susan, born Sept. 17, 1768, married —— Duncan.

64

227 Jireh, born Oct. 1, 1770, went to Maine.
228 Elisha, born July 31, 1772, went to Maine.
 Desire, born Sept. 15, 1774, died Oct. 9, 1802, married Hezekiah Wilber, Nov. 20, 1794.
 Patience, born Aug. 6, 1776, died Aug. 19, 1847, married Elisha Clapp, Nov. 5, 1797.
 Bathsheba, born Sept. 7, 1778, married Stephen Peckham, 1803. He died May 6, 1853.
 Rebecca, born Jan. 6, 1780, married 1st, Lemuel Martin, 2nd, Emerson Brown. He died May 13, 1850.
 Lois, born Dec. 3, 1783, married James Weston, Sept. 3, 1805. He died Jan. 9, 1863.
 Abigail, born Aug. 12, 1785, died Jan. 17, 1858, married Winchester Mathewson, Nov. 7, 1804.
 Lucinda, born Aug. 22, 1787, died 1796, age 9 years.
 Ruth, born Dec. 2, 1788, died Aug. 22, 1867 (?), married 1st, Benjamin Freeman, 2nd, Aaron Burr.

106 PAUL, fourth son of Jireh, Jr., and Deborah Swift (47), born 1753, married Jemima —— and died Nov. 16, 1810, age 57. Jemima born 1748, died Jan. 20, 1821, age 73. No record of any child.

106a JOSHUA, eldest son of Job and Sarah Swift (48), born Aug. 28, 1744, married Mary Hewins at Sharon June 14, 1769. Sergeant in 3rd Co. in Col. Gaston's Regiment of Mass. Militia. The children were:

 Sarah, born Sept. 28, 1771
 Mary, born June 6, 1773, died Aug. 16, 1838, married Nathaniel Simonds at Oxford, N. H.
 Hannah, born April 9, 1775.
228a Joshua, Jr., baptized June 1, 1777.
228b Joseph, baptized March 25, 1781.
 Demaris, baptized May 16, 1779.
 Patience, baptized Aug. 22, 1784, married Jeremiah Pierce.
 Abigail,   married —— Hewins at Walden, Vt.
 Rebecca,   married —— Martin of Haverhill, N. H.

106b JOB, second son of Job and Sarah Swift (48), born Sept. 5, 1746, married 1st, Rebecca Cummins, Sept. 14, 1768, 2nd, Elizabeth Guild. Rebecca, born Oct. 14, 1746, was mother of three children. Job was a member of 4th Co. Minute Men, a part of Col. Robinson's Regiment, Militia of Mass. The children were:

  228c Job, born March 12, 1769 (?), went to Readfield, Mass.
  228d Samuel, born June 28, 1771, married Anna Hewins, May 18, 1797.
  228e Elisha, born April 5, 1799, of Hamilton, N. Y.
  228f Philip of Elmira, N. Y.
  228g Amos,   married Hulda Holmes, born 1783.
    John, baptized Oct. 10, 1784, died unmarried at Sharon.
  228h David, born Oct. 8, 1786, of Hamilton, N. Y.
  228i Asa, baptized 1788, of Hamilton, N. Y.
    Susan, baptized 1790, married Major John Parks, Dorchester, before 1823.
    Betsy, married at Hamilton, N. Y.

106c JIREH, third son of Job and Sarah Swift (48), born June 4, 1748, married Waitstill Lyon, July 31, 1769. She died at Sharon. Jireh was a private in the 3rd Co. of Col. Groton's Regiment of Mass. Militia. He died before July, 1797. Children:

  228j Jireh, born June 23, 1770, lived at Sharon.
    Zilpha, born Jan. 3, 1772, died at Foxboro, Mass., 1795.
  228k Wyeth (Wyatt), born April 27, 1774, lived at Whately, Mass., 1795, married Martha Campbell.
  228l Azel, born Feb. 23, 1776, lived at Northampton, Mass.

107 "DEACON" CHARLES, second son of Silas and Abigail Swift (49), born March 16, 1742, at Lebanon, Conn., married May 26, 1763, Deborah Clark, born 1742, and lived in the same town until his death, June 19, 1824. Deborah died March 31, 1813. Their children were:

    Deborah, born Aug. 20, 1764, married Eliakim Thacher, Dec. 8, 1785, Sharon, Mass.

229 Silas, born Jan. 3, 1767, married Sally Parmalee, Bethlehem, June 1, 1796.
Pamela, born June 25, 1769, married Eliphaz Clark, Tolland, died Sept. 5, 1854, without issue.
Abigail, born April 18, 1772, died unmarried.
230 Charles, born Dec. 31, 1774, married Sept. 1798, Eunice Young, born Windham, Conn., Sept. 14, 1776, died at Cumbridge, Vt., Dec. 10, 1845.
231 Nathan, born Oct. 6, 1777, married 1st, Nancy Calkins, 2nd, Charity Elizabeth Reid, Nov. 8, 1810.
232 Eliphalet, born July 6, 1780, married 1st, Abigail Jesup, Jan. 13, 1806. 2nd, Mrs. Esther Jesup, July 15, 1820, 3rd, Mrs. Maria Church Eldridge.
233 Zephaniah, born July 15, 1786, married Nelly M. Everett, Winchester, Sept. 17, 1811.

108 JIREH, eldest son of Isaac and Susanna Swift (51), born in 1749 at Bridgewater, married Lucy Keith of that place in 1772 and died in 1828. Their children were:

Lois, born April 24, 1773, died Dec. 1, 1851, married Walter Keyes, 1793.
234 Isaac, born Oct. 12, 1775, married Sarah Pratt, 1797.
Clarissa, born July 22, 1777, died unmarried in 1865.
Marlborough, born Jan. 4, 1779, died April 15, 1796, unmarried.
235 Martin. born June 9, 1781, married Sarah Ames, 1809.
Jireh, Jr., born April 30, 1783, died Sept. 5, 1800, unmarried.
236 Sion, born March 29, 1785, married Mrs. Susanna (Washburn) Hall, 1818.
Washington, born March 9, 1787, died May 4, 1787.
237 Reuel, born May 22, 1788, married Mary Borden, 1821.
238 Warren, born Aug. 6, 1790, married ———, no children.
Thomas, born July 14, 1793, died Feb. 9, 1812, unmarried.
Rachel, born Oct. 14, 1796, died Aug. 1, 1830, married Charles Brett, 1822.

109 WILLIAM, second son of Isaac and Susanna Swift (51), born

1752, married Rachel Leonard in 1795 and died without issue May 14, 1839. Rachel died April 9, 1827.

110 BARZILLAI, eldest son of Rowland and Mary Swift (52), born Jan. 9, 1747, married Sarah Fearing of Wareham, Dec. 21, 1769. He removed when married, to Mansfield, Conn., and died in Tolland. Their children were:

 Hannah, born   , married Job Cushman.
 Lucy, born   , married Jabez Adams.
 Cynthia, born   , married Origen Storrs,
 Sarah, born   died a babe.

239 George, born Sept. 28, 1779, married Eunice Storrs, Jan. 26, 1804.
240 Washington, born Sept. 17, 1781, married 1st, Hannah Aspinall, Dec. 11, 1805, 2nd, Mary Storrs Burrows, 1839.
241 Dr. Earl, born April 8, 1784, married Laura Ripley, Windham, April 18, 1810.
242 Fearing, born Aug. 20, 1787, married Lucy Stowell, Middlebury, Vt.

111 ROWLAND, JR., second son of Rowland and Mary Swift (52), born Dec. 10, 1753, married Betsey Larned of Lebanon, removed in 1796 to Western New York and died at De Ruyter in Madison County, Jan. 20, 1849, age 96. Their children were:

 Lewis, born 1781, died at Lebanon, Jan. 17, 1784, age 2 years.
243 Gen. Lewis, 2d, born March 31, 1784, married Anna Forbes, Jan. 12, 1809.
 Mary, born 1785, died at Lebanon, Aug. 21, 1794, age 9 years.
 Sabrina, born 1789, died in 1842.
 Betsey, born 1791, died in 1855.
 Sophia, born 1793, died in 1831.
244 Heman, born 1798, died in 1860, married Althea Thornton, May 23, 1826.
245 Sherman, born 1797, died in 1827.
246 George W., born 1805, died in 1833.

112 JIREH, third son of Rowland and Mary Swift (52), born Dec. 6, 1755, drowned at sea, unmarried.

113 ZEPHANIAH, fourth son of Rowland and Mary Swift (52), born Wareham, Feb. 27, 1759, married Jerusha Watrous of Colchester, Conn., and had by her one son. After her death he married Lucretia Webb of Windham, May 14, 1794, born May 8, 1775, who bore to him seven children. He was a very prominent man in Connecticut, an L. L. D., a judge of the Supreme court, and author of a digest of Connecticut laws, which is a standard work to this day. He was chief justice in Connecticut, 1806-1819. He died at Warren, Ohio, Sept. 27, 1823. Lucretia returned to Connecticut after his death, and died at Lebanon in May, 1843. His children were:

 Henry, born , died a babe.
 George, born Dec. 29, 1795, died April 3, 1796.
247 George, 2d, born June 20, 1797, married Olive Kinsman.
 Edward, born April 29, 1799, died Aug. 15, 1825, unmarried.
 Lucretia, 2d, born Nov 11, 1801, died Feb. 21, 1850, married Rufus Spalding.
 Emily, born Jan. 15, 1804, died March 10, 1866, married Elijah Chapman, June 23, 1830.
248 Lucien, born June 2, 1808, married Sarah S. West, April 17, 1841.
248a Mary A., authoress (?)
 Julia, born May 9, 1810, married 1st, —— Babcock, 2nd, Dr. Huntington.

114 WILLIAM, youngest son of Rowland and Mary Swift (52), born Jan. 19, 1764, married Abigail Clark, who died 1855, and lived in Windham until his death in 1830. Their children were:
249 Justin, born Nov. 3, 1793, married Lucy Lathrop, Windham, Nov. 8, 1819.
 Abigail

115 JESSE, eldest son of Josiah, Jr., and Mary Swift (55), born Oct. 3, 1739, married Elizabeth Swift of Sandwich, April 7, 1763.

No clue to Elizabeth's descent is found. They settled in Wareham, where their children were born. They were:
- Abia, born April 12, 1765, married Benjamin Morey, Jr., Sandwich, March 30, 1786.
- 250 Josiah, born June 20, 1769, married Polly Ellis, Plymouth, Nov. 8, 1798.
- Mercy, born Sept. 5, 1772, married Jesse Wing, Sandwich, Sept. 27, 1790.
- 250a Silas, born Feb. 20, 1774, married Sally Ellis, Sandwich Jan. 29, 1800.
- Elizabeth, born Dec. 9, 1779.
- Hannah, born Jan. 15, 1781.
- 250b Jesse, Jr., born April 24, 1783, married Mrs. Hannah Hathaway, W., March 8, 1810.

116 ELISHA, second son of Josiah, Jr., and Mary Swift (55), and twin to Benjamin, born Jan. 31, 1747-8, married Martha Briggs of Rochester Dec. 18, 1775. See will of Asa 2nd and letter of M. G. Wing.
- 250c Samuel, born Sept. 22, 1778, married Mary Gibbs.
- 250d Asa, born Sept. 1780, died 1816, married Sarah ——, 1806.
- Mary, born Jan. 11, 1782, married —— Tobey.
- Martha, born Dec. 23, 1785, married —— Gibbs.
- 250e Elisha, born March 22, 1795.

117 BENJAMIN, twin to Elisha and third son of Josiah, Jr., and Mary Swift (55), born Jan. 31, 1747-8, leaves no other trace upon the record. He seems to have "died and made no sign."

No. 16.

LIBRARY of
Cape Cod
HISTORY & GENEALOGY

Old Shipmasters
BY ALEXANDER B. CHASE

YARMOUTHPORT, MASS.:
C. W. SWIFT, Publisher and Printer,
The "Register" Press,
1924

OLD SHIPMASTERS

(From The Barnstable Patriot.)

In March, 1910, I wrote an article for the Patriot about coasting and deep-water captains, of whom in the 40s and 50s there were some 200 from the Yarmouth line thro Hyannis and the port. Mentioned at that time as living were Capts F. G. Lothrop, Wm J. Wyer, Myron R. Peak, Frank Lothrop, Geo H. Hallett, John H. Frost, Reuben Baker, Wendell L. Hinckley, Joseph Hinckley, Centerville, John A. Peak, George E. Easton, J. P. H. Bassett, Willis L. Case Allen Brown, Albert Bragg, Horace K. Hallett, Eleazer Baker, C. Howard Allyn.

Capt Frank Lothrop was a native of Hyannis, now in Texas. His father was John Lothrop, who lived near the Howard Crowell place. His other sons were Asa, John Atwood, Henry Allen, and Joshua, all ship and deep water captains.

Those captns now living are Geo H. Hallett, now in his 95th year, J. H. Frost, C. Howard Allyn, Reuben Baker, Wendell L. Hinckley, John A. Peak, George E. Easton, J. P. H. Bassett, Willis L. Case and Allen Brown.

I would mention Capt Elkanah Crowell, who was born and was formerly a resident of West Yarmouth, and his brother, Capt Sturgis Crowell, both of whom were deep sea captains. Capt Crowell some years ago moved his house to Railroad avenue, Hyannis, and is one of the oldest shipmasters living in this vicinity. The following is an extract from a letter written by Capt Crowell to Mr F. W. Sprague and published in Mr Sprague's book, "Barnstable and Yarmouth Sea Captains and Owners":

"I started out quite young, for a short time hand line fishing, and later deep sea voyages. When in Boston I went into the ship chandlery store of J. Baker & Co., Commercial street. They told me the new clipper ship Spitfire was loading for San Francisco and the captain, John Arey, is a driver. He wants a mate who can jump over the foreyard every morning before breakfast. I said, 'I am

290

the man for him if it lies on deck.' "

At the age of 26 Capt Crowell was master of ship Boston Light, later of ships Fair Wind, Galatea, Carrie Reed, barques Gerard C. Tobey and George S. Homer, later an auxiliary sail and steam vessel owned by himself, W. H. Besse and others of Wareham, completing 29 years as master.

Capt John H. Frost went to sea quite young and was soon master of ships Agenor and Conqueror, and went to all parts of the globe. He retired some few years ago, and is now pilot commissioner in Boston.

I must not forget my genial friend, Capt C. Howard Allyn, formerly of West Barnstable, now a resident of Hyannis. I imagine he started out with a common school education, quite young, and went in coasting vessels hailing from Cotuit and later was master of the schr Hattie Baker, a fine schooner of 335 tons, built in 1862 in East Boston for J. Baker & Co., and Capt Allen Crowell, as owner and captain. Capt Allyn went with him as mate for a few years, when William Allen, Capt Crowell's son, took charge and soon after was killed accidentally in Mobile bay on a gunning expedition.

Then Capt Allyn took charge for several years, later going on deep sea voyages when he was master of ships Gold Hunter, Importer, and Titan. The latter was wrecked in a severe gale, but captain and crew were all saved. Capt Allyn was accompanied by his wife on this voyage. They then returned home and the captain retired from the sea. At that time (about 20 years ago) the foreign trade for sailing ships had seen its best days and steam took the place of sailing vessels.

Capt Andrew B. Chase, formerly of West Yarmouth and Hyannis, sends me notes in regard to vessels which went to Ireland in 1847 to carry grain.

Capt Chase now lives in Portland, Me. He was a deep water captain and followed the sea for 50 years and has been master of several vessels, schooners and barques. His last command was barque Normandy of Portland.

I am reminded of a young man, my neighbor, who went to New York to ship as a mate. He was there for some time and to his relatives here, who wrote to inquire what he was doing he replied: "A man here now wants quite a number of influential friends to get a job before the mast."

Late in the 40s Capt Lemuel B. Simmons had the schrs Croton and Isis built. Capt Luke Chase, Jr., commanded the Croton, and the Isis was built for Capt Anthony Chase, for the coasting trade. The Louisa was built at the same time by Capt Heman Chase for Capt Joshua, his son. At the time of the great famine in Ireland in 1847, Capt Jehiel Simmons of Hyannisport sailed in the Croton, as master, with a cargo of grain. When a few days out, in a rough sea, the jib boom was carried away and hung by the rigging and stays, swinging alongside, and was in danger of doing much damage. No one seemed to want to go out and clear the wreckage, so Capt Simmons took r wood saw and went out and with one hand on the bobstays, sawed the boom off.

The schr Cabot, a fine schooner, built for Capt John Nickerson of Chatham, sailed at the same time. Capt Nickerson was not in her. Both vessels went out and came back. The Cabot was in the New York line for a long time and had several captains, one of whom was Capt Eli Phinney of Centerville, and later Capt William B. Parker of Osterville.

Capt Lemuel Simmons was master of ship War Hawk and several others, and in 1853 had the schr Alice B. built on the lake at Cleveland for Capt Luke Chase.

Several other vessels were built at the same time. Capt Owen Bearse built the Owen Bearse for Capt Prince Bearse of Centerville, schr Ira Laffrienier for Capt Fred Coleman, also of Centerville, and Capt George P. Bearse had the schrs Claribel and George P. Bearse, Capt Z. D. Bassett the schr Paige.

Freights were very high at that time, and paid good dividends.

Capt Rodney Baxter, a pioneer sea captain, was in the 40s commander of the topsail schr Benjamin Bigelow, one of the several schooners in the New York line of packets and a very fast sailer. I remember these schooners well: Pequot, Joshua Baker; Renown, Zadock Crowell, West Yarmouth; Charles G. Baker, Frederick Lovell, Hyannisport; Excel, Gerry Bassett, Hyannis; Victor, J. P. Hallett; Friend, Alex. Lovell; William Roscoe, Albert Chase; Splendid, Orin Crowell; Red Rover, Sylvanus Bacon; Fancy, H. B. Chase, West Yarmouth; later H. B. Chase, Jr., West Yarmouth.

Capt Baxter purchased in the 40s the schr American Belle, nearly new. She was a fine schooner of 160 tons. He loaded her in New York in 1847 with grain for Ireland and made a very quick passage. On her trip back in ballast she was only 17 days—a record breaker.

I have seen a painting of the Belle on her passage across the Atlantic under her four lower sails in a rough sea.

Later Capt. Baxter was in the ship Flying Scud of some 2000 tons, and was in the steamer South Carolina, running from Boston to South Carolina. The stmr Massachusetts was built at the same time, but was not successful, and was soon out of commission.

In the 40s and 50s in the little village of South Hyannis, there were 25 men, most of them very young, who left their homes and followed the sea deep water and coasting.

I had two brothers who when 21 years of age were masters of vessels, who later left foreign ports for home and neither were ever heard from. Alex. Crocker, my nephew, when 12 years of age left school, and went up the Mediterranean, shipping as cabin boy with Capt Joseph H. Parker of Hyannis, in barque Wild Fire, and was master quite young of schrs New York and Bay State, packets of the Commercial line. Later he sailed on foreign voyages in barques Sarah Hobart Nash and Alice, new, both hailing from Salem.

There have been many changes since that time. I am reminded of the good old times when coasting was at its best; many of the smaller vessels were built at Osterville by Oliver Hinckley and Deacon Samuel Crosby of Centerville and were built to last.

Vessels coming in here for a harbor had plenty of bunting displayed— American flag, burgee, and pennant fore and aft, and the New York packets, which were many, the names of which I knew well. Some few were named for presidents: The John C. Calhoun, Capt Philander Case of Centerville; Millard Filmore, Joshua Chase; Abraham Lincoln, Henry Davis, Centerville; John Quincy Adams, Capt John Norris, Hyannis. Now for 25 years or more I have seldom seen the American flag displayed.

In looking over the Bath Daily Times, an item appears regarding ship building: In the year 1914 the total merchant tonnage that has been launched from the shipyards of Bath has been 1137 tons, the poorest year since 1813. The best year since was 1900, which had a record of 41,352 tons of merchant shipping.

The prospects for sailing vessels for the future are very poor. Some of the larger vessels, 5 and 6 masters, have been lying idle this past season, freights being so low.

The big steamers and barges that have been built of late are driving the sailing vessels to the wall.

I can look from my lookout and see in fairly good weather, every day in the year, steamers and ocean tugs passing through the South channel with a string of barges in tow. The Crowley fleet of Taunton have had many steamers built of late with a capacity of 7000 tons or more, also other parties, such as Crowell & Thurlow, Boston. Is it any wonder there is nothing for vessels?

There is also a big difference in the wages paid then and now. If I remember rightly the sailors' wages in the 40s and 50s were $15 per month, now they are $30.

Then New York packets with vessels of any small tonnage carried four men before the mast and second mate with general cargoes and two men to the fall, discharging cargoes by hand. Now barges require a very small crew to man them.

I might go on and tell of the changes in this village since the 40s, but will say but a few words. In my recent writings I have said that Hyannis is second to none in the country, with its churches, schools, etc. The Normal school, for which much credit is due to the late Franklin Crocker for the interest he manifested, being at the State House most of the time for one winter, and the interest the whole community showed in raising $11,000 for the location and the mansion occupied by Principal Baldwin.

In closing I would say that probably I have made some errors in my reminiscences. I have but given notes and have had to trust to my memory. In the words of an old song, "The mistakes of my life have been many;" who has not made mistakes?

A. B. C.

No. 17.

LIBRARY *of*

Cape Cod

HISTORY & GENEALOGY

CHURCH COUNCILS

BY WILLIAM C. SMITH

YARMOUTHPORT, MASS.:
O. W. SWIFT, Publisher and Printer,
The "Register" Press,
1924

CHURCH COUNCILS

Mr Editor:

In early times the usual practice among the churches was to settle their troubles and difficulties by means of church councils, composed usually of the pastors and deacons of the neighboring churches. The records of these councils, not a few of which were held on the Cape, are not now easy to find, there having been no regular way for preserving them. For this reason, the following report of a council held at Chatham on Nov. 24, 1715, is of special interest. It was discovered by Mr Stanley W. Smith of Boston, to whom I am indebted for a copy, in a collection of papers in the Library of the Massachusetts Historical Society:

"We the Elders and Messengers of ye next neighbouring Churches to Chatham being invited by ye disagreeing parties to sit in Counsell in a Case of difference relating to ye Ministry there, and to give our Advice thereon according to ye Rules contained in yo Divine Oracles, are now accordingly met, and having considered wt has been laid before us, and finding yt the differences are irreconcilable; together with other things then and there considered; Our Result is as followeth:

1. That ye Towne of Chatham doe give ye Revnd Mr Adams and his Heirs forever wt interest they have in ye House and house lot where he dwells now, he paying to ye Towne fifty pounds of ye hundred mentioned in ye Con hundred mentioned in their Con-

2. that Mr Adams hence forward

296

doe wholly desist from any part of his ministeriall work here.

3. that his Salary, so much of it as is behind for ye time past be paid in fully to him in all convenient time.

4. Yt each party henceforward, under a sense of duty and impressions of ye fear of God, doe carefully avoid any reflections on, or recriminations toward one another, and yt all their differences and discords be buried in oblivion, as being most conducive to ye glory of God, ye good of both parties and leading to ye obtainmnet of another minister to settle in ye Towne.

5. Yt ye Inhabitants of ye Towne doe unite in love, under a sense of duty to their own and children's eternall soules, to invite and bring in a Gospell Minister of suitable qualifications to dispence ye ordinances of Christ to ym as soon as possible may be.

Chatham Nov. 24
    1715.
    Samll Treat
    Nathll Stone
    Danll Grienloaf
    Joseph Doane
    Peter Thacher
    Thomas Freeman
    Chillingswth Foster

Rev Mr Adams, above referred to, was Rev Hugh Adams, a graduate of Harvard College, sometime pastor in South Carolina and after leaving Chatham, pastor for twenty years of the church at Dover, N. H.

    WILLIAM C. SMITH.
Chatham, Mass.
April 15, 1915.

No. 18.

LIBRARY of
Cape Cod
HISTORY & GENEALOGY

HOMER

BY AMOS OTIS

YARMOUTHPORT, MASS.:
C. W. SWIFT, Publisher and Printer,
The "Register" Press,
1924

HOMER

BY AMOS OTIS

CAPTAIN JOHN HOMER, born in England, was the emigrant ancestor of the family.

He was master of a ship trading between Boston and London and came to Boston about 1672. He married in Boston, July 13, 1693, Margery Stephens, and had:

1 John, born Aug. 8, 1694; married 1st, Anne Moster, 1716; 2d, Mary Belknap, 1726; died without issue.
2 Mary, born May 7, 1696; died young.
3 Benjamin, born May 8, 1698; removed to Yarmouth.
5 Michael, born Sept. 26, 1703; married ——, had four sons; died 1760, age 57.
6 Robert, born Mar. 29, 1706, merchant at Honduras; married and left issue.
7 Thomas, born May 6, 1707; married Lydia Kill, June 10, 1736.
8 Mary, born Aug., 1708.

Capt. John Homer died in Boston Nov. 1, 1717, age 70 years. Mrs. Margery Homer died in Yarmouth in 1762, age 95 or over.

BENJAMIN HOMER, son of Captain John, removed to Yarmouth, was a tailor, and resided at Hockanom. He married, Dec. 22, 1721, Elizabeth, daughter of John Crowel, and had:

1 Bethyah, born March 18, 1722; married Benjamin Cobb of Boston.
2 John, born Sept. 29, 1724; married 1st, Abigail Osborne, 1749; 2d, Hannah Carnes, 1772, had issue. Removed first to Boston and thence to Barrington, N. S.; died 1799, age 74.
3 Margery, born June 13, 1727; married 1st, Willard Sears, by whom she had one daughter who married Levi Crowell and removed to Vermont; 2d, —— Higgins.
4 William, born July 14, 1729, a loyalist; died unmarried.
5 Benjamin, born Aug. 5, 1731. Removed to Boston; married, Oct. 23, 1759, Mary Parrott, had issue; died March 30, 1776.
6 Stephen, born April 13, 1734.
7 Thomas, born March 21, 1735-6, "The Valiant Captn."
8 Elizabeth, born Nov. 18, 1738.
9 Robert, born Jan. 28, 1742.

Mrs. Benjamin Homer died in Yarmouth Oct. 24, 1776, age 78. Mrs. Elizabeth Homer died ——.

JOHN HOMER, eldest son of Benjamin, had eight children born in Boston, five dying in infancy. His son John, born July, 1755, died unmarried at Mirrimachi, July 4, 1812; Joseph, born March, 1757, married, had issue, died at Barrington, May 14, 1837, aged 80; and Samuel, born Jan. 15, 1759, married Sarah Smith and had issue.

BENJAMIN HOMER, son of Benjamin, removed to Boston, married Oct. 23, 1759, Mary Parrott, and had:

Benjamin, born June 30, 1761, who married and had issue.
Ruth, married M. P. R. Arsouneau.
Elizabeth, married Judge Amasa Paine.
Mary, married Judge Lot Hall of Westminster, Vermont.
Bethia Cobb, married Col. Oliver Gallup.

STEPHEN HOMER, son of Benjamin, married March 25, 1758, Elizabeth, daughter of —— Chapman. Children born in Yarmouth:

1 Chapman, born Sept. 22, 1758, removed to Kennebec, had issue.
2 Bethia, born Aug. 17, 1760, married Elisha Miller.
3 Betty, born Feb. 6, 1762, died young.
4 Stephen, born July 14, 1763, married Thankful Chapman.
5 Abigail, born May 24, 1765, died young.
6 William, born Dec. 11, 1766, removed to Bucksport, had issue.
7 Zenas, born Dec. 2, 1768.
8 Joshua, born June 2, 1770. Lost at sea. No issue.
9 John, born Feb. 6, 1772. Lost at sea. No issue.
10 David, born Feb. 6, 1773, married Anna Berry.
11 Abigail, born Feb. 20, 1775, died young.
12 Joseph, born July 11, 1777. Lost at sea. No issue.
13 Benjamin, born June 23, 1779, married.
14 Betty, born Jan. 12, 1781, married —— Clough.

The nine sons of Stephen and Elizabeth all lived to mature age and were remarkably tall, the nine averaging six feet three inches. David was the tallest, being six feet, eight or nine inches. All excepting Benjamin went to sea. Stephen Homer's house stood in the low ground east of his father Benjamin's, at Hockanom.

No. 19.

LIBRARY of
Cape Cod
HISTORY & GENEALOGY

The SOUTH DENNIS
MEETING HOUSE

YARMOUTHPORT, MASS.:
C. W. SWIFT, Publisher and Printer,
The "Register" Press,
1924

The SOUTH DENNIS MEETING HOUSE

———

Compiled by
WILLIAM B. BRAGDON

THE SOUTH DENNIS MEETING HOUSE.

In 1674 Daniel Baker built a home in the south part of the Township of Yarmouth, and became the first settler on record of the present village of South Dennis. As others joined him and a small community grew up, the inhabitants were compelled to journey to Yarmouth each Sunday for worship, as they had no church of their own.

When the Rev. Josiah Dennis was ordained pastor of the east part of the town of Yarmouth in 1727, in order to become the minister of the first meeting house erected in the present town of Dennis, he assumed the duties of spiritual adviser of the inhabitants of the south village as well. So the worshipers of this south precinct flocked to the north village.

For 38 years Josiah Dennis devotedly remained the pastor of this district, until his death in 1763, and 30 years later, in 1793, the Township of Dennis was incorporated under the name of this well remembered and well loved man.

The Rev. Nathan Stone succeeded him as pastor, and continued in that office for 40 years, until his death in 1804, but in the meantime the people of South Dennis had decided to erect a meeting house of their own. This was accomplished in 1795 after 121 years had elapsed since Daniel Baker first settled in this section.

The only description we have of this church is from a visitor who briefly remarked, "They have an elegant meeting house with a steeple." But we do know that the building contained 48 pews on the floor and 20 above in the galleries which were on three sides.

Nathan Stone dedicated this meeting house, but neither he, nor his successors, Rev. Holmes and Rev. Haven, preached here more than once in every three weeks.

It was not, however, until Dec. 30, 1817, that South Dennis

3

had a pastor exclusively her own. Then the Rev. John Sanford was ordained as the regular preacher and the church organized. Of the original 29 members, the majority brought letters from the North village. They were the following:

Gorham Baker, Bethia Baker, Susannah Baker, Experience Baker, Sally Baker, Thankful Baker, Rhoda Baker, Mary Baker, Betsy Baker, Polly Baker, Rebecca Bangs, Elizabeth Burgess, Polly Chase, Rhoda Collins, Elisha Crowell, Sarah Crowell, Desire Crowell, Esther Kelley, Thankful Kelley, Thankful Marchant, Anne Matthews, Simeon Nickerson, Keziah Nickerson, Mary Nickerson, Sally Nickerson, Thankful Nickerson, Mehitable Nickerson, Ruth Nickerson and Achsah Robbins.

John Sanford preached in South Dennis for 18 years, when, the population increasing and the meeting house not considered adaptable to enlargement, it was decided in 1835 to tear down the old building and erect a new one.

Accordingly an appraisal was made of the old pews, as follows:

"South Dennis, Feb. 16th, 1835. We the Subscribers being called upon to appraise the South Congregational Meeting House in South Dennis, we do agree in our opinions the Meeting House as it now stands to be worth three hundred and fifty dollars and fifty cents and have leveled the same on the pews as follows viz,

No.					
1	Pew on Lower floor			Cornelius Baker	$4.50
2	"	"	"	"	Jonathan Bangs	5.00
3	"	"	"	"	Samuel Rogers	5.00
4	"	"	"	"	Seth Baker	5.00
5	"	"	"	"	Edward Sears	5.25
6	"	"	"	"	Benj. & Lothrop Thacher	5.50
7	"	"	"	"	Caleb S. Nickerson	5.50
8	"	"	"	"	Jona Bangs & L. Studley	5.50
9	"	"	"	"	Seth & Miller Whelden	5.50
10	"	"	"	"	Gorham Baker	5.50

11	"	"	"	"	Barna & Browning Baker	5.50
12	"	"	"	"	Minister	0.00
13	"	"	"	"	Eleazer Nickerson	5.00
14	"	"	"	"	Elijah Nickerson	5.50
15	"	"	"	"	Samuel Chase	5.50
16	"	"	"	"	Nehemiah Baker	5.50
17	"	"	"	"	Shubael & Obed Nickerson	5.50
18	"	"	"	"	Obed Baxter	5.50
19	"	"	"	"	Polly Nickerson	5.50
20	"	"	"	"	Elisha Crowell & A. Kelley	5.25
21	"	"	"	"	Samuel & Richard Nickerson	5.00
22	"	"	"	"	Samuel Baker	5.00
23	"	"	"	"	Samuel Small & S. Studley	5.00
24	"	"	"	"	Eldridge Baker	4.75
25	"	"	"	"	Ebenezer Baker	7.00
26	"	"	"	"	Jonathan Nickerson	7.50
27	"	"	"	"	Rebecca Baker	8.00
28	"	"	"	"	Eleazer Nickerson	8.50
29	"	"	"	"	Asa Payson	8.50
30	"	"	"	"	John Baker	8.00
31	"	"	"	"	Tho. Crowell	7.00
32	"	"	"	"	Gideon Harden	7.00
33	"	"	"	"	Eleazer Nicks & Gorham Baker	7.00
34	"	"	"	"	Isaiah & Absa Nickerson	7.00
35	"	"	"	"	Benoni Baker	6.50
36	"	"	"	"	Reuben Baker	6.50
37	"	"	"	"	James Nickerson	6.50
38	"	"	"	"	Maj. Maxter (probably Baxter)	6.50
39	"	"	"	"	James Small	7.00
40	"	"	"	"	Sally Baker	7.00
41	"	"	"	"	Dea Elisha Crowell	7.00
42	"	"	"	"	Peter Baker	7.00
43	"	"	"	"	Judah Baker Decd.	8.00
44	"	"	"	"	Isaiah Nickerson	8.50
45	"	"	"	"	Levi Crowell	8.50

5

46	"	"	"	"	Freeman & Uriah Baker	8.00
47	"	"	"	"	Allen Bangs	7.50
48	"	"	"	"	Nehemiah Crowell	7.00
No. 1	"	in gallery	Jediah Burgess Decd.			2.50
2	"	"	"	John Nickerson		2.50
3	"	"	"	Samuel Baker		2.50
4	"	"	"			2.50
5	"	"	"	Nehemiah Baker		2.50
6	"	"	"	Isaac Crowell & others		2.75
7	"	"	"	Eleazer Nickerson		2.75
8	"	"	"	Eleazer Nickerson		2.75
9	"	"	"	Lewis Sears		2.75
10	"	"	"	Shubael Baker Decd.		2.75
11	"	"	"	John Taylor		2.75
12	"	"	"	Ed. Sears		2.75
13	"	"	"	Joseph Crowell decd.		2.75
14	"	"	"	John Baxter		2.75
15	"	"	"	Elisha & Tho. Crowell		2.75
16	"	"	"	Peter Baker		2.50
17	"	"	"	Harden Nickerson		2.50
18	"	"	"	Barnabas Baker		2.50
19	"	"	"	Samuel Chase		2.50
20	"	"	"	Eldridge Baker		2.50

$350.50

And we do likewise give our opinions that it will be the interest of whom it may concern to pull down and build a new one.

South Dennis   February 16th, 1835.
                               John H. Dunbar
                               John Gorham
                               Reuben Ryder."

In order to guarantee the expense of the proposed undertaking of erecting a new church building, voluntary subscription of shares of stock by the parishioners was proposed, and issued as follows:

"We the Subscribers hereby promised and agree to take the number of Shares in the Stock of the Proprietors South Congregational Meeting House in the town of Dennis, as set against our respective names, and to pay all such assessments, as may from time to time be made thereon, agreeable to a note of said Proprietors for the purpose of defraying the expenses of buying and taking down the old Meeting House, and building a new one, contemplated, and paying all lawful charges, and expenses incidental thereto, at such times and in such amounts as said proprietors, at any legal meeting or their officers thereto duly appointed and authorized shall determine. The Stock of said House shall be divided into one hundred shares and no individuals, may subscribe for more than two shares each until all the Parishioners shall subscribe that shall feel disposed and then if the stock of said house is not all taken up the balance to be disposed of in such a manner as may be agreed upon by a note of said Proprietors.

South Dennis February 1835.

Proprietors Names.

Eleazer Nickerson	two shares
Obed Baxter	two shares
Jonathan Bangs	two shares
Barnabas Baker	two shares
Samuel Rogers	two shares
Lathrop T. Thacher	two shares
Obed Baxter, Jr.	two shares
Samuel Nickerson	two shares
Seth T. Whelden	two shares
Howes Baker	two shares
James Nickerson	two shares
John Nickerson	two shares
Ebenezer Baker	one share
Nehemiah Crowell	two shares
Theophelus Nickerson	two shares

7

Miller W. Nickerson	two shares
John Baxter	one share
Samuel Smalley	one share
John Bangs	one share
Isaac Burgess	one share
Samuel Smalley, Jr.	two shares
Alvah Nickerson	two shares
Uriah Baker	one share
Joseph Baker, 2d	two shares
Thomas W. Baker	two shares
Nehemiah Baker	two shares
Freeman Baker	one share
Benjamin Thacher	two shares
Seth T. Whelden, Jr.	two shares
Alexander Nickerson	one share
Ezra H. Baker	two shares
James Learned	two shares
Joel Nickerson	one share
Moses Smalley	one share
Colman Smalley	one share
Elizah Nickerson	one share
Herman Baxter	one share
Atherton H. Baker	one share
Arunah Smalley	one share
Milton Kelley	one share
William Baker	two shares
Warren Crowell	one share
David H. Smalley	one share
Elizah Baxter	one share
Eleazer Baker	one share
Francis Baker	two shares
Nathan Nickerson	one share
Jothan Nickerson	one share
Joseph C. Baker	one share
Grafton Sears	one share

Harvey Crowell	one-half share
Caleb B. Howes	one-half share
James Baker	one share
Watson Baker	two shares
Peter Baker	two shares
Ahirah Baxter	one share
Israel Nickerson, Jr.	one share
Elizah Nickerson, Jr.	one share
Peter B. Harden	one share
Collin C. Baker	one share
Samuel Baker, Jr.	one share
Alpheus Baker	two shares
Freeman Davis	one share
Francis Smalley	one share
Joseph Smalley	one share
Shubael Nickerson, Jr.	two shares
Moses Nickerson	one share
Abigail Smalley 2d	one share
Polly Nickerson	one share
Obed N. Baker	one share
Alpheus Baxter	one share
John W. Williams, Jr.	two shares
Edward T. Williams	two shares
Varenus Harden	one share
John Sanford	two shares
Alfred Swift	one share
Zeno Crowell	one share
Frederick Nickerson	one share
Henry Bangs	one share
Peter Baker, Jr.	two shares
Philander Baker	one share
Isaiah Nickerson, Jr.	one share
Jothan Nickerson	one share
Alvira Kelley	one share
Samuel Chase, 3d	one share

Benjamin Hallet	one share
Lucinda Baker	one share
Wid Mercy Baker	one share
Peleg Howes	one share
Samuel Crowell	one share
Shubael Nickerson	one share
Eleazer Nickerson, Jr.	one share
Simeon Nickerson	one share
Colemon Nickerson	two shares
Harden Nickerson	one share
Otis Baker	one share
Seth T. Nickerson	two shares
Alvin Smalley	one share
Solomon Thacher	two shares
Caleb S. Nickerson	two shares
Wilber Harden	one share
Francis Smalley, 2d	one share
Reuben Cash	one share
Miller Whelden	one share
Barnabus Baker Jr.	two shares
Oren Lewis	two shares
Isaiah Nickerson	one share
Sylvanus Crowell	one share
Freeman Baker, Jr.	one share
Levi Crowell	two shares
Julius Baker	one share

As soon as a guarantee fund had thus been established by this allotment of shares of stock, a Committee of the Proprietors was appointed, composed of Obed Baxter, Luther Child, Nehemiah Crowell, Eleazer Nickerson, Samuel Small, Peter Baker, Samuel Rogers, James Baker and Nehemiah Baker, who entered into a contract on May 11, 1835, with Whittemore Peterson of Duxbury, Mass., for building the new meeting house at a cost of $3,730.00.

The contract was drawn up as follows:

"Be it remembered that on this eleventh day of May in the year of our Lord one thousand eight hundred and thirty-five it is agreed between Obed Baxter, Luther Child, Nehemiah Crowell, Eleazer Nickerson, Samuel Small, Peter Baker, Samuel Rogers, James Baker and Nehemiah Baker all of Dennis in the County of Barnstable a Committee of the Proprietors of the South Congregational Meeting House in said Dennis and Whittemore Peterson of Duxbury in the County of Plymouth Carpenter in manner and form following (to wit) The said Peterson for the consideration hereafter mentioned doth for himself his heirs executors and administrators covenant with the said Committee that he the said Peterson or his assigns shall and will within the space of six months next after the date hereof in a good and workmanlike manner, at Dennis well and substantially erect build and finish one Congregational meeting House according to the dimensions following viz. Forty-four feet in front and sixty-five feet in the rear with twenty-three feet posts and compose the same of the following materials, white hemlock timber and cover said House with hemlock merchantable boards clapboard the front end and sides with best clapboards shingles or clapboards the back end paper the seams roof to be shingled with best pine shingles door steps of yellow pine plank gothick windows glass nine by thirteen imitation heads with blinds and weights a projecting tower belframe ball, spear, vane pointers and stone chimney paint said House inside and out with three coats for the sum hereafter named if said Committee may so direct pews settee backs and arms with mahogany capping ivory buttons on the scroll and brass buttons on the Pew doors pews of such width and length as said committee may order mahogany desk and columns like the Sandwich new meeting house entry in such a form and width as said committee may hereafter direct Plastering to be of the hard finish with a center piece and said Peterson further agrees to furnish all the materials as aforesaid for building said house above the foundations at his own expense of such quality as good judges shall say it is equal to the Sandwich Meeting House in every respect except-

11

ing what is above specified and the clock and aparatus   In consideration whereof the said Committee doth for themselves and said proprietors Covenant with said Peterson his heirs and assigns well and truly to pay unto the said Peterson the sum of thirty-seven hundred and thirty dollars providing said Peterson paints said house as aforesaid otherwise the sum of thirty-five hundred and fifteen dollars in manner and form following (to wit) one half thereof when said house is raised one fourth part thereof when said house is plastered the remaining part thereof in full for said work in thirty days after the same shall be completed finished. And also they the said committee shall and will provide a place for the erection of said house on or before the tenth day of July next And said Peterson further agrees to risk said house after it shall be plastered until it shall be delivered to said committee To the true and faithful performance of the several articles and agreements above mentioned the said committee and Peterson do hereby respectfully bind themselves their heirs executors administrators and assigns firmly by these presents each to the other in the penalty sum of three thousand dollars.   In witness whereof they have interchangeably set their hands and seals the day and year above written seventeenth line from top on second page interlined before signing.

Signed sealed in	Whittimore Peterson L. S.
presence of us	Eleazer Nickerson L. S.
Seth T. Nickerson)	Obed Baxter L. S.
Jotham Nickerson)	Luther Child L. S.
	Nehemiah Baker L. S."

The building was raised in August, completed in November and dedicated in December, 1835.

Mr. Peterson attached his final receipt to the contract when the church was finished and turned over to the committee, as follows:

"South Dennis, Nov. 21, 1835.
Recd pay for the within agreement and given up said house to the

12

Committee viz; Obed Baxter, Nehemiah Baker and James Baker who gave a note to Balance of $988. as per bill.

Whittemore Peterson."

On Jan. 11, 1836, an auction sale took place of the pews for the new meeting house. The sale was made in two hours and ten minutes and yielded $6006.00, to cover the sum of about $4600.00 which was the entire cost of the new building.

The record of this sale is as follows:

"Conditions of Sale and payments of the pews in the New South Congregational Meeting House in South Dennis are as follows, viz, The highest bidder of the South Congregational Parishinors are to be the purchasers. They are as follows viz, Cash at the Signing of the deed by Obed Baxter Eleazer Nickerson and Peter Baker a Committee chosen for that purpose—Any person wishing credits on one half for twelve months can be accommodated by paying Bank interest with good Security.

South Dennis, Jany. 11, 1836.

Francis Wood Auctioneer.

Howes Baker, Pew No. 45,	$ 95.00
Miller W. Nickerson, Pew No. 47.	108.00
Theophelus Nickerson, Pew No. 49,	130.00
Nehemiah Baker, Pew No. 51,	121.00
Shubael Nickerson, Jr., Pew No. 53.	116.00
Caleb S. Nickerson, Pew No. 55.	105.00
Milton Kelley, Pew No. 57,	96.00
Frederick Nickerson, Pew No. 59,	82.00
William Baker, Pew No. 61,	77.00
Allen Bangs, Jr., Pew No. 63,	65.00
Harden Nickerson, Pew No. 65,	55.00
Harvey Crowell, Pew No. 67,	51.00
Obed Baker, 2d, Pew No. 69,	40.00
Rev. John Sanford, Pew No. 73.	19.00
Francis Smalley, Pew No. 71,	27.00
Obed Baxter, Pew No. 38.	100.00

13

Eleazer Nickerson, Pew No. 39,	120.00
Eleazer Nickerson, Pew No. 40,	98.00
Barnabus Baker, Pew No. 41,	80.00
Nehemiah Crowell, Pew No. 42,	77.00
Uriah Baker, Pew No. 43,	100.00
Shubal Nickerson, Pew No. 44,	102.00
Freeman Baker, Jr., Pew No. 46,	87.00
Colman Nickerson, Pew No. 48,	85.00
Ezra H. Baker, Pew No. 50,	88.00
Joseph W. Jones, Pew No. 52,	94.00
Levi Crowell, Pew No. 54,	86.00
Obed Baxter, Jr., Pew No. 56,	86.00
Barnabus Baker, Jr., Pew No. 58,	85.00
Peter Baker, Pew No. 60,	80.00
Ebenezer Baker, Pew No. 62,	80.00
Peter Baker, Jr., Pew No. 64,	71.00
John Baxter, Pew No. 66,	60.00
Samuel Smalley, Pew No. 68,	51.00
Israel Nickerson, Jr., Pew No. 70,	41.00
Sylvanus Crowell, Pew No. 72,	29.00
Arunah Smalley, Pew No. 74,	22.00
Isaac Burgess, Pew No. 29,	130.00
Samuel Rogers, Pew No. 27,	115.00
Samuel Nickerson, Pew No. 25,	116.00
Benjamin Hallet, Pew No. 23,	115.00
Seth T. Whelden, Pew No. 21,	106.00
Watson Baker, Pew No. 19,	110.00
Alvah Nickerson, Pew No. 17,	91.00
Philander Baker, Pew No. 15,	91.00
Seth T. Whelden, Jr., Pew No. 13,	86.00
Benjamin Thacher, Pew No. 11,	83.00
Varenus Harden, Pew No. 9,	71.00
John Bangs, Pew No. 7,	64.00
Warren Crowell, Pew No. 5,	41.00
Reuben Cash, Pew No. 3,	30.00

Miller Whelden, Pew No. 37,	100.00
Isaiah Nickerson, Pew No. 36,	126.00
Eleazer Nickerson, Jr., Pew No. 35,	100.00
Lothrop Thacher, Pew No. 34,	95.00
Seth T. Whelden, Pew No. 33,	88.00
Elijah Baxter, Pew No. 32,	101.00
Jonathan Bangs, Pew No. 30,	101.00
Elijah Nickerson, Pew No. 28,	100.00
Wilber Harden, Pew No. 26,	96.00
Alexander Nickerson, Pew No. 24,	91.00
Peter Harden, Pew No. 22,	92.00
Freeman Rogers, Pew No. 20,	93.00
Samuel Chase 3d, Pew No. 18,	91.00
John Nickerson, Pew No. 16,	90.00
Alvin Small, Pew No. 14,	80.00
James Leonard, Pew No. 12,	87.00
James Smalley, Jr., Pew No. 10,	80.00
Julius Baker, Pew No. 8,	59.00
Lothrop Thacher, Pew No. 6,	60.00
Richard Nickerson, Pew No. 4,	49.00
Colman Smalley, Pew No. 2,	43.00
James Rogers, Pew No. 1,	26.00
	$6,006.00"

The following is a detailed account of the financial transactions relating to the demolishing of the old meeting house and the completion of the new:

"An Account of Sales of old Meeting House, as follows:
1835, Dec. 28

Sold at auction,	$210.36	
Due from Lewis Sears,	2.05	
	$212.41	$212.41

Sold at private sale to the following persons:
John W. Williams,	$24.57

Ebenezer Ryder,	3.60	
Benjamin Howland,	2.50	
Elkanah Howland,	21.18	
Judah Baker,	2.24	
Nehemiah Baker,	1.50	
Ezra H. Baker,	4.93	
Cahim Conant (980 ft. board $7½)	14.85	
" " Tunber,	6.61	
Peter Baker,	16.81	
Samuel Baker, Jr.,	3.04	
John Baxter,	5.52	
Israel Nickerson, Jr.,	4.28	
A. J. Hinkley,	1.05	
Henry Nickerson,	1.20	113.88
		$326.29

An account of sales of old pipe and other articles, July 18, 1837.

To Benj. Thacher,	$7.49	
Peter Baker,	2.88	
Allen Bangs, Jr.,	.14	
Allen Bangs,	.21	
M. W. Nickerson,	.30	
Howes Baker,	.81	
N. Baker,	.85	
Milton Kelley,	.36	
F. Nickerson,	3.12	
	$16.16	

Account of cost of Old Meeting House as follows, viz:

Old meeting house as appraised,	$350.50	
Appraisers Bill, (Paid by Samuel Nickerson)	7.00	
	$357.50	$357.50

Paid by Maj. Baxter

Cost for taking down old house,	$65.00	
Dr. Swift work removing do.,	7.50	
Simeon Nickerson, do.,	2.00	
Samuel Moody, do.,	1.25	
Maj. O. Baxter, do.,	10.00	
Gideon Harden, do.,	1.50	
	$87.50	87.50
Miller Whelden bill,	9.00	
Eleazer Nickerson, do.,	4.37	
	$13.37	13.37
		$458.12

Account of cost of New Meeting House

Peter Baker, bill,	$8.00
Benjamin Thacher, do.,	6.50
Whittemore Peterson, do.,	3,785.53
Samuel Small, do.,	21.00
Coleman Small, do.,	5.24
Samuel Small, Jr., do.,	22.32
Maj. Obed Baxter, do.,	475.52
Maj. Obed Baxter, cash paid interest on bank note,	45.00
Maj. Obed Baxter, on int. on cost 13M,	6.00
Samuel Small, Jr., bill,	1.09
James Leonard, bill,	1.10
Eleazer Nickerson, bill for cushion,	36.38
James Baker, bill for buttons,	1.00
Nehemiah Baker, bill,	18.48
Samuel Rogers, bill,	3.72
	$4,457.58

Whole cost of old Meeting House as appraised, Expense of taking down and removing included	458.12	
	$4,915.70	
Contra Cr.		
By sales of old house,	326.24	
	$4,589.41	
John Baxter, bill,	$1.00	
Nehemiah Baker, paid auctioner,	1.50	
	$2.50	2.50
		$4,591.91
Benjamin Hallet, bill,	$1.00	
Watson Baker, bill,	2.00	
Miller W. Nickerson, bill,	2.00	
Samuel Nickerson, interest on 7$ for yr.,	.42	
Samuel Nickerson, for candles,	.04	
Miller W. Nickerson, bill,	1.50	
Miller Whelden, bill,	6.75	
Mistake in Ezra Baker bill,	1.24	14.95
		$4,606.86
Dec. 1836		
Samuel Small, bill,	$14.33	
Almond G. Hinckley, do.,	9.15	
Samuel Small, Jr., do.,	36.28	
James Leonard, do.,	.52	
Benjamin Thacher, do.,	40.07	
Coleman Small, do.,	4.50	
John Baxter, do.,	12.75	
Allen Bangs, Jr., bill,	14.07	
Joshua B. Bangs, bill,	.67	
David Kelley, bill,	1.08	

Allen Bangs, bill,	2.75	
William Baker, bill,	24.06	
Gideon Harden, bill,	6.12	
Varanus Harden, bill,	1.08	
Samuel Chase, Jr., bill,	.50	
Alvah Nickerson, bill,	3.75	
Heman Baxter, bill,	6.00	
Peter Baker's bill of paints of Akins,	43.30	
Caleb S. Nickerson, 30 feet board,	.60	
Josiah Foster, bill,	180.39	
H. Underwood, bill,	23.74	
Miller Whelden, bill,	1.17	
Bill of carpets,	23.27	
Bill of pulpit lamps,	36.50	
Bill of curtain,	101.25	
Bill of chandelier,	100.00	
Bill for springs for doors,	2.62	
John B. Doane, bill,	14.49	
Joseph C. Baker,	.50	
Joshua Baker, bill,	.84	
Miller W. Nickerson, bill,	.94	
Samuel Nickerson, bill,	2.09	
Peter Baker, bill,	27.80	
Obed Nickerson,	1.58	
Joshua Robbins, bill,	20.42	
Samuel Small, bill for taking down chimney etc.,	8.00	
Nehemiah Baker's bill for cash paid, etc.,	10.50	
Reserved for repairing vane,	30.00	
Reserved, one Bible for pulpit,	8.00	
Reserved, three lamps,	6.00	
Reserved, shovel, tongs and bellows,	1.25	822.91
		$5,429.77
Money paid Jonathan Nickerson for Grave Yard,	$20.00	
For recording a deed of do.,	.50	

Maj. O. Baxter's bill of sundries,	10.36
Falling short on money,	.47
Samuel Smalley, bill for services,	8.00
Peter Baker, bill for services,	9.70
Samuel Rogers, bill for services,	5.00
Nehemiah Baker, bill for services,	15.00
Nehemiah Crowell, bill for services,	5.00
Obed Baxter, bill for services,	15.00
Eleazer Nickerson, bill for services,	10.00
Miller W. Nickerson, bill for services,	1.00
Two earthen pots for stoves,	.20
Samuel Small, Jr., bill for chest,	1.50
Clerk and Treasurer's fees,	2.00
	$5,733.50
Divided amongst proprietors,	370.87
	$6,104.37

Contra Credit

Amount of sales from pews,	$6,006.00
Interest on 763$ notes,	45.78
Interest from Peter Baker,	23.83
To 12 gals. Linseed oil, Maj. Baxter,	12.60
Account of sales of materials left of the Meeting House,	16.16
	$6,104.37"

In the year 1874, the Rev. Wm. C. Reed, the eighth pastor in succession from John Sanford, compiled an alphabetical list of the members of the South Dennis church from its organization June 16, 1817, to January 1, 1870, which contained the names of 301 persons, including the 29 original members. From 1850 to 1875 the church membership was at its highest.

On Sunday, August 14, 1910, the Rev. John C. Labaree, who was then pastor, preached a most interesting "Historical Sermon" for the seventy-fifth anniversary of the erection of the meeting house. As he mentioned many names bearing upon the life of the church and the community, it is not out of place to quote from a portion of his address:

"Over against the preacher's lofty desk rose the still loftier choir-gallery, where presided as chorister, Mr. Benjamin Thacher, Sen., supported in the service of song by Joseph and Edward, Joshua and Laban Baker, Elijah Baxter, Colman Small, Marshall S. Underwood, and yet others, on the men's side; and of the women might be heard Mrs. Theophilus Nickerson, Mrs. Sarah Baker Covill, Mrs. Mercy Baxter, Miss Lizzie Small, and still others; while the stringed instruments were served by Reuben Baker, father and son, Benjamin Thacher, Jr., Jonathan and Henry Bangs, and probably others.

"Elisha Crowell stands at the head of the list of deacons, with Simeon Nickerson as his associate in office. Then follow John Bangs and Nehemiah Crowell; Moses Baker and Samuel Small, Jr. These are especially the deacons of the olden time, the last named having been born in 1802 and was a member of the church 57 years. . . . Then came C. M. Hulbert and A. J. Hersey. . . .

"The Sunday school and Bible class were evidently born in the old church. Deacon Samuel Small, Jr., Theophilus Nickerson, and Benjamin Thacher are said to have been the founders of the school. Among the early teachers were Deacon Small, Miss Polly Bangs, Susan Hallet Nickerson, and Miss P. Annie Wheldon, and Mrs. Sarah Wheldon. . . .

"It is well to recall and put on record the names of some of the humble and devoted women 'who served God and fell on sleep.' The name of one such angel of light as Miss Polly Bangs is a more precious possession to a church than stocks and bonds. She was the first president of the Sewing Circle. She read her Bible through once a year for forty years, and in every way was a help and blessing to the entire community. . . .

21

"Nor will the 'Angel over the Right Shoulder' suffer oblivion to cover the names and deeds of such mothers in Israel as Mrs. Gorham Nickerson, Mrs. Hannah Baker, Mrs. Miller Nickerson, Mrs. Ann Collins, with others from the West village—a goodly company—Mrs. Amanda S. Baker, Mrs. Reuben Baker.

"In the dry and monotonous catalogue of names, one comes occasionally upon such a bright line as this—'Keziah Nickerson,' an original member, wife of James Nickerson, Sr., who died, 1823, aged 73 years; 'venerated for her piety.' Brief but beautiful eulogy."

The dedication sermon by Rev. John Sanford in December, 1835, concluded with these words:

"To the only living and true God, the Great Jehovah, the Father, the Son and the Holy Ghost, we do joyfully and reverently dedicate this House.

"To Him we dedicate this Pulpit.

"To Him we dedicate these Pews.

"To Him we dedicate this Communion Table.

"To Him we dedicate these Walls.

"To Him we dedicate this entire Building.

"And now what wait we for but thy blessing. This House, O God, is thine. Here record thy name; here meet thy waiting people. Here may this people of every age and class, through many passing years, repair and be fed with living bread. May the glory of this latter House far exceed the glory of the former House. May it remain from generation to generation as a token that the Lord is among this people; that the church of the Redeemer, which is gathered here, is the object of His care, and shall remain so, as long as the sun and the moon shall endure."

William B. Bragdon

22

No. 20.

LIBRARY *of*
Cape Cod
HISTORY & GENEALOGY

Old Indian Meeting House at Mashpee

YARMOUTHPORT, MASS.:
C. W. SWIFT, Publisher and Printer,
The "Register" Press,
1923

OLD INDIAN MEETINGHOUSE AT MASHPEE REOPENED

After a lapse of more than twenty years, the old Indian chapel at Mashpee, near the old Barnstable road, has been opened again for worship. The service of rededication took place Sunday, Sept. 9, 1923, at 1:30 in the afternoon, and the president of Harvard university, which has for years paid an annual sum to the Indians of Mashpee towards the support of their chapel, was among the speakers. President Lowell, in fact, is a summer neighbor of those Indians, for his lands in Cotuit are not far from the Indian town.

In 1711 "a pious man, named Daniel Williams, died in England and in his will made the following provision: 'I give the remainder of my estate to be paid yearly to the College at Cambridge, or to such as are employed to manage the blessed work of converting the poor Indians there, to promote which I design this part of my gift.'"

The income of this fund is now about $700 a year, but living expenses are such that the Mashpees have to supplement this sum with enough to bring the total to $1000 for the support of a preacher. Just now this preacher is Rev George W. LaFlush, and these Christian Indians are Baptists and have been so for many years.

According to the records, the Indian chapel was built in 1684, and a glance at its wide floor boards of soft pine, its narrow-seated box pews and the high risers to the stairs leading to the gallery assures one of the age of the building.

Cyrus Edwards, the tax collector of Mashpee and a master carpenter, has recently put the chapel to rights, for in the twenty years of neglect it had become dilapidated enough, and many visitors have wondered at its abandoned appearance.

Mr Edwards is not only a master carpenter, but a stone mason, a painter and a general handy man. He and three helpers did the work, which included several branches of the building trades.

Although a pure-blooded Indian, this handy man is entirely modern in his conversation, and is less reticent than his forefathers. "Gee whiz," he remarks, "it was some job. The sills were gone, and although I put jacks under each corner and relaid the foundation where it was necessary (the building has no cellar) I couldn't make the floor level, and I don't think it ever was level. After jacking up the corners, the roof had to be trussed and a new roof put on, then we built a new chimney, using most of the old bricks, and we painted outside and inside and kalsomined all through."

So the chapel stands now clean and fresh. Half of an old millstone is before each of the entrance doors, the same millstones which have stood before the chapel for years; the outside is of the usual white paint and green blinds appearance, and inside the restoration includes painted floor and stairs of light blue, with canary-colored pews and black walnut rails. The gallery is shallow, and in the accustomed place opposite the pulpit, on the front of the gallery, is a good-sized clock. A wood-burning stove of heroic proportions is in the centre, with a pipe stretching to a flue behind the pulpit platform. Thus

3

the worshippers are likely to be warmer than their forefathers were, warmer during their devotions, in fact, than the forefathers of the white man—and a cold church is a sad detriment to spiritual reflection. Indeed it is not planned to have service in this restored chapel in midwinter on stormy days, but services will be held hereafter during the spring, summer and fall months, and at other times weather permitting. The parish has a comfortable parsonage in the village.

The Indian chapel has not always been where it is today. It is now in the midst of an Indian graveyard, and it is fair to say that instead of starting a graveyard around a church, as in most cases, this is an instance where the church has been moved to the graveyard.

And it is literally true. The Indian chapel was built at Briant's Neck, in the east part of the town, on the road from Cotuit to Sandwich. A man named Coleman built it for the Mashpees and in exchange they gave him all the land extending for half a mile from the big pond.

In 1854 the chapel was moved three miles to its graveyard site; and the graveyard, at upwards of 250 years of age, is somewhat older than the chapel.

The reason for the removal was economic. In former days, the Indians lived mostly near the ponds. Fishing and hunting were their vocations; but more recently they have taken to farming and have made new homes away from the ponds. They still have their fishing privileges, however, which they hold under a permanent grant.

From all directions the people gathered on Sept. 9, the day of rededication, nearly every village from Hyannis to Wareham being represented in the congregation of some 500 persons who had come together for the service of reopening. So great was the crowd that the little meetinghouse could not begin to hold them and the services were held in the grove in front.

The exercises were as follows:
Organ prelude.
Doxology.
Invocation, Rev Mr LaFlash.
Scripture reading, Lawrence D. Hinckley, pastor at Cedarville.
"The Church in the Wildwood," Mashpee choir.
Historical address, Dr A. Lawrence Lowell, president Harvard university.
Cornet solo, Gabriel Frazier.
"Praise His Name Forever," choir.
Prayer of Consecration, Mr LaFlash.
Dedication sermon, Rev Frank W. Dunham, pastor Cotuit Federated church.
Duet, "Ever Near," Mr and Mrs Laurie Green.
"How Firm a Foundation," choir.
Dedication prayer, Rev Edwin B. Dolan, missionary Massachusetts Baptist convention.
Duet, "Steer for the Harbor," Rev G. R. LaFlash and Rev Elizabeth B. LaFlash.
Unveiling of Tablet, address by Dr Alfred Johnson of Brookline.
America.

The tablet which marks the renewal of the use of the old chapel as a house of worship, has been placed on a small boulder in front of the meeting house and bears this inscription:

OLD INDIAN CHURCH
Built in 1684
Remodeled in 1717
Rededicated in 1923
In Memory of Friends Who Labored
Among the Indians
To the Ones Who Gave More
Grounded Hopes of Adoration
To the Things of God
In 1711 Daniel Williams Left a Trust Fund in Charge of Harvard College for the Perpetuation of Preaching to the Indians

Indian Preachers
Simon Popmonet
Solomon Briant
William Apes

Joseph Amos, the Blind Preacher That it may stand in all the future years the indestructible Record of a Rugged Race

Now to their gentle memory be naught but kind regards and to their quiet ashes—Peace

A unique feature of the occasion was the appearance of Chief Nelson Simons (Wabin Annung) and a few other full-blooded Indians in Indian costume.

The history of Mashpee seems to have centered around the chapel life, for its leaders were identified not only with civic affairs but with the religious life of the community.

In 1658, Richard Bourne effected a settlement of the boundary line between the Indian settlement and the town of Barnstable, and soon afterwards secured a patent for the Indians. In 1693 the government appointed guardians for the Indians, but affairs went poorly until in 1760 Reuben Cognehew went to England and in person presented to the king complaints against the Colonial government, and permission was given the Mashpees to choose their own officers. Dissatisfaction continued, however, and in May, 1833, a council in Mashpee sent resolutions to the legislature. The leaders were Ebenezer Attaquin, Daniel B. Amos, Ezra Attaquin, and others. They were imprisoned, but in March, 1834, Mashpee was incorporated as a district, and the Indians began to manage their own affairs, assisted by a state commissioner.

They chose their own selectmen and school committee, land was partitioned among proprietors, and deeds were recorded. The first selectmen, chosen in 1834, were Ezra Attaquin, Isaac Coombs and Israel Amos. Charles Marston of Barnstable was the first commissioner.

Returning briefly chronologically, the History of Barnstable County states that in 1767 there were 21 shingled houses in Mashpee; that in 1500 there were 50 houses, and that wigwams had practically disappeared. In the late eighties the Indian population was 311, with 79 voters. There are fewer male voters today.

Richard Bourne set out to evangelize the Indians in 1661—they were then called South Sea Indians as well as Marshpees—and in 1670 was ordained pastor, "assisted by Mr Eliot and Mr Cotton, who came from Plymouth."

They were succeeded by Simon Popmonet, an Indian; Rev Joseph Bourne, Solomon Briant and Rev Gideon Hawley. In 1811, Rev Phineas Fish of Sandwich succeeded Hawley. Fish was a thorn in the flesh of the Indians, who maintained that he took the salary and held church for the white people, and discouraged the attendance of the In-

5

diana. William Apes, a Pequot preacher, was adopted by the Mashpees in 1833.

Meantime, "Blind Joseph" Amos had started a society in opposition to Mr Fish. The parish was organized in July, 1840, resolutions hostile to Mr Fish were adopted, and at the close of the meeting Mr Fish was forcibly ejected, and the lock on the door of the chapel changed. There followed a succession of white preachers down to the present day.

There has been public instruction in Mashpee since 1831, when the legislature appropriated $400 for two schools—one at North Village and one at South Village. There has been a postoffice there since 1870, and it is in a small ell attached to the house in which Chief Simons lives.

The war record of the Mashpees is good. Seventy men were killed in the Revolution, and a number in the Civil war, both army and navy. With a diminished population, the Mashpees still sent 24 men to the World war, and most of them went across.

Nelson Simons, the chief, says that in spite of all equalities of civilization granted his people, the tribal form persists, though it is more traditional than official. Nevertheless, matters come up which are settled in council, apart from town meeting, and thus Simons is a leader of some 250 souls. He is a pure type of Indian—serious, slow of speech, dignified. He is studying law at Boston university, and has one more year there. He says: "I hope some day to be a student at Harvard college; it would be the joy of my life if I could do that."

Chief Simons became head of the Mashpees by inheritance from his great-uncle, Watson Hammond, who, in the past century, was a member of the state legislature. Simons is 37 years old, is not married, and in summer works to earn the money for his winter schooling. He is known to many sportsmen as a guide.

Roughly sketching the history of Mashpee, Chief Simons says: "After many troubles, both in church and civil affairs, a system of partial self-government was installed in 1834, but it was not until 1870 that a charter of incorporation as a town was granted. In later years, the inhabitants of Mashpee have improved their condition greatly, particularly since the introduction of the cranberry culture. They soon fell into the ways of their white brothers who follow the sea and you will find in almost every house in Mashpee someone who can tell you of voyages which kept him away for three or four years on a trip.

"As the town is located ten miles from a railway station, it makes transportation an expensive problem, therefore we have no manufacturing, and the people have their individual farms and raise enough to carry them through the winter. Hunting and fishing are an important part of their livelihood as there are plenty of wild animals, which, when caught serve both for food and the income that the furs bring in. Fishing is excellent at all seasons of the year. Today we manage our own town affairs, have our own schools and church.

"The most interesting thing about the Indian is that which at first we are likely to think of, his humanity—his quality of being human. In all respects he is like the average human being. Intimate relations with him show us that in him may be found the same good qualities that our white brothers possess. Many of you are disposed to think of the Indian as irresponsible, acting only on the whims and emotions of the moment, but as a matter of fact, the Indian is conservative.

"I might mention their way of travelling. It was a custom of the Indian to go ahead of his wife and children. One Indian was asked why he went ahead of his wife and children, while they trailed behind. The Indian replied by asking: 'Why do you always walk beside your wife?' The white man explained: 'It is the survival of an old custom when a man had to have his right hand free to protect her against attack.' The Indian nodded and brought out this explanation—his custom also was one of protection in the wilderness. He walked ahead to hold back the underbrush and clear the way for the women, and also to be on guard against wild animals or attack. For safety the woman carried the pack, and, shielded by her also from the unknown, came the children last of all.

"One injustice to the Indian is due to a sort of national hostility in the American people of the older generation by the school books and teachings of their youth. They teach one to know the Indian only by his occasional and natural revolt against the process of extermination, which he foresaw and struggled against. Not once in those books do I remember of a reference to the attitude of the Indians towards those early explorers, who, from the settling of New England in 1620, were so completely at their mercy. At that time the Indians met the pioneers with friendliness, gave them food, helped them to find their way through the forest, and parted from them with regret. It was not until the Indians began to doubt the good faith of the early settlers, not until they found themselves taken as prisoners to be sold into slavery, that they began their frantic warfare for self-preservation. They had then and still have certain fundamental racial characteristics. They are loyal, proudly dignified and very generous to their fellow men. Today there is no grievance held against the Indian on account of his past history. He fought against conquest in his own fashion, as weak nations have always fought against the strong. No method of his was worse than the tortures devised by civilized men in the recent war.

"There should be a vast pride in these people who go back to the original American stock, who descend from people who were mighty hunters, brave fighters, and whose original creed for simple honesty and dignity, and the unbroken work stands today for a code by which a people must stand or fall.

"The Indians of today do not lead the life of their forefathers. They do not follow the trails as in the days of the past. Instead of wigwams and teepees, we now live in modern houses with all the conveniences that circumstances allow. The Indians of today face a very serious problem—that of upholding the race. This problem cannot be solved by them alone. There must be nation-wide understanding of our needs. Serious thinking, patriotic American men and women must understand the conditions that surround us. It is our idea

7

to enlighten the people on the present-day Indian and by sane, impartial methods to obtain the corrective measures necessary to give the American Indian the rightful place in modern society.

"It matters not whether we can agree with their theology or with their form of government. That which was of the greatest importance then, and now, is that they place the spiritual above the material, the possessions of the mind and heart above those of the body, qualities which make life richer and more comfortable. Today we cannot better express ourselves here than by sweeping away our errors, and plan here for our great country, the standard of justice and real human brotherhood, a noble spirit for all mankind, the spirit of America."

Thus does Chief Simons speak of "My People," and with great pride.

And he sums up with several stanzas under the heading, "Thoughts of Mashpee," which express the spirit and the romance of these original citizens—citizens now of the state:

Oh! dear little hills of my people,
What long ago secrets art hiding?
What fears and hopes long expended
When all the forests were virgin?

Only my little village—the woods
Unbroken for ages surrounding—
Lies as it lay in the long ago,
The Indian village of Mashpee.

Long past is the struggle barbaric—
Long since has the hatchet been buried—
But ever the deeds of our warriors
Shall live in the garden of mem'ry.

Shall blossom again in full splendor—
In deeds of a valorous merit,
By warriors of now-a-day living
In acts of Faith and of Kindness.

No. 21.

LIBRARY of
Cape Cod
HISTORY & GENEALOGY

The Revolutionary War Service of Nathan Crosby

YARMOUTHPORT, MASS.:
C. W. SWIFT, Publisher and Printer,
The "Register" Press,
1923

THE REVOLUTIONARY SERVICE OF NATHAN CROSBY.

(From The Yarmouth Register.)

To the Editor of The Register:

I was in Yarmouth the latter part of June last and had a talk with Mr Albert Taylor and his sister about Cape Cod ancestry, particularly the Taylor and Crosby families.

On my return to Washington, D. C., I looked the matter up and send you the following which I trust will be of interest to your readers.

The Revolutionary records of the War department show:

"Nathan Crosby, private, served in companies commanded by, or designated as, Capt Isaac Warren, Major Andrew Peters, Capt Seth Drew and Capt Luther Bailey, 2d Regt Massachusetts commanded successively by Col John Bailey and Lieut Col Sprout. He enlisted April 20, 1777, for 3 years and his name last appears on the company muster roll for April, 1781."

The Pension Office shows his application for pension, the granting thereof and certificates attached which I give in full as they are of exceptional interest.

Certificate No. 1: "I was a Lieutenant in Capt Luther Bailey's Co. in the 2d Massachusetts Regiment of the Revolutionary War from the first of June 1781 about two years and that Nathan Crosby was a soldier in his Co. for the duration of the war with Great Britain. He did his duty faithfully during that time and continued unto the end of the war."

William Taylor, Lieut.
November 6, 1809.

Certificate No. 2: "I hereby certify that Nathan Crosby, the person alluded to by the certificates of Capt Luther Bailey and Lieut William Taylor, was a soldier in the 2d Massachusetts Regiment during the late Revolutionary War, that he served in said capacity faithfully till the close of said war and was regularly discharged with the Badge of Merit. His discharge was signed by that Excellent man, the late General George Washington and was countersigned in the books of said Regiment by me."

William Torrey,
late Adjutant of 3d Regt
Pembroke, Mass., Sept. 6, 1814.

Certificate No. 3: "I hereby certify to the integrity of Nathan Crosby and that he has been a faithful Revolutionary soldier and that while in the Defense of his Country, by some misfortune received an unhappy wound on his head, the bad effects of which in my opinion entitles him to the commiseration of everyone."

Rufus King, Physician
Ware, Octo. 11, 1815.

Certificate No. 4: "I certify that Nathan Crosby is a resident of the Town of Ware and has been for more than 25 years—when not journeying—and is esteemed for his fidelity and strict regard for the truth, but in very indigent circumstances, and from the best information that I can obtain is entitled to some compensation or pension from the General Government."

William Bowdoin,
Justice of the Peace.
Hampshire s.s. Aug. 24, 1816.

Certificate No. 5: "I hereby certify that Nathan Crosby, the person alluded to in the above certificate, was in a platoon under my command at the battle of Monmouth and that from the extreme heat and fatigue of the day he was in consequence thereof much debilitated."

John Alden, late Capt
in 2d Massachusetts Regt.
Duxbury, Oct. 18, 1816.

Capt Luther Bailey adds to his certificate this poetic stanza:

"Our God and soldiers alike we adore,
Just at the brink of ruin and not before.
After deliverence both alike requited,
Our God forgotten, our soldiers slighted."

John Reed, in the House of Representatives February 14, 1817, certifies that Nathan Crosby, applicant for pension, received injury at the memorable battle of Monmouth and recommends that he be allowed a half pension, viz: $4 per month. This was referred to the Committee on Pensions and Revolutionary Claims on Feb. 15, 1817.

The Pension Office brief of the case shows:

Nathan Crosby, private, Capt L. Bailey's Co., 2d Mass. Regt, during Revolutionary War.

Inscribed on the Mass. roll at $4 per month to commence Feb. 14, 1817.

Certificate of pension issued March 24, 1817, and sent to Benjamin Austin, Esqr., agent for Invalid Pensions, Boston, Mass.

L. M. Mooers,
Washington, D. C.
July 20, 1923. Takoma Park Station.

No. 22.

LIBRARY *of*
Cape Cod
HISTORY & GENEALOGY

The Revolutionary War Service *of* Ansel Taylor

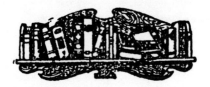

YARMOUTHPORT, MASS.:
C. W. SWIFT, Publisher and Printer,
The "Register" Press,
1923

THE REVOLUTIONARY SERVICE OF ANSEL TAYLOR.

Ansel Taylor of Yarmouth was born Nov. 10, 1748. His wife was Azuba Hallett, born Dec. 4, 1752, daughter of Jonathan Hallett and Thankful Crowell.

Azuba died June, 1832. Ansel died July 11, 1850, at the age of 101 years, 8 months, 1 day.

Their children were Josiah, Betsey, Elsy, Lettis, Olive, Nancy, Mercy, Mary. The son Josiah was lost at sea. The daughter Olive married James Mooers of Pittston, Maine, July 2, 1810, and died Feb. 22, 1874. She was the mother of ten children, the last survivor of whom was James, Jr., who died Feb. 13, 1917, at the age of 97 years.

Ansel Taylor was the son of Daniel, son of Ebenezer, son of Richard, Jr., son of Richard called "Rock Richard," the first of the Yarmouth family.

He was a soldier of the Revolutionary war and served in the Massachusetts militia according to the military rules of the times.

The official records show him as sergeant in Capt Ebenezer Baker's company, Col Freeman's regiment, marched Oct. 4, 1777, service 28 days. Company marched to Tiverton, R. I., on a secret expedition. Also in Capt Elisha Hedge's company, Col Freeman's regiment, on an alarm to Dartmouth in Sept. 1778. Also private same company in Nov. 1778, guarding prisoners belonging to the British ship "Somerset;" all sworn to at Yarmouth, Jan. 1, 1779.

His service therefore covered the period from Oct. 4, 1777, to Jan. 1, 1779, during which time he was continually under arms either in active service or awaiting orders.

The Pension office has no record that he ever applied for or received a pension. His family urged him to do so but he refused, saying he was not disabled and could do his part without being paid for it.

I have heard my grandmother Olive say he was "terrible set in his ways." It would have been better if he had not been quite so "set" when in his last years he found himself disabled by old age and imagined himself a burden.

L. M. Mooers.

Sept. 7, 1923.

No. 22a

LIBRARY of
Cape Cod
HISTORY & GENEALOGY

The Oldest Public Library Building in the United States.

YARMOUTHPORT, MASS.:
C. W. SWIFT, Publisher and Printer,
The "Register" Press,
1923

THE OLDEST PUBLIC LIBRARY BUILDING IN THE UNITED STATES

From the delicate and dangerous inquiry—"Which was the first free public library in the United States?"—not all the gunpowder has been burnt or blown out yet. Dublin and Peterborough, N. H., may each be said to have had one good keg exploded in its honor, but there are more to come. The Librarian knew as much when he started. He knew it the moment he first mentioned the subject to his distinguished and omniscient colleague, the Nomad, and received the reply: "Oldest free public library in the United States?— Why, I had an idea it was down on Cape Cod. Mind you, I don't feel sure of this; but it is an idea I have."

From this source, as from others, the Librarian knew there was dynamite in the subject. If the Nomad possessed so much as "an idea" that Cape Cod had some form of claim in the premises, then one might be sure that some form of claim would soon be presenting itself to justify even this fleeting memory. Well, the bomb has exploded—and in an odd quarter, to wit, Logan, Utah. There dwells an esteemed contributor to the Transcript, Mr Frank R. Arnold. And he writes to the Librarian that the true and proper seat of the oldest public library building in the United States is the town of Barnstable, County of Barnstable, Province of Cape Cod, Commonwealth of Massachusetts.

Members of the TNT Squad note well the words, "oldest public library building." Mr Arnold does not allege that Barnstable has the oldest free public library as an institution. He merely says it has the oldest building, and by this the Librarian believes the writer means, more exactly, the oldest building now used—and for a long time used—as a free public library. Certainly it is on this general understanding that the Librarian, after some investigation into the subject, now offers his readers Mr Logan's article, setting it forward in the writer's own text and without the use of inverted commas, as hereinafter follows.

The oldest public library building in the United States is the one in Barnstable down on Cape Cod. You would never know from the outside that it is a public library if it were not for the sign, Sturgis Library, over the front door, though you might wonder why even an old-fashioned dwelling place should have six granite hitching posts along the sidewalk. It may look like an old colonial residence on the outside but the moment you are inside you are convinced you are in a library, though never was there a more attractive combination of private home and public institution. Also never were you in a more inflammable library, but as the librarian has her home with the books the danger is lessened though the responsibility is great.

The building was the family dwelling of Captain William Sturgis who began his business life in the counting house of Russell Sturgis in Boston and was for many years occupied in trade with China. Shortly before his death in 1863, he conveyed to the trustees of the Barnstable public library the house and land of his birthplace, together with the sum of $15,000. The trustees, who, Poole says, were first organized in the same year as the bequest, 1863, had the house altered to suit the wants of a library by converting a portion into a library hall and fitting up the remaining part as a residence for the librarian.

The house was orginally built for the Reverend John Lothrop in 1644, five years after his arrival in Barnstable from Scituate. It followed then the general plan of a New England farmhouse with a hip roof, a big kitchen at the rear in the middle, and with bedroom and shed at either side. One of the front rooms was "sufficiently large to accommodate members of the church at their meetings," and this room today is the workroom of the librarian, Miss Elizabeth C. Nye. It is sixteen feet square with a beamed ceiling and deep, broad window seats. It is furnished with old-fashioned mirrors, rockers and Windsor chairs, has ivy in vases over the fireplace as well as a beautiful photograph of the West Barnstable marshes, and so charming is the room that you would almost think you had strayed into some private library. This room is still unchanged from Lothrop days, but the rest of the house is much modified. Like a modern lady, the building has lost its hips and is now a two-story colonial house. The kitchen bedroom is transformed into a travel library room and the two stories on the west have been made into the large library hall. This large room is the main library but the books overflow into the rest of the house.

The library is homelike to its core. When you visit it you visit a charming colonial home as well as a public library. Biography lines the vestibule. Essays cover the dining room walls, and what was formerly a little bedroom is now a Cape Cod sanctum full of books on navigation and travel, a perfect retreat for a ship captain. Think of having Pepys's Diary smile at you in the vestibule, or being able to reach back for a volume of "Wisdom and Destiny" as you sit at breakfast, or imagine yourself loitering of a Sunday morning with the "Varieties of Religious Experience" instead of going to church. The library helps give the home distinction and the home gives the library charm. It is a happy combination for both librarian and visitor.

Any library, public or private, offers as many surprises as a new acquaintance. It has accumulated traditions, individual traits, a soul, and above all certain books that set it apart from all other libraries and make it almost holy ground.

At present the trustees of the Barnstable library are trying to build up the library in history, essays, and biography, rather than fiction, as they argue very sensibly that people will get hold of fiction anyway, and so have greater needs in other directions.

The library has many other distinctive features. First, it has inherited many of the books of Captain Sturgis, which form a library to delight the heart of a seafaring man. Captain Sturgis is reported to have been a man of bookish tastes and a master of many languages including Latin, but judging from his literary vestigia in Barnstable his master passion was the sea. Here are the names of some of his books that are in the library: "Oriental Commerce" by William Milburn. London, 1813; "Physician for Ships" by Usher Parsons; "American Coast Pilot" by Captain Lawrence Furlong, Newburyport, 1808; "Treatise in Law Relative to Merchant Ships and Seamen" by Charles Abbott, Newburyport, 1810; "Cleveland's Voyages;" "Adolphus Slade's Records of Travel," London,

1833; "John Martin's Natives of the Tonga Islands," London, 1818; "Tschudi's Travels in Peru;" Olmstead's "Journey in the Back Country;" "Two Years in Ava;" Selkirk's "Recollections of Ceylon." Most New England towns have their historical societies, but Cape Cod towns like Barnstable or Yarmouth with books of travel so easily accessible and sea captains on every hand should have geographical societies even more active than those of Paris or London.

The biggest treasure of the library, the unreplaceable book, is the handwritten pamphlet containing the "Laws and Regulations for the Second Social Library in Barnstable." This was written in 1796 and also contains a list of the new books purchased on Sept. 6, 1796, from Eben Larkin at a total cost of seven pounds, eight shillings and ten pence. Here is a quotation which will show the Yankee shrewdness and individuality of the document:

"Article 3. Each subscriber shall have liberty to take out about seven-eighths of the property which they subscribe, that is, to take as near as the books they want will come to it. If they want one book that costs more money than they subscribe they shall not be deprived of taking it, or if one book that was a little less they shall take it, so as to come as near the sum as convenient. They may take such books as they may choose, if in the library, which they may keep from four to eight weeks according to the size of book to be marked on it, and no longer, without giving a reason satisfactory to the librarian."

As each member of the society had subscribed at least two dollars and the whole new library had not cost over forty dollars, a subscriber had much range, even if he were circumscribed by article three.

Here is the list of new books mentioned above. The spelling is that of Barnstable and Boston in 1796 and from the list we may safely conclude that the literary spokes of Boston already were reaching into the cranberry bogs:

Morse's Universal Geography, 2 vols.
More's Travels
Zeluco
Dignity of Human Nature
Lathrop's Sermons
British Plutarch, 3 vols.
Cecilia
Fool of Quality, 3 vols.
Blairs' Sermons
Beauties of History
Williams' Letters
Mirror
Evelina
Hervey's Meditations
Franklin's Works
Julia de Roubigne
Goldsmith's Essays and Poems
Pelen Islands
Price's Sermons
History of England
Bennett's Letters
Hannah Mores' Sacred Dramas
Howard's Life
Vicar of Wakefield
Berthier's Evidences
Chesterfield's Principles
Ladies Advice

—The Librarian, in Boston Transcript.

No. 23.

LIBRARY of
Cape Cod
HISTORY & GENEALOGY

THE GEOLOGICAL FORMATION OF CAPE COD

By
Winthrop Packard

YARMOUTHPORT, MASS.:
C. W. SWIFT, Publisher and Printer,
The "Register" Press,

THE MAKING OF CAPE COD.

At least two glacial periods went to the making of Cape Cod. One of those left the masses of pebbly till at Nauset Head, the Gardiner Clay in the "Clay Pounds" at Highland Light and some other material near by. Then it went its way for I do not know how many thousand years and we know nothing about what did happen, so far as the Cape is concerned. But the ice came down from the north again. Miles deep it covered New England. Moving in majestic grandeur it flowed down hill, seaward, taking the hill with it, leaving only striated remnants of the great uplands it ground over. The slow momentum of its irresistible mass cracked mountains and ground their fragments underfoot, loaded and transported parts of them on the ice, 100-ton bowlders, rocks, gravel and sand, an endless transportation line from the frigid north toward the warm winds of tropic seas to southward.

These warm winds met the ice not far from the latitude where previous glacial action had deposited the tills and clays already mentioned. They melted it in an age-long battle and stopped it; pushed it slowly back. From beneath the melting glacier flowed a thousand streams laden with clay, sand and gravel which they deposited in broad levels on the outwash plains that stretch from Orleans on the east to Falmouth on the west all along the southern half of the Cape. This is the fertile land of the region having enough clay in its composition to hold the humus of decayed vegetation deposited there through the centuries.

There were three lobes to the southern edge of this melting ice which had to do with the shaping of Cape Cod. One of these was a broad one to the eastward. It dropped the long ridges of sand and gravel which lie today beneath the sea and are known as Nantucket Shoals and Georges Banks. These shoals so swarmed with codfish that Bartholomew Gosnold, who visited the region in 1602, called it Cape Cod. The name, brief, descriptive, somehow appealing, has stuck, though Gosnold's predecessors had given other names, possibly as appropriate. Champlain called it Cap Blanc because of its white sands. Capt John Smith came in 1614 and named it Cape James in honor of this English King. Long before these were the Norsemen, who named it in their own language Wonderstrand. And before them were the Phoenicians — we think — whose name for it we do not know.

The part of the Cape which runs north and south, from Orleans to Provincetown, was built by this same lobe of the glacier, between it and the next lobe, which filled Massachusetts bay, was an indentation in the ice where the melting masses spilled great stores of gravel, sand and clay; part of it on the clay and gravel left by the preceding glacier, and we have thus the highlands of the outer Cape, the land on which stands North Truro, Truro, Wellfleet and Eastham. The curved hook of the Cape where stands Provincetown was an afterthought, to be dealt with later.

In the same way the middle lobe of the glacier, melted back toward the north by the south wind, pushing against it with the mighty weight of its ice, dropped long ridges of rocks and sand along its front from Orleans to Sandwich. The third lobe of the glacier lay across the land from Buzzards Bay north. On its front fell the great terminal moraine which is the Elizabeth Islands, from Cuttyhunk to the west end of Naushon. Between this and the middle lobe of ice lay another indentation running narrowly northward of Plymouth. Prodigious amounts of gravel and great bowlders were dropped here, building the hills about Plymouth, Manomet and the long line of highlands that run down the east shore of Buzzards Bay all the way to Falmouth. In places there are great aggregations of granite bowlders, tossed indiscriminately together, making a considerable portion of the highest hills, such, for instance, as Telegraph Hill in Bourne, whose summit rises 260 feet above the tide.

The material of which Cape Cod is built, practically all granite, has been traced to its native quarries in the White Hills in the Laurentian Highlands far to the north of that, and in nearer lands as well. In some cases it is easy to trace special rocks from their very point of origin. Iron ore, for instance, from Diamond Hill in Rhode Island; is scattered all along its southward route in recognizable bowlders to and over the seaward rim of Martha's Vineyard. So plentiful is this Cape Cod granite that in the early days it was exported from Falmouth to England and was reckoned one of the valuable products of the Old Colony. The same type of rock, rich in red feldspar, porphyritic, shows all through the moraine which extends along the eastern end of Buzzards Bay.

So much for the glacial making of the Cape, which took place we do not know how many thousand years ago. The feat, a great one indeed, had no more than been finished when other mighty but less steadily acting forces took up the work of finishing what the glacier had begun. The ocean currents the waves and the wind the rain and the sun, have been at it over since. Yet, through thousands of years, the great outstanding aspects and conditions of the region have been little affected. Such changes as are most marked have come through the erosion of coastline by the ocean currents and the deposition of the eroded material on other portions of the outline. Thus the great seasonal cyclonic storms, known to the Cape people as northeasters, beat yearly upon the great "Clay Pounds" at North Truro and take away the face of the cliff, there 150 feet high. The rate at which they remove this lofty, tremendously hard structure varies from year to year. It averages 1½ feet yearly. That is not much, but when it is multiplied by the centuries passing down time in endless procession it counts for a good deal. It means that in perhaps 10,000 years the cliffs will have disappeared.

You and I need not worry about that. The material thus excavated goes north and south, mingling with the loose sands cast up by the sea and building extensions to the Cape in each direction. The sandhills on which Provincetown stands were thus carried north in ocean currents and built into the hook of the Cape, being raised in dunes and shifted by the sea winds of the centuries. Peaked Hill bar, which lies off shore there, is thus being built. Some day no doubt, it will be a refuge and perhaps a homestead for landsmen instead of a menace to sailors as it is at present. In the change and counterchange of ocean currents some of this sand and clay material goes south as well as north, and is building up Monomoy year by year. How far south Monomoy may thus extend no man can say. Probably the south channel currents, growing stronger as the barriers build, may always keep a passage open for ships which thus pass, safe from Nantucket Shoals to the southward.

The great arctic current which swings into Massachusetts Bay has bent the tip of the Cape far around, south and then east. Because of this process Provincetown harbor, land-defended from all winds today as it was when the adventuring Pilgrims found refuge there, may in time become completely land enclosed and from a salt sea harbor become a fresh water pond. All along the southern shore of the Cape the sea has done this with what were once long bays, running far into the land, by building barrier beaches across them. Such waters are especially numerous in the town of Falmouth. From Provincetown south to Monomoy the work of the wind with the sand is everywhere conspicuous. It builds dunes that bury trees and buildings, then it moves them on, leaving the sanded wood smothered or worn away with the continual attrition of moving particles. Beach grass alone stops this movement. It grows with the growing dune, lacing its internal texture with stems and roots and holding it in place for other vegetation. To the beach grass is due such permanency as this portion of the land has.

As for man, the established work of his hands, great as it often seems to him, has only in a tiny part affected the region. His railroads, his slender black tarred highways, his meandering byways, his farms and sandpits and dredged channels have neither marred nor beautified a thousandth part of the surface. The forests and the dunes, the free winds and the sea in a thousand phrases of beauty and change, invite today just as they did before Gosnold or Champlain, the Norsemen or the Phoenicians found it, just as they did, very likely, before the first men of any kind came there.

—Winthrop Packard in Christian Science Monitor.

No. 24.

LIBRARY of
Cape Cod
HISTORY & GENEALOGY

Fast Runs of Clipper Ships

YARMOUTHPORT, MASS.:
C. W. SWIFT, Publisher and Printer,
The "Register" Press,
1922.

FAST RUNS BY CLIPPER SHIPS.

(From As the World Wags, Boston Herald.)

Some days ago Mr Halliday Witherspoon questioned the accuracy of a statement made by Mr Hergesheimer in his "Java Head" concerning a sailing vessel making the run from Bombay to Liverpool in 24 days, and again from Madeira to Colombo, a distance of 1100 nautical miles, in 20 days. As a result, The Herald has received several letters about fast runs made by American clipper ships which we now print.

Mr Heywood Broun of the New York World published recently in his entertaining column a letter in which the writer pointed out incredible, grossly inaccurate statements, according to the letter, made by Mr Hergesheimer in a story published in the Saturday Evening Post of Oct. 22. For example, the cargo carried by a ship. "At the date of this story—the middle of the last century—there wasn't a hull afloat equal to a cargo of that size" (800 tons).

All this does not prevent us from enjoying Mr Hergesheimer's stories when he does not strain himself to write well. We know nothing about vessels, nothing about sailing, though we have wondered at the peculiar construction of the Flying Dutchman as represented on the operatic stage. Our knowledge of sea-life is derived chiefly from novels by Melville, Marryat, Cooper, Clarke Russell—and other old-fashioned writers: also from the Psalmist's description of those that do business in great waters: "They reel to and fro, and stagger like a drunken man."

But these letters will surely interest many.

FAST CLIPPERS.

The Northern Light built in 1851 by Briggs Bros. at South Boston, made in 1851 the record passage from San Francisco to Boston, viz: 76 days, 6 hours. This has never been equalled by a sailer. A detailed account of this passage is given in "The Clipper Ship Era" by Arthur H. Clark.

The famous marine artist of that time, William Bradford, painted two pictures of the Northern Light, one of which was for the owner, Mr James Hucknis, and the other for the builder. The latter I now have.

The record passage from San Francisco to New York is 76 days made in 1854 by the Comet, built in 1851 by William H. Webb at New York. Both these records are faster than any ever made from either Boston or New York to San Francisco.

Boston.   F. H. B.

FLYING CLOUD.

The Flying Cloud, constructed in 1851 by Donald McKay, bore as a figurehead, a winged angel with a

speaking trumpet in her hand. The mainmast of this clipper, including the topmast and skysail pole, rose to 200 feet; her main yard measured 82 feet and her bowsprit and jibboom extended 58 feet. She was a rakish craft, to be sure; her masts canted 1¼ inches to the foot. On that memorable voyage in 1851, from New York to San Francisco, under the command of Captain Josiah Perkins Cressy, she covered the distance in 89 days and 21 hours. In one day she made 433½ statute miles, 42 miles faster than any steamship of that period. For a number of days, indeed, she averaged 13½ knots, sailing 5912 miles on an average of 227 miles a day; and this in spite of the fact she sprung her mainmast, split her staysails at both fore and maintopmasts and lost her fore topgallantmast. The Flying Cloud established the record in 1854 by making the passage from New York to San Francisco in 89 days and 8 hours. The Andrew Jackson by dint of good fortune made the voyage in 89 days and 4 hours in 1860. She was not, however, a consistently fast performer, like the Flying Cloud.
Allston. William L. Robinson.

DR CROCKETT NAMES TWO.

How about the Red Jacket in 1854? Thirteen days and one hour from New York to Liverpool. Or the Live Yankee at the same time, sailing from New York three days before the Red Jacket? On the passage from Liverpool, when near the Grand Banks, with a smooth sea and a sharp northwest wind the live Yankee logged 17 knots close hauled and sharp at it, for a time, which under that way of sailing is remarkable. I was there. I know of no craft under sail that ever beat this record. About 1833 the schooner Cirlue (I do not know if I have spelled this correctly) of about 60 tons, loaded with a cargo of lime made the run from Rockland, Me., to New York in 48 hours. My father was in command. This was the craft that was run down by an excursion steamer. The steamer was sunk; the passengers were saved by the schooner's crew.
Boston. Dr W. E. Crockett.

QUICK WORK IN '49.

In looking over some of my ship cards of Glidden and Williams I came across a very interesting piece signed "R. T. P." in 1908 on "Signal Flags of Former Bostonians."

Glidden and Williams's flag was white and yellow with red star. In 1849 Messrs Glidden and Williams started the first California line and did an enormous business. Clippers were built and loading in their line at Lewis wharf in 90 days from the stretching of their keel. They were brought to the wharf immediately after launching, masted and rigged while loading and in many instances were fully loaded and already cleared before they were rigged. It was not an unusual circumstance to see four, five and six vessels at their piers in various stages of loading. Sole owners of many vessels and interested in others, their flag was over all, and designated one of, if not the most honorable and successful of California shipping lines.

Captain William T. Glidden and

Hon John M. S. Williams started the firm, and my father, Mr John A. Glidden, went into the firm in 1853. Brookline.   Jennie M. Glidden.

FOUR FAST CLIPPERS.

While the world prays for peace, I am thirsting for the blood of anyone who claims that any sailing vessel ever made a greater day's run than the Lightning's of 436 nautical miles.

In the research for my "Maritime History of Massachusetts," I found but four authentic records of day's runs of more than 410 miles by sailing vessels. They were made, of course, by Yankee clipper ships:

Sovereign of the Seas, Captain Lauchlan McKay, March 17-18, 1853, 411 miles.

Red Jacket, Captain Asa Eldridge, Feb. 27-28, 1854, 413 miles.

Lightning, Captain James N. Forbes, Feb. 28-March 1, 1854, 436 miles.

Donald McKay, Captain Henry Warner, late February or early March, 1855, 421 miles.

The Red Jacket was designed by Samuel Hartt Pook of Boston, and built by George Thomas of Rockland, Me. The other three were designed and built by Donald McKay at East Boston. All four records were made at the same time of year; those of Red Jacket and Lightning on succeeding days. The Sovereign's run was made in the roaring forties in the South Pacific; the other three in the North Atlantic. All four were made on eastward runs; consequently the sea day, from noon to noon, was less than 24 hours long, and the "corrected" day's run would read considerably higher: 424 miles for the Sovereign, and probably more in proportion for the others. These records are derived from abstracts of the ships' logs, printed in newspapers immediately after they were made, and, in the case of the Sovereign at least, reprinted in Maury's "Sailing Directions." There are plenty of phoney clipper ship records to be found, in nautical almanacs of the latter 19th century, and in letter columns in New York papers. One set of records was constructed by measuring degrees of longitude in the 40's as if they had been on the equator.

I challenge anyone to produce an authentic contemporary record to beat that of the Lightning; and I doubt whether any sailing ship other than the above-mentioned unless it be McKay's other masterpieces, the James Baines and the Flying Cloud, ever made a day's run of over 410 miles. Nautical miles of 6080 feet, mind you. The greatest day's run by a British-built clipper, mentioned in Basil Lubbock's book, is a beggarly 363 miles.

Cambridge.   S. E. Morison.

THE CHAS. C. LEARY.

I think the quickest time made from Singapore to Boston was by the "Chas. C. Leary," Captain Baker. In the captain's report I read: "I was writing in my cabin when the wind suddenly veered in right direction and I closed my letters, sent them ashore by boatman and cast off for home. I passed Aujer Head in 50 hours, and on voyage I ran seven weeks without changing sails, and here I am in Boston, 81½ days from sailing." It proved to be the last voyage of the captain. The longest voyage between same ports was by the "Nehemiah Gibson," 165 days, partly caused by her going into Vineyard Haven, where she was detained 21 days. The last sailing vessel loaded at Singapore for any port was the "Manuel Llaguno," she having safely arrived here in about 100 days.

Boston.   Everott F. Sweet.

QUICK PASSAGES.

In 1853 the ship Trade Wind of New York made the passage east, San Francisco to New York, in 75 days.

In 1855 (I am not sure of the year) the ship Lightning of Boston made the passage from Melbourne to Boston in 64 days. I believe, the record.

The writer has seen in the log of the American ship John Ena, record of a day's run in the Pacific in 1906 of 378 knots and of 2142 knots in seven consecutive days. The John Ena was Scotch built, port Glasgow. She was given American registry when the Sandwich Islands came under our control. She was lost two years ago, going into Wellington, N. Z. There are records of fast passages from India to Great Britain. Few from Bombay to an American Atlantic port.

Henry Sargent.
Lower Pawcatuck (Stonington), Ct.

ABERDEEN CLIPPERS.

Chambers's Edinburgh Journal of Aug. 21, 1852, has an extended article on nautical matters, of which the following relating to fast clipper ships of that period is an interesting excerpt: "One of the Aberdeen clippers, the Chrysolite, built for a Liverpool firm, made the run from Britain to China in 104 days, and traversed 320 nautical miles (nearly 370 statute miles) in 24 hours, and the Stornoway, built at the same place for a London firm, has accomplished the distance in 103 days. Three American clippers were sighted during these voyages and were distanced by them, if newspaper reports tell truly. But the United States attained a high ship speed before Britain had thought of the matter, and Baltimore clippers had long been known as dashing, rapid little vessels. Let us take two instances that 1852 has afforded,—one by Britain and one by America. The Aberdeen clipper-built barque Phoenician arrived at Plymouth Feb. 3, having left Sydney Nov. 12, and performed the voyage in 83 days. The American clipper Witch of the Wave, a fine vessel of 1400 tons, left Canton on Jan. 5, and arrived at the Downs on April 4, a period of 90 days. Her greatest speed was 338 nautical miles in 24 hours—equivalent to about 389 English miles. Thus it is, we find, that in one voyage we beat the Americans and in another they outstrip us. There seems at present no reason why either country should fail in making still further advances."

No. 25.

LIBRARY *of*
Cape Cod
HISTORY & GENEALOGY

- - *The* Romance *of* - -
A BARNSTABLE BELL

YARMOUTHPORT, MASS.:
C. W. SWIFT, Publisher and Printer,
The "Register" Press,
1922.

THE ROMANCE OF A BARNSTABLE BELL.

It Now Reposes In the Court House and Is Thought to Be the Oldest Church Bell in America.

The Pilgrim, when he came to these shores, possessed, in addition to other qualities, a genius for hard work. Which was perhaps fortunate, for the country which he had to subdue was not going to yield without a struggle. Closely allied to this genius for hard work is the genius for adventure, and this, too, was a fortunate endowment of the Pilgrim, for the subjugation of Cape Cod needed this spirit of progress in addition to the spirit of striving. Because he was a believer in repression of the emotions, however, the Pilgrim gave little evidence of the turmoil of achievement which surged within him.

This passion for work is evidenced in the stern life of the Mayflower passengers and their descendants and persists to this day in the conservatism and plodding, slow advance of the Cape communities. The drift toward the unexpected, though not always given the freedom of the rover, crops out in the remarkably full lives of some of the men and women who seldom journey far from the homes of their youth.

No outsider, however, can guess the joys and sorrows, the turmoils and tragedies which these Cape dwellers have experienced from their calm and repressed appearance. This restraint is evidenced even in the architecture. No Georgian frills or "Colonial" embellishments adorn the plain and substantial houses, built to stand against time and weather. The atmosphere about them diverts speculation from the happenings within their walls, and their very similarity tends to preserve their secrets.

Occasionally you will find a Cape Cod man or woman who has rubbed up against the world enough to loosen the tongue a little, and then you are in for tales and reminiscences which give you an insight into the Cape and its spirit of adventure which you never had before.

Alfred Crocker's grandsons are a fortunate pair, for they are of the age which delights most in a "story" and their grandfather is the man to tell them. Out of a long and varied life he has stored up a vast amount of experience, his own and others, and he possesses both the ability and the willingness to tell a tale. In the pursuance of his duties as clerk of courts of Barnstable county he has obtained a fund of anecdote and reminiscence. In his comfortable office in the Court House at Barnstable he is always ready to lay this at the disposal of the seeker for information.

One of the treasures of the building

is an old bell, which Mr Crocker thinks is the oldest church bell in America. It is kept carefully on a standard in a corner of his office, and is regarded with reverence and handled with care, for its history is interesting.

As Mr Crocker tells the tale, a vessel went ashore in 1697 off Sandwich in a severe storm. The vessel soon pounded to pieces, and all hands were drowned. The bodies were rescued as they drifted ashore and carried to the church, where a public funeral was held next day, and they were given decent burial.

From letters found in the pockets of the captain it was learned that his name was Peter Adolph. The minister of the parish sent an account of the accident, together with words of comfort, to Captain Peter Adolph's widow, and out of gratitude to him and to the people of Sandwich, she bought the bell, which now rests honorably in the clerk of courts' office, and presented it to them to be hung in the church.

The parish voted in 1703, however, that the bell was too small, and authorized the minister, Benjamin Fessenden, to sell it to the Courts of Sessions, Barnstable, which was done, and it was hung in the county court house, next the library, where it was used to call the jurors and court officers when time to open court arrived.

This county house was of brick, with wooden floors and roof, and in it were the offices of the registrar of deeds, the registrar of probate and the clerk of courts. On Oct. 22, 1827, a fire started, which burned out the entire inside and the walls and belfry caved in. The belfry, however, fell away from the burning ruins and the bell was rescued, none the worse except for a few nicks.

The present court house of stone was started in 1833, and the old bell was hung in the belfry and was rung when the judge and sheriff came from the hotel and were ready to resume court.

The fourth of July, 1872, marked another epoch in the old bell's life, for on the night before the fourth the boys of Barnstable, bent on making as much noise as possible, rang it till they tired, and then, to make more noise, climbed to the belfry and began striking it with a hammer.

Of course the bell protested this kind of treatment, and soon it cracked. It was kept in the belfry, however, and offered the courtesy of being allowed to do its feeble best, until 1874, when a new bell was bought.

Then the relic was pensioned for its long and honorable service, and brought down into the clerk of courts' office, where Mr Crocker, whenever he raises his eyes from his desk, may see it in its corner, and if he be so inclined, may meditate on the things of the past, which the old bell recalls.

He has plenty to meditate on. Born on the Cape, he went to sea when he was fifteen, and after that he worked with his father in the salt works. This is an industry which has disappeared from the Cape altogether. Then the spirit of adventure of his forbears would not be denied, and he became a mail clerk, running between Boston and Wellfleet. After that he settled down more or less, except for various trips around the country, and is now in the comfortable office of the clerk of courts. True to the Cape traditions, however, a kindly, humorous, even jocose exterior covers the memory of many a hard experience but his repression is the repression of sorrow, not of joy.

—Transcript.

No. 26.

LIBRARY *of*
Cape Cod
HISTORY & GENEALOGY

GLASS-MAKING in SANDWICH

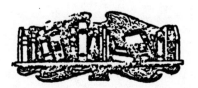

YARMOUTHPORT, MASS.:
C. W. SWIFT, Publisher and Printer,
The "Register" Press,
1922.

GLASS-MAKING IN SANDWICH.

The Growing Favor with Which Collectors Regard Pressed Glass of the Early Nineteenth Century and the History of the Cape Cod Industry Which Labor Troubles Forced to Suspend.

From attics, from closets, from dark and dusty reaches of long-untouched shelves, even from woodsheds and barns, the people who have saved things in the belief that they might come handy some day are digging out old pieces of glass, dusting them off, giving them a bath and a polishing, and setting them aside where they can be got at easily when the glass collector comes around, as he is sure to do, with an offer many times the price they originally sold for and far beyond their intrinsic value.

Gradually the collector of antiques has been awakening to the fact that American glass is interesting. Stiegel glass made near Philadelphia and dating from the eighteenth century, has for a long time commanded large prices, and collections of it have been deemed worthy of a place in the larger museums. Cut glass has of course an intrinsic value which age enhances, and that, too, has had its share of attention. But the ordinary pressed glass, the kind our grandmothers had when they went to housekeeping, has only lately been looked at twice by collectors.

The collector of antiques lives in a peculiar state of mind. He may be actuated by the desire to possess things simply because they are old, but if he is a true collector this romantic period does not last long, or he may like them because of their historical associations, or he may work from the standpoint of beauty and gradually weed out of his accumulations the commonplace, the ugly and the imperfect. The glass which is now being sought belongs mostly in the historical class. There are collectors of bottles and flasks which were made with devices on them commemorative of some notable event, or for some such purpose such as a presidential campaign. Others go in for the little cup plates, on which well-bred persons set their cups after they had poured their tea into the saucers to drink from. Still others affect the sauce dishes and the glass plates which were pressed in intricate and sometimes beautiful design.

The chief point of interest in this sudden access of interest in glass collecting, however, is the fact that it removes into the realm of the so-called antique another class of objects which have heretofore been considered as modern. Thus is an era made in collecting.

Those who take up the fad of collecting glass will often hear of Sandwich glass, the wares which were made in Sandwich, Mass., beginning in 1825. This factory prided itself in making a fine grade of flint glass, though glass cutters will tell you that it was sometimes too hard to work well, that the glass made at the New England Glass Works in East Cambridge would work better. The Sandwich works used good lead for metal, and the result was a clear ring when the manufactured article was struck.

During its long career—from 1825 to 1888, the works at Sandwich turned out glass of all sorts for all sorts of uses. In the early days came the pressed articles which are now in demand, and indeed it has been said that this factory was the first in the United States to make pressed glass. Also some of the curious millefiori paper weights. Later it made full sets for the table—goblets, tumblers and all kinds of wine glasses, with finger bowls and other accessories. These were plain, cut, etched or engraved. About 1860 the management sent a man to Europe to study the process of acid etching, and he brought back a machine which was used to the company's profit both for table ware and commerical uses. At one time the factory was turning out gas shades in between forty and fifty patterns, and many of these were etched.

Glass in various colors was also made, and many articles of opal glass were sent out, among them lamp shades, from six to sixteen inches across, very difficult to blow. Besides the opal there was much ruby glass turned out, which is colored through the use of gold, and also blue, canary and black. A few ruby lantern globes were made.

In the later years of its existence the company did a large export business, especially in kerosene lamps. For certain styles brass standards were bought and the bowls and chimneys fitted at Sandwich, while others were all of glass. There were also cruets for various uses made as well as tumblers—at one time 500 tumblers every five-hour shift—and jars and bottles of all sizes.

These later manufactures, however, are of too recent a date to have the interest for collectors that the old productions have. Maybe some time in the future the vessels of ordinary use in our day will be carefully collected by the antique hunters or their equivalents of the future. Meanwhile the searcher for the glass of the first half of the nineteenth century rejoices when he finds a piece which he thinks is from the factory at Sandwich.

During the eighties, the little town of Sandwich was congratulating itself on its prosperity and its glowing future. The Boston & Sandwich Glass company was employing something like three hundred men and boys, and these workers were making wages of from four to six dollars a day. Most of the men owned their homes, there was plenty of work and they had con-

2

fidence that the Flint Glass Workers union, to which they belonged, would insure them a continuance of this prosperity for an indefinite time.

Today a wrecking company is rapidly removing a monument to union labor troubles which has stood since Jan. 1, 1888, a daily reminder to the little town of the prosperity which once belonged to it and which it cast away over night. For on Jan. 1, 1888, the glass works were closed, the affairs of the Boston & Sandwich Glass company were wound up, and thus perished the one industry which had been the chief support of the town since 1825.

But for a certain ill-advised strike Sandwich might have advanced to be one of the major manufacturing towns of the state, instead of standing still, or worse, retrograding for the last thirty-two years. Certainly it might have been more prosperous than it is today.

This little known chapter of Massachusetts industrial history runs somewhat as follows:

Early in 1825 a Boston man named Deming Jarves, who is said to have had a great fondness for that part of Cape Cod, called a meeting of the citizens of Sandwich and told them that he had recently been on a trip through the West and had observed among other interesting things that the men working in the glass works of Pittsburgh were making from two dollars to two dollars and a half a day and that the labor was neither arduous nor dangerous. Mr Jarves told the meeting that if there were sufficient interest manifested in Sandwich he would build a glass works there in order that the citizens might profit by the employment. Now two dollars a day was a high wage in those times and Sandwich proceeded to show that it was interested and the glass works were built.

As Mr Jarves himself writes of it: "Ground was broke in April, 1825, dwellings for the workmen built and manufactory completed; and on the 4th day of July, three months from first breaking ground, commenced blowing glass."

The beginning was modest, just an eight-pot furnace, holding 800 pounds each, which melted 7000 pounds weekly. The location at Sandwich was not on account of the sand there—there is sand at other places on Cape Cod—but there was a large amount of timber available near by and the works used wood for fuel. The policy of Mr Jarves was to buy land with timber on it, and the agent who was in charge of the works, besides having authority to buy land, had also the duty of seeing to the erection of houses for the workmen. It seems that he exceeded his authority somewhat, and soon Mr Jarves found that he needed more capital than he possessed to carry out the ambitious plans which had been developed. He therefore formed a stock company, and the Boston & Sandwich Glass company was incorporated on Feb. 22, 1826, by Deming Jarves, Henry Rice, Andrew T. Hall and Edward Monroe. At this time from sixty to seventy men were employed and the manufactured goods produced yearly amounted to about $75,000 worth.

3

The glass works prospered from the start and regularly and gradually expanded, employing more and more men and turning out more and more glass. Other factories sprang up in New England and the other Atlantic states and competition apparently was a benefit to all. By 1854 the capitalization had reached $400,000 and 500 men and boys were employed. The value of the goods manufactured each year was $600,000.

It was a time of great prosperity for Sandwich. The company laid out lots and built houses which were sold to the workers and which they were allowed to occupy at once and to pay for in instalments. The company opened stores and purchased more and more land, thus affording employment to others beside those who were at work in the glass works. From 1825 to 1858 the finished product was transported to Boston entirely by water and the company owned the sloop Polly, which was able to come up a small creek almost to the door of the factory. In 1858 what is said to be the first railroad of its kind in the United States was built to carry the barrels of finished goods from the factory to the wharf, farther away than the landing on the creek, for that was to be negotiated only at high tide, and the growing business of the company demanded more frequent transportation than the tide afforded. In later years the company bought the steamer Acorn and used it to compete with the Old Colony railroad, doubtless holding an efficient club thereby to drive freight prices down.

In 1858, after a quarrel among the directors, Deming Jarves left the company and formed the Cape Cod Glass Works, to run in competition with the factory he started, but it was never a great factor in the glass industry of the Cape and continued only a short time after the death of Mr Jarves in April, 1869.

Things ran smoothly both for town and works until a delegation of workers from Pennsylvania visited the plant and urged the workmen in Sandwich to form themselves into a union. This was an idea new to the Cape, and in perplexity the men sought the advice of Mr Jarves, who had been their friend and patron for so many years. He told them that he did not know what the union was for and he did not care. He was concerned only with getting a fair day's work for a fair day's pay. He could not see what advantage a union would be to them, for their wages were satisfactory and their living conditions were better than those of the operatives in Pittsburgh or any other glass centre.

However, the men were swayed by the smooth-tongued organizers, and they formed their union, and from that time things began to go less smoothly. There were numbers of rules and regulations they found which they had to abide by, and which had never been found necessary before. For instance, the union headquarters stipulated the number of boys who should be employed in each gang. Then there were rules as to the number of hours which should constitute a day's work. Finally the number of lamp chimneys or tumblers

4

that should be turned out in a day was limited. An expert could get through with his day's work in four hours, and for this he drew four dollars pay. Sometimes a man could get in two days' work in one. The shifts were of five hours each.

The company made no complaint about the restrictions imposed, but met all the demands of the men and watched its profits being cut down and its production slowed up.

For mutual protection and trade advantage the Sandwich company had formed a working agreement with other glass manufacturers of the country and the combination was called the Flint Glass Manufacturers' association. At the end of December, 1887, the association presented a new scale, which was uniform in all the factories, and contained among other technical details the demand that the right of the manufacturer to employ or discharge employees must be acknowledged, and that employers or employees must not discriminate for or against any individual because of his membership in any organization. There were other rules affecting only the operation of a glass factory. It was explained that under the new rules some of the men would receive more pay, others less, but that the average would be the same as under the old scale. At once there was a clamor from very glass works where it was proposed to put the new rules into effect. The company at New Bedford did not agree with the other manufacturers, and was not insistent on the adoption of the new scale, consequently there was no trouble there. The other workers saw an effort to squeeze out the union, and there were immediate threats of a strike, which were carried out in many plants.

The refusal to accept the manufacturers' demands was made also by the men at Sandwich, and there, too, were heard threats of a strike if the demands were imposed.

The company got wind of this approaching trouble and called a meeting of the workers to inquire if it were true. The union leaders corroborated the report, whereupon the company announced that it had been running for several years with little or no profit, and offered to open its books to a committee of the union to prove its statement. It said that it could not continue under the new scale and besides, it had on hand an order for a large number of lamps for which the materials were all ready. If the men would only finish this order they might strike for as long as they wished, and the plant would be closed until they returned. Otherwise, if unable to make the lamps the company would have to buy them in the market to fill the order, which would mean the loss of several thousand dollars.

The spokesman for the company asked the men who they considered their best friend, himself or the union. There could be but one answer to that, but they said that they had been ordered to strike, and they would have to obey the union.

Then the glass company issued an ultimatum of its own. If the fires were allowed to go out they would

5

362

never be built again. There was not enough profit in the business as it was run under existing conditions for them to continue, and if there was a strike, they would close the plant. One big fellow intimated that it was a bluff, that the company could not afford to close the plant, and all the workers had to do was to stand firm and they could call the bluff. So the strike was on.

The bluff was called by the other side, though, and when on Jan. 1, 1888, the plant was closed, it was not reopened. The company wound up its affairs and went out of business, and Sandwich lost its one industry.

There is another side to the story of the closing of the works. George T. McLaughlin, the postmaster of Sandwich, who worked in the glass factory till he was twenty years old, lays the blame squarely at the door of the stockholders of the company. According to his version there was a combination of glass manufacturers, which included those of Philadelphia, Brooklyn, Pittsburgh, New Bedford, Sandwich and several other places. This association made demands on the glass blowers, the nature of which Mr McLaughlin is unable to remember, that they do certain things in a certain time. They asked time to consider them which was not given. They stated that they would make any concessions that the union would permit, as they had done on two occasions previously, and the head of the union came to Sandwich to try to settle the difficulty, but the owners were firm, and drew the fires. It was a lockout, Mr McLaughlin affirms and not a strike, that closed the plant.

The closing of the works wrought a great hardship on the men who owned their homes. So much real estate thrown on the market at one time forced the prices down, and the men found that they could obtain but a small part of what their property was worth, much less what they had put into it. During the year 1888 some ten of the workers who did not leave Sandwich formed the Sandwich Co-operative Glass company and put up a building and started the manufacture of glass. The venture did not succeed, however. During the sixty-three years of its existence the Boston & Sandwich Glass company had paid out in wages about $22,000,000 and had produced about $30,000,000 worth of glass. After the strike its land was sold and the buildings remained idle. Now they are being torn down to make room for another industry which is to start the manufacture of wood pulp and soap. The old building of the Cape Cod works is being transformed into a plant for cutting veneer. Maybe Sandwich has learned its lesson.

—Boston Transcript, August, 1920.

No. 27.

LIBRARY *of*
Cape Cod
HISTORY & GENEALOGY

THOMAS FOSTER *of* Weymouth *and* His Cape Cod Descendants

YARMOUTHPORT, MASS.:
C. W. SWIFT, Publisher and Printer,
The "Register" Press,
1922.

THOMAS FOSTER OF WEYMOUTH AND HIS CAPE COD DESCENDANTS.

By Amos Otis

Revised and edited by C. W. Swift

I THOMAS FOSTER of Weymouth, had three sons:
(1) Thomas, born 18 Aug. 1640, who is supposed to be the Doct. Thomas Foster who died in Cambridge 28 Oct. 1679, at the age of 39 years, and
(2) John, born 7 Oct. 1642, whom we suppose to be the Deacon John Foster, named below.
(3) Increase,

II DEACON JOHN FOSTER settled early in Marshfield and married Mary, daughter of Thomas and Joanna Chillingsworth, by whom he had ten children. His wife died 25 Sept. 1702. He then married 2d, Sarah Thomas, who died 26 May, 1731, aged 85. Deacon Foster died 13 June, 1732, aged 90, according to the record made by his son Thomas, (who was town clerk,) or 91, according to the inscription on his headstone standing in the Winslow burying ground. But if he was son of Thomas of Weymouth he lacked a few months of 90 years. The children of Dea. John and Mary Foster were:

1 Elizabeth, born 24 Sept. 1664, married William Carver, the centennarian, 18 Jan. 1682-3, and died in June 1715.
2 John, born 12 Oct. 1666, married Hannah Stetson of Scituate, resided in Plymouth, was a deacon, and died 24 Dec. 1741.
3 Josiah, born 7 June, 1669. Resided in Pembroke.
4 Mary, born 13 Sept. 1671, married John Hatch, died in Marshfield 3 April 1750.
5 Joseph, born about 1674, resided at Barnstable and Sandwich.
6 Sarah, born about 1677, died unmarried, 7 April 1702.
7 Chillingsworth, born 11 June 1680, resided in Harwich.
8 James, born 22 May, 1683, died 21 July 1683.
9 Thomas, born 1686, resided in Marshfield, was a deacon, town clerk, etc. Married Lois Fuller Nov. 25, 1725, had Gershom at Barnstable, Sept. 23, 1733; died 6 Feb. 1758, aged 72.
10 Deborah, born 1691, died unmarried 4 Nov. 1732, aged 41.

CHILLINGSWORTH FOSTER, son of Dea. John and Mary, resided in Harwich, of which town he was many years Representative in the General Court. His first wife was Mercy Freeman, by whom he had seven children. She died 7 July, 1720, and he married for his second wife Widow Susanna Sears, Aug. 10, 1721, who died Dec. 7, 1730; by whom he had four children. He died about 1764.

The children of Chillingsworth Foster were:

By first wife:
1 James, born Monday, January 21, 1704-5, resided in Rochester, married Lydia, daughter of Edward Winslow, Esq., 10 July 1729. He was deacon. His age was over 80 years. He latterly resided with a son in Athol, where he died.
2 Chillingsworth, born 25 Dec. 1707. Resided in Harwich; many years Representative; he married Mercy, daughter of Edward Winslow, Esq., of Rochester, 10 Oct. 1730; she died and he married 2d, Ruth Sears of Harwich 7 Dec. 1731. Children born Barnstable, by wife Mercy, were Mercy, May 2, 1735; Chillingsworth, July 17, 1735.
3 Mary, born Thursday, 5 January 1709-10, married David Paddock of Yarmouth, 12 Oct. 1727.
4 Thomas, born Saturday, 15 March, 1711-12, married Mary Hopkins of Harwich 11 July 1734, and had: Joseph, March 27, 1735; Thomas, June 22, 1736; James, Febraury 18, 1737-8; Mary, July 18, 1740.
5 Nathan, born Friday, 10 June 1715, married Sarah Lincoln of Harwich 14 June 1739.
6 Isaac, born Tuesday, 17 June 1718, married Hannah Sears of Harwich 2 Nov. 1738.
7 Mercy, born Wednesday, 30 March 1720, and died 28 Aug. 1720.

By 2d wife:
8 Mercy, born Sunday, 29 July 1722.
9 Nathaniel, born Saturday, 17 April 1725.
10 Jerusha, born Saturday, 9 Dec. 1727.
11 A son, stillborn, March 1729-31.

CHILLINGSWORTH, JUNIOR.
His children were:
1 Thankful, born in Harwich 14 June 1733.
2 Mercy, born in Barnstable May 2, 1735.
3 Chillingsworth, born in Barnstable July 17, 1737.
4 Mehitabel, born in Harwich April 18, 1746,
5 Sarah, born in Harwich Nov. 26, 1747.

ISAAC had:
1 Isaac, May 29, 1739, married

Eunice Freeman June 10, 1762. She was born May 1, 1730, gem.
2 Samuel, May 31, 1741.
3 David, Nov. 24, 1742-3.
4 Lemuel, Feb. 24, 1744.
5 Seth, March, 1747.
6 Hannah, March 4, 1749.
7 Nathaniel, April 8, 1751.

JOSEPH FOSTER, son of John, married Rachell Bassett of Sandwich.
Children born in Barnstable and Sandwich:
1 Mary, born 1 Sept. 1697, at Sandwich, married Moses Swift of Sandwich Dec. 24, 1719.
2 Joseph, born 19 Sept. 1698, at Barnstable.
3 Benjamin, born 16 Nov. 1699, at Barnstable, married Maria Tobey at Sandwich Dec. 31, 1724.
4 William, born 31 March 1702.
5 Thankful, born 3 Nov. 1703, married Sept. 23, 1725, Nathan Tobey.
6 John, born 12 April 1705.
7 Nathan, born 3 January 1707-8.
8 Abigail, born 17 Feb. 1708-9, married May 15, 1735, Zaccheus Swift.
9 Deborah, born 18 January 1710-11, married May 10, 1733, Isaac Freeman.
10 Ebenr, born 10 May 1713.
11 Solomon, born 4 Sept. 1714,
12 Rachell, born 30 Oct. 1716, married Dec. 10, 1743, Jonathan Churchill.
13 Sarah, born 23 Sept. 1721, married Nov. 11, 1742, Nath Nye.
14 Solomon.

NATHAN FOSTER resided in the Timothy Crocker house at West Barnstable. He was a hair dresser and wig maker by trade and died aged. He married 1st, Mary Lothrop, May 21, 1753; 2d, Mercy Smith, 1766. Children born in Barnstable:
1 Abigail, Sept. 24, 1756.
2 John Burnley, June 11, 1758.
3 Mary, Oct. 4, 1765 (?)
4 James, Feb. 8, 1767.
5 Mercy, March 7, 1768.
6 Thomas, March 4, 1771.
7 Nathan, March 19, 1773.
8 Abigail, Jan. 4, 1775.
9 Joseph, July 16, 1776.
10 John, July 15, 1778.
11 Abigail, May 6, 1780.
13 Elizabeth, Feb. 16, 1783.

No. 28.

LIBRARY of
Cape Cod
HISTORY & GENEALOGY

THE ROBBINS FAMILY OF CAPE COD.

Compiled by H. N. Latey.

YARMOUTHPORT, MASS.:
C. W. SWIFT, Publisher and Printer,
The "Register" Press,
1917.

THE ROBBINS FAMILY OF CAPE COD.

Compiled by H. N. Latey.

Note.—The following data have been collected from many sources, the most important of which is a manuscript record compiled by the late Mr. I. Gilbert Robbins of Boston, now in the possession of Mr. William A. Robbins of New York. The late Hon. Josiah Paine had collected a considerable amount of data on this family and supplied much information to both Mr. Robbins and the writer. Nearly all of the earlier records are found in the published vital records, in the Mayflower Descendant and elsewhere, but most of the later records are from Mr. Robbins's manuscript, which does not state where the information was obtained. The matter is published in its present incomplete state hoping that someone interested may continue the work and publish a complete and accurate genealogy. It doubtless contains many errors and omissions and the publisher will be glad to receive corrections and additions.

Only two references have been found regarding John Robbins, who is believed to have been the first of that name in Harwich; the first, a transcript of a deed in the papers of Hon. Josiah Paine dated Oct. 30, 1713, in which Samuel Robbins transfers fifty acres of land, in what is now North Harwich, to his brother James on condition that the latter maintain and care for John and Sarah Robbins, their parents, for life. According to this deed Samuel had obtained this land from his father, who had purchased it from one John Pugsly, who died before 1711. It is probable, therefore, that John Robbins was in Harwich before 1711.

The other reference to John Robbins is in the will of James Robbins filed at Barnstable, dated Nov. 6, 1717, in which are mentioned wife Thankful, father John and brother Nathaniel Higgins, the latter being a brother of Thankful Higgins, wife of James.

These records prove that John and Sarah were the parents of Samuel and James, and it is assumed that Roger, the only other Robbins in this district at this time, was also a son of John, although no proof has been found of this.

In the Marblehead vital records is found a marriage of John Robbins and Sarah Childs dated Oct. 13, 1680, and a record of an unnamed child born the same year. It has not been possible to connect this record with John and Sarah of Harwich, but no records to the contrary are found and the connection is considered probable.

As to the probable ancestry of John, a careful study of all available early records eliminates all of the various Robbins families except the following:

1st. Mr. I. Gilbert Robbins in his manuscript record refers to one Nathaniel Robbins, who married in Barnstable in 1641 Mary Hinckley,

THE ROBBINS FAMILY

daughter of the first Samuel of that name. Mr. Robbins assumes that John might have been a child of this marriage. Inasmuch as there was at this time a family named Childs in Barnstable in which Samuel and Richard were family names, this line if proved may clear up the uncertainty as to the maiden name of Sarah, wife of John Robbins.

2nd. The frequent use of the name Richard in the Cape Cod family suggests the descent from Richard of Cambridge, who had a son John born at Charlestown May 31, 1640, not accounted for in the records, although mentioned in the will of his father. This man appears somewhat old but the deed above referred to would seem to indicate that in 1713 John was old and infirm and unable to take care of himself.

If he is not descended from one or the other of the above it is believed he was an emigrant from England and had no known connection with other American families.

FIRST GENERATION.

JOHN[1] Robbins, born probably before 1655 and alive in 1717. No record of birth or death. Married Sarah ———, possibly Sarah Childs at Marblehead Oct. 13, 1680.

He probably lived in Harwich before 1711 and may possibly have lived in Eastham before that date.

No record of children is found but he is believed to have been the father of the following:

    Roger, mar. (1) Mercy Blackman 1710, mar. (2) Hannah Crowell 1758.

    Samuel, mar. Desire Chase 1713.

    James, mar. Thankful Higgins 1713.

Note—Sarah Robbins, who was in trouble with the church at Brewster about 1740, may have been a daughter.

SECOND GENERATION.

ROGER[2], possibly son of John[1], born before 1690, mar. (1) 1710, Mercy Blackman, prob. dau. of Peter. She died Mar. 7, 1753. Mar. (2) Aug. 26, 1758, Hannah Crowell, dau. of Joseph and Sarah, born Aug. 25, 1734. He lived at Yarmouth but owned property in Maine on which he gave quitclaim deed to brother Thomas Blackman Sept. 19, 1732, wife Mercy signing with him.

Children, all recorded at Yarmouth except first two:

    Richard, born about 1712, mar. Hannah Berry 1733.

    Eleazer, born about 1715, mar. (1) Mehitable Weeks 1736, mar. (2) Mary Bassett 1753, mar. (3) Thankful (Baker) Butler 1760.

    James, born Mar. 16, 1717, prob. died young.

    Eleanor, born Mar. 16, 1717.

    John, born July 19, 1719, mar. (1) Elizabeth Downs 1750, (2) Abigail Rogers 1758.

    Lydia, born April 24, 1721, mar. Beriah Broadbrooks 1737.

    Timothy, born June, 1724, mar. Jane Laha 1753.

SAMUEL[2], son of John[1], born prob. about 1690, mar. June 18, 1713, Desire Chase. He lived in Yarmouth, where his wife joined the church Jan. 8, 1713. Family prob. moved away. It is hoped that future search will discover records of this family.

Children at Yarmouth:

    Hannah, born Nov. 6, 1713.

Priscilla, born Mar. 5, 1715, mar. James Cowen 1736.

Thankful, born Feb. 12, 1718, mar. Simeon Covel 1746.

Seth, born Sept. 14, 1720.

Desire, born Sept. 10, 1723, prob. died young.

Joseph, born Oct. 4, 1727, mar. Rose Covel 1749.

Jonathan, born Jan. 21, 1730.

Desire, born April 18, 1733, died July 10, 1742.

Martha, born Aug. 18, 1735.

Mary, born Aug. 23, 1736.

JAMES², son of John¹, born prob. about 1690 and died at Eastham before Jan. 22, 1718, mar. April 15, 1714, Thankful Higgins at Eastham. She mar. (2) June 7, 1720, Samuel Doane and by him had five children, and died before 1741. He prob. lived in Eastham, where he left will dated Nov. 6, 1717, proved Jan. 22, 1718, mentioning wife Thankful, father John and brother Nathaniel Higgins. His one child is, however, recorded at Yarmouth.

Child at Yarmouth:
Joseph, born May 1, 1714, poss. mar. Desire Homer 1754.

THIRD GENERATION.

RICHARD² (Roger², John¹), born about 1712, died Nov. 7, 1748, mar. June 28, 1733, Hannah Berry, dau. of John, at Yarmouth. Lived both in Yarmouth and Harwich and owned land in both places.

Children recorded at Yarmouth:
William, born Mar. 22, 1734, mar. Hannah Vincent 1757.

Heman, born Feb. 24, 1736, mar. Rebecca Hall 1761.

Zilpha, born Nov. 2, 1738, mar. Jeremiah O'Kelley 1768.

Thomas, born July 22, 1741, poss. of Maine.

Jedidah, born April 5, 1745, mar. Anguish McCloud 1772.

Richard, born 1749, mar. Elizabeth Ellis 1773.

ELEAZER² (Roger², John¹), born about 1715, died July 15, 1785, mar. (1) Oct. 28, 1736, Mehitable Weeks, dau. George, d. June 24, 1750; mar. (2) July 11, 1753, Mary Bassett, pub. (3) June 28, 1760, Thankful (Baker) Butler, dau. of John. She survived him and died Nov. 9, 1809, aged 97. He lived at Brewster, where he was admitted to the church Aug. 22, 1742, but was dismissed to the South Parish church Nov. 8, 1747.

Children, first four at Brewster:
Eleazer, bapt. Jan. 9, 1740, prob. died young.

Nathaniel, bapt. 1742, mar. Lydia Broadbrooks 1766.

Abigail, bapt. Nov. 6, 1743.

James, bapt. Mar. 15, 1746, mar. Abigail Phillips 1766.

Amiell, mar. (1) Abigail Broadbrooks, (2) Phebe Smalley.

Thomas, born July, 1765, mar. Anna Rogers 1793.

Eleazer (prob. second of name), mar. Anna Chase 1790.

Thankful, mar. Joseph Walker 1794.

JOHN² (Roger², John¹), born July 19, 1719, mar. (1) Feb. 8, 1750, Elizabeth Downs, mar. (2) Feb. 23, 1753, Abigail Rogers. Lived at Yarmouth but probably moved away.

Children at Yarmouth:
Sarah, born Mar. 22, 1751, mar. William Garrock 1776.

James, born Sept. 17, 1752, mar. Dorcas Linnell 1776.

Mercy, born July 5, 1754, mar. Nathan Chase 1782.
Elizabeth, born Nov. 7, 1756.
John, born Oct. 12, 1758, soldier in Revolution.
David, born Dec. 11, 1760, of Barnstable.
Ruth, born Aug. 16, 1763.
Josiah, born Aug. 9, 1766.
Deborah, born Dec. 18, 1768.
Thankful, born Dec. 18, 1768.
Thomas, born May 14, 1771.

TIMOTHY³ (Roger², John¹), born June, 1724, died before 1790, mar. Mar. 9, 1753, Jane Laha. He was published to Mercy Laha Aug. 10, 1751, but married Jane. Jane was a widow in Yarmouth in 1790 census. Children recorded at Dennis:
James, born Dec. 25, 1753.
Mercy, born Sept. 24, 1755.
Richard, born Sept. 5, 1757, died Apr. 5, 1758.
Richard, born Mar. 21, 1759.
John, born Dec. 25, 1760.
Henry, born Mar. 13, 1763, mar. Elizabeth Crowell 1785.
Samuel, born July 21, 1765.
Tamson, born July 11, 1767, mar. Jonathan Tripp 1790.
Timothy, born Nov. 25, 1769.
Mary, born July 21, 1772, mar. Lemuel Studley 1794.
Eli, born June 26, 1773, mar. Achsah Kelley 1798.
Eliphalet, born Dec. 26, 1776, mar. Betty Rogers 1802.
Abigail, born Dec. 26, 1776, mar. Abner Studley 1799.

FOURTH GENERATION.

Note.—Inasmuch as all of the following are descendants of Roger², John¹, these names will not be repeated in the indication of descent.

WILLIAM⁴, son of Richard³, born Mar. 22, 1734, died 1814; mar. Mar. 5, 1757, Hannah Vincent, dau. Isaac. Lived in Yarmouth and Harwich and died at Brewster, where his estate was admin. June 28, 1814, and an allowance granted Hannah, his widow, Oct. 11, 1814. In 1790 census he had listed three sons under 16 and five females.
Children, part at Yarmouth and part at Harwich:
Abner, born July 10, 1758, mar. Jenkins 1778.
Enoch, born about 1760, moved to South Carolina.
William, born 1763, mar. Thankful Clark 1785.
Hannah, mar. Thomas Robbins.
Thankful, born Aug. 13, 1768, mar. Benjamin Walker 1793.
Anna, mar. Nathan Robbins 1796.
Judith, born Oct. 17, 1775, mar. (1) Samuel Cash, (2) Richard Robbins.
Thomas, born Aug. 11, 1781.
Jonathan, born May 17, 1785, mar. Rachel Newcomb 1804.

HEMAN⁴, son of Richard³, born Feb. 24, 1736, died in Me. 1815; mar. Oct. 2, 1761, Rebecca Hall, dau. Josiah, born July 8, 1737. Lived at East Yarmouth, from where his wife was dismissed to the church in Maine Oct. 14, 1787. He moved to Maine with his family about 1775 and settled first at Dresden, but moved to Vassalboro in 1777, where he took lot No. 53 and built a home. Became a prominent man in this district.
Children, all at East Yarmouth except the last:
Margery, born Aug. 3, 1762, bapt. May 12, 1765.

Thomas, born Aug. 17, 1765, mar. Hannah Robbins.

Isaac, bapt. Sept. 27, 1767, mar. Rebecca Adams 1799.

Nathan, bapt. June 11, 1769, mar. Ana Robbins 1796.

Rebecca, bapt. Sept. 22, 1771.

Huldah, bapt. Mar. 13, 1774.

Heman, Jr., born about 1776, mar. Desire Mathews.

Note.—The East Yarmouth published records give another son, Howes, bapt. Oct. 13, 1765, but not again referred to. It is assumed that this was Thomas, who was born two months earlier and is the only one of this family without record of baptism.

RICHARD[4], son of Richard[3], born 1749, died Dec. 13, 1819, age 70, mar. July 8, 1773, Elizabeth Ellis. He lived and died in Harwich, where he was a deacon in the Baptist church. His name is in the 1790 census with two sons under 16 and four females. He served in the Revolution.

Children, order uncertain:
Richard, born Sept. 30, 1774, mar. (1) Judith (Robbins) Cash 1802, mar. (2) Roxanna Ellis 1816.

Seth, mar. Sarah Robbins 1794.

Judith

Jerusha, mar. Richard Chase.

Hannah, mar. William Walker 1822.

Note.—The above does not agree with Mr Robbins' manuscript, which states that Richard married Judith Cash and Judith mar. Samuel Cash.

NATHANIEL[4], son of Eleazer[3], bapt. 1742, died Feb. 9, 1810, age 68. Pub. Mar. 22, 1766, Lydia Broadbrooks, dau. Ebenezer and Lydia Winslow. She died Sept. 11, 1820. His name appears in 1790 census with 1 son over 16, four sons under 16 and one female. Lived at Harwich Centre, where he was a member of the Congregational church.

Children at Harwich:
Mehitable, born Mar. 27, 1767, mar. (1) Reuben Tripp 1786, mar. (2) Ebenezer Weeks 1803, mar. (3) Seth Nickerson.

Nathaniel, born May 31, 1769, died young.

Lydia, born Mar. 27, 1771, mar. Thomas Smalley 1789.

Nathaniel, born Sept. 24, 1774, mar. Bathsheba Nickerson 1796.

James, born Feb. 24, 1776, mar. Hannah Nickerson 1795.

Kimbal, born April 8, 1779, mar. Sally Berry 1802.

Freeman, born June 15, 1782, mar. (1) Polly Nickerson, mar. (2) Deborah (Mayo) Eldridge.

Nathan, born May 30, 1784, mar. Lucy Phillips 1808.

JAMES[4], son of Eleazer[3], bapt. Mar. 15, 1746, prob. died before 1790, mar. Dec. 3, 1766, Abigail Phillips. Lived at Harwich until about 1778, when he moved to East Greenwich, R. I., and soon after to Warren, Litchfield Co., Conn., where he held several minor town offices 1786 to 1791. Not in 1790 census but town of Warren agreed to pay his doctor's bill in 1792, at which time he was probably deceased. Served in Revolution in Capt. James Davis' Co. and with Capt. Mathias Tobey at Ticonderoga in 1777.

Children at Harwich:
Eleanor, born Oct. 24, 1768.
Mary, born Oct. 11, 1770.
Abigail, born Feb. 16, 1773.
Thankful, born June 22, 1775.

THE ROBBINS FAMILY

James, born Feb. 7, 1777. and possibly others at Warren.

AMIEL⁴, son of Eleazer³, born prob. died in Maine; mar. (1) Mar. 3, 1770, Abigail Broadbroks, dau. Beriah, mar. (2) Apr. 22, 1779, Phebe Smalley, dau. Jonathan. He lived at Harwich but moved to Maine about 1796 and settled at Swansville. He appears in 1790 census with 3 sons under 16 and 4 females. On Feb. 8, 1785, he was appointed guardian of his three minor children. In Capt. Smalley's Co. in Revol.

Children at Harwich, order uncertain:
Mary
Sarah, mar. Seth Robbins 1794.
Desire, mar. Zenas Ellis 1796.
Elisha
Elijah
Ammiel
Eleazer

THOMAS⁴, son of Eleazer³, born July, 1765, d. Mar. 5, 1841, age 75. Pub. Mar. 31, 1794, Anna Rogers, dau. Eleazer, d. Nov. 8, 1846. He lived at Orleans, where his estate was admin. April 21, 1841, his widow Anna assenting.

Children at Orleans:
Mehitable, born Aug. 8, 1795, mar. David Eldridge 1837.
Anna, born Dec. 23, 1796, mar. (1) Phineas Phillips, (2) Freeman Hayden.
Sally, born Jan. 30, 1799, died unmarried 1882.
Thomas, born Dec. 18, 1800, mar. (1) Elizabeth Eldridge, (2) Delilah Butler.
Child, born 1803, died infant.
Abigail, born Oct. 1, 1806, mar. James Smith 1842.

ELEAZER⁴, son of Eleazer³, born , lost at sea 1798; mar. 1790, Anna Chase, dau. Daniel, who mar. again Feb. 28, 1805, Daniel Kelley. He lived at Harwich, where his estate was settled Aug. 4, 1798, Daniel Chase being admin. He was a petitioner from Harwich Jan. 16, 1746.

Children at Harwich:
Nehemiah, born Oct. 16, 1792, mar. Zipporah Brooks 1816.
Thankful, born Oct. 1, 1794, mar. Kimbal Eldridge 1816.
Eleazer, born Mar. 14, 1795, died Nov. 14, 1798.
Sylvia, born Nov. 21, 1796, mar. (1) Nathaniel Tripp 1816, (2) Freeman Taylor, (3) Barnabas Wixon.

JAMES⁴, son of John³, born Sept. 17, 1752; mar. Aug. 1, 1776, Dorcas Linnell. He lived at Yarmouth, where his name appears in 1790 census with five females. Served in Revolution with Capt. Joseph Pilmer, Capt. Jose Silvester and Capt. John Chadwick.

Children at Yarmouth:
Elizabeth, born Oct. 17, 1776, mar. Heman Linnell.
Susanna, born Aug. 25, 1778, mar. Robert Phinney 1807.
Lucy, born Nov. 17, 1782.
John, born Mar. 20, 1784, mar. Zerviah Burgess.
Deborah, born June 1, 1787, mar. James Crowell 1810.
William, born Oct. 1, 1790, mar. Betsey Cahoon 1816.

JOHN⁴, son of John³, born Oct. 12, 1758, possibly had wife Mable and son Samuel, who died May 10, 1775, age 9. He was a soldier in the Revolution.

DAVID⁴, son of JOHN³, born Dec.

11, 1760, married and had a family at Barnstable, of whom only one son is found.

Child at Barnstable:
David, born Jan. 14, 1802, mar. Mary Gross 1830.

JAMES⁴, son of Timothy³, born Dec. 15, 1753, married and had family, of whom no records are found. He is believed to have had Rufus, who mar. Letitia (Doane) Wyman at Salmon River:'

RICHARD⁴, son of Timothy³, born Mar. 21, 1759. Married and had family at Harwich but no records found. Name appears in 1790 census with two sons under 16 and five females.

JOHN⁴, son of Timothy³, born Dec. 25, 1760, died June 18, 1844, aged 83. Married but wife not known. She came from Nantucket. Moved to Fairhaven, where both he and his wife died same year.

HENRY⁴, son of Timothy³, born Mar. 13, 1763, died Aug. 4, 1829, aged 68; mar. Oct. 25, 1785, Elizabeth Crowell. He lived at Harwich. He does not appear in the 1790 census, but apparently lived there at time of his death. Will dated April 12, 1729, proved Mar. 29, 1830, mentions only his wife Elizabeth but refers to sons and daughters.

Children at Harwich:
Tamson, born June 19, 1786.
Arethusa, born Nov. 22, 1787, mar. James Baker 1810.
Elizabeth, born Nov. 2, 1789, mar. Allen Studley 1816.
Henry, born May 16, 1792, mar. (1) Priscilla Baker, (2) Ruana Eldridge.

Nathan, born Oct. 15, 1794, mar. Phebo Hopkins 1819.
Mary Crowell, born June 20, 1797, mar. William Ryder.
John, born July 16, 1803, mar. (1) Data Eldridge 1824, (2) Christian Cahoon 1851, (3) Sally Kelley 1866.
Zenas Crowell, born Jan. 14, 1807, mar. (1) Ruth Clark 1828, (2) Fanny Cahoon 1862.

ELI, son of Timothy⁴, born June 26, 1773. Pub. Jan. 19, 1798, Achsah Kelley of Dennis.

Children at Dennis:
Polly, born Aug. 28, 1799.
Achsah, born July 10, 1801.
Sylvester, born Aug. 26, 1803, mar. Betsey
Truman, born July 26, 1805.
Jonathan, born Jan. 30, 1809.
Patty K., born Mar. 15, 1811.
Nathan C., born Sept. 29, 1812.
Betsey R., born Mar. 11, 1814, mar. John Land of Philadelphia.
Alexander, born Feb. 9, 1817, mar. (1) Lucinda Brown 1841, (2) Deborah Baker 1850.

ELIPHALET⁴, son of Timothy⁴, born Dec. 26, 1776, died 1810; mar. 1802, Betty Rogers. Lived at Dennis, where his estate was admin. Mar. 19, 1810, his widow Betty being adminst. On Oct. 9, 1810, she was appointed guardian to two children, then minors.

Children at Dennis:
Samuel, born Sept. 3, 1804, mar. Huldah Studley 1824.
Eliphalet, born April 7, 1807, mar. Lydia Hall 1827.

FIFTH GENERATION.

ABNER⁵ (William⁴, Richard³), born July 10, 1758, died 1825; mar. Aug. 25, 1778, Judith Jenkins, dau. Thom-

THE ROBBINS FAMILY

as of Barnstable. He lived at Brewster, where he was a deacon in the Baptist church and from where he is listed in the 1790 census with family of two sons under 16 and three females. He was a fisherman by trade, a soldier in the Revolution in Capt. Harwood's Co. and a pensioner. His will, dated Dec. 18, 1824, proved April 22, 1845, mentions wife Judith, children Bethiah "Spindle," Nathaniel and Alexander and grandchildren Sally Crosby and Lydia Robbins.

Children at Brewster:
Bethiah, born May 7, 1779, mar. Manuel Aspendelo 1797.
Abner, born April 16, 1781, mar. Mehitable Clark 1806.
Nathaniel, born Aug. 1, 1786, mar. Anna Freeman Clark 1810.
Mercy, born Aug. 13, 1788, mar. Barnabas Crosby 1815.
Alexander, born Nov. 27, 1790, mar. Eunice Sears 1816.

WILLIAM⁵ (William⁴, Richard³), born 1763. Pub Dec. 23, 1784, to Thankful Clark. He lived at Harwich, where he appears in the 1790 census with one son under 16 and three females.

Children at Harwich:
Thankful, born   , mar. Nathan Robbins of Maine.
Ebenezer, born Jan. 11, 1788, mar. Phebe Chase.
Dorcas, born Nov. 15, 1789.
Enoch, born May 9, 1792, mar. Polly Hinckley 1818.
Polly, born Nov. 9, 1794.
David, born Mar. 13, 1797.
John, born Aug. 8, 1798, mar. (1) Rhoda Long, (2) Mahala (Briggs) Robbins.
William, born Mar. 8, 1802.

Note.—Brewster record says John was son of William and Hannah. If this record is correct it indicates William had 2nd wife named Hannah ———.

———

JONATHAN⁵ (William⁴, Richard³), born May 17, 1785, died before 1822. Pub. Nov. 17, 1804, to Rachel Newcomb, dau. Jeremiah, who married 2nd Jan. 11, 1822, Joshua Avery.

Children at Harwich:
Rachel
Thomas, born Oct. 31, 1806, mar. Jane E. Nye 1840.
Isaac,   mar. Mary Shepard.
Freeman,   mar. Ruth Crowell 1830.

———

THOMAS⁵ (Heman⁴, Richard³), born Aug. 17, 1765, mar. Hannah Robbins, dau. William⁴, his cousin. He lived at Vassalboro, Me., where he had a family, of whom only the following is found.

Child at Vassalboro:
Howes, born 1812, married

———

ISAAC⁵ (Heman⁴, Richard³), bapt. Sept. 27, 1767, died July 12, 1832; mar. 1799, Rebecca Adams, dau. Edward. She died May 3, 1865. He lived at Vassalboro, Me.

Children at Vassalboro, order uncertain:
Edward,   died in Texas.
Sarah,   mar. Reuben Fairfield.
Harriet,   mar. Isaac Fairfield.
Caroline,   mar. Hartshorne Burgess 1840.
Isaac
Hiram
William A., born 1806, mar. Mary Wales Tilden.
Charles B.
Mary,   mar. James Courage.
Margaret,   mar. Francis Tabor.

———

NATHAN⁵ (Heman⁴, Richard³),

bapt. June 11, 1769, mar. July 1796, Doane 1844, (2) Almira Chase 1864.
Anno Robbins, dau. William⁴, his
cousin. He lived in Maine but no SETH⁶ (Richard⁴, Richard³), mar¡
records of children found. He prob- 1794, Sarah Robbins, dau. Amiel.
ably had Nathan, who mar. Thank- It is believed he moved to Swans-
ful Robbins, and possibly others. ville, Me., where he had descendants
not yet identified.
HEMAN⁶ (Heman⁴, Richard³), born Probably had at Swansville:
about 1776, in Dresden, Maine, mar. Seth, who mar. Alice Seekins
Desire Mathews, dau. of James. 1826.
Lived at Vassalboro, Me., and prob- John N., who mar. Sarah W——.
ably died there.
Children in Maine, order uncertain: NATHANIEL⁶ (Nathaniel⁴, Elea-
Stillman, died aged 6. zer³), born Sept. 24, 1774, died Oct. 7,
George A., born 1812, mar. Ros- 1822, aged 47; mar. Dec. 22, 1796,
etta Donney 1834. Bathsheba Nickerson, dau. of Seth.
James, born 1813, mar. (1) Mar- She died at Harwich Aug. 2, 1853,
tha Turner, (2) Harriet Turner 1844. aged 76. He lived at Harwich Centre.
Isaiah Nathaniel Underwood admin. estate
Almira Nov. 12, 1822. Allowance given wid-
Rebecca, mar. James A. ow Bathsheba Dec. 10, 1822.
Engley. Children at Harwich:
Mehitable, born Sept. 4, 1797,
RICHARD⁶ (Richard⁴, Richard³), mar. Simeon Jones 1822.
born Sept. 30, 1774, died at Brewster; Betsy, born July 29, 1799, died
mar. (1) June 25, 1802, Judith (Rob- Nov. 2, 1826.
bins) Cash, dau. William, mar. (2) Nathan, born June 2, 1801, mar.
Jan. 5, 1816, Roxanna Ellis, dau. Polly Nickerson 1821.
Phillip. She died at Brewster Aug. Nathaniel, born Oct. 25, 1805, died
5, 1873, aged 83 years. young.
Children by first wife at Brewster: Nathaniel, born June 8, 1807, mar.
Seth, mar. (1) Olive Ellis (1) Cynthia Kelley 1828, (2) Huldah
1825, (2) Eunice Higgins 1830. Howes 1848, (3) Hepzibah Kelley
Samuel, mar. (1) Nancy 1864.
Cash, (2) Betsey Cahoon 1828, (3) Bathsheba, born Aug. 18, 1810.
Rebecca Dennis 1837. Love, born Oct. 5, 1811, mar. (1)
Richard, mar. Mahala —— Jones, (2) John Tuttle 1857.
Briggs 1828. Joshua Homer, born May 2, 1815,
Thankful, mar. William mar. Olive B. Harding 1836.
Cahoon 1826. Mary Mitchell, born Feb. 18, 1821,
Anne died Oct. 9, 1822.
Children by second wife:
Lettice, born 1818, died infant. JAMES⁵ (Nathaniel⁴, Eleazer³),
Kimbal, born Sept. 27, 1819, mar. born Feb. 24, 1776, died at Barnsta-
(1) Mary Frost 1838, (2) Lydia B. ble; mar. 1795, Hannah Nickerson,
Fish 1850. dau. of Seth. He lived at Harwich,
Gilbert, born 1823, mar. (1) Sarah where most of his children were

THE ROBBINS FAMILY

born, but moved to Cotuit after 1810.
Children:
Lydia, born Nov. 27, 1795, mar. Alvan Coleman 1816.
Polly, born June 7, 1797, mar. Pardon Burlingame.
James, born Dec. 17, 1798, mar. Sally Bearse 1821.
Clarissa, born Oct. 2, 1801, mar. Seth Goodspeed 1819.
Eleazer, born Dec. 2, 1803, died Dec. 8, 1803.
Hannah, born Dec. 2, 1804, mar. Ira Hinckley 1821.
Joseph, born July 8, 1807, mar. Persis H. Waite 1837.
Eliza, born Oct. 29, 1810, mar. John A. Blossom 1834.
Julia, born prob. at Cotuit, mar. Lot Phinney.

KIMBAL⁵ (Nathaniel⁴, Eleazer³), born April 8, 1779, died Aug. 1, 1855; mar. Nov. 1802, Sally Berry, dau. of Jonathan. She died at Brewster Aug. 25, 1855. He lived at Brewster, where he had children:
Kimbal, born Sept. 16, 1803, died Oct. 1803.
Kimbal, born Oct. 23, 1804, mar. Melinda Ellis 1831.
Eliza, born Dec. 21, 1807.
Eleazer, born Sept. 23, 1808, died 1832.
Sally, born Feb. 28, 1812, mar. Amos Kelley 1838.
Luther, born Mar. 14, 1814, mar. Sabrina Doane 1838.
Leonard, born June 21, 1817, mar. (1) Desire Allen, (2) Julia Allen 1888.
Deborah, born Jan. 17, 1820, mar. William Bassett.
Cynthia C., born Aug. 18, 1823, mar. Daniel Twyer.

FREEMAN⁵ (Nathaniel⁴, Eleazer³), born June 15, 1782, died Nov. 5, 1854,

aged; 72 mar. (1) Dec. 4, 1806, Polly Nickerson, who died June 23, 1812, (2) Dec. 20, 1812, Deborah (Mayo) Eldridge, dau. of Paul, who died Nov. 5, 1864.
Children at Harwich:
Freeman, born Aug. 28, 1807, mar. Lydia Rogers.
Hiram, born April 6, 1810, mar. Irene Eldridge.
Shubael, born July 2, 1811, mar. Eliza Ellis 1831.
Elisha, born Nov. 3, 1813, mar. (1) Desire Ellis, (2) Sarah E. Snow.
Polly, born Sept. 2, 1815, mar. Joseph Craibe 1850.
Allen, born Sept. 4, 1817. Lost at sea while young.
Alvah, born Aug. 8, 1819, mar. Ardelia Brown.
Louan, born June 15, 1821, died Sept. 26, 1822.
Benj. Franklin, born Nov. 12, 1823, mar. Emily Chism 1852.
Charles P., born Feb. 3, 1826, mar. Phebe H. Ryder 1850.
Clarington E., born June 26, 1828, mar. Dorcas D. Hammond 1855.
Harriet N., born Sept. 16, 1831, mar. John W. Dow.

NATHAN⁵ (Nathaniel⁴, Eleazer³), born May 30, 1784, died April 29, 1860, aged 75; mar. Mar. 9, 1808, Lucy Phillips, who died Oct. 6, 1848, aged 59. He lived at Harwich, where the following children are recorded:
Nathan, born Nov. 5, 1808, mar. Rose Nickerson 1833.
Rhoda, born Dec. 9, 1809, died April 10, 1818.
Almira, born Mar. 7, 1812, mar. Cornelius Eldridge.
Eliza B., born Oct. 13, 1813, mar. David Harding.
Marshall, born Sept. 11, 1815, mar. Rebecca Ryder 1840.

Lydia, born Sept. 5, 1819.
Polly, born Feb. 13, 1822, mar. William Robbins.
Sanford, born Feb. 8, 1824, mar. (1) Roxanna Buck 1851, (2) Maggy McCoy 1881.
Susan, born Feb. 4, 1827, died Mar. 2, 1836.

THOMAS[5] (Thomas[4], Eleazer[3]), born Dec. 18, 1800, died July 2, 1890; mar. (1) May 13, 1836, Elizabeth Eldridge, dau. David, died Oct. 12, 1840, (2) Jan. 17, 1842, Delilah Butler, dau. Samuel, died Mar. 19, 1878. He lived at Orleans, where he was appointed guardian of Eleazer and Joseph, two minor children, April 16, 1855.

Children at Orleans:
Eleazer F., born Aug. 6, 1837, mar. (1) Jerusha G. Eldridge 1856, (2) Anna E. Lantry.
Joseph F., born May 25, 1840, mar. (1) Abbie C. Nickerson 1865, (2) Harriet Snow 1870, (3) Almena Small 1881.
Elizabeth E., born Dec. 8, 1845, mar. (1) Joseph H. Garison 1871, (2) Wm. W. Ellis 1890.

NEHEMIAH[5] (Eleazer[4], Eleazer[3]), born Oct. 16, 1792, prob. died at Clinton; mar. April 25, 1816, Zipporah Brooks, dau. of Nathan. He lived at Harwich but moved to New Haven, Bridgeport and then to Clinton, Conn. He is said to have had 15 daughters and one son, of whom only the following is found.
The son married and had one or two children but died early.
Daughter Ruth, born Sept. 28, 1820, mar. David C. Wright 1845.

JOHN[5] (James[4], John[3]), born Mar. 20, 1784, died Feb. 11, 1859, aged 74; mar. Zeruriah Burgess, dau. Timothy.

Children at Yarmouth:
Sarah, born Aug. 14, 1815.
Child, born Aug. 24, 1817, died Oct. 1, 1817.
Azubah, born Oct. 16, 1818, mar. Lockwood Baxter.
William, born Nov. 28, 1820, mar. Sally W. Baker 1844.
Nelson, born Dec. 29, 1822, mar. Kezia Crowell 1845.
Timothy, born Dec. 12, 1825, mar. Emily Baxter 1849.
Pauline S., born April 16, 1831, died July 13, 1846.
Asa, born Jan. 18, 1834, mar. (1) Mary E. Broad 1860, (2) Ann R. Wild 1867.

WILLIAM[5] (James[4], John[3]), born Oct. 1, 1790, died 1844; mar. 1816, Betsey Cahoon, dau. Peter. He lived at Harwich, where his estate was settled Dec. 10, 1844, mentioning only his widow Betsey.

Children at Harwich:
William, born 1822, mar. Polly Robbins.
Hiram H., mar. Nancy L. Davis.
Elizabeth, mar. Stephen Cahoon.
Phebe, born June, 1834, died May 6, 1853.

DAVID[5] (David[4], John[3]), born Jan. 14, 1802, died Nov. 18, 1880, aged 78; mar. 1830, Mary Gross, who died Dec. 23, 1860, aged 52. He lived at Augusta, Me., where he died.

Children at Augusta:
John W., born May 23, 1834, mar. Angelissa Hussey.
Warren W., born April 18, 1837, mar. Ann Springer 1862.
Allen T., born July 25, 1847.

HENRY[5] (Henry[4], Timothy[3]), born

THE ROBBINS FAMILY

May 16, 1792, died Dec. 25, 1871, aged 79; pub. (1) Mar. 16, 1816, to Priscilla Baker, who died Aug. 1, 1849; mar. (2) Feb. 14, 1850, Ruana Eldridge, dau. of Freeman, who died June 6 or July —, 1866. He lived at Harwich. Cyrus Weeks appointed admin. of estate of Ruana Sept. 1, 1866, and mentions daughters Huldah C., wife of Darius Hall, and Saloma, wife of Albert Allen. No birth records of these children have been found.

Children at Harwich:
Isaiah, born Sept. 11, 1811, mar. (1) Bethania Young 1835, (2) Fanny Cahoon 1851.

Huldah C., mar. Darius Hall.
Saloma, mar. Albert Allen.
Henry C., born Aug. 11, 1821, mar. (1) Sarah S. Chase, (2) Sarah K. Sylvester 1866.

Freeman, born July 19, 1824; not married.

Roland H., born Aug. 25, 1828, mar. Bathsheba Robbins 1848.

Nehemiah B., born 1830, mar. Melissa D. Ryder 1853.

NATHAN⁶ (Henry⁴, Timothy³), born Oct. 15, 1794; pub. July 2, 1819, to Phebe Hopkins. He lived at Dennis and Brewster.

Child at Brewster:
Mary Crosby, born June 16, 1822, died Mar. 7, 1842.

JOHN⁶ (Henry⁴, Timothy³), born July 16, 1803, died May 21, 1878, aged 74; mar. (1) Sept. 28, 1824, Data Eldridge, dau. Seth, who died Nov. 26, 1850, (2) June 15, 1851, Christiana (Cahoon) Kelley, died 1851, (3) April 11, 1866, Sally (Kelley) Wixon.

Children at North Harwich:
James E., born 1830, died Aug. 2, 1837, aged 7.

Betsey, born 1833, mar. Ross G. Chase 1850.
Data, born 1838, mar. Joshua S. Baker 1855.
Amanda, born 1840, mar. Freeman D. Chase 1858.
John, born Mar. 25, 1847, died young.
John Wesley, born 1849, mar. Sarah H. Sears 1873.

ZENAS CROWELL⁵ (Henry⁴, Timothy³), born Jan. 14, 1807, died April 11, 1873, aged 66; mar. (1) 1828, Ruth Clark, dau. Heman, who d. May 20, 1862, (2) Sept. 11, 1862, Fanny (Cahoon) Robbins, dau. Heman. She mar. (3) William Ryder, who had as his first wife Mary, sister of Zenas C.

Children at North Harwich:
Laura Ann, born Jan. 1, 1827, mar. Simeon Young 1844.
Ruth Crowell, born Dec. 20, 1830, died Aug. 28, 1843.
Zenas C., born Jan. 1833, died May 10, 1834.
Freeman Studley, born Aug. 31, 1834, mar. Laura A. Atwood 1856.
Tamson Studley, born Oct. 15, 1836, mar. Leonard Clark.

SYLVESTER⁵ (Eli⁴, Timothy³), born Aug. 26, 1803, died April 7, 1860, aged 56; mar. Betsy ——.

Children at Yarmouth:
Huldah, born Nov. 6, 1835, mar. Henry Blachford 1858.
Alexander, born Dec. 23, 1837.
Thomas D., born July 1, 1840, died Oct. 11, 1847.
Stephen T., born Jan. 2, 1843.
John K., born Aug. 5, 1845, mar. Cordelia C. Baker 1872.

ALEXANDER⁵ (Eli⁴, Timothy³)), born Feb. 9, 1817, died June 13, 1893, aged 76; mar. (1) Dec. 2, 1841, Lucinda Brown, who died about 1843, (2) July 7, 1850, Deborah Baker, dau. Crowell.

Children at Yarmouth:
Child, born Sept. 6, 1843, died Oct. 1, 1843.
Foster Stafford, born Aug. 19, 1850.
Clara L., born 1853, mar. Benj. F. Dray 1871.
Elizabeth Parker, born Dec. 15, 1858.

SAMUEL⁵ (Eliphalet⁴, Timothy³), born Sept. 3, 1804, died Jan. 22, 1860, aged 55; mar. Oct. 7, 1824, Huldah Studley.

Children at Dennis:
Eliphalet H., born June 17, 1825, mar. Ann L. Chase 1847.
Rebecca, born June 24, 1828, died Mar. 28, 1829.
Samuel, born Oct. 22, 1831, died June 8, 1833.
Emeline W., born Sept. 24, 1834, mar. Joseph A. Baker 1853.
Mary E., born Oct. 2, 1837, mar. Michael McNeil 1853.
Samuel, born July 3, 1842, mar. Cordelia F. Luce 1871.
George G. H., born Dec. 27, 1844, mar. Ellen G. Thacher 1869.
Huldah M., born Mar. 3, 1846, died July 22, 1864.

ELIPHALET⁵ (Eliphalet⁴, Timothy³), born April 7, 1807, died May 14, 1864, aged 57; mar. Nov. 29, 1827, Lydia L. Hall, dau. Jonathan. She died Dec. 8, 1893, aged 85.

Children at Harwich Centre:
Betsey Rogers, born Sept. 29, 1828, mar. John G. Lucas 1853.
Priscilla L., born Mar. 21, 1830, mar. James H. Crittenden 1847.

Jonathan Hall, born Dec. 25, 1831, died Sept. 26, 1833.
Eliphalet, born Nov. 30, 1835, mar. Anna E. Coombs 1856.
Elizabeth, born 1839, mar. Rowland W. Snow 1855.

SIXTH GENERATION.

ABNER⁶ (Abner⁵, William⁴, Richard³), born April 16, 1781, died before 1817; mar. Feb. 17, 1806, Mehitable Clark, who mar. (2) at Brewster June 21, 1817, John Smith of Harwich. Estate adm. Aug. 12, 1817, and Silvanus Bangs appointed guardian of minor child Lydia. On Oct. 14, 1817, an allowance is granted to Mehitable Smith.

Child at Brewster:
Lydia, of whom nothing further is found.

NATHANIEL⁶ (Abner⁵, William⁴, Richard³), born Aug. 1, 1786, died Nov. 24, 1868; pub. Aug. 22, 1810, to Anna Freeman Clark, who died April 27, 1857, aged 66.

Children at Brewster:
Fanny, born July 20, 1812, mar. Moses Hopkins 1833.
Nathaniel, born Jan. 29, 1815, mar. Sarah Williams.
Eliza Ann, born Aug. 22, 1820, died Jan. 3, 1823.
Joseph Henry, born May 12, 1823, mar. Sarah Joy 1843.
Joshua Clark, born May 1, 1826, mar. (1) Delilah Maker 1847, (2) Anne Revolle 1862.

ALEXANDER⁶ (Abner⁵, William⁴ Richard³), born Nov. 27, 1790, died Nov. 19, 1876, aged 86; mar. Nov. 23, 1816, Eunice Sears, dau. Christopher. She died Jan. 22, 1867, aged 70, and is buried with her husband at Cohasset. He lived at Brewster until

THE ROBBINS FAMILY

about 1850, when he moved to Plymouth, where he died. He was a mariner.

Children at Brewster:

Alexander, born Jan. 19, 1813, mar. Eliza A. Chapman.

William S., born Oct. 2, 1819, drowned Dec. 26, 1832.

Mary Snow, born Sept. 18, 1822, mar. Capt. Cyrus W. Gammons 1838.

Eunice Sears, born Nov. 7, 1824, mar. Capt. Nelson T. Spoor 1849.

Abner, born July 14, 1826, died Dec. 1826.

Mercy A., born Sept. 5, 1828, mar. Capt. Benj. R. Pegram.

Lot S., born Jan. 9, 1830, died unmarried in Cal.

Infant, born Aug. 22, 1831, died same day.

Abner R., born Sept. 24, 1832, mar. Catharine Pratt 1852.

William, born July 1, 1835, died in Californie 1860.

Cyrus, born Nov. 1, 1837, mar. Almina (Bartlett) Jeffries.

Emma Smith, born June 17, 1841, mar. Frank Davenport.

EBENEZER[6] (William[5], William[4], Richard[3]), born Jan. 11, 1788, died 1825; mar. Phebe Chase. He lived at Harwich, where his estate was admin. Mar. 8, 1825. He was a mariner.

Children at Harwich:

Freeman, born 1812, mar. Mercy Hayden.

Nathan, born 1821, mar Emeline Eldridge.

Rosalinda, born Mar. 22, 1822, mar. —— Ryan.

and doubtless others.

ENOCH[6] (William[5], William[4], Richard[3]), born May 9, 1792, died 1826; mar. May 14, 1818, Polly Hinckley. He lived at Dennis, where his estate was admin. Dec. 12, 1826, but wife or children not mentioned. He is possibly the father of Enoch who mar. Ruth and had Erastus Mar. 25, 1844.

JOHN[6] (William[5], William[4], Richard[3]), born Aug. 8, 1798, died April 6, 1879, aged 80; pub. Mar. 13, 1821, to Rhoda Long. She died Feb. 20, 1842, mar. (2) July 6, 1843, Mahala (Briggs) Robbins, widow of Richard. The Brewster records give his age at time of second marriage as 45 and state he was son of William and Hannah. He was a farmer and lived at Brewster, where are recorded:

Children:

William, born Sept. 3, 1821, mar. Fanny G. Rogers 1842.

Silvanus, born Sept. 24, 1824, mar. Clarissa Long 1844.

Polly A., born Nov. 28, 1826, mar. Charles Spinney 1851.

John C., born July 9, 1829, mar. Typhosa Brown 1851.

Eliza Ann, born Sept. 12, 1831, mar. John F. McLane 1852.

Clarissa, born May 3, 1833, mar. Joshua Howland 1857.

Daniel H., born Feb. 3, 1837, mar. (1) Jedidah Sears 1857. (2) Louisa H. Chapman 1869.

Henry, born Oct. 3, 1839, died Feb. 20, 1842.

Rhoda Ann, born Sept. 3, 1841, mar. Amos Ayer 1859.

Henry Nelson, born Dec. 27, 1843.

Lydia Frances, born Feb. 21, 1850, mar. Alfred Gould 1871.

Mary E., born Nov. 28, 1851.

HOWES[6] (Thomas[5], Heman[4], Richard[3]), born 1812, died in Maine 1889; married but name of wife not found. He lived at Vassalboro, Me., and had

at least one child:
 Oliver P., born 1838, mar. Martha T. Pierce.

WILLIAM A.⁵ (Isaac⁴, Heman³, Richard²), born 1806, died July 15, 1848, aged 42; mar. Mary Wales Tilden, who died Dec. 2, 1867, aged 61. He lived at Vassalboro, Me., where he had:

Children:
Augustus, born Jan. 4, 1838, mar. Jennie A. Burke 1866.
Mary W., born May 29, 1842, mar. Andrew Tilden 1864.
Phebe N., born May 29, 1842, prob. died young.
William Atherton, born Sept. 10, 1844, mar. Lucy Kent 1868.

CHARLES B.⁵ (Isaac⁴, Heman³, Richard²), born at Vassalboro, Me., married but name of wife not found. He had at Vassalboro:
 Sumner, born 1844, died in California 1878.
 Smith born 1846, mar. Florence Hawes.

GEORGE A.⁵ (Heman⁴, Heman³, Richard²), born 1812, mar. Oct. 26, 1834, Rosetta Bonney in Maine. He lived at Vassalboro, but had no children.

JAMES⁵ (Heman⁴, Heman³, Richard²), born 1813, mar. (1) Martha Turner and (2) Harriet C. Turner about 1844. He lived at Vassalboro, where he had:
 Daughter by first wife, mar. Hartwell Churchill.
 Julia D., born about 1846.
 George A., born about 1848, mar. Anna B. Randall 1872.
 Albert, born about 1850.
 Ira J.

SETH⁵ (Richard⁴, Richard³, Richard²), born prob. about 1803, died July 11, 1885; mar. (1) Oct. 27 1825, Olive Ellis, dau. Charles, pub. (2) Nov. 6, 1830, Eunice Higgins, dau. Elkanah. She died April, 1883, aged 83.

Children at Brewster:
Seth G., born Sept. 19, 1827, mar. Patience W. Crowingshield 1849.
Albert, born Sept. 29, 1831 mar. Sally D. Willmarth 1858.
Olive, born Aug. 15, 1833, mar. Nathan Kenney 1855.
Isaiah, born Aug. 8, 1835, mar. Mary H. Higgins 1857.
Freeman, born Sept. 11, 1837, mar. Deborah Crosby 1860.
Eunice H., born 1841, mar. Asa Higgins 1865.
Anna, born 1844, mar. Warren Parker 1862.

SAMUEL⁵ (Richard⁴, Richard³, Richard²), born prob. about 1805, mar. (1) Nancy Cash, who died before 1826, (2) Feb. 12, 1826, Betsey Cahoon, who died Nov. 4, 1836, pub. (3) Feb. 10, 1837, Rebecca Dennis.

Children at Brewster:
Ellen
Richard, born May 30, 1827, mar. Mrs. Kate Knowles 1857.
Harriet, born Sept. 22, 1828.
Ann, born Jan. 10, 1832.
Elizabeth, born Feb. 1839, mar. John Brown 1856.
Amber J., born June 10, 1843, mar. Samuel Newcomb 1865.
Emily H., born 1846, mar. George W. Walker 1863.
Mary Hallett, born Feb. 11, 1850, mar. Joseph P. Ellis 1863.

RICHARD⁵ (Richard⁴, Richard³, Richard²), born about 1807, died Oct. 1841; pub. Jan. 19, 1828, to Mahala

Briggs of Dennis. She mar. (2) July 6, 1843, John Robbins. He lived at Brewster, where his estate was admin. Feb. 8, 1842, and Stephen Homer was appointed guardian of Eliza Jan. 13, 1846. Dower allowed to Mahala April 19, 1842.

Children at Brewster:
Eliza Ann, born April 10, 1828.
Samuel F., born July 16, 1830.
Richard H., born Aug. 6, 1832.
Thankful, born Oct. 9, 1834.
Nelson F., born Oct. 10, 1836.
Franklin F., born Aug. 3, 1839.
Mahala F., born July 16, 1841, died July 19, 1843.

KIMBAL[6] (Richard[5], Richard[4], Richard[3]), born Sept. 27, 1819, mar. (1) 1838, Mary Frost, who died Mar. 20, 1880, (2) Nov. 25, 1880, Lydia B. Fish, dau. Jehiel.

Children at Harwich:
Kimbal, born Sept. 13, 1838, died young.
Lettice D., born Sept. 27, 1840, mar. (1) Charles B. Megillion 1860 (2) William Garfield 1897.
Kimbal W., born Sept. 27, 1842, mar. Jennie Ricketts.
Mary E., born Aug. 19, 1845, mar. Lorenzo F. Cahoon 1866.
Martin Luther, born Sept. 30, 1848, mar. Bertha E. Baker 1877.
Isaac E., born Mar. 5, 1850, died April 1, 1852.
Ellen A., born Sept. 3, 1852, mar. Nehemiah B. Robbins 1870.
Isaac E., born Sept. 10, 1854, died May 12, 1857.
Sarah E., born May 11, 1857, mar. Herbert F. Robbins 1878.
Bathsheba G., born Dec. 25, 1859, mar. Henry B. Enos 1878.

GILBERT[6] (Richard[5], Richard[4], Richard[3]), born 1823, mar. (1) Feb. 22, 1844, Sarah Doane, dau. Freeman, who died June 1862, (2) June 15, 1864, Almira Chase, dau. Ensign.

Children at Harwich:
Roxanna, born Sept. 23, 1844, mar. Joseph H. Cahoon.
Gilbert, born June 18, 1849, mar. Eliza E. Bearse 1869.
Meranda D., born Sept. 6, 1851, mar. Richard Gray.
Samuel F., born 1854, mar. Mercy Gray 1874.
Nelson W., born Sept. 26, 1855, mar. Lizzie C. Silver 1874.
Christal W., born Sept. 8, 1856, mar. (1) Ada Baker 1879, (2) Mary E. Fish 1881.
Edith, born Mar. 26, 1858, died young.
Edith E., born 1861, mar. Joseph Swears 1878.
Sarah D., born May, 1862, died Aug. 16, 1862.
Charles E., born May 13, 1862, mar. Sheba S. Ellis 1888.
Pamelia C., born 1864, mar. (1) Wendell F. Robbins 1882, (2) Charles B. Nickerson 1888.

SETH[6] (Seth[5], Richard[4], Richard[3]), poss. mar. Oct. 25, 1826, Alice Seekins at Swansville, Me. No record of children.

JOHN N.[6] (Seth[5], Richard[4], Richard[3]), born 1809, died at Swansville; mar. Sarah W——.

Children at Swansville, Me.:
William H., born June 6, 1845, mar. Lillian F. Walton 1870.
Martin, born 1853, mar. (1) Louisa Jenkins 1877, (2) Ella O. Colby 1884.
And doubtless others.

NATHAN[6] (Nathaniel[5], Nathaniel[4], Eleazer[3]), born June 2, 1801, died May 14, 1847, aged 45; mar. April 12, 1821,

Polly Nickerson, dau. of Silas, who survived him and mar. (2) Judah Chase. She died Aug. 19, 1860.

Children at Harwich:
Nathaniel, born Oct. 17, 1822, mar. (1) Meribah P. Rogers 1847, (2) Lydia D. Williams 1855, (3) Louisa (Chase) Baker 1881.

Sally W., born Dec. 15, 1824, mar. Sylvester Nickerson.

Sidney N., born June 20, 1829, mar. Esther A. Small 1851.

Nathan A., born Oct. 8, 1831, mar. Sophronia E. Miles 1856.

Orrick N., born Nov. 15, 1833. Lost at sea Sept. 1, 1851.

Silas N., born Sept. 21, 1835, mar. Loretta G. Bassett 1858.

Polly N., born Dec. 15, 1837, mar. Otis M. Cahoon 1858.

Marion M., born Sept. 25, 1843, died Jan. 1, 1865.

Delia W., born 1846, mar. Augustus Baker 1866.

NATHANIEL[5] (Nathaniel[4], Nathaniel[3], Eleazer[2]), born June 8, 1807, died Dec. 1, 1888, aged 81; mar. (1) April 10, 1828, Cynthia Kelley, dau. Patrick, died Dec. 4, 1847, aged 38, (2) Nov. 14, 1848, Huldah (Howes) Kelley, dau. Ezra, died July 27, 1863, (3) July 7, 1864, Hepzibah (Kelley) Chase, dau. Patrick.

Children at Harwich Centre:
Nathaniel, born Sept. 5, 1829, mar. Hannah D. Nickerson 1848.

Bathsheba, born Nov. 20, 1832, mar. (1) Roland H. Robbins 1848, (2) Isaac Bea 1880.

Love C., born Nov. 10, 1835, mar. (1) Ebenezer Smalley 1858, (2) Cyrus Howes.

Wendell P., born Aug. 23, 1849.

Joseph K., born Sept. 20, 1853, mar. Helen C. Paine 1877.

Rebecca H., born Oct. 9, 1855, died Sept. 9, 1857.

JOSHUA HOMER[5] (Nathaniel[4], Nathaniel[3], Eleazer[2]), born May 2, 1815, killed at Harwich April 8, 1865, firing a cannon in celebration of a Union victory. Mar. Aug. 16, 1836, Olive B. Harding, dau. of Veranus; she survived him and mar. (2) Jan. 14, 1871, Charles Lincoln. His estate was admin. Oct. 30, 1865, his widow Olive being named administrator, mentions his three children alive at that date.

Children at Harwich:
Ferdinand, born Dec. 30, 1836, mar. Eliza N. Burgess 1859.

Gustavus C., born June 13, 1840, mar. Mary G. Thacher 1865.

Mary E., born April 30, 1842, died May 13, 1843.

Mary C., born Nov. 13, 1845, mar. Henry J. Higgins 1864.

Olivia F., born Sept. 12, 1846, died Oct. 31, 1847.

Eliza H., born Mar. 27, 1849, died Dec. 25, 1856.

George T., born Nov. 10, 1851, died Dec. 25, 1856.

Olivia F., born Dec. 20, 1852, died Dec. 22, 1856.

Daughter, born Nov. 22, 1857, died same day.

JOSEPH[5] (James[4], Nathaniel[3], Eleazer[2]), born July 8, 1807, died Mar. 2, 1888, aged 81; mar. 1837, Persis Hallet Waitt.

Children at Barnstable:
Medora M., born Nov. 5, 1837, mar. (1) Isaac Hedges 1858, (2) Horace S. Lowell 1872.

Joseph A., born April 24, 1839, died April 24, 1841.

Emeline C., born April 17, 1841, mar. John H. Cammett 1864.

Laura A., born Nov. 17, 1843, mar. Eugene F. Blossom 1874.

Everett Clinton, born July 31, 1845.

Adeline, born Oct. 25, 1846, died Aug. 22, 1848.

Atteresta W., born Aug. 23, 1848, mar. Andrew Johnson 1871.

Persis E., born Nov. 14, 1850, died Feb. 2, 1855.

Abbott Lawrence, born Sept. 10, 1852, mar. Fanny Austin Lowell 1886.

Sophrina G., born May 24, 1854, died Feb. 14, 1855.

Edith M., born Dec. 14, 1856, mar. Charles H. Crosby 1877.

Penelope, born Mar. 29, 1860, died May 14, 1860.

Geneva C., born Sept. 6, 1861, died Aug. 7, 1862.

KIMBAL⁵ (Kimbal⁵, Nathaniel⁴, Eleazer³), born Oct. 23, 1804; mar. 1831, Melinda Ellis, dau. Henry, who died Mar. 21, 1886, aged 77. Lived at Brewster but moved to New Bedford.
Children:
Bethiah Hall, born Oct. 14, 1832, died July 28, 1832.
Bethiah Hall, born 1835, mar. Abiathar Rogers 1852.
Albert Loring, born Mar. 25, 1837.
Daughter, born Nov. 2, 1846, at New Bedford.

LUTHER⁵ (Kimbal⁵, Nathaniel⁴, Eleazer³), born Mar. 14, 1814, died 1840; mar. Mar. 15, 1838, Sabrina Doane. He lived and died at Harwich, where his estate was admin. April 20, 1840. Widow Sabrina appointed adm. but no children are mentioned.

LEONARD⁵ (Kimbal⁵, Nathaniel⁴, Eleazer³), born June 21, 1817, died Nov. 6, 1890; mar. (1) Desire Allen, dau. James, died Sept. 26, 1887, (2) Dec. 17, 1888, Julia Allen, dau. Zephaniah, who survived him and mar. (2) Alixi Nickerson Dec. 1, 1893. No records of children.

FREEMAN⁶ (Freeman⁵, Nathaniel⁴, Eleazer³), born Aug. 28, 1807, lost at sea 1844; mar. Lydia Rogers, dau. of Edmund and Thankful. She survived him and mar. (2) David Harwood of Manchester, N. H., at Brewster, Nov. 27, 1845. No record of children.

HIRAM⁶ (Freeman⁵, Nathaniel⁴, Eleazer³), born April 6, 1810, died in Cal.; mar. Irene Eldridge. He lived in Sandwich but moved to Wareham and then to California.
Children at Sandwich:
George Henry, born Nov. 5, 1833, mar. (1) Desire G. Pierce 1854, (2) Eunice C. Pierce 1857.
Darius Eldridge, born May 28, 1835, mar. (1) Christina McCullen 1853, (2) Mary J. Harris 1872, (3) Mary Ellen ———.
Bethiah K., born Feb. 14, 1840.
Freeman Allen, born Aug. 11, 1841.
Charles Albert, born Nov. 19, 1844, did not marry.
Hiram, born Feb. 13, 1847, died Feb. 22, 1847.
Thomas M., born 1848, mar. Martha E. Francis 1870.

SHUBAEL⁶ (Freeman⁵, Nathaniel⁴, Eleazer³), born July 2, 1811, died Dec. 24, 1887, aged 76; mar. 1831, Eliza Ellis, dau. Henry, who died June 22, 1893, aged 81.
Children at Harwich:
Joseph, born Sept. 12, 1832, mar. Laura A. Ellis 1854.
Shubael, born Dec. 13, 1834, died June 11, 1857.

Freeman T., born June 28, 1838, mar. Sarah F. Phinney 1861.

Elizabeth M., born Dec. 26, 1842, mar. Amos Kelley 1861.

Elisha E., born May 12, 1846, mar. Jane A. Howland 1867.

Mary Ann F., born April 15, 1848, mar. Simeon S. Kendrick 1866.

Jervis N., born Aug. 30, 1851, died Nov. 30, 1851.

Ellen M., born Feb. 6, 1853, died May 11, 1853.

ELISHA[6] (Freeman[5], Nathaniel[4], Eleazer[3]), born Nov. 3, 1813; mar. (1) Desire Ellis, dau. Henry, who died May 6, 1850, aged 32, (2) Sarah E. Snow, dau. Nathaniel, who died 1882, aged 59.

Children at Harwich:

Deborah A., born Oct. 11, 1835. mar. (1) Darius Rogers, 1851, (2) Nathan C. Robbins 1855, (3) Nathan Smith 1878.

Abbie G., born Oct. 13, 1837, mar. Richard S. Handy 1857.

Washington E., born June 14, 1840, mar. Rebecca G. Nickerson 1861.

Elisha F., born Sept. 17, 1842, mar. Charlotte B. Rogers 1863.

Job Chase, born April 20, 1845, died aged 5 or 6.

Desire, born May 2, 1850, died next day.

Henry C. W., born Aug. 30, 1853.

Wm. Lloyd Garrison, born 1855, mar. Mary C. Savery 1877.

Annie Gertrude, Sept. 11, 1856, mar. Simeon F. Holman 1879.

Jessie, born July 25, 1858

ALVAH[6] (Freeman[5], Nathaniel[4], Eleazer[3]), born Aug. 8, 1819, died Jan. 20, 1891, aged 71; mar. Ardelia Brown. Moved to Mansfield, Conn., where he had:

Francis B., born 1845, mar. Narzette F. Mason 1880.

Thomas S., born July 4, 1846, mar. Fanny J. Smith 1875.

Sarah, m. Francis Bunker.

Abby

And probably others.

BENJAMIN FRANKLIN[6] (Freeman[5], Nathaniel[4], Eleazer[3]), born Nov. 12, 1823; mar. Nov. 4, 1852, Emily F. Chism of Maine, who died July 9, 1870. He was a mariner and sailed his ships all over the world.

Children at Harwich:

Charles B., born Jan. 11, 1854, not married.

Emily F., born Dec. 15, 1857, died Oct. 24, 1858.

Carrie A., born July 11, 1861.

Hattie V., born Jan. 1, 1870.

CHARLES P.[6] (Freeman[5], Nathaniel[4], Eleazer[3]), born Feb. 3, 1826; mar. (1) Jan. 16, 1850, Phebe H. Ryder, dau. William, died May 6, 1853; (2) Susanna B. Kendrick.

Children at Harwich:

Clarington E., born Nov. 23, 1851. died 1859 or 1860.

Sarah Doane, born July 22, 1858.

Cynthia C., born July 2, 1864, mar. Lewis Johnson 1883.

CLARINGTON ELDRIDGE[6] (Freeman[5], Nathaniel[4], Eleazer[3]), born June 26, 1828; mar. Jan. 18, 1855, Dorcas D. Hammond, dau. of John, who died Aug. 23, 1888, aged 57. She was from Chatham. He was a mariner and captain of over twenty vessels, and was commissioned capt. in the Civil war.

Children, probably at Harwich:

Susan Jeanette, born Nov. 8, 1855, died Dec. 16, 1856.

THE ROBBINS FAMILY

Mercy Claringtina, born Aug. 2, 1859.

NATHAN⁶ (Nathan⁵, Nathaniel⁴, Eleazer³), born Nov. 5, 1808, died Jan. 3, 1837; mar. Jan. 15, 1833, Rose Nickerson, dau. Sylvanus. He lived at Harwich, was a mariner and was lost at sea. Estate admin. Aug. 8, 1837, widow Rose assenting. Widow mar. (2) Elias Crowell Dec. 1, 1844.

Children at Harwich:
Lucy Phillips, born Sept. 2, 1834, mar. George V. Mecarta 1855.
Ruth Crowell, born Oct. 9, 1836, mar. Hezekiah Mooney 1861.

MARSHAL⁶ (Nathan⁵, Nathaniel⁴, Eleazer³), born Sept. 11, 1815, died Nov. 21, 1869, aged 54; mar. Nov. 28, 1840, Rebecca Ryder, dau. Samuel.

Children at Chatham:
Susanna, born 1840, mar. Zoeth Nickerson 1866.
Rufus M., born Aug. 20, 1845, died July 1, 1846.
Ann Rebecca, born June 12, 1847, mar. Luther A. Sears 1869.
Rufus M., born Feb. 3, 1850, mar. Susanna Graves 1872.
Isaac E., born Nov. 6, 1851, mar. Mehitable Graves 1874.
Jedidah R., born Jan. 5, 1854, mar. William F. Handren 1877.
Nathan C., born May 4, 1855, mar. Alice Baker 1877.
Lewis R., born June 2, 1857.
Everett E., born July 9, 1859, mar. Cora B. Eldridge 1881.
Edrick S., born July 9, 1859, mar. Abbie C. Nickerson 1887.

SANFORD⁶ (Nathan⁵, Nathaniel⁴, Eleazer³), born Feb. 8, 1824; mar. (1) April 9, 1851, Roxanna Buck, dau. Joseph, died Mar. 2, 1880, (2) Nov. 9, 1881, Maggie McCoy, dau. Alex.

Children at Harwich:
Emogene B., born July 15, 1852, mar. Isaac Small, Jr., 1871.
Lucy S., born July 22, 1853, mar. Samuel A. Ellis 1873.
Albert M., born Jan. 21, 1855, mar. Emma L. Smith 1881.
Son, born May 4, 1859, died June 20, 1859.
Lowell M., born Dec. 24, 1861, died Sept. 30, 1881.

ELEAZER F.⁶ (Thomas⁵, Thomas⁴, Eleazer³), born Aug. 6, 1837, died Feb. 5, 1882, aged 44; mar. (1) Nov. 27, 1856, Jerusha G. Eldridge, dau. Solomon, (2) Feb. 1870, Anne E. Lantry, dau. Thomas. She survived him and mar. (2) Eleazer Rogers Nov. 19, 1891.

Children at Harwich:
Frank Herbert, born 1857, mar. Almena F. Chase 1880.
Paul Curtis, born Jan. 1, 1860, not married.
Abby E., born May 18, 1863, mar. (1) Isaiah S. Chase 1878, (2) William Cahoon 1885.
Jerusha E., born May 6, 1866, mar. Joshua A. Chase 1882.
Ella N., born Jan. 20, 1874, mar. Carl B. Harvey 1895.

JOSEPH F.⁶ (Thomas⁵, Thomas⁴, Eleazer³), born May 25, 1840; mar. (1) Mar. 12, 1865, Abbie C. Nickerson, dau. Zenas, (2) Oct. 31, 1870, Harriet Snow, dau. John, (3) Feb. 24, 1881, Almena Small, dau. Aaron. No record of children.

WILLIAM⁶ (John⁵, James⁴, John³), born Nov. 28, 1820, died April 17, 1892, aged 71; mar. 1844, Sally W. Baker, dau. Nathan, who died Mar. 27, 1893, aged 69.

He had, probably at Yarmouth:

Alice Jane, born Oct. 18, 1845, mar. Prentice Linnell 1864.
William Allen, born Aug. 12, 1848, died Dec. 13, 1862.
James H., born Dec. 5, 1850, mar. Mary E. Chase 1876.
John W., born Aug. 5, 1853, died Nov. 17, 1883.

NELSON[5] (John[4], James[3], John[2]), born Dec. 29, 1822, died before 1862; mar. Dec. 14, 1845, Kezia Crowell, dau. Judah, who survived him and mar. (2) Lockwood Baxter Nov. 30, 1862.
Children at Yarmouth:
Alwilda, born Mar. 29, 1846, died Nov. 12, 1851.
Irving, born April 27, 1852, died Nov. 27, 1886.
Nelson Francis, born May 21, 1858, mar. Eliza F. Robinson 1883.

TIMOTHY[5] (John[4], James[3], John[2]), born Dec. 12, 1825; mar. April 15, 1849, Emily Baxter, dau. Isaac. He lived at Yarmouth but probably moved to Maine.
Children at Yarmouth:
Edith, born Oct. 26, 1849, mar. Eli A. Leighton 1870.
Abby A., born Oct. 2, 1851, mar. Lemuel Merchant 1870.

ASA[5] (John[4], James[3], John[2]), born Jan. 18, 1834; mar. (1) June 23, 1860, Mary E. Broad, dau. William, (2) May 16, 1867, Ann Rebecca Wild, dau. Washington.
Children at Dorchester:
Emily Jane, born Dec. 9, 1861, died April 7, 1862.
Ella Medora, born Dec. 27, 1868.
Edith Sophia, born April 19, 1871.
William Allen, born July 4, 1874.

WILLIAM[5] (William[4], James[3], John[2]), born 1822; mar. about 1849, Polly Robbins, dau. Nathan. She died at Falmouth in 1897.
Children at Falmouth:
William Nelson, born Oct. 21, 1850.
Son, born Sept. 15, 1852, died infant.
Martin Luther, born Dec. 10, 1854, mar. Lizzie M. Chase 1880.
Sophia Louise, born April 13, 1856, mar. William Rogers 1877.
Zenas Eldridge, born Jan. 7, 1860, died Oct. 10, 1861.
Zenas Eldridge, born 1863, mar. Cordelia A. Ireland 1884.
Abbot L., born Dec. 25, 1864, died June 5, 1889.
Louisa P., born Dec. 7, 1868, mar. Loring C. Swift 1888.
Hiram E., born May 1, 1871.

HIRAM H.[5] (William[4], James[3], John[2]), born about 1825; mar. (1) about 1846, Nancy L. Davis, (2) about 1853, Elizabeth F. Holmes at Bridgewater.
Children:
Hiram, who died at Wareham Feb. 22, 1847.
Nancy E., born Sept. 17, 1849, mar. Briggs H. Emery 1866.
Myron Forrest, born June 30, 1854, died Oct. 30, 1854.
Fannie Eveline, born May 7, 1860, died same year.
Wendell Freeman, born Sept. 14, 1862, mar. (1) Panelia C. Robbins 1882, (2) Josephine K. Davis 1894.

JOHN W.[5] (David[4], David[3], John[2]), born May 28, 1834, died Jan. 4, 1893, aged 58; mar. Angelissa Hussey.
Child at Melrose:
Eugene, mar. Stella M. Gerrish 1884.

WARREN W.[5] (David[4], David[3],

THE ROBBINS FAMILY

John²), born April 18, 1837; mar. 1862, Ann Springer.
Children at Augusta, Me.:
Frank N., born Aug. 29, 1867.
Annie G., born May 25, 1869, mar. W. C. Miller 1890.

ISAIAH⁶ (Henry⁴, Henry⁴, Timothy³)), born Sept. 11, 1811, died April 10, 1858, aged 39; pub. (1) Sept. 30, 1835, Bethania Young, died April 5, 1850, mar. (2) July 23, 1851, Fanny Cahoon, dau. Heman, who mar. 2nd Zenas C. Robbins.
Children at Harwich:
John Y., born Feb. 21, 1839, died June 20, 1854. "
Priscilla B., born Oct. 22, 1840, died May 8, 1855.
Bethania, born Nov. 6, 1844, died Sept. 28, 1845.
Mark, born Jan. 8, 1846, died May 18, 1870.
Adeline F., born June 2, 1848, mar. Joshua Paine 1865.

HENRY C.⁶ (Henry⁴, Henry⁴, Timothy³), born Aug. 11, 1821; mar. (1) 1842, Sarah S. Chase, (2) 1866, Sarah K. Sylvester.
Children at Harwich:
Harriet N., born 1842, died Jan. 24, 1864.
Child, born Mar. 30, 1844, died infant.
Sabra, born Jan. 12, 1847, died Oct. 26, 1849.
Howard, born May 24, 1853, died July 6, 1854.
Theodore P., born Aug. 27, 1855, mar. Aggie B. Kelley 1877.
Cyrus A., born July 15, 1859, mar. Ella Mary Lucas of Taunton.

ROWLAND H.⁶ (Henry⁴, Henry⁴, Timothy³), born Aug. 25, 1828; mar. Nov. 30, 1848, Bathsheba Robbins, dau. Nathaniel. He was drowned, his former wife marrying again, Isaac Bea.
Children at Harwich:
Hannah F., born Sept. 12, 1850, mar. Rufus Ellis 1869.
Love C., born April 29, 1853, mar. George W. Martin, Jr., 1871.
Merwyn, born Oct. 20, 1860, died Sept. 14, 1878.
Rowland M., born Sept. 19, 1861, prob. died young.

NEHEMIAH B.⁶ (Henry⁴, Henry⁴, Timothy³), born 1830, died 1872; mar. April 24, 1853, Melissa D. Ryder, who survived him and mar. 2nd Zenas Doty June 1, 1873. He was lost at sea on the schooner Olive G. Tower.
Children at Harwich:
Nehemiah B., adopted 1849, mar. Ellen D. Robbins 1879.
Herbert F., born Mar. 19, 1854, mar. Sarah E. Robbins 1878.
Child, born Aug. 1, 1856, died infant.
Joseph S., born 1861, mar. Martha E. Baker 1882.
Daughter, born Mar. 14, 1863, died young.
Leban J., born Jan. 22, 1866, mar. Lizzie Upham 1881.

JOHN WESLEY⁶ (John⁴, Henry⁴, Timothy³), born 1849; mar. Feb. 20, 1873, Sarah H. Sears, dau. Samuel, died May 2, 1885, aged 37.
Children at Brewster:
Son, born May 19, 1876, died infant.
Samuel J., born Mar. 20, 1879.

FREEMAN STUDLEY⁶ (Zenas C.⁵, Henry⁴, Timothy³), born Aug. 31, 1834, died Dec. 27, 1916; mar. Mar. 4, 1856, Laura A. Atwood, dau. Joseph.

Child at Harwich:
Freeman, born 1857, died Dec. 1, 1881, unmarried.

ELIPHALET H.⁵ (Samuel⁴, Eliphalet³, Timothy²), born June 17, 1825, died Nov. 9, 1875, aged 50; mar. Feb. 14, 1847, Ann L. Chase, dau. Judah. He lived and died at Dennis, where he had:
Son, born Mar. 13, 1847, died infant.
Anna W., born Aug. 2, 1855, mar. Henry M. Olmstead 1873.

SAMUEL⁵ (Samuel⁴, Eliphalet³, Timothy²), born July 3, 1842, died Feb. 29, 1880, aged 38; mar. Oct. 10, 1871, Cordelia F. Luce, dau. Freeman. He lived and died at New Bedford. His widow mar. (2) William J. Macy Nov. 24, 1895. No record of children.

GEORGE GUSTAVUS HOWE⁵ (Samuel⁴, Eliphalet³, Timothy²), born Dec. 27, 1844, died Sept. 19, 1874, aged 30; mar. April 30, 1869, Ellen G. Thatcher, dau. Prentice.

Children at Dennis:
Samuel P., born Aug. 18, 1872, died same day.
Mary T., born July 18, 1874.

ELIPHALET⁵ (Eliphalet⁴, Eliphalet³, Timothy²), born Nov. 30, 1835, died May 18, 1866, aged 31; mar. Jan. 20, 1856, Anna E. Coombs, dau. Benjamin.

Child at New Bedford:
Clara A., born Mar. 28, 1859, mar. Ezra F. Chase 1877.

No. 29.

LIBRARY *of*
Cape Cod
HISTORY & GENEALOGY

BANGS FAMILY PAPERS

YARMOUTHPORT, MASS.:
C. W. SWIFT, Publisher and Printer.
The "Register" Press.
1917.

SIXTH ANNUAL CONVENTION
OF THE EDWARD BANGS DESCENDANTS, JULY 28, 1917.

(Reported for the Yarmouth Register by Michael Fitzgerald, East Brewster)

Brewster was honored this year by being chosen as the meeting place of this convention. On last Saturday descendants of Edward Bangs, the Pilgrim, met in the First Parish church (Unitarian) and were cordially welcomed by the pastor, the Rev. Adam J. Culp, and his talented wife. Associated with Mr. and Mrs. Culp in Brewster's greeting were Thomas D. Sears, Esq., chairman of the board of selectmen, and other prominent Brewster people. Also among those present was Nathan Clark, Esq., chairman of the Eastham board of selectmen, who brought the best wishes for the success of the convention from Eastham, the "mother town," of which Edward Bangs was one of the founders in 1644.

The visitors were hospitably entertained during their stay by Mr. and Mrs. Thomas P. Consodine of the Consodine House.

The meeting was called to order at 1.30, and Mr. Culp in graceful words expressed his pleasure at the presence of the distinguished guests. They had come, he said, from far away towns and cities to do honor to the memory of their ancestor, one of that hardy band of adventurers who sought in this land the opportunities denied them at home. The Pioneers of New England faced a big problem when they sailed westward to the strange shores of the new world, then very little known to Europeans. But they never quailed under the most trying circumstances, and the New England of today, and indeed the whole of this vast country, is the lasting monument to their unconquerable perseverance and unflinching spirit. Within the grounds of that old church was buried Captain Jonathan Bangs, son of Edward the Pilgrim, and it was indeed an appropriate place for his descendants to meet and pay a tribute to his worth.

After Messrs. Sears and Clark had spoken for the inhabitants of Brewster and Eastham, the retiring president of the society, Francis Sedgwick Bangs of New York city, addressed the assemblage. He was listened to with rapt attention. Mr. Bangs is one of New York's leading lawyers and an orator of renown. He reviewed the early history of the settlement of this country and the hardships which the Pilgrims had to endure in their efforts to establish a system of government suitable to their new conditions. They had, he said, a clean sheet on which to write. The wildest dreams of the most rabid Socialist never pictured a state of affairs so congenial to his theories as that in which the Pilgrims found themselves situated. How did they meet the problem of government? The immortal Compact drawn up in the cabin of the Mayflower answered that question. In that document could be found the germ of the democracy which is the cornerstone of our present system. These Pilgrims were not men of the narrow Puritan type found later in the neighboring colony of Massachusetts Bay. Strong as was their faith in the righteousness of their own creed, they show no hatred of others in the declaration of their principles embodied in the Compact. They desired to live in peace with all men, and through all the trials and sufferings of their first years in the new land they clung steadfastly to this ideal. He was proud to claim descent from this pioneer stock. He thanked the members of the society for their loyal friendship during his year of office as their president, and he was sure that his successor would meet the same kindly treatment. He had much pleasure in introducing the president-elect, Col. Frederick A. Bangs, who nobly sustained the traditions of the family in the great city of Chicago.

Col. Bangs thanked the meeting for its hearty welcome. He would have to work hard to keep up to the high standard of efficiency set by his predecessor in the president's chair, but he hoped to get along all right with the generous help of his fellow-members. On an occasion like the present he thoroughly appreciated the privilege of being a descendant of Edward Bangs, for this privilege brought him into close communion with the patriotic men and women who compose their society. Most of them passed their lives far removed from each other, but their annual convention brought them together as one family and gave them an opportunity to feel the clasp of kindred hands and the warmth of kindred hearts. He hoped that during his year of office there would be no weakening of this spirit of fraternity and that each individual member of the Bangs Descendants would live up to the high level of citizenship which characterized the career of Edward Bangs.

Mr. Gay Estey Bangs of Chicago, chairman of the Committee on Genealogical Research, read a most interesting memoir of the Bangs family in England.

The company then visited the grave of Captain Jonathan Bangs in the cemetery adjoining the church. Here for nearly two hundred years the bodies of Captain Bangs and two of his three wives have rested. The old headstones of slate that recorded briefly their births and deaths were securely embedded in a block of granite, erected by the society. The graves of some fifty of the Bangs family were decorated with the Stars and Stripes. Standing beside the granite monument, Mr. George Dennis Bangs of Huntington, N. Y., read a paper on the life of Jonathan Bangs. It was a fine tribute to the gallant soldier and sterling citizen who died in 1728 in his 88th year.

A professional photographer then took a picture of the society and the gathering dispersed.

The success of the convention is in a large measure due to the work of the indefatigable and efficient secretary of the society, Dr. Charles H. Bangs, one of Boston's eminent physicians. Dr. Bangs may rightly be called the father of the society. From small beginnings he has seen it grow into national proportions, and he has good reason to be satisfied with the result of the time and labor which he has given to its organization.

On Sunday forenoon services in connection with the convention were held in the First Parish church. There was a large attendance of members of the church and visitors. The Rev. William W. Bellinger, vicar of St Agnes' chapel, Trinity parish, New York city, was the preacher. The rev. gentleman delivered a splendid sermon on the duties of citizenship, and his appeal for the full performance of these duties was very impressive.

Among those at the convention were Mr. Francis Sedgwick Bangs of New York, retiring president; Col. Frederick A. Bangs of Chicago, president-elect, and Mrs. Bangs; Mr. and Mrs. George D. Bangs of Huntington, N. Y.; Dr. Charles H. Bangs of Boston, secretary; Mr. William Parcher Bangs of Swampscott; Mrs. Lydia M. B. Fisher of Hyde Park; Mrs. Adelaide Bangs Walker, historian, of Needham; Mrs. Nellie Doane Dunning of Boston; Mrs. Josephine Brooks of Fitchburg; Miss Mary Freeman Bangs of Hamilton; Mr. Clarendon Bangs of Atlanta, Ga.; Mrs. Caroline Adele Leighton of Cambridge.

Col. Frederick Augustus Bangs, the new president of the society, is a notable figure in the public life of Chicago, a member of the bar who has achieved distinction in his profession, and an ex-president of Chicago's famous political organization, the Hamilton club.

ADDRESS

By Francis Sedgwick Bangs, Esq., of New York City
President The Edward Bangs Descendants.

The generous interest which you, Mr. Culp, and the members of your parish have shown in this meeting, has done much to make the meeting practicable, and has been the forerunner of the very kindly welcome which you and Mr. Clark and Mr. Sears have just given to us.

If our thanks are brief, it is because words in greater number could no more adequately express the gratitude we feel.

We who have come together here from widely separated places have at least one tie in common. We honor that courageous and adventurous company of the sturdy Anglo-Saxon race, which braved the sea and in Plymouth Colony founded a nation upon principles of self-discipline, self government, mutual concessions and just and equal laws, and we pride ourselves upon an ancestry which goes back to the creation of an upbuilding American democracy.

The Pilgrims of the Mayflower, in their famous compact, signed at sea a month before they landed upon these shores, composed the earliest written constitution in history. They landed at Plymouth against their will. They held a charter from the Virginia Company, and Virginia was their intended destination. Winter storms drove them to a haven they had not sought and forced them to occupy lands to which at first they had no title, but which they afterward acquired by honorable purchase, even from the Indians. They had gone from their English homes first to Holland, where the Dutch love of liberty was unconquerable, and thence set out for the western world in their quest for political and religious freedom. The intolerance of the Puritan had no place among them. They touched American soil as men absolutely free, with nothing but a common desire to live together in harmony, with industry and for the common good. They were bound by no laws except such as they should choose to make and they had agreed that those laws should be just and equal, a quality which belonged to the body of the law nowhere else in the world. They were in a condition of unconscious socialism, with an opportunity such as the socialist of today, however visionary, might envy, but which will not be seen again.

The socialism of modern times is on exhibition in action in Russia. It stands for disorder, for loyalty to no person, cause or country, for the meanest demands of the individual against the state, for confiscation, for dishonor, treachery and the depths of human degradation. The socialistic opportunity of the Pilgrims counted for the supremacy of equal rights under the law, for justice and for order, and out of it they and those who joined them, and those who in the passage of time followed their example, built a free government of the people. In what they did Edward Bangs filled out an honorable share. He was a shipwright, who, if the story be true, three years after the sailing of the Mayflower, was summoned to the Ann to repair and fit her for the voyage, to the end of which he stayed. He was a worker with his hands and evidently with his heart, and he must have believed that effective industry was the chief dignity of labor. The chronicle of his life is one of valued service to the people of the colony and he was an honored member of the community of the voyagers of the Mayflower, the Fortune and the Ann. These people made democracy as we know it, and it cannot be said of them, as has been said of the ancient Greeks and their ancient republics, that they were "eager for liberty without that discipline which liberty requires."

As we meet here in this peaceful atmosphere of the Cape it is hard to realize that the liberty which our forefathers created, fought for and maintained, and which we have believed to be eternal, is at death grips with a cruel, monstrous, blasphemous despotism, which claims God for a partner and commits murder in His name. The struggles and the hardships of the Pilgrims, which they overcame in this colony, meant life or death for them. The struggle of today means either world tyranny or world freedom. The hardships, the darkness and the sorrows which we must foresee in the new fight for liberty on the battlefields of Europe and in the paths of ships, multiply a million fold the cares, the dangers and the sorrows of colonial days. We need God's help, and with that help we see ahead the light of peace and liberty, but peace after a fight for it and liberty only when those who would destroy it have themselves been destroyed. As our forefathers fought, so must we for life and for freedom on both land and sea, for liberty in our homes and in our relations to the state, for the liberty of a free people.

THE BANGS FAMILY IN ENGLAND.

By Gay Estey Bangs, Chicago.

It is the purpose of this article to give a fairly comprehensive view of the family in England to which our Pilgrim ancestor, Edward Bangs, belonged, and to connect him with the earliest personages of the name of which we have found reference. It is unfortunate that the war has closed up, we hope only temporarily, some avenues of research, which give indication of resulting in unquestionably interesting data.

Until recently but little of anything was known as to the antecedents of Edward Bangs. Traditions held in several branches of the family made up for the lack of absolute knowledge—no one taking the trouble to investigate the truth or falsity.

Hon. Edward D. Bangs, Secretary of State of Massachusetts, in his family record, written about eighty years ago, stated that Edward Bangs was a native or inhabitant of Chichester, in the county of Sussex, England, according to his family tradition; in the family of Rev. Nathan Bangs it was claimed that the Bangses came from Isle of Man, but later investigations seem to indicate that they came from an entirely different part of the country.

Then again he was considered a member of some Banks family, the illiteracy of the time carrying him down as Bangs in the public records.

King in his history of the Norman people, published in London in 1874, is good enough to credit us as a family name in England, but says that Bangs is from Banks, but as he gives no authority for his statement, we can only take it for its face value and no more.

The origin of the name Bangs then remains an unsolved problem, and its antiquity uncertain. It is generally considered a rare name in England, and it certainly is in comparison to Banks, which is noted in nearly every county. However, as we unlock the musty records of the past, we find Bangs a name of some distinction and fairly diversified, giving it a standing as a separate family from a time not long after the Norman conquest.

Walter Rye of Norwich, the well-known authority on Norfolk and North England names, says the name Bangs is from Banges, meaning son of "Bange."

It may be noted here that there was a certain French family of Bange; one Col. de Bange was a prominent French artillery officer and inventor in the 19th century.

Bangs appears under the spelling of Bannges, Banges and Bangs.

Banges appears more often in the ancient English records and the early colonial ones than any other, and some time after 1700 was discontinued in both the English and American branches of the family—the shorter form "Bangs" taking its place. It will be remembered that Edward signed his name, "Edward Banges" to public documents and to his will in 1677.

The records show wonderful persistence in the use of Banges; Bangs throughout the centuries showing no interchanging of Bangs and Banks, a contingency which might be expected, allowing for the illiteracy of the prevailing periods.

The name Bangs appears more largely in the counties of Norfolk, Essex and Hertford than any other. It is known in London, though not earlier than the 18th century. In Norfolk it existed parallel with "Bange," though apparently distinct, but here, no doubt, was the earlier home of the family of Edward Bangs.

In Norwich one Augustine Bange was made a freeman 1395. His widow Alice made her will in 1445. Robert Bange was in Blofield in 1428. Henry Bange in Strumpshaugh, 1461. Robert Bange, same place, 1434. John Bange, 1477. Katherine Bange, Acle, 1469. Henry Bange, Acle, 1509, in Glentworth, Lincolnshire. Robert Bange and son William Bange are referred to as early as 1327.

The earliest instance of the name yet found is in the year 1297, when one Thomas Bannges (so spelled) was mentioned in the records of Thorpe-le-Soken in Essex. This is taken from the records of the visitation of the Dean and Chapter of St. Paul's Cathedral, published by the Camden society.

This could not have been much after the time that surnames came to be used by the common people, but to establish an unbroken line to this Thomas Bannges can hardly be expected.

Thorpe-le-Soken was attached to the jurisdiction of St. Paul's Cathedral by King Athelstane in 941. Even now it belongs to the diocese of London.

The official records of Norfolk contain many records of the Bangses, but only now are not available.

John Bangs was of Scarning. He made his will in 1416, and proved in 1427. This could carry us back into the 1300's. John Bang or Bangs of Smallburg made his will 1460, proved 1509. William Bangs, Smallburg, 1547, proved 1549. Robert Bangs of Hingham, 1501, proved 1507. These are a few of the records of the names on the Probate Registry of Norwich.

The definite records from which we trace the source of the stream are in Norwich. Here in 1547, Richard Banges, whom I believe to be the grandfather of Edward Banges, was made a freeman as a tanner in the first year of Edward VI. He evidently was not a native of that city, but may have been a son or grandson of William Bangs, who died at Smallburg, about 12 miles from Norwich, in 1547. The records of that parish give baptism of a Richard Banges, son of Thomas Banges, in 1563—29 Oct.—probably a nephew of the Norwich Richard.

Richard Bangs prospered in his trade as tanner, so that in 1569 he was the owner of property in the parish of St. Mary and St. Martins of Coslaney, which he and his wife disposed of, probably not all, in 1586, to Thomas Norforth, Junior, for £440, which shows him to have been a man of some wealth for those days, as he was styled Richard Banges, gentleman, and Margaret, his wife.

The house in which Richard Bangs has been identified, was torn down in 1914, and a Tudor mantlepiece, having in it the initials of one of the earlier owners, was found and placed in the museum at Norwich.

Richard Banges died in 1586, leaving a wife, Margaret, and several children. His widow Margaret married the next year, 1587, Mr. John Kinge of Norwich, and resided in St. Martins, Coslaney. She died in 1592. Her will was proved 21 February same year, and mentions sons Robert and Edmund, daughters Sarah and Elizabeth Bangs, Hall, Ixworth, and sons-in-law Robert Claphamson and Henry Paman. She does not mention as son John Banges, but we know that he was her son, and probably had been taken care of during his father's lifetime.

The eldest son of Richard Bunges was John Banges. The chancery suit of Bangs vs. Pendleton says that "John Banges, son and heir of Richard Banges, late of the City of Norwich, tanner, deceased" 21 Nov. 1586. John Banges was born probably about 1560—no doubt in Norwich —and married soon after his father's decease, about 1587 or 1588. In 1590 John Banges and wife disposed of certain property in the parishes of St. Marten and St. Mary, Coslancy, to Nicholas Palmer, and he is heard of no more in that locality.

In 1596 we have certain evidence of the residence of a John Banges in Hempstead, County of Essex, though he was probably there earlier, but in 1596 and 1600 the records at Chelmsford "Liber Actium" show that John Banges was church warden at Hempstead, and John Luddington vicar, indicating that he must have been there long enough to establish a standing in the parish.

I have no doubt that John Banges of Norwich and John Banges of Hempstead are one and the same parties.

It is unfortunate that the church registry at Hempstead does not begin till 1665—too late to be of much help to us.

That John Banges was the father of Edward Banges is just as certain, as all evidence seems to corroborate the claim.

John Banges in his will states his desire not to be buried by the side of his parents or ancestor, but by the side of his two children, proving conclusively that he was not a native of Hempstead, and there is no evidence in the other parishes of that locality of residence of any Bangs prior to him. It would appear then strongly that Norwich was his birthplace.

John Banges was a resident of Hempstead many years. He was of that hardy and self-reliant class of Englishman, the yeomanry, that have always been the bulwark of Anglo-Saxon liberties. He was a member of the church of England with puritanical leanings—a man of education, and character as a layman to hold the position of church warden in the parish, which was also held by subsequent members of his family, as Thomas Bangs, a grandson, in 1667, and still later a Thomas and Uriah Bangs at Hempstead.

John Banges during his lifetime prospered as any man of discretion, sobriety and energy might be expected to do, so that in his old age he was able to remember his children, and leave them well taken care of, each of his sons being left £40 apiece, besides certain lands and houses to his wife, who survived. As money at that period was four or five times its present value, we can get a good idea of his worth.

He died at Hempstead 11 February,

1632, and was buried in the churchyard there. His wife, Jane, died shortly after, not proving the will, which was done at Dunmow by the son James. An inquisition was taken at Stratford Longthorne, Essex, February following, and decided that the property should descend to Thomas Banges, grandson, born 1619, son of John Banges, deceased, the eldest son.

This property was transmitted by Thomas Banges at his death in 1703 to his son John, who died in 1725, leaving no children, and his brother Thomas became the possessor, dying in 1747-8, at which the male line of the Hempstead family became extinct.

The children of John and Jane Banges were all born, I believe, at Hempstead, with, perhaps, the exception of the eldest. The baptismal font still is used that may have witnessed the baptism of Edward Bangs and his brothers. They were John, who died shortly before his father; Edward, undoubtedly, our ancestor; James, of whom little is known, but who executed the will and inherited certain property, presumably the father of Thomas and Uriah Bangs, as they came into possession of property which James Bangs secured; Sampson, who was at Hempstead in 1633; Jonas, settled at Fryerning, Essex, in 1640, married then and died at Ingatestone in 1664, leaving a son, Jonas Bangs, Jr.,—the descendants of Jonas still live at Ingatestone and vicinity.

Joshua Bangs, a younger son, married the daughter of Rev. Thomas Greene, of Royston, Hertfordshire, but settled at Longhem in Norfolk, where he died in June 1661. He was the father of nine children. The youngest son, Benjamin Bangs, though brought up in the Established church, became a member of the Society of Friends or Quakers, and traveled for more than fifty years over the United Kingdom as a preacher. He died at Stockport in 1740, at the good age of 89 years. His biography published in 1797 is to be found in the British Museum. Members of the Bangs family still residing at Mildenhall, Suffolk, retain traditions of their Quaker ancestry.

Jane, the daughter, married a Mr. Payne, and was probably a widow.

That there was another son John— as there were often two sons of the same name in the same family at that period—appears certain and the will and post-mortem can be interpreted in no other way. Hempstead is a small parish about 60 miles from London, in the north part of Essex. The church, an ancient one, dedicated to St Andrew, is still standing. It contains the burial place of Dr. William Harvey, who discovered the circulation of the blood.

John Bangs wrote his name Banges, and was, I believe, the common ancestor of all the living members of the Bangs family in England and America, though of course it is not always possible to trace the direct ancestor. Hertfordshire, England, has had Bangses living in its boundaries many years at Standon. Thomas, William and Edward Bangs were there shortly before 1700. Evidently they were brothers. In Chesthunt another family is found; John and William Bangs were there about 1760. From this line was descended Charles Edward Banges of London, who has contributed much to our English history. At Great and Little Munden were still others. As they are all subsequent to the Hempstead Bangs, it is reasonable to suppose they are a branch of the old stock, though proof as yet is lacking.

An old Bible of date 1693 has been found, which was once the property of Joshua Bangs, the brother, and contains records of his descendants down to 1746, at Braintree, Essex. The present owner, Mr. Percy J. Bangs, of Frinton-on-Sea, Essex, seems not to have a clear record of his descent from the original owner.

The name is scattered through England, though in America and Canada it has reached its most affluent state. Yet a branch is to be found in Australia—a strange coincidence. An Edward Bangs went from London to Melbourne in 1852 or 53 and founded the family there.

Thus do we find a few of the references to our common ancestry. Much yet is to be written. In England "they are people of clean mind," writes one. In America they have maintained the high honor of the family name. May its lustre be never dimmed.

I have yet to find one among all the vast hosts of Edward Bangs descendants who has proved recreant to the high Pilgrim ideals held by him.

CAPTAIN JONATHAN BANGS.

By George Dennis Bangs, Huntington, N. Y.

The Edward Bangs Descendants entitled to the name of our ancestor had a narrow escape from extinction in 1640, for, had not Captain Jonathan Bangs been born two centuries and more ago, there would have been none of us entitled to that honorable name.

Contemplate, if you will, the loves and friendships, the trials and triumphs we would have missed but for him! He was the only son of Edward Bangs, the Pilgrim, having male children, namely, Captain Edward, Captain Jonathan, Jr., and Captain Samuel, and from whom the Bangses have multiplied and scattered throughout these United States and into Canada. The survivors, and they are not few in numbers, doubtless, in some way or other, all are doing their "bit" to serve humanity in the world struggle of today, with the same patriotism as did Edward Bangs, the Pilgrim, and Captain Jonathan, his son, in their day to help set the foundations of a democracy that is rapidly encompassing the world.

Gathering the limited fragments of Captain Jonathan Bangs' history, we find him the same type of man as was his father, respected and trusted by his fellowmen, a freeman doing public service for the community in which he from his early years was evidently prominently active.

Captain Jonathan's father was Edward Bangs, our ancestor, who came to America in the "Anne" in 1623, the third vessel to arrive at Plymouth from England.

As to his mother's maiden name, beyond the recorded fact that her name was Rebecca, there has been until now some uncertainty, and the query has been with our historian, "Who was Rebecca?"

Doan Dudley in his "History and Genealogy of the Bangs Family" establishes the fact that Lydia Hicks was the first wife of Edward Bangs, doubtless wedded later than 1627, as in that year Lydia Hicks is named as one to whom was apportioned part of the property brought over in the "Anne."

He also establishes that John Bangs was born to Edward and Lydia Bangs, and then argues that the others were children of Rebecca, including the daughter Lydia as named after his first wife. It is possible that the identity of Rebecca can be established to a reasonable certainty; that the mystery of Rebecca may be solved by an entry claimed to be in some journal of the Rev. Peter Hobart stating that he went to Eastham to attend his sister Bangs' funeral, and by other circumstances, possibly not all authentic, but enough to establish the probability.

The Rev. Peter Hobart had a sister Rebecca born in 1598, who came to Charlestown, Mass., in 1633 from Norwich, County Norfolk, England, with their father, Edmund Hobart, and in

1635 they moved to Hingham, Mass. Rebecca's sister's name was Sarah, and she had a brother Joshua.

Edward and Rebecca Banges' first children were named Joshua and Sarah, names not unlikely selected from Rebecca's family.

Mrs. Lydia M. B. Fisher, a Bangs descendant, and one of our members, remembers very distinctly that, when she was a child at the christening of Walter Matthew Bangs, also one of our members, now of Bridgeport, Conn., her grandmother Bangs told her that Edward Banges' wife was Rebecca Hubbard.

In Orleans, are records of Josiah Hubart, in 1661 and 1665, carrying away horses on order from Edward Banges, and in 1668 it is recorded that a horse was sold to Josiah Hubbard of Hingham. Hubart, Hubbard and Hobart are claimed to be synonymous. It is quite consistent that Josiah Hobart traveled from Hingham to Eastham on three occasions to visit his sister, Rebecca Banges, and incidentally indulged in horse-trading.

In the Bangs genealogy we find that John Doane, a grandson of Edward and Rebecca, married Hannah Hobart, daughter of Joshua Hobart of Hingham, undoubtedly Rebecca Hobart's brother.

The statement is made, although not verified by the Bangs genealogy, that Captain Jonathan's grandson named a son Hobart, who died in infancy.

These circumstances all tend to verify the probability that the second wife of Edward Banges, the Pilgrim, was Rebecca Hobart. Their marriage, though, must have been soon after 1635, for Captain Jonathan was born in 1640, and he was preceded by Captain Joshua in 1637, and possibly by one of his three sisters, Rebecca, Sarah or Lydia; the date, though, and order of their births is uncertain.

It may be, and it is not at all unlikely, that Edward Banges and Rebecca Hobart were friends and, possibly, sweethearts in England, for according to our research committee, there is a record in Norwich, county of Norfolk, from which the Hobarts came, of Augustin Bangs being made a freeman in 1385.

True, Edward is believed to have been born in County Essex, but the Bangses evidently lived in Norfolk for many generations and must have had family connections there. What could have been more natural than that Edward and Rebecca should have renewed an attachment temporarily suspended by separation and distance?

So let us believe that Edward Bangs, after a separation of ten years or more from his first love, whom he left behind in England and may not have expected to meet again, and after becoming widowed, was reunited to the sweetheart of his youth, who had failed to reciprocate the affections of other men, as she was 37 years of age when her father moved to Bear Cove, near Hingham. Most girls in those years were married before they were twenty. Let us suppose that she remained steadfast in her love for Edward, while he, none the less faithful to his early affection, after four years' sojourn in Plymouth, succumbed to the custom of his surroundings and married first for convenience and then for love.

This ought to satisfy the Bangs family of today, as but for Rebecca, Jonathan would not have been born, and were it not for Jonathan there would be no Bangses to meet here to revere his memory.

So, first to Edward and Rebecca, who begat Jonathan, and then to Jonathan and his wife, Mary Mayo, mother of all his children, must we be thankful for our existence, and for the tribal feeling that brings us together today in Brewster. Here those ancestors lived their simple, though rigorous lives, full of love for family and friends, amid the privations and perils of a new country, doing their duty to God and their fellowmen, according to their enlightenment, that the generations following should benefit and the world grow better from their having been in it.

Captain Jonathan Bangs, whose memory we are revering by our gathering here in Brewster, where he lived and died and lies buried, forever resting, with two of his three wives on either side, and whose graves we are marking against the erosions of time, was born in Plymouth in 1640, and was four years of age when, in 1644, his father's family moved to Nauset.

It is an interesting fact that on the gravestones for Jonathan's two wives buried in 1711 and 1719 the name is spelled B-a-n-g-e-s, while in 1728 on his stone it is spelled B-a-n-g-s.

Jonathan must have been early a leader in military affairs. In 1658, at the age of eighteen, he became ensign of a military company, his father supplying him with a horse and equipment. In 1670, he is recorded as a sergeant; in 1675, a lieutenant; again in 1690, an ensign; and by the title of captain he is designated on the stone marking his grave in the old burying ground at Brewster.

In the civic affairs of Eastham in 1658 he was made a rate-maker for the term of one year, beginning with 1659; in 1670 he was appointed to act in the matter of "Pine Knots"; in 1674 he was elected a selectman for three years, as well as a deputy to the Old Colony Court at Plymouth, serving as such also in 1676, 1682, 1683, 1687 and 1688; in 1676 he was empowered to act for the town in reference to a misunderstanding between Eastham and other towns on the Cape growing out of the war.

In 1692, he must have been one of the foremost citizens of Eastham, for under a new charter and authority from the new governor of the United Plymouth and Massachusetts Bay Colonies, Sir William Phipps, Ensign Bangs was chosen one of the two representatives to serve the town of Eastham in the General Court held at Boston. To have been selected one of the first representatives of the town under that new charter, must have been an honor in those days.

The last public service by Captain Jonathan, of which record has so far been found, was in 1706, when he was one of four appointed from Harwich to meet a like number selected from Eastham to settle the bounds between the two towns, "the matter being in controversy." The agreement was signed and sealed on "the 16th day of October in the fourth year of the reign of our Gracious Lady, Queen Anne."

Through Jonathan comes one fact to link as of common ancestry, somewhere in the so far impenetrable past, the Bankses of England and our ancestor, Edward Banges, for Jonathan used as a seal a part of the crest of the Banks family.

At Plymouth, July 7th, 1680, eight men, including Jonathan Bangs, signed a document agreeing that all the tract of land known as Satucket, bought by them, would be equally divided, etc. That document has on it, so Dean Dudley proves, the seal mentioned.

The Banks crest used by Sir John Banks of London in the time of the Stuarts, according to Burke, was a Moor's head, full faced, couped at the shoulders, on the head a cap of maintenance, turned up adorned with a crescent, issuant therefrom a fleur-de-lis.

Dean Dudley says that the seal used by Jonathan "is the same as this, but very poorly engraved and shows no helmet."

The seal was evidently brought from England, for we have no reason to believe that there were any makers of seals in Plymouth at that date.

Evidently Edward the Pilgrim and Captain Jonathan were not the sort to make a claim to which they were not entitled. The fact that Jonathan possessed the crest claimed by the Bankses must satisfy the Bankses that he had a right to it; also that we, his descendants, have the same right if we may wish to use it, and that somewhere in the centuries the now two families were but one.

Captain Jonathan, for the period in which he lived, must have had considerable wealth, especially in land, for besides a large inheritance from his father, mainly in that part of Eastham which in 1694 was incorporated into Harwich and in 1805 became part of Brewster, he was one of the "original proprietors" or land owners of Truro, and also possessed property in what now remains of Eastham and in Orleans.

His father's (Edward Banges) home is believed to have been in that part of Eastham now known as Orleans on the further side of the Town Cove on the hill, and this is doubtless where Jonathan lived until he married Mary Mayo, the daughter of Captain Samuel, son of Rev. John Mayo, who came to Eastham as the first minister of that community.

There seems to be some uncertainty as to just when Captain Jonathan became a resident of Harwich. Dean Dudley states the date as 1694, the year Harwich was incorporated. The Rev. Enoch Pratt of Brewster in his history of Eastham, which bears every evidence of careful research, states the date as about 1674. It seems probable that the latter date is more nearly correct, for Dean Dudley contradicts himself by stating that Captain Jonathan's son, Captain Jonathan, Jr., was born in Harwich May 4, 1673, and his son, Captain Samuel, as born there in 1680. The completeness with which he states the date of Captain Jonathan, Jr.'s birth, indicates the correctness of the statement, but doubtless the naming by Dean Dudley of Harwich as the birthplace was in deference to locality, as Harwich in 1673 and until 1694 was still a part of Eastham.

A verification that it was before 1694 is in a statement made by Dean Dudley that a daughter, Mary, was born to Captain Jonathan's son, Edward, in Harwich in 1692.

It may be, therefore, that Captain Jonathan took up his home in that part of Eastham which is now Brewster, soon after, if not at the time of his marriage, and that all of his children were born in this town.

Eastham, described in 1644, when the forty-nine settlers came from Plymouth, as only suitable for about twenty-five families of the Plymouth Colony, according to Pratt, had increased in 1676 to 520 inhabitants. Pratt also says:

"Eastham was the only township below Yarmouth on Cape Cod until 1694, when the tract of land granted to the purchasers or old comers of Plymouth Colony being inhabited by a competent number of families, many of whom removed from this town, petitioned the Court for an act of incorporation by the name of Harwich, which was granted."

It is not unreasonable that Captain Jonathan was among the many from Eastham who early took up their homes in that section of the town, which by its incorporation in 1694 became Harwich, and not unlikely that he settled on the tract of land purchased by his father, Edward, at Namskekett, called Situate or Satuckquett, lying between Namskokett and Satucket brook, and afterward willed to Jonathan by his father, together with other nearby land at Rock Harbor. To Jonathan he also gave land at Pocomotte, but the principal bequests to Jonathan were about Satucket, which was a part of Eastham until 1694, when it was incorporated into Harwich and into Brewster in 1805.

As Jonathan Bangs's last public service to Eastham was in 1692, he might have lived in Satucket, as the facts seem to indicate, and still have performed that service; and so we may conclude that Edward Bangea, the Pilgrim, and his wife, Rebecca, passed their declining years in what is now Brewster, with their favorite and most trusted son, Jonathan, for such he evidently was, as Jonathan was designated by Edward in his will as his executor. That Edward Banges, the father, was living with Jonathan when he made that will in 1677 cannot be doubted, for Edward bequeathed to him, "All those things which I have at this house," while to his son, Captain Joshua, he gave, stated in his own words, "The house that I lived in and all the housing belonging to it."

Therefore Edward, living with his son Jonathan's family in Satucket when he made his will in 1677, no doubt died there in 1678, and if not buried in the old cemetery at Eastham may lie somewhere within the bounds of Brewster.

Captain Jonathan Bangs and his first wife, Mary Mayo, brought into the world twelve children. Mary Mayo Bangs died January 26th, 1711, in the sixty-sixth year of her age. Subsequently Captain Jonathan married Sarah, maiden name and date not stated, who died June, 1719, aged seventy-seven years. One year later, in 1720, he married Mrs. Ruth Young, nee Cole, of Eastham, who survived him, when he died November 9th, 1728, aged 88 years.

What a privilege it is to us, the descendants of Edward Banges, the Pilgrim, to meet in this church as we do today, to honor Captain Jonathan, his son, our ancestor, who with his three successive wives, his children and his grandchildren, worshipped here two hundred years ago, and of which his eldest son, Captain Edward, in 1700, was one of the founders, and whose grandson, David, son of Captain Samuel, married Eunice Stone, the daughter of its first pastor, the Rev. Nathaniel Stone, who officiated here for fifty-five years. As we gather about the resting place of Captain Jonathan in the adjoining burying ground, surrounded as he is by many of his loved ones, of family and friend, we can look back and know him as soldier and patriot, public servant and legislator, father and friend, a respected, trusted, God-fearing man of his time, Captain Jonathan Bangs, son of Edward Bangs, the Pilgrim, both of them our ancestors.

The fragile slate that has preserved his memory so safely for nearly two hundred years, we have embedded in the more enduring granite that shall retain its legend for many centuries.

The incidents of his life, gathered from the perishable annals of tradition and gleaned from the scattered fragments of early and poorly guarded records, we have collected here today for the first time, and we commit them to the custody of the undying pages of written history.

There they shall stand as a memorial, a pen portrait of the living, vital, throbbing life that wrought itself into the foundation of our nation.

ADDRESS OF GEORGE D. BANGS PRESENTING TABLET IN MEMORY OF EDWARD BANGES TO EASTHAM, MASS.

August 26, 1916.

The descendants of Edward Banges are gathered here today to unite with the descendants of other Pilgrim forefathers, to do reverence to the founders of this town.

It is most fitting in this new Town hall, to perpetuate the memory of those sturdy pioneers who braved the tempestuous ocean journey from England to this wondrously beautiful New England coast, and there faced the perils of hostile natives and hardships of rigorous winters.

We, their descendants, are favored when we can come together, as we do on this occasion, to honor those men and women who not only founded Plymouth Colony and settled Nauset —otherwise Eastham—but contributed so largely to the principles of enlightened free government. They endowed posterity with a patriotic fervor that needs to be continued, as it has been in the past; a patriotism that has been the mainstay of this great republic, a nation among nations, that might, and should, take lead in establishing universal arbitration for the peace of the world.

There is no egotism in our pride of this ancestry, so long as we live up to their high standards.

I have been honored in being chosen to speak of Edward Banges, one of the seven founders of the town named by the Indians "Nauset."

He came to Plymouth in the year 1623 in the "Anne," the third vessel that brought from the old world those people who formed the Plymouth colony. Born in England, he was of good old British stock, according to records of the family, dating back to 1297.

Historians tell us very little of Edward Banges; not a mention is made by Governor Bradford in his history of the Plymouth Colony, and very little is said of him by the writers of those times, but from the records of Plymouth and Eastham, the records that historians do not write about, because they tell of no valorous deeds, or striking romances, we are able to get an insight as to the type of man that Edward Banges was known to be.

His first recorded public service was in 1627, when he was appointed "in a full court" as one of the "layers out" of land, an appraiser of land by court appointment, as also a builder of wolf traps, and as overseer or captain of the guard against the Indians.

In those early days the church was the governing power, and membership in the church was necessary to citizenship.

Edward Banges was made a "Freeman," or citizen; in 1633, and from then to his old age, he was evidently almost continuously in some public service.

In 1633 he was appointed with Captain Miles Standish, John Doane, Stephen Hopkins, Joshua Pratt, Jonathan Brewster and Robert Hicks, to divide meadow ground in the "bay." In 1634 Governor Prence appointed him on a committee for laying out highways; he was an assessor in 1634, 1635 and 1636, and in the latter year serving as juror to try "actions and abuses."

In 1635 he was on Governor Bradford's staff with Captain Miles Standish, Thomas Prence, Mr. Howland, John Alden, Stephen Hopkins, William

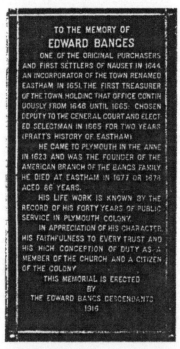

Tablet Placed in Town Hall, Eastham, August 26, 1916.

Collier, Manasseh Kempton, Joshua Pratt and Stephen Tracy.

Five times, in 1636, 1637 and 1638 and again in 1640 and 1641, he served as one of the Grand Inquest or Grand Jurymen "sworn to inquire of all abuses in the body of the government."

Evidently he was a diplomat, for in 1639 he was an arbitrator in some dispute between two neighbors, always a difficult task.

In 1641 and 1642 he contributed one-sixteenth part of the money to build a barque of forty or fifty tons burden to cost £200, and is said to have superintended the building of this, the first vessel constructed at Plymouth.

In 1657 he was licensed as a merchant in Eastham, and is reputed to have been engaged for many years, quite extensively, in trade.

Edward Banges must have become one of the leading citizens of the Colony, for, in 1644, when it seems to have become fully realized that the territory about Plymouth was insufficient for their increasing numbers, he was chosen as one of the commission to investigate Nauset.

When the church, on the report of this commission, decided to give permission to those to settle in Nauset, who would pay for the land purchased from the Indians, but seven families, totalling forty-nine souls, according to Pratt's History, made the move, the family of Edward Banges being one of them.

Just where the Edward Banges family made their home is not certain, but, from a record, we are led to believe it was "on the further side of the Cove," adjoining land "upon the hill" granted to Daniel Cole.

When Nauset was incorporated in 1646, Edward Banges became the first town treasurer, holding that office for twenty years until 1665, inclusive.

During these years he also served four terms as deputy of the General Court at Plymouth, and, at times, as surveyor of highways, constable, and selectman; his last recorded service being in 1667 on a coroner's jury in the case of the death of David Doane.

His patriotic zeal is illustrated in the record that in 1643 he was in the list of those able to bear arms, and that in 1659, the military being required to arm and equip for service and three "troop horses" being protioned to Eastham, Edward Banges united with Governor Thomas Prence in each paying the expense of a man and horse.

That Edward Banges was held in high esteem is shown by records referring to him as "Mr. Banges," the "Mister" in those days, so authorities claim, being applied to yeomen of the higher class—men of considerable wealth, intelligence and local influence.

In the records of his community service, he is shown to have been associated with leading men of Plymouth Colony: Governors William Bradford, Edward Winslow and Thomas Prence, as also Captain Miles Standish and others prominent in the government affairs.

In his home life we must look for him to have been a good provider and an affectionate husband and father. Edward Banges was twice married and raised a family of ten children, his name being perpetuated through his son, Jonathan.

He was modest, not a seeker of glory, but an intelligent, upright, faithful, conscientious, public-spirited citizen of the times, revered and trusted by his fellow men.

That our ancestor was tender and kind, and held to be worthy to care for the welfare of the unfortunate, may be inferred from that in 1658 he was designated with Nicholas Snow and Richard Higgins for "oversight and disposal of poor children."

He passed from his earthly labors in the year 1678. It is not known where his body was laid to rest. He left a record of usefulness in Eastham as well as in Plymouth.

So we get a fair insight into the business, political, community and domestic life of Edward Banges, the Pilgrim, and as we find him, so, may we claim, is the general history of his descendants.

We find them scattered throughout this great republic in all spheres of life, from the farmer and mechanic to the merchant and the professions, as well as office-holder and soldier, and in whatever may be their chosen vocation, is it not true that they, in the large majority, are as was our revered ancestor, Edward Banges, honest, faithful, conscientious, public-spirited and useful citizens in their community life, and true and affectionate in their home life?

We may be justly proud that we are descendants of Plymouth Pilgrims, for they were, with scarcely an exception, of the same type, and most of us here can claim kinship to many of them.

I presume that the majority of the descendants of the founders of Eastham are in some way connected with one another.

The Banges genealogy shows that early male members of the Banges family took as their wives descendants of three of the founders of Nauset, Governor Prence, John Smalley and John Doane, and that sons of Richard Higgins and John Doane married daughters of Edward Banges, the Pilgrim.

Does it not seem especially appropriate that representatives of families, who were so closely related in the early days of Nauset, not only by mutual interests, but by friendships and family ties, should now be united in honoring the founders of Eastham, on what, to them, should be hallowed ground?

No. 30.

LIBRARY of
Cape Cod
HISTORY & GENEALOGY

PUDDINGTON—PURRINGTON—PURINTON.

By Evelyn Rich.

YARMOUTHPORT, MASS.:
C. W. SWIFT, Publisher and Printer,
The "Register" Press,
1917.

PUDDINGTON—PURRINGTON—PURINTON.
By Evelyn Rich.
Copyright, 1917,
by Charles W. Swift

Exeter, England, known as the London of the West, was early interested in the cloth and serge industries. About thirteen miles away from Exeter is Tiverton, an ancient borough, which sent two members to Parliament, and was likewise an important centre of the cloth and weaving interests. Here, in 1588, died Andrew Puddington, weaver, who left a bequest in his will for the benefit of the poor of the town. In connection with his family name it is suggestive to note that the parish of Puddington lies nearby Tiverton. Whether this parish took its name from the family, or the family from the parish, does not appear. Whatever the origin of the name that Andrew Puddington left to his sons, they continued to carry it on as weavers and clothiers in their home town.

Robert Puddington, presumably a grandson of the above Andrew, dying in Tiverton in 1631, named his three sons Joshua, George and Robert, all weavers and clothmakers, as the executors of his will.

The years that followed marked sorry times in Tiverton. The Stuart despotism in religious, political and financial matters had begun to make life a hardship for thinking men. Added to this came disasters by flood and fire for the Puddington brothers.

Joshua removed his business to London. The hold on the old home was shaken, and George, with his brother Robert and their families, crossed the sea to settle in New England.

In April 1640, George bought land at York, first called Gorgeana, that dream city of Sir Ferdinando Gorges. (York Deeds, 3, 84.) (Putnam's Magazine.) Here George Puddington threw himself into the life of the place, serving as one of the original Aldermen, Deputy to the General Court and Juryman. When he made his will, June 1647, his family consisted of his wife Mary, and their five children all under age: 1 John, 2 Elias, 3 Mary, 4 Frances, 5 Rebecca. He named his brother Robert one of the supervisors of the will. (Maine Wills 289, recorded at York 1695.)

In the list of debts due the estate of Isaac Gross, 1649, Boston, appears the name "Widdow Puddington of Agamenticus" "for £22, owed by her husband before his death." There were many other names from the same region on the list, for Gross had a large trade there. The date serves to show that Mrs. Puddington had not then made her second marriage. In 1654 Mary Puddington was witness to a deed for three men of Dorchester. (Suffolk 2, 116.) This Mary may have been the widow of George Puddingtin or their daughter Mary², or even a daughter-in-law. March 15, 1661, appear "John Davis and Mary, his wife, formerly wife of George Puddington deceased." (York Deeds 1, 119.) She outlived Davis, who d. 1691.

John² Puddington, b. Eng. (George¹) From various data in his life it is inferred that he was born about 1630. 6 Oct. 1668, his name with that of his wife Mary, occurs in a foreclosure. (York Deeds 2, 98.) 2 Nov. 1674, John Purrington of York to his brother-in-law John Penvill with the consent of Mrs. Mary Davess, the mother of John Purrington. (York Deeds 2, 160.) Also 1674, John Daviss of York to his son-in-law John Penwell. (York Deeds 2, 164.) This complicates the clearness of family relationships, leaving the term "brother-in-law and son-in-law" open to different interpretations.

About 1678 he had become a Lieutenant, which title is often used to distinguish him from his cousin of the same name. He removed from York to Cape Porpoise, where he was town clerk until its destruction by the Indians, 1690. Deeds and other papers show him to have lived in various places of that region. During his life the family name had softened to Purrington and has since with slight variations kept this form among the descendants of George Puddington. Lieut. John² d. about 1692-3. His children, as far as known, were

James³, b. about 1663, m. 1st Elizabeth   ; 2d Lydia Muzzey.

John³,   m. Sarah   . He lived at Salisbury.
Joshua³,   m. ——— dau. of Phillip Durrell of Hampton.
George³,   d. Jan. 1692, at Cape Porpoise.
Elizabeth³,   m. John Connors. (York Deeds 13, 131.)
Mary³,   m. Sanders Carr. (York Deeds 13, 131.)

James², b..1663 (John¹, George¹) m. 1st Elizabeth   ; 2nd Lydia Muzzey. He was Adm. of the estates of his father and of his brother George, 1692-1693. He claimed land at Cape Porpoise by an Indian deed dating from 1672.

Robert² Puddington, who came to N. E. with his brother George, settled at Portsmouth, N. H., where he was one of the committee, 1645, to assign land for the parsonage house." (Portsmouth Records.) In 1660 Robert Purinton agreed to care for Robert Davis, who deeded to him his house at Sagamore Neck. (Salisbury Families.) This gives color to the belief that he married Amy Davis. Among the marriages recorded by Rev. John Pike of Dover, was that of Amy Puddington "widdow," to Francis Graves 17 Aug. 1689. Ham says she was the widow of Robert Puddington of Portsmouth but does not indicate which Robert was her husband, Senior or Junior. (Ham Dover Records.)

John², b. 1635 (Robert¹) was 43 years of age in 1678. (N. E. His. and Gen. Reg. 8, 161.)

Robert², b. 1638 (Robert¹) was 40 years of age in 1678. (N. E. His. and Gen. Reg. 8, 161.)

John², b. Eng. 1635 (Robert¹) was, it is claimed, father of Hezekiah³, b. 1674-5, who removed to Truro, Cape Cod, about 1704. He was a deacon in the Truro church, and died in that town 8 Jan. 1717, in his 42d year. (Gravestone, Truro.) He had been a soldier at Wells in 1696, and belonged in the region of Dover or Kittery. His wife was Mary², daughter of Humphrey¹ Scammon of Kittery, whose will of 12 March 1713, named her as Mary Pudinton. (Me. Wills.) When he died 7 Jan. 1727, she was the wife of Jonathan Paine of Truro, to whom she had been married 29 June 1719. (Truro Record.) Therefore she received her portion of her father's estate under the name of Paine. She died in Truro 17 May 1760, in her 79th year "relict widow of Jonathan Paine," hence born 1682. (Truro gravestone.)

Hezekiah³ Purington, b. 1674-5 (John², Robert¹) m. Mary Scammon about 1702.

Children:

Humphrey⁴, b. 31 Jan. 1703, Kittery, m. 25 June 1724, Thankful Harding.

Mary⁴, b. 20 Oct. 1706, Truro, m. 25 June 1724, Barnabas Paine.
Sarah, b. 6 Oct. 1709, Truro, m. 3 June 1725, Solomon Lombard.
Mercy, b. 10 Nov. 1711, Truro, m. 28 June 1730, Nathaniel Harding, Jr.
Elizabeth, bap. 1713, probably died young.
Hezekiah, bap. 1715, m. 7 Oct. 1735, Mercy Bates of Middleboro.
Abiel (dau.) bap. 1718.   (Truro Records.)

With the exception of Elizabeth, all the above are named in the settlement of Hezekiah Purington's estate, 1718. (Barnstable Probate Rec.) In connection with the family relationship it is interesting to find that Humphrey Scammon was a Selectman of Pamet (Truro) in 1709. (Hist. Truro, p. 100.)

Humphrey⁴ Purington, b. 31 Jan. 1703, Kittery, (Hezekiah³, John², Robert¹) m. Thankful Harding 25 June 1724, both of Truro.
Hezekiah⁵, bap. 1727, Truro.
Humphrey, bap. 1729, Truro.
David, bap. 1731, Truro.
Mary, born 11 June 1734, Truro, bap. 1734.
Nathaniel, bap. 1736. Truro.
Abiel (dau.) bap. 1738, Truro.
Joshua, bap. 1740. Truro.
James, born 9 april 1742, Truro, bap. 1742.

This family removed later to Bath, Maine, and their further history is to be found in that state.

Hezekiah Purington and Isabel Smalley were married in Truro 2 March 1748. This could be the eldest son of Humphrey⁴ and his wife Thankful. There is nothing in the record itself to show this. It might also be a second marriage of his uncle Hezekiah³.

Robert¹ Puddington of Portsmouth.

Robert², b. 1638, either elder brother or father of Elias below.

"Elias Purrington, son of Robert Purrington, deceased, late of Portsmouth, now of Boston, blacksmith, sells house and land at Portsmouth 4 April 1694." (Deeds Rockingham Co., N. H.)

Elias was married in Boston 7 July 1694. (Boston Records.)

No. 31.

LIBRARY of
Cape Cod
HISTORY & GENEALOGY

THOMAS' HOWES OF YARMOUTH, MASS., AND SOME OF HIS DESCENDANTS, TOGETHER WITH THE REV. JOHN MAYO, ALLIED TO HIM BY MARRIAGE.

By JAMES W. HAWES, ESQ.

YARMOUTHPORT, MASS.:
C. W. SWIFT, Publisher and Printer,
The "Register" Press,
1917.

THOMAS¹ HOWES OF YARMOUTH, MASS., AND SOME OF HIS DESCENDANTS, TOGETHER WITH THE REV. JOHN MAYO, ALLIED TO HIM BY MARRIAGE.

By JAMES W. HAWES, ESQ.

Copyright, 1917, by C. W. Swift.

HOWES.(a)
FIRST GENERATION.

I. THOMAS¹ HOWES, b. in England; m. there Mary ____ ; came to America about 1637; d. between Oct. 6, 1665 (date of acknowledgement of his will), and Oct. 13, 1665 (date of his inventory). His widow m.(b-d) 2d before Aug. 1, 1668, and probably before Feb. 9, 1667-8, as his 4th wife, Gov. Thomas Prence of the Plymouth Colony, and d.(e) in Yarmouth Dec. 9, and was buried Dec. 11, 1695. Gov. Prence d.(f) in Plymouth March 29, 1673.

The will(f1) of Gov. Thomas Prence, dated March 13, 1672-3, contains the following reference to his wife:

"And Respecting my temporall estate wherwith the Lord hath blessed mee my will is that Mary my beloved wife shall have such household goods of Any kind as were hers, before wee married, Returned to her againe, after my Decease and if any of them, be much Impared or be wanting, that shee shall make it good out of my estate in such goods as shee Desireth;

"Item I give unto my said loveing wife my best bed and the furniture therunto appertaining and, the Court Cubberd that stands in the new Par-

---

(a) Bardsley, in his Dictionary of English and Welsh Surnames (p. 402), derives the name from two sources: 1st from the Christian name "Hugh," mentioning the South of England, and 2d from the local word "how," meaning a mound or a hill, giving instances in Cambridgeshire, the counties of Cumberland and Norfolk, and elsewhere. The name will be found in early records spelled Howe, Hows, House, &c. See "Note as to Howes," infra, p. 32.

(b-d) Proved by Miss Ella F. Elliot of Somerville, Mass., in 6 Mayflower Descendant (hereinafter cited as Mf.), 127, 230-235; 59 N. E. Reg. 217, 218; 61 ib. 200.

(e) 3 Yar. Recs. 328; 6 Mf. 230. Swift in Old Yarmouth, 117, says she died at the house of her son-in-law Jeremiah Howes. He was also her own son.

(f) 3 Mf. 203.

(f1) 3 Mf. 204, 205. (3 Plym. Col. Wills, pt. 1, p.p. 58-70.)

lour with the Cloth and Cushen that is on it, and an horse and three Cowes such as shee shall make Choise of, and foure of my best silver spoones and alsoe During her Naturall life. I give her the Rents and proffitts of my prte of the mill att Satuckett; and of the lands adjoining, and my Debts and legacyes being first payed; I Doe further give unto my said wife a full third prte of my prsonall estate that Remaines." He made her sole executrix of his will.

His inventory,(f2) dated April 23, 1673, contains a list of the "goods mistris Mary Prence had before Marriage." She swore to the inventory June 5, 1673.(f3)

Thomas¹ Howes was first in Lynn and afterward settled in Yarmouth, of which he was one of the three original proprietors. He settled at Nobscusset on the north side of Cape Cod, which afterwards became a part of the town of Dennis.(g) He was one of those in August, 1643, between 16 and 60 years of age, able to bear arms in Yarmouth.(h) He was one of the deputies from Yarmouth to the General Court at Plymouth for six years, commencing in 1652.(i) The tax of his widow (then also the widow of Gov. Prence) in 1676 "towards the charges of the late war" was £1 3s. 4d.(j)

The first mention of Thomas' Howes is in the court records of Essex county in September, 1638. At the 10th Quarter Court, held at Salem Sept. 25, 1638, in the suit of Mr. Holgrave against Thomas Howes for trespass, the jury found for the plaintiff seven bushels and a half of corn and four shillings costs.(k) At the same court Abram Temple obtained a verdict for two bushels of corn, five shillings damages and four shillings costs against Mr. John Humphreys, Mr. Howes and Mr. Hawks for trespass done by their horses; Hugh Browne, a verdict for three bushels of corn, seven shillings and sixpence damages and four shillings costs against Thomas Howes for trespass; James Molton, a verdict for eleven bushels and one peck of corn and four shillings costs against Mr. Howes and Mr. Hawks for trespass; James Hinds, a verdict against the same two for four bushels and a half of corn and four shillings costs for trespass; and Henry Skerry, a verdict against the same two, also for trespass, for the same amount of corn and costs.(k)

He is first mentioned in the Plymouth Colony records in December, 1638. Mr. John Crow and Mr. Thomas Howes, of Mattacheese, otherwise called Yarmouth, took the oath of allegiance to the King and of fidelity to the government December 18, 1638.(l) At the court held January 7, 1638-9, it appears that a grant of land at Yarmouth had been made to Mr. Anthony Thacher, Mr. Thomas Howes and Mr. John Crow, together with John Colte "to be enquird of," and that Mr. Howes proposed to take up his freedom at Yarmouth.(m)

(f2) Ib. 213, 214.
(f3) Ib. 216.
(g) Swift's Old Yarmouth, 24.
(h) Ib. 34, 35; 3 Plym. Col. Recs, 194.
(i) Plym. Col. Recs.
(j) Swift 105; 2 Freeman's Cape Cod, 195.

(k) 7 Essex Inst. Hist. Colls. 187, 188; 3 Essex Antiquarian, 31, 35, 126.
(l) 1 Plym. Col. Recs. 107.
(m) Ib. 108.

Feb. 29, 1638-9, Richard Walker, planter, of Lynn, appointed Edward Dillingham, gentleman, of Sandwich, his attorney, to sue Howes, planter, late of Lynn and then of Mattachecso, for damages sustained by him as surety for Howes for a debt to Samuel Smith. Smith had sued Walker and Howes before the Governor, Council and Assistants of Massachusetts and Jan. 4, 1638-9, had recovered against them 30 bushels of corn and 10s. costs, whereupon Walker had been compelled to pay the sum of £9 10s. and had been put to other charges to the amount of 12s.(n) March 5, 1638-9, it was "ordered by the Court that Mr. Nicholas Sympkins, William Palmer, Phillip Tabor, and Josuah Barnes, of the towne of Yarmouth, shalbe added to Mr. Anthony Thacher, Mr. Thom Howes, & Mr. John Crowe, comittees of the said place, to make an equall division of the planting landes now to be devided at this first division there, to eich man according to his estate and quallitie, and according to their instruccons; and that Josuah Pratt, of Plymouth, and Mr. John Vincent, of Sandwich, shall view the landes there, and make report thereof unto the Court, that if those proporcons wch Mr. Andrew Hellot hath assumed to himself there shalbe so pjudiciall to the whole, that then some just and equall order maybe taken therein, to pvent the evell consequence it may

(n) Lechford's Notebook, 7 Tranactions of Am. Antiquarian Soc. [31] 50, 51. The editor seems to think there was a Samuel Howes in Yarmouth at this time, but there was not. There was a Samuel House in Barnstable, but he lived most of his life in Scituate and died there.

be to the whole plantacon."(o) Sept. 3, 1639, Mr. Thomas Howes, of Yarmouth, was proposed to be a freeman at the next court.(p)

At the court held March 3, 1639-40, the following record appears: "Whereas Mr. Thacher, Mr. Crowe, & Mr. Howes, the committees of Yarmouth, were complayned of to have made unequall divisions of lands there, whereupon the said comittees have exhibited a very formall division of the said lands unto the Court, wch is well approoved of, and the Court doth further order, that the said comittees shall receive no more inhabitantes into the said towne, except they bring certificate from the places whence they come, under sufficient mens handes of the sd places, of their religious and honest carriage, wch certifycate shall first be allowed by the govnr and assistantes before such psons be admitted there."(q) June 17, 1641, "a warrant [was] granted to distraine xij s upon Emanuel White for keepeing cowes, and upon Mr. Sympkins xvj s, and Mr. Howes 16s, if Mris Fuller will not pay the sd 16s for Howes."(r) From the same record it appears that he and William Chase and Joshua Barnes had incurred expenses as a committee. for the town, and a rate was ordered to defray them. June 7, 1642, Mr. Thomas Howes of Yarmouth, planter, was surety for the appearance at Court of Joshua Barnes in the sum of £40. The bond was afterwards released.(r1)

(o) 1 Plym. Col. Recs. 117.
(p) Ib. 132.
(q) Ib. 142.
(r) 2 ib. 20.
(r1) 2 ib. 41.

June 5, 1644, he is named as constable of Yarmouth.(s) August 20, 1644, "Mr. Anthony Thacher, Mr. Thomas Howes, & Mr. Willm Lumpkin, of Yarmouth, or any two of them, are appoynted by the Court to lay forth the farm land graunted to Nathall Sowther neere Billingsgate; and the Court confirmes the same unto him.(t)" March 3, 1644-5, it was "ordered by the Court, that Mr. Thomas Starr shall have psently layd forth for him at Yarmouth fifty acrees of upland, either next to Elder Hores or Mr. Howes landes at Seahewit, on wch side he will, so that it adjoyne to one of them."(u) June 2, 1646, Mr. Thomas Howes was foreman of the grand jury.(v) June 1, 1647, Thomas Howes was admitted a freeman and sworn.(w) June 7, 1648, Mr. Thomas Howes was foreman of a jury.(x)

Captain Standish, who had been appointed by the Court March 7, 1647-8, to have a hearing "and to put an end to all differences as doe remayne in the towne of Yarmouth," made his report May 14, 1648, which included the following: "whereas Mr. Thatcher, Mr. Howes, and Mr. Crow, comittees of this plantation of Yarmouth, in consideration of thayer charges about the discovering, purchas, and other charges by them disbursed, about the same, have clamed and taken up. viz, Mr. Thatcher, 130 acars of upland, and twenty six acres of meadow for a farme, and Mr. Howes 100 acars of upland, and 20 acars of meadowe for his fearme, or great lot,—the towne hath alowed Mr. Thatcher an hundred and tenne acares of upland, and his twenty-six acares of meadowe, and hee hath layed downe to the towne the other twenty acares of upland, and likewise the towne have graunted unto Mr. Howes fourscore acars of upland, and twenty acares of meadow, and hee hath layed downe to the towne, in liew of the other twenty acares of land by him taken up in his great lot, twenty acars lying in Rock Furland, next on the west side of Edward Sturges land, bought of Gabriell Wheildin; and lickwise the towne hath allowed unto Mr. Crow 4 score acars of upland, and twenty acars of meadowe, wherof som part is taken up allredy, and the rest to bee taken up by him where hee shall find it convenient, and twenty acars hee remits to the towne, which the towne accepts, and is satisfyed in full in respecte of any differences yt hath been betwext the towne and them, and everyone of them, in respecte of theire farmes or great lots, or any greewances about the laying out of lands from the begining of the plantation to the 13th day of May, 1648, aforsaid. Also, Mr. Thatcher and Mr. Howes hath layed down to the use of the town, viz, Mr. Thatcher 12 acares of upland neare the Great Basse Pound, and Mr. Howes hath layed downe 10 acares of upland in Nobscussett, lying there in a furland called Rabbits Ruine, in liew of 12 acares a peece claimed by them, and taken up heertofore, in consideration of charges about the laying out of lands in the winter 1638, which apeers in thayer acompte given into Court, ano 1640, which the towne hath otherwise satisfied upon agreement."

"It is lickwise granted yt Mr. Howes

(s) Ib. 72.
(t) Ib. 76.
(u) Ib. 81, 82.
(v) Ib. 102.
(w) Ib. 114.
(x) Ib. 126.

shall have 17 acars in the Eastern Meadow, and at the easterne end in the Swan Ponds, in liewe of 17 acars of meadow Mr. Howes hath taken up in Nobscussett, als Sassuett Necke, and sould to Thomas Burman: hee hath layed downe to the townes use 7½ acars of meadowe, late Mr. Hallotts, lying at the lower end of the rocke tree furland, and eight acares of meadow, late William Chases, lyeing next unto Edward Sturges meadow, between the river and Mr. Simkins necke."

"The 15th day of May, 1648. It is agreed by Captain Standish, Mr. Crow, Mr. Thatcher, and Mr. Howes, the comittees of this plantation of Yarmouth, and Richard Hore, Mr. Hawes, William Nicorsone, William Pallmer, and Robert Dennis, in the behalfe of the towne, that Mr. Staare, William Nichorsone, and Robert Dennis shall bee joyned to the comittees for this psent year, and thence after by tho towne: thay have thayer liberty to choose other three to the comittees aforsaid, so yt the comittees shall not heerafter dispose of any lands, either uplands or meadow, without the consent of those three or tow of them, and if any difference arise between them which they cannot compose themselves, yt thay repayer to Captain Standish for his dyrection."(y)

June 5, 1650, Mr. Thomas Howes, with Samuel Mayo, was appointed administrator of the estate of Samuel Hallet, deceased.(z)

Oct. 2, 1650, Mr. Thomas Howes with a number of others had a suit against William Nickerson for slander, claiming £100 damages, which was referred to the magistrates, to decide and compose the controversy. The decision was: "The Court doe judg yt the said Willam Nickarson, in regard of his offencive speaches against sundry of the towne, to have carried himselfe therin unworthyly, and desire him to see his evell therin, and to bee redy to acknowlidg it; and yt those hee hath offended in that behalfe should rest therin."(a)

June 7, 1651, he was on a jury.(b) Oct. 14, 1651, Mr. Howes had in his keeping belonging to John Barnes of Plymouth a pied cow, "the said Cow being put forth to the said Mr. Howes to halfe the encreas," which had produced two heifers and a steer calf.(c) June 7, 1652, Mr. Thomas Howes is named as a deputy to the General Court from Yarmouth.(d) Oct. 5, 1652, it appeared that Mr. Howes had been appointed for Yarmouth by the Colonial Treasurer to receive the oil for the county.(e) June 7, 1653, Mr. Thomas Howes was named as one of the deputies to the General Court from Yarmouth.(f) June 6, 1654, he was on the grand jury.(g) It appears March 5, 1656-7, that he and Mr. Anthony Thacher had purchased lands of Janno, an Indian sachem, and, as the Indian claimed, had not paid for them. Mr. Thacher was directed to appear and answer at the next May court.(h) May 8, 1657, Mashantampaine, Sagamore of Yarmouth, acknowledged that he had

(y) Ib. 128-130.
(z) Ib. 156.

(a) 7 ib. 50.
(b) Ib. 54.
(c) 12 ib. 215.
(d) 3 ib. 9.
(e) Ib. 17.
(f) Ib. 32.
(g) Ib. 49.
(h) Ib. 113.

received full compensation from Antony Thacher, Mr. John Crow and Mr. Thomas Howes for land he had sold to "Mr. William Bradford, Esq."(i) June 1, 1658, he is named as a deputy from Yarmouth.(j) May 14, 1658, Mr. John Alden and Capt. Josias Winslow, having been appointed arbitrators by the court, agreed with Janno upon the amount due him and decided that of that amount Mr. Anthony Thacher, Mr. Howes and Mr. Crow should pay one half and the town of Yarmouth the other half and the sum of £6 in charges which the town had been to about the business, should be borne, £4 by the town and 20s. each by Mr. Thacher and Mr. Howes, "old Mr. Crow" being excused from paying any part of it.(k)

It appears that Capt. Myles Standish with the consent of Mrs. Barbara Standish, his wife, had sold to Thomas Howes a farm lying in the liberties of Yarmouth, the deed being recorded Oct. 5, 1658.(l) June 7, 1659, Mr. Howes is named as a deputy from Yarmouth;(m) also, June 6, 1660.(n) June 13, 1660, he was a deputy to consider the trade at Kennebeck and met in conference on the subject.(o) Oct. 2, 1660, Mr. Howes attended a special session of the General Court.(p) On March 5, 1660-1, the following entry was made:

"Whereas this Court is given to understand that there are sertaine cottages to bee erected, or in erecting, within the towneship of Yarmouth, contrary to order of the Court, the Court ordereth Mr. Anthony Thacher and Mr. Thomas Howes, Senir, that they take dilligent care henceforth, from time to time, that noe more houses bee erected there contrary to the said order; and incase any after theire prohobition shall psist soe to doe, then they to signify the same to the Court, and attend their further order."(q)

April 1, 1661, he witnessed a deed by Indians to John Howland, Sr., of Plymouth, and others.(r) June 3, 1662, Mr. Thomas Howes is named as a deputy from Yarmouth to the General Court.(s) He was appointed June 10, 1662, one of the committee to take the account of the Colonial Treasurer.(t) June 9, 1662, he was on the committee to take the Colonial Treasurer's account and signed the report.(u) March 3, 1662-3, he and Robert Dennis obtained judgment for £10 damages and the costs of the suit against William Nickerson, Sr., they complaining "in the behalfe of themselves and the rest of theire naighbours, whoe by towne order are to have theire shares of the whales this yeare, wh by Gods providence are or shalbee cast up within theire townshipes," "for unjust molestation in unjust attachment of the blubber of a whale belonging to the complainants."(v) June 7, 1665, the Court

(i) Swift, 95, 96; 2 Freeman, 292.
(j) 3 Plym. Col. Recs. 135.
(k) Ib. 146.
(l) 13 Mf. 142, 143; 2 Plym. Col. Deeds, pt. 2, p. 11.
(m) 3 Plym. Col. Recs. 162.
(n) Ib. 187.
(o) Ib. 194, 195.
(p) Ib. 198.

(q) Ib. 207.
(r) 2 Plym. Col. Deeds, pt. 2, p. 61; 16 Mf. 78.
(s) 4 Plym. Col. Recs. 14.
(t) Ib. 21.
(u) 8 Ib. 106. No doubt the same occasion as the next above.
(v) 7 Ib. 106.

ordered that whereas William Nickerson had illegally purchased of the Indians a certain tract of land at "Mannamoiett" (now Chatham), he should have 100 acres thereof at or near his house, and the rest of the land was granted to nine persons, including Thomas Howes, Sr., who were to pay Nickerson their equal proportions of what he should show he had paid for the land, and they were given liberty to purchase other land there not to exceed 100 acres apiece.(w) March 6, 1665-6, Mistress Howes complained that some Indians had sold her a parcel of sturgeon and had not delivered them, whereupon the court ordered the Indians to make satisfaction unto her for the same.(x) On the same date, letters of administration were granted unto Mistress Mary Howes on the estate of Mr. Thomas Howes, deceased.(y)

The will of Mr. Howes is printed in 6 Mayflower Descendant, 157. It was dated Sept. 26, 1665, and proved March 7, 1665-6. It was witnessed by Thomas Thornton and Anthony Thacher. The record(z) states that after its date it was read over to him and acknowledged to be his last will Oct. 6, 1665, in the presence of his

---

(w) 4 Ib. 96, 97, 101, 102.
(x) Ib. 115.
(y) Ib. 117.
(z) 2 Plym. Col. Wills, pt. 2, p. 31.
The Rev. Dr. Reuben Wing Howes of New York city informs the compiler that the original will of Thomas' Howes is at "Morningthorpe," Brewster, Putnam county, N. Y., an estate in the possession of the widow of Seth B. Howes, which upon her death will pass to her late husband's grandnephew, Leander Townsend Howes, a son of Dr. Howes.

wife and of Mr. Anthony Thacher and the latter's wife Elisabeth. He made his wife Mary executrix and his friends Mr. Anthony Thacher and Robert Dennis "feofees in trust to see to the prformance of this my last will." He gave certain lands to his eldest son Joseph, his second son Thomas and his youngest son Jeremiah, after his and his wife's decease. He willed that his three sons should have and hold the upland and meadow he had given them and placed them in possession of. To his wife he gave his dwelling house, his outhouses and all the land then in his possession during her life, but if she married, she was to have only the thirds of them.

"And my will is that shee alsoe have all my moveable goods both within and without after my Debts bee payed att her Dispose for her use and benifitt; provided shee Dispose and give the remaine of them; att her Decease or marriage unto my said Children but in such and such proportions as shee shall see meet."

All the rest of his lands he gave to his wife "to bee Desposed of and given unto my said Children as shee pleaseth att or before her Decease." He also provided that his son Thomas, in consideration of his gifts in the will, was to teach his grandson Samuel the trade of a cooper, to give Samuel when twelve years old a mare of three years, and to keep the dwelling house in repair during the life or widowhood of his wife. The will mentions six acres of land that had been William Nickerson's.

The inventory of his personal estate, taken Oct. 18, 1665, was sworn to by the widow Feb. 26, 1665-6. It amounted to £242 14s., and mentioned £23 19s. 3½d. of debts to be paid. Included in the inventory were two Bibles and other books, appraised at £2.(a) By deed dated Feb. 9, 1667-8, his three sons made division of his real estate.(b) Dec. 23, 1695, the inventory of the personal estate of the widow (then Mrs. Prence) was taken by John Miller and Thomas Folland. It was sworn to Dec. 31, 1695, by her son, Mr. Jeremiah Howes, Sr. It mentions Thomas and Jonathan Howes, a cow at Jeremiah Howes's, a debt of £7 8s. due to Jeremiah Howes, Jr., an old chest and a cupboard at Prence Howes's, and an old Bible, appraised at 4s. The inventory, less debts, amounted to £42 2s. 7d.(c) Swift in "Old Yarmouth" (p. 47) says respecting Thomas' Howes:

"Nothing is known of Mr. Howes before his coming to this country, neither have we any knowledge in what part of England he originated. He was in Salem in 1635."(d)

"That he was a man of much influence, great maturity of judgment, and of considerable importance in the Colony, is sufficiently attested." (p. 48).

"It need not, however, be inferred from the fact that the first dwelling houses of the settlers were small and unpretentious, that they were necessarily an indigent and humble class of people in point of worldly fortune. In respect to some of them we know

---

(a) Ib. 33; 6 Mf. 159.
(b) 3 Plym. Col. Deeds, 106, 167; 6 Mf. 232.
(c) 2 Barn. Prob. Recs. 12; 6 Mf. 234.
(d) There is no proof nor is there reason to think that he was in this country as early as 1635 or that he ever resided in Salem.

this would not be a correct estimate. Anthony Thacher, Edmund Hawes and Richard Sears were certainly men of education and social standing in England, and Thomas Howes, John Crow, Edward Sturges, Andrew Hallet, Nicholas Simpkins and others appear to have belonged to the substantial middling class, either staunch yeomen or educated gentlemen. They built such houses as their condition required of them as pioneers of a new country; whose first care was to shelter their families while they were preparing the soil, making roads and enclosing their plantations. The next generation saw a great change in their style of living, as well as in their habitations."(pp. 79, 80.)

Thomas' Howes and Samuel House of Scituate were not brothers and there is no evidence that they were related.(e)

Children.(f)
II. Joseph
III. Thomas
IV. Jeremiah

(e) 66 N. E. Reg. 357, 358; 67 ib. 261; 69 ib. 284; 2 Otis's Barn. Families, 54-57.

(f) It is not known whether he had other children who died before him nor whether he left one or more daughters, but, in the absence of all mention of them, we must assume that he did not. It is, therefore, probable that Austin is in error in assuming in "Allied Families" (pp. 53, 136, 137) that Elizabeth Howes who, as he says, according to the Friends' records, married June 28, 1665, Daniel Butler of Sandwich and Falmouth and died in 1717, was his daughter.

8

SECOND GENERATION.

II. JOSEPH² (Thomas¹) Howes; b. in England in 1634 or before; m.(g) Elizabeth² (Rev. John¹) Mayo; d.(h) Jan. 19 and buried Jan. 21, 1694-5. She d.(h) March 12 and was buried March 16, 1700-1. He was brought to New England by his parents and resided in the part of Yarmouth now Dennis. In 1676 in the rate "towards the charges of the late war" his tax was £7 11s.(i) In 1698 his widow was taxed £4 4s. 6d.(j) June 3, 1655, Joseph Howes was propounded to take up his freedom.(k) June 3, 1657, he was admitted and sworn.(l) June 4, 1661, he was on the grand jury.(m) June 7, 1665, he is named as constable of Yarmouth.(n) The same date he was appointed one of three persons to lay out the 100 acres of land granted to William Nickerson at Monomoy (later Chatham) and to place in possession the nine grantees of the lands not allowed to Nickerson. The warrant was dated June 30, 1665.(o) March 6, 1665-6, as constable of Yarmouth, he complained that Thomas Starr had opposed him and used threatening language against him in the execution of his office. The case being tried before a jury, Starr was found guilty and the court fined him £5.(p) The same date he was approved as one of the selectmen of Yarmouth.(q) June 5, 1666, he was one of the selectmen of Yarmouth approved by the court.(r) June 30, .1667, he signed a paper to the General Court in favor of the Rev. Thomas Thornton against an attack by Nicholas Nickerson.(s) June 5, 1671, he was one of the surveyors of highways of Yarmouth.(t) June 5, 1672, he was on the grand jury,(u) and the same date he is mentioned as a surveyor of highways for Yarmouth.(v) In 1679 Joseph Howes and two others were appointed a committee to collect the residue of the salary due the minister.(w) In February, 1680, the town agreed upon him, with Samuel and Jeremiah Howes, to secure to it all such whales as should be cast up between Sawsuit Harbor mouth and Yarmouth Harbor, for £4 a whale.(x) July 7, 1681, he was on the jury in several suits.(yz) June 6, 1682, Joseph Howes was on the grand jury.(a) June 6, 1683, June 2, 1685, and June, 1686, he is mentioned as one of the selectmen of Yarmouth.(b)

Joseph² Howes left a will, dated

(g) 1 Otis, 25, 220, 222.
(h) Yarmouth Recs,; 2 Freeman, 202, 203.
(i) Swift, 105.
(j) Records of Superior Ct. of of Judicature, No. 4600; Rec. Book, 1686-1700, p. 297; Supremé Ct. Clerk's Of., Boston.
(k) 3 Plym. Col. Recs. 78.
(l) Ib. 117.
(m) Ib. 215.
(n) 4 Ib. 91.
(o) Ib. 96, 97, 101, 102, 135.
(p) Ib. 115.
(q) Ib. 117.
(r) Ib. 124.
(s) Swift, 90, where a reduced facsimile of his signature may be seen. See "Edmond Hawes," 139, by the compiler.
(t) 5 Plym. Col. Recs. 53.
(u) Ib. 91.
(v) Ib. 93.
(w) Swift, 108.
(x) Swift, 109.
(yz) 7 Plym. Col. Recs. 241-243.
(a) 6 Ib. 35.
(b) Ib. 108, 163, 186.

Jan. 7, 1694-5, and proved Feb. 7, 1694-5.(c) He mentions his wife Elizabeth, his sons Samuel, Joseph, John, Nathaniel, Thomas and Amos, and his daughters Mary Hallett, Elizabeth Myrick and Hannah Howes. His sons Nathaniel, Thomas and Amos and his daughter Hannah were under the age of 21 years. He named his wife and his son Joseph his executors, and his brothers Jeremiah Howes and John Mayo to advise and help them. The inventory of his estate, taken Jan. 30, 1694-5, and sworn to Feb. 7, 1694-5, amounted to £288 in real estate and £166 18s. in personal property; total, £454 18s.(d) Included in his inventory are the following items:

A share in a whale boat	£1 0s.
A try pot and materials belonging to it,	3 0
A great pewter platter	0 15
Four platters	1 0
Books	2 12
Arms and ammunition	3 6

The will of his widow Elizabeth Howes, dated Feb. 7, 1694-5, and proved April 1, 1701, gave her dwelling house, barn and homestead to her sons Nathaniel, Thomas and Amos, and the rest of her estate to be divided between all her surviving children. She made her sons Samuel and Joseph executors.(e) Her inventory, dated March 26, 1701, and sworn to April 1, 1701, by her sons Lieut. Samuel Howes, Joseph Howes, Thomas Howes and Amos Howes, amounted to £125 19s. 10d. in personal property.(f) Included in her inventory are the following items:

(c) 1 Barn. Prob. Recs. 108.
(d) Ib. 109.
(e) 2 ib. 121.
(f) Ib. 122.

One pair of Oxen	£ 7	15s.	0d.
Other cattle	27	17	0
Four horses	5	15	0
16 sheep	6	10	0
8 swine	2	2	0
A silver cup	3	15	0
A gun	0	15	0
A cutlas	0	3	0
A rapier	0	6	0
A bible	0	5	0
Other books	0	7	6

Children

as given in the will. The actual dates and order of births are not known, except the order of the sons among themselves and of the daughters among themselves:

1. Samuel, b.
2. Joseph, b.   ; m.(g) Mary Vincent(g1) Nov. 28, 1689; d.(h) Dec. 24, 1743. His children appear on the Yarmouth records, the oldest b. in September, 1690, and the youngest May 25, 1705.(i) In 1693 he was one of a committee to agree upon

---

(g) Yar. Recs.; 2 Mf. 209; J. C. Howes, Gen. of the Howes Family, 12.
(g1) J. C. Howes, 12, says that, according to the record, she d. March 24, 1776, in the 100th year of her age. He, however, thinks it was Sarah (Hedge), wife of Thomas, son of Jeremiah' Howes, who thus died, "as," he correctly says, "appears upon her gravestone." But the last mentioned Thomas Howes did not marry Sarah Hedge. His p. 15 is erroneous. It was Thomas, son of Thomas², who married her. Howes's statement of the record is also incorrect. The town record reads that widow Mary Hewes departed this life March 24, 1776, in the hundredth year of her age.
(h) J. C. Howes, 12. 2 Freeman, 216, says he d. then "in a good old age."
(i) 11 Mf. 112.

some fit person to teach school.(j) In the rate of 1698 the tax of Joseph Howes was £2 3s. 6d.(k) In the division of the common lands in 1712 Joseph Howes had 30½ shares.(l) The church in the East Precinct of Yarmouth, later Dennis, held its first meeting the last of February 1721-2, and Joseph Howes, Sr., signed the covenant.(m) In 1739 he was among the proprietors of the common lands in Crocket Neck.(m1)

3. John, b. ____ ; m.(n) 1st Elizabeth Paddock Nov. 28, 1689, and 2d Mary Matthews July 8, 1691; d.(o) April 30, 1736. His 2d wife d.(o) April 8, 1746. In 1693 he was one of a committee to agree on a fit person to teach school.(o1) In 1698 Mr. John Howes was chosen by the town of Yarmouth as one of its representatives in the Massachusetts Legislature, but declined to serve.(o2) In 1698 his tax in the rate of that year was £2 3s. 8d.(o3) He was town clerk and treasurer three years, commencing in 1695,(p) and one of the selectmen 8 years, commencing in 1707.(q) In 1710 he was chosen one of a committee to report a list of persons entitled to a portion of the public lands and the number of shares each was entitled to, according to a plan previously adopted. The report of the committee was confirmed and John Howes was on the relief committee to hear and report on grievances, which committee reported but few changes.(r) On the division of the common lands in 1712 he received 28 shares.(s) In 1716 a new meeting house was built and Mr. John Howes was one of the building committee chosen to determine the dimensions and contract with the workmen.(t) In 1721 a committee was appointed to devise some plan for disposing of the town's share of £50,000 issued by the Province and loaned to the towns. Mr. John Howes was one of the committee.(u) His will(u1) was dated Feb. 18, 1734-5, and proved July 7, 1736. He mentions his wife Mary and his children John, James, Elizabeth, and Sarah Eldredge.(u2)

4. Nathaniel, b. ____ ; m.(v) Esther Ryder Feb. 22, 1704-5; d.(v) July 26, 1745. She d.(v) Nov. 27, 1763. His will,(v1) dated June 10, 1745, and proved Oct. 9, 1745,. mentions his wife Esther, his children Nathaniel,

---

(j) Swift, 116.
(k) Recs. of Superior Ct. of Judicature, No. 4600; Rec. Book 1686-1700, p. 297.
(l) Swift, 126, 128.
(m) Deyo's Barnstable County, 516, 517.
(m1) Swift, 141, 142.
(n) 2 Freeman, 215; J. C. Howes, 13; Yar. Recs.; 2 Mf. 209; Yar. Reg, Dec. 3, 1846.
(o) 2 Freeman, 215; J. C. Howes, 13; 2 Mf. 209.
(o1) Deyo, 520.
(o2) Swift, 118.
(o3) Superior Ct. Recs. as above, p. 9.
(p) Swift, 238.

(q) Ib. 237.
(r) Ib. 125.
(s) Ib. 127.
(t) Ib. 136.
(u) Ib. 137.
(u1) 5 Barn. Prob. Recs. 272, 273.
(u2) Austin's Allied Families, 187, makes his 1st marriage Jan. 28, 1689-90, and his death June 30, 1736.
(v) 2 Freeman, 216; J. C. Howes, 13; Yar. Recs.
(v1) 6 Barn. Prob. Recs. 449, 450.

Zaccheus, Hannah Sears, Rebecca Hall and Esther Howes, and his grandsons Nathaniel Sears and Nathaniel Hall. In the rate of 1698 his tax was £2 and over.(w) In the division of the common lands in 1712 he had 25 shares.(x) The first meeting of the church in the East Precinct of Yarmouth, later Dennis, was held in his house.(x1)

5. Thomas, b. about 1680; m.(y) in Eastham Dec. 11, 1701, Content⁸ (Daniel², Ralph¹) Smith; d. between May 29, 1736 (date of his will), and Oct. 19, 1738 (date of probate).(z) The will mentions his wife Content and his children Daniel, Joseph, Thomas, Elizabeth (wife of Samuel Stewart), Mary Howes, Thankful Howes, and Hannah Howes. The inventory, sworn to March 9, 1741-2, amounted to £2353 1s. 6d.(z1) The real estate was divided Jan. 4, 1769, 1-3 to Capt. Daniel Howes, 1-3 to Joseph Howes and 1-3 to the heirs and legal representatives of Thomas Howes, deceased.(z2) His wife had survived him. He purchased land in Monomoit (later Chatham) in 1703 and settled there. He was the ancestor of the Howes family in that town. He was one of the selectmen two years and town treasurer two years. He was successively ensign, lieutenant

(w) Superior St. Recs. as above, p. 9.
(x) Swift, 127.
(x1) Deyo, 517, 518.
(y) East. Recs.; will of Daniel² Smith, 3 Barn. Prob. Recs., 63; 7 Mf. 18. J. C. Howes erroneously says (p. 13) that he married Rebecca Howes.
(z) 5 Barn. Prob. Recs. 366, 367.
(z1) 6 ib. 111.
(z2) 13 ib. 410.

and captain of the military company.(a) March 13, 1715-16, he with others signed a paper in behalf of Ebenezer Hawes in the suit of the Rev. Hugh Adams against the latter.(a1)

6. Amos, b.   ; m.(b) Susannah Hedge May 22, 1701; d.(b) Feb. 16, 1717-18. She d.(b) Jan. 24. 1755. His children or some of them appear on the Yarmouth records, the oldest b. in April, 1702.(c) In the division of the common lands in 1712 he had 25 shares.(d)

7. Mary, b.   m.(e) John Hallett Feb. 16, 1681-2.

8. Elizabeth, b.   ; m. Joseph Merrick of Eastham May 1, 1684.(f,g)

9. Hannah, b.   ; m.(h) William Matthews Dec. 15, 1693.

Will of Joseph² Howes.

I, Joseph Hows of ye Town of Yarmouth in ye County of Barnestable in ye Province of ye Massachusetts in America being weak in body but of sound and disposing mind and memory and not knowing ye day of my death do make. constitute and ordaine this my last will and testa-

(a) Early Chatham Settlers, by Wm. C. Smith, in Yarmouth Register. 1915.
(a1) Files 10812, Superior Ct., Supreme Ct. Clerk's of., Boston.
(b) J. C. Howes, 13; Yar. Recs.
(c) 10 Mf. 245.
(d) Swift, 127.
(e) Yar. Reg. Dec. 3, 1846; Yar. Recs.; 2 Mf. 207.
(f,g) 7 Mf. 12; 6 N. E. Reg. 169; 3 Savage's Genealogical Dictionary of New England, 198; Merrick Geneal. 18 and 2 Freeman, 391 n., erroneously say that they were m. May 8, 1684.
(h) J. C. Howes, 11.

ment in manner following and do hereby anul and mak void all other and former wills whatsoever viz:

Imprimis I do give myself wholy and intierly unto ye Lord my God to be his alone both in life and death and unto Eternity to God ye father to be my God and Father in and through ye Lord Jesus Christ; to ye Lord Jesus Christ my dear Lord and Redeemer to ye holy Ghost my Blessed Comforter I give my soul unto God that gave it and my body to decent burial as to my Executors hereafter named shall seem convenient in firm hope of a glorious resurrection that I may meet and be ever with ye Lord. And as for that portion of worldly goods which God of his grace has been pleased to bestow upon me an unworthy worm far above my desarts I do dispose of ye same in manner following I do confirm to my loving son Samuel Howes all those lands I have formerly given him as his childs portion with all ye ways priviledges and easements thereto belonging to be to him and his heirs forever.

Item I do give and confirm to my loving son Joseph Howes all those lands both upland and meadow which I have formerly given him as his child's portion both upland and meadow to be to him and his heirs forever with all ye ways easements and priviledges thereto belonging.

It. to my loving son John Howes I do confirm all those lands which I formerly gave unto him boath upland and meadow with all ye ways easements and priviledges thereunto belonging to be to him and his heirs forever.

It. To my other three sons Nathaniel Thomas and Amos Howes I do give all ye rest of my lands to be equally divided between them by my executors to be to them and their heirs forever with this proviso that if my loving wife Elizabeth shall have occasion for it shee shall have liberty during her widdowhood to make use of one third part of it and if eather of these my three sons shall dy before they come of age such part shall be divided equally between all my surviving sons And as they come to ye age of twenty one years so they shall possess their part only except as hereafter excepted.

It. To my daughter Mary Hallett I give twenty shillings in household goods as they shall be apprized.

It. To my daughter Elisabeth Mirrick I give Twenty shillings in household goods as they shall be apprized.

It. To my daughter Hannah Howse I give thirty pounds to be paid to her by my executors on her marriage or at ye age of twenty-one years

It. I do give to ever one of my grandchildren which I now have a Bibble to be paid them by my executors soone after my death

It. I do give my house and homestead lands chattels plate money and all other my estate whatever it be I do give it to my dear and loving wife Elizabeth to be to her use and behoof during her widdowhood And if shee live and dye a widdow to be by her disposed to my children as she shall see meet. but if she shall marry again after my decease then one third part of it to be her own proper estate and ye rest to be equally divided between all my children.

It. I do appoint constitute and ordaine my loving wife Elisabeth and my loving son Joseph Howse executors of this my last will and testament and I do desire my loving brother Jeremiah Howse and John Mayo to be overseers to take care of advise and help, for performing of this my last will and testament January 17, 1694-5.

Joseph Howes (seal)
Signed sealed and delivered as my last will and testament
In presence of
Jonathan Russell
Thomas Sturgis
John Paddoke

Will of Elizabeth Howes.

I, Elizabeth Howse of Yarmouth In the County of Barnstable In ye Province of the Massachusetts wid. Relict of Joseph Howse late deceased being weake in body but of good and disposing minde and memory and calling to minde the frailty and uncertainty of my present life, do for the setting my house in order make constitute and ordain this my last Will and Testament hereby anuling and making void all other wills whatsoever.

Imps. I do give up myself intirely unto God as being my God and father to the Lord Jesus Christ as my Lord and Redeemer and the holy Ghost as my Comforter, I give my spirit unto God that gave it and my body to desent burial as to my Executors hereafter mentioned shall sem meet In firm hope of a blessed Resurrection att the great Day to be then forever with the Lord and as for that portion of worldly estate which God of his Grace has been pleased to bestow uponme I do dispose of it in manner following.

It. I do give and confirm to my three sons Nathan Thomas and Amos Hows my now Dwelling house, barn and homestead with all ye priviledges and appurtinances thereto belonging to be equally divided between them after my death according as I know it was my late dear husbands minde

Item. My will is that all the rest of my estate of what kind soever it bee shall be equally divided between all my children sirviving at my death.

It. I do make constitute and ordain my loving sons Samuel & Joseph Hows my executors of this my Last Will Testament In witness whereof I have hereunto sett my hand and seale this seventh day of February one thousand six hundred ninety and foure five

Elizabeth X Hows (seal)
Signed sealed and declared to be my last Will and Testament
In presence of
Jonathan Russell
Thomas Sturges
John Paddocke

III. THOMAS[2] (Thomas[1]) Howes; b. probably in England ; m.(i) in 1656 Sarah[2] (Edward[1]) Bangs ; buried(j) Nov. 20, 1676. She d.(j) the last of February, 1682-3. He was brought to New England by his parents and resided in the part of Yarmouth now Dennis. He took the oath of fidelity· in 1657.(k) He was one of the selectmen of Yarmouth for 6 years, commencing in

---

(i) 14 Mf. 199, 200; 1 Savage 111; 2 Freeman, 194. See will of Edward Bangs (3 Plym. Col. Wills, pt. 2, p. 106; 14 Mf. 193, 197), where it appears that his daughter Rebecca m. Jonathan Sparrow. 10 N. E. Reg. 157 erroneously gives the year of the marriage as 1756.

(j) Yar. Recs.; Yar. Reg. Nov. 26, 1846.

(k) 8 Plym. Col. Recs. 185, 186.

1668.(l) He was a deputy to the General Court at Plymouth for seven years, commencing in 1668.(m) He was appointed captain of the military company June 3, 1674(n), and is usually called Capt. Thomas Howes. In 1742 Ebenezer Goodspeed, then 86 years old, swore that he was a soldier in the Narragansett wars so-called under Capt. Thomas Howes.(o) Capt. Howes served in the 3d expedition in King Philip's war with eight one month's men and in the fifth expedition with 21 men. His wages on the third expedition were £6.(p) June 1, 1663, he was on the grand jury.(q) April 2, 1667, he was appointed one of the council of war for Yarmouth.(r) June 5, 1667, he was sworn as constable of Yarmouth.(s) June 30, 1667, he signed a paper to the General Court in favor of the Rev. Thomas Thornton against an attack by Nicholas Nickerson.(t) Oct. 30, 1667, at the request of the town, the Court added Andrew Hallett, Thomas Howes, and John Thacher to the committee of Yarmouth for the disposing of lands in that town.(u) June 3, 1668, he is mentioned as one of the deputies to the General Court.(v) The same date he was one of the selectmen of Yarmouth.(w) At the same date also he complained against William Nickerson, Sr., Nathaniel Covel, Samuel Nickerson, Joseph Nickerson, and William Nickerson, Jr., for affronting him in the execution of his office while he was constable of Yarmouth and offering divers abuses to him. They were convicted and punished.(x) June 1, 1669, he is mentioned as a deputy to the General Court.(y) In 1670 he was collector of minister's rates.(z) May 29, 1670, he was one of the freemen of Yarmouth.(a) June 7, 1670, he was a deputy;(b) also, June 5, 1672, when he is styled Ensign Howes.(c) The same date he was one of the selectmen of Yarmouth,(d) and also, June 3, 1673, when he was also a deputy.(e) April 28, 1672, he was on a jury of inquest to inquire into the death of a child in Yarmouth, and signed the verdict.(e1) Oct. 30, 1672, he owned one-third of a parcel of nets and of a boat in partnership with Thomas Doten and Lt. Morton, together with a third of the rodes, anchors and sails appertaining to the boat.(f) June 7, 1673, and June 9, 1676, he was on the committee that took the Colonial Treasurer's account, and signed

(l) Plym. Col. Recs.
(m) Ib.
(n) Bodge's King Philip's War, 455; 5 Plym. Col. Recs. 146.
(o) Bodge, 441.
(p) Swift, 99, 100, 102, 103.
(q) 4 Plym. Col. Recs. 37.
(r) Ib. 145, 146.
(s) Ib. 148.
(t) Swift, 90, where a reduced facsimile of his signature may be seen; "Edmond Hawes" (139), by the compiler.
(u) 4 Plym. Col. Recs. 167.

(v) Ib. 180.
(w) Ib. 182.
(x) Ib. 183, 184.
(y) 5 ib. 17.
(z) Ib. 37.
(a) Ib. 274, 276.
(b) Ib. 34.
(c) Ib. 90.
(d) Ib. 92.
(e) Ib. 113, 114.
(e1) 5 Plym. Col. Recs. 95.
(f) 7 ib. 173.

the report.(g) July 4, 1673, he was appointed guardian of Mercy Hedge, daughter of Capt. William Hedge, late of Yarmouth. He is here styled Lieutenant.(h) Sept. 15, 1673, he was a deputy.(i) June 3, 1674, he is named as one of the selectmen of Yarmouth.(j) June 1, 1675, he was one of the selectmen of Yarmouth and a deputy. He is here and subsequently styled Captain.(k) The same date the court appointed Mr. Hinckley, Mr. Gorham and Jonathan Sparrow to fix the bounds of the lands in Monomoy between William Nickerson and the purchasers, and if Mr. Hinckley could not attend, then Capt. Howes was to take his place.(l) June 7, 1676, he was one of the selectmen and a deputy for Yarmouth.(m) The same date he was one of a committee of three to take the Colonial Treasurer's account.(n) In the rate of 1676 "towards the charges of the late war" Capt. Howes's tax was £6 7s. 3d.(o) His will,(p) dated Jan. 15, 1675-6, and proved Aug. 14, 1677, is printed in 6 Mayflower Descendant, page 160. He made his wife Sarah executrix and requested his friends and brethren Jonathan Sparrow, Jonathan Bangs, Jeremiah Howes and John Thacher to be helpful to her. The witnesses were Benjamin Howes and John Thacher. He mentions his sons Thomas and Jonathan, his daughters Rebecca and Sarah, an unborn child, Elizabeth (daughter of "my brother Sparrow") and his mother Prence. The will recites as follows:

"Being Called and Desired to Goe forth to warr in the praent expedition; against the Indians Called Narragansetts; and forasmuch as such a servis exposeth prsons to Danger of life I doe therfore make and Declare my last will."

He willed "That Sarah my Loveing wife shall have the sole Disposing of my whole estate; both of Lands housing and Goods During the time of her widdowes estate to her owne use and benifitt; shee Giveing out and paying such portions and legacies to my Children in time and manor heer specifyed."

He gave to his sons Thomas and Jonathan equally all his "estate of lands and housing" and in case either of them should die before coming of age unmarried, his share should go to his brother. If either of his sons should die without issue, then he was to dispose of his share to his brother or the latter's sons. He gave to his two sons and two daughters £20 apiece. If either of his daughters were to die before marriage, her legacy was to go to her sister, and if either of his sons should die before attaining the age of 21 years, his legacy should go to his brother. He also provided as follows:

"I give to Elizabeth the Daughter of my brother Sparrow which Liveth in my family the sume of fifteen pounds; and incase shee Die before shee be married or attaine to twenty years of age then her Legacye to returne to my Daughters;

"Be it Knowne that my will is that my Loveing wife shall have and Injoy

(g) 3 ib. 139, 140, 145.
(h) 5 ib. 124.
(i) Ib. 135.
(j) Ib. 143.
(k) Ib. 164, 165.
(l) Ib. 171.
(m) Ib. 195, 196.
(n) Ib. 200.
(o) Swift, 105.
(p) 3 Plym. Col. Wills, pt. 2, p. 85.

the one halfe of my Now Dwelling house; with the benifitt of one halfe of my lands orchyards and meddowes; That is to say the house Lotts and the Meddowes and Lands on Simpkins Necke; During the time of her widdowhood; But be it alsoe Knowne; that if my wife Change her widdowhood and Marry againe, then I Doe Give to her the sole Dispose of one third prte of my movable estate and the benifit of halfe my lands orchyards and meddowes; That is my Dwelling house lott; and the Land and Meddow; In Simpkins neck as is above expressed; but not then to hold; the possession of the halfe of the house; unliesse my children & frinds betrusted, see it most Convenient; and what shall remaine of the other two third prtes of my estate after Debts and legacyes are payed shalbe Devided equally amongst my Children;

"Be it alsoe Knowne that my will is that my Mother Prence Injoy without molestation During her Naturall life the house whee Now lives in with the orchyard belonging therunto; and to pay a bill my mother hath under my hand bearing Date the 15th of the 11th 1675."(q) He also provided that the legacies should be paid to the legatees either at marriage or at the age of 21 years.

The inventory(r) of his personal estate, taken Dec. 26, 1676, by Joseph Howes and Gershom Hall, and sworn to by his widow June 19, 1677, amounted to about £518. Feb. 26, 1679-80, his nephew Samuel Howes, with the consent of his father Joseph Howes, released his estate from his grandfather's requirement that he (Thomas) should teach him the trade of a cooper, and acknowledged that he had received a mare out of the estate of his Uncle Thomas as specified in his grandfather's will.(s) The will(t) of the widow of Thomas' Howes, dated Feb. 26, 1682-3, and proved April 3, 1683, is printed in 6 Mayflower Descendant, page 163. The witnesses were John Thacher and Jonathan Russell. Her brethren Jeremiah Howes and Jonathan Bangs were made executors. She mentions only the four children named in her husband's will. Elizabeth Sparrow who lived with her was to have 20s. Her young son Jonathan was to have 40s. to be improved for his teaching to read, write and cypher and in convenient time at the discretion of the overseers of her late husband's will he was to be put to learn some suitable trade. Her young daughter Sarah was to reside with her sister Rebecca and to have 20s. to be improved "for her more perfecting in reading." Her four children were to have the rest of her estate equally. The inventory(u) of Mrs. Sarah Howes's personal estate, taken March 17, 1682-3, by Joseph Howes and Gershom Hall and sworn to by Jeremiah Howes, amounted to £189 3s. 11d., less debts due from the estate. It included books, appraised at 7s., and "several things she brought from Boston when she was last there for her selfe unmade up", appraised at £3 11s. 7d.

(q) Jan. 15, 1675-6.
(r) 3 Plym. Col. Wills, pt. 2, p. 86; 6 Mf. 162.

(s) 6 Plym. Col. Recs. 30, 31.
(t) 4 Plym. Col. Wills, pt. 2, p. 37.
(u) Ib.; 6 Mf. 164.

Children.(v)
11. Rebecca,(v1) b. Dec. 1657.
12. Thomas, b. May 2, 1663; m.(v2) Sarah Hedge June 23, 1698; d. Nov. 22, 1737, in his 74th year.(v3) His will(w) mentions his wife Sarah, his daughter Mary, his son-in-law Joseph Howes, grandson of Joseph (my No. II), his grandsons Thomas, Isaac and George Howes, and his granddaughters Sarah, Thankful and Abigail. He was called Thomas Howes, Sr. His daughter Mary was born in December, 1702.(w1) J. C. Howes (14) is erroneous. The Thomas there numbered 11 was son of Jeremiah² and not Thomas² Howes, and should be his number 15. His number 15 (on p. 15) should be this number 12 of mine, except that there probably should be no son Thomas. J. C. Howes in his No. 19 (p. 17) gives the daughter and son-in-law (and their children) of Thomas² Howes, Sr. He says correctly on p. 15 that Thomas's wife Sarah appears from her gravestone to have died March 24, 1776, in the 100th year of her age. In 1698 the tax of Thomas Howes, Sr., in the rate of that year was £2 4s. 3d.(w3) Thomas Howes, Sr., was town clerk and treasurer in 1698.(w4) In the division of the Common lands in 1712 Thomas Howes had 34½ shares.(w5)

13. Jonathan, b. Feb. 25, 1669-70; m. Sarah about 1694; d.(x) Jan. 5, 1750-1. His children appear on the Yarmouth records, the eldest being b. the last day of June, 1695.(y) His will, (z) dated May 12, 1742, and proved Jan. 17, 1750-1, mentions his wife Sarah, his children David, Thomas, Sarah (wife of Peter Paddock), Joshua, the latter's daughters Sarah and Mary, and his deceased brother Thomas. May 8, 1684, he chose his uncle Mr Jeremiah Howes to be his guardian, who accepted.(a) He was a selectman for three years, commencing in 1707.(b) In 1712 he (styled lieutenant) received 32 shares of the Common lands of Yarmouth.(c)

14. Sarah, b. Oct. 29, 1673; m.(d) 1st Stephen⁴ (Stephen³, Giles², Stephen¹) Hopkins, of Eastham and Harwich, May 19, 1692, and 2d as his 3d wife, Joseph² (John², Edmond¹) Hawes of Yarmouth, July 3, 1746. She survived him and left issue by her 1st husband.

IV. JEREMIAH² (Thomas¹) Howes, b. about 1637 ; m.(d1) Sarah²

(v) Yar. Recs.; 2 Mf. 207.
(v1) She perhaps married her cousin Samuel, son of her Uncle Joseph. His wife was Rebecca and she survived him. (Infra, p. 20.)
(v2) J. C. Howes, 15; Yar. Recs.
(v3) Gravestone in old Howes burying ground; 2 Freeman, 215.
(w) 5 Barn. Prob. Recs. 379, 380. The will was dated June 15, 1737, and proved Jan. 19, 1737-8.
(w1) 10 Mf. 245.
(w3) Superior Ct. as above, p. 9.

(w4) Swift, 238.
(w5) Swift, 127.
(x) J. C. Howes, 14.
(y) 11 Mf. 112.
(z) 8 Barn. Prob. Recs. 440, 442.
(a) 6 Plym. Col. Recs. 134.
(b) Swift, 237.
(c) Ib. 126.
(d) Boston Eve. Transcript Oct. 26, 1914; "Edmond Hawes," by the compiler, p. 164; Har. Recs.; East. Recs.; 8 Mf. 16. J. C. Howes, 11, erroneously says she m. Daniel Sears Feb. 12, 1708.
d1) 6 Mf. 233.

(Thomas¹) Prence; d. Sept. 9, 1708, aged about 71 years.(e) She d. March 3, 1706-7, in the 60th year of her age, having been born about 1648.(e) They were buried and have stones in the old Howes burying ground in Dennis.(e1) Sarah's father was long governor of Plymouth Colony. Her mother was Mary² (William¹) Collier of Duxbury, her father's second wife.(f) Swift, in "Old Yarmouth," (g) says: "He was a son of the first Thomas, and a prominent and influential citizen." He was a deputy to the General Court at Plymouth for seven years, commencing in 1677; and for eleven years one of the selectmen, commencing in 1677.(h) June 1, 1663, he was admitted a freeman and sworn.(i) June 30, 1667, he and his brothers Joseph and Thomas signed a paper to the Governor and Assistants in favor of the Rev. Thomas Thornton against an attack by Nicholas Nickerson.(j) June 3, 1668, he was on the grand jury.(k) March 2, 1668-9, John Mocoy had an action against Jeremiah Howes for taking up and detaining from him without his leave or order complainant's horse, which was nonsuited because the letter of attorney by the plaintiff to Elisha Hedge "was found to be illegall."(l) April 28, 1672, he was on a jury of inquest to inquire into the death of a child in Yarmouth and signed the verdict.(m) March 13, 1672-3, Gov. Thomas Prence by his will gave to his daughter Sarah Howes (wife of Jeremiah) his biggest beer bowl and a share of the residue of his estate.(n) Feb. 29, 1675-6, Jeremiah Howes was appointed on the council of war for Yarmouth.(o) June 7, 1676, he is mentioned as constable of Yarmouth.(p) June 10, 1676, the following heirs, individually or through their attorneys, sold land of Gov. Thomas Prence's estate, viz.: Susannah Prence, single, of London; Capt. John Freeman in behalf of his wife

---

(e) J. C. Howes, 11, erroneously says he d. Jan. 5, 1705-6, which was the date of death of his son Jeremiah. See 59 N. E. Reg. 217.

(e1) The Yarmouth town records say that Jeremiah² Howes died Dec. 9, 1708, but the tombstone is evidently correct as his will was proved Oct. 6, 1708 (infra, p. 21). The town records also say that Sarah, his wife, died March 3, 1703-4. The tombstone is no doubt the better evidence.

(f) 6 Mf. 127; History of New Plymouth, by Francis Baylies, pt. 2, p. 70n.

(g) Page 122. He gives erroneous dates for the deaths of him and his wife.

(h) Plym. Col. Recs.; Swift, 116, 122, 236, 237, gives the periods differently, and says that he was for two years a representative in the legislature at Boston, commencing in 1692, the first year of the union of the two colonies, but 7 Province Laws of Massachusetts (p. 8) gives the name of the representative in 1692-3 as "Mr. Jeremiah Howes, jun."

(i) 4 Plym. Col. Recs. 38.

(j) Swift, 90, where a reduced facsimile of the signatures may be seen. See also "Edmond Hawes," by the compiler, pp. 128, 138, 139.

(k) 5 Plym. Col. Recs. 180.

(l) 7 ib. 153.

(m) 5 ib. 95.

(n) 3 Plym. Col. Wills, pt. 1, pp. 58-70; 3 Mf. 204, 205.

(o) 5 Plym. Col. Recs. 185, 186; Swift, 104.

(p) 5 Plym. Col. Recs. 195.

Mercy; Jonathan Sparrow and his wife Hannah; Nicholas Snow and his wife Jane; Jeremiah Howes and his wife Sarah; John Tracy and his wife Mary; and the widow Mary Prence.(q) In the rate of 1676 "towards the charges of the late war" the tax of Jeremiah Howes was £7 14s.(r) June 5, 1677, Mr. Jeremiah Howes is mentioned as one of the selectmen of Yarmouth and as one of the deputies to the General Court from that town.(s) June 3, 1679, and June 1, 1680, Jeremiah Howes was one of the selectmen of Yarmouth.(s1) Sept. 28, 1680, he was added to the committee to dispose of the Yarmouth lands, succeeding his brother Joseph.(s2) In February, 1680-81, the town agreed that Jeremiah Howes, with Joseph and Samuel Howes, should secure for it all such whales as should be cast up between Sawsuit Harbor mouth and Yarmouth Harbor for £4 a whale.(t) June 7, 1681, June 6, 1682, June 6, 1683, June 3, 1684, June 2, 1685, June, 1686, June, 1689; and June 3, 1690, Jeremiah Howes is mentioned as one of the selectmen of Yarmouth.(t1) June 7, 1681, June 6, 1683, June 3, 1684, June 2, 1685, June, 1686, and June, 1689, he was mentioned as one of the deputies from Yarmouth to the General Court.(t2) Feb. 6, 1682-3, Mr. John Miller and Jeremiah Howes of Yarmouth were appointed to sell the house and lands of Richard Berry, deceased, to pay his debts, there being no other estate to pay them.(t3) May 8, 1684, Mr. Jeremiah Howes was chosen by his nephew Jonathan (youngest son of Capt. Thomas Howes, deceased), as his guardian, and accepted.(t4) Gov. Prence had with others purchased land on the N. side of Titticut river near Bridgewater. This land was bounded Dec. 24, 1686, and then divided into ten lots of 100 acres each. Jeremiah Howes had the 10th lot.(t5) In 1692 Jeremiah Howes bought land in South Harwich of John Skinnaquit, an Indian.(u) March 22, 1693-4, Jeremiah Howes, with John Thacher and John Miller, fixed the bounds of certain land belonging to John Hawes.(u1) In the rate of 1698 in Yarmouth the tax of Mr. Jeremiah Howes was £4 8s. 6d.(v) In 1698 Mr. Jeremiah Howes was chosen one of the representatives in the legislature, but declined.(w) In 1701 Mr. Jeremiah Howes was chosen one of a committee to make out a list of such persons as were rightful proprietors of the commons.(x) In 1703 he was one of a committee appointed to "seat persons in the meeting-house."(x) Af-

(q) Supplement to Pope's Pioneers of Mass., p. ix.
(r) Swift, 105.
(s) 5 Plym. Col. Recs. 230, 231.
(s1) 6 ib. 10, 35.
(s2) Ib. 50; Swift, 124.
(t) Swift, 109.
(t1) 6 Plym. Col. Recs. 59, 84, 108, 129, 168, 186, 207, 241.
(t2) Ib. 61, 106, 127, 164, 186, 205.

(t3) Ib. 101.
(t4) Ib. 134.
(t5) Nos. 2439, 162 and 243, Records of Superior Ct. of Judicature, Supreme Ct. Clerk's of., Boston.
(u) Deyo's Barnstable Co. 827.
(u1) Book of Grants of Yarmouth, 164, 165.
(v) Records of Superior Ct. of Judicature, No. 4600; Rec. Book 1686-1700, p. 297; Supreme Ct. Clerk's of., Boston.
(w) Swift, 118.
(x) Ib. 119.

ter the death of his brother Thomas, he became one of the committee to make grants of the common lands, his father having been an original member.(y)

His will, dated August 14, 1708, and proved Oct. 6, 1708, was witnessed by Thomas Howes, John Howes and Nathaniel Howes.(z) He mentions his eldest son Jeremiah, deceased, the latter's son Jeremiah, his daughters Hannah, Sarah, Mary and Martha, and his widow Mary. The will then names the testator's sons Prince, Ebenezer, Thomas (deceased), the latter's son Thomas, and testator's eight daughters: Elizabeth Bacon (and her son Joseph Bacon), Sarah Mayo, Mary Hawes, Bethiah Hawes, Mercy Sturgis, Susannah Bassett, Thankful Miller and Rebecca Howes. He made his sons Prince and Ebenezer and his son-in-law Samuel Sturgis executors of his will. "A true Inventory of all and singular the Goods chattels and Credits of Mr. Jeremiah Howes Deceased September the 9th 1708: prized by Joseph Hall and John Howes at Yarmouth September 23d 1708," and sworn to by his executors Oct. 6, 1708, amounted to £1463 13s. 5d., of which £100 consisted of land at Middleborough and Bridgewater and £950 of "housing and land" at Yarmouth and Harwich.(a)

Children.

15. Jeremiah, b. ; m.(b) after Oct. 18, 1693, Mary, daughter of Thomas Daggett of Edgartown; d.(b)

(y) Ib. 124.
(z) 3 Barn. Prob. Recs. 174.
(a) Ib. 177.
(b) 2 Barn. Prob. Recs. 213, 222; 55 N. E. Reg. 112, where the date of his death is given as Jan. 5, instead of Jan. 6. See 59 N. E. Reg. 217, 218.

Jan. 6, 1705-6. He had Jeremiah, Hannah, Sarah, Mary and Martha. He was a representative of Yarmouth in the legislature at Boston in 1692-3.(c) His tax in 1698 was £2 2s. 6d.(c1) J. C. Howes (pages 11 and 15) is erroneous.

16. Prence, b. about 1671; m. Dorcas Joyce about 1695; d. Oct. 2, 1753, in his 84th year.(d) His children appear on the Yarmouth records, the eldest born May 22, 1696.(e) His will,(f) dated Feb. 18, 1739-40, and proved Oct. 16, 1753, mentions his wife Dorcas and his children Desire Hallett, Dorcas Matthews, Prince, Jeremiah, Thomas and Lot. His inventory,(f) dated Jan. 15, 1754, amounted to £696 5s. 4d. in real estate. In 1698 his tax amounted to £2 2s. 4d.(f1) In 1712 he received 36 shares of the common lands of Yarmouth.(g) In 1739 he was one of the proprietors of the common lands of Crockett Neck.(h)

17. Ebenezer, b. about 1674; m.(i) 1st Sarah Gorham, April 20, 1699 (who d.(j) Sept. 9, 1705), and 2d(j) Lydia Joyce Nov. 20, 1706; d.(k) Jan. 8,

(c) 7 Prov. Laws of Mass. 8.
(c1) Super. Ct. as above, p. 9.
(d) Gravestone; 59 N. E. Reg. 217, 218. J. C. Howes (14), erroneously gives the marriage as Aug. 8, 1698. He says the wife d. Nov. 14, 1757.
(e) 10 Mf. 242.
(f) 9 Barn. Prob. Recs. 65, 66, 67.
(f1) Superior Ct. as above, p. 9.
(g) Swift, 127.
(h) Ib. 141, 142.
(i) 52 N. E. Reg. 359; J. C. Howes, 16.
(j) J. C. Howes, 16.
(k) Gravestone; 59 N. E. Reg. 217, 218.

1726-7, aged about 53. His will,(l) dated Dec. 3, 1726, and proved Feb. 13, 1726-7, mentions his wife Lydia and his children Lydia, Thankful, Mercy, Anna, Susannah, Mary, Samuel and Prince (youngest sons), Thomas (eldest son), Ebenezer, Sarah Sears, and Elizabeth Howes. His inventory,(l) taken Feb. 22, 1726-7, amounted to £532 15s. 10d. in personal property and £1920 in real estate. In 1712 he received 47½ shares of the common lands of Yarmouth.(m) Dec. 28, 1714, he was a witness to the will of John Joyce of Yarmouth.(m1)

18. Thomas.(m2) b.   ; m.(n) Abigail Hussey in Nantucket April 5, 1700; d.(o) Aug. 8, 1700. His father Jeremiah Howes was appointed administrator Oct. 8, 1700, and after his death the widow Abigail was appointed Oct. 7, 1708.(n) He appears to have no child born at the time of his death, but a son Thomas was born March 6, 1700-1.(p) In 1698 his tax was £2 1s.(p1)

(l) 4 Barn. Prob. Recs. 379, 382; 11 Mf. 113, 114.
(m) Swift, 127.
(m1) 3 Barn. Prob. Recs. 344; 9 Mf. 123.
(m2) J. C. Howes (14) is erroneous.
(n) 2 Barn. Prob. Recs. 111, 114, 118; 3 ib. 55; 7 N. E. Reg. 262.
(o) 2 Barn. Prob. Recs. as above; 7 N. E. Reg. 324, which says Thomas Howes of Yarmouth was drowned between Nantucket and the Main Aug. 1, 1700.
(p) Yar. Recs.; 7 Mf. 248; 7 N. E. Reg. 262, where the date of birth is erroneously given as March 6, 1701-2.
(p1) Super. Ct. as above, p. 9. He appears to have been the one then called Thomas Howes, Jr.

19. Elizabeth, b.   ; m.(q) Dec. 10, 1786, Jeremiah Bacon of Barnstable and had issue.
20. Sarah, b.   m.(r) Daniel Mayo of Eastham.
21. Mary, b. about 1672; m.(s) as his 1st wife about 1695 Joseph² (John² Edmond¹) Hawes of Yarmouth and d.(s1) Jan. 10, 1728-9, in her 58th year, leaving issue.
22. Bethiah, b.   ; m.(t) 1st Jan. 8, 1700-1, Isaac² (John², Edmond¹) Hawes and had issue in Yarmouth and Chatham. He d. about 1731. She m. 2d as his 2d wife John Smith of Eastham in 1741 and 3d Nov. 16, 1743, as his 2d wife Rev. Joseph Lord of Chatham, where she d. before July 7, 1748.
23. Mercy, b. about 1682; m. Oct. 17, 1700, Samuel Sturges, she being in her 19th year and he in his 35th. They had issue.(u)
24. Susannah, b.   ; m.(v) Joseph Bassett Feb. 27, 1706-7.
25. Thankful, b.   ; m.(w)

(q) Barn. Recs.; 2 Mf. 215; 1 Otis's Barnstable Families, 28, 29; 59 N. E. Reg. 217.
(r) 59 N. E. Reg. 217, 218. J. C. Howes (12) erroneously says she m. Cornelius Higgins.
(s) 61 N. E. Reg. 200, 322; "Edmond Hawes" by the compiler, p. 163.
(s1) Yar. Gravestone Recs. 21; 62 N. E. Reg. 202; 29 Plym. Col. Deeds, 121; 5 Mf. 162; "Edmond Hawes" by the compiler, p. 164.
(t) Yar. Recs.; 61 N. E. Reg. 200, 322; "Edmond Hawes" by the compiler, pp. 167-170; 2 Otis, 36, 37.
(u) Yar. Recs.; 10 Mf. 243; 59 N. E. Reg. 217, 218.
(v) 59 N. E. Reg. 217, 218.
(w) 51 ib. 33, 224; 59 ib. 218; 3 Savage, 210.

22

John Miller Jan. 23, 1706-7.
26. Rebecca, b.   ; m.(x)
Aug. 14, 1712, Ebenezer Hallett.

Copy of Will* of Jeremiah* Howes.
(From Probate Records of
Barnstable Co., Vol. 3, p. 174.)

To all people To whom these presents shall concern The fourteenth Day of Agust In the Year of our Lord Annoque Domi one Thousand seven hundred and eight, Know ye That I Jeremiah Howes of Yarmouth in the County of Barnstable in the Province of the Massachusetts Bay in New England Yeomau; Being but weak in body but of perfict mind and memory. Thanks be Given to God therefor: Calling unto mind the mortality of my Body, and knowing that it is appointed for all men once to Dye—Do make and ordaine this my Last will & Testiment (That is to say) Principally and first of all I Give & Recommend my sole Into the hands of God that Gave it, and my Body I Recomend unto the Earth to be buried in Decent Chrisdan burial att ye Discretion of my Executor. Nothing Douting but att the General Resurrection I shall Receive it again by the mighty power of God: and as Touching such worly Estate wherewithall it Hath pleased God to bless me with in this Life—I Give Demise and Dispose of the same In ye following manner and form

first 1 Give unto my Grandson Jeremiah Howes the son of my Eldest son Jeremiah Howes Deceased: All

---

(x) 59 ib. 217, 218.
*There are two other copies, in No. 7536 of the records of the Superior Court of Judicature, now on file in the clerk's office of the Supreme Court, Boston, Mass. The original will is not known to be in existence.

that my Land and meadow & beach & creek stuff that I bought of Mr John Sunderlin: Excepting what I sold to Jeremiah Crow and all the housing now upon it: And also I Give to this my Grandson Jeremiah Howes a piece of meadow Lying to the Westward of Simkins neck bounded by Thomas Howes meadow on the Southeastward side and by ye upland northard as the fence now Rangeth to a pare of barrs: and from them barrs unto the meadow southerly or thereabouts to a stake standing between Two ponds and from thence near the same Range to a stake standing by a creek; and from thence to ye meadow I sold to John Howes, and if this my Grandson Should Dye without Issue then this Land and meadow to be eaquely Divided to his Sisters surviving; and my Will is is that my Daughter Mary Howes Relict to my son Jeremiah Howes shall have the use of this Land and meadows and housing untill my Grandson Jeremiah Howes comes to the age of Twenty and one years or at marrage Day if before (only it is Reserved to his mother the use of one third part of this housing and Land to his mother after his possession During her widowhood.

2ly It. I Give unto my son Prince Howes all my homested of Housing and Land excepting a piece of upland taken off of that corner called the nine acres beginning upon the south side where Jonathan Howses fence and mine Joyns in ye Range betwixt us and then straight over to the marsh near the north end of a Ditch that Rangeth northerly from the meadow barrs where an old fence Joyned within ye ehd of the Ditch about a Rod and from thence northerly as the fence Rangeth betwixt

23

the upland and meadow bounded by Jonathan Howes land on ye Eastard side all this piece about twelve acres I Give eaquely to be Divided betwixt my too sons Prince Howes and Ebenezer Howes; and all my meadow on ye westerly side of my Land called my homested; Excepting that peice before Given to my Grandson Jeremiah Howes I Do Give to my Two sons Prince Howes and Ebenezer Howes to be eaquely Divided betwixt them, and the fence that now Divides the upland from the meadow shall be the bounds betwixt the upland and medow, and after that peice of meadow Lying in my calves pasturo I Give to my son Prince Howes.

3ly It. I Give unto my son Ebenezer Howes his hom Lott he now Lives upon with all the housing upon it home to the Ditch that parts betwixt him and the house Lott Prince Howes Lives upon with the meadow at the foot of it: And also all that my piece of Land and meadow that Lyes below Jonathan Howeses house Lott betwixt that and the house lott of Samuel Eldreds Deceased and all that my piece of Land Liying in the Indian field so called Lyeing betwixt the Land of Zachariah Paddock and the Land of Jeremiah Crowels: to be Ebenezer Howeses forever.

4ly It I Give unto my Two Sons Ebenezer Howes and Prince Howes to be Eaqully Divided betwixt them all that my Housing that Prince Howse Livis in Togather with the out housing and the Houslott of Land and meadow att the foot of it so far as the fence and Ditch parts betwixt Prince Howses Lott and Ebenezer Howeses Lott; and also a peice of Land Lying above the widow Eldreds House Lott betwixt the Land of Joseph Hows and Jonathan Howes and also a peice of Land Lying & near the Coy pond so called onely I Do order my Two sons Ebenezer Howes and Prince Howes to pay a Leagsy of forty(y) pounds appiece of money or money worth unto my four Grandaughters my son Jeremiah Howeses children to wt Hannah Howes Sarah Howes Mary Howes and Martha Howse the which will be twenty(z) pounds appiece to be paid unto him at the age of eighteen years or upon marrage Day if before; and if either of these four geirls should Dye before they Receive their portions yt ye survivors to have their part betwixt them.

5ly It. I Give unto my Grandson Thomas Howes the son of my son Thomas Howes all that my Land and meadow I bought of Josephas Quason Contained in one Deed: the Land Lying near Joseph Sevrances Joyning to a Great pond, and the meadow Lying below on the South side so called but in case this my Grandsons Thomas Howes should Dye without Issue then then this Land & meadow to be Eaquely amongst all my Children now Living or their heirs: and also I Do give unto this my Grandson Thomas Howes my Silver Tanker.

6ly my will is that my Children Shall Have a Convenient way to come at their meadow with a Cart where it is below my Land

7ly I Do Give out of my movable Estate to my Daughter Rebeka Howes thirty pounds

It I do give unto my Two sons Prince Howes and Ebenezer Howes all my Right in the Comon Land betwixt Garshom Halls and monomoy to be eaquely Divided between them;

(y) Sic.
(z) Sic.

and all my wearing Clothes to be Divided Eaquely betwixt my Two sons Prince Howes and Ebenezer Howes

It I Give unto my Grandson Joseph Bacon out of my moveable Estate Ten pounds

It I Do Give unto my Eight Daughters Elizabeth Bacon Sarah Mayo Mary Howes(z1) Bethiah Howes(z1) Marcey Sturges Susanah Bassett Thankfull Miller and Rebekah Howes out of my movable Estate the sum of six score pounds that will be fifteen pounds appiece to each of them.

It I Give unto my five Grandchildren the children of my son Jeremiah Howes, the eleyenth part of all my movable Estate that is not herebefore Disposed of to be Eaquely Divided betwixt them; And as for the Rest of my movable Estate Togather with all my Land and meadow Lyeing in Bridgewater and Midelburough or thereabouts Lyeing or falling in the neighbouring Towns thereabouts I Do Give and bequeath Eaquely to be Divided betwixt all my Children now In being: to wit: Prince Howes Ebenezer Howes Elizaboth Baken Sarah Mayo, Mary Hawse Bethiah Hawse Mercy Sturgis Susanah Bassett Thankfull Miller and Rebeka Howse to be Eaquely Divided betwixt them all; I Likewise I Do order Constitute and appoint my Two sons Prince Howse and Ebenezer Howes Togather with my son Samuel Sturgis these three to be sole Executors of this my Last will and Testiment and I Do hereby uterly Disalow Revoke Disanul all and every other former will & Testament any wayes before named Ratifying and confirming this to be my Last will and Testiment and no other In

(z1) So in the record, no doubt an error of the recorder or draftsman.

Witness whereof I have hereunto sett my hand and seal the Day and year above written

Jeremy Howes (seal)
Signed Sealed Published pronounced and Declared by ye sd Jeremiah Howes as his Last will and Testiment In the free sence of us ye subscribers:

Thomas Howes
John Howes
Nathll Howes.

THIRD GENERATION.

V. (1) Samuel^3 (Joseph^2, Thomas^1) Howes, b. in Yarmouth ; m. about 1678(a) Rebecca(a1) ; d. in Yarmouth Jan. 10, 1722-3.(a2) He resided on the N. side of Cape Cod in the present town of Dennis. He was in King Philip's war, starting on the expedition June 24, 1675. His pay amounted to £1 16s.(b) In the rate of 1676 "towards the charges of the late war" his tax was £2 6s. 9d.(c) In May, 1678, he was a freeman present at the town-meeting.(d) In 1679 he is styled "sergeant".(d1) In February, 1680, with his father, Joseph, and his uncle, Jeremiah, he

(a) March 8, 1677-8, the town gave him a house lot containing six acres more or less adjoinidg his father's land. (Land Grant Book of Yarmouth, p. 7.)
(a1) Perhaps his cousin, daughter of his uncle Capt. Thomas^2 Howes.
(a2) Howes Genealogy, by Joshua C. Howes, p. 12; 2 Freeman, 213, which says erroneously that he d. Jan. 10, 1723-4.
(b) Swift, 100.
(c) Ib. 105.
(d) Ib. 108; 2 Freeman, 196.
(d1) Yar. Recs.
(e) Swift, 109.

25

was appointed by the town to secure for it all whales that might be cast up between Sawsuit Harbor mouth and Yarmouth Harbor, for £4 a whale.(e) June 9, 1683, Samuel Howes is mentioned as a surveyor of highways for Yarmouth.(f) Feb. 11, 1685-6, Samuel Howes was a witness to the will of Capt. James Forster and swore to it July 13, 1686.(g) June 24, 1690, he took the oath of a freeman at a county court at Barnstable.(h) April 13, 1690, Samuel Howes was a witness to the deed of partition of the estate of Thomas Crowell, Sr., of Yarmouth, deceased.(i) In the rate of 1698 in Yarmouth the tax of Samuel Howes was £4 4s. 3d.(j) In 1695 the town's meadow at Simpkins Neck, Nobscusset, was leased to Samuel Howes.(k) In 1704-5 he was a representative in the legislature at Boston.(l) In the division of the common lands in 1712 he received 32 shares, and is styled Captain.(m)

His will was dated June 7 and a codicil Dec. 14, 1722. They were proved Jan. 29, 1722-3, and are recorded in 4 Barn. Prob. Recs. 90. They mention his wife Rebecca, his grandson Samuel Sears (son of Josiah), his son Joseph, his daughters Experience Howes, Hope Sears, Sarah Sears, Mercy Sears, deceased, and his grand-

(f) 6 Plym. Col. Recs. 111.
(g) 1 Barn. Prob. Recs. 1; 2 Mf. 177.
(h) 6 Plym. Col. Recs. 257.
(i) 11 Mf. 26.
(j) Recs. of Superior Ct. of Judicature, No. 4600; Rec. Book 1686-1700, p. 297; Supreme Ct. Clerk's Of., Boston.
(k) 2 Freeman, 202.
(l) Swift, 236; 8 Prov. Laws of Mass. 62, 63.
(m) Swift, 126.

daughters (daughters of Mercy) Mercy Sears and Hannah Sears. The inventory(m1) of Capt. Samuel Howes, taken Jan. 22, 1722-3, amounted to £1446 19s. 9d., of which £1190 represented real estate.

Children,(n)
born in Yarmouth, order of birth uncertain:

27. Joseph, b.   ; m.(o) Elizabeth Paddock Nov. 2, 1710; d. between July 13, 1750 (date of his will(p)), and Jan. 1, 1750-1 (date of probate). His will mentions his wife Elizabeth, his children Samuel,(q) Edward, Joseph, Zachariah, Barnabas, Elizabeth and Rebecca, and his grandson Samuel.

28. Hope, b.   ; m.(r) 1st at Yarmouth May 15, 1706, Richard Sears   , who moved to Chatham, and 2d John Rich of Eastham, and had issue by both.

29. Sarah,(r1) b. about 1686; m.(r) Feb. 12, 1708-9, at Yarmouth, Daniel Sears   , (who moved to Chatham) and had among other children Sarah, b. April 11, 1714, who m. Joshua⁴ (Thomas³, Henry¹) Atkins August 1, 1734, and d. April 30, 1751, leaving among other children Susannah (b.

(m1) 4 Barn. Prob. Recs. 92.
(n) J. C. Howes, 12, says Samuel⁶ Howes had also Samuel, who d. March 18, 1705-6. He was probably the Samuel Howes who m. Mehitable Goodspeed Dec. 18, 1705 (Yar. Recs.; 14 Mf. 88).
(o) J. C. Howes, 12. He says (p. 16) that he d. Dec. 6, 1750; Yar. Recs.
(p) 4 Barn. Prob. Recs. 436-8.
(q) Joseph and Elizabeth Howes had Samuel, b. Oct. 12, 1712, and other children recorded in the Yarmouth records (13 Mf. 227). See J. C. Howes, No. 18, pp. 16 and 17.

March 6, 1738-9) who m. 1st Aug .17, 1756, William⁴ (William³, Joseph², Robert¹) Eldredge, and had by him among other children Sarah (Sally), b. Sept. 13, 1761, who m. Reuben C. Taylor and was the grandmother of the compiler of this article.(s) Sarah (Howes) Sears, wife of Capt. Daniel Sears, d. in Chatham Nov. 9, 1748, in her 63d year.(t)

 30. Mercy, b.   ; m.(r) Josiah Sears at Yarmouth April 3, 1702. She had issue.

 31. Experience, b.

  Will of Capt. Samuel Howes.

In the name of God Amen the seventh day of June in the eighth year of his majtes Reign 1722, I, Samuel Howes of Yarmouth in the County of Barnstable and province of the Massachusetts Bay In New England being at present Time In helth of body and of Disposing mind and memory blessed be God for it, but not knowing how soon my Change may come by death and being minded to settle my Temporal affairs in order thereunto; Do make ordaine & appoint this to be my Last will and Testament. And first I Recomend my Soul Into the hands of God that gave it me hopeing thro' the merrits Death &c. of Christ to have the free and full pardon of all my sins, and to Inherit Life Eternal thro' him and my body to the Dust

(r) Sears Genealogy by May, 11, 59, 60, 63, 68.

(r1) J. C. Howes (p. 11) is in error in making her the daughter of Thomas' Howes.

(s) Sears Geneal. by May, 60; "Atkins" by the compiler, 9, 10, 16, 17; "Eldred, Eldredge" by the compiler, 17, 18, 28, 29; "Richard Taylor, Tailor," by the compiler, 31, 35.

(t) Gr. St.; 8 Mf. 239.

from whence it came to be buried in such Decent manner after my decease as my Executors hereafter named shall think fit; And as for such worly goods or Estate as it hath pleased God to bless me with; I give and Dispose of the same as followeth. And first I will that all my Just debts and funeral charges shall be paid In convenient Time after my decease out of my moveable estate by my sd Executors

Imp. I give and bequeath unto my loving wife Rebeckah the one third part of all my moveable Estate without Doors and within Doors, which shall be left after my debts and the legacies herein given are paid; to be at her own Dispose forever and the other two thirds thereof to be for her use and improvement untill her death or marrage; and then to be dispoesing of as followeth and also one third part of the proffits use or improvement of all my Lands and meadows & the use and improvement of the wester end of my dwelling house from the ground upward and the use of half my shop & sollor under it and also half my barn and half the fruit of my orchard all so as she shall continue my widow

Item I give and bequeath unto my grandson Samuel Sears son of Josiah Sears (In case he continue to dwell with and serve me or my said wife until he arive to the age of Twenty and one years) all my parcell of Lands at the Black Earth so called and half a Lot of Land lying above Skargo hill in Yarmouth and all my brocken meadow at grays beach only if he shall see cause to sell said Lands or meadow or any part thereof my will is that he Tender the same unto my son Joseph Howes he giving as much as another for the same.

Item I give and bequeath unto my son Joseph Howes and to his heirs and assigns forever all my houseing Lands and meadows whatsoever & wheresoever the same is or may be found at my decease as an estate of Inhabitance forever excepting what is Allredy given and granted unto my wife and my grandson.

Item I give and bequeath unto my Daughter Experience fourty pounds to be paid to her out of my moveable Estate as it shall be prized and ye privilege to Live in the western end of my house untill she shall marry. And I do give unto my Daughter hope Sears besides what she hath allredy Received, the sum of fourty shillings out of my moveable estate, and to my Daughter Sarah Sears besides what she hath allredy Received of me Twenty shillings out of my moveable estate as it shall be prized.

Item I give unto my three grandchildren Samuel Sears Mercy Sears and Hannah Sears children of my Daughter Mercy Sears deceased the one quarter of all my moveable estate which shall be remaining after my wifes Decease or marrage to be equally divided between them or to those of them yt shall be then liven, but if none of them shall Live so long then the same to be equally Divided between my said three Daughters now Living or to yr heirs.

Item I give the remainder of the two thirds of my moveable estate not alredy herein Disposed, which shall be Left at my wifes Decease or marrage to be equally Divided between my three Daughters hope sears Sarah sears and Experience or to their heirs.

And I do hereby make nominate and appoint my sd wife Rebekah my son Joseph Howes and my Loveing brother John Howes to be Executors to this my Last will and Testament. And I do hereby Renounce and make void all other wills hear tofore made by me Declearing this to be my Last will & Testament In witness whereof I have hereunto set my hand and seal the Day and year above written. Signed sealed pronounced and Decleared by the above named Samuel Howes to be his Last will and Testament In Presence of us Witnesses

    Samuel Howes (seal)

Peter Thacher
Ebenezer Baker
Thankfull Thacher
John Howes
Ebenezer Howes

For explanation of the above written my will is that my wife's Interest in my Real Estate granted to her as aboveed shall returne to my son Joseph Howes and to his heirs and assigns forever at her decease or marrage and that if my sd grandson Samuel Sears shall Dy before he come to the age of twentyone years or shall Leve serving my sd wife that then the Lands and meadow above granted to him shall allso, return unto my said son Joseph Howes and to his heirs and assigns forever as witness my hand & seal Decbr ye 4th 1722 In presence of us

    Samuel Howes (seal)

MAYO.

JOHN" MAYO, a clergyman, came from England in 1638. He was in Barnstable in 1639 before the Rev. John Lothrop came, who arrived Oct. 11, 1639. Mr. Mayo then had a frame house there and acted as teaching elder of the church, of which the Rev. Joseph Hull acted as pastor.(a) Dec.

(a) 1 Otis, 333; 2 ib. 190, 201, 202, 204, 220-222.

11, 1639, Thanksgiving was held at Mr. Hull's. The praises of God being ended, they "divided into three companies to feast together, some at Mr. Hull's, some at Mr. Mayo's, some at Brother Lombard's, Senior."(b) April 15, 1640, Mr. Mayo was ordained as teaching elder.(c) He went to Eastham in 1646 and took charge of the church, remaining till 1655, when he went to Boston and was settled over the Second or North church, remaining till 1673, when he was dismissed on account of age. He was ordained in Boston Nov. 9, 1655. The church records (in the handwriting of the Rev. Increase Mather) in the beginning of 1672, say: "Mr. Mayo, the Pastor, likewise grow very infirm, insomuch as the congregation was not able to hear and be edified." The congregation therefore desired a new minister and he consented. "On the 15th of the 2d month [April] 1673, removed his person and goods also, from Boston to reside with his daughter in Barnstable where (and at Yarmouth) since he hath lived a private life, as not being able through infirmities of old age to attend to the word of the ministry. The day of the 3d [May] month 1676 he departed this life at Yarmouth, and was there buried." His widow Tamison (Tamsen) died also at Yarmouth, Feb. 26, 1682-3. After he left Boston, the congregation continued to contribute to his support until his death.(d) The Rev. Increase Mather was associated with him in Boston as teaching elder from 1664 and succeeded him as pastor.(e) He preached the election sermon in June, 1658.(f) March 3, 1639-40, he was admitted a freeman at Barnstable and sworn.(g) June 17, 1641, he and Mr. Thomas Dimmack were by consent of the parties made arbitrators of the differences between Nicholas Simpkins and William Chase.(h) In August, 1643, he was one of those in Barnstable between 16 and 60 years of age able to bear arms, his name being 2d on the list, following that of Rev. John Lothrop.(i) In 1675 Christopher Gibson of Dorchester by his will made a bequest to Mr. Mather and Mr. Mayo.(j) Before May 12, 1655, John Morton of Plymouth had bought land in Eastham of the Rev. John Mayo, formerly of that town.(k) Oct. 2, 1660, Rev. John Mayo was one of the witnesses to the will of William Paine and swore to it in Boston Nov. 14, 1660.(l) Dec. 22 and 29, 1670, Mr. John Mayo (described as elder), with other elders and named first among them, and with the selectmen, magistrates and governor, was present in Boston when Ezekiel Cheever was made head master of the free school.(m) In the Yarmouth rate in 1676 "toward the charges of the late war" Mr. Mayo's tax was £2 4s. 3d.(n) He died in 1676.(o)

(b) 2 ib. 21, 204.
(c) 2 ib. 21, 207; 2 Freeman, 247.
(d) Pratt's Eastham, 23; The Preble Family, by G. H. Preble, 259, 260; 3 Savage, 187.
(e) Winsor's Boston, 188.
(f) 2 Freeman, 358.
(g) 1 Plym. Col. Recs. 140.
(h) 2 ib. 20.
(i) 8 ib. 193.
(j) 65 N. E. Reg. 63; 6 Suffolk Prob. Recs. 64.
(k) 9 Mf. 233.
(l) 10 N. E. Reg. 85, 86.
(m) 33 N. E. Reg. 171, 172.
(n) Swift, 105.
(o) Swift, 107.

Under date of June 7, 1676, the following entry appears:(p) "Mr. Hinckley, Mr. Freeman, and Mr. Huckens are appointed by the Court to take course about the estate of Mr. John Mayo, deceased, to make devision and settlement of the said estate, both with reference unto his wifes pte and amougst his children, and therin to acte. If it may be, to theire satisfaction; and incase they can not, then to make report therof to the next Court, that soe further maybe taken for settlement therof."

The inventory of Rev. Mr. Mayo's personal estate, taken June 1, 1676, by Edmond Hawes and Thomas Huckins, amounted to £111 4s., including £10 for books.(q) June 15, 1676, his heirs settled his estate by agreement, which was signed by Tamsen Mayo, widow, John Mayo, son, Joseph Howes, son-in-law, and by Thomas Huckins in behalf of Hannah Bacon, daughter. John Mayo and Joseph Howes were made administrators. There were three grandchildren mentioned, Samuel Mayo, Hannah Mayo, and Bathsheba Mayo, children of his son Nathaniel Mayo, deceased.(r)

Children,(s) born in England.
1. Samuel[2]; m. Thomasin (or Tamsen), daughter of William Lumpkin of Yarmouth(t); d. early in 1664, being a mariner. In August, 1643, he was one of those between 16 and 60 in Barnstable able to bear arms.(u) His wife joined the Barnstable church Jan. 20, 1649-50.(v) He removed later to Boston, where his estate was settled, his inventory being taken April 25 and his father being appointed administrator April 26, 1664, his widow declining to act.(w) She m. 2d, Mr. John Sunderland of Boston, who later was a citizen of Eastham.(w1) June 7, 1648, he had a suit of trespass on the case against John Williams, Sr., for £40 damage. Not appearing, he was nonsuited and ordered to pay the charges of the court.(x) June 4, 1650, he was propounded to take up his freedom.(y) June 5, 1650, he and Mr. Thomas Howes were appointed administrators of Samuel Hallett, deceased.(z) Oct. 2, 1652, Samuel Mayo was one of the witnesses to a deed at Barnstable,(a) and Jan. 29, 1657-8, he also witnessed a writing.(b) In 1653 Peter Wright, Samuel Mayo and William Leveridge bought of Assiapum alias Moheness, an Indian sachem, the land now the village of Oyster Bay on Long Island. The three grantees by endorsement on the deed gave to seven other persons equal rights with themselves in the land purchased.(c) William Leveridge had been the first pastor of the church in Sandwich, Mass., and employed Samuel Mayo, who owned the

(p) 5 Plym. Col. Recs. 200.
(q) 3 Plym. Col. Wills, pt. 1, p. 165; 9 Mf. 120.
(r) 3 Plym. Col. Wills, pt. 1, p. 175; 9 Mf. 119, 121, 122. See also 6 N. E. Reg. 168, 174; 1 Otis, 25, 220, 222.
(s) 6 N. E. Reg. 168.
(t) 3 Savage, 130, 188.

(u) 4 N. E. Reg. 258.
(v) 9 N. E. Reg. 281.
(w) 13 N. E. Reg. 332, 333.
(w1) Josiah Paine.
(x) 2 Plym. Col. Recs. 125.
(y) Ib. 154.
(z) Ib. 156.
(a) 1 Mf. 139.
(b) 12 ib. 81.
(c) History of Queen's Co., N. Y. (1882), 469, 470.

vessel named Desire, to transport his goods to Oyster Bay. This vessel was captured by one Thomas Baxter in Hempstead Harbor under pretense of authority from Rhode Island, but Mayo recovered a judgment against Baxter because of the capture. Mayo was at Oyster Bay for some time, but did not settle there, and the statement that he died at that place in 1670 is erroneous.(d) If a Samuel Mayo died there at that time, it may have been the son of the grantee.

Samuel[2] Mayo and his wife had six children:(e) Mary, who was baptized(f) in Barnstable Feb. 3, 1649-50, and married(g) Capt. Jonathan Bangs July 16, 1664, who lived in Eastham and Harwich (now Brewster); Samuel, baptized in Barnstable Feb. 3, 1649-50;(f) Hannah, b. Barnstable Oct. 20, 1650;(h) Elizabeth, b. Barnstable May 22, 1653, who m. March 16, 1674-5, the Rev. Samuel Treat, who had become minister of Eastham in 1672;(i) Nathaniel, b. in Boston April 1, 1658;(j) Sarah, b. in Boston Dec. 12, 1660;(k) the 2d wife of Lt. Edward Freeman of Eastham. Mr. Paine gives Samuel[2] and his wife a daugh-

(d) Ib. 471.
(e) 6 N. E. Reg. 168, 169.
(f) 9 N. E. Reg. 284.
(g) 8 N. E. Reg. 368 (sheet); 3 Savage, 188; Bangs Geneal. by Dudley, 22.
(h) 3 Savage, 188.
(i) East. Recs.; 8 Mf. 243, 244. See also Pratt's Eastham, 36, 37, and Rich's Truro, 97. The last-mentioned works erroneously make this Elizabeth the daughter instead of the granddaughter of the Rev. John Mayo.
(j) Births, Marriages and Deaths of Boston, 1630-1699, p. 64.
(k) Ib. 74; Mr. Paine.

ter Mercy who m. Capt. Samuel Sears of Harwich, and a son John, who m. Hannah Freeman (daughter of Major John) and settled in Harwich.

2. Hannah[2], b. ; m. in Barnstable Dec. 4, 1642, Nathaniel Bacon.(l)

3. Nathaniel[2]; m. Feb. 13, 1649-50, Hannah Prence, daughter of Gov. Thomas Prence and granddaughter of Elder Brewster;(m) d. in Eastham about the end of 1661. His will was dated Dec. 19, 1661, and his inventory was filed March 4, 1661-2.(n) His widow married as his 2d wife Capt. Jonathan Sparrow.(m) Nathaniel and Hannah had the following six children:

Thomas, b. Dec. 7, 1650; m. June 13, 1677, Barbara Knowles of Eastham; d. April 22, 1729.

Nathaniel, b. Nov. 16, 1652; m. 1st January 28, 1678-9, Elizabeth Wixam,(o) and 2d June 10 1708, Mercy, widow of Nathaniel Young; d. Nov. 30, 1709.

Samuel, b. Oct. 12, 1655; m. twice; d. Oct. 29, 1738.

Hannah, b. Oct. 17, 1657.

Theophilus, b. Dec. 17, 1659. Mentioned in the will of Gov. Prence, his grandfather. He died without issue.(p)

Bathsheba.

June 5, 1651, Nathaniel[2] was propounded to take up his freedom.(q) He was announced as surveyor of highways for Eastham June 1,1658.(r) Mar.

(l) 1 Otis, 25, 220, 222; 9 Mf. 119; 6 N. E. Reg. 168, 174.
(m) 6 N. E. Reg. 234; 1 Brewster Genealogy, 21, 22; 14 Mf. 2, 193, 194.
(n) 6 N. E. Reg. 93.
(o) 4 Mf. 32.
(p) 3 Mf. 204, 205; 14 Mf. 198.
(q) 2 Plym. Col. Recs. 167.
(r) 3 Ib. 136.

4, 1661-2, he having died, his widow Hannah was appointed administratrix.(s) In August, 1643, he was one of those in Barnstable between 16 and 60 able to bear arms.(t) He was admitted a freeman and sworn June 3, 1652.(u)

    4. John²; m.(v) at Eastham Jan. 1, 1651-2, Hannah Lecraft; d. before Oct. 28, 1706, at Eastham.(w) He was surveyor of highways for Eastham June 3, 1656.(x(June 1, 1658, he was a constable at Eastham.(y) Nov. 14, 1676, he was one of the overseers of the will of Nicholas Snow.(z) John² Mayo and his wife had nine children(a):

    John, b. Dec. 15, 1652.
    William, b. Oct. 7, 1654.
    James, b. Oct. 3, 1656.
    Samuel, b. April 2, 1658
    Elisha, b. Nov. 4, 1661.
    Daniel, b. June 25, 1664.
    Nathaniel, b. April 2, 1667.
    Thomas, b. June 24 and d. Aug. 11, 1670.
    Thomas, b. July 15, 1672.

    5. Elizabeth²; m. Joseph² Howes of Yarmouth; d. March 12, 1700-1, leaving issue. See supra, p. 9.

(s) 4 ib. 3.
(t) 8 ib. 194.
(u) 3 ib. 7.
(v) East. Recs.; 6 Mf. 205. 8 Plym. Col. Recs. 26 gives the name of his wife as Hannah Reycraft and the date of marriage as Jan. 1, 1650-1.
(w) His will, dated June , 1702, was proved July 8, 1707. His inventory, dated Oct. 28, 1706, was sworn to Nov. 4, 1706. (3 Barn. Prob. Recs. 324, 326.)
(x) 3 Plym. Col. Recs. 101.
(y) Ib. 136.
(z) 3 Mf. 169.
(a) 6 Mf. 205; 14 ib. 117.

Note as to Howes.

The "Genealogy of the Howes Family" (1892), by Joshua C. Howes, gives the name of the wife of Thomas¹ Howes as Mary Burr,(b) but no proof of her surname can be found. Mr. Howes says that the emigrant came from the County of Norfolk, England, but here again there is no proof that the emigrant had any connection with the Norfolk family or was entitled to the coat of arms given in the book. Burke's General Armory, 513, gives the arms of Howes or Howse (Morningthorpe, Co. Norfolk), without indication of date, from which those in this book of J. C. Howes are taken, but Burke gives two different sets of arms without indication of place or date, and also gives the arms of Joan Howes, heiress of the family in the time of Henry VIII, Co. Essex. He also gives different sets of arms for various families named Hughes, Hugh, Hewes and for others having similar names. At the time of the emigration of Thomas¹ Howes the name was not uncommon in various parts of England.

The author also says (p. 7) that "they [Thomas¹ and his wife] were in Salem, Mass., two years before, or in 1637, where they first landed. They brought with them three sons, Joseph, Thomas and Jeremiah, the last born on the passage over, or soon after arrival." There is no evidence that they had lived in Salem. There is evidence that they had lived in Lynn. The date and place of their arrival in America nowhere appear. They may have landed in Boston or Salem and in view of the litigation he was en-

(b) Austin's Allied Families, 136, gives the same name, probably taken from J. C. Howes.

gaged in in 1638, no doubt as early as 1637. Jeremiah was born about 1637, but whether in England, on the passage over or in America is not known. There is no proof of the age of Thomas' Howes at his death. This genealogy by J. C. Howes contains many errors and is imperfect. He appears not to have consulted the Barnstable Probate Records, only a few miles away from him. I have not relied on him except in a few instances where other authority was lacking. Otis seems to think that the principal settlers of Yarmouth came from Norfolk County. In the 2d volume of his Barnstable Families, p. 190, he says:

"The leading men among the first settlers [of Yarmouth] were from Norfolk county, of which Yarmouth was the principal seaport, hence the name."(c) Swift, however, takes the opposite view. In his Old Yarmouth (published in 1884), 23, he says: "The first mention of the name Yarmouth, as applied to this township, is found in the court record of January, 1639, in connection with the grant to Thacher, Howes and Crow. From the fact that this name was selected, it has been inferred that the settlers of this town came from Yarmouth, in England. This may have been true of some individual, but does not apply to the settlers as a body. They did not come from any single locality. Some were Eastern County men, some were from the Midland Counties, some from Wales, and others from the South of England. Yarmouth, the principal seaport on the eastern coast of England, was the place of embarkation and debarkation between that country and Holland, and was naturally associated in the minds of the Pilgrims with their experiences in the mother country. Hence, perhaps, the name." H. H. Sanford, who wrote on a branch of the Howes family in 1893, evidently derived his information as to the early generations from Joshua C. Howes. Pelletreau, in his history of Putnam Co., N. Y. (501-505), no doubt derived his early information from a common source, while Thomas Prince Howes in his genealogy from Jeremiah[5] Howes (pub. by Charles W. Swift, Esq., of Yarmouthport, Mass., in 1914) also followed J.,C. Howes, and in his early generations has similar imperfections and errors.

Swift, in his Old Yarmouth, 47, also says: "Nothing is known of Mr. Howes before his coming to this country, neither have we any knowledge in what part of England he originated. He was in Salem in 1635,(d) and in Yarmouth in 1639, as one of the original grantees of the town, where in connection with Mr. Thacher and Mr. Crow, he commenced the settlement, establishing himself in that part of the present town of Dennis, called 'New Boston'."

Mr. Howes's authority for the coat of arms and the English genealogy is the Rev. Dr. Reuben[6] Wing Howes of New York city, whose line is Reuben[5] Wing, Daniel[4], Moody[3], Thomas[2], Ebenezer[2], Jeremiah[2], Thomas[1] Howes. Moody[3] Howes removed to what is now Putnam County, N. Y., about 1750. Reuben[6] Wing Howes was the founder and first president of the National Park Bank in New York city and afterwards head of the banking firm of Howes & Macy there. The compiler has had interviews with Dr. Howes and has been received with

---

(c) Written before 1875.   (d) No proof of this.

much courtesy. Dr. Howes visited about 1874 or 1875 the Rev. Thomas G. F. Howes of the Morningthorpe family, who was rector of Belton parish in Suffolk in or near Yarmouth, for many years. On that occasion the rector produced papers and documents that showed a Thomas Howes of his family of the time of Thomas' Howes who could not be accounted for, and whom the rector thought to be the emigrant. The compiler cannot concede to this suggestion the force of proof, especially as in seeking the English origin of his ancestor Edmond Hawes he at first found a Hawes family in Sussex, which it seemed must include his ancestor, but subsequently proof was found that he came not from Sussex, but from Warwickshire. With reference to the claim of a Norfolk origin for Thomas' Howes, the best we can say therefore is that he may have come from that county.

In 1834 a monument was erected in the Howes burying ground in Dennis carrying the following inscription: (e)

"Here Lies
Mr. Thomas Howes,
and on his right, his wife, Mary Burr.
She adorned her character by a discreet and virtuous life.
They were natives of England, and emigrated in the year 1637.
Their births, deaths and marriages unknown.
We, their descendants, from a sense of filial duty, consecrate
This stone to the first Howes that came to America.
'Twas from the central part of Briton's Isle they came,
And on Columbia's soil did propagate a name;
We their descendants the Patriarch own
And to the first Howes, do dedicate this stone."

Swift's Old Yarmouth (p. 48) gives the inscription somewhat differently. He says the stone is on the E. declivity of a hill to the N. E. of his family seat, where he and many of his descendants are buried.

(e) J. C. Howes, 200.

No. 32.

LIBRARY of
Cape Cod
HISTORY & GENEALOGY

FOUNDERS' DAY EDITION
AUGUST 26, 1916.
of the
EARLY SETTLERS OF EASTHAM
Containing Sketches of all Early Settlers of Eastham
By Josiah Paine, Esq., of Harwich
IN TWO NUMBERS: BOOK 2

Book 1: Thomas Prence, Nicholas Snow, John Doane, Edward Bangs, Richard Higgins, John Smalley, Samuel Hicks, John Jenkins, Robert Wixon, Josiah Cooke, Joseph Rogers, John Freeman, John Mayo, Thomas Williams, Thomas Roberts; 32p.

Book 2: Richard Knowles, Richard Sparrow, Job Cole, Daniel Cole, Giles Hopkins, Ralph Smith, William Walker, William Merrick, Richard Bishop, William Sutton, William Twinning, George Crisp, Richard Rich, John Young, Thomas Paine, Joseph Collins, Thomas Bills, Henry Atkins; 31 pages.

YARMOUTHPORT, MASS.:
C. W. SWIFT, PUBLISHER AND PRINTER,
THE "REGISTER" PRESS,
1916.

EARLY SETTLERS OF EASTHAM.

By Josiah Paine of Harwich.

RICHARD KNOWLES.

Richard Knowles was early settled in Plymouth. At that place he had land granted him in January, 1638-9, and there he was married to Ruth Bower, August 15 following. He appears to have been a sea-faring man. He was at Eastham in 1653. At that date he is mentioned as being in command of a barque which the government had secured to transport military stores, in case such were needed, the colony then expecting trouble with the Dutch. He was a surveyor of highways in 1669-70. He held no other offices in town it appears, though a man of standing. The time of his death does not appear. There appears no perfect record of his children. It is certain he had James, who died about 1682; John, who was slain in the Indian war in 1675; Mercy, who married Ephraim Doane; Samuel, born at Plymouth in 1651; Mehitable, born in Eastham, 1653, and Barbara, born in 1656.

John Knowles, son of Richard, married Apphia Bangs, Dec. 28, 1670. He was slain near Taunton by the Indians, in 1675, as above stated. By wife Apphia he had two sons, viz: Edward and John, who were prominent men in their day. Edward was a deacon, and for some years a selectman of the town. He died ―― 16, 1740. Col. John Knowles, his brother, was father of Col. Willard Knowles, a prominent citizen of Eastham. who somewhat exasperated the Revolutionary patriots of Eastham at the beginning of the conflict, by dealing in tea, and whose daughter Temperance was the first wife of Rev. Jonathan Bascom, minister of the South society. It is understood that Col. Willard resided in the north precinct. He was a man of considerable influence before the Revolution. His tombstone standing in the burying ground at Eastham, says: "After a life of virtue and various usefulness, attended with prosperity and reputation, died Mar. 11, 1786, in the 75 year of his age." He had before the

Revolutionary war been a colonel of the second regiment, a selectman and a representative.

Samuel Knowles, son of Richard, married Mercy Freeman, daughter of Major John Freeman, in December, 1679. He was a very prominent citizen. He was many years a representative and selectman. He died June 19, 1737, aged 85 years, and lies buried in the old cemetery in Orleans. He had a large family. His son Samuel, born in 1683, was a man of some notoriety. He was at one time a colonel in the militia. He served his townsmen as selectman and representative. He was taken sick in Boston and died there Jan. 30, 1750, at the age of 67 years. He lies buried in the Granary burying-ground in that city, where a stone with inscription marks the spot. His son Samuel, the third one of the name, was also a man of distinction. He was much in military service. He led a company of militia against Crown Point, and Fort William Henry, in the year 1756, under Col. Josiah Thacher of Yarmouth, and was in command of a company under Col. Doty against the French in 1758. He was in service a considerable length of time.

RICHARD SPARROW.

Richard Sparrow was in Plymouth as early as 1633. In 1638, he had forty acres of land granted him on the north end of Fresh lake. The same year he was one of those who investigated the cause of the death of John England, whose body had been found upon the flats about Plymouth. In 1639 he was one of the grand jurors for Plymouth; and is mentioned as having taken a fatherless girl as an "apprentice" for nine years, her former friend and stepfather consenting. The same year, he is reported as having had four steers sold him, by John Barnes, which were being wintered at Yarmouth, where they were to be delivered. In 1640, he was a constable and surveyor at Plymouth, and had meadow granted him at that place. In 1643, he was a grand juror, and in 1647 a surveyor at Plymouth. In 1650 he was a resident in that town, and had a cow stolen by one called in the record Thomas Sherne. He was in Eastham in 1655, and a surveyor. In 1656 he represented Eastham in the Colony court, showing that after

2

so short a residence the good people of Nausett had full confidence in his abilities, and that they were willing to entrust him with official honors. In 1657, with John Doane, Josiah Cooke, Richard Higgins, and John Smalley, he had land granted him between Bridgewater and Weymouth. The same year, with Thomas Clark, he was appointed by Plymouth court to make arrangements for the accommodation of Mr. Prence, who had been chosen governor, while on business at the seat of government, and also in going to and from court, while he had his home in Nausett. He was a surveyor in 1658, and a grand juror in 1659. He died at Eastham, "the 8th of Jan. in the year one thousand six hundred and sixty" say the Eastham records. His will was made Nov. 9, 1660, and presented at Plymouth March 5, 1660-1. It was witnessed by Samuel Freeman and Josiah Cooke. He mentions wife Pandora, son Jonathan, granddaughters Priscilla and Rebecca, and a grandson, John Sparrow. He gave to the church at Eastham "one ewe sheep," which his executors were to dispose of to the best advantage. He gave his place, etc., to his wife during her life, and at her decease, to his son Jonathan. This place was situated in the present town of Eastham, near the old burying-ground of the first settlers. A short time after his death, the mother and son sold out to Mr. Thomas Crosby, the religious teacher, and removed to the highlands of Porchet, within what is now called East Orleans, where the son Jonathan had made several purchases. Here the widow, it is supposed, lived until her death. He had a son but no daughters to survive him. The son, Captain Jonathan Sparrow, was a prominent man in Eastham. In 1876, the descendants of Richard Sparrow erected in the old yard at Eastham, a stone, with inscription, to his memory.

JOB COLE.

The Coles were among the early settlers of the Old Colony. John, Job and Daniel were brothers, and came over from England quite early. John settled at Plymouth, and died testate about the year 1637. Job and Daniel finally settled in Eastham, where they died.

Job Cole married Rebecca, daughter of Mr. William Collier,

a resident of that part of the Old Colony now Duxbury, May 14, 1634. He lived for awhile near Mr. Collier. In 1638, Mr. Cole had 40 acres of land granted him at Green Harbor, now Marshfield. He was propounded at Plymouth court March 4, 1638-9, and admitted a freeman March 3, 1639-40. It is recorded in 1639 that he paid the passage to this country of Thomas Gray, and found him apparel afterwards and before he became the indentured apprentice of Mr. John Atwood of Plymouth. Mr. Cole's name appears in the list of those who were able to bear arms in Yarmouth in 1643, which indicates that at that date he was a resident of Yarmouth; but if he were a resident it seems quite certain that he was not long at that place.

In 1648, he was residing in Eastham, and was that year chosen constable, and was ordered by the Old Colony court to take the oath at home. In 1650, he conveyed land at Marshfield to Thomas Chillingsworth, a shoemaker. In 1654, he was again constable of Eastham. In 1657, August 13, he sold his house and land at Duxbury to Christopher Wadsworth, for £17 sterling. After this date but little appears concerning him, and it is supposed that he died not far from this period.

His widow Rebecca died at Eastham Dec. 29, 1698, aged "about 88," and there was doubtless interred. Of the children of Job and Rebecca Cole, there appears no full list. It is quite certain he had three children, viz: Daniel, Samuel and Rebecca. Daniel Cole, the son, it is supposed is the one mentioned in the settlement of Mr. Collier's estate as receiving a portion of the estate, and the one who died in Eastham in 1713, leaving a wife Mercy and daughters Elizabeth, Mercy and Abigail.

Samuel Cole, son of Job, conveyed in 1682, meadow at Billingsgate which had been granted to his father, to Samuel Smith of Eastham. He settled in Harwich before 1694, and died in December, 1717, leaving children.

Rebecca, daughter of Job Cole, born in 1654, probably married Robert Nickerson of Chatham. It seemed that with this daughter lived the mother (the widow of Job) in her last years. Rebecca Nickerson was living as late as 1710, and received a small parcel of land at Billingsgate, towards what she had done in supporting her deceased mother during the closing years of her life.

Job Cole appears to have been a man of good standing in Eastham, though not much honored in public positions. His brother Daniel was the more noted man and of greater influence in the town and colony.

DANIEL COLE.

Daniel Cole, a brother of Job Cole, of whom a sketch has already been given, was born in England in 1615, and found his way to Plymouth when a young man. He was a tailor by trade, and as early as 1640 had a large lot of land granted him in Duxbury, near William Bassett's and Edmund Hawes's land. He was at Marshfield as early as June, 1642, and his name appears upon the list of those able to bear arms in Yarmouth in 1643, but he seems not to have been a resident. He was admitted a freeman June 4, 1645, and one of the Grand Inquest that year. In 1649 he was a resident of Eastham and an accepted townsman, and sold his land in Duxbury to Mr. Edmund Weston. In 1650, he sold to the same gentleman his land at Marshfield. He soon became prominent in municipal affairs at Eastham, and in 1653 was one of the Grand Inquest. In 1654 he was sent a deputy or representative to the Colonial court at Plymouth, and represented Eastham in 1666, '67, '68, '69, '70 and '72. He was a selectman in 1668, '71, '72 and '74. In 1667 he was allowed to look out land for his accommodation, and in 1668, with Thomas Hinckley, Nathaniel Bacon, Constant Southworth, John Alden, John Chipman and Lieut. Morton, was appointed by the Old Colony court to purchase for Gov. Prence the place at Plain Dealing in Plymouth, which had been selected for the residence of the governor.

Mr. Cole, with Mr. Thomas Prence and Mr. John Freeman, was appointed by the town to use his "best endeavors to put forward or encourage the Indians" or the "English to kill the wolves," which at this time, and for more than thirty years afterwards, were numerous and troublesome within the precinct. As late as 1690 the Indians were encouraged to hunt and capture them. Manassan, an Indian, carried in to the clerk of the town, in the spring of that year, four young wolves, which he affirmed he

5

caught in the vicinity of "Cliff pond." In 1661, he had liberty granted him "to draw and sell strong water and wine at Eastham, provided that he always be furnished with good wine for the supply of those that are in need amongst them." Whether he followed the instructions and allowed the wine to be sold without being adulterated, we have no knowledge. It is presumed that the art of adulteration at that period was known, and that liquor selling was a lucrative business, as all kinds of liquors were in common use. The early settlers were very careful in allowing the sale, and none were appointed to draw strong water but men of character. Illegal traffic in liquors was not allowed, and all violaters, of whatever standing in society, were dealt with according to law when caught. But with all their strictness and watchfulness, there were violaters that escaped punishment, as now, and intemperance not much prevented.

Mr. Cole died at Eastham Nov. 20, 1694, aged 79 years. His wife Ruth died Dec. 16, following. Mr. Cole had twelve children, viz: John, Timothy, Hepsibah, Israel, James, Mary, Ruth, Hester, William, Thomas and Daniel. From him have descended, it is supposed, all the Coles of the Cape.

John Cole, son of Daniel, born in 1646, married Ruth Snow in 1666, and died in Eastham Jan. 6, 1725-6. He was a large land owner in Truro, Eastham and Harwich. He left John, Joseph, Ruth, Hepsibah, Hannah, Mary and Sarah, children.

Israel Cole, son of Daniel, married Mary Rogers in 1679. He was a trader in Barnstable, where he died about 1724. He had two children, Hannah and Israel.

Mary, daughter of Daniel, married Joshua Hopkins, son of Giles, a large land owner of Eastham; died in 1734.

Daniel Cole, Jr., son of Daniel, died at Eastham, June 15, 1736, aged 69 years. He left no children. His wife, Mercy, died Sept. 25, 1735, aged 64 years. He was a man of means. He gave his property to his relatives.

GILES HOPKINS.

Giles Hopkins was the eldest son of Mr. Stephen Hopkins of Plymouth. He was born in England, and came over with his father's family in the Mayflower in 1620, and with the other members of his father's family survived the first winter's sickness, which swept off so many of that company. Of his boyhood days, but little appears. He appears to have been of a retiring disposition, only forward when duty impelled. When, in 1637, the Pequots, a tribe of brave Indians inhabiting the eastern part of Connecticut, commenced war with the English in that region, and Plymouth Colony concluded to send a company to assist in the overthrow of the Indians, he, with his father and younger brother Caleb, volunteered to go out in the company in the defence of his Connecticut neighbors, but happily for the company, before ready to go forth, the troops under Captain Mason had "vanquished" the enemy, and the company was not needed. The next year, Mr. Stephen Hopkins having been allowed by the Old Colony court "to erect a house at Mattacheese" now Yarmouth, "to cut hay there" and "to winter his cattle," it is supposed his son Giles went down there and had charge of his cattle. At any rate, he was at Yarmouth in 1639, and with Hugh Tilley and Nicholas Sympkins, "deposed" to the last will and testament of Peter Warden, the elder, deceased, and also courted and married Catherine Whelden, daughter of Gabriel Whelden, who was licensed to build at Mattacheese the year preceding. The house he occupied while a resident of Yarmouth stood a little to the northwest on the declivity or knoll, and the site was pointed out to the writer by the late Amos Otis a few years before his death. It is believed by Mr. Otis to have been the first house built below Sandwich, and certainly it must have been, if it were the one built by Stephen Hopkins by order of Plymouth court. Mr. Otis, in his account of Andrew Hallett, Jr., says it was sold by Giles Hopkins in 1642 to Mr. Hallett. It would seem that Mr. Hopkins was not a resident of Yarmouth in 1643, as his name does not appear in the list of those able to bear arms that year in the township, but evidence is quite conclusive that he was a resident June 6, 1644. At that date his father made his will, and several times speaks of Giles being at Yarmouth in charge of the cattle. It is probable he was not enrolled on account of being physically unable to do military duty. In what year he removed to Nausett or East-

7

ham, is not known. He was there in 1650, occupying the position of surveyor of highways, which he subsequently occupied several years. For some reason, now inexplicable, his father, by will, made Caleb, his younger son by second wife, the "heir apparent," and consequently the whole of the real estate, which was large, passed into the hands of Caleb at his death. Caleb Hopkins, soon after his father's death in July, 1644, gave up a very large tract of land to Giles, his only surviving brother, lying in what is now Brewster. Upon the death of Caleb, who was a seaman, and who died single at Barbadoes before 1657, Giles came into possession of large tracts. In 1659, Mr. Hopkins had land granted him in Eastham. In 1662, with Lieut. Joseph Rogers and Josiah Cooke, he had liberty allowed him by the Colony court to look out for land for his accommodation between Bridgewater and Bay Line. In 1672, with Jonathan Sparrow and Thomas Mayo of Eastham, he purchased Sampson's Neck in what is now Orleans, then called by the Indians Weesu Neck in what is now Orleans, then called by the Indians "Weesquamseutt." The tract was a valuable one; it embraced the territory between Higgins's river on the north, and Potonumecot river on the south. He seems to have been a very quiet man, caring but little for public positions. He was in 1654 drawn into a lawsuit by the noted William Leveridge, who had defamed him. Mr. Hopkins claimed damages to the amount of £50. Mr. Leveridge was ordered to pay £2 and some shillings for the offence.

The will of Giles Hopkins bears date Jan. 19, 1682; the codicil March 5, 1688-9. The former was witnessed by Jonathan Sparrow and Samuel Knowles, and the latter by Mark Snow and Jonathan Sparrow, and was presented for probate April 22, 1690, Stephen Hopkins, son, executor. There are no daughters mentioned. Sons mentioned are: Stephen, Caleb, Joshua and William. The widow was alive at the date of the codicil, and Mr. Hopkins had become unfit for labor and held out inducements to his son Stephen to supply his wants. It seems quite certain that his farm was in that part of Eastham now Orleans, and some part of it joined Town cove. According to the records, Mr. Hopkins had ten children, five of whom were daughters. They were Mary, born November, 1640, who married Samuel Smith; Stephen, born September, 1642; John, born in 1643; Abigail, born in 1644; Deborah, born in 1648, who married Josiah Cooke, Jr.; Caleb, born January, 1650; Ruth, born in 1653; Joshua, born June, 1657; William, born in 1660, and Elizabeth, born in 1664. Stephen Hopkins, the eldest son, removed to Harwich, now Brewster, and settled, having all his father's possessions there, where he died Oct. 10, 1718, aged 76 years. He was twice married and had eight children. Caleb Hopkins, the third son, removed to Truro, where his father had tracts of land, and died there about 1725, intestate, leaving four sons and one daughter, viz: Caleb, Nathaniel, Thomas, Thankful and Constant. Some of his grandsons lived to great ages. Isaac Hopkins, born in Truro March, 1725, died Jan. 6, 1814, was the oldest person native of the town that had died during the pastorate of Mr. Jude Damon up to that date. Mr. Samuel Hopkins, who died aged ninety-two years, eleven months, in July, 1820, was the eldest person who died in Truro between December, 1786, and September, 1828.

Joshua Hopkins, the third son of Giles, married Mary, daughter of Daniel Cole, May 26, 1681, and settled on the east side of Town cove, near his father's house. His house stood near or on the spot where the house of the late Isaac Seabury now stands. He was a very wealthy man. Much of his landed estate he inherited. He had eight children, viz: John, Abigail, Elisha, Lydia, Mary, Joshua, Hannah and Phebe. Hannah of this family died in Harwich, Oct. 24, 1793, in her 94th year. Mr. Hopkins was a farmer and shoemaker, it is understood. He owned land in Eastham, Harwich and Chatham. His wife Mary died March 1, 1734; he died in 1738. Many of his descendants have lived to great ages. Priscilla, a granddaughter, died in 1818, aged 90. Deacon Asa Hopkins, a great-great-grandson, died a few years since in Orleans, aged above 90 years.

William, the youngest son of Giles Hopkins, was never married. He was living in 1690. He seems not to have been capable of looking out for himself, and his father made ample provision for his support during life, leaving the matter of his support with Stephen, the executor, who, it is presumed, strictly carried out his father's plans in relation to his maintenance.

9

RALPH SMITH.

Ralph Smith appears to have been the first of the surname who settled in Eastham. He was there as early as 1657. He came from Hingham, where he had been a resident many years. He was originally from Hingham in England, it is understood, not far from the year 1633. While a resident of Eastham, he occupied no important official position. It is inferred from the Colonial records he was not a quiet citizen. He probably was twice married. His death occurred at Eastham in the year 1685. That year, October 27, letters of administration were granted to his widow, Grace, and son, Samuel. There appears no full record of his children, but as far as can be learned they were: Samuel, baptized at Hingham July 11, 1641; John, baptized July 23, 1644; Daniel, baptized March 2, 1647; Deborah, born in 1654, and Thomas. The date of the death of his wife Grace is not known.

Samuel Smith, son of Ralph, married Mary, daughter of Giles Hopkins of Eastham, and settled in that town. He early engaged in the whale and mackerel fishery, and was very successful. The latter years of his life he engaged in agriculture. He was owner of very large tracts of land, his largest tract containing over four hundred acres, situated in that part of Eastham now Orleans, and extending over to Baker's pond, from a line running northerly from Potonumecot river over Island pond to the mouth of the rivulet at the cove, near the house formerly occupied by Vickery Sparrow, which he sold November 1, 1684, to a large number of his townsmen. The tract for many years after this period was known as "Smith's Purchase." His death occurred March 20, 1696-70. His estate, both real and personal, was valued over twelve hundred pounds. He had beside his farm at Eastham, parts of two at Monomoy, now Chatham. The inventory of his estate shows that he was in possession of over fifty head of neat cattle, sixty sheep, and a number of horses at the time of his decease. Mr. Smith had six children; but only Mary, who married Daniel Hamilton, and John, survived him. They went to Chatham and settled. Samuel Smith, the oldest son, married Bashsheba Lothrop. of Barnstable, and died Sept. 22, 1692, leaving Samuel and Joseph, who had their father's share of the estate. Mr. Samuel Smith held no office of importance in the town. He appears to have been a determined and resolute man. He doubtless resided in that part of the town of Eastham now Orleans. The date of his widow's death does not appear.

John Smith, son of Ralph Smith, settled in Eastham. He married probably twice. His first wife, Hannah, was daughter of Thomas Williams, whom we noticed sometime since. They were married May 24, 1667. They had a son John, it is certain, as he was mentioned in the will of Thomas Williams, which bears date 1692. He probably had other children, but the writer has not investigated the records regarding them. There were several John Smiths contemporary with John, the grandson of Thomas Williams, and it would require considerable time to give their lives and descent.

Daniel Smith and Thomas Smith, sons of Ralph, married and settled in Eastham, where some of their descendants reside.

The Smiths are numerous on the Cape; but it is not known that they are all descendants of Ralph of Eastham. A branch of the family of this name, residing in Harwich, claims to descend from an Englishman of the surname who came to this country about the first of the last century, and settled at the west part of the town.

WILLIAM WALKER.

William Walker, the first of the name who settled on the Cape, came from England in 1635, in the Elizabeth, Captain Starr. He found his way to Eastham after the settlement had commenced, courted and married Sarah Snow, daughter of Nicholas, and settled near his wife's father, in Gov. Prence's neighborhood, on the west side of Town cove. He seems to have been a man of character and of education, but not inclined to give great attention to seeking official honors. He was undoubtedly a mariner in early life. In 1653 he was impressed to do duty as a seaman on board of the barque commanded by Richard Knowles, in anticipation of trouble with the Dutch, to carry the military stores. In 1664, with Mr. John Doane, he was appointed to report the amount of liquor brought within the precincts of Eastham. In 1667, he was appointed to receive excise. He was a surveyor of highways in Eastham in 1668, '69, '78, '79 and '93. In 1685, the Colony court, in consideration of his "having two natural sons in the training band, and one killed in the wars," and having "some weakness and infirmity of body," relieved him from "training." In 1686, he was appointed to assist in collecting the ministerial tax due Mr. Treat, and in October following, attended the court in Barnstable as a petit juror. He was a grand juror in 1690 and 1694; a petit juror in 1693; and a tithing man in 1695. He was not so large a land owner in Eastham as some of his contemporaries in the settlement. At different periods he received grants of land from the town to meet his wants. He was living in 1699. His wife was Sarah Snow, a daughter of Nicholas. He was married to her, according to the Eastham records, Jan. 25, 1654. His children were: John, born Nov. 24, 1655, who fell in the battle with the Indians at Rehoboth, under Captain Pierce, on March 26, 1676; William, born Oct. 12, 1637, who died in infancy; William, born August 2, 1659; Sarah, born July 30, 1662; Elizabeth, born Sept. 28, 1664; Jabez, born July 8, 1668. From Jabez, the youngest son, descended most of the Walkers upon the Cape. Jeremiah Walker, son of Jabez, married Esther Tomlin or Tumblen in 1724, removed to Harwich and settled, where he died in 1734. From him descended Jonathan Walker, the well-known Abolitionist, a native of Harwich, who died a few years since in Michigan.

WILLIAM MERRICK.

William Merrick was an early resident of Eastham. He came over to this country before 1636; settled first within the limits of Old Duxbury, and had land granted him by the Colonial court near the path to "Green Harbor" in 1637; also land granted him adjoining Mr. William Collier's, in 1630. In 1643, he was a juror for Duxbury, and in 1646 was a surveyor of highways. In 1648, he was on the jury that tried Mrs. Alice Bishop for the murder of her little daughter at Plymouth, whom, with her husband, we shall have occasion to notice in a future article. In 1652, he was admitted a freeman, and not long after moved to Eastham. He was among the settlers there May 2, 1655, as appears by the ancient records of that township. He settled within the limits of the present town of Orleans, in that part called Skaket. Among his neighbors were Richard Knowles, John Freeman and Robert Wixon. The date of the earliest entry respecting granting of land to him at Eastham is not clear. In 1659, the records show that he had a lot granted him of about four acres adjoining "Robard Wixon," denominated a "house lott" by the highway, with the small piece of meadow within his fence, showing he had improved the lot previous to the grant; also this year a tract of upland at Pocke, near "Robard Wixon's" tract, containing about fifteen acres, was granted him; also meadow at "Little Namskaket," "Rock Harbor," and at "Boat Meadow;" together with another tract of eight acres, as "his great lot," on the south side of the "Cove." In 1662, he was, with "other ancient freemen and old servants," chosen to look out for land for his accommodation, provided Saconet Neck was not purchased, in another locality. In 1666, he was allowed to purchase land. Mr. Merrick was appointed in 1663 lieutenant of the trained band at Eastham, an office which had long been held by Lieut. Joseph Rogers. He was succeeded by Lieut. Rogers in 1664. Mr. Merrick at this date was beyond the age of 60, and was thereby disqualified by law to do military duty. He had been ensign of the trained band for some time. He is mentioned in the records as "Ensign Merrick." He held no other important office while a resident of Eastham. He was a surveyor in 1665, and receiver of excise in 1668.

The date of his marriage does not occur in the Plymouth Colony records or the ancient records of Eastham. He undoubtedly was married in this country some few years after his arrival. His wife at the time of his death was Rebecca, but whether she was the mother of all of his children, the writer is not informed. He died at Eastham the last of the year 1688, or the beginning of 1689, as his will was presented for probate at Barnstable in March, 1689. He was about 86 years old when he made his will, the year previous. Mr Merrick, as far as is known, had ten children: six sons and four daughters.

Of his children, William was the oldest. He was born in

Duxbury in 1643, went to Eastham with his father, and married Abigail Hopkins, daughter of Giles, May 23, 1667. He moved to the north precinct of Harwich, now Brewster, before 1694, and there resided until his death, at the great age of 90 years, in 1732. He was very prominent in the settlement of Harwich. He was one of the seven who established the church at Harwich, now Brewster, in 1700, and one of the petitioners for the incorporation of the town in 1694. He was selectman of the town consecutively from 1702 to 1709. He was a representative to the General court at Boston in 1719. He had, certainly, eight children. Nathaniel, his son, born in 1673, was a very prominent man in Harwich. He survived his father about eleven years, dying "at noon," Nov. 13, 1743. William, the son of Nathaniel, married Elizabeth Osborn in 1734, and was lost at sea, leaving three children, viz: William, Gideon and Elizabeth. The mother, Elizabeth, was daughter of Rev. Samuel Osborn of Eastham, and married William Paine, Esq., for her second husband, and for her third husband married Edmund Doane. She died at Barrington, Nova Scotia, in 1797, where she had been living since 1761.

William Merrick, or Myrick, son of William and Elizabeth (Osborn) Myrick, born Oct. 26, 1734, (and a half-brother of William Paine, the distinguished teacher, and father of John Howard Paine) settled in Orleans. Among his descendants are W. P. Myrick, late clerk of Orleans, and Rev. O. Myrick.

Joseph Merrick, son of William of Eastham, born in 1662, settled in that town. He married Elizabeth Howes of Yarmouth, May 1, 1684. He died June 15, 1737. He was probably twice married. He had several children.

Stephen Merrick, son of William of Eastham, married Mary Bangs in 1670. He, it is thought, was the one of the name who settled in Norwich, Conn. He had a son Stephen, born in Eastham in 1673.

The Merricks of the Cape are descendants of the Eastham settler. They are not numerous, however. They write their name Myrick.

RICHARD BISHOP.

Richard Bishop was an early resident of Eastham. He came to Plymouth some time prior to 1654, but how long he resided in the latter place, records do not clearly show. He was there, however, in 1638, in the employ of Love Brewster, son of Elder William Brewster of the Mayflower band of Pilgrims. Some time previous to the year 1648, he was married to a widow whose name was Alice, a very singular woman, it is evident. On the 22nd of July, 1648, she took her 14-year-old daughter, Martha Clarke, into the chamber of her house, cut her throat, and left her dead upon the floor, in an almost nude state, admitting she did the cruel deed to some of the Grand Inquest, when an inquiry was being made to learn the particulars concerning her death. Her trial for murder was commenced Oct. 8, 1648, at Plymouth, and she was adjudged guilty and sentenced to be hanged. She was accordingly hanged. Two of the jurors, Richard and William Merrick, were from Eastham. After this affair, which gave him some notoriety, he continued his residence in Plymouth, and the year following, in March, he was up before the court for taking a spade from Andrew King, one of his townsmen, and was fined. He had tracts of land allowed him in 1654 at Nausett or Eastham, by the proprietors, and while there gave his attention to agriculture as a principal means of support. His propensity to purloin seems not to have left him after his removal to Eastham and associating with the good settlers there. He was allured by the nice fleece Goodman George Crisp had taken from the sheep, in 1670, and entered his premises and helped himself. He was arraigned and ordered to settle, which he did, paying the sum of thirty shillings. He, soon after this affair, left the township with his family. His place was sold in 1673, by his order, to Thomas Cole. The records point to his place of residence in Eastham, in what is now East Orleans, in the vicinity of Tonset. The Coles, Twinnings and Higginses were his neighbors. Upon his farm at "Pocha," was a hole in the earth, called for many years after his removal, "Bishop's Butter Hole." The records give Bishop no children. It is believed, however, he had several. The Damaris Bishop who married William Sutton in 1666, is thought was his daughter.

WILLIAM SUTTON.

Of William Sutton, but little appears. He was in Barnstable in 1666, and was up before the court for entering the meetinghouse, taking away the Bible, and denying having taken it, and was fined for both offences. What led him to take away the Bible from Mr. Walley's pulpit is not stated by the records. Sutton was not long a resident of Eastham. He had, born in Eastham: William, May 13, 1668; Thomas, Nov. 11, 1669; Marah, Oct. 4, 1671. He appears not to have been either a land owner or townsman of Eastham.

WILLIAM TWINNING.

William Twinning, the ancestor of the Cape family of the name, was in Yarmouth in 1643, and went forth a soldier in 1645 against the Indians. The precise date of his removal to Eastham with his family, the Eastham records do not show, but he was there located before 1651, as that year he was constable of the place. His place of residence, it is understood, was on "Poche Neck," now called East Orleans, but the particular spot is not known to the writer. He was a considerable land owner, though not of the class called "Town-purchasers." His days in Eastham were few. He passed away April 15, 1659. His wife, Anne, survived him, and died Feb. 27, 1680. His children are not all known. Some of them, doubtless, crossed the ocean with him. Isabel married Francis Baker of Yarmouth, the ancestor of the Baker family, in 1641; Elizabeth married John Rogers of Eastham in 1669; and William married Elizabeth, daughter of Stephen Deane, whose widow married Josiah Cooke of Eastham.

William Twinning, the son, who married Elizabeth Deane, came with his father's family to Eastham, and settled near his father, their land adjoining. He was a considerable land owner. He had a three-acre lot, called a house lot, granted him in 1659, adjoining his father's land; a ten-acre lot granted at Poche; meadow at Great Namskaket, Billingsgate and Boat Meadow in 1659. He had twenty acres of land at Poche granted in 1664, which was formerly possessed by Josiah Cooke and Francis Baker; and also meadow granted him the same year, which was located at Namskaket. In 1668, he again was put into legal possession of some swamp land near his garden, which adjoined Richard Bishop's land. He was a quiet and peaceable man, and occupied but a few official positions in the town. He was a deacon of the church in Eastham as early as 1677. The date of his death does not appear. He had, it is certain, two sons, Stephen and William. His daughter Joanna, born May 30, 1657, married Thomas Bills, March 2, 1676, who had, it is reported, in 1673 married her sister Anne, and who died Sept. 1, 1675. He also had a daughter Susannah, born Feb. 25, 1654, who probably died young. He doubtless had other children.

William Twinning, of the third generation, and grandson of the settler, married Ruth Cole, March 20, 1688-89, settled in the eastern part of Orleans. He had seven children. His sons were William and Barnabas. William Twinning, the son, born in 1704, married Apphia ——, settled near his father's place, and died about 1769, leaving wife Apphia, and sons Thomas and Elijah. Thomas removed to Sandesfield, Mass., in 1787, with his family. Elijah, brother of Thomas, married Lois Rogers, and removed from town.

The son William, of the fifth generation, brother of Thomas and Elijah, born March 25, 1739, died March 26, 1759, some ten years before his father's death. The mother Apphia, was a member of the Orleans church, and was living in 1773. As her death was not recorded by Mr. Bascom in his register, it is supposed she died abroad with one of her sons. It is believed the name is extinct on the Cape.

GEORGE CRISP.

George Crisp was in Eastham in 1650, acting in the capacity of a constable, but the precise year of his settlement is not known. Though a townsman, he was not of the class called Town-purchasers, and had no legal right to the common land. What his vocation was, is now unknown. His townsmen, who had the disposal of the common land, were very liberal in their allowance to him. He was, it is supposed, a resident in that part of Eastham called by the Indians Poche, and now denominated East Orleans.

In 1658, in that vicinity, near his house, he had a swamp and upland allowed him, near John Young's. Under date of April 27, 1659, he was allowed 17 acres of land near William Twinning, Jr.'s, in Poche, and also three acres of meadow on the south side of Boat Meadow, or as the Indians called it, Onoscotist. He was the fortunate possessor of a horse, and he is set down as having one as early as May 30, 1660. In 1662, he appears to have brought upon himself some trouble, by receiving for sale liquor illegally, which he claimed was received without knowledge of doing an unlawful act. He was favorably considered by the court. The report of some little disorder at his house in consequence of the sale, was investigated. Mr. Crisp was a grand juror in 1672 and 1678. He died at Eastham, July 28, 1682.

Mr. Crisp was twice married. His first wife, Mary, by whom he had no children, died Feb. 20, 1676. His second wife, Hepsibah, was daughter of Daniel Cole, to whom he was married May 24, 1677. By her he had Mary, born Dec. 9, 1678, and Mercy, born Oct. 15, 1681.

Mr. Crisp attempted to adopt a son of Richard Berry of Yarmouth, in 1660, a lad of some six years of age called Samuel. He became "stubborn and rebellious and went away against" Mr. Crisp's protest "before his lawful time." In conseuence Mr. Crisp ordered the executor to pay him the small sum of "twelve pence and no more." Mr. Crisp, it will be seen, could not tolerate stubbornness and rebellion.

Mr. Crisp's widow Hepsibah married Deacon Daniel Doane, a neighbor many years her senior, and had children. Her daughter, Mary Crisp, married Samuel Gold of Topsfield, Dec. 1, 1700. Mercy Crisp married, as is understood, George Williamson. From her descended the late Judge William D. Williamson of Maine. George Williamson settled in Eastham. He was there in 1722. It is said he had seven children, two sons and five daughters. George and Caleb were the sons. George was murdered by a highwayman, and Caleb married and settled in Middleboro. The name of Crisp is extinct in Eastham, also in Barnstable county.

RICHARD RICH.

Richard Rich, the ancestor of the Rich family of the Cape, came to Eastham from Dover, New Hampshire. He was a mariner, say the records, and admitted a townsman Aug. 23, 1681, it being the first notice of him upon the record of Eastham. He appears to have been a man of standing, and entitled to the prefix of "Mister." The particular spot he selected for his house lot, the writer is not informed. He evidently was married before his settlement here. His wife was Sarah Roberts, it is said by his descendants. But very little is said of him in the records. He had the description of his cattle marks entered April 12, 1686. He is mentioned as buying rights to undivided land known as "Smith's Purchase." The right of William Mayo he purchased June 3, 1686, and the right of Stephen Atwood he purchased June 29 of the same year. The tract of land known as "Smith's Purchase," and sometimes called the "Ten Pound Purchase," estimated to contain 1,000 acres, was bought of John Sipson, an Indian of Potonumecot, by Samuel Smith in behalf of the town proprietors in 1684. It extended northerly nearly across the present town of Orleans, from an east and west line between Kescayogansett and Potonumecot rivers.

Mr. Rich died early in the autumn of 1692, evidently not a very aged man. An inventory of his effects was taken by John Doane, Isaac Pepper and Richard Rich, Oct. 5, 1692. Letters to administer upon the estate were granted to Isaac Pepper and Richard Rich, the eldest son, Oct. 19, the same year. A settlement was effected April 8, 1697

The children mentioned in the settlement as surviving are Richard, the eldest son, John, Sarah, Thomas, Samuel and Lydia. At this date none of the daughters had been married. Richard Rich, the son, born in 1674, went to Truro and settled. He died May 3. 1743, in the 69th year of his age. His wife Anna died May 11, 1754, aged 74. They had nine children.

John Rich, the younger brother, and son of Mr. Richard Rich, married Mary Treat, daughter of Rev. Samuel Treat, Dec. 10, 1700. She died Jan. 4, 1722-23. He, the same year, married Mrs. Hope Sears, widow of Richard Sears of Chatham. He settled in

19

that part of Eastham now Wellfleet, where he died of the small pox in 1747, which was prevalent there that year. Mr. Rich was deacon of the church and a prominent man. His daughter Hope, by second wife, born May 7, 1725, was the wife of Col. Elisha Doane, a well-known citizen of Wellfleet, who amassed wealth in the whale fishery, and was thought to have been the richest man of his time in Massachusetts. Deacon Rich had 8 children by his wife Mary. His son John, born in 1706, married Thankful Sears, daughter of Richard and Hope Sears, in 1727.

Thomas Rich, the third son of Mr. Richard Rich, married Mercy, daughter of Samuel Knowles, Esq., of Eastham, July 23, 1702, and settled in that part of the town now Orleans, near the late John Doane's house. He had nine children. His sons were Thomas, James, Joseph, David, John and Samuel. He died the middle of the last century. He had land granted by the town, in 1702, on the south side of the way, near the cedar swamp and pond.

Sarah Rich, daughter of Mr. Richard Rich, married, Feb. 25, 1702-3, Isaac Baker of Eastham, and settled at Billingsgate, now Wellfleet. They had six children, viz: Simeon, Samuel, Isaac, Joseph, Richard and Sarah.

JOHN YOUNG.

John Young came to Eastham before 1659. He was a resident of Plymouth in 1643, and his name appears that year among those liable to do military duty. So far as can be now ascertained, his place of residence was in what was called by the Indians, Pochet or Poche, and now called East Orleans. He was a planter, and had but very little to do with town affairs while a resident of Old Eastham. He was not of that class called town purchasers. The old records of Eastham show he was a considerable land holder, and that some of his land was obtained by purchase. He had ten acres at Poche, as early as 1659, adjoining George Crisp's land, the purchase of which was confirmed by the town. His purchase of five acres between "Young's Cove and the highway yt goeth at the end of Richard Sparrow's ground," this year was confirmed also, by the town. In 1676, he bought of Thomas Paine, for £9, fifteen acres of upland on the westerly side of "Young's Cove."

According to the records, he died Jan. 25, 1690, and his wife Abigail, April 7, 1692. No stones with inscriptions mark their resting places. "Goodman" Young died testate, and his will is on record at Barnstable. He had eleven children, two of whom died in infancy. His children that survived were John, born 1649, at Plymouth; Joseph, born in 1654; Nathaniel, born in 1656; Mary, in 1658; Abigail, in 1660; David, in 1662; Lydia, in 1664; Robert, in 1667; Henry, in 1672. These all survived their parents.

John, the eldest, died in 1769, leaving nine children. His wife was daughter of Daniel Cole, and at the decease of her husband, John Young, she married Jonathan Bangs of Harwich.

Joseph Young, son of John, married Sarah Davis of Barnstable, Oct. 25, 1679, and had four children. Nathaniel Young, his brother, married Mercy Davis of Barnstable.

David Young, born in 1662, married Ann Doane of Eastham, Jan. 20, 1687, and had eleven children. His son, John Young, married Widow Dinah Baker, daughter of Joseph Harding, and settled in the western part of Chatham on the old road to Harwich. He died April 20, 1788, aged 93. His wife Dinah died Jan. 3, 1779, aged 78. They lie interred in the old burying ground at Chatham. He had several children. His son, Prince Young, removed to Harwich and settled. He was the first of the name who settled within the limits of the present town of Harwich. There appears to be no full record of the children of John Young, son of David.

THOMAS PAINE.

Eastham had been settled but a very few years when Thomas Paine became a resident. He was born in England, but the particular place is not known with certainty. Credible traditionary accounts that came down several branches of the family, and committed to writing before and soon after the commencement of the present century, have it that he came over when a lad of about ten years of age, with his father, Thomas, and married Mary Snow and settled in Eastham. But as to the father, Thomas, beyond that he settled in Plymouth Colony, tradition is silent. It has been supposed the father was the Thomas Paine who settled in Yarmouth, and the first representative to the Colony court in

1639, but the evidence to establish the fact is yet wanting. It has also been supposed that the lad, the subject of this article, was the Yarmouth Thomas, and that he removed to Eastham from that town. Of this there is no evidence. If he were the man he must have reached a great age at his death in 1706. That Thomas Paine, the lad, did marry Mary Snow and settle in Eastham, as tradition has it and accepted by his descendants, the records clearly show.

His name first appears upon the records as a constable of Eastham in 1653. He was in that town in 1655, and is mentioned as one of the nineteen men then townsmen. He was propounded at the Colony court at Plymouth in 1658, and June 1, that year, was admitted as freeman. In 1662 he was appointed, with Nicholas Snow, Jonathan Sparrow and Giles Hopkins, to view and lay out the meadow between Namskaket and Silver Springs, then within the limits of Eastham, to those of the inhabitants that were entitled to the same; and the same year, with Giles Hopkins, was selected a surveyor of highways. In 1664, for the first time, he was chosen deputy to the Plymouth Colony court, and a juryman. In 1667, with eleven others, he was called to investigate the cause of deaths of Robert Chappell, James Nichols and James Pidell, of Captain John Allen's company, who were put ashore at Cape Cod. The same year he was allowed by the Colonial court to select a tract of land for his use, and in June, 1669, he was allowed, with Experience Michell, Henry Sampson and Thomas Little, to purchase land at Namaskat, now Middleboro. With these persons, July 20, the same year, he purchased of Tuscaquin, the Black Sachem, and his son William, for £10 sterling, their right to the grant. This land adjoined John Alden's tract, at the famous Assawamsett pond. In 1670, with Jonathan Sparrow, he was appointed an inspector of the ordinaries in town, to see that there was no excessive drinking; and the same year, one of the Grand Inquest.

In 1670, Mr. Paine became interested in purchasing land in what is now Truro, of the proprietors. His first purchase was made of Gov. Prence of Plymouth, May 2, 1670, of his "half share" lying between "Bound Brook" and "Eastern Harbor," or "Lovell's Creek," paying the sum of £20. This tract some twenty years after, he sold to his eldest son, Thomas, for the same sum,

22

together with the tract he had bought of Jabez Howland in 1673, in the same vicinity for the same amount. In 1670, he was appointed to the office of "bayle by land & water," an officer created to "demand and receive for the Colony's use" the fines of those who disregarded the laws regulating the fishing at the head of the Cape, now Provincetown, and the territory adjacent, now Truro. This office he held many years, giving entire satisfaction. While acting as bailee, he resided during the fishing season in that region. In 1671, he represented Eastham in the Colony court at Plymouth; also in 1672, '73, '76, '78, '80, '81 and '90. He was selectman of Eastham in 1671 and several years afterwards. In 1676, he was one of the committee to collect a debt of Sandwich and to superintend the building of the meetinghouse in Eastham. This meetinghouse was the second one built there and stood near the ancient burying ground. The first one was thatched roof and stood nearby, and had been erected many years. It was now considered unsuitable for the congregation of their minister, Mr. Samuel Treat, who was now regularly settled. Mr. Paine was clerk and treasurer of Eastham, it is understood; but how many years in service is not clear from the record. Mr. Pratt says he was treasurer of the town for nineteen years, and Mr. Freeman says twenty-four years. The sources from which they derive the information the writer cannot find. The early records of the town, covering the years of his active public life, certainly give us but little as to the clerks and treasurers of the town. Mr. Paine was many years a "rate maker" or assessor. In 1685, with Rev. Samuel Treat, Captain Jonathan Sparrow, John Mayo, Sen., and Jabez Snow, he was chosen by the town "to hear and determine the difference between those called the purchasers and the town," respecting land within the limits of Eastham.

In 1667, together with Thomas Huckens of Barnstable, Edward Gray of Plymouth, and Mr. Constant Southworth, the Colonial treasurer, he hired the "fishing privileges and profits" at the head of the Cape for the period of seven years, for which was given £30 a year. By trade he seems to have been a cooper and millwright. He built mills in various parts of the county. In 1683, he conceived the importance of a mill in the southern part of the town, at a place called by the Indians Kescayogansett, and laid his plan before the town of erecting a mill on the river leading out of the cove. The town entered into an agreement with him, and two mills were built by him; in consideration of which, he had a large tract of land granted him, extending northerly from Kescayogansett cove and river, containing upwards of twenty-six acres, early in the year 1684, together with meadow on Sampson's Island. Whether both of the mills he built were tide mills, we are unable to learn. One was, it is certain, and the millstones from near site many years since, are pointed out. The land given by the town to Mr. Paine for his building the mills, was the parcel claimed by Jefferie and Sampson, Indians, and which the town laid out for them in June, 1682, and afterwards bought of them for the town's use. The tract, upon Mr. Paine's death, passed into the hands of his son, Nicholas, who occupied it until his death. It passed out of the possession of Mr. Paine's heirs about the year 1743. Sometime previous to 1695 he removed to Boston, where the records say he purchased of Thomas Stableford of Philadelphia, March 14, 1694, a homestead at the South end, paying the sum of £130. Here he was residing in 1697. Selling out this year to Eleazar Darby, he returned to Eastham, to his house at Kescayogansett, where he spent, it is supposed, the remainder of his life, passing away Aug. 16, 1706. He appears to have been a man of more than ordinary education. He was an excellent penman. Specimens of his chirography, when "well in years," are yet preserved. His wife Mary, daughter of Nicholas Snow and granddaughter of Mr. Stephen Hopkins, one of the Pilgrims who came over in the Mayflower in 1620, to whom he was married in 1650, was a woman of whom much has been said in her praise. She was "a faithful wife," "a careful mother," "a good quiet neighbor," "a diligent reader of God's hold word," and "a lover of, and attendant at God's house of worship." Her son, Deacon John Paine, thus gives in his diary an account of her last hours and death: "On the 28th day of April, 1704, my honored mother, Mary Paine, departed this life, being suddenly taken and struck with death, she having reasonable health all day, was taken ill about sunset, so she never after spoke reasonable; but decaying gradually, gave up the ghost about the dawning of the day."

The will of Thomas Paine bears date May 12, 1705. It was presented for probate Oct. 2, 1706. He mentions seven sons: Samuel, Thomas, Elisha, John, Nicholas, James and Joseph; two daughters: Dorcas, wife of Benjamin Vickery of Hull, and Mary, wife of Israel Cole. To Nicholas Paine, his fifth son, he gave all his "lands, mills, house and house at Keaskokagansett, in the town of Eastham," with all his "right title to all town's privileges," etc. He appointed his two eldest sons, Samuel and Thomas, executors. His house at Keaskokagansett stood between the cove and Fresh pond, near where the house of James Percival now stands. His son Nicholas occupied it until his death, when it passed into possession of his daughter Patience, and her husband, William Norcot; and upon their removel to Connecticut after 1740, it passed into the hands of Mr. Samuel Knowles, and became the residence of Mr. Enos Knowles.

The first place of Mr. Paine's residence in Eastham, it is understood, was within the limits of the present town of Eastham, near the Prence place, and not far distant from the residence of his father-in-law, Nicholas Snow. It is supposed he conveyed much of his real estate to his sons by deeds, before he made his will; but to what extent cannot now be ascertained, as all the books of records of deeds of the county were destroyed by fire in 1827. A deed of gift of meadow to his son Thomas, in his own handwriting is yet extant, bearing date 1684, and witnessed by his two sons, Nicholas and James.

Samuel Paine, the eldest son, married Patience Freeman, daughter of Major John Freeman of Eastham and granddaughter of Gov. Prence, Jan. 31, 1687. He settled within the limits of the present town of Eastham, near the house of the late Deacon Joshua Paine. He was much employed in public affairs. He was six years selectman of Eastham, and for some time lieutenant of the military company. He was cut down by a fever, Oct. 13, 1712. He left a wife and nine children. Only two of his sons left descendants, and they are widely scattered. Hon. Samuel James Bridge, who recently caused to be placed on the college ground at Cambridge, Mass., the statue of John Harvard, the founder of the college, is one of the descendants.

25

Thomas Paine, the second son, born in 1657, was a man of prominence. He succeeded Mark Snow, as clerk of Eastham, in 1695, and was yearly elected until 1701, when he was succeeded by his younger brother, John. He was an excellent clerk. He was a selectman of Eastham seven years. He became a landholder at Pamet, now Truro, and removed there and settled on the north side of Little Pamet river, where the house spot is yet to be seen. He was clerk of the proprietors many years. He was selectman of Truro seven years, representative five years, and town clerk several years. He was justice of the peace, deacon of the church, captain of the military company, and a special justice of the court of common pleas, to which office he was appointed July 5, 1713. He died June 23, 1721, in the 65th year of his age. He was twice married, and father of fourteen children. His descendants are widely scattered, numerous and highly respected. From his daughter Hannah descended the late Hon. Horace Binney of Philadelphia.

Elisha Paine, the third son, married Hannah Doane, daughter of John Doane of Eastham, Jan. 5, 1685. In 1689, he was a resident of Barnstable. He removed back to Eastham, and resided in "Little Skaket Neck" until 1703, when he bought a tract of 500 acres of wild land in that part of Plainfield now Canterbury, Conn., and removed thither. Here he took an active part in public affairs. He was one of the founders of the first church in that town in 1711. He died Feb. 7, 1736. His wife died very aged, Dec. 19, 1758. He was the father of ten children. His sons, Elisha, Solomon and John, were ministers. The two former were leaders of the Newlights in Connecticut, and distinguished preachers of that denomination. Among his descendants is the author of "Cape Cod Folks."

Deacon John Paine, the fourth son, settled in that part of Eastham, now Orleans. He was a prominent man in the town. He succeeded his brother Thomas as clerk in 1701, and held the office until ill health compelled him to decline an election in 1730. He was several years selectman and seven years representative to the General court. He was treasurer of the town for more than thirty years, being first elected in 1696. He was twice married, and father of thirteen children. His first wife, Benner, was daughter of Major John Freeman. He died in 1731. He was great-grandfather of John Howard Paine, author of "Home, Sweet Home." His descendants are widely scattered. He was of a literary turn of mind, and some of his spare moments were devoted to literary pursuits. A portion of a diary kept by him in which are entries as early as 1695 and 1717, is yet extant.

Nicholas Paine, the fifth son, married Hannah Higgins, daughter of Jonathan, and settled at Keaskakogansett. He was a miller and farmer, and had not much to do with public affairs. He died in the autumn of 1733. He was the father of seven children. His only son, Philip, died unmarried, April 10, 1725, aged 20 years and 5 months. Hannah, his mother, died Jan. 24, 1731-2. He had his father's place and a large share of his property.

James Paine, the sixth son, born July 6, 1665, married Bethiah, daughter of Col. John Thacher of Yarmouth, April 9, 1691. He went to Barnstable to reside in 1689. He was a school teacher, miller, cooper and clerk. He was in Captain John Gorham's company at the expedition against Canada in 1691, as "clerk." For his services, his heirs in 1736 received a grant of land in Maine. He was the first clerk of the East precinct or parish in Barnstable. He died at Barnstable, Nov. 12, 1718, and lies buried in the old cemetery, where a headstone marks the spot; he also was a man of a literary turn of mind. He was a member of the Barnstable church. He had seven children. Thomas, his only son, was educated at Harvard college, graduating in 1711. He married Eunice Treat, and had Robert Treat Paine, the distinguished lawyer, who signed the Declaration of Independence and was the first attorney general of Massachusetts under the Constitution. Mr. James Paine resided, at his death, in the house now occupied by Mr. Gray in Barnstable. It was built for Mr. Paine in 1717. The frame was cut in Scituate. Dr. Samuel Savage bought it in, or about, 1776, of Mr. Paine's heirs.

Joseph Paine, the seventh and youngest son, married Patience Sparrow, daughter of Jonathan Sparrow of Eastham, May 27, 1691. He removed from Eastham to Harwich, now Brewster, before 1700. He was one of the founders of the Brewster church,

Oct. 17, 1700. He was selectman of the town in 1701, and by successive elections until 1711. He was chosen town clerk in 1706, and annually chosen until his death, Oct. 1, 1712. He appears to have enjoyed athletic feats in his youthful days. His nephew in his journal says: "He was very stout, and flung Col. Thacher, the Champion of Bay State, at Commencement." He was an exemplary member of the church. His wife was a granddaughter of Gov. Prence. She married for her second husband, John Jenkins of Barnstable in 1715; she died Oct. 28, 1745. Joseph Paine was the father of eleven children. Prof. John K. Paine of Harvard college is a descendant. Most of his descendants are in Maine.

JOSEPH COLLINS.

Joseph Collins was the first of the name in Eastham. Of his ancestry the writer knows nothing of certainty. Some writers have it that he was from Lynn and son of Henry Collins, a starch maker of that place, who came from Ireland, but fail to give authority for their statements. He married Ruth, (not Duty Knowles, as is given by some writers) daughter of Richard Knowles, March 20, 1672. He died at Eastham about 1724. He appears to have been married twice. He mentions Sarah as his wife, in his will in 1723. He was a member of the North church in Eastham, and ordered that his "dragon table-cloth be delivered to the deacons for the use of the church." He had nine children, viz: Sarah, John, Lydia, Joseph, Hannah, Jonathan, Jane, Benjamin and James.

John Collins, his eldest son, born in Eastham Dec. 18, 1674, married Hannah Doane, daughter of John Doane, Jr., Feb. 22, 1701-2, and settled in what is now Wellfleet, having had land laid out to him there in 1698. He removed to Chatham, where he resided till his death, May 24, 1765, in the 92nd year of his age. His grave is marked in the old cemetery at Chatham by a half-sunken slate stone with inscription. He was a man of importance in Chatham. Most of his children were doubtless born in Eastham. They were Solomon, Samuel, Martha, who married Moses Godfrey, John, Hannah, Joseph, David, Jane and Anna. Hannah, wife of

John Collins, died June 6, 1765, aged 85. From John Collins descended Hon. Enos Collins, a distinguished merchant, who died in Liverpool, Nova Scotia, 1871, aged 97 years, very wealthy. His wife was daughter of the late Sir Brenton Haliburton, chief justice of Nova Scotia.

Joseph Collins, fourth child and second son of Joseph Collins, married Rebecca Sparrow, March 25, 1703. He had children. His oldest child, Lois, was born in 1704.

Jonathan Collins, born Aug. 20, 1682, and third son, married Elizabeth Vickery, probably daughter of Rev. Jonathan Vickery, some time preacher at Chatham. He settled in Truro.

Benjamin Collins, born Feb. 1, 1687, married and settled in Truro, where he died Dec. 23, 1756. He had nine children recorded.

Joseph Collins, Sen., the progenitor of the Cape family, had land granted him by the town. In 1681, he had twelve acres laid out near "Spactacle Pond." He is not much mentioned in the records of Eastham as taking active part in town affairs. He was several times juror, and in 1700 constable of the town.

THOMAS BILLS.

Thomas Bills was an early resident of Eastham. He married Anne Twinning, Oct. 3, 1672, for his first wife. She died at Eastham Sept. 1, 1675. For his second wife he married Joanna Twinning, probably her sister, May 2, 1676. By both wives he had: Anna, Elizabeth, Nathaniel, Mary, Mehitabel, Thomas, Gershom, Joanna, all born in Eastham. He had land granted him at various times in Eastham. He had, with several others in 1681, the "dry swamp" granted him, provided it was cleared within six years. The "dry swamp," it is understood, is the swamp northeast of the meetinghouse in Orleans, now mostly covered with cranberry vines. It is not known that he and his partners attempted to clear off the brush. He removed to the west side of Bass river, within the present town of Yarmouth, sometime about 1690, near the house of his brother-in-law, Francis Baker, who had also resided in Eastham. He was alive in 1693, and witnessed the will of Francis Baker. The time of his death is unknown, no male descendants in the country bearing the surname. His place of residence in Eastham was in that part now East Orleans. His eldest daughter, Anna, born in 1673, married David O. Kelley of Yarmouth, March 10, 1692.

HENRY ATKINS.

Henry Atkins came from Plymouth to Eastham sometime before 1655. He was a quiet man, and had but little to do with town affairs. He doubtless was engaged in tilling the soil. He bought much of his real estate in Eastham of Mr. John Mayo, who for awhile was a resident of Eastham and engaged in ministerial work. The town confirmed his purchase of a lot of 5 acres lying near John Mayo, Jr., which he had purchased of Mr. Mayo April 21, 1659; also at the same date confirmed his purchase of 4 acres of cedar swamp of Mr. Mayo, and a lot of meadow at the harbor's mouth toward Rock harbor. His other purchases, a piece of meadow at Great Meadow, and Boat Meadow, were confirmed April 25th, the same year. He was twice married. His first wife, it is said, was Elizabeth Wells, who died at Eastham in 1662. His second wife was Bethiah Linnell, to whom he was married, say the Eastham records, March 25, 1664. By his wife Elizabeth he had Mary, born at Plymouth March 13, 1647, who died young. By his wife Bethia he had Isaac, born in Eastham June 15, 1657; Desire, born May 7, 1665; John, born Dec. 15, 1666, who died in infancy; Nathaniel, born Dec. 25, 1667; Joseph, May 4, 1669; Thomas, June 19, 1671; John, Aug. 1, 1674; Mary, Nov. 24, 1676; Samuel, June 25, 1679. Henry Atkins died in 1700. His widow married Stephen Hopkins, and with him removed to Harwich, that part now Brewster, where she died March 25, 1726.

Mr. Atkins made his will. It was witnessed by Samuel Treat and Jonathan Sparrow. It was proved Oct. 13, 1700. His estate was valued at £181 11s. The inventory was presented in August, 1700. He desired to be buried in "ye burying at Eastham." He remembered his children in his will, but did not give each a great sum. Wife Bethia was named as executrix of his will.

Mr. Atkins's eldest son, Samuel, fell in the war with the Indians, June 4, 1675, and he named his youngest son Samuel, who was born four years after the death of the eldest son.

Isaac Atkins settled in Harwich, where he died in 1729, leaving a son, Samuel. Joseph Atkins, his brother, married and settled in Eastham, where he had eight children. Nathaniel Atkins married and settled in Truro, where he had six children. Thomas Atkins removed to Chatham before 1700, where he died, leaving children. John Atkins married at Edgartown Elizabeth Newcomb, and settled in Chatham, where he died in 1733, leaving no issue. Samuel Atkins married Emblem Newcomb of Edgartown, and settled in Chatham, leaving issue.

No. 33.

LIBRARY *of* Cape Cod
HISTORY & GENEALOGY

FOUNDERS' DAY EDITION
AUGUST 26, 1916.
of the
EARLY SETTLERS OF EASTHAM
Containing Sketches of all Early Settlers of Eastham
By Josiah Paine, Esq., of Harwich

IN TWO NUMBERS: BOOK 1

Book 1: Thomas Prence, Nicholas Snow, John Doane, Edward Bangs, Richard Higgins, John Smalley, Samuel Hicks, John Jenkins, Robert Wixon, Josiah Cooke, Joseph Rogers, John Freeman, John Mayo, Thomas Williams, Thomas Roberts; 32p.

Book 2: Richard Knowles, Richard Sparrow, Job Cole, Daniel Cole, Giles Hopkins, Ralph Smith, William Walker, William Merrick, Richard Bishop, William Sutton, William Twinning, George Crisp, Richard Rich, John Young, Thomas Paine, Joseph Collins, Thomas Bills, Henry Atkins; 31 pages.

YARMOUTHPORT, MASS.:
C. W. SWIFT, Publisher and Printer,
The "Register" Press,
1916.

EARLY SETTLERS OF EASTHAM.

By Josiah Paine of Harwich.

EASTHAM.

Eastham was the fourth town settled on the Cape. The first settlers were principally from Plymouth, and were persons of character. Pratt, in his history of the town, and those who have written subsequently about its history, state that the settlement began in April, 1644. The authority for the statement is not given. Dr. James Freeman's historical account, in the eighth volume of the collections of the Massachusetts Historical Society, from which Mr. Pratt obtained much of his information for his work, and the Old Colony Records as printed, do not sustain the statement. The evidence is conclusive that at the period Pratt mentions, no white person had attempted a settlement within what was afterwards the township of Nausett or Eastham. From the best authorities, it appears, the first purchase of the Indians was made in June, 1644, by a committee of the Plymouth church, consisting of "Mr William Bradford, Mr. Thomas Prence and divers others," and confirmed unto the Church of New Plymouth or "those that go to dwell at Nausett," March 3, 1644-5.

It was the intention of the Plymouth church when they sent out the committee to make a thorough survey of the territory at Nausett, if found sufficiently large for their accommodation, to remove in a body. But as the committee found the place not large enough to accommodate the whole church, "much less to afford room for future increase," it was judged not proper to remove in a body. Liberty was given, however, to such members as were desirous of going to attempt a settlement, provided they agreed to pay for the purchase which had been made in the name of the church.

The territory purchased of the Indians, for which they paid "moose-skins, Indian boats, wampam, little knives," etc., embraced the greater part of Orleans and the towns of Eastham and Wellfleet. The deed from the Indians, confirmatory of the purchase, was given Nov. 9th, 1666.

How long after the grant, March 3rd, 1644-5, that Gov. Prence, John Doane, Nicholas Snow, Joshiah Cook, Richard Higgins, John Smalley and Edward Bangs, the pioneers, went thither to locate, it is not certain, but doubtless not long, as by the Court records of Plymouth Colony, under the date of June 2nd, 1646, we find "Nausett is granted to be a township, and to have all the privileges of a township as other towns within the government have," and Samuel Hicks, constable of the place, the only person reported as an officer of the town.

Nausett is an Indian name and was applied to some particular locality in the present town of Eastham by the aborigines. Our forefathers gave the name to the whole purchase, and so it was called until 1651, when for some unassigned cause, the court at Plymouth promulgated an order that henceforth Nausett should be known as Eastham. That order has never been revoked, though the ancient township has been shorn of territory both on the north and south. The good old Indian name, however, has never been allowed to be forgotten, nor will it be, so long as the beach and harbor, bearing the name, remain. Long before the Pilgrims set feet upon its soil, Nausett was known, and the Indians inhabiting the regions about the famous place had become acquainted with the white man and had suffered from his hands. It is doubtless true that the "First Encounter" the Pilgrims had in 1620, near the Great pond in the present town of Eastham, was on the part of the Indians to gratify feelings of revenge which had been engendered by the perfidy of Hunt, in the employ of Captain John Smith, by entrapping the natives and carrying them off to Spain and selling them. Aspinet was the first sachem of the Nausett tribe known to the English. He did not survive long after the Pilgrims had settled at Plymouth. He joined the conspiracy in 1623 to extirpate the English, but the death of the principal conspirators at the hands of Captain Standish so terrified him that he lived concealed in unhealthy places and died from disease there contracted.

2

THE SETTLERS.
THOMAS PRENCE.

Thomas Prence was the most distinguished of the settlers of Eastham, though not the best educated. At the time of his removal in 1645, he was holding the position of an assistant to Gov. Bradford, and had twice been chosen governor of the infant colony —first election in 1634, and second election in 1638. He was a native of Lechlade, a parish in Gloucestershire, England, it is understood, and born about the year 1600. He came to Plymouth in the ship Fortune, in November, 1621. At the time of his removal he was residing in Duxbury. His farm at Eastham contained many acres. It was situated northwest of Town cove, in that part now included within the present town of Eastham. His house stood on the east side of the county road, near where Mr. E. Doane's house now stands. It is said his farm comprised the "richest land" in the place. The famous old pear tree planted by him while a resident, and which was blown down in 1849, stood but a few rods westward from the site of his house. He was a large land-owner. He owned land in what became afterwards Harwich and Truro, besides tracts at Tonset and other localities in the Colony. He disposed of most of his landed estate before his death. His tracts at Sauquatucket, now Brewster, which came to him by grant, on the account of having been a "Purchaser or Old-Comer," he sold to his son-in-law, Major John Freeman, in 1672. His "half share" at Paumet, both "purchased and unpurchased," lying between "Bound Brook," at Wellfleet, and "Eastern Harbor or Lovell's Creek," he sold to Mr. Thomas Paine in 1670.

Mr. Pratt, in his History of Eastham, says the homestead of Gov. Prence was given by will to his son-in-law, Samuel Freeman, but the statement is not supported by documentary evidence. Records show that Gov. Prence did sell to his "beloved son-in-law, Mr. Samuel Freeman, Jan. 12, 1671, for thirty pounds" his "house lot situated and being in the town of Eastham" and "containing eighteen acres of upland, be it more or less," bounded "at the northeasterly end" by a creek, together with other upland and meadows in other parts of the town. Records also show that Gov. Prence provided a place of abode for his son-in-law, Samuel

Freeman and Mercy his wife, soon after their marriage, and that in December, 1662, it was conveyed to them. They were then residing upon it. It was the place the governor purchased of Mr. Josiah Cook, a "gentleman" of Eastham. The position of this house lot the writer cannot give, but undoubtedly it was near Gov. Prence's place.

Gov. Prence continued in the office of an assistant by successive elections till 1657, when he was unanimously elected to the office of governor, as successor to Gov. Bradford, who died that year. As the law required the governor to reside at the seat of government, a dispensation was obtained for him, and he was allowed to remain at Eastham, as he desired. Mrs. Bradford was engaged to entertain him and his assistants while at Court; an attendant was appointed to attend him in his journey to and from Plymouth, and Mr. Allyn of Barnstable was engaged to accommodate him and his attendant in his house with private rooms when passing "to and fro." In 1665, Gov. Prence removed to Plymouth, and occupied the place provided by the government at a place called Plain Dealing, which the late Judge John Davis, a native of Plymouth, says was "nearly two miles from the centre of the town on the road to Boston." The late William Russell in his Guide to Plymouth, says the place called Plain Dealing "extended it is believed to Kingston line"; and that Gov. Prence's house was near "Mr. Hedges," and in the vicinity of "Starts Hill." At this place, while occupying the gubernatorial chair, he died March 29, 1673, in his 73d year. He was "honorably interred at Plymouth, April 8th." Judge Davis says: "The Plymouth church records, in expressing Mr. Prence's character and his amiable and pleasant conversation, depart from their usual course by an indication of his personal appearance, from which it may be supposed that it was peculiarly dignified and striking. He was excellently qualified for the office of governor. He had a countenance full of majesty, and therein, as well as otherwise, was a terror to evil doers. Besides holding the office of governor, Mr. Prence was a great number of years an assistant of Gov. Bradford. He was one of the commissioners of the United Colonies many years; colonial treasurer and one of the council of war. He

4

was one of those who stood bound to the adventures for the payment of the sum they demanded for their interest in the stock, trade, etc., of the Colony, when the purchase was made in behalf of those who came in the three first ships, viz: Mayflower, Fortune and Ann.

The first marriage of Gov. Prence was with Patience, daughter of Mr. William Brewster, the elder of the Plymouth church, who came in the Mayflower in 1620. It occurred August 5, 1624, and was the ninth marriage in Plymouth Colony, according to the accurate chronologist, the Rev. Thomas Prince. Miss Patience Brewster did not come over in the Mayflower, with her father, but deferred her coming till 1623, when with her sister, Fear, she arrived in the Ann. Mrs. Patience (Brewster) Prence, it is reported, died in 1634, leaving children. Among them it is certain, were Thomas, Rebecca, Mercy and Hannah. The governor again united in marriage with Mary Collier, according to the Old Colony records, April 1, 1635. It has been asserted that he was subsequently married, but there appears no conclusive proof of the fact. The assertion rests upon two significant declarations which are yet inexplicable. First, the declaration of Gov. Prence in 1662 and 1671 that Samuel Freeman of Eastham was his "beloved son-in-law," and secondly, upon the injunction of Captain Thomas Howes of Yarmouth, in 1676, upon going forth in the expedition to the Narraganset country to fight the Indians, to allow "Mother Prence to enjoy without molestation, during her natural life, the house she now lives in."

The births of the children of Gov. Prence, by his wives Patience and Mary, are not recorded either at Plymouth or Eastham. Besides those already mentioned, viz: Thomas, Rebecca, Mercy and Hannah, his children were (though we know not the order of their nativity), Jane, Mary, Judith, Sarah and Elizabeth. Thomas was born before 1627 and went to England early, where he died. He left a widow and a daughter, Susanah. Rebecca, also born before 1627, married Edmond Freeman, Jr., of Sandwich, April 22, 1646, who died soon after. Mercy, born about 1631, married John Freeman of Sandwich, Feb. 13, 1649-50, and settled at Eastham, where she died Sept. 28, 1711, aged 80 years. Hannah married first, Nat. Mayo of Eastham, Feb. 13, 1649-50; second, Captain Jonathan Sparrow of Eastham. Jane, born November, 1637, married Mark Snow of Eastham, Jan. 9, 1660; she died in Harwich, now Brewster, in 1712. Mary married John Tracy of Duxbury. Judith married Isaac Barker of Duxbury, Dec. 28, 1665. Sarah, born in Eastham about 1646, married Jeremiah Howes of Yarmouth and died, according to grave stone, in 1706, aged 60 years. Elizabeth married Arthur Howland, Jr., of Marshfield, a son of a Quaker, much against the feelings of the puritanical governor, Dec. 9, 1667.

Soon after the death of Gov. Prence, the widow removed to that part of Yarmouth now North Dennis, and occupied a house belonging wholly or in part to Captain Thomas Howes, brother of Jeremiah Howes, who married Sarah Prence. Here she died. The Yarmouth book of records has this entry respecting her death: "Mrs Mary Prence wife of the late Governor Thomas Prence, died upon the ninth day of December, 1695, and was buried upon the eleventh day of ye said 1695.' It is not known where she was interred; if at Yarmouth, doubtless in the old Howes Yard at North Dennis.

Gov. Prence's will bears date March 13th, 1673, and codicil March 28th, 1673. He appointed his wife, Mary, executrix, and desired that his brother, Thomas Clark, and Mr. Josiah Winslow be her advisers. To his wife Mary, he gave the profits of his part of the mill at Sauquatuckett, now West Brewster, with the land adjacent to it, which he desired at her death to go to his grandson, Theophilus Mayo, who was living with him. This, he said, he gave him for his encouragement to proceed in learning. He also gave him all his "books fit for him in learning." He enjoined him to "carry it well with his grandmother," and, in case he did so, to have a "bed." How dutiful he was to his aged grandparent, we have no means of knowing. He doubtless removed with her to Yarmouth. From what can now be gathered he did not survive her. His death, it is supposed, took place about 1678. He was the youngest son of Nathaniel and Hannah (Prence) Mayo, and it would seem, at the death of his father, was taken by the governor into his family. The governor also gave him one-half of his land and meadow near Namassakett, in Middleboro, which if he died without descendants, would be equally divided between Gov. Prence's daughters. Of his books he gave, among others, "to Maj John Freeman, of Eastham, Speeds', Church's and Wilson's Dictionary; Simpson's History of the Church, and Newman's Concordance." He made other bequests, but we cannot mention them all.

The inventory of the governor's estate shows he owned on the Cape, "one fourth of the mill and land adjoining to it at Satuckett," now West Brewster; twenty acres of land and three acres of meadow at Tonsett in Eastham, and eighteen acres on Porchy Island. Before his death Gov. Prence disposed of most of his estate by deeds. Thomas Prence's descendants are numerous upon the Cape. Thomas Prence, the only son of the governor, died in England, leaving no sons, consequently he has no descendants of the patronymic living.

NICHOLAS SNOW.

Nicholas Snow, one of the first seven who settled at Nausett, was a man of sterling worth and very prominent in the settlement. He came over from England, a passenger in the Ann, in the latter part of July, 1623, and at first located in the township of Plymouth, where he soon married. The Ann brought over many of the near relatives of the Pilgrims, besides quite a number of other passengers to settle with them, among whom might be mentioned Thomas Clarke, Anthony Anable, Edward Bangs, Experience Michell and George Morton. The settlers of Plymouth at the arrival of Nicholas Snow and other passengers of the Ann, were sadly destitute, not only of apparel, but of food to eat. The new comers were "diversely affected" to behold "their low and poor condition." "The best dish," says Bradford, the renowned leader of that settlement, "they could present their friends with was a lobster or a piece of fish without bread or anything else but a cup of fair spring water." Bradford farther says, "Some of the passengers wished themselves in England again; others fell aweeping, fancying their own misery in what they saw now in others; some pitying the distress they saw their friends had been

7

long in and still were under; in a word, all were full of sadness." In this ship it may be well to state, came Mrs. Alice Southworth, to become the wife of the renowned leader, and they were married shortly after.

What were the feelings of the subject of this sketch upon knowing the sufferings of these poor ragged and half-fed Pilgrims, we are not told, but from what we can gather relative to the character of the man, we are led to believe he regretted their condition, cheerfully lent them a helping hand and prayed for better times, which, according to both Bradford and Morton, came at harvest time.

Nicholas Snow, not long after his arrival, became acquainted with Miss "Constanta" or Constance, an elder daughter of Mr. Stephen Hopkins, who had but a few years before braved the dangers of the Atlantic in the Mayflower and escaped the first winter's distress, and took her for his wife, who, before 1650, had borne him twelve children, all then alive. The date of his marriage does not appear; but he was married before 1627, as by the record of the division of the cattle, May 22nd, he and his wife Constance received their share, they belonging to Mr. Stephen Hopkins' company, which was composed of thirteen persons. In 1633 he was a freeman and a tax payer in Plymouth. The following year, with Edward Bangs, he was appointed to lay out roads in Plymouth. In 1636, he was one of the arbitrators to settle the difficulty between Joseph Beadle and Edward Dowty. In 1638, he was one of the jurors appointed to investigate the cause of the death of John England, a lad found dead on Plymouth flats. In 1640, he was one of the surveyors of highways at Plymouth. In 1645, with Gov. Prence, Josiah Cooke and others, he removed to Nausett; and when that place became a municipality, to him was assigned the duties of town clerk, an office he held until about 1663, when his son Mark succeeded him. He was surveyor of highways at Eastham in 1647; a deputy to the Colony court in 1648, also 1650-52-57. He was a selectman in 1668-71-72-74-75. He also held other offices in town. His death occurred at Eastham, according to the records of that town, November 15th, 1676. His will bears the date November 14th, 1676. It was witnessed by his pastor, Mr. Samuel Treat, and his son-in-law, Thomas Paine, Sen. His wife, Constance, survived him and died in October, 1677. The settlement of the estate he entrusted to his fellow townsmen, Deacon Samuel Freeman and John Mayo. He remembered the Eastham church and left a small sum towards furnishing "the furniture of the table of the Lord with pewter or otherwise."

The children of Mr. Snow are not recorded, and consequently the names cannot all be given. Gov. Bradford says he had twelve children in 1650, all alive. He mentions no daughters in his will, though it is certain he had several then alive. His sons mentioned were Mark, Joseph, Stephen, John and Jabez. He was a large land owner. He had land in Harwich, Eastham and Truro. Mark, Joseph and Stephen came into possession of his landed estate in Harwich, then Satucket; John, of that in Paomet, now Truro, and Jabez of that in Eastham, including the homestead. His "moveable goods," at his wife's decease, he ordered divided among all his children equally. His residence was in that part now Eastham, not far from Gov. Prence's homestead, as far as it can be ascertained from the records. He undoubtedly was buried in the old yard at Eastham, though no stone with inscription marks the place. His son Mark, who married Gov. Prence's daughter Jane, and his son-in-law, Mr. Thomas Paine, were distinguished men in their day. The descendants of Mr. Nicholas Snow are numerous, and an effort by them should be made to erect a monument to his memory in the old yard, that the future generations may know where their Pilgrim ancestor lies buried.

JOHN DOANE.

Mr. John Doane was the eldest of the seven first settlers, and undoubtedly next in rank to Gov. Prence. They were the only persons of that band whom the records of that period honor with the prefix of Mister, which in those days was only given to men of means, magistrates and ministers. At what time he arrived at Plymouth, it does not appear. Mr. Pratt, the Eastham historian, was certain he came over in one of the three first ships, his authority he does not state. This, however, is certain:

he did not come over in the Mayflower, Fortune or Ann. His name appears as a freeman and tax payer at Plymouth in 1633, and that year is mentioned as being with Mr. Wm. Bradford, Capt. Miles Standish, Mr. John Howland, Mr. John Alden, Mr. Stephen Hopkins and Mr. Wm. Gilson, an assistant of Gov. Edward Winslow; but having been chosen deacon in the church at Plymouth, "at the request of the church and himself, was freed from the office of assistant in the Commonweale," January 2, 1633-4. In 1633, with others, he was appointed to divide meadow at Plymouth. He is also mentioned in the records as presenting the inventory of the estate of Martha Harding, Oct. 28, 1633, who in behalf of her son, was appointed administrator. In 1635, at the July court, the Colony agreed "to build a mill" at Plymouth, and a committee consisting of Capt. Miles Standish, Mr. Collier, Mr John Doane and John Winslow, was "appointed to collect, etc., money for the building of the same," and to engage the workmen. In 1636, December 24, he sold his house and land at Plain Dealing, which he held in common with John Atwood, late of London, for £60. In 1637, June 7th, the court was called upon to regulate the trade in "beaver, corn, beads," etc., which was "likely to go to decay," and "Mr. Doane," with others, was appointed to aid the governor and council in considering the way to regulate it. In 1637, he had land granted him near his house, also one hundred acres granted him at Jones river, in Plymouth. This year, he was appointed by the court, with others, to view and lay out hay ground between Eel river and South river, at Plymouth. With Nicholas Snow, Richard Burne, Richard Sparrow, Josiah Cooke, John Smalley, "honest and lawful men," and others, whose names we omit, he examined into the cause of the death of a lad found dead on the flats near Plymouth. In 1639, he was again allowed "to draw wine" at Plymouth; and appointed, with three others, to assist the governor and council to revise the laws of the Colony, which was the first revision since the settlement of the Pilgrims at Plymouth. In 1640, "Mr. John Doane" was of the Grand Inquest, and a deputy for Plymouth in 1642-43. In November, 1644, he was licensed "to draw wine" at Plymouth, but in January, 1644-45, the court agreed to allow James Cole, the

10

keeper of the ordinary or tavern at Plymouth, to take the wine Mr. Doane had on hand. It is evident that Mr. Doane was closing up his business in Plymouth, in view of the removal to Nausett of himself and family. It will thus be seen by these transactions, that Mr. Doane did not go to Eastham to settle in 1643 or 1644, as many of our local historians have stated, but in 1645 (N. S.) as we have heretofore stated, upon authority of the Colony records.

Mr. Doane was appointed, March 3rd, 1644-5, with others, to take the account of the colonial treasurer under consideration, in order for the annual settlement. In 1649, "Mr John Doane" and his son-in-law, Samuel Hicks, were deputies from Nausett or Eastham to the Plymouth court. He was also elected in 1650, 1651, 1653 and 1659. In 1663, he was appointed by the Colony court to solemnize marriages, administer oaths to witnesses, etc., in Eastham.

Mr. Doane held other offices in town and colony. Mr. Pratt, and other historical writers, say he was fourteen years selectman, but they are not sustained in their statement by the Colony records. The office of selectman was created in 1663. The first notice in the Colony records of those chosen in Eastham was in 1666, next in 1668, and then in 1670. After this date they are noticed regularly for many years. Mr. Doane's name is not among them. Possibly he held the office, but it is certain he did not hold it that period of time. In 1663, Mr. Doane was seventy-two years of age, and if their statements are correct, Mr. Doane was near eighty-four years of age when he retired from the board.

Although Mr. John Doane was not one of the purchasers or old comers, yet he was a large land owner. At various periods he had land granted him by the court. In 1657, with Josiah Cooke, Richard Higgins, Richard Sparrow and John Smalley, he had land granted him between Bridgewater and Weymouth; in 1666, a tract of one hundred acres in "Potonumequot Neck;" and in 1681, sixty acres "out of land that was Mauamwed or Takamanuckes, if to be had there." This appears to have been the last grant from the Colonial court.

Mr. Doane, it is understood, settled to the north of Town Cove, in the present town of Eastham, where the site of his house is pointed out, and stone monuments erected by him are to be seen upon land he formerly owned and occupied. Mr Pratt, in his history of Eastham, published in 1844, says Mr. Doane "took possession of about two hundred acres" in the vicinity, and that his house stood "near the water, and the remains of the cellar" were then visible.

Rev. Mr. Pratt says, Mr. Doane "was forty-nine years old when he came here, and lived sixty years afterwards, being one hundred and ten years old when he died, in 1707." Upon what authority he makes the statements we do not know, but it is clearly evident they are unreliable. Mr. Doane, May 18, 1678, declared his age to be "88 or thereabouts," which shows he was born about 1590. Consequently, in 1645, when he came to Eastham, he was not far from fifty-five years of age. Mr. Doane, it is certain, died in 1686, having lived here about forty-one years, and not sixty-four, as Mr. Pratt has it. If Mr. Doane's statement made in 1678 is reliable, at his death in 1686 he was about ninety-six years of age. Tradition, says Mr. Pratt, in 1844, has it, "that he was rocked in a cradle several of his last years."

He made his will May 18, 1678. It was presented to probate June 2, 1686. His wife mentioned was Abigail. Whether she was the mother of his children or not, the writer has not been able to ascertain satisfactorily. They, too, were undoubtedly interred in the old cemetery at Eastham. No correct record of the children of Mr. John Doane appears; but it is certain he had Abigail, Lydia, John, Daniel and Ephraim. From these three sons have descended the Doanes of the Cape, Connecticut, Ohio, and of other places in the United States.

EDWARD BANGS.

Edward Bangs, one of the seven who began the settlement at Nausett in 1645, came over from England in the Ann in 1623, a fellow passenger with Nicholas Snow, whom we have already noticed. At this period he was about thirty-two years of age, but whether a married or single man is not positively known. In the beginning of the year 1624, it having been decided to allow each person who came over in the first three ships, one acre apiece to be laid out near the settlement as possible, for planting land, which each was to use for seven years, the records show that "Bangs" was assigned four acres "towards Eel River," while Nicholas Snow was allowed the use of one acre. From this fact, it has been supposed Mr. Bangs was a married man with children at this early date. Mr. Bangs is mentioned in the records as being of John Jenney's company, which numbered thirteen persons, and to which "the twelfth lot" of cattle fell at the division, May 22, 1627. To this company "fell," says the record, "the great white back cow, which was brought over with the first in the Ann." Both Bradford and Morton say the first neat cattle were brought over in the year 1624.

It having been decided at a court, Jan. 3rd, 1627-8, to allow every person twenty acres of land, besides the land each person had already, and Mr. Bangs, with Gov. Bradford, Edward Winslow, John Howland, Francis Cook and Joshua Pratt, was chosen with instructions to lay out the land near the water on both sides of the settlement, and to lay the lots out "5 acres in breadth by the water side, and 4 acres in length." These twenty acres laid out for each person were for tillage. At this period, no meadow ground had been divided in Plymouth. Each year the planters were shown where to cut their hay and how much, by men appointed. They now continued the same rules relative to this matter, which were satisfactory.

Mr. Bangs was a tax payer in Plymouth, March 25, 1633, and his tax is put down as twelve shillings. The same year, with Mr. John Doane, he was appointed to divide meadow, and in 1634, with Nicholas Snow and others, to lay out roads at Plymouth. In 1634 and 1635, he was one of the assessors of Plymouth. In 1637, "for Eel River" he was appointed one of the committee to view the hay ground and assist in laying it out. Among others appointed with him were Mr. Wm. Brewster, Mr. Stephen Hopkins, Mr. John Doane of Plymouth, and Jonathan Brewster of Duxbury. He was one of the grand jury the same year, also in 1638 and 1640. In 1639, he was an arbitrator to settle a case between Samuel Gorton and Thomas Clark. In 1642, he was employed to superintend the building of a barque at Plymouth, to which he

13

contributed one-sixteenth part of the amount raised for its construction. This vessel is supposed to have been the first built in the Colony.

Mr. Bangs was the first treasurer of Eastham, after the settlement in 1645. He was a surveyor of highways in 1647, 1650 and 1651, and perhaps a deputy to the court in 1652, which year he was also of the Grand Inquest. In 1657, he was allowed "to draw wine" and strong water at Eastham, with instructions not to sell to the Indians. In 1658, he agreed to find "2 horses and 2 men for the country's service," upon the town providing "sufficient furniture for them." In 1659, he "promised freely" to find "a man and horse with complete furniture, for the term of one year for the country's service." Upon an order of the court to appoint overseers of the poor, with Nicholas Snow and Richard Higgins, he was appointed for Eastham in 1659. After this he took but little interest in public matters.

Whether Mr. Bangs was more than once married, it is impossible to determine. His wife, in 1651, was called Rebecca. If she were his only wife, she was a daughter of Robert Hicks, who died at Scituate in 1647, as he mentions his grandson, John Bangs, in his will, which would indicate that John Bangs' mother was a daughter, and that she had been or was the wife of Edward Bangs.

Mr. Bangs died at Eastham, about the last of February in the year 1677-8, at the age of about 86 years, leaving no wife. His will, a lengthy document, in which he makes known his age, bears date Oct. 19, 1677. It was presented for proof at Plymouth, March 5, 1677-8, Mr. John Freeman and Mr. Thomas Crosby upon oath, testifying as to its being his last will. Mr. Bangs' younger son, Jonathan, was appointed the "whole and sole executor," who, it would appear, was somewhat of a favorite with his father, from whose hands he received a good share of his landed estate, which was considerable, he having been of that favored number called "Purchasers or Old Comers." Mr. Bangs undoubtedly resided with Jonathan the last years of his life.

The children of Edward Bangs, as far as can be ascertained, were John, Joshua, Jonathan, Rebecca, Sarah, Lydia, Hannah,

Bethiah, Apphia and Mercy. John and Joshua were married but left no descendants. Jonathan settled finally in Harwich, where he died in 1728. He had three wives and twelve children. From him have descended all the Bangses in the United States, it is supposed. He was a prominent man in his day, and died at the age of 88. From his daughter, Tamsin Burgess, descended that distinguished orator, the late Tristam Burgess of Providence.

JOSIAH COOKE.

Josiah Cooke was born in England in or about the year 1610, and it appears was a servant to some one of the early planters of Plymouth during his minority. The first notice of him that appears upon the records is under the date of Jan. 2, 1633-4, when he and Edward Dowty were before the court at Plymouth to answer for a breach of the peace in having a fracas, in which Mr. Cooke was roughly handled. They were both amerced in the sum of six shillings, although "Dowty drew blood from sd Josias." Dowty had been the servant of Mr. Stephen Hopkins, and was one of those who came over in the Mayflower. He seems to have been a very passionate man, and fond of settling difficulties without due recourse to law. Between Dowty and Lester, the first duel in New England was fought. Lester was also a servant of Mr. Hopkins. They fought with sword and dagger, and both were wounded. This occurred June 15, 1622. They were both punished for the offence, but not so severely as was intended, on account of their master's humble plea in their behalf, and they promised to reform, after being tied head and foot an hour.

In 1638, Mr. Cooke was living in Plymouth, and had forty acres of land granted him on the north side of Fresh lake and also made a purchase of land of Mr. Stephen Hopkins. He was this year one of the grand jurors, and one of those appointed to examine into the cause of the death of John England. In 1640, he was surveyor for Plymouth, and in 1641 and 1642, constable. In 1645 he went to Nausett, and in 1647 was a deputy to the Colony court from that place. He was a deputy or representative in 1651, 1652, 1658, 1659, 1661, 1662, 1663, 1664, 1666 and 1671. In 1648, he was surveyor at Nausett, and that year appointed to

15

sell wine, and to be a "Register Keeper." Mr. Cooke was a grand juror for Eastham in 1656, and a selectman in 1666 and 1671. In 1664 he was appointed to solemnize marriages in Eastham, succeeding Mr. John Doane. He was one of the Colonial auditors in 1659 and 1661. He was one of the five chosen by the town of Eastham "to survey all the lands granted or laid out to the several inhabitants of the township" in 1659. As Mr. Cooke was not one of those called Purchasers or Old Comers, he was often favored by special grants from the court, of land in various parts of the Colony, upon his application. In 1658, with Mr. John Doane, Richard Higgins, Richard Sparrow and John Smalley, he had land granted between Bridgewater and Weymouth. In 1662, as one of the old servants, he had land allowed him. In 1665, he had a large tract granted him at Eastham, in that part now South Orleans but then known as Pottonumequot, which he purchased of the Indians the same year, and in 1669 exchanged it for land in another part of the town, with Major John Freeman. It was upon this tract the first settlement in this part of Eastham was attempted.

He married, September 16, 1635, Mrs. Elizabeth Deane, widow of Stephen Deane, an early resident of Plymouth, who came in the Ann, in 1623, and had Ann, who married Mark Snow; Josiah, who married Deborah Hopkins, and Bethiah, who married Joseph Harding. He died, say Eastham records, Oct. 17, 1673. His widow survived him several years. His will was exhibited at Plymouth court for probate, Oct. 29th, and letters testamentary were issued to Wid. Elizabeth. The widow, by her former husband, Stephen Deane, had several children, among whom were Elizabeth, who married Wm. Twinning, the first of the name in Eastham; Susannah, who married Joseph Rogers and Stephen Snow, and Miriam, who when aged, married John Wing, Sen. of Harwich. It is quite certain that Mrs. Cooke was somewhat older than her last husband.

Mr. Cooke was a very energetic man, and appears to have given much more attention to material things than his compeers in the early settlement of the place. He was an impulsive man, and often in imbroglios with some of his worldly neighbors of impetuous temperaments. Some notice of his cases of litigation are upon record. They are principally of a defamatory character, and show unmistakably that Mr. Cooke had some very implacable neighbors, who delighted in giving him trouble, not caring whether their slanderous charges could be sustained or not. The many public positions he held in town from the settlement in 1645 to his death in 1673, show that he was a man that the majority of his townsmen had confidence in and respected. Of the religious life of Mr. Cooke we have nothing positive. It is inferred he was a member of the church.

RICHARD HIGGINS.

Richard Higgins was in Plymouth in 1633, and is mentioned as being one of the freemen and tax payers of that town, his rate being nine shillings. He was a tailor by trade, and married Lydia Chandler, daughter of Edmund of Scituate for his first wife, Dec. 11, 1634. He purchased of John Barnes of Plymouth, the 13th day of January following, the twenty acres of land and dwelling house on it, belonging formerly to Edward Holman, and doubtless at once commenced business, as by record on April following, he is mentioned as having had bound to him, Samuel Godbarson, as an apprentice. In 1639, with Josiah Cooke, he had land granted him at Plymouth. In 1644, he was of the grand inquest and then a resident of Plymouth.

In 1645, he went to Nausett, with the other pioneers, and in 1647, with Josiah Cooke was sent to the Colony court at Plymouth, as representative, or deputy as they were at that time called. He was again chosen to represent Eastham at the same court in 1653, 1655, 1657, 1658, 1660 and 1665, according to the Colonial records. In 1651, he was a surveyor for Eastham, and in 1666 and 1668 a selectman. He was one of the first overseers of the poor appointed by Eastham in 1658, and one of those this year who agreed with the town to furnish men and equipment for "the troop of horse." He agreed to furnish "one man and a horse for the country's service," upon condition the town furnished the "furniture," so long as he was able.

At different periods, while a resident in the Colony, he had

17

land granted him for his use. In 1657, he was granted a tract thirteen miles from Rehoboth, and in 1658, with four of his associates in the settlement, he had a grant of land between Bridgewater and Weymouth.

Mr. Higgins, it appears, was not satisfied with his situation at Eastham, as in November, 1672, he was residing in "New Pascataway in the province of New Jersey," a place some thirteen miles northeast of Princeton, which had been settled but a few years, and mostly by New England people. At this place it is supposed he died soon after. He was dead, it is certain, in 1675, as that year his son, Benjamin, applied to the Colony court for land in right of his father, Richard Higgins, deceased, and provision was made for him in land at Saconct.

The second and last wife of Richard Higgins was Mary, widow of John Yates of Duxbury, to whom he was married October, 1651. By her former husband, John Yates, she had one son, John, who came with her to the Cape. She survived her husband, and it is thought she returned to Eastham after her husband's decease. She is mentioned upon the Plymouth record in 1682, as Richard Higgins' widow. By both wives, as far as is known, he had Jonathan, Benjamin, Mary, Eliakim, William, Jadiah, Zerviah, Thomas and Lydia.

The place of Richard Higgins in old Eastham has not been pointed out. He sold in 1667, a large tract to Jonathan Sparrow, in what is now East Orleans, and possibly it was in that section he resided when he removed to New Jersey. The Higginses of the Cape are his descendants. Whether any of his children settled in New Jersey we have not ascertained.

JOHN SMALLEY.

John Smalley, an associate of Richard Higgins and the other pioneers in the settlement at Nausett, was neither freeman nor tax payer at Plymouth in 1663. He was, however, at Plymouth as early at 1638. By trade he was a tailor. He seems to have taken but very little part in public affairs. He was admitted a freeman at Plymouth in 1642. He was a constable at Nausett in 1646, a surveyor in 1649, and of the Grand Inquest in 1654, 1660 and 1665. He was specially favored by the court, and had land granted him in 1658 between Bridgewater and Weymouth, and in 1662 near Taunton.

Mr. Smalley was married at Plymouth to Ann Walden, Nov. 9, 1638. No full list of his children appears. He had Hannah, born at Plymouth, June 14, 1641; John, at Plymouth, Sept. 8, 1644; Isaac, Dec, 11, 1647, and Mary, Dec. 11, 1647. The time of his death is not known, and we fail to find any settlement of his estate... He was living in January, 1668, and had a ward some six years of age, who wandered six or seven miles from his house into the woods and died from exposure.

Mr. Smalley was undoubtedly a man who did not seek notoriety. He seemed to enjoy the quietness of his farm more than the honors and troubles of office. He lived in peace with all men, there can be no doubt, and was gathered to his fathers in peace. Many have supposed that from him descended the Smalleys of Smalls of the Cape. The writer also entertained a similar opinion until quite recently. Investigations by the writer of ancient documents, show that one branch of the Harwich Smalls, at least, descended from one Francis Small, a fisherman of Casco Bay, who, as early as 1657, purchased the land of Scitterygussett, the Sachem, near the site of the city of Portland, and that he assigned a portion of it to Mr. Jno. Phillips, in 1659. Family tradition is that the Smalls laid claim to land near Portland, and attempts at law to recover it were early made. The tradition is sustained by documents that not long since came to light, in which it appears that an attempt was made in the year 1764.

SAMUEL HICKS.

Samuel Hicks was among the first who went to Nausett after the settlement commenced. He came over with his mother, Margaret, in the Ann in 1623, to meet his father, Robert, who had previously come in the Fortune. His age at the time is not known. He was in Plymouth in 1643 and able to bear arms. He went to Nausett and was the constable in 1646. He was a representative to the Colony court in June, 1647, and also in 1649 with

Mr. John Doane. He did not long remain in Eastham. He was a resident of Barnstable as late as 1662, and an inhabitant of Dartmouth in 1670, where the family was interested in some landed estate. His wife was Lydia Doane, daughter, it is understood, of Mr. John Doane, to whom he was married Sept. 11, 1645. Among his children were Dorcas, born 14th of February, 1652; Margaret, born 9th of March, 1654.

Robert Hicks, the father of Samuel, came to Plymouth in 1621, without his family, from London, where he had been engaged in the business of a fellmonger. His wife came over with the children in the Ann, in 1623. He died in 1647, leaving his wife Margaret and four children, viz: Samuel, Ephraim, Lydia and Phebe.

JOHN JENKINS.

John Jenkins was an early resident of Nausett, and a contemporary of Mr. Hicks and had land laid out to him, but he early removed from town. He came from Plymouth, where he had been a resident, and where he had been admitted a freeman in 1637. He appears to have been a resident of Barnstable in 1652. He was a volunteer in 1637 to fight the Pequots, and in 1645 a soldier against the Narraganset Indians. He came over in 1635, it is understood, in the Defense of London. Of his life after his removal from Eastham, we have not an accurate account. He had children born at Barnstable and at other places where he resided. There was a John Jenkins in Sandwich early, friendly to the Friends or Quakers, and one at Succanesset or Falmouth.

ROBERT WIXON.

Robert Wickson, or Wixon, was a resident of Eastham in 1648. He came from Plymouth, where he had been a constable in 1647. He was an indentured apprentice of Wm. Edge, or Hedge, of that town in 1638, but at the desire of Hedge, Gov. Prence took him in November of that year, and with him, undoubtedly, he spent the remaining years of his minority. It is inferred that the governor had something to do in his settlement at Nausett. The settlers in 1648 chose him a surveyor with Josiah Cooke. At the

June session of the Old Colony court at Plymouth, in 1651, he was made a freeman. He was chosen a surveyor in 1655, 1674, 1675 and 1676. He was a constable in 1666. With Mr. John Doane and Jonathan Bangs, of this town, he was on the jury that tried Tobias and other Indians, for the alleged murder of the famous John Sasamon, in Middleboro in 1675, whose dead body was found under the ice in Assowamsett Pond. The trial, conviction and execution of the supposed murderers of Sasamon greatly exasperated King Philip, and undoubtedly caused that warrior to commence the meditated acts which resulted so disastrously to the Colony, and brought sorrow to so many homes.

Robert Wickson died at Eastham in October, 1686. His widow was Alice. His will bears date Oct. 1, 1686, and was presented for probate at Barnstable, Oct. 23, 1686. He had Jemima, born in 1655; Titus, in 1657; Elizabeth, in 1660, and Barnabas. From Barnabas, the son, have descended the Cape Wixons. The sons of Barnabas Wixon were Barnabas, Joshua, Robert and Prence. Joshua, Robert and Prence settled in that part of Yarmouth now Dennis, where they married early in the last century. About 1760, Reuben, Robert and Pelick Wixon removed from the Cape to that part of the Oblong now in Putpam County, New York. This surname was sometimes written Vixon, Wixam, Wickson and Wixon. The prevailing mode is Wixon.

JOSEPH ROGERS.

Lieut. Joseph Rogers went to Eastham soon after the settlement opened, paid his proportion of the purchase money, and at once took a leading part in the affairs of the new township. He came over in the Mayflower, with his father, Thomas Rogers, and appears to have been the only member of his father's family that ventured in that famous vessel. At the time, it appears, he was a lad. He doubtless was the eldest of his father's children, and, perhaps, came to have care of his father, who, it is inferred from what Bradford has stated, was a widower. His father did not survive the first winter; he took the distemper which carried off so many of that noble band, died, and was buried, as is supposed, with the other victims on Cole's Hill. Some years afterwards the remaining portion of his family found their way to this country, where they married and settled. With whom Lieut. Joseph lived during that terrible winter and spring, after burying his father, does not appear. It certainly must have been a dreary winter to him as well as to the other survivors. The bill of mortality as given by Prince, the chronologist, as gathered from Bradford's papers, shows that the little band of worthies was incapable of doing much more than to attend to the sick and to bury the dead, for the first four months. The number of deaths occurring in December was six; January, eight; February, seventeen, and in March thirteen. Elder Brewster and Captain Standish were amoug the very few that escaped the sickness. They have been highly spoken of by the Pilgrim historian for their great services during the sickness.

In the allotment of land in 1623 to those who came over in the Mayower, Joseph Rogers had two acres allotted him; and in the division of the cattle in 1627, he had his portion in the eleventh lot, which fell to Gov. Bradford's company, of which he was one. From the fact of his being in this company, it is thought that he was a member of the governor's household. He was a resident of Plymouth in 1633, a tax payer and married man. His rates this year were nine shillings. In 1636, he was located near Jones' River in that part afterwards Duxbury, and was allowed to establish a ferry near his house, and to take one penny from each person who took passage. In 1637, Duxbury became a township, and in 1639, with John Washburne, he was surveyor of highways for that town. In 1640 he was again surveyor. While a resident of Duxbury he had large tracts of land granted him. In 1638, he had sixty acres of land granted him, and in 1640, he and his "brother John Rogers" had each a tract of land of forty acres granted them at North River, in what is now Marshfield. In 1645, he was one of the six appointed by the court to lay out land at Duxbury, at a place called Saughtuckett.

In 1647, at the June session of the Old Colony court, he was proposed as a suitable person for a lieutenant at Nausett to "exercise the men" in arms, and was appointed. He held this position till 1661, when his lieutenancy was revoked, and he was released from further duty as militia officer. He was, however, reappointed lieutenant of the Eastham Company in 1664, succeeding Lieut. Wm. Merrick or Myrick. In February, 1652, with other persons from various parts of the Colony, he was appointed to lay out the way from Sandwich to near Eel River in Plymouth. In 1658, he was one of the Council of War, and that year had liberty to purchase tracts of meadow at Pottonumecot, near the mouth of the river.

In 1661,.with Giles Hopkins, who was a passenger with him in the Mayflower, and Josiah Cooke, he had liberty to look out for land between Bridgewater and the Bay line. In 1663, he was on the jury from Eastham, and in 1665, with Lieut. John Freeman, was appointed to view certain land petitioned for by Richard Higgins, and to purchase the same if he thought proper. The same year he was made a grantee of land at Manomoyick, now Chatham, which had been illegally purchased by the first settler of that place, Wm. Nickerson; and also liberty with the other grantees to purchase the unpurchased land there. In 1670, he was allowed to purchase more meadow at Pottonumecot near his former purchase. In 1672, he disposed of a large tract in what is now Brewster, which came to him at the division of the "Purchasers or Old Comers reserve," he having been one of that favored number. Lieut. Rogers died the latter part of the winter 1677, and undoubtedly was buried in the old yard at Eastham, which is

"A lonesome acre thinly grown
With grass and wandering vine."

His wife Hannah survived him, but how long is not known. His children were, Sarah, born in 1633; Joseph, in 1635; Thomas, in 1638; Elizabeth, in 1639; John, in 1642; Mary, in 1644; James, in 1648; and Hannah, in 1652.

Joseph, the eldest son, married Susannah Deane, in 1660. In December following, he fell from his horse with such violence that his death took place within forty-eight hours. A prominent citizen of Yarmouth was arraigned for being in some way the cause of his death; he left no issue. Thomas married Elizabeth Snow in 1665, and died in 1678, soon after his father. Elizabeth

23

married Jonathan Higgins, son of Richard. John married Elizabeth Twinning in 1669, and settled in South Eastham. John had a large family, and from him have descended the South Orleans Rogers. He died about 1724. He was a large land owner. James, the youngest son of Lieut. Joseph, married Mary Paine, Jan. 11, 1670. He died April 11, 1677; he left no sons.

The will of Lieut. Joseph Rogers was witnessed by John Bangs and Wm. Twinning, and was presented at Plymouth court March 5, 1677-8. He mentions sons Thomas, Joshua and James; daughters Elizabeth Higgins and Hannah Rogers, and grandson Beniah Higgins, who resided with him. Thomas was the executor, but died before the final settlement of his father's estate. To James was given the homestead. To Beniah he gave one-third of his purchased and unpurchased land at Pamet, now Truro, provided he continued to live with him until his death. Lieut. Rogers gave the church at Eastham ten shillings.

The spot where he resided has not been indicated to the writer; but the records point to that part of Orleans called Barley Neck, as the place where this pioneer and passenger in the Mayflower located upon his removal to Nausett plantation. It is probable he was the first who settled in that vicinity. Tradition has it that in early times a house in that locality was palisaded, to protect the occupants (as well as those who sought it in time of danger) from the hostile Indians then lurking around to get recruits for King Philip's army. It is probable that this house was Lieut. Rogers's, as he had been long active in military matters in the town.

JOHN FREEMAN.

Next in prominence to Thomas Prence of the early settlers of Nausett, was his son-in-law, John Freeman. He was the youngest son of Edmund Freeman, the Sandwich settler, and was born in England. He came over with his father's family when a lad, in the ship Abigail, Captain Hackwell, in 1635. Upon his marriage with Mercy, Gov. Prence's daughter by wife Patience Brewster, Feb. 13, 1649-50, he removed from Sandwich to that part of Nausett called Namskecket, now within the limits of Orleans, and located,

24

having paid his part of the purchase money. He was admitted a freeman in 1651, and the same year was one of the Grand jury from Eastham. In 1652, he was chosen to represent Eastham in the Old Colony court, and also elected in 1654, '56, '62, '63, '64, '65 and '66. He was chosen an assistant to the governor in 1666-7 in place of Mr. William Collier of Duxbury, and re-elected at every yearly election thereafter, until 1692. He was elected a selectman several years, but not as often as has been reported by some who have written concerning him. He was early connected with the militia. In 1665, he was the ensign of the company at Eastham, and in October, 1659, confirmed as lieutenant of the "troop of horse" by the Colonial court. This was the only company of mounted soldiers in the Colony at this date. Command was given to Capt. William Bradford of Plymouth.

Robert Stetson was cornet or color bearer. For this company of mounted soldiers, Eastham was required to furnish three troopers; and Thomas Prence and Edward Bangs each "freely" agreed to furnish a man fully equipped. After this period he was captain of the military company. Upon the division of the Colony into three counties in 1685, the militia was divided into three regiments. The Barnstable county regiment was placed under the command of Captain John Freeman, who was now commissioned major. At that period there were no regimental officers known as colonel and lieutenant colonel. The highest commanding officer of a regiment then known was major. The Plymouth county regiment was placed under the command of Major William Bradford, and the Bristol regiment under Major John Walley. For many years after the union of Plymouth with Massachusetts Colony, there was but one regiment of militia in this county. Upon the division into two regiments, the militia of the towns below Dennis, then Yarmouth, composed the second regiment.

In 1665, to settle the difficulty at Monomoy, now Chatham, between William Nickerson and the Colonial government respecting the illegal purchase of land of the Indian sachem there, Nickerson was allowed one hundred acres of the purchased land, and Major Freeman, with Thomas Hinckley, William Sargeant, Anthony Thacher, Nathaniel Bacon, Edmund Hawes, Thomas

25

Howes, Sen., Thomas Folland, Sen., and Lieut. Joseph Rogers, was allowed a grantee of the remaining portion, with the privilege with the above named to purchase adjacent land. Major Freeman, in 1672, disposed of his right to William Nickerson; and in 1674 Major Freeman and Captain Jonathan Sparrow were appointed to lay out Nickerson's land with instructions, but for some cause the work was not accomplished by the committee until 1692.

He was one of the Council of War, and, it seems, had seen some of the dangers of camp life during the war with King Philip. In a letter from Taunton, under date of June 8, 1675, to Gov. Josiah Winslow, to whom he was an assistant, he writes: "This morning three of our men are slain close by one of our court of guard; houses are burned in our sight; our men are picked off at every bush. The design of the enemy is not to face the army, but to fall on us as they have advantage." Two of the men who fell as above mentioned were from Eastham, viz: Samuel Atkins and John Knowles. The major in the same letter expressed his fears as to the people of Eastham defending themselves in case of assault, and urged the governor "to give instructions how to manage things for their security," as he was of the opinion that the town had "not twenty good arms in it." It is probable the major was forced to believe that the place was not free from the emissaries of Philip, and that an attack was not impossible. Tradition has it that the people of Eastham apprehended attacks and had palisaded houses for refuge erected. Two of them, it is reported, were in East Orleans, one of them near the house of Mr. J. L. Sparrow, and in charge of Captain Jonathan Sparrow, the owner, which we may notice more fully in a future article; and also one at Barley Neck, or vicinity. It is certain, had not Bourne, Treat and others instructed the Cape Indians and influenced them to remain friendly, the English in the Cape towns would have severely suffered, and the result of the conflict been serious to the infant colony. At the period of the war, Eastham was the only incorporated town below Yarmouth, and the whole territory from Dennis bounds to the head of the Cape was considered under the municipal control of the town.

Major Freeman has been very justly regarded as one of the

"fathers of the town." No one of the early residents was held in higher esteem, and it is certain no one was longer in public employment and performed his duties so acceptably. Excepting Gov. Prence, none held a higher public position. His education, it is true, was inferior to several of his contemporaries in the little settlement; but in point of ability he was inferior to none in the township. Upon the union of the two colonies in 1692, he was appointed, with Barnabas Lothrop, Barnstable, John Thacher, Yarmouth, and Stephen Skiff, Sandwich, a justice of the Court of Common Pleas. He held the office until "infirmaties of age" rendered "him incapable" of further service, and he was succeeded by Captain Jonathan Sparrow of Eastham, March 6, 1695. After the commencement of the eighteenth century he gradually gave up public employment, and on the 19th of October, 1719, passed away, in the 98th year of his age, according to the headstone in the old burying-ground at Eastham, where his friends and neighbors lie buried. His wife, Mercy, preceded him to her rest, having died Sept. 28, 1711, in her 81st year.

Major Freeman was a man of some means. He was quite a large landholder, not only in Eastham, but in Harwich, at an early period. He bought out Gov. Prence's right to land he held as a "Purchaser or Old Comer," in the latter town early, and much of it he deeded to his sons, Thomas and John, after their settlement in that part of Harwich now Brewster.

He had, so far as is known, eleven children.. They were John, who died in infancy; John, 1651, who settled in Harwich; Thomas, 1653, who also settled in Harwich and was a prominent man; Patience, who married Lieut. Samuel Paine of Eastham; Hannah, who married John Mayo; Mercy, who married Samuel Knowles, Esq.; William, who married Lydia Sparrow; Prence, who died young; Nathaniel, 1669, who married Mary Howland of Quaker parentage, and who was a man of note in Eastham, and who died at a great age; and Bennet, who married Deacon John Paine, whose great-grandson was the brilliant John Howard Paine, author of "Home, Sweet Home."

The will of Major John Freeman bears the date June 1, 1716, and was presented for probate Nov. 4, 1719.

27

JOHN MAYO.

The first who went to Eastham as a religious instructor, as far as can be ascertained, was Mr. John Mayo. He was from England, it is understood, and came over quite early. He was at Barnstable, said the late Amos Otis, as early as 1639, and there when Mr. Lothrop and company came from Scituate. Mr Mayo "was ordained teaching elder of the Church" over which Mr. Lothrop was pastor, on Fast day, April 25, 1640. His stay here was not long, as Nov. 9, 1665, he was inducted to the pastoral office of the Second church, in Boston, which had been gathered June 5, 1650. Here he preached until the beginning of the year 1672, when he became "very infirm insomuch as the congregation was not able to hear and be edified," and concurring with his brethren, in the proposal to secure another, he retired from the ministry soon after, and in 1673, moved "his person and goods" to Barnstable to reside with his daughter. He afterwards resided at Yarmouth, where he died in May, 1676, and was buried.

Of his ministry at Eastham, but very little is certainly known. It is evident he was not a settled minister there. The settlers, at the time of his removal to the place, were in no condition apparently to hold out great inducements, and it is probable for their failure in that respect, that Mr. Mayo left the town and colony.

Of his children there appears no complete record. It is certain he had Samuel, Hannah, Nathaniel, Elizabeth and John.

The wife of Mr. Mayo survived him, it is supposed, as a "Ma Mayho" died at Yarmouth, according to the records of that town, Feb. 26, 1682.

Samuel, their son, born in England, married Thomasin Lumpkins of Yarmouth, and at first located at Barnstable. From there he went to Oyster Bay, L. I., it is stated in 1653, and purchased land of the Indians. He sold out his land there in 1658, and resided in Boston. He died there the latter part of the year 1663, or the beginning of 1664. He seems to have been a sea-faring man. His father settled the estate. He left a wife, Thomasin or Tamzin, and several children. The widow married Mr. John Sunderland of Boston soon after. Mr. Sunderland was a citizen of Eastham as early as 1678, when the town was thrown into excitement on account of the appearance of the smallpox. Mr. John Cotton, under the date of Aug. 26, this year, in a letter to Mr. Increase Mather, reports the disease increasing and four or five sick; that one man had died, and that Mr. Sunderland's son and grandson had each had it. Mr. Sunderland was a school teacher many years, and was admitted townsman of Eastham in 1695. He died testate, Dec. 26, 1707, aged 84 years; and she died, aged 84, June 13, 1709. They both lie buried at Brewster, where stones with inscriptions mark the spots. Samuel Mayo's daughter Elizabeth was the first wife of Mr. Samuel Treat, the first settled minister of the town; daughter Mary was the first wife of Jonathan Bangs of Harwich; their daughter Sarah, the second wife of Lieut. Edward Freeman of Eastham; their daughter Mercy Mayo married Captain Samuel Sears of Harwich; and their son John Mayo married Hannah Freeman, daughter of Major John Freeman, and settled in Harwich. He was the first representative from that town.

Hannah, the daughter of Mr. John Mayo, married Nathaniel Bacon of Barnstable in 1642. He was the first of that name in the county.

Nathaniel Mayo, son of Mr. John Mayo, married Gov. Prence's daughter Hannah, Feb. 13, 1649-50, and removed to Eastham, where he was somewhat of a prominent man. He died at that place, the beginning of the year 1662. He made his will Jan. 10, 1661-2, and it was presented in March following. He left Thomas, Nathaniel, Samuel, Theophilus, Hannah and Bathsheba. He desired that all of his children should be "brought up to read and write." His son Theophilus went to reside with Gov. Prence, but died when a young man. Hannah Mayo married for her second husband Captain Jonathan Sparrow of Eastham.

Elizabeth Mayo, daughter of Mr. John Mayo, married Joseph Howes of Yarmouth.

John Mayo, Jr., married Hannah Reycraft of Eastham, Jan. 1, 1650-1. He made his will in 1702. It was presented for probate May 4, 1707. He had eight children.

After the removal of Mr. John Mayo to Boston, in 1655,

Mr. Thomas Crosby was engaged as a religious teacher to carry on the Sabbath services, at a salary of £50. Mr. Crosby was a graduate of Harvard college in 1653. He was an author, and his works have been noticed by Mr. Sibley, late librarian of Harvard college. He seems not to have been a settled preacher. While at Eastham, he was engaged in trade. He resided near the old burying-ground at Eastham, on the place he bought, in 1665, of Jonathan Sparrow and Pandora, his mother. After Mr. Crosby's release as preacher at that place, which was about 1670, he removed to Harwich, now Brewster, and located. Here he was also engaged in trade. He was one of the eight who formed the church at that place in 1700. He died at Boston, while on business, June 13, 1702. Mr. Crosby's wife Sarah, by whom he had twelve children, married John Miller of Yarmouth, April 28, 1703. None of Mr. Crosby's children settled in Eastham. His descendants are widely scattered.

THOMAS WILLIAMS.

Thomas Williams was at Eastham in 1649, and that year a road surveyor. He was at Plymouth in 1635, in the employ of Mrs. Richard Warren, and having said to someone that he neither "feared God or the Devil," was arrested for making a "blasphemous" speech and brought before the court, and though the governor thought that he was deserving of corporal punishment, was easily let off. In 1637, he was eager for a brush with the ferocious Pequots, and offered to go with others, under Mr. Prence and Lieut. Holmes, to fight them, but when upon the point of embarking, word came not to proceed, as the "enemy was as good as vanquished and there would be no need" of the company's service. He married Elizabeth Tart at Plymouth, Nov. 30, 1638. He resided in Eastham, on the north side of Town cove, in Gov. Prence's and Nicholas Snow's neighborhood. He survived his wife, and died aged in 1696. There appears no record of his children. His will bears date May 10, 1692, and was presented for probate Oct. 22, 1696. He had, it is certain, five daughters; four only survived him. He had no sons that survived him, or descendants bearing his surname. Among his grandchildren mentioned in his will were John Smith and William Nickerson. John Smith seems to have been a favorite. Two of Goodman Williams's daughters married sons of William Nickerson of Chatham, then Monomoy or Monomoiet. Mercy, who married William Nickerson, Jr., about 1670, died in Chatham, very aged, April 7, 1739. Rev. Joseph Lord, pastor of the Chatham church, thus speaks of her:

On the "7 (2.) 1739, died here Mrs. Mercy Nickerson (commonly written here Nickerson) aged 90 years, or more as is judged,—and some say 95,—for she could not tell her own age. She was born in Eastham, and has left a numerous posterity, 146 being now living in this land, besides which there was a daughter of hers that about twenty years ago went to a place called Duck Creek, either in Pennsylvania or West Jersey, of whose posterity her relation here cannot inform who are living; but she carried away eleven children with her when she went." Mr. Lord was afterwards informed by her son that he found 157 of her posterity living here in this country; "and Duck Creek," says Mr. Lord "I am informed is in Penn. on the borders of Maryland."

Mr. Lord was nearly right in his location of "Duck Creek." That part of Pennsylvania now is included in Kent county, Delaware; and the creek flows easterly into Delaware bay. The particular place where this granddaughter of Thomas Williams settled is not now known with certainty. It is probably in the vicinity of Salisbury—a settlement a few miles north of Dover. To this region about 1711, more than thirteen families removed from Monomoy or Chatham. In this county and Queen Ann's in Maryland, are families of Nickersons now residing, whose ancestors undoubtedly went there at that period or afterwards from the Cape. At Lewes, (in Sussex county) a place south of "Duck Creek," on the eastern coast of Delaware, was residing Captain Nathaniel Hall in 1716. He was from Yarmouth, and had been a brave soldier in the Indian wars, and many years a licensed keeper of a house of public entertainment before his removal.

The other daughters who survived Thomas Williams were Sarah, wife of John Nickerson of Monomoy; Mary Hopkins, probably wife of Caleb of Truro, and Elizabeth, an unmarried daughter.

Thomas Williams was a proprietor of land at Saconett, which he sold to Joseph Howland of Duxbury, Nov. 9, 1683.

THOMAS ROBERTS.

Thomas Roberts was an early resident of Eastham. He came from Plymouth. He was a servant of Mr. John Atwood of that township in 1637. He married Mary Paddock, March 24, 1650-1. He resided in that part of Eastham now East Orleans. He sold to Captain Jonathan Sparrow a large tract of land, about 1667. He was not long a resident of Eastham after that date. He was a surveyor of highways in 1657.

No. 34.

LIBRARY of Cape Cod HISTORY & GENEALOGY

NICHOLAS[1] SNOW of Eastham

AND SOME OF HIS DESCENDANTS, TOGETHER WITH SAMUEL[1] STORRS, THOMAS[1] HUCKINS, ELDER JOHN[2] CHIPMAN, AND ISAAC[1] WELLS, ALLIED TO THE SNOWS BY MARRIAGE.

By JAMES W. HAWES.

YARMOUTHPORT, MASS.:
C. W. SWIFT, Publisher and Printer,
The "Register" Press,
1916.

NICHOLAS[1] SNOW of Eastham

AND SOME OF HIS DESCENDANTS, TOGETHER WITH SAMUEL[1] STORRS, THOMAS[1] HUCKINS, ELDER JOHN[1] CHIPMAN, AND ISAAC[1] WELLS, ALLIED TO THE SNOWS BY MARRIAGE.

By JAMES W. HAWES.

Copyright, 1916, by Charles W. Swift.

NICHOLAS[1] SNOW OF PLYMOUTH AND EASTHÄM, AND SOME OF HIS DESCENDANTS.*

FIRST GENERATION.

Nicholas[1] Snow was b. in England and came to Plymouth in the Anne in the latter part of July, 1623.(a) He m. between 1623 and May 22, 1627, Constance, daughter of Stephen[1] Hopkins by his first wife, who came with her father on the Mayflower.(b) He d. in Eastham Nov. 15, 1676; she d. there about the middle of October, 1677.(c) He resided in Plymouth until early in 1645, when with Mr. Thomas Prence (previously and afterward Governor), John Doane, Josias Cook, Richard Higgins, John Smalley and Edward Bangs, he settled Nauset (afterward called Eastham). In 1646 the place was made a town.(d) The same year he was elected town clerk. He served as such for 17 years. He was a deputy to the General Court for three years from 1648 and one of the selectmen for 7 years from 1663.(e) He resided at Skaket, now Orleans.(e1) In the casting of lots in 1623 his premises fell "on the other side of the towne towards the eeleriver" and butted against Hobbs Hole.(f)

May 22, 1627, in the division of the cattle, he with his wife formed part of the seventh company, headed by his father-in-law, Stephen[1] Hopkins. This company

---

*An account of him and some of his descendants is given by Mrs. Charles L. Alden in the New England Historical and Genealogical Register (hereinafter cited as N. E. Reg.), vol. 47, pp. 81, 186, 341; vol. 48, pp. 71, 188; vol. 49, pp. 71, 202, 451; vol. 51, p. 204.

(a) 2 Mayflower Descendant (hereinafter cited as Mf.), 179; New England's Memorial, 47, 48; 12 Plym. Col. Recs. 5, 6.

(b) 1 Mf. 148-154; 2ib. 118.

(c) Eastham Recs.; 3 Mf. 167.

(d) 2 Plym. Col. Recs. 81, 102.

(e) Deyo's Barnstable County, 728-730.

(e1) Ib. 722.

(f) 12 Plym. Col. Recs. 5 and 6.

obtained two she goats and a black weaning calf, to which was to be added that year's calf of the black cow which fell to John Shaw and his company.(g)

Nicholas¹ Snow was a freeman of Plymouth in 1633.(h)

In 1633 he was rated at 18 shillings, payable in corn at six shillings per bushel,(i) and in 1634 at 12 shillings.(j)

Oct. 1, 1634, Nicholas¹ Snow was one of seven men appointed to lay out highways in Plymouth before November 15 next.(k)

He evidently assigned his servant to John Cooper, for on Jan. 5, 1634-5, the servant expressed his willingness to serve out his time with Cooper, according to the tenor of his indenture.(l)

Twiford West, a servant of Governor Edward Winslow under an indenture for six years, was assigned to Nicholas Snow, but after some trial he disliked to be with Snow and proposed to Winslow if he would take him back that he would serve him an additional year. Thereupon Winslow compounded with Snow, and an indenture for seven years from the date of the first indenture was entered into between Winslow and West and agreed to by Snow Feb. 12, 1635-6.(m)

March 14, 1635-6, it was arranged that Nicholas Snow should mow at Wollingsley and have "one small jag of hey" from the marsh assigned to John Faunce and Mr. Coomb.(n)

Oct. 5, 1636, he was appointed one of three arbitrators to settle the controversy between Joseph Biddle and Edward Doty, they having brought cross actions against each other, "their matters being raw & impfect."(o)

March 7, 1636-7, he was one of the freemen at the court then held.(p)

March 20, 1636-7, he was given the same hay ground at Wollingsley as the year before.(q)

His house was east of the way to Eel river from Plymouth laid out by a jury and confirmed by the court July 7, 1637. It seems to have been between the houses of Edward Bangs and Stephen¹ Hopkins.(r)

Oct. 2, 1637, Nicholas¹ Snow was on a jury. Also, March 6, 1637-8; March 3, 1639-40; Sept. 1, 1640; June 1, 1641; Sept. 6, 1641; March 7, 1642-3, and June 6, 1643.(s)

May 7, 1638, Nicholas¹ Snow desired land towards the Six Mile brook.(t)

June 5, 1638, he was on the grand jury.(u)

The same day he was on a jury of inquest upon the body of John

(g) Ib. 11.
(h) 1 Plym. Col. Recs. 4.
(i) Ib. 9, 10.
(j) Ib. 26, 27.
(k) Ib. 31.
(l) Ib. 33.
(m) Ib. 37.
(n) Ib. 40, 41.
(o) Ib. 44.
(p) Ib. 52.
(q) Ib. 57.
(r) Ib. 58, 59.
(s) 7 ib. 7, 8, 16, 17, 20, 23, 34, 35.
(t) 1 Plym. Col. Recs. 83.
(u) Ib. 87.

England found dead on the Plymouth flats. They found he was drowned while sailing in a canoe, that the canoe was the cause of his death, and that it should be forfeited to the King.(v)

By deed dated July 6, 1638, he sold to Samuel Eddy the house and garden where he dwelt in Plymouth, with the fence in and about the same, for the consideration of £12 sterling, to be paid in forty bushels of good merchantable Indian corn at current rates, and if it should fall short, then Eddy was to make up the sum in money or other commodity. The price was to be paid and delivery given by the last day of the following October.(w)

July 2, 1638, Mr. Snow requested more hay ground and was allowed to cut hay that year upon the meadow reserved for the town of Plymouth.(x)

August 7, 1638, he desired five or six acres of land lying on the N. side of the land lately granted to Mr. Atwood.(y)

March 3, 1639-40, he is mentioned as one of the surveyors of highways for Plymouth.(z)

March 3, 1639-40, by act of the General Court, it was provided that "the purchasers, or old comers" should make choice of two or three plantations for themselves and their heirs, and on Dec. 1, 1640, they gave notice that they had chosen three places, of which one was on Cape Cod from Yarmouth from sea to sea to three miles east of Namskaket, and the others on the mainland, all the rest of the land in the colony being surrendered "to the body of freemen," except such as had been already granted to plantations or individuals. Nicholas Snow was one of the purchasers.(a)

May 5, 1640, he was one of a committee of five appointed to view all the meadows at Greens Harbor that had not been granted, to measure them and report to the next court.(b)

June 2, 1640, he is mentioned as one of the surveyors of highways for Plymouth.(c)

Nov. 2, 1640, he was granted ten acres of meadow "in the South Meddows towards Aggawam, Colebrook Meddowes."(d)

Dec. 1, 1640, with two others he was presented for not mending the highways at the "Second Brooke, Smylt River, New Bridge, and other places." They were discharged upon condition "that they shall repaire the heigh wayes this yeare."(e)

Feb. 1, 1640-1, with Edward Bangs and Joshua Pratt he was appointed to lay out Sarah Morton's lot at the Eel River.(f)

He was one of those in Plymouth in August, 1643, between 16

(v) Ib. 88.
(w) 12 Plym. Col. Recs. 31.
(x) 1 ib. 90.
(y) Ib. 93.
(z) Ib. 141.

(a) 2 ib. 4, 5, 177.
(b) 1 ib. 151.
(c) Ib. 155.
(d) Ib. 166.
(e) 2 ib. 5.
(f) Ib. 7.

and 60 years of age, able to bear arms.(g)

June 6, 1644, by his will Stephen¹ Hopkins gave his mare to his daughter Constance, wife of Nicholas¹ Snow.(h)

Probably in 1646 he sold to Thomas Morton for twelve pounds, the payment of six pounds whereof is acknowledged and the other six pounds were to be paid at the next harvest in good merchantable corn or cattle, all his house, buildings and the upland thereunto belonging and adjoining, with two acres of meadow lying at the High Pines and ten acres of upland meadow lying at Colebrook Meadows, containing in all 52 acres more or less, with the fencing in and about the same, said premises being in the town of Plymouth.(i)

March 10, 1645-6, he sold to Nathaniel Morton for ten shillings to be paid in merchantable corn at the next harvest one acre of upland lying at or near Wellingsley Brook in Plymouth.(j)

June 1, 1647, he and Edward Bangs are mentioned as surveyors of highways of Nauset.(k)

June 7, 1648, he was a committee or deputy to the General Court from Nauset.(l) The same date he was appointed "to take up the excise" at Nauset.(m)

June 4, 1650, with Mr. John Doane he was a deputy from Nauset to the General Court.(n)

June 3, 1652, he was one of the deputies to the General Court from Eastham.(o)

June 7, 1653, he is mentioned as one of the surveyors of highways for Eastham.(p)

In 1655 he and his son Mark signed the call to the Rev. John Mayo to become the minister of Eastham.(q)

June 3, 1657, he was a deputy to the General Court.(r)

July 9, 1660, Nicholas Snow, Edward Bangs and Josias Cook took oath before Gov. Prence as to Cook's share of the South meadow.(r1)

Nicholas¹ Snow was one of those who took the inventory of Richard Sparrow Jan. 22, 1660-1.(s)

June 3, 1662, he is mentioned as constable of Eastham.(t)

Nov. 28, 1664, Nicholas Snow brought into Eastham a gallon and a half of liquor.(u)

March 5, 1667-8, a shipwrecked carpenter, Crispen Wadlen, having stayed about three weeks at Ralph Smith's house in Eastham, complained that Smith oppressively kept a certain parcel of tools of his. Smith was ordered to deliver the tools to Nicholas Snow

---

(g) 8 ib. 189.
(h) 2 Mf. 12.
(i) 12 Plym. Col. Recs. 134.
(j) Ib. 135.
(k) 2 ib. 115.
(l) Ib. 123.
(m) Ib. 125.

(n) Ib. 154.
(o) 3 ib. 9.
(p) Ib. 33.
(q) 47 N. E. Reg. 82.
(r) 3 Plym. Col. Recs. 115.
(r1) 15 Mf. 30.
(s) 12 ib. 58.
(t) 4 Plym. Col. Recs. 15.
(u) Ib. 100.

to be sent to Wadlen, and was allowed to keep a parcel of cotton wool which he had of Wadlen as compensation for his entertainment.(v)

June 3, 1668, he is mentioned as one of the selectmen of Eastham.(w) Also, June 7, 1670;(x) June 3, 1671;(y) June 5, 1672;(z) June 3, 1673;(a) June 3, 1674;(b) June 1, 1675.(c)

Nicholas¹ Snow, April 5, 1669, was witness to a deed of land in Yarmouth.(c1)

June 5, 1671, he is mentioned as one of the surveyors of highways of Eastham.(d)

He having died, on March 6, 1676-7, letters of administration on his estate were granted to his widow Constant and his sons Mark and John Snow.(e) His will is dated Nov. 14, 1676, and was witnessed by the Rev. Samuel Treat and by Thomas Paine, Sr. It was proved at Plymouth March 5, 1676-7. The inventory of the personal estate, amounting to £102 10s. 9d., was sworn to by the widow March 22, 1676-7, before John Freeman, Assistant. The inventory included two oxen, appraised at £7 10s.; four cows, £7 5s.; £2 5s. in silver

---

(v) Ib. 175, 176.
(w) Ib. 182.
(x) 5 Ib. 35.
(y) Ib. 57.
(z) Ib. 92.
(a) Ib. 113.
(b) Ib. 144.
(c) Ib. 164.
(c1) 15 Mf. 51.
(d) 5 Plym. Col. Recs. 58.
(e) Ib. 220.

money; a psalm book and another book, 1s. each; a parcel of old books, 4s.; 27 sheep, £9; 59 lbs. of wool, £2 10s.; 3 hives of bees, £1 10s.; 4 swine, £1 6s.; horses, £4 10s.; 1 five year old steer, £2 10s.; young cattle, £4 1s.; Indian corn, £5 8s.

In his will he gave to his son Mark Snow 20 acres of upland at Namskaket (Orleans) where his house then stood and two acres of meadow and all his broken marsh there; also two-thirds of his great lot at Satucket (Brewster) lying next to the Indians' ground.

He gave land to his sons Joseph, Stephen and John. His youngest son Jabez was living with him and to him he gave most of the residue of his land. To his wife Constant Snow he gave all his cattle, horses, sheep and swine, with all his movable goods, "to be att her Disposall for the Comfort and support of her life," and after her decease to be equally divided amongst all his children. To his wife he also gave the use and disposal during her life of the part of his house she was dwelling in and after her death to his son Jabez. He gave to his wife ten acres of upland at Pochet (East Orleans), "for her Desposall for the Comfort of her life, but if shee need it not, and leave it undesposed; I Give it then to my son Steven Snow." He also upon like conditions gave 20 acres of upland at Billingsgate (Wellfleet) to his wife, but if she left it undisposed of, then to his son Jabez Snow. He gave out of his estate after his wife's death ten shillings "to the Church of Eastham for the furniture of the Table of the Lord, with pewter or other Necessaries." He named Deacon Samuel Freeman and John Mayo as overseers of his will.

His will and inventory are recorded in Vol. 3, pt. 2, pp. 71-77, of Plym. Col. Wills. They are printed at length in 3 Mayflower Descendant, 167-174.(f)

Children.

Mark, b. in Plymouth, May 9, 1628.(g)

Mary, b. ; m.(i) Thomas Paine about 1650; had 10 children and d. in 1704.(h) John Howard Payne, author of "Home, Sweet Home," was a descendant.(j)

Sarah, b. ; m.(k) Jan. 25, 1654-5, in Eastham William Walker. She had children born in Eastham.(l)

Joseph, b. ; m. Mary ; d. Jan. 3, 1722-3.(m) She d. after 1717. They had 11 children.(n) He left a will. Oct. 2, 1689, the choice of Joseph Snow as lieutenant of the military company of Eastham was approved.(o)

(f) His will also appears in 47 N. E. Reg. 83.
(g) East. Recs.; 7 Mf. 14.
(h) 22 N. E. Reg. 61, 62; 2 Paine Family Records (edited by Henry D. Paine) 43.
(i) 3 Mf. 168; 8 ib. 230; 15 ib. 189, 190.
(j) 8 ib. 180; 2 Paine Family Records, 87, 164-166, 224-232, 259, 272, 285-287.
(k) 8 Plym. Col. Recs. 15.
(l) 6 Mf. 206.
(m) 3 ib. 231.
(n) Ib. 230.
(o) 6 Plym. Col. Recs. 218.

Stephen, b. ; m.(p) in Eastham 1st Oct. 28, 1663, Susannah Rogers, widow of Joseph Rogers and daughter of Stephen and Elizabeth (Ring) Deane; and 2d April 9, 1701, Mary Bigford;(p) d. Dec. 17, 1705. His children were born in Eastham and were by his first wife.(p) In 1684 he was a freeman of Eastham.(q) He left a will. See also 15 Mf. 34 and 51, and 3 Plym. Col. Deeds, 334.

John, b. ; m.(r) in Eastham Sept. 19, 1667, Mary Smalley; d. 1692. She m. 2d Ephraim Doane and d. 1703. John Snow's children were born in Eastham.(r) In 1684 he was a freeman of Eastham.(q) He was sworn as such June 5, 1684.(s) See also 12 Mf. 190, and "The Doane Family," 30.

Elizabeth, b. ; m. Dec. 13, 1665, in Eastham, Thomas Rogers; d. June 16, 1678, leaving children.(st)

Jabez, b. ; m.(t) before Oct. 29, 1670, Elizabeth, daughter of Ralph Smith; d. Dec. 27, 1690. His children were born in Eastham.(u) June 1, 1680, Jabez Snow was on the grandjury.(v) The same day he was propounded to be a freeman and took the oath of fidelity.(w) June 7, 1681, he was one of the surveyors of highways for Eastham, and was ad-

---

(p) Eastham Recs.; 8 Mf. 15.
(q) 8 Plym. Col. Recs. 208, 209.
(r) Eastham Recs.; 7 Mf. 17.
(s) 6 Plym. Col. Recs. 130.
(st) East. Recs.; 6 Mf. 14.
(t) 5 ib. 51.
(u) 4 Mf. 32; 5 ib. 22.
(v) 6 Plym. Col. Recs. 36.
(w) Ib. 42, 43.

mitted a freeman.(x) June 6, 1682, he is mentioned as a surveyor of highways for Eastham.(y) March 5, 1684-5, Elizabeth Snow, wife of Jabez Snow of Eastham, was fined ten shillings for using railing expressions on a Lord's day to the Rev. Samuel Treat.(y1) June 3, 1690, he is mentioned as one of the selectmen of Eastham.(z) June 5, 1690, he was chosen one of the lieutenants for the expedition to Canada.(a) His inventory is printed in the Mayflower Descendant.(b)

Ruth, b. ; m. at Eastham Dec. 10, 1666, John Cole; d. Jan. 27, 1716-17, leaving children.(b1)

Three other children of Nicholas Snow, numbered by Gov. Bradford, are not accounted for. Probably they died young.

SECOND GENERATION.

Mark² (Nicholas¹) Snow, b.(c) in Plymouth May 9, 1628; m. 1st Anna, daughter of Josiah Cook, in Eastham, Jan. 18, 1654-5.(f) She d.(g) July 24, 1656, and he m.(h)

(x) Ib. 61, 62.
(y) Ib. 88.
(y1) Ib. 152, 153.
(z) Ib. 212.
(a) Ib. 251.
(b) 12 Mf. 39.
(b1) 8 Plym. Col. Recs. 57; 5 Mf. 196, 197.
(c) East. Recs.; 7 Mf. 14.
(f) 8 Plym. Col. Recs. 15; Eastham Recs.; 5 Mf. 23; 7 ib. 14; 15 ib. 34.
(g) 8 Plym. Col. Recs. 30; East. Recs.; 5Mf. 23; 7 Mf. 14.
(h) 8 Plym. Col. Recs. 28; Eastham Recs.; 7 Mf. 14.

2d in Eastham, Jan. 9, 1660-1, Jane, daughter of Gov. Thomas Prence and granddaughter of Elder William Brewster, a Mayflower passenger. He d. in Eastham between Nov. 23, 1694 (date of his will), and Jan. 9, 1694-5 (date of his inventory). His widow d. in Harwich between Dec. 21, 1703 (date of her will), and June 28, 1712 (date of her inventory). She was admitted to the church there in April, 1701.(i) She was born in Plymouth Nov. 1, 1637.(j)

Mark Snow was one of those in Plymouth stated to be between 16 and 60 able to bear arms in August, 1643.(k) He removed with his father to Eastham, where he was town clerk 14 years from 1663, succeeding his father; one of the selectmen 18 years from 1667; and a deputy to the General Court 6 years from 1675.(k1) He was captain of the militia company in 1659.(k2)

June 8, 1655, Mark Snow was propounded to take up his freedom and is mentioned as constable of Eastham.(l)

June 3, 1657, he is mentioned as one of the surveyors of highways for Eastham, and on the same date he was admitted and sworn as a freeman.(m)

(i) Brewster church recs.; 4 Mf. 245.
(j) Eastham Recs.; 7 Mf. 14; 6 ib. 230.
(k) 8 Plym. Col. Recs. 189.
(k1) Deyo, 728-730.
(k2) Deyo, 727.
(l) 3 Plym. Col. Recs. 78.
(m) Ib. 110, 117; 8 ib. 202.

June 4, 1657, and July 7, 1668, he was on a jury.(n) June 5, 1667, he was on the grandjury.(o)

Dec. 24, 1667, Mark Snow and Joseph Snow signed at Eastham a verdict of a jury of inquest, their names being the first two of the subscribers.(p)

June 5, 1671, he is mentioned as one of the selectmen of Eastham.(q) Also, June 5, 1672;(r) June 3, 1673;(s) June 3, 1674;(t) June 1, 1675;(u) June 7, 1676;(v) June 5, 1677;(w) June 5, 1678;(x) June 3, 1679;(y) June 1, 1680;(z) June 7, 1681;(a) June 6, 1682;(b) June 6, 1683;(c) June 3, 1684;(d) June 2, 1685;(e) June, 1686;(f) June, 1689;(g) June 3, 1690.(h)

Feb. 21, 1675, Mark Snow was witness to a deed of John Doane, Jr., to Jonathan Sparrow.(i)

(n) 7 ib. 83, 147.
(o) 4 ib. 148.
(p) Ib. 176.
(q) 5 ib. 57.
(r) Ib. 92.
(s) Ib. 113.
(t) Ib. 144.
(u) Ib. 164.
(v) Ib. 195.
(w) Ib. 230.
(x) Ib. 257.
(y) 6 ib. 10.
(z) Ib. 35.
(a) Ib. 59.
(b) Ib. 84.
(C) Ib. 108.
(d) Ib. 129.
(e) Ib. 108.
(f) Ib. 186.
(g) Ib. 207.
(h) Ib. 242.
(i) 14 Mf. 176. His signature is

Gov. Thomas Prence March 13, 1672-3, in his will, gave to his daughter Jane, wife of Mark Snow, his silver tankard, and in his codicil March 28, 1673, a bed. She also had one-eighth of the residue of his estate.(j)

June 1, 1675, he was a deputy from Eastham to the General Court.(k)

Feb. 29, 1675-6, he was appointed one of the council of war for Eastham.(l)

March 6, 1676-7, he was appointed an administrator of the estate of his father, Nicholas Snow, deceased.(m)

Mary Ingham, wife of Thomas Ingham, of Scituate, was indicted for having through witchcraft caused Mehitable Woodworth to fall into violent fits and to suffer great pains. On March 6, 1676-7, she was tried and found not guilty, Mark Snow being on the jury. He was also on the jury that the same day tried three Indians, Timothy Jacked (alias Canjuncke), Nassamaquat and Pompacanshe, who were indicted for murdering John Knowles, John Tisdall, Sr., and Samuel Atkins. The verdict as to Jacked and Nassamaquat was: "Wee find they are very suspicious of the murder charged on them," and as to Pompacanshe: "wee find nothing against him." The Indians were sent out of the country, the last named be-

---

reproduced on a page fronting 129 in that volume.
(j) 3 ib. 204, 205.
(k) 5 Plym. Col. Recs. 165.
(l) Ib. 186.
(m) Ib. 220.

cause he was a prisoner taken in war.(n)

June 5, 1677, he was a deputy from Eastham to the General Court.(o)

Oct. 30, 1678, he was with John Rogers made administrator of the estate of Thomas Rogers, late of Eastham, deceased.(p)

Feb. 26, 1679-80, with Jonathan Sparrow he was a witness to an agreement of Samuel³ Howes (son of Joseph² and grandson of Thomas¹ Howes) with his uncle Thomas² Howes.(q)

In June, 1686, he was a deputy to the General Court from Eastham.(r) Also, in June, 1689, and Aug. 14, 1689.(s)

Mark Snow was witness to the will of Robert Wixam of Eastham Oct. 1, 1686, and Oct. 11, 1686, he was one of those who took his inventory.(t)

Mark Snow was one of those who took the inventory of William Freeman of Eastham in 1687.(u)

March 5, 1688-9, Mark Snow witnessed the codicil of Giles Hopkins. He made oath to it April 16, 1690.(v)

His will is printed in full in 47 New England Historical and Genealogical Register, at page 85. It was proved Jan. 16, 1694-5, and is recorded in 1 Barnstable Probate Records, page 111. Letters testamentary were granted to his widow April 13, 1695.(w) The inventory of his estate amounted to £86 14s. for real estate and £45 16s. 1d. for personal property.(x) He does not name his daughters in his will.

He made his wife Jane Snow executrix and gave to her his entire personal estate after his debts and funeral charges were paid. He gave his real estate to his three sons Nicholas, Thomas and Prence. The last named obtained the testator's dwelling house after his wife's decease or widowhood and all the land adjoining and 15 acres of land "above ye common road," three acres of meadow lying "below my now dwelling house," and after his wife's decease "ye remainder of my lot of land in ye before specified Indian fields," at Satuckett, of which Nicholas received one half. He also gave Prence after his wife's decease an acre and a half of meadow "in Namskaket meadow," and one third of the land lying undivided after his wife's death. He also gave him "my musket cat-box and cutlass and one pistol." He gave to his son Thomas "my back sword and one pistol" and to his grandson Jonathan Snow "my carbine." The witnesses were Samuel Knowles, Thomas Crosby, Jr., and Jonathan Sparrow.

The will of his widow, Mrs Jane Snow, of Harwich, is printed

(n) Ib. 223, 224.
(o) Ib. 232.
(p) Ib. 271.
(q) 6 ib. 30, 31.
(r) Ib. 186, 187.
(s) Ib. 206, 211.
(t) 2 Mf. 177, 178.
(u) 1 Barn. Prob. Recs. 9; 3 Mf. 177; 13 ib. 19.
(v) 1 Barn. Prob. Recs 113.

(w) 1 Barn. Prob. Recs. 110.
(x) Ib. 112.

10   NICHOLAS¹ SNOW OF EASTHAM

in full in 47 New England Historical and Genealogical Register, at page 186, and is recorded in 3 Barnstable Probate Records, page 271. It was proved July 2, 1712. She makes her son Nicholas and her brother Jonathan Sparrow executors. She gives articles to her three sons Nicholas, Thomas and Prence, to her daughter Anne Atwood and to her grandchildren Jane Nickerson and Jane Snow. Her cattle she divides equally among all her children. The rest of her moveable estate she divides equally between her two daughters Mary and Sarah. The witnesses to her will are Mary Sparrow and Martha Cobb. She signs with a mark. Her inventory amounted to £39 16s. 8d. in personal property.(x1)

Children,
all born in Eastham.(y)
By 1st wife:
Anna, b. in Eastham July 7, 1656; m.(z) Eldad Atwood in Eastham Feb. 14, 1683-4. Her children were born in Eastham.(z)

By 2d wife:
Mary, b. Nov. 30, 1661; m. in Eastham Jan. 22, 1690-1, William² (Nicholas², William¹) Nickerson. Her children were born in Eastham.(a)
Nicholas, b. Dec. 6, 1663; m.(b) in Eastham Lydia Shaw April 4, 1689. He moved to Harwich in 1706 and about 1729 to Rochester, where he d. about 1754, leaving a will. His children were mostly born in Eastham.(b) June 3, 1690, he was admitted a freeman of Eastham.(c)
Elizabeth, b. May 9, 1666; d.(d) Jan. 18, 1675-6.
Thomas, b. Aug. 6, 1668; m.(e) 1st Feb. 8, 1692-3, Hannah, daughter of Lt. Silas Sears, who was b. in December, 1672,(e) and 2d(f) Sept. 30, 1706, Lydia Hamlin, widow of Eleazer Hamlin, and daughter of Paul Sears; d. after 1732. He had children by both wives born in Eastham.(g) See Sears Genealogy, 42, 43, 48.
Sarah, b. May 10, 1671.
Prence, b. May 22, 1674.
Elizabeth, b. June 22, 1676; d. March 22, 1677-8.
Hannah, b. Sept. 16, 1679.

THIRD GENERATION.
Prence³ (Mark,² Nicholas¹) Snow, b. in Eastham May 22, 1674; m. Hannah, daughter of Samuel Storrs of Barnstable;(h) d. in Harwich July 7, 1742, in his 69th year. He was first ensign and then lieutenant of the military company.
Prence Snow's wife was admitted to the Harwich church March 6, 1708-9. His children, Jabez, Samuel, Prence, Hannah and Mercy, were baptized March 20, 1708-9.(i) He

---

(x1) 3 Barn. Prob. Recs. 273.
(y) 8 Plym. Col. Recs. 30, 58; Eastham Recs.; 5 Mf. 23; 7 ib. 14, 15; 15 ib. 36, 37.
(z) 4 ib. 141.
(a) Ib. 33.
(b) Har. Recs.; 4 Mf. 207.

(c) 6 Plym. Col. Recs. 239.
(d) East. Recs.; 7 Mf. 14.
(e) 8 ib. 13.
(f) 4 ib. 177.
(g) Ib. 175, 177, 178; 8 ib. 13.
(h) Brewster Gravestone Recs. 57.
(i) 4 Mf. 247; Brewster Ch. Recs.

was admitted July 17, 1720.(j) She d. in Harwich between Oct. 19, 1751 (date of her will), and Dec. 19, 1751 (date of probate).

Prence Snow was chosen one of the selectmen in 1718 and served for 13 years.(k)

May 18, 1711, Prence Snow was one of the purchasers from John Quason and other Indians of a large tract of land in what is now Harwich and Brewster, besides Monomoy Great Beach and Strong Island in Chatham.(l)

April 19, 1714, the proprietors met in the house of Nicholas Snow within the present limits of Brewster, and divided the lands in Harwich. Of the portion N. of the road from Chatham to Yarmouth Prence Snow obtained the 19th lot, and of the portion S. of that road, the 5th lot.(m)

In 1713 he was a lot owner in "Sipsons Land" in what is now East Brewster.(n)

Prence Snow of Harwich, March 23, 1720-1, conveyed to Jonathan Sparrow of Eastham for £14 10s., his half of a lot of land in Harwich in the tract lately purchased of the Sipsons and called the 17 shares purchase.(o)

In 1724 Ensign Prence Snow bought one of the 23 spots for a pew in the new church for £6.(p)

In the drawing of the "Little Division" in the Quason purchase Oct. 14, 1730, he drew the 20th lot.(p1)

Prence Snow left a will, dated Jan. 13, 1740-1, and proved July 20, 1742.(q) He made his son Jabez sole executor, and mentions also his wife Hannah, his daughter Mary Burgess, his granddaughter Hannah Snow, his grandsons Mark and Prence Snow, his granddaughter Mary Snow, and his son Jonathan Snow. His sons Jabez and Jonathan were residuary devisees of his real estate. The inventory of his real and personal estate was dated June 17, 1742, and amounted to £1515 5s. 6d.(q1) His widow March 23, 1746-7, joined in an agreement with her sisters dividing the land her father, Samuel Storrs, had left them, she obtaining one-fifth.(q11) She left a will, dated October 19, 1751, and proved Dec. 19, 1751.(q2) The inventory of her estate, taken Jan. 14, 1751-2, amounted to £66 5s. 10d. in personal property.(q3) She mentions her daughter Mary Burgess, her granddaughter Hannah Snow (daughter of her deceased son Samuel), her grandson Prince Snow, her granddaughter Mary Snow (daughter of her deceased son Prince), and her sons Jabez and Jonathan, who with her

---

(j) 5 Mf. 18.
(k) 2 Freeman, 532, 759.
(l) Deyo, 832; Old Superior Ct. Recs. No. 63,883.
(m) Deyo, 533, 534.
(n) Deyo, 834, 835.
(o) 14 Mf. 179, 180.
(p) 2 Freeman, 504.

(p1) Deyo, 834; Old Superior Ct. Recs. No. 30,339.
(q) 6 Barn. Prob. Recs. 227.
(q1) Ib. 230.
(q11) 5 Mansfield (Conn.) Land Book, 174; 51 N. E. Reg. 76.
(q2) 8 Barn. Prob. Recs. 480.
(q3) Ib. 505.

daughter Mary Burgess are her residuary legatees. Her son Jabez is made sole executor. The will is signed with a mark.

Children,
born in Harwich:(r)
Jabez, b. Nov. 11, 1699.
Hannah, b. Nov. 29, 1701.
Samuel, b. Dec. 16 1703; m. Mary, daughter of Stephen and Sarah (Howes) Hopkins March 6, 1729-30; d. July 26, 1730.(s)
Mercy, b. Nov. 18, 1705.
Prence, b. Oct. 26, 1707; m. Jane ; d. May 24, 1740.(t)
Jonathan, b. Dec. 22, 1709.
David, b. Dec. 22, 1709.
Mary, b. Sept. 10, 1712; m. Burgess.

Copy of
WILL OF PRENCE SNOW.

In the Name of God Amen January the thirteenth 1740 I Prence Snow of Harwich in the County of Barnstable within the Province of the Massachusetts Bay in New England Gentlemn being weak in body but of Perfect mind and memory thanks be given to God therefore calling to mind the mortality of my Body and knowing yt it is appointed for all men once to Dye do make & ordain this my Last will and Testament that is to say principally and first of all I Give and recommend my Soul into the hands of God yt Gave it and my body I recommend to the Earth to be buried in Decent Christian burial at the Discretion of my Exectr herein after named Nothing doubting but at the Resurrection I shall receive ye same again through ye mighty Power of God and as Touching such worldly Estate wherewithall it hath pleased God to bless me in this Life I Give Demise and Dispose of the same in the following manner and form.

Imprimis I will that all my Just Debts and funeral charges be well and truly paid out of my moveable or personal estate and then I Give and bequeath unto Hannah my well beloved wife the use and Improvement of the one third of all my upland and meddow During her Natural Life Also my will is yt my. wife have the whole and sole Disposal of all the Land her Father gave her Lying in Mansfield in Connecticut further I Give to my wife all my Personall or moveable estate after my Debts and ye Legacies herein given out are all paid out I also give unto her the use and Improvement of my three eighths in ye wind Gristmill whh I own in partnership with my Neighbours during her Life I also give and bequeath to my well beloved wife ye use and Improvement off of ye Westerly half of my Dwelling house with half my Barn so long as she shall remain my widdow.

Item I give and bequeath to my well beloved and Natural Daughter Mary Burg ye southerly part of a half a Lot of Land that I bought of my brother Nicholas Snow scituate in Harwich at ye southerly from Samuell Crosbey Land near the Clift pond from ye middle of a Deep Valley yt comes

---

(r) Har. Recs.; 4 Mf. 176, 177.
(s) Brewster Gravestone Rec. 58; Har. Recs.; 8 Mf. 35.
(t) Har. Recs.; 13 Mf. 71; Brewster Gravestone Recs. 57.

up from ye Clift pond and runs across ye said half lot to ye south end of said half lot to her her Heirs and assigns forever and also I give unto her my said Daughter Mary one hundred pounds worth of ye old Tenor out of my moveable Estate with what she hath had since marriage.

Item I Give and bequeath unto my Granddaughter Hannah Snow fifty pounds in bills of credit of ye old Tenr or ye value of fifty pounds in Land out of my Real Estate to her her heirs & assigns forever.

Item I Give and bequeath unto my Grandson Mark Snow my Gun and Cuttlass and Catouch-box.

Item I Give and bequeath to my Natural Grandson Prence Snow that Lot of Land that I bought and hold by Deed from Jacob Davis and another half Lot that bought and hold by Deed from Paul Sears and John Wing and my part of a Lot whh I hold in Partnership with Edmund Freeman Esq. being on the Long pond and a piece of meddow yt I bought of Jonathan Bangs & a half share Lot of meddow yt I had of Thomas Clarke, Esqr. to him his Heirs & assigns forever he my said Grandson Prence Snow paying out to my Granddaughter Mary Snow a Legacie of fifty pounds in full for her Portion out of my Estate which I will and bequeath to her.

Item. I Give to my Natural son Jabez Snow Ten acres of Land where his Dwelling house now stands and one quarter of the wind grist mill after his mother's Decease to him his Heirs and assigns forever.

Item I Give and bequeath to my Natural son Jonathan Snow & to his Heirs and assigns forever my other half Quarter of the wind grist mill

Item I Give and bequeath unto my Natural & well beloved sons Jabez Snow and Jonathan Snow equally between them & to their Heirs & assigns forever all the Remainder of my upland and meddow with the fences to ye same belonging only Reserving to my wife the Use and Improvement of one third as aforesd during her Life & then the whole to the said Jabez Snow and Jonathan Snow as abovesaid and I do hereby constitute make appoint and Ordain by above named son Jabez Snow to be my whole and sole Execr. of this my Last Will & Testament and I do hereby utterly disallow revoke and Disannull all & every other former Testaments wills Legacies & bequests & executors by me in any wise before named willed or bequeathed Ratifying and Confirming this and no other to be my Last will will and and Testament In witness whereof I have hereunto set my hand and seal the day and year above written

Prence Snow (Seal)

Signed Sealed Published Pronounced & Declared by the said Prence Snow to be his Last Will and Testament in the Presence of us the Subscribers

Joseph Payne
John Crosbee
Chillingth Foster.

Copy of
WILL OF HANNAH SNOW.

In the Name of God Amen this 19th day of Octor. Anno Domini 1751 I Hannah Snow of Harwich in the County of Barnstable Within the province of the Massachusetts Bay in New England being the widdow of Prince Snow of said Harwich Deceased being week in body and well stricken in years but of Disposing mind and memory Thanks be to god therefore calling to mind the mortallity of my body and knowing that it is appointed for all men once to die do make and ordain this my Last will and Testament That is to say Principally and first of all I give and Recomend my Soul into the Hands of God that gave it and my body I Recomend to the Earth to be buried in Decent Christian Burial at the Discretion of my Execr. hereinafter named & nothing doubting but at the General Resurrection I shall Receive the same again by the mighty power of God and as Touching such worldly Estate wherewith it hath pleased God to bless me in this Life I give Demise and Dispose of the same In the following manner and form.

Imprimis I will that my Just Debts and funeral Charges be well & Truly paid by my Execr. and then I give and Bequeath unto my well beloved Daughter Mary Burge and to her Heirs and assigns forever six pounds Thirteen Shillings and four pence Lawfull money of New England to be Leivd. out of my Estate as also my best Feather Bed Bedstoad and Curtain and also the furniture belonging to it and my Brass Kittle and my Pewter Platter marked with the Letters S. S. M. on it and all my wearing apparel.

Item I Give and Bequeath to my Grandaughter Hannah Snow Daughter to my son Samuell Snow Deceasd & to hir heirs and assigns forever the sum of two pounds Thirteen Shillings and four pence Lawfull money of New England to be Leivd. out of my Estate.

Item I Give and Bequeath to my Grandson Prince Snow my Deceasd Husbands Silver Shoo Buckels.

Item I Give and Bequeath unto my two sons Jabez and Jonathan Snow and to their Heirs and Assigns forever all that Hundred pounds Old Tenor which my sd Deceased Husband sold a piece of Land for to James Ellis and Then I give and Bequeath unto my above named two sons and to my above named Daughter Burgis and to their heirs and assigns forever all the Rest of my moveable Estate both indoors and without to be equally divided among them three or among their Heirs or assigns and I do hereby utterly disallow Revoke and Disanul all and every other former Testaments wills Leagucies and Bequests and Execrs by me in any ways Before named willed and Bequeathed Rattifying this and no other to be my last will and Testament and do constitute make and Ordain my son Jabez Snow to be my whole and sole Execr. of this my last will and Testament In Witness whereof I have hereunto set my hand and seal the day and year above written.

hir
Hannah X Snow (Seal)
mark

Signed Sealed Published Pronounced and Declared By the said Hannah Snow to her last will & Testamt. In presence of us &c
John Snow
Thomas Crosby
Philip Selew

* Item I Give and bequeath to my Grandaughter Mary Snow Daughter of my son Prince Snow Deceased one silver spoon marked P. S. H.

FOURTH GENERATION.

Jabez⁴ (Prence,⁵ Mark,² Nicholas¹) Snow, b. Nov. 11, 1699; m.(u) April 2, 1724, Elizabeth⁴ Lewis, b. August 28, 1701, daughter of Deacon John³ (Edward,² George¹) Lewis, of Barnstable, and Elizabeth Huckins, his wife; d. probably shortly before 1770.

In 1725 he dwelt at Namskaket.(v)

He was chosen one of the selectmen in 1730 and sorved for 20 years.(w)

In 1742 he was executor of his father's estate and in 1751 of his mother's.

Feb. 13, 1741-2, Jabez Snow and his wife, signed a release for her portion of her father's estate.(x)

Oct. 22, 1742, he was appointed

(u) 2 Otis's Barnstable Families, 139.
(v) 2 Freeman, 500.
(w) Ib. 532, 759; Deyo, 845.
(x) Barn. Prob. Recs.

guardian of Prince Snow and Mary Snow, children of his brother Prince Snow, Jr.,(y) and Dec. 9, 1756, he rendered his account as guardian of Prince.(z)

In 1743 Jabez Snow and William Freeman were appointed agents to agree with the agents of Eastham respecting the rates of persons in either town owning lands or meadows in the other.(a)

Oct. 10, 1758, Mr. Jabez Snow was chosen by the legislature one of the guardians of the Indians of Harwich, Yarmouth and Eastham, but by inadvertence the resolve was not laid before the governor. Therefore a resolve was passed Jan. 3, 1759, re-electing them and ratifying their acts.(b)

In 1760, when the meeting house was repaired, Jabez Snow was one of the precinct committee.(c)

Children,
born in Harwich:(d)
Elizabeth, b. Nov. 12, 1724.
Mark, b. Oct. 13, 1727.
Sarah, b. July 12, 1729.
Mehitable, b. April 22, 1731; bap. April 25, 1731.(e) She m.(f) 1st Aug. 23, 1753, Samuel⁵ (Nathaniel,⁴ Stephen,³ Giles,² Stephen¹)

(y) 6 Barn. Prob. Recs. 187, 188.
(z) 9 ib. 264.
(a) Deyo, 510.
(b) 16 Mass. Prov. Laws (Appendix, vol. 11), 241; 16 Mf. 241.
(c) Deyo, 903.
(d) Har. Recs.; 8 Mf. 162.
(e) Brewster Church Recs.; 6 Mf. 217. John Snow had a daughter Mehitable, b. Jan. 16, 1733-4 (8 Mf. 163), but she d. in May, 1755 (10 Mf. 124).
(f) Har. Recs.

Hopkins of Harwich, who d. Nov. 15, 1761;(g) 2d Reuben Ryder, of Chatham, Oct. 16, 1766,(h) who d. before April 30, 1773; and 3d Deacon Paul Crowell, of Chatham, May 4, 1775.(h) She d. before June 29, 1813. She had children by all three husbands. Her daughter Mercy Hopkins m. John[6] (John,[4] Isaac,[3] John,[2] Edmond[1]) Hawes, of Chatham.(i)

    Samuel, b. Jan. 31, 1735-6.
    Mercy, b. Nov. 22, 1739.
    Hannah, b. March 5, 1741-2.

STORRS.

Samuel[1] Storrs(k) was born in the parish of Sutton cum Lound,(l) Nottinghamshire, England, shortly before Dec. 7, 1640; m. 1st Dec. 6, 1666, in Barnstable, Plymouth colony, Mary, daughter of Thomas Huckins, who d. there Sept. 24, 1683, and 2d Dec. 14, 1685, widow Hester Egard, who d. in Mansfield, Conn., April 13, 1730, aged 88 years. He d. there April 30, 1719.

He was a resident of Barnstable in 1663 and removed to Mansfield about 1698. His 1st wife was a member of the Barnstable church in 1683. He was admitted a member March 8, 1685-6. His will was dated May 22, 1717, and was proved July 7, 1719. He had been possessed of considerable property. By his will he gave his five daughters, Sarah, Hannah, Elizabeth, Lydia and Esther, 160 acres of land at Corry Rock in Mansfield equally, and after his wife's decease all his movables and household stuff within doors and cattle if there were any, Lydia to have the feather bed he lay on with the furniture thereof over and above the rest.

    Children,(m)
    all born in Barnstable:
    By 1st wife:

Mary, b. Dec. 31, 1667; not mentioned in her father's will and probably d. before him.

Sarah, b. June 26, 1670.

Hannah, b. March 28, 1672; m. Prence[2] Snow, of Harwich.(m1)

Elizabeth, b. May 31, 1675.

Samuel, b. May 17, 1677.

Lydia, b. June, 1679.

Mehitable, (bap.) Sept. 16, 1683; d. in infancy.

    By 2d wife:

Thomas, b. Oct. 27, 1686.

Hester, b. about the middle of October, 1688.

Cordiel, b. Oct. 14, 1692.

Who Hester Egard or her 1st husband was is not known. Her name may also have been written Agard. She had a son John by her 1st husband who went to Mansfield and married.(n) She may also have had a daughter

---

(g) Brewster Gravestone Recs. 57.
(h) Chat. Recs.
(i) See "Edmond Hawes" and "Stephen[1] and Giles[2] Hopkins," by the compiler.
(k) Also written Stores, Storr, and the like.
(l) Composed of the villages of Sutton and Lound. The church was in Sutton.

(m) Barn. Recs.; 12 Mf. 154; 4 Savage's Geneal. Dict. of N. E. 211.
(m1) 51 N. E. Reg. 76.
(n) Ancient Windham, by Weaver, 30.

Esther who d. young. The Boston town records give the birth July 16, 1683, of Esther, daughter of John and Esther Agard.(o)

Charles Storrs, in "The Storrs Family," pp. 19-38 and 75-83, gives an account of Samuel[1] Storrs and his ancestors, printing several wills.

The will of William Storrs (No. 1), of Lound of the parish of Sutton was dated Aug. 3, 1557, and was proved at York Oct. 6, 1557. He mentions his wife Dorothy and the following children:
Robert. (No. 2)
William.
Elizabeth.
Dyonice.
Ellen.

He directs his body to be buried in the church of St. Bartholomew of Sutton.

The will of Robert Storrs (No. 2), husbandman, of Lound in the parish of Sutton and county of Nottingham, was dated May 16, 1588, and proved at York, Feb. 5, 1588-9. He had been twice married. His 2d wife Mabel survived him. He names the following children:
By his 1st wife:
Cordall. (No. 3)
By his 2d wife:
Robert. (A)
John.
Dorothy.
Anne.

He directs that his body shall be buried in the church or church yard "of Sutton and Lound aforsaid."

(o) Boston Births, Baptisms, Marriages and Deaths, 159.

The will of Cordall Storrs (No. 3) of Lound in the county of Nottingham was dated Feb. 23, 1615-6, and proved at York Oct. 10, 1616. He names his wife Isabel, his mother Mabel, his brothers Robert and John, and his sisters Dorothy and Anne. He names the following children:
Thomas. (No. 4)
William.
Mary.

He directs that he be buried in the church or church yard of Sutton.

No will of Thomas Storrs (No. 4) has been found. He was baptized April 25, 1605, in the parish of SuttoncumLound, and married Mary   . Their children were baptized in the parish church as follows:
Thomas, Jan. 27, 1632-3.
Cordall, Sept. 21, 1635.
George, April 29, 1638; d. April, 1653.
Samuel (No. 5), Dec. 7, 1640; the emigrant.
Joseph, Aug. 20, 1643.
Elizabeth, Feb. 8, 1648-9.
Mary, Nov. 2, 1650.

The will of Robert Storrs (A) "of Lound in the Parish of Sutton upon Lound in the Countie of Nottingham," great-uncle of Samuel (No. 5), was dated July 12, 1658, and proved at York March 29, 1662. He was buried in Sutton Dec. 23, 1661. He mentions his deceased brother Cordall Storrs (No. 3), his nephew Thomas (No. 4), son of Cordall, and Thomas's children Thomas, Cordall, Samuel (No. 5) to whom he gives £13, Joseph, Elizabeth and Mary. He directs that he be buried in the parish church of Sutton.

The wills of William Storrs, uncle, and Cordall Storrs, brother, of Samuel (No. 5), style the testators yeomen. All the above testators had considerable property.

HUCKINS.

Thomas[1] Huckins(p) was born in England about 1618 and came over to New England before he was 21; m. 1st in 1642 Mary (daughter of Isaac[1] Wells of Barnstable), who was buried July 28, 1648,(q) and 2d Nov. 3, 1648, Rose, widow of Hugh Hillier of Yarmouth,(r) who d. in 1687, aged about 71 years. He was cast away in his vessel in a gale and perished Nov. 9, 1679, in his 62d year.(r1)

He resided first in Boston or vicinity.

In 1637 a military company was formed, and Thomas Huckins was the 6th signer of the roll. March 13, 1638-9, it was incorporated as The Military Company of Massachusetts. It was afterward called The Ancient and Honorable Artillery Company of Massachusetts. In 1639-40 he was chosen ensign.(s)

Mr. Otis, in his "Barnstable Families," vol. 2, pp. 58-65, gives an account of him. He styles him Mr. Thomas Huckins.

He was an exemplary member of Mr. Lothrop's church. His lot in Barnstable was granted Sept. 14, 1640, and Mr. Otis thinks he was one of the earliest settlers. "As a business man he perhaps had no superior in the colony, certainly not in the town. . . . . Mr. Huckins had a landing place or wharf near his house, where he discharged and received freights. He was one of the 'farmers' or partners that hired the Cape Cod fisheries. In 1670 considerable quantities of tar were manufactured in the colony, and he was appointed one of the purchasers." Oct. 4, 1675, he was appointed Commissary General of the colony.(t) He held various colonial and town offices, each for several years, to wit: constable, selectman, deputy to the colony court, member of the council of war for the colony and for the town, member of the committee to audit the colony accounts, surveyor of highways, and member of the grand and petit juries. In 1670 and 1671 he and Mr. Thomas Hinckley were appointed "to look after the minister's rate," and in 1677 he was on a committee to adjust the claims against the col-

---

(p) Also written Huckens, Huckings, Huggins, and the like.

(q) 8 Plym. Col. Recs. 44, 45; 6 Mf. 138, 139.

(r) 8 Plym. Col. Recs. 45.

(r1) 2 Otis, 62, 63, 64.

(s) 1 Roberts's History of The Ancient and Honorable Artillery Co., 9, 10, 12, 28, 84, 130, 234. Roberts says it is known that he was one of the number who went to England, and under command of Col. William Rainsburrow of the above company, fought for Cromwell, returning to New England, but he gives no authority, and his statement is at least doubtful.

(t) 5 Plym. Col. Recs. 175; Bodge's King Philip's War, 183, 439.

ony for expenses incurred in King Philip's war.

March 1, 1652-3, he was licensed "to sell wines and strong waters until the next June court." June 1, 1663, "his former liberty [was] renewed to keep an ordinary at Barnstable." He had probably been authorized to keep an ordinary, or public house, during the previous ten years. He was for several years receiver of the excise imposed on the importation of wines and liquors and powder and shot. In the last mentioned year he was captain of the packet, and he brought into the town for himself 35 gallons of wine and 9 of brandy, besides liquors and powder and shot for other persons. Mr. Otis says:

"After the death of Mr. Lothrop the Barnstable church ceased to act in harmony. Mr. Huckins adhered to the party that invited Mr. William Sergeant to become its pastor. This faction belonged to the political party that in 1656 had become dominant in the colony, and had adopted the narrow sectarian policy that had always ruled in Massachusetts. That Mr. Huckins adopted the intolerant policy of the party to which he belonged does not appear. Though constable in 1657, he lived on friendly terms with his neighbor Nicholas Davis [of Quaker sympathies], and as the notorious Barlow of Sandwich was employed to search the house of Davis, it may be inferred that Huckins declined to act officially in the case. In 1662 Mr. Huckins cordially united with the other faction of the church in the settlement of Mr. Walley, a man of peace and an able advocate of the tolerant principles of the Rev. Mr. Lothrop." He was a large land owner.(u)

Children,
born in Barnstable:(v)
By 1st wife:
Lydia, b. July 4 and buried July 28, 1644.
Mary, b. March 29, 1646; m. Dec. 6, 1666, Samuel¹ Storrs.
Elizabeth, b. Feb. 27, 1647-8; buried Dec. 28, 1648.
By 2d wife:
John, b. about Aug. 2, 1649.
Thomas, b. April 25, 1651; m. 1st May 1, 1680, Hannah, daughter of John Chipman, and 2d Aug. 17, 1698, Sarah, widow of Samuel Hinckley; left issue.
Hannah, b. Oct. 14, 1653; m.(w) Feb. 24, 1674-5, James Gorham.
Joseph, b. Feb. 21, 1655-6; lost with his father Nov. 9, 1679.

SECOND GENERATION.

John² ('Thomas¹) Huckins, b. about Aug. 2, 1649; m. Aug. 10, 1670, Hope, daughter of Elder John¹ Chipman; d. Nov. 10, 1678. His widow m. March 1, 1682-3, Jonathan Cobb, and removed to Middleboro. He was constable in 1672.

Children,
born in Barnstable:
Elizabeth, b. Oct. 1, 1671; m. June 4, 1695, Deacon John² Lewis; d. July 12, 1741.
Mary, b. April 3, 1673; m. in 1690 Nathan Bassett of Sandwich.

(u) See Plym. Col. Recs., vols. 2-8, passim.
(v) 8 Plym. Col. Recs. 44, 45; Barn. Recs.; 6 Mf. 138, 139.
(w) Barn. Recs.; 5 Mf. 72.

Experience, b. June 4, 1675; m. Thomas Lewis Sept. 28, 1699. Hope, b. May 10, 1677; m. Thomas Nelson. She d. in Middleboro Dec. 7, 1782, aged 105 years, 6 mos. and 20 days, "the longest liver of any of English descent born in Barnstable."

HILLIER.

Rose Hillier was the widow of Hugh Hillier (or Tilly),(x) who came to Salem from Dorchester, England, or its vicinity, in 1629, in the Lyon's Whelp, under the auspices of the Rev. John White of Dorchester, to serve Sir Richard Saltonstall.(y) He afterward settled in Yarmouth. March 5, 1638-9, with Mr. Nicholas Simpkins and Giles Hopkins he deposed to the will of Peter Werden, the elder, of Yarmouth.(z) March 1, 1641-2, he was with Thomas Starr and another complained of as a scoffer and jeerer at religion and as causing disorder at town meetings, and was ordered to answer at the next court.(a) June 7, 1642, styled planter, he appears on a bond in the sum of £40 that Thomas Starr shall appear at the next court, shall be of good behavior in the meantime and forbear attending town meetings during the pleasure of the court. In the margin it is noted that the bond was released.(b) In August, 1643, he was one of those in Yarmouth between 16 and 60 able to bear arms.(c) June 5, 1644, he is mentioned as one of the surveyors of highways of Yarmouth.(d) His wife's maiden name is not known. They had Deborah, b. in Yarmouth Oct. 30, 1643, and Samuel, b. there about July 30, 1646.(e) He d. in Yarmouth Jan. 28, 1647-8, and was buried the next day.(f)

CHIPMAN.

Elder John¹ Chipman(g) was the only son of Mr. Thomas Chipman of Brinspittal near Dorchester, Dorestshire, England, who had had an estate there; b. about 1621. He had two sisters Hannah and Tamson, who remained in England. His father d. before he left Eng-

---

(x) In the Plym. Col. Recs. the name is sometimes Tilly and sometimes Hillier. In some places it is Hugh Tilly, alias Hillier. It has been erroneously stated that before his death he was of Barnstable.
(y) 1 Felt's Annals of Salem, 36, 99, 112, 170; 1 Hist. Colls. by Ebenezer Hazard, 280; 4 Savage, 302; Pope, 455, who says he was appointed to help in setting up a sawmill in Salem.
(z) 1 Plym. Col. Recs. 117.
(a) 2 ib. 36.

(b) Ib. 41.
(c) 8 ib. 194.
(d) 2 ib. 73.
(e) 8 ib. 45; Barn. Recs.; 6 Mf. 138, 139; 12 ib. 154.
(f) 8 Plym. Col. Recs. 4. See also Swift's Old Yarmouth, 65. Pope says the Scituate Church Recs. show the m. of the widow Tilly at "Nocett" Nov. 3, 1648, to Thomas "Higgins." This should be Huckins.
(g) Mr. Otis (v. 1, pp. 153-161) has an account of him. See also Plym. Col. Recs. vols. 2-5, passim.

land and his mother before 1642. He came to New England in May, 1637, in the service of his cousin Mr. Richard Derby, who settled in Plymouth. He had the trade of a carpenter. March 2, 1641-2, Ann Hinde, the wife of William Hoskins, aged about 25 years, being examined before Mr. Edward Winslow in a case between John Darby(g1) and John Chipman, made oath that she lived in the house of Mr. Darby's father with John Chipman at the time when "the said John Chipman came from thence to New England to serve Mr. Richard Darbey, his brother." That she afterwards came over also to serve the said Richard Darby, "when old Mr. Darbey requested this deponant to comend him to his cozen Chipman, and tell him if hee were a good boy hee would send him over the money that was due to him when hee saw good; and further, wheras this deponant heard the said John Darbey affeirme that his money was paid to John Chipmans mother, shee further deposeth that his said mother was dead a quarter of a yeare or therabouts before her old master sent this message to his cozen Chipman."(h)

Feb. 8, 1657-8, he made a declaration(i) that he supposed himself to be about 37 years old and that the following May it would be 21 years since he came from England. He was the only son and heir of Mr. Thomas Chipman, late deceased, at Brinspudel, about 5 m. from Dorchester, Dorsetshire, and he had two sisters, Hannah and Tamson. His father had entailed to him and his heirs a tenement or tenements with a mill and other edifices belonging thereto in Whitchurch of Marshwood Vale near Bridport in Dorsetshire, worth £40 or £50 per annum. His father, while single, had sold them, he thinks about 60 years before, to his kinsman Mr. Christopher Derby of Sturhill near Bridport for only £40 and the agreement to maintain him during life with diet, apparel, &c. Derby gave him only a poor cottage and garden spot. John Derby, late deceased, of Yarmouth, had acknowledged to him (John Chipman) that his father Christopher had done him (John) much wrong.

In August, 1643, he was not on the list of those between 16 and 60 able to bear arms. In 1646 he m. 1st in Plymouth Hope,* second daughter of John¹ Howland and Elizabeth,* (daughter of John¹) Tilley, his wife, Mayflower passengers. He was of Barnstable in 1649. His wife d. there Jan. 8, 1683-4, aged 54 years, and is buried in the ancient burying ground on Lothrop's hill, where her gravestone was standing in 1860.

He m. 2d Ruth Bourne, daughter of Mr. William Sargeant, b. in Charlestown Oct. 25, 1642, who had m. 1st Jonathan, son of Josiah Winslow of Marshfield and 2d Mr. Richard Bourne of Sandwich. Elder John Chipman d. in Sandwich April 7, 1708. His 2d wife

---

(g1) Usually written Derby.
(h) 4 Plym. Col. Recs. 98.

(i) 1 Otis, 153; 35 N. E. Reg. 127, 128; 4 ib. 251.

d. at Sandwich in 1713, leaving no issue. His will and inventory are printed in full in 3 Mayflower Descendant, 181-185.(j) His 2d wife's will appears in the same volume, pp. 185, 186. He later resided in West Barnstable (also called Great Marshes), and about 1680 removed to Sandwich. His 1st wife had joined the Barnstable church Aug. 7, 1650, and he joined Jan. 30, 1652-3. He was chosen one of the Ruling Elders of that church and was solemnly invested with the office April 14, 1670. He was the last Ruling Elder. Upon his removal to Sandwich strong, but ineffectual, efforts were made to retain him in Barnstable. He was a freeman in 1649. He served several terms as deputy to the colony court and as one of the selectmen and in other important public capacities. June 5, 1663, he was one of those taking the Colonial Treasurer's account.(k) "For his public services the court in 1669 granted him one hundred acres of land, between Taunton and Titicut, which was afterwards confirmed to him."

March 7, 1675-6, the court, considering the estate of Capt. John Gorham, ordered Mr. Hinckley, Mr. Chipman and Mr. Huckins "to take Care that such prte of the said estate which belongeth unto his youngest Children be prserved and Disposed of to them as they Come to be of age."(l)

He left a considerable estate.

Children, (m) all by his 1st wife and all born in Barnstable except the 1st, who was born in Plymouth:

Elizabeth, b. June 24, 1647; m. as his 2d wife, Hosea Joyce of Yarmouth.

Hope, b. Aug. 13, 1652; m. 1st John[3] (Thomas[1]) Huckins, who d. Nov. 10, 1678. Their daughter Elizabeth, b. Oct. 1, 1671, m. Deacon John[3] Lewis June 4, 1695. She m. 2d March 1, 1682-3, Jonathan Cobb.(n) June 3, 1703, she was dismissed from the church in Barnstable to the church in Middleboro. From there the family removed to Portland, Me.

Lydia, b. Dec. 25, 1654; m. as his 3d wife John Sargeant, removed to Malden, and d. March 2, 1730-1, leaving no issue.

John, b. March 2, 1656-7; d. May 29, 1657.

Hannah, b. Jan. 14, 1658-9; m. Thomas[3] Huckins May 1, 1680; d. in Barnstable Nov. 4, 1696, leaving issue.

Samuel, b. April 15, 1661; m. Dec. 27, 1686, Sarah, daughter of Elder Henry Cobb; d. in 1723, leaving issue. She d. Jan. 8, 1742-3.

Ruth, b. Dec. 31, 1663; m. April 7, 1682, Eleazer Crocker; d. April 8, 1698, leaving issue.

Bethia, b. July 1, 1666; m. Shubael Dimmock and d. early, probably leaving two children.

Mercy, b. Feb. 6, 1668-9; m.

(j) 3 Barn. Prob. Recs. 228-231.
(k) 8 Plym. Col. Recs. 108.
(l) 4 Mf. 153.

(m) 8 Plym. Col. Recs. 4, 42, 43; Barn. Recs.; 4 Mf. 121.
(n) Barn. Recs.; 3 Mf. 149.

Deacon Nathaniel Skiff and removed to Chilmark.

John, b. March 3, 1670-1. He was thrice married. He removed to Sandwich and thence to Chilmark and later to Newport, R. I. He left issue.

Desire, b. Feb. 26, 1673-4; m. Hon. Melatiah Bourne of Sandwich Feb. 23, 1695-6;(o) d. March 28, 1705, leaving issue.

WELLS.

Isaac[1] Wells,(p) of Scituate, took the oath of allegiance Feb. 1, 1638-9;(q) m. (probably his 2d wife) Margaret ; d. between June 5, 1673 (date of his will), and Dec. 24, 1673 (date of his inventory).(q1) She d. before Aug. 24, 1675, when her inventory was made.(q2) Oct. 27, 1675, administration on her estate was granted to Mr. John Miller and Isaac Chapman, nearly related to her and entitled to her property.(q3)

Oct. 11, 1639, he was among the members of Rev John Lothrop's church who with him came from Scituate to Barnstable with his family.(r)

He was a grandjuryman March 7, 1642-3.(s) He was admitted to the Barnstable church May 27, 1643.(t)

He was among those between 16 and 60 years of age able to bear arms in Barnstable in August, 1643.(u) June 2, 1649, his land in Barnstable is referred to.(v)

The estate of Anthony Gilpin of Barnstable was indebted to him April 2, 1655, he being styled "goodman Wells."(w) The estate of John Darby of Yarmouth was indebted, Feb. 22, 1655-6, to "goodman Wells."(x)

March 15, 1657-8, he signed the verdict of a jury of inquest with a mark.(y) Oct. 18, 1665, the estate of Mr. Thomas Howes, Sr., of Yarmouth, was indebted to him in the sum of £1.(z)

Deane(a) says that Joseph Wells who m. in Scituate in 1666 Grace Dipple, was probably his son. His daughter Mary m. in Barnstable in 1642 Thomas[1] Huckins.(b) His

---

(o) At p. 115 (vol. 1) Otis gives another date, viz. 1692-3.

(p) Also written Weels and Welles.

(q) 1 Plym. Col. Recs. 110; Pope, 486.

(q1) 3 Plym. Col. Wills, pt. 1, p. 90.

(q2) 3 Plym. Col. Wills, pt. 1, p. 166.

(q3) 5 Plym. Col. Recs. 180, 181.

(r) 2 Freeman, 243, 244.

(s) 2 Plym. Col. Recs. 53.

(t) Barn. Church Recs.; 9 N. E. Reg. 280.

(u) 8 Plym. Col. Recs. 193; 4 N. E. Reg. 258.

(v) 12 Plym. Col. Recs. 180.

(w) 2 Plym. Col. Wills, pt. 1, pp. 6-8; 11 Mf. 21-23.

(x) 2 Plym. Col. Wills, pt. 1, p. 29; 11 Mf. 112.

(y) 3 Plym. Col. Recs. 146, 147.

(z) 2 Plym. Col. Wills, pt. 2, p. 33; 6 Mf. 160.

(a) History of Scituate, 379.

(b) 2 Otis, 62, 63, 64.

daughter Lydia m. in Duxbury Nov. 23, 1642, Ralph Chapman. They had a son Isaac, whose house and shop later stood in Barnstable on the lot formerly owned by Isaac¹ Wells.(c) As we have seen, Isaac Chapman was one of the heirs of the estate of Margaret, widow of Isaac¹ Wells.(d)

(c) 1 ib. 151.

(d) Winsor's Duxbury 244, 1 Savage 362, and Pope 94, say that Ralph Chapman married Lydia Wills or Willis; but the compiler judges that Otis is correct in making his wife the daughter of Isaac¹ Wells.

No. 35.

LIBRARY *of*
Cape Cod
HISTORY & GENEALOGY

EDWARD KENWRICK
The Ancestor of the Kenricks or Kendricks of Barnstable County and Nova Scotia and His Descendants

YARMOUTHPORT, MASS.:
C. W. SWIFT, Publisher and Printer,
The "Register" Press.
1915.

EDWARD KENWRICK

The Ancestor of the Kenricks or Kendricks of Barnstable County and Nova Scotia and His Descendants

Copyright, 1915, by Charles W. Swift.

By
JOSIAH PAINE, Esq.,
of Harwich.

EDWARD KENWRICK, the ancestor of the Kenricks or Kendricks of Barnstable County and Nova Scotia, came, according to tradition, from the "West of England;" but at what place he first came and the date of his landing, as yet nothing has been shown with certainty. By a few it has been thought that he came to the Cape from New Hampshire. He was in Harwich in 1704, as this year the records of the town show that he married for his first wife, Elizabeth Snow. Early in 1705, he was in town prospecting in that part now South Orleans, between the head of Arey's pond, which at that period was known as Potonumocot Saltwater pond, and the fresh pond called by Indians Poponessett, now called Baker's pond, for a tract of land suitable for a farm. He finally selected a parcel of nine acres in the primeval forest on the west side of the old line between Eastham and Harwich established in 1682. The parcel adjoined the line and stretched up from John Yates' land to Poponessett, or Baker's pond as it is now called. It belonged to that noted Indian landholder, John Sipson, who resided at Potonumecot and within the limits of the old town of Harwich.* On the 27th of June, the parcel, "out of ye love" he had for "Mr. Edward Kindwrick, weaver" and for other "valewbel considerations" was conveyed to Mr. Kenwrick by Sipson, with the "liberty" of grazing, cutting timber and fire wood on any of his land "within ye township of Harwich." This tract was his first purchase so far as his deeds that are extant show. Upon a small parcel of land adjoining it, which he purchased of "Mr. John Paine," he erected his first house. In what way Mr. Kenwrick befriended the grantor, as to gain his esteem in so short a period, would interest many of his descendants at this day to know. The Indians had their likes and dislikes, and when once befriended it was never forgotten. The Sipsons, especially John and Thomas, or "little Tom," as he was sometimes called, were large owners of land which came to them by inheritance in Harwich and Eastham, and when Mr. Kenwrick made his purchase but a small portion of it had been sold to the white men. It was well that friendship existed between the two. John Sipson was an Indian of note, and had an influence among the Indians which was helpful to Mr. Kenwrick in many ways.

*The old town of Harwich included South Orleans, which was set off to Eastham in 1772, and Brewster, which was set off as a town in 1803.

Mr. Kenwrick purchased at times many acres of upland of the Indians. Among the Indian grantors that his deeds show were John Laurence, Jacob Jacob, Stephen Jacob, Amos Quason, Rebecca Quason, Lusty Tom, Amos Larrance, Samuel Quog, Joseph George, Thomas Boreman and Matthias Quansit. In their deeds they call Mr. Kenwrick a "dealer," which shows he was a "shop keeper" or "trader," and confirms the tradition that he was engaged "in trade." He purchased of Peepen and Joshua Ralph, Indians, large tracts in Harwich between Muddy Cove river and Round cove; but no deeds are found showing the dates of the sales, yet other evidence is conclusive of the fact. Mr. Kenwrick had meadow at the Great beach which he bought of Judah Hopkins; meadow in Gregory's neck at Matchapoxit,* and meadow at Chequeset near Pleasant bay. He had at the time of his death a tract of twenty acres in Truro, which he had of Experience Turner. He was clerk of the proprietors of the Great beach meadow in 1729, and for some years after. The Great beach was included in the Quasons' deed to the purchasers in 1711.

Mr. Kenwrick after 1725, changed his place of residence. He built a house on the west side of the public road now leading from Orleans to Harwich and Chatham, a short distance southwesterly of the residence of John Kenrick, Esq., at South Orleans. It was erected upon a lot of land that belonged to "Mr. Tom," the "Indian minister," then deceased, and conveyed by his sons, Lusty Tom, Abel Tom and John Tom, to Mr. Kenwrick. At that period the locality was within the limits of the old town of Harwich. The house he built, according to tradition, was of good size, and in style of those erected by the more wealthy class of that time—two stories in front and one story in rear. A few of this kind of a house are yet seen in Yarmouth. Here he continued in the same business as in the Baker's pond neighborhood— being yet a "dealer." This part of the town now his home, was as sparse in population as the locality he had removed from, but he doubtless saw advantages in moving which would be beneficial to his business, besides living near a much travelled road. In his new home prosperity attended him. Acres were added to his estate and money to his coffer.

Like most of men in different kinds of business, and in easy circumstances, at that period, he had colored servants to help in and out of the house. At the time of his death, he had three colored men and the same number of colored woman servants. They were all valued at ninety-eight pounds in the inventory of his personal property. Some of them lived in cabins on his land. When he removed to his new home near Potonumecot, the old

*This was the Indian name of Taylor's pond at South Chatham.

forest there had been but little disturbed by the white men. The pines and oaks yet their giant branches tossed, shook and creaked in the wind; the red men yet, though civilized, roamed in the woods, fished in the inlets, entrapped the fleet-footed deer, and mingled with the settlers as occasion required. The bays, ponds, inlets, streams and localities yet bore their Indian names. Some of them were euphonic and easily pronounced, while others were long, harsh and almost unpronounceable by the settlers.

On the east side of the main road northeasterly, about two hundred rods from Mr. Kenwrick's new house, on the westerly slope of a triangular piece of land which Eastham, through the efforts of the Indians, had set apart for the purpose of setting their meeting house upon, and north of the way leading down to the Saltwater pond, stood the house of their solemnities, and near it, on the same slope, their place of burial in which, until about 1830, mounds of the graves were made invisible by the plow. This house of worship of the praying Indians was here before the advent in old Harwich of Mr. Kenwrick, and remained on the spot some years after his decease it is understood. When he came, the praying Indians of Potonumecot were quite numerous, and had religious instructors. Among them during Mr. Kenwrick's time, were "Minister Tom," Jabez Jacob, an educated Indian and a native of the place; and John Tom, also an Indian of the neighborhood, whose death occurred in 1730. As Mr. Kenwrick was a friend to the natives, and they friends to him, it is quite probable that he occasionally attended their meetings, and perhaps gave them pecuniary aid in sustaining religious services. Up to the time of his death in 1743, there had been a slight decrease in their number in that part of the old town. When Rev. Ezra Stiles visited Potonumecot in 1762, he found there thirteen heads of families, eleven widows, besides a a number of children. At this time, John Ralph was their minister, and so far as known, the last of the Indian preachers there.

The records of Harwich give Mr. Kenwrick two wives. His first wife was Elizabeth Snow, to whom he was married December 24, 1704. She was probably a daughter of Lieut. Jabez Snow, who was with Capt. John Gorham in the expedition to Canada in 1690 under Sir William Phips. She died before 1713, leaving two sons.

For his second wife, he married Deborah Tucker of Harwich, April 30, 1713, whose parentage has not yet been determined. She was a strong minded woman, and known among her neighbors and townspeople as "a doctress." There is evidence that she knew the art of bleeding, indicating that she had a knowledge of surgery. She had many appreciative friends among her relation and acquaintances. In 1719, Lieut. Thomas Clarke, a prominent citizen of Harwich, residing in that part of the town now West Brewster, made her a gift of the parcel of land about one mile southeasterly of her home at Baker's pond, bordering the Potonumecot Saltwater pond on the north, which he had purchased of John Tom, an Indian, in 1717. The parcel was a valuable one, and contained by estimation about fourteen acres. This gift, he affirms, was "in consideration of that love, good will and affection" he bore "towards" her. This parcel caused him much vexation, from the time she obtained her title. Her husband was put to much trouble and expense by the "herbage men," who claimed prior right to it from the Indians. He had to have lawsuits to establish the title and keep off intruders. He began its clearing soon after 1719.

By his two wives he had four children. His children by his first wife, Elizabeth, were:

2. i Solomon,* born about 1705 or 1706.
3. ii Thomas,* born about 1708.

By second wife, Deborah, his children were:

4. iii Susanah,* born January 24, 1713-14.
5. iv Jonathan,* born Nov. 14, 1715.

Edward Kenwrick died early in the year of 1743, well stricken in years, leaving a good estate. His will bears date Nov. 30, 1742. It was witnessed by Joseph Doane, Maziah Harding and John Whitney, and was presented for proof, February 18, 1742-3. After providing for his wife, Deborah, he divided his estate among his four children: Solomon, Thomas, Susanah Wing and Jonathan. He appointed his son, Jonathan, executor, to whom he had given his homestead at his mother's death. His six colored servants with him at his death: Phillip, Zilpha, Cuffee, Barbara, Joseph and "Luce," he mentioned. Phillip he gave to Solomon, his son, and Zilpha to Susanah Wing, his daughter. The others he left with his wife. He remembered his grandson, Edward Kenwrick, a lad of seven years, son of Thomas of Harwich, and gave him twenty-five acres of land in Truro which he had purchased of Experience Turner.

His wife, Deborah, survived him and died late in fall of 1746. She made her will November 26, 1744, and her codicil July 8, 1745. They were proved December 3, 1746. The executrix was her daughter, Susanah Wing. To Solomon and Thomas, sons of her husband by his first wife, she gave the sum of five shillings each. To her daughter, Susanah Wing, she gave her wood lot southwest of Ralph pond, and her colored servants, excepting Joseph, Barbara and her little daughter. To her son, Jonathan, she gave Joseph, her negro servant, and her interest in the grist mill near Joshua Higgins's. To her little grandsons, Samuel and Anson, she made suitable presents. She gave to her faithful colored servant, Barbara, her freedom, and an enclosed piece of land for her use and improvement during life. She gave her a cow; a pair of steers; a bed and linen wheel; and her little negro daughter Barbara her freedom.

The place of burial of Mr. Edward Kenwrick and his second wife, Deborah, is not with certainty known; but as their son, Jonathan, was buried in the old Orleans cemetery, it is believed that their dust lies there.

A part of the old homestead of Edward Konwrick, with the house upon it, built in 1792, for (and occupied by) his great-grandson, Jonathan[4] Kenwrick, and yet standing, is now in possession of John Kenrick, Esq., of South Orleans.

The surname of "Kenwrick" has been indifferently spelled in the records. The three sons of Edward Kenwrick spelled their surname "Kenwrick." Some of their descendants have eliminated the w and placed in its stead d, while others have dropped both w and d, and spell it "Kenrick," deeming them as superfluous.

2. SOLOMON[2] KENWRICK (EDWARD[1]) was born in Harwich about 1706, and married Elizabeth Atkins, daughter of Samuel and Emblem (Newcomb) Atkins of Chatham, May 25, 1727. He first settled in the eastern part of Harwich, near Pleasant bay, near or upon a parcel of land his father had purchased of Joshua Ralph, an Indian. His house stood near or upon the site of the one now occupied by Andrew Kendrick. He was a mariner and farmer. He became interested in the settlement of Barrington, of which place he was one of the original grantees, and went thither with his family in or about 1762. He there took part in the meetings of the proprietors, and had an interest in shaping the start of the place. In 1768, he and his son of the same name had lots laid out to them, located and described. In 1784, the second division of land was made and his name appears in the records for the last time as a grantee. There is no record of his death at Barrington. It is thought, however, that his death occurred not far from the year 1790. His wife is reported to have been buried on Sharoes Island, Barrington, N. S., which must have been after 1769. His occupation after leaving Harwich is not shown, but from the fact he had a very large tract granted him in Barrington, it is evident farming was his business to some extent. The place he left in East Harwich was occupied by his nephew, Edward, and today by a great-grandson. He has the honor of being the father of Capt. John Kendrick, the noted navigator and discoverer of the Columbia river on the northwest coast of America. All of the children of Solomon and Elizabeth Kenwrick were born in Harwich, but only one was recorded. The following is a list of them so far as is known with certainty, though not sure as to their order of birth:

6. i Solomon,[3] born in 1731.
7. ii Elizabeth,[3] born Aug. 29, 1736; mar. Elkanah Smith of Chatham Jan. 24, 1754. They removed to Barrington.
8. iii John.[3]
9. iv Benjamin.[3] He doubtless went to Barrington.

3. THOMAS² KENWRICK (EDWARD¹) was born in Harwich, in the year 1708. He married Anna Atkins, dau. of Samuel Atkins of Chatham. He settled near his brother, Solomon, near or upon land which his father, Edward, purchased of Peepen, an Indian. His house stood near or upon the spot where the house of the late Isaiah Kendrick stood. He was a mariner and farmer. He was a man of prominence in that section of Harwich. The South precinct records of Harwich show that he was a precinct assessor in 1752 and 1753, and the records of the town show that he was a selectman in 1760. He was a large land holder in town. He died at his home in East Harwich, March 13, 1783, in his 75th year. His wife, Anna, died Oct. 31, 1799, at the age of 95. They lie buried in the old cemetery at Chatham, where stones with inscriptions mark their resting places. There is no list of his children in the records of Harwich, but the following is the list given in his will, made in 1783:

10. i Edward,⁴ born in 1735; mar. for first wife, Zelpha King, July 6, 1761; for his second wife he mar. Mary Nickerson. He had children. He died in Harwich Nov. 17, 1821. He resided on the spot where his cousin, Capt. John Kendrick, was born.

11. ii Jonathan,⁴ born about 1740; mar. Mary Bassett of Chatham August 28, 1765. He died in Harwich Sept. 17, 1823, aged 83. His wife died June 20, 1824, aged 77 years. They had children.

12. iii Thomas,⁴ mar. Phebe Smith of Chatham, Nov. 6, 1766. He settled in Harwich; died in 1826. Had children.

13. iv Henry,⁴ mar. Susan Harding of Chatham in 1776. He died in 1819. Had children.

14. v Stephen,⁴ mar. Sarah Nickerson of Chatham in 1775 for his first wife; and for second wife mar. Ziporah Harding of Chatham. He lived in Harwich and had children.

15. vi Levi,⁴ never married. He was a mariner. He went on a voyage with his cousin, the noted mariner, it is said, and never returned.

16. vii Emblem.⁴
17. viii Anna.⁴
18. ix Abigail.⁴

Thomas Kenwrick made his will February 27, 1783, and was proved March 6, 1783. He gave his eldest son, Edward, the place he had bought of his brother, Solomon Kenwrick, and other parcels of land. His homestead he gave to his sons, Edward, Henry and Stephen. He remembered his daughters, Emblem Buck, Anna Nickerson and Abigail Smith.

He had large tracts of land. His estate was valued at £471, 10 shillings. A few of his descendants of the surname are living in the town.

4. SUSANAH² KENWRICK (EDWARD¹), daughter of Edward and

Deborah (Tucker) Kenwrick, was born in that part of Harwich now South Orleans, January 24, 1713-14. She was the only daughter and married Joseph Wing, youngest son of Ananias of Harwich, February 17, 1736-7. They resided in the north precinct of Harwich. They had three children. They were:

 19. i Deborah,⁶ born Dec. 16, 1737; died Jan. 13, 1737-8.
 20. ii Elnathan,⁶ born Oct. 4, 1739.
 21. iii Deborah,⁶ born Feb. 13, 1740-1; mar. Jabez Hinckley of Barnstable Nov. 22, 1764, grandfather of the late Josiah Hinckley of Barnstable, where they resided. Jabez Hinckley was son of Deacon John Hinckley, and born Oct. 24, 1741. He died in February, 1817. The children of Jabez and Deborah Wing Hinckley were James, Josiah, Anna, Joshua, Vicy, Abiah and John.

 5. JONATHAN⁵ KENWRICK (EDWARD¹), was the youngest son by second wife, Deborah Tucker, and born November 14, 1715. He was educated for a physician and was a successful practitioner. He married Tabitha Eldridge, daughter of William Eldridge of Chatham, about 1739, and continued his residence on his father's place with his mother, until her death in 1746, when by will of his father, he became the sole owner and occupant, and here he continued to live till his death. He was a very active man and gave attention to his farm, besides attending to his professional duties. His death occurred at the age of 38, July 20, 1753. He was buried in the old cemetery at Orleans, where some years since a stone was standing with inscription, marking the place of his burial.

He died intestate, and his widow was appointed administratrix in 1753. He left a personal estate valued at £189 11s. 2d. and had considerable real estate, which by deed, July 16, 1753, he gave to his "three beloved sons Samuel, Anson and Jonathan," for an equal division. At the time of his death he had only one negro servant, whose name was Joseph, being the one his mother gave him, who lived upon the farm. His inventory shows that he had three horses, forty-five sheep and a number of neat cattle. His surgical instruments, showing he was somewhat skilled in surgery, were valued at £7 14s. 8d.

His widow, Tabitha Kenwrick, married Theophilus Hopkins of Harwich, July 24, 1754, and died in the year 1775, leaving children by second marriage. Theophilus Hopkins died early in the winter of 1819, aged 91 years. They had a son, Theophilus, who was a physician.

The children of Jonathan⁶ and Tabitha (Eldridge) Kenwrick were:
 22. i Samuel,⁶ b. 1741.
 23. ii Anson,⁶ b. 1743.
 24. iii Jonathan,⁶ b. 1745.

 6. SOLOMON⁵ KENWRICK (SOLOMON,² EDWARD¹), was born

in Harwich in 1731. He was a mariner and went with his father's family to Barrington, Nova Scotia, and there he was a proprietor of land in 1768. Here he was also a mariner as well as a farmer. He, as reported, was twice married, but no record so far learned, has been found showing the date of his first marriage. His second wife was Martha Godfrey, to whom he was married November 30, 1769. He had children but the writer has no correct list of them.

8. JOHN[5] KENDRICK (SOLOMON,[2] EDWARD[1]), the noted navigator, was born about 1740. Though his birth date is not shown upon the books of record of Harwich, yet it is certain that he first saw light in the eastern part of Harwich within a short distance of the beautiful sheet of salt water known as Pleasant bay, at his father's house—the site of which is yet pointed out. Like most of the boys of that period, he went early to sea and continued going to the end of his eventful life. In the spring of 1760, we find him in the employ of Benjamin Bangs, a hand on board of a whaling schooner of Harwich, of which Judah Hopkins was skipper, Scotto Clarke, Elisha Clarke and David Quansett "ends men;" Peres Bangs "ship keeper;" and Samuel Sears, Jr., Nathaniel Cahoon, John Cahoon, Abijah Bangs, Amos Lawrence, Micah Ralph and John Sequattom were hands, bound on a whaling voyage to Canada river, now the St. Lawrence. The voyage was a most successful one to all concerned notwithstanding four of the crew were Indians. In 1762, he chose rather to try martial duties on the land than chasing whales in the waters of St. Lawrence or on the banks of Newfoundland, and enlisted for service in Capt. Jabez Snow's company for service against the French on the frontier, serving a few days over eight months. Tradition fails to report anything in regard to his services; but it seems evident that the tented field and routine of military duty had not the charms for him as the vessel's deck and sailing on the rough sea.

After his return from the army he again went to sea, and soon rose to the command of merchant vessels sailing out of Boston to distant ports. For some time before the Revolutionary war he was in command of packets between Southern ports and Boston. During the Revolutionary conflict he was in command of armed vessels, annoying the British and preying upon their commerce.

In the summer of 1787, a voyage of trade and discovery to the northwest coast of America was planned by Messrs. Barrel, Brown, Bulfinch, Darby and Pintard, merchants of Boston, and Capt. Kendrick, now a noted navigator, was given command of the two vessels they had fitted out for the enterprise. The two vessels were Columbia, a ship of two hundred and fifty tons, and Washington, a sloop of ninety tons, a tender. The Columbia was an armed vessel, built at Hobarts Landing on North river, in the present town of Scituate, in 1773, and in her outward passage was in command of Capt. Kendrick in person. The Washington in the outward passage was in command of Capt. Robert Gray. They sailed from Boston on the 30th of September, 1787, around Cape Horn for the northwest coast, and arrived at Nootka Sound in September, 1789, where they spent the winter, having on the way discovered the river between Oregon and the state of Washington, which Capt. Kendrick called Columbia in honor of his ship which first entered it. While at Nootka Sound the sloop Washington was rigged into a brig and taken charge of by Capt. Kendrick, who ordered the Columbia to proceed to Canton in command of Robert Gray, and from thence to Boston. In the Lady Washington, the intrepid navigator now visited many places on the coast and some of the nearest islands to trade with the natives. While he lay at anchor in 1791, at Queen Charlotte's Island, his vessel was visited by a large number of natives pretendedly to trade but really to capture the vessel, and had it not been for the great bravery and coolness of Capt. Kendrick, when the savages made their attack with knives upon his men, the vessel would have fallen into their hands, and death dealt to the whole number of the crew. The fight, as narrated in the ballad written by one of the sailors after the terrible skirmish, was indeed a warm one, and the Captain shown up as a bold leader. The ballad says the deck was cleared of the dead, and the living landed, and the good vessel was upon her passage to China.

It has been clamied that he purchased of the natives large tracts of land on both sides of the Columbia river at the mouth, and that he determined that Vancouver's land was an island by sailing around it, which, up to that time, was supposed to be united to the main.

While his vessel in 1793, was lying in one of the harbors at Owhyee (now Hawaii), one of the Hawaiian Islands, he died from the effects of a "ball accidentally fired from a British vessel while saluting him," about two hours after the occurrence.

Thus fell the distinguished navigator who had commanded the first expedition to the northwest coast from the United States in the interest of trade and discovery, and who first hoisted the nation's flag in the Straits of San Juan de Fuca and in the Straits of Georgia, which separate Vancouver's Island from the mainland.

The tidings of Capt. Kendrick's death did not reach his widow in Wareham, it is traditionally reported, for a long time after its occurrence. This was due to the infrequency of vessels on that coast and at the far off isles at that time. Vessels were relied on for conveyance of letters to and from friends, and the senders and receivers were satisfied, even with this privilege of a slow transmission, if good or bad news could be received from absent ones at home or abroad. The news of his sad end must have been severe to his family and kindred, especially so when the circumstances of his death and the knowledge of his intention at the end of the voyage to leave the sea for the quiet of home, were made known to them.

Although Capt. Kendrick's parents removed to the township of Barrington, Nova Scotia, and made that place their home, yet there appears no positive evidence that he lived with them there before his marriage when not at sea. It is very probable the newly settled place and its surroundings, away from the stir of business, did not appeal to him as a place of abode.

At Edgartown in Marthas Vineyard, Capt. Kendrick met Miss Huldah Pease, who became his wife Dec. 28, 1767. She was a daughter of Theophilus Pease of that place, and was baptised April 20, 1744, while an infant. She became a member of the church in that town early in life, and when her husband became a resident of Wareham, she united with the church there. She was a gentle woman, "lovingly mild and amiable," and a devoted wife to the bold mariner.

After marriage he made Marthas Vineyard his home, living most of the time in Edgartown, until 1778, when he sold out and removed to Wareham, Mass., where he purchased a large parcel of land, building upon it a costly gambrel roof house, finished internally in accordance to "foreign order of archetectural designs." From this old house, he went forth to take command of the expedition to the northwest coast. It was standing a few years ago, and is now probably standing.

Capt. Kendrick visited the Cape in 1781, to see his relatives and renew acquaintance with the friends of his boyhood: At the house of his cousin, Jonathan Kenwrick,* in what is now South Orleans, he found an unnamed infant of his cousin which he desired should bear his name. This infant grew to manhood, and was the grandfather of the present John Kenrick, who lives upon the old homestead, and third in the line bearing the name.

Capt. Kendrick, it has been said, was a very large man, possessing great strength and courage.

The children** of Capt. John Kendrick and Huldah, his wife, were:
25. i John,⁴ born at Edgartown, and baptized April 12, 1772.
26. ii Solomon,⁴ born at Edgartown, and baptized Nov. 15, 1772.

---

*From a statement made in 1846 by John Kenrick, Esq., who was born in 1781 and died in 1849.

**From information furnished the writer by the late Greene Kendrick, Esq., of Connecticut.

27. iii Benjamin,⁴ born about 1776; was a mariner and lost at sea; was never married.
28. iv Alfred,⁴ born at Wareham Oct. 20, 1778.
29. v Joseph,⁴ born at Wareham July 29, 1779.
30. vi Huldah,⁴ born at Wareham in 1781; married Rev. Jonathan Gilman at Starks, Mo., in 1803. They had children.

22. SAMUEL³ KENWRICK (JONATHAN,² EDWARD¹) was born in that part of Harwich now South Orleans in the year 1741. He was a physician. He studied with Dr. Nathaniel Breed, a physician of Eastham, who practiced in that town several years before 1760 and who removed to Sudbury not long after this time, and from there to Nelson, N. H. Dr. Kenwrick married Esther, daughter of Israel and Mercy (Rider) Mayo, Feb. 21, 1761. She was a great-granddaughter of Rev. John Mayo. Dr. Kenwrick was very skillful in his profession and had a large practice in the adjoining towns. He occupied his father's place, which was his grandfather's also. He made many improvements on it. He added many fruit trees to the old orchard, some of which were standing within the remembrance of the older men now living. He died February 10, 1791, at the age of 49. He was buried in the old Orleans cemetery, where a slate stone marks the spot bearing the following inscription:

"Erected in memory of Doct. Samuel Kenwrick, eldest son of Dr. Jonathan Kenwrick, who lived beloved and died lamented, Feb. 10, 1791, aet 49."

> "How loved, how valued once, avails thee not,
> To whom related or by whom begot;
> No longer thy all-healing art avails,
> But every remedy its master fails."

His wife, Esther, survived him thirty-six years, dying early in the year 1827, at the age of 86 years. She was a woman of intelligence and helpful to the doctor in many ways in his business. She was a practitioner in the obstetric art. After her husband's death, she continued to reside in the old house, and after it was taken down and the new one built in 1792, she occupied rooms in the new one till her death. She was a woman well spoken of.* She had rare conversational gift and a genial disposition. She was admitted to church June 26, 1791.**

The birth dates of the children of Samuel Kenwrick and wife, Esther, do not appear upon the records. They had an infant that

---

*The mother of the writer, a great-granddaughter on the maternal side, well remembered her as a most amiable woman, indulgent and entertaining.
**Orleans Chh. Records.

died in 1780. Their children, however, that grew up, were as follows, though they may not all be in order of birth:

31. i Jonathan,[4] born in 1761; mar. Betsey Rogers; d. in 1839.
32. ii Warren Anson,[4] born in 1763; mar. Ruth Gould; d. in 1808.
33. iii Samuel,[4] never married; died in 1784.
34. iv Cynthna,[4] married 1st Paine Gould, Dec. 6, 1789. He died 1794; she then mar. 2d David Twining, April 13, 1799.
35. v Sabrina,[4] mar. Jona. Higgins of W. Nov. 27, 1794.
36. vi Tabitha,[4] mar. Samuel William Kenwrick of Barrington, Nova Scotia, April 17, 1800, and removed to the western country after marriage.

23. ANSON[3] KENWRICK (JONATHAN,[2] EDWARD[1]), second son, was born in that part of Harwich now South Orleans in September, 1743. He was a boy of about ten years when his father died. In early life he was by occupation a carpenter. At some period between 1765 and 1770, he removed to the township of Barrington, N. S., settling near a place called Shag harbor, where he spent his days in fishing, farming and other business. He married before his removal, Azubah Sears, daughter of Josiah of Eastham, Mass., October 29, 1765. He lost his life by drowning. With his youngest daughter, Abigail, her husband, Mr. Bradford, and their two children, in going from an island to Shag harbor in a boat, it was capsized by a heavy sea on a bar, throwing all on board into the surging water. Mr. Bradford and the two children were immediately drowned. Mr. Kenwrick started to swim ashore, but returning to aid his daughter, was drowned. The daughter with the courage of a heroine clung to the up-turned boat in its various motions and successfully reached the shore after a great struggle. The year this sad occurrence happened is not reported.

The following is the list of the children of Anson and Azubah (Sears) Kenwrick, his wife:

i Tabitha,[4] born July 29, 1766; mar. James Smith.
37. ii Edward,[4] born May 9, 1768; mar. Rebecca, daughter of Jonathan Smith. Their children were: Jonathan, Edward, Cynthia and Abigail.
38. iii David,[4] born Nov. 13, 1770; mar. Jedidah, daughter of Ansel Crowell. They had David, Judah, Seth, Anson, Samuel, Edward, Rebecca, Azubah, Via and Eliza.
39. iv Anson,[4] born Dec. 2, 1772; never married; in the naval service; died in a hospital in London.
40. v Martha,[4] born Nov. 16, 1774; mar. Simeon Nickerson of Cape Sables.
41. vi John,[4] born Nov. 3, 1776; mar. Letitia Atwood. Their children: Jacob,[5] Anderson,[5] Joseph,[5] Hepsibah,[5] Tamsin, Dianna, John[5] and Mary Ann.

42. vii Samuel,⁴ born September 22, 1778; mar. Tabitha, dau. of Dr. Samuel Kenwrick of Orleans, April 17, 1800. They removed to Ohio, is the tradition.
43. viii Azubah,⁴ born April 1, 1781; mar. 1st Jonathan Smith, 2d Samuel Watson, a Scotchman.
44. ix Josiah Sears,⁴ born April 17, 1783; was twice married. He married 1st Hannah Weekes of Harwich; married 2d Lydia Allen. He resided in many places in Nova Scotia. He died at Yarmouth, N. S. He had children by last wife. Among them, David, Huldah, Arvin William.
45. x Seth,⁴ born April 26, 1785.
46. xi Huldah,⁴ born May 18, 1787; married John Bennison, an Englishman.
47. xii Phebe,⁴ mar. Joshua Nickerson of Cape Sables, a brother of Simeon Nickerson.
48. xiii Abigail,⁴ mar. 1st a Mr. Bradford; 2d Thomas West of Queens Co., N. S. She narrowly escaped drowning by the capsizing of the boat she was in with her father, husband and children.

24. JONATHAN³ KENWRICK (JONATHAN,² EDWARD¹) was born in that part of old Harwich, now South Orleans, February 29, 1745. He was the youngest of his father's family, and was eight years of age when his father died. His wife was Hannah, a daughter of Mr. Isaac Cole, who removed from Eastham to Ashford, Conn., before 1786. His intention of marriage to her bears date Aug. 5, 1771. She was born June 21, 1749, in East Orleans, where her father then possessed a large farm. She became a member of the Congregational church in that town Aug. 24, 1794. Her death occurred at the house of her son, Nov. 2, 1837, at the age of 90 years, surviving her husband 28 years.

Mr. Kenwrick was a mariner and farmer. He had large tracts of land, much of which is now held by his descendants. He resided near or on the spot where the house of John Kenrick, Esq., now stands. He died November 9, 1809, aged 64 years. They lie buried in the Orleans cemetery, where stones mark the spots.

Their children were:
49. i Lucy,⁴ born Dec. 6, 1772; mar. Nathan Kendrick of Harwich, October 26, 1793. They lived in Harwich. Had a large family.
50. ii Seth,⁴ born Aug. 17, 1775; died at San Cruz, Cuba, Nov. 30, 1797.
51. iii Calvin,⁴ born in 1777; lost at sea July 30, 1795; age 18 years.
52. iv Arvin,⁴ born in 1780; mar. Tabitha Sparrow, dau. of Dea. Richard Sparrow, Jan. 13, 1803. He was lost at sea Jan. 1, 1822. Left children. Among them was Alexander Kenrick.
53. v John,⁴ born May 18, 1781.

54. vi Carlton,⁴ born in 1784; died at Havana, Cuba, Sept. 14, 1815.
55. vii Alexander,⁴ born ——; died at sea in 1822.
56. viii Hannah,⁴ born ——; died

31. JONATHAN⁴ KENWRICK (SAMUEL,³ JONATHAN,² EDWARD¹) was born in that part of Harwich, now South Orleans, in 1761. His father's intention was to educate him for a physician, but he showed a fondness for seafaring life and was allowed his choice and went to sea. He was a master mariner for many years. He married Betsey Rogers of Eastham, daughter of Moses and Elizabeth (Smith) Rogers, November 13, 1783. She was a lineal descendant of Joseph Rogers, who came over on the Mayflower from England in 1620, and was born August 8, 1764. She died Sept. 14, 1852, at the age of 88 years. Capt. Kenwrick resided on his father's place with his mother. He took down the old house built for his great-grandfather, and in 1792 built a new house, which is yet standing upon the site, or near it, of the old house. He had a retentive memory and colloquial talents of high order. His last days were spent with his youngest daughter, Caroline, at whose house he died of consumption, at the age of 78, June 4, 1839. He had the distinction of residing in Harwich, Eastham and Orleans, without changing his place of residence. The singularity was owing to change of town lines; the portion of Harwich in which he was born was set off to Eastham in 1772, and in 1797 became a part of the town of Orleans. Capt. Kenwrick removed to Smithfield, R. I., at the beginning of the last war with England, returning at the close to Orleans.

The children of Jonathan⁴ and Betsey (Rogers) Kenwrick were:

57. i Samuel,⁵ born November 10, 1784; mar. Eunisa, dau. of William Eldredge, Esq., of Harwich, Nov. 24, 1812.. He was a mariner and died at Port au Prince, March 6, 1822. They had one son, Jonathan.

58. ii Warren Anson,⁵ born Oct. 12, 1786, who died in January, 1788.

59. iii Betsey,⁵ born May 29, 1788; mar. twice. She had children. Died in 1872.

60. iv Warren Anson,⁵ born July 24, 1790; married Abigail, dau. of Heman Snow, Oct. 23, 1813. He was a master mariner and resided in Orleans. He had children. Among them were: Samuel, born in 1814, who died at St. Jago, March 21, 1835, at the age of 20, from the effects of a fall out of the rigging to the deck of a vessel in command of his uncle Alfred; Polly, the wife of Isaiah Young; Warren, born in 1824, who died Sept. 24, 1843, aged 19 years; and Albert, born in April, 1831, who died Oct. 29, 1850, aged 19 years and 6 months. Capt. Kenrick died at his home in Orleans, Feb. 12, 1842. His wife survived him many years.

61. v Mercy,⁸ born Aug. 12, 1792; married Matthew Kingman, son of Simeon Kingman, Esq., of Orleans, Nov. 30, 1808. They resided in Orleans. Their children were Rebecca F.,⁸ Betsey K.,⁸ Freeman,⁸ Overy,⁸ Simeon,⁸ Alfred,⁸ Seth,⁸ Isabel M.,⁸ Alonzo,⁸ Eliza M., and Matthew. Overy and Alfred died young. She died Sept. 17, 1857, at the age of 65. He died October 20, 1848, very suddenly, aged 58. A man greatly respected by all who knew him.

62. vi Esther,⁸ born April 18, 1794; married Luther Nickerson of Orleans. They resided in Orleans. He was a mariner. They had Freeman S., Louiza, Mary, Mercy, Caroline and Esther. Freeman S. was lost at sea. He was in command of the ship Alice Gray, which sailed from Philadelphia for Londonderry with a cargo of corn and flour, April, 1848. She was never heard from after leaving the Capes of Delaware. Mrs. Esther Nickerson died in Orleans.

63. vii Jonathan,⁸ born Jan. 29, 1796; married Abigail Taylor of Orleans, Jan. 24, 1818. They had sons and daughters. He was a master mariner. He resided in Orleans.

64. viii Eliza,⁸ born Feb. 18, 1798; married Edward Hall, Jr., of Harwich, April 9, 1820. They removed to Providence. He was a master mariner. Their children were: Alfred K., Abner, Abira, Eliza K. and Edward W. He died Aug. 21, 1841. She died Aug. 2, 1839.

65. ix Alfred,⁸ born May 30, 1800.

66. x Seth,⁸ born July 16, 1803; died of a fever Dec. 12, 1821. He was a mariner. Unmarried.

67. xi Frederick,⁸ born October 14, 1805; married for his first wife, Eliza, daughter of John Myrick of Orleans. She dying Sept. 11, 1835, he married her sister, Lucy Myrick. He had children by both wives, but they died young. He was a seafaring man and resided in the western part of Orleans. He died in 1892. He was a highly respected citizen, and of a quiet disposition; he was a good conversationalist. Had seen much of sea life.

68. xii Caroline,⁸ born October 30, 1809; was twice married. Her first husband was Nathan Cole of Orleans, who died at sea. By him, she had two children. Edward H., the eldest, was the well-known merchant of New York, who will be long remembered for his gifts. For her second husband, she married Heman Snow, son of Robert, of Brewster. For awhile after marriage they lived in Orleans. About 1850, they removed to West Harwich, and afterwards removed to Dennisport. By the second marriage, she had three sons. They were Nathan C., William B. and James. She died in April, 1883, and was buried in Dennisport. She long was in ill health. Her husband survived her a few years.

32. WARREN ANSON⁴ KENRICK (SAMUEL,⁸ JONATHAN,⁸ EDWARD¹) was born in Harwich, that part now South Orleans, in 1763. He was educated for a physician, and finally settled in

Wellfleet, where he was a successful practitioner, and died there, February 10, 1808, aged 44 years. He married in Eastham, that part now Orleans, Ruth Gould, daughter of Thomas, November 18, 1784. She died May 10, 1801, at the age of 33. They lie buried in the Duck Creek cemetery. They had children. Among them were Thomas G.,⁵ Samuel,⁵ Overy,⁵ Warren A., Franklin and Ruth,⁵ who died young. His second wife, Sally, survived him.

53. JOHN⁴ KENRICK (JONATHAN,³ JONATHAN,² EDWARD¹) was born in that part of old Harwich, now South Orleans, May 18, 1781. He early went to sea and continued in the seafaring business until the breaking out of war between the United States and England in 1812, when he left the sea on account of it, and began business on the land, in which he was as fully successful.

His first command as master was given him in 1804, when he was twenty-three years old, of the schr. Primrose of Boston on a trading voyage to Curacoa, W. I., and to the Madeira isle on the African coast, taking an assorted cargo and returning with hides, salt and Madeira wine. His next voyage was in 1805 in command of the schr. Three Friends, owned by William Colman Lee of Boston, to Havana, where he obtained a cargo of sugar and molasses for Boston.

In 1806, he was given command of the ship Cecelia, owned by William Colman Lee of Boston, for a voyage to Campeache for a cargo of logwood and fustic or yellow wood for dyeing. The same year he commanded the same ship on a voyage to San Sebastian, Spain, but it was an unfortunate one. The ship encountered, August 28, a terrific gale of wind off Cape Ontegal in the Bay of Biscay of two days' duration, which smashed the stern boat, carried away the ship's quarter boards, and caused the death of a seaman by falling from aloft. To save the ship a part of her cargo of cocoa was thrown overboard. She was brought into San Sebastian after five days in a bad condition, and upon a survey is said to have been condemned and sold. With his boy and negro man, he found a passage to United States on the brig Harlequin of Stonington, Conn., in command of Capt. Dickens.

Capt. Kenrick's next voyage was in command of the brig Maria Caroline, from Boston to Cadiz, Spain. This was in 1807. He took out tar, pitch, turpentine and resin as a cargo, and consigned to the "Widow of Maurice Roberts & Co." In 1808, he was in command of the brig Eliza of Boston, carrying freight to and from ports in Virginia; and from Boston to St. Vincent. At the latter place in the month of November he sold flour and tobacco amounting to the sum of $18,373 to William Durham.

In 1810, he was master of the brig Alert on a voyage to Barbados from Boston, with a cargo of flour, provisions, lumber, etc., which he sold for Fenno & West of Boston. In 1811, he took command of brig Constellation of Boston, owned by Isaac Winslow of Boston, for a voyage to Lisbon with a cargo of flour consigned to William Jarvis. The same year he commanded the brig Enterprise on a voyage to Cadiz, Spain, with an assorted cargo. It is probable during his seafaring life, Capt. Kenrick commanded other vessels than those named. It is a tradition among his descendants that he was in command of a vessel to Europe that was seized under the Berlin and Milan decrees, yet there is nothing found to verify it among his papers.

Upon leaving the sea, Capt. Kenrick turned his attention to farming, salt-making and trade. In all of the patriotic movements in his town during the war, he took an active part. With others of his townsmen, he "was instrumental in saving his town from the heavy exactions of the British cruisers in 1812."

He was selectman, assessor and overseer of the poor for thirteen years from 1818, and a representative to the General Court at Boston in 1830 and 1831. He was a justice of the peace for many years after 1818.

He was one of the founders of the Baptist church in Orleans in 1826, having asked dismission from the Brewster Baptist church June 10, 1826, for the purpose of being one of the founders, of which he and his wife were members. Becoming an Universalist he helped organize the Orleans church, April 21, 1833, of which he was a member at his death. He was a lay preacher of that denomination, and left in manuscript many sermons he had delivered in various places between 1833 and 1839. His death occurred at his home, May 24, 1849.

Mr. Kenrick married, December 4, 1804, Rebecca, daughter of Dea. Richard Sparrow of Orleans, who was born April 25, 1779, and was baptized by Rev. Jonathan Bascom, May 2, 1779. They were both members of the Orleans Congregational church up to April 6, 1826, when they asked for dismissal in order to unite with the Baptist church at Brewster. She died at Orleans, June 1, 1843, at the age of 64 years.

Their children, all born in Orleans, were:

68½. i Sophia,[5] born Oct. 29, 1805; married Elisha Cobb of Eastham, November 13, 1828; died Oct. 23, 1823.

69. ii John,[5] born October 9, 1819.

70. iii Rebecca,[5] born July 15, 1822; married Mitchel F. Anderson of Boston, and died Dec. 6, 1897.

65. ALFRED[5] KENRICK (JONATHAN,[4] SAMUEL,[3] JONATHAN,[2] EDWARD[1]) was born in Orleans in the old Kenrick house, May 30, 1800. He went with his father's family to Smithfield, R. I., at the beginning of the last war with England, where he worked in a cotton factory; and at the close of the war he commenced his sea life. He rose from an ordinary seaman to a master of a ship at

the age of twenty-seven years. During his long sea life he visited many ports of the world. He crossed the Atlantic one hundred and eight times. In 1853, in command of the bark Osmanlie on a voyage to Melbourne and Callao he circumnavigated the world, arriving in Boston in June, 1854. This was his last voyage at sea. But few masters of his time had traversed more miles upon the ocean, or had been more fortunate in avoiding the dangers of the sea. He was upright in all his business affairs with his employers and by them held in high esteem.

Capt. Kenrick never sought office, yet he was called to fill official positions many times. He represented Barnstable county, (with Sylvester Baxter), in the state senate in 1856. He served his town as selectman, school committee, and upon important committees. He was a justice of the peace and for a period a deputy sheriff.

Capt. Kenrick was one of the number who was instrumental in forming the Universalist society in Orleans in 1825, and who was an active member thereafter until his death.

Capt. Kenrick was twice married. He married for his first wife, Almina, daughter of David Taylor of Orleans, Jan. 4, 1825. She died Jan. 11, 1879. For his second wife, he married Mrs. Adeline Walker in 1880, who died in 1889. He died January 18, 1896, in his 96th year.

Capt. Kenrick by his wife, Almina, had seven children, but only four reached adult age. They were:

71. i Alfred,* born in 1825; mar. Sarah B. Gleason. He resided in Brookline, and died in 1885. Had sons.

72 ii David T.,* born in 1830; mar. Amanda Gibbs. He resided in Brookline. Now deceased.

73 iii Mary T.,* born in 1841; mar. George H. Moss. Now deceased.

74. iv Eliza F.,* born in 1844; mar. Asa Smith. She is now deceased.

After 1835, Capt. Kenrick resided in the northwest part of the town near Rock Harbor, he having purchased of Prence Snow of Boston the Snow estate in that neighborhood in 1834.

69. JOHN* KENRICK (JOHN,* JONATHAN,* JONATHAN,² EDWARD¹) was born in Orleans, August 9, 1819. He was educated in the public schools. He became early interested in educational matters and was a school teacher at the age of nineteen. He was on the school board of Orleans twenty-five years and the superintendent of the schools eight years from 1880. He was interested in farming, arboriculture and pomology all through life. He was a member of the Barnstable County Agricultural society and a delegate to the state board in 1866. He was in mercantile business in his native village from 1867 to 1891. He was thirty-three years

postmaster of the place; was selectman, assessor and overseer of the poor of Orleans fourteen years; was a trial justice in 1850; was a representative in the legislature in 1852 and 1853; was a member of the governor's council in 1855 and 1856; was a notary public and justice of the peace, and from 1876 to 1898, a trustee of the Cape Cod Five Cents Savings bank. He occupied the place of his father. He died December 26, 1898, at the age of 79.

Mr. Kenrick was twice married. He married for his first wife Thankful Crosby, dau. of Joshua of Orleans, July 30, 1843, who died March 14, 1886. For his second wife, he married Catherine A. M. Crosby of Brewster, dau. of Nathan Crosby, Nov. 17, 1891.

The children of John and Thankful (Crosby) Kenrick:
75. i Sophia,* b. Jan. 23, 1845; d. Nov. 26, 1845.
76. ii Emma,* b. March 28, 11850; d. Dec. 7, 1892.
77. iii Clara,* b. Dec. 16, 1847; d. June 10, 1903.
78. iv Rebecca,* b. March 16, 846; d. Feb. 18, 1847.
79. v, Eva,* b. Nov. 22, 1852; d. Feb. 22, 1853.
80. vi Alice T.,* b. July 30, 1854; d. Nov. 21, 1887.
81. vii John,* b. Oct. 25, 1857. He resides at South Orleans and occupies the old homestead. He is engaged in mercantile business. He has held many official positions. He was two years a representative in the House, and two years in the state Senate. He was a selectman, assessor and overseer of the poor of Orleans many years. He is now postmaster, and one of the trustees and vice president of the Cape Cod Five Cents Savings bank.

No. 36.

LIBRARY of
Cape Cod
HISTORY & GENEALOGY

EARLY CHATHAM SETTLERS
By William C. Smith, Esq.,
Author of a History of Chatham.

Early Settlers, 1690, 1711—Atkins, Bassett, Covell, Eldredge, Godfrey, Hamilton, Harding, Howes, Lumbert, Nickerson, Paddock, Phillips, Sears, Smith, Stewart, Tucker.

Later Settlers—Collins, Crowell, Doane, Eldredge, Farris, Hawes, Knowles, Mayo, Mitchell, Ryder, Smith, Stewart, Taylor.

YARMOUTHPORT, MASS.:
C. W. SWIFT, Publisher and Printer,
The "Register" Press,
1915.

EARLY CHATHAM SETTLERS
By William C. Smith, Esq.,
Author of a History of Chatham.
Copyright, 1915, by
William C. Smith.

EARLY CHATHAM SETTLERS.*
ATKINS.

Capt. John Atkins, son of Henry and Bethiah (Linnell) Atkins of Eastham, born August 1, 1674, married Elizabeth, daughter of Lieut. Andrew Newcomb of Edgartown, March 5, 1699-1700. He lived a few years in Eastham, removing to Monomoit about 1705. It is not certain where his farm was located. He was active in local affairs, being selectman five years, treasurer two years, etc. He became lieutenant of the military company under Capt. Ebenezer Hawes in 1715 and was appointed captain in 1720. He was one of the first seven members of the church organized in 1720, and was prominent in the controversies, which arose with Rev. Hugh Adams and Rev. Samuel Osborne, the Eastham minister.[1] He died January 30, 1732-3, leaving no descendants. His widow was living as late as 1743, when she conveyed land in Edgartown.[2]

Samuel Atkins, brother of John, born at Eastham June 25, 1679, married Emlen[3] [Emeline] Newcomb, a sister of his brother's wife, April 3, 1703, and settled at Monomoit soon after. He probably bought a tract of land of the Indians, adjoining the shore and bounded south on the Sears farm. This tract after his death fell to his only son Henry.[4] He was selectman in 1737 and 1738. His name does not appear on the tax lists or records of the town after 1755, but his estate was not administered upon till August 26, 1768. His widow was not then living. The entire estate was assigned to the son Henry, he paying his sisters certain sums of money.[5]

Dea. Thomas Atkins, an older brother of John and Samuel, born at Eastham June 19, 1671, removed to Monomoit as early as 1694. The name of his first wife is not known. He bought of the Nickersons and Covells 10 acres of land lying between Lord's pond and the highway, which became his homestead. The house and four acres of this land, lying north of the meeting house, he sold in 1718 to the town for the use of the ministry and the remaining six acres he sold in 1729 to Thomas Doane.[6] After the sale to the town, he appears to have lived on the Vickery homestead, which he had bought of the Vickery heirs in 1714.⁷ With Capt. Joseph Harding he bought Sept. 7, 1707, of Josephus Quason all the interest of the latter in the Quason lands in the south part of Old Harwich and later, in 1713, in the division of these lands, received one-sixteenth part, which he later sold.⁸ He was clerk of the proprietors of these lands. He was one of the leading men of the town, being selectman 21 years, town clerk 14 years, and holding other offices. He was a leader in the church and a firm friend and confidant of the ministers. He was the first deacon of the church. He married 2nd, June 28, 1739, Hope (Horton) Snow, widow of Ebenezer Snow of Eastham. Administration on his estate was granted Jan. 16, 1750-1, to his son Joshua. Although town clerk many years, he failed to record any information about his own family.⁹

NOTES.

*The author is indebted to Mr. Josiah Paine of Harwich, Mr. Stanley W. Smith of Boston and Mr. William E. Nickerson of Cambridge for helpful genealogical information respecting some of the families mentioned in these articles.

(1) Rev. Samuel Treat of Eastham writes of him in 1716 as follows: "He is a person born in our town of godly parents who gave him a religious education and he early expressed a pious inclination to the ways of God and a religious profession and has for many years been entertained in our church, adorning his profession by a very laudable conversation and so esteemed by the adjacent towns, to many of whom he is well known." Adams v Hawes, Files Superior Court of Judicature, No. 10,812.

(2) Newcomb Genealogy, 20.

(3) She is called Emlen in the will of Capt. John Atkins. The name has caused trouble for genealogists. In the Newcomb Genealogy she is called Emblem, elsewhere Embling. The forms Embling and Emblen (not Emblem) are old forms for Emlen (Emeline), just as we have Hamblen for Hamlin, Tombling and Tomblen for Tomlin, Hambleton for Hamilton, etc.

(4) By deed dated July 29, 1783, Henry Atkins sold to Isaac Howes and John Harding the following tract in Chatham, doubtless his father's farm: "where my dwelling house stands, beginning at a stake and stone at the westerly end of the Pond near my Dwelling house aforesaid in Mr. Paul Sears his range, thence Westerly as the fence now stands to the highway, thence northerly to Thomas Bee's range, being about twenty-five feet, thence Easterly in said Bee's range till it comes to the Partition fence between the aforesaid Bee and Atkins, thence Northerly as the fence now stands till it comes to the land of Seth Smith, thence Easterly in said Smith's range as the fence now stands till it comes to the land of Constant Nickerson, thence still Easterly as the fence now stands till it comes to the corner of the fence to a stone in the ground, thence Northerly in the aforesaid

Nickerson's range as the fence now stands till it comes to another corner to a stone in the ground, thence Southeasterly in the range of the land that was Solomon Collings, as the fence now stands, till it comes to a Ditch near the fore side of the aforesaid John Harding's now Dwelling house, thence Easterly as the Ditch now runs to low water mark, thence Southerly by the water till it comes to Mr. Richard Sears his range, thence Westerly in said Sears his range, as the fence now stands, till it comes to the aforesaid Pond, thence Westerly through the Pond to the first specified bounds * * * exclusive of 5 or 6 acres which belong to said Atkins his sister." Seth W. Hammond papers.

(5) Children of Samuel and Emlen (Newcomb) Atkins (from Probate Records, order uncertain): 1 Eunice, b. 1705; m. Solomon Collins, son of John, about 1726. 2 Elizabeth, b.__ ; m. 1st Daniel Eldredge of Eastham Jan. 31, 1727-8, (East. Rec.) who was "supposed to be deceased" Jan. 1732-3; m. 2nd about 1735, Solomon Kendrick, son of Edward of Harwich; removed to Barrington, N. S., about 1762. 3 Desire, b. ; m. Sylvester. 4 Anna, b. 1714; m. Thomas Kendrick, son of Edward of Harwich (int. Jan. 27, 1734-5, East. Rec.). 5 Bethiah, Jr., b. ; m. Christopher Taylor, son of Abraham of Barnstable, Feb. 3, 1757 (Chat. Rec.); d. before 1769. 6 Tabitha, b. ; m. Southworth Hamlin, son of Joseph of Barnstable, May 12, 1757 (Chat. Rec.). 7 Henry, b. (not. of age Jan. 1733); m. Deborah Lothrop, dau. of Joseph of Barnstable, Dec. 8, 1768 (Barnst. Rec.); after selling his farm in 1783 as above, he probably moved to south part of Eastham, where his widow died Nov. 22, 1822, aged 85 (Hdstn.).

(6) Town Records; M. L. Luce papers.

(7) Page 124, note 86, Smith's History of Chatham.

(8) Files Superior Court of Judicature, Nos. 7,626, 9,537, 66,388, 30,339; Osborn Nickerson papers.

(9) Children of Thomas and ( ) Atkins (order uncertain): 1 Thomas, b. ; m. 1st Elizabeth Nickerson, dau. of William, about 1726. She died before Sept. 13, 1739, (date of her father's will) and he m. 2nd Thankful Snow, dau. of Ebenezer of Eastham, May 14, 1741 (East. Rec.). 2 Joshua, b. ; m. Sarah Sears, dau. of Daniel, Aug. 1, 1734 (Chat. Rec.). She died April 30, 1751, and he m. 2nd Mary (Freeman) Doane, widow of Benjamin (int. Oct. 5, 1751, Chat. Rec.). 3 Susanna, b. about 1717; m. Reuben Ryder, son of John, Oct. 26, 1740 (Chat. Rec.); d. Aug. 9, 1743, aged 26. 4 Bethiah, sen., b. ; single in 1757. (See marriage of Bethiah Jr., note 5 supra. Bethiah, sen., considering the known facts, could have been no one but a dau. of Thomas.) 5 Possibly other daughters not identified.

BASSETT.

Nathan Bassett, son of Nathaniel and Mary or Dorcas (Joyce) Bassett of Marshfield and Yarmouth, born , married Mary, daughter of Thomas and Deborah Crow of Yarmouth, March 7, 1709, and

EARLY CHATHAM SETTLERS.

settled at Monomoit soon after. He bought of one of the Covells (probably Joseph) an interest in the common land and settled on that part of it on the south side of the road to Yarmouth, opposite the farm of Joseph Nickerson. In the division of the common land in 1713, he had all the land between the ponds and the road, from the Indian meeting house nearly to Harwich line, assigned to him.¹⁰ He died in 1728, but his estate was not settled. His widow died in 1742, leaving a will dated Nov. 5, 1741, proved May 6, 1742, disposing of her husband's property. She gave the homestead to her sons Nathaniel and Samuel.¹¹

NOTES.

(10) A Proprietors' Book for Chatham, town clerk's office.
(11) Children of Nathan and Mary (Crow) Bassett (from Probate Records, order uncertain): 1 Dorcas, b.   ; m. John Nickerson, Jr., son of William of Harwich, March 14, 1727-8 (Har. Rec.). 2 Nathan, b.   ; m. Elizabeth Rogers, dau. of Eleazer of Harwich, Jan. 2, 1734-5 (Har. Rec.). 3 Mary, b.   ; single in 1741. 4 Thomas, b.   ; m. 1st Deborah Godfrey, dau. of Moses; 2nd, Mary Newcomb, widow of Joseph of Wellfleet, Sept. 15, 1763 (East. Rec.). 5 Hannah, b.   ; m. 1st Joseph Covell, son of Joseph, who died before 1741, and she m. 2nd Asa Mayo of Eastham July 23, 1756 (East. Rec.). 6 Nathaniel, b.   ; m. Sarah Chase, dau. of Thomas of Yarmouth, Aug. 23, 1730 (Yar. Rec.). 7 Samuel, b.   ; living in 1741.

COVELL.

Nathaniel Covell, son of Nathaniel and Sarah (Nickerson) Covell, born about 1670, married March 1, 1696-7, Judith Nickerson, dau. of William and Mercy. He lived on or near his father's farm between Crow's pond and Ryder's cove at Chathamport.¹² He was selectman two years and treasurer two years. His will, dated Sept. 19, 1746, was proved March 13, 1746-7. He had previously disposed of his real estate to his children. His widow, daughter Elizabeth and granddaughter Daty Nickerson each received one-third of his personal estate.¹³

William Covell, son of Nathaniel and Sarah (Nickerson) Covell, was born at Monomoit about 1673. His wife was Sarah, but her parentage is not known. His homestead, bought of Joseph Nickerson about 1695, was at Chathamport, bounded "Easterly by Ensign William Nickerson, Southerly by the land of Jehosaphat Eldred, Southerly, Southwesterly and Westerly by ye land of Jeremiah Nickerson's to ye Bank or Clift neer ye Wading place, and Northerly by ye Clift," containing 60 acres. On November 28, 1710, he bought of Jeremiah Nickerson a tract of 20 acres adjoining the above on the west. All his lands and right at Chatham, he sold by deed dated September 10, 1716, to John Crowell, Jr., of Yarmouth¹⁴ and removed to Harwich, where he purchased of his brother Ephraim the easterly part of the latter's farm, lying on the southwest side of Flax pond. It was conveyed to him by deed dated February 9, 1718-9, after he had built a house upon the tract.

This farm of 40 acres he sold by deed dated August 17, 1725, to Jonathan Smalley of Harwich[14] and removed to that part of Eastham now Wellfleet. He died there January 18, 1760, aged 87.[15]

Joseph Covell, son of Nathaniel and Sarah (Nickerson) Covell, born at Monomoit about 1675, married first Lydia Stewart, daughter of Ensign Hugh of Monomoit, about 1700. She died not long after and he married second Hannah Bassett, daughter of Nathaniel of Yarmouth and sister of Nathan of Monomoit, March 1, 1703-4. His farm was on the east side of Muddy Cove and extended east to the present road from the old cemeteries over to the late Rufus Smith's. It was a part of the old William Nickerson farm. There is no record of his death or of his children and no settlement of his estate. He was living as late as 1732,[17] but does not appear in the tax list of 1755.[19]

Ephraim Covell, youngest son of Nathaniel and Sarah (Nickerson) Covell, born about 1677; married, first, Mercy , who died Feb. 1, 1727-8; second, Abigail Ellis of Yarmouth Feb. 4, 1729-30, and after her decease, third, Mary Taylor of Chatham (intent. Sept. 20, 1746), who survived him.[19] By deed dated May 19, 1699, he received from his mother one-fourth part of all her interest in his grandfather Nickerson's home, farm and in all his other land at Monomoit, his brothers probably receiving their respective shares at the same time.[20] His part of his grandfather's farm lay between the two ponds (which are next the Stephen Smith place) and the road past the late Dr. Clifford's and extended easterly nearly to the head of Ryder's Cove. This property he sold in 1712 to Edward Bangs of Harwich, receiving in exchange the farm of 300 acres on the south side of Harwich, formerly belonging to Joseph Severance and Manoah Ellis, which lay between Grassy pond, Flax pond and the sea, and bounded west on land of Isaac Atkins and east on land of Scotto Clark.[21] His house was on the south side of Grassy pond. He sold the easterly part of this farm to his brother William in 1719. In the latter part of his life he was reputed to be a Quaker.[22] His will, dated July 14, 1749,[23] was proved Sept. 10, 1753.[24]

NOTES.

(12) Town Records, 1734.
(13) Children of Nathaniel and Judith (Nickerson) Covell (from Probate Records, order uncertain): 1 Jane, b. ; m. Jonathan Nickerson, son of Thomas, about 1718. 2 John, b. ; m. Thankful Bangs, dau. of Jonathan of Harwich, Aug. 16, 1721 (Har. Rec.). 3 Nathaniel, b. ; m. Keziah Tucker, dau. of Samuel, April 14, 1727 (Chat. Rec.). 4 Seth, b. ; m. Sarah Hurd, dau. of John of Harwich, Nov. 22, 1732 (Har. Rec.); removed to Ridgefield, Conn., about 1747. 5 Hannah, b. ; m. Alexander Cunningham of Nantucket, Feb. 8, 1732-3 (Nan. Rec.). 6 Simeon, b. ; m. Thankful Robbins of Yarmouth, probably dau. of James, Aug..26, 1746 (Yar. Rec.); removed to Ridgefield, Conn. 7 Elizabeth, b. ; died single about 1770. This Nathaniel Covell

did not settle in the north part of Eastham as stated by Pratt (Hist. of Eastham, 113); it was his brother William who is referred to.

(14) M. L. Luce papers.

(15) Files Superior Court of Judicature, No. 62,800.

(16) Children of William and Sarah (   ) Covell (order uncertain): 1 Nathaniel, b.   ; m. Esther Atwood, dau. of Medad of Eastham (int. July 29, 1724, East. Rec.). Their children probably were Esther, Sarah, Reuben, Philip, Jedidah and Priscilla. 2 Ephraim, b.   ; m. Mercy Brown of Eastham, July 9, 1730 (East Rec.). Their children were Amy, Phobe, Zeruiah, Ephraim, Amy, Solomon, Daniel, Mary, Mercy. 3 William, b.   ; m. 1st Joanna Atwood, widow of Eleazer of Eastham, June 27, 1734 (East. Rec.). She died Jan. 16, 1736-7, in her 44th year (Hdstn.) and he m. 2nd Elizabeth Webber of Eastham Feb. 16, 1737-8 (East. Rec.). Children: Joanna and David. 4 Propably a son, b.   ; m. Mary   , and d. young, leaving a widow and dau. Mary. 5 Prob. a dau., b.   ; m. before 1726 Daniel Eldridge of Eastham and d. young. (Files Sup. Ct. of Judicature, No. 19,310.) Other children not identified.

(17) M. L. Luce papers.

(18) Children of Joseph Covell: By wife Lydia: 1 Lydia, b. July 12, 1701 (Chat. Rec.), m. Thomas Nickerson, Jr., May 16, 1716 (Chat. Rec.). By wife Hannah: (order uncertain) 2 Sarah, b.   ; m. William Nickerson ("Red Stockings"), son of William, about 1723 (Osborn Nickerson papers). 3 James, b.   ; m. 1st Mehitable Nickerson, dau. of Samuel of Harwich, Aug. 4, 1727 (Har. Rec.). She died Nov. 26, 1761, and he m. 2nd Ruth (Crowell) Kelley, widow of Amos Kelley of Yarmouth. 4 Nathaniel, b.   ; m. Mary Chase, dau. of Isaac of Yarmouth (int. July 20, 1740, Yar. Rec.). 5 Joseph, b.   ; m. Hannah Bassett, dau. of Nathan, and died not long after marriage, leaving widow and dau. Hannah. 6 Possibly a dau. Constant, who. m. Ebenezer Nickerson, son of Thomas. 7 Possibly a dau. Dorcas, who m. James Nickerson, son of William.

(19) The Harwich records give the name of the second wife as Mrs. Abigail Ellis and of the third wife as Mrs. Mary Taylor, yet one and perhaps both were unmarried. Mary Taylor was dau. of John Taylor of Yarmouth and Chatham. Her brother, Seth Taylor of Chatham, in his will in 1762 mentions "my sister, Mary Covell, which now liveth with me."

(20) The description in this deed is as follows: "All that part & share of land situate, lying & being in Manamoyet aforesaid bounded viz: ye estern corner a stone marked E near ye harbor, from sd stone Westerly to a stone marked E on ye Southerly side of ye Buriing place hill & so from sd stone Westerly to a rock marked C & so westerly to a stone marked E on ye Southerly side of the Comon road wich is ye bounds between sd lands & Joseph Covel's land & so ranging on ye Southerly side of sd Comon highway to another stone marked E & from sd stone Southerly to a white oake tree marked on four sids nere a pond called by

EARLY CHATHAM SETTLERS.

ye Indians Nespoxet and so ranging by ye North side of sd pond Easterly to a pond called ye pasture pond to ye old bounds & so by sd pond untill it come to ye land wich was Abraham Johnson's. [Also a parcel of meadow adjoining meadow of Joseph Covell, imperfectly described.] With one quarter part of a small neck of land in said Manamoy comonly called ye short neck, with one quarter part of all my share of the undivided land with all woods, fencings, with whatsoever ys standing, lying or growing on sd lands." Reservation made for "William Nickerson Senr to have a convenient highway from his now dwelling house to ly open to his land at Manamoyet." (Files, Superior Court of Judicature, No. 3,919.)

(21) Files, Superior Court of Judicature, No. 144,324.

(22) Freeman, History of Cape Cod, II, 512.

(23) On a stone erected to his memory in Harwich Centre cemetery by his grandson, the date of his death is given as Aug. 23, 1748 (13 Mayflower Descendant, 239.) This is obviously a mistake, as his will is dated in 1749.

(24) Children of Ephraim and Mercy   Covell (from his will, order uncertain): 1 Thankful, b.   ; m. Edward Nickerson, son of Thomas of Chatham, Feb. 24, 1724-5 (Har. Rec.). 2 Mercy, b.   ; m. Samuel Burge, son of Samuel of Yarmouth, Sept. 25, 1730 (Har. Rec.). 3 Sarah, b.   ; m. Benjamin Nickerson, son of Samuel of Harwich, Oct. 13, 1741 (Har. Rec.). 4 Mary, b.   ; m. Thomas Burge, son of Samuel of Yarmouth, July 28, 1742 (Har. Rec.).

ELDREDGE.

Lieut. William Eldredge, son of Robert and Elizabeth (Nickerson) Eldredge, married first,   ; second, Sarah (Newcomb) Conant, widow of Joshua of Salem and later of Truro, Jan. 30, 1706-7. She was born about 1670. As early as 1700 he had a sloop or small vessel used in coasting trips.[25] He acquired his father's farm at West Chatham in the John K. Kendrick neighborhood, lying between the highway and Oyster pond river, besides considerable adjacent land. This property, consisting of about 200 acres, he sold by deed dated December 18, 1711, to Mr. Seth Taylor of Yarmouth, a real estate trader,[26] and removed to Monomoit Beach, where he had bought land of Joseph Stewart and others. He built a house here and opened a tavern for the entertainment of sailors and others seeking a temporary harbor at or near Wreck Cove. After a few years he sold this place to Morris Farris and returned to the main land.[27] He was selectman for seven years between 1697 and 1727 and lieutenant as early as 1713. His death, which occurred April 27, 1749, is the only one recorded in the first book of town records. There is no settlement of his estate and no list of his children.[28]

Serg. Joseph Eldredge, son of Robert and Elizabeth (Nickerson) Eldredge, perhaps married first a daughter of Teague Jones, a neighbor at Monomoit from 1675 to 1683. He acquired land and prob-

8 EARLY CHATHAM SETTLERS.

ably lived for a time in the south part of Yarmouth on the west side of Bass river. His land adjoined land of Teague Jones and his sons, and the circumstances indicate that it was a family community.* The Boston records give the marriage of a Joseph Eldredge and Elizabeth Gross October 9, 1695. He was living at Monomoit again before 1698, where he settled on a tract of 50 acres on the south side of the Oyster pond, extending from the head of the pond westerly along the pond and river. William Nickerson, son of John, owned and lived upon the farm next southerly, and the present road from Atwood's corner westerly, known as Cedar street, is the old cart way which separated these two farms. His house stood at the east end of the farm in the present John Emery neighborhood.* He was selectman in 1710. His will, dated August 27, 1728, was proved September 24, 1735. His wife Elizabeth survived him and was living probably as late as 1755. His farm passed to his three sons, subject to the dower of the widow.*

Jehoshaphat Eldredge, son of William and Anne (Lumpkin) Eldredge of Yarmouth, born in that town about 1658, married Elizabeth , probably daughter of Nathaniel and Sarah Covell.* He settled on a portion of the old Nickerson or Sarah Covell farm at Chathamport. His house stood on the west side of Crow's pond, near and south of the William Covell (later Paul Crowell) farm. His will, dated Feb. 9, 1731-2, was proved Nov. 29, 1732. He had a house and lot of land at Red River neck, which was given to his son Elisha, a neck of land at Chathamport called Short neck, meadow at Ragged neck, meadow at Matchapoxett and woodland near the Red river. His dwelling house and land near Paul Crowell were given to his sons Ebenezer and Barnabas. His wife survived him, and was probably living as late as 1755.*

NOTES.
(25) Town Records, 1700.
(26) Deed from Seth Taylor to Thomas Doane dated March 20, 1718-9. M. L. Luce papers.
(27) See page 200, note 29, Smith, History of Chatham.
(28) Children of William and Eldredge (order uncertain):
1 Rebecca, b.   ; m. Ebenezer Berry of Harwich, son of John, Oct. 13, 1713 (Har. Rec.). 2 William, b.   ; m. Thankful Crowell, dau. of John of Yarmouth, March 20, 1718 (Yar. Rec.); lived at Harwich. Their children were Reuben, Rebecca, Sarah, Thankful, Bridget, William, Isaac, Jeremiah. 3 Isaac, b.   ; m. Dorothy   ; lived at Harwich. Their children were Jerusha, Monica, Mary. 4 Prob. a son Joshua, b.   ; m.   (taxed in 1755). 5 Other children, if any, not identified.
(29) See a deed from Teague Jones to his son Jeremiah, dated May 29, 1691, conveying land on the west side of Bass river, Yarmouth. Files, Superior Court of Judicature, No. 9,838.
(30) See a deed from Samuel Sprague to Richard Sears dated March 3, 1707-8. Josiah Paine papers.
(31) Children of Joseph and

Eldredge (from the will, order uncertain): 1 William, b. ; m. Hannah Taylor, dau. of John, Oct. 1, 1713 (note 45, page 188, Smith, Hist. of Chatham). 2 Tabitha, b. ; m. William Mitchell, son of William, March 19, 1712-3 (note 45, page 188, Smith, Hist. of Chatham), and died not long after. 3 John, b. ; m. Ruhamah Doane, dau. of Thomas, Sept. 26, 1728 (Chat. Rec.). 4 Jeremiah, b. ; m. 1st Lydia Hamilton, dau. of Daniel, before 1720. She died before Jan. 28, 1735-6, and he m. 2nd Thankful   , perhaps his first wife's sister.

(32) James Covell mentions Barnabas Eldredge as his cousin.

(33) Children of Jehoshaphat and Elizabeth (Covell) Eldredge (from the will, order uncertain): 1 Nathaniel, b. ; m. Sarah Conant, dau. of Joshua of Truro, Sept. 4, 1712 (East. Rec.). She was b. in Salem April 12, 1695. 2 Elnathan, b. as early as 1694; m. 1st at Yarmouth, Hannah O'Kelley, dau. of Jeremiah of Yarmouth, where he was living in 1723; m. 2nd Deliverance, probably dau. of Caleb Lambert; removed to Dartmouth about 1740. 3 Elizabeth, b. ; single 1732. 4 Edward, b. July 17, 1702 (Chat. Rec.); m. Mary, dau. of Thomas Nickerson. 5 Elisha, b. ; m. Fear Nickerson, dau. of Robert. 6 Ebenezer, b. about 1707, m. Deliverance, dau. of William and Sarah Nickerson (tradition through Mr. Josiah Paine), about 1742. 7 Barnabas, b. ; m. Mary   , about 1735.

GODFREY.

George Godfrey, oldest son of George and   Godfrey of Eastham, born January 2, 1662-3, settled at Monomoit about 1690. There is no record of his marriage. He owned land, probably his homestead, near and north of Ragged Neck.[64] He was chosen in 1700 with William Nickerson, Sen., to have charge of the building of the first meeting house. There is no mention of him in the town records after this date.[65]

Moses Godfrey, son of George and   Godfrey of Eastham, born Jan. 27, 1667-8, married Deborah Cook, daughter of Josiah and Deborah (Hopkins) Cook of Eastham. He settled at Monomoit about 1695, in that part called Cotchpinicut (Old Harbor) in the vicinity of the farm of William Nickerson, son of the first William.[66] He was early interested in religious affairs and was a special friend of Rev. John Latimer, who remembered him and his wife in his will.[67] When the church was organized in 1720, he and his wife were among the first to join. He soon, however, found himself at odds with Rev. Joseph Lord, the pastor, on account of the attitude of the latter towards Rev. Samuel Osborn and the church at Pochet (now Orleans) and was excommunicated, together with Mr. Elisha Mayo. They both were at once received again by the Pochet church, to which they had formerly belonged. Mr. Godfrey was selectman in 1710 and held other offices. He was a substantial citizen and reared a large family, which furnished energetic citizens to the town for nearly two centuries. He died April 16, 1743, aged 75 years, and his wife died seven days later, aged 64. He left a will, dated Feb. 1741-2, proved May 21, 1743, leaving his large property to his seven living sons, Samuel, Moses, David, George, Benjamin, Joshua and Richard, they paying certain legacies. A son Jonathan had died.[*]

Jonathan Godfrey, son of George and Godfrey of Eastham, born June 24, 1682, married Mercy Mayo, daughter of Thomas and Barbara (Knowles) Mayo of Eastham, October 30, 1707, and settled at Monomoit soon after. The location of his farm is not known. He appears to have been a worthy citizen, but not prominent. He had an interest in the Common land and was one of those who took pew ground in 1742. His will, dated March 7, 1765, was proved April 23, 1765, and divided his property equally among his children and the heirs of deceased children.[*]

NOTES.

(34) See deed from William Nickerson and others to Michael Stewart dated Oct. 12, 1702, and deed from Samuel Eldredge to Seth Taylor dated May 15, 1711. M. L. Luce papers.

(35) It is not known whether or not he had any children.

(36) See Smith, Hist. of Chat. page 142, note 30.

(37) See Smith, Hist. of Chatham, page 166.

(39) Children of Moses and Deborah (Cook) Godfrey (from the will, order uncertain): 1 Jonathan, b.   ; m. Mercy Nickerson, dau. of Robert, Sept. 2, 1725 (Chat. Rec.). (Admn. on his estate March 18, 1729-30. Children, Caleb, Jonathan, Rebecca.) 2 Samuel, b.   ; m.   . 3 Moses, b.   ;m. Martha Collins, dau. of John, about 1726. 4 Desire, b.   ; m. Nathaniel Ryder, son of John and Esther of Yarmouth, Sept. 26, 1728 (Chat. Rec.). 5 George, b. about 1706; m. 1st Mercy Knowles, dau. of Richard, Nov. 1, 1733 (Chat. Rec.). She died May 14, 1758, and he m. 2nd Jane (Collins) Bearse, widow of Prince Snow, Jr., and Benjamin Bearse, Nov. 9, 1758 (Chat. Rec.). 6 David, b.   ; m. Priscilla Baker, dau. of   of Yarmouth, Oct. 14, 1731 (Yar. Rec.). 7 Mary, b. Sept. 4, 1711 (old Bible record); m. 1st Caleb Nickerson, son of William, about 1732. He died Dec. 18, 1749 (Chat. Rec.), and she m. 2nd Seth Smith, son of John, Nov. 18, 1756 (old Bible record). 8 Deborah, b.   ; m. Thomas Bassett, son of Nathan. 9 Benjamin, b.   ; m. Elizabeth Hopkins, dau. of Elisha, Aug. 23, 1738 (Chat. Rec.). 10 Elizabeth, b. about 1717; m. Benjamin Bearse, son of Benjamin of Barnstable, May 31, 1733 (Chat. Rec.). 11 Joshua, b   ; m. Phebe Gould, dau. of Nathaniel of Harwich (Int. Dec. 17, 1742, Har. Rec.). 12 Richard, b.   ; m. Azubah Collins, dau. of Solomon, Jan. 10, 1750-1 (Chat. Rec.). He died in 1759, leaving Enoch, b. April 20, 1752, and Warren, b. April 6, 1757 (Liverpool, N. S. Rec.).

(40) Children of Jonathan and Mercy (Mayo) Godfrey (from the will, order uncertain): 1 Hannah,

b.   : m. James Rogers, Jr., of Eastham May 21, 1730 (East. Rec.). 2 Mercy, b.   ; m. 1st Ebenezer Burgess, son of Thomas, of Yarmouth (Int. Feb. 22, 1734-5, Yar. Rec.); m. 2nd Elkanah Rogers, son of Joseph, of Eastham (Int. June 25, 1748, East. Rec.). 3 Thomas, b.   ; m. 1st Bethiah Eldredge, dau. of Nathaniel, June 7, 1733 (Chat. Rec.); m. 2nd Mrs. Mary Covell of Eastham, March 8, 1753 (East. Rec.). 4 Ruth, b. about 1719; m. 1st John Gould, son of Nathaniel of Harwich (Int. Aug. 18, 1737, East. Rec.); m. 2nd Thomas Myrick of Harwich. 5 Lydia, b.   ; m. 1st Joseph Myrick, son of   of Eastham (Int. Feb. 5, 1742-3, East. Rec.); m. 2nd Samuel Smith, Jr., of Eastham (Int. July 3, 1756, East. Rec.). 6 Jephthah, b.   ; m. Bathsheba Eldredge, dau. of Nathaniel (See deed dated April 19, 1759, Warren J. Nickerson papers). 7 Mehitable, b.   ; m. Nathaniel Hamilton, son of Thomas, Sept. 7, 1749 (Chat. Rec.). 8 Anna, b.   ; m. 1st   Eldredge; m. 2nd James Freeman Dec. 8, 1763 (Chat. Rec.). 9 Barbara, b.   ; m.   Young; died before her father.

HAMILTON.

Serg. Daniel Hamilton, probably son of Thomas and Lydia Hamilton of Rhode Island, Sandwich and Eastham,[] born in 1670, married at Eastham Mary, daughter of Samuel Smith, about 1693 and resided there till after the birth of their second child. By the will of her father, who died in 1697, his wife came into possession of one-half of two farms at Monomoit located at Tom's Neck, and the family removed thither. His first wife having died, he married second August 5, 1708, Sarah (Smith) Snow, widow of Joseph Snow of Eastham,[] and daughter of John and Hannah Smith of Eastham. His third wife was Desire Springer, widow of Edward Springer of Newport, R. I., and daughter of James Gorham of Barnstable, whom he married at Barnstable Dec. 15, 1715. His fourth wife, who survived him, was named Elizabeth, perhaps daughter of John Taylor. Serg. Hamilton, with his brother Thomas, served under Capt. John Gorham in the expedition to Canada in 1690 and received therefor a share of land at Dunbarton, N. H., in 1735.[] He was active in local affairs, being selectman three years, constable several years and holding other positions. He was styled Sergeant as early as 1710. Through his first wife, he was interested not only in the farm at Tom's Neck, but in the Common lands and the Great Beach. He died December 8, 1738, aged 68 years. His will, written by Rev. Mr. Lord, dated January 20, 1735-6, was proved March 22, 1738-9. In it he calls Sarah, Elizabeth and Thankful his three youngest daughters.[]

NOTES.

(41) Note the following entry in the Sandwich town records: "Thomas Hambleton, the son of Thomas Hambiton and Lidia his wife was bourne the 17 of Febuary 1671, borne at Rohd Iland." 14 Mayflower Descendant, 170.

(42) "Nathaniel Snow of Lawful Age Testifieth and Saith that on

or aboute yo year 1709 I went to Chatham to Live with my Father in Law, Daniel Hambleton, Late of said Chatham, Deceased, and I saw my said Father, John Atkins, Theophilus Mayo, Thomas Mayo, John Smith and Joshua Higgins Mow and Carry of hay from Monomoit Great Beach, so called, for seven years together without Molestation. Sworn in Court July 1753. Att. Saml Winthrop Clerk." Files, Superior Court of Judicature, No. 71,149.

(43) State Archives, vol. 114, page 116; petition of Shubael Gorham June 12, 1735. Acts and Resolves of Mass.

(44) Children of Daniel Hamilton (from the will and Eastham records). 1 Grace, b. Aug. 3, 1694; d. Aug. 20, 1694 (East. Rec.). 2 Thomas, b. Sept. 1, 1695, m. Rebecca Mayo, dau. of Nathaniel of Eastham, May 3, 1716 (East. Rec.). 3 Lydia, b.   ; m. Jeremiah Eldredge, son of Joseph, about or before 1720. 4 Mary, b.   ; m. Judah Mayo, son of Thomas, of Eastham (Int. Jan. 27, 1721-2, East. Rec.). 5 Samuel, b.   ; m. 1st Bethiah Stewart, dau. of Michael, May 25, 1727 (Chat. Rec.); m. 2nd Mrs. Mercy Ellis of Harwich, Oct. 3, 1741 (Har. Rec.). 6 Daniel, b.   ; m. 1st, Abigail   , about 1729; m. 2nd Mrs Sarah Lewis of Harwich (Int. July 21, 1750, Chat. Rec.). 7 Sarah, b.   ; m. Theodore Harding, son of Joshua, of Eastham, Jan. 23, 1728-9 (Chat. Rec.). 8 Joseph, b.   ; m. Martha Atkins, dau. of Joseph, of Eastham, Jan. 22, 1731-2 (East. Rec.); lived at Eastham. 9 Elizabeth, b.   ; m. Seth Taylor, son of John, about 1730. 10 Thankful, b.   ; single in 1736; perhaps m. Jeremiah Eldredge as 2nd wife after sister's death. The last four children were by wife Sarah.

HARDING.

Capt. Joseph Harding, eldest son of Joseph and Bethiah (Cook) Harding of Eastham, born July 8, 1667, married Dinah   , probably daughter of Tristram Hedges, and settled at Monomoit prior to 1693 in the southwest quarter of the town. He was selectman seven years, treasurer two years and held other local offices. He became lieutenant of the military company as early as 1702 and captain as early as 1706, holding that position till 1715. He was probably one of the first members of the church. He had interests in the Common lands and with Thomas Atkins, bought of Josephus Quason in 1797 the interest of the latter in the Quason lands in Harwich, later receiving one-sixteenth part in the division of these lands.⁴⁵ In 1721 he took the contract to build a new parsonage for Rev. Mr. Lord, but later, after he had begun, the town cancelled the agreement and controversy ensued. He lived on the neck southeast of Cockle Cove, then called Ragged Neck, the whole of which he owned at his death. Harding's Beach, which adjoins this neck, was named for him. His wife Dinah died January 28, 1738, aged 76 years. He died early in 1745, leaving a will dated February 16, 1738-9, proved May 8, 1745. The homestead at Ragged Neck was given to his son Nehemiah. His son Maziah had a homestead and land on each side of the road

EARLY CHATHAM SETTLERS.

leading out of the neck to the highway, bought by the testator of Samuel Taylor in part and of Michael Stewart in part."

NOTES.

(45) Files, Superior Court of Judicature, No. 7,626.

(46) Children of Joseph and Dinah [Hedges(?)] Harding (from the will, order uncertain): 1 Joseph, b.   ; m. 1st Jane Adams, dau. of John of Boston and sister of Rev. Hugh Adams, July 23, 1713 (note 45, page 188, Smith, Hist. of Chatham); m. 2nd Mary Stewart, widow of Michael, betw. 1716 and 1720. 2 Maziah, b. about 1693; m. Bethiah Hawes, dau. of Isaac, about 1721. 3 Dinah, b. about 1700; m. 1st, William Baker, Jr., of Yarmouth, who d. soon after marriage; m. 2nd John Young, son of David of Eastham (Int. March 10, 1721, East. Rec.). 4 Bethiah, b.   ; m. William Nickerson, son of Thomas, before Oct. 1725. 5 Priscilla, b.   ; m. Joseph Howes, son of Thomas, Feb. 2, 1726-7 (Chat. Rec.). 6 Grace, b.   ; m.   ; d. before her father, leaving dau. Mary. 7 Mary, b.   ; m. John Buck, son of   , after 1726. 8 Nehemiah, b. about 1708; m. Priscilla Collins, dau. of Joseph of Eastham, Jan. 14, 1730-1 (East. Rec.). The Harding Gen. by Rev. Abner Morse mentions a son John who m. a Deborah Nickerson, but the will of Joseph Harding does not mention him or any children of his. Sylvanus Harding, a grandson of Joseph, had a son John who m. Deborah Nickerson, Jr., Sept. 15, 1767 (Chat. Rec.).

HOWES.

Capt. Thomas Howes, son of Joseph and   Howes of Yarmouth, born about 1680, married at Eastham Dec. 11, 1701, Content Smith, daughter of Daniel and Mary (Young) Smith of Eastham." By deed dated April 8, 1703, he purchased of William Griffith, Sen., all the real estate of the latter at Monomoit, consisting of a homestead lot of 26 acres in the Christopher Smith neighborood, one-half of 20 acres on the Great Neck and some meadow land (in all about 40 acres)." Two years later by deed dated October 22, 1705, he purchased of Philip Griffith a lot of four acres adjoining the homestead, the other half of the 20 acre lot on the Great Neck and another lot of meadow."

Still later, by deed dated April 6, 1713, he purchased of James Eldredge, the farm inherited by the latter from his father, Nicholas Eldredge, which adjoined a portion of the Howes farm." He was selectman two years and treasurer two years. He was ensign of the military company in 1715, later lieutenant and then captain. His will, dated May 29, 1736, was proved October 19, 1738. His widow survived him. His real estate was divided between his three sons."

NOTES.

(47) The Howes Genealogy by Mr. J. C. Howes is incorrect in giving the wife of Thomas as Rebecca Howes. See the will of said Daniel Smith in Barnstable Probate Records.

(48) "Thirty acres, of which Farm or Tenement is yt on which ye dwellinghouse now stands,

which hath a highway through it down to ye Inlands so Called, ye land on ye North side of sd way where ye house stands was bought of William Nickerson deceased, with ye priviledge of Comon for Cutting wood feeding or grasing as pr deed expressed under hand of ye sd William Nickerson; and ye land on ye South side of sd way bought of James Maker, excepting four acres of sd Tract which was formerly disposed of to my son Philip Griffeth x x x and also one half of a twenty acre lot upon ye Great Nock & is Called ye fourth lot, my son Philip Griffeth owning ye other half—with two acres of salt and fresh meadow, one acre bought of Trustrum Hedges & one acre bought of Samuel Nickerson, joyning both together & lyeth on ye South side of ye Oyster pond & is on ye Easterly side of ye meadow of Lieut Eldred deceased. With ye Interest in ye Meeting house according to charge paid in building ye Same by ye said William Griffeth." Old Barnstable Deeds, book 4, page 87. M. L. Luce papers.

(49) Forty acres more or less, bounded "beginning on ye south side at a stone next ye lands of ye sd Thomas Howes & on ye west side it is bounded by ye sd Howeses land & John Paddock's land, from sd stone to a red oak tree, thence to ye Corner of ye fence, thence to a red oak tree by ye Cart way, thence by a sett off Easterly to a pine tree marked, thence a little Southerly to a white oak tree by a swamp side & so through ye Swamp to another white oak tree & thence by ye swamp to ye Indian bounds, leaving ye highway to ye Jury way, thence by ye sd Jury way Westward to ye first mentioned stone. And also ye one half of a twenty acre lot on ye Stage Neck, ye other half of said lot is now in ye tenure & possession of ye sd Thomas Howes. And also half an acre of meadow, lying in Grigeries Neck adjoining to David Melvels meadow & was formerly William Griffith Junrs meadow." Old Barnstable Deeds, book 5, page 49. M. L. Luce papers.

(50) Sixteen acres, "bounded on ye Southwest by an old ditch & post & rail fence down to ye White Pond so called & then bounded Northwest by sd Pond down to ye land of John Eldredg which was set out to him as a part of his Father's farm to a Beach tree marked, thence Easterly to a markt red oak tree near ye head of a swamp & stone set in ye ground & thence upon ye same range straight over a fresh pond to ye other side thereof. And then bounded by sd Pond down to meet with ye other land of ye sd Thomas Howes: Then it is bounded Easterly by ye land of ye sd Thomas Howes up to ye land now in occupation of Lieut. Seth Taylor which he bought of Lieut. Eldredge (excepting only ye highway or road throu) And then by ye land of sd Taylor to ye first mentioned ditch & post & rails (only still allowing to Elizabeth, ye mother of ye sd James to gather cherrys & other fruit for her spending in ye summer time & ye sd James to take off ye timber & old bords of ye old house thereon)." Old Barnstable Deeds,

EARLY CHATHAM SETTLERS.

book 6, page 513, Luce papers.
(51) Children of Thomas and Content (Smith) Howes (from the will, order uncertain): 1 Daniel, b. about 1702; m. Elizabeth Doane, dau. of Thomas, about 1723. 2 Elizabeth, b.   ; m. Samuel Stewart, son of Hugh, as his 2nd wife about 1730. 3 Mary, b.   ; single in 1736; m. Zachariah Sears of Yarmouth, as 2nd wife, Dec. 14, 1768 (Chat. Rec.) 4 Joseph, b. about 1708; m. Priscilla Harding, dau. of Joseph, Feb. 2, 1726-7 (Chat. Rec.). 5 Thankful, b.   ; prob. m. Paul Ryder, son of of Yarmouth (Int. Oct. 1, 1742, Yar. Rec.). 6 Thomas, b. about 1712; m. 1st Rebecca Sears, dau. of Daniel, about 1730. She died of smallpox Dec. 10, 1765, and he m. 2nd Hope (Sears) Doane, widow of Nehemiah, 7 Hannah, b.   ; prob. m. Joseph Harding, son of Maziah, Sept. 17, 1747 (Chat. Rec.).

LUMBERT.

Caleb Lumbert, son of Caleb and Lumbert of Barnstable and Monomoit, born   ; married Sept. 1, 1704, Elizabeth Small, daughter of Edward and Mary (Woodman) Small. By deed dated Feb. 22, 1709-10, he purchased of Joseph and Ephraim Covell all their interest in the Common lands at Red River Neck and was the first to settle there.[52] In the division of the Common lands in 1713, a considerable tract in this neck was laid out to him, on which he had, no doubt, previously settled. He had trouble with the adjoining owners. In 1722 he was sued by Robert Nickerson, son of William, for cutting wood over the line, but successfully defended himself on appeal.[53] In or about 1733 he was attorney for Katherine, widow of Nathaniel Nickerson, having charge of her property in the town in her absence.[54] By deed dated Feb. 14, 1739, he conveyed to Shubael Gorham, Jr., his rights in Narragansett Township No. 7, (Gorham, Me.) derived from his father.[55] In 1741 he brought suit against Ebenezer and Barnabas Eldredge on account of the adjoining meadow land of said Eldredge.[56] He appears to have moved from town or to have died soon after this date, there being no further mention of him.

NOTES.

(52) "All that our right & Interest in & to a neck of land called the Red River Neck in said Manamoy, that is, our right in & to the upland in said neck, being two fifths parts of one third of sd neck, the whole of sd neck is bounded viz: at the Northeasterly corner where a spring Issues out into the pond thence running on a straight line to the cartway to a little swamp neer adjoining to said Cart way to the Easterly side of said Swamp, thence running Westerly by said Cartway as [it] runs to the head of the Red River hollow." Old Barnstable Deeds, book 5, page 563. Files, Superior Court of Judicature, No. 8,005.

(53) Records, Superior Court of Judicature, vol. 5, page 171; files of said Court, No. 19,259.

(54) Files, Superior Court of Judicature, Nos. 37,166 and 38,588.

(55) York, Me., Deeds, book 27, page 78.

(56) Files, Superior Court of Judicature, No. 55,602.

(57) Children of Caleb and Elizabeth (Small) Lumbert (Chat. Rec.): 1 Mary, b. June 4, 1705. 2 Deliverance, b. April 4, 1710; m. probably Elnathan Eldredge, son of Jehoshaphat. 3 Elizabeth, b. April 1, 1714; m. Seth Hammond of Dartmouth Aug. 23, 1738 (Chat. Rec.), and lived there. 4 Caleb, b. Sept. 20, 1717; m. . 5 Edward, b. March 11, 1721-2; m. . One of these sons m. Nelly Eldredge, dau. of Nathaniel.

NICKERSON.

William Nickerson, son of John and Sarah (Williams) Nickerson, married Hannah . He settled on the Great Neck (Stage Neck) probably on the lot conveyed to his father Nickerson in 1674 (see note 83, page 124, Smith, History of Chatham). His house stood on the west side of the road to the wharf near the present Davis place and his land extended west along the south side of Cedar street to and beyond the Cedar Swamp." He also had land on the east side of the road near the Joseph Atwood place. He was selectman two years and treasurer one year. He and some of his children signed their names Nicholson, doubtless through the influence of Rev. Mr. Lord, who evidently considered it the proper spelling. His will, written by Mr. Lord, was dated August 6, 1735, and proved Oct. 19, 1738. His wife Hannah survived him and was living as late as 1755. He gave the land on the east side of the road to his son David, that on the west side, with the dwelling house and outbuildings, to his son William. He had land at Seaquan-set, which he gave to Thomas Bea, son of his daughter Martha, deceased, also meadow land bought of David Melvil at a place called Melvil's flats."

John Nickerson, son of John and Sarah (Williams) Nickerson, married Mary July 11, 1706. He lived on his father's farm between the White pond and Emery's pond near the centre of the town at that time. He was selectman three years and held other offices. His will, dated May 27, 1762, was proved Sept. 7, 1762. His only son Elisha having removed to Nova Scotia, he gave his farm and other property to his maiden daughters, Mary and Elizabeth. He had meadow bought of David Melvil and land and meadow adjoining John Buck's."

Lieut. Thomas Nickerson, eldest son of William and Mercy (Williams) Nickerson, born at Monomoit about 1670, married Mary, daughter of Jonathan Bangs of Harwich. She was born April 14, 1671. He settled at Cotchpinicut Neck (Old Harbor) on land lying just west of his father's farm there. He was selectman two years, town clerk twice for short periods and held other offices. His wife joined the Harwich church Nov. 14, 1708, and he and his children were all baptized Oct. 9, 1709. His wife was dismissed to the church in Chatham July 7, 1728." He was lieutenant of the military company as early as 1708. By deed dated July 11, 1700, he acquired the interest which his mother had by foreclosure in the land adjoining him on the west and in the possession of Dogamus, Stephen and Mortiquit, Indians. They disputed his title and successfully defended themselves in the courts." There were about 100 acres in this tract, which bordered on Ryder's cove and Pleasant bay." His will, dated August 4, 1735, was proved August 3, 1736. He devised his dwelling house and land connected with it and one-half of Ram Island to his nephew, Samuel Hinckley, who lived with him. His son Nathaniel received the other half of the island. His other sons had already received their portions."

Ensign William Nickerson, second son of William and Mercy (Williams) Nickerson, born about 1675, married first Deliverance, probably daughter of Caleb Lumbert, Sen., of Monomoit. She died probably about 1716 and he married second Anna Atwood, daughter of Eldad Atwood of Eastham, October 24, 1717." By deed dated March 25, 1697, he purchased of John Quason a lot of land at Cotchpinicut, on which he probably lived." His father, by deed dated October 13, 1702, conveyed to him the land at Monomesset Neck." He was plaintiff for the "proprietors" in the dispute over the division of the Common lands. He is styled Ensign as early as 1706. He was selectman two years and for many years carried on the business of tanning hides. There was a demand for leather in those days not only for shoes but for making the leathern trousers which nearly everyone wore at his work. About 1740 he bought of the heirs of his brother Nathaniel a part of the real estate of the latter. He took pew ground in the church in 1742. He died between October 19, 1742, date of the codicil to his will, and November 15, 1742, date of its probate. His wife Anna survived him and married August 25, 1747, Benjamin Bearse, Sen., of Barnstable, who died the following year. He gave the tan house and tanning business to his sons Caleb, Nathaniel and Eldad."

Nathaniel Nickerson, son of William and Mercy (Williams) Nickerson, born about 1680, married Katherine Stewart, daughter of Hugh, May 13, 1702. He settled at Chathamport on the west side of Frostfish creek. His homestead is described in 1728 as bounded "by Capt. Thomas Howes' land on ye South side and by Elisha Mayou's land on ye west and north side and by a salt creek on ye East side."" He was town treasurer in 1723 and 1724. Administration on his estate was granted to his widow Katherine, May 20, 1725. He left, beside the homestead held by deed from his father, a parcel of upland, meadow and woodland held by deed from Ebenezer Stewart, upland at "the Stage" by deed from William Mitchell, and land at Cotchpinicut by deed from his father. Elisha Mayo was appointed guardian of his daughter Mercy Sept. 8, 1726. His widow leased the homestead in 1728 to Samuel Godfrey" and probably removed with most of the family to Falmouth, where her daughter Experience had married. She appointed Caleb Lumbert an attorney for her, who had trouble with Godfrey, and in 1733 leased the property to Elisha Hopkins." The widow Katherine died

EARLY CHATHAM SETTLERS.

about 1740. There is no list of the children."

Robert Nickerson, youngest son of William and Mercy (Williams) Nickerson, born about 1684, married Rebecca Jones, daughter of Jeremiah of Yarmouth, March 28, 1706-7. He lived on his father's farm and came into full possession of it on the death of his father in 1719, subject to the life estate of the widow. By deed dated May 15, 1729, he conveyed all his property to his sons James, Robert, Sylvanus and Elkanah, reserving the use and improvement to himself and wife." Soon after this his creditors became more pressing. Richard Knowles, Thomas Doane, Samuel Godfrey, Benjamin Ashton and others secured judgments against him about 1730." His will, dated January 16, 1755, and proved February 4, 1755, mentions no other son but Elkanah. His widow died about 1765."

NOTES.

(58) A deed dated March 16, 1767, from William Nicholson to Joseph Atwood gives the following description of this land: Thirty acres bounded "Easterly by the Road to Stage Harbour Northerly by the land of John and Jeremiah Eldredge, Westerly by land of Solomon Eldredge as the fence stands and by other land of the grantor and in ye Swamp, Southerly by land of Seth Eldredge's heirs." Joseph Atwood papers.

(59) Children of William and Hannah ( ) Nickerson (from the will, order uncertain): 1 Martha, b. ; m. John Bea of Eastham March 30, 1729 (East. Rec.). 2 Hannah, b. ; single in 1735. 3 David, b. ; m. Elizabeth Mayo, dau. of Nathaniel, of Eastham, Aug. 7, 1731 (East. Rec.). 4 Elizabeth, b. ; single in 1735. 5 Sarah, b. ; m. Thomas Ash before 1735. 6 William, b. ; m. Hannah Baker, dau. of Jonathan(?) of Yarmouth (Int. Jan. 28, 1738-9, Yar. Rec.). 7 Ruth, b. ; single in 1735. 8 Zilpha, b. ; m. Thomas Baxter, son of Thomas, of Yarmouth (Int. Nov. 8, 1740, Yar. Rec.).

(60) Children of John and Mary ( ) Nickerson (from the will, order uncertain): 1 Elisha, b. March 7, 1706-7 (Chat. Rec.); m. Desire ; moved to Harwich and about 1761 to Liverpool, N. S., thence to Argyle, N. S. 2 Mary, b. ; single in 1762. 3 Elizabeth, b. ; single in 1762. 4 Bethiah, b. about 1715; died Aug. 7, 1759, aged 44 (Hdstn.). 5 ; m. Prince Young, son of John, and died leaving a dau. Patience.

(61) Harwich Church Records; IV Mayflower Descendant, 247; VI ib. 155.

(62) Files, Superior Court of Judicature, Nos. 7,043 and 13,779; Records, Superior Court of Judicature.

(63) Page 99, note, Smith, History of Chatham.

(64) Children of Thomas and Mary (Bangs) Nickerson (all baptized at Harwich Oct. 9, 1709, by Rev. Nathaniel Stone, who records their names in the following order, doubtless according to age): 1 Jonathan, b. ; m. 1st Jane Covell, dau. of Nathaniel, about 1718. She died about 1728, and he m. 2nd Sarah Collins, dau. of

EARLY CHATHAM SETTLERS.

Jonathan of Chatham and Truro; moved to Harwich about 1735 and to Provincetown about 1742. 2 Mercy, b.   ; m. Seth Crowell, son of Thomas of Yarmouth, March 23, 1714 (note 45, page 188, Smith, History of Chatham). 3 Thomas, b. Dec. 24, 1696 (Chat. Rec.); m. 1st Lydia Covell, dau. of Joseph, May 16, 1716 (Chat. Rec.). She died Oct. 18, 1750 (Chat. Rec.), and he m. 2nd Mrs. Sarah Crowell, widow of John (Int. July 5, 1751) (Chat. Rec.); m. 3rd Mrs. Bethiah Harding, widow of Maziah, Dec. 26, 1763 (Chat. Rec.). 4 William, b.   ; m. 1st Bethiah Harding, dau. of Joseph, before Oct. 1725; m. 2nd Sarah Bassett; moved to Ridgefield, Conn., in 1747. 5 Ebenezer, b.   ; m. Constant, prob. a dau. of Joseph Covell. 6 Edward, b.   ; m. Thankful Covell, dau. of Ephraim of Harwich, Feb. 24, 1724-5 (Har. Rec.); lived in Harwich. 7 Nathaniel, b.   ; m. Hannah   ; moved to Ridgefield, Conn., in 1747, thence to Putnam Co., N. Y. 8 Mary, b.   ; m. Edward Eldredge, son of Jehoshaphat. 9 Thankful, b.   ; prob. m. Nathaniel Nickerson, son of William, about 1738.

(65) "William Nickerson and hannah Elis ann atwood were joyned in marriage on the 24th day of october 1717 at Chatham by Peter Thacher jus. of peace." (Yar. Rec.) This entry probably means "Hannah alias Ann Atwood," "alis" and possibly "elis" being a common spelling for "alias." The marriage to Deliverance appears from Osborn Nickerson papers.

(66) Note 13, page 137, Smith, History of Chatham.

(67) Osborn Nickerson papers.

(68) Children of William Nickerson (from the will, order uncertain). By wife Deliverance: 1 William, b. May 15, 1701 (O. Nickerson papers); m. Sarah Covell, dau. of Joseph, about 1723. 2 Deliveranse, b.   ; m. Abraham Chase of Harwich; moved to Tisbury before 1744. 3 Mercy, b .   ; m. Seth Paddock, son of Robert, April 13, 1727 (Chat. Rec.); died before her father, leaving two children. 4 Elizabeth, b.   ; m. Thomas Atkins, son of Thomas, about 1726; died before her father. 5 Caleb, b.   ; m. Mary Godfrey, dau. of Moses, about 1732. 6 James, b.   ; m. Dorcas   , prob. dau. of Joseph Covell; moved to Ridgefield, Conn., about 1747. 7 Joshua, b. (of age in 1734) living in 1739. 8 Nathaniel, b. (under age in 1734); m. prob. Thankful Nickerson, dau. of Thomas, about 1738. By wife Anna: 9 Anna, b.   ; m. Jonathan Crowell, son of Isaac of Yarmouth, July 13, 1738 (Chat. Rec.); moved to Barrington, N. S., about 1762. (Their children, according to Barrington records, were David, Joanna, Deborah, Azubah, Mary, Jonathan, Ruth, Sylvanus and Freeman. They did not have a son Samuel, who went to Connecticut, and other children, as given in Freeman's History of Cape Cod, II, 598, in Crowell Genealogy, etc. These latter were children of Jonathan Crowell (son of Paul) and Anna (Collins) Crowell, who moved about 1762 from Chatham to Liverpool, N. S.) 10 Deborah, b.   ; m. William Padishall between Sept. 1739, and Oct. 1742. 11 El-

dad, b. about 1723; m. Mary Cahoon, dau. of James of Eastham, Oct. 31, 1744 (East. Rec.); moved to Barrington, N. S., about 1762.
(69) Files, Superior Court of Judicature, No. 21,870.
(70) Files, Superior Court of Judicature, No. 21,870.
(71) Files, Superior Court of Judicature, No. 37,166.
(72) Children of Nathaniel and Katherine (Stewart) Nickerson (order uncertain): 1 Experience, b. ; m. Thomas Parker of Falmouth Feb. 12, 1726-7 (Chat. Rec.). 2 Mercy, b. about 1709; m. Abraham Chase in Falmouth March 5, 1732 (Falmouth Rec.), and lived in Tisbury. (Their children according to Tisbury records were Valentine, Zaccheus, David, Waitstill Mercy, and Margaret.) 3 Nathaniel, b. about 1718; m. Ruth Young of Falmouth (Int. Jan. 21, 1742, Fal. Rec.). 4 Samuel (probably) b. ; m. Jane Hunt, dau. of William of Chilmark, July 5, 1744 (Chil. Rec.). (They had children: Jane, Beriah and Nathaniel.) 5 Shubael, b. ; m. Mary Hamilton, dau. of Samuel of Chatham, Dec. 23, 1748 (Chat. Rec.), and removed to Tisbury. He, his wife and children, Katherine, Samuel and Job, were warned from Boston July, 1753 (Files, Superior Court of Judicature, No. 71,573). 6 Other children, if any, not known.
(73) M. L. Luce papers.
(74) Records, Superior Court of Judicature.
(75) Children of Robert and Rebecca (Jones) Nickerson (order uncertain): 1 James, b. ; grandjuryman 1732. 2 Mercy, b. ; m. prob. 1st Jonathan Godfrey, son of Moses, Sept. 2, 1725 (Chat. Rec.). He died in 1730 and she m. 2nd Stephen Kidder. 3 Robert, b. ; m. Mercy Cole, dau. of Daniel of Eastham, Sept. 17, 1728 (East. Rec.). 4 Fear, b. ; m. Elisha Eldredge, son of Jehoshaphat. 5 Sylvanus, b. ; (taxes abated 1742). 6 Elizabeth, b. ; m. 1st, Sept. 19, 1733, Peter Ray, son of Peter of Edgartown, and had children Joseph, Peter, Elizabeth. He died before 1741 and she m. 2nd Alexander (?) Cunningham and died before 1755. 7 Elkanah, b. Feb. 14, 1721-2 (Chat. Rec.); m. Bathsheba Snow, dau. of of Eastham, Oct. 18, 1741 (East. Rec.); moved to Liverpool, N. S., about 1762. 8 Rebecca, b. ; m. John Hopkins, son of Elisha, about 1741; moved to Dartmouth, Mass., about 1750, and to Liverpool, N. S., about 1762.

PADDOCK.

Serg. Robert Paddock, son of Zachariah and Deborah (Sears) Paddock of Yarmouth, born January 17, 1670-1, married Martha Hall, daughter of John and Priscilla (Bearse) Hall of Yarmouth, March 6, 1701-2. He moved to Monomoit soon after the birth of his second child in 1705 and settled on a farm in the north part of the town near Great Hill. He was selectman in 1720 and 1721, and was living at Chatham as late as 1730, but removed soon after to Mansfield, Conn., where Joseph, William and Benjamin Hall of Yarmouth and other relatives of his wife had settled. He probably died there before 1750 and his children or most of them removed

NOTES.

(76) Children of Robert and Martha (Hall) Paddock (order after third child uncertain): 1 son, unnamed, b. Feb. 2, 1702-3; d. seven weeks later. 2 Seth, b. March 13, 1704-5 (Yar. Rec.); m. 1st Mercy Nickerson, dau. of William, April 13, 1727 (Chat. Rec.). She died leaving children Deliverance and Zachariah, and he m. 2nd Zeruiah Storrs, dau. of Capt. Thomas Storrs of Mansfield, Conn., Oct. 10, 1735. She died Jan. 3, 1737-8; and he m. 3rd Ruth Arnold, dau. of Lieut. Robert Arnold of Mansfield, Feb. 17, 1744-5 (Mansfield Rec.). 3 Deborah, b. about 1706; m. Joseph Doane, Jr., of Eastham, Sept. 30, 1725 (Chat. Rec.). He died in 1745 and she moved to Middletown, Conn., where she died of small pox Aug. 27, 1752. 4 Zachariah, b. ; m. prob. in Chatham, moved to Mansfield, Conn. 5 Bethiah, b. ; m. Nehemiah Easterbrook, son of Rev Samuel of Mansfield, Sept. 2, 1736 (Mansfield Rec.). She died about 1743. 6 Martha, b. ; m. Elnathan Doane, son of Israel of Eastham, Feb. 25, 1737 (East. Rec.); moved to the "Oblong" about 1754. 7 Robert, b. ; m. Ruth Fletcher, dau. of John of Mansfield, June 19, 1740 (Mansfield Rec.). 8 Priscilla, b. ; m. Elisha Eldredge, son of Elisha of Mansfield, Jan. 1743 (Mansfield Rec.). 9 Eunice, b. ; m. Thomas Storrs, Jr., of Mansfield, Feb. 27, 1742-3 (Mansfield Rec.). 10 Silas, b. ; m. Abial Russ, dau. of Nathaniel of Coventry, Conn., Nov. 5, 1747 (Mansfield Rec.)

PHILLIPS.

Benjamin Phillips, probably son of Thomas Phelps or Phillips of Yarmouth, whose estate was settled in 1674 by Hugh Stewart, (who may have brought Benjamin with him to Monomoit) married about 1696 , daughter of Nathaniel and Sarah Covell. He received from his mother-in-law a lot of land near and east of the head of Muddy Cove, whereon he erected a house." It is supposed that his wife died in a few years and that he married second Temperance Stewart, daughter of Hugh of Chatham,[18] and removed to Harwich. He sold his place at Monomoit to Ebenezer Hawes between 1706 and 1713. He was of Harwich as early as 1712, having located at East Harwich near the house lately of James T. Smalley. In deeds of land in 1713 Briggs pond, East Harwich, is described as "the pond southward of Benjamin Phillips." He was living as late as 1744.[19] His widow Temperance married Beriah Broadbrooks in 1747. There is no settlement of his estate and no record of his children.[20]

NOTES.

(77) See note 23, page 84, Smith, History of Chatham.

(78) Temperance and her sister Joanna were unmarried in March, 1711, the date of their father's will, but it is believed that they married soon after, Joanna becoming the wife of one Oaker. The widow Joanna Oaker is mentioned in the Chatham records. Note that

two of the children of Benjamin Phillips are named Joanna and Oaker.

(79) 8 Mayflower Descendant, 119.

(80) Children of Benjamin Phillips (order uncertain): By 1st wife probably: 1 Anna, b. ; m. Samuel Atkins, son of Isaac of Harwich, Feb. 23, 1720-1 (Har. Rec.). 2 Henry, b. ; estate settled in 1725. 3 Micah, b. ; m. Joanna Baker of Yarmouth, dau. of William, Aug. 25, 1726 (Yar. Rec.). 4 Jane, b. ; m. Gowell Chase, son of Isaac of Yarmouth, Nov. 1727 (Har. Rec.). Probably by wife Temperance: 5 Benjamin, b. ; m. Maria Broadbrooks, daughter of Beriah of Harwich, Aug. 23, 1735 (Har. Rec.). 6 Joanna, b. ; m. Ebenezer Berry of Yarmouth as 2nd wife Dec. 20, 1738 (Har. Rec.). 7 Oaker, b. about 1720; m. Mary Small or Smalley Dec. 4, 1741 (Har. Rec.). 8 Joseph, b. about 1721; m. Mercy Small or Smalley Nov. 8, 1744 (Har. Rec.). 9 Hannah, b. ; m. Samuel Nickerson, Jr., of Harwich Dec. 6, 1745 (Har. Rec.).

SEARS.

Richard Sears, son of Paul and Deborah (Willard) Sears of Yarmouth, born in 1680 or 1681, married May 15, 1700, Hope, daughter of Samuel and Rebecca Howes of Yarmouth. By deed dated March 3, 1707-8, he bought of Samuel Sprague of Marshfield all the lands and rights of the latter at Monomoit. This included a farm, formerly of Joseph Quason, Indian, extending from the head of the Oyster pond east to the bay or salt water, and from the Black pond south to the head of the Mill pond, also one-third interest in the undivided lands.[81] He settled at Monomoit soon after this purchase. He was treasurer in 1713, constable in 1714-5 and selectman in 1717. He died May 24, 1718, at the early age of 37 years. His gravestone is the oldest in the old cemetery. His widow married, second, Dea. John Rich of Eastham (Int. Aug. 2, 1723) and his children were brought up in that place, but Paul, the son, returned to Chatham, and settled upon the real estate assigned to him out of his father's estate.[82]

Capt. Daniel Sears, brother of Richard, born 1682 or 1683, married Feb. 12, 1708-9, Sarah Howes of Yarmouth, sister of his brother's wife. He became interested in the farm at Monomoit bought by his brother and removed thither. The purchase was doubtless made on their joint account. After the death of Richard, the management of the whole farm doubtless fell upon Daniel. During his long career he was one of the leading citizens of the town, being town clerk 24 years between 1715 and 1753, selectman 8 years, and holding other offices. He was ensign as early as 1722, lieutenant as early as 1733 and later captain of the local military company. He died August 10, 1756, aged 73, leaving a will dated January 30, 1753. His wife died November 9, 1748, aged 62. He gave all his real estate to his son Daniel. His descendants have probably attained more wealth and distinction than those of any other Chatham family. His grandson, David Sears, long a prominent merchant and financier of Boston, director of the first Bank of the United States, was accounted at his death the richest man of that city and founded a family long and prominently known. His grandson Richard of this town also attained a local prominence, which the family maintained till its extinction here about 50 years ago."

NOTES.

(81) "All those my land and rights of land I now have or of right I ought to have within the precinct or Village of Monomoy in the County of Barnstable aforesaid, that is to say more particularly all that my farm or tract of land which I lately purchased of Joseph Quason, Indian of Monomoy aforesaid. The said farm being bounded towards the east by the Bay or Salt Water & towards the north by certain boundaries that that is to say ptly by the ditch called Indian Nicks ditch so extending westerly over a pond w----oak tree marked so continuing the same range westerly till it comes to a tall pine tree marked which is the corner boundary of the farm and bounded towards the South by the land lately John Cussens, Indian, as an old fence & dry ditch directs to a pine tree near the house of Joseph Eldridges & is bounded towards the West partly by the Oyster pond & ply by the lands of particular persons, That is to say all my lands pertaining to said farm & not formerly sold or passed away by the said Joseph Quason before the 12th day of October A. D. 1702 as in & by one instrument or deed of feofment of the date aforesaid given me under the hand and seal of said Quason may appear at large, referance thereto be had for the westerly bounds of the said farm --And also my two parcels of meadow land, The one called Stumpy Marsh esteemed at eight acres more or less environed with upland and meadow of the heirs of Samuel Smith deceased. The other being a small piece of marsh esteemed at one acre more or less bounded westward by a creek southward by a pine tree standing on the upland which tree is the Northerly bounds of the meadow of the heirs of the said Samuel Smith, Eastward by the upland till it comes to point thereof near ye creek, together also with my one third part of all the common or undivided land within the limits of Monomoy aforesaid, excepting such priviledges of herbage or feeding for cattle & firewood as hath been formerly granted to any person or persons in or on the said Commons or undivided land by Mr. William Nickerson deceased or by his son William Nickerson, Sarah Covel & her children or myself or any one of us." March 3, 1707-8, Samuel Sprague acknowledged before Elikem Brett, Justice Peace. Witnesses, Abraham Samson and John Murdo. Recorded July 6, 1708, William Bassett Reg. (Josiah Paine papers.)

(82) Children of Richard and Hope (Howes) Sears: 1 Thankful, b. at Yarmouth March 18, 1706-7; m. April 13, 1727, John Rich, Jr., of Eastham (East. Rec.). 2 Paul, b. at Chatham about 1710, m. Anna Atkins, dau. of Joseph of

Eastham (Int. Jan. 31, 1729-30, East. Rec.). 3 Samuel, b. at Chatham about 1712; d. Dec. 21, 1738, aged 26 (Hdstn.). 4 Hannah, b. at Chatham about 1717; m. Feb. 23, 1737-8, Zoheth Smith of Eastham (East. Rec.).

(83) Children of Daniel and Sarah (Howes) Sears (Chat. Rec.): 1 Rebecca, b. March 19, 1701-11; m. Thomas Howes, son of Thomas, about 1730. 2 Daniel, b. June 1, 1712; m. Fear Freeman, dau. of Benjamin of Harwich, Oct. 31, 1745 (Har. Rec.). 3 Sarah, b. April 11, 1714; m. Joshua Atkins, son of Thomas, Aug. 1, 1734 (Chat. Rec.). 4 Mercy, b. July 17, 1716; m. Stephen Ryder, son of John, about 1738. 5 Richard, b. April 26, 1718; died unmarried in 1746. 6 David, b. April 21, 1720; died unmarried in 1746. 7 Deborah, b. Oct. 13, 1722; m. Joseph Atwood, son of Joseph of Eastham (Int. April 14, 1742, East. Rec.).

SMITH.

John Smith, son of Samuel and Mary (Hopkins) Smith of Eastham, was born May 26, 1673, and married Bethiah Snow, daughter of Stephen and Susanna (Dean) Snow, May 14, 1694. He resided at Eastham till after the birth of his second child. Having received by the will of his father one-half of two farms at Tom's Neck, Monomoit, he removed thither and became one of the substantial citizens of the place. The boundaries of the two farms are described in the note on page 90, Smith, History of Chatham. He was selectman one year and held other offices in the town. In 1716 he testified against Rev. Mr. Adams in the suit of Adams vs Hawes." He was a large owner in the Great Beach. He died in middle life, administration on his estate being granted to his son Samuel, Feb. 25, 1717. His widow was living as late as 1734,* when his estate was finally settled among the children.

NOTES.

(84) Page 183, Smith's Chatham.

(85) Children of John and Bethiah (Snow) Smith (from Probate and Eastham Rec.): 1 James, b. Feb. 13, 1694-5; died May 27, 1696. 2 Samuel, b. May 25, 1696; m. Mercy Higgins, dau. of Isaac of Eastham (Int. July 19, 1718, East. Rec.). (He did not m. 2nd Sarah Snow of Eastham, Sept. 25, 1730, and have children born in Eastham, as frequently stated. See N. E. Hist. Gen. Reg. [1897] 204, "Wellington Smith and his Family" etc. He lived at Chatham, was selectman there in 1736 and 1743, member of the church, and so far as known, had but one wife and ch.: Samuel, Eleanor and Bethiah, all baptized at Chatham May 25, 1742. N. E. Hist. Gen. Reg. [19]). 3 Deane, b. about 1698; m. Esther Ryder, dau. of John of Yarmouth, Oct. 17, 1720 (Yar. Rec.). 4 Mercy, b. betw. 1698 and 1702; m. Nathan Kenney of Chatham, Sept. 24, 1729 (Chat. Rec.). 5 Mary, b. about 1702; m. m. Obediah Chase, son of Isaac of Yarmouth, about 1732; died about 1767. 6 John, b. April 7, 1703 (old Bible rec.); m. 1st Elizabeth Brown, dau. of George of Eastham, Sept. 21, 1727 (East. Rec.); m. 2nd Lydia Snow, wid. of Ebenezer of Eastham, April 7, 1763 (Chat. Rec.); moved to Eastham after second marriage. 7

Stephen, b. about 1700; m. 1st Hannah Collins, dau. of John, about 1727; m. 2nd Bathsheba Brown, dau. of George of Eastham, April 9, 1729 (East. Rec.). 8 Bethiah, b. about 1708; m. Elisha Young, Jr., Dec. 15, 1731 (Chat. Rec.). 9 David, b. about 1711; living in 1734. 10 Seth, b. about 1713, acc. to Probate Rec.. (Nov. 13 or 14, 1711, old Bible rec.); m. 1st Elizabeth , March 15, 1737 (old Bible rec.). She was b. March 15, 1718 (old Bible rec.), and died April 12, 1756 (Hdstn.). He m. 2nd Mary (Godfrey) Nickerson, wid. of Caleb, Nov. 18, 1756 (Chat. Rec.).

STEWART.

Michael Stewart, eldest son of Hugh and Wait Stewart, born in Yarmouth probably about 1670, married Mary . He was a mariner. By deed dated October 12, 1702, he bought of the then proprietors of Monomoit, viz: William Nickerson, Sen., Nathaniel Covell, William Covell, Joseph Covell, Ephraim Covell and Samuel Sprague, a large irregular tract at what is now West Chatham, on both sides of the highway, lying between the ponds there and Ragged Neck and extending from the present Doane neighborhood westerly to the present George Buck neighborhood.⁸⁵ The easterly end of this tract at Ockpesett he sold in part. by deed dated March 31, 1703, to William Eldredge, receiving in exchange a parcel of meadow near his own land "at or near a place commonly called Nick's place," and in part by deed dated May 22, 1708, to James Eldredge."⁷ That part

on the south side of the highway between it and Ragged Neck appears to have been sold to Samuel Taylor, son of John, before 1711.⁸⁸ He died in middle life. Administration was granted on his estate to his brother Samuel September 26, 1716. His widow married Joseph Harding, Jr., before 1720.⁸⁹

John Stewart, probably son of Hugh and Wait Stewart, married Elizabeth . He was tithing man in 1702, but appears later to have moved away, returning to the town again about 1715.⁹⁰ Administration on his estate was granted to his widow July 11, 1722. He left an estate valued at £360, of which £290 was in real estate. His widow was left with several small children, among whom was probably a son John, who married Jenny, daughter of Joseph Harding, Jr., and was a resident of the town as late as 1744, and perhaps Elizabeth, who married Seth Smith.

NOTES.

(86) This tract is described as follows: "Beginning at ye Northerly Corner of ye land of Hugh Stewart thence ranging Easterly to a fresh pond, so ranging further Easterly by ye sd pond on thwart a neck of land to a Run or flow of water that runs into a pond Called ye white pond & bounded westerly by ye lands of ye sd Hugh Stewart & Southerly partly by ye meadow sometime of Robert Eldredge deceased & partly by ye upland of George Godfree & partly by ye land formerly reputed to be ye land of John Downing deceased & Easterly by

ye reputed lands of ye sd Robert Eldredge & Northerly by ye reputed lands of Teague Jones deceased x x reserving a Convenient highway through sd land & a way issuing out of ye sd highway to ye six acre lots so called & another way to ye neck of land called ye Ragged Neck." Recorded Book 4, folio 86, Old Barnstable Deeds. (M. L. Luce papers.)

(87) M. L. Luce papers.

(88) See "A Proprietor's Book for Chatham" and deed from Samuel Eldredge to Seth Taylor of Yarmouth dated May 15, 1711. (M. L. Luce papers.)

(89) Children of Michael and Mary Stewart (Chat. Rec.): 1 Bethiah, b. Sept. 21, 1704; m. Samuel Hamilton, son of Daniel, May 25, 1727 (Chat. Rec.). 2 Patience, b. Aug. 27, 1713; prob. m. at Liverpool, N. S., Dec. 25, 1760, George Winslow (Liverpool Rec.).

(90) See page 190, Smith, History of Chatham.

TUCKER.

Samuel Tucker, probably son of John and Susanna Tucker of Tisbury and brother of John Tucker of Harwich, married Hannah Mayo, daughter of William and Elizabeth (Ring) Mayo of Eastham, about 1706 and settled at Monomoit soon after." On May 17, 1713, he joined the church at Harwich and his children, Keziah, Elizabeth and Thankful, were baptized there July 3, 1715, and his daughter Hannah, July 29, 1716." Later he doubtless joined the Chatham church under Mr. Lord. He had the care of the church building for many years, receiving an annual stipend from the town "for his paines of swepen the meten hous." He was often chosen tithingman and in 1750 was the town schoolmaster. He died about 1765, leaving no estate. His wife died a few years before him."

NOTES.

(91) 14 Mayflower Descendant, 117; 6 ib. 95.

(92) Harwich Ch. Rec.; 4 Mayflower Descendant, 248, 249; 5 ib. 17.

(93) Children of Samuel and Hannah (Mayo) Tucker (Chat. Rec.): 1 Keziah, b. Nov. 1707; m. Nathaniel Covell, son of Nathaniel, April 14, 1727 (Chat. Rec.). 2 John, b. Sept. 1709; died Sept. 1709. 3 Thankful, b. Sept. 1710. 4 Elizabeth, b. Sept. 1712. 5 Hannah, b. Sept. 1714; prob. m. Isaac Hawes, Jr., and moved to the Oblong about 1747. 6 John, b. March 20, 1715-6. 7 Samuel, b. March 16, 1719-20. 8 Eunice, b. June 12, 1722.

COLLINS.

The foregoing families all settled in or became connected with the village between 1690 and the emigration of 1711. After that emigration the following new families came in, completing the settlement of the town. By 1725 the period of settlement may be said to have ended. Very few new families came in after that date.

John Collins, son of Joseph and Ruth (Knowles) Collins of Eastham, born December 18, 1674, married Hannah Doane, daughter of John of Eastham, February 12, 1701-2. He lived for some time at Eastham, selling his farm there by deed dated Sept. 5, 1715, to Ichabod Higgins." The same year he purchased land at Tom's Neck, Chatham, of John Smith or Daniel Hamilton or both and settled there. He was interested in the church and was one of the earliest pew owners. He was a man of energy and ability and accumulated considerable property. Although not the richest man in the place, he and his children together formed by far the wealthiest family in the place in the period before the Revolution. His oldest son, Solomon, became in time the largest taxpayer, and several of his other sons had large properties for the time. From him, through his son Joseph, who went to Nova Scotia, descended Hon. Enos Collins, a distinguished merchant of Liverpool, N. S., who married a daughter of Chief Justice Brenton Haliburton of that colony. From him, through his daughter Anna, who married Jonathan Crowell, descended Hon. John Crowell of Ohio, member of Congress in 1816, and prominent in Ohio in his time. Although he lived to be very old, he left a large estate for his time. He died March 24, 1765, at the age of 91. His widow died June 6, 1765, aged 85. His will dated March 12, 1749, with codicil of later date, was proved June 28, 1765. It divides the real estate among his sons and shows that he lived in the easterly part of Tom's Neck."

NOTES.

(94) Stanley W. Smith papers.

(95) Children of John and Hannah (Doane) Collins (all born in Eastham except the last two): 1 Solomon, b. Feb. 6, 1703-4; m. Eunice Atkins, dau. of Samuel, about 1726. 2 Samuel, b. Nov. 26, 1705; m. 1st ; m. 2nd Patience (Howes) Eldredge, widow of Jonathan and of Seth Eldredge, Oct. 19, 1758 (Chat. Rec.). 3 Martha, b. Jan. 26, 1707-8; m. Moses Godfrey, son of Moses, about 1726. 4 John, b. Nov. 2, 1709; m. Thankful Taylor, dau. of Samuel, about 1740. 5 Hannah, b. Nov. 2, 1711; m. Stephen Smith, son of John, about 1727; died young leaving child Stephen. 6 Joseph, b. Aug. 14, 1713; m. Abigail Crowell, dau. of Paul, about 1737; moved to Liverpool, N. S., about 1760. 7 David, b. April 20, 1715; m. Desire . 8 Jane, b. at Chatham about 1717; m. 1st Prince Snow, Jr., of Harwich (Int. Sept. 10, 1737, Har. Rec.); m. 2nd Benjamin Bearse of Chatham, son of Benjamin of Barnstable, about 1743; m. 3rd George Godfrey, son of Moses, Nov. 9, 1758 (Chat. Rec.). 9 Anna, b. at Chatham; m. Jonathan Crowell, son of Paul, about 1740; moved to Liverpool, N. S., about 1760. (The list of the children of John Collins born in Chatham given by Dean Dudley in his Genealogy of the Bangs Family, p. 39, is wholly erroneous.)

CROWELL.

John Crowell, son of John and Hannah Crowell of Yarmouth, born December 5, 1689, married Alice Gross, daughter of Simeon and Mary (Bond) Gross of Hingham (published Aug. 21, 1714). He was a carpenter by trade. He lived at Hingham a year or two, removing to Eastham about 1716 and to Chatham two or three years later. His house was at the head of

Muddy Cove, near the Harwich line and opposite the Indian meeting house.⁹⁵ Administration on his estate was granted to his son Jabez July 9, 1746. In the inventory of his estate appears the following item: "Cash being the dec'ds wages at Cape Breton £44-06-04." His widow, whose name was Sarah, a second wife, married second Thomas Nickerson, Sen., July 5, 1751.⁹⁷

Col. and Dea. Paul Crowell, second child of John and Bethiah (Sears) Crowell of Yarmouth, born April 20, 1687, married first Elizabeth, daughter of Jonathan Hallett of Yarmouth, October 21, 1714. She died November 17, 1723, aged 34 years, and he married second Margery Hall, daughter of Dea. Joseph Hall of Yarmouth, February 15, 1724-5. He settled at Chatham in 1717 on the farm at Chathamport purchased for him by his father of William Covell.⁹⁸ The house of the late Osborn Nickerson, Esq., stands on this farm, which bordered on Pleasant Bay. He soon became an active and highly respected citizen. He was town treasurer seven years and selectman six years. He became a deacon of the church as early as 1738. He was first a lieutenant (1739) and then captain (1744) of the local military company, then major (1749) and finally colonel of the county regiment of soldiers. From him, through his son Jonathan, is descended Hon. John Crowell, member of Congress from Ohio in 1846.⁹⁹ Col Crowell died October 11, 1705, aged 78 years. He left a large estate, most of which was divided by his will among his three sons. The homestead was given to his son David. The widow, Margery Crowell, died May 26, 1773, aged 78.¹⁰⁰

NOTES.

(96) Town Records—renewals of boundary with Harwich.

(97) Children of John and Alice (Gross) Crowell: 1 Abigail, b. at Hingham June 3, 1715 (Hing. and East. Rec.); m. Hincks Gross, son of Thomas of Eastham, July 25, 1734 (Chat. Roc.). 2 Jabez, b. at Eastham June 4, 1717 (East. Rec.); m. Lydia . 3 Jonah, b. ; mentioned in the list of his father's creditors; perhaps d. young. 4 John (?) (a John Crowell removed from town or died in 1763).

(98) See account of William Covell, Smith, History of Chatham.

(99) Hon. John Crowell, member of the Ohio state Senate and elected to Congress in the fall of 1846, was born at East Haddam, Conn., Sept. 15, 1801, son of William and Ruth (Peck) Crowell of East Haddam. His grandparents were Samuel and Jerusha (Tracy) Crowell, of whom Samuel was born at Chatham, Mass., March 16, 1742-3, removed with his parents about 1760 to Liverpool, N. S., and thence removed to East Haddam, Conn., where he was married about 1770. (For evidence of this removal see land records of Queens Co., N. S.) The parents of Samuel were Jonathan and Anna (Collins) Crowell of Chatham and Liverpool, N. S.

(100) Children of Paul Crowell (from family Bible): by wife Elizabeth: 1 Abigail, b. Sept. 13, 1715; m. Joseph Collins, son of

John, about 1737; removed to Liverpool, N. S., about 1760. 2 Paul, b. April 4, 1717; m. 1st Rebecca Paine, dau. of Ebenezer, about 1738. She died Dec. 30, 1746, and he m. 2nd Reliance Cobb, dau. of Eleazer of Barnstable, April 27, 1747 (Barn. Rec.). She died Nov. 9, 1774, and he m. 3rd Mehitable (Snow) Ryder, widow of Samuel Hopkins of Harwich and of Reuben Ryder of Chatham. 3 Jonathan, b. Feb. 25, 1718; m. Anna Collins, dau. of John, about 1740 (not Anna Nickerson, as stated II Freeman, Hist. of Cape Cod, 598); removed to Liverpool, N. S., about 1760. By wife Margery: 4 Elizabeth, b. April 7, 1726; m. Hezekiah Doane, son of of Eastham, Oct. 25, 1750 (Chat. Rec.). 5 David, b. Aug. 3, 1730; m. Thankful Atwood, dau. of James of Eastham, Dec. 6, 1759 (East. Rec.).

DOANE.

Thomas Doane, son of Ephraim and Merry (Knowles) Doane of Eastham, born September 4, 1674, married Patience Mulford, daughter of Thomas and Hannah of Eastham, February 28, 1700-1. He learned the trade of a blacksmith, but early engaged in whaling. He removed his family to Chatham in or before 1719, where he purchased by deed dated March 20, 1718-9, of Seth Taylor of Yarmouth, a large farm of about 300 acres at West Chatham lying between the Oyster pond river and the White pond.¹⁰¹ He was for many years one of the leading citizens and the largest land owner and tax payer of the town. He was selectman ten years between 1725 and 1745, frequently moderator of town meetings and often chosen to serve the town in other capacities. He was one of the first to take pew ground in the church in 1742. He was often engaged in litigation. His deeds and papers (herein referred to as the M. L. Luce papers) have come down to us and throw a flood of light on the early history of the town. His wife died February 8, 1744, aged 70, and his death occurred May 3, 1756, at the age of 82 years. His will, dated March 17, 1756, was proved September 21, 1756. His three sons had died before him and his real estate went to his grandsons. His youngest child, Anna, married Dr. John Osborn, son of the minister at Eastham, a graduate of Harvard college, a poet, physician and man of talent, and lived at Middletown, Conn., where there was a colony of Cape settlers.¹⁰⁰

NOTES.

(101) "All that my Messuag, Tenement, Dwelling House and house lot of land situate in Chatham x x with all my Lands and Meadows lying in sd Chatham, Together with all the Right and Interest that I have Devided & undevided in the bounds of Harwich, being all my Housing, Lands & Meadows, Rights & Interest, acording as they are expressed In & by one Deed Pole of Conveyance from William Eldred of Manemoy now Chatham, Planter, bearing date the 18th day of December 1711 Recorded in the Registry of sd County in the sixth book of Evidences of Lands, folio 300, to me given & Granted, signed sealed & delivered: sd Granted premises

Containing by estimation two hundred acres more or less. Together with all my Rights in & to the Lands lately Divided or to be Divided in sd Chatham so far as my Right extends by virtue of what I bought of Capt Ebenezer Hawes of sd Chatham. Together with all that my parcel & parcels of Land & Meadow lying in Chatham above sd, being by estimation forty acres more or less, which is all the Lands that I have in sd Chatham & all the Meadows there that I have & hold by Deed from Samuel Eldredg of Manamoy formerly so called & is buted & bounded as by one Deed Pole under the hand & seal of sd Samuel Eldrege to me signed, sealed & Delivered may appear baring date the 15th of May 1711 Recorded in the Registry of sd County in the sixth book of Evidences of Lands in folio 49 & 50 & 51: Together with all that my parcel of Land Messuage or Tenement lying in sd Chatham which I have & hold by one Deed Pole from under the hand & seal of Robert Nickerson of Harwich in the County abovesd son of Robert Nickerson Deceased baring Date the 22nd Day of July 1713 Recorded in Seventh book of Evidences of Lands page 97 buted & bounded as in & by sd Deed is expresst: Together with all that my parcel of meadow & sedge ground lying in sd Chatham which I have & hold by one Deed Pole from under the hand & seal of John Eldredg of sd Chatham, Labourer, baring Date the 7th day of June 1716 Recorded in the Eighth Book of Evidences of Lands folio 195 buted & bounded as in & by sd Deed is expresst." M. L. Luce papers.

(102) Children of Thomas and Patience (Mulford) Doane (all born at Eastham): 1 Thomas, b. Jan. 10, 1701; m. in 1729, Sarah Barnes, dau. of Jonathan of Plymouth. 2 Elizabeth, b. Feb. 5, 1703-4; m. Daniel Howes, son of Thomas, about 1723. 3 Reuben, b. March 21, 1705; m. Sarah Haugh, dau. of Samuel of Boston, (Doane Gen.) about 1730. 4 Abigail, b. March 28, 1708; m. John Hawes, son of Isaac, about 1735., 5 Ruhama, b. about 1709; m. John Eldredge, son of Joseph, Sept. 26, 1728 (Chat. Rec.). Benjamin, b. Dec. 26, 1710; m. Mary Freeman, dau. of Nathaniel of Harwich, Nov. 7, 1734 (Har. Rec.). 7 Anna, b. ; m. Dr. John Osborn, son of Rev. Samuel of Eastham. He died May 31, 1753, and she m. 2nd Thomas Smith of East Haddam, Conn.. May 27, 1756.

ELDREDGE.

James Eldredge, eldest son of Lieut. Nicholas and Elizabeth Eldredge, married Ruth . He lived at West Chatham on the John Downing farm set off to him in the division of his father's estate in 1708. By deed dated May 22, 1708, he bought of Michael Stewart, a tract of 10 acres between the highway and the White pond.¹⁰⁰ This he sold, together with six acres more inherited from his father, to Thomas Howes by deed dated April 6, 1713.¹⁰¹ He died July 19, 1757. He gave his homestead by will to his sons James and Abner. His widow Ruth removed with several of her children in 1762 to Liverpool, N.

EARLY CHATHAM SETTLERS.

S., but returned in a few years.[103]

NOTES.

(103) Described as follows: "Bounded Southerly by ye land of ye sd James Eldredge, & at ye Easterly end is bounded by ye land of William Eldredge & is bounded Northerly by ye land of Nicholas Eldredge [deceased] & is bounded westerly by ye Rellict of an old fence called ye General fence near a little pond runing into ye white pond or adjoining to ye white pond, containing ten acres more or less." M. L. Luce papers.

(104) See note 50, supra, for description.

(105) Children of James and Ruth ( ) Eldredge: 1 Seth, b. ; m. ;lived in R. I. 2 Mary, b. ; single in 1757. 3 Zephaniah, b. Dec. 2, 1733; m. Phebe Eldredge Nov. 29, 1752 (Chat. Rec.). 4 Rebecca, b. Nov. 16, 1735; m. Cyrenus Collins, son of Solomon, July 13, 1756 (Chat. Rec.). 5 Ruth, b. Feb. 16, 1737; m. Jonathan Bearse May 19, 1755 (Chat. Rec.). 6 Abner, b. Oct. 11, 1738; m. Sarah Eldredge, April 19, 1762 (Chat. Rec.). 7 James, b. April 8, 1742; m. Hannah Collins, dau. of , March 2. 1771 (Chat. Rec.).

FARRIS.

Morris Farris, whose origin and parentage is unknown, married at Nantucket June 18, 1708, Mrs. Orange (Rogers) Cartwright, widow of Nicholas of Nantucket. He was a resident of Chatham as early as 1715,[106] living first on Quituessett (Morris) Island[107] and later keeping tavern on Monomoit Beach. This tavern he sold to Joseph Stewart about 1728.[108] It is supposed that he died not long after, leaving a son William, who was of Chatham in 1736, a sea faring man, and gave bond on that date to Sylvanus Bourne of Barnstable.[109] In 1745 William Farris was one of the creditors of the estate of Elisha Hopkins.[110] It is supposed that this William (or a son William) removed to Falmouth, where he was living as late as 1790.[111]

NOTES.

(106) See page 190, Smith, History of Chatham. His stepson, Nicholas Cartwright, came with him.

(107) See page 92, note 38, Smith, History of Chatham.

(108) See page 200, note 29, Smith, History of Chatham.

(109) Bourne Mss. Harvard Coll. Library.

(110) Barnstable Probate Rec., est. of Elisha Hopkins.

(111) See U. S. census, 1790. In Dec. 1784, William Farris and others, described as of Falmouth, signed an inquest on the body of Elizabeth Cator of Mashpee. Files, Superior Court of Judicature, No. 144,470.

HAWES.

Lieut. Isaac Hawes, son of Captain John and Desire (Gorham) Hawes of Yarmouth, born March 9, 1679-80, married January 8, 1700-1, Bethiah Howes, daughter of Jeremiah of Yarmouth, and lived there till about 1712, when he removed to Chatham. He purchased a part of the interest of the

Covells in the common land and received in the division of 1713 a tract on each side of the road which runs from the late Samuel D. Clifford's to the late Rufus Smith's. His house was in or near this tract. In the latter part of his life he lived in or near the place late of Ephraim Steele.[113] He was sergeant of the military company as early as 1720 and later lieutenant. Administration on his estate was granted to his widow Bethiah March 16, 1730-1. She married second John Smith of Eastham, son of John (Int. April 11, 1741). He died in 1742 and she married third November 16, 1743, Rev. Joseph Lord of Chatham. She died between March 7, 1746-7, when she is named as one of the executors of Mr. Lord's will, and June 30, 1748, when the will was proved and she was not appointed with the others.[114]

NOTES.

(112) See a deed dated July 30, 1750, from John Hawes, administrator of Isaac, to Ebenezer Paine of a tract of land "where the dwellinghouse of the late Isaac Hawes last stood, containing six acres more or less, bounded Westerly on the said Ebenezer Paine, Southerly on the way untill it comes to the land that James Covell bought of Simeon Covell, then Northerly to the pond and Westerly by the pond to James Covells land where the fence stands and by the fence and James Covells land to said Paine's land." Josiah Paine papers.

(113) Children of Isaac and Bethiah (Howes) Hawes: 1 Bethiah, b. July, 1701; m. 1st Maziah Harding, son of Joseph, about 1721; m. 2nd Thomas Nickerson, Sen., Dec. 26, 1763 (Chat. Rec.). 2 Isaac, b. April, 1703; m. Hannah, prob. dau. of Samuel Tucker; removed to the "Oblong," N. Y., about 1747, and thence to Kent, Conn. 3 Thankful, b. March, 1705; m. Moses Young, son of Henry of Eastham (Int. March 6, 1724-5, East. Rec.). 4 John, b. Jan. 22, 1706-7; m. Abigail Doane, dau. of Thomas, about 1735. 5 Desire, b. Jan. 14, 1708-9. 6 Jeremiah, b. April 5, 1711; m. Phebe Young of Eastham, prob. dau. of Jonathan, Aug. 8, 1734 (East. Rec.), lived at Eastham. (The foregoing children were born in Yarmouth). 7 Hannah, b. at Chatham; m. 1st John Slater, Feb. 21, 1749-50 (Chat. Rec.). 8 Sarah, b. May 31, 1719 (Bible record); m. Cornelius Higgins, son of Ebenezer of Eastham, Sept. 29, 1743 (Bible record), int. of m. Feb. 19, 1742-3 (East. Rec.); removed to Haddam, Conn., about 1747.

KNOWLES.

Lieut. Richard Knowles, son of Samuel and Mercy (Freeman) Knowles of Eastham, born July, 1688, married Martha Cobb, daughter of James and Sarah Cobb of Barnstable, about 1712.[114] He came to Chatham about 1719 and succeeded Capt. Ebenezer Hawes as the tavern-keeper of the place. He undoubtedly bought of Hawes the tavern and land adjoining owned by the latter, and carried on the business for many years. He was selectman three years and treasurer two years. He was active in local affairs, but appears

EARLY CHATHAM SETTLERS.

to have lost his property in his old age. His wife died October 31, 1763, aged 81. He died about 1769, leaving no estate.¹¹⁴

NOTES.

(114) See Barnstable Probate Rec., estate of Jane Snow.
(115) Children of Richard and Martha (Cobb) Knowles (Chat. Rec.): 1 Martha, b. Jan. 28, 1713-4; m. John Shaw of Eastham (Int. Nov. 10, 1729, East. Rec.). 2 Richard, b. March 26, 1715; died Aug. 20, 1736, aged 21 (Hdstn.). 3 Mercy, b. Aug. 9, 1717; m. George Godfrey, son of Moses, Nov. 1, 1733 (Chat. Rec.). 4 James, b. Nov. 11, 1719; m. 1st Sarah Doane of Eastham, dau. of Joseph, Nov. 25, 1742 (East. Rec.). She died Dec. 26, 1748, aged 28 (Hdstn.), and he m. 2nd Ruth Mayo, dau. of Theophilus of Eastham, July 20, 1749 (East. Rec.). She died Sept. 17, 1766, aged 45 (Hdstn.), and he m. 3rd Sarah (Linnell) Mayo, widow of Gideon of Eastham, Nov. 19, 1767 (East. Rec.). She died about 1774 and he m. 4th Alice Paine, dau. of John of Eastham, Dec. 12, 1775 (East. Rec.). She died April 18, 1777, and he m. 5th Hannah _____, who survived him. 5 Cornelius, b. April 10, 1722; m. Mary, prob. dau. of Elisha Hopkins; removed to Liverpool, N. S., about 1760. 6 Rebecca, b. March 2, 1723-4; died unmarried about 1784.

MAYO.

Elisha Mayo, son of Nathaniel and Elizabeth (Wixon) Mayo of Eastham, born April 28, 1695, married Hannah Linnell, daughter of Jonathan of Eastham, Feb. 20, 1717, and settled in Chatham soon after. He was one of the seven first members of the Chatham church, which was organized in 1720, but with Moses Godfrey soon got into a controversy with Rev. Mr. Lord, who excommunicated them.¹¹⁶ They were at once received into the church at Orleans. His wife died about 1727 and he soon after removed with his family to Provincetown, a more convenient place for the fishing industry, selling out to Elisha Hopkins of Eastham. His second wife was Martha ¹¹⁷

Judah Mayo, son of Thomas and Barbara (Knowles) Mayo of Eastham, born November 25, 1691; married Mary Hamilton of Chatham, daughter of Daniel by his first wife, Mary Smith (Int. Jan. 27, 1721-2). He settled at Chatham on a farm lying between the farm of Menekish, the Indian sachem, and that of Samuel Atkins and probably bounding east on the salt water.¹¹⁸ His will, dated December 5, 1758, was proved October 6, 1761. He gave all his real estate to his surviving son Judah.¹¹⁹

NOTES.

(116) See chapter xiii, Smith, History of Chatham.
(117) Children of Elisha Mayo: by wife Hannah: Elizabeth, b. at Chatham. By wife Martha (Prov. Rec.): Lemuel, b. Sept. 11, 1729; Jerusha, b. Oct. 21, 1733; Sarah, b. July 11, 1736; Elisha, b. July 3, 1738; Martha, b. July 31, 1743, baptized at Truro Sept. 4, 1743.
(118) See will of Menekish, Barnstable Probate Rec.
(119) Children of Judah and Mary (Hamilton) Mayo (from the will, order uncertain): 1 Lydia, b.

Jan. 23, 1722-3 (East. Rec.); m. Prince Young, son of John, as second wife. 2 Mary, b. about 1725; m. 1st Joseph Doane, son of Hezekiah of Truro, about 1744; m. 2nd Freeman, before 1758; removed to Liverpool, N. S., about 1762. 3 Richard, b. ; m. Mary Ann Hale of Boston, June 14, 1750; died before 1758, leaving child Augustine. 4 Barbara, b. ; m. George Smith, son of Stephen, Oct. 16, 1755 (Chat. Rec.). 5 Ruth, b. ; m. Benjamin Gardner of Nantucket Nov. 3, 1756 (Chat. Rec.). 6 Elizabeth, b. ; m. Caleb Nickerson, son of Caleb, May 4, 1758 (Chat. Rec.). 7 Judah, b. about 1736; m. 1st Mary Rogers, dau. of of Harwich Dec. 21, 1758 (Har. Rec.). She died about 1776 and he m. 2nd Mrs. Sarah Fuller in 1779; removed to Rutland, Mass., about 1780 and to Woodstock, Vt., about 1797. 8 Hannah, b. ; m. William Mitchell, son of William, at Liverpool, N. S., Sept. 11, 1761 (Liverpool Rec.). 9 Sarah, b. about 1742; m. Benjamin Godfrey, son of George, April 26, 1764 (Chat. Rec.). 10 Priscilla, b. ; m. Eleazer Simmons of Northfield at Chatham April 2, 1767 (Liverpool Rec.); removed to Liverpool, N. S.

MITCHELL.

William Mitchell, only child of William and Mercy (Nickerson) Mitchell, born about 1691, married first Tabitha Eldredge, daughter of Joseph, March 19, 1712-3. She died in a few years, probably without children, and he married second Sarah Higgins of Eastham, probably daughter of Isaac, April 10, 1717. He inherited his father's farm on the west side of Mitchell's river, but sold it in part to Nathaniel Nickerson before 1725 and in part to Richard Knowles before 1740.[1] Nothing more is known about him.[1]

NOTES.

(120) See page 153, note 66, Smith, History of Chatham.
(121) Children of William and Sarah (Higgins) Mitchell (Chat. Rec.): 1 James, b. Nov. 4, 1718. 2 Tabitha, b. July 19, 1720. 3 Mercy, b. May 4, 1722. 4 William, b. June 31, 1725; m. Hannah Mayo, dau. of Judah, at Liverpool, N. S., Sept. 11, 1761 (Liverpool Rec.).

RYDER.

John Ryder,[1] son of John and Esther (Hall?) Ryder of Yarmouth, born May 28, 1692, married Mehitable Crowell, daughter of John and Bethiah Crowell of Yarmouth, May 20, 1713. He settled at Chatham as early as 1715 on land formerly the homestead of William Nickerson, Sen. This farm appears to have extended from Muddy Cove across to Herring river (later called Ryder's Cove) and to have bounded north on land of Paul Crowell and of Jehoshaphat Eldredge. He and his wife both died in the great small pox epidemic of 1766, which fell upon this family with unexampled severity. Not only did the father and mother succumb to this disease, but a daughter Bethiah, a son Zenas and his wife, a son Stephen, his wife and nine of his ten children, and the wife of a son Reuben making in all seven-leon people out of this one family.¹⁵⁵ Mr. Ryder died January 10, 1766, and his wife March 26, 1766, aged 76. His will dated March 30, 1762, was proved March 11, 1766, the son Reuben being the only surviving executor. He gave the homestead to his son Zenas and equivalent property to his other two sons in Chatham. Two other of his sons had removed to the "Oblong," nearly twenty years before.¹⁵⁶

NOTES.

(122) He is not styled "Col." in the town or probate records or elsewhere, and is not entitled to that designation, given him by some writers.

(123) See account of this epidemic, chapter xiv, Smith, History of Chatham.

(124) Children of John and Mehitable (Crowell) Ryder: 1 John, b. about 1715; m. Mary Paine, dau. of Ebenezer of Chatham, and removed to the Oblong about 1747. 2 Reuben, b. about 1717; m. 1st Susanna Atkins, prob. dau. of Thomas, Oct. 26, 1740 (Chat. Rec.). She died Aug. 9, 1743, aged 26, and he m. 2nd Hannah Paine, dau. of Ebenezer. She died of smallpox Jan. 11, 1766, aged 42, and he m. 3rd Mehitable (Snow) Hopkins, wid. of Samuel of Harwich, Oct. 16, 1766 (Har. Rec.). 3 Stephen, b. about 1718; m. Mercy Sears, dau. of Daniel, about 1739. 4 Simeon, b. April 4, 1720; m. , and removed to the Oblong about 1747. 5 Mehitable, b. Jan. 27, 1724-5; m. Samuel Taylor, son of Samuel, about 1743. 6 Zenas, b. April 27, 1726; m. Elizabeth Howes of Yarmouth, dau. of , March 30, 1749 (Yar. Rec.). 7 Bethiah, b. Sept. 11, 1728; d. unmarried Jan. 17, 1766, of smallpox. 8 Zeruiah, b. Jan. 12, 1733-4; m. 1st Reuben Collins, son of Solomon, July 11, 1751 (Chat. Rec.). He d. Feb. 4, 1762 (Hdstn.), and she m. 2nd Joseph Harding, son of Maziah, Oct. 2, 1766 (Chat. Rec.). 9 Esther, b. March 4, 1734-5; m. Joshua Nickerson, son of Caleb, Dec. 15, 1754 (Chat. Rec.), removed to Barrington, N. S., about 1763.

SMITH.

David Smith, son of Thomas and Mary Smith of Eastham, born in the last part of March, 1691, married Sarah Higgins of Eastham, daughter of Jonathan (Int. Feb. 26, 1717-8.). It is believed that he is the David Smith who was of Chatham in 1716 and again in 1723,¹⁵⁵ and that he had the children given below. Very little is known about him.¹⁵⁶

NOTES.

(125) See page 190, Smith, History of Chatham.

(126) Children of David and Sarah (Higgins) Smith: 1 David, b. ; m. 1st Sarah , who died March 20, 1750, aged 28 (Chat. Rec.). He m. 2nd Thankful (Godfrey) Reynolds, widow of John Reynolds and dau. of Samuel Godfrey, and removed to Barrington, N. S., about 1762 (B. Bangs Diary). 2 Solomon, b. ; m. Rebecca Hamilton, dau. of Thomas and Rebecca, removed to Barrington, N. S., about 1762. 3 Jonathan, b. ; m. Jane Hamilton, dau. of Thomas and Rebecca, Nov. 9, 1752 (Chat. Rec.), removed to Barrington, N. S., about 1762. 4 Elkanah, b. about 1734; m. Elizabeth

Kendrick, dau. of Solomon and Elizabeth (Int. Nov. 17, 1753, Har. Rec.), and removed to Barrington, N. S., about 1762. 5 Daughters not known. According to the notes of Mr. Arnold Doane, late of Barrington, N. S., these four Smiths were brothers.

STEWART.

Joseph Stewart, son of Hugh and Wait Stewart, born   , married Mary   about 1712. He kept a tavern on Monomoit Beach near Wreck Cove for about 25 years, beginning about 1725.[127] The starving immigrants of Charles Clinton landed at his tavern in October , 1729, and were saved, as also were many shipwrecked sailors, cast ashore on the beach from time to time. In or about 1753 his house there, which he had left some time before, was either blown down or torn down by maliciously disposed persons.[128] At that time he appears to have been living in Harwich or Yarmouth, but later returned to Chatham, where he and his wife were living as late as 1763. He left no estate.[129]

NOTES.

(127) See page 209, note 29, Smith, History of Chatham.

(128) Files, Superior Court of Judicature, Nos. 70,958, 27,319 and 71,055.

(129) Children of Joseph and Mary (   ) Stewart (Chat. Rec.): 1 Temperance, b. March 15, 1713-4; m. William Penney, prob. son of John of Harwich (Int. March 15, 1734-5, Har. Rec.). 2 Prob. Lydia, b.   ; m. Shubael Baker of Yarmouth, son of Samuel, June 19, 1733 (Chat. Rec.). 3 Prob. Hugh, b.   ; tax abated 1741 and 1745. 4 Prob. Michael, b.   ; tax abated 1740 and 1741. 5 James, b. May 9, 1722. 6 Mary, b. March 26, 1724; m. Hezekiah Baker of Yarmouth, son of Samuel, Sept. 2, 1744 (Yar. Rec.). 7 Abigail, b. March 15, 1726. 8 Samuel, b. Oct. 25, 1727. 9 Alice, b. Feb. 19, 1729. 10 Mercy, b. July 17, 1735; m. Thomas Crowell, son of John of Yarmouth, June 25, 1753 (Yar. Rec.)

TAYLOR.

John Taylor, son of Richard and Ruth (Whelden) Taylor of Yarmouth, born about 1652, married Sarah Matthews, daughter of James of Yarmouth, December 15, 1674. He was a soldier in King Philip's war, going out on several expeditions.[130] He lived most of his life at Yarmouth. There is no evidence of his removal to Monomoit till the year 1711. As he owned land adjoining Tumblen's or Tomlin's Cove and came to Monomoit about the time the Tomlons appear to have moved away, it is supposed that he bought the farm of Nathaniel Tomlon, which was doubtless located on the east side of Taylor's pond, now so called, formerly known as Tomlin's Cove.[131] He also had an interest in the common lands both at Yarmouth and at Monomoit. His will, dated June 23, 1718, was proved January 18, 1721-2. He devised his real estate to his son Seth.[132]

NOTES.

(130) Freeman, Hist. of Cape Cod II, 193; deed from Samuel

Taylor to Shubael Gorham, Jr., York (Me.) Deeds, XXVII, 75.

(131) The exact location of this farm appears to a deed from Seth Taylor, grandson of John, to Sears Atwood, David Atwood, John Taylor and Elizabeth Howes, dated June 30, 1821, as follows: "All my real estate situate in the south west quarter of the town of Chatham, consisting of upland and meadow ground with the buildings thereon standing, bounded, Beginning at the Northeast corner of the premises at a drain of water near the old Bridge so called in the range of Mathis Taylor and Stephen Smith, thence Westerly in said Mathis range to a corner of fence near my dwelling house, thence Northwesterly by said Mathis to another corner of fence, thence Northerly by said Mathis Taylor, as the fence stands to the Public Road, thence Westerly by the said Road to Enoch Bassett his land, thence Southerly by said Bassett to Taylor's Pond so called, thence Southeasterly in a straight line to Nathaniel Bassett and Ebenezer Barse's range at the Pond, then Easterly a short distance by said Bassett and Barse to a fence, thence Southerly and Southwesterly by said Bassett and Barse as the fence now stands to the Eldredge meadow so called, thence Southerly and Westerly by the meadow round points of land and nooks of meadow into Chatham Bay at the Southwesterly part of Taylors Neck socalled, thence Easterly by said Bay to a Harbor or Neck near Fox hill socalled, then Northerly through the middle of the main Creek to Edward Kendrick his meadow, then Westerly by said Kendrick to the upland or fence, thence Northerly by said Kendrick and Barse's meadow to an old Watering place and the main Creek near by, thence Northerly and Easterly by said Creek which parts my meadow from Stephen Smith and others to the first mentioned bounds." Joseph Atwood papers.

Dea. Samuel Taylor, eldest son of John Taylor above, born December 14, 1675, at Yarmouth, married Elizabeth . His farm was at West Chatham between the highway and Buck's Creek, bounding west on Hugh Stewart's farm and east on the cartway to Ragged Neck.[138] He is styled Deacon as early as 1734. He was selectman seven years and frequently moderator of town meeting. He received an interest in the Narragansett lands on account of his father's service in King Philip's war. He was living in 1756, but died before 1761, when his son is no longer called Samuel Jr. in the town records. There is no settlement of his estate.[131]

NOTES.

(132) Children of John and Sarah (Matthews) Taylor (all born at Yarmouth, order uncertain): 1 Samuel, b. Dec. 14, 1675; m. Elizabeth about 1713. 2 John, b. June 15, 1678; m. Hannah ; d. 1734. 3 Hannah, b. ; m. William Eldredge, son of Joseph, Oct. 1, 1713 (page 188, note 45, Smith, History of Chatham). 4 Elizabeth, b. ; single in 1722; perhaps m. Daniel Hamilton as fourth wife. 5 Mary, b. : m. Ephraim Covell of Har. (Int. Sept. 20, 1746, Har. Rec.) 6 Seth,

b.   ; m. Elizabeth, dau. of Daniel Hamilton, about 1730.

(133) See "A Proprietor's Book for Chatham," and a deed from Samuel Eldredge to Seth Taylor dated May 15, 1711. (M. L. Luce papers.)

(134) Children of Samuel and Elizabeth (   ) Taylor: 1 Joseph, b. Jan. 22, 1713-4 (Chat. Rec.); m. Hannah   ; removed about 1747 to the "Oblong," N. Y., and thence to Kent, Conn. 2 Thankful, b.   ; m. John Collins, son of John, about 1740. 3 Samuel, b. about 1722; m. Mehitable Ryder, dau. of John, about 1743. 4 Matthews, (commonly written "Matthes") b. May 15, 1724 (Chat. Rec.); m. Desire Harding, dau. of Maziah, Aug. 3, 1747 (Chat. Rec.). 5 James, b. about 1732; died May 19, 1758, aged 26 (Hdstn.).

No. 37.

LIBRARY of
Cape Cod
HISTORY & GENEALOGY

STEPHEN[1] and GILES[2] HOPKINS
Mayflower Passengers
and Some *of* Their Descendants
INCLUDING AN ELDREDGE LINE

By James W. Hawes

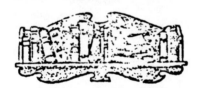

YARMOUTHPORT, MASS.:
C. W. SWIFT, PUBLISHER AND PRINTER,
THE "REGISTER" PRESS,
1915.

STEPHEN[1] *and* GILES[2] HOPKINS
Mayflower Passengers *and* Some *of* Their Descendants
INCLUDING AN ELDREDGE LINE

By James W. Hawes

Copyright, 1915, by Charles W. Swift.

FIRST GENERATION.*

Stephen[1] Hopkins, born in England, came over in the Mayflower in 1620, bringing with him Giles and Constanta (Constance), children by a first wife whose name is not known, a second wife Elizabeth whose maiden name is not known,(a) two children by her, Damaris and Oceanus (born on the passage), and two servants, Edward Doty and Edward Litster. He d. between June 6, 1644 (date of his will), and July 17, 1644 (date of his inventory).(a1) His 2d wife d. in Plymouth between 1640 and 1644.(a2)

In 1651 Mr. Hopkins and his wife were dead. They had had a son and four daughters born in Plymouth. The son became a seaman and had died in Barbados, one daughter had died in Plymouth, two daughters were married, one of them having two children, and one was unmarried. His son Giles was married and had four children. His daughter Constanta was also married and had 12 children, one of them being married.(b)

*Acknowledgment must be made for valuable aid rendered by the writer's nephew, William C. Smith, Esq., author of "History of Chatham."

(a) She was not the daughter of Francis[1] Cooke (2 Mf. 63).

(a1) 2 Mf. 12-17.
(a2) 2 ib. 117.
(b) Bradford's History of Ply-

"All that we know of Stephen Hopkins and his family before they arrived at Cape Cod is contained in these brief statements from Mourt's Relation and Bradford's History. He came from London, had been married twice, had two children by each wife and brought two servants. These meagre facts are the only ones yet discovered which are supported by absolutely trustworthy contemporary evidence. Much speculation regarding his early life has been indulged in by various writers, but all have failed to produce from contemporary sources conclusive evidence of the soundness of their claims."(c)

His bringing two servants shows that he was one of the well-to-do of the pilgrims. The facts hereinafter given from contemporary records will show that he was a man of energy, courage and ability and one of the most prominent and useful men in the colony. He was one of the earliest freemen of Plymouth(c1) and was one of the assistants to the governor from 1633 to 1637. He was engaged in trade, selling liquors and various other articles. He was charged at times with abuse of his traffic in liquors and with selling liquors and other articles at excessive rates, according to the views of the period, but he never lost the confidence of the leading men. He was not without kindness of heart, as appears from his petitioning for the release of his servants from cruel punishment.(c2)

---

mouth Plantation, Davis's edition, 408, 411, 412; 1 Mayflower Descendant (hereinafter cited as Mf.), 10, 13, 14, 163; 3 ib. 40; 5 ib. 47-53. Gov. Bradford's account of the Mayflower passengers and their issue was written between Feb. 24 and March 24, 1650-51 (1 Mf. 161-163). See also 2 ib. 114-119, for Stephen¹ Hopkins and some of his children. Mourt's Relation (Dexter's ed., 1865), 44; 3 Mf. 46; 5 ib. 47.

(c) 5 ib. 47.

(c1) 8 Plym. Col. Recs. 173.

(c2) June 18, 1621, Doty and Litster fought a duel with sword and dagger. Both were wounded, one in the hand and the other in

He apparently boarded the Mayflower in London with his family about the end of June, 1620, for on the arrival of the Speedwell at Southampton from Holland about July 2 she found the Mayflower there, having arrived with her passengers from London. They sailed from Southampton August 5, but by reason of the claimed unsafety of the Speedwell, they put into Dartmouth. After some repairs, they put to sea again, but after they had got "above 100 leagues without the Lands End", the master of the Speedwell complained that his ship was very leaky, and after consultation, both ships put into Plymouth. Here it was decided that the Speedwell should not proceed. Some of the passengers returned to London, and the rest sailed on the Mayflower on the 6th of September, reaching what is now Provincetown harbor on the 11th of November.(d) On that day he signed the compact of government on board the Mayflower, his name being 14th on the list of signers.(e)

Nov. 15, 1620, 16 armed men were set ashore, "under the conduct of Captaine Miles Standish, unto whom was adjoyned for counsell and advise, William Bradford, Stephen Hopkins, and Edward Tilley." They made a voyage of discovery, saw some Indians who fled from them, obtained some corn that had been buried in the earth, and found a the thigh. They were sentenced by the whole company to have their heads and feet tied together and so to lie for 24 hours without meat or drink, "but within an hour, because of their great pains, at their own & their master's humble request, upon promise of better carriage, they are released by the governor." (Chronological History of New England, by Thomas Prince, ed. of 1826, 190, 191.) Doty d. at Plymouth Aug. 23, 1655, leaving issue. (3 Mf. 87.) Litster, after the termination of his service, went to Virginia and d. there before 1651. (Bradford, 414.)

(d) New England's Memorial (Lord's ed., 1903) 5, 6, 10, 11. Mourt's Rel. 1, 3; Bradford, 78–80, 87, 88; 1 Mf. 80.

(e) Mourt's Rel. 6–8; 1 Mf. 79.

trap for deer, as Stephen Hopkins informed them, in which William Bradford was caught. They returned to the ship on the 17th.(f)

On the 6th of December Stephen Hopkins (described as of London) in the company of 17 other men, Capt. Standish at the head, started on a second voyage of discovery, with the shallop, which lasted five or six days, during which they had an encounter with the Indians. They entered Plymouth bay and landed on the 11th of December.(g)

The Mayflower went to Plymouth on December 16, and shortly thereafter the work of erecting buildings and landing the passengers and goods was started.(h)

February 17, 1620-21, two Indians appeared on the top of a hill and signalled for the settlers to come to them. Capt. Standish and Stephen Hopkins were sent towards them, but the Indians disappeared.(i)

March 16, 1620-21, Samoset came into Plymouth and that night was lodged and watched in Stephen Hopkins's house.(j)

July 2, 1621, Stephen Hopkins and Edward Winslow were sent by Gov. Carver on a mission to Massasoit, with whom the governor had made a treaty. They visited the chief at his residence within the ancient territory of Swansea, Mass., and in the present town of Warren, R. I., and had a satisfactory interview. They had the assistance of Tisquantum (Squanto). On their return, after considerable hardships, they arrived at Plymouth on the 7th of July.(k)

In 1623 Stephen Hopkins received 6 acres in the division of lands, his allotment lying on "the

---

(f) Mourt's Rel., 13-27.
(g) Ib. 43-59.
(h) Mourt's Rel. 60, et. seq.
(i) Mourt's Rel. 81.
(j) Ib. 82-85.
(k) Ib. 98-111; New England's Memorial, 31; Bradford, 117.

South side of the brook to the woodward opposite to tho" lots "on the South side of the brooke to the baywards." Between him and John Howland were the lands of "Hobamak," an Indian.(l)

May 22, 1627, it was decided that the cows and goats belonging to the company should be divided and kept for 10 years at the care and expense of those to whom they were allotted, and that the old stock and half the increase should remain for common use to be divided at the end of the term "or otherwise as ocation falleth out." The other half of the increase was to belong to the allottees.(m)

The 7th lot fell to Stephen Hopkins and his company, which besides himself consisted of his wife Elizabeth, his children Giles, Caleb and Deborah, Nicholas and Constance Snow, William and Frances Palmer, William Palmer, Jr., John Billington, Sr., Helen Billington and Francis Billington. To this lot fell a black weaning calf and the calf "of this yeare to come of the black Cow, wch fell to John Shaw & his Companie." The company was to have no interest in these two calves, but only half their increase. This lot also received two she goats, "which goats they posses on the like terms which others doe their cattell."(n)

Damaris Hopkins was the 13th in Samuel Fuller's or the 8th company. This company received a red heifer and two she goats.(o)

Mr. Edward Winslow, who had returned to England on business of the colony, came back on the Charity in 1624, bringing three heifers and a bull, the first cattle in the colony.(p)

Gov. Bradford speaks of this division of the cattle as follows:

(l) 12 Plym. Col. Recs. 4; 1 Mf. 227-230; New England's Memorial, 31.
(m) 12 Plym. Col. Recs. 9; 1 Mf. 148-154.

(n) 12 Plym. Col. Recs. 11.
(o) Ib. 11, 12.
(p) Bradford, 117, 166.

"And first accordingly the few catle which they had were devided, which arose to this proportion; a cowe to 6. persons or share, and 2. goats to the same, which were first equalised for age and goodnes, and then lotted for; single persons consorting with others, as they thought good, and smaler familys likewise; and swine though more in number, yet by the same rule."(q)

In 1627, before the division of the cattle, an agreement was made by which William Bradford, Capt. Miles Standish and Isaac Allerton and such as they should join with them were among other things to discharge the colony of all debts due by it and to have for six years the trade of the colony. Among 27 who signed this agreement on the part of the colonists, the name of Stephen Hopkins stands second, following that of William Brewster.(r)

Jan. 2, 1631-2, he was appointed one of the assessors of taxes.(r1)

In 1633 Stephen Hopkins is named in a list of the freemen of Plymouth.(s)

Jan. 1, 1632-3, he was chosen one of the council for the ensuing year, Edward Winslow being chosen governor.(t) Jan. 10 of the same year he was a member of a court that tried a servant who had run away. The servant was privately whipped before the court.(u)

In 1633 he was assessed to pay a tax of £1 7s., only five persons being assessed at a greater sum, of whom Isaac Allerton was to pay £3 11s. and Gov. Edward Winslow, £2 5s.(v)

July 1, 1633, it was ordered that at or before the last of the next August Stephen Hopkins divide with six others "the medow ground in the bay equally, ac-

---

(q) Bradford, 217.
(r) 6 Mf. 145, 146; Gov. Bradford's Letter Book, Colls. of the Mass. Hist. Soc., 1st ser., vol. 3, pp. 59-61; 5 Mf. 5-7.

(r1) 1 Plym. Col. Recs. 9.
(s) Ib. 3.
(t) Ib. 5.
(u) Ib. 7.
(v) Ib. 9.

cording to the proporcon of shares formerly devided to the purchasers." It was also provided that he mow where he did the last year.(w)

Oct. 24, 1633, Mr. Stephen Hopkins with Mr. John Doane took an inventory of the kins was appointed with Mr. John Doane to take an inventory of the goods and chattels of Godbert Godbertson and Zarah, his wife, deceased.(x)

Nov. 25, 1633, with Capt. Miles Standish he was made administrator of the estate of John Thorp of Duxbury,(y) who owed him £5 7s. for various particulars.(z)

Jan. 1, 1633-4, he was chosen assistant to the governor.(a)

Jan. 2, 1633-4, he and John Jenny were the appraisers of the estate of Samuel Fuller, the elder, which included about thirty books.(b)

In 1634 he was one of the assessors of taxes and was to pay £1 10s., only two persons being assessed to a higher sum, viz. Edward Winslow and Mr. William Collier £2 5s. each.(c)

Oct. 1, 1634, he was appointed the first of a committee to treat with the existing partners as to the future management of the trade.(d)

Oct. 2, 1634, he and Robert Hicks took the inventory of the goods of Stephen Deans.(e)

Jan. 1, 1634-5, he was chosen an assistant, and entered upon his office the 3d of March.(f)

Jan. 5, 1635-6, he was chosen assistant, and took the oath March 1.(g)

(w) 1 Plym. Col. Recs. 14, 15.
(x) Ib. 19; 1 Mf. 154.
(y) Ib. 20.
(z) 1 Mf. 160.
(a) 1 Plym. Col. Recs. 21.

(b) 2 Mf. 8; 1 Plym. Col. Wills, 22.
(c) 1 Plym. Col. Recs. 20, 27.
(d) Ib. 31.
(e) 2 Mf. 87; 1 Plym. Col. Wills, 26.
(f) 1 Plym. Col. Recs. 32, 33.
(g) Ib. 36, 37.

March 14, 1635-6, he was authorized to mow the marsh between Thomas Clarke and George Sowle, and it was ordered that he and Clarke have the marsh up the river as formerly.(h)

June 7, 1636, John Tisdale, yeoman, brought an action of battery against Mr. Hopkins, assistant to the government, by whom he alleged he was dangerously wounded. Hopkins was fined £5 sterling to the use of the King, "whose peace he had broken, wch he ought after a special manner to have kept," and was adjudged to pay 40s. to the plaintiff.(i)

Nov. 7, 1636, a way between his land and that of Thomas Pope, Richard Clough and Richard Wright, "at the fishing point, neer Slowly Field," is mentioned.(j)

In a list of freemen, dated March 7, 1636-7, he is styled gentleman.(k)

Stephen Hopkins was an assistant Jan. 3, 1636-7. On the same date he was made one of a committee to arrange an agreement with "those that have the trade in theire hands" and report to the court.(l)

March 7, 1636-7, it was ordered that those who then had the trade of beaver, corn and beads, etc., with the Indians should hold it until the beginning of June, and in the meantime a committee was appointed, of which Mr. Hopkins was one, to consider propositions and ways "so as the said trade may be still continued to the benefit of the collony'.'(m)

March 20, 1636-7, action was taken as to the use of the hay grounds and Mr. Hopkins was made one of a committee to view those grounds between the Eel river and the town of Plymouth, that each man might be assigned a proper portion. He and Thomas

---

(h) 1 Plym. Col. Recs. 41.
(i) Ib. 41,42.
(j) Ib. 46.
(k) Ib. 52.

(l) 1 Plym. Col. Recs. 25, 26.
(m) Ib. 54.

Clark were given the hay ground they had the past year.(n)

May 10, 1637, a jury impanelled for the purpose rendered a verdict (which was delivered to the General Court July 7, 1637) laying out highways to the Eel river from Plymouth, which mentions Mr. Hopkins's house, one of the ways passing it on the west.(o)

June 7, 1637, he with the governor and assistants and other persons formed a committee to consider how the trade in beaver, etc., (which was likely to go into decay) might be upheld.(p)

On the same date the committee of which Mr. Hopkins was a member reported that the expenses of the Pequot service would amount to £200, of which £100 was to be paid by Plymouth and £50 each by Duxbury and Scituate.(q)

Among the names of those entered June 7, 1637, who willingly offered themselves to assist the people of Massachusetts Bay and Connecticut "in their warrs against the Pequin(ql) Indians, in reveng of the innocent blood of the English wch the sd Pequins have barbarously shed, and refuse to give satisfaccon for," were Mr. Stephen Hopkins and his two sons Caleb and Giles.(r) The soldiers who volunteered for the Pequot war were, however, not required to take the field.

On the same date Mr. Hopkins for the town of Plymouth was one of two men who, together with the governor and assistants, were to form a board to assess the inhabitants for the expenses of that war.(r)

July 17, 1637, Stephen Hopkins sold for £60 lawful money of England, to be paid one half on May 1, 1638, and one half Sept. 29, 1638, to George Bonre of Scituate his messuage, houses, tenements

---

(n) 1 Plym. Col. Recs. 55, 57.
(o) Ib. 59, 60.
(p) Ib. 62.
(q) Ib.

(ql) Pequot.
(r) 1 Plym. Col. Recs. 61.

and outhouses at the Broken wharf towards the Eel river, together with the six shares of land thereunto belonging, containing 120 acres.(s)

October 2, 1637, he was appointed one of a committee for the town of Plymouth to act with the governor and assistants and a committee from Eel river, Jones river and Duxbury in agreeing upon an equal course in the division of about 500 acres of meadow between the Eel river and South river.(t)

On the same date he was on a jury.(u)

Oct. 2, 1637, he was charged with suffering men to drink in his house on the Lord's day before the meeting was ended, and also on the Lord's day, both before and after the meetings, servants and others to drink more than for ordinary refreshing. This complaint was adjourned to the next court and was subsequently withdrawn. On the same day he was fined 40s. for suffering servants and others to sit drinking in his house contrary to the orders of the court and to play at "shovell" board, and to commit similar misdemeanors. This fine was subsequently released.(v) Nov. 13, 1637, the estate of William Palmer owed him £1 12s.(w) Jan. 2, 1637-8, he was presented by the grand jury for suffering excessive drinking in his house and was acquitted.(x)

Feb. 5, 1637-8, he requested a grant of lands towards the Six Mile brook.(y)

June 5, 1638, he was presented and fined for selling beer for 2d. a quart not worth one penny a quart, and also for selling wine "at such excessive rates, to the oppressing & impovishing of the colony."(z)

August 7, 1638, the following entry appears:

"Liberty is granted to Mr. Steephen Hopkins to erect a house at Mattacheese, and cutt hey there this yeare to winter his cattle, pvided that it be not to wthdraw him from the towne of Plymouth."(a) Mattacheese was afterwards called Yarmouth.

Sept. 4, 1638, he was fined £5 upon two presentments against him the last court and three this court, for selling wine, beer strong waters and nutmegs at excessive rates.(b)

Nov. 30, 1638, for £6 sterling he sold to Josias Cooke his 6 acres of land "lying on the South side of the Towne brooke of Plymouth to the woodward."(c)

Feb. 4, 1638-9, it was ordered concerning Mr. Stephen Hopkins and his servant Dorothy Temple that as by her indenture she had about two years to serve him, he

(s) 12 Plym. Col. Recs. 21.
(t) 1 Plym. Col Recs. 67.
(u) 7 Plym. Col. Recs. 7.
(v) 1 Plym. Col. Recs. 68.
(w) 2 Mf. 148, 151; 1 Plym. Col. Wills, 29.

(x) 1 Plym. Col. Recs. 75.
(y) Ib. 76.
(z) Ib. 87.
(a) Ib. 93.
(b) Ib. 97.
(c) 12 Plym. Col. Recs. 39.

should keep her and her child, or provide that she should be kept with food and raiment, during said term. If he refused to do so, the colony was to provide for her and Mr. Hopkins was to pay it. He evidently refused, for the same day he was committed to ward for contempt of the court, to remain committed until he should either receive his servant Dorothy Temple or provide for her elsewhere at his own charge during the term she had yet to serve him.(d)

It appears that the father of Dorothy Temple's child was Arthur Peach, who had been executed for murder and highway robbery before its birth, and that Feb. 8, 1638-9, John Holmes of Plymouth agreed with Mr. Hopkins to hold him and the colony harmless from the said Dorothy Temple and her child, she to serve with him the residue of her time as provided in her indenture with Mr. Hopkins. Mr. Hopkins seems to have paid Mr. Holmes three pounds sterling and other considerations for the agreement.(d1)

Dec. 3, 1639, he was presented for selling a looking glass for 16d., which could be bought in Massachusetts for 9d., and the matter was held over for further information. On the same date he was fined £3 for selling strong water without license.(e)

June 1, 1640, he appears to have received a grant of land.(f)

Nov. 2, 1640, he was granted 12 acres of meadow in the North meadow by Jones river.(g)

March 3, 1639-40, the General Court had granted to the "purchasers or old comers" the privilege of making choice of two or three plantations for themselves and their heirs, and on Dec. 1, 1640, the said "purchasers or old comers" announced that they had chosen three tracts, one of which stretched across Cape Cod from Yarmouth to 3 miles east of Namskaket. Among the 53 purchasers or old comers of Plymouth Colony was Stephen Hopkins.(g1)

Dec. 7, 1641, he had a suit against James Luxford for £12 10s.(h)

Jan. 4, 1641-2, he is mentioned as one of the contributors (a sixteenth part) to the "building of a Bark of 40 or 50 Tunn, estimated at the Charge of 200li."(i)

April 5, 1642, this entry appears: "Jonathan Hatch, by the consent of the Court, is appoynted to dwell wth Mr. Steephon Hopkins, & the said Mr. Hopkins to have a speciall care of him."(j)

June 8, 1642, William Chase mortgaged to him his house and 8 acres of upland in Yarmouth "and six acres more lying at the Stony Cove," to secure the pay-

---

(d) 1 Plym. Col. Recs. 111, 112.
(d1) Ib. 113.
(e) Ib. 137.
(f) Ib. 154.

(g) 1 Plym. Col. Recs. 166.
(g1) 2 Plym. Col. Recs. 4, 177; 11 ib. 34, 35.
(h) 7 Plym. Col. Recs. 27.
(i) 2 Plym. Col. Recs. 31.
(j) Ib. 38.

ment to Hopkins of £5 Nov. 1, 1642.(k)
Nov. 7, 1643, Mr. Stephen Hopkins was the foreman of a jury.(l) August 20, 1644, Capt. Miles Standish and Mr. William Bradford deposed to his will, and his son Caleb Hopkins, appointed executor, produced an inventory on oath of his goods and chattels.(m)
Nov. 21, 1644, Caleb Hopkins as executor received the mortgage of a black cow from Francis Billington to secure the payment of £3 sterling on or before Dec. 1, 1645, which Billington owed the estate of Stephen Hopkins.(n)
Sept. 26, 1645, Josias Cooke sold six acres of land which he had lately bought of Mr. Stephen Hopkins.(n1)
June 29, 1652, provision was made for the public use of the house that was Mr. Hopkins's.(o)
Land that Mr. Stephen Hopkins had owned in Plymouth is referred to in a deed dated June 24, 1685.(p)
His will was proved August 20, 1644.(q) In his will he mentions his deceased wife and requests to be buried near her. He mentions his son Giles Hopkins, who he says is in Yarmouth, and the latter's son Stephen, his daughters Constance, wife of Nicholas Snow, Deborah, Damaris, Ruth, Elizabeth, and his son Caleb, whom he makes his heir.

He gives Giles his great bull then in the hands of Mrs. Warren(r) and to his grandson Stephen 20s. due from Mrs. Warren for its hire, to Constance his mare, to Deborah a cow and her calf and half of another cow, to Damaris a cow and a calf and half of another cow with Deborah, to Ruth a cow and her calf, a bull and half of another cow and to Elizabeth a cow and her calf, the other half of the cow with Ruth, and a yearling heifer. To his four unmarried daughters he gave equally all the movable goods in his house, including a silver spoon to each, and provided that if any one of them should die unmarried, her share should go to the survivors. To Caleb he gave all his right, title and interest in and to his house and lands in Plymouth and in and to any lands that might come to him or he might have the right to by reason of being one of the first comers. He also gave Caleb a yoke of oxen then in the hands of Richard Church and their hire, and all the debts due him. He provided that his said four daughters should have the right to remain in his house in Plymouth till married. He made his son Caleb his executor and Caleb and Capt. Miles Standish jointly supervisors.

(k) 12 Plym. Col. Recs. 83.
(l) 7 Plym. Col. Recs. 36.
(m) 2 Plym. Col. Recs. 75.
(n) Ib. 78, 79.
(n1) 12 ib. 114.
(o) 3 Plym. Col. Recs. 14.
(p) 6 Plym. Col. Recs. 162, 163.
(q) 1 Plym. Col. Wills, 61-63; 2 Mf. 12-17.

(r) Widow of Richard Warren, a Mayflower passenger (2 Mf. 12; 3 ib. 48, 49).

The will also provides:
"It is also my will that my Executr & Supervisor shall advise devise and dispose by the best wayes & meanes they cann for the disposeing in marriage or other wise for the best advancnt of the estate of the forenamed Deborah Damaris Ruth and Elizabeth Hopkins."

The witnesses were Capt. Miles Standish and Gov. William Bradford.

The inventory of his goods and chattels, taken by Capt. Miles Standish, Mr. Thomas Willet and Mr. John Doane, amounted to £128 16s. 7 d., and included a mare, household goods, wearing apparel, cattle, two pigs, some poultry, 6d. in money, "Divers bookes" valued at 12s., debts due him amounting to £17 6s., &c.

His will and inventory are printed in full in The Mayflower Descendant (vol. 2, pp. 12-17).

The movable estate of Mr. Stephen Hopkins was apportioned to his four daughters by Capt. Miles Standish and Caleb Hopkins in 1644. Deborah, Damaris and Ruth's shares, consisting of various articles, are set out.(s)

Children.

By his first wife, born in England:
Giles,(t) b. .
Constanta (Constance), b. ; m. at Plymouth between 1623 and June 1, 1627, Nicholas Snow, who came over in the Anne in the latter part of July, 1623,(u) and who d. in Eastham Nov, 15, 1676. She d. in Eastham about the middle of October, 1677.(v)

By his second wife:
Damaris, b. in England ; d. in Plymouth before her father and after the division of cattle, May 22, 1627, when she was in Samuel Fuller's company, which drew the 8th lot.(w)

Oceanus, b. on board the Mayflower between Sept. 6 and Nov. 11, 1620; d. before the division of cattle, May 22, 1627.(x)

Caleb, b. in Plymouth probably before June 6, 1623; became a seaman and died at Barbados before 1651.(y) He was made the residuary devisee and legatee and executor by his father's will in 1644. Caleb Hopkins was one of those in Plymouth between 16 and 60 able to bear arms in August, 1643.(z) In 1637 he volunteered in the Pequot war, as above stated. In 1644 he conveyed a part of his father's lands to his brother Giles, as seen below.

Deborah, b. in Plymouth, possibly before Caleb; m. Andrew Ring, April 23, 1646.(a) She consented to a conveyance of land by her husband Feb. 13, 1659-60.(a1)

will and inventory are in 3 Mf. 167-174.
(v) 3 ib. 167.
(w) 1 Mf. 152; 5 Mf. 47-52.
(x) 5 Mf. 48, 50.
(y) Bradford, 411, 412; 1 Mf. 13, 161-163; 4 ib. 114; 5 ib. 50, 51.
(z) 8 Plym. Col. Recs. 187, 188.
(a) 2 Plym. Col. Recs. 98. See 4 Mf. 193-198; 6 ib. 95-97; 13 Mf. 86.
(a1) 14 Mf. 142.

(s) 1 Plym. Col. Wills, 65; 4 Mf. 115, 116.
(t) Also written Gyles.
(u) 1 Mf. 229, 230; 2 ib. 170. His

Damaris, b. in Plymouth ; m. there Jacob⁸ (Francis¹) Cooke after June 10, 1646, date of his marriage settlement;(b) d. before Nov. 18, 1669, when Jacob Cooke married again.(c)

Ruth, b. in Plymouth ; d. unmarried before Oct. 1, 1659, the date of the settlement of her

(b) June 10, 1646, the settlement of Jacob Cooke, in view of his intended marriage to Damaris Hopkins, was made by his parents, Francis Cooke and Hester, his wife. They gave their son upon his marriage about 100 acres of land with meadow lying at the North river, ½ of the land that shall fall to Francis by any division of the Purchase Land or that shall be due him as one of the first comers, one ox, one cow, one calf and the foal of Francis's mare. It was also provided that Jacob might build a house on Francis's land at Rockynook and if he should think it convenient or should be compelled to remove, the said Jacob "at the Judgment of honest and Judicial men shall have satisfaction for any building or buildings fence or fences which otherwise might prove Damage to the said Jacob." It was also provided that upon the decease of the longer survivor of Francis and his wife "the said Jacob or his heires shall have the teame with all the furniture belonging thereunto." Witnesses: Miles Standish, James Hurst and John Howland. (2 Plym. Col. Deeds, 35; 2 Mf. 27, 28; 5 ib. 51.)

(c) 3 Mf. 101, 105.

sister Elizabeth's estate, and before Gov. Bradford wrote in 1651.(d) Oct. 15, 1644, Richard Sparrow acknowledged that he had received one-half of a cow from Capt. Standish which belonged to Ruth Hopkins and agreed at the expiration of three years or sooner to pay Capt. Standish for Ruth Hopkins two year-old heifers or two year-old steers. On May 19, 1647, Capt. Standish acknowledged that he had received two young steers in full settlement.(e, f)

Elizabeth, b. in Plymouth ; d. presumably before Sept. 29, 1659, when her cattle were valued by John Freeman and Edward Bangs.(f1) It was agreed Nov. 30, 1644, between Capt. Standish and Caleb Hopkins of the one part and Richard Sparrow of Plymouth of the other part that Sparrow should have her until she should marry or reach the age of 19 years. This provision was included in the agreement: "2ly. In consideracon of the weaknes of the child and her inabillytie to prforme such service as may acquite their charges in bringing of her up and that shee bee not too much oppressed now in her childhood wth hard labour It is agreed that Richard Sparrow shall have putt into his hands her whole estate and to have the use of yt for the tyme of her continuance wth him. Onely one heiffer reserved wch is

(d) 5 Mf. 52.

(e, f) 1 Plym. Col. Wills, 66; 4 Mf. 117.

(f1) 4 Mf. 119.

now in the hands of Gyles Hopkins of Yarmouth."(g)

It was further provided that if "Goodwyfe Sparrow" should die, then Elizabeth Hopkins and her estate should be free to be disposed of as Capt. Standish and Caleb Hopkins should think best, but if Mrs. Sparrow's death should occur within three years, then Sparrow was to have 12 months within which to return the estate, and if after three years, then 9 months. It was further agreed that if Elizabeth should die, her estate was to return to Capt. Standish and Caleb Hopkins to be disposed of among the rest of her sisters according to the will of Mr. Hopkins, provided that Sparrow should have 12 months to return it if her death occurred within three years, and nine months if it occurred after three years.

The estate to be returned was £15 1s. 2d. and was to be returned in the following form: a milch cow, a feather bed and things belonging thereto, of the same value as they were delivered, and the rest, one half in wheat and one half in Indian corn. The agreement was witnessed by William Paddy and Thomas Willett.

Oct. 5, 1656, Capt. Myles Standish complained against Richard Sparrow of Eastham in behalf of Elizabeth Hopkins, demanding £20 damages for breach of an agreement made with Sparrow concerning said Elizabeth Hopkins. The parties settled the suit by an agreement in writing.(i)

On Oct. 10, 1657, Elizabeth Hopkins sold to Jacob Cooke of Plymouth "in consideration of a valluable sume to her alreddy satisfyed and fully paid" "all that her portion or preell of meddow that shee hath in the great meddow att Joanses river viz ten acres of ffresh meddow bee it more or lesse lying betwixt the meddow of Capt: Thomas Willett and Mr. John Done runing from woodside to woodside."(j)

An inventory of her estate in the hands of Jacob Cooke and Andrew Ring was taken Oct. 6, 1659, and verified by them, amounting to £26 14s. There was a small matter in the hands of Mrs. Standish.(k) Sept. 29, 1659, John Freeman and Edward Bangs appraised in the hands of Giles Hopkins, belonging to Elizabeth, one half of three steers, a poor calf, one very small poor cow and an old defective cow at £14 5s.(k1)

On Oct. 5, 1659, it was agreed by Andrew Ring, Jacob Cooke and Giles Hopkins and ordered by the court "that in case Elizabeth hopkins Doe Come Noe more", the above mentioned cattle at their valuation should be the portion of Giles Hopkins in the estate of

(g) On the margin of the page is this note: "the tearmes of this agreement are fully prformed by Richard Sparrow."

(h) 1 Plym. Col. Wills, 65; 4 Mf. 116, 117.

(i) 7 Plym. Col. Recs. 80.

(j) 2 Plym. Col. Deeds, pt. 1, p. 196; 4 Mf. 118.

(k) The last known mention of Barbara Standish.

(k1) 4 Mf. 119.

Elizabeth and that Andrew Ring and Jacob Cooke should remain in peaceable possession of what they had of her estate.(l)

SECOND GENERATION.

Giles² (Stephen¹) Hopkins, b. in England ; came over in the Mayflower in 1620; m. Oct. 9, 1639, Catherine(m) Whelden, probably daughter of Gabriel Wheldon;(n) d. in Eastham between March 5, 1688-9 (date of the codicil to his will), and April 10, 1690 (date of probate). His wife d. after the date of his codicil. He lived at first in Plymouth. In the latter part of 1638 or very early in 1639 he removed to Yarmouth, where his father had erected a house and pastured cattle.(o) This house was the first one known to have been built by a white man in Yarmouth.(p) His house in Yarmouth was in the extreme N. W. of the town (now Yarmouthport) not far from the Barnstable line. Going E. from that line, it was the third house on the N. side of the road.(q) He took the oath of fidelity in Yarmouth.(r) He was of Yarmouth Oct. 28, 1644, when his brother Caleb conveyed land to him.(s) He later and probably shortly after removed to Nauset (later Eastham). He settled in the part of Eastham which is now Orleans.(t)

June 7, 1637, while in Plymouth, he with his father and brother volunteered to serve in the Pequot war, but his services were not required.(u)

Giles Hopkins Feb. 9, 1638-9, was one of the witnesses of the will of Peter Worden, Sr., of Yarmouth, with Nicholas Simpkins and Hugh Tilly, and swore to it March 5, 1638-9, at Plymouth.(v)

May 3, 1642, Walter Devell of Plymouth owed Giles Hopkins of Yarmouth 9 bushels of corn, for which suit was brought and execution taken out for £3 17s. 2d., which included 14 bushels due Mr. Hedge of Yarmouth and the costs of the suit.(w)

May 12, 1642, Giles Hopkins of Yarmouth, planter, sold to Andrew Hallett, Jr., 10 acres of upland in the west field between the land of Nicholas Simpkins on the N. E. and the land of Robert Dennis on the S. W., with two acres of meadow adjoining at the N. W. end, "for and in consideration of two acres of upland and four acres

(w) 7 Plym. Col. Recs. 29, 30. of meddow . . . lying and being in the prime feild in a furlong there called by the Name of

---

(l) 2 Plym. Col. Wills, pt. 1, pp. 90, 91; 4 Mf. 118, 119.
(m) Also written Katherne and Catorne.
(n) 1 Plym. Col. Recs. 134; 13 Mf. 85. See "Early Wheldens of Yarmouth," by the compiler.
(o) Aug. 7, 1638, Stephen Hopkins obtained the right to do so.
(p) Swift's Old Yarmouth, 51.
(q) 1 Otis's Barn. Families, 484, 486.
(r) 8 Plym. Col. Recs. 185.

(s) 12 Plym. Col. Recs. 104.
(t) Josiah Paine, Esq.
(u) 1 Plym. Col. Recs. 61.
(v) 1 Plym. Col. Wills, 33; 3 Mf. 75, 76; 1 Plym. Col. Recs. 117.

Jack Daw furlong late in the tenure and possession of yelverton Crow of yarmouth aforsaid and two steer calves to mee in hand paied att the sealling of these prsents and eighteen bushells of good and marchantable Indian Corne to bee paied, ten bushels therof att in or upon the last Day of November now next ensewing the Day of the Date heerof and the other eigh bushells att in or upon the last Day of November thence next enswing."(x)

March 7, 1642-3, Giles Hopkins is named as one of the surveyors of highways for Yarmouth.(y)

Oct. 28, 1644, Caleb Hopkins, son and heir of Mr. Stephen Hopkins, conveyed to Giles Hopkins of Yarmouth, planter, 100 acres of those lands taken up for the purchasers of "Satuckquett,"(z) which lands accrued to said Stephen as a purchaser.(a)

June 4, 1650, he is named as one of the surveyors of highways for Nauset (later Eastham).(b)

Oct. 3, 1654, Giles Hopkins in an action of defamation against William Leverich obtained judgment for £20 and 10s. 6d. costs of the suit.(c)

He had owned about three acres of marsh meadow lying next to Green Harbor (Duxbury), which he had sold to Thomas Clarke before Feb. 13, 1659-60.(d)

June 3, 1662, and June 5, 1671, he is named as one of the surveyors of highways for Eastham.(e)

In 1662 with Lt. Joseph Rogers and Josiah Cooke he had liberty to look out for land between Bridgewater and the bay line.(f)

June 5, 1666, the court granted to Giles Hopkins, the Widow Mayo and Jonathan Sparrow a parcel of land near Eastham, being a small neck called Sampson's Neck, and the waste land lying between the head of the fresh water pond and the westerly bounds of the Widow Mayo's land and so down to the cove.(g) June 5, 1667, the court ordered Lt. Freeman to purchase this land, or hire it for the grantees.(h)

He had the 8th lot in a tract in what is now West Brewster, east of Quivet, which he owned as early as 1653 and which he sold Nov. 9, 1666, to John Wing of of Yarmouth in consideration of a mare, colt and other land.(i)

Jan. 1, 1667-8, Giles Hopkins was on a jury of inquest upon the death of a child in Eastham and signed the verdict.(j)

(x) 2 Plym. Col. Deeds, pt. 1, p. 171; 10 Mf. 140.
(y) 2 Plym. Col. Recs. 53.
(z) Later in what is now Brewster.
(a) 12 Plym. Col. Recs. 104.
(b) 2 Ib. 155.
(c) 7 Plym. Col. Recs. 71, 72.
(d) 14 Mf. 143; 2 Plym. Col. Deeds, pt. 2, 31.
(e) 4 Plym. Col. Recs. 15; 5 ib. 58.
(f) Josiah Paine.
(g) 4 Plym. Col. Recs. 129.
(h) Ib. 152.
(i) 3 Plym. Col. Deeds, 91; Deyo, 893, 894.
(j) 4 Plym. Col. Recs. 177.

Aug. 21, 1672, he conveyed land in Eastham.(k)

He owned at his death 1-3 of meadow or sedge ground in Eastham "on Pochey sedge flats or low medows neer Hog Iland." Lt. Joseph Rogers and James Rogers owned the other 2-3.(l)

His will was dated Jan. 19, 1682-3. Both the will and codicil are signed with a mark. They are recorded in the Barnstable County Probate records,(m) and are printed in full in the Mayflower Descendant.(n)

He mentions his wife Catorne, his sons Stephen, William, Caleb and Joshua. His will gave to Stephen all his upland and meadow lying within what was later Harwich and half his cattle, on condition that he should after his (testator's) decease "take ye care and oversight and maintaine my son William Hopkins during his natural Life in a comfortable decent manner."

Lands N. and E. of those given to Stephen he gave to his sons Caleb and Joshua equally, but if either died without issue, his share was to go to the survivor.

He gave to his wife and his son William the improvement of two acres of meadow lying at the head of Rock Harbor during the life of his wife and after her decease, he gave one half of it to his son William for his life, and after the death of his wife and his son William, he gave the two acres to his son Joshua and his heirs.

He also gave to his son Joshua a parcel of meadow lying at the mouth of Rock Harbor and to his son Caleb a parcel of meadow lying at Little Namskaket.

He gave one half of his land and orchard by his house to his son Joshua and the other half and his dwelling house to his wife for her life and after her death to Joshua.

He gave a pair of plow irons to his son Caleb and another pair and his cart and wheels to his son Joshua.

The will also contained the following provision:

"I give unto my wife ye other half of my stock and moveables I say to my wife and my son William or what part of ye moveables my wife shall see cause to bestow on my son William Hopkins."

He made his son Stephen executor.

His codicil declared that whereas by the Providence of God his life had been prolonged and by reason of age and disability of body he was incapacitated from providing for the support of himself and wife, "my son Stephen Hopkins from this time and forward shall possess and Injoy all my stock and moveable estate provided he take effectual care of mine and my wifes Comfortable Support during our natural Lives."

The witnesses to the will were Jonathan Sparrow and Samuel Knowles and to the codicil, Mark Snow and Jonathan Sparrow.

(k) 5 Plym. Col. Deeds, 252.
(l) 11 Mf. 5.
(m) Vol. 1, p. 32.
(n) Vol. 1, pp. 110-113.

Children,(o) born no doubt the first four in Yarmouth and the rest in Eastham:

Mary, b. in November, 1640; m.(p) Jan. 3, 1665-6, Samuel* (Ralph¹) Smith; d. July 2, 1700.(q) d. July 2, 1700.(q)

Stephen, b. in September, 1642. John, b. in 1643; d. being 3 months old.

Abigail, b. in October, 1644; m. William Merrick (Myrick) in Eastham May 23, 1667.(r)

Deborah, b. in June, 1648; m. Josiah Cooke in Eastham, July 27, 1668.(s) He was not the son of Francis Cooke of the Mayflower.(t)

Caleb, b. in January, 1650-1; m. Mary Williams, daughter of Thomas Williams of Eastham; d. before May 22, 1728, at Truro, leaving issue.(u)

Oct. 28, 1684, Caleb Hopkins was fined 20s. and the costs of prosecution for breaking the King's peace by striking John Smith in his own house on a Sabbath evening.(v)

June 12, 1685, the Colonial treasurer was debtor to the colony for a fine of £1 from Caleb Hopkins of Eastham.(w)

At the July Court, 1685, Caleb Hopkins of Eastham, being accused of supplying the Indians with strong liquor and "refuseing to give his oath for his clearceing according to law," was fined £5 silver money, to be committed to prison until the same should be paid. Afterward he requested to put in "security to traverse his conviction of said fact the next Court, & bee tryed by a jury," whereupon he was permitted to give bond in the sum of £10 with the security of William Ring of Plymouth in the sum of £5, conditioned that he would appear on the last Tuesday of the next October. He was then found guilty, and paid his fine of £4 10s. in money.(x)

Ruth, b. in June, 1653; perhaps m. Job Winslow.(y)

Joshua, b. in June, 1657; m. May 26, 1681, Mary Cole, who d. March 1, 1733-4.(z) He d. about 1738. He was admitted a freeman June 3, 1690.(a) His son Elisha, b. in 1688, lived in Chatham.(b)

William, b. Jan. 9, 1660-1.(c)
Elizabeth, b. in November, 1664, and d. being a month old.

THIRD GENERATION.

Stephen* (Giles², Stephen¹) Hopkins, b. in September, 1642; m.(d)

(o) Eastham Recs.; 7 Mf. 236, 237.
(p) 8 Mf. 17, 18.
(q) 12 Mf. 116. See also ib. 112-117, 236-239.
(r) 8 Plym. Col. Recs. 56.
(s) 5 Mf. 185, 186; Eastham Recs.; 8 Mf. 88.
(t) 3 Mf. 97, 103.
(u) 8 Mf. 240-243.
(v) 6 Plym. Col. Recs. 145.
(w) 8 ib. 164, 165.

(x) 6 ib. 171, 172, 175.
(y) 45 N. Y. Genealogical and and Biog. Record, 8.
(z) 6 Mf. 204; 7 ib. 15.
(a) 6 Plym. Col. Recs. 239.
(b) 21 N. E. Reg. 213; 7 Mf. 15; 16 ib. 35-39, 105. See 15 ib. 175.
(c) 8 Plym. Col. Recs. 28.
(d) Eastham Recs.; 7 Mf. 16; 8 Plym. Col. Recs. 58.

STEPHEN¹ AND GILES² HOPKINS

1st in Eastham Mary (dau. of Wm.) Myrick, May 23, 1667; d. in Harwich Oct. 10, 1718.(e) He married 2d Bethiah Atkins April 7 or 9, 1701.(f) She d. in Harwich March 25, 1720.(f1) He is styled Mr. in the town records.

Nov. 28, 1664, Stephen Hopkins brought into Eastham two pounds of powder and one gallon of liquor.(g)

In 1675 Stephen Hopkins, Sr., was a freeman of Eastham admitted since 1655.(h) Stephen Hopkins was a freeman in Eastham in 1683-4.(i) In 1695 he was an inhabitant of Eastham.(j) His wife was admitted to the Harwich church Sept. 14, 1701.(k) He was admitted Dec. 26, 1708, and baptized Jan. 2, 1708-9.(l)

After the death of his father and before 1701 he moved to land left by his father in Harwich, now the eastern part of Brewster.(m) In 1713 he was a lot owner in "Sipsons Land" in East Brewster.(n) May 18, 1711, he was among the purchasers from John Quason and other Indians of a large tract of land in Harwich and Brewster and on Monomoy (Chatham) Great Beach, which purchase also included Strong Island in Pleasant Bay, now within the jurisdiction of Chatham. March 24, 1713-14, he was named as one of a committee to lay out the Harwich tract into lots and to pass on the rights of those who claimed prior title to lots therein. April 19, 1714, they met at the house of Nicholas Snow in Brewster and drew lots. In the region N. of the road from Chatham to Yarmouth Stephen Hopkins obtained the 5th and 10th lots and S. of that road the 10th and 13th lots.(o) In 1703 he was one of a committee to determine the boundaries of Harwich and Monomoyick (now Chatham) and he signed the report dated May 28, 1703.(p)

Children,(q) born in Eastham:

Elizabeth, b. the last week in June, 1668.

Stephen, b. July 15, 1670; m. May 19, 1692, Sarah Howes.(q1) They had issue.(q2) He d. April 9, 1733,(q3) and she m. 2d Joseph Hawes of Yarmouth.(q4)

Ruth, b. about the beginning of November, 1674.

Judah, b. about the middle of January, 1677-8.

(e) Har. Recs.; 6 Mf. 56.
(f) Eastham Recs.; 7 Mf. 16; 9 Ib. 9.
(f1) Har. Recs.; 8 Mf. 35.
(g) 4 Plym. Col. Recs. 100.
(h) 2 Freeman's Cape Cod, 367.
(i) 8 Plym. Col. Recs. 202, 208.
(j) 2 Freeman, 374.
(k) 4 Mf. 245.
(l) Ib. 247.
(m) Deyo's Barnstable County, 895, 898, 909.
(n) Ib. 834, 835.
(o) Deyo, 832-834; Records of Old Superior Court, No. 63,888.
(p) 2 Freeman, 496.
(q) Eastham Recs.; 7 Mf. 16; 8 Plym. Col. Recs. 58.
(q1) Eastham Recs.; 8 Mf. 16.
(q2) Har. Recs.; 6 Mf. 82.
(q3) Brewster Gravestone Records, 63.
(q4) Har. Recs. Int. June 14, 1746.

Samuel, b. the middle of March, 1682-3.
Nathaniel, b. about the middle of March, 1684-5.
Joseph, b. in 1688.
Benjamin, b. the middle of February, 1690-1.
Mary, b. April 15, 1692.

FOURTH GENERATION.

Nathaniel⁴ (Stephen³, Giles², Stephen¹) Hopkins, b. about the middle of March, 1684-5, in Eastham;(r) m. Mercy, daughter of John and Hannah (Freeman) Mayo, May 26, 1707;(s) d. Sept. 13, 1766, in his 82d year. She was born April 23, 1688.(t)

In 1725 he resided east of the meeting house in the part of Harwich now Brewster.(u) In 1732 he was one of the selectmen of Harwich.(u1)

His will, dated March 25, 1765, and proved Oct. 21, 1766, mentions his wife Mercy, his daughters Elizabeth Crosby and Mercy White, his son Nathaniel, the two children, James and Mercy, of his son Samuel, deceased, and his sons David, Reuben and Theophilus.

(r) 7 Mf. 16. John⁵ Mayo was son of Capt. Samuel³ and grandson of Rev. John¹ Mayo. Hannah Freeman was the daughter of John³ (Edmund¹) Freeman. Her mother was a daughter of Gov. Thomas Prence and granddaughter of Elder William Brewster.
(s) Har. Recs.; 4 Mf. 178, 179.
(t) Brewster Gravestone Recs. 62.
(u) 2 Freeman, 506.
(u1) Deyo, 815.

Theophilus was made executor.(v)
Children:(w)
David, b. July 13, 1707.
Jeremiah, b. March 14, 1708-9.
Elizabeth, b. April 21, 1711.
Nathaniel, b. Sept. 1, 1713.
Bethiah, b. Aug. 19, 1715.
Nathaniel, b. Sept. 15, 1717.
Mercy, b. Feb. 21, 1719-20.
Reuben, b. April 4, 1722.
Samuel, b. Aug. 30, 1724.
James, b. March 20, 1726-7.
Theophilus, b. March 13, 1728-9.(x)

Will of Nathaniel Hopkins.

In the Name of God Amen this 25th Day of March Anno Domini 1765 I Nathaniel Hopkins of Harwich in the County of Barnstable within the Province of the Massachusetts Bay in New England yeoman being in an advanced age but of perfect mind and memory Thanks be to God therefore but calling to mind the mortality of my body and knowing that it is appointed for all men once to Dye Do make and Ordain this my last will and Testament, That is to say, principally and first of all I give and Recommend my soul into the hands of God that Gave it and my body I Recommend to the Earth to be Buried in decent Christian manner att the discretion of my Executor nothing Doubting but att the General Resurrection I shall Receive the same again by the mighty Power of God and as touching such worldly estate wherewith it hath pleased God to bless me in this Life I Give

(v) 13 Barn. Prob. Recs. 246.
(w) Har. Recs.; 4 Mf. 178, 179.
(x) Har. Recs.; 13 Mf. 56.

Demise and Dispose of the same in the following manner and form.

Imprimis, I will that all my Just debts and funeral Charges be well & truly paid out of my moveables or personal estate and then I Give and Bequeath unto Mercy my well beloved wife one good feather bed & suitable Furnature for the same and other household stuff sufficient to keep house withall and all the provision that shall be in my house att my decease and two cowes and my horse or mare and the Improvement of all my Real Estate so long as she shall Remain my widow

Item. I Give to each of my Daughters and to their heirs and assigns forever The sum of fourty shillings viz to my daughter Elizabeth Crosby forty shillings Lawfull money of New England and to my Daughter Mercy White forty shillings to be paid to each of them by my Excer six months after my Decease.

Item I Give and bequeath to my son Nathaniel and to his heirs & assigns forever one shilling he having received sufficient for his portion already by his own choice and the remainder of my moveables or personal estate after the payment of my Just Debts and Funeral charges and the above mentioned Legacies I give and bequeath to my other three sons and to my Grandchildren viz the two children of my son Samuel Deceasd to be equally Divided among them all as followeth viz to my son David and to his heirs and assigns forever one quarter to my son Reuben one quarter and to his heirs and assigns forever, to my son Theophilus and to his heirs and assigns forever one quarter, and the other quarter to my two grandchildren above named as followeth viz my grandson James to have two thirds of said quarter to him his heirs & assigns forever and the other third of sd quarter I Give and bequeath to my grandaughter Mercy and to her heirs and assigns forever and I also Give and bequeath unto my three sons above mentioned and to my two grandchildren above named and to their heirs and assigns forever all the rest of my estate att my wives decease or marriage to be divided in proportion as above written.

And I do hereby constitute make and ordain my son Theophilus aforenamed to be my whole and sole executor to this my last will and Testament and I Do hereby uterly disallow revoke and disannull all and every other former Testaments Wills Legacies and Bequests and Executors by me in any wise before named willed and bequeathed Ratifying and confirming this and no other to be my Last will and Testament

In witness whereof I have hereunto sett my hand and seal the day and year above written

Nathaniel Hopkins (L S)

Signed sealed Published Pronounced & Declared by the said Nathaniel Hopkins to be his Last Will and Testament in presence of us

Eleazer Crosby
Mercy Hinkley
Phillip Selew

FIFTH GENERATION.

Samuel[5] **(Nathaniel**[4]**, Stephen**[3]**, Giles**[2]**, Stephen**[1]**) Hopkins**, b. in Harwich (the part now Brewster) Aug. 30, 1724; m.(y) there Aug. 23, 1753, Mehitable[5](y1) (Jabez[4], Lt. Prence[3], Mark[2], Nicholas[1]) Snow; d. there Nov. 15, 1761, in his 38th year.(z) He was received into full communion in the church June 7, 1761, and June 21 the same year he was baptized.(a)

Children:
James, b. April 24, 1755.(b)
Huldah, bap. July 3, 1757;(c) d. before March 25, 1765, the date of her grandfather's will.
Mercy, bap. June 3, 1759;(c) m. John Hawes of Chatham, Jan. 5, 1777;(d) d. Jan. 27, 1834, leaving issue.(e)
Eunice, bap. June 24, 1761;(a)

(y) Harwich Records. The declaration of intention was Aug. 4, 1753.
(y1) She was b. in Harwich (Brewster) April 22, 1731 (8 Mf. 102), and baptized April 25, 1731 (6 Mf. 217). There was a Mehitable, daughter of John Snow, b. in Harwich Jan. 16, 1733-4 (8 Mf. 163), but she d. in May, 1755 (10 Mf. 124).
(z) Brewster Gravestone Records, 57. According to the Bangs Diary, he died of consumption.
(a) Brewster Church Recs.; 12 Mf. 53.
(b) Har. Recs.
(c) Brewster Church Recs.; 10 Mf. 251, 253.
(d) Chat. Recs.
(e) Chat. Recs. See Hawes genealogy by the compiler.

d. before March 25, 1765, the date of her grandfather's will.

His will dated Feb. 25, 1761, and proved March 16, 1762, makes his wife Mehitable executrix and leaves her his estate, but provides that if she should marry, then what is left shall go to his children.(f)

Nov. 11, 1766, Reuben Ryder of Chatham was appointed guardian of his children, James Hopkins and Mercy Hopkins.(g)

Samuel[5] Hopkins's widow Mehitable m. 2d. Reuben Ryder of Chatham Oct. 16, 1766.(h) By him she had two daughters, Susannah, who m. Isaac Smith of Chatham, and Mehitable, who m. Nathaniel Snow of Chatham.(i) These daughters left issue. Nov. 11, 1766, Reuben Ryder was appointed guardian of her children, James and Mercy Hopkins.(j)

Reuben Ryder died before April 30, 1773, when letters of administration on his estate were granted to his widow Mehitable.(k) Nov. 29, 1774, she was appointed guar-

---

(f) 12 Barn. Prob. Recs. 279.
(g) 14 Barn. Prob. Recs. 166, 167.
(h) Har. Recs. The record of the marriage calls her Mehitable Snow, but the declaration of intention Sept. 27, 1766, both in Harwich and Chatham gives her name as Mehitable Hopkins.
(i) Information from the compiler's Aunt Patia (Hawes) Howes in 1877.
(j) 14 Barn. Prob. Recs. 166, 167.
(k) 16 Barn. Prob. Recs. 40.

dian of Susannah and Mehitable.(l)

April 11, 1785, division of his lands was made to his widow, then Mehitable Crowell, and to his two daughters Susannah and Mehitable.(m)

The widow Mehitable Ryder mar. 3d Deacon Paul Crowell of Chatham May 4, 1775,(n) by whom she had one daughter, Betsey, who mar. Solomon Smith of Barnstable.(o)

Deacon Paul Crowell died Nov. 10, 1808, in his 92d year.(o1) His will mentions his wife Mehitable, his sons Hallett, Thomas, Joseph, Ezra and Paul, his daughters Patience Ryder, Reliance Hopkins and Betsey Smith, and his grandchildren Betsey Knowles, Paul Sears and Betsey Sears.(p)

His widow Mehitable died before June 29, 1813, when the division was made of her thirds as widow of Reuben Ryder to Mehitable, wife of Nathaniel Snow, and to Ryder Smith, James Smith, Priscilla Smith, Hannah Smith, Susannah Smith, Freeman Smith and Molly Smith, children of Susannah, late wife of Isaac Smith.(q)

(l) 15 Barn. Prob. Recs. 200, 201.
(m) 26 ib. 24.
(n) Chat. Recs.
(o) Information from the compiler's Aunt Patia (Hawes) Howes in 1877.
(o1) Gravestone; 8 Mf. 237.
(p) 32 Barn. Prob. Recs. 237; 33 ib. 83; 35 ib. 71, 246.
(q) 37 Barn. Prob. Recs. 458-460.

Will of Samuel Hopkins.

In the Name of God Amen February 25th 1761 I Samuel Hopkins of Harwich in the County of Barnstable in the Province of the Massachusetts Bay in New England being weak in body but of Perfect mind and memory Thanks be Given to God therefore Calling to mind the mortality of my Body Do make and ordain this my Last will and Testament that is to say Principally and first of all I Give and Recommend my soul Into the Hands of God that gave it and my Body I Recommend to the earth to be buried in Decent Christian Burial at ye Discresion of my Executor hereinafter named; and as Touching such worldly estate wherewith it hath pleased God to bless me in this life I Give demise dispose of the same in the following manner and form.

I will That my Just Debts and funeral charge be well and truly paid out of my Estate Real or Personal as my Executor hereafter Named shall think proper then I Give and bequeath unto Mehitable my well beloved wife all my Real and Personal or Moveable Estate to be at her own Dispose as she shall think proper to Enable her to pay my Just Debts as abovesaid and to bring up our Children but if she should marry again and any of said estate should —— My Will is that it be equally divided amongst all my children and I Do hereby Constitute make appoint and ordain my above named wife Mehitable to be my whole and sole Executor of this my Last Will and Testament and I Do hereby utterly Revoke and disannull all and every other or former Testament Will Legacies and Bequests and Executors by me in any wise before named Willed or Bequeathed Ratifying and Confirming this and no other to be my Last Will & Testament In witness whereof I have hereunto set my hand and seal the Day and year above written Signd Seald Published and Declared by sd Samll Hopkins to be his Last Will and Testament in presence of us the subscribers

<pre>
                         his
          Samuell X Hopkins (L S.)
                        mark
Nathaniel Hopkins
Theoplilus Hopkins
Jabez Snow.
</pre>

SIXTH GENERATION.

James[6] (Samuel[5], Nathaniel[4], Stephen[3], Giles[2], Stephen[1]) Hopkins, b. April 24, 1755, in Harwich (the part now Brewster);(r) m. in Chatham Reliance, daughter of Deacon Paul Crowell, March 7, 1776;(s) d. before March 20, 1820, when letters of administration were granted on his estate to his brother-in-law Ezra Crowell.(t)

The inventory of his estate amounted to $499.00 in real estate and $93.08 in personal property. The estate appears to have been insolvent.(u)

He served in the Revolutionary war. "Massachusetts Soldiers and Sailors of the Revolutionary War"

(vol. 8, p. 238) contains the following:

"Hopkins, James, Chatham. Private, Capt. Thomas Hamilton's Co.; enlisted July 10, 1775; service to Dec. 31, 1775, 6 mos. 7 days; company stationed on the seacoast in Barnstable Co.; also, Capt. Benjamin Godfrey's Co., Col. John Cushing's regt.; service from Sept. 23, 1776, 60 days, at Rhode Island; roll dated Newport and sworn to in Barnstable Co.; also, Capt. Benjamin Godfrey's Co., Col. Josiah Whitney's regt.; arrived at destination May 10, 1777; discharged July 10, 1777; service, 2 mos. 12 days, at Rhode Island, travel (12 days) included; 108 miles reported as distance from Chatham to place of destination; enlistment, 2 months; roll dated Boston Neck, South Kingston."

According to the U. S. census of 1790 for Massachusetts (p. 13,) his family consisted of one adult male, two males under 16 and three females.

Children, born in Chatham:(v)

Huldah, b. April 22, 1778; m. Oct. 4, 1808, William Bea.

Samuel, b. July 18, 1780; m. Abigail Crowell Feb. 17, 1806. They lived in Chatham and had Sept. 23, 1807, Lucinda, and July 9, 1810, Huldah.

Rebecca, b. May 21, 1785; m. 1st Nov. 23, 1806, John Howes, and 2d(w) Hamilton; lived in Chatham.(w)

James, b. June 1, 1787; m.

(r) Har. Recs.
(s) Chat. Recs.
(t) 36 Barn. Prob. Recs. 450.
(u) 43 Barn. Prob. Recs. 100, 288.

(v) Chat. Recs.
(w) Information from the compiler's oldest sister (b. 1826), Mrs. Sally T. Smith.

March 8, 1808, Cynthia Snow.
Eunice, b. Oct. 6, 1790; m. Lendal Nickerson March 12, 1807.(x)
Nathaniel, b. Sept. 24, 1792.
Mercy, b. Nov. 18, 1794; m. Dec. 2, 1819, James Eldredge, Jr.(y)
Reliance, b. Nov. 2, 1796; m. Nov. 4, 1819, James Eldredge, Sr.
Mehitable, b. Nov. 8, 1798; m. 1st Abijah Eldredge and 2d Christopher Smith,(w) the 2d wife of both husbands.
Betsey, b. Feb. 2, 1800.

The compiler's Aunt Patia (Hawes) Howes informed him in 1877 that James⁶ Hopkins's sons left no male issue.

SEVENTH GENERATION.

Reliance⁷ (James⁶, Samuel⁵, Nathaniel⁴, Stephen³, Giles², Stephen¹) Hopkins, b. in Chatham Nov. 2, 1796; m. there Nov. 4, 1819, James Eldredge; d. Oct. 18, 1860, aged 63 years and 11 months. He d. March 12, 1858, aged 63 years and 5 months.(z) They lived in West Chatham.
Children, born in Chatham:(a)
Elisha, d. young.
Elisha, b. Jan. 31, 1822.
Lucina, d. young.

(x) Mrs. Smith thought her husband was Leonard Nickerson and that they lived in Dedham.
(y) Mrs. Smith, who said that they lived in North Chatham and that two sisters, Mercy and Reliance, married men of the same name.
(z) Gravestones in Baptist cemetery in Chatham.
(a) Information as to these and

Daniel Webster, b. Nov. 5, 1835.

EIGHTH GENERATION.

Elisha⁸ Eldredge, son of James and (Reliance⁷ Hopkins) Eldredge; b. Jan. 31, 1822; m. 1st in 1849 Betsey Ann, daughter of Zenas Eldredge of South Chatham, 2d in 1856 Elizabeth, daughter of Ephraim Eldredge of South Chatham, and 3d in March, 1863, Marion W. Lothrop, widow of James D. Lothrop (son of Rev. Davis Lothrop) and daughter of Nehemiah D. Kelley of West Harwich; d. Oct. 31, 1878.
Children, by 3d wife, born in South Chatham:
a. Nehemiah D., b. Sept. 4, 1864; m. April 25, 1888, Sadie Brooks of Boston; d. in April, 1907, leaving two children, Charles, b. March 16, 1894, and Josephine D., 15 years old in 1915, who live with their mother at 316 Newbury St., Boston, who married 2d Charles W. Warner.
b. Mary Doane, b. Aug. 12, 1869; m. William E. Howes of Dennisport, who live in Malden and have Victor E., 19 years old, and Emily M., 8 years old.
c. Victoria, b. in March, 1874; d. in 1888.

Daniel⁸ Webster Eldredge, son of James and (Reliance⁷ Hopkins) Eldredge; b. Nov. 5, 1835; m. Oct. 12, 1858, Eliza Ann, daughter of Captain Hiram Small of Harwich; d. May 26, 1870.

---

their descendants from the widows of Elisha and Daniel W. Eldredge.

His widow m. Luther Eldredge, now deceased.
Children, born in South Harwich:
a. Hiram J., b. November, 1859; d. young.
b. Effie Mabel, b. January, 1864; m. Eugene C. Ellis, who is postmaster in East Wareham. They have three children: Harold Merwin, Eugene Webster and Doris Amelia.
c. Hiram Webster, b. October, 1866; m. Jan. 24, 1889, in Harwich, Rebecca Mayo Snow. They have three children: Henry Burr, b. in Barnstable; Cranston Daniel and Mabel, b. in Antrim, N. H., where he is the editor and publisher of The Antrim Reporter.

ELDREDGE LINE.

The Eldredge line is as follows:(b)
Robert¹, first mentioned in the Colonial record in 1639, lived some 10 years in Plymouth and then removed to Yarmouth, where in 1649 he married Elizabeth, daughter of William¹ Nickerson. About 1666 he followed his father-in-law to Chatham, where he died about the beginning of 1683. He left among other children
Lt. Nicholas², b. in Yarmouth Aug. 18, 1650. He came with his father to Chatham, where he died

April 30, 1702. He left among other children
James³, who died July 19, 1757, leaving among other children Abner⁴, who m. Sarah Eldredge April 19, 1762;(c) d. before May 12, 1772.(d) His children Dorcas, Abner⁵, Daniel⁵ and Desire had their uncle, Zephaniah⁴ Eldredge, termed a mariner, appointed their guardian April 11, 1774.(e)
Daniel⁵ (Abner⁴, James³, Nicholas², Robert¹) Eldredge, m. in Chatham Tabitha Howes (intention Oct. 6, 1787).(f)
Children, born in Chatham:(g)
Elisha⁶, b. Sept. 23, 1788; killed by lightning while at sea. He m. Patience Young and had one child, Mary, who m. Philip Small, of Harwichport, and has a son, Frank Small, living there.(h)
Abner⁶, b. Jan. 22, 1791. He was a sea captain in his early life, married and had issue.(h)
James⁶, b. Oct. 4, 1794; m. Reliance Hopkins, as above stated.
Sarah, b. April 14, 1798. She m. Jeremiah Kelly, of Centerville; no children.(h)
Tabitha, b. Feb. 22, 1807; m. Jabez Crowell of East Harwich.(h)

(b) See "Eldred, Eldredge" by the compiler, published by C. W. Swift, Yarmouthport, Mass.

(c) Chatham Recs. See 15 Mf. 133.
(d) 16 Barn. Prob. Recs. 26.
(e) 15 ib. 188-191.
(f) 2 Chat. Recs. 314.
(g) 3 Chat. Recs. 267.
(h) Family information.

No. 38.

LIBRARY *of*
Cape Cod
HISTORY & GENEALOGY

OLD QUAKER VILLAGE
South Yarmouth, Massachusetts
Reminiscences Gathered and Edited by

E. Lawrence Jenkins

1915

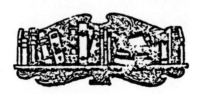

YARMOUTHPORT, MASS.:
C. W. SWIFT, Publisher and Printer,
The "Register" Press,
1915.

Copyright, 1915,
By Charles Warner Swift.

OLD QUAKER VILLAGE

South Yarmouth, Massachusetts

No land of beauty art thou, Old Cape,
But a prouder name we crave,
The home of the purest, bravest hearts,
That traverse the dark blue wave.
Then cherished for aye shall thy mem'ry be,
For where'er through life I roam,
My heart will turn, like a wearied bird,
To my own, my Cape Cod home.
—E. J. Dudley.

Reminiscences Gathered and Edited by

E. Lawrence Jenkins

1915

BASS RIVER.

There's a gently flowing river,
  Bordered by whispering trees,
That ebbs and flows in Nobscussett,
  And winds through Mattacheese.

Surely the Indians loved it,
  In the ages so dim and gray,
River beloved of the pale-face,
  Who dwell near its banks today!

They pass on,—the generations—
  Thou stayest, while men depart;
They go with thy lovely changes
  Shrined in each failing heart.

Beautiful old Bass river!
  Girt round with thy murmuring trees;
Long wilt thou flow through Nobscussett,
  And wander through Mattacheese.
            —Arethusa, South Dennis.

BASS RIVER.

At the sound of thy name, what fond mem'ries arise
Of the scenes of my childhood, 'neath soft summer skies!
At each sail on thy surface, or walk on thy shore,
Thy quaint beauty impressed me as never before.

Of the Afton and Tiber the poets have sung;
For the Avon and Danube their harps they have strung.
May the the singer be blest, whosoe'er he may be,
Who shall sing the just praises, dear river, of thee!
            —Daniel Wing.

—OLD QUAKER VILLAGE—

The idea of putting upon paper various items of information and interest that might be gathered of South Yarmouth, formerly known as "Quaker Village," was suggested by a former resident of the place who had been greatly interested in a conversation with the late Orlando F. Wood, then one of its oldest residents. Recognizing the fact that our old men are one by one passing away and much interesting and valuable information is being lost, I suggested to Mr. Wood that he describe the village as it was when he was a boy and I would write it down. So, seated in his big chair in the cozy quarters which he liked to designate as the "O. B. S. club," and surrounded by a few congenial listeners and good friends, he took each street and described its appearance at that early period.

I wish to state at this point, however, that I have not relied entirely upon Mr. Wood's account, but have had valuable assistance from Mr. Daniel Wing, who has for years made a study of the history of South Yarmouth.

One is apt to think that these country villages change but little, but he has only to let his mind wander back even so short a time as twenty-five years to see that many changes have taken place, and that the Quaker Village of that period was a far different place than that of today; fifty or seventy-five years have brought about great changes.

There is one thing that I cannot but remark, and that is the "youngness" of the present day residents. Even when I was a boy, a man or woman who had reached the age of fifty years was considered "old;" now, he or she is simply in the prime of life and best able to enjoy it. And still more strange, none of those whom I considered old in my boyhood days ever seemed to grow any older! In those days, a man who had reached the age of fifty no longer thought of mingling with the young in society. It was his duty to set the example of sedateness and propriety, as if it were a sin to grow young in heart as he grew older in years. My father was fifty years old when I was born, and he was considered so old a man that his friends told him he would never live to see me grown up. And yet he did live to see me pass my thirtieth birthday. I remember that he was a much younger man at heart when he was eighty than he was at sixty, and grew far more liberal in his views during the last twenty years of his life. In these days it is rarely we find a man under seventy-five who cares to be thought "old."

Before taking up the appearance of the village, street by street, as described by Mr. Wood, it would be well to give a bit of the history of South Yarmouth, gathered from various sources, particularly from a series of articles by Mr. Daniel Wing, a former resident, which were published in the Yarmouth Register.

According to Mr. Wing, the town of Yarmouth, in 1713, set off a tract of land "for ye Indian inhabitants to live upon," which included the land from Long pond to Bass river, and from the old Yarmouth road to the lands now owned by Joseph Chase; in fact, what is now the most populous section of the village. The Indians having been killed off by small pox, the town authorized the selectmen in 1778 to sell these lands, reserving a tract for Thomas Greenough, one of the survivors. Greenough afterwards sold more or less of this land, the first of which was to David Kelley, great-grandfather of the present David D. Kelley, in 1790, and was about two acres; on the southwesterly corner of which the structure now known as the "cellar house" was erected.

In 1713, when the town of Yarmouth reserved for the native Indians 160 acres, the Indians, according to Mr. Alden in his "Memorabilia of Yarmouth," equalled the whites in population, but disease thinned their ranks and in 1767 there were but six wigwams inhabited in the whole township. In 1787 but one wigwam was inhabited and that was on the grounds now owned by the Owl club.

Speaking of Indians reminds me that "Nauhaught, the Deacon," the subject of Whittier's poem of that title, lived in South Yarmouth on the south side of Long pond, near the Yarmouth road, and the swamp on the opposite side is today known as "Sarah's swamp," being named for the Deacon's daughter. All are familiar with the story of how he was attacked by several black snakes that began to twine about his legs. One of them reaching his head, Nauhaught opened his mouth, and the snake putting his head inside, the Indian bit it off, whereupon the blood streaming down from the decapitated snake alarmed the rest and they fled. Even to this day traces of an old trail may be seen in the vicinity of Swan pond, where an Indian meeting house once stood. "It is probable," says a writer, "that it was on this path that Nauhaught had his encounter with the snakes." Mr. Alden visited him in his last days and asked him if he was resigned. "Oh yes, Mr. Alden," he replied, "I have always had a pretty good notion of death."

Upon the records of the town of Yarmouth may be found under date of November 17, 1778, "Voted, that the charge made by the

Indians having the small pox, be paid out of the town treasury.

"5th. Then voted that all their effects be sold to pay their charge of having the small pox, and the land formerly belonging to the Indians to live upon be sold or leased.

"6th. Concerning the Indian land—Voted that the town impower the selectmen to lease or sell the Indian land or reserve a piece for Thomas Groenough as they shall think proper."

Some of the Indians of South Yarmouth were first buried on land afterwards owned by Robert Homer, but when it was proposed to use the land for salt works, it so grieved Cato, a negro, whose wife Lucy was an Indian, who occupied the last wigwam in South Yarmouth, that the bodies were disinterred and buried with the others on a hillside near Long pond, which spot is now marked by a monument of boulders bearing the inscription:

"On this slope lie buried
the last native Indians
of Yarmouth."

When the bank back of the monument was dug away for the purpose of making a cranberry bog, several skeletons were found, together with pieces of coffins, showing that the burial place was comparatively modern, although the general idea remains that it was also an ancient burial place as well. Certainly it must have been a part of their old hunting grounds, those old woods, bordering upon the largest pond in the vicinity, which was full of fish and the resort of water fowl, and we can well imagine that it would be an ideal spot for the last resting place of the members of the tribe that once held possession of all these lands.

At the time of Orlando Wood's first recollections, there were but few trees in the village excepting wild cherry trees that bordered the streets, and here and there an apple orchard, evidences of which may now be seen in the yard of Captain Joseph Allen, which trees, although at least one hundred years old, still bear fruit of excellent quality. The cherry trees in front of what is known as the "Katy Kelley house" on Bridge street, I am informed by Seth Kelley, were old trees when his father was a boy, which would be very nearly if not quite a hundred years ago. Trees for ornamentation evidently were thought to be too worldly for those old Friends; to them, there was no place for a tree unless it bore fruit, and the idea of ornamenting streets or grounds with trees was something not to be thought of.

Beginning at Bridge street, Mr. Wood says there was no dwelling beyond it. The "rope-walk" extended to the Friends meeting house on the main road, but all below it, to the river, was given over to fields and gardens, large portions being used for corn-fields. The present street leading to the David Kelley house was not opened, nor were any of the present houses on that street built. The "toll-house" of course was not built, nor even thought of, and the first house on the street, from the river, was the house in which Mr. Wood was born, on the spot where now stands the paint shop of Manton H. Crowell. The garden of this house was the spot where the bank building now stands. This house was undoubtedly the residence of the first David Kelley, who died in 1816, an enterprising man who bought several acres of the Indian lands. It was a one-story house, with a large unfinished chamber on the second floor, in which were several beds, as was the custom in those days. Mr. Wood remembers that a storm blew out one side of the house and he saw some of the neighborly women standing in the breech admiring the view of the river.

Mr. Wood's father was Zenas Wood and his mother was Mercy Hawes of Yarmouth. He tells a story of his grandmother Lydia, or "Liddy" as she was called, that shows that even in those early days "love laughed at locksmiths." It seems that her parents were strict Quakers, and Liddy, against their objections, had met and fallen in love with a young man of West Barnstable. There was evidently no objection to the young man except that he was not a Friend, and Liddy's parents could not be reconciled to her marrying "out of the meeting." But love will find a way, and when the old folks went to monthly meeting one day, Liddy quietly packed up some of her belongings in a bundle, mounted a horse and rode away to West Barnstable, hiding there in an old grist mill—which was standing up to a few years ago—where the young man met her and took her to the parson's. Her father refused for a long time to forgive her, but the mother finally brought about a reconciliation and Liddy went back to her meeting. This old grist mill was the same that received a grant from the town of Barnstable in 1689 of eight or ten acres at Goodspeed's river and the benefit of the stream forever on condition that the parties interested "should set up a fulling mill on the river and maintain the same for twenty years and full and dress the town's cloth on reasonable terms."— (D. Wing.) The story is told that Aunt Liddy dreamed one night, during her last years, that she saw the vessel on which had sailed a favorite grandson, coming up Boston harbor with the flag at half mast and that the boy was dead. A few days later brought tidings that her dream was but the forerunner of sad news.

I remember, rather vaguely, Zenas Wood as a man of whom the school boys stood in awe, because they imagined that he possessed certain authority and power to arrest them for any misdemeanors of which they might be guilty. I also remember that he had a tall flag pole in his garden and a flag which he used to raise upon patriotic occasions, even as Mr. Wood delighted to do later. Mr. Wood informed me that he, Orlando, was born upon a day of general muster, and that upon that eventful occasion, Uncle George Baker shot off one of his arms by a careless handling of his musket. I can just remember the old man myself. The stump of his arm was a great curiosity to me, and the deft way in which he managed to saw wood, which he used to do for my father. In this old house on Bridge street the late David Kelley lived after he was first married, and later Zeno Baker and others. At the foot of Bridge street was a wharf, to which large vessels were often moored.

The next house on Bridge street was that owned by the late Thomas Collins, then belonging to Abiel Akin, blacksmith, grandfather of the late Peleg P. Akin, who came from New Bedford previous to 1800. He had formerly owned the "cellar house," where the late David K. Akin was born. Previously it was occupied by a potter named Purrington, and the second story was used as a sail-loft. After Abiel built the Collins house and moved into it, the "cellar house" was occupied by one of his children, and during a storm the good woman of the house used to take her children and go to her father's to stay, for fear that the house would blow over! However, the old house has weathered many a storm since those days and still stands as probably one of the most substantial dwellings in the village. Certainly it is one of the most interesting old landmarks of the place. The Collins house was also known as the "Amos Kelley house."

The only other house standing at that time on Bridge street, according to Mr. Wood, was that known as the "Kate Kelley house." It was built by the father of the late David Kelley, and afterwards became the home of his daughter Catherine, of whom the older portion of the community have many pleasant memories.

As has been said, back of these houses, on the right hand side coming from the river, was nothing but open fields excepting upon the road leading to the Friends meeting house, where stood the "rope-walk," which extended from the head of Bridge street to the meeting house grounds. For a description of this old business enterprise I am indebted to the late Stephen Sears and to Mr. Wing, although Mr. Wood recalled the old building because he worked there when he was a boy. It was built in 1802 by David Kelley the first and Sylvanus Crowell, and the business of making rope was carried on for a number of years,—more than twenty-five at least. At that time there was a large fleet of coasting and fishing vessels that sailed from Bass river, and there was a great demand for the product of the rope-walk. The "walk" was, perhaps, twelve feet wide and seven feet high, with port holes that could be closed by inside shutters. At the north end was the power house, operated by horses to do the heavy work, such as the making of cables and standing rigging. At the opposite or south end was the store house for manufactured goods, etc. Mr. Sears recalled a visit to the place when a lad, and seeing two men and a boy spinning. The men had large wisps of hemp about their waists which they attached to the twisting machine, kept in motion by the boy, and walking with their backs to the machine, paid out the material for some two or three hundred feet, and then returned to the wheel, hanging the newly spun thread to hooks. Mr. Sears thought that the men received two cents a thread for spinning and the boy forty cents a day. The tarring plant was outside the main building. When the business of rope making became no longer profitable, the building was occupied for the making of oil cloth, a man by the name of Jacob Vining being the manager, and Stephen Wing the designer and pattern maker. He (Wing) had always a taste for artistic work of a like nature, which showed itself in the painting of signs, lettering and designing. When this business was given up the structure was taken down and the land gradually sold for building purposes, and on the site of the old rope-walk stand today the dwellings built or occupied by Morris Cole, James F. Kelley, William Haffards, Joseph Crowell, Bartlett White, Charles Farris, Nelson Crowell, the dry goods store of E. D. Kelley and the grocery store of David D. Kelley. In those early days the rope-walk was a convenient passageway to the meeting house in stormy weather and as the owners were themselves Friends, they allowed the worshippers to pass through it, a favor I fear no one of the present day would offer if the building still stood and was owned by other parties.

In looking back to those days I am struck with the fact that there were many opportunities offered to keep the young men at work and at home. The Quakers were not a sea-going people as a rule, but they were full of business ideas and promoters

—OLD QUAKER VILLAGE—

of many industries. In addition to rope making, there was the salt industry, the fishing business was excellent on our coast, shoe making establishments employed many young men, as did a tailoring shop, a magnesia factory, a tannery, and other opportunities were not wanting; while on the other hand, today there is hardly anything for a young man to do who wishes to live in his native place.

On the opposite side of the road from the rope-walk was a "stretch" of pine woods; tall large trees such as one rarely sees now. These woods extended down to the "flatiron" in front of the house known as the "David Chubbs house."

When the old David Kelley house on Bridge street was torn down a portion of it was used in building that now owned by Frank Crosby, and about the same time the house of Charles Baxter was built, and here he lived and died as did his wife, Aunt Betsey. At present it is occupied by Mrs. Hathaway. Next to it was the house in which Mr. Tripp, one of the earlier school teachers lived, now occupied by Mrs. Crowell, the mother of our postmaster, who at this date is ninety-four years old, and in excellent health.

And now, while we are in the vicinity, it is well to speak of the Friends meeting house, which was then the principal place of worship, and to within a few years of the birth of Mr. Wood, the only place of worship in South Yarmouth. It was built in 1809. Nearly one hundred years before, the society built a meeting house in what is now South Dennis, on a hill overlooking the river. Dennis then being a part of Yarmouth, the old meeting house was that of the Yarmouth Quakers, and more particularly those of South Yarmouth. All the Quakers from the country round, says Mr. Wing, used to attend services there, those from Harwich coming on what is still known as "Quaker path," while those from the vicinity of "Indian town," now known as "Friends village," came on the road leading by "Dinah's pond" and crossing at the "second narrows" in a boat kept there for the purpose. When the present structure was built the old meeting house was sold and floated down the river to its mouth and converted into a dwelling house. It is now standing and is known as the "Waterman Baker house." Its age of nearly two hundred years makes it an object of interest to all.

In those early days the Friends meeting was largely attended, both sides of the house being filled at every service, on Sundays and Thursdays, for it was considered an inexcusable neglect of duty not to be present. On Fifth day, or Thursday, the children in the schools were excused for the purpose of attending meeting, and the young men left their work to attend.

It is told of the late David Kelley, that when a young man and working in the rope-walk, one Fifth day he did not attend meeting as usual. There was much whispering and smiling among the others, and it turned out that on that particular day his proposed marriage to Phoebe Dudley was announced. She was a niece of Robert and Daniel Wing, senior, and came from Maine to teach school in South Yarmouth, and it was here he first met her. If I am not mistaken, the last marriage ceremony performed in the old meeting house was that of the oldest daughter of the late Henry G. Crowell. A visitor to the old cemetery is struck with the simplicity and neatness of the enclosure, the care taken of the grounds and graves, and above all with the fact that there all are equal; there are no costly monuments proclaiming to the world the wealth of him who sleeps beneath, no carved eulogies reciting the worldly deeds of the sleeper; only a simple stone with the name and date of birth and death, and each stone is like every other in size; the richest man in the place—when he was living—having no more costly stone than his neighbor who had to toil early and late to support his family. I think there are few more impressive resting places for the dead than this little cemetery of the South Yarmouth Quakers.

My own memories of Quaker meeting are very tender. My father did not belong to the meeting, although he always attended, and in his later years sat upon the second seat facing the congregation, an honor accorded him because of his life-long attendance and because of the great respect with which he was held by the members of that meeting. As a boy, I was required to attend on First day, and I remember well how long that hour of quiet seemed to me, and how the sighing of the pines back of the meeting house would often lull me to an inclination to sleep, and with what interest I watched Uncle David Akin and Aunt Ruth Baker to see if they showed any signs of shaking hands, which was the closing ceremony.

The old meeting house is closed; all the old Friends are sleeping in the little cemetery. Only a few of the younger members of the meeting remain, and they are so few that to hold services could only cause feelings of sadness as they sit there in solemn silence while their minds harken back to the years that are not, and to the faces of those who once filled the seats.

Facing the "gridiron" was the house of David Chubb, a portion of which was the tailor shop of Alexander Hillman, attached to the house now occupied by Frank Collins, of which I shall have more to say later on. The house has been added to from time to time until it reminds one now of the "house of the seven gables," although how many more gables than seven it has I am still at a loss to say. A large barn is near it, and when I was a boy there used to be a stencilled notice facing the door bearing this information:

> "My will is good,
> My word is just,
> I would if I could,
> But I cannot trust."

David Chubb drove the stage coach for many years and was a well-known personage in the vicinity. And speaking of the stage coach, reminds me that within my recollection the stage coaches ran down the Cape from Hyannis on the south side, and from Yarmouth on the north, and I can see them now, lumbering through the village. I used to envy the driver holding the reins of his four horses and snapping his long whip as he dashed around the corner, with almost invariably a boy clinging to the trunk rack, while some less fortunate urchin sang out, "Whip behind!" To me it seemed like a bit of the circus outside the tent. There are men living in the village who can remember going all the way to Boston in the stage coach, a journey which consumed a whole day. Sometimes passengers went by vessel from Yarmouth, a ball on the top of a flag pole on one of the hills, which could be seen from the village, announcing the departure of such a vessel.

Daniel Wing in a recent article to the Register speaks of the great severity of the weather in those days and of hearing older people tell of walking to the roof of the rope-walk upon frozen snow drifts on the way to the schoolhouse, which stood on the left hand side of the road near the village of Georgetown. I remember hearing similar stories of big snow drifts; one of which was near the foot of Bridge street, so high that an arch was cut into it, through which the stage coach passed. Even within my own recollection the winters were much more severe than those of the present time.

Going back to Bridge street, we come to the street that runs past the house of Thomas Collins to that of the late Peleg P. Akin. There was no building opposite the Collins house, nothing but an open field; but on the corner of the next street leading to the river and to the "cellar house," or near the corner, stood the grocery store of Thomas Akin and the postoffice. There were but two mails a week and these came by the way of Yarmouth and were brought over by carrier. Postage was higher in those days and I have in my possession letters, without envelopes, with postage marked twelve and a half cents. Mr. Wing writes me, "I remember very well the Thomas Akin store when it was on the site here described. The stone wall was very much the same as now, except in front of the store it was removed so as to allow of passage under the store piazza and into the basement. I used to think, when a boy, that the incline leading up to the store on the other side, together with the stone wall and the stairs, was a very grand combination and looked upon it with greater wonderment than I experience now in viewing structures twenty times as high."

Next to Thomas Akin's store, this side of it I think, nearer the corner, was David Akin's jewelry store, one part of which was used by Alexander Hillman as a tailor's shop until he moved across the street to the house now occupied by Frank Collins. Later this little building of David Akin's was moved to Bridge street and used as a postoffice. It is now the dwelling house of Uriah Sears. Thomas Akin was succeeded as postmaster by David Akin, who in turn gave way to John Larkin. Peleg P. Akin was postmaster when the postoffice was in the grocery store, now used as a library room, and he in turn gave place to Bernard L. Baker, who held the office for many years. In the meanwhile, however, the little building had become the postoffice again and continued so until the appointment of the present postmaster, J. W. Crowell, who moved into new quarters.

Down this street, leading to the "cellar house," at the wharf, was the blacksmith shop of Charles and Timothy Akin, the village blacksmiths.

"Uncle Timothy," said Mr. Wood, "was a very keen and witty old Quaker, and very fond of a joke. One day he came to my grandmother's house and said. 'Liddy, I want thee to get thy potatoes and dumplings all ready tomorrow and I will bring thee a goose.' My grandmother thanked him for his kindness, and the next day Uncle Timothy appeared and said, 'Liddy, here is thy goose; it is rather tough and will need a deal of cooking.' And he pulled out from under his coat a tailor's iron goose! I don't know what my grandmother said, but she kept the goose and it was in the family for many years."

Uncle Timothy was a practical joker and many were the pranks he played upon one and another of the villagers. Although some of his jokes resulted in a sacrifice of material, he was always ready to make good the loss, and seemed to count himself the gainer though the fun cost him several hours of labor. "On a certain occasion he partly filled a gun barrel with water, securely closing the muzzle and inserting a plug in the tube so slightly as to allow of its removal by a slight pressure from within. One day Uncle Robert, a boat builder and intimate friend and frequent visitor of Uncle Timothy, called at the smithy and entertained himself, while engaged in conversation, by blowing the huge bellows at the forge. Just then it occurred to the smith that it was a favorable opportunity to try that gun barrel, so, with other irons, he carefully laid it on the fire, and going out of the shop he took a position where he could watch the development of events within; Uncle Robert, meanwhile, ignorant of the preparations, blowing away as if great results depended upon his diligence. As the heat increased, the water in the gun barrel began to boil and the pressure of steam became so great that the plug was forced from the tube, and the issuing steam, after the manner of Hero's engine, caused the gun barrel to leave the fire, sending it in the air in so zig-zag a course as to defy all attempts at predicting where or when it would finally alight. Uncle Robert, who was somewhat corpulent, was entirely taken by surprise, and not knowing what the infernal machine might do next in its mad career about the shop, crawled under the bellows to get out of the way, in which awkward position he was found by the blacksmith, who just then happened(?) to come in to see what on earth was to pay!" (Cape Cod News, 1887.)

Across the street from Thomas Akin's store was the house of Alexander Hillman, (now occupied by Frank Collins) and attached to it was his tailor's shop in which he employed a dozen or more women and boys, the latter being apprentices who were learning the trade, among them being Mr. Wood. Asking Mr. Wood who worked there at that time, I found that many of the women I knew as wives of prominent men in the village were among the number, and others came from Yarmouth, Dennis and Brewster. Evidently some of them were not satisfied with their boarding places, as the following prayers were written by two of the tailoresses, who possessed a streak of humor in their make-up:

"Lord of love, look down from above
And pity us poor creatures;
Give us some meat that is fit to eat,
And take away the fish and potatoes!"

"Lord make us able
To eat all that is on the table,
Except the dish cloth and ladle!"

Alexander Hillman afterwards removed to New Bedford, where he continued the tailoring business.

Next to this house was that of Cyrenus Kelley, grandfather of William R. Farris, a former resident of this place. It later on became the property of William White, and is now occupied by his son, Edwin M. White. Cyrenus Kelley was a carpenter by trade, and had a shop back of his house. William White was one of a large family that descended in direct line from Peregrine White, the first white child born in New England, and one of the sons, I think Captain Osborn White, has in his possession the cane that belonged to the said Peregrine. William White's direct line from the "Mayflower" is as follows:

1 William White with his wife Anna came over in the Mayflower.
2 Peregrine, first white child born in New England.
3 Jonathan White.
4 Joseph White.
5 Deacon Joseph White.
6 Peregrine.
7 Alfred, William, Perry, Rufus, etc.

On the opposite side of the street was the house of Zeno Kelley, now occupied by Mr. G. W. Tupper. Mr. Wood remembers Uncle Zeno very well because he gave him five dollars a year to milk his cow, and he remembers that one night he forgot to milk. How little things remain in our memories— things that happened long years ago— while events of yesterday are even now forgotten! Uncle Zeno also built and occupied for awhile the house opposite, known as the "Edward Gifford house," one of the most picturesque old houses in the village. He conveyed the premises, says Mr. Wing, in 1805, so that the building is somewhat over a hundred years o.d. Uncle Zeno also built the house formerly used as a Methodist parsonage, standing opposite the church on Main street, but which when erected occupied the present site of the late Mrs. Sarah Bray residence.

Uncle Edward Gifford had a large family. One of them—his daughter Sarah R.— I remember quite distinctly as the village dressmaker; a very bright and witty old maid and a great favorite with all who knew her. I recall that at one time, I think it was during the Civil war she had company to tea and her mother, a hospitable old Quaker lady, said to the young women present at the table, "Girls, eat all the butter thee wishes, but I'm dreadful afraid it will hurt thee." And the eating of too much did hurt the pocketbooks of many of our parents during those times when everything was high and money scarce. Mr. Wing has sent me some of the bills received by Wing & Akin in those days for goods from the wholesalers, and from them I find that the consumer must have paid about sixty cents a pound for butter, one dollar a gallon for kerosene oil, thirty-five cents a pound for sugar, and other things in proportion. It is a wonder that our fathers were able to live and bring up large families of children. Evidently they were living the "simple life."

The street to the water from Edward Gifford's was then a private way and led to the ferry landing which was near the cooper shop of Frederick P. Baker. This cooper shop was built about seventy years ago and was at one time the scene of great industry. One of the sights of my boyhood days was to watch the cooper as he fashioned his barrels, which seemed more wonderful in the various stages than most anything within my experience. I look back to my recollections of Mr. Baker with a great deal of pleasure. He was always one of the most cordial in greeting me when I came home on my vacations from the city, and I recall many a pleasant chat with him in those days when it meant so much to a boy to be noticed by an older man.

The charter for the ferry was granted to David Kelley, and the boats later on were run by "Uncle" Elihu Kelley, who lived on the opposite side of the river. The rates were two cents for a single passenger and twenty-five cents for horse and carriage, which were taken across the stream in a flat bottom boat. "He had a skiff for passengers and a scow for teams," said Mr. Wood, "and a conch shell was tied to a post at the landing, which was blown when the services of the ferryman were needed. The mischievous boys would often blow the conch to get the old man out." Mr. Wing has this to say of Uncle Elihu:

"Although Uncle Elihu's accustomed place in the Friend's meeting, which he regularly attended though not a member, was upon the 'rising seats,' he was evidently averse to talking much of his religious views, for it is related of him that, when questioned upon that subject by a travelling preacher while the ferry boat was in mid-stream, the old man pretended to be very hard of hearing and replied as he poled the boat vigorously, 'Yes, about half way across; and upon a repetition of the inquiry, he said, 'Yes, yes, about half way across, half way across,' and so evaded the question."

He was very much opposed to the building of a bridge, declaring that he could see no sense or reason in such a thing; but the bridge was built and the old ferryman's occupation was gone. The bridge was built in 1832, and as the old man lived until October, 1841, he had many chances to cross it if he so wished. Mr. Wing further says, "The several roads leading from the main highway to the river had been but private ways, but even the one leading to the ferry had a gate across the upper end, upon which Tom Lloyd, the schoolmaster, had painted the words, "To the Ferry,' but the establishment of a bridge necessitated the laying out of a public way, and to this need the Bridge street of today doubtless owes its origin."

As I have said, the bridge was built in 1832, and the late Peleg P. Akin told me that he was the first to cross it, being carried in the arms of his nurse across a planking. Mr. Wing, in one of his Register articles, gives an interesting account of the old toll-house and also of the present building, which I copy in full, as probably no better account could be written.

"Relegated to a position in the back yard near the river's edge, the original toll-house connected with the Bass river lower bridge now serves as a general storehouse. Its successor, moved a little back from the site occupied by it previous to the time when by action of the state legislature the bridge was made free, is a more pretentious building, which furnished a residence for the toll-keeper. It formerly had an extension of the roof over the side walk. Upon this projecting roof was a large sign giving the rates of toll for all possible combinations of vehicles, passengers and quadrupeds. The first toll-keeper whom I remember was Micajah Baker, who also served in later years as telegraph operator. The toll-house was a favorite resort evenings for men and boys. On three sides of the room were wooden benches which were generally filled, while Mr. Baker occupied a chair tipped back, in the part of the room farthest from the outer door. A stone water pitcher always stood upon the shelf close by, which was exceedingly popular, especially when the tobacco smoke was thicker than usual; Mr. Baker used to declare that boys walked all the way from Provincetown to drink out of that pitcher. The writer well remembers one evening when the pitcher seemed to be neglected more than usual; but the cause was apparent when it was learned that there was no water in it. After a time a schoolmate volunteered to fill it. He took the pitcher, was gone about the usual length of time, returned and set it in its accustomed place. The first one who sampled the contents, made a wry face, quite perceptible to the knowing ones, but said nothing and resumed his seat. The explosion came when the second person stepped forward, and then the fact developed that the pitcher had been filled with salt water from the river. The joke was greatly appreciated, but that boy wasn't asked for a long time to fill the pitcher again. Occasionally, during the long winter evenings, the shrewd boy trader having molasses candy and cornballs for sale came in, and trade in that line was generally lively for a time. As the hour for the coming of the evening mail drew near, the attendance in the room gradually diminished, and when word came of its actual arrival, there was a general rush for the postoffice. David Smith, a Mr. Cahoon and another person whose name I do not now recall served as toll keepers after Mr. Baker."

Of course the river has always entered largely in the life of the village, but even this has changed in the course of years. Bass, which were once plentiful in the river, have long since passed it by, and within my recollection one could catch quantities of bluefish with a hook and line from the banks at the mouth of the river. Clams, quahaugs and oysters were once to be had in return for a little labor; now even the clam is found in small numbers, while the other two are almost strangers. The "oldest inhabitant" can remember when the river was almost devoid of eel-grass that makes it now so shallow, while the salt marshes were not in evidence to a great extent, the shores being clear white sand.

On the street leading to the ferry lived Captain Benjamin Tripp, and his son, Joseph Tripp, lived in one half of the house or in the ell. Captain Tripp commanded the schooner "Polly" and was in the lumber business.

The street beginning at the residence of the late Peleg P. Akin, now owned by his daughter, Mrs. G. W. Tupper, and continuing down to what is known as the "magnesia factory street," was then merely a passage way and was called "Cat alley." On one side was Uncle Zeno's apple orchard, and below the Edward Gifford house were salt works as far as what is now called the "red house," and on the shore were two salt mills, one owned by Edward Gifford and the other by Prince Gifford, his brother.

The Lewis Crowell house came next. The "red house," also known as the "witch house," was built, says Mr. Wing, by Joseph Crandon, generally known as "Old Cran," and sold afterwards to Samuel Farris, great-grandfather of William R. Farris. Captain Isaiah Crowell bought the place in 1808 with a strip of land extending from the river to Main street, the northwesterly portion of which is now owned by the Owl club, the building now their headquarters having been erected in 1827.

An interesting story is told of the porch of the "red house." It seems that in 1812 the owner desired to build a porch as an addition to his house, and sent to New Brunswick for the lumber. When the vessel bringing the lumber reached Chatham it was pursued by a British privateer. The captain ran his vessel ashore and he and his crew escaped in boats. The privateersmen, seeing that the cargo was only lumber, sailed away, having first, however, set fire to the vessel. The captain and crew of the burning vessel, seeing the enemy disappear, returned to it, put out the fire, floated the craft and proceeded on the voyage, delivering the cargo in due time. Some of the timbers were charred, but were used and may be seen to this day if one is inquisitive; at least they were seen by the men who were working upon the house a few years ago. Lewis Crowell lived in this house until he died, and after him, his son, Captain Hatsel Crowell, who was lost at sea. Hatsel had three children; the oldest became a sailor and disappeared, no one ever knowing his fate; the other two grew up and both died of consumption. Since that time the house has had many occupants but at present is the summer residence of Charles D. Voorhis.

Mr. Wood says he well remembers when the Isaiah Crowell house was built, (1839) as he and another boy were sent to Dennis to inform the Friends that there would be a "raising" in the morning and a Friends meeting in the afternoon. It was Isaiah Crowell's grandchild who was the last person to be married in the meeting house. He was captain of a ship in early life, and in the war of 1812 his vessel was captured off St. Johns, Newfoundland, by a British cruiser. He had made several successful voyages previously, which had brought him in a large amount of money, so that, for the days and the place, he was considered a wealthy man. He was for thirty-seven years director of the Yarmouth National bank, and for eighteen years its president. His son, Henry G. Crowell, lived at the old homestead for many years. He was a successful business man in Boston and held many positions of trust under both state and city governments.

Coming back now to the street that runs past the front of the Peleg P. Akin house to Main street, we find that the spot now occupied by the dwelling of Captain Joseph Allen was Uncle Zeno Kelley's apple orchard, and the space was filled with trees, which, as a lady who well remembers them said, were full of pink and white blossoms in the spring time, and she never passes the spot but she seems to see them and smell their fragrance, as she did in the days of long ago. As I have said before, these trees, or those that remain, though very old, still give forth fruit in their season.

Pointing out the house now occupied by C. F. Purrington, Mr. Wood said that when he was a boy it was owned and occupied by Robert Wing, a boat builder. His shop is now Mr. Purrington's woodshed. "The land was bought of David Kelley, senior, in 1810. The frame of the building was originally intended to be erected on the old ferry road in West Dennis." (D. W.) His barn then stood near Main street, nearly opposite the town pump, and was moved to its present location by Mr. Fearing, who owned the place later on. He was a large, stout man of rather genial disposition, I believe. He had a fine garden and grapery in which he took much pride. A man told me that when he was a boy, Uncle Robert hired him to take away a pile of stones from one end of his garden and place them at another spot, and when he had finished the work to the old man's satisfaction, he told him to take them back and place them where he found them; this was his way of helping a boy to earn a little spending money. The house remained in the Wing family for many years, and was at one time the home of Franklin Fearing, who married Maria Wing, a sister of Stephen and Daniel Wing. Mr. Fearing was the proprietor of the magnesia factory, of which I shall have more to say later on. He was a man of more than ordinary education for this section in those days; a man of great intelligence; a man of genial disposition, kind-hearted and a thorough gentleman. He served as a member of the school board for many years.

Opposite the Robert Wing house and next to the orchard was the pump and block shop of Prince Gifford, which was afterwards made over into a dwelling house in which Captain Jonathan Sears lived, and later on Bernard L. Baker, for many years the village postmaster. Prince Gifford was a very stern and austere Quaker with—as was not uncommon with the Friends in those days—but little sympathy for other religious beliefs than his own. It was this rigidness that was, in my opinion, the main reason why the Friends have gradually lost their footing in this country; it did not appeal to the young, and when the religious world became more liberal the Friends found it hard to give way. It is true that they too have grown more liberal, that the Friends do not insist upon the strict observances and penalties of years ago, but the change came too late. And yet after all, to me there are no sweeter memories than those of the old Friends and of their meetings. When Prince Gifford built his shop, he insisted that it should be built close to the line of the orchard and of the sidewalk, and so it was built, as may be seen today. The house next to the shop was built by Uncle Zeno, who lived there for awhile, but it afterwards became the property of Prince Gifford and his children still occupy it.

Next to this house was a little country store kept by Silas Baker and later still by his brother, Braddock Baker.

Next to the store and on the corner of Main street was a small house also built by Uncle Zeno. Afterwards it was purchased by the Methodists for a parsonage, although previously it was owned by David Wood, who was the village blacksmith and whose first shop was near the cellar house, but afterwards he used his barn for the purpose. Mr. Wing recalls his business advertisement, which read somewhat as follows:

"Diamonds of the finest water.
Horses shod on scientific principles
at the shop of David Wood."

He moved to New Bedford and was for many years a letter carrier in that city. Previous to its removal, this house was, according to Mr. Wing, occupied by "Jim Hudson," later by Timothy Akin, David K. Akin and his wife Rachel, Doctor Green, and Silas Baker and his wife Ruth H.

Silas Baker piloted the first steamboat that ever sailed into Boston. It was a sort of scow, with no deck, and wood was used for fuel. Coming from the westward and arriving off Bass river, Captain Baker was taken on board as pilot around the Cape. My own recollections of Silas Baker are not very clear, but I remember his wife, Aunt Ruth, who was the principal speaker at the Friends meeting for a great many years. She was a kindly old lady, and at New Years used to have a liberal supply of cornballs and other tempting things for the children who came to wish her a "happy new year." I can remember seeing her walking to Quaker meeting leaning on the arm of Uncle Silas; and I can remember her speaking in meeting and how I used to watch her as she deliberately untied her Quaker bonnet of drab, passed it to the one sitting next to her, and then rising and in a voice of remarkable clearness spoke the words that came to her mind. I remember that she very often had something to say to "my dear young friends." I recall them all now,—Aunt Betsey Akin, Aunt Rhoda Wing, Aunt Tamsen Gifford, and afterwards Aunt Lizzie Stetson,— as they sat upon the "high seats." To me there were never such beautiful women to look upon, excepting my own mother; they always gave me the impression that they indeed communed with God. We have all remarked the beautiful countenances of the Sisters of Charity that we have seen upon the streets; they may not have regular features, they may not possess the physical lines of beauty, but there is something in their faces that makes one think them beautiful; and that was the impression upon my young mind when looking at those older women of the Friends in their quaint but becoming attire. I could not tell you why it was so, but the impression has always remained in my memory.

To the outsider, the men of the Quaker meeting always appeared stern and sedate, but they were by no means free from the spirit of life and enjoyed their jokes and bits of humor as well as anyone. They were just, but sharp in business and generally got the best of a bargain. At the same time, they were full of kindness and hospitality and I think this world, bounded by the limits of South Yarmouth, was better, morally and socially, at that time than it will ever be again.

Before leaving the house of Silas Baker, later the property of Mrs. Sarah Bray, I wish to speak of Aunt Fanny Whelden, a relative of Aunt Ruth's who lived with her many years. Aunt Fanny was what many call a "shouting Methodist," and seemed to enjoy her religion in proportion to the noise she could make in expressing her feelings. Undoubtedly she was a very excitable woman by nature and found in this way an escapement valve for her pent up feelings. I have sometimes thought that living in a quiet Quaker family was too much for her and that after repressing her emotions for a whole week she let them flow forth at the regular Sunday night prayer meetings. I well remember her as an old woman, going to meeting in winter with her foot stove in one hand and a huge muff and cane or umbrella in the other. She sat in one of the side pews near the pulpit and was always present at prayer meetings, for in those days there were preaching services morning and afternoon and prayer meeting in the evening on the Sabbath. At these latter services Aunt Fanny was in her element and her "amen!" and "bless the Lord!" were interjected at all times. I am sorry to say that those of the younger generation saw much to smile at, and I suppose I was not any better than the other unregenerates, who did not understand that it was simply her way of expressing her joy and happiness. One of her favorite expressions was "Praise be to God!" and one evening while she was speaking some young people, unable to restrain their mirth, left the church, whereupon Aunt Fanny, pointing her finger at them, cried out, "There they go, straight to hell! Praise be to God!"

Going back to "Cat alley" and to the new house built by Isaiah Crowell, we find but three houses on the street leading to Main street, the first being that occupied by the Owl club, which was built in 1827 by Daniel Wing, senior, the father of the present Daniel Wing. The ell of the house has been raised since those days, and the present social hall of the Owl club was formerly a barn. Daniel Wing, senior, was born in East Sandwich in 1800. He was the youngest of ten children of whom four have lived in South Yarmouth, viz.: Rose, wife of Zeno Kelley, Robert, George and Daniel. Daniel came to South Yarmouth in 1823 or 24 and tended salt works. In later years he associated himself with Silas Baker under the firm name of Baker & Wing and was interested in several fishing vessels that fitted out from Bass river. They also carried on the business of general country store in the building between the Prince Gifford house and that of Silas Baker. He was a very popular man in his day and had many friends. He died in 1842.

Mr. Wing gives the following description of the country store spoken of above:

"They dealt in grain and must have had the usual difficulty in getting back sundry bags iohned to customers, for a notice posted in this store by a young clerk, Joseph Dudley by name, ran as follows:

'No bags to lend; no bags to let;
You need not tease; you need not fret;
You need not twist; you need not wring;
For you'll get no bags from Baker & Wing.'

This clerk, who was quite a mechanical genius, devised a plan for keeping loafers from sitting on the dry goods counter, which was at once original, unique and decidedly effective. Certain needles connected with levers were concealed below the field of action, and the apparatus could be set in motion by a person sitting at a desk near the front window."

Opposite the Daniel Wing house is one now occupied by Frank L. Baker. When Mr. Wood was a boy, Doctor Green, one of the two physicians of the place, lived there, and I am of the impression that he built it. He used to go about the country on horse back, his medicines in his saddle bags, and was a most popular physician and man, I should imagine from what I have been able to learn. The house afterwards came into the possession of Loren Baker and later still into the hands of his son, A. H. Baker, a man of whom those who knew him will always have the kindest of memories.

Between this house and that of David K. Akin, Mr. Wood told me, used to stand the little schoolhouse maintained by the Friends, although previously it stood on the land now occupied by Captain Whittemore (formerly Elisha Taylor's). Among the teachers were H. P. Akin, Rebecca Akin, Mary Davis, Sylvia G. Wing and Elizabeth Sears. I remember the little building when it stood on the road leading to the magnesia factory. It was afterwards taken by Peleg P. Akin and used in the making of additions to his house. I do not know whether there are any photographs of the little building in existence, but it was very small with an entry on the front, and I should imagine could not contain more than twenty-five pupils at the most.

On the corner of the street, facing Pleasant street which runs now to the lower village but at that time only as far as the house of Orlando Baker. stood and still stands the residence of the late David K. Akin, (now the property of Captain Joseph M. Lewis) a staunch old Quaker and a man for those days of wealth and

—OLD QUAKER VILLAGE—

importance. He was president of the Yarmouth National bank for many years and one who commanded the respect and trust of the community. As his residence was next to that of my father's, I have most vivid recollections of him as a kindly, genial gentleman, who was always a warm friend of all the members of my father's family. I have previously spoken of the little jewelry store that he kept on the street leading to the collar house, which building is now standing on Bridge street. I have most interesting recollections of a pear tree that stood in his garden, near to the line of my father's fence, which, when I was a boy, was loaded down with tempting fruit, which he liberally gave to me from time to time.

His son, Peleg P. Akin, lived in the Zeno Kelley house on the road leading to the ferry, where he died in January, 1903. The present generation is familiar with his life and it is not necessary for me to insert any eulogies of him in this place. He was a man of a naturally retiring disposition, never coveting honors, and yet never shirking the duties of public trusts thrust upon him. The savings bank of the place owes much to his fidelity and because of the fact that the depositors had the utmost confidence in his word. It was not his money that made people speak well of Peleg P. Akin; it was the worth of the man and the man himself.

Opposite the house of David K. Akin was and is an open field, and at the lower end, near the river, was a public "pound" in which were put stray cattle, but that disappeared years ago, as there were no cattle to put in it, but in those days there were large droves of cows that were driven to different places for pasturage; one place in particular I remember being "old field," formerly called "Kelley's Neck," in West Dennis. Every morning a boy collected the cows from different parts of the village and drove them over to that place and every night went for them, always finding the cows patiently waiting at the gate to be driven home.

Before leaving the David K. Akin house I would speak of three negroes who were at one time brought from the South by this old Friend and who for years lived in South Yarmouth. Eli and Noah Morgan and their cousin, Dempsey Ragsdale, were slaves, whom their master wished to set free. (This was of course before the war.) David Akin brought them North and took charge of the two Morgan boys, who were at that time 16 or 18 years of age, while David Kelley took Dempsey, who was nearly white. They all attended school in the village, made rapid progress in their studies, and at length started out to make their own ways in the world. Dempsey went to sea and from what I can learn, was soon lost to view; Eli became master of a vessel, and Noah went into business in New Bedford, and both became men who were greatly respected wherever they were known. Previous to this, David K. Akin had taken into his house a young colored girl named Lizzie Hill, who was a great favorite with everyone who knew her. She grew up with the other young people and in later life married and went as a missionary to Africa, where she died.

The next house to David K. Akin's was that of Elisha Jenkins. This house was probably built by Cyrenus Kelley, at least it was of him that my father bought it. It is with some hesitation that I write of my father, as my account might be tinged and biased by the deep affection I have for his memory, but in another place I shall take the liberty of inserting one of Mr. Daniel Wing's letters to The Register, that, coming from one outside the family, may be taken for an honest opinion of my father as a man and as a citizen. He was born in West Barnstable, and in his early life worked at his trade in the South, but eventually drifted to South Yarmouth, where he set up the business of shoemaking. He married Mary G. Crowell of West Yarmouth; her two sisters, Sophie and Harriet, married South Yarmouth men, and the three houses or homes were on the same street. In his early days my father was considered an excellent singer; he was always very fond of music, and it is from him that I get my taste for the same art. Both my father and mother were exceedingly fond of reading, which taste was handed down to all of the children.

I have only one story to tell of my father, which I heard from my mother:

One winter's day a man came home with him to stop all night. I do not recall his name, but I think he was one of the many who had worked for my father. Anyway, he was going out to join the Mormons and evidently hoped to secure a convert. He and my father sat up all night discussing and arguing religious questions, while at the same time, the guest was trying to convince his host of the truth of the new doctrine and urging him to leave all, go with him and become a Latter-Day Saint. "And that," said my mother, "is as near as we came to becoming Mormons." Not very near, for I fancy that my father did not get the worst of the argument.

Nearly opposite my father's house was that of Captain Emery

Sears, according to Mr. Wood, which later on became the property of Zeno Baker. Mr. Wood could tell me no particulars of Captain Sears, but I recall Zeno Baker very well. He was a man of excellent education and in winter, when he did not go to sea, he taught school. He taught in the present building, in the old red schoolhouse, in Dennis and other places, and was, for those days, an excellent teacher of the commoner branches. He was also a superior penman and the pages of the secretary's records when he was on the school board are beautifully written.

I remember two stories he used to tell of his experiences as a teacher; one was of a note he received from the parent of one of the pupils, which read:

"plcs smiss Mary to recis."

The other was of a boy who had two brothers, Coley and Luke. One day they were all absent, and the next day upon being questioned as to the reason, the boy replied, "Coley, Luke and I, sir, we stayed home from school, sir, 'cause Sally had a sore toe, sir." But why Sally's infirmity should prevent the boys from attending to business I never learned.

It was from a tree in the corner of the lot next to Zeno Baker's that all the so-called "silver leafs" came. I think the original was brought from Maine. We acknowledge they are often a nuisance, but at the same time what would the village have been without them? They are handsome trees, they grow rapidly, they have done much to beautify our streets; we wanted just such a tree, but we did not want so much of them.

Next to Zeno Baker's was the house of George Wing, a brother of Robert and Daniel Wing, senior, now the property of Mrs. Chase. Its appearance then was much like that of its neighbors. At one time it was occupied by Joseph Howland, who came from New Bedford, believing that one could find peace and an absence of temptation in a village of Quakers.

Then came the house of James Davis, recently moved nearer the river and changed beyond recognition of its former self. He had an adopted daughter, Amelia D. Russell; a son, Russell Davis, and a son, William P. Davis, for many years cashier of the First National bank of Yarmouth. Russell Davis was one of those eccentric people who are found in every country village. He was known as "Lord Russ," and stories told of his eccentricities would fill a book. In appearance he was short and thick set, with a merry, laughing face and the rolling gait of a sailor. He was an old bachelor, but report said that he had had his romance like most others. After the death of his father he built himself a house in the fields near the river, half way between the upper and lower villages. The living room was decorated or papered with pictures cut from magazines and illustrated papers, which were not inartistically arranged or grouped. In one corner of the room was his berth or bunk, similar to those on board ship, for although he had never been to sea, he delighted in everything pertaining to it, and in his leisure hours fashioned some of the most beautiful of miniature ships. He was a great reader; one might say of him that he devoured books, often sitting up all night to finish a story that particularly pleased him. One of his peculiarities was to imagine himself a poet, and as the result, he wrote so called poems without number. Unfortunately, he had no idea of rhyme or rhythm, which at times resulted in making his effusions rather amusing reading. He was always ready to read them at the meetings of the "Lyceum" and they were published in the local papers from time to time, which gratified his pride and really hurt no one.

Across the road from the James Davis house was that of Orlando Baker, which Mr. Wing considers as one of the oldest in the place, 116 years at date of writing. According to Mr. Wing, it was built by Michael Crowell, and conveyed to Benoni Baker and his uncle, Obed Baker, in 1799, the former of whom lived there when he was first married. Michael Crowell was in active business in 1792. He was an uncle of Lewis Crowell and lived in a hollow between Captain Zeno Baker's and the river. He also owned the tract between Main street and the river and between the town landing and a line not far from the old magnesia street. Lewis Crowell lived there before he moved to the "red house." Orlando Baker's garden came across the present street leading to the lower village, for Pleasant street ended at his garden and the street leading to the magnesia factory. His farm sheds were down that street on the other side of his garden. He was one of the original members and a pillar of the Methodist church; a man who lived, to the best of his ability, upright before God and man; more than that none of us can do.

Between the two houses of Orlando Baker and Elisha Jenkins, who by the way, married sisters, was an open piece of land just wide enough for a building and Elisha Taylor of West Yarmouth, who also married a sister, purchased the same and built the house now owned by Captain James L. Whittemore. 'Squire Taylor, as he was called, never did any manual labor in his life; his father

—OLD QUAKER VILLAGE—

left him a little money and by a life of almost penurious saving he accumulated a fair fortune, the income of which supported him and his wife. For many years he was a victim of the "shaking palsy," which affected both his limbs and his speech, so that it was almost impossible for a stranger to understand a word he said. In his younger days he was considered a man of sound judgment and just. He served the town as selectman for twenty-six years, which showed that his townspeople appreciated his worth, or else showed that in those days there was no great desire for office, and considering that there was no money in it and very little glory, it is not to be wondered at that men were kept in office for a quarter of a century. A position of that kind in these days carries with it precious little glory, but the financial reward is by no means small in proportion to the amount of work it entails.

Leading from the Orlando Baker house was a road to the river, and at the foot of it was the magnesia factory, but not in Mr. Wood's boyhood days, for it was not built until 1850. The first factory was burned two years later and then the second structure was erected by its owner, Franklin Fearing. After his death the Wing brothers carried on the business for a time, but the rapid diminishing of the salt works made it impractical to continue it and the building was taken down.

From this point until we come to the place where now stands the summer residence of Freeman C. Goodeno, there were no dwellings, excepting upon the main street. All the land was covered with salt works, which business, as far as South Yarmouth is concerned, must have begun about 1811, according to estimates made by Mr. Wing, although the making of salt by solar evaporation dates back to 1776, and in 1802, according to the reports of the Massachusetts Historical society, over forty thousand bushels of salt were thus made on Cape Cod, several, years before South Yarmouth had built its first vat. In 1837, 365,000 bushels of salt were manufactured in the town of Yarmouth valued at $110,000, so that it can be easily seen that when the industry got fairly on its feet it increased rapidly and was a financial success.

From the house of Selim Baker (now Osborne White's) to the house of Hatsel Crosby, there were no houses, but a large area of salt works extended to the river, not to mention many other "stretches" of works farther down, even to the lower village and on the other side of Main street clear to the woods. It was—or rather would be today—a novel sight: those long lines of covered vats containing salt water in various stages of evaporation, while

—OLD QUAKER VILLAGE—

on the shores were at one time eight mills, whirling and pumping water from the river.

It is a great pity that a few of the salt works and at least one mill could not have been preserved. Few have any idea of the picturesqueness of the river at that time; artists were not long in finding it out and for awhile they were often seen in this region. Then came the era for improving things, and, as is generally the case; the improvements have cost far more than could ever be realized at the time. The actual value of an old mill as a marketable piece of property was not great, but its value in attracting people to the village and in making it something different from other villages was untold. The salt works were a never-failing source of pleasure to the boys; they furnished "slides," to the detriment of one's clothes; they furnished fascinating places to play robbers and pirates; the "coolers" in which salt was handled made splendid canoes, and there were almost a thousand and one entertainments that the salt works and the surroundings furnished.

Having made our tour of the side streets of the village, we come back to the corner of Main and Bridge streets. On the Long pond road, the left hand side going to Yarmouth, was the house of Amos Farris, but on the right hand side there was nothing but pine woods down to the house of David Chubb; then we came to the house of James Covill (later Isaiah), where Sidney Chapman now lives.

Next to it was Reuben Farris's house. He was the miller. It is a low one story house, with a kitchen that goes the whole length of it, and other smaller rooms on the same floor. It was thought in those days that the kitchen was the principal and most important part of the house, and in some respects it is still. Uncle Reuben was a Universalist, and naturally in a community of Friends and Methodists he was not religiously at home, so when the Universalist church was built in South Dennis he attended services there. The next tenant of the house was his son Samuel, who also succeeded him as miller, and later on his grandson, William R., lived there for a number of years.

The next house, that of Mrs. R. D. Farris, was not built until 1856, and the store not until 1866. R. D. Farris was, in the earlier days, a successful merchant. He learned the trade of harness maker of Benjamin Hallett in Yarmouth, the old shop now being next to A. Alden Knowles's store, I believe, and used by Mr. Knowles as a carriage house or barn. His first store or shop was a little building now used by Mrs. Phoebe Farris as a woodhouse.

He gradually added tinware, stoves, etc., and finally groceries. He was naturally a trader, being shrewd and watchful to keep up with the various changes. His first wife was Mercy Easton, and, as he has often told, they went to housekeeping in one room of his father's house. Later on he built the Mrs. Phoebe Farris house and later still the one next to the store.

At the head of Bridge street on Main, was a house occupied by Richard Kelley and later by the Widow Hovey, who kept a boarding house, and later still by William Crocker, Loren Baker and then by Braddock Baker, whose heirs owned it until it was bought by Abiel Howard, torn down and the present house erected. Braddock Baker kept the general store previously run by Baker & Wing. He was a short, heavy man, with stooping shoulders which impressed him firmly in my boyhood mind. He was one of the original members of the Methodist church, and undoubtedly did much to put it on its feet when it was young and struggling. I can remember that both he and his wife were speakers at the prayer meetings, and I also remember that when I was a boy, on being sent to his store in the morning and not finding him in, I would go to his house and generally find him at family prayers. My errand or presence never shortened the service, and I had to wait until the last verse had been read and the last "amen" said. He had several children, among them Darius Baker, judge of the Supreme court of Rhode Island, who at one time was my school teacher. One little thing I remember in connection with the Judge was that one day I took up a volume of Shakespeare which he had been reading, and being too young to know anything of the merits of the great bard, although a book of any kind possessed a fascination for me, I asked if it was "good." He turned to me and said very impressively, "We do not speak of Shakespeare as 'good'; it is very interesting." That was a lesson for me, and I never forgot it.

In the late Mrs. Delyra Wood's house lived William Farris, father of Allen Farris, who lived farther down the street. His wife, Aunt Liddy, was a large woman, a good, motherly soul, who was one of the greatest talkers I have ever known. She would come over to my mother's house as far as the door, in too much of a hurry to come in, and there she would stand and talk for half or three-quarters of an hour. Her daughter, also named Liddy, and wife of Zeno Baker, was one of the smartest women to work and one of the kindest of neighbors. I shall never forget Aunt Liddy Baker, for she spanked me for stealing her pears, and strange to say, my mother whipped me for the same offense when I got home!

The present Methodist church is but little over sixty years old, so that we can hardly speak of it as "old." It was not standing when Mr. Wood was a boy, and was built after I was born, so we will simply say it is growing old.

But in the yard or enclosure leading to the present schoolhouse there was a building, "the little red schoolhouse," the old district schoolhouse, which now stands back of the bank and is used as a storehouse. Here Mr. Wood went to school; here Mr. Wing went to school, to Zeno Baker as teacher. Mr. Wood remembers David Kelley as his teacher at one time, and Sophia Crocker of West Barnstable. The curriculum was not extended, but the "three Rs" were well taught and the ground work well laid for a higher education if the pupil was ambitious to go farther than the district school could take him. Spelling schools and spelling contests were popular in those days, and the old schoolhouse witnessed many an exciting time in such diversions.

The present schoolhouse, built in 1855, ended the usefulness of the old building, which was removed to another location and used for more ignoble purposes. The marks of the seats, the depressions in the floor, the names written on the plastering, are still there. The fiftieth anniversary of the opening of the present schoolhouse took place in June, 1905, and was participated in by all the pupils of the public schools of the town.

The house of Zenas Wood, in which his son, Orlando Wood, lived during the last years of his life, stood next to the schoolhouse grounds, and was built by Moses Burgess. He came from West Barnstable, worked at his trade, that of a carpenter, and built for himself this house. Later, he moved back to his old home. Orlando F. Wood was a notable example of a young old-man. He was born in the village in 1825 in a house that stood upon the spot now occupied by the paint shop of Manton H. Crowell. As a boy he attended school in the little old red schoolhouse which stood on the present school grounds, at the little Friends' schoolhouse which stood on land of the late David K. Akin, between his house and that now occupied by Frank L. Baker, and at the "academy." He went to sea when a boy, the principal incident of which was that he fell from aloft and narrowly escaped death. He worked in the "rope-walk" and later learned the tailor's trade in South Yarmouth, which trade he practised in New Bedford and Boston, eventually returning to his native village, where he lived until his death in 1911, at the age of 86.

—OLD QUAKER VILLAGE—

Next to the Zenas Wood house stood the shoe shop of Elisha Jenkins, my father, and it is to Mr. Wing that I am indebted for the following, which was published in the Yarmouth Register: "The shoe store now owned and occupied by Mr. E. T. Baker and situated on Main street, is an enlargement of the long, low building where, some years ago, shoes were both made and sold. At one time a number of young shoemakers from Lynn were employed there. They were full of fun and frolic, and in those days of practical jokes, if a neighbor's horse was found in the morning, gaily striped with bright colors, or if some sailor man was unable to open any of his outwardly swinging doors because of a chain cable passed entirely around his house and attached to an anchor set deep in the lot on the opposite side of the street, the mischief was quite likely to be charged to the shoe-shop employes.

"So far back, however, as the memory of the writer reaches, Elisha Jenkins was the proprietor and sole occupant. A man of more than ordinary intellectual power, a deep thinker, possessed of a wonderful memory, a reader of good books, a lover of history, intensely patriotic, fond of young people, instructive in conversation, the writer will always feel indebted to him for the pleasure of many an hour spent in his company. All through the Civil war, when news of more than ordinary interest was expected, the arrival of the evening mail would almost invariably find an attractive audience assembled at his shop, listening with breathless interest as some one read aloud the latest news from the seat of war.

"I can see now the rack of lasts at one end of the room, with a wooden bench in front of it; cases of boots (long-legged ones) standing here and there; the cobbler's bench of the proprietor in the southwest corner, with its depressed seat and its square compartments for wooden pegs, iron nails, shoemaker's wax, bundles of bristles, and its usual assortment of awls, hammers, etc., while the drawer beneath contained pieces of leather and supplies of sundry sorts.

"The Thanksgiving proclamation of Governor George N. Briggs with 'God save the Commonwealth of Massachusetts' in bold type at the bottom, hung on the south wall for years and seemed to become one of the fixtures of the place. The wooden post in the centre of the room, close by the wood burning stove, was used when a customer came in and ordered a new pair of boots or shoes to be made expressly for him. With his heel against the post, the length of the foot was marked on the floor with a knife. Close by was the tub of water in which the pieces of leather were soaked to make them pliable. The north room contained a stock of boots, shoes and rubbers, mostly arranged upon shelves on two of the side walls. Congress boots were unknown to the earlier times, and as a boy, the writer can remember with what pleasure he went there each autumn to be fitted to a pair of long-legged boots, having square patches of red morocco at the top in front, and with a stout strap on either side of each. No costlier pair since has ever quite equalled in splendor those specimens of long ago. Such were some of the attractions for a boy; the features which in later years made deepest impressions upon the memory were the conversations with the genial proprietor."

Ebenezer Hallett's house and tannery stood on the spot where now stands the house of Reuben K. Farris. It was a low, double house, and back of it was a tannery. Later on, Leonard Underwood, a Friend, purchased it and the tannery was discontinued. He was a carpenter and lived there but a few years, moving to Fall River. When the house was torn down Allen Farris built the large double house still standing.

There was nothing in the way of buildings until we came to "Mill lane." The Isaiah Homer house had not at that time been moved from Yarmouth, but there were two houses on the northeasterly side of the lane. One of these was occupied by Samuel Eaton Kelley, and was afterwards moved to the corner of Main street, and is now the home of Captain Alonzo Kelley; the other is still standing and was occupied by James Covill and others.

Isaiah Homer moved from Yarmouth and was one of our most respected of citizens. He had a little shoe shop in one corner of his yard on Main street and there he worked for years. He was a man who, even in his old age, showed remarkable powers of physical endurance and I have often watched him with admiration as he walked off as smartly and lightly as would a much younger man; there was no sign of physical decrepitude. He was born on the North side in an old house that was undoubtedly the first church built in Yarmouth, that is, the framework was the same if nothing else: it is known now as the "Hannah Crowell house" and is one of the historical relics on the north side of the town. The family possesses many old relics of the Homer family, but none of them more curious than a bill of sale of a negro, dated Feb. 20, 1776. In it F. W. Homer acknowledges receiving from his father, Benjamin Homer, forty pounds for two-thirds of a negro named

"Forten." According to the late Charles F. Swift, "Forton" lived to see his race declared free.

On the opposite side of Mill lane, on the corner, lived Josiah Baker, James Lewis, "Uncle Levi" and others. Of these and their families I have nothing to say.

The old grist mill that stood at the head of the lane was run in Mr. Wood's early days by Reuben Farris and in my early days by Samuel Farris, his son, and by Homoglo Lewis. It was originally on the north side of the Cape and was moved to its present location in 1782. The people of South Yarmouth made a great mistake when they allowed it to be sold and taken from the village. It is now in West Yarmouth on the land of the late Mr. Abell and attracts much attention from visitors from all parts of the country. A similar mill stands in the lower village.

Coming to the house now occupied by Ernest P. Baker, Mr. Wood said, "In my day old Cato, a negro, had a small house on that lot, in which he lived with his daughter. His wife was a full-blooded Indian, and at one time they had a wigwam on the land which was the garden of David K. Akin, and next to the house of Elisha Jenkins." Alden, in his "Memorabilia of Yarmouth," speaks of old Cato as living in a wigwam there in 1797, and he also says that in 1779 there was a small cluster of wigwams about a mile from the mouth of Bass river. According to Mr. Wing, Cato was living in 1831.

Daniel Weaver's house (now Mrs. Matilda Smith's), was then standing. He was a weaver by name and by trade, and wove carpets, probably the once favorite rag carpet. I thought it was he, but have since been corrected, who invented a perpetual motion machine, which he exhibited to a select company in the academy. The company assembled, the machine was produced, but somehow it refused to work; the exhibition was a failure and the machine went the way of thousands of similar inventions.

I do not know how old the Homan Crowell house is, which when Mr. Wing was a boy was occupied by Minerva Crowell, who had three children; Laban Baker owned the other half of the house.

The Frank Homer house was occupied by John Cannon and by Venny Crowell, grandfather of the late Mrs. Henry Taylor. It is related that it was here that his son, Venny Crowell, met his wife. She was passing through the village and stopped to get a glass of water; the son saw her, and afterwards married her. Both father and son were tall, spare men of rugged frames and great endurance. Once upon a time, at a revival meeting, one of the women exhorters and. singers asked Uncle Venny if he did not like music? He was honest, and replied that he liked singing but he hated to hear it murdered!

In the present house of Mrs. Albert White, although now much changed of course, lived Dr. Apollos Pratt, an eccentric old country practitioner. The stories told of the old man are without number, many of them very amusing. He had two daughters; one became the wife of Captain Soleck H. Matthews, and the other the wife of Freeman Matthews. The doctor was given to telling wonderful yarns; among others, he told of a patient of his who had been given up as incurable, but he disemboweled him, killed a sheep and substituted the intestines, and the man got well. On being asked how it seemed to affect the man afterwards, he said, in no way particularly, except that "he had a h——l of a hankering for grass!" One evening while talking with one of his familiars, they agreed to see who could tell the biggest lie. The other man said he could see the man in the moon. "Well," said the doctor, as he gazed earnestly at the sky, "I can see him wink;" which certainly required the better eyesight. Mr. Wood said he had frequently seen the old man sitting in a rocking chair by the window, the floor being worn in ridges where he had rocked back and forth, year after year. He died in 1860, aged 83 years.

On a short street in the vicinity of the present Standish hall was a little house belonging to Ormond Easton, which was later moved to the river opposite the magnesia factory, and was known as the "Noah Morgan house."

There was no house from Dr. Pratt's to that of Barnabas Sears, the space being filled with salt works. The Isaiah Crocker house was not built then nor was that of David Sears.

The Barnabas Sears house, according to Mr. Wing, originally stood in a field near James pond and was built by Ebenezer Baker. It was moved to its present location in 1753 by John Kelley, senior. This is the second oldest house in the village; its curved rafters, low eves and ancient appearance make it an object of great interest to visitors. Barnabas Sears had five sons: Seth, who died while a young man, John, Stephen, Barnabas and David, all of whom lived near the old homestead, and for years his daughter, Elizabeth Stetson, lived in the house. Aunt Lizzie, as she was called, was the last of the Quaker preachers of the South Yarmouth meeting, and to hear her prayers brought me as near the throne of God as I ever expect to be in this world. Her words were earnest and simple, but her very earnestness, and her firm belief that her words were heard by the Father, impressed me greatly. She was a large woman, and tall, almost masculine in many ways, and when she was a girl it is said that she was equal to any man in riding a horse or managing one. Of her the following story is told:

When she was a young woman, she was riding through the woods one day when she came upon a minister leading his horse from the blacksmith's. "Why don't thee ride thy horse instead of leading him?" she asked. "Because," said the minister, "he won't allow me to put the bridle over his head, and he bites and kicks so I am afraid of him." "Give it to me," she said, with a look of contempt at his ignorance, and jumping from her horse she whipped off her apron and flinging it over the horse's head deftly adjusted the bridle. "There, friend, a little brains used intelligently may be useful in other ways than in writing sermons," she said. "True," replied the minister, "but unfortunately, I do not wear aprons."

Although the houses of the sons of Barnabas Sears were not in existence seventy-five years ago, they were men who were looked up to in the community. Barnabas, Jr., and John K. were carpenters and builders, and at one time they had a steam sawmill back of their house near the woods, called the "Pawkunnawkut mill." Stephen was for many years a teacher, and served the town as selectman and as school committee. David, "Uncle David" as most of us called him, was one of the most genial souls among us and needs no words of introduction to those for whom these pages are written.

The next house from Barnabas Sears, senior, was that now occupied by Charles I. Gill, who purchased it from the estate of Reuben J. Baker. Mr Baker, familiarly known as "Blind Reuben" because of his loss of eyesight when a boy, was the son of Captain Reuben Baker, whose wife, Louisa, afterwards married William Gray. In many respects he was a remarkable man, for in spite of his blindness he carried on a successful grocery business for years.

Next to this house was that of Captain Freeman Baker. Mr. Wing says that opposite this house, in the middle of the main road, was a house belonging to the Widow Marchant, the travelled roadway passing on either side.

The Baptist church was then standing, but it bore no resemblance to the church of today. It stood with its eaves to the street and had no belfry or steeple. It bore no evidence of paint without and was very plain within, as plain as the Friends meeting house. Aunt Lizzie Stetson named it "The Lord's barn." Mr. Wing has this to say of it:

"At times there was no regular service there, but the young people of the village nearby could count with a certainty upon the annual temperance meeting as long as Barnabas Sears, senior, was living, for his interest in the temperance cause was deep and abiding, as indeed it was in the religious society of which he was a devoted member. Either side of each aisle was a row of old-fashioned pews with high backs. The pulpit was a long, box-like affair, some two and a half or three feet above the floor level, with steps leading up to it on its righthand corner. A door at the head of the steps kept out those not eligible to that enclosure, and a seat along the front of the pulpit was known as the "deacon's seat." The pews at the lefthand side of the pulpit faced the front of the building, while those in the opposite corner faced the pulpit. A lot of lighted tallow candles placed in different parts of the room did their best to overcome the natural darkness of the place, and when with blackened wicks hanging to one side they seemed ready to give up the task, the ever-watchful Father Sears, even then an old man, would go around with a candle snuffer and carefully remove the charred portions of the wicks and so brighten up the place until his services in that line were again needed.

"Father Sears was a thoughtful, earnest man, highly respected by both old and young, and although his quaint language would provoke a smile, it was not a token of disrespect, but often of pleasure, caused by the reviving of features that all realized were rapidly passing away. On one occasion, when some of the smaller portion of the audience became somewhat restless and began to leave the room, Mr. Sears stopped the exercises and in his usually dignified manner said, "All those who want for to go out will go out, and all those who want for to stay in will stay in." I think there was no more passing out until the close of the meeting, and the quaint language and impressive manner remain in my memory as a pleasing feature of the occasion.

"The Baptist church in South Yarmouth was organized in 1824. The structure itself dates back to the year 1826, when it was built at a cost of $600, the whole amount being paid by Rev. Simeon Crowell and Captain Freeman Baker, the former being the first pastor there."

In 1860 extensive alterations were made in it, and in 1891 it was again remodeled and put in its present shape. Mr Wood spoke of the church as "Uncle Sim's church," and says that he attended Sunday school there and that Lurania Lewis was his teacher.

He also attended Sunday school at the old Methodist meeting house which stood farther up the road towards West Yarmouth, and of which the only present reminder is the cemetery. This church, which Mr. Wood calls "Uncle Siley's church," was built by Silas Baker, senior, who came from Harwich. He died in 1844, aged 78 years. In a measure, Uncle Siley ran the church to suit himself during his life, as, having built it, he thought he had the right to do. The Rev. Mr. Winchester was the preacher and Elisha Parker was Mr. Wood's Sunday school teacher. The worshippers who came from any distance brought their luncheons and made it an all-day duty. On one occasion Mr. Wood had his lunch stolen from the pew, which awful crime he remembered all his life, for he had to go hungry. The choir was in the long gallery at the back of the church, and a big bass viol was the accompaniment for the singers.

There were two little schoolhouses a little way below or beyond the church; one of them near the residence of Jerry Eldridge, the other I cannot place, but they were not more than a hundred yards apart.

Returning up Main street on the opposite side, Mr. Wood said there were no houses until we get to that of Mrs. Cyrus White, formerly occupied by her father, Captain Barnabas Eldridge, who died in 1846, aged 46 years, and then a long strip of field land until we came to the little old house that was always known as "the old maids'." The occupants of the house were known as "the three old maids" although two of them had been married. Robert Homer married one of them after a courtship of forty years, and it is said that he remarked that he wished he had courted forty years longer. These old ladies had very amusing ways and were the victims of many practical jokes at the hands of ungodly boys. On one occasion they were routed out of bed in the middle of the night by some young men who asked if they had seen a red and white cow pass that way. They had not, and the young men were advised to go over to "Brother Freeman's and ask him." The young men retired, the door was shut and the old ladies presumably had returned to their beds, when again came loud rappings at the door; another procession from the bedrooms, and there stood the same young men, who said that they thought they would come back and tell them that "Brother Freeman" had not seen the cow!

I have thought it a great pity that those old ladies could not have sought comfort in a few swear words. When the last of this trio died, the contents of the house were sold at auction and among other things an old bureau, in the lining of which the purchaser found a $100 check which proved to be good and was collected.

The present building of Mrs. Sturgess Crowell was then standing, occupied by Captain Elisha Baker, as was the house occupied by Elisha T. Baker. Of the latter, Mr. Wood said that he remembered that Solomon Crowell had a little dry goods store in one of the front rooms; later it became the property of Mrs. Baker's father, Captain Frederick White.

Then we come to the old house known as "Major Dimmick's," formerly owned by Major D. Baker, "Major" being his name and not his title as one might infer. Old Uncle Amos Baker lived there, but what relation he was to Major I do not know.

The house of Peter Goodnow was not standing, but his father had a house by the river exactly upon the spot where is now the summer residence of his grandson, Freeman C. Goodnow.

The Hatsel Crosby house was built with the front door on the side, the carpenter, Job Otis of New Bedford, who drew the plans, having the idea that Main street ran north and south ordered the front door on the south side, supposing that it really would be facing Main street and upon the front side of the house. It was built by Uncle Russell Davis, who lived there with his wife Phoebe. He was a brother of James Davis, and a Quaker preacher. Hatsel Crosby came from Brewster and went into the salt making business. He married several times and had a large family of children, none of whom, however, live in South Yarmouth. He died in 1890, aged 89 years.

From this point to the house of Selim Baker the section was given up to salt works, and all of the houses on this side of the street are comparatively new. Selim Baker's house was built some years before the salt works were taken down. He was a carpenter by trade, a man prominent in church affairs and much respected. His daughter, Mrs. Osborne White, lives in the house, which has been greatly changed.

The Academy came next; it sat well back from the street. It had a belfry and a bell—the only school building in South Yarmouth that ever did—and was quite an imposing looking structure. It was built in 1844 and owned by the citizens of the place, and was used as a private school, the idea of its promoters being to furnish better educational facilities for their children than could be found at the district school. That its reputation during its short career was high was shown by the fact that a large number of pupils came from away. It ceased to exist as a school when the present public schoolhouse was opened in 1855, and was converted into a dwelling house in 1862, after having been moved close to the street, by the father of the present Zenas P. Howes. Mr. Alonzo Tripp was the first teacher, and Mr. Adams the last.

The house formerly belonging to Mrs. Elisha Parker and now to the heirs of Benjamin Homer, was built by William P. Davis, but he did not live in it many years; for he accepted a position in the Yarmouth National bank and was cashier of that institution from 1875 to 1895. He also was town treasurer for over fifty years. Elisha Parker, who bought the house of him, was then living in the lower village. He was at one time in the shoe business, and later during the Civil war was very successful in the wool business.

The next house was that of Aunt Mima Wood, which stood near the spot where now stands the house formerly occupied by Dr. E. M. Parker. She was the widow of Tilson Wood, and her son David used to wheel her to Friends meeting in a wheelbarrow; she died in 1841. Frank Wood built the present house. He was a stone mason, and did the stone work on the abutments of the Bass river bridge, and split the stone for the foundations of his own house from boulders on Town Hills. He died in 1853, aged 56.

We now come to the place from which we started, the corner of Main and Bridge street. The house on the corner was built in 1831 by Abiel Akin for his son Joseph, who was a brother of David K., and like him interested in salt making. Joseph Akin had three children, Catherine, Frederick and Charles, the last of whom only is living. Catherine Akin was a remarkable woman in many respects and especially in the ambition she possessed and in the power of will that enabled her to fit herself for a position in the world which she occupied. When hardly more than a girl she began to teach in the little district school in Georgetown, studying nights to keep ahead of her classes. Later she was the principal of a boarding school which became famous as "Miss Akin's school" in Stamford, Conn. Throughout her life her friends remained loyal to her and her pupils loved her and became her friends. She was always very fond of her native village, and it is in the old Quaker cemetery, within sight of the river she loved, and where the ever murmuring pines sing a requiem, that she sleeps.

QUAINT STORIES.

One old Quaker forbade his son to go upon the ice, but in coming from school they passed the pond, and his companion, venturing upon the ice, fell through and would have been drowned but for the aid of the boy who had been forbidden to go. He did not dare to tell his father about it for fear of the consequences, but the old gentleman heard of it, and while commending his son for saving his companion's life he thrashed him soundly for disobedience.

The old Quakers were averse to worldly music; to them it was one of the snares of the evil one. It is related that one of them beat his son soundly for playing upon a jews-harp, and when some of the apprentices in a neighboring shoe shop got possession of a fife and drum he closed all the windows and doors to keep out the sinful sounds.

Another good old Quaker lady was so worked up over the singing of hymns at the Methodist church, which she could hear from her house, that she declared she "had rather hear it thunder."

Two young men who did not possess as much of the Quaker sanctity as they should, considering their bringing up, but who did possess a deal of worldly desires, shut themselves up in an old salthouse and while one played on an old flute the other danced a breakdown. Then they came forth, feeling that for once they had been like other fellows and thoroughly wicked!

The late Catherine Akin used to delight in telling the following story, and although it loses much of the real humor it possessed when told by herself, for she was an inimitable story teller, it will give one an idea of the strictness of those early Friends.

It seems that Miss Akin had a piano in her father's house, an innovation looked upon with a great deal of disfavor by the old Quakers, and while they did not openly make objections, it was known that they thoroughly disapproved of it. Miss Akin's mother had a gathering of the Friends to tea, and on that occasion it was thought best to close the piano, so that even the sight of it might not cause offense; its cover was put on and books and other things arranged so that it would not be too noticeable. In the evening someone, probably more worldly minded, asked Miss Akin to play something, which she of course declined, evidently having been coached by her parents, and her father said that perhaps the others would not approve of it. "Well," said Aunt Ruth, after a pause, "thee might play something if thee played it very slow." What she played, whether it was a quick-step in the time of "Old Hundred" or the "Dead March" from "Saul" I do not know, but it evidently gave satisfaction. Someone told Miss Akin that they saw Uncle Silas and Aunt Ruth, at another time, standing by the window while she was playing, but what they thought of it she never knew.

As in all country villages, occasionally there has been one whose mind has given away, and years ago there was a man who went insane upon religion. One of the pleasures of the boys in the country is the ringing of the bells the night before the Fourth of July, being unable to restrain their patriotic feelings longer than the last stroke of the bell at midnight. One night they had stolen into the Methodist church, made their way up the dark stairs and begun to ring the bell, when in walked the aforesaid "crazy man" carrying a long butcher's knife with which he threatened the boys. He told them to kneel down while he prayed, and said that if they attempted to leave he would cut their ears off. And there he kept them for hours, kneeling in fear and trembling, while he prayed for them, knife in hand, glancing about from time to time to see that the boys were properly devout and attentive. It was the most quiet "night before the Fourth" that had been known for several years, for the boys were in no mood to continue the bell ringing when the last "amen" was said and they were released.

THE BREAKWATER.

Quoting again from Mr. Wing:
"The breakwater was built about the year 1837 from material which came mostly from Dinah's pond. A continual hawser of about four and a half inch size was stretched from the mouth of the river to the breakwater site and by its help the scows were pulled to and fro. This undertaking proved a failure on account of the formation of sand bars on the in-shore side.

"Work was suspended and the structure has never been completed according to the original plans. A wooden building which was erected upon the central portion of the breakwater was set on fire and destroyed by sailors some years ago.

"According to tradition both the old pier and the breakwater have received great quantities of smuggled goods in the years of long ago.

"During the war of 1812-15 some of the smaller vessels of the English fleet visited this part of the coast and demanded a thousand dollars as tribute money. A committee endeavored to raise the money by subscription and at last succeeded in securing the whole of the amount required. This they sent to the English in two installments by a citizen known as "Uncle Abner." The object of the business portion of the community was to impress upon the minds of the enemy that none but poor ignorant fishermen dwelt thereabouts, in order that they might escape the requisition of a larger sum. The messenger was well chosen, and an address was sent to the "Commander of the British Squadron on the coast of Boston Bay" etc. On returning to shore the messenger stated that he had been kindly received; was taken to the cabin and that he not only delivered the written address but spoke to some length to the assembled officers, who listened respectfully, evidently much moved by his words of pleading for the poor fishermen. Before leaving, the British agreed not to molest any fishing vessel that could show a license from Uncle Abner. The English kept their word and vessels having the requisite permit from Uncle Abner were not disturbed."

OLD PIER.

The following extract from the "Collection of the Massachusetts Historical society," Vol. VIII, which is headed "A Description of Dennis in the County of Barnstable. September, 1802," has been handed to me by Mr. Freeman C. Goodnow, a former resident of the village and at the present time the owner of a summer cottage here, will be found of interest as it gives a good description of the old pier as it was in 1802, and judging from it we should infer that the pier was built in the vicinity of 1800.

"Half way between the river's mouth and the end of the bar, stands a pier 37 feet long and 31 feet broad, on which is a store. There is good anchorage 2 cables length east of it and 12 feet of water at low tide. Common tides rise here 4 feet. Such is Bass river. The harbor which it affords might be improved by art. Mr. Sylvanus Crowell, who lives in Yarmouth and who built the pier, has endeavored to confine the water of the river within the main channel and to prevent it flowing through the marsh on the eastern side, but his laudable attempts have hitherto failed of success. Persevering labors may perhaps, in time, effect the wished for object."

When the old pier disappeared I do not know, but the irregular piles of rock were a guide to those entering the river, for if the rocks could not be seen then there was sufficient water to enter. During the War of 1812 it must have been a busy place. vessels discharging cargoes, fishermen taking in salt, and purchasing supplies.

From this same article quoted above:

"On the Yarmouth side (of Bass river) there are six wharfs, three near the mouth of the river and three north of it. There are here twenty-one vessels, one brig sails immediately for the West Indies, ten coasters from 30 to 40 tons burden sail to Boston, Connecticut or the Southern states and thence to the West Indies. The other ten vessels are fishermen, one of a hundred tons, the rest are smaller. The fishing vessels go to the Straits of Belle Isle, the shoals of Nova Scotia or Nantucket sound. On a medium, a fishing vessel uses 700 bushels of salt in a year. One or two vessels are annually built in Bass river, chiefly on the western side."

The article closes with these words:

"These facts in addition to those which have been made already, and which will hereafter be mentioned in this volume, show the present flourishing state of the South shore of the county of Barnstable, a part of Massachusetts not often visited and little known."

FIFTIETH ANNIVERSARY
of the
Methodist Episcopal Church.
Sept. 3 and 4, 1902.

The exercises began on the evening of Sept. 3 with a social gathering of welcome to the visitors and the friends of the society. The pastor at this time was Rev. A. J. Jolly, who made the opening address of welcome. Addresses were made by several of the former pastors, and letters read from many who were unable to be present. Members of the choir and others furnished enjoyable music.

The celebration was continued on Wednesday afternoon, and in the evening there was a religious service at which the Rev. L. B. Bates, D. D., preached the sermon, music being furnished by members of the choir in former days.

—OLD QUAKER VILLAGE—

FIFTIETH ANNIVERSARY
of the Erection of the Present School Buildings.
June 9, 1905.

The celebration took place in Lyceum hall, Yarmouthport, in the afternoon, and all the children of the schools were present and took part in the exercises. The speakers were Mr. George H. Cary of Boston and Mr. Stephen Sears of South Yarmouth. Prayer was offered by the Rev. Arthur Varley, Mr. E. W. Eldridge presided, Mr. W. A. Schwab gave the address of welcome, and an original poem, of which the following is a part, was read by Mr. E. Lawrence Jenkins:

The Old School Buildings.

Fifty years the staunch old buildings
   Weathered have the rain and snow;
Stood amid the storm and sunshine,
   Watched the seasons come and go.

Fifty years within those class rooms,
   Children have been taught to climb
Up the grand old path of knowledge,
   Leading to the heights sublime.

Fifty years of grand, brave service,
   Teaching thousands ow to live;
Storing in their minds the knowledge
   That to others they might give.

Fifty years have seen the passing
   From their portals to the world,
Thousands of young men and maidens,
   With their banners bright unfurled.

And they stand today, those buildings,
   Just as strong and true as then;
They were builded upon honor,
   They were built by honest men.

And a thought it is most pleasant,
   They were builded thus to last,

E'en as character was builded
By those pupils in the past.

* * * *

Fifty years have others labored
At the tasks now set for you;
Many more will follow after,
Many more these tasks will do.

May you then strive in the doing
Just the very best you can;
Study hard, each day improving,
Each for each, as man for man.

* * * *

Honor to those staunch old buildings,
Honor for the work they've done
For our fathers and our mothers,
And their children, every one.

The anniversary hymn was written by Mr. E. F. Pierce, principal of the high school.

FIFTY YEARS AGO.
Tune: "Fair Harvard."

Far, far through the mists of the hurrying years,
  Away to those days ever dear,
Fond memory guides us and sings to our ears
  Of that work, sure, far-seeing and clear.
And shall we forget in this circle so bright,
  Those builders of fifty years gone?
With steadfastness, foresight, with eyes toward the light,
  They builded for children unborn.

We breathe the same air of the murmuring seas;
  We tread paths that their footsteps have worn;
These loved scenes, this dear schoolhouse, these whispering trees,
  Speak to us, as to them, of life's dawn.
So, while onward we press, life's full duties to meet,
  Wheresoever our lot may be cast,
We remember in honor, in gratitude sweet,
  The brave work of the men of the past.

The following interesting article has been received from Mr. Daniel Wing which gives valuable information.

THE FRIENDS' BURIAL GROUNDS IN YARMOUTH.

About the year 1714 there stood on the highway a short distance north of Kelley's bay in what is now a part of Dennis, but was then within the boundaries of Yarmouth, a small building owned and occupied by the Society of Friends or Quakers as a meeting house.

For about a century, possibly more, the meetings there were attended by members coming from various directions; some of them from sections quite distant from the place of worship; and there is yet an old roadway in that vicinity known to the older generation as "the Quaker path."

With the opening up of the Indian reservation in South Yarmouth for settlement by whites, the centres of population were affected somewhat, and the present Friends' meeting house was built in 1809 for the better accommodation of the generation of that time.

In accordance with the custom prevailing in those days, the burial place was located in each case upon the grounds adjacent to the place for worship.

In 1875 the grounds of the old site were surrounded by a neat wooden fence; but in 1901 the writer received a letter saying, "Alas! the fence has fallen; who will restore it?" In 1903 a new wooden fence was built, enclosing, however, only that portion of the grounds which had been used for burial purposes.

And now the question forcibly presents itself: Who will, in the coming years, see that this ancient cemetery is properly cared for and protected?

For many years the grounds of the South Yarmouth meeting house were enclosed by a wooden fence; but this was eventually replaced by a more durable construction of stone and iron.

The earlier Friends nowhere showed their traits of modesty and simplicity more prominently than in their meeting houses and burial grounds. The former were marked examples of architectural simplicity and the latter showed a complete abstinence from ostentation and vain glory.

To these early Friends, Death leveled all human distinctions, and in the grave, sinner and saint rested alike so far as outward manifestations were concerned. A simple mound of earth marked the last resting place, and no tablet was allowed to distinguish one burial from another.

Years passed, and a rule was adopted allowing the placing of headstones not exceeding eighteen inches in height, with simple inscription showing name and age. This occurred not far from the middle of the last century. Today although

> "No storied urn nor animated bust
> In grandour stands above their silent dust,
> The lowly headstones, standing row on row,
> Reveal to us all that we need to know."

From the earliest days, this place of burial, although owned and controlled by Friends, has been essentially a village cemetery. Of the first thirty-one adult burials there, less than one-half were members of the Friends' society, and when the number of burials reached two hundred and sixty-six, less than one-third were members by birthright or otherwise.

The privilege thus extended to persons not connected with them by ties of religious belief, shows great neighborliness of feeling and emphasizes the thought so prominent in the minds of the early Friends, that at the grave human judgment should end, and that the merits or demerits of the deceased should be left to God, who judgeth not as man judgeth.

Each succeeding year the membership grows perceptibly less, and to one who remembers events connected with those honored people of the past during a period of nearly seventy years, a review of the former days brings a feeling of deep sadness.

> It seems but yesterday those scenes were laid,
> And yet it needs no prophet's wondrous aid
> To show us that those goodly scenes of yore
> Have long since passed and will return no more.

Maywood, Ill., 1915.   Daniel Wing.

—OLD QUAKER VILLAGE—

And now we come to the last words. The editor confesses that there is much more that might be said; there are many names that might claim a place within those pages,—men who were an active part of the building up of the village, and who occupied positions that entitle them to the remembrance of the public, but the plan of these reminiscences is to picture the earlier aspect of Quaker village, rather than to form a series of biographies, although the editor confesses that at times he has been led away from the original idea. He also is well aware that more information could have been procured if he had known where to apply for it, but a public appeal through the Yarmouth Register failed of responses except in one instance. He has done what he could, only regretting that much that is of value and interest must, in the course of years, be hopelessly lost. The errors that may occur in any of the statements are such that could only come from incorrect information; the editor has presented it as given to him by various people, as they have heard it or it has been handed down to them.

No. 39.

LIBRARY *of* Cape Cod HISTORY & GENEALOGY

WEST YARMOUTH HOUSES
Seventy-Five Years Ago
From Parker's River Westward

By DANIEL WING.

YARMOUTHPORT, MASS.:
C. W. SWIFT, Publisher and Printer,
The "Register" Press,
1915.

WEST YARMOUTH HOUSES
Seventy-Five Years Ago
From Parker's River Westward
By DANIEL WING.

"I do not envy any man, that absence of sentiment which makes some people careless of the memorials of their ancestors, and whose blood can be warmed up only by talking of horses or the price of hops."
Blades, in Enemies of Books.

It has been asserted by some historian that the Crowels or Crowells of the Middle states were originally Cromwells and that they dropped the letter M about the time they dropped their anchor in a harbor of the American continent. It requires but little knowledge of history to convince one that in many instances, during the political struggles between England and France, hundreds of years ago, it was advisable for the safety of one's person to change the family name. For a long period the relations between England and Normandy were intimate and more or less complex.

The Norman French name Le Crochere (pronounced Cro share) was easily abbreviated by dropping the first syllable and the final e. This left Crocher, which, in English, would be pronounced Crocker: hence the changes in spelling and pronunciation. Another change was effected by eliminating the final syllable of Crochere altogether: hence the names Cro, Crow and Crowe, which by the process of evolution have become Crowell.

It was natural that the descendants of John Crowe, who lived near Follens pond, should establish their residences along the northern shore of the Cape; and that those of Yelverton should settle on the southern coast near the home of their paternal ancestor, where there was an abundance of land suitable for tilling and a natural growth of salt grasses for their cattle.

The woods furnished an abundance of timber for the construction of dwellings and barns, and the waters, both fresh and salt, yielded considerable food for their tables.

In later years the coasting trade furnished employment for many, and a goodly number of those who afterwards became masters of merchant ships, took their first lessons as cooks and "hands" on board the small craft which were largely owned and sailed by their fathers or near relatives.

The boys of those days, instead of wasting their time in pursuit of pleasure, worked on the home lands, hoeing corn and potatoes, cutting wood for fuel, milking the cows morning and night, going to the district school for a few weeks in the winter and so keeping up the round of duties throughout the year. Those indeed were strenuous times, the like of which the rising generation knows but little from personal experience. But there was a compensaion in the fact that in that way were produced men of sturdy character, energetic, self-reliant, persistent. Some of them have gained an enviable reputation as ship masters, while others have attained success in other departments of human endeavor.

The exact spot on which Yelverton's dwelling stood is not known; but is supposed to have been in the vicinity of the residences formerly owned and occupied by the late Captains Elkanah Crowell and Zadok Crowell. The building may have been constructed of logs from the adjacent woods. Here Yelverton lived forty-four years. His wife Elizabeth survived him twenty years and died in November, 1703. The will of the former is dated Dec. 23, 1681, and is signed "Yelverton Crowell alias Crow," which seems to indicate the period in which the final change in surname was made.

The site of the residence of John, son of Yelverton Crowe, is known. A great-great-grandson of the latter showed it to a descendant in the seventh generation and he in turn pointed out the spot to one now living. The old Yelverton farm has been occupied and worked by his descendants in all the successive generations down to the present time. Captain Elkanah Crowell¹, (Elkanah⁶, Elkanah⁵, Simeon⁴, Ephraim³, Thomas², Yelverton¹) now living in Hyannis at the age of 85 years, has kindly furnished the writer of this article with a list of householders along the line of what is now known as South Sea avenue in the order in which they were located 75 years ago.

The writer has looked up the male ancestral line of some of these worthies and offers the same in the hope that it will be acceptable to some at least who have not the time or the inclination to unravel the intricasies of genealogical history.

Commencing at Great Island, the first residence to be named was that of Captain Nehemiah Crowell⁵ (Abner⁴, Thomas³, Thomas², Yelverton¹), who died about the year 1819, leaving the house to be occupied by his son Robert.

The next was the residence of John Hallet, who married Rachel Crowell of the sixth generation from Yelverton. This house was moved from its original site many years ago and now stands upon land on the county road owned by the heirs of the late F. A. Abel. In still earlier times there had been a dwelling on the "Island" occupied by the family of Freeman Hallet, and later by his widow; but which was removed longer ago than Captain Crowell can remember, and became the residence of the late B. K. Chase, who married a daughter of the former owner.

Near the Island fence, on the mainland, were a lot of saltworks and an establishment where lampblack was made. Salt was made in this vicinity as early as 1839, by Gorham Crowell and Ezekiel Crowell. The lampblack was manufactured by a man named John Bangs, who lived in the house later occupied by Timothy Lewis on the easterly side of the highway, now serving as a summer residence.

Then, on the west side, was the home of the late Alexander Crowell, a son of Nehemiah, already mentioned, now also a summer residence. Back in the fields was the ruins of an old cellar on the estate of Ezekiel Crowell, where a house had been located; by whom it was built and occupied is beyond the knowledge of any one now living. A little farther north was an old, low, double house, owned by Captain Ezekiel Crowell[5] (Jeremiah[4], Joseph[3], John[2], Yelverton[1]). This place was occupied by Joshua Hallet and Arven Baker some seventy or more years ago; also by a family of Winslows from Brewster who tended saltworks near by. The building was subsequently torn down and Captain Ezekiel Crowell, son of Jeremiah, built a residence near the site of the old house. One of the daughters of the former married the late Frederic P. Baker; one, Captain Edward Lewis, and the third, still living at the advanced age of eighty-nine and one-half years, is the widow of the late Heman Chase of West Yarmouth. This building was moved about 30 years ago to South Yarmouth.

Next in order stood the low, double house of Timothy Crowell[5], son of Jeremiah[4], previously named in this article. This house in later years was the home of Zenas Wood, who married Sarah Ann, daughter of Timothy, July 1, 1838. Mr Wood's family moved West many years ago, and finally the house was taken down.

The late Captain Zadok Crowell[6] built a house close by the site of that of his father Timothy[5], and occupied the same with his family for many years. This house, now known as Creltholme, has been for several years past the residence of Joshua F. Crowell[7] (Isaiah[7], Elkanah[6], Elkanah[5], Simeon[4], Ephraim[3], Thomas[2], Yelverton[1]). The present owner is also a descendant of Yelverton in the eighth generation in the line coming down from Thomas[2], the fourth son of Yelverton, born about the year 1647.

On the east side of the way nearly opposite the last named, stood the house of Captain Ebenezer Crowell[5] (Solomon[4], Joseph[3], John[2], Yelverton[1]) who was lost at sea in February, 1828, when about 42 years old. His widow survived him many years. None of their children are now living, but there are grandchildren. The old dwelling was bought by Reuben Blachford and went into the construction of a new house on Main street, opposite the late Isaac Crowell's, now occupied by Addie F. Crowell.

On the west side of the Lane, as it was formerly called, once stood the residence of Captain Elkanah Crowell², son of Simeon. This building was taken down about the year 1843 and a new structure was erected by Captain Elkanah of the sixth generation near the site of his father's house. Of the children who grew up in this home, Captain Elkanah Crowell of the seventh generation, heretofore named in this article, and a sister living in the West are the sole survivors. The last-named dwelling is located near the spot once occupied by the residence of John, son of Yelverton, and presumably quite near also to that of Yelverton himself.

Almost directly opposite the residence of Captain Elkanah Crowell of the sixth generation from Yelverton, the pioneer of 1639, there had stood for a number of years the district schoolhouse, to which we presume the description of one elsewhere by Whittier would apply:

"Within, the master's desk is seen,
  Deep scarred by raps official;
The warping floor, the battered
  seats,
The jack-knife's carved initial;
The charcoal frescoes on its wall;
The door's worn sill betraying
The feet that, creeping slow to
  school,
Went storming out to playing."

About the year 1839 or 40 this building of an early period in the educational history of this section was moved farther north and became a part of the residence of Captain Zenas Crowell. A new schoolhouse was built on the same site about the year 1839; but that too was sold when the larger building now in use superseded it on Main street, and it was used as a storehouse for a time on the opposite side of the street by Elkanah Crowell, the 6th.

Again it was sold and removed to Main street near the old cemetery and converted into a dwelling house by George Taylor, a citizen of the village.

On the west side of South Sea avenue, next north of Captain Elkanah Crowell's, stood the residence of the late Captain Henry Crowell⁵ (Nehemiah⁶, Abner⁴, Thomas³, Thomas², Yelverton¹). This dwelling has been removed south, to a site nearly opposite that formerly occupied by the home of the late Alexander Crowell previously mentioned.

Next in order came the residence of the late Davis Crowell, on the east side of the street, now owned and used as a summer residence by Edward Brown.

Again, on the west side of the highway, stood the chimney stack of an old dwelling, the original builder of which cannot now be certainly known.

Mrs. Martha Chase (daughter of Captain Ezekiel Crowell of the fifth generation from Yelverton), now living at the advanced age of ninety years, remembers distinctly that her grandfather, Jeremiah, who died in 1827, once lived there.

It is quite possible that the building itself was erected by Joseph, the father of Jeremiah, and a grandson of Yelverton, the pioneer. This house was locally known as the Molly Gamie house. Jeremiah married Mary Hallet in 1778, and Mary was frequently called Molly in the early days.

Then came the home of the late Captain Henry Taylor with its large family of boys and girls, most of whom have passed away.

Next came Captain Zenas Crowell's, where were four daughters and five sons, only one of whom, the youngest daughter, is now living.

Thus ends the panorama of South Sea avenue as it was seventy-five years ago. What changes have taken place since then! Quite a number of the dwellings still remain upon the sites they occupied in the long ago; but the occupants are not the same. Children have been born, have attained their three score years and ten, and have passed away, leaving their places to be filled by others, who, in their turn will occupy for a more or less brief period.

"Like to the falling of a star,
Or as the flights of eagles are;
Or like the fresh spring's gaudy hue,
Or silver drops of morning dew;
Or like a wind that chafes the flood,
Or bubbles which on water stood:
E'en such is man, whose borrowed light
Is straight called in and paid tonight.
The wind blows out, the bubble dies;
The spring entombed in autumn lies;
The dew dries up, the star is shot;
The flight is past, and man forgot."
—H. King.

The last line often becomes true sooner than it should.

The body of land known as Great Island has been doubtless, in the long ago, an island in fact, as well as in name; but the mighty forces of wind and wave which have extended seaward the bar off Bass river and formed Dogfish bar farther west, have formed a sandy beach which transforms the one time island into a peninsula. It is true that the highway leading to it is bridged over an arm of Lewis bay; but this is because the line of the highway, as established, is more direct than the route nearer the sea shore.

It is reasonable to presume that this peninsula was a part of the tract taken up by Yelverton Crowe, the pioneer, in 1639.

The fact that it would make the area of his territory possibly as great as three square miles is no argument against its probability. In Middleboro, as well as on the Cape, in the early days, large tracts of land were purchased from the Indians and were known as the Twelve Men's Purchase, Five Men's Purchase, Sixteen Shillings Purchase, etc., and the last named seems to indicate the consideration paid.

The southeastern point of the peninsula was formerly known as Fox point; the southernmost extremity still bears the name Point Gammon. Why this name, which intimates imposture, delusion, trickery, was applied to this headland is somewhat difficult to ascertain with any degree of certainty; but some investigation by correspondence and a study of maps new and old, has convinced the writer that it originated with mariners and not with landsmen. The writer, in a former article, was led into error by a statement made to him in good faith, that a tradition had been handed down to the effect that a few generations ago, cattle were driven across a narrow channel to Bishop and Clerk's and pastured there. He invited criticism and suggestions from others, and has received letters from several parties which have convinced him that the following statements can be relied upon.

A great many years ago the Bishop and Clerk's ledge was an island about five miles in circumference, and sheep used to be scowed across the channel and pastured there. The channel at that time must have been considerably narrower than now; but never, since the advent of white men in New England, has it been shallow enough to admit of its being forded.

The native Indians accounted for the islands Nantucket and Marthas Vineyard by a mythical story which ran somewhat in this wise:

A great many moons ago there lived upon the Cape a giant named Maushop. One day he waded out into the South sea to a great distance, for his legs were exceedingly long and his bodily vigor wonderful. After a time his moccasins became full of sand, which made walking painful. Thereupon he emptied one, and the island of Nantucket appeared above the surface of the water, while the sand which he poured from the other formed the island known as Marthas Vineyard. He lighted his pipe and volumes of smoke arose, obscuring the vision for miles around. Ever afterward, when fog appeared over the water, the Indians would exclaim in their native tongue, "Here comes old Maushop's smoke."

The government lighthouse was established on Point Gammon in 1816 and was kept by Samuel Peak until 1826. He was succeeded by his son, John Peak, who officiated until the light was discontinued in 1859, when the Bishop and Clerk's lighthouse, which had been in process of construction for several years, was put to service.

Hyannis Harbor light was established in 1849; the Range light on Railroad wharf in 1885; the line of the two serving as a guide in entering Hyannis harbor.

Captain Elkanah Crowell, who hoed corn and dug potatoes near Fox point and Point Gammon, when a boy, estimates the area of cleared land on the southern and western portions of "The Island" at that time to have been twenty acres or more, and that probably there were thirty to forty acres of woodland. This territory was owned by some dozen or more proprietors, and when the wood was big enough to convert into firewood the area was laid off into lots and the proprietors bid for choice. Captain Crowell himself drew a plat of the woodland for that purpose about forty years ago.

The body of water north of Great Island, known as Lewis bay, doubtless received its name from some family residing in that neighborhood.

The late Amos Otis, Esq., is authority for the statement that the "South Sea men" of Barnstable in 1696 included Thomas, Edward and John Lewis, and that the last named fell in battle in the war with the Indian chief, King Philip. The name Lewis does not appear on the Yarmouth tax list for 1676. Additional facts along this line would be welcome, to show the origin of the name and period in which it was applied to this beautiful body of water. It may be that, forming, as it does, a portion of the eastern boundary of Hyannis, it received its name from the Lewis families of Barnstable.

About a hundred years ago, "there were in this bay four coasters of about forty-five tons each, and ten fishing vessels of from forty to fifty tons each." The lampblack and salt making industries added to the volume of business in this section. Today these are all gone and their places taken by summer cottages and pleasure craft.

Farming, too, except on a very small scale, has become a thing of the past; although the raising of vegetables is carried on to some extent. A lady is still living who remembers riding home from a party in an oxcart; but oxcarts have been succeeded by carryalls and truck wagons, and they, in turn, are being supplanted by automobiles and power trucks.

However, the old days were good old days of peace and comparative contentment; and we of the living should not lose sight of them in our scramble for that which is just ahead of us.

To the section of which we write, in 1639, nineteen years after the landing of the Pilgrims at Plymouth, and one year after the incorporation of the town of Yarmouth, came Yelverton Crowe, the pioneer, who was not only a man respected by his fellow citizens, but one who accepted and performed well his duties as a citizen. He not only served his town in several official capacities, but served, too, as a soldier in King Philip's war.

It would be exceedingly appropriate to erect some memorial to his memory in the cemetery where so many of the early settlers quite probably including himself are buried, and to mark the historic sites of the neighborhood, before they are altogether lost to human knowledge.

With suitable inscriptions, no other material would seem to be as appropriate for this purpose as the massive boulders of the town which he and his descendants have done so much to establish and perpetuate.

The writer has several times mentioned this name and has diligently sought a reason for its bestowal upon the southern headland of Great Island. He, himself, has at sundry times, when sailing in Nantucket sound, seen a mirage in that vicinity which so distorted the shore outline as apparently to make it possible to sail through several channels, where, in fact, there was no water at all.

When the Bishops was an island of considerable extent, as it was a few generations ago, and Great Island extended farther south, a mirage or a more or less dense mist or fog may have made that portion of the coast even more deceptive than now. Hence the name, as applied by mariners who were gammoned by it— Point Gammon.

As particularly interesting in this connection I quote a passage from Thoreau's "The Maine Woods," page 227, descriptive of a canoe trip on Moosehead lake in Maine with one white companion and an Indian guide. "Looking northward from this place," writes Thoreau, "it appeared as if we were entering a large bay, and we did not know whether we should be obliged to diverge from our course and keep outside a point which we saw, or should find a passage between this and the main land. I consulted my map and used my glass, and the Indian did the same; but we could not find our place exactly on the map, nor could we detect any break in the shore. When I asked the Indian the way, he answered, 'I don't know,' for he had never been up this side. It was misty, dogday weather. . . It seemed that, if we held on, we should be fairly embayed. Presently, however, the mist lifted somewhat, and revealed a break in the shore northward, showing that the point was a portion of Deer Island, and that our course lay westward of it. Where it had seemed a continuous shore even through a glass, one portion was now seen by the naked eye to be much more distant than the other which overlapped it, merely by the greater thickness of the mist which still rested on it." Another Point Gammon.

Captain Loring Fuller of South Yarmouth, who has sailed along the coast of Great Island more than a thousand times, offers no solution of the problem as to the origin of the name Point Gammon; but gives a version of the old Maushop myth that is new to the writer of this article. It runs thus:

"A very long time ago there lived a great Indian giant named Maushop, who could wade up and down Vineyard sound without finding the water more than knee deep. His home was in a cave called the Devil's Den on Gay Head. He used to sit on a boulder in the sound to smoke, and the ashes from his pipe, taken away by the currents, formed the island of Nantucket. He undertook to build a bridge from Gay Head to Cuttyhunk by filling one of his shoes with sand and wading out to empty it on the intended line; but a crab bit him on his uncovered foot and made him so angry that he broke off a portion of the cliff and threw it southward, thus forming the island called No Man's Land. He flung his five children into the sea and they were transformed into fishes. His wife remonstrated with him and he tossed her across the channel to Seaconnet." There! if that does not equal, in vivid imagination, the myths of the Israelites, the Assyrians and Babylonians of four thousand years ago, then the writer is no judge.

This subject (Point Gammon and vicinity) will be continued in No. 9 of this series.

Meantime, will those persons who have either fact or tradition bearing upon the topic referred to, kindly forward same to the writer, who will serve as a sort of "clearing house" to receive, assort and publish later on. Names will not be printed if anyone objects.

The result of correspondence now at hand will be given from time to time.

The writer has no pet theories which he is trying to maintain; but is anxious to ascertain facts, before it is too late, and tradition is often helpful.

Traditions grow and change as the years pass. As one reaches the three score years and ten of human life he is sometimes temporarily in doubt whether certain events that occurred in his early lifetime were actually witnessed by himself, or were so vividly portrayed to him by another as to leave upon his mind and memory an impression as strong and enduring as that produced by personal experience.

A correspondent regrets that the writer doubts the fording of the channel between Point Gammon and Bishop's since the advent of the white man in New England; and states that a worthy citizen of say three generations ago said in his hearing that he, himself, "as a boy, waded across." Now, there is no intention on the part of anyone to insinuate wilful misrepresentation by any person. The writer for many years believed as did his correspondent; but accumulating evidence shook his faith in the fording; although he still believes that sheep and possibly larger animals were taken across the channel to pasture on the Bishop's island by means of scows.

In reply to a query on this subject he received the following from the U. S. Coast and Geodetic survey, bearing date Sept. 9.

"There is nothing on file in this department or bureau" (Department of Commerce) "to indicate that the locality about Bishop and Clerk's lighthouse was ever an island of any greater extent than at present shown upon the charts. The earliest survey by the coast survey was in 1847, and at that time the water north of the lighthouse was too deep to be forded. The earliest chart of the locality is that of 'Nantucket shoals' by Captain Paul Pinkham, 1791. It shows several rock symbols where Bishop and Clerk's lighthouse is located and three and one-half fathoms of water between there and Point Gammon. We have no information regarding the origin of the name Point Gammon."

A U. S. chart of "Hyannis harbor" whose hydrography is based on surveys made between 1888 and 1902 with certain corrections to Sept. 14, 1914, shows the distance from Point Gammon to the lighthouse on Bishop's to be about 2½ statute miles. There is a channel a little more than three-fourths of a mile wide, in which the water is more than 18 feet deep at its "mean low water;" the depth in that vicinity being from 19 to 26 feet.

Summing up, we have as follows:

Depth of channel in 1791, 3½ fathoms (21 feet).

Lighthouse established on Point Gammon in 1816.

U. S. survey in 1847 shows channel "too deep to be forded."

Latest chart shows channel 19 to 26 feet deep at low water.

Tradition says that a man born in 1801 waded across this channel when a boy.

There is no doubt that the wearing away of this portion of the coast during the last three centuries has been very great. It has been estimated that the wearing away of the east coast of Nantucket in recent times has been as great as a foot per annum, and on parts of the south coast, three feet.

Geologists suppose that at least three to four miles have been washed into the sea from the east coast of Cape Cod in ages past. The waste from the land has greatly extended the bar off Bass river.

The question under discussion, however, is whether or not the channel referred to has, within a century or two, been shallow enough to be forded.

No. 10 of this series will review the residences along the county road from Parker's river bridge westward, covering a period of seventy years.

On the northerly side of the county road westerly from the bridge and distant from it, say fifteen rods or thereabout, there stood about eighty years ago a low double house occupied by the widow of Simeon Lewis, who was the sister of Elkanah Crowell 1st, born in 1757. Of their children, Mehitable married Isaiah Parker and Simeon married Thankful, sister of John Hallett.

Some twenty rods farther west on the same side of the road and about the same time, was the residence of Captain Winthrop Sears; a building of similar design to the one first named. In fact, that was the style of architecture that prevailed a century or more ago. It was the custom to have the front toward the south, having no reference to the location or direction of the nearest highway. In South Yarmouth representatives of this class are the Reuben Farris house and the Amos Baker house, the second dwelling south of the Hatsel Crosby place. The Baker house originally had the front door toward the river instead of on the street side. The most of such homes had a large room each side of the front door; the kitchen in the rear, with pantry and bedroom at one end and cellarway and bedroom at the other, and an immense chimney stack and brick oven directly back of the "front entry."

Captain Sears married first Betsey Crowell, and second Susannah Crowell. The children of the second marriage were Odlin, Susan, Abbie, Winthrop and Mary. The house is now occupied by Mrs Irene Taylor, widow of the late Roland Taylor. Still farther on was the low, double house of John Gorham, where he with his mother and sister lived some seventy-five or eighty years ago. This building was torn down many years since; but the writer remembers its ancient appearance, its white plastered chimney of ample dimensions bearing evidence of its having been used as a target by passing gunners. Mr Gorham, who married late in life, was a very pious old gentleman, who used to lead the singing at prayer meetings, and who, the writer thinks, was a pensioner of the war of 1812, having served on the watch for the enemy along the coast from his station on Great Island.

It was in that war that the English armed vessel Nymph demanded a "ransom" of South Yarmouth to the amount of one thousand dollars, which was paid in two instalments.

Nearly opposite the site of the John Gorham house was a small house occupied by Warren Lewis, whose wife's name was Diantha. Their children were Phebe, Alfred, Edwin, Ruth and Thatcher, the last named living at present in Dennisport. This house was moved a number of years ago to South Yarmouth.

Still farther west on the north side of the road formerly stood the meeting house of the west precinct, built in 1794, in which the Rev Timothy Alden preached every fourth Sabbath for many years. About the year 1832 this structure was replaced by a more modern one; and this newer building was moved a few years ago to the south side of the highway near the schoolhouse.

In the early days many worshippers came from "Gray's country" and the Matthews settlement near the mouth of Bass river.

A little farther on, upon the same side of the street, was the home of Captain Odlin P. Sears, who married Thankful, daughter of Captain Elnathan Lewis, Senr. Their children were Cyrus and Richard. The old house was torn down and a new house erected on the same site. This is now owned and occupied by the heirs of the late Captain William Peak, son of John Peak, a onetime keeper of the lighthouse on Great Island.

Next on the south side of the road was the home of Thomas Crowell, who married Lydia, sister of Jabez Lewis. Their children were Serena, Eliza, Warren and Lydia. This residence stood just east of the cross roads leading to South Sea avenue on the one hand and North Lane on the other, the place being known as "The Four Corners." The dwelling was taken down some years ago and moved to Hyannis by George Miller. Thomas was of the seventh generation from "John Crowe of Bass Ponds."

On the northerly side of the highway and across North lane from the Odlin P. Sears homestead, stood the residence of Jabez Lewis, which was probably occupied by his father at a still earlier date. This also was a "low double house" corresponding to the style of architecture of the period when it was built. By his first wife, Thankful, the children were William, Thankful and Prentiss; by his second wife, Rebecca Howland, Edgar, Lothrop, Leonidas, Irene, Amelia, Elizabeth, Melora and George. The dwelling was burned some twenty-five years ago.

The ancient cemetery is located just beyond the site of the Jabez Lewis home and is bounded on the west side by a road which leads to the former site of the town house. In the days when this cemetery was laid out, it was customary to have the burial ground in the immediate vicinity of the meeting house; but at that time the people of "South Sea" attended service on the north side of the town, hence the desirability of a burial place nearer the home village.

It seems a pity that so few of the earlier burials are marked by headstones; but this lack is easily accounted for by the fact that most of the pioneers were people of limited means, and the needs of the living were rather to be looked after than the marking of the resting places of the dead.

The old wooden fence which had heretofore enclosed the grounds was replaced in 1884 by a substantial stone and iron fence at a cost of $1755.23, the funds being raised by subscription, under the devoted management of the late Captain Sturgis Crowell, of the sixth generation from Thomas, son of Yelverton.

The town of Yarmouth contributed $300.00 and the following named persons each gave $100.00 or more: Captain Sturgis Crowell, Elisha Taylor, Esq., Elkanah Crowell, Jr., and Mrs Albert Chase. In addition to cash donations, many persons gave their labor and the use of their teams to forward this worthy object.

Across the highway from the cemetery are the recently built residences of Lothrop and Ferdinand Baker, and across a way which connects with South Sea avenue is that of Joshua Baker.

A short distance west from the residence last named, stands a small concrete structure recently built for the use of Christian Scientists. Opposite this is the home of George Taylor. The building was formerly the district schoolhouse located on South Sea avenue, which was referred to in No. 5 of this series.

Next west, stands the low double house formerly occupied by John Seymour and later by the late Benjamin Blachford. This dwelling has had many occupants, is in a good state of preservation and is now owned by Rev Lester Lewis, a descendant of Jabez Lewis hereinbefore mentioned.

Nearly opposite the place last named there stood many years ago an old-time dwelling known as the "Aunt Brown house." Aunt Brown was the mother of Blind Frank, a character known for miles around.

At the annual sheep washings and sheep shearings on Nantucket in the first half of the last century, Blind Frank filled the position of chief "fiddler" for the dancing in the evenings. In those days, as many as seven thousand sheep were pastured on Nantucket and the annual sheep shearing was an occurence of great interest.

Close by, Benjamin Blachford, who married Lydia Seymour, built a small house of more modern style. His children were Henry, John, Benjamin, Reuben, Frederic,

Lydia and Elizabeth.

The late Henry Blachford of the Yarmouth board of selectmen, was the last survivor of this large family.

Still farther west on the north side of the county road, was the low double house of Captain Elnathan Lewis, who used to have charge of the West Yarmouth postoffice when the stage brought the mail from Plymouth, not very regularly, some seventy-five or eighty years ago. The original dwelling was taken down some sixty-five years ago and a more modern structure built by Captain Lewis, who occupied it during the remainder of his life. This house came into possession of Captain Elkanah Crowell, 3d, and was moved in 1894 to Railroad avenue, Hyannis, where it is now occupied by him.

Captain Lewis owned a large tract of land extending from the county road to Lewis bay, a distance of more than half a mile, together with salt works near the shore. A road to the saltworks was laid out just west of the house. His children were Christopher, Thankful, Betsey, Phebe, Joseph and Edward. Captain Christopher Lewis married Susan Sears and established his home about seventy years ago directly opposite his father's. Christopher's children were Elnathan, Susan and Adelbert. The dwelling is now occupied by Mr E. B. Matthews, who married the daughter.

A little distance west from Captain Elnathan Lewis's old house, Captain Edward Lewis built a more up to date residence on the same side of the highway. He married Lucretia, daughter of Captain Ezekiel Crowell. Their children were Mary, Martha, Lavinia and Joseph. The last named, now living in Boston, is the sole survivor of that family. A fire in the woods, some fifteen years ago, kindled by sparks from a locomotive on the railroad caused the complete destruction of this fine residence.

Nearly opposite the Edward Lewis home, there stood for many years one of the old district schoolhouses which were superseded by the three larger structures now in use, and this one was moved about a half mile farther west to the woods back of the Downs cottage.

On its former site, Captain Joseph Bourne, who married Sarah, the daughter of Sylvanus Crowell, built a house. One son, Joseph, now resides in Boston, and the cottage is occupied by the superintendent of the Barnstable Water Co. When the late C. B. Corey bought Great Island, he purchased a right of way across the old fields in this vicinity, of Elnathan and John Lewis, the same extending to South Sea avenue, as it now lies open to travel.

A few rods farther west, and on the same side of the county road, the Congregational church built a parsonage not far from sixty years ago, which was afterward sold to Captain Arthur P. Blachford and occupied by his father, Captain Henry Blachford. Captain Blachford's first wife was Mary, daughter of the late Rev. Enoch F. Chase. Two children were the result of this marriage, both of whom died in their youth. The

WEST YARMOUTH HOUSES

captain married for his second wife Huldah Robbins. They also had two children. None of the members of this family are now living.

On the north side of the highway was the low, double house of John Lewis, which was probably owned by his ancestors before him, for it had the appearance of being very old. Many different tenants have resided in it during the last fifty to sixty years. John's wife was Ruth, daughter of Joyce Taylor, and their children were Simeon, Isaiah, Alice and Dora. The dwelling is now occupied by Anthony Montcalm.

Still farther west, Captain Arunah Whelden built a house some sixty years ago. He married Serena, daughter of Daniel Hallet. Of their two children, James and Carrie, the latter is still living. The dwelling was burned down about ten years ago.

Upon the same side of the highway, a little farther on, Captain Zimri Whelden, an older brother, established a fine residence. His first wife, who died young, was Mary, daughter of Captain Winthrop Sears, Senr. His second wife was Betsey, daughter of Captain Charles Baker, who lived a short distance east of Parkers river bridge. They had one son, Captain Charles Whelden, who married Hattie May, daughter of the late Captain Elbridge Crowell of South Yarmouth. Connected with this couple, who are now living, there are many memories which are exceedingly pleasant to the writer.

The dwelling last named was later owned and occupied by the late Captain Ephraim Crowell, and now by his son Julius, a former postmaster in that locality.

A short distance west from the home of Julius Crowell we see a small house, which, some seventy-five years ago, was the residence of Captain Hiram Crowell, born Jan. 12, 1804, who married Betsey, daughter of Captain Elnathan Lewis, in January, 1828. Christopher, a son of the above, died at sea some years ago. The house has of late been occupied by Mr Thacher.

Next, on the south side of the road, stands the small structure used for some ten or twelve years past for postoffice purposes and kept by Captain Richard Sears, the present postmaster.

Next comes a dwelling erected about sixty-five years since by Captain Benjamin Crowell, in which Postmaster Sears and wife, a daughter of the captain, now reside.

Still farther on, Captain Erastus Chase built a house of the same type as the one last mentioned. He married Betsey, daughter of Captain Higgins Crowell, Senr. Of the children, Alonzo, Erastus and Susan, the second son, a sea captain, died some years ago.

On the north side of the road, about opposite the Benjamin Crowell house, stands the home formerly of David Downs, Senr., now occupied by a son bearing the same name.

Back of the last named place, the old district schoolhouse stood for a time in the woods, as stated in a previous article. It was transformed into a hall and was subsequently destroyed by fire.

Close by, on the same side of the highway, was the old house of Sylvanus Crowell, who was born July 11, 1786, married Susan Baker in 1809 and died April 17, 1856. He was a lineal descendant of John Crowe of Bass Ponds in the eighth generation. His children were Freeman H., Lot, Sylvanus, Betsey, Susan, Sarah, Christina and Orlando. This old house was torn down about forty-five years ago and to its site, Freeman H., the oldest son, who married Olive, the daughter of Captain John Hallet of Great Island, moved the Captain Hallet house as mentioned in the fourth chapter of this series. The premises finally passed to the ownership of the late F. A. Abell of Pawtucket. By him, the dwelling was enlarged and the grounds extended and greatly improved and beautified. Both Mr and Mrs Abell have recently died and this fine estate is now held by their heirs.

Next to the Abell estate, on the corner at the junction of the county road and an old road leading to the "North side," stands a small house which has changed owners several times and is now occupied by the heirs of the late Dustin Baker.

On the diagonal corner, next to Berry avenue, so called, Captain Higgins Crowell, Jr., established his residence. He was a descendant of John Crowe of Bass Ponds in the 8th generation, was born in 1809, and married Abigail, daughter of Captain Winthrop Sears, Senior, in 1835, whose children were Odlin, Susan, Abbie, Winthrop and Mary. The dwelling was destroyed by fire several years ago and a new house erected on its site by Mr Chester Stacy.

Across the highway and a short distance west, Captain Kelley H. Crowell, who also was descended from John of Bass Ponds in the eighth generation, built a residence similar to that of Captain Higgins Crowell. His wife was Mary Lee, daughter of Anthony Chase. Their children were Howes and Ella. The last named married Dr W. J. Nickerson, formerly of South Yarmouth. None of this family are now living. The dwelling is now owned and occupied by Miss Flora Baker.

Next, on the same side of the road, is the low, double house of Thomas[5] Crowell— Abner[4], Thomas[3], Thomas[2], Yelverton[1]. Thomas was born in 1766 and married Mary, daughter of Gorham Crowell, in 1789. Mary survived her husband, dying in 1853 at the age of 81 years. The residence was known for many years as "the Molly Thomas house" to distinguish it from "the Molly Crowell house" down "the Lane," now South Sea avenue. The children of Thomas and Mary were Washington and Mary Ann. The last named married Jabez Perry and the old home is occupied during the summer season by their heirs.

Across the county road, nearly opposite the old "Molly Thomas house, stands a dwelling formerly occupied by Leander Crowell and subsequently by the late Captain Washburn Baker, who married Cordelia, daughter of Anthony Chase, in 1834. Their children, none of whom are now living, were Albert, Delia, Howard and Edward. The house is now owned and occupied by Prescott H. Baker, son of the late Isaiah F. Baker, and in the sixth generation from Silas Baker, Senior, who was born not far from the year 1700.

Still farther west on the same side of the highway, and on the hill a short distance from it, is the two story schoolhouse erected in, or about, the year 1854. On account of the small number of attending pupils, one of the lower rooms has been used for library purposes.

There is considerable contrast between the methods of instruction now prevailing and those in 1693 when it was voted to divide the town into "five squadrons," of which "South Sea" was to be known as No. 5, the boundaries to be as follows: "Beginning at Thomas Bills', all the west side of Bass River and South Sea, and to Thomas Batter's." A committee was appointed "to agree with some fit person to teach school" and South Sea's share of his labors was to extend "from July 15, to last of August" annually.

"In 1712, Mr. Jaquesh, school master, was allowed £24 salary, and 5 shillings per week additional for board." He was to teach children to read, write and cypher and to give them some knowledge of grammar and Latin.

Close by the schoolhouse stands the meetinghouse, which was moved from its former site a half-mile farther east, about eight years ago.

Across the road is the low double house of the late James Crowell or "Squire James" as he was popularly known. The squire was born in 1767, was of the fifth generation from Yelverton, the pioneer, in the line of Thomas, son of the latter. He married, first, Ruth Howes, by whom he had two children: Marten, who died at sea at the age of twenty-one years, and Ruth H., born in 1798, who married Silas Baker of South Yarmouth, and was well known locally for many years as a preacher in the Society of Friends or Quakers. For his second wife, Squire James married Deborah Robbins, generally known in that community as "Aunt Deborah." To her were born the following named children: Harrison, Russell, Lucy Ann, James, Rufus, Winslow, Alger, Olive A., Edwin, Randall, Mary H., and one other who appears to have died young. None of this large family are now living, and the dwelling is now owned by a family from Pawtucket.

About sixty-five years ago Captain Benjamin Adams Crowell of the eighth generation from John Crowe of Bass Ponds (vicinity of Follens pond) purchased the building which previously had been the store of Deacon Anthony Chase, moved it to a site a little west from the Congregational meetinghouse, and converted it into a dwelling. The captain was born in 1813 and married Cyrene Crowell in 1838. Their children were Philena, Herbert and Goodrich. The house is now occupied by the widow of Herbert, above named, who after his decease married Lewis Taylor.

Next to the residence of Mr. and Mrs. Lewis Taylor, Captain John Orlando, a native of Sweden, erected his dwelling. Captain Orlando married Betsey, widow of Solomon Howes of Dennis and daughter of George and Olive Crowell. Captain Orlando was an able mariner and became master of a fine large schooner, which was wrecked on a voyage from Boston to South America. The captain was four days on the wreck, and by exposure became paralyzed to such an extent that he was unable to walk. His ingenuity came to his assistance, and he constructed a vehicle propelled by hand power, which enabled him to go about the village quite freely. He also built a large boat, so arranged as to have every rope within easy reach as he sat in the stern. He could make sail, weigh anchor, reef sails, and come to anchor without moving from his seat; and he even went to Marthas Vineyard summers and took parties out for a sail upon the "briny deep." Since his decease his residence has been sold and is at present occupied by strangers.

About opposite the former home of Captain Orlando stands a low single house which was once the residence of Ebenezer Crowell, commonly known as "Ebenezer Daniel" to distinguish him from Captain Ebenezer who lived on South Sea avenue. He was the brother of Squire James, was born in 1784 and married Dorcas Lewis. Their children were Benjamin, Ann and Ephraim. The former occupants have all passed away and the old home is owned and occupied by strangers.

A little beyond, on the same side of the highway, Osborn, son of Captain Lysander Chase, erected a structure to be used for store purposes below and for a dwelling on the second floor. This property was later sold to the late Isaiah Crowell, son of Captain Elkanah, 2d, who carried on the grocery business there for some twenty years or thereabout, and about fifteen years ago was bought by the late Winchester Johnson.

The dwelling next to the store, in which Captain Daniel Taylor now lives, was once the home of Amos Crowell, a descendant in the seventh generation of John Crowe of Bass Ponds. He married Rhoda, daughter of Judah Crowell of Bass Ponds ancestry, in 1817. Their daughter Ruth became the wife of Lysander Chase, Senior, and the last named and their children, Amanda, Osborn, Ruth and Lysander, occupied the premises for a number of years.

Just opposite the last mentioned place is the house of Captain Reuben Blachford, built some twenty-five years ago.

It is the old Captain Ebenezer Crowell house moved from South Sea avenue, as stated in No. 4 in this series, and rejuvenated. It is now owned and occupied, the writer is informed, by Mrs. Addie F. Crowell, one of his contemporaries in the early school days in the new schoolhouse in South Yarmouth. He recalls the time when the upper room was so crowded that several of the boys were obliged to sit on the girls' side, himself being one of the number; and now after some sixty years have passed, he still lives to testify to the uniformly good nature and genial disposition of his nearest neighbor and to express the wish that years of happiness and comfort yet await her. Her husband was the late Orris B. Crowell, son of Captain Elkanah, 2d, formerly of South Sea avenue.

On the north side of the road and a little to the west is the fine two story house built by Captain Heman B. Chase, a grandson of Anthony, Senior. By his first wife, Emily F. Hinckley of Barnstable, he had one son, Heman B., and by his second, Clarence, Edward, Emily and Walter. The fine homestead later became the property of Isaiah, a brother of Orris B. Crowell named above. He married Mercy B., daughter of Captain Zadock Crowell of South Sea avenue, their children being Joshua F., Thomas and Isaiah.

Beyond, on the same side of the highway, still stands the low double house of Captain Heman Chase, who, with his family, occupied it for many years. His children were Lysander, Joshua, Heman B., Mary, Abbie, Davis, Andrew and Louise. Later, the house was owned by David Merchant and now by his heirs.

Opposite is the former home of Luke Chase, son of Deacon Anthony. The building was moved from Hyannis some seventy years ago. Since the decease of Mr Chase in 1855 the place has been owned by several parties, is still in good condition and occupied by strangers.

Crossing a narrow road that extends southerly to Lewis bay, we come to a house that is "an old timer," indeed. With its low underpinning and its curb roof it is calculated to attract more than a passing notice from the stranger who travels that way. The building has within a few years been considerably enlarged but the shape of the original structure can still be traced. The writer remembers very distinctly taking a long walk in that vicinity in 1878, and of meeting Rev. Knoch E. Chase, who then lived in the old house referred to above. He said that his father, Deacon Anthony, moved to that home in 1799 and that he himself was born there in 1804 and had resided there ever since. In reply to an inquiry concerning Indians who had lived thereabout two centuries or more previously, the rev. gentleman pointed out the old Indian burial place which the town had reserved in the early days, and which is located on a peninsula of upland extending into the low ground on the east side of Chase's brook, so called, on the northerly side of the county road. The peninsula, which is about ten rods in width, was partly covered with a small growth of wood, mostly pine, with a clump of oaks on the easterly part. Mr Chase said that the burial place had been encroached upon by cultivation of the adjoining field. At a town meeting, possibly thirty-five years ago, at which it was proposed to place stone bounds upon each one of the town's reservations, this old burial place being one, Mr. Chase said that his father and himself had occupied the premises for many years; but if the town had any Indians to be buried, they could be brought along and he should not object to their burial near the graves of their fathers. The children of Deacon Anthony Chase by his second wife, Mary Eldridge, were Enoch E. and a son who was lost at sea. The children of Rev. Enoch E. Chase were Mary, George, Rebecca and Alexander.

Opposite this ancient structure stands a small house owned formerly by Anthony Chase, Jr., whose children were Albert, Erastus, Cordelia, Leonard, Mary, Anthony and Benjamin.

Crossing the brook already mentioned, which unites with the Baxter's mill stream before reaching Lewis bay, we come to the small dwelling formerly the residence of Captain William Howes, a successful skipper in the mackerel fishery. This home has changed owners several times and is now owned and occupied by Mr. Lysander Chase.

On the opposite side of the highway Captain Leonard Chase, a son of Deacon Anthony by his first wife, Keziah Baker, built a house which was owned and occupied by himself and family. Later this dwelling came into the posession of Captain Gorham Crowell of the sixth generation from Yelverton the pioneer.

Some forty years ago an attempt was made to establish a trout hatchery in the brook close by. The pools were carefully laid out and kept in excellent condition for some years by Mr. Eben Perry, a son of Jabez Perry; but were finally abandoned as the venture proved unsuccessful. Without any special information as to the cause of failure, one might easily conceive it to be a lack of pure, cold spring water, which seems to be the natural habitat for brook trout. Mr. Perry was certainly entitled to much credit for the time, energy and funds which he expended upon this experiment.

A short distance west of the William Howes residence lived, some sixty years ago, Mr. Asa Crocker with his large family. He was a shoe cobbler and worked for Mr. Daniel Crowell in Hyannis.

About a quarter of a mile still farther west, on the south side of the highway, on Eleazer's hill, so called, stands the old-time home of Eleazer, a brother of Captain Timothy Baker, Senr., and in the fifth generation from Francis, a pioneer. Eleazer, or "Uncle Eleazer" as he was called, was miller in the "Baxter's mill" near by, some seventy-five years ago, and for many years after the "Little mill" in West Yarmouth ceased its labors. The dwelling has had many different tenants during the long period of its existence.

Away back "in the forties," on the left hand side of the highway, stood the residence of Captain Alexander Baxter, quite an extensive owner in shipping, who married Sophronia, a half-sister of the Rev. E. E. Chase. Some years later this building was moved farther west to the corner next to a road leading to Lewis bay, and a large double house

WEST YARMOUTH HOUSES

was erected on the old site. Here the captain and his good wife resided for many years, and after their decease the property came into the possession of Captain John A. Baxter, a brother of Captain Alexander, who occupied the premises for some years. In 1876 this fine residence was destroyed by fire. Captain Crowell, in writing of this event, says: "It was a beautifully clear night. The moon casting its golden rays over the old mill pond upon the high land in the background, formed a picture which it would be difficult for an artist to equal in the beauty and grandeur of its scenic effect. But, mingled with the beauty of the scene was the sadness of such an ending of so beautiful a place."

The old gristmill directly opposite the Captain Baxter residence was known as Baxter's mill. It was at one time owned by Captain Timothy Baker, Senr., (born in the first half of the eighteenth century) and later by his son, Captain Joshua Baker, born in 1766. The mill pond was fed by several streamlets which came down from the north; but, its work having been completed, the dam has been allowed to wash away; and, there being some question as to ownership, we learn that this once beautiful and interesting spot is now grown up with rushes. It seems as if the water power here might, in this day of improved machinery, be made again to serve a useful purpose.

Returning now to the "Four Corners" at the head of South Sea avenue, we take the North lane, so called, and proceed northerly. This roadway was doubtless, in the early days of the settlement, an Indian trail, which, with its branches, led to Bass river and the Indian settlements lying northerly and easterly.

Near the Corners, on the left hand side, stood the home of Jeremiah Gorham, generally known as Jeremy, a brother of John, heretofore mentioned.

On the same side of the way, a little farther north, was the residence of James Whelden, whose sons, Zimri and Arunah, became prominent masters both of sailing ships and steamers. Several other members of the same family became officers of steam vessels.

Nearly opposite was the home of Thomas Sherman, who married Rebecca Burgess, a daughter of Isaiah Burgess. Their children were Stephen, Mary, Thomas and Lydia. The father of Thomas, Senr., was Ichabod Sherman, a blacksmith, who came to Indian town (South Yarmouth) from New Bedford not far from the year 1790 in company with Captain Benjamin Tripp and Abiel Akin, father of the late David K. Akin. He died in 1844. Isaiah Burgess and his wife Nancy were near neighbors of Thomas Sherman, Senr.

A little to the north, and on the west side of the lane, we come to the site of the old house of Higgins Crowell, Senr., whose children were Higgins, Ruth, Betsey and Benjamin. His second wife was Patience Coleman.

On the east side of the road which led from North lane directly to the "little mill," more than eighty years ago lived Mr. Joyce

Taylor, father of a large family. Several of the sons were noted skippers of mackerel catchers fifty to sixty years ago. Joyce, Freeman, Henry and Dustin, who became captains, were worthy of their ancestry. The little mill ceased its labors more than thirty years ago.

North lane proper extends across the mill stream just north of the site of the little mill and was, in the early days, bordered by homesteads as far as Long pond; for this was the main highway until Parkers river bridge was built. Now, we believe, not a single building remains on this once frequented way.

The fact that the site of the John Crow house is several rods west of South Sea avenue has led some people to suppose that the highway has been relocated. To the writer of this article, the evidence points to the contrary. In the earliest days of settlement, when the danger of attacks by Indians was great, the pioneer who wished to establish a home at a distance from his neighbors, so placed his dwelling within his clearing as to have an open space on all sides, in order that he might more easily detect the presence of an enemy and also to diminish the danger from forest fires.

When Yelverton came to this locality in 1639 or 40 his nearest neighbors were probably located some four miles or more distant. About ten years later his nearest neighbor on the east was Richard Berry, who established a home near the mouth of Bass river. At the time of his decease, in 1683, his son John was forty-one years old, and he had but two grandchildren living in Yarmouth, the elder being less than two years of age.

It is quite reasonable to suppose that the spot known by reliable tradition as the site of John's residence, marks also the location of the home of his father, Yelverton. One other reason for locating the residence at a distance from the well marked trail might have been that water was more easily to be obtained from a spring or shallow well on the ground near at hand.

In closing this series, the writer would earnestly invite any information respecting the Baxter's mill and the little mill; the dates of their establishment and of their falling into disuse; together with any other facts relating to the history of the section in which they are located; and especially does he invite correction of any errors which may have appeared, and a criticism of any portion of the series; for in this way is gained a more definite knowledge of historic facts.

No. 40.

LIBRARY *of*
Cape Cod
HISTORY & GENEALOGY

A MAYFLOWER LINE

Hopkins--Snow--Cook

By Grace Fielding Hall

YARMOUTHPORT, MASS.:
C. W. SWIFT, Publisher and Printer,
The "Register" Press,
1914.

A MAYFLOWER LINE
Hopkins--Snow--Cook
By Grace Fielding Hall

Copyright, 1914,
by Charles W. Swift.

STEPHEN[1] HOPKINS.

Stephen[1] Hopkins came in the Mayflower with his second wife, Elizabeth   , and three children born in England, one child, Oceanus, born on the voyage over. Stephen[1] Hopkins was born in England in 1580; died in Plymouth in 1644.

Children of first wife.

Gyles[2], born in England about 1605; m. Katherine Whelden.

Constanta[2], Constance, b. in England about 1608; m. Nicholas Snow.

Children of second wife.

Damaris[2], b. in England; m. Jacob Cooke.

Oceanus[2], b. on the voyage, Oct. 1620; died 1627.

Deborah[2] b. in Plymouth 1622; m. Andrew Ring.

Caleb[2], b. in Plymouth.

Ruth[2], b. in Plymouth; died an infant.

Elizabeth[2], b. in Plymouth.

GYLES[2] HOPKINS.

Gyles[2] Hopkins was born in England about 1605; married, 1639, Katherine, daughter of Gabriel Whelden of Yarmouth. Gyles[2] died 1690.

Children.

Mary[3], b. 1640, probably in Harwich.

Stephen[3], b. 1642, probably in Harwich; m. Mary Myrick.

John[3], b. 1643; died in infancy.

Abigail[3], b. 1644.

Deborah[3], b. June 1648, in Eastham; m. Josiah Cooke.

Caleb[3], b. 1650; m. Mary Williams.

Ruth[3], b. 1653.

Joshua[3], b. 1657; m. Mary Cole.

William[3], b. 1660.

Elizabeth[3], b. 1664; d. in infancy.

CONSTANTA OR CONSTANCE HOPKINS.

Constance[2] was born in England about 1608; married Nicholas Snow of Plymouth (probably son of Nicholas Snow and wife Mary of London). Constance died Oct. 1677; Nicholas, 15 Nov. 1676.

Children.

Mark[3], b. 9 May 1628, in Plymouth; m. 1st Anne Cook, 2nd Jane Prence.

Mary[3], b. about 1630, in Plymouth; m. Thomas Paine.

Sarah[3], b. about 1632, in Plymouth.

A Mayflower Line.

Joseph³, b. 1634, in Plymouth.
Stephen³, b. 1636, in Plymouth.
John³, b. 1638, in Plymouth.
Elizabeth³, b. 1640.
Jabez³, b. 1642.
Ruth³, b. 1644.
Hannah³, b. 1646, probably at Eastham.
Rebecca³, b. 1648, probably at Eastham.

MARK² SNOW.

Mark², son of Nicholas and Constance (Hopkins) Snow, born in Plymouth, 9 May 1628; married 1st 18 Jan. 1655, Anne Cook, daughter of Josiah Cook. She died 25 July 1656. He married 2nd 9 Jan. 1660, Jane Prence.

Children.
Anne³, b. 7 July 1656, in Eastham; m. Eldad Atwood.

JOSIAH¹ COOK.

He is first mentioned in the Plymouth Records in 1633, was rated as a tax payer in 1634, was married 16 Sept. 1635, to Elizabeth (Ring) widow of Stephen Deane and daughter of the widow Mercy Ring, who came to Plymouth in 1629. He died in Eastham 17 Oct. 1673. His widow Elizabeth administered on his estate.

Children.
Josiah², born ; m. Deborah Hopkins.
Ann², b. ; m. Mark Snow.
Bethia², b. ; m. Joseph Harding.
Davis of Plymouth says there were seven other children.

JOSIAH² COOK.

Son of Josiah¹ and Elizabeth (Ring) Cook, married 27 July 1668, Deborah³, dau. of Gyles² and Katherine (Whelden) Hopkins.

Children.
Elizabeth³, b. 12 Oct. 1669; died March 1670.
Josiah³, b. in Eastham 12 Nov. 1670; m. Mary .
Richard³, b. 4 Sept. 1672.
Elizabeth³, b. 16 June 1674; m. Oct. 1693 Thomas³ Newcomb.
Caleb³, b. 28 April 1679.
Joshua³, b. 4 Feb. 1683.
Benjamin³, b. 28 April 1687.

JOSIAH³ COOK.

Son of Josiah² and Deborah (Hopkins) Cook. Born in Eastham 12 Nov. 1670. Moved to Truro, married Mary . He served the town of Truro in many public offices. The last mention of him is in Aug. 1718, as present at a public meeting. There is no date of death or burial.

Children.
Desire⁴, b. 1694.
Deborah⁴, b. 1696.
John⁴, b. 1698.
Mary⁴, b. 1700.
Solomon⁴, b. about 1708, baptized 18 Nov. 1711; died 21 Nov. 1781; residence, Provincetown; m. 4 June 1733, Rebekah Cowell.

SOLOMON⁴ COOK.

Son of Josiah³ and Mary Cook. Born about 1708, m. 4 June 1733, Rebekah, dau. of Edward and Rebekah (Broughton) Cowell of Boston. She was born 1713-14, bap. 3 Dec. 1727. He died 21 Nov. 1781. She died 19 Aug. 1788.

Children.
Mary*, b. 1735; m. Doty of Plymouth.
Solomon*, b. 12 Sept. 1737.
Rebecca*, b. 1740.
Barnabas*, b. ; m. Sarah Whorf.
Edward*, b. 29 April 1746.
Elisha*, b. ; m. Susan Atwood.
Jonathan*, b. 22 July 1753; m. Mercy Tilton.
Samuel*, b. 29 Aug. 1756; m. Jane Nickerson.
John*, b. ; m. Mary Newcomb.
Lemuel*, b. ; died young.

JONATHAN* COOK.
Son of Solomon⁴ and Rebecca (Cowell) Cook. Born in Provincetown 22 July 1753; m. 16 April 1773, Mercy, dau. of Phillip and Desire Tilton.
Children.
Patty*, b. 27 Aug. 1773; m. Joshua F. Grozier 24 March 1793.
David N.*, b. 29 Aug. 1776; m. Salome Lombard 23 Nov. 1800.
Jonathan*, b. 23 Feb. 1780; m. Sabra Brown 26 March 1802.
Philip*, b. 15 Oct. 1781; m. Anna Smith.
Bethiah*, b. 14 Oct. 1784; m. Thomas Sparks.
Lemuel*, b. 13 Sept. 1786; m. Rebecca Whorf 29 Dec. 1807.
{ Edward*,
b. 16 March 1789; died
Sally*, in infancy.
Sally*, b. 3 Sept. 1792.

PATTY* (MARTHA) COOK.
Daughter of Jonathan and Mercy (Tilton) Cook. Born in Provincetown 27 Aug. 1773; m. 24 March 1793, Joshua Freeman Grozier, born in Truro 2 April 1769, son of John and Mercy (Hopkins) Grozier. She died
Children.
William⁷, b. 17 April 1794.
{ Joshua⁷,
b. 7 July 1796.
Freeman⁷,
Freeman⁷, b. 27 Nov. 1798.
Mercy⁷, b. 22 July 1800; m. Patty⁷, b. 20 Feb. 1802.
Sally⁷, b. 28 Aug. 1803; m. Saloma⁷, b. 14 Oct. 1805.
Caleb Upham⁷, b. 7 Jan. 1808; m.
Rebecca Atkins⁷, b. 4 Oct. 1810.

DAVID* NEWCOMB COOK.
Born 29 Aug. 1776; m. 23 Nov. 1800, Salome Lombard, born 23 Jan. 1782. He died 18 May 1856. She died 26 March 1845.
Children.
Rebecca⁷, b. 7 Sept. 1801; d. 15 March 1802.
Patty⁷, b. 9 Jan. 1804; m. James Stanford.
Rebecca⁷, b. 8 July 1806; m. Thomas Lothrop 30 April 1826.
Salome⁷, b. 31 Dec. 1808; d. 2 Oct. 1823.
Lemuel⁷, b. 2 Nov. 1811; m. Mary J. Weeks.
Rosetta⁷, b. 31 May 1814; m. Enoch Hall.
Thomas Dunlop⁷, b. 15 Jan. 1817; d. 6 Sept. 1823.
Benjamin Lombard⁷, b. 6 Oct. 1819; m. 1st Anne E. Hammersley, 2nd Mary J. Trask.
Eliza Bryant⁷, b. 26 Feb. 1822; m. Peter E. Dolliver.

JONATHAN* COOK.
Son of Jonathan and Mercy (Tilton) Cook. Born in Provincetown 23 Feb. 1780; m. 26 March 1802, Sabra Brown.

A Mayflower Line.

LEMUEL⁵ COOK.
Son of Jonathan and Mercy (Tilton) Cook. Born in Provincetown 13 Sept. 1786; m. 29 Dec. 1807, Rebecca Whorf, born 20 July 1790. He died in St. Iago De Cuba 25 Jan. 1828. She died 27 Sept. 1849.

Children.
David⁷ b. 15 Oct. 1808; m. ; lost at sea 7 Dec. 1849.
Tilton⁷, b. 10 July 1810; m. Clarinda Cook.
Charles Dyer⁷, b. 12 June 1813; m. Ellen
Emily⁷, b. 12 Oct. 1815; m. Jairus H. Hilliard.
Ephraim Ryder⁷, b. ; m. Abbie Conant; d. 29 Oct. 1867.
Lemuel⁷, b. 31 March 1828; m. Rebecca Morgan; d. 30 Nov. 1885.

SAMUEL⁵ COOK.
Son of Solomon⁴ and Rebecca Cowell Cook. Born 29 Aug. 1756; died Feb. 1825; married Jane, dau. of Phineas and Susannah (Smith) Nickerson.

Children.
Eleanor⁶, b. Jan. 19, 1778; m. Cyrenius Brown.
Ephraim, b. Feb. 4, 1779; m. Rebekah Lombard.
Samuel, b. Oct. 17, 1781; m. Tamsin Brown.
Jesse, b. June 13, 1783; m. Thankful Smith.
Stephen, b. Oct. 29, 1786; m. Delia Cornwell.
Ebenezer, b. Oct. 21, 1788; d. Aug. 30, 1810.
Jane, b. June 24, 1791; d. Feb. 28, 1796.
Betsey, b. April 12, 1794; m. Epaphras Kibbe.
James T., b. April 10, 1796; m. Phebe Nickerson.
Jane, b. July 21, 1799; m. Abraham Small.

No. 41.

LIBRARY *of*
Cape Cod
HISTORY & GENEALOGY

ATWOOD GENEALOGY

By Grace Fielding Hall

YARMOUTHPORT, MASS.:
C. W. SWIFT, Publisher and Printer,
The "Register" Press,
1914.

ATWOOD GENEALOGY.
By Grace Fielding Hall

Copyright, 1914,
by Charles W. Swift.

The name Atwood occurs early in England and was probably given in the first instance to one whose residence was in or near a forest. It is not likely that so descriptive a name would escape repetition in its use, so that the Atwoods may not have originally sprung from a common stock.

Probably the name Atwood and Wood have been more or less interchangeable from the first. That this is the case in modern times we shall see later. (The name Forest and DeForest are instanced as being analogous in this respect.)

There have been many Atwoods in England and there are now many in America. In the Herald's college in England, sixteen families of the name have recorded the coats of arms.

The Atwood race from whom we came probably originated in Sanderstead, a parish in Surrey county, about twelve miles south of London. It was first spelled Atte Wode. The first record of this name is one buried in the church at Sanderstead, A. D. 1520.

From the Atwoods of Sanderstead, the Atwoods of America have undoubtedly descended.

The Atwoods of America, so far as is known, are not one stock.

The pioneers of the name are:

1 PHILLIP ATWOOD, who came over from England a boy of 12 or 13 years, in either the "Susan and Ellen" or the "Planter," (the name appears in both passenger lists by some mistake or other) in 1635. His name occurs in the records of Lynn and Bradford. He married and had children and grandchildren; but the female sex predominated among them, and it is not supposed that he now has many descendants of the name.

2 JOHN ATWOOD came from London previous to 1635 (when he was made a "freeman") with a considerable estate. He was assistant governor of Plymouth for several years, and the treasurer of the colony from 1641 to 1644, when he died, leaving a wife Ann (Lee) but no children.

3 JAMES ATWOOD was made a freeman in Massachusetts May 22, 1639. Nothing further is known of him.

Atwood Genealogy.

John⁴, b. Sept. 25, 1725; m. Abigail Freeman Feb. 13, 1755.
Thankful⁴
Ephraim⁴, b. March 9, 1728; m. Bethiah
Timothy⁴, b. July 5, 1731.
Simeon⁴, b. Nov. 3, 1733.

ELEAZER⁴ ATWOOD.

He was born in 1681, probably a grandson of Stephen¹ of Eastham but no proof of it can be found. His father's name may have been Joseph or Daniel. Eleazer died May 25, 1729, 48 years old, according to the inscription on his tombstone, which is still standing (1885) in the neglected old burying ground at Mayo's Neck, Wellfleet. Beside it is the tombstone of his wife Joanna (Stout) whom he married in Eastham May 31, 1709. She survived him and married, second, William Covell June 27, 1734, and died Jan. 16, 1736; was buried beside her first husband, Eleazer Atwood.

Children, born in Eastham.
Thankful⁴, b. June 30, 1711; m. Seth Hinckley Oct. 10, 1727.
Eleazer⁴, b. Sept. 15, 1713; m. Rebecca Young Feb. 1735 or 6.
James⁴, b. Aug. 31, 1715; m.
Richard⁴, b. March 31, 1717; m. Mary⁴ Atwood Oct. 27, 1748.
Jesse⁴, b. July 28, 1720.
Christopher⁴, b. April 4, 1724.
Joshua⁴, b. Sept. 23, 1729; d. March 31, 1736.

RICHARD⁴ ATWOOD.

Born March 31, 1717; m. Mary⁴ Atwood, daughter of John and Thankful (Williamson) Atwood, Oct. 27, 1748.

Children.
Mary⁵, b. Aug. 16, 1749.
Lucy⁵, b. Aug. 17, 1751.
Richard⁵, b. May 27, 1753; m. Elizabeth Rich.
Deborah⁵, b. Aug. 16, 1755.
Isaiah⁵, b. July 11, 1759.

RICHARD⁵ ATWOOD, JR.

Wellfleet.
Born May 27, 1753; m. Elizabeth Rich of Truro, probably July 1781. Richard⁵ died May 20, 1809. His wife died Aug. 17, 1836.

Children.
Uriah Atkins⁶, b. July 15, 1782; m. Mary Newcomb.
Richard⁶, b. July 31, 1784; m. Cynthia Gross.
Ruth⁶, b. Feb. 24, 1787; m. Joseph Cobb.
Daughter⁶, b. May 5, 1789; d. May 19, 1789.
Jesse⁶, b. June 23, 1790; m. Henry⁶, b. Sept. 26, 1793; m. Polly
Infant daughter, b. Sept. 26, 1793; d. Oct. 1, 1793.
Son, b. May 15, 1796; d. same day.
Elisha Rich⁶, b. July 15, 1797; m. Polly Lombard.
Levi Young⁶, b. Sept. 18, 1799; m. Nancy Dyer.

URIAH⁶ ATKINS ATWOOD.

Born July 15, 1782; m. Mary Newcomb March 12, 1808. Uriah died July 23, 1856. His wife died Nov. 27, 1831 or 32.

Children.
Eliza⁷, b. Nov. 13, 1810; d. Aug. 28, 1867.
Mary Higgins⁷, b. Feb. 23, 1813; m. Isaac Ryder.
Sally Rich⁷, b. March 23, 1815; m. Richard Rich.
Betsey Newcomb⁷, b. Dec. 15, 1816; m. Amos P. Fielding.
Bethiah Gross⁷, b. Nov. 2, 1819; m. Bartholomew O. Gross.

Atwood Genealogy.

4 HARMAN ATWOOD, who came from Sanderstead, County Surrey, England, in the employ of Theo. Buttolph, settled in Boston, Mass. He married Ann Copp, Aug. 11, 1645, and died 1651. His son John, born Oct. 5, 1647, had several children, and probably there are a goodly number of descendants from this branch.

5 JOHN ATWOOD or WODD first appears in Plymouth, Mass., in 1643. He married Sarah Masterson and was the ancestor of the Atwoods of Plymouth and neighboring towns. (See Davis's "Ancient Landmarks of Plymouth.")

6 STEPHEN ATWOOD or WODD (very likely a brother of John) was also in Plymouth in 1643. He married Abigail Dunham Nov. 6, 1644, and settled in Eastham. From him are descended the Atwoods of Cape Cod. The Atwoods of Maine are largely if not entirely from this stock. A considerable immigration from the Cape towns to Maine occurred in the latter part of the last century.

7 DR. (sometimes Capt. from a tradition that he was in Cromwell's army) THOMAS ATWOOD was in Hartford, Conn., in 1664, and settled in Wethersfield, Conn., about 1667; died in 1682, leaving children from whom are descended the Atwoods of Connecticut.

8 The Taunton Atwoods are descended from JOSEPH ATWOOD or WOOD, who married Esther Walker Jan. 1, 1680.

STEPHEN ATWOOD[1].

Was probably born in England about 1620. He is first heard of in Plymouth, Mass., in 1643. He married Abigail Dunham, daughter of John Dunham of Plymouth, Nov. 16, 1644. Soon after he removed to that part of Eastham set off in 1763 as Wellfleet, and resided there until his death in February, 1694.

Children.
John[2]
Hannah[2], b. Oct. 14, 1649.
Joseph[2], m. Mrs. Apphiah Knowles (widow of John), who was born Oct. 15, 1651. She was a daughter of Edward Bangs.
Daniel[2]
Eldad[2], b. probably 1660; m. Anna Snow.
Stephen, Jr.[2], m. Esther

ELDAD[2] ATWOOD.

Born in Eastham about 1660; m. Feb. 14, 1683, Anna Snow, daughter of Mark and Anna (Cook) Snow. She was born in Eastham July 7, 1656. He died 1715.
Children.
Mary[3], b. Nov. 4, 1684.
John[3], b. Aug. 10, 1686; m. Thankful Williamson Sept. 28, 1719.
Ann[3], b. Jan. 1688.
Deborah[3], b. March 1690.
Sarah[3], b. April 1692; m. Elisha Hunter May 17, 1726.
Eldad[3], b. July 9, 1695; m. Mary Snow Feb. 15, 1727.
Ebenezer[3], b. March 1697; m. Hepzibah Williamson Feb. 3, 1725.
Benjamin[3], b. June 1701.

JOHN[3] ATWOOD.

Son of Eldad[2] Atwood, b. Aug. 10, 1686; m. Sept. 28, 1719, Thankful Williamson.
Children.
William[4], b. April 11, 1721; m. 1st Bathsheba Smith, 2nd Mrs. Mary Newcomb Nov. 28, 1765.
Mary[4], b. Feb. 15, 1723; m. Richard Atwood Oct. 27, 1748.

Cordelia Studley', b. July 24, 1822.
Frederick Upham', b. Dec. 11, 1824; m. Sarah Hatch.

Deaths.
Cordelia died Feb. 9, 1834.
Sally d. Jan. 15, 1854.
Betsey d. June 20, 1861.
Frederick d. July 6, 1861.
Eliza d. Aug. 28, 1867.
Mary d. Feb. 25, 1874.
Bethiah d. Sept. 20, 1891.
Sarah (Hatch) Atwood d. Mar. 29, 1862.
Frederick W.' d. June 9, 1876, age 26 years, 9 months.

BETSEY' NEWCOMB ATWOOD.
Born Dec. 15, 1816; m. Amos Paine Fielding April 8, 1838. She died June 20, 1861. He died Dec. 10, 1848.

Children.
Warren⁸, b. Oct. 3, 1841; m. Rebecca C. Lathrop Dec. 7, 1865.
Cordelia Studley⁸, b. July 13, 1845; m. Solomon T. Atwood.
Betsey Jane⁸, b. Aug. 5, 1847; m. Jonathan Freeman.

MAYFLOWER ANCESTRY OF ELDAD ATWOOD.

Among the passengers who came to this country in the Mayflower, arriving at Plymouth Dec. 22, 1620:

Francis Cooke.
He was one of the signers of the Mayflower compact. There came with him a son, John. His wife came in the "Ann," 1623, with other children. His son Josias married in 1635 Elizabeth, widow of Stephen Deane, and moved to Eastham. They had among other children Anne or Anna.

Stephen Hopkins.
He was one of the signers of the Mayflower compact. With him came in the Mayflower his second wife, Elizabeth, with her two children and two servants, Edward Doty and Edward Lister, also two children by a former wife, Giles and Constanta or Constance. Constance in 1627 married Nicholas Snow, who came in the "Ann," 1623. They had Mark, born 1628. Anne or Anna Cooke and Mark Snow m. Jan. 18, 1655. Among other children they had Anne or Anna, b. July 7, 1656. She married Eldad Atwood Feb. 14, 1683.

NO. 42.

LIBRARY of Cape Cod
HISTORY & GENEALOGY

NEWCOMB GENEALOGY

By Grace Fielding Hall

YARMOUTHPORT, MASS.:
C. W. SWIFT, Publisher and Printer,
The "Register" Press,
1914.

NEWCOMB GENEALOGY.
By Grace Fielding Hall

Copyright, 1914,
by Charles W. Swift.

CAPTAIN ANDREW[1] NEWCOMB.

Of the early history of Andrew Newcomb little is known. That he was born in England is quite certain; that he migrated from the west of England, perhaps Devonshire or Wales, nearly all traditions declare.

The date of his arrival in this country is not definitely known, but it is quite probable that he was among the earliest settlers of New England.

First mention of him is made in 1663 in Boston, Mass., when and where he married his second wife, Grace, widow of William Rix or Ricks.

He was at that time a mariner or sea captain. The name of his first wife has not been found. His second wife, Grace , born about 1620 to 1625.

Suffolk Deeds contain copy of agreement, date Feb. 1645-46, in which Andrew Newcomb and wife Grace are to enjoy during life the old dwelling house "now in the tenure and occupation of the same Newcomb," formerly of William Ricks, deceased, John and Thomas Ricks, sons of William, to have the new dwelling house adjoining the same, etc., near the water mill in Boston.

Andrew Newcomb's will, filed among the Probate papers of Boston, made 31 Jan. 1682. Will is upon Suffolk Probate, Vol. II, page 48. That he died in Nov. 1686, is inferred from the date of admission of his will to probate. That he was a man of education is shown from the specimen of his writing still extant.

Children by first wife.

Andrew², b. about 1640; m. 1st Sarah   , 2nd Anna Bayes.

Susannah², b. between 1640 and 1650; m. Phillip Blague of Boston, 2nd Pritchett or Pritchard.

Children by 2nd wife, Grace.

Grace², b. Oct. 20, 1664; m. James, son of Stephen and Jane Butler, Boston, 2nd Andrew Rankin of Boston.

LIEUT. ANDREW² NEWCOMB.

Andrew² Newcomb was residing in this country as early as July 1666, as at that date he attended a meeting at Isles of Shoals, near Portsmouth, N. H. Probably born about 1640. Appears to have moved from Isles of Shoals about 1675, and settled same year at Edgartown, Mass., where he lived until his decease, which took place between March 7, 1703-4, and Oct. 22, 1708, aged about 64 to 68 years.

He lived many years in the village of Edgartown and owned the land upon which the Court house now stands.

Mr. Newcomb was chosen lieutenant April 13, 1691, and in the same year was in command of the fortification, having such number of men under him as were ordered by the chief magistrate. Spelled name Nucomb. M. 1st Sarah   , 2nd Anna Bayes, daughter of Capt. Thomas and Anna (Baker) Bayes. She was born about 1658; died summer or Sept. 1731.

Children by 1st wife, Sarah.

Simeon³, b. about 1662; m.

Andrew³, b. about 1664; d. in Edgartown, June 1678.

Simon³, b. 1664; m. Deborah .

Thomas³, b. 1668; m. Elizabeth Cook.

Sarah³, b. 1670; m. Jan. 9, 1690 or 91, Joshua Conant; moved to north part of Eastham, which is now Truro.

Mary or Mercy³, b. about 1672; m. Oct. 4, 1694, Capt. Thomas Lumbert of Barnstable; removed to Truro 1669; d. Nov. 13, 1736.

Peter³, b. about 1674; m. Mercy Smith.

Children by 2nd wife, Anna Bayes.

Anna³, b. 1677; m. Lieut. Matthew Mayhew of Edgartown.

Elizabeth³, b. 1681; m. Capt. John Atkins.

Joseph³, b. 1683; m. Joyce Butler.

Emblem³, b. 1685; m. Samuel Atkins.

Tabitha³, b. 1688; m. Peter Ray.

Hannah³, b. 1694; m. Thomas Dureary.

Zerviah³, b. 1698 or 99; m. Josiah Bearse.

Mary³, b. 1700; m. Jonathan Pease.

THOMAS³ NEWCOMB.

Born at Kittery, Maine, or vicinity about 1668; m. at Eastham Oct. 1693, Elizabeth, dau. of Josiah and Deborah (Hopkins) Cook. She was born June 16, 1674.

Children.

Edward⁴, b. Aug. 3, 1695.

Thomas⁴, b. Aug. 13, 1697; m. Hepzibah, 2nd Mary Tilton.

Simon⁴, b. Nov. 30, 1699; m. Lydia Brown, 2nd Sarah .   .

Deborah⁴, m. Jan. 28, 1729, Thomas Larkin.
Mary⁴, m. April 11, 1723, Luke Stubbs.
Josiah⁴, bap. June 2, 1717.
Elizabeth⁴, m. July 24, 1729, Joshua Pierce.
Ebenezer⁴, m. Thankful Freeman, 2nd Experience Brown.
Joseph⁴, m. Mary Eldredge.

SIMON⁴ NEWCOMB.

Born in Eastham Nov. 30, 1699, yeoman; m. April 5, 1722, Lydia, daughter of Samuel and Susannah (Harding) Brown, b. April 30, 1702, 2nd Sarah ... Lived in that part of Eastham which was set off in 1763 as the town of Wellfleet.
Children.
Simeon⁵, b. about 1723; m. Mercy Brown, 2nd Experience Arey.
Susannah⁵, m. Oct. 8, 1747, Joseph Pierce.
William⁵, b. 1727; m. Vashti Cole.
Simon⁵, b. Jan. 25, 1735; m. Harding, 2nd Rebecca Smith.
Lydia⁵, m. Aug. 18, 1772, Isaac Hopkins of Truro.

SIMON⁵ NEWCOMB.

Born in Eastham, now Wellfleet, Jan. 25, 1735; m. April 12, 1757, Grace Harding of Chatham, by Rev. Stephen Emery. She died in Wellfleet June 16, 1785, in her 52nd year. He m. 2nd Rebecca Smith of Eastham, to whom he was published Aug. 20, 178-. She died Oct. 2, 1807, in her 73d year. He died May 20, 1808.
Children.
Thomas⁶, b. May 30, 1758; m. Jemena Newcomb.
Jeremiah⁶, b. April 2, 1760; m. Mary Higgins, 2nd Sarah Lombard.
Zerviah⁶, b. March 16, 1762; m. Reuben Covell, Jr.; d. Feb. 25, 1843.
Huldah⁶, b. Nov. 28, 1763; m. David Atkins.
Grace⁶, b. March 4, 1765; m. Joshua Young, Jr., 2nd Samuel Pierce.
Seth⁶, b. March 3, 1768; m. Abigail Snow.
Simon⁶, b. March 16, 1770; d. young.
Priscilla⁶, b. Feb. 18, 1772; m. Solomon Holbrook, 2nd, Joseph Hatch.
Theophilus⁶, b. Feb. 6, 1774; m. Dorcas Young.
Simon⁶, b. Oct. 5, 1778; m. Sarah Cole, 2nd Polly (Rich) Cobb.
Simon's daughter Grace m. Elijah Atwood.

CAPT. JEREMIAH⁶ NEWCOMB.

Born in Eastham, now Wellfleet, April 2, 1760; m. March 18, 1784, Mary⁷ Higgins, dau. of Enoch and Mary, b. July 7, 1764, d. April 16, 1814. He m. 2nd Aug. 16, 1814, Sarah Lombard, who died Nov. 18, 1831, aged 67. He died Feb. 20, 1842, in Wellfleet.
Children.
John⁷, b. March 25, 1786; m. Hannah Lombard, 2nd Sally Lombard.
Mary⁷, b. March 20, 1788; m. Uriah A. Atwood.
Nancy⁷, b. Aug. 27, 1791; m. Aug. 27, 1808, Elisha Higgins. He was lost at sea. She died in Wellfleet March 26, 1829.
Hannah Atkins⁷, b. Nov. 1, 1793; m. Ebenezer Freeman, 3rd. She d. July 7, 1870.
Betsey⁷, b. Dec. 3, 1798; m. April 18, 1817, Samuel P. Snow of Truro.

Jeremiah⁷, b. Nov. 15, 1802; m. Abigail Harding.

Capt. Jeremaih Newcomb entered service in the Revolutionary war March, 1776, in Capt. John Gill's company of Wellfleet; sailed to Plymouth, thence marched to Boston, where he was stationed with troops under Gen. Putnam. Discharged about May 1, 1776, when he entered service as matross in artillery company for twelve months, Capt. John Gill, Col. Craft's regiment or battalion. Remained during the winter at Castle William, building the fort; passed daily in flat-bottomed boat to Boston and back; dragged cannon to top of hill to place in fort; stocked and bedded those injured by the English and received passports of vessels passing the fort. Procured a mortar, stationed it in north side of Long Island head with breastwork and 6 pounder cannon on Nantucket or Nantasket hill, to play across the head onto the shipping of the enemy. The throwing of the third bomb caused the vessels to drop down near the lighthouse, which they blew up. Was discharged at end of year. He was of the brig Resolution, was taken prisoner Nov. 28, 1780, and committed to Old Mill prison Jan. 22, 1781. He was also out at other times during the war.

Capt. Newcomb received pension under the Act of 1832. He was selectman and treasurer, 1813-14; town clerk, 1814, and coroner, 1822.

LEMUEL NEWCOMB⁵.

Born in Truro July 27, 1724; m. Nov. 28, 1751, Phebe Atkins, 2nd Dec. 12, 1765, Elizabeth Wood. The 2nd wife may have been the widow Elizabeth Newcomb, who died March 5, 1806, if she was Elizabeth N. whose estate was administered upon in 1766; then Mr. N. must have died soon after his second marriage. He was dead before July 24, 1787. He lived in Wellfleet.

Children.

James⁶, b. Nov. 11, 1754; m. Tabitha Nickerson.

Phebe⁶, m. Nov. 3, 1785, John Pierce.

Margery⁶, m. Sept. 12, 1786, Zephaniah King Pierce, 2nd A. Blake.

Hannah⁶

Joshua⁶, said to have left no descendants.

Lemuel⁶, b. April 7, 1757; m. Lucy Holbrook.

CAPT. JAMES NEWCOMB⁶.

Born in Eastham, now Wellfleet, Nov. 11, 1754.

Children.

Lucy⁷, b. Aug. 29, 1776; m. Sept. 22, 1796, Benjamin Coan of Truro; resided in Wrentham.

James⁷, b. June 12, 1778; d. Sept. 19, 1796.

Lemuel⁷, b. Sept. 16, 1782; m. Hannah Doane, 2nd Mary Rich.

Sally⁷, b. Oct. 30, 1784; d. Nov. 29, 1784.

Phebe Atkins⁷, b. Aug. 15, 1786; pub. Dec. 12, 1801, to John Pococh, m. 2nd Feb. 8, 1810, Elisha Newcomb, 3rd Oct. 16, 1829, or Dec. 18, 1831, John Young.

Betsey⁷, b. June 4, 1788; m. Oct. 23, 1808, Jeremiah Atwood and died 1866 in Wellfleet.

Hannah⁷, b. Nov. 10, 1791; m. Rev. James Burnett, had two children, resided in Charlestown.

Lydia⁷, b. June 8, 1794; m. April 6, 1813, Freeman A. Baker.

No. 43.

LIBRARY of
Cape Cod
HISTORY & GENEALOGY

EARLY WHELDENS OF YARMOUTH

By James W. Hawes

YARMOUTHPORT, MASS.:
C. W. SWIFT, Publisher and Printer,
The "Register" Press,
1914.

EARLY WHELDENS OF YARMOUTH.

By James W. Hawes.

Gabriel[1] Whelden,(a) b. in England, was in the Plymouth Colony in 1638. The date of his arrival in America and the place of his landing are not known. He probably came from Nottinghamshire. His children were no doubt born in England and were probably by a first wife. When he died in 1654 his wife was Margaret, who, it seems clear, was his second wife and not the mother of his children. He apparently came to Yarmouth about 1639 with a family of grown children. He left Yarmouth about 1648.

Pope(a1) says he removed to Lynn and then to Malden, where he died between Feb. 11, 1653-4, (date of his will) and April 4, 1654, (date of probate). He gave 10s. to the church in Malden and the rest of his estate in that town, consisting of house, lands, cattle and corn, together with the money due him from William Crofts, to his wife Margaret. His will mentions no children. The inventory of his goods, chattels and cattle amounted to £40 11s. 8d.(b)

Gabriel Whelden, Sept. 3, 1638, was licensed by the Plymouth court to dwell at Mattacheese (Yarmouth), with the consent of the committee of the peace, and to have land there.(c)

June 17, 1641, the court ordered William Lumpkin and Hugh Tilly to pay 15s. to Gabriel Whelden for his third part of a skiff or boat they were partners in and for his damage sustained in the want thereof to fetch fish to fish his corn with, the boat or skiff to be theirs.(d)

In 1642 he was surveyor of highways for Yarmouth,(e) and June 1, 1647; he was presented and sworn for the same office.(f)

It appears that before May 14, 1648, he had sold land in Yarmouth to Edward Sturgis.(g)

Oct. 21, 1653, Gabriel Whelden and his youngest son John sold lands in Arnold and elsewhere in Nottinghamshire, England, to William Crofts of Lynn, New England.(g1) After Gabriel's death his sons Henry and John in 1655 brought suit for their portions of his estate.(h)

Children, order uncertain.

Ralph, probably; m.

Henry, m.

John, m. Mary, dau. of Thomas Folland, Sr.(h1)

Catharine, probably; m. Giles Hopkins Oct. 9, 1639.(i)

Ruth, m. Richard Taylor after Oct. 27, 1646.

Oct. 9, 1639, Gyles Hopkins and Katherne (Catharine) Whelden were married at Plymouth.(i1)

Oct. 27, 1646, the record(j) of the court reads: "In the case betweene Gabriell Whelding and Richard Taylor, about his daughter Ruth, the said Gabriell pmiseth his free assent and consent to theire marriage."

In August, 1643, Henry Whelden is mentioned as one of those between 16 and 60 able to bear arms in Yarmouth.(k) August 23, 1645, he was one of five men who went from Yarmouth against the Narragansets and their confederates.(l) Jan. 25, 1647-8, he was married at Yarmouth, the name of his wife being effaced.(m) June 21, 1650, Sarah Whelden, who may have been his daughter, was born.(n) June 30, 1667, he signed a letter to the court in support of the Rev. Thomas Thornton.(o) He died Oct. 28, 1694.(p)

July 7, 1646, a suit between Teague Jones and Ralph Whelden and the latter's daughter was adjourned.(q)

John Whelden of Yarmouth took the oath of fidelity in 1657.(r) Oct. 30, 1677, he was exempted from training because he had three sons fitted with arms.(s) He died Nov. 20, 1711.(t)

Hannah, daughter of John and Desire Gorham, married a Whelden and removed to Cape May.(u)

NOTES.

(a) Also spelled Whelding and Wheldon and without the "h" in the old records.
(a1) Pioneers of Mass. 489.
(b) Pope, 489; 4 Savage, 504; 16 N. E. Reg. 75.
(c) 1 Plym. Col. Recs. 95.
(d) 2 ib. 21.
(e) Ib. 34, 41.
(f) Ib. 115.
(g) Ib. 129.
(g1) Pope, 489; 1 Essex Deeds, 24.
(h) Pope, 489; Middlesex Files.
(h1) Will of Thos. Folland, Sr., in 1686; Pope, 235, who calls the testators Holland erroneously and not Folland; 3 Mf. 176; 1 Barn. Prob. Recs. 5.
(i) The Bangs Family by Dean Dudley, Ancestral Chart bet. pp. 314 and 315, pp. 318 and 320.
(i1) 1 Plym. Col. Recs. 134.
(j) 2 ib. 110.
(k) 8 ib. 194.
(l) 2 ib. 90-93.
(m) 8 ib. 4.
(n) Ib. 12.
(o) Swift, 90.
(p) 2 Freeman, 202.
(q) 2 Plym. Col. Recs. 104.
(r) 8 ib. 186.
(s) 5 ib. 246.
(t) 2 Freeman, 210.
(u) 7 Mayflower Descendant, 177.

No. 44.

LIBRARY of
Cape Cod
HISTORY & GENEALOGY

CAPTAIN WILLIAM HEDGE OF YARMOUTH

By James W. Hawes

YARMOUTHPORT, MASS.:
C. W. SWIFT, Publisher and Printer,
The "Register" Press,
1914.

Descendants of William Hedge of Yarmouth.

A correspondent in the Boston Transcript, under date of March 23, says: I have read with considerable interest the many notes in these columns on the Hedge family and the descendants of William Hedge of Yarmouth, but I have never seen an account of his father, his grandfather and grandmother. While perhaps it is well known and common knowledge—too much so to take up space in this valuable paper—I will call the attention of the readers who are interested in this family to the will of Thomas Hedge of London, merchant tailor, proven April 10, 1623 (see Waters' "Gleanings of England," page 1440), in which he speaks of his wife Alice, sons Elisha and Abraham, daughter Rebecca and grandson William Hedge, "Thomas Hedge, his (Elisha's) eldest son," and "William Hedge, another of the sons of said Elisha" (1)—Thomas also speaks of his brothers and sisters, etc. The William here spoken of is the William of Yarmouth, no doubt. Thomas (1) Hedge and wife Alice therefore had children: Elisha, Abraham and Rebecca. Elisha (2) and wife had Thomas and William (3), John and Rebecca. Abraham)2(, son of Thomas (1), was apprenticed in the Merchant Tailor Company in March, 1605-6 and married Deborah Peacock of St Dionis Back Church, December 10, 1611, from which church she was buried March 24, 1622-3, the same church from which she was married. Deborah was daughter of Elizabeth Peacock, widow, who was buried from the same church March 24, 1622.

Abraham died while on the way to this country on the "good ship Reformation." His will is dated July 6, 1629, on the ship Reformation, and proved June 16, 1631. In that will he left, after a few bequests, the bulk of his property to his mother, Elizabeth Rennick, whom he appointed sole executrix. She being a widow in 1623, had married Rennick. Abraham had daughters Deborah and Elizabeth. All of the above can be found in Waters's "Gleanings of England." I have never heard of any one finding the name of the wife of William (1) of Yarmouth, whom we generally call William (1). She was the mother of his children. He must have married in this country, as he was less than 20 years of age in 1634, and his brother, John, somewhat younger. By the way, what became of John? He was in Lynn in 1634 and have never heard from him since.

There was a William Hedge who married Mary Andrews of Taunton, but this could not be our William, as the William of Taunton, who lived there, owned a house and died there in 1654. Our William of Yarmouth died in 1670. In a letter which I received from an official of the Old Colony Historical Society of Taunton, in answer to my inquiry on this point, he said the husband of Mary Andrews was William Hodges, not Hedge. The records of the Massachusetts Historic Genealogical Society say William Hedge, not Hodges. William Hedge of Yarmouth married Blanch Hull in 1655. So she could not have been the mother of his children.

There was also a William Hedge of Plymouth (History of Plymouth.) Hedge Pond in that place was given that name from the fact that William Hedge, an Indian, lived on the banks. So we find three William Hedges in Plymouth about this time, for the Indian could not have been husband of Mary Andrews, nor our William of Yarmouth. I have the names of the children of Isaac Gorham Hedge, Jr., and wife Eliza (Cobb) Hedge, married April 24, 1825, which I will gladly give if any of our friends want them. I think I have asked before for the children of Elisha (5), (John 4, John 3, Elisha 2, William 1) Hedge and Mary Gorham, daughter of Isaac Gorham and Hannah Hallet. Isaac and Hannah married Jan 24, 1737. Isaac Hedge, who married Thankful Thacher, November 7, 1793, was one of them. Who were the others?

No. 45.

LIBRARY of Cape Cod HISTORY & GENEALOGY

THOMAS CLARKE, The PILGRIM

And His Descendants

By Amos Otis

YARMOUTHPORT, MASS.:
C. W. SWIFT, Publisher and Printer,
The "Register" Press,
1914.

THOMAS CLARKE, The PILGRIM
And His Descendants
By Amos Otis

Copyright, 1914, by Charles W. Swift.

Thomas Clarke, who was buried on the hill, in Plymouth, came over in the Anne, in 1623, being then 23 years old.

He was probably a seafaring man, as well as carpenter. It is recorded that in 1635, he lost a boat worth £15 in a great storm in Eel river.

He had for his garden plot in 1623, one acre on the south side of the brook. In 1637, he was the first to volunteer to go against the Pequot Indians. In this roll are Mr Stephen Hopkins and his two sons, Caleb and Giles. At this date he dwelt at Eel river, and was styled "yeoman."

In 1642, he was surveyor of Plymouth; in 1651, one of the Plymouth committee. He appears to have been a very active, trading, speculating man. In 1629, he bought an acre of land on the south side of the town for 30 pounds of tobacco and the next day sold it to Governor Bradford. He purchased a lot of land at Eel river in 1630, for £10. He resided at Plymouth in 1643 and 58. December 3, 1639, he was fined 30 shillings for extortion, in that he sold a pair of boots and spurs for 15 shillings which he had purchased for 10 shillings. Before 1631, he had married Susanna, daughter of widow Mary Ring. Stephen Dean married another of Mrs. Ring's daughters.

Mr. Clarke was elected one of the deputies of Plymouth in 1655, and again in 1656.

In 1654 Thomas Clarke purchased a large tract of land in Brewster from Experience Mitchell of Bridgewater. This name of Mitchell does not occur in Freeman's History; but the purchase was made, as evidenced by the warrantee deed, in which Mr. Mitchell says: "I, Experience Mitchell, formerly of Duxbury, but now of Bridgewater, in the Government of New Plymouth &c., one of the purchasers of the lands of said Plymouth Colony, in consideration of a certain competent sum of current pay to me in hand, at, and many years before, the ensealing and delivery of these presents, by Mr. Thomas Clarke of the town of Plymouth, &c., one other of said purchasers, well and truly paid, have in the year 1654, given granted, bargained, sold, aliened, enfeoffed, and confirmed, and absolutely do confirm &c., unto said Thomas Clarke his heirs and assigns forever, all that tract or tracts of uplands and meadows, that I had or have, as purchaser, lying and being from the bounds of Yarmouth, ranging three miles to the Eastward of a place called Namskeekitt, quite across the neck from sea to sea, and from the bounds of Eastham to a place called the Eastern Harbor, as more fully may appear pr. Court Records, excepting always reserved out of this present grant one small lot of upland with some meadow laid out to me adjoining or near unto Mr. William Bradford's lot, near Bound Brook, as may more fully appear by the Records of said lots; which lot I gave my son-in-law, John Washburn, who sold it to said Bradford; but all the rest of my lands within the bounds above mentioned, I have sold as aforesaid, with all the rights and appertenances thereto belonging."

March 6, 1654-5, he was presented before the grandjury for taking six pounds for the bare loan of twenty pounds one year, which the jury "conceived to be great extortion, contrary to the law of God and man." At his trial the traverse jury cleared him. It was probably a false charge.

The wife of Samuel Jenney dying about 1659, left a legacy to her daughter, and placed the child and her portion in the custody of Mr. Clarke. But on petition of Mr. Jenney, the court delivered to him his child, but allowed the property to remain in custody of Mr. Clarke.

He died at Plymouth, March 24, 1697, aged 98 years.

Andrew Clark, son of the Pilgrim, Thomas Clarke of Plymouth, was living in Boston before 1676. He married Mehitable, daughter of Thomas Scottow of Boston. She was baptised 11 Feb. 1649. They had Thomas, born in 1672, Susanna, born in 1674, married John Gray, and other children. Mr. Clark removed to Satucket, which was the Indian name of the western part of Brewster, about 1676. His father, Thomas Clarke, in 1693, conveys lands in Satucket, for love and affection, to his sons and grandsons, viz.: Thomas, son of his son Andrew, a piece of land at Satucket, already laid out and in his tenure and occupancy, bought of Sachemus, Indian sachem, in 1653, with rights of meadows lying by the meadows of Mark Snow, also ten acres lying by lands of William Myrick, and 5 acres lying with lands of Daniel Cole; "also one moiety of my meadows lying at Nameskeket now in the tenure of Mr. Thomas Crosby, with all my purchased lands that were purchased in 1674, and 1675, by the water side between the lands in the occupation of Thomas Freeman and the land that Mr. Prence obtained of Sachemus, both land and marsh: also my land which I purchased of an Indian called Keencomset, which John Freeman, Jr., hath enclosed for a pasture; also that my land and pasture lying by the mills on the Eastward side of Satucket river, that Mr. Thomas Prence purchased of Sachemus in the year 1663, and also half my grist mill standing on Satucket river but not to have the profits of said mill till the term of seven years after the date of these presents. As also one half my meadows lying by John Dillingham's house.

"Next I give to my son Andrew Clark and to Mehetabel his wife for their lives, all my dwelling house and land that is within fence on the westerly side of Satucket river, where said Andrew Clark now lives, and also half my meadows lying by John Dillingham's, and after the decease of him, my said son Andrew Clark and Mehetabel his wife or her marriage again, I give the above said lands and meadows unto Andrew, Scotto and Nathl., the sons of my said son Andrew Clark to be equally divided between them. I further give and grant unto my said grandson Thomas Clark all my ten acres and ¾ of land, that I purchased of an Indian named Wequam, and also those lands I bought of an Indian called Joseph Shantom, with free liberty to my said grandson, to purchase what lands yet remain unpurchased of said Indians, viz., Wequam and Shanton. All the rest of my lands in Barnstable county, that I have now or may have, hereafter I give to my sons and grandsons, viz., William Clark, James Clark, and Nathaniel Clark, and to the sons of said William, viz., James, John and Andrew, except his son Thomas above said."

Scottow Clark, son of the first Andrew, was a miller, and lived on Stony river, otherwise called Satucket river. A grist mill on this river was sold in 1677, by William Griffith of Harwich, to Thomas Clarke the Pilgrim. This, or another, was part of the inheritance of the heirs of Gov. Prence. In 1696-7, John Tracy, Jr., of Duxbury, conveyed his share of it with the land adjoining, viz., 100 acres which he had from his mother Mary, daughter of Governor Prence, to John Gray, for £3; and in 1700, Jeremiah Howes and Sarah his wife, and Jean Snow, widow of Mark, sold their shares to said John Gray of Harwich, for £6, 11s.

Andrew Clark's brother Nathaniel was for a long time secretary of the colony.

Descendants of Thomas Clarke, Senior, of Plymouth:
William.
James, b.   , m. Abigail Lothrop, Oct. 7, 1657.
Scottow, d. at Harwich 1706.
John, b.   m.
Nathaniel, b. 1644, the Secretary.
Susannah, b.   m. Barnabas Lothrop, Esq., of Barnstable Nov. 13, 1658.
ANDREW Clark of Harwich, son of Thomas Clarke, Senr., of Plymouth, m. Mehitable Scottow 1676. He d. 1706, and his widow Mehitable survived him. He had children:

THOMAS CLARKE, THE PILGRIM,

Andrew.
Scotto, or Scottoway.
Nathaniel m. Abigail Hedge 1720.
Thomas, b. 10 July 1672. He was called Lieut. Thomas. He m. 1st Rebecca, d. of John Miller.
Susannah, b. 12 March 1673-4.
Mehitable, b. 8 Dec. 1676, m. John Haskel Dec. 5, 1705. Mehitable is recorded as born in Boston Dec. 8, 1676 (daughter of Mehitable and Andrew). He removed to Harwich that year.
JOHN Clark of , son of Thomas Clarke, Senr., of Plymouth. Children:
Thomas, b. , of Nantucket.
ANDREW Clark, son of Andrew, and grandson of Thomas Clarke, Senr., of Plymouth, m. Elizabeth Winslow Aug. 9, 1711, and had children born in Harwich, namely:
Mehitable, b. Oct. 29, 1712.
Elizabeth, b. May 25, 1714, d. young.
Elizabeth, b. Jan. 18, 1716-17.
Thankful, b. Nov. 18, 1721.
Eunice, b. Oct. 28, 1724.
Hannah, b. June 13, 1726.
SCOTTOWAY Clark, son of Andrew and grandson of Thomas Clarke, Senr., of Plymouth, m. Mary and had children b. in Harwich, namely:
Andrew, b. Dec. 1, 1707, m. Bethia Hall Aug. 20, 1729.
Scotto, b. Nov. 8, 1709, m. Thankful Crosby March 22, 1732-3.
Mary, b. April 17, 1712, m. Edmund Freeman, Jr., Oct. 7, 1731.
Joseph,
b. Jan. 8, 1714-15.
Benjamin,
Benjamin m. Mehitable Crosby Feb. 22, 1738-9.
Lydia, b. March 7, 1716-17, m. Berry.
Nathaniel, b. June 10, 1719, m. Mary North of B. Oct. 26, 1739.
Sarah, b. Sept. 18, 1721.
Ebenezer, b. June 2, 1723.
Seth, b. June 19, 1726.
THOMAS Clark, son of Andrew and grandson of Thomas Clarke, Senr., of Plymouth, m. 1st Rebekah, daughter of John Miller of Yarmouth, Feb. 15, 1681. Children:
Susannah, b. Feb. 21, 1683-4, m. Samuel Hallet of Yarmouth June 15, 1720.
Thomas, b. Dec. 25, 1685.
Mrs. Rebekah Clark d. April, 1688, and he m. 2d . Children:
Hannah, b. , m. Jonathan Lincoln April 26, 1711.
Rowland, b. , had sons Edward, Isaac and Dillingham.
A daughter, m. Maccarthy.
Mehitable, b. m. Joshua Bangs, June 18, 1713.
Mary, b. about 1700, m. Jonathan Cobb?
Sarah, b. 1702, m. Edward Bangs Feb. 11, 1719-20, d. Aug. 8, 1727?
He m. 3d Sarah . Children:
Seth, b. May 9, 1709, m. Huldah Doane of E. 1728.
Isaac, b. Aug. 18, 1710, m. Lydia
Content, b. April 23, 1712.
Elizabeth, b. , d. April 24, 1715.
He m. 4th Patience, widow of Hall.

No. 46.

LIBRARY *of* Cape Cod HISTORY & GENEALOGY

BURGESS

By Amos Otis

YARMOUTHPORT, MASS.:
C. W. SWIFT, Publisher and Printer,
The "Register" Press,
1914.

BURGESS--By Amos Otis.

Copyright, 1914, by Charles W. Swift.

The two first of the name of Burgess, mentioned in the records of the town, are Samuel and John. They were in Harwich as early as 1726, and belonged to the "Sixth School Remove," which then constituted nearly all the South parish now Harwich. Of their marriages, families and deaths the records make no mention. But from tradition, which I think reliable, Samuel had sons Samuel and Thomas, and perhaps Ezekiel.

The records say "Samuel Burgess, Jr.," married Mercy, daughter of Ephraim Covil, "Sept. 25, 1730." Who his family was the records are silent. It is probable the "Samuel Burgess, Jr," who married "Bethiah Clark," "January 15, 1761," was his son; and the "Samuel Burgess" who married "Dianna Ellis, January 12, 1793," his grandson.

Thomas Burgess, who is reputed to be the son of the first Samuel, was born, as nearly as can be ascertained, about the year 1720. He was married several times. His first wife was Mary, daughter of Ephraim Covil, to whom the records say he was married "July 28, 1742." Tradition (which is reliable) says he had sons Thomas, Jonathan, Nathaniel, Philip and Covil; but there is no record of them as being his sons upon those of the town. "Thomas Burges Jr." married "Elizabeth Nickerson Oct. 3, 1765." His family is not recorded. Jonathan, his brother, born Feb. 19, 1748, married Mehitable Chase. His family is recorded.

Nathaniel, brother of the above Jonathan, married "Mercy Crowell" daughter of Jabez of Chatham, in 1746. He went to Sandwich.

Covil Burgess married a daughter of Jabez Crowell and went to Sandwich.

Philip Burgess married and had a family which is recorded. He died in 1794.

Of Ezekiel Burgess but little is known. His birth, marriage and death is not recorded. His family, recorded, is as follows: Ezekiel Burges, by his wife Sarah, had Catherine, born 1737; Jeremiah, Jan. 25, 1739; Sarah, 1744. He resided in the South Parish; was living in 1747.

The David Burgess, who lived in that part of Harwich now known as Brewster, married Mercy Snow in 1748, had Prince, born April 18, 1741; Hannah, 1742; Sarah, 1744; Mercy, 1746; Mary, 1748; Huldah, 1751; and Jane, 1752. To what family he belonged the town records are silent.

The following is a list of those of this name whose marriages are recorded in the first and second volumes of our early records, and not mentioned in the foregoing paragraphs:

Nicholas Cartwright of Chatham married Patience Burgess of Harwich, Feb. 1730.

BURGESS.

Daniel Cole of Eastham m. Thankful Burgess of Harwich, Sept. 19, 1738.
Sylvanus Harding of Chatham m. Kesiah Burgess, May 10, 1744.
John Burgess, Jr., of Harwich m. Sarah Rogers, Jan. 20, 1756.
Benjamin Berry m. Mercy Burgess, April 29, 1762.
Moses Hopkins, Jr., m. Mary Burgess, 1765.
Jacob Burgess m. Rebecca Hopkins, Nov. 6, 1766.
Judah Eldredge m. Mercy Burgess (daughter of David of Brewster), June 11, 1775.
Stephen Burgess of Harwich m. Temperance Wing, Feb. 18, 1778.
Joshua Burgess of H. m. Hannah Smith, Feb. 5, 1795.
Joseph Smith of Eastham m. Huldah Burgess of H., April 10, 1796.
Sylvanus Studley m. Rebecca Burgess, March 9, 1793.
Nathan Burgess m. Abigail Wing, 1794.
Jabez Crowell m. Rebecca Burgess, Feb. 1, 1787.
Bani Eldridge m. Ruth Burgess, Jan. 25, 1787.
Ebenezar Killey m. Hannah Burgess, Dec. 28, 1788.
Sparrow Nickerson m. Abigail Burgess, Feb. 11, 1762.
Seth Hall m. Elizabeth Burgess, June 27, 1756.
Edward Hall, Jr., intended marriage with Mercy Burgess, 1760.
Hezekiah Eldridge m. Jane Burgess, Feb. 26, 1785.
Oker Phillips m. Mercy Burgess, March 16, 1785.

JOHN Burgess of Y. m. Mary Warden, 8 Sept. 1657. (Sandwich Recs.)
Children.
(Yar. Recs. p. 7 is gone.)
John, eldest son.
Thomas.
Martha, m. Samuel Stoors, Jr., of Windham, 31 Oct. 1700.
Joseph.
Samuel.
Jacob, b. 1681; d. Aug. 15, 1772, age 91.
He had five daughters.

THOMAS Burgess, son of John, m. Sarah Stoors of B. Feb. 26, 1695-6, and had children born in Yarmouth, viz.:
(Recs. p. 36.)
Mary, b. 27 Nov. 1696, m. Elnathan Ellis, Mar. 2. 1715-16.
Thomas, b. 8 Aug. 1698, d. young.
Hannah, b. 20 May 1701.
Martha, b. 15 Feb. 1703, d. Feb. 9, 1717-18.
Sarah, b. 4 Jan. 1704, d. young.
Thankful, b. 10 June 1707, m. John Blossom April 6, 1727.
Ebenezer, b. 13 June, 1709, m. Marcy Godfrey, 1735.
Matthias, b. 4 Mar. 1711, m. Dorcas Cobb of E. 1737.
David, b 23 Aug. 1713, m. Mary Snow of H. 1740.
He d. Dec. 1720.

SAMUEL Burgess, son of John, m. Elizabeth and had children born in Y., viz.:
(Y. Recs. p. 37.)
Patience, b. 16 Sept. 1706, m. Nicholas Cartwright of C. May 1730.

BURGESS.

Elizabeth, b. 30 Mar. 1708, m. Saml. Burgis, Nov. 10, 1726.
Abigail, b. 5 Sept. 1710.
Jacob, b. 10 Oct. 1712, m. Ruth Wood Nov. 28, 1738.
Remember, b. 23 June 1714.
Thomas, b. 7 June 1721.
Martha, b. 23 Sept. 1723.
He d. Sept. 26, 1753.

JOHN Burgess, eldest son of John, m. Sarah   (she d. 4 Feb. 1722-3) and had children born in Y., viz.:
(Y. Recs. p. 38.)
  Marcy, b. 25 Dec. 1695, m. Elnathan Ellis Mar. 2, 1715-16.
  Elizabeth, b. 12 Oct. 1697, m. Prince Wixson April 1, 1720.
  Joseph, b. 9 July 1699.
  Benjamin, b. 3 May 1701, m. Thankful Nickerson.
  Samuel, b. 3 Feb. 1702-3, m. Elizabeth Burgess Nov. 10. 1726; m. 2d, Mary Taylor May 1733.
  Ezekiel, b. 19 Aug. 1705, m. Catharine Oakes June 1, 1732; 2d, Sarah Baker Sept. 8, 1736.
  Thankful, b. 7 June 1708, m. Daniel Cole 1728.
  John, b. Oct. 1710, m. Alice Baker Feb. 20, 1734-5?

JOSEPH Burgess, son of John, m. Tameson   and had children born in Y., viz.:
(Y. Recs. p. 38.)
  Joseph, b. 26 Feb. 1701-2.
  Lydia, b. 2 May 1704, m. Jona. Luce of Tisbury April 14, 1724.
  John, b. 5 April 1706.
  Jonathan, b. 5 May 1708.
  Marcy, b. 1 Jan. 1711-2, m. Judah Baker Feb. 15, 1727-8.
  Remember, b. 21 June 1716, m. Israel Cole, Jr., of E. Mar. 11, 1736-7. She is called of E.

JACOB Burgess, son of John, m.   . He d. Aug. 15, 1772, in the 92d year of his age. (Gravestones.)
A Thankful Barge of H. m. Daniel Cole of E. Sept. 19, 1728.

JOSEPH Burgess, son of   , m. Thankful Snow of Eastham April 11, 1723. They had children born in Y., viz.:
(Y. Recs. p. 96.)
  Lydia, b. 18 April 1724.
  Hannah, b. 24 April 1726.
  Phebe, b. 2 April 1728.

BENJAMIN Burgess, son of John, m. Thankful Nickerson of Harwich June 15, 1726. They had children born in Y., viz.:
(p. 101.)
  William, b. 12 June 1728, m. Hannah Sears, 1751.
  Sarah, b. 31 July 1731.

JOSEPH Burgess, son of   , m. Desire   , and had children born in Y., viz.:
(Y. Recs. p. 104.)
  Robert, b. Jan. 6, 1725-6.

SAMUEL Burgess, son of John, m. his cousin, Elizabeth Burgess Nov. 10, 1726. They had children born in Y., viz.:
(Y. Recs. p. 120.)
  Surviah, b. 30 Sept. 1727, d. 19 April 1759.
  Thaddeus, b. 19 March 1728-9, m. Martha Lewis, 1750.
  Benjamin, b. 1 Nov. 1732.

BURGESS.

By his 2d wife, Mary Taylor: Jonathan, b. 31 Jan. 1734-5.

JOHN Burgis, son of , m. Alice Bacon Feb. 20, 1734-5, (she d. Mar. 21, 1771) and had children born in Y., viz.:
(Y. Recs. p. 123.)
John, b. May 21, 1736.
Hannah, b. Sept. 16, 1737.
Joseph, b. Nov. 17, 1739.
"Zilpha," b. April 16, 1742, m. Samuel Chase, 1758.
Alice, b. Aug. 12, 1744.
Mary, b. May 20, 1749.

EBENEZER Burgess, son of Thomas, m. Mercy Godfrey. He d. Oct. 3, 1744. They had children born in Y., viz.:
(Y. Recs. p. 140.)
Sarah, b. Aug. 15, 1737.
Mercy, b. Mar. 3, 1739-40.
Ruth, b. April 2, 1742.
Hannah, b. May 29, 1744.

MATTHIAS Burgess, son of Thomas, m. Dorcas and had children born in Y., viz.:
(Y. Recs. p. 143.)
Priscilla, b. Nov. 17, 1737.
Mary, b. Aug. 17, 1739.
Dorcas, b. Sept. 13, 1741, drowned Sept. 13, 1745.
A daughter, b. Mar. 1743-4, d. Mar. 1743-4.
Thomas, b. Feb. 27, 1744-5.
Dorcas, b. June 3, 1749.

BENJAMIN Burgess, son of Samuel, m. Rebecca Parker 1755 and had children born in Y. viz.:
(Y. Recs. p. 207.)
Thankful, b. Aug. 1756.
Elizabeth, b. Nov. 20, 1757.
Benjamin, b. June 23, 1763.
Parker, b. June 24, 1767.
David, b. Aug. 28, 1769.
Thomas, b. Jan. 26, 1772.
Rebecca, b. July 26, 1774.

THADDEUS Burgess, son of Samuel, m. Martha Lewis 1750 and had children born in Y., viz.:
(Y. Recs. p. 223.)
Timothy, b. Aug. 15, 1751, d. Feb. 14, 1816.
Samuel, b. July 23, 1756, d. abroad 1811.
Martha, b. June 3, 1759.
Thaddeus, b. June 29, 1766, d. Jan. 3, 1797.

JOSEPH Burgess of Y., son of John, m. Deliverance, daughter of Silas Baker of H., 1759, and had children born in Y., viz.:
(Y. Recs. p. 223.)
Deliverance, b. Dec. 13, 1760.
Sarah, b. Feb. 1, 1762.
Abigail, b. Aug. 11, 1763.
Joseph, b. July 30, 1765.
Anthony, b. Oct. 26, 1767.

JONATHAN Burgess, son of Samuel, m. Elizabeth and had children born in Y., viz.:
(Y. Recs. p. 223.)
Desire, b. Oct. 27, 1759.

JOHN Burgess, Jr., m. Sarah Rogers of Harwich and had children born in Y., viz.:
(Y. Recs. p. 216.)
Hannah, b. Nov. 10, 1758?
John, b. June 10, 1759.
Jonathan, b. Feb. 3, 1761.
Ezekiel, b. Aug. 28, 1763.

No. 47.

LIBRARY of
Cape Cod
HISTORY & GENEALOGY

The Yarmouth Families *of*
E L D R E D G E
By Amos Otis

YARMOUTHPORT, MASS.:
C. W. SWIFT, Publisher and Printer,
The "Register" Press,
1914.

The Yarmouth Families of
ELDREDGE
By Amos Otis

Copyright, 1914, by Charles W. Swift.

This name is variously written on the records, Eldred, Eldredge, Eldritch, Aldredge, Alderedg. Two of the name were among the early settlers in Yarmouth, Robert and William.

Robert, May 25, 1639, is named as a kind servant of Captain Nicholas Sympkins, who at that date assigned his services to Mr. Thomas Prence for the term of three years from the following July. As seven years was the usual term of apprenticeship, the above facts indicate that Robert came over in 1635. In 1643 he was of Plymouth, and soon after removed to Yarmouth. The last week in October, 1649, he married Elizabeth, daughter of William Nickerson of Yarmouth. She was born in old Norwich, England, and came over with her parents and grandparents in 1637. He probably resided in Yarmouth till about the year 1663, when he removed with his father-in-law to Chatham. He died in 1683, and his widow and his son Nicholas administered on his estate.

His son Nicholas was born in Yarmouth 18 Aug. 1650. He is named as one of the grandjury in 1682, freeman in 1690, and first representative under the new charter, 1692. He died 30 April, 1702, leaving widow Elizabeth, James, eldest son, John, Nicholas,

ELDREDGE.

Mary, Elizabeth, Martha and Desire.

William Eldredge does not appear to have been a resident in the Plymouth colony in 1643. March 3, 1645-6, he and his wife Ann resided in Yarmouth. He was surveyor of highways in 1662, 1674, '75 and '77. He married Anne, daughter of William Lumkin.

ROBERT Eldredge m. Elizabeth, daughter of William Nickerson of Yarmouth, the last week in October, 1649. He d. 1683. His widow Elizabeth (a member of the Barnstable church) d.

Children, born in Yarmouth.
Nicholas, b. 18 Aug. 1650.
Mary.

WILLIAM Eldredge m. Anne, dau. of William Lumpkin (or Ludkin). Her father came over in 1637. The wife of William Eldredge was buried Nov. 1, 1676.

Children, born in Yarmouth.
Ann, b. 16 Dec. 1648.
Sarah, 10 Oct. 1650.
Bridget,   m.   Long.
Elisha.
Bethia.
Jehosaphat,   m. Elizabeth.
Joseph,   m. Elizabeth.
Samuel,   m. Keziah Taylor, 6 Feb. 1680-1.
John.
William.

JOSEPH Eldredge, son of William, removed to Chatham. He was a farmer and accumulated a large estate. In his will, dated 27 Aug. 1728, proved 24 Sept. 1735, he names his wife Elizabeth, and brother William and sister Bridget Long,

son William, m. Hannah Taylor, Oct. 1, 1713, m. Thankful Crowell March 20, 1718-19, d. 1753, children, Seth, Joseph, Hezekiah, Solomon, William, Tabitha (Kenrick);

son John, m. Ruhannah Doane, Sept. 26, 1728;

son Jeremy,

g. son Joseph Eldredge,

g. daughter Tabitha Eldredge, m. William Mitchell, 19 March,

ELDREDGE.

1713, at the house of his grandfather, Mr. William Nickerson, Sr., before many witnesses; g. daughter Elizabeth, dau. of Jeremy.

JEHOSAPHAT Eldredge, son of William, removed to Chatham. He had a good estate. His wife was Elizabeth. In his will, dated the 9th day of the 12 mo., commonly called February, 1731-2, proved 29 Nov. 1732, he names his wife Elizabeth;

dau. Elizabeth, unmarried, for whom he provides;

son Edward, b. in Chatham 17 July 1702, m. Mary , d. 1730, leaving two children, Mercy and Anna;

son Nathaniel, m. Sarah d. 1729, leaving seven children, Jonathan, Nathaniel, Bathsheba, Bethia, Nelley and Mehetabel;

son Elisha,

son Elnathan,

son Ebenezer,

son Barnabas.

SAMUEL Eldridge son of William, m. Keziah Taylor, 6 Feb. 1680-1. He d. 3 Jan. 1705-6. She d. 30 March 1733-4.

Children, born in Yarmouth.

Samuel, b. 25 Sept. 1681, m. Mary Bates of Lynn, Jan. 26, 1703-4.

Jehosaphat, 12 Oct. 1683, m. Thankful Rider, Feb. 10, 1708-9.

Mehetabell, Jan. 1686-7, m. Ebenezer Hall, 27 Sept. 1705.

Ezekiel, March 1689, m. Bethia Rider, 21 Jan. 1714-15.

Ann, April 1691, m. Samuel Rider, 17 Feb. 1713-14.

John, Feb. 1692-3, m. Sarah Howes, 29 Aug. 1722.

Keziah, March 1695, m. John Crowell, 23 Oct. 1718.

Mary, March 1697, m. John West, 26 April 1720.

All the above children are named in the will of widow Keziah, dated 15 Oct. 1722.

In the division of the common lands in Yarmouth 1710, all of the name of Eldredge, entitled to shares, were Samuel, dec'd and

ELDREDGE.

his sons Jehosaphat and Ezekiel.
EZEKIEL Eldredge, son of Samuel, m. Bethia Rider 21 Jan. 1714-14.
Children, born in Yarmouth.
Ann, b. 23 Aug. 1717.
Samuel, 31 July 1717.
Ezekiel, 2 April 1722.
JOHN Eldridge, son of Samuel, m. 1st Mary , 2nd Sarah Howes, 29 Aug. 1722.
John, b. 22 Jan. 1715-16, at Kittery in the county of York.
Born in Yarmouth.
Lemuel, b. 25 June 1723.
Samuel, b. 30 June 1726.
Sarah, b. 24 Aug. 1738, d. 21 Feb. following.
John, b. 28 Aug. 1741, d. April 9, 1742.
JOHN Eldridge, Jr., m. Betty Gorham, July 20, 1737.
Children, born in Yarmouth.
Barnabas, b. May 9, 1738.
Mary, b. June 28, 1739.
Dorcas, b. July 10, 1742.
John, b. Feb. 14, 1742-3.
Elizabeth, b. Feb. 3, 1744-5.
David, b. Dec. 24, 1746.
Gideon, b. May 31, 1749.
Ann, b. Feb. 26, 1750-1.
LEMUEL Eldridge, son of John, m. 1st Reliance Mayhew of H., 1745, 2d Mary Tobey.
Children, born in Yarmouth.
David, b. Sept. 4, 1746.
Jonathan, b. March 24, 1748.
SAMUEL Eldridge, son of John, m. Sarah
Children.
Levi, b. Sept. 27, 1753.
Eli, b. Aug. 12, 1756.
Sarah, b. Dec. 28, 1757.
Lydia, b. Sept 2, 1760.
Keziah, b. March 13, 1764.
Reliance, b. April 5, 1762.
Samuel, b. March 18, 1762.
Daniel,
b. July 3, 1769.
Rebecca,
Mary, b. Feb. 14, 1773.
Annah, b. Feb. 25, 1776.
BARNABAS Eldridge, son of John,
Children, born in Yarmouth.
Sarah, April 5, 1763.
John, Sept. 7, 1764.
Gideon, Nov. 9, 1766.
Kelley, Aug. 19, 1768.
Barnabas, Feb. 24, 1771.
Reuben, Nov. 1, 1773.
Joseph, Sept. 20, 1775.
Anna, May 27, 1777.
Patience, Jan. 4, 1779.
Asa, Nov. 27, 1782, d. July 1, 1791.

No. 48.

LIBRARY *of*
Cape Cod
HISTORY & GENEALOGY

RICHARD TAYLOR, TAILOR
and Some *of* His Descendants

By James W. Hawes

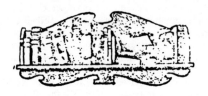

YARMOUTHPORT, MASS.:
C. W. SWIFT, Publisher and Printer,
The "Register" Press,
1914.

RICHARD TAYLOR, TAILOR
and Some of His Descendants

By James W. Hawes

Copyright, 1914, by Charles W. Swift.

FIRST GENERATION.

Richard[1] Taylor married Ruth, daughter of Gabriel Whelden, who gave his consent Oct. 27, 1646.(b) She died before Dec. 4, 1673. He died before Dec. 13, 1673. He

---

(a) There were two men in Yarmouth in early times named Richard Taylor, the one, who appears to have been the older, was called Richard Taylor, tailor, from his trade, and the other, Richard Taylor of the Rock, from having built his house near a large rock near the boundary between Hockanom and Nobscusset in the northeastern part of the town. The latter, it is said, married Ruth, probably daughter of Thomas Burgess, although neither the will of Thomas Burgess nor of any contemporaneous Burgess mentions her nor any Taylor. His wife died June 9, 1693. He died Aug. 1, 1703. To his will, dated Sept. 2, 1693, and to a codicil dated Oct. 28, 1699, he made his mark. The will and codicil were proved Oct. 3, 1703. (2 Barn. Prob. Recs.

262.) He is mentioned in the records March 1, 1663-4, when it is stated that Thomas Starr had taken a piece of timber from "Richard Tayler, of the Rocke," and was ordered to give him another piece and pay damages, or pay him £3. (4 Plym. Col. Recs. 53.)

Richard Taylor, tailor, died in 1673. After his death there are only two mentions of Richard Taylor in the Colony records: one, Jan. 21, 1679-80, when the bounds of his land near Nobscussel were fixed, and the other, June 2, 1685, when he was on the grandjury. This last mention probably refers to his son, Richard Taylor, Jr. (12 Plym. Col. Recs. 142, 143; 6 ib. 166. See also Land Book of Yarmouth, pp. 31-34.)

The fact that his will was made

RICHARD TAYLOR, TAILOR,

came from England, but the date of his arrival and the particular place of his birth are not known.

ten years before his death and was not signed by him indicates that he was unable to write, although sometimes aged and infirm persons made a mark who were not illiterate. This fact, and the fact that practically no mention of the name is made after the death of Richard Taylor, tailor, indicate that it is correct to award the mentions of the name, when the individual is not distinguished, to the latter, as the writer has done in the text.

Richard Taylor of the Rock had in 1677 seven children (3 Mf. 246):

Richard, b. June 9, 1652;
Mehitable, b. July 23, 1654;
Keziah, b. Feb. 18, 1655-6;
Jasher, b. May 9, 1659;
Hannah, b. Sept. 17, 1661;
Elisha, b. Feb. 10, 1663-4;
Mary, b. June 12, 1667.

The late William P. Davis, long the town clerk, gives the birth of Richard as above, and the fact that the calculation in the record where not worn out is from 1677, accounts for the year of Mary's birth. Davis says that Mehitable married Jonathan Smith; Keziah, Samuel Eldredge; and Hannah, Job Jenkins.

The will of John Joyce of Yarmouth, dated Nov. 20, 1666, and

He lived in the N. W. part of Yarmouth.(c)

proved March 5, 1666-7, contains a provision giving to Richard Taylor at the Rock, "because a poor man, in corne or in some beast, the sume of twenty shillings, provided that he vindecate my name and acknowledge the wronge that hee hath done mee about a calfe, to be passed him when hee hath done the same." (2 Plym. Col. Wills, pt. 2, p. 35; 6 N. E. Reg. 188.) In the volume of recopied Colonial wills in the Barnstable Probate office he is called Richard Taylor at the Neck, but there was no person in Yarmouth so generally known and the Register of Deeds at Plymouth informs me that in the original record the first letter looks more like R than N although the second letter looks more like e than o. As Richard Taylor of the Rock was known and frequently so called, we may safely assume that John Joyce so named him in his will.

The "Taylor Family," by Rev. B. S. Taylor, who derived his information from Wm. P. Davis, gives some of the descendants of Richard Taylor of the Rock, but contains many errors.

The writer printed in the Chatham Monitor of Sept. 19, 1882, a notice of Richard Taylor, tailor, and some of his descendants. The

759

He is first mentioned in the Colonial records as among those in Yarmouth between 16 and 60 years of age able to bear arms in August, 1643.(d)

June 7, 1648, he was a surveyor of highways for Yarmouth.(e) June 5, 1651, he was sworn as a member of the grandjury.(f)

May 30, 1656, with Edmond Hawes, Richard Taylor was witness to a deed of Samuel Mayo to John Phinney of Barnstable.(g)

June 3, 1656, he was constable of Yarmouth.(h) June 3, 1657, he was one of the surveyors of highways there.(i) That year he took the oath of fidelity.(j)

The will of William Chase of Yarmouth, dated May 4, 1659, appointed his neighbors Robert Dennis and Richard Taylor, tailor, overseers. With Edmond Hawes Taylor took the inventory Sept. 14, 1659.(k)

In October, 1659, he signed the verdict as one of a jury of inquest on the death of Mary Chase of Yarmouth.(l) Oct. 6, 1659, he had custody of a firkin of butter

---

present notice omits some of the descendants, but makes some additions and corrections.

(b) The Plymouth Colony Records (v. 2, p. 110), under date of Oct. 27, 1646, say: "In the case betweene Gabriell Whelding and Richard Taylor, about his daughter Ruth, the said Gabriell pmiseth his free assent and consent to their marriage." "Bearse Family," by John B. Newcomb, at p. 5, erroneously states that this Taylor's wife was a Burgess. The accounts of him in Swift's "Old Yarmouth" (p. 62) and 2 Free-

man's "Cape Cod" (p. 207) are not entirely correct.
(c) 2 Plym. Col. Wills, 63; Swift, 56, 60.
(d) 4 N. E. Reg. 258; Swift, 35; 8 Plym. Col. Recs. 194.
(e) 2 Plym. Col. Recs. 124.
(f) 1b. 168.
(g) Hinckley's Transcripts of Plym. Col. Deeds.
(h) 3 Plym. Col. Recs. 100.
(i) Ib. 116.
(j) 8 ib. 185, 186.
(k) 5 N. E. Reg. 388; 2 Plym. Col. Wills, 63; Barn. Prob. office, recopied Wills, 296, 297.
(l) 3 Plym. Col. Recs. 172.

RICHARD TAYLOR, TAILOR,

formerly belonging to William Norkett and claimed by Robert Dennis.(n) March 6, 1661-2, as one of the agents of Yarmouth he signed a statement to the Court in settlement of the town's demand for oil from whales.(n)

June 4, 1661, the Court enacted "That a sufficient man in every towne; bee appointed to take up what excice shalbee due to the Countrey whether Iron Tarr boards oysters &c. and that the said men bee under oath and that they shall have power to make serch and what forfeites they find they shall have the one halfe therof; and out of the said excice evidenced to have three shillings upon the pound; and that they give a Just account To the Treasurer the first of November and the first of May Annually; The Names of such as are apointed are as followeth . . . . . For Yarmouth Rich: Tayler Tayler."(o)

June 8, 1664, the excise on strong drink, wines and liquors was added to the duties of the office and the two commissioners were Mr. Edmond Hawes and Richard Taylor.(p)

March 3, 1662-3, Mr. Anthony Thacher, Robert Dennis and Richard Taylor were sureties for the town in the suit of Nickerson v. Yarmouth.(q)

Richard Taylor was one of those who took the inventory of John Joyce Feb. 18, 1666-7, and he signed the document.(r)

June 30, 1667, he was one of the signers of a paper in support of the Rev. Thomas Thornton.(s)

June 3, 1668, Richard Taylor was constable of Yarmouth.(t)

(m) Ib. 174.
(n) 8 ib. 194; Swift, 88.
(o) 11 Plym. Col. Recs. 133.
(p) 4 Plym. Col. Recs. 67; 11 ib. 186, 187.
(q) 7 Plym. Col. Recs. 106.
(r) 2 Plym. Col. Wills, pt. 2, p. 35.
(s) Swift, 90.
(t) 4 Plym. Col. Recs. 181.

Dec. 11, 1668, with Edmond Hawes, John Gorham and Barnard Lambert, Richard Taylor was appraiser of the estate of William Clarke.(u)

The will of Capt. William Hedge of Yarmouth, dated June 30, 1670, names his beloved friends, Mr. Edmond Hawes and Richard Taylor, tailor, as overseers.(v)

March 8, 1670-1, "Richard Tayler Tayler," for being in company with John Sprague and others about the beginning of December in the house of James Cole of Plymouth the greatest part of the afternoon, "and siting tippling with them, and by his psence abeting them in theire evill practices," was fined 10 shillings. The record states that Sprague gamed and brought a mare into the parlor, and that it was "near unto or on the evening before the Sabbath day."(w)

In the Land Book of Yarmouth (p. 20) appears the following:

"Given and granted to Richard Tailor; Tailor his heirs & assines forever this 4th day of Feb. 1672 two small ilands of Creeke thach one lying against ye said Tailors Meddows ye other against ye Meddows of Samuell Riders these islands lying in ye creeke northerly from Hosiah Joyces Medows."

His wife perished shortly before Dec. 4, 1673, in the wreck of a boat in which she had probably intended to go from Yarmouth to Plymouth or Duxbury. A jury of inquest was formed in Duxbury, where the boat appears to have been found, which rendered its verdict on the last-mentioned date. The following was the verdict: The jury of inquest appointed "to view a corpes found in a boate now racked, and being supposed

(u) Barn. Prob. office, Recopied Wills, p. 295.
(v) Plym. Col. Wills, v. 3, pt. 1, p. 20; Barn. Prob. office, Recopied Wills, pp. 299, 300.

(w) 5 Plym. Col. Recs. 53.

to be the wife of Richard Tayler, somtimes of Yarmouth, and to make dilligent serch how the said woman came by her death, doe judge, that the boate being cast away, the woman was drowned in the boate." (x)

Mr. Taylor died before Dec. 13, 1673. It seems probable that he was at an advanced age and that his decease was hastened by the tragic death of his wife.

The Court Mch. 4, 1673-4, made the following order: "Mr. John Gorum and Mr. John Thacher are joyned with John Tayler for the disposing of the estate of Richard Tayler to his children, and for the paying and receiving of debts, according to order of Court.

Concerning the estate of Richard Tayler, late of Yarmouth, deceased, this Court doth order, first, that the eldest son of the said Tayler shall have his fathers housing, and two thirds of the land, both upland and marsh, and the rest of his portion out of what of the estate Mr. Gorum and Mr. John Thacher shall judge most suitable for him, hee being by order of Court to have a dubble portion.

2condly, it is ordered, that the hay, and what provisions was or is upon the invoice of the estate that is now spent, or shalbe judged convenient for the family to spend betwixt this and the first of the next Augst, shall not be accounted to the estate, as likewise what woole and flaxe hath bin spon by the daughters sence theire parents death shalbe accounnpted theires that spon it.

The rest of the estate to be devided betwixt the second son and the five daughters, everyone an equall proportion, to bee sett out to them as maybe most suitable for them, by the discretion of theire eldest brother, and Mr.

(x) 5 Plym. Col. Recs. 123.

John Gorum, and Mr. John Thacher.

The second son to have the other third of his father's land, besides his portion equall to his sisters.

Lastly, that nothing that hath bin alreddy given or bestowed by the said Taylor on any of his children, shall not be considered in the devision, but every one to have an equall proportion, after the payment of debts due from the estate." (y)

His inventory, taken Dec. 13, 1673, and submitted to the Court under oath March 6, 1673-4, amounted to £199 4s. 11d. The debts of the estate were £18 1s. 2d. Included in the inventory were 12 acres of upland, nine of meadow and three of marsh, which together with houses and some grain sown amounted to £60. The children named are John, Joseph, Martha and Mary. (z) The inventory shows that he possessed a considerable many cattle, sheep and hogs, one horse, corn, wheat, flax, provisions, 21 yards of cloth, lumber and household articles. There were due to him 38½ barrels of tar, and John Blake of Boston owed him money. Some things had been given to the children in his life time.

Children, born in Yarmouth.

Ruth, b. July 29, 1647; buried in 1648. (a)

Ann, b. Dec. 2, 1648; buried March 29, 1650, aged about 1½ years. (b)

Mary, b. in 1649; m. Merchant. (c)

(y) 5 Plym. Col. Recs. 137, 138.

(z) Plym. Col Wills, v. 3, pt. 1, p. 96; Barn. Prob. office, Recopied Wills, p. 307.

(a) 8 Plym. Col. Recs. 3, 7; 15 Mayflower Descendant (hereinafter cited as "Mf."), 26, 29.

(b) 8 Plym. Col. Recs. 7, 12; 15 Mf. 29.

(c) 4 Savage, 263. Pope (p. 310) gives Abijah Merchant of Yarmouth, b. Jan. 10, 1650-1. Swift (p. 105) and 2 Freeman (p. 185) give Abisha Merchant as taxed in Yarmouth in 1676.

RICHARD TAYLOR, TAILOR.

Martha, b. Dec. 18, 1650;(b) m. Joseph Bearse of Barnstable Dec. 3, 1676;(d) d. Jan. 27, 1727-8, aged 77, leaving issue.(d)

2 John, b. about 1652.

Elizabeth, b. about 1655; m. Dec. 20, 1680, Samuel Cobb of Barnstable;(e) d. May 4, 1721, aged 66, leaving issue.(e)

Hannah, b. about 1658; m. as his 2d wife July 19, 1680, Deacon Job Crocker of Barnstable;(f) d. May 11, 1743, in her 85th year,(f) leaving issue.

Ann, b. about 1659; m. Josiah

(d) Barn. Recs.; 2 Mf. 214; 4 Savage, 263; 1 Otis, 55. 1 Savage, 148, erroneously states that the marriage took place in 1675.
(e) 1 Savage, 413, 414; 4 ib. 263; 1 Otis, 173. Savage (414) says: "Descendants are very numerous, of whom Ebenezer, that d. at Kingston, 8 Dec. 1801, at the age, as was said, of more than 107 and ½ years, was, perhaps, the oldest man who ever was born and lived on the soil of Mass."
(f) Barn. Recs.; 3 Mf. 151; 1 Savage, 474; 1 Otis, 215.

Davis, of Barnstable, June 25, 1679,(g) and had issue.

3 Joseph, b. about 1660.

Sarah, b. ; d. unmarried July 31, 1695.(h) The inventory of Sarah Taylor of Barnstable was taken Aug. 16, 1695, and amounted to £34 19s.(h) Deacon Job Crocker and Samuel Cobb, brothers-in-law, were made administrators Sept. 23, 1695.(h) The estate was, Sept. 13, 1695, ordered equally divided between the brothers and sisters of the deceased, given in the following order, to wit: John Taylor, Joseph Taylor, Mary Marchant, Martha Bearse, Elizabeth Cobb, Hannah Crocker and Ann Davis.(h) The inventory consisted of wearing apparel, five pounds of worsted yarn, a Bible, cattle, sheep and lambs, cash, moneys due from Samuel Cobb and Joseph Bearse, &c.

(g) Barn. Recs.; 4 Mf. 223; 2 Savage, 19; 1 Otis, 280.
(h) 2 Barn. Prob. Recs. 6.

SECOND GENERATION.

2 John² (Richard¹) Taylor, b. about 1652; m.(i) Dec. 15, 1674, Sarah, daughter of James¹ Matthews; d. before Jan. 18, 1721-2, when his will was proved. March 6, 1665-6, John Crow, son of Yelverton, was fined 3s. 4d. for striking John Taylor.(j) In 1675 he served in King Philip's war.(k) In 1676 his rate for the expenses of that war was £3 8s. 10d.(l) John Taylor, Oct. 29, 1677, as one of a jury of inquest, signed the verdict on the death of the wife of James Claghorne of Yarmouth.(m) In the Scrap Book in the Registry of Deeds at Plymouth, p. 111, is the original bond of John Taylor, John Gorham and John Thacher, administrators of Richard Taylor, deceased (not signed by Thacher), dated March 4, 1673-4.

John Taylor June 28, 1680, received the following grant from the town:

"Given and granted to John Tailer his heirs and assignes forever six acers of planting land on ye south side of ye roade waye allowing 4 pols for the breadth of the said road from the said Taillers field fence this said six acers lying at the north west and even with ye old field fence extending by the road neere south east 40 pols thence on a set of towards the wods 24 pols; and 24 pols on ye westside; and 40 pols on ye south side."(n)

In 1695 he was appointed to take care of the meetinghouse for

---

(i) Yar. Rees.; 2 Mf. 208.
(j) 1 Plym. Col. Rees. 117.
(k) Bodge, 439-441; 16 N. E. Reg. 146; 114 Mass. Arch. 103-110; Swift, 141.
(l) 2 Freeman, 194; Swift, 105.
(m) 5 Plym. Col. Rees. 250.

(n) Land Book of Yarmouth, p. 27.

one year for the compensation of one pound.(o)

In 1698 his tax in Yarmouth was £4 2s. 10d. No tax equalled £5 except that three persons paid between £6 and 7 and one person between £8 and 9.(p)

In 1712 he received 23 shares in the division of the common lands of Yarmouth. A plan of division had been adopted in 1710 and a further plan in 1711.(q) In 1713-14 a final division was provided for, which was made by lot July 14, 1715, when it appears that Samuel Sturges chose lot 29, 7½ acres, being John Taylor's right. John Taylor had lot 23, 17½ acres.(r) Shortly before this he had removed to Chatham, where his son Samuel had probably preceded him. He purchased land and resided in South Chatham near Taylor's pond.

In the division of the common lands of Chatham in 1714, John Taylor as a "priviledged" man received lot 38, which lay N. W. of Taylor's pond.(s)

March 13, 1715-16, he was one of those who signed a paper in behalf of Ebenezer Hawes in the suit of the Rev. Hugh Adams v. Hawes.(t)

His cattle mark appears in the Chatham town records May 18, 1716.

His will dated June 23, 1718, was proved Jan. 18, 1721-2.(u) He gave to his wife Sarah the use of

---

(o) 2 Freeman, 202, 203; Swift, 117.
(p) Files of Superior Ct. of Judicature, 4600; Record Book 1686-1700, p. 297.
(q) Swift, 124-126.
(r) Swift, 130; Yarmouth Recs.

(s) Smith's Chatham, 201, and map at p. 132. Smith says: "As he owned land adjoining Tumblen's or Tomlon's Cove and came to Monomoit about the time the Tomlons appear to have moved away, it is supposed that he bought the farm of Nathaniel Tomlon, which was doubtless located on the east side of Taylor's pond, now so called."
(t.) Files, 10,812.
(u) 4 Barn. Prob. Recs. 26.

one-third of his "houseing, lands and meadows" during her widowhood, his best bed and the furniture belonging to it, and the sum of £10 to be paid out of his movable estate; to his son Samuel, 20s.; to his son John, 20s. besides what he gave him in land by a deed bearing even date with the will; to his daughter Mary Taylor, £26; to his daughter Elizabeth Taylor, £20; to his daughter Hannah Eldredge, 8s. besides what she had already received as her portion. He made his son Seth residuary devisee. He named his wife and his son Seth as executors of his will. His inventory, taken Jan. 25, 1721-2, amounted to £185 15s. 6d., of which £150 represented real estate.(v)

Children, no doubt all born in Yarmouth.

4 Samuel, b.(w) Yarmouth Dec. 14, 1675.

(v) Ib. 31.
(w) Yar. Recs.: 2 Mf. 208.

5 John, b.(w) Yarmouth June 15, 1678.

Mary, b.   ; m. as his 3d wife Ephraim Covel of Harwich (int. Sept. 20, 1746).(x)

Elizabeth, b.   .

Hannah, b.   ; m. in Chatham William Eldredge, son of Joseph, Oct. 1, 1713.(y)

6 Seth, b.   .

Will of John⁸ Taylor.

In the Name of God amen. I John Taylor of Chatham In the County of Barnstable In New England, being aged & under bodily Infirmity, tho of Good and Disposing mind and memory at this Present Time through the mercy of God, and calling to mind ye uncertainty of my Natural life and the certaintie of my death, I do make ordaine & appoint this to be my Last Will and Testa-

(x) Harwich Recs.; her brother Seth's will, 13 Barn. Prob. Recs. 68.
(y) 23 N. E. Reg. 178.

ment In manner and forme following, that is to say first and principally I give and bequeath my soul to God that gave it to me and my body to the Earth to be buried In such Decent manner after my decease as shall be thought good by my Executor hereafter named; and as for such worldly goods and Estate as God has given me My will is that all those Debts and dues which I owe to any person, shall be paid In convenient Time after my decease.

Imps. I give and bequeath unto my Loveing wife Sarah the use and improvement of one third part of my houseing Lands and meadows so long as she shall continue to be my widdow, and I give unto my sd wife my best bed and the furniture belonging to it, and ten pounds more to be paid to her out of my moveable estate as it shall be apprized to be at her Dispose

Item I give and bequeath unto my son Samuel Taylor Twenty Shillings to be paid to him out of my Estate by my Executor hereafter named

Item I give to my son John Taylor Twenty Shillings to be paid to him out of my estate besides what I have given to him my sd son in Lands as appears by one deed bareing equal date with these presents.

Item. I give to my Daughter Mary Taylor Twenty & six pounds out of my estate.

Item I give to my Daughter Elizabeth Taylor Twenty pounds to be paid out of my estate.

Item. I give to my Daughter Hannah Eldredge eight shillings besides what she hath allredy Received for her portion.

Item. I give and bequeath unto my son Seth Taylor and to his heirs and assigns forever all my houseing Lands and meadows whatsoever and wheresoever the same is or may be found (except-

ing the Privilege In my sd house
& Lands above given unto my
wife) which is also to returne to
him my sd son Seth or his heirs
when she shall sease to be my
widow—and my will is yt the debts
and Legacees above given, shall be
paid out of my moveable estate
as it shall be prized so far as yt
will do, and ye Remainder to be
paid by my sd son Seth In Consideration
of what I have given to
him In this my will, And to pay
yt part weh must be paid out of
my sd sons Sethe estate within
four years after my Decease.

Lastly I do hereby impower
nominate and appoint my wife
Sarah and my son Seth Taylor to
be Executors to this my Last Will
and Testiment hereby Revocking
and Disallowing all former will
heretofore made by me, and declearing
this to be my Last Will
and Testament In witness whereof
I have hereunto set my hand and
seal the Twentythird Day of
June 1718.

     his
John X Taylor (seal)
    marke
Signed sealed and Decleared
In presence of
Peter Thacher
Joseph Stewart
   her
Mary X Stewart
   marke
Proved Jan. 18, 1721-2.

---

3 Joseph[2] (Richard[1]) Taylor, b.
about 1660; m.(z) April 25, 1684,
in Marshfield Experience Williamson;
d.(a) there Sept. 13, 1727,
aged 67 years.

He had chosen Mr. John Miller
as his guardian, and on June 3,
1674, the choice was approved by
the Court.(b) In 1683-4 he was a
freeman of Marshfield.(c) In 1697
Experience, his wife, was admitted
to the church there and his children
Richard, Joseph, Marah and

(z) Marshfield Recs.; 2 Mf. 183.
(a) Gravestone inscription
('Thomas's Marshfield, 95), styling
him "Mr."
(b) 5 Plym. Col. Recs. 146.
(c) 8 ib. 208.

RICHARD TAYLOR, TAILOR,

Ebenezer were baptized.(d) His son Samuel was baptized April 12, 1700; his daughter Experience March 28, 1702; and his son Timothy Dec. 3, 1704.(e) Savage says he was the son of Richard Taylor of Yarmouth(f) and this is undoubtedly correct. His will, dated Aug. 31, 1727, and proved in Plymouth County Oct. 30, 1727, mentions his wife Experience, his sons Ebenezer, Samuel and Timothy and his daughter Mary Taylor.

THIRD GENERATION.

4 Samuel² (John², Richard¹) Taylor, b. Dec. 14, 1675; m. Elizabeth   , perhaps his 2d wife; d. in or after 1756.(g) In 1698 his tax in Yarmouth was £2 1s.(h)

(d) 11 Mf. 37.
(e) Ib. 122, 123.
(f) 4 Savage, 262,709.
(g) His son Samuel is called Jr. in the Chatham records in 1756.
(h) Files 4600.

The inventory of Lt. Silas Sears of Yarmouth, verified May 2, 1698, shows him indebted to Samuel Taylor in the sum of £1 10s.(i)

In 1712 in the division of the common lands of Yarmouth he received 7½ shares.(j)

About 1711 he removed to Chatham.

He located on land probably bought of Michael Stewart, who had purchased it by deed dated Oct. 12, 1702, of William Nickerson, Sr., Nathaniel Covel, William Covel and Ephraim Covel, of Chatham, and Samuel Sprague, of Northfield, Plymouth Co., who had succeeded to the right of the original William Nickerson, purchaser from the Indians.(k) His house was on or not far from the site of what was long the almshouse of Chatham, W. of Capt. Ephraim Smith's and N. W. of

---

(i) 2 Barn. Prob. Rees. 70.
(j) Swift, 124-126.
(k) Thos. Doane Papers.

Richard Young's. This was where his son Samuel lived.

The 10th lot of the common lands of Chatham comes down to a point or corner at the road nearly opposite Ebenezer Hawes's and nearly opposite the w. boundary of Samuel Taylor's purchase.(l). A settlement of boundaries between Samuel Taylor and Samuel Stewart, dated March 20, 1722-3, is recorded in the Chatham records. Stewart was on the W. of the boundary, Taylor on the E. and N. The boundary commenced near Taylor's house and ran as far S. as the Cove and meadows. Seth Taylor was to have a way to the salt water pond. In the Chatham records in 1725 a road between William Nickerson and Samuel Taylor is mentioned.

In the division of the common lands of Chatham in 1714, he received as a "priviledged" man lot 26, which lay some distance from Cockle cove in a direction a little W. of N.(m)

In a deed of Samuel Eldredge to Seth Taylor, dated May 15, 1711, conveying a parcel of land consisting of 12 acres of upland and 2 acres of meadow at or near the Oyster pond, the tract is bounded northwesterly by land of Samuel Taylor.(n)

In the Chatham town records Samuel Taylor is first mentioned March 19, 1712-13, when he was chosen grandjuryman. In May, 1711, his cattle mark is recorded. March 21, 1714-15, he was chosen one of the selectmen, and the following year one of the selectmen and assessors. Jan. 24, 1715-16, he was one of the appraisers of the estate of Hugh Steward of Chatham.(o) March 13, 1715-16,

---

(l) Proprietors' Book of Chatham.

(m) Smith, 201 and map at p. 132.
(n) Thos. Doane Papers.
(o) 3 Barn. Prob. Recs. 358.

RICHARD TAYLOR, TAILOR,

he was one of those who signed a paper in behalf of Ebenezer Hawes in the suit of the Rev. Hugh Adams v. Hawes.(p) In 1718 he was one of the selectmen and constable. April 28, 1720, he was named as a committee to consider with the Rev. Mr. Lord the building of a new house or the repairing of the old one. The old one was repaired. May 14, 1722, he was moderator of the town meeting, and was chosen to petition the General Court to exempt the town from a fine for not keeping a school master, but only a school dame. In 1723 it was voted to pay him £1 6s. for serving the town. May 17, 1725, the town voted that the roadway between Samuel Taylor and William Nickerson be "turned" provided Taylor should dig up the stumps and make it a good passible road for travellers.

March 26, 1726, he was chosen trial juryman. March 23, 1726-7, he was made town treasurer. June 24, 1728, he was chosen one of the trustees "to fetch our Money made by ye Province at Boston." July 17, 1728, Samuel Taylor with others was appointed "to take an account of all ye Constables beginning at John Ryder & since." July 24 and Sept. 24, 1728, he was moderator of town meetings. In 1729 and 1730 he was chosen one of the selectmen. Jan. 14, 1729-30, Mr. Samuel Taylor was appointed agent "to keep our Meeting house in order and repair until we can procure another." July 6, 1731, he was one of the appraisers of the estates of three Indians.(q) March 26, 1733, he was elected one of the selectmen. Jan. 25, 1733-4, he was chosen trial juryman. In 1734 he is styled Deacon. March 12, 1733-4, he was made one of the selectmen. May 10, 1736, he was appointed to hire a schoolmaster for

(p) Files, 10,812.

773

one quarter of a year. In 1736 he took the oath as selectman. From the last-mentioned date to 1749 he was moderator of town meetings 15 times and is usually styled "Deacon."

Jan. 29, 1741-2, he was a witness to the will of Elisha Hopkins of Chatham.(q1) By deed dated and acknowledged March 18, 1741-2, he conveyed to Shubael Gorham of Barnstable, for the consideration of five pounds, the lot in Gorham (now in Maine), containing the one hundred and twentieth part of the township, which had been granted by the General Court of Massachusetts on account of the services of his father, John Taylor, in King Philip's war.(r) According to the law, the eldest male heir was to have the land, paying to the other heirs such portions of £10 as they respective-

(q) 5 Barn. Prob. Recs. 117, 118.
(q1) 16 Mf. 36, 37.
(r) York Co. Registry, Book 27, p. 75.

ly would have had of the land if it had descended on the intestacy of the ancestor.(s)

Oct. 17, 1748, Deacon Samuel Taylor was placed on a committee to engage the Rev. Stephen Emery.

Deacon Samuel Taylor is mentioned April 17, 1749, and he was living as late as March 2, 1756, when, as also March 13, 1755, his son Samuel Taylor, Jr., is mentioned in the town records.

Children, born in Chatham.

7 Joseph, b. Jan. 22, 1713-4, perhaps by a first wife.

8 Samuel, b. about 1722.

9 Matthews, b. May 15, 1724.(t)

Thankful, b.   ; m. John Collins, Jr.(u)

(s) 16 N. E. Reg. 143.
(t) Chat. Recs.; 10 Mf. 197.
(u) John Collins died before Jan. 29, 1772, when letters of administration were granted to his brother. (16 Barn. Prob. Recs. 19.) His inventory, taken March 6, 1772, amounted to £216 11s. 4d. He had land in partnership with his brother Samuel and others and land on Tom's Neck and Morris

James, b. about 1732; died May 19, 1758, in his 27th year.(v) Probably Samuel, born in Yarmouth, who died young and who was perhaps by a first wife.(s1)

Island. (12 ib. 497.) The dower of his widow Thankful was set off April 6, 1772, by James Covel, Nathan Bassett and John Hawes. (17 ib. 113.) According to the town records, Matthews Taylor on July 21, 1774, agreed to keep his sister Thankful Collins. She had died before April 8, 1777, when the account of the administrator was dated. A second inventory dated April 15, 1777, amounted to £160 13s. 4d. The decree of settlement was entered July 8, 1777, the distribution being to brothers and sisters and their issue. (20 ib. 93-96.) The children of John Collins, Jr., and Thankful his wife are given from the Chatham records in 10 MF. 197 and 198, viz.: Thankful, b. May 16, 1742; Elizabeth, b. Feb. 29, 1744, and d. Aug. 25, 1744; John, b. Oct. 8, 1745, and d. July 31, 1746; Elizabeth, b. Dec. 8, 1747. All were deceased before their father.

(v) Gravestone; 8 Mf. 239.
(s1) Swift (p. 126), among those in 1712 entitled to the common lands of Yarmouth, names "John Taylor, Senr., Samll Taylor, Senr., John Taylor, Jun'r, John's son."

5 John⁵ (John², Richard¹) Taylor, b. in Yarmouth, June 15, 1678; m. Hannah ; d. before Oct. 30, 1734, when letters of administration were granted to his widow Hannah Taylor.(w).

In the division of the common lands of Yarmouth in 1712 he received 7½ shares,(x) and in the final division in 1715 he had 7 acres in lot 113.(y) He removed to Chatham with his father in or about 1712.

March 13, 1715-16, he signed a paper in behalf of Ebenezer Hawes in the suit of the Rev. Hugh Adams v. Hawes.(z)

Children, b. in Chatham.

Barnabas, b. ; m. Bethiah, widow of Elisha Howes and daughter of John Hawes. He d. between May 25 (date of his will) and July 9 (date of probate),

(w) 5 Barn. Prob. Recs. 242. She is described as spinster, but it is believed she was his widow.
(x) Swift, 126.
(y) Ib. 130; Yar. Town Recs.
(z) Files, 10,812.

1776, leaving a daughter Rhodia, who m. Seth Ryder, July 3, 1797.(a)

Abigail, b. ; m. Joshua Ellis of Harwich, Jan. 15, 1769.(b) These are most probably the children of John² and Hannah Taylor, although they may have been of Samuel² and Elizabeth.

6 Seth² (John², Richard¹) Taylor, m. Elizabeth, daughter of Daniel Hamilton.(c) He died 1764.

Children.

Sarah, b. ; m. Daniel Howes, Jr., Nov. 28, 1754.(d)

Mary, b. ; m. 1st Solomon Collins, Jr., Nov. 16, 1758, who died before June 25, 1762, and 2d, after that date, Elijah Smith.(e)

Tabitha, b. ; m. Isaac Howes, Sept. 20, 1753;(d) d. April 25, 1759, aged 24.(e1)

(a) 17 Barn. Prob. Rees. 349; Chat. Rees.
(b) Har. Rees.
(c) His will, dated Jan. 20, 1735-6, 5 Barn. Prob. Rees. 369.
(d) 7 Mf. 141, 142; Chat. Rees.
(e) 9 Mf. 35; Chat. Rees.
(e1) 8 Mf. 239.

Seth, b. June 11, 1747; m. Rebecca Mayo, March 3, 1768; d. Sept. 10, 1829; she d. Oct. 16, 1831. Among their grandchildren were Miss Polly Taylor, well-versed in the family history of Chatham, and Ephraim Taylor, a prominent citizen of the town.

Seth² Taylor left a will, dated June 25, 1762, and proved Dec. 4, 1764.(f) He mentions his wife Elizabeth, daughters Sarah Howes and Mary Collins (widow), son Seth, granddaughter Tabitha Howes, and sister Mary Covel, "which now liveth with me."

FOURTH GENERATION.

7 Joseph⁴ (Samuel³, John², Richard¹) Taylor, b. Chatham, Mass., Jan. 22, 1713-14; m. Hannah   . He removed, probably about 1740, to that part of Dutchess Co., N. Y., now included in

(f) 13 Barn. Prob. Rees. 68. Much information was obtained about 1880 of Miss Polly Taylor.

the town of Southeast, Putnam Co., (then known as the "Oblong"), and from there about 1770 to the part of Kent, Conn., now included in the town of Warren.

In 1754 and 1768 he was a tenant in possession on the Philipse Patent in Putnam Co., N. Y., with other persons bearing Chatham or Cape Cod names.(g)

He and his wife are buried in the ancient burying ground of Warren.

The inscriptions on the gravestones of Joseph Taylor and his wife read as follows:

"In Memory of Mr. Joseph Taylor, who died June 15, 1792, AE 79."

"In Memory of Mrs. Hannah Taylor, wife to Mr. Joseph Taylor, who died Sep. 7, 1804. AE 83."

Oct. 12, 1880, the Rev. John L. Taylor, who graduated at Yale college in 1835, wrote:

(g) Pelletreau's History of Putnam Co., 418, 419.

"Fifty years ago I had from my father this acct. of our ancestors, viz.:

1 Samuel, coming over from England and settling in Chatham, Mass., date not known.

2 Joseph, son of Samuel; his wife's name, Hannah. Joseph and Hannah moved from Chatham to the town of Southeast in N. Y., lying west of Danbury, Conn.; date of this removal not given; but, "about the time of the revolution," they again moved, going up from Southeast in N. Y. to Warren, Ct. At this time they had a family of four sons and one daughter, viz.: John, David, Reuben, Joseph and Hannah.

3 Joseph Jr. (his wife, Mercy Lord) lived with his parents on the Warren homestead and had there a family of twelve children: Sarah, John, Matilda, Sears, Joseph L., Enoch, Sears 2d, Phebe, Philemon, Zenas, Hannah, Laura.

4 The John of this list was my father; who died 20 years ago,

aged 74, in Warren, near the old homestead. He had a family of 4 sons and 1 daughter: Cyrus C., John L., Anna M., Franklin B. and Henry J.

5 John L., born (son of John and Anna) May 20, 1811.

The graves of Joseph and Hannah, Joseph and Mercy, John and Anna, with many others of the family line, are all in a group within the old Warren graveyard, which I have often visited. My residence, for 41 years, has been in Andover, first as pastor of its old South Church, and next in connection with the Theol. Semy."

Franklin B. Taylor, a brother of the Rev. John L. Taylor, was living in Thomaston, Conn., in 1882. Under date of Aug. 3 of that year, he sent the following, stating that the figures before the names of the children of Joseph Taylor, Jr., indicated the number of their children respectively:

"1st Samuel Taylor, who came over and settled in Chatham, Mass., near Cape Cod.

2 Joseph, his son, born in Chatham Jan. 22, 1714, removed to Southeast near the S. W. part of Conn., (the date not known). Afterwards removed with his family to Warren about the time of the Revolutionary war. He had four sons and one daughter, viz.: John, David, Reuben, Joseph and Hannah.

1st John, born May 22, 1746; died Oct. 4, 1776, and leaving three children: Edmund, Anna and Elizabeth.

2d David, born May 18, 1752; died Dec. 31, 1828. He had 9 children, viz.: Reuben, Harvey, Seth, Elisha, Lauren, David Lerrett,(g1) Jerusha, Polly and Asuba.

3d Reuben, born Aug. 25, 1754; died Sept. 2, 1776, at White Plains, N. Y., of camp distemper.

4th Joseph, born Oct. 10, 1760; died in Warren Dec. 23, 1825. He

(g1) Perhaps Serrett.

had 12 children, viz: ⁸Sarah, ⁹John, Matilda, ⁴Joseph L, Sears, ⁴Enoch, ⁴Sears, ⁵Phebe, Philemon, ⁷Zenas, ³Hannah, ¹Laura. [5th] Hannah, married Luther Comstock and died in Hardwick, N. Y., leaving children.

Joseph married Mercy Lord Aug. 28, 1782.

John, son of Joseph, born Feb. 22, 1785, married Anna Beardsley Sept. 18, 1805. They had 5 children: ⁵Cyrus C., ⁴John L., ³Anna M., ²Franklin B., and ¹Henry J. (C. C. and A. M. are dead.)

Cyrus C. left 8 children; Anna M., 1."

As we see above, the family tradition was that Samuel, the father of the Joseph Taylor who died in Warren, came from England, but as there was only one Samuel Taylor in the early history of Chatham, who was the son of John and born in Yarmouth, he must be the father of Joseph of Warren.

8 Samuel⁴ (Samuel³, John², Richard¹) Taylor, b. about 1722; m. about 1743 Mehitable⁵ (John⁴, John³, John², Samuel¹) Ryder; d. Dec. 29, 1787, in his 66th year. She d. May 9, 1788, in her 64th year.(h)

He was chosen hog reeve March 16, 1752, and tithingman March 5, 1754; March 13, 1755; and March 2, 1756. On the last-named date he with others took the oath prescribed in "An act intitled an act for the effectual preventing the currency of the bills of credit of Connecticut, New Hampshire and Rhode Island within the Province."

March 17, 1756, he was a witness to the will of Thomas Doane, which he signs as Samuel Taylor, Jr.(i) March 12, 1761, he was chosen fence-viewer and surveyor of highways, and March 8, 1762, fence-viewer. Aug. 19, 1765, he was moderator of the town meet-

---

(h) Gravestone; 13 Mf. 179.
(i) Doane Geneal. 61.

ing. March 18, 1767, he was elected constable, but agreed with Barnabas Eldredge to act for him for the usual bounty. In 1768 he and John Hawes were to arrange for a school in the S. W. quarter of the town. In 1769, 1771, and 1774 he was a grandjuryman. Nov. 28, 1769, he was chosen warden and took the oath. June 19, 1771, he was one of the witnesses to the will of Joseph Howes.(j) In 1772 he had land near James Ryder's.(k) May 25, 1776, he was one of the witnesses to the will of his cousin Barnabas Taylor.(l) Aug. 16, 1779, he was appointed on a committee to visit the Rev. Mr. Emery, who could not live on his salary, and see if he would accept private subscriptions and to tell him of the many poor people in town. The committee were unable to reach an agreement with him, and on Sept. 28,

(j) 12 Barn. Prob. Recs. 445.
(k) 17 ib. 49.
(l) 17 ib. 349.

1779, Mr. Taylor with others was empowered to make him a second visit, discourse with him and see if he would take money by subscription or any other way. Aug. 7, 1780, Mr. Taylor was placed on a committee to raise men for the government service. April 2, 1781, he agreed to keep Hannah Eldredge one year for £50 old tenor, 45 shillings to the dollar. In 1781, 1782 and 1783 he was a grandjuryman. Jan. 28, 1783, he was appointed on a committee to arrange the settlement and salary of the Rev. Mr. Roby. The salary was fixed at £75 together with four loads of salt hay hauled to his barn and 18 cords of good wood, half oak and half pine, carried to his door.

His will, dated August 13, 1783, was proved Jan. 8, 1788. It mentions his wife Mehitable, his sons Thomas, Samuel, Simeon, Seth, Christopher, James, Reuben Collins, and Zenas, daughter Susannah Smith, and grandson Joseph

RICHARD TAYLOR, TAILOR,

Harding (son of his deceased daughter Mehitable Harding).(m)

The inventory of his personal estate(n) was taken Feb. 8, 1788, by Nathan Bassett, James Eldredge and John Hawes, and amounted to £93 2s. 4d.(a) It included his wearing apparel, appraised at £4, beds and bedding, household utensils, looking glass, six silver teaspoons, 18 lbs. of flax, 55 hogsheads of Indian corn, 17 bushels of potatoes and turnips, ¾ of a barrel of pork, a barrel of beef, a mare appraised at £6, "his old oxen" £8 8s., "his young oxen" £6 12s., "his stears" £5 10s., "his red farow cow" £2 8s., "his brown cow with calf" £3 12s., "his young [cow] with calf" £3, "two heffers" £4 4s., "two young swine" £1 10s., carts and farming utensils including saddle and pillion, "his great Bible" 16s. Reference is made to his east bedroom and his west bedroom. His real estate was appraised by the same men at £275, divided as follows:

His east field, about 18 acres, £13 10s.

His land north of the road, about 19 acres, £22 16s.

His field east of the dwelling house, about 7 acres, £10 0s.

His rye field adjoining the dwelling house, about 7 acres, £14 0s.

"His upland ajoining the meadow home to the rie field including a peace of meadow they used to Pasture with the upland," about 23 acres, £48 6s.

"His home meadow and part of two Islands of Salt meadow and one peace of meadow purchased of Samuel Hamilton all abought of hay ajoining the Cockel Cove," £77 0s.

About 20 acres of woodland in Harwich, including "one peace of Paul Harding abought 3 acors" and "one peace of Lot gray Jur 3 acors," £24 0s.

(m) 26 Barn. Prob. Recs. 380.
(n) 24 Barn. Prob. Recs. 324;
26 ib. 452.

His dwelling house, £58 0s.
His barn, £ 5 0s.
His corn house, £ 1 4s.
His "draw" house, £ 1 4s.

Children, born in Chatham.(o)

Susannah, born Sept. 6, 1744; married Obediah Smith Jan. 15, 1767. He d. Feb. 15, 1814, aged 79. She d. Feb. 4, 1823, aged 79.

10 Thomas, born Dec. 27, 1746.

Mehitable, born Jan. 20, 1748; d. July 18, 1748.

11 Samuel, born July 25, 1750.

12 Simeon, born July 12, 1752.

Mehitable, born Feb. 14, 1755; married Amos Harding Oct. 17, 1777; d. June 1, 1783, leaving a son Joseph.

A daughter, born Jan. 2, 1757; d. Jan. 10, 1757.

13 Seth, born Oct. 13, 1757.

14 Christopher, born Nov. 27, 1759.

15 James, born April 28, 1762.

(o) Family record of Samuel Taylor in possession of writer; Chat. Recs.; 10 Mf. 198; 13 Mf. 179.

16 Reuben Collins,(o1) born Feb. 25, 1764.

17 Zenas, born Feb. 24, 1766.

Will of Samuel Taylor.

In the name of God amen I Samuel Taylor of Chatham in the County of Barnstable and Commonwealth of Massachusetts Yeoman in consideration of my own mortality and how soon I shall depart this life I have thought it my duty to settle my estate what God has pleased to give me while I am in some good measure of health and altho I am advanced in years yet I am of a sound disposing mind and memory and first I do give my soul to God that gave it in hopes of his gracious acceptance through Jesus Christ and my body to the earth to be decently buried after my decease by my executor after named in hopes of a glorious resurrection at the last day.

(o1) Named for his aunt, Thankful Collins.

First I give to my beloved wife Mehitable Taylor the whole improvement of all my real estate so long as she remains my widow my will is that she do not make sale of any wood no more than for her comfortable support of life.

2dly, I do give to my eldest son Thomas Taylor a point of upland a little to the southwest of his dwelling house adjoining the meadow to a stone in the ditch together with my great Bible to him and his heirs forever.

3dly, I do give to my eight sons all the rest of my upland and meadow and woodland excepting what I have given as above mentioned to my eldest son Thomas to be equally divided amongst and with them if they do live to the time of division if any of them should be taken away by Death before Division without heirs for their part to be divided equally between the surviving brothers, that is to say, Thomas, Samuel Simeon Seth Christopher James, Reuben Collins Zenas Taylors and as Seth is now absent and I cannot tell whether he is alive or not my will is if he should not return again for his part to be divided equally with the other brothers as above mentioned and to their heirs forever

4thly, I do give all my buildings as House and Barn with all other buildings to my four youngest sons as Christopher, James, Reuben Collins and Zenas Taylor to be equally divided between them at the time when a legal division may be made after my decease to each of the four last mentioned sons and to their heirs forever and further my will is that the Legacies after mentioned to my eldest daughter Susannah Smith and to my grandson Joseph Harding is to be paid by and out of my four youngest sons part or portion abovementioned

5thly, I do give to my eldest Daughter Susannah Smith ten

pounds lawfull money to be paid her or her heirs after my decease and further my will is that there be paid to my little grandson, son of my youngest daughter deceased, Joseph Harding five pound lawfull money as above mentioned by my four youngest sons to him and to his heirs and assigns forever.

6thly My will is that my youngest son Zenas Taylor to have all my wearing apparel after my decease if he survives me to him and to his heirs forever and my will is if my youngest son Zenas deceases before me for my son Simeon Taylor to have all my wearing apparel to him and his heirs forever.

7thly I give to my beloved wife Mehitable Taylor one full third part of all my household goods and furniture for her own proper use and improvement and to take her choice of one cow out of my live stock before any division for her sole use to her and her heirs forever.

8thly & Lastly I do constitute and appoint my two older sons (viz) Thomas Taylor and Samuel Taylor to be sole executors to this my last will & testament and do order them to pay all my just debts and funeral charges with the remaining part of the two thirds of my household Goods and the live stock above mentioned the cow above mentioned excepted and with my farming tools and tackling and if there is any remains over for that to be equally divided amongst all my sons or their heirs that survive me and to their heirs forever. In witness whereof I have hereunto set my hand and seal this thirteenth day of August annoque Domini 1783 and do look on myself to be of a sound disposing mind and memory and declare this to be my last will and testament.

Samuel Taylor. (L.S.)

RICHARD TAYLOR, TAILOR

In presence of us
James Eldredge
Jonathan Kenwrick
Nathan Bassett.

9 Matthews⁴ (Samuel³, John², Richard¹) Taylor, b. May 15, 1724; m. Desire, daughter of Maziah Harding, Aug. 3, 1747; d. in 1811.(p) The writer's mother and father informed him that this man lived near Taylor's pond and was the brother of her grandfather.

While he is usually called Mathes and his will is so signed, it appears that his name was really Matthews, given to him in remembrance of his grandfather James Matthews. James Covel, town clerk, calls him Matthews in the record of the town meeting of April 16, 1765, when he agreed to keep Nicholas Eldredge one year for £4 2s. 8d.(q) He is called Matthews Taylor in the division of the estate of Thomas Howes Jan. 4, 1769, and Jan. 5, 1770, and in the will of Joseph Howes June 19, 1771. James Covel probably wrote these documents. He was a witness to the will and a commissioner on the divisions.(r) The name is also given as Matthews Taylor in 1811.(s) Later the name was supposed to be Matthias and later generations were so called.

Matthews⁴ Taylor left a will, dated Feb. 17, 1797, and proved March 18, 1811.(t) It is signed "Matthes." He mentions his wife Desire, daughters Bethiah Crowell, Hannah King, Elizabeth Paine and Desire Young, and son "Matthes."

Children, born in Chatham.(u)

Bethiah, born Aug. 27, 1748; married Zenas Crowell, Feb. 20, 1772.

Hannah, born Sept. 12, 1750; married Nath'l King, Jr., of Har-

(p) Chat. Recs.; 4 Mf 182; 10 Mf. 197.
(q) 2 Chat. Rees. 175.

(r) 12 Barn. Prob. Recs. 445; 13 ib. 411, 496.
(s) 32 ib. 266.
(t) 32 Barn. Prob. Recs. 366.
(u) Chat. Recs.; 10 Mf. 197.

(now Brewster), Nov. 26, 1771.
 Elizabeth, born   ; married John Paine, June 15, 1772.
 Desire, born   ; married Simeon Young of Harwich. (intention Nov. 13, 1779).
 "Matthes," born   ; m. Rebecca Snow (int. June 9, 1786).

. FIFTH GENERATION.

10 Thomas⁵ (Samuel⁴, Samuel³, John², Richard¹) Taylor, b. Dec. 27, 1746; m. 1st. Rebecca Godfrey Feb. 13, 1772, who d. Sept. 24, 1775, in her 30th year, and 2d Sarah Harding Oct. 26, 1778; d. 1828.(v) Children, born in Chatham.
By first wife.
George, b. .
Rebecca, b. : m. Zenas Ryder (int. Dec. 20, 1794).
By second wife.
Seth, born .
Christopher, born July 27, 1781.

(v) Chat. Rees.; Gravestone Rees.; 8 Mf. 239; personal information.

Hannah, born June 12, 1784; married Henry Eldredge, Dec. 10, 1806.
Jane, born   ; married Reuben Eldredge (int. Nov. 6, 1805).
Thomas, born June 21, 1791.
11 Samuel⁵ (Samuel⁴, Samuel³, John², Richard¹) Taylor, b. July 25, 1750; m. Eunice Ryder, March 25, 1773. Soon after the birth of his last child he removed with his family to Readfield, Me., where he died March 5, 1816. His wife died in Jay, Me., Dec. 5, 1845. His brother Simeon and his son-in-law, Levi Eldredge, accompanied him to Maine.(w)
Children.
Susan, b. Nov. 24, 1775; probably died young.
Mehitable, b. Nov. 11, 1778; m. Levi Eldredge (brother of Sally Eldredge, who m. Reuben⁵ C. Taylor), Nov. 4, 1794.

(w) Chat. Rees.; information from his grandson Levi Eldredge about 1880.

Bathsheba, b. Sept. 18, 1780; m. Reuben Bean of Jay, Me.

Eunice, b. Jan. 25, 1786; m. James Bean of Jay, Me.

Sally, born Nov. 16, 1788; m. Greenleaf Bean of Jay, Me.

James, b. May 11, 1791; m. Rhoda Chandler; d. in Jay, Me., Oct. 4, 1845.

Samuel, b. July 6, 1794; m. Jemimah Gould, d. in Vienna, Me., 1856.

George, b. March 12, 1797; d. unmarried about 1825.

Rufus Taylor, a son of James, resided in Jay in 1882.

12 Simeon[6] (Samuel[4], Samuel[3], John[2], Richard[1]) Taylor, b. July 12, 1752; m. Tabitha Howes, Jan. 14, 1779. He removed to Readfield, Me., and died about 1825. His wife died about 1820. His children were all born in Chatham.(x)

Children.

Elizabeth, b.   ; m. John Dellof of Mt. Vernon, Me.

Esther, b.   ; m. Zebulon Gilman of Readfield, Me.

Sally, b.   ; m. Jones of Greene, Me.

Simeon, b.   ; d. 1814, aged 20 years.

13 Seth[6] (Samuel[4], Samuel[3], John[2], Richard[1]) Taylor, b. Oct. 13, 1757. He went away during the Revolutionary war and never returned.(y)

14 Christopher[6] (Samuel[4], Samuel[3], John[2], Richard[1]) Taylor, b. Nov. 27, 1759; m. Mercy Godfrey (int. April 17, 1784).(z) He was lost at sea with the vessel and entire crew in 1786 while on a voyage to the banks. Verses on the calamity by Isaiah Young, dated Nov. 20, 1786, are in the writer's possession.

Child, b. in Chatham.

Christopher, b. Feb. 24, 1786.

15 James[6] (Samuel[4], Samuel[3], John[2], Richard[1]) Taylor, b. April

---

(x) Chat. Recs.; Levi Eldredge.
(y) Miss Polly Taylor.
(z) Chat. Recs.

28, 1762; m. Susannah Smith Nov. 8, 1787; d. Sept. 15, 1843, aged 81 years. She d. May 13, 1855, aged 92 years.(a)

Child.

Elizabeth, b.   ; m. Lothrop Howes of Dennis, Jan. 24, 1813.

16 Reuben⁶ Collins (Samuel⁴, Samuel³, John², Richard¹) Taylor, b. Feb. 25, 1764; m. Sally⁵ (Sarah) daughter of William⁴ (William³, Joseph², Robert¹) Eldredge (int. Jan. 17, 1789);(b) d. June 7, 1827. She died May 1, 1842, aged 80 years. He was one of the selectmen nine years, from 1804, and town clerk and treasurer three years, from 1823.(c) He resided in West Chatham near the Oyster Pond river a little east of where it turns to the south around the head of Stage Neck.

(a) Chat. Recs.; his grandson, James S. Howes of Dennis.
(b) Chat. Recs.; gravestone recs.; 13 Mf. 179; family record of Sally Taylor in writer's possession.
(c) 2 Freeman, 614.

Dec. 10, 1788, Obediah Smith and Susannah his wife gave him a receipt for £2 10s., being one-fourth of what her father Samuel Taylor had left her in his will.(d)

Oct. 4, 1790, he was drawn as petit juryman, and March 6, 1797, he was chosen tithingman. Sept. 29, 1795, Levi Eldredge gave him a receipt for £23 9s. 10d., which had been left for Samuel Taylor to pay him.(d)

By deed dated Sept. 15, 1804, his brother-in-law William Eldredge, for the consideration of $50, conveyed to him 4 1-3 acres of land on Stage Neck.(e)

By a deed of Jonathan Nickerson and Susannah, his wife, dated Dec. 26, 1804, and acknowledged by him April 7, 1808, Reuben C. Taylor for $450 bought all their real estate on Stage Neck in Chatham, with a dwelling house

(d) Receipt in writer's possession.
(e) Barn. Recs., 2 Chat. Deeds, 106.

and barn, including premises lying in partnership with the heirs of William Eldredge, deceased, and premises bought of Solomon Eldredge in 1793 and of Daty Eldredge, his widow, in 1799.(f)

April 27, 1805, Joseph Otis, collector of the district of Barnstable, certified that Reuben C. Taylor, an American seaman, aged forty-one years, or thereabouts, of the height of five feet ten inches, and having a dark complexion, black and gray eyes and black hair, was an American citizen.(g)

March 22, 1808, Ezra Crowell for $195 sold to him a tract of land bounded W. by James Ryder, S. by the road from Hezekiah Doane's to Samuel Doane's, E. by Moses Ryder and N. by the white pond and ponds W. of it.(h) The road above mentioned was the main road.

March 7, 1812, the heirs of Joseph Howes sold to him upland and meadow on Harding's Neck, and March 10, 1819, Mulford Howes sold him other land there.(i) This land was S. of the Cove.

He was appointed administrator of the estate of Jonathan Nickerson (2d husband of his mother-in-law) Jan. 11, 1814. He swore to his account (dated March 8, 1814) May 9, 1815. The estate had owed him $42.10.(j)

By deed dated March 14, 1814, Jonah Crowell, administrator of Nathaniel Butler, deceased, for the consideration of $358, conveyed to him Butler's house and 20 acres of land on the Oyster Pond river E. of and adjoining Taylor's place, reserving the dower of the widow Achsah Butler.(k)

(f) Barn. Co., 2 Chat. Deeds, 103.
(g) Protection paper in writer's possession.
(h) Barn. Rees., 2 Chat. Deeds, 102.

(i) Id. 134, 135.
(j) 36 Barn. Prob. Rees. 160; 39 ib. 105, 106.
(k) Barn. Rees., 2 Chat. Deeds, 132.

By deed dated Sept. 15, 1814, William Eldredge, for the consideration of $30, conveyed to him 3½ acres of land in Chatham.(l)

Dec. 2, 1814, William Eldredge, for the consideration of $85, conveyed to him land on Stage Neck.(m) By deed dated Dec. 3, 1814, William Eldredge and Reuben C. Taylor, for the consideration of $35, conveyed to Richard Sears the right of their father, William Eldredge, in Monomoy Great Beach.(n)

By deed dated May 18, 1816, Reuben C. Taylor and wife, for the consideration of $350, conveyed to their son Samuel Taylor a three-fourths interest in a house, land and meadow on Stage Neck.(o) April 3, 1820, for the consideration of $70, they also conveyed land to him on Stage Neck.(p)

(l) Ib. 105.
(m) Barn. Recs., Chat. Deeds.
(n) 2 ib. 301.
(o) Id. 130.
(p) Id. 131.

Aug. 18, 1826, Stephen B. Wiggins gave him a receipt for £8, being for two shares of meadow that belonged to their mother Betsey Wiggins, one share for the signer and one for Rhoda N. Wiggins.(q) Betsey Wiggins was Taylor's sister-in-law.

While he had been a seafaring man, soon after 1800 he settled down to farming, trading and public office. He taught school many winters. Not seldom he was employed to calculate the profit and loss of fishing voyages and to apportion the gains to the owners of the vessels and the members of the crew, to "settle the voyages" as the phrase was.

His account book in the writer's possession shows transactions with George Taylor, Lemuel Hunt, James Harding, Squire Joseph Doane, John Eldredge, Doane Ryder, Thomas Taylor, Enoch Bas-

---

(q) Receipt in writer's possession.

RICHARD TAYLOR, TAILOR,

sell, Nathaniel Eldredge, Willis Berry, Seth Harding, Dr. Daniel P. Clifford, John Young, Samuel Eldredge, Jesse Harding, Benjamin Buck, Edmund Young, James Taylor, Reuben Rogers, Zaddock Bearse, Josiah Ryder, Zoeth Nickerson, Reuben Eldredge, Susannah Eldredge, Nathaniel Ryder, Stephen Emery, Seth Taylor, Elisha Eldredge, Daniel Harding, Prince Young, Joseph Eldredge, Daniel Eldredge, Widow Susannah Smith, and others, consisting of sales of articles, work of teams, etc., from 1808.

His will was proved from memory by John Seabury, a witness, a certificate by him being dated March 5, 1828. A petition by his son Samuel Taylor, named as executor, states that the testator died the previous June, that the petitioner on the 2d Tuesday of June deposited the will in the probate office, and that it was burned with the Court House on the night between Oct. 22 and 23, 1827. The will was dated March 10, 1827, and proved the last Monday of March, 1828. It gave his son Samuel land on Stage Neck and mentions his granddaughter Mary B. Taylor, daughter of his son William, deceased.(r) The greater portion of his estate was given to his son Reuben C. Taylor. The inventory of his estate amounted to $2,953.75, of which $2,519 represented real estate and $434.75 personal property.

The will of his widow Sally Taylor, dated May 15, 1841, was proved Oct. 13, 1842. She made her son Samuel executor and gave him all her right and title to land on Stage Neck. She gave her son Reuben C. Taylor $5, and to her grandchildren Mary B. Collins (daughter of her deceased son William) $12, John W. Atwood (son of her deceased daughter

―――――――――

(r) Barn. Prob. Rees. No. 251; vol. 47, p. 205.

Mehitable) $12, and Mehitable Atwood (daughter of her deceased daughter Mehitable) $25. All her wearing apparel was given to her daughter Susannah Hawes, and the rest of her estate to Susannah Hawes and Samuel Taylor equally. (s)

Children, born in Chatham.

18 Samuel, b. May 3, 1790.

19 William, b. Oct. 31, 1792.

Mehitable, b. April 6, 1795; m. John Atwood; d. July 31, 1832.

Susannah, b. March 25, 1798; m. James Hawes, Dec. 13, 1821; d. March 17, 1856. See "Edmond Hawes," by the writer.

Rhoda, b. March 25, 1798; d. Dec. 28, 1800.

20 Reuben Collins, b. Aug. 17, 1800.

17 Zenas⁵ (Samuel⁴, Samuel³, John², Richard¹) Taylor, b. Feb. 24, 1766; m. Rebecca Crowell, April 10, 1792; d. May 2, 1838.(t)

(s) Barn. Prob. Recs. No. 1672.
(t) Chat. Recs.; personal information.

Children, born in Chatham.
Joseph, b. March 7, 1794.
Thankful, b. July 9, 1796; m. Ephraim Taylor.
Marcy, b. Jan. 27, 1800; m. Thatcher Ryder.
Zenas, b. July 26, 1806; m. Lavinia Ryder.
Liza, b. March 20, 1808; m. Solomon Howes.

SIXTH GENERATION. (u)

18 Samuel⁶ (Reuben⁵ Collins, Samuel⁴, Samuel³, John², Richard¹) Taylor, b. May 3, 1790; m. 1st Betsey Smith Oct. 27, 1815, and 2d Mrs. Lurany Howes Nov. 4, 1846. He d. June 20, 1870.

Children by 1st wife, born in Chatham.

David Smith, b. June 29, 1817; m. Hannah Taylor.
Rhoda, b. Oct. 24, 1818; m. Amon Hammond.
Hiram, b. Aug. 6, 1820; m. Elizabeth Nickerson.

(u) Chat. Recs. and personal information.

RICHARD TAYLOR, TAILOR,

William, b. Nov. 7, 1821; d. June 14, 1844.

Betsey Smith, b. Feb. 6, 1823; d. Nov. 20, 1844.

Thankful, b. Nov. 17, 1824, m. James A. Stetson; resides in Gloucester.

Marinda, b. Aug. 6, 1826; d. Feb. 10, 1850.

Sally E., b. Dec. 12, 1828; d. May 7, 1842.

Caroline, b. June 26, 1831; d. Aug. 14, 1847.

The children are all deceased except Thankful. David S. and William left issue. Thankful has issue.

19 William⁶ (Reuben⁵ Collins, Samuel⁴, Samuel³, John², Richard¹) Taylor, b. Oct. 31, 1792; m. Betsey Buck Dec. 9, 1815; d. March 20, 1821, drowned on Pollock Rip out of the schooner George. His widow m. Elisha Crosby of Brewster.

On the 2d Tuesday of March, 1828, administration on the estate of William Taylor, deceased, was granted to David Kendrick. His widow Betsey is mentioned.(v)

Children, born in Chatham.

Levi Eldredge, b. Dec. 14, 1816; d. young.

(v) Barn. Prob. Recs. No. 254; vol. 42, p. 302.

Mary Buck, b. July 2, 1819; m. Richard Collins and had issue.

20 Reuben⁶ Collins (Reuben⁵ Collins, Samuel⁴, Samuel³, John², Richard¹) Taylor, b. Aug. 17, 1800; m. Nabby (Abigail) C. Baker of Dennis, Mar. 20, 1823; d. Feb. 4, 1843, in Georgetown, S. C., killed on a vessel by the fall of a block from aloft, which struck him on the head.

Children, born in Chatham.

Levi, b. Aug. 20, 1824; m. Martha B. Howes.

Barnabas Baker, b. July 23, 1827; lost at sea April 1, 1846.

Mercy Baker, b. Oct. 27, 1829; m. Reuben L. Bearse.

Reuben Collins, b. Feb. 24, 1832; m. 1st Clarissa S. Nickerson, 2d Mrs. Phebe Lewis of Dennis

Samuel, b. Dec. 13, 1834; d. Sept. 12, 1858.

Erastus, b. Oct. 1, 1837; lost at sea, Jan. 1857.

Abby Lucretia, b. May 4, 1840; m. 1st Alpheus Myrick of Brewster, 2d Reuben Loveland.

Infant son, b. and d. Oct. 18, 1842.

These children are all deceased. Levi, Mercy Baker and Reuben Collins left issue. Abby Lucretia left issue by Mr. Loveland.

No. 49.

LIBRARY of
Cape Cod
HISTORY & GENEALOGY

THE GROSS FAMILIES OF TRURO AND WELLFLEET

By SHEBNAH RICH.

YARMOUTHPORT, MASS.:
C. W. SWIFT, Publisher and Printer,
The "Register" Press,
1914.

THE GROSS FAMILY OF TRURO.

By Shebnah Rich.

Gross, Grosse and Groce; by American genealogists are regarded the same family, the variations being only the accidents of the times and of emigration.

It has been accepted as good history, I know not from what authority, that the Cape Cod family of Gross were Huguenots, and that the name not many generations back was De Gross. My theory does not disprove this statement. Gross is evidently a French name. They may have been Huguenots, but probably of Norman stock. The American family were indisputably from England. The Harlian Society publications speak of "Grosse who came out of Norfolk and lived at Liskard." "The visition of Cornwall. Echiell Grosse, of Cambourne, 7 Sonnes. Frances, dau. of Echiell Grosse, esq. and Margarett bap. 10 Aug. 1610 at Probus Joan dau. of E. G. m. at St Ives 7 mar. 1623 to Tho. Tremwirth of Tilmuth." Also Grose. "Wm. Grose, gent and Alice dau of Wm Norseworthy, mar 1639." "Edward Grosse and Anna Kulthmans m. 7 April 1611. Truro Par. Reg. Jonathan Grosse & Kathren Polsewe m. 1619." These last are Cornish names.

Dr. Savage gives "Grosse" only. "Isaac, born in England, was a brewer, m. before 1619. Son Clement b. in Boston. Isaac, son of Clement, cordwainer in Boston." Savage evidently does not quote all the issue, but is content to give the connecting links. Barry's History of Hanover gives Edmund Gross in Boston, 1642, died there 1655. Also Clement, who left son Isaac, brother of Matthew. This must be the same Isaac referred to by Savage as son of Clement, cordwainer, showing conclusively that they are the same family. Clement left son Simon, who in 1675 m. Mary Bond in Boston and settled Hingham. No male of this name was a taxable inhabitant of Boston in 1695. This fact cuts us clear of the Boston family.

Simon and Mary Bond, m. 1675, are unquestionably the ancestors of the Truro and Wellfleet families, and reasonably of all on Cape Cod, and gives us the following well-sustained connection:

Simon(4) —Isaac(3), Clement(2), Isaac(1)— m. Mary Bond, 1675. Children:
  i. Simon, b. 1676.
  ii. Thomas, b. 1678, m. —— Hinckes of Dover Neck.
  iii. John, b. 1681.
  iv. Josiah, b. 1683.
  v. Misah, b. 1685. The Truro patriarch; m. Mary ——. 2d H. Freeman.
  vi. Alice, b. 1689.
  vii. Abignil, b. 1692.

Micha(5) —Simon(4), Isaac(3), Clement(2), Isaac(1)— b. 1685, m. Mary ——, d. 1724, aged 35. Second, Hannah Freeman, dau. of Constant and Jane Treat, d. 1758, aged 54. He d. 1753, aged (by gravestone at the Old North) 68,

proving him to have been b. 1685, the same year as Micah, son of Simon; thus establishing his identity by the Hingham record. Collateral proof is the names of his children b. at Truro, which in the old record are almost infallible. The first-born Simon, Josiah, etc. Children:
i. Simon, b. 1709, m. Phebe Collins. 2d Lydia Hinckley, 1755.
ii. Ebenezer, b. 1713.
iii. Israel, b. 1718, m. Eliz. Rich, 1740. 2d Lydia, dau. of Dea. Moses Paine.
iv. Mary, b. 1720, m. Richard Stevens, Jr., 1741.
v. Micah, b. 1726, lost at sea.
vi. Jonah, b. 1728, m. Dorcas Dyer, 1749, dau. of Ebenezer.
vii. Joseph, b. 1731, lost at sea.
viii. Benjamin, b. 1733, m. Ruth Dyer, 1757, dau. of Jonathan.
ix. Hannah, b. 1740.
x. John, b. 1741, m. Eliz.——. 2d Mrs. Susannah Snow, dau. of Ephraim Lombard. Her son was Captain Nath'l Snow, the father of Nath'l, late merchant of Boston, extensively engaged in the Russian trade, d. at France, left a large estate.

Israel(6) —Micah(5), Simon(4), Isaac(3), Clement(3), Isaac(1) - - b. 1717, m. Eliz. Rich and Lydia Paine. Was a prominent man. First lived near the valley south of the old graveyard, still known as the "old orchard." Then built the large flat house at the village, where lived Captain John Collins. In this house were born Captains Israel Gross, John and Edward Knight Collins. Children:
i. Israel, b. 1741, d. young.
ii. Samuel, b. 1743, m. Apphiah Freeman, 1768, 2d Mary Lewis, 1776.
iii. Jaazaniah, b. 1745, m. widow Sarah Snow, was the father of Captain Jaazaniah.
vi. Elizabeth, b. 1748, m. Isaiah Atkins, Jr., 1764.
v. Mary, b. 1749, m. Barzillai Smith, 1719.
vi. Joseph, b. 1751, m. Deliverance Dyer, 1773.
vii. Dilla or Delia, b. 1755, m. John Collins, 1774, d. 1811.
viii. Micah, b. 1764, m. Eliz. By Lydia Paine:
ix. Lydia, b. 1769.
x. Israel, b. 1772.

THE GROSS FAMILY OF WELLFLEET:

Strange as it may seem, I have found no person able to tell me the grandfather of Deacon Thomas Gross. There is a tradition that his name was Thomas; that he went from Hingham to Piscataqua, or Dover Neck, and there married daughter of Gov. or Judge Hincks; that she died at the birth of her first-born, who received the maternal family name, a custom then not uncommon. Touching the after life of the father tradition is silent. There are indications that he moved to Nova Scotia, which we shall consider later. In proof of the tradition I find in the Dover Neck records:

"Hincks married, date unknown, ——— Gross, and had Hincks Gross, who lived in 1729 at Billingsgate (Wellfleet) on Cape Cod," also find "Hincks Gross, who lived for awhile in the British Provinces, and afterwards removed to Wellfleet and m. Abigail Crowell." This Hincks is the father of Dea. Thomas. The history is straight enough in him. In the records of the First Church of Charlestown is the following: "John Hincks, Chief Justice of the Supreme Court of New Hampsire, came from England 1670 [Savage 1673]. He lived in Great Island, Portsmouth, now Newcastle, remained in office councillor C. J., and captain of the King's fort till 1707; was living in 1722; d. before 1734." This was the maternal grandfather of Hincks Gross. Samuel Hincks, the Truro schoolmaster referred to, was the son of Samuel and grandson of John, b. in Portsmouth, 1711, moved with his parents to Boston. So Hincks Gross and Samuel Hincks were cousins.

We have yet to account for the father of Hincks. We have stated that there is, or was, an understanding that his name was Thomas. Dr. O. R. Gross understood from his father that his grandfathers, Deacon Thomas and Israel of Truro, were cousins. They could not be cousins-german, but it denotes recognized relationship. The second son of Simon and Mary Bond, b. 1678, was Thomas, a brother to Micah. Nothing is now known of his history. But the traditions, the fact that the first child of Hincks received the name of Alice, another Abigail, and the first son the name of Thomas, all the dates, and acknowledged relationship with the Truro branch, are the links in the chain of evidence that point unmistakably to Thomas as the man The fact that a large family of Gross with the marked Yankee family characteristics are known in Nova Scotia, and that Hincks "lived for a time in the British Provinces," makes it presumably certain that Thomas went thence from Dover Neck, where he married and died. This then is the line:

Hinckes(6) —Thomas(5), Simon(4), Isaac(3), Clement(2) Isaac(1)— b. about 1705, m. Abigail Crowell of Chatham in 1734, perhaps before; the date of all his children not known, but as Deacon Thomas was b. 1740, and was the 7th child, it would denote considerable despatch if m. 1734. His house was east of the Gull pond, not far from the little neck that divides the ponds. His second m. is noticed under the "bans" as follows: Jan. 27, 1756, Mr. Hinckes Gross of Eastham to Mrs. Bethiah Rich of Truro. I found the gravestone of the last named, at the Old North, in Truro, near the Gross neighborhood, entirely overgrown by a clump of brush, in good condition, with the following inscription:

In memory of
Mrs. Bethiah Rich,
widow of Mr. Hinckes Gross,
who died Jan. 5, 1789,
In the 82d year of her age.

Mr. Gross is often mentioned in the Wellfleet records; held various offices and was quite prominent in business affairs; not known to the writer when he died, or where buried. Children:
i. Alice, b. ——, m. Thomas Paine of Truro, 1759.
ii. Azubah, b. ——, m. John Wetherell, of Wellfleet, 1765.
iii. Sally, b. ——, m. Crowell Lombard of Eastham.
iv. Huldah, b. ——, m. Josiah Rider of Chatham.
v. Hannah, b. ——, m. Reuben Rich of Truro.
vi. Elizabeth, b. ——, m. David Newcomb.
vii. Dea. Thomas, b. 1740, m. Abigail, 1765, dau. John and Rebecca (Harding) Young.
viii. Jabez, b. ——, m. Dorothy Ellis of Provincetown. Settled in Maine.

Dea. Thomas(7) —Hinckes(6), Thomas(5), Simon(4), Isaac(3), Clement(2), Isaac(1)— b. 1740, m. Abigail Young, 1765. House not far from his father's; about midway of the Gull pond; so near the margin that all the water was taken from the pond as needed. A few apple-trees still stand in the old orchard. Children:
i. Laurania, b. 1767, m. Captain Eleazer Higgins, d. 1856.
ii. Abigail, b. 1769, m. Wm. Barge of Boston, d. 1851.
iii. Hinckes, b. 1770, d. in infancy.
iv. Sarah (Sally), b. 1773, m. Joseph Rider, 2d John Chipman, d. 1807.
v. Bethiah, b. 1775, m. Micah Dyer, d. 1867.

vi. Thomas, b. 1778, m. Betsey Millne of N. Y., drowned, 1828.
vii. Hinckes, b. 1780, m. Betsey Snow of Truro, d. 1861.
viii. Rebecca Young, b. 1783, m. Capt. John Barnacoat of Charlestown, d. 1862.
ix. Polly Stickney (Mary) b. 1785, m. Captain Frank Cartwright, 2d Rev. Bartholemew Otheman, d. 1878.
x. Cynthia, b. 1786, m. Richard Atwood, d. 1805.
xi. Thankful, b. 1788, m. Rev. Elijah Willard, d. 1872.
xii. Deborah, b. 1708, m. Daniel Paine, 2d Richard Paine of Truro, d. Sept. 11, 1882, the last of the family.
xiii. Jonathan, b. 1791, m. Cynthia ——, of Duxbury, d. 1871.
xiv. Miriam (Maria), b. 1794, m. Freeman Atkins of Provincetown, d. 1873.

Of this family, like many others here introduced, much might be said. I find others of the name which I cannot connect. Mrs. Phebe Gross, daughter S. Penhallow, was 2d wife of Leonard Vassall, the wealthy planter who built the first house in Summer street, Boston, a man of great wealth, who lived like a nabob. Lieut. Gross was in the Expedition to Louisburg in 1745. "April 20th, Lieut. Gross with about seventy men to go on board ye Superbe." "Aug. 19, about 12 of the clock, died Lieut. Jonah Gross in Louisburg." "'Two o'clock p. m., Lieut. Gross was buried. Fired 14 guns as he was carried to his grave."—Abdonajah Bidwell, Chaplain of the Fleet.

NO. 50.

LIBRARY of
Cape Cod
HISTORY & GENEALOGY

THE MAYO FAMILY OF TRURO

By SHEBNAH RICH.

YARMOUTHPORT, MASS.:
C. W. SWIFT, Publisher and Printer,
The "Register" Press,
1914.

THE MAYO FAMILY OF TRURO.

Dr. Savage thinks Mayo or Mayhew the same, and remarks what all have discovered who have read old records, that "Very little attention was paid in those times to orthography of proper names." We, however, incline to the opinion that in this case they are distinct names, and represent entirely different families. I fail to find any connection between Mayhew, the missionary, and Rev. John Mayo from whom, I understand, all the Mayos on the Cape descended. Through an Irish name, he was born in England, graduate of an English university. Was at Barnstable 1639; ordained a teaching elder; moved to Nauset, 1646, had charge of the church the 1646, had charge of the church there, though not a settled minister til 1655. Settled over the old North Cong. in Boston; ordained Nov. 9, 1665. On account of age and infirmities, removed to Yarmouth in 1673; lived with his daughter Elizabeth till his death, 1676; buried in B. Preached the annual election sermon, June, 1658. Wife, Tamosin or Tamsin; d. Yarmouth, 1682. His children were all b. Eng. Son John m. Hannah Lacroft, 1651; had 8 sons; 6th son, Daniel, settled in Wellfleet; dau. Bethiah m. Ebenezer Lombard, 1727; Sarah, Jonathan Paine, 1709; Margery, m. Deacon Moses Paine 1720. All of Truro. The first Noah Mayo, father of this Truro family, came through Thomas, g. s. of Rev. John, as follows:

Noah (4) —Thomas (3), John (2), Rev. John (1)— m. Mary Cushing, 1742-3, removed to Provincetown. Son Noah, b. 1743-4, brought up in Truro, m. Hope Rich, 1764. Children:

i. Noah, b. 1767; m. ——, moved to Harpswell, d. and buried in T., 1809.

ii. Nehemiah Doane, b. 1769, m. Malatiah Rich.

iii. Thomas, b. 1772, m. Sabra Rich.
iv. Mary, b. 1772, m. Zoheth Smith.
v. John, b. 1776, m. Hannah Rich, 1798.
vi. Jane, b. 1784, m. Moses Paine.
vii. Samuel, b. 1787, m. Tirzah Wiley, 1810, of Wellfleet.

The Provincetown branch came through another channel from the same head.

Joshua Atkins(6) —Thomas(5), m. Bethiah Atkins, Truro, Jeremiah(4), Daniel(3), John(2), Rev. John(1)— went to Provincetown when 12 years old, from Chatham; m. Martha Nickerson, 1779.

i. Bethiah, b. 1782, m. Isaiah Nickerson, 1800.
ii. Joshua Atkins, b. 1786, m. Betsey Small.
iii. Thomas, b. 1789, d. 1808.
iv. Joseph, b. 1792, m. Joanna Small, 1817; 2d Deborah Rich, 1824.
v. Stephen Atwood, b. 1796, m. Jerusha Sawtelle, 1824.
vi. Patty, b. 1798, m. Robert S. Miller, 1820, d. 1822.

Isaac, son of Thomas, g. s. of Joseph, the Rev. soldier, m. Hannah Cahoon, 1780; removed from Boston to Provincetown, from thence to Brownville, Me., where he became a "devout and zealous" Methodist preacher; his sons, Allan, Reuben and Jacob, raised very large families.

No. 51.

LIBRARY *of*
Cape Cod
HISTORY & GENEALOGY

DEACON JOHN DOANE
and The Doane Family

By HON. JOHN DOANE.

YARMOUTHPORT, MASS.:
C. W. SWIFT, PUBLISHER AND PRINTER,
THE "REGISTER" PRESS,
1914.

DEACON JOHN DOANE

And Some Account of the Genealogy of The Doane Family.

A meeting of the Doane family of Eastham and the adjoining towns was held on the 10th of September, 1869, at the place where stood the residence of Deacon John Doane, one of the seven first settlers of the town, to witness the erection of a memorial stone by Hon. John Doane of Orleans, and hear an address by a member of the family.

The site of the stone is on the eastern side of the town, near the "Backside" and the head of Nauset bay. The stone is a block of granite, and bears the inscription:

Dea.
John Doane,
Born, 1590
Here, 1644
Died, 1685
1869.

ADDRESS, BY HEMAN DOANE.

Ladies and Gentlemen of the Doane Family, and all present:— We deem a few words of address to be appropriate on this uncommon occasion; and if you will now give me your attention, I hope not to weary your patience, or keep you standing very long.

A glance backward by the light of history, through the vista of time, to "long, long ago," if our hearts are in their right places, methinks will be profitable to us in this fast driving age, when mortals seem in such hot haste to get through the world, that they can hardly spare a moment of time to look behind them. Absorbed in the all engrossing concerns of the present, and anticipations of the future, they have no time or taste for contemplation of the past. But these are the exceptions and not the rule. Veneration for men and things of antiquity, conspicuous in the world's history, seems to have been instinctive in the people of all ages and nations, whether civilized or barbarian. "I remember the days of old," said the Psalmist, and with what pathetic eloquence did Israel, while sojourning in a strange country, discourse concerning the land and sepulchres of his fathers! "Bury me not, I pray thee, in Egypt; but I will lie with my fathers, and thou shalt carry me out of Egypt, and bury me in their burying place." He, too, remembered the days of old.

Imbibing, I trust, some of the spirit of the old patriarch, we, a few of the descendants of Deacon John Doane, our common progenitor, have come hither today, and to his worthy memory set up this humble stone. In the year 1644, according to the records, he, with Gov. Prince, and five other "prominent men" of the Colony and church of Plymouth, came to this place and commenced its settlement; became one of the fathers and founders of the town, and here lived till 1685, when, after a long and well-spent life, he died, full of years and honors, far away from the land of his birth.

This act of filial duty in which we are now engaged, seems the more appropriate at this time,— and by the hand of our venerable kinsman from Orleans,—as no monument has been found indicating the place of his burial. In the ancient burying ground near the Cove, there is a rough stone, the inscription of which is entirely obliterated by the hand of time, which we suppose to be his, but are not certain. Hence the propriety of this memorial, with a brief inscription, on the spot where no doubt exists in regard to his residence while living.

In briefly contemplating the life and character of our great ancestor, let us turn to the page of truthful history, and see what it has to tell us about him. Secretary Morton, in his "New England Memorial," says of those who had liberty from the church of Plymouth to go out in search of a more eligible place of settlement, that "many of the town of Plymouth by reason of the straights that were upon them, took up thoughts of removing to some other place for their better accommodation; and for that end made a more exact and particular discovery of a place called by the Indians Nauset; which place being purchased by them of the Indians, divers of the considerablest of the church and town removed thither, and erected a town which is now called Eastham."

This little company of Plymouth emigrants at first consisted of Gov. Thomas Prince, Deacon John Doane, Edward Bangs, Nicholas Snow, Richard Higgins, John Smalley and Josiah Cooke. "The church of Plymouth," says another historian, "regretted their departure; for they who went out from her were among the most respectable of the inhabitants of Plymouth."

By reference to the Plymouth Colony Records, we find the name of John Doane associated with the most conspicuous men of the infant colony, being placed in various civil offices, the most responsible and important. Evidently he was no ordinary man in the elevated sphere in which he moved.

Tradition says Deacon Doane was from Wales, west of England. At what time he came over I am unable to state. Gov. Prince, we are told, came in the Fortune, the next ship after the Mayflower; and being intimate friends and associates, it is probable that they came in company in 1621, the next year after the Pilgrims. Mr Freeman, the historian of Cape Cod, says "he (Deacon Doane) was in Plymouth in 1630. Assistant to the Governor in 1633, but declined civil office after being chosen deacon."

After removing to this place in 1644 we find him actively and acceptably engaged in promoting the interests of the young town, of which he was one of the fathers and founders, being successively chosen to the highest offices in the gift of the town, and performing also important services abroad. Did any controversies arise, between the town and individuals, Deacon Doane was pretty sure to be placed at the head of a committee to settle the trouble. He was chosen deputy to the Colony court for several years, until the infirmities of age forced him to ask the town to be relieved of that duty, but so confiding was the town in his ability, wisdom and integrity, that they unanimously voted him additional compensation to induce him to continue to serve them in that capacity. What a contrast to the wire-pulling, scheming and chicanery mixed up in the elections of our modern times! In those days their best men were selected for public servants, the highest moral character, to say nothing of the religious, was strictly required of all whom they clothed with responsible trust, when parties, party machinery, and party corruption, were things unknown, "How has the gold become dim, and the fine gold changed!" With the life and character of Deacon John Doane his descendants ought to be better acquainted. A few traditional accounts that such a man once lived here and that he was nearly a hundred years old when he died, is about all that many of them know about it.

Although we can point to no monumental stone where his ashes have slept for nearly two centuries, there are still standing in this vicinity several of the boundstones to his large farm, bearing the initials of his name—chiselled perhaps by his own hands—relics more interesting to the Christian antiquarian than monuments of sculptured marble that tell of the deeds of heroes and conquerors, whom the world calls great. To live backward, in imagination, two hundred years, and see Deacon John Doane cultivating these Nauset fields in peace with God and all mankind, with a well ordered, virtuous and happy family around him, brings infinitley more pleasurable emotions to my mind than to contemplate the bloody work wrought by the Napoleons, the Caesars and Alexanders of the world.

Truly the poet says:

"Blest are the sons of peace."
His life well spent, the good man dies
And lays him down to rest;
His children talk his virtues o'er,
And call his mem'ry blest.

Some account of the genealogy of the Doane family I think will be interesting to those of us who have not made it the subject of investigation. Nothing is known, I believe, of Deacon Doane's ancestral pedigree— nothing beyond himself. Mr. Freeman in his "Annals of Eastham," says he was born in 1590 and died in 1685, at the age of 95 years. He had by his wife Abigail, children: Abigail, John, Daniel, Ephraim and Lydia.

John, Jr., (son of Deacon John) like his father, was a prominent man in the early history of the town. He married Hannah, daughter of Edward Bangs, and had John, Anna, Rebecca, Isaac and Samuel. He died March 15, 1707.

Daniel, (2d son of Deacon John) married Hepsabeth Cole and had Constant, the only child found recorded to them. He was a physician, and resided in this vicinity.

Ephraim, (3d son of Deacon John) married Mary Knowles, and had Patience, Apphia, Hezekiah, Thomas, Ebenezer, Nehemiah and Ruhamah.

Abigail, (daughter of Deacon John) married Mr. Samuel Lothrop of Barnstable, and lived to the great age of 102 years. Her sister Lydia married Samuel Hix of Eastham.

Samuel, (son of John, Jr.,) married Martha Hamblen, and had Samuel, Sarah, Dinah, Dorcas, Solomon and Simeon.

Deacon Samuel, (son of Samuel) married Dorcas Cole, and had Ruth, Joel, Martha and Mercy.

Solomon, (son of Samuel) married Alice Higgins, and had Solomon, Noah, Sarah, Dorcas, Nehemiah, Joseph, Isaac, Betsy and Joshua.

Simeon, (3d son of Samuel) married Apphia Higgins, daughter of Elisha, and had Ruth, Abigail,

Benjamin, John, Isaiah, Phebe, Ephraim and Ebenezer who died young. Deacon Samuel Doane's and his brother Simeon's names figure conspicuously in the town records. He first served for several years in the office of town treasurer, and the latter in that of selectmen and other offices. Other worthy names of this family might be mentioned in this connection. Joseph Doane, Esq., whose parentage I am unable to state, was a prominent man in the early history of the town. He was called to the highest offices of the town, was town clerk and selectman for a succession of years, and did much legal business in various parts of the county. Not a few of the marriages of his time were celebrated, in the language of the records, by "Mr. Justice Doane." Thomas and Israel Doane were active and influential townsmen; and later, Jonathan and Nathan Doane (sons of David) appear in the foreground. Jonathan was a justice of the peace and the father of Sylvanus, who was the father of the late Captain Obadiah. Nathan, his brother, represented the town for several years in the General Court.

The Wellfleet Doanes came from John, son of John, Jr., and grandson of Deacon John, who settled at Billingsgate; and the Chatham Doanes also owe their origin to Deacon John of Plymouth memory.

Returning again to Deacon John, and following the line of descent from him through John, Samuel, Simeon, John and Timothy, we come down to the present generation, where we find a living John of the sixth generation, whose presence we have with us, and by whose suggestion this memorial is placed here. Having had the pleasure of pointing out to him this consecrated spot of earth, it is gratifying to me to assist him in his old age in this act of filial regard and respect for the memory of the great ancestor and good man whose name he bears. And may his years be prolonged to visit occasionally this interesting locality, bringing with him some stray member of the Doane family— once numerous on the Cape, but now widely scattered from Maine to California—inquiring for the place where lived and died the associate of Governors, one of the fathers of this ancient town, a "good man and a just," in his day and generation.

We have thus passed in rapid review the life, character and genealogy of the common head of our family, of whom the history of his colonial life in Plymouth and the record of this town make the most honorable mention. We are satisfied with the record and the retrospect.

Standing here today, a few of his numerous descendants of the sixth generation, on the very spot where his children gathered around the paternal hearthstone in days of "lang syne," let us fitly impress our minds with the lesson that such an occasion ought to teach us—that it is a sacred duty to cherish and perpetuate the memory, and imitate in our lives the examples of the "ancient worthies" to whom under God we are indebted for life and being, our Godly heritage, our country, government and institutions;—and thus verify the scriptural saying, that "the memory of the just shall be blessed"—"the righteous shall be had in everlasting remembrance."

No. 52.

LIBRARY of
Cape Cod
HISTORY & GENEALOGY

A Brief Sketch of The Life of George Webb

A Cape Cod Captain in the Revolutionary War.

By Josiah Paine, Harwich, Mass.

YARMOUTHPORT, MASS.:
C. W. SWIFT, Publisher and Printer,
The "Register" Press,
1914.

A Brief Sketch of The Life of George Webb

A Cape Cod Captain in the Revolutionary War.

By Josiah Paine, Harwich, Mass.

Copyright, 1914, by Charles W. Swift.

This brave officer who served throughout the Revolutionary war, who participated in seventeen engagements, and who was considered by his superior officers a trusty captain, was a Cape Cod man, and was born in that part of old Yarmouth, now Dennis, June 9, 1740. He was the eldest of the two sons of John and Betsey (Sears) Webb. His father was a mariner who had for some time been connected in some way with the British navy. Some few years after the birth of his youngest son, John, he went on a sea voyage and never returned. The sons, George and John, hardly remembered him; but their recollection of him was such as to establish in their minds an opinion of his regular nautical training and his ability as a disciplinarian that was never forgotten. The mother died at the age of 35, in September, 1755, and lies buried in old Winslow burying ground in East Dennis, a stone with an inscription marking the place of burial. She was a daughter of John and Priscilla (Freeman) Sears, born about 1720,* and married John Webb, Aug. 23, 1739.

In 1760, it appears, Capt. Webb had his first experience as a soldier in active service. At that time he was not twenty years of age, yet he felt it his patriotic duty to heed the call of the Provincial government for volunteers to re-enforce Gen. Amherst's army now preparing for the final ending of the French control of Canada, and bringing to a close the long war for that end, for which, from its beginning, the Cape towns had furnished many soldiers; so he enlisted to serve in Capt. Thomas West's company, and was mustered in at the North parish, in Harwich, March 18, 1760. Capt. West was a young man then residing in Chatham, and his company was made up mostly by young men of about young Webb's age, recruited in the Cape towns.

Capt. West had seen much of martial life. He was at the taking of Cape Breton in 1745, and had served as a corporal nearly a year, in a company against the French and Indians, led by Capt. Peleg West of Tisbury, in 1757. He had also served as a first lieutenant in the company led by Capt. Samuel Knowles of Eastham, in 1758. This company was in Col. Doty's regiment under Gen. Abercrombie, and participated in the disastrous attempt to take Ticonderoga from the French.

---

*The old house occupied by her father was, a few years since, standing in East Dennis, just west of the Brewster line and southwesterly of the old Sears burying ground in West Brewster. It was built, it is supposed, about the year 1705.

Capt. Thomas West's company took up its line of march from the public house* of "Widow Howes" in Harwich, April 26, for the rendezvous in Worcester by the way of Boston. From Worcester, the company proceeded to the frontier, and joined the "Western Army." Its term of service expired the last of December following, and Capt. West returned to Chatham. But becoming interested in lands in Barrington, Nova Scotia, as a proprietor, he went to that place and settled upon his land, and there died about the year 1769. He was a fearless, self-reliant man and a good soldier.

Upon the disbandment of the company, young Webb returned to his home; but of his subsequent life to the beginning of the Revolutionary war, very little is known. It is thought he became engaged in seafaring business, as his brother, John, was a master mariner before his removing to western Massachusetts. The Harwich records show he intended marriage with Ann Sears, Aug. 22, 1761, and that his marriage to her, by Rev. Isaiah Dunster of Harwich, took place October 29 following. He undoubtedly was at this time a resident. In 1771, his name appears as a tax payer in Harwich. His place of residence was in that part of old Harwich, now Brewster.

When the Revolutionary war broke out it found him on the right side, against England, fired with ardent patriotism, ready to

---

*This "public house" was situated in North Harwich on the north side of the way from Chatham to Yarmouth, close to the west side of the Herring river, and had been known as "Downes' tavern."

3

take the field and fight against England with the same zeal he had fought when a lad of twenty for England in the French and Indian war. By the record it appears his first service in the cause of liberty as an officer was as first lieutenant of the company of coast guards, commanded by Capt. Seth Clark of the North precinct of Harwich. The company numbered about fifty men, who were chiefly residents of the town. It was raised principally to observe the movements of the British war vessels upon the southern coast of the Cape, and in case of any attempt of landing men to oppose it. It was on duty from July 1, to December 31, 1775, when it was disbanded, having performed efficient duty. Some of these men afterwards served in the Continental army at various times.

Early in the year 1776, Lieut. Webb became the first lieutenant of Capt. Peter Harwood's company of light infantry in the Continental army under Washington. In this company he served more than a year, when he was promoted to the captaincy of a company in Col. William Sheperd's regiment of light infantry which was known as the Massachusetts Fourth, ranking from January 1, 1777. While lieutenant in Capt. Harwood's company he participated in several engagements among which were Trenton and Princeton.

Capt. Webb's company was composed of young men chiefly enlisted in Barnstable county. Twenty-two of them were enlisted in Harwich and were mustered by Gen. Joseph Otis of Barnstable, the muster master. Some of the company were enlisted for nine months, some for three years and a few for the war.

While in command of his company, Capt. Webb was in many

4

of the battles that gave our arms the victory. He was in Glover's brigade and Sheperd's regiment in the two engagements that preceded the surrender of the army of Burgoyne at Saratoga, Oct. 17, 1777, and was present at the capitulation. He was with Washington and his army in the winter quarters at Valley Forge during the intensely cold winter of 1777-78, which followed Burgoyne's surrender, where he and his men, and other soldiers in the snow covered encampment, spent indeed a trying period. It was surely his winter of discontent, as well as that of Washington and his army in the encampment. Well could these soldiers—hungry, ragged, shoeless and shivering in their poorly constructed log huts during that rigorous winter—have said with the foremost political writer in America in 1776 when our arms were suffering repeated defeats and gloom hung over the colonies—"These are the times that try men's souls."

The encampment at Valley Forge was on the west side of the Schuylkill river in Pennsylvania and about twenty miles northwest of Philadelphia. This position for an encampment was taken by Washington for the purpose, says Marshall, "of covering the country of Pennsylvania, protecting the magazines laid up in it and cutting off those supplies to the British in Philadelphia which many of the people were disposed to furnish them." It was "a very strong and commanding piece of ground for the purpose," but weakly situated for winter headquarters. The army entered it from Whitmarsh, a place not far distant, December 11, and at once commenced building huts for occupancy during its stay. The snow was upon the ground, and during the march many of the soldiers left bloody footprints in the snow, they being without shoes. Both Marshall and Thacher give a deplorable condition of the army in this place.

During the six months at Valley Forge Capt. Webb's company was not free from sickness and death, nor from diminution in number through expiration of enlistment. The terms of two of his men from Eastham, John Myrick and Amos Doane, who had enlisted for nine months, expired here in midwinter. The former rather than to suffer longer here, upon his discharge, returned to his home, while the latter chose to re-enlist for another nine months, probably on account of sickness, as he was sick in camp about three months "of a fever and the smallpox," all probably the result of innoculation. John Young and Crocker Young, both of old Harwich, in the company, doubtless found resting places here, as they were reported in March as being dead. Haskell Freeman, Watson Freeman and Edward Nickerson, with others, all young men from old Harwich, were in the company, and survived the terrible winter, and had the privilege to be at the battle of Monmouth and Rhode Island the same year and test their bravery.

Capt. Webb was with his company in Sheperd's regiment, and Glover's brigade at the battle of Monmouth, June 28, 1778, when Washington turned defeat into victory. The day was excessively warm, and his men suffered intensely from heat and thirst. The day was Sunday and the conflict continued from nine in the morning till darkness. At night the men lay upon their arms on the warm ground expecting a renewal of the fight in the morning, but when it dawned there was no British army in sight, and Washington with his army proceeded on to White Plain on the Hudson for headquarters. The day at Monmouth was never forgotten by the old soldiers when telling stories by the fireside of the capture of Burgoyne, and of their stay at Valley Forge.

Soon after returning to the Hudson, Capt. Webb's company was sent to Rhode Island, and there under Gen. Sullivan, took part in the battle fought at Quaker Hill, August 29, 1778. In this battle Capt. Webb had two of his men, belonging to old Harwich, severely wounded. They were Haskell Freeman and Watson Freeman. The former was unfit for duty for sometime on the account of his wound, and was given a furlough for recuperation. He was promoted to the lieutenancy, Nov. 26, 1779, but resigned Aug. 24, 1780, on the account of ill health, due to the wounds he had received at Rhode Island.

Capt. Webb was on duty in Col. Sheperd's regiment at the hanging of Maj. John Andre, the spy, Oct. 2, 1780, at Tappan, N. Y.

With his command, he was in the detachment under Lafayette, sent by General Washington from the main army to strengthen the continental force in Virginia early in the spring of 1781, in protecting that colony from the depredations of Cornwallis's army then centering there. It was in May, following the arrival of the detachment, that he had a brisk and successful skirmish with the enemy while out on an important excursion with his command. The defeat of the enemy by the bravery of Capt. Webb greatly pleased Gen. Lafayette, and he sent to his trusty captain a letter,* assuring him that the "successful skirmish" had "afforded" him "the greatest pleasure," and desired him to accept his "best thanks" and convey the same to his company "on this occasion."

At other times afterwards, while Lafayette's division was watching the movements of Cornwallis's detachments, and badgering them at every point about Richmond, Petersburg and places north and south of James river and other points in that part of Virginia, he was sent out on secret service and was equally as successful in good results.

When the seige of Yorktown commenced, he held his command in Gen. Lafayette's division, and was given an active part in the intrenchments before that doomed place with his brave men, and was present when it fell and the British army under Cornwallis surrendered. In his company in the trenches before the illfated place, in uniform, with blistered hands, displaying great gallantry, enduring hardship, and daring to follow where her brave captain dared to lead, was the noted heroine, Deborah Sampson of Massachusetts, a new recruit, bearing the name of Robert Shurtliffe, the story of whose life in the sacred cause of liberty has so often been read.

Capt. Webb after the surrender of Cornwallis remained in Yorktown until the middle of November following, when, with his company in the detachment in which he had rendered such important service, returned to the headquarters of Washington's army

---

*History of Holden, Mass.

on the Hudson, where he was on duty until the middle of January, 1782, when Gen. McDougal gave him a furlough to visit Massachusetts. After an absence of seven months he reported for duty at Westpoint and again entered service, August 15. In January, 1783, independence of the United States being well assured, no active duty seemed to be in sight; the routine of camp life having lost some of its charms, and longing to be again with his family in a new home, he resigned his commission, returned his sword to the scabbard, bade adieu to his old comrades in arms, and returned to his family at the new home he had provided in Holden, Worcester county,—Harwich being no longer his place of abode,—where he continued to reside the closing years of his eventful life, commanding the respect of the people of the place.

There were many interesting incidents in the life of Capt. Webb while in his long and continuous service of seven and one-half years in the cause of liberty that were known to his family, to the children of his brother, John, and to those who served under him that period of time, showing his adroitness and intrepidity in charge of hazardous enterprises; his dexterity as a submarine leader; summary dealings with pugilists and political carpers of tory proclivities. But it is a matter of regret that these incidental relations have not all reached our time.

An incident related by one of his kinsmen serves to show the valor and firmness of Capt. Webb in an emergency, and how he, by proper maneuvering of his men, escaped capture when unexpectedly met by the enemy. He was out on a foraging expedition which had required the greatest precaution to insure success, but

9

which on this occasion was without avail. While on his march he was intercepted by a large party of English, and shortly was ordered to surrender. Although greatly outnumbered and hard pushed, he scornfully resented the command and laconically replied, "Come and take me if you can!" So fighting and retreating, each man doing his very best for some hours, at last a relief party from the main army met him, and his command was saved from capture though hotly pressed.

The year in which Capt. Webb had his family removed from the old home in Harwich to Worcester County is not yet precisely known. It is a matter of record, however, that he began to purchase land in Holden in 1780 while yet in the army. His first purchase there was made of Simeon Lyons of that town of a very large tract of land, June 12, that year. At this time he claimed Harwich as his place of residence. His next purchase there was December 25, 1782, of John Jolls of several large parcels, amounting to many acres. At this date he is mentioned as of Holden. Subsequently he made more purchases of land in that town; and upon his leaving the army, as already stated in January, 1783, he went to Holden* and became a citizen. His removal from Harwich to that town was probably encouraged by his only brother, John Webb, who had left the seafaring business and made Hardwick, a town near by, his home. The house occupied by Capt. George Webb is yet standing in Holden and known as the "Webb house."

---

*In 1913, a Chapter of the D. A. R. was instituted in Holden which bears his name.

10

The death of Capt. Webb occurred August 25, 1825, at the age of 85. He lies buried in Holden and the grave is marked by a stone with inscription. His widow, Ann, died August 2, 1827, at the age of 85 years. Under the pension act of 1818, he applied for and received a pension, which he continued to receive as long as he lived.

Capt. Webb was held in high esteem by his townsmen and at times selected for official positions. He was early a member of the "Society of the Cincinnati" of Massachusetts, which was formed in 1783, and was such at the time of his death.

Capt. Webb was a man of great valor and resolution, which were tempered by good judgment. He was cautious when it was necessary and resolute when resolution was needed. No duty assigned him was neglected. By nature he was fitted for a higher position in the army of patriots than a captain, but he would not allow promotion. He was contented with his captain's commission. When once asked if he would accept a colonel's commission, his answer was, "It's a pity to spoil a good captain to make a poor colonel."

No. 53.

LIBRARY of
Cape Cod
HISTORY & GENEALOGY

GENEALOGICAL SKETCH *of*
DESCENDANTS *of* JEREMIAH
HOWES *of* DENNIS, MASS.
By Thomas Prince Howes

YARMOUTHPORT, MASS.:
C. W. SWIFT, Publisher and Printer,
The "Register" Press,
1914.

GENEALOGICAL SKETCH of DESCENDANTS of JEREMIAH HOWES of DENNIS, MASS.

By Thomas Prince Howes

Copyright, 1914, by Charles W. Swift.

Thomas Howes, the progenitor of the Howes family of Yarmouth, according to the best information so far obtained, arrived in New England sometime in 1635. There is evidence of his residence for awhile in Essex county.

He appears in Yarmouth in 1639 as one of the grantees of the town in company with Mr. Anthony Thacher and Mr. John Crow. He took the oath of alliegiance the December preceding.

Mr. Howes was one of the committee to divide the planting lands at the first division, a constable in 1644, and of the Council of War in 1658. He was frequently one of the deputies to the Colony Court.

His death took place in 1665. His widow, whose name was Mary, survived him as appears by his will. No family records tell us at what age this couple died. Tradition has preserved the knowledge of their graves.

There is hardly room to doubt but what Thomas Howes, and family, came from Norfolk County, England. The name has been a common one in that region for centuries.

It is claimed to have descended from one John de Huse, who, as far back as 1065, had a large manorial property in Basthorpe, Norfolk. The name has, through changes in spelling, come to be "Howes".

The coat of arms of the Howes family was first granted by Henry 8th in 1519. Be that as it may, there are plenty of people of that name living in Norfolk county, England, now, and about the neighborhood of Yarmouth, and it is fair to assume that our ancestors came from that section of the county.

He was a good, sturdy, honest Englishman of the best type extant in the early part of the seventeenth century.

He came with his wife and two sons, Joseph and Thomas. Jeremiah must have been born soon after their arrival, as his grave stone in the Howes burial ground says his age was about 71 years. He died 1708, consequently Jeremiah Howes must have been born

SKETCH OF DESCENDANTS OF JEREMIAH HOWES.

after the family arrived in America.

How old the other sons were at that time we have no means of ascertaining. Neither of them have grave stones. They were both, doubtless, under 21 years of age when they settled with their father at Yarmouth.

Joseph, the eldest, married Elizabeth, daughter of Rev. John Mayo of Eastham. He died in 1704 at a good old age. His branch of the Howes genealogical tree is like that of Joseph, the son of Jacob.

"Joseph is a fruitful bough, even a fruitful bough by a wall, whose branches run over the wall."

The descendants of Joseph are scattered through all parts of the country.

Thomas, the second son, commonly called in the records, "Captain", married Sarah Baugs. He died in 1676. He frequently commanded the Yarmouth company of soldiers, when sent on any expedition from the Cape against the Indians. His branch of the genealogical tree is the smallest of the three. He left only one son, Jonathan, Lieutenant Jonathan.

Jeremiah, youngest son of Thomas, born on the soil of America in 1637, died 1708, married Sarah Prince, daughter of Governor Thomas Prince. She died in 1706 at the age of 60, as her grave stone asserts. Jeremiah was a prominent citizen of Yarmouth. He was 10 years deputy to the Colonial Court and two years representative, after the union with Massachusetts. He was selectman for 20 years; evidently a man of position and influence. His house was near where Mr. Harvey Howes now lives.

Mr. Joseph probably lived somewhere in Indian Fields, as his property was largely about that region.

Thomas, I judge, lived in his father's house, until his death, with the widow of Thomas, Senior. He only survived his father 11 years. His son, Jonathan, was left to the guardianship of his uncle Jeremiah during his minority, and afterwards built a large house opposite the house of his grandfather, Thomas, then deceased.

This house, built about the year 1700 by Lieutenant Jonathan, was in the possession of his descendents for five generations. A part of the frame forms a portion of the house of David Howes on South street.

Thomas, the grantee, built his house in the field ever since called the Fort, on the easterly side of what is now New Boston brook. His landed estate included a large part of the village of Nobscussett, Indian Fields and Suet Neck. Besides, he had land in Harwich, and meadow at mouth of the Bass river, and large lots of woodland.

His three sons were well supplied with property in land when he died in 1665. Meantime, they had all taken

SKETCH OF DESCENDANTS OF JEREMIAH HOWES.

root in the soil, and flourished. The land, sub-divided among the descendants through seven and eight generations, is still, to a great extent, owned by the posterity of the original proprietors.

SECOND GENERATION.

Jeremiah, youngest son of Thomas, Senior, married Sarah Prince, and had four sons and one daughter, Sarah.
Prince, married 1695, Dorcas Joyce.
Jeremiah married Sarah.
Thomas married Sarah Hedge.
Ebenezer 1st married Sarah Gorham.
Ebenezer 2nd married Lydia Joyce.
Sarah, the daughter, married Cornelius Higgins, and disappeared from our knowledge.

THIRD GENERATION.

Prince, eldest son of Jeremiah, born 1659, married 1695 Dorcas Joyce of Yarmouth, died 1753, was named for his maternal grandfather, Governor Thomas Prince, who died at Plymouth when his grandson was about two years old. Whether the governor ever saw his young namesake we have no means of ascertaining, although it is not unlikely that he would call on his journey from Eastham to Plymouth, and spend the night with his daughter, as he might cross the bay in a shallop, and save the tedious land journey. However, the boy, Prince, could not have remembered his grandfather, if he did receive the patriarch's blessing. He grew up for all that, and married Dorcas Joyce.

The Joyce name is now extinct on Cape Cod, but was in early times quite prominent.

Prince, soon after his marriage, built the house in New Boston, still standing. It was the first house erected on that side of the brook and meadow.

For the first century and half there was no cart bridge over the stream. There was a foot-bridge only, within the memory of persons with whom I have conversed. The road all the way to the upper end of the lane was, in rainy weather, a perfect quagmire, since my remembrance.

What education young people received when Prince Howes was a child must have been of the most elementary sort. An old Almanac, and account book of his, printed in 1706, shows that his penmanship was very rudimentary.

It will be seen that Prince had three brothers. Jeremiah, next in order, married a woman named Sarah. That is all we know of her except that she brought forward a claim upon certain lands that Prince had bought of her husband. Right of dower it was, I presume, as she claimed to have never signed the purchase deed. However, it appears that she never obtained anything.

Jeremiah removed, date unknown, to Pemmaquid, Maine, where he died.

The next brother, Thomas, married a woman named Sarah, and

had one son whose name was Thomas. There the line stops on the genealogical tree.

However, this year in looking over the American Genealogist in Albany, I found several names of Howes who traced their genealogy back to a Thomas Howes of Austerlitz, Columbia County, New York.

A correspondence with one of these gentlemen, Dr. Edward W. Howes of Chatham, N. Y., convinces me of the Thomas being son of Thomas, brother of my great great grandfather, Prince. That Thomas of Austerlitz who died in 1760, and beyond whom these descendants of his in Columbia County could not trace, was cousin to my great grandfather, Lot. He probably left the Cape when a great many people were emigrating to "Oblong", as it was called.

The youngest brother of Prince was Ebeneazer. He held the rank in the militia of captain. His first wife was Sarah Gorham. Second, Lydia Joyce, sister of his brother Prince's wife.

Ebeneazer lived and died on the ancestral acres. Both he and his wife, Lydia, have grave stones in the Howes burial ground.

Ebeneazer lived where Captain Almond T. Howes now lives, or a little back of his house. He owned a large property in land, and was a prosperous and influential man. Being the youngest son of Jeremiah, he retained the homestead of his father, as was the custom in those days.

The property, a good deal of it, still belongs to his descendants.

Prince Howes lived to a good old age, and passed his life on the farm he inherited from his father, Jeremiah. It does not appear that he held any public office, or was much of a factor in public affairs.

His wife outlived him only a short time. They had a family of six children who lived to grow up; viz.:

Desire, born May 22, 1696, married Jonathan Hallett, 1716.

Prince, born Feb. 1, 1700, married Thankful Hedge, 1735.

Dorcas, born March 11, 1702, married James Matthews, 1723.

Jeremiah, born April 26, 1704, married Sarah, moved to Plymouth.

Thomas, born June 27, 1706, married Hannah Sears, 1734.

Thomas, born June 27, 1706, married Bethiah Sears, 1711.

Lot, born September 24, 1709, married Thankful Smith, 1743.

This was the family of Prince Howes that survived him.

The two daughters, Dorcas and Desire, married in Yarmouth, and were remembered by their father in his will.

Two of the sons removed from the Cape, Prince and Jeremiah. Prince to Putnam County, N. Y., and Jeremiah to Plymouth, Mass.

Several letters from Prince, after he removed to Oblong, are in my possession. They are dated somewhere between 1742 and 1744.

Prince went by the name, among his contemporaries, of

SKETCH OF DESCENDANTS OF JEREMIAH HOWES.

"Hero". There was an old ditty preserved when I was a boy, "Prince, the Hero, bound for Banks of Quero, owes no man a penny."

His nephew, Jonathan Howes, who was my great-uncle, could remember his uncle, the "Hero", coming to the Cape from his western home for a visit.

He told me that he was dressed with a "ruffled shirt, and ruffles at the wrist as well as bosom." Jonathan was a mere child at that time, but was impressed with the fine appearance of his uncle.

Prince had been a sea-faring man. One of his letters is dated, 1739, from St. Eustasia, one of the English West India Islands. He had commanded vessels in the whale fisheries. Quite a stirring, hustling man in his day.

The date of his death is to me unknown. It is doubtful if he left any children. He mentions none in his letters.

Jeremiah, second son of Prince, Senior, appears to have removed to Plymouth sometime before his father's death which occurred Oct. 2, 1753.

Jeremiah was, with his brother Lot, an executor of his father's estate. Several letters, soon after his death, were written by him to Lot which are still extant. They relate mainly to the disposal of his property, with some allusions to the health of his family.

He seems to have had one son, Sylvanus, but all traces of his descendants, if he had any, are lost. The date of his death is uncertain.

Thomas, son of Prince, was born June 27, 1706. He appears, if we can trust the records, to have been twice married.

First, Hannah Sears, July 4, 1734.

Second, Bethiah Sears, Oct. 15, 1741.

I am inclined to believe that Thomas had two wives with the above names, as he had granddaughters who bore the same names.

Thomas remained upon his portion of the farm inherited from his father.

As middle names were not common for ordinary individuals in those days, and as so many persons bore the same names, christian as well as surnames, it was usual to resort to nicknames to distinguish these of the same family name. There were, at the time I am writing, four men of the name of Thomas Howes.

The one who is the subject of this sketch went by the absurd name of "Tom Severns". There was a man known, at the same time, by the familiar appelation of "Tom Sailor". He resided in the house now owned by the present writer, but subsequently removed with his family to Ashfield.

Another Thomas, also, lived beside the New Boston brook in the house before spoken of as built by Lieutenant Jonathan Howes, was called "Tom Tupper".

The Thomas now spoken of,

"Tom Severns," built the house on the hill now occupied by Charles and James O. Howes. It was built in 1742. They are his great grandsons.

Thomas was married first in 1734. Where he lived before he built his house is not known, but perhaps with his father, keeping house in the upper chambers as was quite common. What little we know of "Uncle Thomas" he was an easy-going sort of person. My great-uncle Jonathan used to talk about his uncle occasionally. He used to say that he would drop in to talk with his brother Lot, and his wife, Thankful, and tell what he heard; after he had left, his brother Lot would say, "His stories are about as near the truth as 'chalk is like cheese'." He was fond of his joke, I judge.

I have heard Uncle Jonathan relate that Uncle Thomas would say to his sister-in-law, that was Uncle Jonathan's mother, "I am going to make my will." "Are you? How are you going to dispose of your property, Uncle Thomas?" "Well, I am going to give my son so much, and my daughter so much, and leave so much to my widow." "But, Uncle Thomas, you have not so much property as that." "Well," he would say, "it is my will they should have it, and if they want it, they must go to work and get it."

This story shows the antiquity of the joke about leaving property to a person, and if he wants it, go to work and get it.

The house that Thomas built was built of timber from our own woods. The boards, probably, came from Plymouth. The bricks were burned in a kiln where the garden of the late Nehemiah Hall is now.

My great-grandfather Lot, brother of Thomas, kept a memorandum for a number of years of his expenses and his father's also. He notes when this house was built, and that his brother made use of his father's team to cart brick and other material for building his house. Also the fact that he had the use of the old man's horse for various purposes without giving any credit to his father for it.

Thomas died in 1764. His widow, Bethiah, died in 1788. His successor was Solomon, born Aug. 18, 1744, whose descendants will be noticed in another place in my narrative.

Lot Howes, born Sept. 24, 1708, took for his wife Thankful Smith, 1743. She was the daughter of Jonathan Smith, who lived a short distance from the main road on the county highway, just before the Yarmouth is reached. His house has been torn down within thirty years or so. It was the residence of Gamaliel Howes, father of Philip Howes.

Jonathan Smith was a carpenter by trade, and a man of some property.

In my boyish days there was in our family an old saw which Father said was Grandfather Smith's.

SKETCH OF DESCENDANTS OF JEREMIAH HOWES.

He left, when he died, a black boy named Eleazer whom he had bought when young of one Hannah Thorpe. This slave was left as a charge in the care of Grandfather Smith's two daughters, Thankful and Martha. He was then old and blind.

Martha was the wife of Isaac Vincent, who lived somewhere near where Mr Jesse Hall's house now is. That Martha is the person to whom the name of Martha in our family owes its origin.

Old Eleazer died on his way to one of these houses, either Vincent's or Howes's.

Lot lived in the house with his father Prince, until the old man died on Oct. 20, 1753. His mother lived with him until her death, 1759.

Lot was, judging from what his children and grandchildren remembered of him, and the testimony of his memorandum books, a hard-headed, literal minded, square dealing sort of a man. He was in office at times, constable, selectman and the like. He had a good estate, lived in comfortable style, and kept maid servants to help do the housework.

He was somewhat stern in his manners and not much given to jesting, and children stood rather in awe of him. That is the impression that his grandchildren had of him.

His wife must have been of a more lively disposition, judging from the temper of his two sons, Jeremiah and Jonathan, who are both of a jocose disposition.

There was another one named Lot who was weak minded. He died when some forty years old. It is said he was injured by lightning which impaired his mind.

Grandfather Lot died in 1791, July 1. His wife, Thankful, died the year previous, 1790, July 21. Their children were:

Jeremiah, born Dec. 26, 1743, married Priscilla Hall, Nov. 2, 1767.

Martha, born May 29, 1746, married Anthony Howes, 1769.

Lot, born September 14, 1748, bachelor.

Jonathan, born July 27, 1752, married Susanna Matthews, Dec. 28, 1774.

Having described the children of Prince, we now take up those of Lot.

His eldest son was, as above, Jeremiah. He lived until 1824 and I can well remember him, being seven years of age when he died. He married when 24 years old Priscilla Hall. She was of the same age as her husband.

Her father was Joseph Hall, Merchant Hall he was called. He built the house where Cerenias Hall lived.

She was one of a large family, and through her I am related to many of the Halls. She died on Lord's day, July 6, 1783, as her husband records with his own hand, giving the respective ages of their children at their mother's death.

Sylvia, 15.
Jabez, 13.
Rebecca, 11.
Prince, 9.

SKETCH OF DESCENDANTS OF JEREMIAH HOWES.

Oren, 7.
Priscilla, 5.
Martha, 2.
Jeremiah's children were born on the following dates:
Sylvia, Sept. 17, 1768, died unmarried.
Jabez, Aug. 1, 1770.
Rebecca, Aug. 1, 1770.
Rebecca, Aug. 21, 1772.
Prince, July 27, 1774.
Oren, July 7, 1776.
Priscilla, Dec. 6, 1778.
Martha, Oct. 16, 1781.
Jeremiah was an active citizen of Yarmouth. Before its division he was moderator of the meeting held to consider the subject of division. He wrote a copy of the petition for the separation. He was ten years one of the selectmen of Yarmouth, and eleven years selectman in the town of Dennis. For many years he was the only justice of the peace in Dennis. He held in 1776 the rank of lieutenant in the militia, and marched with Captain Abijah Bangs's company to Dorchester where he was during the summer of 1776. Was there when the news came of the retreat of Washington with the continental troops from Long Island.
Lieutenant Howes was a man very much alive when times were stirring, and had a hand in what was going on. He was, for many years, called to act as moderator at town meetings. A genial, pleasant person, fond of his joke, and withal had a good opinion of himself.
After his first wife's death in 1783, he married Mrs. Tempy Hedge, widow of Captain John Hedge of Yarmouth, who had died on board the prison-ship in New York harbor.
His widow, Tempy Hedge, was before her marriage Tempy Thacher, sister of Judge George Thacher of Biddeford, Maine, and Col. Thomas Thacher of Yarmouth. She had three children by John Hedge:
Mary, who married Silas Lee, afterwards member of Congress from Maine.
Lucy, who married Capt. Daniel Howes.
Daniel, who was grandfather to Milton and Daniel Hedge of East Dennis.
He was lost at sea in the schooner Hannah, with all his crew, in 1804, I think bound for North Carolina with a cargo of grind-stones. His wife was Mehitable Vincent, daughter of one David Vincent.
This second wife of Grandfather Jeremy brought him into relationship with the Thacher family of Yarmouth, and much correspondence with them.
His wife's oldest daughter, Mary, went to live with her uncle, Judge Thacher of Biddeford, Maine, and he had a young student of law in his office named Silas Lee. He married Mary and removed to Wiscasset, and went to Congress. I can remember Mrs. Lee. She came to our house to see his step-father's folks. I suppose Grandmother Howes, nee Tempy Thacher, died about 1806. She

SKETCH OF DESCENDANTS OF JEREMIAH HOWES.

was buried under a marble slab in our cemetery. The slab was placed there by her son-in-law, Silas Lee. Grandfather lived eighteen years or so after his last wife's death. He had many different girls to keep house for him. Mrs. Judah Sears, Prissa, kept his house for awhile. The house is the one now owned by Calvin C. Howes which was built by my grandfather somewhere about 1780.

The last twenty years or so of his life my father lived in the house with him, having enlarged it by building to it a large front room. Grandfather occupied the north room, where I remember him sitting in his armchair. I was seven years old when he died in 1824, but I remember him very distinctly.

He used to call me "good boy." He wore out of doors a soft felt hat with round crown. In the house in winter he wore a red woolen cap. Wigs had gone out of fashion. He used on evenings when I sat by the fire with him, and no one being with us, to tell me stories, mostly fables out of the spelling-book. A pleasant old age he seemed to enjoy. He had no care, apparently, about providing for his wants. His sons, Prince and Oren, looked after his comforts, and he at the age of 81 went to his grave like a "shock of corn fully ripe." His first wife was buried at the Howes burying ground, but for the reason of some want of room, he was buried beside his last wife at the Dennis cemetery. His oldest son Jabez had been dead twenty years or more.

So he left two sons, Prince and Oren, and one daughter Priscilla living. Priscilla married Enos Howes and moved to Lennox about 1801.

Now I will take up the other children of Grandfather Lot. It will be seen that he had only one daughter, whose name was Martha. She was named for her mother's sister, who married Isaac Vincent. There is where we first meet with the name of Martha; Martha Smith, daughter of Jonathan Smith, as I have remarked before.

Lot's daughter Martha married Anthony Howes in 1769. He was son of Daniel Howes of Suet Neck, and lived in the small, old fashioned, low shingle house near the Suet Neck bridge. I don't know the date of her death, but surmise it to be about 1788. Her husband was one of the deacons of the church, and had been master of whaling vessels. Martha had two daughters, Sabra and Maria. After her death, Deacon Anthony removed to Ashfield, where he had another wife. He must have married her before he left the Cape. Her name was Bethiah Howes.

His daughter Maria, cousin to my father, I saw in Hawley in 1859. I have heard my father tell of his going to Suet Neck with his grandmother, Thankful, to visit her daughter. They rode horse-back, as wheel carriages were extremely scarce at that time. Father went to open the bars. The open highway there only went as far as where Calvin Crowell lives. Below was through gates and bars. The county road was through Scargo.

The next child of Lot's was a son who bore the name of his father, and who died at somewhere about the age of forty. He was hardly "compos mentis," but was able to be of some service on the farm. He had no idea of numbers and could not count. I imagine Uncle Jonathan used to tell many anecdotes of his brother Lot. He was buried in the old Howes burying ground, and has a grave stone beside his parents in the southwest corner of the ground. His brother Jonathan is one that I remember distinctly.

He was born 1752 and died 1834. His wife was Susannah Matthews of Yarmouth. They were married in 1774 when the people were much excited over the question of the tax on tea. I have heard him tell how careful he had to be to get a pound or so of the "tabood" herb to serve his wedding guests. I forgot what seaport he was in, but think it was Plymouth, where someone directed him to a lone widow who sold it on the "sly" to those she could trust.

I remember Aunt Susie well. She died when I was ten years old. A pleasant old couple, Uncle Jonathan and Aunt Susie. They were fond of chaffing each other, getting the best of the joke on April Fool's day, and the like.

Uncle Jonathan was a large man with good lungs. In his old age, I remember him, sitting in his back door, hailing the passers by. His house was quite a resort for young people, whose company he enjoyed. In his youth he had made a number of voyages to the Labrador coast for whales. This gave him endless subjects for story telling, and many a story have I heard from his lips.

He lived with his father, or in the same house, after his marriage, and built on that "lean-to" where Mr. Freeman G. Hall now lives.

When he was about eighty years old, his son Alexander took him to his house to live with him. The old house was sold to Captain Freeman Hall, and passed out of the line of Prince Howes, its builder.

From Uncle Jonathan I heard much of the old times. He was very fond of hearing of foreign countries, and never having read much, was somewhat credulous. He was not a man upon whom public business could be thrust, but he was eager to know what was going on in town affairs. When my father had been to town meeting over to Barnstable, to court, or anywhere out of town, Uncle Jonathan was sure to come in and talk it over. "Now begin to talk" would be his first salutation as he entered the house. He was a sort of "ready money jack" in his characteristics, barring his ready money. Always at all public gatherings, where people congregated, this Uncle Jonathan was in his element. At launchings and raisings he was on hand. A whole-souled man was Uncle Jonathan. His children were:

Thankful, born Nov. 22, 1777.
Sarah, born Dec. 22, 1781.
Alexander, born July 12, 1784.
Eben, born March 19, 1788.
Lot, born July 2, 1793.
Willie, born about 1798.
Serviah.

This family will be treated of in a subsequent chapter of my genealogy.

I will now resume the line of Thomas, brother of Grandfather Lot.

Solomon was the only son of whom we have any distinct account, and he is not very discernable owing to his comparatively short career. He was born Aug. 18, 1744, married Abigail Howes Dec. 30, 1773. His death occurred May 24, 1785. Their children were:

Bethiah, born Aug. 13, 1775.
Hepsibah, born Feb. 13, 1778.
Hannah, born May 17, 1780.
Abigail, born March 4, 1782.
Ira, born Feb. 26, 1784.

Solomon's wife, Abigail, was the daughter of Samuel Howes, "Great Sam" he was called, and who lived in a house that stood back of Capt. Almond S. Howes's. Harvey Howes's house is a part of "Great Sam's" house which was moved off to where it now stands, and the eastern half built by Harvey Howes's grandfather, "Great Sam's" youngest son Obed.

I can remember Aunt Nab, as she used to be called, Charles and James Otis's grandmother. Her husband, Solomon, died in 1785 and 1789 she married Ezra Howes of Indian Fields and went to live with him. Ira, her only son by her first marriage was then five years old, Bethiah, the oldest child, 14, and Hepsibah, 11. Their mother used to come to see them every Saturday night, I have been told, and perhaps more often. It was a singular arrangement. There was considerable property in land, and the house where Charles and James now live. Who carried on the farm would be hard to say now. Things must have been left to run themselves.

The line of Jeremiah is now resumed. It will be seen that he had by his wife, Priscilla, seven children. I purpose to give a brief account of them without giving dates which are not important in this statement.

The eldest child of Squire Jeremy, as he was called by his contemporaries, was Sylvia, Aunt Sylvia I used to hear her called in my childhood. It is my impression that she was a very amiable person who was for several years an invalid, and confined to her room in Grandfather's house. She died in 1813, aged 45 years, with consumption.

The next of Grandfather's family was Jabez, born 1770. He went to sea, and appears to have been an active, competent man, but

somewhat irritable in his disposition. This, however, was explained to have been caused by his having been subject to attacks of chills and fever, or fever and ague, which he contracted by going on voyages to North Carolina. I think he never went on foreign voyages. He married Huldah Crowell, daughter of Aaron Crowell. They had children:
Annah.
Betsey.
Jabez.
Priscilla.
Annah married Reuben Clark, and died about 1821. Then this same Reuben Clark married Betsey, who died when I was a boy of 7 or 8 years, and left a boy named Reuben, who was a source of much care and grief to his grandmother, Huldah, and his Aunt, Prissa, and finally took himself off to sea and never turned up after.

Uncle Jabez built a house in new Boston, now moved off on South street and the residence of Edwin Whittemore. Uncle Jabez died while on a voyage in the schooner Victory, I think her name was, to the Straits of Belle-Isle, where they used to go for codfish. This was in 1804 or so.

His only son, Jabez, was a smart sailor, and was mate to the schooner Napoleon in 1824 with Joshua Hall, brother to Capt. Christopher Hall and Aunt Eliza, when the crew mutineered and murdered Capt. Hall and Jabez. This was just outside the harbor of Madeira, which port they had just left, being bound to St Ives for a load of salt. There was a passenger on board, and a cabin boy. The crew of three or four more proceeded to get drunk on some wine which was on board, when the passenger took charge and sailed the vessel back towards the port, so at daylight next morning she was under the guns of the fort, and signals which he made brought assistance from the town, and the mutineers were arrested and taken out of the vessel. They were, as near as I could ascertain, subsequently sent to some Portuguese penal station.

The vessel belonged to South Yarmouth owners who soon recovered her back, so I have been told. I can remember the Sunday morning when the messenger came from South Yarmouth with the bad news.

Aunt Huldah and Prissa and the New Boston people were on their way to meeting when they met the messenger bearing the fatal letter. I well remember the day, a bright morning in spring. The friends all came into our house and gathered in Grandfather's room to hear Uncle Oren read the letter. Uncle Jonathan, Aunt Susie, his wife; Aunt Dinah, Uncle Oren's wife, and my friends; in fact about all the New Boston population were in the room to listen to the melancholy news. It was a bad time. Aunt Huldah and Prissa were, of course, the chief mourners. Jabez was related to them all, and all wept for his sudden taking off. In a few

13 SKETCH OF DESCENDANTS OF JEREMIAH HOWES.

months his chest and personal effects came home, and gave occasion for another outburst of grief. Jabez, I can well recollect although he was most of the time at sea. He had made some voyages in square rigged vessels, and had served as mate of a ship, I believe. He once presented me with a two-bladed knife. I was hardly seven years old when he died. His mother and sister and cousin Prissa, who still lives, Feb. 1890, upon Grandfather's death shared equally with Father and Uncle Oren in the division of his property. It was valued, I believe, at $9000. His sons had paid his bills and charged the amount against the estate, and that was the residuary balance.

Prissa married in 1828, I think it was, Mr. Judah Sears, and soon after they sold their house to Mr. Judah Howes, and removed to Suet Neck, East Dennis, and six or seven years after removed to South Boston, where she still lives at the ripe age of 84 years. Her mother always lived with her until her death at the age of 83. Cousin Prissa lived with Grandfather in his old age, and was 19 years old at his death. She remembers Judge George Thacher coming to visit him, and Mrs. Lee, his wife's daughter, and many things concerning his personal traits. It seems he had a weakness in favor of New England rum which he had in common with his many contemporaries. It was necessary to limit his allowance of that liquid to one quart a week.

It was not considered strange for an old man to take his dram during the day in grandfather's time. I have remarked that the old gentleman had quite a good opinion of himself. One anecdote I have heard related will show this weakness of his.

Obed Howes, Harvey Howes's grandfather, kept a tavern, and Grandfather called in of an evening and stayed so late that my father came to look him up. The old man had taken enough to raise his spirits a little above the ordinary level. However, he went along with his son towards home, muttering as he went, so the story went, "I am a man of greater parts than Prince or Oren, so now." But it is evident by the letter addressed to him that he was regarded as an honest, correct man of business, and fully entitled to the estimate he put upon himself.

The next child of Grandfather's to Jabez was Rebecca, who married Mr. Noah Howes. She died young and no child of hers grew up. Noah Howes was father by another wife to Polly, Mr. William Crowell's mother. This Aunt Rebecca, my father's sister, I know scarcely anything of. Her husband Noah I well recollect. An excellent old man. When I was a boy he lived where Abijah Collins now lives.

Prince Howes, my father, was born, as you will see, July 25, 1774, the year before the Revolutionary war commenced. He could remember the Dark Day in 1781 when the fowls went to roost and people were wondering what was to happen. He was two years old when Col. Enoch Hallett sent his father's notice in a letter which I still have that a company of men was to go from Yarmouth to Dorchester and he could go as lieutenant if he wished. He did go. Of course, Prince could hardly have remembered much of what occurred during the war.

Who he went to school to I have no recollection of hearing him say.

He had no ear for music, neither could he dance, but he was willing to pay his share for the fiddler who furnished music for the village frolics as they were called. His education was of the most elementary kind, reading, writing and arithmetic. This was about the sum of schooling to be had in the school in his day. The Westminster Catechism was the only lesson which had to be committed to memory, except the multiplication table. However, such education had to suffice for lads of his time.

How early he went to sea no one knows. His voyages were to Cape Sable and Straits of Belle Isle, fishing. The vessels were from 50 to 100 tons burden. In 1798 he had a vessel built at Pembroke, Mass., of about 48 tons. Her name was the "Dolphin." I can remember the schooner. She was lost in 1839 on a voyage to Mobile. Father commanded this vessel for a number of years, fishing summers and making trips to Virginia winters.

Captain Elisha Howes, father of Mr. Osborn Howes of Boston, my honored friend and former employer when he was senior member of the well-known firm of Howes & Crowell, was his mate in some of those winter cruises. Many fireside stories I have heard Father tell of those voyages south. They used to take out "Yankee notions." New England rum was one of the commodities they sold. In exchange they took grain. It was a barter trade.

I fancy Father did not go to sea after he was 35 years old. They used to quit going to sea at a much earlier age than nowadays. When a man got to be 70 or even younger it was thought he ought to quit work and sit in the sun and enjoy himself. They have different views now.

When the manufacture of salt came to be a productive industry, middleaged men, like Father, built as many salt works as they had means to construct, and if they owned land enough, bought a pair of oxen and bade farewell to the sea. This salt making business commenced in good earnest about 1800. Salt brought a good price, sometimes as high as $1 per bushel. In my boyish days it reached its height. Salt works lined the shores of Cape Cod from Sandwich to Provincetown. When Father stopped on shore, he built three strings of salt works, about 1400 feet. I suppose he made 400 bushels of salt in a summer, $300 income from that source. This was ready money, and he owned a part of the "Dolphin." He was quite comfortably fixed. In 1801 he married Temperance Crowell of Quivet Neck. She was the daughter of Mr. William Crowell, a descendant of John Crow, one of the grantees of Yarmouth. She had two brothers and one sister. The brothers were William, father of Daniel, and Paul, who removed to West Sandwich and had a numerous family of whom only Hiram and Calvin survived. The sister of Mother was Molly, who married Elijah Howes of Indian Fields. They lived where Walter C. Hall's widow now lives. Aunt Molly was a woman of most excellent character and highly esteemed. She had a large family of children, three sons and five daughters; beautiful girls and handsome boys, all long since gone. Father regarded this family with great affection. Uncle Elijah got into a melancholy frame of mind and attempted suicide, and soon after died. I was perhaps a boy of ten at the time. Aunt Molly's youngest child was a boy of near my own age, Lewis. He was a boy of wonderful brightness and beauty. We were much together considering that we lived a mile apart. His mother died when he was perhaps 12 years old. He was obliged to go to sea to earn something to help support the family.

The oldest son died of consumption. His name was Amasa. The second son, named Elijah, one of the handsomest men I ever saw, was master of a brig called Pocket. He married in New York and getting dissipated finally jumped overboard from a schooner in which he was a passenger, somewhere in the Gulf of Mexico, and was drowned.

The five daughters, one after another, all died with consumption, and poor Lewis, who was a sailor on board a barque called the Fanny of Boston, fell from the fore topsail yard while reefing topsails and was killed. This was in 1834. Lewis was then 16 years old. So disappeared, from Indian Fields, Aunt Molly's family.

No descendants of his are alive today. In my boyhood there was constant intercourse between our families. Saturday afternoon Lewis was at our house, or I was with him. The names of Aunt Molly's daughters were:
Phoebe,
Tempe,
Hannah,
Typhosa,
Tryphina.

Phoebe married Dean Sears of East Dennis, and lived only about six months after her marriage. Hannah married Ansel Crowell of West Dennis. Tryphosa married Elnathan Crowell of Crow Town. None of them left any children. None of the girls. Amasa left one son, William, who died in Key West sometime in the fifteens. Elijah had a daughter whose

SKETCH OF DESCENDANTS OF JEREMIAH HOWES.

name was Mary Abbie. She was born in New York, and married there to a Mr. Damon, I think. She is dead. I was well acquainted with Elijah's wife. She was Miss Harriett Gorham, daughter of Mr. Allen Gorham, a native of Barnstable. Many pleasant hours I have passed at Mr Gorham's house in Grand street, New York, in 1812, 1843, 1844 and 1845, and perhaps later. He had a son, Leonard, who was master of ship Albany. A smart fellow. He died years ago. They made much of me always at Mr. Gorham's.

My father was married in 1801. In Feb. 1802, my brother Jeremiah was born. In Sept. 1809, sister Martha was born, and Sylvia in the same month 1813, and in 1807, Sept. 28, I was born.

Mother, from all that I have heard and from my own recollection of her, was a woman of much sweetness of temper and kindnses of heart. Children loved Miss Tempe, and she was a fond and indulgent mother. She had a vein of humor and was inclined to see the ludicrous side of things. When the great religious revival shook the Cape churches (1821) and Father experienced religion, as the term was, Mother could not see the same light that Father did, and for four or five years was under a mental cloud. She fell into a melancholy state, and was harassed with doubts and fears. Her condition was something like that of the poet Cowper. She feared she had committed the "unpardonable sin" and sinned away the day of grace. However, she emerged from that cloud two or three years before her death, which occurred in 1828. Her death was on Sunday, in June. I was not 11 years old until the next September. She had been violently seized with typhus fever and only lived a few days. It was a day of great grief in New Boston, the recollection of which is still vivid in my mind. Mother, I judge, was not graced with personal beauty. She was tall and had large teeth, and dark brown hair. When I was a boy people would say, "How much you look like your mother." As for education, she could read, and write a very poor hand. That was all that girls were expected to acquire in her day. The female mind was supposed to depend upon the masculine for what information it might need. I doubt if she ever read anything besides the Bible or some religious book.

During the revival of 1821 and 1822, Father was converted. He had been considered a man of great moral character, and when he came out as a converted Christian, it was thought to be a great acquisition to the church. His experience was something like St. Paul's, sudden and effective. He wrote out an account of his experience, and it is among my papers, in his own handwriting. I have been told by several of his contemporaries that when at a prayer meeting he arose and told the story of his conversion, it made a profound impression on his hearers. He soon after joined the church and had his three younger children baptized. I can remember my being led up to the deacon's seat to be sprinkled by Mr. Haven, the minister. I had no sort of an idea of what it was all about. Not long after, Father was chosen a deacon. His colleague was Deacon Nathan Hall, grandfather of the present Nathan Hall. I recollect that I was ridiculed by the boys upon being the son of a deacon, and felt some mortification in consequence.

Father was one of the pillars of the church. He was full of religious fervor, and kept his zeal alive by attending all the devotional exercises common among Christians at that time. He read the scriptures morning and evening, and prayed after the reading. He invoked the Divine Blessing at every meal. He kept the Sabbath day after the rigid order.

Father's brother Oren lived next house to ours, and they carried on much of their work together. They owned a pair of oxen and a horse in common. The most perfect harmony existed between them, only they differed in religious matters. Uncle Oren was inclined to liberal views, never experienced religion, but was a very popular man in town. However, I will speak more fully of him further on.

Father was high in the councils of the church and his advice much respected. He never had any quarrels or squabbles with his neighbors; was eminently a peace-maker. No one questioned his integrity when he spoke in town meetings or elsewhere in public. His words were listened to and bore the weight which his personal character gave them. He was plain in his dress, and plain in appearance, of a grave countenance, blue eyes and brown hair with heavy eyebrows. He was about 5 feet, 10 inches in height, 168 pounds in weight, industrious in his habits and frugal in his expenses. He managed to live in comfort and die free from debt. He was 58 years old at his death in 1832. His last sickness commenced sometime in summer and lasted until sometime in October. It was considered a great loss to the community when he died. I was then 15 years old, and received his last advice to be "steady and good."

My brother Jeremiah was away on a trip to the South, but my sisters and Uncle Oren were with him in his last moments and I think Uncle Jonathan and other friends, full of grief at his death. Uncle Oren survived him four years. He was two years younger, being born in 1776, July 7. He was a man of more popular manners than his brother Prince. He was a seafaring man in his younger days. In 1805 or 6 he had command of a two topsail schooner called the Enterprise. This vessel was built at Hockonom by the Brays, who had a ship-yard at that place and built schooners there for several years. This En-

SKETCH OF DESCENDANTS OF JEREMIAH HOWES.

terprise was a vessel of some 100 tons. Uncle Oren made several voyages to the south of Europe in her. One voyage in particular I have heard related by several men who formed part of the crew. The vessel returned in the spring from Lisbon, I think, where she had carried a load of codfish, and fitted out for a fishing trip to the Straits of Belle Isle. Her crew consisted of Oren Howes, master, and Ezra Hall, mate. The hands were William Hall, Henry Hall, Eben Hall, Shear Jashup Howes, John Howes, Moody Sears, Elnathan Lewis, cook, John Gorham. There was another man among the hands whose name I have forgotten. The voyage was a successful one, and ten of the crew were alive 55 years after the event. Now as I write I remember the name of the tenth man,—Abner Howes.

Somewhere about 1811, Uncle Oren had a full rigged brig called the Only Son built by the Brays, in which he only made one voyage when the war of 1812 compelled him to haul her up in Philadelphia, where she lay until the peace in 1815. This was bad business for owners of vessels. The brig, after the peace, made one voyage to St. Helena. Soon after that the vessel was sold and Uncle Oren bought a sloop for the coasting trade. After two or three years he quitted the sea and built a couple of strings of salt works, and built a house at New Boston, where his son Oren lived and died. That house was built in 1821. I can remember when the family removed their furniture from the house where Mrs. Lucy B. Howes now lives to the new house in New Boston. I rode down on a load of furniture.

Uncle Oren soon became the most popular man in town. He was elected one of the board of selectmen, and frequently went as representative to the General Court. He was the moderator of most of the town meetings, and employed on all occasions in public affairs. His agreeable manners, his sound judgment and high character commended him to the esteem and confidence of all parties. He was a natural leader of men, and was so acknowledged by his fellow citizens. He excited no envy in others. Everyone was pleased to see him trusted and honored.

In personal appearance, Uncle Oren had the light complexion which was characteristic of the whole of Grandfather's family. Light sandy hair and whiskers, blue eyes, good sound teeth, which my father had also. He was of medium height, perhaps 5 feet, 8 inches, active and alert in his movements, of nervous, sanguine temperament. He was quite high spirited, and at times would give away to bursts of indignation when aroused, but usually he was good natured, and always generous and kind hearted.

In the spring of 1836 he was in Boston attending upon his duties as a member of the legislature when he was taken suddenly ill,

SKETCH OF DESCENDANTS OF JEREMIAH HOWES.

and after a few days he expressed a desire to return home.

His son, Oren, Jr., was master of the schooner North at the time, and arrangements were made to carry him by the packet to Dennis. He was removed from his boarding house to the vessel, but did not live to reach home. I was in Boston when he was taken sick, and went twice to see him. The first time, I think, was on Fast day. I belonged to a vessel, a schooner called Cohassett, loading for New York, Calvin Howes, master.

Uncle Oren's wife was Dinah Hall, daughter of Major Isaiah Hall, who lived where Mrs. Hope Howes now lives, 1890. Her two brothers, Ezra and Eben, sailed with him on several voyages. She outlived her husband nearly twenty years, and to the last cherished his memory as few women do. Talking with me she always called him Uncle Oren. She seldom went out of New Boston after his death, but devoted her time to ministering to the wants of his son Oren, and her granddaughter who bore her name, Dinah.

She prided herself on her family, and her husband, and all her family connections. Many stories she used to tell of her wedding and of our family relations with the Thachers through Grandfather's marriage with the widow, Tempe Hedge, who was a sister of Judge George Thacher and Col. Thomas Thacher of Yarmouth, no small people according to Aunt Dinah's thinking. Altogether she carried her head very high, and considered her family the cream of the best society to be found in Nobscussett.

Aunt Dinah was much beloved by her relatives, and the young people of the neighborhood. She had a heart full of sympathy for all in affliction or trouble of any kind. The young people loved to sit by her fireside, and chat with her of old times. Her son Oren was her idol and to care for him was the chief end of her existence.

I spent almost as much time at her house, in my early childhood, as at home, owing to my mother's lengthy illness, and nothing could exceed the kindness with which I was treated. In fact our two families were so united as to seem like one. It is pleasant to recall the respect which young Oren, as he was called in those days, always showed towards his uncle Prince. We looked upon Uncle Oren with equal regard and affectionate veneration.

Besides his son Oren, there was one daughter, Thankful, who married Harvey Howes. Their union did not prove happy and they separated. She came home, and after a few years died of brain fever. She left three children, Dinah, Dorcas and Harvey, still living.

The next in Grandfather's family was Priscilla, born in 1778. I can remember seeing her when a boy of eight years or thereabouts. She came with her husband on a visit from their home in the

Berkshire Hills in the town of Lenox.

Aunt Prissa married Enos Howes, son of John Howes, who lived in an old house which stood on the spot where Southy Nye now lives.

John Howes was called "John Amey" from being the son of Amos Howes.

This Amos Howes, whose name is in the Howes Tree, had eight sons, many of whom moved away. John went with his family to the town of Lenox. His son, Enos, was, already I think, married to Aunt Prissa. None of the Amey tribe were seamen. Some were mechanics.

Uncle Enos was not much of a driver, I judge. They were not burdened with wealth when they left. Dennis, sometime before the War of 1812 ended. They had pitiful hard times in the country. Aunt Prissa was awfully homesick. I have seen her letters from there for the first few years. They were full of longings for the home of her childhood. Children were born to them in great plenty. Their names were:
Oren
William
Rebekah
Priscilla
Sylvia
Jeremiah
Enos.

Somewhere about 1829 the whole family of the John Amey tribe removed to Geneva County, N. Y., near the city of Rochester. There they suffered from chills and fever and poverty. However, after awhile, things improved, land increased in value, and they got out of log houses into frame buildings, and Aunt Prissa had things quite comfortable. Aunt Prissa died about 1852, perhaps. The husband a few years before. None of the children are now living. Some of Jeremiah's children are in Michigan, and there are quite a number of persons by the same name of Howes in that state who descended from John Howes of Nobscussett.

Father's youngest sister, born 1785, was Martha. She married Abijah Howes, father of the present Abijah. She had no children, and only lived a few years after her marriage. Her death was from typhus fever, so I have been told. I think she never removed from her father's house. The names of their uncles and aunts were familiar to my ears in my young days from hearing them spoken in our house so often.

Having followed the line of Lot Howes's descendants down through to his great grandchildren, we now resume the line through his brother Thomas, who left only one son, Solomon.

Solomon's oldest child was Bethiah, born Aug. 13, 1775. She I can well remember. She was never married, and lived with her brother Ira. She died about 1834. Aunt Thiah, as we used to call her, was a frequent caller at my father's house, and always welcome. She used to smoke, as women often did in her day, but she did not seem to care so much for smoking as she did for the satisfaction she seemed to take in lighting her pipe. Living in her brother's family, where the children were numerous and not always too indulgent to her whims, though never unkind, she was glad to enjoy a quiet chat at our fireside. Sunday evenings were sure to find her there, talking over the sermon; how well Mr. Stearns had preached and other topics suited to Sunday evening's gossip. She was inclined to be somewhat superstitious, I remember; had faith in witchcraft, omens and other supernatural phenomena. I have heard her tell how Horton, long time physician in North and East Dennis, and married Rev. Mr. Nathan Stone's daughter, had declared he saw one night an apparition of some kind on the gloomy road near Scargo hill. Many stories of that sort she would tell us, that is my sisters Martha and Sylvia and myself, when Father was away. Oftentimes when the ground was slippery from ice I have been and escorted her home. Good, simple old soul was Aunt Thiah.

Next in Solomon's family came Hepsey. She married Micah Howes, father to Edmund and Eben Howes. They lived up on the road back near Mr. Jonathan's on the field in the rear of where Abijah Collins now lives. Their house was removed down on the road in 1848, and is the residence of Mr. Albert L. Howes. Their son Joseph then owned it, and Aunt Hepsey died there. They had a large family of sons, now all dead but Eben. A worthy woman was Aunt Hepsey; kind and loving hearted through all her trials and bereavements.

Following Hepsey was Abigail. "Nabby" she was called. She married Mr. David Howes, who went by the name of David Neck from his living in Suet Neck. He built the house where his nephew, David Porter, now lives. His wife Nabby unfortunately became insane. This was before my remembrance. It commenced about the time of the great religious revival of 1821, and was caused by the excitement of that time, so I have heard. I remember her coming to New Boston occasionally when I was young. She lived until 1848, perhaps, cared for by David Porter and his wife. She was a large, formidable looking woman, and Mrs. David Porter had years of anxious service in ministering to her wants.

The youngest of the family we are writing about was the only son, Ira. He was married to Charlotte, daughter of Elisha Howes; "Elisha East" he was styled. He lived where Mr. Thomas Howes now lives in an old, large, two story house which faced to the northwest. It had a lean-to. I have no idea who built it.

When I was a boy, my father and Uncle Oren used to speak of Ira as "Cousin Ira." He was in fact their second cousin. A very

SKETCH OF DESCENDANTS OF JEREMIAH HOWES.

pleasant, compassionate man he was. He married young, and had a large family of children. Their names were as follows:
Emeline,
Nancy,
Charles,
Frederic,
Elisha,
James Otis,
Lucilla.

They never lived to grow up. At the present writing only two survive, Charles aged 77 and James aged 68. Frederic and Elisha were lost at sea in the great gale of 1841, both being in the same vessel. Uncle Ira, as he was called by me, was a person for whom I entertained much esteem and affection. His wife, Aunt Charlotte, was a woman of great sweetness of character. Their house was to me a place where I loved to go, and when away on my early voyages used to dream of, when afflicted with homesickness. They had hard work when the children were young to provide for all their wants, but their trials never made them sour or unpleasant. It was a happy and cheerful home however poverty might distress them. Uncle Ira was always a home-abiding individual. He was seasick the moment he entered a boat or got on board a vessel, and even the motion of the waves as he stood on shore and gazed seaward would excite seasickness. He was also constitutionally cautious, and averse to change. The result was that he never left Cape Cod. The extent of his travels east was as far as Orleans, and west to Sandwich. Nevertheless, he was a man well informed, well read in the topics of the day and conversant with the Scriptures and the doctrines of the different religious sects. Himself, he was contented with the faith as preached by the Unitarians. He was a member of the Unitarian church as was also his wife. His house, in my boyhood, had the old fashioned chimney and fireplace with wide frames where four or five children could sit on each side of the fire. The chimney was a straight shaft. You could see the stars in the evening by looking upwards. There was a chain hanging down from a cross bar upon which a ham could be suspended to be smoked. I can remember Father taking hams there in the fall to be smoked in his cousin Ira's chimney.

One winter's day coming home from school, one of Uncle Ira's boys, Frederic, said to me, "Father and Mother are off visiting at Uncle Perez's, and we have borrowed Aunt Sarah John's spoon mould and are going to mould pewter spoons, and after have some candied corns. You must come up and spend the evening with us." This promised to be a rare treat. The old folks gone and the children, that is the brothers Charles, Frederic, Elisha and James with their little sister Lucilla, then perhaps three years old, were to have full swing. Running spoons was quite good fun and candied corns, that is roasted corns boiled in molasses in an old fashioned iron spider, were not to be desposed. I obtained leave at home, and was their only guest. All went on finely. The spoons were run, and good, bright new specimens turned out of Aunt Sarah John's mould. Then the corns were roasted over the coals and the molasses poured over them and boiled to the right consistency and pronounced to be properly cooked. The spider was placed in a small stand and all hands were helping themselves when little Lucilla, who was an interested party in the proceedings, somehow hit the spider handle and down it went to the hearth. We were badly frightened at this catastrophe, but picked up and examined the spider. We discovered a scratch or crack near the handle, but concluded it might be a streak of molasses. This accident threw a cloud over our jollity, and 1 soon left. The next morning, as I was informed, Aunt Charlotte put a piece of dough in the spider to bake, knowing nothing of the previous evening's transactions. When she lifted the spider out came the handle much to her surprise. No one volunteered an explanation of this occurrance and the spider for many years was used for baking bread, minus its handle.

Many happy hours of my childhood were spent in that old house on the hill. The well was a fine spring at the foot of the hill. Of course, it all had to be lugged up to the house, but no one thought of that. This bringing up of the water was mainly done by the mother, Aunt Charlotte, herself. One can imagine the life of toil she had, but she always seemed cheerful and happy.

The front room with its large fireplace was the living room, cooking room and sleeping apartment for the parents, and the trundle bed which was rolled under the large bed in daytime was the crib for the youngest children to sleep in at night. There slept James and his sister Lucilla in their childhood.

Uncle Ira had quite a knack at rhyming, and was often persuaded by his children to indulge them by making rhymes for their amusement. Some were very ridiculous and made much sport for us children. "Hannah Skipper," so called, had said she was fond of waterpudding. Thereupon Ira, smoking his pipe, responded to a call for a rhyme.

"Water-pudding I do hate
Always when put upon a plate."

He sometimes tried his muse on acrostics. One I remember, upon Sarah Adeline Howes. She was the eldest daughter of his next door neighbor and cousin Alexander, and sister to Mrs Persis Howes, a girl of fine mind and refined tastes, afterwards the wife of Captain N. Crowell.

Uncle Ira was considered, I believe, a good singer and sang in the church choir. He would some-

SKETCH OF DESCENDANTS OF JEREMIAH HOWES.

times sing for our amusement of an evening some old ballads now pretty much forgotten. "The Fair Maid of P—— Hill" and an old song concerning the death of Generals Wolf and Montcalm.

"King George and Louis could never agree
Where their dividing lines should be,
Till they had fought by land and sea,
They both seemed in a flame."

That was the way it commenced. Uncle Ira died in Sept. 1848, at the age of 64. His amiable wife survived him several years. Blessings on their memories! Their last years were made comfortable and happy by the loving kindness and filial offices of their two sons, Charles and James, and daughter Lucilla, and Charles's wife, Priscilla.

The children of Jonathan, youngest son of Lot, will now be mentioned. They were as follows:
Sarah, born 1775.
Thankful, born 1777.
Seviah, born 1781.
Alexander, born 1784.
Eben, born 1788.
Lot, born 1793.
Willis, born 1797-8.

Sarah, the oldest, was never married. She lived to be towards 40 years old. She made some attempts at writing poetry, as I have some lines on the death of a young man supposed to be a lover, who died in Surinam. His name was Enoch Hall and belonged, I judge, in Holland, Conn.

Seviah married Josiah Howes. I remember her well, being a cousin to my father. My sisters used to be invited to all the weddings that occurred in Uncle Siah's family. She was the mother of Jonathan, and had daughters:
Eliza, married David Sturgis of Barnstable.
Elmira, married Isaac White.
Susan, married Barnabas Crocker.
Thankful, old maid.

Seviah's sister Thankful married Judah Howes, father of the present Judah. She had two sons, Judah and Eben, who died young, and Judah, who died in 1842. I have no remembrance of Thankful. She died when the children were young. Besides her two sons, she left a daughter Susannah, who married Nathan Foster Sears of East Dennis and had Judah Howes, Nathan Howes and Susie, wife of Jesse Hall.

Alexander, eldest son of Jonathan, was an active stirring man. He followed the sea, fishing when young and later in coasting vessels. He was of an excitable temperament and put much force into his pursuits. He was somewhat lacking in caution and consequently often met with accidents. His earnestness and enthusiasm sometimes led him to miscalculate the obstacles to be overcome. His mind was active and inquiring and his intelligence beyond the average of his neighbors. He held, after retiring from the sea, the office of selectman for two years, and was twice elected to the General Court.

Alexander married Persis, daughter of Paul Howes of Indian Fields. His home was the one lately occupied by John McDonell.

Paul Howes had six daughters. They lived to be, with one exception, mothers of worthy families. Their names were:

Anna, who married Nathan Myrick.

Persis, who married Alexander Howes.

Susannah, who married Asa Shiverick.

Deborah, who married Elisha Howes.

Sally, who married Freeman Howes.

Myra, who married Willis Howes.

Persis, wife of Alexander

Persis, wife of Alexander, was a woman of estimable character. She was the mother of children that grew up as follows:

Cyrus, who married Hannah Crowell.

Sarah Adeline, who married Nathan Crowell.

Olive, who died at the age of 16.

Persis, who married Laban Howes.

Susannah Matthews, who married Joseph O. Baker.

Deborah, who married William Crowell.

Alexander, who married Emily Crosby.

Persis is the only one of the family now living. Our family was on terms of great intimacy with Captain Alexander's. He and my father were cousins and belonged to the same church. My mother was cousin to Mrs. Persis's mother, who was Sarah Crowell.

Captain Alexander had removed to Maine, where he lived for years in the town of Hallowell, I think. I was some four years old when they moved back, and came to live where Freeman G. Hall now lives. Captain Alexander was then running a coaster to and from Maine. He soon built the house he afterwards lived in, where John G. Rayner now lives, and also built some two thousand feet of salt works. He continued his coasting trips until 1840 when he stopped on shore. I used to be much at his house enjoying the company of his daughters. One summer I went as mate with the captain in the schooner Atlas. He allowed me to go two trips as master. We ran between Boston and New York.

His son, Cyrus, although ten years my senior, was always on intimate terms with me. We met afterwards in foreign ports and always felt great regard and confidence in each other. His attachment has been continued to his son, Barnabas B. Howes, and I trust will be handed down to our posterity.

Alexander was a man of integrity and probity. He was fond of a joke upon occasion, and would preserve a grave countenance when joking. I remember once, some years before he quitted the sea, of his having one of his wife's nephews with him as cook for the coasting season. The lad's

SKETCH OF DESCENDANTS OF JEREMIAH HOWES. 26

name was Asa. He had been engaged with the understanding that his wages should be such as other boys received on similar vessels. Along in the winter Asa had discovered that his uncle had paid him a half a dollar or so less than some other boys had received, so one cold winter's evening he, in company with my cousin Lewis, who lived a near neighbor in Indian Fields, came to New Boston to see if Uncle Alex would not pay him what he thought was his due. Lewis stopped at our house, and Asa went on to confront the captain. Pretty soon he called on us to meet Lewis.

"Well, what luck did you have?" I asked him. "Not very good," said he. "The old man sat dozing in his chair with his newspaper in his hand, and just looked up and said, 'Oh Asa, it is too windy to carry out money tonight'."

That was all the comfort Asa got that night. Afterwards his uncle made inquiry and paid his mother, who was a widow, what was right. I always entertained great affection for Uncle Alex. He died quite suddenly in December, 1849. His wife died the year before, when a great many deaths occurred from dysentery. This is a very imperfect sketch of Uncle Alex and his wife.

His brother Eben, who comes next in Uncle Jonathan's children, was drowned in Hampton Roads, Virginia, and buried at Sewell's Point. I know nothing more of him. His grave stone is in the Howes burial ground.

Lot, the next brother, married when quite young, Deborah Baker, daughter of Archibald Baker of Yarmouth or Dennisport. He worked and served at the ship carpenter's trade. They removed before my remembrance to Ponniquassett, the Indian name for Dartmouth, near New Bedford. They had a large family: eight sons and two daughters. I think only three of their children are now living. They reside in Fairhaven and Vineyard Haven and New Bedford.

Lot's sons took early to whaling voyages. I remember of meeting two of them in Honolulu in 1850. Those were Alexander Matthews and John Fletcher. The eldest, Gorham Baker, and his next brother were soon to become masters of ships. Gorham is living at Fairhaven, and in comfortable circumstances, but has no children. Willis lives in Vineyard Haven, where he is a man of some note.

Lot, the father of these sons, was a man of intelligence, but never filled any public station. He wrought at his trade of ship carpenter, and remained through life a poor man. His sons, in his old age, provided for him, or his wants, and after his death looked well after their mother's comforts. She lived to a good old age and died a few years ago. I remember this couple well. They used to visit their relatives in Dennis occasionally, and I called once, on my way to New York, at their house in New Bedford. That was in 1846.

The youngest son of Uncle Jonathan was Willis. He was born, I judge, in 1798 and lived until 1871. He married Almira Howes, daughter of Mr. Paul Howes of Indian Fields. His house was the one lately occupied by John McDonell. Willis lived, after his marriage, for a short time in the house owned by Mrs. Lucy B. Howes. Then it was the residence of one Mr. Eben Hall. My father and his brother Oren once owned it and lived there together. Subsequently, after Alexander built his house, Willis removed to his father's and lived where Freeman G. Hall now lives. Many different families have made that old lean-to their abode since I can remember:

Alexander Howes,
Willis,
Daniel Hedge,
Freeman Hall,
Franklin Howes,
John Howes,
Oren Howes,
Perez Howes, and I daresay others whom I forget. Loren Howes also lived there and Willard Gorham. It seems to have been a favorite place for young married couples to commence housekeeping. I can remember the wedding of Willis and Myra. Aunt Susie, his mother, gave me a handful of raisins. I remember the carriages drive up to Uncle Jonathan's from Indian Fields for the second day's wedding, as it was once called.

Willis went to sea, first coasting and later on foreign voyages. I recollect his coming home once late in the fall or early winter from Malaga. He brought a keg of Malaga grapes, the first I ever tasted. My cousin, Elijah Howes, had been his mate. The vessel was a topsail schooner, afterwards built into a brig called the Alexander. I heard much of this voyage. I listened to Captain Willis as he talked with his father and heard what Cousin Elijah had to relate to my father. It was quite an event in New Boston when one returned from a foreign voyage and brought the fruits of other countries home. Then Willis brought home a young Spanish boy who was a wonder to us. He did not prove to be much of a protege, for Willis soon got rid of him. Willis followed the sea for several years, removing his residence to South Boston, and somewhere about 1837 went into business with Captain Osborn Howes on Commercial street, under the firm name of Howes & Co. The firm dissolved in 1840 and after a few years Willis was elected to the office of port warden, which he held until his death in 1871.

His widow survived him some years. For many years they lived in Old Harbor street, South Boston, and their house was the seat of a generous and kindly hospitality. They had no children. Captain Willis was, like his father, fond of children, and his house was seldom without a guest under its roof. He was gifted with a kind of humor, was good-natured and had lots of friends. He had a handsome face and form, and bright, pleasant dark eyes. Something of an impediment in his speech at times, rather served to give point to his jokes. He was for many years a notable figure in South Boston circles.

Having now sketched the generations of my great, great grandfather Prince's descendants and given the names of some of the fourth, I will now give a brief description of my father's family. None of them were alive but myself and brother Jeremiah when I married in the fall of 1842 Deborah Bassett. He lived eleven years after that event and possibly may be remembered by my oldest son.

Jeremiah was nearly sixteen years my senior. I saw not much of him in my childhood as he was away to sea a great part of the time. He was a man of a practical turn of mind, very industrious in his vocation. Idleness he regarded almost as a crime. At sea he kept the crew always busy at something. He commenced his sea life with his uncle Oren in a sloop running between New York and Boston. Longer voyages he went on afterwards; one to Copenhagen in the brig Cypher. He did not get command until quite old, 26 or 27, I should say. Then he had command of a schooner of 80 or 90 tons burden, going to West India in winter and coasting in summer. His last command was a full rigged brig called the Democrat. In that vessel he made several voyages to Europe and South America and West Indies. His last voyage was in 1847, when he took a cargo of grain to Belfast, Ireland, in the time of the great famine. This brig came on shore near where the Nobscussett House is, in a great gale in December, 1839. She was got off, and bought by Jeremiah's brother-in-law, Captain Christopher Hall, and he was put in charge.

Jeremiah married in 1821 Eliza Hall of East Dennis, a most worthy person, who survived him eleven years. Jeremiah was a man of integrity and uprightness. He stood four square to all the winds that blew. As he grew old his character grew softened and more indulgent, and children were fond of his company. He liked to tell stories to the boys and what they would encounter if they went to sea in square rigged vessels. He was much beloved and respected by his neighbors.

My sister Martha was a woman of great gentleness and amiability of character. She was the favorite of Father's. Her turn of mind was devotional and religious. She experienced religion and joined the church sometime before Father did. She had the care of the household as soon as she was able to assume the duties, and was tireless in her labors to perform every requirement. A more blameless person it would be hard

SKETCH OF DESCENDANTS OF JEREMIAH HOWES.

to imagine, as I remember her. Her love for me was almost maternal. After Father's death we three children, Martha, Sylvia and myself, kept house together in the north part of Father's house. Jeremiah lived in the other part. A year and a half after Father's death, Martha married Zenas Howes. They went to live in a new house he had built, where Thomas S. Howes now lives. That broke up our housekeeping. I went to sea, but boarded with Jeremiah, and Sylvia boarded with him also. Martha had one daughter, born 1836 or 5, Sylvia Maria. Martha died in 1838.

Sylvia, my sister, four years my senior, was a girl of great brightness and attractiveness. She was a ready scholar and full of humor. Withal, she was a girl of high spirit. She had red hair and blue eyes, while Martha's hair was dark, almost black. Sylvia married in 1838 William Howes of Indian Fields, to whom she had been engaged before Father's death. A fine, handsome, sailor-looking fellow. He was master of brig Omar and died six months after their marriage, in Havannah. This was a death blow to poor Sylvia. She never recovered from that stroke, so sudden and severe, although she lived until 1840.

No. 54.

LIBRARY of
Cape Cod
HISTORY & GENEALOGY

The LUMBERT or LOMBARD FAMILY

By Amos Otis

YARMOUTHPORT, MASS.:
C. W. SWIFT, Publisher and Printer,
The "Register" Press,
1914.

The LUMBERT or LOMBARD FAMILY

By Amos Otis

Copyright, 1914, by C. W. Swift.

This name was generally written by the first settlers Lumbert, sometimes Lumber, which is in accordance with the common pronunciation. Mr. Lothrop wrote the name Lumber, Lumbert, Lumbart and Lumbard; Mr. Russell Lumbert and Lumbart. On the colony and town records, all the above modes are used, but in no instance do I recollect of seeing the name written Lombard, according to the usage of the Truro branch of the family.

Thomas Lumbert, the ancestor, came over early, probably in the fleet with Gov. Winthrop, and was admitted a freeman of the Massachusetts colony, May 18, 1631. At that time he must have been nearly fifty years of age, for his son Bernard was then twenty-three, and it is not certain that he was the first born of the family.

On the arrival of Mr. Lothrop, Bernard removed to Scituate: but the father appears to have removed, direct from Massachusetts to Barnstable. The records of Mr. Collicut and his associates are lost; but there are, circumstances that show that Thomas Lumbert was in Barnstable in the spring of 1639. When Mr. Lothrop arrived in Oct. 1639, Mr. Lumbert had one of the largest and best houses in the plantation, fitted up and designed for an ordinary, or a public house, and which he was licensed by the Court to keep on the third of December following. He was a church member, probably before he came over, certainly in 1631, and was an associate of Mr. Hull, who came to Barnstable in May, 1639. When Mr. Lothrop came, Oct. 11, 1639, the two churches united, and though there is no record of the union at that time, subsequent records show that Mr. Hull, Mr. Dimmock, Mr. Bursley, William Casely, Thomas Lumbert and others of the first comers, were recognized as members of Mr. Lothrop's church, and consequently that there had been such a union.

His house lot was the second west of Rendezvous Lane, contained twelve acres, and was bounded north by the harbor, east by Thomas Lothrop's lot, south by the highway, and west by the house-lot of Mr. Robert Linnell.

April 5, 1656, he sold this lot with the dwelling-house thereon, to Thomas Lewis, for £20 sterling, and removed to his great lot of forty-five acres, near the northeast corner of the town. It was bounded northerly by the highway, easterly by the Hallet farm, south by the wood lots, and west by Bernard Lumbert's great lot. It included the whole of the Dead swamp, one of the largest in town, which was deducted from the lots as described in the records. It would appear by the record of the lot and the deed of Thomas Lumbert of the same dated April 5, 1656, that his lot was of even width from the harbor to the old highway; but it is evident, from subsequent records, that the swamp on the southeast was not included. This was the uniform custom, whether the swamps were valuable for timber or considered worthless for cultivation.

The Lumbert or Lombard Family

In addition to his homestead, which he sold to Thomas Lewis as above stated, for £20 sterling, he owned six acres of planting land in the common field adjoining the Little pond, and a great lot of forty-five acres, bounded northerly by the highway, easterly by the Hallet farm, southerly by the wood lots, and westerly by Bernard Lumbert's great lot. His great lot included the whole of the Dead swamp, which was not included in the measurement.

About the year 1656 he removed to his great lot, and built a house thereon. He had a good estate, and was comparatively a wealthy man. He was not distinguished, and his name rarely occurs on the records.

1 THOMAS Lumbert, d. 1664, m. 1st ———, m. 2d Joyce ——.
Children.
2 Bernard, b. in Eng. 1608.
3 Joshua, b. in Eng.
4 Caleb.
5 Margaret.

6 Joseph, 1638.
7 Jedediah, 20 Sept. 1640.
8 Benjamin, 26 Aug. 1642, d. 2 Aug. 1725.
Margaret, m. Edward Coleman, 27 Oct. 1648.

2 BRENARD Lumbert, m.
Children.
9 Abia.
10 Jemima.
11 Thomas.
12 Mary, bap. 8 Oct. 1637.
13 Martha, 2 Nov. (19 Sept.) 1640.
14 Jabez, 4 July 1642.
Jemima m. Jo. Benjamin, 10 June 1661.
Mary m. Geo. Lewis, Jr., 1 Dec. 1654.
Martha, m. John Manton, 1 July, 1667.

3 JOSHUA Lumbert, m. Abigail Linnel, 27 May, 1651.
Children.
15 Abigail, 6 April, 1652.
16 Mercy, 15 June, 1655.
17 Jonathan, 28 April, 1657.
18 Joshua, 16 Jany, 1660, d. Oct. 1724.
19 Susannah.
20 Hannah(?) 1663, d. 12 July, 1754.
Susanna m. John Lovell, June, 1688.
Hannah m. 1 John Whetsone, 2d Ben Lumbert.

The Lumbert or Lombard Family

4 CALEB Lumbert, m.
Children.
21 Caleb?

7 JEDEDIAH Lumbert, m. 1 Hannah Wing, 20 May, 1668.
Children.
22 Jedediah, 25 Dec. 1669, d. Sept. 10, 1739.
23 Thomas, 22 June, 1671, d. Nov. 13, 1736.
24 Hannah, Aug. 1673.
25 Experience, April, 1675.

8 BENJAMIN Lumbert, m. 1 Jane Warren, 19 Sept. 1672, d. 27 Feb. 1682; m. 2 Sarah Walker, 19 Nov. 1685, d. 6 Nov. 1693; m. 3 Wid. Hannah Whetstone, 24 May, 1694.
Children.
26 Mercy, 2 Nov. 1673.
27 Benjamin, 22 Sept. 1675, d. 13 Jan. 1753.
28 Hope, 26 Mar. 1679.
29 Sarah, 29 Oct. 1686.
30 Bathshua, 4 May, 1687.
31 Mary, 17 June, 1688, d. May 1, 1772.
32 Samuel, 15 Sept. 1691, d. 12 Nov. 1759.
33 Temperance, 25 May, 1695, d. 2 Sept. 1759.
34 Martha, 28 Dec. 1700.
Mercy m. Ebnr. Burges, 20 Ma. 1701.
Hope m. Ben. Goodspeed, 1707.
Sarah m. Job Hinckley, 15 Nov. 1711.
Mary, m. Ben. O'Killey, 2 Aug. 1709.

11 THOMAS Lumbert, m. Elizabeth Derby, 25 Dec. 1665.
Children.
35 Sarah, Dec. 1666, May 5, 1753.
36 Thomas, Mar. 1667, May 30, 1761.
37 Elizabeth, Sept. 1668.
38 Mary, April, 1669.
39 Hannah, Dec. 1671.
40 Jabez, Feb. 1673, d. Feb. 1673.
41 Rebecca, May, 1676.
42 Jabez, June, 1678.
43 Bethia, July, 1680.
44 Bathshua, Aug. 1682.
45 Patience, Sept. 1684.
46 Martha, bap. 1686.
Sarah m. John Phinney, 30 May, 1689.
Mary m. Daniel Parker, 11 Dec. 1689.
Rebecca m. Rev. Parker, 8 Dec. 1698.
Bethia m. Jos. Robinson, 7 Dec. 1704.
Patience m. Judah Rogers, 6 April, 1704.

14 JABEZ Lumbert, aged 18 yrs., 5 mo., m. Sarah Derby, 1 Dec. 1660.
Children.
47 A son, 18 Feb. 1661, d. same day.
48 Elizabeth, June, 1663.
49 Mary, April, 1666.
50 Bernard, April, 1668.
51 John, April, 1670.
52 Matthew, 21 Aug. 1672.
53 Mehetabel, Sept. 1674.
54 Abigail, April, 1677.
55 Nathaniel, 1 Aug. 1679, 18

The Lumbert or Lombard Family

June, 1749.
56 Hepthsibah, Dec. 1681.
Elizabeth m. Ben Gage, 10 Mar. 1684.
Mary m. James Lovell, May, 1686.
Mehetabel m. Wm. Lovell, 24 Sept. 1693.

17 JONATHAN Lumbert, m. Elizabeth Eddy, 11 Dec. 1683.
Children, Barnstable.
57 Jonathan, 20 Nov. 1684.
58 Alice, 19 Oct. 1686.
59 Ebenr., 4 Feb. 1688.
At Tisbury.
60 Abigail, 12 July, 1691.
61 Samuel?

18 JOSHUA Lumbert, m. Hopestill Bullock 6 Nov. 1682, d. April, 1749, aged over 90.
Children.
62 Mercy, 16 Mar. 1684.
63 Hopestill, 15 Nov. 1686.
64 Joshua, 5 Aug. 1688, d. Oct. 1724.
65 Samuel, 1 June, 1690, d. 1771.
66 Abigail, 20 Jan. 1692.
67 Mary, 22 Nov. 1697.
68 Elizabeth, 22 April, 1700.
69 Jonathan, 16 April, 1703, d. June, 1788.
Mercy m. Shobaei Lewis, Dec. 8, 1703.
Hopestill m. 1 Shobael Davis, Sept. 15, 1720; 2 Hamblin.
Mary m. John Robinson, April 11, 1717.
Elizabeth m. John Ewer, July 5, 1716.

4 or 21 CALEB Lumbert, m. Elizabeth.
Children, born in Chatham.
70 Mary, 4 June, 1705.
71 Deliverance, 4 April, 1710.
72 Elizabeth, 1 April, 1714.
73 Caleb, 20 Sept. 1717.
74 Edward, 11 March, 1721-2.
Caleb Lumbert of Truro m. Thankful Rich, Jr., 10 Nov. 1760.

22 JEDEDIAH Lumbert, m. Hannah Lewis, 8 Nov. 1699, d. April 25, 1743.
Children, Barnstable.
Removed to Truro.
75 Solomon, 5 April, 1702.
76 Jonas, 11 Oct. 1703.
77 Ebenezer, 12 March. 1705.
78 Sarah, 4 Aug. 1709.
79 Lewis, 20 Feb. 1711.
80 Ephraim, 18 Aug. 1716.
81 Hannah, 4 Oct. 1718.
Sarah m. Richard Collins, 25 Jan. 1732.
Hannah m. Nathan Paine, Jr., 6 March, 1740.

23 Captain THOMAS Lumbert m. Mary Newcomb, 4 Oct. 1694.
Children, Barnstable.
82 John, 5 Jan. 1695.
83 Jedediah, 16 Feb. 1696.
84 Thomas, 3 Aug. 1698, d. April
85 William, 25 Jan. 1700.
86 Simon, 28 Nov. 1701, d. young.
87 Hannah, 16 Jan. 1703.
88 Keziah, 30 June, 1705.
Hannah m. Conant.
Keziah m. Job Conant, Oct. 18, 1725.

The Lumbert or Lombard Family

27 BEN. Lumbert, m. 1st Hannah Treddeway, 23 May, 1711; 2d Sarah Crocker, 27 May, 1720.
Children, Barnstable.
89 Jonathan, 29 March, 1712.
90 Hannah, 8 Sept. 1714.
Hannah m. Ben. Thacher, Jan. 30, 1735.

32 Captain SAMUEL Lumbert, m. 1st Anna Baker, 17 Oct. 1717, d. May, 1747; 2d Thankful Thacher, 1748.
Children, born in Barnstable.
91 Sarah, 3 Sept. 1718.
92 John, 9 Jan. 1720.
93 Joseph, 8 Jan. 1722.
94 Anna, 26 March, 1724.
95 Benjamin, 4 Dec. 1726.
96 Elizabeth, 25 Feb. 1730.
97 Mercy, 30 Jan. 1733.
Sarah m. John Manning of Windham, June 10, 1744.
Anna m. Sam. Crocker, May 29, 1760; 2d Davis.
Elizabeth m. Davis, April 8, 1757.

36 THOMAS Lumbert, m. 1st Hannah (Parker?); 2d Wid. Patience Coleman, Sept. 10, 1715. She died March 30, 1747.
Children b. Barnstable.
98 Mehetabel, 27 Sept. 1690.
99 Elizabeth, 2 Sept. 1692.
100 John, 19 July, 1694.
101 Thankful, 19 April, 1696.
102 Jabez, 19 Feb. 1698.
103 Gershom, 4 July, 1700, d. 1727.
104 Elihu, 20 May, 1702.

105 Zaccheus, 9 April, 1704.
106 Mercy, 30 July, 1706.
107 Hezekiah, 18 July, 1708.
108 Abigail, 3 April, 1710.
109 Patience, 9 April, 1712.
Elizabeth m. Captain Simon Davis, 12 May, 1725.

50 BERNARD Lumbert, m. Susanna , d. April 4, 1734; 2d Sarah White, 1742, d. Nov. 22,1761.
Children b. in Barnstable.
110 Joanna, Dec. 1692.
111 Mehitabel, 18 Ma. 1694.
112 Matthew, 15 Jan. 1698.
113 Mariah, Oct. 1700.
114 Bethia, Sept. 1702.
115 John, April, 1704.
116 Solomon, 1 March, 1706.
117 Desire, bap. Jan. 1717.
Maria m. Thomas Phinney, Nov. 1731.
Bethia m. 1 James Hadaway, Oct. 8, 1730; 2 James Lewis, 3d, April 24, 1742.

55 Captain NATHANIEL Lumbert, m. Jemimah , d. April 9, 1765, age 78.
Children, b. in B.
Sarah, b. 2 Aug. 1710.
Mary, bap. 1 March, 1713.
Jemimah, 2 Sept. 1716.
Lydia, 7 Sept. 1718.
Lemuel, 31 July, 1720.
Elizabeth, 11 March, 1722, d. young.
Nathaniel, 13 Dec. 1723, d. young.
Nathaniel, 13 June, 1725.
Elizabeth, 23 June, 1728.

The Lumbert or Lombard Family

Sarah m. Solomon Lumbert, 7 July, 1737.
Mary m. Zaccheus Lumbert, 9 July, 1736.
Jemima m. Hezekiah Lumbert, 25 Nov. 1736.
Lydia m. John Bears, Jr., 12 Feb. 1746.
Elizabeth m. Robert Lewis, 7 Nov. 1757.

57 JONATHAN Lumbert, m. 1st Rachel , 1708; 2d Bathsheba , 1734.
 Children, b. in Tisbury.
 118 Benjamin, 22 July, 1709.
 119 Ann, 7 Feb. 1711.
 120 Mary, 15 May, 1715.
 121 Tabatha, 19 Oct. 1718.
 122 Timothy, 25 Nov. 1735.
 123 Moses, 13 Nov. 1737.
 124 Rachell, 20 March, 1741.
 125 Hannah, 8 March, 1744.

61 SAMUEL Lumbert (?) m. Mary . 1716.
 Children b. in Tisbury.
 126 Elizabeth, 10 Oct. 1727.
 127 Gideon, 21 March, 1729.
 128 Elisha, 24 Feb. 1732.
 129 Lemuel, 17 Aug. 1733.

59 EBENEZER Lumbert, m. Bethia Mayo, June 15, 1727.

64 JOSHUA Lumbert, 16 June, 1764, m. Sarah Parker, 14 Dec. 1715, d. Jan. 16, 1719; 2d Hannah , d. May 9, 1796.
 Children b. in B.
 130 Sarah, 28 Sept. 1716,

131 Parker, 24 Dec. 1718, d. 27 Dec. 1754.
132 Samuel, 25 April, 1721, 16 Aug. 1721.
 A daughter, 9 July, 1722, 6 Aug. 1722.
133 Joseph, 10 Jan. 1724.
 A daughter, 28 Jan. 1725, 2 Feb. 1725.
134 Hannah, 31 July, 1726.
135 Ebenezer, 1 April, 1728.
136 Lemuel, 15 Feb. 1731.
137 Hopestill, 17 Oct. 1733.
 Sarah m. Eben Claghorn, Oct. 30, 1735.
 Hannah m. David Dunham of Boston, 29 Oct. 1744.

65 SAMUEL Lumbert, son of Joshua, West Parish, d. 1774, m. Mary Comer, 10 April, 1717; 2d Beulah Lovell, 10 Sept. 1744.
 Children b. in B.
 138 Mary, 1 Feb. 1718.
 139 Abigail, 23 April, 1720.
 140 Joshua, 18 March, 1722.
 141 Samuel, 18 Aug. 1726.
 142 Benjamin, 4 March, 1729.
 Mary m. Lazarus Lovell, Jan. 23, 1726.
 Abigail m. Thos. Phinney, 3d, Nov. 1748.

69 JONATHAN Lumbert m. Martha Phinney, March 10, 1728.
 Children, b. in Barnstable.
 143 Jonathan, 20 Oct. 1729.
 144 Martha, 24 Oct. 1731.
 145 Mercy, 5 March, 1734.
 146 Hopestill, 30 April, 1737.
 147 Sarah, 11 April, 1739.

The Lumbert or Lombard Family

148 Susanna, 9 Jan, 1741, Sept. 19, 1817.
149 Simeon, 18 Oct. 1744.
Jabez, bap. 22 May, 1748.
Martha m. Shubael Hamblin, March 7, 1751.
Mercy m. Barnabas Downes, Sept. 20, 1753.

---

73 The family of CALEB Lumbert is discontinued. Beside those named, there was a Barnabas L. of Yarmouth, whose wife Sarah died March 22, 1761, in the 74th year of her age.

---

75 SOLOMON Lumbert, m. Sarah
Children b. in Truro.
150 Anna, 26 Sept. 1725.
151 Jedediah, 8 April, 1728.
152 Sarah, 8 June, 1730.
153 Hannah, 11 May, 1732.
154 Susanna, 5 Aug. 1734.
155 Salome, 14 June, 1736.
156 Solomon, 15 May, 1738.
157 Mary, 9 Sept. 1740.
158 Richard, 13 Feb. 1744.
159 Ebenezer, 26 March, 1745.
160 Hezekiah, 30 Sept. 1746.
161 Calvin, 25 May, 1748.
Anna m. Simeon Lumbert, Mar. 26, 1747.
Sarah m. Nehemiah Harding, Ma. 28, 1770.
Hannah m. John Pike, Dec. 13, 1757.
Susannah m. Jos. Freeman, April 17, 1772.
Salome m. Austin Alden of Gorham, Maine, Sept. 20, 1756.

76 JAMES Lumbert, m. Elizabeth
Children b. in Truro.
162 James, 21 March, 1731.
163 Sarah, 6 July, 1733, d. Aug. 6, 1734.
164 Elisabeth, 4 July, 1735.
165 Hannah, 15 Nov. 1737.
166 Lewis, 17 March, 1740.
167 Jane, 22 April, 1742.
168 Ephraim, 13 June, 1744.
169 Sarah, 15 Sept. 1745.
170 Rachel, 20 April, 1749.
171 Mehetabel, 20 April, 1751.
Elisabeth m. George Pike, Nov. 23, 1758.
Hannah m. Peter Wells, March 28, 1765.
Jane m. Thacher Rich, April 19, 1764.
Sarah m. Nehemiah Harding, March 22, 1770.
Mehetabel m. Zac. Atkins, March 12, 1772.

---

77 EBENEZER Lumbert, m. Bethia Mayo, June 15, 1727.
Children b. in Truro.
172 John, 3 Aug. 1728, d. 1748.
173 Bethia, 27 June, 1736.
Bethia m. James Webb, April 4, 1764.

---

79 LEWIS Lumbert, m. 1 Sarah Parker of Y., Nov. 16, 1741; 2 Sarah Paine, March 1, 1753; 3 Hannah Pane, April 9, 1761.
Children b. in Truro.
174 Rebecca, 12 Sept. 1747.
175 Sarah, 7 June, 1750.
176 Hannah, 22 Ma. 1755.
177 Lewis, 19 Dec. 1757.

178 Elisabeth, 25 Sept. 1763.
Sarah m. Wm. Myrick, Jan. 4, 1777.
Hannah m. John Selew, July 12, 1774.

---

80 EPHRAIM Lumbert, m. Joanna Vickery, Feb. 27, 1746-7.
Children b. in Truro.
179 Hannah, 16 Oct. 1746.
180 Mary, 17 Dec. 1748.
181 Joanna, 11 June, 1751.
182 Ephraim, 18 May, 1753.
183 Ruth, 12 Aug. 1755.
184 Susanna, 13 Feb. 1758.
185 Salome, 1 May, 1761.
186 Jedediah, 1 June, 1761.
Hannah m. Eph. Rich, April 16, 1771.
Mary m. Thos. Dyer, Ma. 25, 1771.
Joanna m. Jesse Dodge, Oct. 2, 1769.
Ruth m. Sam. Atkins, Feb. 17, 1774.
Susan m. Nathl. Snow, March 29, 1781.
Salome m. Obadiah Rich, Jan. 22, 1781.

---

82 JOHN Lumbert, m. Bethia
Children b. in Truro.
187 John, 22 Jan. 1738.
188 Experience, 18 July, 1741.
189 Hannah, 14 June, 1747.
190 Jemima, 4 Sept. 1750.
Experience m. Simeon Lumbert, April 22, 1760.

---

83 JEDEDIAH Lumbert, m. 1 Mary White, 25 Sept. 1716, d. Dec. 17, 1741; 2 Abigail .
Children b. in Truro.
191 Joseph, 1 May, 1717.
192 Jedediah, 28 June, 1718, d. young.
193 Mary, 4th, 13 Dec. 1719.
194 Susanna, 14 May, 1721, d. May 24, 1721.
195 Benjamin, 23 March, 1722.
196 Susanna, 30 April, 1723.
197 Matthew, 28 Ma. 1725.
198 John, 4 Aug. 1727.
199 Simon, 29 Nov. 1729.
200 Elisabeth, 2 Feb. 1731.
201 David, 24 May, 1732, d. Sept. 7, 1732.
202 Joshua, 13 May, 1733.
203 Rebecca, 26 Sept. 1734.
204 Thomas, 26 Ma. 1737.
205 Ruth, 22 Sept. 1744.
206 Ebenezer.
207 Jesse.
Fourteen living in 1749.
Mary, 4th, m. Sil. Rich, Sept. 18, 1740.
Susan m. Sam. Bassett of B., June 15, 1745.
Rebecca m. Richd. Rich, Nov. 19, 1761.
Ruth m. John Pierce, March 25, 1767.

---

84 THOMAS Lumbert, d. April 20, 1779, age 81, m. Elizabeth Binney of Hull, April, 1721, d. May 21, 1787, age 85.
Children b. in Truro.
208 Elizabeth, 17 Feb. 1723, d. Dec. 17, 1793.
209 Simon, 8 Oct. 1725.
210 Thomas, 16 Nov. 1727.

211 Samuel, 1 May, 1731.
212 Isaac, 5 Aug. 1734.
213 Caleb, 20 Oct. 1736.
214 Peter, 23 March, 1739, d. Jan. 14, 1765.
215 Rebecca, 6 July, 1741.
216 Paul, 16 Aug. 1743.
217 Israel, 17 April, 1746.
Rebecca m. David Smith, April 9, 1767.

85 WILLIAM Lumbert, m. Mary Gains, Aug. 3, 1721.

86 SIMON Lumbert, m. 1, Anna Lumbert, March 26, 1747; 2 Margaret Snow, March 25, 1756.

89 JONATHAN Lumbert, m. 1 Rachell , 1708; 2 Bathsheba , 1734.
Children b. in Tisbury.
218 Benjamin, 22 July, 1709.
219 Ann, 7 Feb. 1711.
220 Mary, 18 May, 1715.
221 Tabatha, 19 Oct. 1718.
222 Timothy, 25 Nov. 1735.
223 Moses, 13 Nov. 1737.
224 Rachell, 20 March, 1741.
225 Hannah, 8 March, 1744.

3 LUMBERT
95 Lieut. BENJAMIN Lumbert, m. Mary Davis, May 23, 1741.
Children b. in Barnstable.
Joseph, 19 March, 1752, O. S.
Martha, 12 March, 1754.
Benjamin.
Davis, bap. 7 Aug. 1768.

100 or 115 JOHN Lumbert, m.

Thankful Revis, March 11, 1731.
Children b. in Barnstable.
Cornelius, bap. 28 Nov. 1731.
Deborah, 18 July, 1736.
Susannah, bap. 5 Aug. 1739.
Sylvanus, 19 Sept. 1742.
Jerusha, 25 Aug. 1745.

103 GERSHOM Lumbert, d. 1727, m. Thankful Lewis, 17 March, 1726. She m. 2d Nathl. Bacon, Sept. 1739; 3d Augustine Bearse, 7 Sept. 1744.
Children.
Hannah, 25 Jan. 1727.

104 ELIHU Lumbert m. Rebecca Taylor, 1728, d. May 5, 1775.
Children
Bapd. in B., June 14, 1747.
David.
Susannah.
Ann.
Rebecca.

107 HEZEKIAH Lumbert m. Jemima Lumbert, Nov. 25. 1736.
Children bapd. in B.
Mary, Jan. 1, 1738.
Ann, Nov. 4, 1739.
Hezekiah, June 10, 1744.
Thomas, June 7, 1747.
Lydia, July 27, 1755.

112 MATTHEW Lumbert, m. Remember Mercy Davis, 1727, d. 12 May, 1758.
Children b. in B.
Davis, 25 May, 1729, 20 June, 1729.
Gershom, 8 July, 1730.

The Lumbert or Lombard Family

Remember, 6 May, 1734, 27 Aug. 1734.
Desire, 19 Dec. 1736.
Desire m. Joseph Cobb, 10 Feb. 1757.

116 SOLOMON Lumbert, m. his cousin, Sarah L., 7 July, 1737.
Children b. in B.
Daniel, 6 Aug. 1741.
Lemuel, 6 Sept. 1743.
Ichabod, 10 Nov. 1746.
Sarah, bapd. 3 Jan. 1750.
Elizabeth, bapd. 5 Aug. 1753.

Tisbury families omitted.
131 PARKER Lumbert, d. Dec. 24, 1754, and leaving no own brothers or sisters gave his real estate to the town.

EBENEZER Lumbert, pub. to Thankful Davis, m. Bethia Smith, 26 Sept. 1751.
May.
bap. 4 May, 1753.
Elizabeth.

140 JOSHUA Lumbert, m. Hannah Fuller, Dec. 23, 1752; 2d Jane Claghorn, Sept. 1755.
Children b. in B.
Timothy, 10 May, 1756.
Sarah, 10 Jan. 1758.
Mary, 7 Feb. 1764.

143 JONATHAN Lumbert, m. Susannah Lewis, Jan. 24, 1750.
Children b. in Barnstable.
Jonathan, 24 Aug. 1757.

Lumbard families that removed to Truro. Jedediah's sons Jedediah and Thomas.
JEDEDIAH, JR." branch:
1 Solomon, 12 children.
2 James, 8 children.
3 Ebenezer, 2 children.
4 Ephraim, 8 children.
5 Lewis, 5 children.
THOMAS'S branch:
1 John, 4 children.
2 Jedediah, 17 children.
3 Thomas, 10 children.
4 William, find no record of children.
5 Simon, died before 1736, probably no issue.
None of the children of Solomon, son of Jedediah, appear on the copy of the Truro records. This family probably removed to Gorham.
JAMES Lombard, son of James, m. Thankful Dyer, March 28, 1754.
Children born in Truro.
Elizabeth, July 9, 1754.
Thankful, June 18, 1756.
Nabbe, Sept. 7, 1758.
Thankful, Nov. 3, 1760.
Jane, March 31, 1763.
Hannah, April 7, 1765.
Mehetable, July 26, 1767.
Aphia, Aug. 25, 1770.
LEWIS Lombard, Jr., son of James, m. Elizabeth Pike, Jr., March 27, 1766.
Children born in Truro.
Lewis, Aug. 10, 1767.
James, May 15, 1769.
Elizabeth, Sept. 12, 1771.
Anna, Aug. 7, 1772, m. Joshua

The Lumbert or Lombard Family

Paine, March 5, 1789.
Sarah, April 11, 1774, m. Zaccheus Knowles, 1791.
Jane, Dec. 23, 1775.
Hannah, Aug. 20, 1779.
EPHRAIM Lombard, son of James, m. Huldah Ryder, Nov. 10, 1768.
Children born in Truro.
Ebenezer, Aug. 22, 1769.
Ephraim, Aug. 3, 1771.
Huldah, July 14, 1774.
Peggy Hopkins, July 3, 1776.
Freeman, May 2, 1779.
EPHRAIM Lombard, son of Ephraim, m. Mehetabel Knowles, Nov. 17, 1774.
Children born in Truro.
Ephraim, Sept. 9, 1775.
James, April 9, 1777.
Mehitabel, Oct. 6, 1778.
Hannah, April 22, 1781.
That Knowels, Nov. 29, 1784.
DANIEL Lombard, son of   , m.
Marcy Avery, July 14, 1748.
Children born in Truro.
Thomas, May 24, 1749.
Daniel, June 22, 1751, m. Tamsin Cobb, April 15, 1779.
Hannah, June 14, 1753.
Mary, Dec. 31, 1757.
BENJAMIN Lombard, son of Jedediah, m. Elizabeth
Children born in Truro.
Elisha, June 3, 1746, d. June 19, 1746.
Mary, in Eastham, Sept. 5, 1748.
Josiah, Truro, April 18, 1751.
Keziah, Truro, June 1, 1752.
Elizabeth, Feb. 27, 1755.
Keziah, Sept. 6, 1756.
A Solomon Lombard m. Rebecca Knowe, 1786, and had Mehetabel, Sept. 1, 1786; Hannah, May 18, 1791; he died Jan. 3, 1793, age 32.

No. 55.

LIBRARY of
Cape Cod
HISTORY & GENEALOGY

EASTHAM and ORLEANS

HISTORICAL PAPERS

By Josiah Paine of Harwich.

YARMOUTHPORT, MASS.:
C. W. SWIFT, Publisher and Printer,
The "Register" Press,
1914.

EASTHAM and ORLEANS HISTORICAL PAPERS

By Josiah Paine of Harwich.

FIRST AND SECOND CHURCH OF ANCIENT EASTHAM.

First Ministers of the Town. The Mayos and Crosbys. The Hero of Cooper's "The Spy."

The year in which the first church of Eastham* was organized is not with certainty known, but there is reason to suppose it was early constituted. The loss of the early church records, and the silence of the old records of the town upon the measures adopted early to sustain public worship, render unavoidable a brief notice of the preachers before the settlement of Mr. Samuel Treat.

As far as it can now be ascertained the first employed by the early settlers of Eastham to conduct the public religious services was Mr. John Mayo. He came over from England, it is understood, about 1638, and he is mentioned by Morton as one of the number of "godly and able gospel preachers" who "gave light in a glorious and resplendent manner." He was at Barnstable in 1639, when Mr. John Lothrop and his company from Scituate arrived, and having been called to the position of "teaching elder" in the church of which Mr Lothrop was pastor, he was ordained Fast day, April 25, 1640, Mr. Lothrop, Mr. Joseph Hull and Elder Henry Cobb assisting. He continued here in connection with Mr. Lothrop's church for some time, when he went to Nausett, or Eastham, and was employed to conduct religious services. The precise date of his removal to Eastham cannot now be given; but it is quite evident it was not long after the settlement, which began in 1645, and not in 1644, as Pratt and Freeman have it. His services, as a religious teacher were ended here before November 9, 1655, as at this date he became pastor of the second church in Boston, which had been gathered June 5, 1650. In 1664, Mr. Increase Mather was ordained his colleague in the

---

*The old township of Eastham embraced what is now Orleans, Eastham and Wellfleet. Wellfleet, known as Billingsgate, was set off in 1763, and Orleans in 1797.

ministry, and remained connected with the church many years after Mr. Mayo retired from the pastoral office. Mr. Mayo's retirement was caused by the "infirmities of age." In the beginning of the year 1672, he became "very infirm, insomuch as the congregation was not able to hear and be edified;" and the brethren, desiring a change in the pastoral office, he consented, and in the summer of 1673 he removed to the Cape, and died at Yarmouth in May, 1676, and was there buried. His widow died at Yarmouth Feb. 26, 1682.

But very little indeed appears relating to Mr. Mayo's ministry in Eastham. It is evident he had no settlement in the ministry there for any period of time. At the time he went there, the settlers were not in condition to sustain a minister, and for lack of proper support, it is probable, he felt compelled to accept the pastorate in Boston, and leave the Colony in which he had been admitted a freeman.

Of Mr. Mayo's children there appears no complete list. It is certain, however, he had Samuel, Hannah, Nathaniel, Elizabeth and John, who, doubtless, were all born in England and came over with him.

Samuel Mayo, the eldest son, was a mariner. He married Thomasine, daughter of William Lumpkins of Yarmouth, who was born about the year 1625. He settled first in Barnstable. In 1653, with some others, he removed to Oyster Bay, Long Island, where he had made large purchases of the Indians. From here, about 1658, he removed to Boston, where he resided until his death in 1663. His father, Mr. John Mayo, was appointed to administer upon the estate the widow declining to take out letters —April 26, 1664. The widow, Thomasine, married John Sunderland of Boston, in or about 1665. She died at the age of 84, June 13, 1709, and lies buried in the Brewster cemetery beside her last husband, Mr. Sunderland, who died December 26, 1709, in his 85th year.

There is no complete list of the children of Samuel Mayo. Recent investigation almost conclusively shows that it was his son, John Mayo, who married Hannah Freeman, daughter of Maj. John Freeman, in 1681, who first settled in Hingham, and after 1700 moved to Harwich, now Brewster, and settled, and was the first representative from Harwich to the General Court in 1711. Some genealogists have put down the Harwich John Mayo as son of John Mayo of Eastham. Mr. Samuel Treat, the first settled minister in Eastham, married Elizabeth, a daughter of Samuel Mayo.

John and Nathaniel Mayo, the other sons of Mr. John Mayo, settled in Eastham. The latter married Hannah, daughter of Gov. Thomas Prence, and died at Eastham in 1663, leaving sons Thomas, Nathaniel, Samuel and Theophilus. The widow, Hannah, married Captain Jonathan Sparrow. There are yet descendants of John and Nathaniel Mayo in the county.

Rev. John Mayo, while in the ministry at Boston, occupied a brick house standing near the northwest corner of Prence and Hanover streets. It was taken down in 1882. Upon his removal to the Cape, after leaving the pastorate, he sold it to Alexander Gording, a mariner. It was occupied after 1688 by Rev. Cotton Mather for some length of time. The lot upon which it stood was near John Sunderland's land. Mr. Sunderland removed to Eastham some time after Mr. Mayo's removal, where he died.

The immediate successor of Mr. Mayo as religious teacher in Eastham is not positively known. The first, however, of whom the ancient records of the town make mention was Mr. Thomas Crosby. It is under date of August 12, 1663, that his salary of "fifty pounds per annum" was established "for carrying on the public service on the Lord's day." He was born in England, and was the son of Simon Crosby, who came to this country in 1634 and settled in Cambridge. He was educated at Harvard college, graduating in 1653.

After leaving college, until he was employed in Eastham, but very little has been said of him. Indeed, but little is known of his services even after he became teacher here. It is claimed that he officiated here as a religious teacher until Mr. Samuel Treat was settled; but the ancient records of the town are silent upon the matter. He early became engaged in trade. In December, 1664, he was reported among those who kept for sale liquor, powder and shot. While a resident of Eastham, he resided near the old cemetery, now included in the present town, near the old meeting-house, in the house occupied by Richard Sparrow till his death, which he bought of the widow, Pandora, and her son, Jonathan Sparrow, in February, 1665. Mr. Crosby, some time after 1695, became a resident of that part of Harwich now Brewster. Here he engaged in the mercantile business. He was one of the founders of the church in that part of the town in 1700, of which Mr. Nathaniel Stone became pastor immediately after its organization. He died in Boston, while there on business, June 13, 1702. By wife Sarah he had twelve children, viz.: Thomas, Simon, Sarah, Joseph, John (who died in infancy), John, William, Ebenezer, Mercy, Anne, Increase and Eleazer. The Johns were twins, and Mercy, Anne and Increase, "born April 14 and 15, in the year 1678," were triplets. The widow, Sarah, became the wife of Mr. John Miller of Yarmouth, April 28, 1703. From Mr. Crosby have descended all of the surname on the Cape.

Thomas Crosby, a grandson of Mr. Crosby, who married Elizabeth Hopkins of Harwich, August 9, 1733, and removed about 1753, with his large family, to what is now Carmel, Putnam county, was the father of Enoch Crosby, the hero of Cooper's novel, "The Spy: a tale of the Neutral Ground," and also hero of the "Spy Unmasked," by H. L. Barnum. Mr. Crosby, the "Harvey Birch" of the tale, was born in what is now Brewster, December 25, 1749, and baptized December 31 following. He was the seventh child. The part he bore in the Revolutionary war in behalf of the Colonies in the secret service, is given in Barnum's "Spy Unmasked, or Memoirs of Enoch Crosby, alias Harvey Birch." Enoch Crosby died near Brewster, Putnam county, N. Y., June 26, 1835, and lies buried in the old Gilead cemetery, where his parents were interred. A marble slab, with inscription, marks the spot.

NO. 2.

Rev. Samuel Treat and His Ministry. His Interest in the Indians. His Farm, now the Knowles Estate, etc.

The first minister after Mr. Crosby, of which any mention is made in the Eastham records, was Mr. Samuel Treat; but the year of his settlement is unknown, as no records of the church of that period are extant. Rev. James Freeman, in his sketch of Eastham, in the eighth volume of the collections of the Massachusetts society, gives the year 1672, and that no one might be misled, in a foot note, gave as his authority Mr. Treat's gravestone, which states he died in 1717, after a "space of forty-five years" in the ministry. From his quoting the statement upon his gravestone, it is evident Rev. Mr. Freeman, in his zealous pursuit after facts for his interesting sketch, found no record of his ministry or any writing extant giving the exact date. Mr Pratt, who drew largely from this sketch for his history of Eastham, and Mr. Freeman, who copied from Pratt and Freeman without giving authority, agree that the year was 1672, while the ancient records of the town are silent as to the precise date, and yet pointing to a date of his settlement in the ministry here several years later. The gravestone inscription is doubtless correct as to the length of time he was in the ministry, but it was not intended to show that was the space of time he was engaged in Eastham. From what has been gathered, Mr. Treat was not settled in Eastham much earlier than the latter part of the year 1673.* The following from the original book of records of Eastham shows that he was not settled April 11, 1673, though the town had evidently expected he might be induced to settle; and what he or any other minister might expect in case of settlement: "1673. At a town meeting the 11th of April, it is agreed by the inhabitants of the town that if it please God to bring Mr. Treat to settle amongst us in respect of carrying on the public worship of God amongst us in an efficient way, they are willing and do promise to allow him fifty pounds and every family a sufficient load of wood brought to his house or place of residence, per annum." At the same meeting the town, as further inducement to the settlement of the minister, agreed to reserve for "the support of such person or persons as" should "be engaged in the work of the ministry amongst" them; the "piece of upland and meadow given to the town by Manaseth Kempton" of Plymouth, lying in Eastham; the upland and meadow bought of John Young;" "three acres of meadow called Mill Meadow;" "the island at Billingsgate, called Lieutenant's Island, with the meadow about it;" the "broken marsh in the great meadow" not laid out; and "twenty acres of upland at the head of the cove called Town Cove."

The Town Cove lot, which is now included in the town of Orleans, was the tract upon which the town intended to build the minister's house, but Mr. Treat upon his settlement, having decided to reside upon another lot which was nearer to the meetinghouse, between the land of Nicholas Snow and Stephen Atwood, he was allowed the privilege, and after many years the town, upon Mr. Treat relinquishing his right, sold it. After 1709 a portion of it was within the limits of Samuel Knowles's farm. Mr. Pratt in history of Eastham states that Mr. Treat settled upon it, and that it became the farm of James H. Knowles. Mr. Pratt was mistaken respecting the location of the tract, though undoubtedly correct in respect to the (then) possessor of Mr. Treat's farm.

At first the parcels of land granted for the minister's use were not given in fee simple to Mr. Treat as has been stated. It was many years after his ordination that full title was given. The upland and meadow given the church by Manasseh Kempton

---

*Since this statement was made, the writer has found that Mr. Treat was ordained March 17, 1675. The Plymouth Church Records have the following entry regarding the ordination: "In March, 1675, the church of Eastham sent to our chh, for messengers, to be with them at their ordination of Mr. Samuel Treat to be their Pastor; the chh sent the Pastor, Elder & Deacon Finney who attended that service, March 17."

in 1662, at the suggestion of his friend, Gov. Prence, was never given in fee simple to him. It being given to the church for the use of the ministry, it was reserved and other ministers, beside Mr. Treat, who labored here, had use of it. It comprised upland and meadow, and contained little over six acres, and according to the records, a little more than one acre was meadow. It is mentioned in the records as lying near "Fort Hill," and undoubtedly was near other parcels of land in Mr. Treat's use included within the limits of the present town of Eastham.

Mr. Kempton, who has been by several local historians called an Indian, was a respectable citizen of Plymouth, of English parentage and was glad, he says in his letter to Gov. Thomas Prence, at whose suggestion the gift was made, of having the opportunity to "be usefull to God's people either in this or any other way."

Mr. Treat was the eldest son of Gov. Robert Treat of Milford, Conn., who was father of twenty-one children, and grandson of Hon. Richard Treat of Weathersfield in that state. He was born in 1648, and was a graduate of Harvard college in 1669. In 1670 he appears to have been a resident of Newark, N. J., where his father was then residing; and as the people of Woodbridge desired their committee to invite either Mr. Peck of Elizabethtown or Mr. Samuel Treat, "to preach six or seven months," it is inferred he had, or well nigh completed his preparatory studies for the ministry.

During the early period of his pastorate at Eastham, Mr. Treat was deeply interested in the temporal and spiritual welfare of the Indians within the township and places adjacent, and when Mr. Richard Bourne, the pioneer in the work, withdrew from the field of labor below Yarmouth, he very zealously continued the work with considerable success, having become, by earnest study, familiar with Indian dialect. For the edification of his converts, "he was at the pains to translate the Confession of Faith into the Nauset language," which was printed. A copy of it was seen by Rev. Dr. Freeman, some time before the commencement of the present century, it being in the possession of Miss Eunice Paine, sister of Hon. Robert Treat Paine, and the granddaughter of the translator. For his services in behalf of the Indians, he was remunerated by the society in England for the propagation of the gospel among the Indians of New England.

Mr. Treat's parish was somewhat extended, but he was enabled by a firm and vigorous constitution to attend to all ministerial duties, and devote time and attention to trade, in which he was engaged, to add to the means of his support. A few years before his death he received a paralytic shock. The second shock terminated his life, March 18, 1716-17, in the 69th year of his age. The snow which had fallen during the succession of remarkable storms of that century, in February, was heaped up to an uncommon height over the whole township at the time of his death, and the time of his burial was postponed till the completion of an arch through the snow drifts, through which to bear his body to the grave. Upon its completion, it is said, the Indians at their request, were permitted to assist in bearing the remains of their friend to the grave as their last tribute of respect. The grave of Mr. Treat is yet marked in the oldest cemetery in Eastham by two stones with inscriptions. The old slate stone erected soon after his death has this inscription:

"Here lies interred ye body of ye late learned and Rev'd Mr. Samuel Treat, ye pious and faithful pastor of this church, who, after a very zealous discharge of his ministry, for ye space of 45 years, and a laborious travail for ye souls of ye Indian natives, fell asleep in Christ, March ye 18th, 1716-17, in ye 69 year of his age."

Mr. Treat was twice married. His first wife was Elizabeth Mayo, to whom he was married March 16, 1674. She died at Eastham, in her 44th year, December 4, 1696. For his second wife he married Mrs. Abigail Easterbrook, daughter of Rev. Samuel Willard of Boston, August 29, 1700. She survived her husband, and died December 27, 1746. It is said she "made the character of her deceased husband a frequent subject of conversation," and it was from her grandchildren, especially from the eldest, Mrs. Abigail Greenleaf, that the late Rev. Dr. Freeman of King's Chapel, Boston, obtained "many of the facts in the life and character of Mr. Treat." Mrs. Greenleaf, at the death of her grandmother, was twenty-one years of age.

The children by the first wife were: Jane, born in 1675, married Oct. 11, 1694, Constant Freeman of Eastham, who settled in Truro; and from whom descended Rev. Dr. James Freeman, a prominent member of the Mass. Hist. society, and a well-known Unitarian minister; Elizabeth, born in 1676, who married ——— Snow of Eastham; Sarah, born in 1678, who married Thomas Rogers of Eastham in 1700, and who settled in Truro; Samuel, born in 1680, who married Joanna Vickerie in 1708 and settled in Truro; Mary, born in 1682, who married John Rich in 1700; Robert, born in 1683, who died of a fever, May 1, 1701; Abigail, born in 1686, who married Richard Stevens in 1708 and resided in Truro; Joseph, born in

1690, who married twice and settled in Boston, where he died in 1756; Joshua, born in 1692, who married Mercy Higgins and died in 1753 in Eastham; John, born in 1693, who married Abigail Young in 1716 and settled in Eastham; Nathaniel, born in 1694, who married Mary Lyons, a lady of English birth who died in 1791, "aged about 95;" Eunice, by second wife, born September 27, 1704, (mother of Hon. Robert Treat Paine, the signer of the Declaration of Independence) who married Rev. Thomas Paine, a native of Barnstable, April 21, 1721, and died Oct. 7, 1747; Robert, born Jan. 21, 1706-7, who died of a fever while an undergraduate of Harvard, at the age of 17 years, Feb. 26, 1724, being the only son of the minister who entered college. From what has been learned, Mrs. Treat and her children removed soon after the minister's death from Eastham.

3 Ministers.

Mr. Treat's farm comprised then, as it does now, the very best land in Eastham. It contained about twenty acres, and is now in possession of Mr. Seth Knowles. The boundaries are yet well defined. A stone marked with the letter T set at the order of Mr. Treat, if not by his own hands, at the northwest corner of his premises, is yet standing. The site of his house is pointed out on the rising ground near the meadow, southeasterly of Mr. Knowles's house, and not a great distance northerly from the "brook" or small stream that flows out of the cedar swamp, which formerly divided the Prence and Treat farms. One standing on the high ground overlooking Mr. Treat's farm and the ocean, and the territory once belonging to Gov. Prence, and after him to Deacon Samuel Freeman, over the "brook," or passing over the productive farms and observing the richness of the the soil, will not longer wonder what led Mr. Treat to choose the tract for his homestead instead of the twenty acres at the head of the Cove which were given him by the town to build upon if he so chose. The whole farm, it is understood, has been in the Knowles's possession since the heirs of Mr. Treat sold it.

NO. 3.

First Place of Meeting. Second Meeting House. Two Places of Meeting Required. Mr. Treat's Deacons. Deacon Twining Joined the Friends.

The meeting-house in which Mr. Treat first held service was the same one in which Mr. Mayo and Mr. Crosby conducted religious services. It was a small structure, twenty feet square, with a thatched roof, and stood not far from the first old cemetery, on the same side of the highway.

The records show, as late as 1677, John Smith was employed "to get thatch" and repair the meeting-house therewith, "where it needed thatching." In 1678, the old house of worship was considered unfit for use, and a committee, consisting of Samuel Freeman, Jonathan Sparrow, Thomas Paine and John Doane, Jr., was chosen by the town to build a new meeting-house. It was erected upon the spot selected by the town "at the head of Goodman Williams's old field," where he then lived, and the town fulfilled its contract with the committee. The house had a belfry added in 1681 "to hang the bell in." It was not a very expensive one, as the sum of only "four pounds" was ordered to be paid for its construction. Whether the town purchased the bell and had it hung, tradition is silent. In the year 1700, the house was enlarged "sixteen feet in breadth," making it square. Mr. Israel Cole and John Paine had the oversight of the work at the expense of the town.

The increase in the number of attendants rendered it necessary in 1718 to make better provisions for their accommodation, which resulted finally in a vote to build two houses of worship; one at Porchet, now East Orleans, and the other at the Herring pond, near the house of James Mayo, then deceased. Upon the erection of the proposed house of worship for the middle parish in 1719 at the Herring pond, the old house was pulled down. It is reported that some portion of its frame was put into the house now occupied by Mr. John Snow of Orleans.

In 1800, the meeting-house of the middle society underwent repairs, and in 1829 it was demolished, the society having built a commodious house some distance northwardly, on the west side of the county road, to better accommodate the whole society.

The old house at the Herring pond stood in the northeast corner of the cemetery. Mr. Heman Doane, the bard of Eastham, who died a short time since, gave in verse a reminiscence of the old house, "time-worn and gray," which fronted east "on the king's highway," in which only Webb, Cheever and Shaw had regularly preached. Its demolition gave rise to deep feelings of regret among the aged parishioners. One of them so filled with reverence, whose memory "so clung to that hallowed spot," could not be restrained from going to the church yard the Sabbath following its removal, to spend the usual devotional hours near the site of his pew. No doubt he felt as did the old bard in after years, at the recollections of the same old church edifice, when he said:

"I have seen splendid temples with lofty steeple,

With soft cushioned seats, filled
with fashion-clad people;
But none on the tablet of memory
will stay
Like that old gray church by the
king's highway."

The deacons who officiated during Mr. Treat's pastorate were, John Doane, Samuel Freeman, Josiah Cooke, Daniel Doane, William Twining, John Paine and Joseph Doane.

The apostacy of Mr. Twining while holding the office of deacon, and his removal with a portion of his respectable family to the banks of the Delaware, in Pennsylvania, to join the Society of Friends and become the exponent of the peculiar views of George Fox, must have given rise to much comment in the puritanical town. What led to his apostacy, and to his removal to the far-off Quaker settlement in his old age, when there were others of his belief in Mr. Treat's parish, is, at this distance of time, past conjecture. But he did not long have the pleasures of his new home, as death closed his earthly career November 3, 1703. His wife, Elizabeth, daughter of Stephen Deane, survived him and died Dec. 28, 1708. His will is dated at New town "ye 26 of fourth month in year 1697." Mr. Twining had two sons, Stephen and William. Stephen with his family of children removed at the time his father went, and became a leading man in the settlement, where he died in 1715. William and a sister, Elizabeth, the wife of John Rogers, remained in Eastham, and their father remembered them in his will, leaving them his estate in Barnstable county. Deacon Twining, it appears, as well as his son Stephen, opposed the liquor traffic in the settlement, and asked that it might be restricted among the Indians.

NO. 4.

Mr. Osborn at the South Parish; His Stirring Career and Varied Labors; His Posterity.

Efforts were made, soon after Mr. Treat's death, to secure the settlement of a minister. Several candidates were heard. Prominent among them were Mr. Joseph Lord and Mr. Samuel Osborn. Mr. Lord had recently returned from his field of labor in South Carolina, where he had been since 1695. He was heard only a few Sabbaths. He was settled in Chatham as successor of Rev. Hugh Adams, where he died in the pastoral office in 1748. Mr. Osborn was heard for several months as a candidate, and a call was extended to him by the church, May 19, 1718, with much unanimity, which he accepted, and he was ordained September 18, 1718. He commenced his labors in the old meeting-house which stood near the oldest cemetery in the present town of Eastham, built in 1678, but in 1719, upon the completion of the meeting-house in South Eastham, upon the site of the present Congregational meeting-house in Orleans, and upon the division of the church, he chose to remove and occupy the new edifice, and become pastor of this branch of the church, it then representing the parent church, liberty having been given him to make his choice. Here he continued actively engaged in the ministry until trouble arose between him and the church, respecting doctrinal points, which finally ended in his formal dismissal by the church, November 20, 1738, after a full trial. His accusers it seems brought nothing to prove any immoral conduct while in the ministry; but they thought, as did the "venerable council" convened June 28, 1738, that his "unguarded expressions" concerning "God and his moral perfections, as also concerning election, redemption, and other like tenets of the holy faith," were enough to disqualify him from holding the pastoral office. The leaders in the trial for heresy appear to have been men of prominence in the town. Two of them—Joseph Doane and Nathaniel Freeman, Esq.,—were men of intelligence and large influence; and it is safe to venture the opinion that, after having so many years listened to so radical an exponent of all the sharp points of Calvinism as Mr. Treat, they should not fail to discover the gradual changing of the doctrinal views of their finely educated minister from those maintained by the strict Calvinists, and his leaning towards Pelagianism, and regret the cause that had compelled them to ask his dismission from the pulpit to which he first came nineteen years before, to lead the parent church, from which time this branch has been known.

After his dismission Mr. Osborn became again a school master, and taught school in Boston and other places. There is a tradition among his descendants in Barrington, N. S., that for awhile he was a resident of that place. In the list of the original proprietors of that township the name of Samuel Osborn appears, as also in the census of 1770, but whether this Samuel Osborn was the ejected minister, it cannot be determined. Mr. Osborn was "a man of wisdom and virtue." He contributed much to the temporal, if he did not to the spiritual wants of his people, "by introducing new improvements in agriculture, and by setting them the example of economy and industry." From him, it is said, his parishioners learned the preparation of peat for fuel.

There are conflicting accounts of Mr Osborn's birthplace and place of education, as well as the time and place of his death. Rev.,

James Freeman, who made a little investigation as to his life before 1802, says "he was born in Ireland and educated in the University of Dublin." Mr. Osborn's grandson, Israel Doane, who died very aged in 1844, at Argyle, Nova Scotia, in his brief and interesting notice of his grandfather Osborn and family, states that "he was born of Irish parents in Scotland, and was educated at Glasgow, and at the age of 22 came over to America," landing "in Boston in New England," and "died in Boston about the year 1774." Dr. Freeman says, at his death—the year he does not give —he was between ninety and a hundred" years old.

It appears that his first engagement to teach school in this county was at Sandwich in 1712, being then "lately of Edgartown." In 1713, he was engaged to teach in Harwich, and while there, with wife, witnessed the will of Kenelm Winslow, which bears date Jan. 12, 1712-13. In the Harwich records his name is written "Asbon." He probably was a schoolmaster after this date in Sandwich. At the time of his call, in the latter part of the year 1717, to the ministry at Eastham, he was a resident of Plymouth, and engaged in school teaching. He gave up his school in order to supply the pulpit as a candidate. Mr. Richard Knowles brought his family and goods from that place, and was allowed two pounds and ten shillings.

Mr. Osborn was twice married. His first wife was Jedidah Smith of Edgartown, whom he married Jan. 1, 1710. His second wife was Experience, widow of Elisha Hopkins, a merchant of Chatham, with whom he was living at Nantucket in 1746, and to whom he was married after 1742, as that year Mr. Hopkins died. Mr. Osborn's children were: Sarah, who married Ephraim Moton of Plymouth; John, born in 1712, who married Ann Doane of Chatham, and died in Middletown, Conn., in 1753, aged 40 years; Mary, bap. in Harwich in 1718; Elizabeth, born in 1716, who was three times married, died in Barrington, N. S., in 1798; Abigail, who married John Homer in 1749; and Samuel.

John Osborn, who it is claimed was born in Sandwich, was educated at Harvard college, and graduated in 1725. He studied for the ministry, at his father's desire, but his "trial sermon, delivered in presence of a number of clergymen, was adjudged not orthodox, though well prepared, and his father encouraged him to prepare for the practice of medicine, as his inclinations were in that direction. Marrying Ann, daughter of Thomas Doane, he moved to Middletown, Conn., where he was a physician of eminence. He was a man of fine scholastic attainments. He had a taste for

HISTORICAL PAPERS

poetry, and several of his poetic effusions gained for him some celebrity as a poet. He died May 31, 1753, and was buried in what is now the Riverside burying ground, in Middletown, where a monument marks the spot. He had six children. John, his eldest son, born in 1711 and dying in 1825, was an eminent physician, as well as his son, Dr. John Chevers Osborn, who married Lucy T. Payne, sister of John Howard Payne, his father's cousin, and died at St. Thomas in 1819, on his passage to St. Croix for the benefit of his health.

Rev. Mr. Osborn's daughter Elizabeth married for her first husband, William Myrick, a master mariner of Harwich, in 1733. He was lost at sea, leaving three children. Her second husband was William Paine, Esq., a merchant at Eastham, whom she married in 1745. He died at Louisbourg in 1746, leaving an infant son, whom she named William, who grew up to manhood, and became an eminent school teacher. He died in 1812, and left a number of children, among whom was the author of "Home, Sweet Home." For her third husband she married Mr. Edmund Doane of Eastham, in 1749, by whom she had a number of children. Her descendants are quite numerous and highly respectable. Mr. and Mrs. Doane died in Barrington, N. S.

Mr. Osborn's place of residence while engaged in the ministry at South Eastham is not now clearly known. The town ordered the building of his house "at Pochy" in 1719, and it was erected and given to him as was agreed, when he consented to the settlement.

NO. 5.
Mr. Crocker's Ministry and Associates.

Mr. Osborn's dismission, it appears, created no schism in the church or society, whatever might have been the feelings of some as to the dismission; and early effort was made to obtain a candidate. Among others Mr. Joseph Crocker of Barnstable was heard. A call was given him to a settlement, April 16, 1739, which was accepted August 14 following. He was ordained pastor of the church, now the first or south church in Eastham, September 12, 1739. Mr. Crocker was the son of Thomas and Hannah Crocker of Barnstable, and was born in 1715. He graduated at Harvard college in 1734. He married twice. His first wife was Reliance Allen of Falmouth, now Portland, Me. He entered his intention of marriage the next day after his ordination, Sept. 13, 1739. She died of a lingering sickness at the age of 44, June 30, 1762, and lies buried in the old cemetery at Orleans, where a stone marks the spot bearing the following inscription: "Here lies interred the remains of Mrs. Reliance Crocker, the amiable and virtuous consort of the Rev. Joseph Crocker, pastor of the first church in this town. She lived desired and died much lamented, in the 44th year of her age. Smitten friends are angels sent on errands full of love; for us they languish and for us they die; and shall they languish and shall they die in vain."

For his second and last wife he married Mrs. Mary Hatch of Boston, widow of James, in 1766. She survived her husband, Mr. Crocker, 35 years, dying Dec. 25, 1807, aged 80 years. She was buried in Brewster, where she spent the closing years of her life with her daughter, Mrs. Benjamin Bangs. Mr. Crocker died March 2, 1772. He lies buried in the old part of the cemetery, beside his former wife. His gravestone bears the following inscription: "The remains of the Reverend Joseph Crocker, the pious faithful pastor Crocker, the pious faithful & much respected pastor of the south church in this town. who, willing rather to be absent from the body and to be present with the Lord, died March 2, 1772, in the 58th year of his age, and the 33d of his ministry. O man greatly beloved, thou shalt rest, and stand in thy lot at the end of the days." In Freeman's History of Cape Cod the inscription is incorrectly given, and also in the Cong. Manual, edition of 1866.

He had, it is certain, nine children by his wife, Reliance. Six of them, however, died in infancy; and each one has a headstone with inscription. They stand in a row at the feet of their parents, time worn and partly sunk. The three children surviving the mother were Josiah, the first born, Lucy and Anne. Josiah Crocker was born in 1740. He graduated at Harvard college in 1760, studied for the ministry, and had a call to settle as pastor of the church in the east precinct of Yarmouth, as successor of Rev. Josiah Dennis, deceased, Dec. 7, 1763, he having supplied the pulpit as a candidate for some time since Mr. Dennis's death, which took place August 31, the same year. Mr. Crocker was never ordained. He died of consumption, after several months of sickness, on the morning of June 20, 1764, in the 25th year of his age. He was "a promising young man, a fluent, lively preacher," and his death was much lamented. He was buried beside his mother, and a stone with a full inscription marks the spot. He frequently supplied Mr. Dunster's pulpit in the north precinct meeting-house in Harwich, during the years 1762 and 1763. When his mother lay dead, at his home in Eastham, and his father was in sorrow over her death, he supplied Mr. Dunster's pulpit, that Mr. Dunster might of—

ficiate in his father's desk. Lucia Crocker married Rev. William Shaw, and was the mother of Rev. Philander Shaw, the last settled minister of Eastham, and of Rev. Josiah C. Shaw of Cohassett. Anne Crocker married Rev. Simeon Williams of Weymouth.

Rev. Mr. Crocker "was a strict Calvinist." As a minister he was prudent and faithful; but was "destitute of popular talents as a speaker." "He was," says the late Dr. Freeman of Boston, "a hard student in theology, but without much information on other subjects; mild in his temper, affectionate in his manners, greatly beloved by his people and exemplarily pious."

The number admitted to the church, and number of children baptized, cannot now be given. The record of the church from Mr. Osborn's dismission to the end of his pastorate, which was extant in 1802, is now lost, together with the records kept by the learned Mr. Osborn, his immediate predecessor.

The house occupied by Mr. Crocker stood about thirty rods southward of the Congregational meeting-house in Orleans, on the north side of the road leading from the main road easterly to the road that leads from the main road southerly, by the house of Thomas Higgins, to what was known in olden times at "Nathaniel Mayo's landing." It was a "two story, single house" while he was an occupant; but in 1829, while in possession of Captain Ebenezer Rogers, the porch of the old meeting-house was moved and joined to it. Captain Rogers occupied the house until his death. It was taken down about twenty years since, and the site is yet visible. Mr. Crocker had a large orchard near by. His farm numbered many acres. He had a large tract of cleared land extending from the main road southerly to the Cove, eastward of his house lot. Beside meadow, he had woodland and cedar swamp. It is said he had a walk from his house to the meeting-house, on both sides of which was thickly set the privet, and known to all his parishioners as the "prim." There are none now living who even remember of seeing a vestige of the famous walk or the beautiful hedges.

Mr. William Paine, the distinguished school teacher, father of the author of "Home, Sweet Home," whose youthful days were spent in the family, and who ever held in loving remembrance his "venerable and beloved master" and the old homestead, years after the decease of Mr. Crocker referred to the "prim" and the "surrounding objects" that pleased him in his youthful days, and often wished to return and behold them as he had left them. It was under the hospitable roof of Mr.

Crocker in 1761, while standing at the window at prayer time, he beheld his stepfather and own dear mother, and other members of the family, pass on their way to the "landing," there to embark for Barrington, N. S., to spend their days in the new settlement.

Mr. Crocker made his will a few days before he died. He made provisions for the education of Joseph Crocker, son of his cousin, Rev. Josiah Crocker of Taunton, at college; mentions wife Mary and her daughters, Mary and Hannah Hatch, and his daughters, Lucia Shaw and Anna Williams. He also mentions William Paine, Jr., to whom he gave "one-half of the third or last division" of his land in Gorham, which contained about "seventy acres." His whole estate was appraised at 681 pounds, 1 shilling, one penny. His dwelling-house, land and outbuildings were valued at 441 pounds, 9 shillings, 4 pence.

The deacons of the First or South church while Mr. Crocker was pastor were Joseph Doane, Esq., John Freeman, Esq., and Jonathan Higgins. Mr. Doane died in 1757, Mr. Freeman died in 1772, and Mr. Higgins in 1792, at the age of 94 years. Mr. Doane had been deacon about forty years.

NO. 6.
Mr. Bascom, Mr. Johnson and Their Associates in South Church.

The successor of Mr. Crocker was Rev. Jonathan Bascom. He was ordained Oct. 14, 1772. He was born in Lebanon, Conn., in 1740, and graduated at Yale college in 1761. When he commenced his ministerial work the church contained one hundred and seventy-three members. Of these only forty-eight were male members. During his ministry of thirty-five years two hundred and forty-five persons became members. He baptized nine hundred and twenty-four children and solemnized three hundred and nineteen marriages, and entered upon his register six hundred and thirty-one deaths which happened within the limits of his parish during his pastorate. He died March 18, 1807, after an illness of some weeks. Mr. Bascom was a man of talents and acquirements; of a kind and facetious disposition, and in manners easy and affable. His death was much lamented. He published a sermon preached Thanksgiving day, Dec. 15, 1774, and discourse upon the death of George Washington. He was three times married. He married for first wife, Temperance, daughter of Willard Knowles, Esq., Dec. 26, 1766. She died April 8, 1782, aged 32 years. For second wife he married Phebe, widow of David Sears, and daughter of John Taylor, in 1782. She died August 16, 1784, aged 38. For his third wife he married Betsey, daughter of Maj. Gideon Freeman, Feb. 10, 1785. She survived him, and died June 6, 1828, aged 74. He had eight children. By wife Temperance he had Timothy, Jonathan (who died young), Abigail, Jonathan, Temperance and William; by wife Phebe, had Phebe; by wife Betsey, had Charles. William Bascom, his son, graduated at Harvard college, studied for the ministry, and was ordained pastor of the Fitchburg church in October, 1805, and installed pastor of the church in Leominster in 1815. Timothy and Jonathan Bascom resided in Orleans for many years and then removed from town.

The house occupied by Mr. Bascom, and in which he died, is yet standing. It is situated on the north side of main street, nearly opposite the house of Bangs Taylor.

The deacons during Mr. Bascom's pastorate were Jonathan Higgins, Solomon Pepper, Joshua Doane, Elisha Smith, Abial Cole, Richard Sparrow, chosen in 1795, Judah Rogers, chosen in 1795, and Abner Freeman, who was chosen in 1806. Mr. Higgins was deacon during the pastorate of Messrs Osborn and Crocker. He died, aged 94, in 1792. Mr. Freeman, becoming a Baptist, was dismissed in 1827.

After the death of Rev. Mr. Bascom, immediate efforts were made to secure his successor. Mr. Jesse Fisher was heard as a candidate, and a call was given him to settle in the ministry, but the offers made did not suit him and he declined a settlement. Mr. Daniel Johnson appeared as a candidate, and, at length, an unanimous call was given him to settle, which he accepted and was ordained March 11, 1808. Among the ministers who took part in the ordaining services were Rev. Dr. John Reed of Bridgewater, father of Hon. John Reed; Rev. Dr. William Shaw of Marshfield, father of Rev. Philander Shaw, and Rev. Philander Shaw fo Eastham. Mr. Johnson continued in the pastorate till March 12, 1828, when he was dismissed at his own request by a council convened for the purpose, and removed to Victor, N. Y., where he preached for some time. He subsequently was pastor of the church in Sweden and Parma in that state. He was a faithful minister. While in the ministry at Orleans, one hundred and fifty-five were admitted members, five hundred and twenty-seven persons were baptized, and two hundred and fifty-six marriages solemnized. His "bill of mortality" during his pastorate shows that four hundred and seventy-nine persons died within his parish. One of these persons —the last one upon his record— Mrs. Susannah (Higgins) Taylor, attained to the great age of one hundred and two years. She was the daughter of Samuel Higgins and widow of Mr. John Taylor; and upon the anniversary of her one hundredth birthday, in 1825, the century sermon was preached by Mr. Johnson.

The last years of Mr. Johnson's pastorate were much disturbed by religious dissensions. Three societies were formed in consequence, and strengthened by deserters from his church and society. These societies were the Methodist, Universalist and Baptist.

Mr. Johnson was born in Bridgewater, Mass., Nov. 5, 1783, and was son of Thomas and Mary Johnson of that town, and was graduated at Brown university in 1806. He married Maria A. Sampson of Plymouth in 1809. His death occurred at Fairport, N. Y., Oct. 11, 1867, in the 84th year of his age. He had five children born in Orleans, viz.: Mary S., in 1810; Simeon S., in 1812; Samuel, in 1815; Daniel, in 1819, and Maria, in 1822. Mr. Johnson first occupied the house of the late Sylvanus Higgins, but upon the removal of Timothy Bascom from town he purchased his place, and there resided till his removal. The old house is yet standing and is occupied by Mrs. Rosanna Higgins.

The deacons who officiated while Mr. Johnson was pastor were Richard Sparrow, Judah Rogers, Abner Freeman, who became Baptist and dismissed in 1827; Prince Twining, chosen in 1812; Isaac Sparrow, chosen in 1823, became a Baptist and dismissed in 1827, and James Rogers.

After Mr. Johnson's dismission no effort was made to settle a minister. The society had now become much disturbed in consequence of the introduction of new views on religious matters, and to settle a pastor as had been done there seemed to be no way opened. In 1829 Rev. John Turner was engaged to supply the pulpit. He was a very zealous preacher, and he very earnestly urged the society to erect a house of worship and he very earnestly urged the society to erect a house of worship and keep up with the societies that had been formed in the town. His appeals were heard with favor, and an unanimous vote was obtained to build. Work was commenced June 29 of this year, and on Sunday, July 12, services for the last time were held in the old house, where the voices of Osborn, Crocker, Bascom and Johnson, the settled pastors, had been heard, and on Monday, the 13th, the work of demolishing began. On the 16th following, the frame of the new house, upon the site of the old one. was raised without the use of "any ardent spirits," or injury to any one. The frame being covered, services were held the 19th, and were continued each Sabbath, with one exception, till completed, Nov. 19. The dedicatory sermon was delivered by Mr. Turner, who had interested himself in its building, and in keeping up the interest of the society. Mr. Turner's services were ended the following year, and he left the town.

The old meeting-house was completed in 1719. It was a small structure, with a hopper-shaped roof, and with a small porch on the south side. It is said the lumber used in its construction was brought from Scituate. In 1734, the house had become too small for the accommodation of the precinct, and a committee was chosen to report what was necessary. The committee recommended the building of a new house of worship upon the old site; but the precinct delayed action, and nothing was done until 1736, when the precinct consented to enlarge the house by carrying out the north or back side, and a committee of seven took charge of the enlargement. In 1800 the old house again underwent repairs. The old porch was taken down and the "high porch" erected in its place, in which the gallery stairs were placed, the doors in the end of the house closed, and new pews built. The cost of the repairs and painting was borne by the precinct, which was defrayed by the amount received from sale of the new pews. There are many now living who remember the old hopper-roof edifice, with its "high porch," two rows of windows, sounding board, deacon's seat, old men's and old women's seats, galleries on each end and front side, and its high back pews. The town held its meeting here after Orleans was set off. The burying ground adjoining the church yard was laid out by the town March 20, 1719-20. It has been enlarged several times, and is now a very large cemetery. The oldest portion has not been disturbed by the association which controls it, only to keep out the bushes. Here lie many of the sons and daughters of the early settlers of this part of old Eastham.

After the removal of Mr. Turner to another field of labor, and before the installation of Rev. Stillman Pratt in 1835, Rev. Mr. Scovel, Rev. Mr. Bartley and Rev. Mr. Boyter supplied the pulpit. Rev. Stillman Pratt was a native of Reading, Mass., and was born April 24, 1804. He graduated at Amherst college in 1831. He was a devoted minister and closed his labors here April 23, 1839, and removed from town. He died at Middleboro Sept. 1, 1862.

Mr. Pratt was succeeded by Rev. Hazael Lucas, who was employed for about two years. His successor was Rev. Jacob White, who was ordained in 1841. Mr. White was a graduate of Brown university. He continued pastor of the church till 1860, when he gave up his pastorate on account of ill health. He died at Lyneboro, N. H., April 13, 1866, aged 60 years.

His remains were brought to Orleans for interment, as requested. Mr. White was a faithful pastor and was greatly esteemed by the people of his charge.

Between 1860, when Mr. White retired, and 1870, the following ministers supplied the pulpit: Rev. William E. Dickinson, Rev. Orlando H. White, Rev. Joseph W. Tarleton and Rev. J. E. M. Wright. Among those since 1870 who have supplied the pulpit a considerable length of time was Rev C. E. Harwood, a graduate of Amherst college, who was ordained June 7, 1871.

The eccentric physician, Dr. Abner Hersey of Barnstable, gave this society by will five fifty-sixths of the income of his estate after his wife's decease. How much of the income the society annually received before the sale of the whole of Dr. Hersey's estate in 1816, it does not appear. It is probable if any was received it was small. Upon the sale of the estate by legislative authority, the society obtained a large sum, which, with its accumulation, was expended in building the minister's house in 1835.

In 1888, the old meeting-house, which had stood since 1829 without much repairs, was renovated; and now it is in condition to stand many years yet, to accommodate the society, and to mark the site of the ancient house of worship of the Congregationalists.

NO. 7.
Mr. Paine, Mr. Webb and Mr. Cheever.

Mr. Osborn's removal to the south precinct of Eastham, now Orleans, in 1719, to have charge of that branch of the old church, as pastor, now to worship in the new meeting-house, necessitated action to secure the settlement of a pastor in the north precinct to succeed him. Mr. Isaac Pepper was appointed by the town to secure a candidate for the ministry. Among those invited was Mr. Thomas Paine, the only son of James Paine, Esq.. of Barnstable, who was a native of the town. Mr. Paine was a graduate of Harvard, of the class of 1717, and was on a visit to uncles and aunts and other relatives in the town. In his interleaved almanac for the year 1719, he speaks of his visit, and regarding an invitation to preach as a candidate he says: "March 1, 1718-19. I preached in Eastham all day." "March 2d. Mr. Pepper being appointed by ye town to look out for a minister, invited me to preach here in order to a settlement; but I gave him no encouragement." Mr. Paine was settled in Weymouth the same year, where he was pastor till 1730, though not formally dismissed till 1734. Ill health was the cause of his leaving the ministry and entering commercial business. Mr. Paine "was a man of great talents, learning, industry and piety." His only son, Robert Treat Paine, was an eminent lawyer, and one of the signers of the Declaration of Independence; and was grandson of Mr. Treat, the minister, of whom mention has already been made in these papers.

Rev. Thomas Paine died in that part of Braintree called Germantown, at his daughter's, Mrs. Abigail Greenleaf's, May 30, 1757, in his 64th year, and was buried in Weymouth, his wife having died October 17, 1747. Mrs. Paine was Mr. Treat's youngest daughter. They were married at Boston, April 21, 1721.

Mr. Benjamin Webb of Braintree, a young man, was invited to preach as a candidate soon after Mr. Paine supplied the pulpit, and May 28, 1719, the town concurred with the church in giving him a call to the ministerial office vacated by Mr. Osborn, who now was pastor of the south church by choice. He accepted the call and was ordained some time during the latter part of the year. Mr. Webb continued in the ministry here until his death, which happened August 21, 1746, in the 52d year of his age. He was buried in the oldest cemetery in Eastham, where stones mark the spot. The headstone is broken and that portion which bore the inscription has been gone for many years. The footstone is in place, and in a good state of preservation. What led to his interment in the oldest burying ground, when there was a burial ground near the meeting-house in which he preached, cannot be learned. Mr. Webb was an excellent man. Mr. Crocker, of the first church, for some time his contemporary, it is said, pronounced him to have been "the best man and the best minister he ever knew." He was graduated at Harvard college in 1715, when twenty years of age.

Mr. Webb married Mehitabel, daughter of Thomas and Mary Williams of Taunton. She was born in 1695. By her he had children. The following are found recorded: Benjamin, born Nov. 2, 1721; Mary, born June 20, 1724; and Thomas, born Aug. 2, 1726. Benjamin became a schoolteacher and moved from town.

The house in which Mr. Webb lived stood near the meeting-house in which he preached. It was built by the town, as was agreed upon at his settlement. He managed to live comfortably from the proceeds of his small farm and yearly salary, and to leave at his death an estate valued at nine hundred and three pounds and four shillings, old tenor. He had servants; two of them at his death were valued at sixty-five pounds. He had a library appraised at seventy-three pounds, three shillings and six pence. He possessed at the time of his decease, a mare, three cows, a calf

EASTHAM AND ORLEANS

and thirteen sheep.

Mr. Webb left no record of his ministry, and it is not known the success that attended his labors.

The successor of Mr. Webb, as pastor of the middle church in Eastham, was Rev. Mr. Edward Cheever, who was settled in 1751. He was son of Thomas Cheever of Lynn, and was born May 2, 1717. He graduated at Harvard college in 1737. He was ordained minister of the third parish in Lynn, now Saugus, December 5, 1739, but for some reason not now known he relinquished his connection in 1747. He died at Eastham, August 17, 1794, in his 78th year, and lies buried in the old cemetery near the site of the meeting-house in which he preached, a slate stone, with inscription, marking the spot. He was twice married. His first wife, Martha, died Feb. 28, 1783, in her 64th year, and lies buried beside her husband. His second wife was Dorcas Cook of Eastham, to whom he was married by Mr. Bascom, June 3, 1788. By his first wife Mr. Cheever had several children. His son, Joshua, died when sixteen years of age, Nov. 24, 1765. His son, Dr. Samuel Cheever, was some years a practicing physician in Eastham. Mr. Cheever's pastorate extended through the stormy period of the Revolutionary conflict. He left no record of the church during his connection with it. That his views upon the great question of separation from the mother country were in accord with a majority of his townsmen there is no doubt.

NO. 8.

Rev. Philander Shaw, Mr. Babcock, Mr. Hardy and Their Successors.

The successor of Mr. Cheever was Rev. Philander Shaw. He was ordained Sept. 23, 1795. He was given 200 pounds as an inducement to settle, and an annual salary of 90 pounds. He was the last settled minister in Eastham. He continued in the ministry here till early in the year 1838, when he asked for his dismissal. The important event of his pastorate was the division of the ancient town.

Mr. Shaw was born in Marshfield, Mass., March 27, 1767. He was the son of Rev. William Shaw, and grandson of Rev. John Shaw of Bridgewater. His mother was Lucia, daughter of Rev. Joseph Crocker of Eastham. He was educated at Brown university and Harvard college. At the former institution he spent two years, and at the latter two years. Among his classmates at Harvard were Rev. Mr. Kirkland and Levi Hedge, Esq. After his dismissal from the pastoral charge, in 1838, he occasionally supplied the pulpit in his own and neighboring parishes. He represented Eastham in the General Court in 1837 and 1838, and preached the funeral discourse, at the invitation of his townsmen, upon the death of President Harrison in 1841. "As a preacher his voice was strong and his articulation clear and distinct." It is said "his talents were of high order and discoverable in all his performances; but seen to the best advantage on great occasions. His sermons were evangelical, generally practical rather than doctrinal, and rich in thought. His style of writing was clear and vigorous, bearing the mark of a scholar." He died after a short illness, October 10, 1841, aged 72 years. Mr. Shaw was twice married. His first wife was Miss Dorcas Doane, to whom he was married by Rev. Jonathan Bascom, November 19, 1795. She died of "a languishment" at the age of nineteen. July 17, 1797. For his second wife, he married Miss Lucy Crocker of Barnstable, in November, 1798. She was the daughter of Alvan Crocker, and by her he had children: his eldest son, Philander, died when seven weeks old, Jan. 27, 1800; his son, Joseph Crocker, fell a victim to the spotted fever, at the age of 13, Feb. 4, 1816; and his son, Oaks, died of the same disease, Feb. 24, 1816, aged 9 years.

The Congregational society at the close of Mr. Shaw's pastorate was not as large and prospreous as it was when he began his labors forty-one years before. It could not now be said, as had been said, "no individual in town but what belongs to the Congregational society." The great falling off was due to the Methodist society, which was formed in 1820. The society in 1839 obtained the services of Mr. Daniel H. Babcock, a native of Ohio, and a student of theology at Andover. He was ordained Nov. 7, 1839. He remained here but a short period, when he went to West Yarmouth, and became pastor of the church there, organized in 1840.

Rev. Solomon Hardy, a native of Hollis, N. H., took charge of the society a short time after the dismission of Mr. Babcock. He died while in the ministry here in September, 1842. Mr. Hardy was a graduate of Middlebury college in 1824, and had preached in various places. He came to this place from South Wellfleet, where he had preached since January, 1838. His death was much lamented by all who knew him.

Rev. Enoch Pratt succeeded Mr. Hardy as pastor and continued several years. He was a native of Middleboro, and graduate of Brown university in 1803. He settled in the ministry at West Barnstable, having been ordained Oct. 28, 1807. He asked for a dismission as pastor of the West Barnstable church in 1835, and removed to Brewster. In 1836 he supplied the pulpit in South Wellfleet, and for several years after supplied pulpits whenever occasion required, until he was called to the Eastham church. While in charge here he applied himself to the examination of records and to the collection of facts for his history of the ancient town of Eastham, which he published in 1844. He died at Brewster, Feb. 2, 1860, aged 78 years. He was three times married, and left children.

Rev. Edward W. Noble supplied the pulpit from November, 1846, to December, 1849, when he went to Truro and was there installed pastor Dec. 26, 1849. Mr Noble was born in Williamstown, Mass., in 1811, and was graduated at Williams college. He preached at Truro until 1883, when he severed his connection with the Congregational society and removed to Cambridge, where he has since died.

Between 1850 and 1851, Rev. John H. Wells and Rev. Stephen Bailey supplied the pulpit. Mr. Bailey had been in the ministry at Truro and Wellfleet. He was a native of New Hampshire. He died at Dorchester, Dec. 30, 1868.

The last pastor of the church was Rev. Ebenezer Chase. He preached from 1851 to 1859. Mr. Chase had been pastor of the Congregational church in West Yarmouth, and had supplied the West Barnstable church.

In 1854 the Congregational society found it impossible to support religious worship, sold the meeting-house, and it was removed for secular purposes. Thus this branch of the old Congregational society of Eastham, first led by Webb, has become extinct.

NO. 9.
The "Cold Plague" and "Spotted Fever."

In the beginning of the year 1816 a malignant febrile disease, called the "cold plague" and also the "spotted fever," made its appearance in the lower Cape towns. At Orleans, Eastham and Truro it was attended with fatality. The local physicians found it very difficult to control, and very few recovered under their treatment. The disease appeared in Orleans in February and continued its work of prostration and death for several weeks. The whole number of deaths resulting from the fever has never been fully given. Rev. Mr. Johnson of the Congregational society, who kept a record of those who died in his parish that year, fails to designate the disease each person had, so no account of the number can be made up from his record. His "bill of mortality," however, for the year 1816, shows that fifty-two persons—twenty-eight adults and twenty-four children— died, showing an excess of thirty-two deaths over the number in 1815.

In Eastham this disease appeared in January, and it continued for several months. The first three weeks it was attended by great fatality. The physicians here had no success in its treatment. Fortunately for the sick, in the month of April appeared Dr. Samuel Thomson, the founder of the Thomsonian system of practice, in pursuit of vegetable substances for medicinal purposes. He at once made himself acquainted with the nature of the disease, and had many calls to attend the sick during the few days he spent here. His manner of treatment restored each patient to health, and after selling two men "rights" to practice he returned to Boston, the disease appearing to abate. Within a week after his return to Boston, he received a letter from Eastham, strongly inviting him to return as "the fever had made its appearance among the people with double fatality." He took a "stock of medicine," he says, and returned and "soon found enough ready to purchase the twenty rights for which I had offered to sell the right of the whole town. I attended on many of those who had the disease, in company with the two men who had purchased the right of me when there before, and instructed them how to carry a patient through a course of medicine, and they attended and gave instruction to others. When they could meet together I gave information by lectures; those who got the information attended wherever they were wanted. I pursued my usual mode of treatment by giving the medicine to promote a free perspiration, and when necessary steamed and gave injections, cleansed the stomach and cleared off the canker." He says, "The success in curing this alarming disease was very great. I staid about two weeks, during which time there were attended with my medicine thirty-four cases, of whom one died and the rest got well." "At the same time," he says, "of those who were attended by the regular doctor eleven out of twelve died, making in the whole upwards of fifty deaths in a short time in this place, which was about one-twelfth part of the inhabitants who were at home." Dr. Thomson says, "The people generally treated me with great kindness and respect, and took a great interest in my cause; and the success of my system of practice, in relieving them from this alarming disease, gave universal satisfaction."

At Truro the disease commenced the latter part of February or first part of March, and soon became very fatal. Rev. Jude Damon, the pastor of the Congregational church, in his register of deaths kept during his long pastorate, gives the name, time of death and age of each one who was a victim to this malignant fever. The following list of victims is made up from his bill of mortality:

John Atkins, who died March 9, aged 49 years.
Richard Rich's wife, who died March 13.
Joseph Lombard, who died March 14, aged 3 years.
Joseph Higgins, Jr., who died March 11, aged 13 years.
Widow Nancy Brewer, who died March 18, aged 46 years.
Ambrose Collins, who died March 19, aged 20 years.
Widow Ruth Snow, who died March 19, aged 71 years.
Betsey Lombard, who died March 24, aged 18 years.
Widow Betsey Rich, who died March 24, aged 75 years.
Mary Atkins, who died March 25, aged 16 years.
Sarah Knowles, who died March 29, aged 39 years.
Huldah Snow, who died March 29, aged 69 years.
Pauline Paine, who died March 29, aged 2 years.
Jaazaniah Gross, who died March 30, aged 46 years.
Silas Knowles, who died March 31, aged 22 years.
Caleb Lombard, who died April 2, aged 15 months.
Anthony Snow, Esq., who died April 3, aged 71 years.
David Dyer, who died April 3, aged 56 years.
Joshua Hinckley, who died April 7, aged 36 years.
Edwin Lombard, who died April —, aged 17 months.
Thomasin Snow, who died April 11, aged 5 years.
Wife of Caleb Hopkins, who died April 16, aged 70 years.
Wife of Thomas Rich, who died April 16, aged 40 years.
Child of Thomas Peirce, who died April 16, aged 3 months.
Widow Anna Cole, who died April 17, aged 53 years.
Silas Atkins, who died April 17, aged 84 years.
Mrs. Sarah Knowles, who died April 23, aged 49 years.
Mrs. Eliza Rich, who died May 1.
Mrs. Deborah Paine, who died May 1.
Mrs. Susanah Dill, who died May 5.
Isaac Small, who died May 6, aged 61 years.
Widow Christian Coan, who died May 11, aged 76 years.
Widow Thomasin Snow, who died May 15, aged 67 years.
Mrs. Elizabeth Small, who died May 21, aged 56 years.
Jeremiah Knowles, who died May 25, aged 18 years.

NO. 10.
Wreck of Pirate Ship Whidah. Over 100 Lives Lost. Passage Through the Cape.

The loss of the pirate ship Whidah or Whido, and her two consorts, on the eastern shore of Eastham, in April, 1717, with all their crews, with the exception of seven men, was for many years an interesting theme at the evening gathering at the firesides in the lower towns of the Cape; and well it might have been, for never, since the settlement, had there been such destruction of vessels and loss of life on the Cape shores.

The Whidah or Whido was a fine merchant ship, and at the time of her capture by Bellamy in February, 1717, was in command of Capt. Prince, bound from Jamaica to London with a valuable cargo. Bellamy had her armed with 28 guns, and retaining a portion of her crew, with the sloop he lately sailed well manned, as a tender, sailed for the shores of Virginia; but encountering a heavy gale of wind, in which both vessels narrowly escaped destruction, he changed his course for Rhode Island. While nearing the coast, the pirates fell in with a vessel, which they captured and sunk after taking aboard the crew. The Whidah and tender, continuing their cruise off Cape Cod, captured a wine vessel. Williams, who had been engaged with Bellamy in his piratical work from the commencement, was put on board as the prize master with seven other pirates, with instructions to keep the craft with the fleet. After a short cruise off the eastern coast, destroying vessels and detaining crews, the piratical squadron encountered storms, and it was determined to return for a cruise off Cape Cod, where the prospect for their work was better. But their cruise was short. The pilot of the wine vessel, who had been the master before its capture by the pirates, having become exasperated by the ill usage of Williams, the prize master, who kept him constantly at the helm, ran the vessel ashore while Williams and his crew were intoxicated, and was the only one of the crew who succeeded in reaching the shore alive. The night was dark and windy, the waves ran high, and it was remarkable that the pilot escaped death. The Whidah, following the wake of the wine vessel, got into the breakers, turned bottom up and all but two of the crew lost their lives. The other vessel was run ashore and five succeeded in gaining the shore, while the others constituting the crew were drowned. The pirates, upon reaching land, sought a place of safety till morning, when they began their journey to Rhode Island.

Joseph Doane, Esq., one of the justices of the peace for the county, was informed of their passage through the town and immediately started with a deputy sheriff in pursuit. They were overtaken and arrested. After examination they were committed. Two days after, another pirate, who had managed to get ashore from the Whidah, was found, examined and committed for trial. These pirates were tried at Boston in October following, and those found guilty were executed. Esq. Doane attended the trial, upon the command of "His Excellency Samuel Shute, Esq., the Governor and Commander-in-chief," and spent ten days from home. It appears that he was not remunerated for his time and expense until 1727, when upon application to the Great and General court, an order was passed for his pay.

Immediately upon receiving intelligence of the destruction of the pirate vessels in the surf on the eastern shores of Eastham, Gov. Shute ordered Capt. Cyprian Southack to proceed to the place of the disaster in behalf of the government. He took passage in the sloop Nathaniel, hired by the government, commanded by Capt. John Sol, May 1. The next day coming to anchor in "Cape Cod harbor," a whale boat was obtained, and Messrs Cutler and Little of his party were sent without delay to Truro to get horses and proceed to the wreck. Capt. Southack followed the next day, May 3. He found upon his arrival at Truro much trouble to get the horses his business required. He spent some little time at the house of Thomas Paine, Esq., in making arrangements for his journey, etc. Here he met Mr. Caleb Hopkins, an outspoken old settler, grandson of the sturdy old Pilgrim, Stephen Hopkins of the Mayflower band, who "very much affronted" him. From here Capt. Southack proceeded on his journey to Eastham, where it appears he arrived late in the afternoon. At the place of the wreck he found, besides Cutler and Little, Joseph Doane, Esq., and at least two hundred men on the shore, picking up whatever was of any value that floated from the wrecks. Many of these men had come from places twenty miles distant. Capt. Southack, next day after his arrival, posted a notice of his business and ordered all goods taken, belonging to the vessels, to be brought to him at Mr. William Brown's house. The goods recovered, Capt. Southack employed men to take them to Billingsgate, from where they were taken to Boston by Capt. Dogget in a sloop. Great many of the articles picked up were in a very bad condition, which was in consequence of the heavy action of the surf. The poor condition of the goods gave rise to the saying often heard since: "Looks as if it came out of Bellamy's wreck."

Capt. Southack while at this place caused the burial of more than one hundred men that came ashore from the wrecked vessels.

It is stated that during his visit here Capt. Southack went across the Cape in a whale boat. In the State House at Boston there is an old map—"The Sea of New England"— without date or name of publisher, upon which is outlined the channel in which he made his passage. The following inscription, appearing upon the map, shows Capt. Southack was responsible for the outline at least: "The place where I came through with a whale boat, being ordered by ye Governm't to look after ye Pirate Ship Whido, Bellame, command'r, cast away ye 26 of April 1717, when I buried one hundred and two men drowned."

The passage he made across the Cape in his whale boat was doubtless where in 1804 Eastham and Orleans attempted to open a navigable canal between the head of Boat Meadow Creek and Town Cove, but which failed. The channel designated upon the map is certainly in the locality, and was probably what the old people before Bellamy came called "Jeremiah Smith's Gutter," or what is now sometimes called "Jeremiah's Gutter."

No. 56.

LIBRARY *of*
Cape Cod
HISTORY & GENEALOGY

RICHARD RICH OF DOVER NECK

BY SHEBNAH RICH

YARMOUTHPORT, MASS.:
C. W. SWIFT, Publisher and Printer,
The "Register" Press,
1913.

RICHARD RICH OF DOVER NECK

English history abounds with this name. The earliest notice I have seen is Edmund, Archbishop of Canterbury, 1236, referring to an order requiring all fonts to be covered in accordance with a constitution by said archbishop. One of the most remarkable characters of English history is Baron Richard Rich, b. London, 1498, who from a London barrister, without fortune or friends, became the wealthiest nobleman, and founded the most powerful family in England, and known as kingmakers. His sons, Earls of Warwick and Holland, have been mentioned in the colonization of America. The former was president of the Plymouth Council, and Admiral of England. Warwick, R. I., was named for him. The name is found among authors, actors, scholars, ministers, soldiers, travellers, inventors, and courtiers; men of many virtues and not a few vices.

My first knowledge of the name in America occurs in the following Salem notice: "Obadiah Rich married Bethiah Williams, 1667." In 1668 he was a signer of the petition against imports as an inhabitant of Salem. In Judge Sewell's interleaved almanac diary, March 31, 1675, occurs: "No lecture, because Mr. Rich from home." Perhaps the same Obadiah. In 1678, his widow Bethiah administered on a large estate. In 1684, Henry Rich m. Martha Panon. This is the celebrated Martha Corey, alias Martha Rich immortalized by Longfellow:

As for my wife, my Martha, and my martyr,
Whose virtues, like the stars, unseen by day,
Though numberless, do but await the dark
To manifest themselves unto all eyes.
She who first won me from my evil ways,
And taught me how ot live by her example,
By her example teaches me to die,
And leads me onward to the better life.

The following from the Salem records, throw light on this subject:

June 27, 1723. Petition of Thomas Rich of Salem, only surviving child of Martha Corey, alias Martha Rich deceased, praying the compassionate consideration and commiseration of the court for great losses to petitioner in the year 1692, enumerated.

Fifty pounds was allowed to petitioner for goods deprived, mentioned, by illegal action of the the persons charged as witches. Martha Corey alias Martha Rich, one of the victims of the witchcraft delusion. January 29, 1723. The committee reported that in consideration of the loss the petitioner might sustain by being deprived of the goods mentioned in the petition, together with the many illegal actions of the sheriff and his officers respecting the persons charged as witches, they are hereby of the opinion that the sum of fifty pounds be allowed and paid out of the public treasury to the petitioner, Thomas Rich, which was done.

Richard, of Dover Neck, is the ancestor of all the Cape Cod family, by far the largest branch, but not all of the old English stock in America. The first notice of Richard is found in the old Portsmouth records. "Samuel Treworgey, with the consent of Dorcas Treworgey (Cornish names), his wife, conveys the above land to Richard Rich of Dover, Nov. 6, 1674." How long he had then been at Dover I am unable to say. "Philip Demon of Dover Neck, d. June, 1676; by will, May 1676, makes son Evans and Richard Rich, my kinsman, executors." Mr. Rich seems to have been a man of some prominence; his name appears considerably in the records. Married Sarah, dau. of Gov. Thomas Roberts.

Son Richard(2) first appears at Eastham 1665, taxed 1671; freeman, Aug. 23, 1681, d. 1692. Children:

i. John(3), b. 1665, m. Mary, dau. Rev. Samuel Treat.

ii. Thomas(3), I think, settled in Connecticut or New York, and the founder of the old families found in New York City.

iii. Richard(3), b. 1674, m. Anne, b. 1680, in E., held lots in Truro, 1703, moved few years later.

iv. Samuel(3), b. 1684, m. Elizabeth ——; was tything-man in Truro 1711, d. 1752.

v. Sarah(3), m. Samuel Treat, son or g. s. of Rev. Samuel, 1741.

vi. Lydia(3).

vii. Joseph(3), among the Eastham voters, 1695.

The majority of this family settled in Truro; though not the first in town, they early became the most populous, and in a representative sense, more particularly local than any other in the country. Comparatively few of the name are found who did not originate here. From 1720 to 1780 the name increased rapidly, became by intermarriage, and duplicating christian names, greatly involved and interwoven, so that it is almost impossible to locate the family lines, or trace the lineal branches, without making a complete family history. In '75 there was Richard 4th, and in '98 there were five householders Richard, besides juniors and bachelors. Obadiah, John, Samuel, Benjamin, Joseph and Isaac are some of the other oft-repeated names. Richard's family seem to be the best defined. Thomas was a surveyor in 17211, and John m. Lydia Collins, 1727. Samuel was a tything-man in 1711; it is said had 24 children.

Richard (3) —Richard (2), Richard (1)— b. 1674, and wife Anna were baptized as adults by Mr. Avery in Truro, 1726. Children:
  i. Sarah, b. 1696.
  ii. Richard, b. 1699, m. Hannah — , Feb. 26, 1725, by Mr. Avery.
  iii. Rebecca, b. 1704.
  iv. Zaccheus, b. 1704, m. Ruth Collins, 1727.
  v. Obadiah (4), b. 1707, m. Polly Cobb.
  vi. Priscilla, b. 1710, d. young.
  vii. Huldah, b. 1712.
  viii. Joseph, b. 1720, m. Susannah Collins, 1742.
  ix. Sylvanus, b. 1720, m. Mary Lombard, 1740.

Inscription on gravestones in the old churchyard:

Here lies buried
the body of
Mr. Richard Rich,
who died May ye 3d,
1743, in ye
69th year of his age.

Here lies the body of
Mrs. Anna Rich,
wife of Mr. Richard Rich,
who died May ye 11, 1754.
Aet. 74.

Richard (4) Richard (3), Richard (2), Richard (1) m. Hannah, 1726. Children:
  i. Josiah, b. 1724, m. Ann Knowles.
  ii. Uriah, b. 1723.
  iii. Matthias, b. 1725, m. Mercy Paine, 1751, 2d, Kezia Orcott, d. 1792.
  iv. Hannah, b. 1729, m. Samuel Rider of P., 1746.
  v. Obadiah, b. 1730, m. Ruth Dyer, 1756.
  vi. Peggy, b. 1733.
  vii. Richard, b. 1740, I think Capt. Richard (Buzzy Dick).

Matthias (5) —Richard (4), Richard (3), Richard (2), Richard (1)— m. Mercy Paine, 1751, dau. of Barnabas, d. 1758, 2d, Mrs. Kezia Orcutt. Children:
  i. Joshua, b. 1752, m. Mary (Molly) Dyer, April, 1775, bap. June, 1775.
  ii. Mercy, b. 1754, m. Jonathan Collins.
  iii. Matthias (Beau Flash), b. 1756, lived in Boston, d. at Baltimore about 1810.
  iv. Margarette (Peggy), b. 1758, m. Wm. Tufts of Boston, where she d. about 1735.
  v. David, by K. O., b. 1764, m. Nabby Cook of Provincetown, lost at sea.
  v. Sally, by K. O., b. 1769, m. Jeremiah Gooding.

Joshua (6) —Matthias (5), Richard (4), Richard (3), Richard (2), Richard (1) m. Molly Dyer. Children:
  i. Joshua, b. 1776, lost on passage from Liverpool to Boston, 1799.
  ii. Mercy, b. 1777, m. Joseph Higgins, d. 1855.
  iii. Mary (Polly), b. 1779, m.

Captain Ephraim Snow, moved to Cohasset, died there.

iv. Shebnah, b. 1782, m. Belinda Higgins of Wellfleet, Dec. 1808, d. Oct. 29, 1843.

v. Hannah Dyer, b. 1784, m. Joshua Atwood of Wellfleet, d. Brooklyn, N. Y., about 1866.

vi. Sarah Dyer, b. 1786, m. Francis Pascal, 2d Jedediah Dyer, d. 1849.

vii. Thankful, b. 1788, m. John Gill of Wellfleet, 2d Isaac Smith of Provincetown, d. P., 1830.

viii. Matthias, b. 1791, m. Delia Pike, 1814, d. March 21, 1864.

Rebecca, b. 1796, m. Elijah Dyer, for many years keeper of Race Point lighthouse, d. at Provincetown, 1847. The only living of this family in 1883 was Mrs Delia Rich.

Shebnah(7) —Joshua(6), Matthias(5), Richard(4), Richard(3,) Richard(2), Richard(1)— m. Belinda Higgins, Dec. 10, 1807, dau. of Capt. Eleazer and Laurania (Gross), b. August 2, 1788, at Wellfleet, d. Nov. 27, 1878. Children:

i. Charles Higgins, b. Feb. 1809, m. Eliza Carpenter, 1838, Strafford, Vt., d. Boston, July, 1863. Son, Rev. Charles E. of Cal.

ii. Adeline, b. Feb. 1811, m. Joshua Smith, 1830, d. March, 1866. He d. 1841.

iii. Eleazer Higgins, b. Sept. 1813, m. Mercy Collins, Provincetown, 1836, d. March 12, 1875.

iv. Abigail Harding, b. Sept. 1815, m. Daniel P. Higgins, 1836.

v. Belinda, b. Sept. 1819, m. Isaiah Snow, Dec. 1840, 2d James C. Lombard, June, 1845. Isaiah Snow d. Oct. gale, 1841, James C. Lombard d. 1879.

vi. Maria Atkins, b. July 19, 1821.

vii. Shebnah, b. Aug. 7, 1824, m. Delia C. Knowles, Dec. 19, 1847.

viii. Elizabeth, b. Dec. 1828, m. Josiah Snow, Provincetown, d. July, 1857.

Shebnah(8) —Shebnah(7), Joshua(6), Matthias(5), Richard(4), Richard(3), Richard(2), Richard(1). Children:

i. Eliza Evelyn, b. Boston, Oct. 11, 1848.

ii. Delia Collins, b. Boston, Jan. 24, 1851.

iii. Irving Hale, b. Boston, May 22, 1853, m. Sept. 1878, Mrs. Mary W. Lewis, St. Louis.

iv. William Arthur, b. Boston, July 11, 1856.

v. Albert Smith, b. Boston, May 10, 1859, d. St. Louis, May 25, 1862.

Zaccheus(4) —Richard(3), Richard(2), Richard(1)— b. 1704. m. Ruth Collins, was the father of a wonderful posterity. He settled at the extreme south part of the town. Some say that he and his brother Obadiah settled on Beach Hill; had eleven children; Ann(5), Sarah(5), Zaccheus(5) m. Rebecca Collins or Harding, 1753. Jesse(5) m. Hannah Smith, 1757; Benjamin(5) b. 1737, m. Mrs. Lucy Somes. Son, Capt. Benj.(6) of Boston; dau. Huldah m. Richard Baker; Hannah m. Capt. John Rich; Nehemiah settled in Maine.

4

I think. Thatcher(5) b. 1739, m. Jane Lombard. Son Thatcher(6) b. 1770, m. Hope Smith, 1797. Richard(5) b. 1741. Son Richard(6) (Uncle Hunn), dau. Mehitable m. Jonah Atkins, 1795. Ephraim(5) b. 1746. Sons Mulford(6), and Ephraim(6), Elisha(5), b. 1758, Priscilla(5). I am not positive that Richard(6), b. 1741, is not "Uncle Hunn," instead of son Richard(6).

Thatcher(6) —Thatcher(5), Zaccheus(4), Richard(3), Richard(2), Richard(1)— b. 1770, m. Hope Smith, 1797. Children: Thatcher, Daniel, Richard, Zaccheus, Zobeth, Benjamin, Betsey, m. Thomas Rich; Susan m. Richard Cobb; Hope m. Samuel Rich.

Richard(5) — (4) ?, Richard(3), Richard(2), Richard(1)—b. 1741, m. Rebecca Lombard (?), 1761. Children: John(6), b. 1763. m. Hannah Rich, dau. Benjamin(5). Sons, Capt. Richard, Abram and Joseph of Hallowell, Me., dau. Lucy. 2d Sarah Hatch. Children: Lombard, Michael, Jacob, Nehemiah, Hannah and ——. Richard Sears(6), b. 1766, m. Mary Rich, dau. Jesse. Sons, Captain Sears and Thomas Smith. Peter(6), b. 1763; Thomas(6), b. 1770. Sons, Thomas, Samuel; dau. Rebecca(6), b. 1773; Samuel(6), 1775; Reuben(6), b. 1777; Ephraim Doane(6), b. 1782. Sons, Atwood, Capts. Ephraim Doane, Richard, Eleazer and Zenas.

Samuel(3) —Richard(2), Richard(1)— b. 1684, m. Elizabeth. 2d Bethiah. It is said had 24 children. I find 11 only. Jerusha(4) m. Lieut. Hugh Paine, Deliverance(4) m. Jonathan Collins; Dinah(4) m. George Lewis; Mary(4) m. Elkanah Paine; Bethiah(4) m. Nicholas Sparks of P.; Rachel(4) m. Jonah Stevens; Dea. Ebenezer(4) m. Ruth Paine, moved to Enfield with brother John(4); Apollos(4) m. Abigail Collins, moved to Ware. Son Elkanah(5), g. s. Apollos(6) m. Bethiah Banister. Sons Lyman(7) and Henry(7) of Hyde Park, Dwight R.(7) of Boston; dau. Martha(7) m. Amasa Brown of Mayflower line; son, Wm. F.(8), the Boston printer. Aquila(4) m. Ruth Avery. Sons, Obadiah(5) and Aquila(5), through whom, I think, came Obadiah(6) of Woburn, and sons Obadiah(7) of Boston, and Aquila(7) of New York, but there are so many Obadiahs, I am not clear. Three of the sisters moved to Enfield. Obadiah Rich, the great American bibliographer and antiquarian, was b. Truro; I am not able to connect his family of birth. Was elected member of the Mass. His. Soc. March 5, 1805, whom the Soc. mentions as "our great bibliographer." He is also mentioned "As a critic of high authority, has borne off rich spoils from those dark and dusty repositories of antiquarian lore." Washington Irving acknowledges his valuable and genial co-operation at Madrid, and Longfellow compliments him for wonderful accomplishments and distinguished services. His name appears probably in more libraries than any other American scholar; London. O. Rich was commander of brig Intrepid, 4 guns, 1787.

Obadiah(4) —Richard(3), Richard(2), Richard(1)— b. 1707, m. Polly Cobb. Children, Jonathan(5) m. Thankful Newcomb; Deborah(5) b. 1739; Joseph(5) b. 1741; Rebecca(5) b. 1743; Ruth(5) b. 1745; David(5) b. 1753; Isaac(5) b. 1756, settled on Great Island, Me. Large family. Sons, David(6), Zoheth(6), Isaac(6); all large families. Reuben(6) settled in W. Bath, Me.; David(6), b. 1735; dau. Betsey, m. Micah Talbot of Machias, Me., mother of Rev. M. J. Talbot of N. E. S. Con., and Mrs. B. J. Pope of Boston. I think Revs. A. J., of Hyde Park and J. A. L., of N. E. Con. are of this family.

Ephraim(6) —Ephraim(5), Zaccheus(4), Richard(3), Richard(2), Richard(1). Children: Samuel Brown(7), m. Bicknell, son, Abner Bicknell(8) of Provincetown, Ephraim(7), Hannah(7), Benjamin(7), Chloe(7), David(7).

Mulford Treat(6) —Ephraim(5), Zaccheus(4), Richard(3), Richard(2), Richard(1). Children: Zephaniah(7) —sons Capt. Lyman B.(8), Hiram— Mulford(7) of Wellfleet, Joshua(7), Ruth(7), Betsey(7), Jerusha(7) m. James Grove.

Capt. Napthali(7) —son of James(6)— b. about 1800, m. Anna Rich, dau. Capt. Reuben. Son Napthali(8) of South Boston.

Lemuel(5). Sons Ezekiel(6) b. 1738; Lemuel(6) b. 1740; Zephaniah(6), 1746; James(6), 1748, and daughters; moved to Gorham, Me., with sons Ezekiel(7) and Lemuel(7), ancestor of all that family inMaine; all large families. Also Ezekiel moved to N. H.; son Henry Holmes m. Mary Atkins of Truro; bro. Timothy moved to Medford, son Edward Ruggles, S. Boston; Esquire Solomon to Provincetown.

Nathaniel(6) —Obadiah(5), Josiah(4), Richard(3), Richard(2), Richard(1)— b. m. Martha Atkins. Children: Nehemiah(7), Atkins(7) m. Susan Mayo. William(7) —sons Napthali(8), Boston Highlands, Atkins(8) of Cambridge— Henry(7), Polly(7), Deborah(7) m. Joseph Mayo of Provincetown; Peggy(7) m. Nath. Pierce. Other descendants of Obadiah are Joseph, Jonathan, Isaac, all of whom had large families, which I cannot well trace.

Isaac(6), b. about 1760, sons, Theophilus(7) Isaac(7) m. Mercy Pike; Samuel(7) m. Polly Rich, and Seth(7), sons Seth(8) and Elisha Demondrel.

Samuel(6) —James(5) b. 1748, Joseph(4) b. 1720, Richard(3), Richard(2), Richard(1)— b. 1780. Son Samuel(7), b. 1807, of Provincetown, m. Polly Gross, dau. Alexander.

Captain Richard(5) (Buzzy Dick) —Richard(4) b. 1699, Richard(3),

Richard(2), Richard(1)— b. 1740, m. Betty (Betsey) Snow (?) about 1764. Children: Richard, b. 1765, lost at sea; Phebe, b. 1667, m. Silas Knowles, 1787; Zuruiah, b. 1769; Snow, b. 1771, lost at sea; Hannah, b. 1773; Capts. Obadiah, b. 1775; Heman Smith, b. 1777; Doan, 1779; Ruth m. Shaw; Mary m. John Cassell; perhaps Betsey m. Thomas Williams; am not certain of order or dates or number.

Dea. John (3) —Richard(2), Richard(1)— b. 1665, m. Mary, dau. Rev. Samuel Treat, to whom have referred in history of Isaac Rich, is the ancestor principally of the Wellfleet branch. Children: Mary, b. 1701; Robert, b. 1703; John J., b. 1705; Reuben, b. 1707, d. 1714; Joshua, b. 1710; Moses, b. 1712; Reuben and Thankful, twins, b. 1715; Sarah, b. 1720, m. Isaac Baker. Through these descended a numerous race. Hope, dau. of John and Thankful, b. 1742, m. Col. Elisha Doane of Wellfleet; a woman of vigorous mind. Mr. Pratt says, "strong and benevolent." Col. Doane left 120,000 pounds sterling; was the richest man in Mass. 2nd Hope m. Dr. Samuel Savage; 3d Hope m. Chief Justice Shaw.

Capt. Robert Rich, b. 1762, d. at Charlestown, aged 90 years; was among the first who established the market fishing trade in Boston; was highly esteemed. Many of his descendants are now engaged in the business he began. His large posterity revere the name of Robert Rich. Son Samuel had sons Joseph Smith, m. Maria M. of Truro, and Samuel, both of Charlestown, a member of the famous 3d Mass. Battery, escaped unharmed from 28 fights, in which one half the company were left behind.

7

No. 57.

LIBRARY *of*
Cape Cod
HISTORY & GENEALOGY

JOHN ROBINSON OF LEYDEN

AND HIS DESCENDANTS TO THE
SIXTH GENERATION

Jenkins, John

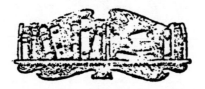

YARMOUTHPORT, MASS.:
C. W. SWIFT, Publisher and Printer,
The "Register" Press,
1913.

JOHN ROBINSON OF LEYDEN

JOHN ROBINSON OF LEYDEN and His Descendants, to the 6th Generation.

The substance of the following memoir copied from a manuscript of Mr. Freeman Robinson of East Falmouth, is understood to have been compiled by the late Hon. John Jenkins of Falmouth, a descendant of the Puritan pastor.

Rev. John Robinson was born in England, in the year 1576, admitted to Christ Church college, Cambridge, 1592, took the degree of A. M. and became a Fellow of said college in 1598. He lived for some time in Norwich, County of Norfolk, Eng., "a man worthily reverenced of all the city for the grace of God in him," and in 1606 was chosen pastor of the Puritans gathered at the residence of William Brewster, at the village of Scrooby in the County of Nottingham. He removed with the church in the winter 1607-8 to Amsterdam, and in 1610 to Leyden, and witnessed the departure of a portion of the church to America in 1620. He died in Leyden, March 1, 1625, in the 50th year of his age. Thirty-five families of his congregation in Leyden were brought over to Plymouth in 1629, and in 1630 another company came over, both at the expense of their brethren in the colony. In one of these companies were the wife and children of John Robinson. [Mr. Jenkins is in error in saying that the wife of John Robinson came over. She was in Leyden as late as 1629, and there is no evidence that she or any of the family but Isaac did come over.]

Isaac Robinson came over in 1631, was a freeman in Scituate in 1633, in Barnstable in 1639. He was an influential man, an assistant in the Sacrament for some years. Prince in his New England Chronology says of him, in speaking of John Robinson: "His son Isaac came over to Plymouth colony, lived above ninety years of age, a venerable man whom I have often seen, and has left male posterity in the Co. of Barnstable." Isaac sold his house in Scituate to one John Twisden, and removed to Barnstable in 1639. He was disfranchised by Gov. Prince in 1659 on account of his opposition to the laws against the Quakers, and for his sympathy with that sect, but was restored to his civil rights by Gov. Winslow in 1673. He married Margaret Handford, June 27, 1636. She died June 1649. His second wife's name was Mary. He removed from Barnstable to Succanessett and was one of the thirteen who made the first purchase of lands from the aborigines, and commenced the settlement of Falmouth 1660. The first house built at Falmouth was Isaac Robinson's, and was situated near the south end of "Fresh pond."

Dr. Thacher in his history of Plymouth, gives an account of the connection of Isaac Robinson with the Quakers, and his disfranchisement by Gov. Prince. It is probable that the views of the settlers of Succanessett were somewhat in advance of other Christians in respect to religious toleration, and it was for this cause that he was probably led to commence a settlement at this place. A "meeting" of Friends had been early established here, Isaac Robinson having early embraced some of the peculiarities of that sect before leaving Barnstable, and it is not improbable that a knowledge of this fact (he being a man of considerable influence in the colony) led members of that sect to look to this place as a favorable place for the establishment of this worship. From the records of the Friends' Monthly Meeting, it appears that a meeting for discipline was established in Falmouth in 1719, and a meeting for worship had existed here for many years previously. Isaac Robinson, Jr., grandson of the first Isaac, married Hannah Harper, whose father, Robert Harper, was a Quaker, and Isaac Robinson, Jr.,'s name is found on the early records of the Friends' Monthly Meeting.

Isaac Robinson removed from Falmouth to Tisbury, was proprietor's clerk in 1673, selectman 1678-84, and died in Barnstable in 1704.

Children of ISAAC Robinson(2) and Margaret and Mary, his wives:

Susanna(3), bap. Jan. 21, 1637.

JOHN(3), bap. April 5, 1640, m. Elizabeth Weeks, May 1, 1667.

Isaac(3), bap. Aug. 7, 1642, m. Ann, d. Tisbury, 1728.

Fear(3), bap. Jan. 26, 1644, m. Samuel Baker, without issue.

Mercy(3), bap. July 4, 1647, m. William Weeks, March 16, 1669.

—— Stillborn child, June 1649, and mother died.

Israel(3), bap. Oct. 5, 1651.

(Children of Mary Faunce.)

Jacob(3), bap. May 15, 1653, m. Experience, d. 1733.

Peter(3), removed to Norwich, Ct.

Thomas(3), bap. March 6, 1666, removed to Guilford, Ct.

Children of JOHN Robinson and Elizabeth Weeks:

John(4), born 1668.

ISAAC(4), born 1669, m. Hannah Harper, 1690; Alice Dexter, Sept. 9, 1744.

Timothy(4), b. Oct. 30, 1671, m. Mehitable Weeks, May 3, 1699.

Abigail(4), b. 1674, m. Jos. Percival, 1699.

Joseph(4), b. 1679, m. Bethiah Gall, Oct. 22, 1700; Bethia Lumbert, Dec. 7, 1704.

Mercy
Mary(4), m. Benj. Davis,
1704.
Love(4), b. Dec. 12, 1683, died Dec. 16, 1683.
Love(4), b. May 1, 1688, died Aug. 8, 1688.
Children of JACOB(3) and Experience Robinson:
Jacob(4)
Isaac(4)
Mary(4) m. Jonathan Weeks, 1704.
Children of ISAAC Robinson(4) and Hannah Harper:
Sarah(5), b. Jan. 4, 1691, m. Solomon Hoxie.
Elizabeth(5), m. M. Price.
Abigail(5), b. Nov. 18, 1694.
Experience(5), b. Jan. 4, 1696, m. Amos Landers.
JOHN(5), b. Nov. 16, 1699, m. Rebecca Robinson, Nov. 21, 1727, Jane Gifford, April 25, 1740.
Peter(5), b. Dec. 15, 1701, m. Martha Green.
Mary(5), b. May 5, 1704, m. Thomas Robinson, Sept. 1725.
Prudence(5), b. July 1, 1707, m. Eben Chadwick, Sept. 1727.
Hannah(5), b. Oct. 1, 1709, m. Nathan Rowly, Nov. 24, 1726.
Isaac(5), p. b. Aug. 11, 1713, m. Esther Nye, Nov. 13, 1735, Jane Hatch, Dec. 23, 1742.
Children of TIMOTHY Robinson and Mehetable Weeks:
Mehetable(5), b. Feb. 28, 1700.
Thomas(5), b. April 3, 1703, m. Mary Robinson, Sept. 23, 1725.
Rebecca(5), b. June 9, 1706, m. John Robinson, Nov. 2, 1727.
Timothy(5), b. June 13, 1713.
John Jr.(5), b. Aug. 30, 1716,
m. Keziah Hatch and Anne Hoxie.
William(5), b. Aug. 10, 1719, m. Addie Gifford, Aug. 1737.
Children of JOSEPH Robinson(4) and Bethiah Gall and Bethiah Lumbert:
Rowland(5), b. May 27, 1701, m. Thankful Dimick, 1723.
Bethiah(5), b. Aug. 23, 1705, m. John Hinckley, Nov. 1726.
Martha(5), b. Dec. 8, 1706, m. Benj. Gifford, June 22, 1727.
Joseph(5), b. March 13, 1708, m. Hannah Ryder, July 1731.
Jabez(5), b. March 12, 1711, died Jan. 7, 1740.
Elizabeth(5), b. Feb. 13, 1712, m. Abigail Turner, Scituate.
Abigail(5), b. Jan. 27, 1714, died Jan. 12, 1739.
Mercy(5), b. March 24, 1716, died March 5, 1739.
Anna(5), b. Nov. 23, 1718, m. Eph. Swift, Feb. 1736.
Children of JOHN(5) and Rebecca Robinson.
MICAH(6), b. Sept. 28, 1729, m. wid. Love Mayhew, June 23, 1780.
Ezekiel(6), b. June 24, 1731, m. Hannah Gifford, 1750.
Daniel(6), b. Oct. 15, 1735, d. Feb. 1, 1736.
Children of PETER Robinson and Martha (Green):
Jabez(6), b. June 9, 1726, m. Tabatha Green, Jan. 7, 1748.
Hannah(6), b. Oct. 23, 1728, m. Eben Dimmock, Dec. 1744.
Jeremiah(6), b. Feb. 10, 1732.
Susanna(6), b. Sept. 23, 1735, m. Paul Green, 1755.
Fear(6), b. March 10, 1738(?)
Elihu(6), b. Aug. 15, 1741, m. Huldah Gifford, Sept. 1779.

908

Martha(6), b. Sept. 1743.

Children of ISAAC Robinson, Jr.(5), and Esther and Jane:
Sarah(6), b. Aug. 17, 1706.
Katharine(6), b. Oct. 10, 1708.
Benjamin(6), b. March 24, 1740.
Esther(6), b. Aug. 10, 1742, m. Nathan Dexter, Feb. 15, 1764.

Children of THOS. Robinson(5) and Mary Robinson:
Deliverance(6), b. Jan. 12, 1725.
Zephaniah(6), b. July 26, 1729, m. Anna Hatch, Feb. 27, 1757.
Paul(6), b. Aug. 11, 1730, died Sept. 7, 1736.
Rhoda(6), b. Feb. 17, 1732, m. Braddock Dillingham, Jan. 1763.
Paul(6), b. April 20, 1734.
Mary(6), b. Feb. 12, 1738.
Thomas(6), b. June 13, 1744.

Children of JOHN Robinson, Jr.(5), and Keziah and Anne:
Zenas(6), b. Nov. 25, 1740, m. Mary Childs, Dec. 1763.
Seth(6), b. June 24, 1742.
Solomon(6), b. April 1744.
Bartlett(6), b. July 12, 1746.
John Jr.(6), b. Feb. 4, 1747, died March 27, 1805.

Children of WILLIAM Robinson(5) and Addie Gifford:
Daniel(6), b. March 22, 1737.
Lucy(6), b. Sept. 26, 1739.
Rebecca(6), b. June 1, 1741.
Timothy(6), b. March 20, 1743.
Joseph(6), b. Feb. 25, 1735.
Mercy(6), b. Feb. 25, 1735.

Children of ROWLAND Robinson(5) and Thankful:
Mary(6), b. July 4, 1724, m. Moses Swift, Sandwich.
Bethiah(6), b. July 20, 1726, m. Thos. Jones.
Susanna(6), b. Nov. 3, 1738, m. Timothy Crocker.

Children of JOSEPH Robinson(5) and Hannah:
Martha(6), b. Aug. 26, 1734, m. David Shiverick, 1752.
Zepbiah(6), b. Feb. 11, 1736, m. Jos. Gifford.

Children of JABEZ Robinson(5) and Hannah:
Jabez(6), b. Nov. 14, 1737.
Tabitha(6), b. July 21, 1739, m. Eben Dimmick, 1757.

Child of MICAH Robinson(6) and Love (Mayhew):
Mehitable, bap. April 21, 1782, m. John Swift, June 28, 1798, d. Jan. 25, 1845, at Fairhaven.

No. 58.

LIBRARY *of*
Cape Cod
HISTORY & GENEALOGY

THE YARMOUTH FAMILY OF GRAY

YARMOUTHPORT, MASS.:
C. W. SWIFT, Publisher and Printer,
The "Register" Press,
1913.

THE YARMOUTH FAMILY OF GRAY

Memoranda Respecting the Family of Gray.

In the list of those able to bear arms in the town of Yarmouth, dated Aug. 1643, is the name of John Gray.

Wm. Lumpkin in his will calls Wm. Gray his grandson.

John Gray's Inventory. Estate appraised 10th of Feb. 1674, by John Thacher and John Miller, 82 pounds, 16 shillings, 8 pence. Old Colony Recd. p. 109, vol. 3.

May 13, 1648. "Granted to Mr. Gray about 6 years since being 10 acres of upland and 4 acres of meadows lying there (at Sasuet Neck in Y.) betwixt the great Rock and Harbour's mouth the upland and the creek." Old Colony Records.

1642. "Mr. John Gray of Yarmouth presented for swearing and committed to prison." O. C. Rec.

1645. "presented for abusing Ann the wife of Wm. Eldridge in an injurious manner." ib:

EDWARD GRAY, gent., d. at Plymouth the last of June 1681, aged 52 years. He was a younger man than John Gray Senr. of Yarmouth.

THOMAS GRAY of Plymouth was of age in 1645.

JOHN GRAY was of Yarmouth in 1642. He m. Hannah d. of William Lumpkin of Y. He died in 1674. The record of his children on the Y. records is lost. He had

Benjamin, b. Dec. 7, 1648.

William, b. Oct. 10, 1650. He was a seargent under Capt. Gorham in King Philip's war. He removed to Harwich.

Mary, p. his daughter, m. Benjamin Rider, June 13, 1670.

Edward, p. his son, was of Yarmouth June 19, 1684.

Gideon, p. his son.

John, prob. his son, of Yarmo. Mar. 26, 1679.

WILLIAM GRAY, son of John of Y., m. Rebecca Dillingham; d. in 1723 at Harwich. He names in his will recorded in the 4 vol. p. 128 of the Barnstable Probate Records his children living in 1723, viz.:

William, m. Deborah Sears, Oct. 8, 1719.

Hannah, m. Wm. Penney of H. 1715.

Dorothy, m. Josiah Swift June 25, 1719.

Sarah, m. Eldad Atwood Oct. 23, 1718.

Mehitable, m. Isaac Atwood Oct. 23, 1718.

Rebecca, m. Samuel Berry Oct. 16, 1712.

EDWARD GRAY, p. son of John, m. 1st   She d. 29 of Mar.

1692, and he m. 2d, Melitiah Lewis July 16, 1684, and had children born in Yarmouth, viz.:

Benoni, b. Mar. 15, 1681. Also recorded as born at Eastham. He m. Sarah and removed to Falmouth where he d. 1733.

Presilah, b. Oct. 8, 1686.
Gideon, b. Sept. 6, 1688, m. Dorcas Eldridge July 26, 1716.
John, b. July 26, 1691, m. Hannah Taylor Dec. 25, 1721.
Melatiah, b. June 6, 1694, m. Elisha Smith Jan. 3, 1716-7.
Mercy, b. April 13, 1696, m. Ebenr. Hallet May 30, 1737.
ANDREW, son of John of H., m. He removed to North Yarmouth, Maine, where he d. He had sons, John, Andrew, Thomas and Joshua and a daughter who m. Cutter. After his decease his family returned to Harwich, and his widow m. Thomas Hallet of Yarmouth, who d. April 10, 1772, in the 82d year, leaving his estate to his adopted son, Joshua Gray. (From Chandler Gray, son of Joshua.) See Alden' Colls. Vol. 1, No. 129.
Mr. JOHN GRAY of Harwich, p. son of John of Yarmouth, m. Susannah (Clark), granddaughter of Mr. Thomas Clark, Senr., of Plymouth, and had children born in Harwich, namely: Pro. Rec.

Lot, m. 1st Bethia Paddock Oct. 1718, 2d, Jenney Otis.
Susannah, m. 1st, Nathl. Sears Oct. 10, 1712, and 2d, C. Foster.
Hannah, m. Thomas Hallet of Y. Feb. 8, 1721-2.

Lydia, m. aniel Hall May 18, 1721.
Sarah, m. Watson Freeman Jan. 30, 1723-4.
Thomas, m. Rachel
Samuel, m. Alice Prince of Middbo. Sept. 23, 1721. Har. Rec.
Mehitable, b. April 7, 1706, m. John Dillingham, Jr., Dec. 29, 1726.
Andrew, b. Sept. 29, 1707, m. Anna, b. Aug. 31, 1709,
Elisha, b. Nov. 29, 1711, m. Miss Susanna Davis of B. July 28, 1739.
Joshua, b. Oct. 19, 1713, d. unmarried Sept. 2, 1735.
Anna, b. Nov. 30, 1714, m. Thacher Freeman Jan. 27, 1731-2.
Mr. John Gray d. Mar. 31, 1732.
Mrs. Susanna Gray d. Sept. 10, 1731.
WILLIAM GRAY, son of William and g. son of John, m. Deborah Sears Oct. 8, 1719, and had eight children born in Harwich, viz.:

William, b. Feb. 13, 1720-
Rebecca, b. June 16, 1723, m. Jabez Berry, 1744.
Thankful, b. Jan. 14, 1724-5.
Sarah, b. Dec. 19, 1726.
Thomas, b. Nov. 19, 1728.
Anna, b. Oct. 16, 1730.
Mary, b. Jan. 22, 1732.
Deborah, b. Oct. 21, 1734.
JOHN GRAY, son of Edward, m. Hannah Taylor, Dec. 25, 1721, and had seven children born in Yarmouth, viz.:

Oliver, b. Feb. 4, 1721-2, m. Sarah Hallet, 1746.
Meletiah, b. Jan. 22, 1723-4.
Edward, b. Mar. 24, 1725-6.

Lydia, b. May 25, 1728.
John, b. Oct. 31, 1730, d. in Boston, 1805.
Gideon, b. April 23, 1732.
Richard, b. April 27, 1734.
This family removed to Boston about 1745.
Descendants of Mr. John Gray of Harwich.

LOT GRAY, son of John, kept a public house in Harwich. He m. 1st, Bethia, d. of Paddock, Oct. 1718; she died Oct. 16, 1728, and he m. 2d, "Genney" (Jane) d. of Nathl. Orris of Barnstable, 1730. Children born in Harwich:
John, b. July 27, 1719.
Lydia, b. May 22, 1722.
Mary, b. Feb. 28, 1724-5.
Mehitable, b. Feb. 20, 1726-7.
Nathaniel, b. Oct. 5, 1723.

THOMAS GRAY, son of John, m. Rachell . Children born in Harwich:
Susannah, b. Oct. 18, 1732.
Betty, b. Sept. 6, 1734.
Joshua, b. Sept. 18, 1736.
Hannah, b. April 27, 1739.
Sarah, b. Oct. 8, 1741.
Rachell, b. April, 1744.
Mehitable, b. April, 1747.
Mary, b. April 20, 1749.

July 25, 1733, Thomas Gray and John Dillingham, Jr., were appointed guardians of their brother, Samuel Gray of Harwich, who had been distracted about one year.—Probate Records.

SAMUEL GRAY, son of John, m. Alice Prince of Middleboro, Sept. 23, 1721.

ANDREW GRAY, son of John, m. . He removed to North Yarmouth, Maine, where he died, and his family returned to Harwich. Children:
John
Andrew
Thomas
Joshua
Daughter, m. Cutter.

EDWARD GRAY, m. Hannah Godfrey, July 3, 1727, and had born in Harwich:
Mary, b. Oct. 18, 1728.

No. 59.

LIBRARY of
Cape Cod
HISTORY & GENEALOGY

THE YARMOUTH FAMILY OF CHASE

YARMOUTHPORT, MASS.:
C. W. SWIFT, Publisher and Printer,
The "Register" Press,
1913.

THE CHASE FAMILY OF YARMOUTH.

THOMAS and Sarah Chase.
Children.
Guell, b. Jan. 22, 1707-8; m. Jane Phillips, 1727.
Hannah, b. May 24, 1712.
Phebe, b. July 4, 1713; m. Thomas Baker, Aug. 2, 1733.
Richard, b. March 3, 1714-15; m. Widow Thankful Chase, Jan. 21, 1734-5.
Joseph, b. March 17, 1718-19; m. Sarah O'Kelley, Jan. 19, 1743-4.
Priscilla, b. April 10, 1720; m. Christopher Ellis, Oct. 12, 1739.
Sarah, b. May 20, 1722; m. Nathaniel Basset of Chatham, Aug. 23, 1739.
Abner, b. June 22, 1729; m. Deborah Baker, Oct. 27, 1748.

GOUELL Chase, son of Thomas, m. Jane Phillips, 1727.
Children.
Thomas, b. July 20, 1728; m. Martha Rogers of Harwich, 1751.
Gouell, b. Feb. 7, 1729-30; m. Basheba Nickerson, 1752.

ISAAC Chase m. Mary Berry, May 23, 1706.
Children.
Hezekiah, b. Dec. 9, 1706.
Obadiah, b. Sept. 16, 1708; m. Mary Smith of Chatham, 1832.
Thankful, b. Feb. 14, 1711-12; m. Jacob Baker, Oct. 19, 1732.
Isaac, b. March 28, 1714; m. Thankful Maker, 1737.
Lot, b. March 11, 1716; m. Rebecca Wing, 1738.
Hannah, b. Sept. 27, 1718.
Nathaniel, b. May 1724.
Mary. b. Jan. 9, 1720-21; m. Nathaniel Covil of Chatham, 1740.
Judah, b. Oct. 24, 1726.

ISAAC Chase m. Charity O'Kelley, Aug. 3, 1727.
Children.
Barnabas, b. April 29, 1731; m. Lydia Ryder, 1748-9.
Temperance, b. March 4, 1731-32; m. Nathaniel Baker, Jan. 23, 1745.
Charity, b. July 15, 1736; m. Sylvanus Chase of Harwich, 1757.
Mehitable, b. Aug. 9, 1740; m. Isaac Eldridge of Harwich, Jan. 5, 1756.
Desire, b. March 6, 1741-2; m. Archelus Chase, 1764.

JOHN Chase m. Thankful Berry, 1733. Thankful m. Richard Chase, Jan. 21, 1734-5.
Children.
Marcy, b. Feb. 11, 1733-4. Her father died suddenly by a fall from his horse on the first day of the same month.

WILLIAM Chase, son of John, m. Dorcas Baker, Sept. 20, 1715; m. 2, Patience

Children.
Lydia, b. March 27, 1716; m. Leonard.
Elizabeth, b. Oct. 6, 1718; m. Wixon.
JONATHAN Chase, son of John, m. Sarah
Children.
Joshua, b. Nov. 16, 1709.
Eunice, b. July 15, 1711.
Caleb, b. Sept. 25, 1713; m. 1, Priscilla Godfrey, 1834; m. 2, Mary Wixon, Sept. 8, 1736.
Jonathan, b. Aug. 10, 1716; m. Experience Arey, Harwich, 1752.
JONATHAN Chase, son of Jonathan, m. Elizabeth Smith of Harwich, 1752.
Children.
Elizabeth, b. Jan. 8, 1756; m. David Basset, Chatham, Nov. 28, 1782.
Nathaniel, b. March 24, 1759.
JEREMIAH Chase, son of John, m. Hannah Baker, Sept. 11, 1719.
Children.
Jeremiah, b. Aug. 28, 1720.
Ebenezer, b. Sept. 25, 1722.
Jabez, b. March 15, 1726-7.
David, b. March 15, 1728-9; m. Susanna Baker, 1752.
Elizabeth, b. July 1, 1731; m. Joseph O'Kelley, Jr., 1750.
RICHARD Chase, son of Thomas, m. Thankful, widow of John Chase, Jan. 21, 1734-5. Richard died Jan. 14, 1794.
Children.
John, b. Feb. 2, 1735-6; m. Thankful Smith of Harwich, 1757.
Samuel, b. Feb. 11, 1737-8; m. Zilpha Burgess, 1759.
Archelus, b. May 17, 1740; m. Desire Chase, 1764.

Berry, b. July 23, 1742; m. Mercy Baker, Dec. 2, 1763.
Richard, b. July 21, 1745; m. Mary Chase, 1768.
Rebecca, b. Aug. 1747; m. Shubael Baker, Nov. 15, 1764.
Thankful, b. March 8, 1750-51; m. Eleazer Nickerson, Jr., 1769.
Huldah, b. Feb. 21, 1751-2; m. Sparrow Howes, June 10, 1777.
Abigail, b. May 1, m. Eliphax Chapman, 1773.
Phebe, b. June 3, 1760; m. Sylvanus Baker, Aug. 31, 1780.
ISAAC Chase, son of Isaac, m. Thankful Maker of Harwich, Oct. 22, 1737.
Child.
Reuben, b. Nov. 24, 1738.
JOSEPH Chase, son of Thomas, m. Sarah O'Kelley, Jan. 19, 1743-4.
Children.
Joseph, b. Nov. 17, 1744; m. 1, Phebe Bassett of Chatham, 1766; m. 2, Hannah Chase of Harwich, 1767.
Daniel, b. April 13, 1746; m. Hannah Broadbrook, Harwich, 1773.
Hannah, b. m. Elkanah Chase, Oct. 29, 1766.
Lot, b. June 30, 1750; m. Lydia Chase, Jan. 25, 1770.
BARNABAS Chase, son of Isaac and Charity, m. Lydia Rider, March 17, 1748-9.
Children.
Sarah, b. Dec. 6, 1750; m. Eleazer Kelley, 3d, 1770.
Isaac, b. Feb. 15, 1752.
Lot, b. Nov. 24, 1755.
Reuben, b. June 8, 1761; m. Polly Nickerson, Dec. 22, 1816.
ABNER Chase, son of Thomas, m. Deborah Baker, Oct. 27, 1748.

Children.
Priscilla, b. July 1, 1750; m. Joseph Baker, Jr., Oct. 13, 1765.
Lydia, b. May 16, 1752; m. Lot Chase, Jan. 25, 1770.
Elizabeth, b. May 29, 1754; m. Shubael Baker, July 5, 1787.
Nathan, b. Jan. 10, 1756; m. Mercy Robbins, Jan. 26, 1782.
Anthony, b. July 8, 1758; m. Keziah Baker, Oct. 3, 1780; lived in Yarmouth.
Deborah, b. Dec. 26, 1760; m. Enos Nickerson, 1780.
Abner, b. Jan. 1, 1764.
Thomas, b. Nov. 13, 1769; m. Abigail Small of Harwich, 1790.
Owen, b. Sept. 13, 1771; m. Penina Bassett, 1790.

THOMAS Chase, son of Gowel, m. Martha Rogers, 1751.
Children.
Jane, b. July 7, 1752; m. Richard Baker, Nov. 7, 1771.
Sarah, b. Nov. 21, 1753; m. Eleazer Kelley, 3d, 1770.
Reliance, b. Nov. 13, 1756; m. Josiah Nickerson, March 1774.
Henry, b. April 7, 1758.
Rachel, b. Sept. 7, 1760; m. Elisha Rogers of Eastham, June 16, 1780.
Martha, b. Sept. 3, 1763; m. Levi Ellis of Harwich, 1792.

GOUEL Chase, son of Gouel, m. Basheba Nickerson, 1752.
Child.
Gouel, b. Oct. 27, 1755; (m. Betsey Kelley, Aug. 30, 1789. Gouel, son of Lot.)

JOHN Chase, son of Richard, m. Thankful Smith of Harwich, 1757.
Children.
Lucy, b. Nov. 15, 1758.
Content, b. Sept. 14, 1761.
Charles, b. July 17, 1763.
John, b. March 24, 1765; m. Salome Chase, Nov. 8, 1787.
Jane, b. Aug. 16, 1767.
Marcy, b. April 29, 1769.

RICHARD Chase, son of Richard, m. Mary Chase, 1768.
Children.
Archelus, b. Oct. 28, 1768; d. Feb. 25, 1770.
Benjamin, b. Dec. 28, 1770.
Thankful, b. March 27, 1773.
Phebe, b. Nov. 29, 1775; m. Thomas Bray, Nov. 13, 1800.
Richard, b. July 15, 1778.
William, b. Feb. 29, 1781.
Mary, b. Dec. 15, 1784.
Elizabeth, b. Oct. 20, 1787.

JOSEPH Chase, son of Joseph, m. 1, Phebe Basset, Chatham, 1766; m. 2, Hannah Chase, Harwich, 1767.
Children, by 2d wife Hannah.
Tamzin, b. Oct. 14, 1768.
Sarah, b. Sept. 19, 1770.
Obed, b. Sept. 6, 1772; m. Phebe Hathaway, 1794.
Joseph, b. Sept. 14, 1774.
Susannah, b. July 11, 1777; m. Judah Berry, 1797.
Betty, b. Jan. 13, 1780.
Lewis, b. July 30, 1782.
Daniel, b. March 6, 1785; m. Rhoda Berry, Yarmouth, 1808.
Happy, b. Aug. 2, 1787.
Enoch, b. Nov. 24, 1790.

EBENEZER Chase, Jr., of Harwich m. Phebe Kelley, Dec. 24, 1769. (Ebenezer Chase, Jr., born Aug. 11, 1747.)
Child.
Ebenezer Chase, b. Sept. 28, 1770.

EDMOND Chase m. Abigail
Children.
Lydia, b. July 1, 1763.
Jeremiah, b. April 5, 1765.
Sarah, b. Aug. 25, 1767.
Hannah, b. Nov. 17, 1767.
DESIRE Chase m. Bachelor Swain, July 30, 1772.
Children.
Judah Chase, b. March 26, 1765.
Abigail Swain, b. June 26, 1773.
DANIEL Chase, son of Joseph, m. Hannah Broadbrook, Harwich, 1773.
Child.
Anne, b. Aug. 10, 1774.

THOMAS Chase settled in Hampden as early as 1639, m. Elizabeth Philbrick; died in 1652. Had five sons:
1 Thomas, b. 1643; d. a bachelor, 1714.
2 Joseph, b. 1645; m. Rachel Partridge, Jan. 31, 1671; d. Jan. 12, 1717-18.
3 James, b. 1646; m. Elizabeth Green; d. 1700.
4 Isaac, b. 1647; m. d. 1727.
5 Abraham, killed in battle, 1674.
2 JOSEPH Chase, son of Thomas, m. Rachel Partridge. Rachel died Oct. 27, 1718, in her 68th year. Joseph's estate was valued at 4,000 pounds. In his will he gives 50 pounds to the people of God called Quakers and a legacy to Elizabeth Chase, daughter of John Chase.
Children.
Hannah, b. June 5, 1672; d. June 10, 1674.
Elizabeth, b. March 11, 1674; d. Sept. 8, 1675.
Jonathan, b. March 14, 1676; drowned Feb. 1, 1696.
Anne, b. March 9, 1677; m. Sinclair.
Rachel, b. April 27, 1678; m. Jacob Frieze.
Elizabeth, b. m. Benjamin Hilliard.
3 JAMES Chase, son of Thomas, m. Elizabeth Green.
Children.
Abigail, b. Aug. 27, 1681; m. John Chase.
Dorothy, b. March 17, 1686; m. John Chapman.
Mary, b. Feb. 8, 1688.
4 ISAAC Chase, son of Thomas, m. moved to the Vineyard and settled at Holmes Hole.
Children.
6 Thomas, b. 1677.
Rachel, b. 1679.
7 Isaac, b. 1681.
8 Abraham, b. 1683.
9 James, b. 1685.
Mary, b. 1687.
10 Joseph, b. 1689; m. Lydia Coffin of Nantucket.
11 Jonathan, b. 1691.
Hannah, b. 1693.
Sarah, b. 1695.
Priscilla, b. 1697.
Elizabeth, b. 1703; d.
10 JOSEPH Chase, son of Isaac, m. Lydia Coffin.
Children.
12 Abel, Priscilla, Lydia, Mary, Damavis, Rachel, Sarah, 13 Joseph, and 14 Thomas.
14 THOMAS, son of Joseph, m. Anna Field, Boston.

Children.

Thomas, father of Major W. H. Chase, March 16, 1846.

Anna

LOT Chase, son of Joseph, m. Lydia Chase, Jan. 25, 1770.
 Gouel, b. Dec. 22, 1771; m. Betsey Kelley, Aug. 30, 1789.
 Lot, b. Dec. 22, 1773; m. Elizabeth Bassett, Chatham, 1794.
 Lydia, b. Jan. 4, 1778; m. Abner Crowell, 1812.
 Daley, b. March 4, 1780.
 Freeman, b. April 4, 1782.
 Daley, b. Oct. 17, 1784.
 June, b. Feb. 19, 1787.
 Amos, b. July 28, 1789.

ELKANAH Chase m. Hannah Chase, Oct. 29, 1766.
Children.
 Rebecca, b. Nov. 4, 1768; m. Reuben Kelley, March 6, 1786.
 Lemuel, b. Jan. 13, 1772; d. 1775.
 Elkanah, b. Aug. 13, 1773.
 Love, b. March 20, 1776; m. Joseph Howland, March 18, 1795.
 Tabitha, b. May 29, 1779.

(Deacon) ANTHONY Chase, son of Abner, m. 1. Keziah Baker, Oct. 3, 1780; m. 2, Widow Mary Eldridge, 1803. This family resided in what is now Yarmouth.
Children.
 Davis, b. March 25, 1781; m. Hannah Baker, 1807.
 Reliance, b. July 25, 1783.
 Ruth, b. July 9, 1785; m. Ulysses Baker, 1806.
 Anthony, b. April 12, 1788.
 Luke, b. June 29, 1791; d. Aug. 3, 1855.
 Leonard, b. Dec. 30, 1793.
 Joshua, b. June 30, 1796.

Heman, b. Feb. 7, 1799; m. Nabby A. Howes, 1817; d. March 31, 1848.
By 2d wife.
 Enoch E., b. March 27, 1804.
 Son lost at sea, 1816.

NATHAN Chase, son of Abner, m. Marcy
Children.
 Polly, b. Aug. 23, 1782; m. Cornelius Baker, 1800.
 Nathan, b. Dec. 19, 1785.
 Timothy, b. Dec. 21, 1787.

SAMUEL Chase m. Mary
Children.
 Samuel, b. Feb. 1, 1785.
 Polly, b. Oct. 10, 1786; m. Samuel Whelden, 1804.
 Warren, b. Jan. 30, 1789.
Children.

DAVID Chase, Jr., of Harwich m. Salome Kelley, March 20, 1780.
Children.
 Jeremiah, b. Jan. 12, 1782.
 Abigail, b. Sept. 23, 1783.
 Hiram, b. Jan 7, 1786.

ABNER Chase, Jr., son of Abner, m. Mary
Children.
 Elizabeth, b. Dec. 11, 1784.
 Abner, b. July 5, 1787.

JOHN Chase, son of John, m. Salome Chase of Harwich, Nov. 8, 1787.
Children.
 Thankful, b. June 10, 1788.

OWEN Chase, son of Abner, m. Pinina
Child.
 Henry, b. Jan. 26, 1790.

DANIEL Chase of Dennis, son of Joseph, m. Rhoda Berry of Yarmouth. She died April 10, 1853. He died June 24, 1858.

Children.
James, b. Jan. 18, 1710; m. Mary Baker, 1828.
Charlotte, b. Dec. 23, 1812; m. 1, Benjamin Stacy, 1832; m. 2, J. N. Cotelle, Oct. 29, 1840.
Rhoda, b. Nov. 27, 1814; m. Ahira Wixon, June 25, 1836.
Daniel b. May 27, 1816; m. Polly Nickerson, 1837.
Betsey Taber, b. July 27, 1718; m. Nehemiah Eldridge of Dennis, 1842.
Lydia B., b. Aug. 5, 1820; m. Samuel Taylor, Nov. 22, 1838.
Caroline, b. Feb. 4, 1823, m. Philip Cotelle, Nov. 8, 1840.
Judah, b. Jan. 15, 1825; d. Sept. 20, 1826.
Lewis, b. June 10, 1827; m. Laura A. Hopkins, Dennis, 1848.
LUKE Chase, son of Anthony, m. 1, Sarah Hall, Barnstable, 1811; m. 2, Olive Clark of Brewster. He died Aug. 3, 1855.
Children.
Sarah Ann, b. Oct. 9, 1812.
Luke, b. June 16, 1818.
Edwin, b. May 1, 1824, in Barnstable.
By 2d wife Olive.
Julia, b. Dec. 28, 1829, in Barnstable; m. Abram Farnsworth, March 4, 1855.
Charles D., b. Sept. 19, 1831, in Barnstable.
Olivia, b. Oct. 8, 1834, in Barnstable; d. in Yarmouth, Oct. 12, 1858.
REUBEN Chase of Dennis m. Polly Nickerson, Dec. 22, 1816. He died Feb. 19, 1847.
Children.
Sukey Blossom, b. April 12, 1817; Sukey Blossom d. Nov. 1, 1819.
Reuben, b. July 3, 1819; m. Sarah Nickerson, April 3, 1851.
ANTHONY Chase, son of Anthony, m. 1, Susannah Baker, 1806; she died Aug. 5, 1823; m. 2, Susannah Studley, 1827; m. 3, Ruth Berry, 1830; m. 4, Hetty Megathlin, Aug. 29, 1850.
Children.
Albert, b. Oct. 18, 1807; m. Elizabeth P. Taylor, Sept. 1830.
Erastus, b. Aug. 13, 1811; m. Betsey Crowell, Jan. 1833.
Son, b. April 7, 1814; d. April 12, 1814.
Cordelia, b. May 18, 1815; m. Washburn Baker, Feb. 1834.
Leonard, b. Nov. 14, 1817; m. Melinda Lawrence, 1842.
Mary Lee, b. June 21, 1820; m. Kelly K. Crowell, March 28, 1839.
Anthony, b. June 17, 1823; m. Clarissa Simmons of Barnstable, 1845.
By 2d wife.
Benjamin Kelley, b. Feb. 22, 1829; m. Eunice A. Hallett, July 3, 1853.
JOHN G. Chase, born in Lynn, June 1, 1800; m. 1, Lucy Hawes, Sept. 1825; she died Feb. 5, 1828; m. 2, Mary Nesbitt, Lebanon, Me., 1828.
Children.
Sarah Allen, b. June 21, 1826.
Lucy Hawes, b. March 18, 1829.
By 2d wife.
Mary Nesbitt, b. June 27, 1830. John G. Chase lived in Yarmouth a few years and moved away.

HEMAN Chase, son of Anthony, Sr., m. Nabby A. Howes, 1817. He died March 31, 1848.
Children.
Lysander, b. May 21, 1819; m. Ruthy Crowell, Jan. 17, 1839.
Mary Thacher, b. Oct. 19, 1821; d. Aug. 7, 1823.
Joshua Atkins, b. July 27, 1823; m. Mary T. Bearse, Barnstable, 1847.
Heman Baker, b. Oct. 3, 1825; 1, Emily F. Hinckley, Barnstable, 1845; 2, Martha Crowell, Dec. 14, 1850.
Mary Thacher, b. May 2, 1828; m. Gorham Crowell, April 27, 1847.
Abigail A., b. Oct. 2, 1831.
Davis, b. July 20, 1834; d. Feb. 16, 1858.
Reliance, b. Aug. 14, 1837; m. Richard Sears, April 11, 1858.
Andrew Baker, b. Aug. 5, 1839; m. Corinna E. Bearse, May 4, 1865.
Loisa, b. July 11, 1841; m. Horatio Baker, Nov. 21, 1858.
Rev. ENOCH E. Chase, son of Anthony, Sr., m. Rebecca
Children.
Mary Hallet Eldredge, b. Nov. 13, 1829, in Dartmouth; m. Henry Blachford, March 10, 1853.
George Sylvester, b. Aug. 21, 1833, in Orleans; m. Susan Baker, Oct. 11, 1855.
Rebecca Baker, b. April 10, 1835, in Orleans; m. Varanus Baker, June 11, 1856.
Alexander Baxter, b. Aug. 9, 1818, in Yarmouth.
LYSANDER Chase, son of Heman, m. Ruth Crowell.
Children.
Amanda Crowell, b. Sept. 28, 1839; m. Zeno T. Gage, Dennis, Dec. 14, 1862.
Osborn, b. April 16, 1842; m. Mary Elizabeth Spear, June 1863.
Ruth, b. Dec. 7, 1843; d. Oct. 27, 1844.
Lysander, b. Jan. 15, 1846; d. June 23, 1846.
Ruth Emma, b. Oct. 2, 1848.
Lysander Amos, b. June 7, 1854.
DANIEL Chase, Jr., m. Polly
Children.
Benjamin Stacy, b. Nov. 12, 1839.
Daniel and family moved to Dennis.
ISAIAH Chase of Harwich m. 1, Rebecca Baker, 1839; m. 2, Patty Robinson, July 17, 1842.
Children, by 2d wife.
Alexander B., b. Dec. 28, 1841; m. Margaret M. Burns, Brewster, Jan. 5, 1866.
G. WASHINGTON Chase, son of Jeremiah, m. Nancy J. Brooks.
Children.
George Washington, b. Jan. 5, 1841; m. Sarah H. Brown, Dennis, July 20, 1861.
Franklin Howes, b. Jan. 25, 1843; m. Julia E. Covil, Dennis, Dec. 21, 1862.
Nancy Jane, b. Feb. 25, 1845; March 14, 1867.
Betsey Nickerson, b. July 15, m. James B. Nickerson, Dennis, 1847.
Mary Ann, b. Oct. 16, 1849.
Timothy Taylor, b. Dec. 14, 1851.
Lucy Williams, b. March 21, 1854.

Luella Augusta, b. March 21, 1859.
Joan, b. July 20, 1861.

JAMES Chase, son of Daniel, m. Mary Baker, 1828.

Children.

Judah, b. Dec. 14, 1828; m. Melissa D. Chase, Pawtucket, Feb. 23, 1851.

Betsey B., b. Aug. 31, 1830; m. John N. Baker, Nov. 22, 1849.

James, b. Nov. 19, 1832; m. Mary E. Chase, Pawtucket, 1855.

Edwin, b. Nov. 26, 1834; m. Ruth Cash, Dec. 21, 1856.

Phebe Ann, b. Aug. 6, 1837; m. Samuel Crowell of Dennis, Jan. 1857.

Lucy Jane, b. Jan. 13, 1839; m. Elkanah H. Baker, Jr., Aug. 4, 1858.

Osborn Howes, b. Nov. 22, 1840.

Alonzo Crowell, b. Sept. 25, 1845.

Female child, b. Aug. 31, 1849; d. Aug. 31, 1849.

WILLIAM Chase, b. in Harwich, June 17, 1809; m. Deliverance Crowell.

Children.

Jerusha Higgins, b. Nov. 14, 1829; d. Nov. 16, 1830.

Achsa Crocker, b. Aug. 25, 1832; d. Oct. 29, 1833.

William Henry, b. June 23, 1834; lost at sea, March 1861.

Luther Crocker, b. Aug. 13, 1840; lost at sea, March 1861.

Joseph Kelley, b. April 12, 1842.

Asenath, b. Aug. 5, 1844; d. June 1853.

ERASTUS Chase, son of Anthony Chase, m. Betsey Crowell, Jan. 1833. Erastus died April 5, 1864.

Children.

Susan, b. Oct. 24, 1833; d. Jan. 25, 1837.

Alonzo, b. July 21, 1835.

Erastus Baker, b. July 10, 1837.

Susan Betsey, b. Jan. 26, 1849.

JEREMIAH Chase m. Betsey from Harwich.

Children, born in Harwich.

Mary Ann Underwood Chase, b. June 9, 1818; m. Edmond Robinson.

G. Washington, b. July 19, 1821; m. Nancy J. Brooks.

Jeremiah, b. May 6, 1829; m. Cordelia Robinson.

GEORGE L. Chase, born in Lynn, m. Mary Ann Bacon, Barnstable, 1836.

Children.

Charles, b. July 3, 1839, in Barnstable.

Betsey Bacon, b. Feb. 2, 1840, in Yarmouth.

Henrietta, b. May 30, 1841, in Yarmouth.

Elizabeth Ann, b. Aug. 18, 1843, in Yarmouth.

b. April 25, 1845, in Yarmouth. Moved off before the name was obtained.

LEONARD Chase, son of Anthony, m. 1, Melinda Lawrence, Barnstable, 1842; she died Dec. 5, 1849; m. 2, Tryphosa Tobey, and lived in Hyannis.

Children.

Edgar, b. Oct. 27, 1842, in Barnstable.

Agnes, b. May 18, 1844; m. Valentine Baker.

Lawrence, b. July 29, 1846.

Rev. EBENEZER Chase, son of Ebenezer and Abigail, b. in Merri-

mack, N. H., May 19, 1785, m. Eliza Patten. He was a Congregational minister at West Yarmouth a short time.
Children.
Nancy U., b. Nov. 27, 1831, in Gilson, N. H.
Edward P., b. Dec. 12, 1834, in Westmoreland, N. H.

JEREMIAH Chase, son of Jeremiah of Harwich, m. Cordelia Robinson, March 23, 1848.
Children.
Edward S., b. 1848; m. Mary Gray, Aug. 5, 1867.
Elvira Dennis, b. Dec. 13, 1850; d. Nov. 1, 1853.
Erastus, b. June 30, 1853; d. Jan. 2, 1855.
Cordelia Emma, b. June 16, 1857.
Jeremiah Williams, b. June 14, 1863.

LEWIS Chase, son of Daniel, m. Laura A. Hopkins of Dennis, 1848.
Children.
Rhoda Anne, b. April 5, 1850.
Elbridge, b. Dec. 20, 1851.
Lewis and family moved to Dennis.

HEMAN B. Chase, son of Heman, m. 1, Emily F. Hinckley of Barnstable, 1845; m. 2, Martha Crowell, Dec. 14, 1850.
Children.
Heman B., b. in Barnstable, Feb. 27, 1849.
By 2d wife.
Clarence, b. in Barnstable, Nov. 4, 1852.
Edward Lewis, b. in Yarmouth, April 28, 1858.
Emily Hinckley, b. in Yarmouth, Oct. 7, 1861.
Walter Burton, b. in Yarmouth, Nov. 8, 1867.

JAMES Chase, son of James, m. Mary E. Chase, daughter of Joseph and Mary Chase, of Pawtucket, R. I., 1855.
James A., b. April 19, 1858; d. June 7, 1862.
David M., b. Oct. 14, 1860.
Hattie Wells, b. Aug. 18, 1863.

JUDAH B. Chase, son of James, m. Melissa D. Chase, daughter of Joseph and Mary, of Pawtucket, Feb. 23, 1851.
Children.
Charles Augustus, b. Aug. 1, 1852.
James, b. Sept. 22, 1856.
Joseph Henry, b. Oct. 1, 1858.
Mary Eliza, b. Feb. 28, 1860; d. Oct. 27, 1860.
Horace Freeman, b. May 1, 1862.
Clara Crocker, b. April 25, 1864; d. April 17, 1866.
Addie E., b. Sept. 11, 1866.
b. Dec. 17, 1868.

EDWIN Chase, son of James, m. Ruth Cash, Dec. 21, 1856.
Children.
Osborn Eddy, b. Sept. 24, 1861.
Anna Lord, b. July 4, 1864.
Moved to Orleans.

THEOPHILUS Chase, son of Sylvester and Sarah of Dennis, m. Sarah K. Crowell of Dennis.
Children.
Lafayette K., b. in Dennis, March 1, 1857.
Hattie C., b. in Yarmouth, Aug. 13, 1860; d. Sept. 21, 1861.
Hattie Crowell, b. in Yarmouth, May 20, 1863.

Phebe Ann,
b. in Yarmouth, Sept. Andrew Almy, 24, 1865. Phebe A. d. Dec. 24, 1865. Andrew A. d. Nov. 18, 1865. Child, b. in Yarmouth, Jan. 2, 1867: d. April 23, 1867.
WILLIAM Chase, son of William, m. Susan A. Stanton in North Carolina.

Child.
William, b. in Hertford, N. C., Nov. 12, 1860.

Rachel Chase, widow of Joseph Chase, died Oct. 27, 1718; in her 68th year. Joseph Chase's estate was valued at 4000 pounds, a large sum for that day. Tradition states that he lived in a painted house and had a paved wharf. In his will he gives 50 pounds to the people of God called Quakers, gives a legacy "to Elizabeth Chase, daughter of John Chase." Query, who was he?

James Chase, son to Thomas, sen., mar. Elizabeth Green. His children were

Abigail, b. 27 Aug. 1681, and mar. John Chase. Who was he?

Dorothy, b. 17 March, 1686, and mar. John Chapman.

Mary, b. 8 Feb. 1688.

The widow of James married James Cass before 3 Aug. 1700, but when James died I know not. Chase, sen., married John Garland in 1654 and by him had three children John, Peter and Jacob. John G. sen., d. 4 Jan. 1671, aged 50. Elizabeth Garland, the widow, then married Henry Roby, (who was a judge in the time of Gov. Cranfield) 19 Feb. 1674. Elizabeth Philbrick Chase Garland Roby died 11 Feb. 1677.

In Winthrop's Journal and in Farmer's Genealogical Register you will find "William Chase, Mass. requested to be made freeman in 1630 and was admitted 4 May, 1634."

Is not all this minute enough? Whatever I obtain I will send you on the same condition that you propose viz. you will make no public use of this letter. As it has cost me some trouble to collect what I have, you and I ought not to give information away.

Please to send me what you can and I will make good use of it. Send also two copies of Yarmouth Register of the same date that you sent week before last.

A friend of mine in town informs me that Nelson Chase of N. Y. is a descendant from Judge Samuel Chase of Maryland and is not related to the New England Chases. He also states that a man named Cromby or Crombie a Scotchman has come from England and wishes to be employed as an agent to receive the money, offering to do it for 5 per cent, and that he "puts up" at Nelson Chase's.

Have you heard of that? I am now trying to find out who John Chase was mentioned in the letter. Perhaps all our enquiries may terminate as the poet Gray says of one of the old feudal castles, which has

10

"Rich windows that exclude the light,
"And passages that lead to—nothing."
Joshua Coffin.
To Amos Otis, Esqr.
Yarmouthport, Mass.

Elisha Chase, Jr., moved one or both of his parents from Swansey to Plainfield, Connecticut, with all their goods and effects. I think the within record was taken from their family Bible. It is evident that it was copied from some other record because it is all of one handwriting and the ink is all of one color. My wife's father, whose name was Grindal Chase, left this record at my house a short time before he died, which was on the 10th of June, 1843. He was buried in Rehoboth in Pecks burying ground so called, where his wife's ancestors have been buried for the last hundred years.
Wm. D. Hunt.

Copy of Family Record.
John Chase born April 6, 1675.
Elisha Chase, the son of John Chase, born Dec. 15, 1712.
Sarah Chase born May 1, 1716.
Elisha Chase and Sarah married Jan. 30, 1733.

Elisha Chase, Jr., born April 18, 1735, on Friday, 2 hours by the sun in the morning.
Mary Chase born Sept. 12, 1736, on Sabbath day.
Sarah Chase born May 21, 1738, on Sabbath day at 10 o'clock in the morning.
Walter Chase b. Oct. 9, 1739, on Tuesday, 4 o'clock in the morning.
Sarah Chase b. May 3, 1741, on Sabbath day at 1 o'clock in the afternoon.
Seth Chase b. Dec. 26, 1742, on Sabbath day at 3 o'clock in the afternoon.
Paul Chase b. July 17, 1744, on Tuesday at 7 o'clock in the forenoon.
Weltha Chase b. April 10, 1746, on Thursday at 11 o'clock in the forenoon.
Prudence Chase b. Feb. 14, 1748, on Sabbath night.
Dean Chase b. April 24, 1750, on Tuesday, 5 o'clock p. m.
Benjamin Chase b. May 21, 1753, on Monday, a little past noon, N. S.
Phebe Chase b. April 8, 1755, on Tuesday, 9 o'clock p. m.
Grindal Chase b. Oct. 1, 1757, on Saturday morning at 2 o'clock.

Sarah Chase died March 5, 1740.
John Chase died Nov. 26, 1755.
Mother Chase died May 1757.
Mother Stephens died April 25, 1759.
Brother Judah died Nov. 7, 1791.

Oct. 16, 1767, Noah and Weltha married.
Dec. 20, 1767, Seth and Mary married.
Aug. 7, 1768, Job and Prudence married.
March 12, 1772, Paul and Betty married.
July 24, 1777, Ephraim and Phebe married.
Sept. 18, 1778, Phebe's son Walter born.

Nov. 20, 1780, Phebe's son William born.
July 22, 1780, Amey's daughter Polly born.
April 24, 1761, Sarah's son Caleb Thurber born.
Feb. 4, 1764, Weltha's son John born.
Seth's son Elisha b. March 24, 1768.
Sarah's daughter Amey Chase b. Jan. 28, 1763.
Phebe's son Walter died Feb. 13, 1781.
Phebe Chase, Walter's mother, died in Warren, Aug. 8, 1844.

CPSIA information can be obtained at www.ICGtesting.com
Printed in the USA
BVOW011659260312

286095BV00005B/42/P